Fodor's Road Guide USA

Florida

First Edition

Fodor's Travel Publications
New York Toronto London Sydney Auckland
www.fodors.com

Fodor's Road Guide USA: Florida

Fodor's Travel Publications
President: Bonnie Ammer
Publisher: Kris Kliemann
Executive Managing Editor: Denise DeGennaro
Editorial Director: Karen Cure
Director of Marketing Development: Jeanne Kramer
Associate Managing Editor: Linda Schmidt
Senior Editor: Constance Jones and Chris Swiac
Director of Production & Manufacturing: Chuck Bloodgood
Creative Director: Fabrizio La Rocca

Contributors
Editor: Douglas Stallings
Editorial Production: Kristin Milavec
Additional Editing: Jeff Boswell, Andrew Collins, Michael de Zayas, Richard Koss, Marylyn Springer, and Susan Walton
Writing: Steven Burris, Andrea Lehman (introductions), Alan Macher, Gloria Quiat, and Mitchell Uscher, with Michele Bloom, Daniel de Zayas, Michael de Zayas, Hannah Fons, William Fox, Nikko Hinderstein, Shari Linnick, Paula Margulies, Ellen McCurtin, Sidharth Murdheshwar, Laurice Nemetz, Jonathan Pelegano, Eric Reymond, Matthew Scheer, Daniel Taras, Sandra Taylor, Ami Trivedi, Karen Tucker, Beth Wolfram, and Mary Woods
Research: Keisha Hutchins, Carla Ranicki, and Amanda Robinson
Black-and-White Maps: Rebecca Baer, Robert Blake, David Lindroth, and Todd Pasini
Production/Manufacturing: Bob Shields
Cover: Laurence Parent (background photo), Bart Nagel (photo, illustration)
Interior Photos: Photodisc

First Edition
ISBN 0–679–00496–3
ISSN 1528–1469

Special Sales
Fodor's Travel Publications are available at special discounts for bulk purchases for sales promotions or premiums. Special editions, including personalized covers, excerpts of existing guides, and corporate imprints, can be created in large quantities for special needs. For more information, contact your local bookseller or write to Special Markets, Fodor's Travel Publications, 280 Park Avenue, New York, NY 10017. Inquiries from Canada should be directed to your local Canadian bookseller or sent to Random House of Canada, Ltd., Marketing Department, 2775 Matheson Boulevard East, Mississauga, Ontario L4W 4P7. Inquiries from the United Kingdom should be sent to Fodor's Travel Publications, 20 Vauxhall Bridge Road, London SW1V 2SA, England.

PRINTED IN THE UNITED STATES OF AMERICA
10 9 8 7 6 5 4 3 2 1

CONTENTS

Great Road Trips

Of all the things that went wrong with Clark Griswold's vacation, one stands out: The theme park he had driven across the country to visit was closed when he got there. Clark, the suburban bumbler played by Chevy Chase in 1983's hilarious *National Lampoon's Vacation*, is fictional, of course. But his story is poignantly true. Although most Americans get only two precious weeks of vacation a year, many set off on their journeys with surprisingly little guidance. Many travelers find out about their destination from friends and family or wait to get travel information until they arrive in their hotel, where racks of brochures dispense the "facts," along with free city magazines. But it's hard to distinguish the truth from hype in these sources. And it makes no sense to spend priceless vacation time in a hotel room reading about a place when you could be out seeing it up close and personal.

Congratulate yourself on picking up this guide. Studying it—before you leave home—is the best possible first step toward making sure your vacation fulfills your every dream.

Inside you'll find all the tools you need to plan a perfect road trip. In the hundreds of towns we describe, you'll find thousands of places to explore. So you'll always know what's around the next bend. And with the practical information we provide, you can easily call to confirm the details that matter and study up on what you'll want to see and do, before you leave home.

By all means, when you plan your trip, allow yourself time to make a few detours. Because as wonderful as it is to visit sights you've read about, it's the serendipitous experiences that often prove the most memorable: the hole-in-the-wall diner that serves a transcendent tomato soup, the historical society gallery stuffed with dusty local curiosities of days gone by. As you whiz down the highway, use the book to find out more about the towns announced by roadside signs. Consider turning off at the next exit. And always remember: In this great country of ours, there's an adventure around every corner.

HOW TO USE THIS BOOK

Alphabetical organization should make it a snap to navigate through this book. Still, in putting it together, we've made certain decisions and used certain terms you need to know about.

LOCATIONS AND CATEGORIZATIONS

Color map coordinates are given for every town in the guide.

Attractions, restaurants, and lodging places are listed under the nearest town covered in the guide.

Parks and forests are sometimes listed under the main access point.

Exact street addresses are provided whenever possible; when they were not available or applicable, directions and/or cross-streets are indicated.

CITIES

For state capitals and larger cities, attractions are alphabetized by category. Shopping sections focus on good shopping areas where you'll find a concentration of interesting shops. We include malls only if they're unusual in some way and individual stores only when they're community institutions. Restaurants and hotels are grouped by price category then arranged alphabetically.

RESTAURANTS

All are air-conditioned unless otherwise noted, and all permit smoking unless they're identified as "no-smoking."

Dress: Assume that no jackets or ties are required for men unless otherwise noted.

Family-style service: Restaurants characterized this way serve food communally, out of serving dishes as you might at home.

Meals and hours: Assume that restaurants are open for lunch and dinner unless otherwise noted. We always specify days closed and meals not available.

Prices: The price ranges listed are for dinner entrées (or lunch entrées if no dinner is served).

Reservations: They are always a good idea. We don't mention them unless they're essential or are not accepted.

Fodor's Choice: Stars denote restaurants that are Fodor's Choices—our editors' picks of the state's very best in a given price category.

LODGINGS

All are air-conditioned unless otherwise noted, and all permit smoking unless they're identified as "no-smoking."

AP: This designation means that a hostelry operates on the American Plan (AP)—that is, rates include all meals. AP may be an option or it may be the only meal plan available; be sure to find out.

Baths: You'll find private bathrooms with bathtubs unless noted otherwise.

Business services: If we tell you they're there, you can expect a variety on the premises.

Exercising: We note if there's "exercise equipment" even when there's no designated area; if you want a dedicated facility, look for "gym."

Facilities: We list what's available but don't note charges to use them. When pricing accommodations, always ask what's included.

Hot tub: This term denotes hot tubs, Jacuzzis, and whirlpools.

MAP: Rates at these properties include two meals.

No smoking: Properties with this designation prohibit smoking.

Opening and closing: Assume that hostelries are open year-round unless otherwise noted.

Pets: We note whether or not they're welcome and whether there's a charge.

Pools: Assume they're outdoors with fresh water; indoor pools are noted.

Prices: The price ranges listed are for a high-season double room for two, excluding tax and service charge.

Telephone and TV: Assume that you'll find them unless otherwise noted.

Fodor's Choice: Stars denote hostelries that are Fodor's Choices—our editors' picks of the state's very best in a given price category.

NATIONAL PARKS

National parks protect and preserve the treasures of America's heritage, and they're always worth visiting whenever you're in the area. Many are worth a long detour. If you will travel to many national parks, consider purchasing the National Parks Pass ($50), which gets you and your companions free admission to all parks for one year. (Camping and parking are extra.) A percentage of the proceeds from sales of the pass helps to fund important projects in the parks. Both the Golden Age Passport ($10), for those 62 and older, and the Golden Access Passport (free), for travelers with disabilities, entitle holders to free entry to all national parks, plus 50% off fees for the use of many park facilities and services. You must show proof of age and of U.S. citizenship or permanent residency (such as a U.S. passport, driver's license, or birth certificate) and, if requesting Golden Access, proof of your disability. You must get your Golden Access or Golden Age passport in person; the former is available at all federal recreation areas, the latter at federal recreation areas that charge fees. You may purchase the National Parks Pass by mail or through the Internet. For information, contact the National Park Service (Department of the Interior, 1849 C St. NW, Washington, DC 20240-0001, 202/208—4747, *www.nps.gov*). To buy the National Parks Pass, write to 27540 Ave. Mentry, Valencia, CA 91355, call 888/GO—PARKS, or visit www.national-parks.org.

IMPORTANT TIP

Although all prices, opening times, and other details in this book are based on information supplied to us at press time, changes occur all the time in the travel world, and Fodor's cannot accept responsibility for facts that become outdated or for inadvertent errors or omissions. So always confirm information when it matters, especially if you're making a detour to visit a specific place.

Let Us Hear from You

Keeping a travel guide fresh and up-to-date is a big job, and we welcome any and all comments. We'd love to have your thoughts on places we've listed, and we're interested in hearing about your own special finds, even the ones in your own back yard. Our guides are thoroughly updated for each new edition, and we're always adding new information, so your feedback is vital. Contact us via e-mail in care of roadnotes@fodors.com (specifying the name of the book on the subject line) or via snail mail in care of Road Guides at Fodor's, 280 Park Avenue, New York, NY 10017. We look forward to hearing from you. And in the meantime, have a wonderful road trip.

THE EDITORS

Important Numbers and On-Line Info

LODGINGS

Adam's Mark	800/444—2326	www.adamsmark.com
Baymont Inns	800/428—3438	www.baymontinns.com
Best Western	800/528—1234	www.bestwestern.com
	TDD 800/528—2222	
Budget Host	800/283—4678	www.budgethost.com
Clarion	800/252—7466	www.clarioninn.com
Comfort	800/228—5150	www.comfortinn.com
Courtyard by Marriott	800/321—2211	www.courtyard.com
Days Inn	800/325—2525	www.daysinn.com
Doubletree	800/222—8733	www.doubletreehotels.com
Drury Inns	800/325—8300	www.druryinn.com
Econo Lodge	800/555—2666	www.hotelchoice.com
Embassy Suites	800/362—2779	www.embassysuites.com
Exel Inns of America	800/356—8013	www.exelinns.com
Fairfield Inn by Marriott	800/228—2800	www.fairfieldinn.com
Fairmont Hotels	800/527—4727	www.fairmont.com
Forte	800/225—5843	www.forte-hotels.com
Four Seasons	800/332—3442	www.fourseasons.com
Friendship Inns	800/453—4511	www.hotelchoice.com
Hampton Inn	800/426—7866	www.hampton-inn.com
Hilton	800/445—8667	www.hilton.com
	TDD 800/368—1133	
Holiday Inn	800/465—4329	www.holiday-inn.com
	TDD 800/238—5544	
Howard Johnson	800/446—4656	www.hojo.com
	TDD 800/654—8442	
Hyatt & Resorts	800/233—1234	www.hyatt.com
Inns of America	800/826—0778	www.innsofamerica.com
Inter-Continental	800/327—0200	www.interconti.com
La Quinta	800/531—5900	www.laquinta.com
	TDD 800/426—3101	
Loews	800/235—6397	www.loewshotels.com
Marriott	800/228—9290	www.marriott.com
Master Hosts Inns	800/251—1962	www.reservahost.com
Le Meridien	800/225—5843	www.lemeridien.com
Motel 6	800/466—8356	www.motel6.com
Omni	800/843—6664	www.omnihotels.com
Quality Inn	800/228—5151	www.qualityinn.com
Radisson	800/333—3333	www.radisson.com
Ramada	800/228—2828	www.ramada.com
	TDD 800/533—6634	
Red Carpet/Scottish Inns	800/251—1962	www.reservahost.com
Red Lion	800/547—8010	www.redlion.com
Red Roof Inn	800/843—7663	www.redroof.com
Renaissance	800/468—3571	www.renaissancehotels.com
Residence Inn by Marriott	800/331—3131	www.residenceinn.com
Ritz-Carlton	800/241—3333	www.ritzcarlton.com
Rodeway	800/228—2000	www.rodeway.com

Sheraton	800/325—3535	www.sheraton.com
Shilo Inn	800/222—2244	www.shiloinns.com
Signature Inns	800/822—5252	www.signature-inns.com
Sleep Inn	800/221—2222	www.sleepinn.com
Super 8	800/848—8888	www.super8.com
Susse Chalet	800/258—1980	www.sussechalet.com
Travelodge/Viscount	800/255—3050	www.travelodge.com
Vagabond	800/522—1555	www.vagabondinns.com
Westin Hotels & Resorts	800/937—8461	www.westin.com
Wyndham Hotels & Resorts	800/996—3426	www.wyndham.com

AIRLINES

Air Canada	888/247—2262	www.aircanada.ca
Alaska	800/426—0333	www.alaska-air.com
American	800/433—7300	www.aa.com
America West	800/235—9292	www.americawest.com
British Airways	800/247—9297	www.british-airways.com
Canadian	800/426—7000	www.cdnair.ca
Continental Airlines	800/525—0280	www.continental.com
Delta	800/221—1212	www.delta.com
Midway Airlines	800/446—4392	www.midwayair.com
Northwest	800/225—2525	www.nwa.com
SkyWest	800/453—9417	www.delta.com
Southwest	800/435—9792	www.southwest.com
TWA	800/221—2000	www.twa.com
United	800/241—6522	www.ual.com
USAir	800/428—4322	www.usair.com

BUSES AND TRAINS

Amtrak	800/872—7245	www.amtrak.com
Greyhound	800/231—2222	www.greyhound.com
Trailways	800/343—9999	www.trailways.com

CAR RENTALS

Advantage	800/777—5500	www.arac.com
Alamo	800/327—9633	www.goalamo.com
Allstate	800/634—6186	www.bnm.com/as.htm
Avis	800/331—1212	www.avis.com
Budget	800/527—0700	www.budget.com
Dollar	800/800—4000	www.dollar.com
Enterprise	800/325—8007	www.pickenterprise.com
Hertz	800/654—3131	www.hertz.com
National	800/328—4567	www.nationalcar.com
Payless	800/237—2804	www.paylesscarrental.com
Rent-A-Wreck	800/535—1391	www.rent-a-wreck.com
Thrifty	800/367—2277	www.thrifty.com

Note: Area codes are changing all over the United States as this book goes to press. For the latest updates, check www.areacode-info.com.

Fodor's Road Guide USA

Florida

Florida

If the nickname the Ocean State weren't being used by Rhode Island, Florida could easily adopt it. Jutting into warm waters at the southeastern corner of the United States, this largely flat, finger-shape peninsula is rimmed by more than 1,200 mi of coastline, attracting beach-goers, water-sports enthusiasts, scenery-gazers, and nature-lovers.

Luckily, its real nickname—the Sunshine State—is every bit as accurate. While much of the rest of the country endures Old Man Winter, most of Florida maintains a pleasant, subtropical climate. The net result is that, for over a century, warm weather (and the bounty that flows from it) has drawn—and continues to draw—hordes of vacationers, snowbirds (winter residents), retirees, immigrants, and other new permanent denizens. Among those who have at one time or another been seduced by its charms (and in some cases seduced others to come to the state) are developers Henry Morrison Flagler and Henry Plant, circus tycoon John Ringling, writers Ernest Hemingway and Marjorie Kinnan Rawlings, singers Jimmy Buffett and Gloria Estefan, and inventors Thomas Edison and Henry Ford.

Fly into any Florida airport during the Christmas season or spring break, and you'll have little doubt as to the economic importance of tourism. Examine the contents of travelers' suitcases—swimsuits, sunscreen, golf clubs, tennis rackets, credit cards—and there's even less doubt about their reasons for visiting: relaxation and recreation.

Of course, the most popular activities center on all that coastline. Florida has a surprising variety of beaches: from the wave-lapped strands along the Atlantic Ocean (east coast) to the sugar-sand, sunset-hung beaches of the Gulf of Mexico (west coast and Panhandle), from people-watcher beaches to family beaches to secluded beaches. For those with sand aversion, there's the largely sandless, coral-reef-lined shore of Florida's Keys and the mangrove-studded margins in places like the Ten Thousand Islands and Biscayne National Park.

CAPITAL: TALLAHASSEE	POPULATION: 14,915,980	AREA: 59,928 SQUARE MILES
BORDERS: AL, GA	TIME ZONES: EASTERN AND CENTRAL	POSTAL ABBREVIATION: FL
WEB SITE: WWW.FLAUSA.COM		

Florida's largest and most cosmopolitan city, Miami, hugs the state's southeastern coast. Whereas Miami Beach has its share of sun and sand, the metropolitan area is equally known for its international trade and international (most notably, Latin) flavor, as well as glitz and celebrity. It seems fitting in this varied state that just a stone's throw away from Miami is one of Florida's other distinctive treasures: the Everglades. This national park—comprising a quiet, slow-flowing river of grass—is home to unusual wildlife, including that quintessential Florida creature, the alligator.

In case you think that Florida action is only on the coasts, travel inland; agriculture flourishes here, unfortunately, however, sometimes at the expense of the natural environment. Citrus fruits like oranges and grapefruit are as synonymous with Florida as pineapples are with Hawaii; but Florida farms and ranches also produce sugarcane and cattle. In one formerly sleepy farming town, the soil seems particularly fertile for growing world-famous amusement parks. In just over a quarter century, Orlando has sprouted eight major theme parks, five water parks, and countless—in fact, uncountable—other attractions, entertainment options, hotels, restaurants, and shops.

History

Almost from its beginnings as a flat, swampy plateau emerging from the ocean, Florida was home to all sorts of animals disinclined to the cold (at that time, glaciated) weather up north. It wasn't until 12,000–10,000 BC that humans, probably hunter/gatherers, arrived. These original Floridians began to farm and develop societies, and their descendants would become Florida's Timucuan (central and north), Apalachee (eastern Panhandle), Seminole (south-central to southwest), Calusa (southwest coast), Miccosukee (south), and Tequesta (southeast) tribes.

As in much of the Americas, the sovereignty of Florida's native peoples did not last. By the 16th century, a succession of Spanish explorers, including Pánfilo de Narváez, Hernando de Soto, Tristán de Luna y Arellano, and Pedro Menéndez de Avilés, arrived with visions of wealth. Though they found little gold and often didn't stay long, they still managed to ravage, enslave, and spread disease among the native population. In 1565 the first permanent European settlement in what is now the continental United States was founded at St. Augustine, and in the years that followed, the Spanish, French, and British all tried to establish Florida footholds. Pensacola, in fact, got the nickname the "City of Five Flags" because at one time or another, it was under the rule of Spain, France, England, the Confederacy, and the United States.

Eventually, Florida became a U.S. territory and state, but that didn't end the struggles. An influx of whites from the north, eager to farm and ranch, created friction with native tribes, and a series of three wars, known as the Seminole Wars, ensued. Led by then-General (later president) Andrew Jackson, the Anglos ultimately drove many Native Americans off their lands and out.

Conflict returned during the Civil War, though to a lesser degree than in the states to the north. In fact, Tallahassee was the only Confederate capital east of the Missis-

FL Timeline

20–30 million years ago	12,000–10,000 BC	5,000 BC	Easter 1513
Florida emerges from the ocean.	First Floridians arrive in the Panhandle region.	Native American groups begin to develop societies along the St. Johns River and north of Tampa Bay.	Spaniard Juan Ponce de León lands in Florida near what is today St. Augustine, naming it *Pascua Florida* (Feast of Flowers).

INTRODUCTION
HISTORY
REGIONS
WHEN TO VISIT
STATE'S GREATS
RULES OF THE ROAD
DRIVING TOURS

sippi not to fall to Union forces. When the South lost the war, however, Florida rejoined the United States.

By the late 19th century, a group of aggressive developers had begun to see Florida's potential as a tourist destination. Henry Plant built a railroad to the west coast as well as the big Tampa Bay Hotel. Henry Morrison Flagler had even grander plans, extending his Florida East Coast Railway to places like St. Augustine, Palm Beach, Fort Lauderdale, Miami, and eventually Key West. Flagler also built opulent hotels that attracted Vanderbilts, DuPonts, Rockefellers, and their confrères. Other developers created their own legacies—Addison Mizner in Palm Beach and Boca Raton, Carl Fisher in Miami Beach, George Merrick in Coral Gables. These names live on today, in everything from island and street names to museums and shopping malls. Unfortunately, their and others' ideas of progress often meant draining swampland, paving or building over animal habitats, and straightening, damming, dredging, or building new waterways, thereby altering the natural environment forever.

The 20th century saw a succession of land booms and busts, as tourists repeatedly rediscovered the appeal of Florida and its climate. The Great Depression of the late 1920s and early 1930s hit tourism hard, as did a 1935 hurricane that cut off Key West from the mainland (except by boat). But this era also brought Art Deco to Miami Beach, whereas the 1950s brought grand hotels, like Morris Lapidus's Fontainebleau and Eden Roc. But by the 1970s and early 1980s, Miami Beach and many other Florida towns had become rundown geriatric centers (sometimes pejoratively referred to as "God's waiting room"); Fort Lauderdale was primarily known as a center for spring break debauchery; and family tourism headed in greater and greater numbers to the new theme parks sprouting up around Orlando.

By the late 1980s, however, towns and cities were beginning to renew themselves. Miami Beach, its Art Deco jewels preserved and restored, became hot again. Miami, with its ever-growing Latin population and flavor, finally began to embrace and even tout its multiculturalism. Fort Lauderdale and West Palm Beach spruced up and added new arts and entertainment attractions. Towns and resorts on both east and west coasts grew, attracting visitors and residents alike. Florida is once again basking in the sunshine.

Regions

1. MIAMI AND MIAMI BEACH

Almost at the end of the line on Florida's east coast, Miami-Dade County throbs with energy. On the mainland is Miami itself, Florida's biggest city. This gateway to Latin America overflows with the food, language, and culture of many ethnic groups, most notably Cuban emigrés. Across Biscayne Bay, to the east, is Miami's island neighbor, Miami Beach. Its boutique Art

Mid-1500s	1565	16th–early 19th centuries	1763	1817–58
Spanish explorers make forays on both east and west coasts.	Menéndez establishes North America's first permanent European settlement, St. Augustine, on a mission to rid the area of the French.	Merchant and treasure ships regularly fall prey to storms and pirates, such as Black Caesar and Gasparilla, who attack from hiding places along the Florida coast.	Spanish cede Florida to the British in return for Cuba, but sovereignty passes back and forth between the major European powers for decades.	Seminole Wars.

Deco hotels and giant luxury resorts, along with a rejuvenated beach and café scene, attract wanna-bes and bona fide glitterati. Other tony and chic towns around Miami, such as Coral Gables and Coconut Grove, add to the allure of this happening corner of the state, while suburban sprawl fills in relentlessly.

Towns listed: Coconut Grove, Coral Gables, Hialeah, Key Biscayne, Miami, Miami Beach.

2. FORT LAUDERDALE AND BROWARD COUNTY

Wedged between Miami-Dade County to the south and Palm Beach County to the north, Broward County has as its hub the canal-laced, boat-friendly city of Fort Lauderdale. Downtown along the New River, Fort Lauderdale has forged a new arts and entertainment district as well as trendy shopping and dining districts, which are matched on the coast by its unobstructed beachfront. To the north and south lie ocean-side communities with varying amounts of view-blocking high-rises, modest family motels, fishing piers, natural areas, and beach-side promenades. Inland are the Western-style town of Davie, that ever-present suburban sprawl, and the eastern fringes of the Everglades (though not the national park).

Towns listed: Dania Beach, Davie, Deerfield Beach, Fort Lauderdale, Hollywood, Hollywood Beach, Lauderdale-by-the-Sea, Pompano Beach.

3. PALM BEACH AND THE TREASURE COAST

North of Broward, in Palm Beach County, are the northern reaches of the aptly named Gold Coast—noted for its golden sun, golden sand, and the golden bank accounts of many of the people who live or vacation here. The centerpiece of tourism is oh-so-ritzy Mediterranean-inspired Palm Beach, while the center of commerce is the larger but lower-crust West Palm Beach. This mainland stepsister has of late strengthened its corporate, artistic, and entertainment life, however. Sophisticated Boca Raton and Delray Beach round out county highlights.

The northern end of Palm Beach County plus the three counties to the north—Martin, St. Lucie, and Indian River counties—make up the area known as the Treasure Coast. Dotted with small, laid-back coastal towns, this area contains fine natural areas. Vero Beach is the region's most upscale town. Inland is Lake Okeechobee.

Towns listed: Belle Glade, Boca Raton, Boynton Beach, Delray Beach, Fort Pierce, Jensen Beach, Jupiter, Lake Worth, Lantana, Okeechobee, Palm Beach, Palm Beach Gardens, Palm Beach Shores, Port St. Lucie, Riviera Beach, Stuart, Vero Beach, West Palm Beach.

4. ORLANDO AND CENTRAL FLORIDA

You can't talk about Central Florida without talking about Orlando, and you can't talk about Orlando without talking about theme parks, along with other attractions from the kitschy to the cultural. Orlando's major theme parks (along with many ancillary attractions, hotels, restaurants, nightlife options, and shops) can be divided into those owned Walt Disney World, Universal, and Anheuser-Busch.

1819	1824	1842	March 3, 1845	January 10, 1861
Spain cedes Florida to the United States.	Tallahassee, midway between the major settlements of Pensacola and St. Augustine, becomes the territorial capital.	Some 3,000 Seminoles travel the "Trail of Tears" to reservation lands in the West.	Statehood is granted.	Florida secedes from the Union.

INTRODUCTION
HISTORY
REGIONS
WHEN TO VISIT
STATE'S GREATS
RULES OF THE ROAD
DRIVING TOURS

Outside Orlando is a mix: Kissimmee, to Orlando's south, is a strip of budget restaurants and lodging places; to its north you'll find tony Winter Park and artsy Mount Dora, an antiques center; and even farther north of Orlando's sprawling reaches you'll find clear springs, pine forests, and scrub in areas like Ocala National Forest. The coastal section of Central Florida, the aptly named Space Coast, is home to NASA's Cape Canaveral facilities and miles of remarkable undeveloped dune-lined coastline.

Towns listed: Altamonte Springs, Bartow, Clermont, Cocoa, Cocoa Beach, Davenport, DeLand, Haines City, Kissimmee, Lake Buena Vista, Lakeland, Lake Placid, Lake Wales, Leesburg, Live Oak, Maitland, Melbourne, New Smyrna Beach, Orlando, Sanford, Sebastian, Sebring, Tavares, Titusville, Walt Disney World, Winter Haven, Winter Park.

5. NORTHERN FLORIDA

Northern Florida is notable for its variety. Bordered by Georgia to the north, the region maintains a decidedly cooler climate than South Florida, so ocean swimming is best reserved for the warmer months. Just below the border is the resort of Amelia Island, the first of many barrier islands that parallel the mainland. Inland, Jacksonville is a major city—the largest, in terms of area, in the United States. St. Augustine adds centuries-old historic charm to the region, while Daytona Beach is known for auto racing, driving on the beach, and spring break madness. Inland is Gainesville, northern Florida's college town and home to the University of Florida.

Towns listed: Amelia Island/Fernandina Beach, Atlantic Beach, Cedar Key, Chiefland, Daytona Beach, Flagler Beach, Gainesville, Jacksonville, Jacksonville Beach, Lake City, Live Oak, Micanopy, Ocala, Ormond Beach, Palatka, Ponte Vedra Beach, St. Augustine, St. Augustine Beach, Starke, White Springs.

6. THE PANHANDLE

This thin wedge that stretches between western Georgia and Alabama on one side and the Gulf of Mexico on the other is as close to the Deep South as you can get in Florida. It simply doesn't feel like the rest of the state: Magnolias, live oaks, and loblolly pines replace palm trees; crowds descend in summer, not winter; drawls thicken; and even the time zone (at least in the western section) is different.

Tallahassee is flavored by the state government, Pensacola has the feel of the historic old port town that it is, and the Air Force maintains a significant presence around Fort Walton Beach. But what the region is most known for is the sugary beaches and bountiful emerald waters that can be found equally alongside tacky tourist areas, old fishing towns, and pristine natural areas. The combination attracts family vacationers, rowdy student revelers, and deep-sea anglers.

Towns listed: Apalachicola, Blountstown, Chattahoochee, Chipley, Crestview, De Funiak Springs, Destin, Fort Walton Beach, Grayton Beach, Gulf Breeze, Marianna, Niceville, Panama City, Panama City Beach, Pensacola, Pensacola Beach, Perry, Seaside, Tallahassee.

March 1865	**1880s**	**Early 20th century**	**1902**	**1912**
During the Civil War Battle of Natural Bridge a Confederate force of old men and boys repels Union troops and prevents the capture of Tallahassee.	Henry Plant builds a railroad to Tampa Bay, while Henry Flagler begins Florida East Coast Railway along the state's east coast.	Florida sees its first tourism boom, with hordes of car- and camper-driving "tin-can tourists."	Cars first race on hard-packed sands of Daytona Beach.	Overseas Railroad to Key West is completed.

7. THE TAMPA BAY AREA

As on the Atlantic, much of the Gulf Coast is known for its barrier-island beaches, and this central section is no exception. At its heart is Tampa Bay itself, with the cities of Tampa and St. Petersburg staring eyeball to eyeball at each other across the water.

Tampa is a bustling commercial city with a significant Cuban district, while St. Pete, a peninsula between bay and gulf, is known for its string of beach communities. Following the coast north on its way to its westward bend, you'll find a much less developed area, dotted with fishing towns and natural areas renowned for manatees and other wildlife. South of the bay, the barrier-island-flanked resorts continue, including the culturally vibrant city of Sarasota.

Towns listed: Bradenton, Brooksville, Clearwater, Crystal River, Dade City, Dunedin, Homosassa Springs, Indian Rocks Beach, Lido Key, Longboat Key, Madeira Beach, New Port Richey, Pine Island, Redington Beach, St. Petersburg, St. Pete Beach, Sarasota, Siesta Key, Sun City Center, Tampa, Tarpon Springs, Treasure Island, Zephyrhills.

8. SOUTHWEST FLORIDA

Between the southern end of Tampa Bay and the northern reaches of the Everglades, the lower gulf coast is another region that serves up what Florida is famous for: a subtropical climate; soft, sandy beaches (some a treasure trove of shells); golf and tennis; and pockets of little-touched Florida beauty—from cypress swamps to mangrove islets. Development is much more recent here than on the east coast, making some of it more informed—there's generally better beach access, for example—and some of it just newer. Resort communities include upscale Naples, often considered the Palm Beach of the gulf coast, and Fort Myers and its nearby barrier islands, Sanibel and Captiva.

Towns listed: Arcadia, Boca Grande, Bonita Springs, Cape Coral, Captiva Island, Englewood, Fort Myers, Fort Myers Beach, Marco Island, Matlacha, Naples, Port Charlotte, Punta Gorda, Sanibel Island, Venice.

9. THE EVERGLADES AND BISCAYNE NATIONAL PARKS

Making up the southern tip of the Florida peninsula, the Everglades are actually much larger than the area contained within the national park. Nevertheless, most people who visit this unique ecosystem will do so within park boundaries via only a few roads that access its western, northern, and southeastern sections. In reality, the Everglades are a 50-mi-wide, shallow, slow-moving "River of Grass," which plays a vital role as a habitat for wildlife and as a filtration system for the water that will ultimately enter Florida Bay. Unfortunately, the Glades have been severely damaged by development and agriculture.

Not far away, on Florida's southeastern tip, is Biscayne National Park, a park that is 96% underwater and that contains the northern extremities of Florida's living coral reefs. Between the two parks is a corridor of "civilization" that provides motels and fast food.

Towns listed: Everglades City, Everglades National Park, Florida City, Homestead.

Late 1920s	Labor Day 1935	1930s	1947	1959
Land boom goes bust.	Hurricane destroys Flagler's Overseas Railroad, which is soon replaced by the Overseas Highway.	Florida begins to recover from the Depression, and Art Deco–style buildings are constructed in Miami Beach.	Everglades National Park is established.	Nation's first domestic jet air service is scheduled between New York and Miami.

INTRODUCTION
HISTORY
REGIONS
WHEN TO VISIT
STATE'S GREATS
RULES OF THE ROAD
DRIVING TOURS

10. THE FLORIDA KEYS

Arcing southwest off the southern tip of the peninsula is this string of mangrove-fringed islands—few beaches here—connected to each other and the mainland by the Overseas Highway. Though all part of Monroe County, the Keys are generally divided into Upper, Middle, and Lower sections for the sake of differentiation. The further south you go, the slower the pace of life seems to flow.

The Keys are at once a huge traffic jam, a rowdy honky-tonk, an angler's and diver's paradise (there are many living coral reefs offshore), and a hideaway for those eager to "get away from it all"—temporarily or permanently. The Keys' main city, Key West, is a funky town that embraces its old-time multicultural and countercultural charm while opening itself to an onslaught of newer, more commercial tourism. Even further west are the atolls of Dry Tortugas National Park.

Towns listed: Big Pine Key, Conch Key/Duck Key, Grassy Key/Crawl Key, Islamorada, Key Largo, Key West, Little Torch Key, Long Key, Marathon, Sugarloaf Key, Summerland Key, Windley Key.

When to Visit

With the exception of the Panhandle and Northeast Florida, winter (roughly November–April) is Florida's busiest season, and for good reason. When it gets cold up north and out west, the weather is nice and warm down south. The farther south you go, the warmer it is. Winter is also when snowbirds (people, mostly retirees, who live in Florida for several months each year) flock south, meaning that Central and South Florida are at their most crowded and most expensive then. However, winter is also the season when there's the most to do. Arts and entertainment calendars are loaded with events, dining and nightlife spots hop, and attractions are fully staffed and fully open.

In spring, when families with school-age children and college students eager to party take advantage of their spring breaks, some weeks are very crowded. By May, the torrent has subsided, and you can often find shoulder-season bargains.

Summer is high season in northern Florida: It's warm enough for sunbathing and ocean swimming. The rest of Florida is less crowded and less expensive than in winter, except for Orlando, which is crammed whenever school is out. Summer is hot and humid, especially inland; fierce, spectacular afternoon thunderstorms are common.

Fall, like spring, is the shoulder season, and you don't have to look hard to find a bargain. The worst heat is past, but not the worst of the storms—this is hurricane season.

The state's record high and low temperatures are 109°F recorded in Monticello and -2°F in Tallahassee, but that doesn't adequately describe the norms. Though the northern part of the state sees temperatures dip into the 20s, frost rarely comes to South Florida. Temperatures here may vary from 40°F to over 90°F, with the Keys about 10° warmer in winter and 10° cooler in summer. The Keys also get substantially less precipitation than the mainland: 30 inches annually as opposed to 55–60 inches, all of it rain. (It did snow in Miami once in the 1970s, but there hasn't been a flurry since.)

1959	1968	October 1, 1971	1980	1980
Fidel Castro stages a revolution in Cuba, leading to the first mass emigration of Cubans to Florida in the 1960s.	Kennedy Space Center, at Cape Canaveral, sends Apollo 7 into space, the first of many manned launches from the facility.	Walt Disney World opens near Orlando and Kissimmee.	Mariel Boatlift: Fidel Castro releases 125,000 immigrants (some of them prisoners) to the United States when he opens the port of Mariel for five months.	Biscayne National Park, a largely marine park, is established.

CLIMATE CHART

Average Monthly Temperatures (in °F) and Monthly Precipitation (in inches).

	JAN.	FEB.	MAR.	APR.	MAY	JUNE
JACKSONVILLE	64/41	67/43	73/49	79/55	85/62	89/69
	3.3	4.0	3.7	2.8	3.6	5.7
	JULY	AUG.	SEPT.	OCT.	NOV.	DEC.
	91/72	91/72	87/69	80/59	74/50	67/43
	5.6	8.0	7.0	2.9	2.2	2.7
	JAN.	FEB.	MAR.	APR.	MAY	JUNE
MIAMI	75/59	77/60	79/64	82/68	85/72	88/75
	2.0	2.1	2.4	2.9	6.2	9.3
	JULY	AUG.	SEPT.	OCT.	NOV.	DEC.
	89/76	89/77	88/76	85/72	80/67	77/62
	5.7	7.6	7.6	5.6	2.7	1.8
	JAN.	FEB.	MAR.	APR.	MAY	JUNE
ORLANDO	71/49	73/50	78/55	83/59	88/66	91/72
	2.3	3.0	3.2	1.8	3.6	7.3
	JULY	AUG.	SEPT.	OCT.	NOV.	DEC.
	92/73	92/73	90/72	85/66	79/58	73/51
	7.3	6.8	6.0	2.4	2.3	2.2
	JAN.	FEB.	MAR.	APR.	MAY	JUNE
TALLAHASSEE	63/38	66/40	74/47	80/52	86/61	91/69
	4.8	5.6	6.2	3.8	4.8	7.0
	JULY	AUG.	SEPT.	OCT.	NOV.	DEC.
	91/71	91/71	89/68	82/56	73/46	66/40
	8.8	7.5	5.6	2.9	3.9	5.0
	JAN.	FEB.	MAR.	APR.	MAY	JUNE
TAMPA	70/50	71/52	77/57	82/61	87/68	90/73
	2.0	3.0	3.0	1.2	3.1	5.5
	JULY	AUG.	SEPT.	OCT.	NOV.	DEC.
	90/75	90/75	89/73	84/65	78/57	72/52
	6.6	7.6	6.0	2.0	1.2	2.2

FESTIVALS AND SEASONAL EVENTS
WINTER

Dec. **Disney Christmas.** Orlando's Magic Kingdom celebrates the season with Walt Disney World's Very Merry Christmas Party,

April 1982

U.S. Border Patrol throws a roadblock across the Overseas Highway south of Florida City, looking for illegal aliens and drug runners. Staunchly independent Key Westers, offended at being treated like foreigners, announce they will secede and form the "Conch Republic."

1980s

The television show *Miami Vice* shows off Miami as hip and trendy.

September 1992

Hurricane Andrew devastates South Florida.

1990s

Rise of eco-tourism and concern for the environmental health of the Everglades.

INTRODUCTION
HISTORY
REGIONS
WHEN TO VISIT
STATE'S GREATS
RULES OF THE ROAD
DRIVING TOURS

while Epcot has the Candlelight Processional and Holidays Around the World. | 407/824–4321.

Dec.–Jan. **Orange Bowl and Junior Orange Bowl Festival.** This Miami-area celebration is best known for the King Orange Jamboree Parade and the Orange Bowl Football Classic, but also includes more than 20 youth-oriented events. | 305/662–1210 or 305/371–4600.

Jan. **Art Deco Weekend.** Miami Beach's historic district is high-lighted with a street fair, a 1930s Moon Over Miami Ball, and live entertainment. | 305/672–2014.

Feb. **Coconut Grove Arts Festival.** This is the state's largest arts fes-tival in the Miami suburb. | 305/447–0401.

Miami Film Festival. Sponsored by the Film Society of Amer-ica, this 10-day festival showcases international, domestic, and local films. | 305/377–3456.

Speed Weeks. This three-week celebration of auto racing culmi-nates in the famous Daytona 500, at the Daytona International Speedway in Daytona Beach. | 904/254–2700 or 800/854–1234.

SPRING

Mar. **Bike Week.** 400,000 riders descend on Daytona for 10 days of races, parades, and even coleslaw wrestling. | 904/255–0981.

Carnaval Miami. During this nine-day Latin blowout, Little Havana turns into Little Rio, and the nation's largest Hispanic celebration culminates in the 23-block-long Calle Ocho Street Party. | 305/644–8888.

Sanibel Shell Fair. For four days starting the first Thursday of the month, Sanibel's largest annual event pays tribute to the island's most famous treasure. | 941/472–2155.

Winter Park Sidewalk Arts Festival. Thousands of art enthusi-asts descend on Winter Park's trendy Park Avenue for one of the Southeast's most prestigious outdoor arts festivals, with internationally known artists. | 407/672–6390.

Late Mar.–Late Apr. **Springtime Tallahassee.** The capital hosts this major cultural, sporting, and culinary event. | 850/224–5012.

Apr. **Delray Affair.** The biggest event in the area, the festival includes arts, crafts, and food. | 561/279–1880.

1998
Walt Disney World opens its fourth major theme park, Disney's Animal Kingdom.

May 1999
Universal opens Islands of Adven-ture theme park and Universal Stu-dios CityWalk enter-tainment complex, to go toe to toe with Walt Disney World.

May **Air and Sea Show.** More than 2 million people descend on the Fort Lauderdale beachfront for performances by big names in aviation, including the Navy's Blue Angels and the Air Force's Thunderbirds. | 954/467–3555 or 954/527–5600.

Tropicool Fest. For two weeks, thousands attend more than 30 concerts, as well as arts and sports events around Naples. | 941/262–6141.

SUMMER

June **Miami/Bahamas Goombay Festival.** Attended by 600,000 participants, this Coconut Grove street party celebrates Miami's Bahamian heritage with parades, a sailing regatta, a beauty pageant, and plenty of Bahamian food. | 305/372–9966.

July **Walt Disney World Fourth of July fireworks.** The Fourth of July is big all over Orlando but perhaps nowhere as big as at WDW. | 407/824–2222 or 407/939–7814.

AUTUMN

Oct. **Fantasy Fest.** Key West stages a no-holds-barred Halloween costume party, parade, and town fair. | 305/296–1817.

Fort Lauderdale International Boat Show. The world's largest boat show (based on exhibit size) has boats of every size, description, and price displayed at the Bahia Mar marina and four other venues. | 954/764–7642.

Nov. **Jacksonville Jazz Festival.** Jazz performances, arts and crafts, food, and the Great American Jazz Piano Competition take up three days. | 904/353–7770.

Miami Book Fair International. The largest book fair in the country is held on the Wolfson campus of Miami-Dade Community College. | 305/237–3032.

State's Greats

It is simply impossible to run out of things to do in Florida, unless your aim is to do nothing at all. Toward that end, Florida's Atlantic and Gulf coasts have some of the best beaches around for sunbathing and people-watching, as well as swimming and water sports. More active sports enthusiasts find plentiful fishing—off piers, in the surf, and from boats offshore—along practically every inch of coastline as well as in freshwater lakes like Lake Okeechobee. Snorkeling and scuba diving are also popular in Florida waters but nowhere more so than in the Keys. Golf courses are found statewide but in particularly large numbers around Naples, Orlando, and Palm Beach. Hikers, canoeists, bicyclists, and others eager to get out into nature can hit the trail through every imaginable environment, and more and more people are doing so, contributing to the growth of Florida's eco-tourism industry. Theme park junkies can find a huge concentration around Orlando, but there are plenty of more modest amusement and marine parks all over the state.

That may take care of the daytime, but at night, Florida can be just as vibrant. Dining is high art here. Fresh seafood is an ever-present menu item from the Keys to the Panhandle. It's also easy to find varied ethnic cuisines, based on who settled the area and who lives there today. Florida's own mark on the culinary world can be found in the frogs' legs and gator tail of Miccosukee restaurants and in the fusion of tropical, Continental, and nouvelle cuisine called "Floribbean." After dinner, party animals have plenty of nightspots from which to choose in resort towns and big cities alike.

INTRODUCTION
HISTORY
REGIONS
WHEN TO VISIT
STATE'S GREATS
RULES OF THE ROAD
DRIVING TOURS

Beaches, Forests, and Parks

Although the question of which beaches are counted among the state's best is largely a matter of personal taste, those in the Panhandle should certainly rank near the top of any list. Because of restrictions against commercial development imposed by Eglin Air Force Base and the Gulf Islands National Seashore, the so-called Emerald Coast has been able to maintain several hundred miles of unspoiled strands. Blue-green water and white sand, often lined with dunes, are found at places such as **St. Joseph Peninsula State Park, St. George Island State Park, Grayton Beach State Recreation Area,** and **St. Andrews State Recreation Area.** On the Gulf coast, shell collectors favor the relatively quiet beaches of Sanibel Island, such as Gulfside City Park and Tarpon Bay Road Beach.

You can find just about any type of beach on the Atlantic coast. Perhaps the best pure beach is the 24 miles of undeveloped coastline at **Canaveral National Seashore,** from New Smyrna Beach to Titusville. Sand runs the entire length of Amelia Island's east coast; its northernmost section is in **Fort Clinch State Park,** which includes a well-preserved brick fort. For more action, head to **Daytona Beach,** where you can drive on the hard-packed sand alongside college students on spring break, or to **Miami Beach,** where families play, would-be models pose, and in-line skaters, parasailers, and volleyball players strut their stuff. On Key Biscayne, the **Bill Baggs Cape Florida State Recreation Area** has a nice beach, an historic lighthouse, and great views of the Miami skyline.

Picture trees in Florida, and chances are you'll think of palms. But northern Florida is home to some genuine forest land ripe for exploration. **Ocala National Forest,** north of Orlando, comprises 366,000 acres with profuse vegetation and natural springs, popular with hikers and water-sports lovers. **Apalachicola National Forest,** southwest of Tallahassee, and the nearby **Edward Ball Wakulla Springs State Park** retain a true southern feel, with cypress, pine, beech, and live oak draped in Spanish moss. In fact, Wakulla Springs is so lush, wild, and jungle-like that Tarzan movies were filmed here in the 1930s.

But Florida's natural areas comprise more than beaches and forests. More than 10 million acres of public and private land are set aside for recreational use, including 3,500 mi of hiking, bicycling, horseback riding, and canoe and kayak trails.

Water is the dominant feature of the state's two national parks, the **Everglades** and **Biscayne**: the former a grassy wetland good for canoeing, kayaking, and wildlife watching, and the latter best known for its coral reefs, which can be seen via snorkeling, diving, or a glass-bottom boat trip. A number of national wildlife refuges also let you see Florida nature up close. Notable is the **J. N. "Ding" Darling National Wildlife Refuge,** on Sanibel Island, where you can view the fascinating wildlife and vegetation from land or water.

Florida's Department of Environmental Protection is responsible for its state park system, which includes 151 state recreation areas, historic sites, botanical sites, archaeological sites, and geological sites. Here's but a sampling of the best the state has to offer: At **John U. Lloyd Beach State Recreation Area,** in Dania Beach, you can sit on a pine-shaded beach, canoe on Whiskey Creek, and watch cruise ships going to Port Everglades. **Sebastian Inlet State Recreation Area,** Melbourne Beach, is one of the most visited state parks, offering great fishing, great views from its tall bridge, and even great waves (by Florida standards). **Homosassa Springs State Wildlife Park,** north of Tampa Bay, is known for the Spring of 10,000 Fish and welcomes manatees, too. **Myakka River State Park,** southeast of Sarasota, has hiking trails, bike rentals, and airboat tours for superb bird-watching and gator sighting. **John Pennekamp Coral Reef State Park,** off Key Largo, contains sea-grass beds, mangrove swamps, and, most notably, coral reefs. **Bahia Honda State Park,** on Bahia Honda Key, has the only natural sandy beach in the Keys.

Additional natural areas are owned and operated by private organizations. For example, the **Corkscrew Swamp Sanctuary,** managed by the National Audubon Society, protects endangered birds and 500-year-old trees.

Culture, History, and the Arts

Sites that preserve Florida history are found statewide. One of the oldest and biggest is St. Augustine, a showcase of more than 60 historic attractions and 144 blocks of historic houses. The history revealed here ranges from the **Castillo de San Marcos National Monument,** a massive fort that's over 300 years old, to the **Lightner Museum,** built by Henry Flagler in 1888 as one of two fancy hotels.

The **Henry Morrison Flagler Museum,** in Palm Beach, tells more of the Flagler legacy through art and railway memorabilia, not to mention the mansion itself. **Vizcaya Museum and Gardens,** in Coconut Grove, is worth visiting for its formal gardens and fountains, as well as its impressive 15th- to 19th-century art and furnishings. Sarasota's Ringling Museums include **Ca'd'Zan** (Ringling's Italianate-style mansion), the **Ringling Museum of Art** (which houses his world-renowned collection of 17th-century paintings by artist Peter Paul Rubens), and the **Circus Museum** (which is home to circus memorabilia).

Other cultural treasures include the **Edison Winter House and Botanical Gardens,** in Fort Myers, seemingly left as it was when the inventor lived there, and Delray Beach's **Morikami Museum and Japanese Gardens,** a leading center for Japanese and American cultural exchange housed in a model of a Japanese imperial villa.

If you tire of museums, walk around towns filled with distinctive Florida architecture. Palm Beach is home to Addison Mizner's Moorish-Gothic creations, while Miami's South Beach is alive with the white and pastel hues of its restored Art Deco jewels. Soak up ethnic culture and food in Tampa's Ybor City (Cuban), Tarpon Springs (Greek), or Miami (Caribbean, Central and South American, European, Middle Eastern, Far Eastern, and then some).

Affluent year-round residents keep the arts flourishing in places like Naples, Palm Beach, Sarasota, and Miami. Performance venues include Miami's stunningly beautiful **Gusman Center for the Performing Arts,** which does a good impersonation of a Moorish courtyard; the **Broward Center for the Performing Arts,** the waterfront centerpiece of Fort Lauderdale's new cultural arts district; the **Raymond F. Kravis Center for the Performing Arts,** a glass, copper, and marble showcase in West Palm Beach; the **Tampa Theatre,** a historic rococo-style 1926 movie palace; and Sarasota's big purple **Van Wezel Performing Arts Hall.**

Sports

With more courses than any other state—1,170 and counting—Florida is a golfing heaven. It's home to the PGA's headquarters in Palm Beach Gardens; the **World Golf Hall of Fame,** part of the expansive new World Golf Village, outside St. Augustine; and some of the most famous courses in the world, including the Blue Monster at the **Doral Golf Resort and Spa.** Many professional events are staged around the state each year. Not far behind in popularity is tennis, and many resorts, such as the **Resort at Longboat Key Club** and Tampa's **Saddlebrook Resort,** have both excellent golf and tennis facilities.

Saltwater fishing is big on practically every inch of the coast. Many seaside communities have fishing piers that charge nominal admission and generally have a bait-and-tackle shop. Deep-sea boat-charter services are similarly plentiful. Destin and Fort Walton Beach, in the Panhandle, have especially large fleets, as do towns in the Keys. Inland, on more than 7,000 freshwater lakes, anglers try for bass, bluegill, speckled perch, and catfish ("sharpies" to locals). The 448,000-acre **Lake Okeechobee** is a favorite for catching bass.

Scuba divers and snorkelers do best in the coral reefs of the Keys, though there is some wreck diving off the mainland's east coast. Great Keys dive spots include **John**

Pennekamp Coral Reef State Park, Looe Key National Marine Sanctuary, and **Content Key.** You can also dive in the crystal-clear springs of northern Florida, but it can be cold.

Canoeists and kayakers paddle Florida's waterways from the Everglades to the Panhandle's Blackwater River and Coldwater Creek, near the town of **Milton,** the self-styled "Canoe Capital of Florida." Canoes and kayaks are also good means to explore the intriguing mangrove-fringed habitats of South Florida's margins.

Spectator sports grab attention, too. Floridians love their pro franchises, and there are several each in football, baseball, basketball, and hockey, as well as beloved college teams and the Boys of Spring (baseball squads who arrive for spring training). Polo is popular around the Gold Coast. Even more unique to Florida, however, are some pari-mutuel (betting) sports. Though horse racing, at famous tracks such as **Hialeah Park** and **Gulfstream Park,** isn't particularly unusual, greyhound racing and jai alai are. Dog tracks and frontons (the stadiums where fast-paced jai alai, originally a Basque game, is played) are found throughout the state.

Theme Parks

Most of Florida's major theme parks are clustered in and around Orlando. The Walt Disney World Resort is the state's biggest but not its first. Disney's four main parks are the **Magic Kingdom,** with rides and shows amid a fantasy world; **Epcot,** an educational theme park divided into two parts—one that looks at many technologies of tomorrow and the other examining the foreign cultures of today; **Disney–MGM Studios,** a park with a movie theme; and **Disney's Animal Kingdom,** which focuses on animals real, imaginary, and extinct. Add to that three water parks: the "snow"-capped **Blizzard Beach,** red-rock **River Country,** and tempest-tossed **Typhoon Lagoon.**

Universal Studios Orlando is anchored by **Universal Studios Florida** (another movie-theme park) and **Islands of Adventure** (populated by a bevy of fictional characters). It also now owns the **Wet 'n Wild** water park.

Anheuser-Busch parks in and around Orlando include the marine-life-theme **SeaWorld Orlando,** which includes the new **Discovery Cove,** where you can swim with dolphins, and the gardens-and-rides complex known as **Cypress Gardens,** famous for its water ski shows and its damsels in hoop skirts, which has been around since 1936. Farther southwest, in Tampa, are **Busch Gardens,** where African and Asian animals meet roller coasters, and **Adventure Island,** Busch's water park.

Other Points of Interest

Other sights worth putting on your itinerary include those you can only find in Florida.

At the **Kennedy Space Center Visitor Complex,** in Cocoa Beach, you can learn about the history of space flight on one of two tours. The complex is one of Florida's best bargains, and if you're really lucky, you might be in town for a space shuttle launch.

Join a nighttime sea turtle walk to look for females who come ashore to lay their eggs in the sand each spring and early summer. Nature centers on the Gold, Treasure, and Northeast Florida coasts (e.g., the **Gumbo Limbo Nature Center,** in Boca Raton) offer walks and encourage the marking of nest locations, so unaware beach frolickers don't ruin the incubating eggs.

Catch a glimpse of the endangered manatee at several places around Florida, depending on the season. A good area is the coast north of Tampa, where you might see manatees at the **Crystal River National Wildlife Refuge.** You can definitely watch the live "mermaids" at the timeless **Weeki Wachee Spring.**

Visit Tarpon Springs to watch sponge diving or **Ybor City,** in Tampa, to see and smell cigars being hand-rolled. Drive through citrus orchard country and taste fresh-squeezed orange juice, and try at least one food you've never had before—perhaps gator tail, Indian fry bread, Florida stone crab, conch chowder, or genuine (yellow) Key lime pie.

INTRODUCTION
HISTORY
REGIONS
WHEN TO VISIT
STATE'S GREATS
RULES OF THE ROAD
DRIVING TOURS

STATE PARKS

State parks are generally open 8–sunset and cost $2–$4 per person or $3.25–$4 per vehicle, depending on the park and its facilities. For further information, call the state park information number (850/488–9872).

Rules of the Road

License Requirements: Prospective drivers must be 15 to obtain a learner's permit, 16 to obtain a license.

Right Turn on Red: Unless posted otherwise, it is legal to take a right turn at a red light in clear traffic *after* a full stop.

Seatbelt and Helmet Laws: All automobile passengers must wear seatbelts, and motorcycle riders must wear helmets.

Speed Limits: Speed limits are 55 mph on state highways, 30 mph within city limits and residential areas, and 55–70 mph on interstates and Florida's Turnpike, unless otherwise posted. Be alert for signs announcing exceptions.

For More Information: Department of Highway Safety and Motor Vehicles | Neil Kirkman Building, 2900 Apalachee Pkwy., Tallahassee, FL 32399.

Gold Coast to Treasure Coast Driving Tour
FROM BOCA RATON TO VERO BEACH

Time: 5 days   Distance: 130 mi
Breaks: 1 night in Boca Raton; 2 nights in Palm Beach; 1 night in Fort Pierce

This tour takes you from Boca Raton to Palm Beach and along the Treasure Coast—one of the wealthiest places in the world. Consider staying an extra night or more in any of the coastal towns to enjoy the beaches. Palm Beach, with its Gatsby-era architecture, stunning mansions, and highbrow shopping is unlike any other place in Florida.

The weather is optimum from November to May, but the trade-off is that facilities are more crowded and prices somewhat higher. In summer you'll need a tolerance for heat and humidity if you want to spend time outside; also watch for frequent afternoon downpours. If you're set on watching the sea turtles come ashore to nest, make sure to visit between mid-May and early August, which is when most of the turtles lay their eggs, and remember that nesting occurs at night. No matter when you visit, bring insect repellent if you plan outdoor outings.

❶ Begin your tour in **Boca Raton** (off U.S. 1, 30 minutes south of Palm Beach). This upscale town at the south end of Palm Beach County reflects the unmistakable architectural presence of Addison Mizner, the principal developer of Boca (and her ritzy Palm Beach neighbor) in the mid-1920s. Visit the **International Museum of Cartoon Art,** showcasing more than 160,000 pieces of art created over two centuries by more than 1,000 artists from more than 50 countries. The permanent collection at the **Boca Raton Museum of Art** includes works by Picasso, Degas, and Matisse as well as notable pre-Columbian art and wonderful metal sculptures on the lawn. Hands-on interactive exhibits make the new **Children's Science Explorium** a definite kid-pleaser. Another big draw for kids is the **Gumbo Limbo Nature Center,** with its four huge saltwater sea tanks and long boardwalk through dense forest. Spend your first night in Boca Raton.

INTRODUCTION
HISTORY
REGIONS
WHEN TO VISIT
STATE'S GREATS
RULES OF THE ROAD
DRIVING TOURS

❷ From Boca Raton, drive 20 mi north on Highway A1A to **Palm Beach,** the indisputable focus of the region. This exceedingly wealthy town was also developed in the 1920s by Addison Mizner, whose Moorish-Gothic style is everywhere evident in the area. The **Henry Morrison Flagler Museum,** the palatial mansion commissioned by the cofounder of Standard Oil, is a must-see. Many of the original furnishings of the 1901 home are on display, and Flagler's personal railroad car, the *Rambler*, is parked behind the building. Originally built by Henry Flagler in 1895 and rebuilt by his descendants after a fire in 1925, **The Breakers,** a large luxury hotel, resembles an ornate Italian Renaissance palace. Walk into the lobby and take a look at the painted arched ceilings hung with crystal chandeliers, and peek into the ornate Florentine Dining Room with its 15th-century Flemish tapestries.

Break for lunch and then head to **Worth Avenue** (between Coconut Row and S. Ocean Blvd.) for some posh, pricey shopping. The ¼-mi avenue is lined with high-end shops and has many examples of Moorish-style architecture. Spend the next two nights in Palm Beach.

❸ On the third day, proceed west for about 2 mi on Royal Poinciana Way to **West Palm Beach.** Far larger than its wealthy neighbor to the east, West Palm has become the cultural, entertainment, and business center of the county and of the region to its north. There's a small but attractive downtown area, which has been spurred on by an active historic preservation movement. Along beautifully landscaped **Clematis Street,** you'll find boutiques and restaurants in charmingly restored buildings and exuberant nightlife that mimics that of South Beach. The **Ann Norton Sculpture Gardens** is a monument to the late American sculptor Ann Weaver Norton, consisting of charming 3-acre grounds displaying seven granite figures and six brick megaliths. The plantings were designed by Norton, an environmentalist, to attract native bird life. The **Old Northwood Historic District** (west of Flagler Dr., between 26th and 35th Sts.) is a 1920s-era neighborhood on the National Register of Historic Places; on Sundays you can take an organized walking tour of the neighborhood. Don't miss the **Norton Museum of Art,** constructed in 1941 by steel magnate Ralph H. Norton. The museum boasts an extensive permanent collection of 19th- and 20th-century American and European paintings with special emphasis on 19th-century French Impressionists.

❹ From West Palm Beach, drive 40 mi west on U.S. 98/441 to **Lake Okeechobee.** Rimming the western shore of Palm Beach and Martin Counties, this second-largest freshwater lake in the United States is girdled by 120 mi of roads; yet for almost its entire circumference, it remains hidden from sight. The Seminole's Big Water and the heart of the great Everglades watershed, Lake Okeechobee measures 730 square mi—roughly 33 mi from north to south and 30 mi from east to west—with an average natural depth of only 10 ft. Numerous small towns dot the lakeshore and offer small museums and dining and lodging options. The Florida Power and Light Company's Martin Power Plan maintains the **Barley Barber Swamp,** a 400-acre freshwater cypress swamp preserve. Here you'll find dozens of birds, mammals, and reptiles, as well as an impressive reserve of bald cypress trees. When you're finished exploring Lake Okeechobee, return east on U.S. 98/441 to Palm Beach and spend a second night.

❺ From Palm Beach, head north on Highway A1A to **Jupiter** (19 mi north of Palm Beach). There are no barrier islands east of Jupiter; the beaches are part of the mainland, and Highway A1A runs for almost 4 mi along the beachfront dunes. Visit the **DuBois House,** a modest pioneer home dating from 1898. Even if you arrive when the house is closed, surrounding Dubois Park is worth the visit for its lovely beaches and swimming lagoons. Permanent exhibits at the **Florida History Center and Museum** review not only modern-day development along the Loxahatchee River but also shipwrecks, rail-

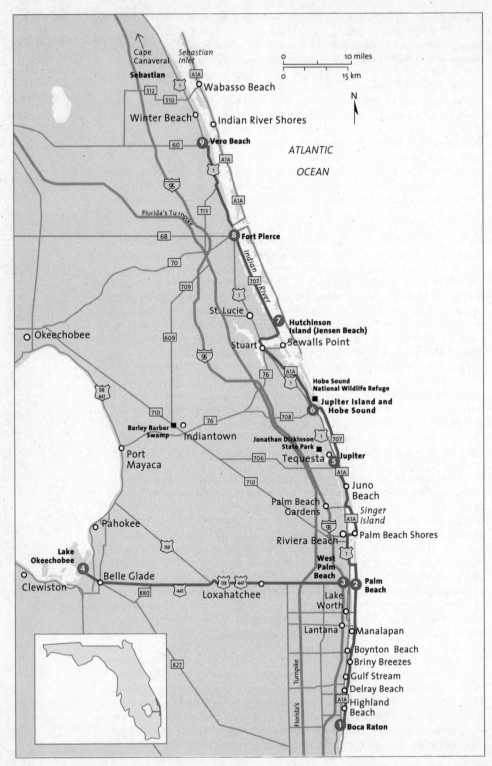

Cape
Canaveral

*Sebastian
Inlet*

Sebastian

A1A

512

510

Wabasso Beach

Winter Beach

Indian River Shores

60

9 Vero Beach

A1A

1

95

ATLANTIC

OCEAN

Florida's Turnpike

713

A1A

Okeechobee

68

70

709

8 Fort Pierce

707

Indian River

609

1

St. Lucie

95

7 Hutchinson
Island (Jensen Beach)

Stuart

Sewalls Point

76

A1A

1

98
441

710

76

Barley Barber
Swamp

Indiantown

Hobe Sound
National Wildlife Refuge

Jupiter Island and
Hobe Sound 6

708

Port
Mayaca

Jonathan Dickinson
State Park

706

1

707

Tequesta

Jupiter 5

710

A1A

Pahokee

Juno
Beach

Palm Beach
Gardens

*Singer
Island*

95

A1A

Lake
Okeechobee

4

Clewiston

Belle Glade

Palm Beach Shores

Riviera Beach

1

West
Palm
Beach

880

441

98

441

Loxahatchee

3

2 Palm
Beach

Lake
Worth

Lantana

Manalapan

Boynton Beach

827

Briny Breezes

Gulf Stream

Delray Beach

A1A

Highland
Beach

Turnpike

Florida's

1 Boca Raton

0 ————— 10 miles
0 ————— 15 km

N

roads, and Seminole, steamboat-era, and pioneer history. The **Jupiter Inlet Lighthouse,** a redbrick Coast Guard navigational beacon designed by Civil War hero General George Meade, has operated here since 1860. Tours of the 105-ft-tall local landmark are given every half hour, and there is also a small museum.

INTRODUCTION
HISTORY
REGIONS
WHEN TO VISIT
STATE'S GREATS
RULES OF THE ROAD
DRIVING TOURS

❻ Five mi north of Jupiter off Highway 707 are Jupiter Island and Hobe Sound. Visit **Blowing Rocks Preserve,** a 73-acre Nature Conservancy holding. The **Hobe Sound National Wildlife Refuge** actually consists of two tracts: 232 acres of sand pine and scrub oak forest in Hobe Sound and 735 acres of coastal sand dune and mangrove swamp on Jupiter Island. Trails are open to the public in both places. Turtles nest and shells wash ashore on the 3½-mi beach, which has been severely eroded by winter high tides and strong winds. Kids will love the baby alligators, baby crocodiles, and scary-looking tarantula at **Hobe Sound Nature Center** (on the grounds of the Hobe Sound National Wildlife Refuge). Once you've gotten to the **Jonathan Dickinson State Park,** follow signs to Hobe Mountain. An ancient dune topped with a tower, it yields a panoramic view across the park's 10,285 acres of varied terrain, as well as the Intracoastal Waterway. The Loxahatchee River, part of the federal government's Wild and Scenic Rivers program, cuts through the park and harbors manatees in winter and alligators year-round. Boat tours leave several times a day.

❼ From Hobe Sound, drive north on Highway A1A for about 15 mi to **Hutchinson Island.** Unusual care limits development here and prevents the commercial crowding found to the north and south, although there are some high-rises here and there along the shore. The small town of Jensen Beach, part of which is in the central part of the island, actually stretches across both sides of the Indian River. Citrus farmers and fishermen still play a big role in the community, giving the area a down-to-earth feel. Its most notable population is that of the sea turtles; between late April and August more than 600 turtles come to nest along the town's Atlantic beach. Built in 1875, the **House of Refuge Museum** is the only remaining building of nine such structures erected by the U.S. Life Saving Service (a predecessor of the Coast Guard) to aid stranded sailors. Exhibits include antique lifesaving equipment, maps, artifacts from nearby wrecks, and boatmaking tools. Run by the Florida Oceanographic Society, the **Coastal Science Center** consists of a coastal hardwood hammock and mangrove forest, a visitors center, a science center with interpretive exhibits on coastal science and environmental issues, and a ½-mi interpretive boardwalk. The pastel-pink **Elliott Museum** was built in 1961 in honor of Sterling Elliott, inventor of an early automated addressing machine and a four-wheeled cycle. The museum has antique automobiles, dolls and toys, and fixtures from an early general store, blacksmith shop, and apothecary shop. **Bathtub Reef Beach** (MacArthur Boulevard off Highway A1A) is a great place to take the kids because the waters are shallow and unusually calm for about 300 ft offshore.

❽ Six mi north of Hutchinson Island on Highway 707, you'll arrive in **Fort Pierce.** This community, about an hour north of Palm Beach, has a distinctive rural feel, focusing on ranching and citrus farming rather than tourism. There are several worthwhile stops here, including those easily seen while following Highway 707. Once a reservoir, 500-acre **Savannahs Recreation Area** has been returned to its natural state. Today the semiwilderness has campsites, a petting zoo, botanical garden, boat ramps, and trails. At the **Heathcote Botanical Gardens,** a self-guided tour takes you through a palm walk, Japanese garden, and subtropical foliage. As the home of the Treasure Coast Art Association, the **A.E. "Bean" Backus Gallery** displays the works of one of Florida's foremost landscape artists. The **St. Lucie County Historical Museum** includes historic photos, early 20th-century memorabilia, and vintage farm tools among other exhibits, while the **UDT-SEAL Museum** commemorates the site where more than 3,000 navy frogmen trained during World War II. Weapons, equipment, and exhibits are on view. Spend a night in Fort Pierce.

◉ Continue north along Highway 707 for about 1 mi to **Vero Beach.** There's a tranquility to this Indian River county seat, an affluent town with a strong commitment to the environment and the arts. At the **Indian River Citrus Museum,** photos, farm tools, and videos tell about a time when oxen hauled the citrus crop to the railroads, when family fruit stands dotted the roadsides, and when gorgeous packing labels made every crate arriving up north an enticement to visit the Sunshine State. The outstanding 51-acre **Environmental Learning Center** has a 600-ft boardwalk through mangrove shoreline and a 1-mi canoe trail. The center is on the north edge of Vero Beach, on Wabasso Island, but it's a pretty drive and worth the trip.

3 To return to Boca Raton, turn around and drive south on U.S. 1, Highway 707, and Highway A1A for approximately 90 mi.

The Florida Keys Driving Tour
FROM KEY LARGO TO KEY WEST

Time: 5 days   Distance: 90 mi
Breaks: 1 overnight in Key Largo; 1 overnight in Islamorada; 1 overnight Bahia Honda Key; 1 overnight Key West.

On this drive, most days you can gaze over the silvery blue and green Atlantic and its still-living reef, with Florida Bay, the Gulf of Mexico, and the backcountry on your right (the Keys extend east-west from the mainland). At a few points the ocean and gulf are as much as 10 mi apart. In most places, however, they are within 1–4 mi, and on the narrowest landfill islands, they are separated only by the road.

YOUR CAR'S FIRST-AID KIT

- ❏ Bungee cords or rope to tie down trunk if necessary
- ❏ Club soda to remove stains from upholstery
- ❏ Cooler with bottled water
- ❏ Extra coolant
- ❏ Extra windshield-washer fluid
- ❏ Flares and/or reflectors
- ❏ Flashlight and extra batteries
- ❏ Hand wipes to clean hands after roadside repair
- ❏ Hose tape

- ❏ Jack and fully inflated spare
- ❏ Jumper cables
- ❏ Lug wrench
- ❏ Owner's manual
- ❏ Plastic poncho—in case you need to do roadside repairs in the rain
- ❏ Quart of oil and quart of transmission fluid
- ❏ Spare fan belts
- ❏ Spare fuses
- ❏ Tire-pressure gauge

*Excerpted from *Fodor's: How to Pack: Experts Share Their Secrets*
© 1997, by Fodor's Travel Publications

INTRODUCTION
HISTORY
REGIONS
WHEN TO VISIT
STATE'S GREATS
RULES OF THE ROAD
DRIVING TOURS

Things to see and do are everywhere, but first you have to remind yourself to get off the highway. You may want to stop to rent a boat and find a secluded anchorage and fish, swim, dive, or simply marvel at the sun, sea, and sky.

High season in the Keys is mid-December through March, and traffic on the Overseas Highway is inevitably heavy. From November to the middle of December, crowds are thinner, the weather is superlative, and hotels and shops drastically reduce their prices. Summer, which is hot and humid, is becoming a second high season, especially among families and Europeans. Key West's annual Fantasy Fest is the last week in October; if you plan to attend this popular event, reserve at least six months in advance. Rooms are also scarce the first few weekends of lobster season, which starts in August.

❶ Begin the tour in **Key Largo** (56 mi south of Miami International Airport on U.S. 1). The first key reachable by car, 30-mi-long Key Largo—named *Cayo Largo* (long key) by the Spanish—is also the largest island in the chain. Most businesses are on the four-lane divided highway (U.S. 1) that runs down the middle, but away from the overdevelopment and generally suburban landscape you can find many areas of pristine wilderness. The 2,005-acre **Key Largo Hammocks State Botanical Site** is the largest remaining stand of the vast West Indian tropical hardwood hammock and mangrove wetland that once covered most of the Keys' upland areas. The site is home to 84 species of protected plants and animals. **John Pennekamp Coral Reef State Park** encompasses 78 square mi of coral reefs, sea-grass beds, and mangrove swamps. Its reefs contain 40 of the 52 species of coral in the Atlantic Reef System and more than 650 varieties of fish, and the diving and snorkeling here are famous. Spend the night in Key Largo so that you can enjoy some of the natural beauty.

❷ The southernmost part of Key Largo is Tavernier. Wood-carver and teacher Laura Quinn brought the **Florida Keys Wild Bird Rehabilitation Center** here in 1991, and nowhere else in the Keys can you see birds so close up. Many are kept for life because of injuries that can't be healed, while others are brought for rehabilitation and then set free.

❸ About 10 miles west of Tavernier is **Islamorada,** a group of islands that includes Plantation Key, Windley Key, Upper Matecumbe Key, Lower Matecumbe Key, Craif Key, and Fiesta Key. In addition, two islands—Indian Key, in the Atlantic Ocean, and Lignumvitae Key, in Florida Bay—belong to the group.

When the Florida East Coast Railway drilled, dynamited, and carved Windley Key's limestone bed, it exposed the once-living fossilized coral reef that was laid down about 125,000 years ago, now visible at the **Windley Key Fossil Reef State Geologic Site.** At **Theater of the Sea,** dolphins, sea lions, stingrays, and tropical fish swim in the 1907 Windley Key railroad quarry, whose huge blasted holes are now filled with seawater. The park has marine-mammal shows, sea-life interaction programs, snorkel ecotours, and cruises. **Somewhere in Time** is a small, unlikely combination museum and antiques and jewelry shop crowded with hundreds of interesting artifacts, including coins from the *Atocha,* rare ceramic containers, original 18th-century maps, cannon, solid silver bars, slave artifacts, religious medallions, rare bottles, and a corny diorama of two infamous English women who were pirates. Spend the night in Islamorada.

❹ **Lignumvitae Key State Botanical Site,** a 280-acre bayside island, punctuated by the home and gardens that chemical magnate William Matheson built as a private retreat in 1919, is still cloaked by a virgin hardwood forest. Access is only by boat—either your own, a rental, or a ferry operated by the official concessioner, Robbie's Marina, which also rents kayaks and boats.

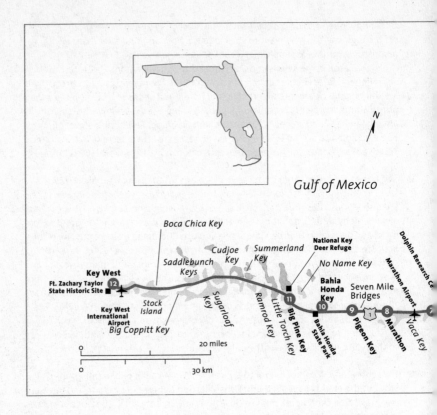

⑤ On the ocean side of the Matecumbe islands, 10½-acre **Indian Key State Historic Site** was inhabited by Native Americans for several thousand years before Europeans arrived. The islet was a county seat and base for early 19th-century shipwreck salvagers until an Indian attack wiped out the settlement in 1840. The island is reachable only by boat—either your own, a rental, or a ferry. To arrange for a ranger-led tour if you're using your own or a rental boat, contact Long Key State Recreation Area.

⑥ **Long Key** is about 10 mi west of Lignumvitae on U.S. 1. The most popular site on this island is **Long Key State Park,** which has a canoe trail through a tidal lagoon and a not-very-sandy beach fronting a broad expanse of shallow grass flats. Bring a mask and snorkel to observe the marine life in this rich nursery area. Hurricane Georges flooded the park's ocean side in 1999 and killed almost all the vegetation. Although the park is open, all repairs and replantings may not be completed by the time you visit.

⑦ Continue west along U.S. 1 for approximately 10 mi to **Grassy Key.** The island is primarily inhabited by a few families who operate small fishing camps and motels. The former home of Milton Santini, creator of the original *Flipper* television series, is now a **Dolphin Research Center** and home to a colony of about 15 dolphins. A not-for-profit organization offers a half-day program called DolphInsight, which teaches dolphin biology and human–dolphin communications and allows you to touch the dolphins out of the water. A 2½-hour instruction-education program aptly called Dolphin Encounter enables you to do just that in the water for 20 minutes.

⑧ Continue west on U.S. 1 for about 10 mi into **Marathon.** This community is the commercial hub of the Middle Keys. Commercial fishing—still a big local industry—began here

INTRODUCTION
HISTORY
REGIONS
WHEN TO VISIT
STATE'S GREATS
RULES OF THE ROAD
DRIVING TOURS

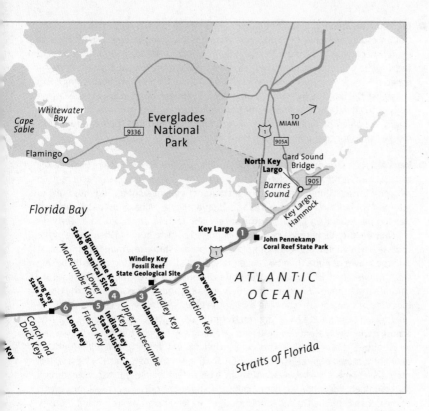

in the early 1800s. The **Museums of Tropical Crane Point**—a 63-acre tract that includes the last-known undisturbed thatch-palm hammock as well as several museums—has several hiking trails that will allow you to explore its area. **Sombrero Beach** has separate areas for swimmers, jet boats, and windsurfers, as well as a grassy park with barbecue grills, picnic kiosks, showers, rest rooms, a baseball diamond, large playground, and volleyball court.

⑨ From Marathon, **Pigeon Key** is about 5 mi west on U.S. 1. This 5-acre island under the Seven Mile Bridge was once the site of a railroad work camp and, later, a fish camp, park, and government administration building. Today it's a park focusing on the history of the Keys. You can tour the museum and historic buildings on your own or take a trolley tour. To reach the island, you can either take the shuttle, which departs from the depot on Knight's Key (MM 47), or walk across a 2.2-mi stretch of the Old Seven Mile Bridge.

⑩ Continuing west along U.S. 1 for 10 mi, you'll come to **Bahia Honda Key.** *Bahia Honda* translates from Spanish as "deep bay," a good description of local waters. The state government owns most of the island, which is devoted to 524-acre **Bahia Honda State Park.** A trail leads through a dense tropical forest where you can see rare West Indian plants and several species found nowhere else in the Keys. The park also contains the Keys' only natural sandy beach of notable size; it extends on both gulf and ocean sides and has deep water close to shore. You can get a panoramic view of the island from what's left of the railroad—the Bahia Honda Bridge. Spend the night in Bahia Honda Key.

⑪ **Big Pine Key,** about 5 mi west of Bahia Honda Key on U.S. 1, is known for its concentration of Key deer and the 2,300-acre **National Key Deer Refuge.** The refuge was established in 1954 to protect the dwindling population of Key deer, a subspecies of the Virginia white-tailed deer. They may turn up along the road at any time of day—especially in early morning and late afternoon. Admire their beauty, but feeding them is against the law. The Blue Hole, a quarry left over from railroad days, is the largest body of freshwater in the Keys. From the observation platform and walking trail, you might see alligator, birds, turtles, Key deer, and other wildlife. There are two well-marked trails for tromping through the area.

⑫ **Key West,** last stop on this tour and in the Keys, is about 20 mi south of Big Pine Key on U.S. 1. Key West has more of a city feel than the other keys. Few open spaces remain, as promoters continue to foster good restaurants, galleries, shops, and museums to interpret the city's intriguing past. As a destination, Key West has a lot to sell—an average temperature of 79°F, quaint 19th-century architecture, and a laid-back lifestyle.

Tour the **City Cemetery,** Key West's celebrated 20-acre burial place, on one of the tours given by volunteers. Among its plots are a bronze statue resembling a ship's mast and the graves of more than two dozen sailors killed in the sinking of the battleship U.S.S. *Maine.* The **Fort Zachary Taylor State Historic Site** (at the end of Southard St., through the Truman Annex) was built between 1845 and 1866 as a base for the Union blockade of Confederate shipping during the Civil War. There's great snorkeling, an uncrowded beach, and a picnic area on the grounds. While in Key West, don't miss the **Ernest Hemingway Home and Museum.** Hemingway bought this house in 1931 and wrote about 70% of his life's work here, including *For Whom the Bell Tolls.* Hundreds of brightly colored tropical fish and other fascinating sea creatures from Key West waters make their home at the **Key West Aquarium.** A touch tank enables you to handle starfish, sea cucumbers, horseshoe and hermit crabs, even horse and queen conchs—living totems of the Conch Republic. Guided tours include shark feedings. If you're into lighthouses, check out the 92-ft **Lighthouse Museum,** built in 1847, and an adjacent 1887 clapboard house, where the keeper lived. Spend the night in Key West.

To return to Key Largo, return north on U.S. 1 for approximately 90 mi.

ALTAMONTE SPRINGS

MAP 3, J5

(Nearby towns also listed: Maitland, Orlando, Sanford, Winter Park)

This upscale residential suburb, 10 mi north of Orlando, is the largest of Seminole County's ten towns. Its population of 40,608 has more than doubled since the early 1980s. Crane's Roost Park, in the middle of town, covers 37 acres, including a mile of lighted boardwalk and covered pavilions. The park is where residents come to relax, and is home to most of the city's major events and festivals. Staying among the housing developments, office parks, and shopping malls of Altamonte Springs may not be as glamorous as dwelling with all the Disney characters, but accommodations here are on average one-third less than comparable lodgings elsewhere in Orlando; Altamonte Springs increasingly offers relief to a growing number of visitors who are trying to escape the frantic tourist scene to the south. The town's name comes from an old spring at Lake Adelaide, discovered in 1887. Though Altamonte means "high mount" in Spanish, the 16-square-mi town is as flat as the majority of central Florida.

Information: Great Seminole/Lake Mary County Chamber of Commerce | 230 N. Westmonte Dr., Ste 1974, Altamonte Springs, 32714 | 407/834–4404.

Attractions

Crane's Roost Lake Park. This 37-acre lakeside park is a great place to spend a day relaxing in the sun. There are a 1-mi lighted boardwalk, covered pavilions, several park benches, and a 900-seat amphitheater. | Shorecrest and Northlake Blvd. | Daily.

Orlando-Seminole Jai-Alai Fronton. Jai-alai matches can be seen live and via simulcast at this stadium 1 mi east of Altamonte Springs. | 6405 U.S. 17/92S, Fern Park | 407/331–9191 | $1 | Daily 11:00 AM–midnight.

Wekiwa Springs State Park. This 7,000-acre park, off I-4 at exit 49, is 6 mi west of Altamonte Springs. If you have time to hike around, you can see how central Florida looked when the Timucuan Indians stalked the uplands and spear-fished in the area's spring-fed creeks. You can canoe, swim, bike, camp, fish, or just picnic for the afternoon. On-site facilities include 13 miles of hiking trails, RV hookups, a concession stand, and a spring for swimming. | 1800 Wekiwa Circle, Apopka | 407/884–2008 | $4 per vehicle | Daily.

ON THE CALENDAR

OCT.: *Taste of Altamonte Springs.* This all-you-can-eat showcase, held behind the Altamonte Mall at Crane's Roost Lake Park, dishes up local restaurants' favorite menu items. | 407/263–3780.

Dining

Amigos. Tex-Mex. Offering some of the best Mexican food in Central Florida, this popular restaurant, part of a local chain, serves up good basics. Order the Santa Fe dinner, and you will be able to sample tamales, enchiladas, and chiles rellenos. | 120 N. Westmonte Dr. | 407/774–4334 | Closed Sun. | $6.95–$11.95 | AE, DC, MC, V.

Bahama Breeze. Caribbean. At this festive restaurant you can sit inside or outdoors on the patio. Part of a small local chain, the Altamonte Springs location serves up to 400 people at a time. You can enjoy such dishes as the jerk chicken pasta or coconut prawns while listening to live Caribbean music. | 499 E. Altamonte Dr. | 407/831–2929 | No lunch | $7–$18 | AE, D, MC, V.

Enzo's Restaurant on the Lake. Italian. Although Enzo's is located on a tacky stretch of highway, this lakefront Italian villa serves up great appetizers, such as antipasti, mussels in white wine sauce, and imported buffalo mozzarella. The food is worth the 30-min trip from I-Drive. | 1130 U.S. 17/92S, Longwood | 407/834–9872 | Closed Sun. No lunch | $15–$30 | AE, D, DC, MC, V.

Gina's on the Water. Italian. The Old World charm of the upstairs patio and a cozy dining room lure the crowds to Gina's, where the view is of tranquil Crane's Roost Lake. Aside from the clay oven–baked individual gourmet pizzas, house specialties include fresh seafood, Tuscan prime rib, and fire-roasted shrimp scampi on rosemary skewers, an excellent follow-up to happy hour in the downstairs lounge (4–7). | 309 N. Lake Blvd. | 407/834–5880 | fax 407/834–6020 | No lunch Sat. | $11–$26 | AE, D, MC, V.

Kobe Japanese Steak House. Japanese. Chefs prepare your meal on a grill right before your eyes at this teppanyaki restaurant with a sushi bar. Kids love watching the action, and even picky eaters might find something on the special kids' menu of non-teppanyaki dishes. Tuna and California rolls are popular orders at the sushi bar. | 468 W. Semoran Blvd. | 407/862–2888 | No lunch | $17–$35 | AE, MC, V.

La Scala. Italian. This restaurant is perfect if you are looking for romantic dining experience. The mirrored walls and crystal chandeliers are only outdone by owner Joseph del Vento's tendency to break into operatic song every so often. Be sure to try the *osso buco* (braised veal shank). | 205 Lorraine Dr. | 407/862–3257 | Closed Sun. No lunch Sat. | $16–$28 | AE, DC, MC, V.

Maison and Jardin. Continental. You dine by candlelight at this romantic restaurant in a faux villa, which is decorated with oriental rugs and antiques. Known for rack of lamb with

Dijon herb crust. | 430 S. Wymore Rd. | 407/862–4410 | No lunch Mon.–Sat. Closed Sun. Closed Father's Day–early Oct. | $20–$35 | AE, D, DC, MC, V.

Pebbles. American. This California-style restaurant is a hit among Orlandoans and now includes five locations in addition to the original in Lake Buena Vista. Entrées include angel-hair pasta with smoked duck and scallops, and Mediterranean salad. | 12551 State Rd., 535 Lake Buena Vista | 407/827–1111 | No lunch | $5–$15 | AE, D, DC, MC, V.

Peter Scott's. Continental. This restaurant has great dinner entrées, such as roast Long Island duck, herb-crusted lamb, and Black Angus New York strip steak. There is live music nightly, including jazz and contemporary selections. In the separate lounge you can enjoy an excellent cigar and cognac. | 1811 W. Hwy. 434, Longwood | 407/834–4477 | No lunch. Closed Sun.–Mon. | $19.95–$36.95 | AE, DC, MC, V.

Romano's Macaroni Grill. Italian. This casual, family-oriented restaurant serves up good but not great pasta and pizza. For a reasonable price you can enjoy Italian entrées, such as *scaloppine di pollo Romano,* which is chicken with artichokes and capers served on angel-hair pasta. | 884 W. State Rd. | 407/682–2577 | $11–$14 | AE, D, DC, MC, V.

Straub's Seafood. Seafood. The emphasis at this well-priced seafood restaurant is on the food, not the atmosphere. Fresh fish, including blackened mahimahi and angel-hair pasta with sautéed shrimp are quite good. The menu even lists the calorie and fat content of every fish item. For a good deal, try the earlybird special from 4:30–6. | 512 E. Altamonte Dr. | 407/831–2250 | No lunch | $12–$22 | AE, D, DC, MC, V.

Lodging

Altamonte Springs/Orlando Travelodge. This three-story hotel is on 8 acres of tropically landscaped grounds. Every room has two double beds, and the executive rooms have sofas. Downtown Orlando is 9 mi away; Walt Disney World is about 30 mi away. Complimentary Continental breakfast. In-room data ports, in-room safes, some microwaves, some refrigerators. Cable TV. Pool. Playground. Laundry service. Business services. | 450 Douglas Ave. | 407/862–7111 or 888/515–6375 | fax 407/862–6663 | www.travelodge.com | 178 rooms | $52–$69 | AE, D, DC, MC, V.

Best Western Altamonte Springs. This three-story motel has a reclining chair in every room. For those planning a large gathering, there is a 600-square-ft meeting room. It's 18 mi from Orlando International Airport, 27 mi from Disney World. Restaurant, bar, complimentary breakfast. In-room data ports, some microwaves, some refrigerators. Cable TV. Pool. Gym. Laundry facilities. Business services. | 150 Douglas Ave. | 407/862–8200 or 800/327–5560 | fax 407/862–5750 | www.bestwestern.com | 144 rooms | $100 | AE, D, DC, MC, V.

Embassy Suites Orlando North. This pleasant all-suites hotel on the shore of Crane's Roost Lake features a landscaped, seven-story atrium lobby with two waterfalls. It's worth taking time out of your schedule to go fishing or jogging around the lake. Plus, it's 22 mi from Walt Disney World. Restaurant, bar, complimentary breakfast, room service. Kitchenettes, microwaves, refrigerators. Cable TV, in-room VCRs (and movies). Indoor pool. Hot tub, sauna. Gym. Business services. | 225 E. Altamonte Dr. | 407/834–2400 or 800/362–2779 | fax 407/834–2117 | www.embassy-suites.com | 277 suites | $109–$169 suites | AE, D, DC, MC, V.

Orlando-Days Inn Altamonte. This three-story motel offers basic rooms about a 30-mi, 45-min drive from Walt Disney World. Complimentary Continental breakfast. Cable TV. Pool. Laundry service. Business services. | 235 S. Wymore Rd. | 407/862–2800 or 800/544–8313 | fax 407/862–2804 | www.daysinn.com | 153 rooms | $89 | AE, D, DC, MC, V.

Hampton Inn Orlando North. This attractive motel built around a courtyard is 20 mi from Walt Disney World, 12 mi from Universal Studios, and 16 mi from SeaWorld. Complimentary Continental breakfast. In-room data ports, refrigerators. Cable TV. Pool. Hot tub. Gym. Baby-sitting. Laundry facilities. Business services. | 151 N. Douglas Ave. | 407/869–9000 or 800/426–7866 | fax 407/788–6746 | www.hampton-inn.com | 210 rooms | $89–$99 | AE, D, DC, MC, V.

Hilton Orlando/Altamonte Springs. It's 32 mi to Walt Disney World and 8 mi to downtown Orlando from this attractive, eight-story concrete and glass hotel. Rooms are spacious, and suites have separate seating areas. Restaurant, bar (with entertainment), room service. In-room data ports, some refrigerators. Cable TV. Pool. Hot tub. Gym. Laundry service. Business services. | 350 S. North Lake Blvd., | 407/830–1985 | fax 407/331–2911 | www.hilton.com | 322 rooms | $165 | AE, D, DC, MC, V.

Holiday Inn of Altamonte Springs. Poolside dining and cocktails, along with beautiful landscaping, make this motel, which is 27 mi from Walt Disney World, stand out. A three-story waterfall cascades into the outdoor, Olympic-size pool. Restaurant, bar (with entertainment), room service. In-room data ports, microwaves, refrigerators. Cable TV. Pool. Gym. Video games. Laundry service. Business services. | 230 W. Hwy. 436 | 407/862–4455 | fax 407/682–5982 | www.holiday-inn.com | 263 rooms | $99 | AE, D, DC, MC, V.

La Quinta Orlando North. This is a pretty hacienda-style motel 19 miles from the Orlando Airport, 18 miles from SeaWorld, and 28 mi from Walt Disney World. Some rooms feature sofa beds and recliners. Complimentary Continental breakfast. In-room data ports, some microwaves, some refrigerators. Cable TV. Outdoor pool. Business services. Pets allowed. | 150 S. Westmonte Dr. | 407/788–1411 | fax 407/788–6472 | www.laquinta.com | 115 rooms | $69–$99 | AE, D, DC, MC, V.

Residence Inn Orlando-Altamonte Springs. Every room in this all-suites hotel has a sofa bed and a full kitchen; some even have fireplaces. Every Monday and Thursday there is a complimentary dinner, which includes free beer and wine. Walt Disney World is about 30 mi away; Universal Studios and SeaWorld are about 20 mi away. Complimentary Continental breakfast. In-room data ports, kitchenettes, microwaves, refrigerators. Cable TV. Pool. Hot tub. Laundry service. Business services. Pets allowed (fee). | 270 Douglas Ave. | 407/788–7991 | fax 407/869–5468 | www.marriott.com | 128 suites | $145–$169 | AE, D, DC, MC, V.

AMELIA ISLAND/ FERNANDINA BEACH

MAP 3, J1

AMELIA ISLAND/
FERNANDINA
BEACH

INTRO
ATTRACTIONS
DINING
LODGING

(Nearby towns also listed: Atlantic Beach, Jacksonville, Jacksonville Beach, Ponte Vedra Beach)

Amelia Island is almost exactly the size of Manhattan (13 mi. long and 2.5 mi. wide at its broadest point), but no one would mistake this Victorian fisherman's village for New York. For starters, the Atlantic washes its entire western length with gorgeous beach backed by huge dunes. The island—named for British King George II's beautiful daughter Amelia Sophia Eleanora—has one town, Fernandina Beach, which boasts an impressive array of Victorian homes. The island is at the northeastern-most point in Florida, 30 minutes from Jacksonville and separated from Georgia by Cumberland Sound.

Bypassed by Henry Flagler's railroad at the tail end of the 19th century, the island was spared early development but still has an interesting history. Eight flags have flown here: the American, British, Mexican, Spanish, French, Union, Confederate, and even the flag of one independent-minded soldier. Fort Clinch, the island's most famous historic site, was used during the Civil War and the Spanish-American War. One of the nation's best-preserved forts, it is now the focal point of a 1,000-acre park.

Charming Fernandina Beach (pop. 12,000), the only town on Amelia Island, has quaint shops and lodging, and good restaurants. Often considered Florida's first resort town, it has over 50 blocks of stately Victorian homes. The rich and famous of yesteryear, including the Vanderbilts and DuPonts, frequented the town's Palace Saloon, which is regarded as Florida's oldest tavern. The Florida House Inn, the state's oldest continuously operating hotel, has housed dignitaries from around the globe, including former President Ulysses S. Grant. Today, luxurious resorts sprawl amid the pines and rise behind the beach dunes. Horseback riding is a common seaside sight.

Information: **Amelia Island-Fernandina Beach-Yulee Chamber of Commerce** | 102 Centre St., Fernandina Beach, 32034 | 904/261–3248 | www.ameliaisland.org.

Attractions

Amelia Island Historic District. More than 50 blocks of Fernandina Beach are a designated historic district, containing 350 ornate Queen Anne, Victorian, and Italianate structures that were built prior to 1927. You can pick up a self-guided tour map at the chamber of commerce, which is in the old railroad depot. | 102 Centre St., Fernandina Beach | 904/261–3248 | www.ameliaisland.org | Free | Office hours Mon.–Fri. 9–5.

Amelia Island Lighthouse This lighthouse was built in 1839 and is the oldest structure on the island. It stands at 107 ft. above sea level and is still functioning today; it's operated by the Coast Guard. You can look, but unfortunately you can't tour the inside. | 1 Lighthouse La. | 904/261–7378 | Daily.

Amelia Island Museum of History. There are two floors to this museum. The first holds the Eight-Flags "spoken history" exhibit, a narrated historical tour that discusses the eight countries that have controlled the island. The second floor holds many exhibits and photographs of the city from the time of the Civil War to the end of the 19th century. | 233 S. 3rd St., Fernandina Beach | 904/261–7378 | Museum free, "Spoken History" exhibit $4 | Weekdays 10–5, Sat. 10–4; "Spoken History" exhibit Mon.–Sat. 11, 2.

Amelia Island State Recreation Area. At the southern tip of the island, the 200-acre undeveloped section of salt marshes and clean, sandy beaches offers opportunities for fishing, hiking, bird-watching, horseback riding, or just relaxing in the Florida sunshine. | Hwy. 108 | 904/251–2320 | www.dep.state.fl.us/parks | Free | Daily.

Kelly Seahorse Ranch. Rent a horse here and go riding on the beach. | 7500 First Coast Hwy. | 904/491–5166 | $35 per hour | Daily, with organized rides every 2 hours from 10–4.

★ **Fort Clinch State Park.** Begun in 1847 on the northern tip of the island, Fort Clinch was never completed: As firearms became increasingly powerful, the fort, with its masonry walls, was obsolete. Still, it was occupied during the Civil War, first by Confederate and then by Union soldiers. Today, you can view artifacts, rifles, uniforms, and cannons from the period. There's camping along the Amelia River and the beach. A fishing pier near the beach has a small observation area where you often see dolphins and manatees. | 2601 Atlantic Ave., Fernandina Beach | 904/277–7274 | fax 904/277–7249 | $3.25 per vehicle; fort $1 | Park daily 8–sunset; fort daily 9–5.

ON THE CALENDAR

APR.: *Bausch & Lomb Women's Tennis Association Championships.* The best players gather each year at the Amelia Island Plantation for singles and doubles play. | 800/486–8366.

MAY: *Isle of Eight Flags Shrimp Festival.* On the first full weekend in May, more than 175,000 shrimp-lovers fill Fernandina Beach for this festival celebrating the area's shrimping industry. | 904/261–0203.

Dining

Beech Street Grill. Contemporary. Bay windows, second-story verandas, and marble mantels give this 1889 home a special charm. You'll enjoy such sophisticated dishes as Parmesan-crusted red snapper with mustard-basil cream sauce, or Mayport scamp grouper with macadamia nut crust and mango chili salsa, in one of the five dining rooms staffed by a courteous and knowledgeable group. There's also an extensive wine list. | 801 Beech St., Fernandina Beach | 904/277–3662 | www.beechstreetgrill.com | No lunch | $13–$25 | AE, D, MC, V.

Brett's Waterway Cafe. American. This nautical-theme restaurant overlooks Fernandina Harbor as well as the Amelia River. There is a porch for open-air dining. Try the steak and shrimp dinner. Pianist nightly. Kids' menu. | 1 S. Front St., Fernandina Beach | 904/261–2660 | No lunch Sun. | $14–$22 | AE, MC, V.

Cinghiale's. Italian. Just beyond the island, on the Intracoastal Waterway by Shave Bridge, this restaurant concentrates in northern Italian fare such as the *zuppa di pesci,* a soup made with shrimp, scallops, calamari, mussels, and snapper, and the scaloppine of yellowfin tuna. Another popular menu item is the roasted cinghiale: roasted wild boar. The deck and dining room overlook the Intracoastal Waterway. | 4768 Wade Pl. | 904/277–2336 | No lunch | $12–$19 | AE, D, MC, V.

Down Under. Seafood. This casual restaurant located on the Intracoastal Waterway serves up gigantic quantities of fried shrimp. The nautical theme is enhanced by the lapping water on the restaurant's floating docks. Some of the house specialties are grouper Monterrey (broiled grouper with sautéed onions, tomatoes, and Monterrey Jack), Dungeness crab boiled in a spicey brew, and their popular Key lime pie. | Hwy. A1A at the Intracoastal Waterway | 904/261–1001 | fax 904/261–1131 | No lunch. Closed Mon. Labor Day–Memorial Day | $14–$23 | AE, DC, MC, V.

Florida House Inn Dining Room. American. This restaurant, one of the oldest in the state, was established in 1865 and once served food to the likes of Andrew Carnegie. Today, the staff dishes up country-style food such as fried chicken, country greens, biscuits, and cornbread to regular folks, as well as beers from 100 different countries. You dine at long tables that seat as many as 12. | 22 S. 3rd St., Fernandina Beach | 904/261–3300 | No lunch. No dinner Sun.–Mon. | $12 prix–fixe | AE, D, DC, MC, V.

Golden Grouper Café. Seafood. Thrilling fresh catches complement the simple decorations of this lunch and dinner joint. The popular red pepper shrimp is served as an appetizer or entrée. Salads and soups are quick lunch ideas that can be enjoyed on the patio. For the deluxe shebang, try the mixed grill or the expertly prepared namesake, grouper. | 201 Alachua | 904/261–0013 | fax 904/261–1191 | Closed Mon. Memorial Day–Labor Day | $11–$22 | AE, MC, V.

The Grill. Contemporary. Fresh, Hawaiian flowers ornament the tables at this restaurant, one of the best in the state, at the Ritz-Carlton Amelia Island. The menu includes such dishes as bison tenderloin with grilled vegetables and salmon escallop with angel-hair pasta in a tomato-basil oil. Sparkling chandeliers add an extra touch of elegance to the ocean-view dining room. A take-out shop sells bottled versions of the restaurant's famous dressings and sauces. Pianist nightly. Sun. brunch. | 4750 Amelia Island Pkwy. | 904/277–1100 | No lunch | $65 prix fixe | AE, D, DC, MC, V.

Horizons Continental. This restaurant features banquettes, terra-cotta partitions, and burgundy and white tablecloths. Popular dishes include roasted duck breast, and sautéed grouper with lobster, Roma tomatoes, and Brie. Pianist Fri.–Sat. | 802 Ash St., Fernandina Beach | 904/321–2430 | $14–$19 | AE, DC, MC, V.

Joe's 2nd Street Bistro. American. Linen tablecloths, candlelight, and ceiling fans adorn the dining room at this romantic restaurant. It is also one of the few restaurants on Amelia Island where you can eat outside. Try the filet mignon with herb sauce or the red snapper with macadamias and sweet potatoes. | 14 S. 2nd St., Fernandina Beach | 904/321–2558 | $14–$21 | AE, D, DC, MC, V.

Le Clos. French. This restaurant, in a 1906 cottage, seats only 44 people for romantic, candlelit dinners. Enjoy light French fare, such as *coquilles St. Jacques* (sea scallops sautéed with shallots) and *confit de canard* (leg of duck with white beans and tomatoes). | 20 S. 2nd St., Fernandina Beach | 904/261–8100 | Closed Sun.; no lunch | $13–$22 | AE, D, MC, V.

O'Kane's Irish Pub. Irish. Authentic shepherd's pie, steak, fish-and-chips, and Guinness pie will fill you up in this traditional shamrock environment. The building is so old you might

AMELIA ISLAND/
FERNANDINA
BEACH

INTRO
ATTRACTIONS
DINING
LODGING

fear it will shake apart with the live music on the weekends (never a cover charge). | 318 Centre St. | 904/261–1000 | fax 904–277–4379 | $12–$20 | AE, MC, V.

Palace Saloon. American. Swagger into the oldest saloon in Florida for a quick bite or to catch a live music show on Friday or Saturday night. The original wooden bar has been here since 1903, though the rest of the building is more than a hundred years older. Lunch is a variety of standard dishes ranging from hamburgers, to deli sandwiches, to fried shrimp. You are at the chef's whims for dinner specials, as they range from fried fish to steak and potatoes. | 117 Centre St., Fernandina Beach | 904/261–6320 | fax 904/261–8855 | $6–$15 | AE, D, MC, V.

Lodging

Amelia Island Plantation. This 1,350-acre resort complex offers a pristine Atlantic-pounded beach and a multitude of activities. Though best known for golf and tennis, the property encompasses forests, marshes, and lagoons, making it an ideal place for hiking and biking. The majority of the standard rooms in the Amelia Inn and Beach Club have private balconies and spectacular ocean views. Suite-style accommodations are also available in the resort's condos. 5 restaurants, 2 bars, picnic area, room service. In-room data ports, some kitchenettes, some microwaves, some refrigerators. Cable TV, some in-room VCRs (and movies). 23 pools. Barbershop, beauty salon, hot tubs, massage. Driving range, 3 18-hole golf courses, putting green, 23 tennis courts. Health club, hiking, horseback riding, beach, boating, fishing, bicycles. Shops. Baby-sitting, children's programs (ages 3–17). Business services, airport shuttle. | 3000 First Coast Hwy. | 888/261–6161 | fax 904/277–5945 | www.aipfl.com | 249 rooms, 418 suites | $172–$215, $225–$334 suites | AE, D, DC, MC, V.

The Amelia Island Williams House. This magnificent B&B 1½ mi from the beach was built in 1856. Wrought-iron gates, sweeping verandas, exquisitely manicured grounds, and one of the most lavishly appointed interiors anywhere in the U.S. make this one of the South's most award-winning inns. Rooms are furnished with 17th-century European antiques and soft, romantic lighting. Several excellent restaurants are nearby. Complimentary breakfast. In-room data ports. Cable TV, in-room VCRs (and movies). Bicycles. No kids under 12. | 103 S. 9th St., Fernandina Beach | 904/277–2328 or 800/414–9257 | fax 904/321–1325 | www.williamshouse.com | 8 rooms (5 with full bath) | $150–$235 | MC, V.

Amelia Surf and Racquet Club. This elegant oceanfront hotel and country club offers charming private villas and a multitude of recreational and sporting activities. The Fernandina Beach golf course is 5 min away. All the units have balconies, and some rooms have ocean views. In-room data ports, kitchenettes, microwaves, refrigerators. Cable TV. 2 pools, wading pool. 4 tennis courts. Gym, beach. Laundry facilities. Business services. | 800 Amelia Island Pkwy. | 904/261–0511 or 800/323–2001 | fax 904/261–0512 | www.surfandracquet.com | 156 villas | $155–$175 | AE, MC, V.

Bailey House. Listed in the National Register of Historic Places, this 1895 Victorian B&B is magnificently decorated with authentic period furnishings. The house is located 1½ miles from the beach and is within walking distance of several excellent restaurants. Complimentary breakfast. Some in-room hot tubs. Bicycles. Business services. No kids under 8. | 28 S. 7th St., Fernandina Beach | 904/261–5390 or 800/251–5390 | fax 904/321–0103 | www.bailey-house.com | 10 rooms | $115–$175 | AE, D, DC, MC, V.

Beachside Motel Inn. This modest but pleasant motel is right on the ocean, the only Amelia Island motel so located. You can have a dip in the seaside swimming pool, or head right down to the beach. All rooms overlook the Atlantic. Complimentary Continental breakfast. Some kitchenettes, some microwaves, some refrigerators. Cable TV. Pool. Beach. | 3172 S. Fletcher Ave. | 904/261–4236 | fax 904/261–8336 | www.beachsidemotel.com | 20 rooms | $96–$165 | AE, D, MC, V.

Elizabeth Pointe Lodge. Built in 1992 in the style of an old Nantucket home, this B&B is right on the ocean. There's a wraparound porch where you can sit in a rocking chair and gaze out at the Atlantic. Each room has an over-size marble bathtub and fresh floral arrangements. Restaurant, complimentary breakfast, room service. In-room data ports, some kitchenettes, some refrigerators, some in-room hot tubs. Cable TV, some in-room VCRs. Business services, airport shuttle. No smoking. | 98 S. Fletcher Ave., Fernandina Beach | 904/277–4851 or 800/772–3359 | fax 904/277–6500 | www.elizabethpointelodge.com | 25 rooms | $160–$270 | AE, D, MC, V.

The Fairbanks House. You'll find 12-ft ceilings and orange wood cabinetry in this ornate 1885 mansion, listed on the National Register of Historic Places. Rooms are appointed with a selection of period antiques and reproductions. Three cottages offer more space than standard rooms, which feature four-poster canopy beds, wing back chairs, oriental rugs, and some fireplaces. Each evening drinks and hors d'oeuvres are served in the rose garden. The entire property is smoke-free. Complimentary breakfast. Some microwaves, some refrigerators, some in-room hot tubs. Cable TV. Pool. Bicycles. No kids under 12. No smoking. | 227 S. 7th St., Fernandina Beach | 904/277–0500 or 888/891–9882 | fax 904/277–3103 | www.fairbankshouse.com | 6 rooms, 3 suites, 3 cottages | $150–$250, $195–$250 suites, $175–$195 cottages | AE, D, MC, V.

The Florida House Inn. Ulysses S. Grant is among those who have spent the night in this inn, built in 1857, which is Florida's oldest surviving hotel. Listed on the National Register of Historic Places, it has second-story verandas, gleaming hardwood floors, and comfortable period antiques. Ten rooms have working fireplaces; five have hot tubs. The inn is especially dog-friendly. Restaurant (Florida House Inn Dining Room), bar, complimentary breakfast. Some in-room hot tubs. Cable TV. Laundry facilities. Business services. Pets allowed (fee). | 22 S. 3rd St., Fernandina Beach | 904/261–3300 or 800/258–3301 | fax 904/277–3831 | www.floridahouseinn.com | 15 rooms | $69–$169 | AE, D, DC, MC, V.

Hoyt House B&B. This beautifully preserved house, built in 1905 by a local tycoon, is an outstanding example of Queen Anne architecture. Rooms are romantic with their original Victorian furnishings. You can relax in the gazebo or sit on the porch swing while enjoying complimentary wine and cheese every evening. Complimentary breakfast. Some in-room hot tubs. Cable TV, some in-room VCRs (and movies). | 804 Atlantic Ave., Fernandina Beach | 904/277–4300 or 800/432–2085 | fax 904/277–9626 | www.hoythouse.com | hoythouse@net-magic.net | 10 rooms | $114–$159 | AE, D, MC, V.

The Inn at Fernandina Beach. Located less than 100 yards from the beach, this two-story motel is adjacent to a Shoney's restaurant. Other restaurants and shopping are within easy walking distance. Restaurant, bar, picnic area. Some kitchenettes, some microwaves, some refrigerators. Cable TV. Pool. Beauty salon, hot tub. Tennis court. Volleyball. Laundry facilities. Pets allowed (fee). | 2707 Sadler Rd., Fernandina Beach | 904/277–2300 | 134 rooms | $49–$89 | AE, D, DC, MC, V.

★ **The Ritz-Carlton Amelia Island.** One of Florida's very best, this resort offers lavish accommodations, complete with stunning antiques and authentic period artwork, with sweeping ocean views, and marble baths. You can spend the day relaxing on 1½ mi of beach, in one of three heated pools, or in a massage or treatment room at the day-spa. However, if you prefer a little exercise along with your relaxation, you can take advantage of one of the ocean-side tennis courts or the PGA Championship golf course. 3 restaurants (The Grill), 3 bars, room service. In-room data ports, minibars, refrigerators. Cable TV, some in-room VCRs. Indoor and outdoor pools. Beauty salon, hot tub, sauna, spa, steam room. Driving range, 18-hole golf course, putting green, 9 tennis courts. Gym. Shops. Children's programs (ages 5–14), playground. Laundry service. Business services, airport shuttle, parking (fee). | 4750 Amelia Island Pkwy. | 904/277–1100 or 800/241–3333 | fax 904/261–9063 | www.ritz-carlton.com | 449 rooms | $279–$525 | AE, D, DC, MC, V.

1735 House. Named for the year Amelia Island was discovered, this modest oceanfront B&B is perfect for a family getaway. One- and two-bedroom suites have ocean views, and breakfast is brought to you every morning in your own private dining area. The Atlantic is only 20 ft away, and you can relax on the patio or sit by the waterfall. Complimentary Continental breakfast. Kitchenettes, microwaves, refrigerators. Cable TV. | 584 S. Fletcher.

AMELIA ISLAND/
FERNANDINA
BEACH

INTRO
ATTRACTIONS
DINING
LODGING

Ave. | 904/261–4148 or 800/872–8531 | fax 904/261–9200 | www.1735house-bb.com | 5 suites (with shower only) | $111–$171 | AE, D, MC, V.

Walnford Inn. This inn, just one block from downtown Centre Street, is framed by a white picket fence. Inside, you'll find hardwood floors covered with oriental rugs; spacious rooms with stained-glass windows are furnished with period antiques and reproductions. One room has a fireplace. Complimentary full breakfast. No smoking. | 102 S. 7th St., Fernandina Beach | 904/277–6660 or 800/277–6660 | www.walnford.com | 10 rooms | $85–$175 | AE, MC, V.

APALACHICOLA

MAP 3, E3

(Nearby towns also listed: Panama City, Panama City Beach, Blountstown, Tallahassee)

Once a cotton-shipping port, sponging center, and ice and lumber manufacturing center, Apalachicola has been reincarnated as a major oyster farming area—in fact, the town calls itself the "Oyster Capital of the World." Nearly half the town's population of 2,700 is employed in the industry, producing 90% of the state oyster supply. Blue crabs and shrimp are also plentiful in Apalachicola Bay, and local seafood restaurants abound. Apalachicola, which meant "land of the friendly people" to the area's aboriginal people, lies on the Panhandle's southernmost bulge. Besides the good eating, historic riverfront warehouses, old inns and churches, secluded beaches, and the porches and verandas of old clapboard houses make the town an intriguing stopover.

Information: Apalachicola Bay Chamber of Commerce | 128 Market St., Apalachicola, 32320 | 850/653–9419 | www.baynavigator.com.

Attractions

Apalachicola Historic District. You'll find fine examples of antebellum architecture in the historic section of Apalachicola. The largest concentration of historic homes is in the area south of Avenue E (Highway 98), between 7th and Market streets. You can pick up a free walking tour map at the Chamber of Commerce during business hours. | 128 Market St. | 850/653–9419 | www.baynavigator.com | Free | Weekdays 9–5.

Apalachicola National Estuarine Research Reserve. The Reserve encompasses 193,659 acres of land and water, including two barrier islands, the lower 52 mi of the Apalachicola River, and the Apalachicola Bay system. The reserve's Visitor and Education Center is in the Robert L. Howell building in Apalachicola, which also runs public exhibits, lectures, education programs, and has an adjoining nature trail. | 261 7th St. | 850/653–8063 | Free | Daily; Visitor Center weekdays 8–5.

Apalachicola National Forest. The largest of Florida's three national forests, Apalachicola National Forest covers 565,000 acres of hardwood hammocks, pine flatwoods, lakes, and rivers. The Florida National Scenic Trail runs 73 mi through the forest. There is also an 8½-mi mountain bike trail and a 31-mi horse trail. Camping, fishing, swimming, and canoeing are all popular. The park spreads north of town and west of Tallahassee and U.S. 319. | 1773 Crawfordville Hwy. | 850/926–3561 | Free | Daily 24 hrs.

Fort Gadsden Historic Site. Fort Gadsden is a requisite tour for Civil War buffs. Built by the British as a base to recruit Native Americans and African-Americans during the War of 1812, the fort was abandoned in 1815 until used as a supply resource by the Confederate Army. It's in the Apalachicola National Forest in a town called Sumatra; follow signs of Highway 65. | 1773 Crawfordville Hwy. | 850/926–3561 or 850/643–2282 | Free | Daily 9–5.

John Gorrie State Museum. This museum honors Dr. John Gorrie, who, while searching for a way to cool the rooms of yellow fever victims, devised an ice machine that led to the invention of the air-conditioner. | 46 6th St. | 850/653–9347 | $1 | Thurs.–Mon. 9–5.

St. George Island State Park. The park occupies 1,962 acres, with 9 mi of undeveloped beaches, dunes, salt marshes, and pine and oak forests. You can camp and hike on 2½ mi of trails, which have observation platforms for bird watching. The park is on 29-mi-long St. George Island, a 20-min drive across the Apalachicola Bay from town. It's home to many of the area's top beach vacation accommodations, though these are primarily rental homes. | 1900 E. Gulf Beach Dr. | 850/927–2111 | fax 850/653–8219 | www.baynavigator.com or www.dep.state.fl.us/parks | Free; State Park $4 per vehicle | Daily 8–sunset.

St. Joseph Peninsula State Park. This pristine 2,516-acre park in Port St. Joe has 20 mi of bay and gulf beaches, but is most famous for its bird watching. Over 200 species have been spotted within the park, and the area is the top spot in the eastern U.S. for observing hawks during their fall migration. There are 119 campsites, luxury furnished bayside cabins, saltwater fishing, boating, canoeing, hiking on two ½–1 mi trails, and seasonal ranger programs. | 8899 Cape San Blas Rd. | 850/227–1327 | www.dep.state.fl.us/parks | $3.25 per vehicle | Daily 8–sunset.

ON THE CALENDAR

APR.: *Historic Apalachicola Antique Boat Show.* New and antique boats are on display in downtown Apalachicola. There are also exhibits which focus on antique outboard engines and model boats. | 850/653–9419.

NOV.: *Florida Seafood Festival.* This family event pays tribute to the Apalachicola Bay's commercial fishermen with arts and crafts, music, and, of course, lots of great seafood. | 850/653–9319.

Dining

Blue Parrot. Seafood. You can order just about any seafood dish under the the gaze of the hanging fish on the walls. Fresh grouper, crab cakes, or the surf and turf are house specialties to be enjoyed either downstairs or on the upstairs patio overlooking the Gulf of Mexico. At night the connected tiki bar livens up the neighborhood. | 68 W. Gorrie Dr. | 850/927–2987 | $7–$20 | AE, D, MC, V.

Boss Oyster. Seafood. Who would have thought oysters could be prepared in over 40 different ways? This place pumps out oysters by the hundreds in original and traditional dishes ranging from raw to baked; they are lathered with spices, cheese, bacon, or jalapeños, for example. Be sure to admire the old oyster boat on the wall, and if you are not into any of the seafood specialties, there is always steak or hamburgers. | 123 Water St. | 850/653–9364 | fax 850/653–2018 | $10–$25 | AE, D, DC, MC, V.

Caroline's Dining on the River. Seafood. This restaurant has great views on the Apalachicola River. You can eat indoors on the patio. There is also a regularly scheduled band upstairs. The seafood is great and includes such selections as shrimp, grouper, shrimp, scallops, and oysters. | 123 Water St. | 850/653–8139 | $15–$25 | AE, D, DC, MC, V.

Chef Eddie's Magnolia Grill. Seafood. The classy and intimate environment here comes complete with a viewable, climate-controlled wine room, a luscious dessert case, and formal gardens with fountains. For a real treat, try the surf and turf dinner of grilled pork tenderloin, crab-stuffed jumbo shrimp, and lobster in *beurre blanc* (white butter) sauce, or the time-tested Apalachicola oyster-stuffed tenderloin served with a Merlot bordelaise sauce. | 99 11th St. | 850/653–8000 | fax 850/653–2490 | Closed Sun. and 2½ weeks following Thanksgiving. No lunch | $12–$24 | MC, V.

Gibson Inn. Continental. Somewhat formal, with polished wooden floors and white tablecloths, this inn's dining room is a great place to stop in for breakfast, lunch, or dinner, even if you are not a guest. The chef conquers seafood, steak, pasta, salad, and dessert with vigor. Stuffed grouper Florentine or veal scaloppine served over fettucine are big hits along with rib-eye steak stuffed with portobello mushrooms and topped with crab meat. | 51 Ave. C | 850/653–2191 | fax 850/653–3521 | $17–$26 | AE, MC, V.

Oyster Cove Seafood Bar & Grill. Contemporary. This is a perfect spot to watch the sunset from the tropical dining room with a wall of windows overlooking Apalachicola Bay. Dining is a unique experience since you never know what accent the food will have on a given evening—Asian, French, Italian, or any other ethnicity is possible on the ever-changing menu. House specialties include a seafood turnover (a 4-inch-tall puff pastry topped with shrimp, scallops, and a roasted red pepper cream sauce), and all you can eat devilled crabs. | E. Pine and E. 2nd Sts. | 850/927–2600 | fax 850/927–3693 | No lunch | $12–$19 | AE, MC, V.

Owl Cafe. Cafe. The crayons and butcher paper on the tables are the casual part of this upscale café, but the extensive wine list is a welcome sight in the land of Zinfandel. Local artists' works hang on the wall and entertain you as you dine on seafood specialties such as crab cakes, fried oyster salad, or crispy Thai snapper served with stir-fried vegetables. | 15 Ave. D | 850/653–9888 | fax 850/653–3698 | Closed Sun. | $10–$22 | AE, MC, V.

Lodging

Best Western Apalach Inn. This dependable national chain motel is popular with families and business travelers. The modern complex is 2 mi from the Gorrie State Museum, 15 mi from St. George Island State Park. In-room data ports, some in-room hot tubs. Cable TV. Business services. | 249 Hwy. 98W | 850/653–2116 | fax 850/653–9136 | www.bestwestern.com | 42 rooms | $63–$85 | AE, D, DC, MC, V.

Coombs House Inn. This inn is housed in a 1905 Victorian-style mansion; the neighboring 1911 Coombs House East is just 80 steps away, and just beyond a separate carriage house. The two may be the most elegant homes in Apalachicola. They have hardwood floors, oak staircases, and nine fireplaces. You can relax on a rocker on the porch or enjoy complimentary wine and cheese weekends evenings in the parlor. Complimentary Continental breakfast. In-room data ports, some refrigerators. Cable TV. Some in-room hot tubs. No smoking. | 80 6th St. | 850/653–9199 | fax 850/653–2785 | www.coombshouseinn.com | 18 rooms (in 3 buildings) | $89–$199 | D, MC, V.

Gibson Inn. This charming four-story, tin roof inn with white wraparound porches is one of a few on the National Register of Historic Places still operating as a full-service facility. The property, built in 1907 and renovated in 1985, overlooks the bay and St. George Island. Guest rooms are unique in size, shape, and color. Furnishings feature Victorian touches such as four-poster beds, antique armoires, brass and porcelain bathroom fixtures, and claw-foot tubs. Restaurant, bar. Cable TV. | 51 Ave. C | 850/653–2191 | fax 850/653–3521 | www.gibsoninn.com | 30 rooms | $75–$125 | AE, MC, V.

St. George Inn. Each of the Old Florida–style rooms in this cozy inn has a unique identity, such as the "Total Escape" or "Dolphin Room." Down comforters keep you in bed; French doors lead out to the bay or the Gulf; and the attentive staff helps you with any special wishes. Boats and bicycles can be rented on the nearby beach. Complimentary Continental breakfast. Some kitchenettes. Cable TV. Pool. | 1305 Franklin Blvd., St. George Island | 850/927–2903 or 800/332–5196 | www.stgeorgeinn.com | 13 rooms | $79–$139 | MC, V.

ARCADIA

MAP 3, I7

(Nearby towns also listed: Lake Placid, Port Charlotte, Punta Gorda, Sarasota)

Arcadia (pop. 6,500), an inland town midway between Sarasota and Ft. Myers, 30 miles east of the Gulf of Mexico, exudes peaceful Old Florida charm. But during the 1890s as a cattle war brewed, it was considered by many to be the wildest town in Florida. Many died in cattle rustling, then a hanging offense. The town was built along the Peace Valley River during early colonial settlements. Today Arcadia still raises cattle in addition to citrus; its river, one of the oldest navigated waterways in the country, offers scenic vistas and canoe trips. It's also a popular fossil-hunting site; with simple tools, you're likely to find Indian beads and shark's teeth. The once desolate downtown area now has over 30 antiques shops, a café, and an ice cream shop under the shade of its many oak trees.

Information: DeSoto County Chamber of Commerce | 16 S. Volusia Ave., Arcadia, 33821 | 863/494–4033.

Attractions

Solomon's Castle. Adding to the list of unusual sites in Florida is this shiny castle constructed of metal printing plates discarded from a local newspaper. Within the castle you will find a museum of works by the sole creator of the castle, artist Howard Solomon, whose family lives within the structure and also runs a restaurant in a 16th-century Spanish galleon (designed after Columbus's *Santa Maria*) built by Solomon as well and moored just outside. The Castle is off Highway 665 between Ona and Gardner, about 20 mi north of Arcadia. | 4533 Solomon Rd., Ona | 863/494–6077 | fax 863/993–0755 | www.solomonscastle.com | $7.50 | Tues.–Sun. 11–4. Closed July–Sept.

ON THE CALENDAR

MAR.: *All-Florida Championship Rodeo.* Florida's oldest rodeo began in 1928 when ranchers came to town to show their skills roping, riding, and bulldogging cattle fresh off the range. In addition to the rodeo at the Fenton Arena off Highway 17S, events include a parade, a mock Wild West shoot-out, and barbecues. | 863/494–2014.

MAR.: *De Soto County Fair.* Local kindergarten through high school students display their work at booths at the fairgrounds south of town. Other displays showcase handicrafts, area businesses, and community organizations. | 863/494–5678.

Dining

Nav–A–Gator Bar and Grill. American. This Peace River restaurant, owned by the same company operating river cruises, offers regular boat trips around lunch and dinner. You cruise down the Peace and return for a meal on land. The restaurant has live guitar music Saturday afternoons, and is known for its grouper sandwich, which comes with fries and coleslaw. | 9700 S.W. Riverview Circle | 941/625–4407 | $9–$24 | AE, D, MC, V.

Paradise. American. Paradise is known for its large portions of catfish and prime rib, and for its seafood platter. Soup and an open salad bar come with every dinner. | 903 N. Brevard Ave. | 863/494–2061 | Breakfast also available. No dinner Sun. Closed Mon. from May–Oct. | $7–$14 | AE, D, MC, V.

Lodging

Best Western Arcadia Inn. This simple, single-story motel is right next to the rodeo, and 20 mi from Solomon's Castle. Complimentary Continental breakfast. Refrigerators, microwaves, some in-room hot tubs. Cable TV. Outdoor pool. Laundry facilities. Business services. Some pets allowed. | 504 S. Brevard Ave. | 863/494–4884 | fax 863/494–2006 | www.bestwestern.com | 38 rooms | $59–$69 | AE, D, DC, MC, V.

Historic Parker House. This B&B was the home of Jasper Newton Parker, one of Florida's original cattle barons, in the late 1890s. Antique Victorian furnishings maintain some of the style of that era. A living room, dining room, and veranda are available for all to use, and all rooms have fireplaces. Complimentary Continental breakfast. Cable TV. No kids under 10. No smoking. | 427 W. Hickory St. | 863/494–2499 or 800/969–2499 | www.desoto.net/parker | 4 rooms | $69–$89 | AE, MC, V.

ATLANTIC BEACH

(Nearby towns also listed: Amelia Island/Fernandina Beach, Jacksonville, Jacksonville Beach, Ponte Vedra Beach)

The towns along Jacksonville's barrier island—which include Atlantic Beach, and to the south, Neptune Beach and Jacksonville Beach—are often grouped together as Jacksonville Beach, but they remain separate municipalities. Atlantic Beach (pop. 13,000) is a laid-back town popular with surfers. Behind the beach's white sand and dunes are eateries and nightspots. Its existence as a resort town began in 1900, when Henry Flagler set up a railway depot on Atlantic Beach. A year later another one of Flagler's enterprises, the Florida East Hotel Company, set up a huge and very popular hotel, which remains today, though various changes in name and ownership, as the Atlantic Beach Hotel. Many residents work in Jacksonville but live here for its quiet, tree-shaded neighborhoods.

Information: **Jacksonville and the Beaches Convention and Visitors Bureau** | 201 E. Adams St., Jacksonville, 32202 | 904/798–9111 or 800/733–2668 | www.jaxcvb.com.

Attractions

Hanna Park. This 450-acre park along the coastline offers 15 mi of biking and hiking trails, pine and oak forests, campgrounds, picnic areas, and beach access. | 500 Wonderwood Dr. | 904/249–4700 | $1 | Daily 8–8.

Dining

Ragtime Taproom Brewery. American. A block away from Atlantic Beach you will find New Orleans flare in this local brewery. Nightly seafood specials are grilled over mesquite, or you can try traditional favorites such as bayou bouillabaisse or ragtime shrimp (beer-battered, rolled in coconut with a honey-mustard sauce). Wash your meal down with any of the six house-brewed beers on tap, or simply view the brewery in action from the glass window in the dining room. | 207 Atlantic Blvd. | 904/241–7877 | fax 904/247–5743 | $11–$22 | AE, D, DC, MC, V.

Sergio's. Italian. The northern Italian cuisine at this restaurant is prepared by the owner, who recommends the veal chops with wild mushrooms and angel hair Portofino. The exposed brick walls, white tablecloths, and flickering candles are perfect for a romantic dinner. If you'd rather sit outside, there's a little Italian courtyard. | 1021 Atlantic Blvd. | 904/249–0101 | Closed Mon. No lunch | $11–$25 | AE, D, DC, MC, V.

Lodging

Comfort Inn Mayport. This three-story branch of the national motel chain is 3 mi from the ocean. The poolside Outback Pub has a few billiard tables inside. Coffee and cookies are served all day. Bar, complimentary Continental breakfast. Microwaves. Cable TV. Outdoor pool. Laundry facilities. Business services. | 2401 Mayport Rd. | 904/249–0313 or 800/228–5150 | fax 904/241–2155 | www.comfortinn.com | 108 rooms | $69–$109 | AE, D, DC, MC, V.

Oceanview Motel. This hotel does indeed have ocean views, from across the street. All rooms have private balconies and full kitchens. Each unit has either a king-size or two twin beds. In-room data ports, kitchenettes, microwaves, refrigerators. Cable TV. | 60 Ocean Blvd. | 904/246–9514 | fax 904/246–9514 | ocvnview@bellsouthnet.com | 16 rooms | $68–$73 | AE, DC, MC, V.

Sea Turtle Inn. This large, eight-story oceanfront hotel has an elegantly tiled white lobby and comfortable, modern rooms with views of the Atlantic. The Plantains restaurant inside the hotel has seaview patio dining. It has 8,000 square ft of banquet space, so you may run into a wedding. Restaurant, bar, room service. Cable TV. Outdoor pool. Beach, bicycles. Laundry facilities. Business services. | 1 Ocean Blvd. | 904/249–7402 or 800/874–6000 | fax 904/247–1517 | www.seaturtle.com | 194 rooms | $139–$169 | AE, D, DC, MC, V.

BARTOW

(Nearby towns also listed: Lakeland, Lake Wales, Winter Haven)

Bartow (pop. 14,300), a small town 8 mi south of Lakeland in central Florida, is the self-styled "City of Oaks and Azaleas," for the proliferation of this flora, though citrus and cattle are its cash cows. Founded as Fort Blount in 1851 as a refuge from Seminole Indians, the town was later re-named after Francis S. Bartow, the first Confederate general to fall in the Civil War. Bartow is seat of Polk County, the state's fifth-largest, which boasts more citrus production than California. Main Street downtown features a stately courthouse, cafés, stately homes with elegant gardens, and an antiques district. You'll find a number of turn-of-the-20th-century homes that are now bed-and-breakfasts. Just south of Bartow on Highway 17 in Homeland, a boardwalk over the Peace River contains markers depicting the area's flora and fauna.

Information: **Greater Bartow Chamber of Commerce** | 510 N. Broadway Ave., Bartow, 33830 | 863/533–7125 | www.bartowchamber.com.

Attractions

Polk County Historical and Genealogical Library. Polk County's classic, white-columned 1908 courthouse was restored in 1997. The east wing houses the Polk County Historical and Genealogical Library, which houses several books on the history and genealogy of the southeastern U.S. | 100 E. Main St. | 863/534–4380 | Free | Tues.–Sat. 9–5.

ON THE CALENDAR
APR.: *Bloomin' Arts Festival and Flower Show.* This downtown festival, one of Florida's premier art events, draws top artists from the Southeast. Besides a huge display of art, there is a flower show, a quilt show, and a classic car display. | 863/534–4030.
DEC.: *The Light Up Bartow Christmas Parade and Promenade.* This parade celebrates the coming holiday season. There are games and food vendors, and Santa Claus attends each year. | 863/533–7125.

Dining

Catfish Country Restaurant. Cajun. This restaurant celebrates Florida's sports teams with booths dedicated to the Seminoles, Marlins, and Hurricanes, among others. The restaurant is known especially for its fried catfish, alligator, and frogs' legs. | 2400 E. Griffin Rd. | 863/646–6767 | $5.95–$14.95 | AE, D, MC, V.

John's. American. This congenial restaurant serves everything from seafood Palermo to Bourbon Street steak. There is an adjacent bar featuring live music most weekend nights. | 1395 E. Main St. | 863/533–3471 | $6–$12 | AE, D, DC, MC, V.

Lodging

Davis Brothers Motor Lodge. This motel is within walking distance of several eateries. Cable TV. Outdoor pool. Laundry facilities. | 1035 N. Broadway Ave. | 863/533–0711 or 800/424–0711 | fax 863/533–0924 | 102 rooms | $40–$55 | AE, D, DC, MC, V.

El Jon Motel. This motel is popular with golfers because greens fees for two people at the Bartow Golf Course are included in the nightly rates. The rooms here all come with Direct TV. Refrigerators, cable TV. Outdoor pool. Golf privileges, golf course. Some pets allowed. | 1460 E. Main St. | 863/533–8191 | 42 rooms | $41–$69 | AE, D, DC, MC, V.

Stanford Inn. This enchanting blue-and-white Georgian Revival cottage was built in 1900 for attorney Thomas Lee Wilson, who came from one of the oldest settler families in central Florida. Some of the original furnishings are still here. Four individually named and styled guest rooms and two separate cottages—originally a servants house and carriage house—are impeccably decorated with period antiques. All rooms have hot tubs and fireplaces. Complimentary full breakfast. Some in-room data ports, some kitchenettes, some microwaves, some refrigerators, in-room hot tubs. Cable TV. Pool. | 555 E. Stanford St. | 863/533–2393 | fax 863/519–0238 | www.wbus.com/stanfordinn | 4 rooms, 2 cottages | $125–$135 room, $145–$165 cottage | AE, D, DC, MC, V.

BELLE GLADE

MAP 3, K8

(Nearby towns also listed: Lake Worth, Palm Beach, Palm Beach Gardens, Palm Beach Shores, Riviera Beach, West Palm Beach)

The motto of this small, close-knit farming community (pop. 18,500), "Her Soil Is Her Fortune," refers to the town's deep agricultural ties. Belle Glade is the eastern hub of the 700,000-acre Everglades Agricultural Area, a crescent of farmland lying south and east of Lake Okeechobee. The town is just a couple of miles from the shore of the "Big O," as locals call the lake. In 1928, the same year as the town's incorporation, a hurri-

HURRICANES

When Hurricane Andrew ravaged areas south of Miami in 1992, Belle Glade residents could sympathize. Though Andrew was the most costly natural disaster in U.S. history—causing over $26 billion in property damage—only 50 people were killed, a toll that seems thankfully low considering the magnitude of its destructive path. That hasn't always been the case. One hurricane that lifted water off Lake Okeechobee in 1928 killed over 1,800 people in Belle Glade and surrounding towns. South Florida and Cape Hatteras, NC, are statistically the most probable spots in the U.S. for hurricanes to come ashore. Preparing for hurricane season—which lasts from June through November—is part of life in Florida.

The Belle Glade hurricane, unlike Andrew, didn't have an official name—this was a time before weather forecasting. Hurricane names, which run alphabetically, alternating now between male and female names, were developed in 1953 by the Tropical Prediction Center, which oversees the National Hurricane Center in Miami. As a tropical depression develops into a tropical storm, it gets the next name on a pre-established list.

The magnitude of a hurricane's power is ranked on an increasing scale of one to five, a system called the Saffir-Simpson Scale, after its meteorological developers. A tropical storm becomes a Category One hurricane if it reaches winds of 75–95 mph. Increasing wind speed—which can create a tidal storm surge, flip cars, and knock over homes and buildings—creates an exponential increase in power. Andrew was a Category Four hurricane. A Category Five hurricane has winds of greater than 155 mph. Only two such hurricanes have landed on the mainland U.S.—one in the Keys in 1935 (again, before naming) and Camille in 1969. Camille had winds gusting to 200 mph and raised water levels 24 ft above normal high tide, killing 143 people along the coast from Alabama into Louisiana.

© Corbis

cane lifted waves off the lake to kill an estimated 2,000 residents, leaving 15,000 families homeless. It stands as the third-deadliest natural disaster in American history.

Besides sugar cane, rice, and vegetables, the soil here produces another bumper crop—football players. Every year, Belle Glade's two high schools contend for state titles, and many players—more than might be expected of a modest town like this—head off with scholarships to play at top Division I universities. A handful have gone on to enjoy stellar professional careers in the NFL.

To the southwest lies Clewiston, the most prosperous lake town. It's known as "the sweetest town in America," thanks to the resident headquarters of the United States Sugar Corporation. Following north along Lake Okeechobee's east side are the towns of Pahokee and Port Mayaca. Indiantown is halfway to Jupiter, 6 mi east from Port Mayaca on Highway 76.

Information: Belle Glade Chamber of Commerce | 540 S. Main St., Belle Glade, 33430 | 407/996–2745 | www.bellegladechamber.com.

Attractions

Barley Barber Swamp. This 400-acre freshwater cypress swamp is cared for by the Florida Power and Light Company, as it is located next to their Martin Power Plant. There is a mile-long boardwalk for a stroll through the watery vegetation. Birds, reptiles, and mammals flourish in this lush environment, but humans are limited to small tours booked at least one week in advance. Special manatee walks are held in January and February, and special turtle walks are held in June and July. Call for schedule information and to make reservations. | Hwy. 710, Indiantown | 800/552–8440 | Free | Park daily, free regular tours Oct.–May, Fri.–Wed. at 8:30 and 12:30.

Clewiston Museum. This museum documents local history, including the growth of the sugar cane and ramie (which makes rayon) industries, to the construction of the Herbert Hoover Dike, to the local British Flight Training school which trained pilots for World War II, and even a WWII German POW camp that existed a few miles outside of town. | 112 S. Commercio St. | 863/983–2870 | Free | Mon.–Fri. 1–5.

Lake Okeechobee. The second-largest freshwater lake in the United States extends over 730 square mi, and has perhaps the best bass fishing in North America. Curiously, most of the lake remains hidden from sight along the length of its circumference. It's girded by nearly 120 mi of roads, a 30-ft-high grassy levee (known locally as "the wall"), and the Lake Okeechobee Scenic Trail, a rough track that is part of the Florida National Scenic Trail.

Lawrence E. Will Museum. The museum in the Belle Glade Library displays extensive materials on the town's history. On the front lawn is a Ferenc Varga mural sculpture of a family fleeing a wall of water that rose from Lake Okeechobee during the catastrophic hurricane of 1928. | 530 S. Main St. | 561/996–3453 | Free | Mon.–Tues. 10–8, Wed.–Sat. 10–5.

ON THE CALENDAR

APR.: *Black Gold Jubilee Celebration.* "Black gold" refers to the region's muck soil, which yields splendid crops of sugar cane and vegetables. This one-day event celebrates the end of the harvest season with entertainment, food, and fireworks. | 561/996–2745.

Dining

Dee Stefanos. Italian. This cozy, family-oriented restaurant is a local favorite best known for hamburgers, pizzas, and subs, as well as an occasional seafood special. | 15510 S.W. Trail Dr., Indiantown | 561/597–5600 | fax 561/597–2145 | $7–$16 | MC, V.

Lodging

Clewiston Inn. Built in 1938, the Inn is now on the National Historical Register and sports a colonial dining room and individually designed, antiques-furnished rooms. Lake Okeechobee is only a mile away, with fishing and boating opportunities. The Everglades Lounge puts you in the spirit of the area with a nature mural drawn by artist J. Clinton Shepherd, which wraps around the room. Weekly rates are available. Restaurant, bar, complimentary breakfast. In-room data ports, some kitchenettes, some microwaves, some refrigerators. Cable TV. Laundry facilities, laundry service. | 108 Royal Palm Ave., at U.S. 27, Clewiston | 863/983–8151 or 800/749–4466 | fax 941/983–4602 | www.clewistoninn.com | 48 rooms | $70–$89 | AE, MC, V.

Okeechobee Inn. This basic, two-story blue motel offers simple rooms with balconies overlooking the pool. Be glad you have a car because Lake Okeechobee is almost 2 mi away. No air-conditioning in some rooms. Laundry facilities. Pets allowed (fee). | 265 N. U.S 27, South Bay | 561/996–6517 | 115 rooms | $45–$75 | MC, V.

Seminole Country Inn. This inn's lobby greets you with cypress wood ceilings and a huge open fireplace, but the staff and the rest of the inn will blow you away with Old Florida charm and southern hospitality. The structure was built in 1926 and retains its tropical, Mediterranean facade. Each room is individually designed with old-fashioned quilts or mosquito netting artfully draped over the bed. The upstairs sitting room is complete with board games, but for more excitement the staff can set you up at a nearby ranch for a day of horseback riding, or fishing in nearby Lake Okeechobee. Special dinners are prepared in-house for Thanksgiving and Christmas. Restaurant. Cable TV. Pool. Laundry service. | 15885 S.W. Warfield Blvd., Indiantown | 561/597–3777 or 888/394–3777 | fax 561/597–2883 | www.seminoleinn.com | 23 rooms | $65–$95 | AE, D, MC, V.

Travel Motor Inn. This motel is about 3 miles from Lake Okeechobee and close to tennis, golf, and bowling. Cable TV. Basketball. | 1300 S. Main St. | 561/996–6761 | 26 rooms | $65–$75 | AE, D, MC, V.

BIG PINE KEY

MAP 3, D6

(Nearby towns also listed: Little Torch Key, Marathon, Sugarloaf Key, Summerland Key)

About half of Big Pine Key is taken up by the National Key Deer Refuge, an 8,000-acre protection zone for the small number of tiny Key deer, a sub-species of the white-tailed deer. In the refuge is Blue Hole, a freshwater lake in an old quarry, where you can spot alligators, turtles, and fish in sparking clear water. Much of the rest of the key is protected wetlands. A population of 4,200—settlement has progressed slowly over the past century, and the key bills itself as the "All-Natural Key"—tends to fishing and diving charters.

Information: **Lower Keys Chamber of Commerce** | MM 31, Drawer 430511, Big Pine Key, 33043 | 305/872–2411 or 800/872–3722 | fax 305/872–0752 | www.lowerkeyschamber.com.

Attractions

Bahia Honda State Park. Bahia Honda is unique among the Keys because of its extensive sandy beaches—probably the best in the Keys—and deep waters close enough offshore to provide good swimming and snorkeling. This 524-acre sun-soaked park sprawls on both sides of the highway, a few miles beyond Big Pine Key. You can do just about everything here, including eat, camp, canoe, dive, fish, walk along great nature trails, and rent boats. | MM 37, OS | 305/872–2353 | $4 per vehicle | Daily 8–sunset.

Blue Hole. This fresh water lake—the biggest in the Keys—is inside the National Key Deer Refuge. A walkway leads to an observation deck, where you can see alligators and turtles in their naturally crystalline habitat. | Key Deer Blvd. | 305/872–2239 | Free | Daily dawn to dusk.

National Key Deer Refuge. This 8,000-acre refuge protects the dwindling population of Key deer, an endangered species that grows only to the size of a dog. Just 250 Key deer are believed to exist. To view the deer, follow the self-guided nature trail off Key Deer Boulevard. Your chances of spotting deer are better at dawn and dusk. | Key Deer Blvd. | 305/872–2239 | Free | Daily dawn to dusk.

ON THE CALENDAR

JULY: *Underwater Music Festival.* In the second week of July, an underwater radio broadcast at Looe Key National Marine Sanctuary focuses attention on reef preservation. | 305/872–2411.

JUNE: *Big Pine and Lower Keys Dolphin Tournament.* Prizes are presented to those anglers who reel in the biggest dolphin (mahimahi) during this three-day fishing tournament. | 800/872–3722.

Dining

No Name Pub. American. The only thing fancy about this casual, old-time standard is getting there—turn north at Big Pine Key traffic light, right at the fork, left at the four-way stop, and over No Name Bridge. The restaurant, known for its fried shrimp, fresh grouper, and pizza, has been open since 1936. The ramshackle walls are covered with dollar bills, and the bar is made from a part of the old Seven Mile Bridge. | N. Watson Blvd. | 305/872–9115 | $7–$12 | D, MC, V.

Lodging

Casa Grande. This B&B is right on the Atlantic. The rooms open onto the patio or the private beach where a hammock is strung between two palms. Each room has a queen-size bed, couch, and Bahama fan. Complimentary full breakfast. Refrigerators. Cable TV. Hot tub. Beach, water sports, bicycles. No kids. | 1619 Long Beach Dr. | 305/872–2878 | 3 rooms | $119 | No credit cards.

Deer Run. This B&B, which has six rooms in two houses, has an acre on the beach all to itself. Some of the rooms have great ocean views, French doors, and Bahama fans; verandas have hammocks and paddle fans. There are also grills and decks overlooking the water. Complimentary full breakfast. Cable TV. Hot tub. Beach, bicycles. No kids. No smoking. | 1985 Long Beach Dr. | 305/872–2015 | fax 305/872–2842 | 6 rooms | $95–$165 | No credit cards.

Looe Key Reef Resort. Think "dive" in the sense that the operators of this resort know everything about diving and have a boat to take you straight out into the wild blue. The two-story hotel has lush gardens in the front and balconies looking over a canal. More pluses are the tiki bar, which rocks on weekend nights with live music, and two complimentary tanks and weights for those into diving. Restaurant, bar (with entertainment). Pool. Boating, diving, fishing. Shop. Laundry facilities. | Oceanside at MM 275, Ramrod Key | 305/872–2215 | fax 305/872–3786 | www.diveflakeys.com | 20 rooms | $70–$150 | MC, V.

BLOUNTSTOWN

INTRO
ATTRACTIONS
DINING
LODGING

BLOUNTSTOWN

MAP 3, D2

(Nearby towns also listed: Chattahoochee, Marianna, Panama City, Panama City Beach)

Blountstown (pop. 2,500), the seat of Calhoun County, lies midway between the Georgia border and the Gulf of Mexico, 50 miles west of Tallahassee in the Panhandle. From Blountstown, you have easy access to the Apalachicola National Forest, a 600,000-acre, wildlife-rich woodland park crossed by canoe trails and footpaths. Blountstown was named after John Blount, a Seminole Indian Chief who, as a guide for General Andrew Jackson, aided in the 1818 invasion of Spanish Florida. Blount visited President Jackson in Washington, D.C., and was rewarded with a reservation on the west side of the Apalachicola River. A restored 1903 courthouse downtown is a registered Florida landmark.

Information: **Calhoun County Chamber of Commerce** | 340 E. Central Ave., Blountstown, 32424 | 850/674–4519 | www.calhounco.org.

Attractions

Torreya State Park. Nineteen mi from Blountstown, this park offers camping, picnic spots, and a number of excellent nature trails. The Apalachicola River Bluffs Trail runs along the river past Confederate gun pits, bluffs, and hardwood forests. The Weeping Ridge Trail heads through one of the park's deep ravines. Rangers offer tours of the 1849 Gregory House and tell stories of river's-edge plantation life. | Hwy. 1641 | 850/643–2674 | $2 per vehicle | Daily 8–sunset.

Dining

Parramore's Restaurant Too. Seafood. This restaurant, which has wooden tables and booths, is the follow-up to the popular restaurant half an hour away in Sneads. The fried catfish and T-bone steak are among diners' favorites. | Chipola Rd. | 850/674–3400 | Closed Sun. | $8–$14 | No credit cards.

Lodging

Airport Motel. Blountville's only motel, named for the now-defunct local airport, sits quietly in the countryside. Cable TV. | Hwy. 20 E | 850/674–8168 | 30 rooms | $35–$40 | AE, D, DC, MC, V.

BOCA GRANDE

MAP 3, 18

(Nearby towns also listed: Cape Coral, Captiva Island, Englewood, Fort Myers, Matlacha, Sanibel Island)

Though Calusa Indians fished here a thousand years ago, only a railroad built in 1907 to transport phosphates led wealthy industrialists to discover Gasparilla Island, a 7-mi-long barrier island on the Gulf of Mexico midway between Fort Myers and Sarasota. Boca Grande became a winter camp for such names as Vanderbilt, Du Pont, Morgan, Astor, and Eastman. Many came to fish for tarpon, a game fish that can weigh up to 200 pounds. The annual "World's Richest Tarpon Tournament" continues that tradition today with a $100,000 first prize. Outfitters and fishing charters translate into a nice living for fishing guides and related industries in Boca Grande (pop. 2,000). Pristine white beaches line the entire Gulf side of the island. The east side faces Charlotte Harbor and Gasparilla Sound, and has a 750,000-acre protected estuary.

Information: **Boca Grande Area Chamber of Commerce** | Box 704, Boca Grande, 33921 | 941/964–0568 | www.bocagrandechamber.com.

Attractions

Gasparilla Island State Recreation Area. The Boca Grande lighthouse, built in 1890, is a focal point of this island park. A museum inside the lighthouse has exhibits on Native American history and fishing. There are many places to picnic, fish, and collect shells. | Gasparilla Island | 941/964–0375 | Free | Daily 8–sunset.

ON THE CALENDAR

JULY: *World's Richest Tarpon Tournament.* This three-day tournament attracts fishers from all over the country. The top prize is $100,000, and there is even a street party in downtown Boca Grande to celebrate the event. | 941/964–0568.

Dining

PJ's Grill. Seafood. For a unique experience you can try this hopping restaurant, which resides in a former theater built in 1927. The theater was active until the 1970s, but now it sports a huge 250-gallon saltwater aquarium and a menu featuring island cuisine. The pan-fried snapper is cooked in white wine and Key lime juice, or you can try the char-grilled filet mignon. Finish up with some white chocolate bread pudding. | Old Theater Mall, 321 Park Ave. | 941/964–0806 | fax 941/964–2860 | Closed Aug.–Sept. | $15–$30 | AE, MC, V.

Lodging

Anchor Inn. Experience downtown Boca Grande as if you actually lived there by staying in this friendly, family-style tropical setting. Golf carts are provided by the inn so you can make easy excursions around the island to explore the nearby marina or beaches in style. Rooms are uniquely set up with bright colors, white-tiled floors, and bamboo furniture. Kitchenettes, microwave. Cable TV. Pool. Laundry facilities. | 450 E. 4th St. | 941/964–5600 | www.bocabeacon.com | 1 efficiency, 1 1-bedroom | $100 efficiency, $185 1–bedroom | No credit cards.

Uncle Henry's Motel. Adjoining the marina of the same name is this little hideaway providing a picturesque backdrop for photos and vacations. The rooms are modern, bright, and surrounded by tropical landscaping. The motel is close to restaurants and shops, not to mention all the boating and fishing you can dream of. Refrigerators. Cable TV. | 5800 Gasparilla Rd. | 941/964–2300 | fax 941/964–2300 | www.bocagrande.com/motel | 16 rooms, 2 suites | $145 room, $225 suite | AE, D, DC, MC, V.

BOCA RATON

MAP 3, L9

(Nearby towns also listed: Boynton Beach, Deerfield Beach, Delray Beach, Pompano Beach)

Call it Boca. This upscale city of 72,500 has its nose in the air, and with reason. Like its ritzy cousin to the north, Palm Beach, Boca Raton was designed in Spanish Revival style by architect and developer Addison Mizner in the mid-1920s. The city was designed to attract the very rich, with landscaped gardens, theaters, and even a cathedral. Mizner Park, a swanky shopping district, bears the architect's name, but shops, galleries, and designer boutiques are scattered all about town. An array of cultural events, fine dining, and recreation makes the city eventful year-round. Boca's beaches epitomize the best of the east coast's ocean-swept, dune-ridged shoreline, where beach-goers descend flights of stairs to reach the sand. Beware of the city's hefty parking fees, designed to keep the beaches safe from the weekend hoi polloi.

Information: Greater Boca Raton Chamber of Commerce | 1800 N. Dixie Hwy., Boca Raton, 33432 | 561/395–4433 | www.bocaratonchamber.com.

Attractions

Boca Raton Museum of Art. This Mizner Park museum boasts a permanent collection with works by Degas, Matisse, Picasso, Klee, and Modigliani, as well as notable pre-Columbian, photography, African, and Oceanic collections. There is an outdoor sculpture garden and an interactive education gallery for kids. | 501 Plaza Real | 561/392–2500 | fax 561/391–6410 | www.bocamuseum.org | $6 | Mon.–Tues. and Thur.–Fri. 10–9, Sat. 10–5.

Children's Museum. This museum explores history, science, and humanities through hands-on exhibits such as Dr. Dig's Back Porch, where kids uncover fossils and win prizes. The museum celebrates Florida's cultural history in The Faces, an exhibit that features crafts, costumes, and storytelling from various countries. | 498 Crawford Blvd. | 561/368–6875 | fax 561/395–7764 | $2 | Tues.–Sat. 12–4.

Children's Science Explorium. In this Sugar Sand Park interactive attraction, kids can create their own laser light shows, explore a 3-D kiosk that illustrates wave motion, and have fun with wind tunnels, microscopes, and microwave and radiation experiment stations. | 300 S. Military Tr. | 561/347–3913 | Free | Weekdays 9–6, weekends 10–5.

Gumbo Limbo Nature Center. This environmental education center has a long boardwalk through dense forest to a 50-ft tower you can climb to overlook the tree canopy. Four huge saltwater tanks house sea turtles, mangroves, and coral. Habitats include a coastal dune, a tropical hardwood hammock, and a sabal palm hammock. From mid-May to mid-July staff members lead nighttime walks to see nesting sea turtles come ashore and lay their eggs. In August, witness hatchlings being released. The center is on an island off A1A, 10 min. from downtown Boca. | 1801 N. Ocean Blvd. | 561/338–1473 | Free | Mon.–Sat. 9–4, Sun. 12–4.

International Museum of Cartoon Art. This Mizner Park museum is the only one of its kind in the world, showing off over 160,000 original drawings by cartoonists from more than 50 countries. The collection embraces every genre of cartoon art, including animation, comic books, editorial cartoons, greeting cards, and computer generated art, as well as a 10,000-volume library, and a film and tape archive. | 201 Plaza Real | 561/391–2200 | www.cartoon.org | $6 | Tues.–Sat. 10–6, Sun. 12–6.

Mizner Park. This 30-acre, open-air shopping village has apartments and town houses among its gardenlike spaces. Some 50 specialty shops include restaurants, museums, outdoor cafés and 12 movie screens. An outdoor amphitheater has occasional ballet productions and performances by the Florida Philharmonic. | N.E. 2nd St., at Federal Hwy. | 561/362–0606 | www.mizner-park.com | Free | Mon.–Sat. 10–9, Sun. 12–6.

ON THE CALENDAR

JAN.–APR.: *Royal Palm Polo.* The sport of kings has been played at this club since 1959. Matches are Sundays at 1 and 3. Brunch and full concessions are available. | 561/994–1876.

MAR.: *Meet Me Downtown.* Some 400 arts and crafts booths line Mizner Park along Federal Highway during Boca Raton's largest arts and entertainment festival. There are also carnival rides, a bevy of food vendors, and stages set up for live music. | 561/395–4433.

Dining

Arturo's Ristorante. Italian. Fettucine with black truffles and torta primavera are two of the most popular dishes at this restaurant. The dining room is formal and quiet; there is also a patio-style room with large windows and a lot of greenery. For private parties, you can use the banquet room, which has a special menu. | 6750 N. Federal Hwy. | 561/997–7373 | Jacket required for formal dining room | No lunch weekends | $25–$37 | AE, D, DC, MC, V.

Carmen's. Continental. This restaurant atop the Radisson Bridge Resort has views of the Intracoastal Waterway. There is a buffet that changes throughout the week between different cuisines. Popular dishes from the menu include filet mignon, veal chops, and fresh grouper. There's live music throughout the week including Sunday brunch. | 999 E. Camino Real | 561/750–8354 | Closed Mon. No lunch Tues.–Sat. | $19–$34 | AE, D, DC, MC, V.

Crab House Seafood Restaurant. Seafood. The front of this lovely restaurant is completely enclosed by huge windows that overlook a small lake. A nautical theme runs throughout, with a wide deck for outdoor dining, a tiki bar, and live music weekend nights. It may be no surprise that the Crab House is known for its crab dishes; the crab cakes may be the best of all. | 6909 S.W. 18th St. | 561/750–0498 | $12–$20 | AE, D, DC, MC, V.

Firehouse. American. When you see the fire engine parked out front, you'll know you're at the right place. Popular dishes at this firefighter's shrine include prime rib and salmon. Old fire extinguishers and patches line the walls. | 6751 N. Federal Hwy. | 561/997–6006 | No lunch Jun.–Oct. | $14–$26 | AE, D, MC, V.

Gigi's. French. This Parisian-style brasserie is popular with locals, who sit at granite-top tables or on the patio. There are an oyster bar and 40 wines available by the glass. There is live music Tues. and Thur.–Sat. | 346 Plaza Real | 561/368–4488 | $13–$29 | AE, D, DC, MC, V.

Guppy's. American. This loud sports restaurant has several TVs tuned in to various sporting events. Fare is simple, but ribs and chicken wings are among the favorites. | 45 S. Federal Hwy. | 561/395–4699 | $8–$14 | AE, D, MC, V.

Kathy's Gazebo Cafe. Continental. This upscale restaurant with a French outlook on cuisine has long been among Boca's most popular restaurants. Highly rated for food, wine list, and service, it's said that Gazebo was serving fresh fish before the rest of Boca caught on. Signature dishes include fresh Dover sole and duck. | 4199 N. Federal Hwy. | 561/395–6032 | Closed Aug.–mid-Sept. and Sun. May–Dec. No lunch weekends | $24–$35 | AE, MC, V.

Ristorante La Finestra. Italian. Nightly piano music and Belle Epoque lithographs on the walls set the mood, but come for the cuisine itself. The portobello mushroom with garlic or roasted red peppers and anchovies are top starters. For the main course, try a pasta dish such as rigatoni *Bolognese* (with ground veal, marinara sauce, and Parmesan). | 171 E. Palmetto Park Rd. | 561/392–1838 | No lunch. Closed Sun. | $18–$34 | AE, D, DC, MC, V.

La Petite Maison. French. The relaxed mood—you can dine in an air-conditioned porch—reflects the owners' French-Caribbean background. The restaurant is known for its broiled lobster with garlic, and its duck magret. Brunch is served Sundays. | 366 E. Palmetto Park Rd. | 561/750–7483 | No lunch | $15–$35 | AE, D, DC, MC, V.

La Tre. Vietnamese. This simple, stylish eatery is popular for its adventuresome menu; Binh Duong has long been considered one of the southeast's top chefs. Vegetarians will appreciate the crispy eggplant and the Happy Pancake (a Vietnamese crêpe stuffed with pork, shrimp, and vegetables). The tamarind squid is another winner. | 249 E. Palmetto Park Rd. | 561/392–4568 | No lunch Sun. | $12–$17 | AE, DC, MC, V.

La Vieille Maison. French. You can dine in one of nine intimate rooms at this Gold Coast culinary temple that evokes dining in southern France. An open-air courtyard has garden tables around fountains and a pond. Prix-fixe and à la carte menus feature Provençal dishes such as *soupe au pistou* (vegetable soup with basil and Parmesan cheese), and venison chop with red currant–pepper sauce and roasted chestnuts. The wine list has over 400 selections. | 770 E. Palmetto Park Rd. | 561/391–6701 | Reservations essential | Closed early July–Aug. | $18–$44 | AE, D, DC, MC, V.

La Villetta. Italian. This family-operated restaurant has been in business for 7 years. Oil paintings hang on the walls and fresh roses adorn every table. The owner prepares excellent Italian cuisine, such as yellow tail snapper encrusted in sea salt. Be sure to make reservations in advance. | 4351 N. Federal Hwy. | 561/362–8403 | No lunch | $25–$37 | AE, MC, V.

Mario's of Boca. Italian. This popular bistro serves up hearty portions of pasta, chicken, and fish. The dining room is laid-back and noisy; an outdoor patio is a refuge. A sampling of vegetarian appetizers alone gives an idea of the range: zucchine fritte, marinated portobello mushrooms, Roman-style baby artichokes, deli-style roast peppers, eggplant pancakes, sautéed spinach and endive, zucchini and mozzarella dumplings, and bruschetta. | 2200 Glades Rd. | 561/392–5595 | Reservations not accepted | $10–$24 | AE, MC, V.

Mark's at the Park. Contemporary. Eclectic styles prevail in the modern and Art Deco furnishings as well as the food. Outdoor seating is available and Thursday nights you can eat while enjoying live jazz. A house appetizer is the carpaccio of Atlantic salmon and tartare of yellow fish served on a bed of mizuna and drizzled with a soy-lime vinaigrette; a killer entrée is the roasted garlic–stuffed beef tenderloin served with baked Gorgonzola polenta, sweet onion confit, sugar snap peas, and rosemary cabernet sauce. | 344 Plaza Real, Mizner Park | 561/395–0770 | fax 561/392–4070 | $16–$32 | AE, D, DC, MC, V.

Max's Grille. Contemporary. This restaurant overlooking Mizner Park has 29 tables and is surrounded by gazebos and flowers. You can dine inside, or on the patio. Popular entrées include lobster boiled with clams and oysters, and meatloaf. Sun. brunch. | 404 Plaza Real | 561/368–0080 | $13–$25 | AE, D, DC, MC, V.

Pete Rose Ballpark Cafe. American. This sports bar and restaurant has 58 TVs tuned into various sporting events. There are three pool tables and a video arcade. Popular dishes include baby back ribs, fajitas, and prime rib. | 8144 W. Glades Rd. | 561/488–7383 | $7–$13 | AE, D, DC, MC, V.

Pete's Boca Raton. Continental. This elegant restaurant (no relation to the sports café above) has three bars, a dance floor, and live music Tues.–Sun. Try the 2-inch-thick swordfish or live Maine lobster. | 7940 Glades Rd. | 561/487–1600 | $15–$40 | AE, D, DC, MC, V.

Prezzo. Italian. A wood-fired brick oven is the centerpiece of this friendly, stylish restaurant. You can eat outside during the winter or sit indoors and watch pizzas being prepared. The baba ghanouj pizza with eggplant puree, pine nuts, spinach, and goat cheese is one of the most popular dishes. | 7820 Glades Rd. | 561/451–2800 | Reservations not accepted | No lunch weekends | $10–$24 | AE, MC, V.

Red Bowl Rice & Noodle Company. American. The vibrant crowd here is lucky to have such good food as well as 16 TV screens on which to watch the day's sporting events. The upscale sports bar dishes out a tasty rack of pork ribs or a hearty 9-oz fillet of beef. After dinner try some chocolate fudge cake before you head over to the pool table or dart boards. Karaoke on Saturday nights. | 22191 Powerline Rd. | 561/394–6699 | fax 561/394–6675 | $10–$15 | AE, MC, V.

Renzo's of Boca. Italian. The southern Italian cuisine at this family-friendly restaurant filled with tapestries includes chicken Gorgonzola, capellini veneziana, and gnocchi with a choice of several cream sauces. | 5999 N. Federal Hwy. | 561/994–3495 | No lunch | $17–$28 | AE, D, DC, MC, V.

Tavern in the Greenery. Continental. The name of this restaurant alludes to the famous eatery in Central Park. While it's not set within a city park, tables are under a six-story glass ceiling in a garden with palm trees, flowers, and a fountain. There is live music daily in winter. The rack of lamb and Dover sole are among the most popular dishes. | 301 Yamato Rd. | 561/241–9214 | $15–$33 | AE, D, MC, V.

Tom's Place. Soul food. A heavenly experience is on hand when you sample a taste of Tom Wright's dripping ribs, pork-chop sandwiches, chicken grilled over hickory and oak in a pepper and mustard sauce, or the sweet-potato pie. The small joint has been blessed by some beefy NFL players, and Lou Rawls, Ben Vereen, and Sugar Ray Leonard to name a few. | 7251 N. Federal Hwy. | 561/997–0920 | Closed Sun., also Mon. May–mid-Nov. | $7–$15 | MC, V.

Uncle Tai's. Szechuan. This fancy restaurant serves some of the best Szechuan of Florida's east coast. House specialties include sliced duck with snow peas and water chestnuts in a tangy plum sauce, and sliced fillet of snapper stir-fried until crispy and then sautéed with pepper sauce, garlic, and orange peel. | 5250 Town Center Circle | 561/368–8806 | No lunch weekends | $13–$22 | AE, DC, MC, V.

Wilt Chamberlain's. American. This family restaurant has a glass-enclosed basketball court where you can shoot hoops to work off calories between courses. There are 48 TVs, video games, and sports memorabilia focusing on Chamberlain's basketball exploits. Try the chicken with penne or the sesame-encrusted tuna, and one of 36 different draft beers. | 8903 W. Glades Rd. | 561/488–8881 | Reservations not accepted | $7–$18 | AE, D, DC, MC, V.

Lodging

Best Western University Inn. This two-story motel features spacious rooms, and a poolside courtyard and patio where breakfast and evening cocktails are served. Restaurant, bar, complimentary Continental breakfast. In-room data ports, microwaves, refrigerators. Cable TV. Pool. Hot tub, sauna. Gym. Laundry facilities. Business services, airport shuttle. | 2700 N. Federal Hwy. | 561/395–5225 or 800/937–8376 | fax 561/338–9180 or 800/528–1234 | www.bestwestern.com | 90 rooms | $59–$120 | AE, D, DC, MC, V.

Boca Raton Marriott. This elegant 11-story hotel is connected to the Boca Center's numerous shops and restaurants. The beach is 2½ miles away. Restaurant, bar (with entertainment). In-room data ports, refrigerators. Cable TV. Pool. Hot tub, sauna. Gym. Laundry facilities. Business services, airport shuttle. | 5150 Town Center Circle | 561/392–4600 or 800/228–2800 | fax 561/395–8258 | www.marriott.com | 256 rooms | $89–$154 | AE, D, DC, MC, V.

Boca Raton Radisson Suite Hotel. Six mi from the beach, this attractive hotel is in a Mediterranean-style business center built around an atrium with tropical gardens and fountains. All the rooms are suites and feature two TVs and VCRs. Complimentary Continental breakfast. Some in-room data ports, microwaves. Cable TV, VCRs. Outdoor pool, lake. Hot tub. Gym. Some pets allowed. | 7920 Glades Rd. | 561/483–3600 | fax 561/479–2280 | 200 rooms | $135–$245 | AE, D, DC, MC, V.

Boca Raton Resort and Club. With a $10 million tennis and fitness center, redesigned golf courses, a beach shuttle, and several restaurants, this resort has some of the best vacation facilities in Florida. Addison Mizner built the Mediterranean-style Cloister Inn in 1926; the resort now has almost 1,000 rooms. Those in the Cloister section are small and warmly traditional, those in the 27-story Tower are similar in style but larger, and rooms in the Beach Club are light, airy, and contemporary. Golf villas near the greens are available as well. 4 restaurants, 5 bars, room service. Some kitchenettes, refrigerators. Cable TV, in-room VCRs. 3 pools. Barbershop, beauty salon, hot tubs, massage. Driving range, 2 golf courses, 2 putting greens, 34 tennis courts. Gym, beach, boating, fishing, bicycles. Shops. Children's programs. Laundry facilities. Business services, airport shuttle. | 501 E. Camino Real | 561/395–3000 or 800/327–0101 | fax 561/447–3183 | www.bocaresort.com | 963 rooms | $250–$495 | AE, D, DC, MC, V.

Boca Raton Town Center. This Mediterranean-style hotel 5 mi from downtown and 6 mi from the beach, has rooms with balconies, an outdoor fountain and a seasonal pool-side bar. Restaurant, bar (with entertainment), room service. In-room data ports, microwaves, refrigerators. Cable TV. Pool, wading pool. Hot tub. Laundry services. Business services. | 1950 Glades Rd. | 561/368–5200 | fax 561/395–4783 | www.holiday-inn.com | 184 rooms | $149–$189 | AE, D, DC, MC, V.

Courtyard by Marriott. A landscaped courtyard distinguishes this four-story chain hotel, which has large rooms with coffee makers among other room amenities. The hotel is 7 mi from the beach and 3 mi from Mizner Park. Restaurant, bar, complimentary breakfast. In-room data ports, kitchenettes, microwaves, refrigerators. Cable TV, in-room VCRs. Outdoor pool. Hot tub. Gym. | 2000 N.W. Executive Center Ct. | 561/241–7070 or 800/331–3131 | fax 561/241–7080 | www.marriott.com | 140 rooms | $143–$189 | AE, D, DC MC, V.

Doubletree Guest Suites. All units are suites in this appealing hotel with a lovely courtyard. Two mi from the beach, and in the heart of the business district, all rooms have two TVs and window views of the courtyard or the pool. Restaurant, room service. In-room data ports, microwaves, refrigerators. Cable TV. Pool. Hot tubs. Laundry facilities. Business services. Some pets allowed (fee). | 701 N.W. 53rd St. | 561/997–9500 | fax 561/994–3565 | www.doubletree.com | 182 suites | $149–$189 | AE, D, DC, MC, V.

Embassy Suites Boca Raton. This all-suites hotel features a tropical atrium, fountains, and lush greenery. At I–95 and Yamato Road, this white, seven-floor hotel 3 mi from beaches and Mizner Park has complimentary evening cocktails. Restaurant, bar, complimentary breakfast. In-room data ports, refrigerators. Laundry services. Pool, lake. Hot tub, massage (fee). Gym. Game room, laundry services. Business services, parking (fee). | 661 N.W. 53rd St. | 561/994–8200 | fax 561/995–9821 | www.embassy-suites.com | 263 suites | $209–$375 | AE, D, DC, MC, V.

Hampton Inn Boca Raton. This hotel has suites and standard rooms, but all units have two double beds or a king-size. The Broken Sound Golf Course is directly behind the hotel, and Mizner Park and the beach are both within 4 mi. Some microwaves, refrigerators. Cable TV. Pool. Gym. Laundry services. | 1455 Yamato Rd. | 561/988–0200 or 800/426–7866 | fax 561/988–0203 | www.hampton-inn.com | 94 rooms | $129–$179 | AE, D, DC, MC, V.

Holiday Inn Express Downtown Boca Raton. This two-story motel facing N. Federal Highway, is 2 mi from downtown and a mile from the beach. While it's by no means a resort, it has a nice Mediterranean look, with bright colors. Complimentary Continental breakfast. In-room data ports, some kitchenettes, some microwaves, some refrigerators. Cable TV. Pool. Laundry services. | 2899 N. Federal Hwy. | 561/395–7172 or 800/465–4329 | fax 561/750–7351 | www.holiday-inn.com | 48 rooms | $119–$129 | AE, D, DC, MC, V.

Holiday Inn West Boca. Seven miles from downtown, this hotel is famous mainly because the Pete Rose Ballpark Cafe (see Dining) is inside. The hotel consists of two-story and four-story structures linked by an interior walkway. Room service. In-room data ports. Cable TV. Pool. Laundry services. Business services. | 8144 Glades Rd. | 561/482–7070 or 800/465–4329 | fax 561/482–6076 | www.holiday-inn.com | 97 rooms | $120–$150 | AE, D, DC, MC, V.

The Inn at Boca Teeca. The small, comfortable rooms at this contemporary inn are popular with golfers at the adjoining Boca Teeca Country Club, otherwise available only to members. Most rooms have a patio or balcony. Cable TV. Outdoor pool. Laundry facilities. | 5800 N.W. Second Ave. | 561/994–0400 or 800/344–6995 | fax 561/998–8279 | 256 rooms | $139 | AE, D, DC, MC, V.

Ocean Lodge. Because its not directly on the water—the beach is across a two-lane road—this is a sound budget choice. The two-story motel has standard rooms and efficiencies, most of which come equipped with kitchenettes and a two-burner stove top. Some kitchenettes, some microwaves, some refrigerators. Cable TV. Pool. Laundry facilities. Business services. | 531 N. Ocean Blvd. | 561/395–7772 | fax 561/395–0554 | 18 rooms | $100 | AE, D, MC, V.

Radisson Bridge Resort. This hotel is right next to the Intracoastal Waterway and its bridge. There is a café by the water, as well as rooftop dining with wide views of the Atlantic. All rooms have balconies with similar views of the beaches and the waterway. Restaurant, bar, dining room, complimentary Continental breakfast. Some microwaves, refrigerators. Cable TV. Pool. Saunas. Tennis. Gym, water sports. Business services. | 999 E. Camino Real | 561/368–9500 | fax 561/362–0492 | www.radisson.com | 121 rooms | $199–$239 | AE, D, DC, MC, V.

Radisson Suite Hotel. This all-suites hotel is on a lake and features a landscaped lobby with pine trees. Each room has a private balcony and living room. | 200 suites. Bar, complimentary breakfast. In-room data ports, kitchenettes, minibars, microwaves, refrigerators. Cable TV, some in-room VCRs (and movies). Pool. Hot tub. Exercise equipment. Laundry facilities. Business services. Some pets allowed (fee). | 7920 Glades Rd. | 561/483–3600 or 800/333–3333 | fax 561/479–2280 | www.radisson.com | 200 suites | $130–$170 | AE, D, DC, MC, V.

Ramada Inn. This contemporary four-floor hotel has nice public zones, like the palm-landscaped pool area. Some rooms have balconies. Restaurant, bar, complimentary Continental breakfast. In-room data ports, kitchenettes, some microwaves. Cable TV, some in-room VCRs. Pool. Hot tub. Laundry services. Business services. Some pets allowed (fee). | 2901 N. Federal Hwy. | 561/395–6850 | fax 561/368–7964 | www.ramada.com | 97 rooms | $105–$135 | AE, D, DC, MC, V.

Residence Inn by Marriott. This two-story hotel 2 mi from Delray Beach has volleyball and basketball courts, an outdoor pool, and two whirlpools. All rooms have full kitchens. Picnic areas, complimentary Continental breakfast. In-room data ports, kitchenettes, microwaves, refrigerators. Cable TV, some in-room VCRs (and movies). Pool. Hot tubs. Driving range, putting green. Basketball, gym, volleyball. Baby-sitting. Laundry facilities. Business services. Some pets allowed (fee). | 525 N.W. 77th St. | 561/994–3222 | fax 561/994–3339 | www.marriott.com | 120 rooms | $149–$199 | AE, D, DC, MC, V.

Sheraton Boca Raton Hotel. This luxury business hotel includes rooms with high-speed Internet access, mahogany furniture and granite bathrooms. Club Level rooms come with cocktails and hors d'oeuvres. The attractive Mediterranean-style pool area has a tiki lounge and a waterfall pool deck. Restaurant, bar (with entertainment), room service. In-room data ports, some refrigerators. Cable TV, some in-room VCRs (and movies). Pool. Hot tub. Gym. Baby-sitting, laundry service. Business services. | 2000 N.W. 19th St. | 561/368–5252 or 800/325–3535 | fax 561/750–5437 | www.sheratonboca.com | 189 rooms | $209–$400 | AE, D, DC, MC, V.

Shore Edge Resort. Just across A1A from the beach, this modest lodging has rooms with microwaves and refrigerators. Hibiscus flowers decorate the lobby; water sports are within walking distance. Some kitchenettes, microwaves, refrigerators. Cable TV. Pool. Beach. Laundry facilities. | 425 N. Ocean Blvd. | 561/395–4491 | www.netcardz.com/shoreedge | 16 rooms | $85–$99 | AE, DC, MC, V.

BONITA SPRINGS

MAP 3, I9

(Nearby towns also listed: Cape Coral, Fort Myers, Fort Myers Beach)

This prosperous southwest Florida community of about 25,000 calls itself the "Gateway to the Gulf," since it lies midway between the resort areas of Fort Myers and Naples. There are several sizeable beaches to the immediate west and south, including Bonita Beach. For thousands of years Calusa Indians paddled the rivers and back bays of this area, until Spaniards arrived in the 16th century. The town took its name in 1912 and began to develop after a road connecting it to Fort Myers was completed in 1917. Long a small farming and fishing community, the area has increasingly developed its residential and business sectors.

Information: **Bonita Springs Area Chamber of Commerce** | 25071 Chamber of Commerce Dr., Bonita Springs, 34135 | 941/992–2943 | www.bonitaspringschamber.com.

Attractions

Corkscrew Swamp Sanctuary. Wander through this 11,000-acre ancient forest on a 2¼-mile boardwalk to explore some of Florida's protected wetland, which is 13 mi east of Bonita Springs (16 mi east of I–75 via Highway 846). In December 2001, the Audubon Society opened its new Blair Audubon Center here, which is a prototype educational facility designed to teach everything there is to know about the swamp to its visitors. Within the center you will find a Swamp Theatre and many exhibits explaining the wonders of the sanctuary. The swamp is a prime bird-watching spot to see pine warblers and painted buntings as well as the largest colony of nesting and fledgling wood storks in the United States. | 375 Sanctuary Rd. W | 941/348–9151 | fax 941/348–9155 | www.audubon.org/local/sanctuary | $8 | Dec.–Apr., daily 7–5; May–Nov., daily 8–5.

Everglades Wonder Gardens. This 5-acre refuge founded in 1936 for injured animals is now home to exotic birds, alligators, Florida panthers, bears, flamingos, tame Florida deer, and otters. Tours, which include alligator feedings, run continuously. Exhibits on Seminole history are in a natural history museum. | 27182 Old U.S. 41 | 941/992–2591 | $9 | Daily 9–5.

Greyhound Racing. There's dog racing year-round at the Naples–Fort Myers Greyhound Track. | 10601 Bonita Beach Rd. | 941/992–2411 | $1 | Racing Mon.–Sat., 7:30 PM, Tues.–Wed., Fri.–Sat. 12:30 PM, Sun. 4:30.

Lover's Key State Park. This park is between Fort Myers Beach and Bonita. The 2½ miles of sandy beach are covered in toppled pine trees, most of which have dried out in the sun. There are a beach pavilion, hiking trails, picnic tables, outdoor showers, and a boat ramp. Make sure you stay for the spectacular sunsets. | 8700 Estero Blvd. | $4 per vehicle | Daily 8–sunset.

ON THE CALENDAR

MAR.: *Bonita Tomato & Seafood Festival.* The Harry Chapin Food Bank sponsors this fundraising event, which is held at the Bonita Springs Recreational Complex. Fried green tomatoes, seafood tastings, carnival rides, games, crafts and continuous live entertainment make this festival as popular as it is worthwhile. | 941/334–7007.

Dining

Café Margaux. French. While it's not exactly fancy, Old Master prints line the walls, and there's a waterfall and a fountain. Popular dishes range from bouillabaisse to French country fare with seafood, to serious steaks dishes such as Chateaubriand. There's a kids' menu, and a twilight special, available daily from 5 to 6 PM, when entrées are priced two for $22. | 3405 Pelican Landing Pkwy. | 941/992–6588 | Closed Sun., Mon. June–Sept. | $25–$35 | AE, D, MC, V.

Jade Island. Chinese. This family-friendly restaurant offers combination platters with fried rice and egg rolls. General Tso's Chicken is a popular choice. | 8951 Bonita Beach Rd. | 941/992–8881 | $7–$15 | AE, D, MC, V.

Lodging

Comfort Inn. Several restaurants are within 2 mi. of this motel, which offers such special amenities as in-room VCRs. Restaurant, complimentary breakfast. Refrigerators. Cable TV, in-room VCRs. Pool. Hot tubs. Laundry facilities. Business services. | 9800 Bonita Beach Rd. | 941/992–5001 or 800/228–5150. | fax 941/992–9283 | www.comfortinn.com | 69 rooms | $98–$104 | AE, D, DC, MC, V.

Days Inn. All the rooms in this single-level motel have two double beds. Downtown is only 4 mi away. In-room data ports, cable TV. Pool. Laundry facilities. | 28090 Quails Nest La. | 941/947–3366 or 800/544–8313 | fax 941/947–6789 | www.daysinn.com | 100 rooms | $89 | AE, D, DC, MC, V.

Hampton Inn Bonita Springs. Two alligators live in a small lake in the front of this inn a mile from Bonita Bay and 2 mi from from gulf beaches. The inn is at the intersection of U.S. 41 and Bonita Beach Road. Complimentary Continental breakfast. In-room data ports, cable TV. Pool. Lake. Laundry service. Business services. | 27900 Crown Lake Blvd. | 941/947–9393 or 800/426–7866 | fax 941/947–3966 | 91 rooms | $129–$139 | AE, D, DC, MC, V.

BOYNTON BEACH

MAP 3, L8

(Nearby towns also listed: Delray Beach, Lake Worth, Lantana, Palm Beach)

This welcoming community of 50,000 lies far enough south of the Palm Beaches to retain a low-key, laid-back atmosphere. It has lovely strands, good shopping, and pleasant restaurants on the mainland and barrier island sides of town. You'll also find some of the best diving on the Atlantic coast here since three major reef systems lie just a few hundred yards from shore. The Gulf is clear, warm, and inviting, and there are numerous dive boat operators in the area.

Information: **Greater Boynton Beach Chamber of Commerce** | 639 East Ocean Ave., Suite 108, Boynton Beach, 33435 | 561/732–9501 | www.boyntonbeach.org.

Attractions

Arthur R. Marshall Loxahatchee National Wildlife Refuge. A portion of the northern Everglades is preserved on this 221-square-mi refuge west of Boynton Beach off U.S. 441 between Boynton Beach Blvd. (Highway 804) and Atlantic Ave. (Highway 806). The Refuge is most important for controlling flooding to the south, but you can canoe, fish, and go wildlife-watching. Two trails lead off from the visitors center. The Marsh Trail takes you to an observation tower where you can get a bird's-eye view of the locals: herons, egrets, ibis, limpkins, anhingas, purple gallinules, vultures, and red-shouldered hawks. | 10119 Lee Rd. | 561/734–8303 | $5 per vehicle | Daily 6 AM–sunset.

Knollwood Groves. These orange groves are a great place to encounter quaint shops filled with local crafts and get a taste of the fresh-squeezed product Florida is famous for. Visitors can wander on their own accord or jump on a tram, which has a guide and leads you to a re-created Hallpatee Seminole Indian Village and an alligator exhibit. A highlight is the Saturday alligator lecture by Martin TwoFeathers. | 8053 Lawrence Rd. | 561/734–4800 | fax 561/737–6700 | www.knollwoodgroves.com | Free for wandering and shopping, $1 for tram tour, $5 for lecture | Open daily 8:30–5:30; show Sat. at 2. Closed Sun. May–Oct.

ON THE CALENDAR

MAR.: *Boynton's G.A.L.A.* Boynton Beach's Great American Love Affair (G.A.L.A.), held downtown on Ocean Avenue, is the city's biggest outdoor family festival, with arts and crafts, games, rides, a picnic area, and an exhibitors' row for businesses and cultural groups. There's also live music on multiple stages. | 561/742–6232.
AUG.: *Taste of Boynton.* Restaurants throughout Boynton gather to provide an all-you-can-eat extravaganza. | 561/732–9501.

Dining

Banana Boat. American. This restaurant on the Intracoastal Waterway has an outdoor bar and dining area. Try the prime rib, Key West dolphin (mahimahi), or the shrimp scampi. There is live music on Wed. and weekend evenings. | 739 E. Ocean Ave. | 561/732–9400 | Reservations not accepted | $7–$29 | AE, DC, MC, V.

Holiday House. American. This casual restaurant offers a large buffet and a menu that includes leg of lamb and fresh roasted turkey. | 710 N. Federal Hwy. | 561/732–6841 | Reservations not accepted | $8–$10 | AE, MC, V.

Mama Jennie's. Italian. This inviting, casual family restaurant serves homemade food, including traditional pizza pies. Spaghetti with meatballs, eggplant parmigiana, and stuffed shells are other good choices. | 706 W. Boynton Beach Blvd. | 561/737–2407 | Reservations not accepted | No lunch | $8–$16 | AE, DC, MC, V.

Two Georges Harbor Hut. Seafood. Try the dolphin (mahimahi) or grouper sandwich at this restaurant on the Intracoastal Waterway, which has a bamboo ceiling and other tropical touches. | 728 Casa Loma Blvd. | 561/736–2717 | $12–$25 | AE, D, MC, V.

Lodging

Ann Marie Motel. This motel offers standard rooms and efficiencies with full kitchens. There's a heated pool outside that has a covered area at one end with a barbecue grill. Say hello to the two parrots in the lobby. Picnic area, complimentary Continental breakfast. In-room data ports, some kitchenettes, some microwaves, refrigerators. Cable TV, in-room VCRs (and movies). Pool. Library. Business services. Pets allowed (fee). | 911 S. Federal Hwy. | 561/732–9283 or 800/258–8548 | www.annmariemotel.com | 16 rooms | $79–$99 | AE, D, DC, MC, V.

Atlantic Lodge. This single-story motel is a 3-min drive from the beach. Both standard rooms and efficiencies are available. The outdoor area has a large pool and a barbecue. Picnic area. Some kitchenettes, some microwaves, refrigerators. Cable TV. Pool. | 2607 S. Federal Hwy./U.S. 1 | 561/732–4446 | fax 561/731–0325 | 31 rooms | $70 | AE, D, DC, MC, V.

Hampton Inn Boynton Beach. There are 77 spacious suites with living rooms, microwaves, and refrigerators at this contemporary hotel. Room service. In-room data ports, some microwaves, some refrigerators. Cable TV. Pool. Hot tubs. Business services. | 1475 W. Gateway Blvd. | 561/369–0018 or 800/426–7866 | fax 561/738–5235 | www.hamptoninn.com | 107 rooms | $109–$149 | AE, D, DC, MC, V.

Holiday Inn Catalina. This four-story chain hotel adjoins the Catalina Shopping Center, a few miles from Boynton Beach and Cypress Creek golf courses. Each room has a private balcony and there is a courtyard fountain. Restaurant, bar (with entertainment), room service. In-room data ports. Cable TV. Pool. Hot tub. Gym. Video games. Laundry facilities. Business services. | 1601 N. Congress Ave. | 561/737–4600 or 800/465–4329 | fax 561/734–6523 | www.holiday-inn.com | 152 rooms | $159 | AE, D, DC, MC, V.

Holiday Inn Express. This four-story slimmed-down hotel just off I–95 is 2 mi from Boynton Beach. There is a complimentary beverage reception each evening. Complimentary Continental breakfast. In-room data ports. Cable TV, in-room VCRs. Pool. Baby-sitting. Laundry facility. Business services. | 480 W. Boynton Beach Blvd. | 561/734–9100 or 800/465–4329 | fax 561/738–7193 | www.holiday-inn.com | 98 rooms, 6 suites | $69–$119 | AE, D, DC, MC, V.

BRADENTON

MAP 3, H7

(Nearby towns also listed: Longboat Key, Sarasota, Siesta Key, St. Pete Beach, St. Petersburg, Sun City Center)

Bradenton, which borders Sarasota to the north on the Manatee River, is Manatee County's largest city, with nearly 50,000 residents. Named after Joseph Braden, an early settler who ran a sugar mill here, it is one of southwest Florida's oldest cities, with fine sand beaches, golf courses, and good saltwater and freshwater fishing access. Some of its old neighborhoods, lined with Spanish moss–draped trees, feel like the Old South.

Manatee Avenue (Highway 64) connects the mainland to the island via the Palma Sola Causeway, next to which is a long, sandy beach fronting Palma Sola Bay. Most beach-goers also head to Bradenton's barrier island to the west, Anna Maria Island. One of Anna Maria's three little towns, Bradenton Beach, has a Historic Bridge District around its popular fishing pier. The Pittsburgh Pirates hold spring training at McKechnie Field on the mainland.

Information: Manatee Chamber of Commerce | 222 10th St. NW, Bradenton, 34205 | 941/748–3411 | www.manatee-cc.com.

Attractions

Anna Maria Island. The barrier island to the west of Bradenton has a few delightful free public beaches bordering both the Intracoastal Waterway and the Gulf. Bayfront Beach is the northern most, followed by Manatee Beach, Cortez, and Coquina. There are also three fishing piers, plenty of boating, and public tennis courts. The island was originally explored by Spanish conquistadors around 1530 and since then the local native tribe, the Timucuans, have died out. The island is 7 mi west of Bradenton. Surrounded by the Gulf on the west, Tampa Bay and Anna Maria Sound on the east, and Sarasota Bay to the south, there are beaches on all sides of the island. It is accessible by Highway 64, over the Manatee Avenue bridge, as well as two other bridges to the south. | Hwy. 64.

De Soto National Memorial. Hernando De Soto, one of the first Spanish explorers, set foot near Bradenton in 1539 with 600 Spanish soldiers. Late December to early April, park employees dressed in 16th-century costumes demonstrate period weapons and exploratory preparations. The visitors center displays replicas of 16th-century arms, shows a De Soto video, and has a short nature trail. | 75th St. NW | 941/792–0458 | Free | Daily 9–5.

Egmont Key State Park. The main resident of this 2-mi-long island off the northern tip of Anna Maria Island is the threatened gopher tortoise. The island can be reached only by boat; the *Miss Cortez* is one of the boats that runs excursions here from Cortez Marina, south of Bradenton. Besides unspoiled beaches and nature trails (don't wander or you'll encounter huge rattlesnakes), you'll find the ruins of Fort Dade, a military installation built in 1900 during the Spanish American War, and an 1848 lighthouse, Florida's sixth-brightest. | Cortez Marina, Cortez | Park 727/893–2627; *Miss Cortez* 941/794–1223 | www.dep.state.fl.us/parks | Park free, boat excursion $15 | Tues., Thurs., Sun. 1–5.

Gamble Plantation and Confederate Memorial State Historic Site. Gamble Mansion is South Florida's only surviving antebellum plantation house, and it still displays some of the original furnishings. The Confederate secretary of state, Major Robert Gamble, took refuge here after the Confederacy fell to Union forces. You can tour his home, headquarters of a 3,500-acre sugar plantation. | 3708 Patten Ave., Ellenton | 941/723–4536 | $3 | Thurs.–Mon. 8–5.

Manatee Village Historical Park. This museum complex at the site of the original county settlement includes a 1860 courthouse, 1912 settler's home, 1903 general store and museum, and a 1887 church. | 604 15th St. E | 941/749–7165 | Free | Mon.–Fri. 9–4:30, Sun. 1:30–4:30, closed Sun. July–Aug.

South Florida Museum and Bishop Planetarium and Parker Manatee Aquarium. Museum exhibits cover South Florida from the Stone Age to the Space Age, with displays relating to Native American life and an excellent collection of Civil War objects. The Mary E. Parker Aquarium is the home to Snooty, the county mascot born here in 1949—he's the oldest living manatee born in captivity. The planetarium has daily star shows and weekend laser light and sound shows. You can use the observatory telescopes Fri. and Sat. 8:30–10 PM. | 201 10th St. W | 941/746–4132 | $7.50 | Tues.–Sat. 10–5, Sun. 12–5.

ON THE CALENDAR

MAR.–APR.: *Spring Training.* The Pittsburgh Pirates have been playing in Bradenton every spring since 1970; McKechnie Field is their spring home. | 941/748–4610 or 941/747–3031.

JULY: *Snooty the Manatee's Birthday Bash.* As part of a Wildlife Awareness Festival, the Parker Aquarium at the South Florida Museum hosts a birthday bash for Snooty, its manatee-in-residence and Manatee County's official mascot. Everyone sings "Happy Birthday" to the manatee, and wildlife organizations stage educational shows with live animals. | 941/746–4131.

Dining

Beach Bistro. Mediterranean. This quaint restaurant seats just 65 people in two dining rooms. One has great views of the Gulf, and the other faces a garden. Popular dishes include jumbo shrimp, char-grilled salmon, and roast duckling. | 6600 Gulf Dr. Holmes Beach | 941/778–6444 | No lunch | $19–$29 | AE, D, DC, MC, V.

The Beachhouse. American. This lively eatery has a huge outdoor deck facing the Gulf. The beechnut grouper and sautéed snapper are two popular choices. There is a sunset contest every evening, with a bottle of champagne to the person who guesses the exact time the sun sets. | 200 Gulf Dr. N | 941/779–2222 | $10–$20 | AE, D, DC, MC, V.

China Palace. Mandarin. This restaurant is known for its bountiful Mandarin buffets. Advance reservations can secure you a lakefront dining spot. The sweet and sour chicken and Szechuan and Mongolian beef are popular choices. | 5131 14th St. W | 941/755–3758 | $5–$15 | AE, D, DC, MC, V.

Gulf Drive Café. American. This restaurant overlooks the Gulf of Mexico with outdoor patio dining. The menu varies from Belgian waffles to fresh sea scallops. Alcohol is not served. | 900 Gulf Dr. N, Bradenton Beach | 941/778–1919 | Reservations not accepted | Breakfast also available | $6–$12 | D, MC, V.

Lee's Crab Trap and Lee's Crab Trap II. Seafood. These casual and very popular restaurants 5 mi north and northwest of Bradenton have rustic furnishings and ultrafresh seafood. The gator tail and wild pig are popular dishes on the more adventurous side. | U.S. 19 at Terra Ceia Bridge, Palmetto | 941/722–6255 | 4815 Memphis Rd., Ellenton | 941/729–7777 | Reservations not accepted | $8–$36 | D, MC, V.

Miller's Dutch Kitchen. American. This delightful Pennsylvania Dutch country dining room has a model train running around its balcony. There are also quilts and other crafts made by Bradenton's Amish community. Popular dishes include meatloaf, breaded veal, and Alaskan codfish. | 3401 14th St. W | 941/746–8253 | Reservations not accepted | Closed Sun. | $6–$15 | MC, V.

Rotten Ralph's Seafood. This restaurant overlooks Bimini Bay and the marina. There are outdoor patio dining and live music in winter. The all-you-can-eat fish and chips meal is popular, as is the escargot. | 902 S. Bay Blvd., Anna Maria Island | 941/778–3953 | Reservations not accepted | $8–$17 | D, DC, MC, V.

Sandbar. Seafood. This popular beachfront restaurant has live music nightly, and is a nice place from which to watch the sunset. Sea glass decorations by local artists hang on the walls. Sandbar is known for grouper "cooked any way you like it." | 100 Spring Ave., Anna Maria Island | 941/778–0444 | $12–$18 | AE, D, DC, MC, V.

Seafood Shack. Seafood. This large, casual waterfront restaurant a few miles west of Bradenton serves a variety of seafood, including fresh blackened grouper and lobster. The first floor dining has a lively bar and grill. | 4110 127th St. W, Cortez | 941/794–1235 | Reservations not accepted | $10–$40 | AE, D, MC, V.

Twin Dolphin Marina & Grill. Seafood. This upscale downtown restaurant looks out onto the Manatee River and Memorial Pier from huge, arched windows. An informal tiki bar overlooks the water, and live music is common. Try the macadamia-encrusted mahimahi or fresh grouper. | 1200 1st Ave. W | 941/748–8087 | $12–$23 | AE, D, DC, MC, V.

Lodging

Best Western Inn Ellenton. This hotel is 5 mi north of Bradenton and 15 miles west of gulf beaches. All standard rooms have a king- or two queen-size beds. Suites with lounging areas are also available. The pool is landscaped with a patio and several palm trees. Restaurant, complimentary Continental breakfast. Some in-room data ports, some microwaves, some refrigerators. Cable TV, some in-room hot tubs. Pool. Gym. Laundry service. Business services. Pets allowed. | 5218 17th St. E, Ellenton | 941/729–8505 | fax 941/729–1110 | $80–$90 | 73 rooms | AE, D, DC, MC, V.

Comfort Inn Bradenton. This hotel is 6 mi from downtown and 8 mi from Bradenton Beach. All the rooms have a queen- or king-size bed. There is a gazebo by the pool. Complimentary Continental breakfast. In-room data ports, some microwaves, some refrigerators, some in-room hot tubs. Cable TV. Pool, lake. Hot tub. Laundry facilities, laundry service. Business services. | 707 E. 65th St. | 941/747–7500 or 800/228–5150 | fax 941/748–8002 | www.comfortinn.com | 70 rooms | $99–$109 | AE, D, DC, MC, V.

Days Inn. This 2-story hotel is 12 mi from the Gulf of Mexico and both the Sarasota Airport and Tampa International are within a 45-mi drive. Rooms have double, queen-, or king-size beds. In-room data ports, refrigerators. Cable TV. Pool. Laundry facilities. Business services. | 644 67th St. | 941/746–2505 or 800/544–8313 | fax 941/745–1839 | www.daysinn.com | 60 rooms | $70–$85 | AE, D, DC, MC, V.

Duncan House. This pink Victorian house is directly on Bradenton Beach and provides guests with picture perfect rooms and tons of hospitality. A full breakfast is served in the main house dining room, though some of the units have their own kitchenettes. Lace curtains and pink floral tones relax your stay here, but if you have the energy to pry yourself off the beach, there are shopping, water sports, and every activity imaginable just down the street. Complimentary breakfast. Some in-room data ports. Some room phones. Pool. Beach. | 1703 Gulf Dr., Bradenton Beach | 941/778–6858 | fax 941/778–2904 | www.duncanhousebb.com | 6 rooms | $79–$139 | AE, MC, V.

Econo Lodge Airport. This hotel is ideal if you need to access the Sarasota–Bradenton Airport, which is 2 mi away. All rooms have double or king-size beds. Free Continental breakfast. Some microwaves, some refrigerators. Cable TV. Pool. Business services. Pets allowed. | 6727 14th St. W | 941/758–7199 or 800/553–2666 | fax 941/751–4947 | www.econolodge.com | 78 rooms | $66–$86 | AE, D, DC, MC, V.

Econo Lodge East. This two-story motel off I–75's exit 42 is a clean, no-frills stay 5 mi from downtown Bradenton and 15 mi from Gulf beaches. One stop further on I–75 is Prime Outlet Mall. Picnic area. Some refrigerators. Cable TV. Laundry services. Business services. | 607 67th St. Cir. E | 941/745–1988 or 800/553–2666 | fax 941/746–9189 | www.econolodge.com | 54 rooms | $75–$79 | AE, D, DC, MC, V.

Five Oaks Inn. This elegant B&B was built in 1912, and is right on the Manatee River across from Bradenton. There is a screened wraparound porch and an oak staircase that leads to all the guest rooms. Complimentary Continental breakfast. Cable TV. Boating, fishing. Library. No kids under 12. | 1102 Riverside Dr., Palmetto | 941/723–1236 or 800/658–4167 | 4 rooms | $100–$125 | AE, D, MC, V.

Holiday Inn Riverfront. This lovely Spanish-style hotel overlooks the Manatee River with fountained courtyards and landscaped grounds. All the rooms have private balconies, most of which overlook the river. Restaurants, bar, room service. In-room data ports, some minibars, some refrigerators. Cable TV. Pool. Hot tub. Gym. Business services. | 100 Riverfront Dr. W | 941/747–3727 or 800/465–4329 | fax 941/746–4289 | www.holiday-inn.com | 153 rooms | $124–$149 | AE, D, DC, MC, V.

Howard Johnson Express. This two-story, limited-service motel on U.S. 41 is 8 mi from Bradenton Beach, 5 mi from Lido Beach, and 3½ miles north of the Sarasota–Bradenton Airport. Complimentary Continental breakfast. In-room data ports, some kitchenettes, some microwaves, some refrigerators. Cable TV. Laundry service. Business service. Pets allowed. | 6511 14th St. W | 941/756–8399 or 800/446–4656 | fax 941/755–1387 | www.hojo.com | 50 rooms | $85–$90 | AE, D, DC, MC, V.

Luxury Inn. The beach is 12 mi away from this inexpensive motel, which caters to families and businesspeople alike. Complimentary Continental breakfast. Cable TV. Pool. Laundry facilities. Business services. Pets allowed (fee). | 668 67th St. Circle | 941/745–1876 | fax 941/747–5046 | 105 rooms | $40–$65 | AE, D, DC, MC, V.

Park Inn Club and Breakfast. This hotel offers packages such the the "Couch Potato," which includes a pizza delivered to your door and two movie tickets for the theater directly behind. Shopping and restaurants are also within walking distance; the beach is 6 mi away. Complimentary Continental breakfast. Some microwaves, some refrigerators, some in-room hot tubs. Cable TV. Pool. Hot tub. Business services. Some pets allowed. | 4450 47th St. W | 941/795–4633 | fax 941/795–0808 | 110 rooms, 20 suites | $104–$134 | AE, D, DC, MC, V.

Quality Inn and Suites. This two-story motel is 8 mi from Bradenton Beach and has a playground for the kids. A shopping mall with a food court is within walking distance. Complimentary Continental breakfast. Some microwaves, some refrigerators. Cable TV. Pool. Playground. | 2303 1st St. E | 941/747–6465 | fax 941/747–1070 | 186 rooms | $65–$95 | AE, D, DC, MC, V.

Silver Surf Motel. The beach and heated pool are right out front this bright white two-story spot on Anna Maria Island, between the Gulf of Mexico and Sarasota. Rooms are simply decorated but comfortable, and many have a great ocean view. Picnic area. Some kitchenettes, some microwaves, refrigerators. Cable TV. Pool. Putting green. Beach. Laundry facilities. | 1301 Gulf Dr. N, Bradenton Beach | 941/778–6626 or 800/441–7873 | fax 941/778–4308 | www.silverresorts.com | 49 rooms | $96–$124 | AE, D, DC, MC, V.

Tortuga Inn. This colorful inn has lush tropical landscaping across the road from its own private beach. There are standard hotel rooms and one- and two-bedroom suites. Some rooms have paddle fans, overstuffed sofas, rocking chairs, and private porches. The swimming pool is fed by a fountain. Picnic area. Some kitchenettes, some microwaves, some refrigerators, some in-room hot tubs. Cable TV, in-room VCRs. Pool. Beach, dock, boating. Laundry service. | 1325 Gulf Dr. N, Bradenton Beach | 941/778–6611 or 877/862–8842 | fax 941/778–6748 | www.tortugainn.com | 62 rooms | $129–$149 | AE, D, DC, MC, V.

BROOKSVILLE

MAP 3, H5

(Nearby towns also listed: Crystal River, Homosassa Springs, Pine Island, Dade City)

Brooksville (pop. 8,000), 15 mi east of the Gulf of Mexico, and about 60 mi from both Tampa and Orlando, is a quiet town with Victorian homes along redbrick and cobblestone streets. A few of these houses have been combined to form the Rogers' Christmas House, which displays year-round yuletide decorations. Main Street has the Hernando County Courthouse and some antiques stores.

During the Civil War, when Union troops started to blockade the Gulf Coast, Brooksville became a key link in the Confederate supply chain. Union forces marched in and plundered the town. The Hernando Historical Museum tells the story through a collection of Civil War artifacts.

Information: Hernando County Chamber of Commerce | 101 E. Fort Dade Ave., Brooksville, 34601 | 352/796–0697 or 800/601–4580 | www.hernandochamber.com.

Attractions

Citrus Attraction at Boyette Groves. The attraction in question at this 20-acre citrus grove and packing site is a small, 2½-acre zoo. There are monkeys, alligators, deer, llamas, and goats. You can tour the grove, 5 mi east of Brooksville, and take some fruit home with you. | 4355 Spring Lake Hwy., Spring Lake | 352/796–2289 or 800/780–2296 | $1.50 | Daily 9–5.

Roger's Christmas House. This shopping village consists of five turn-of-the-20th-century houses selling antiques, dolls, tree lights, decorations, and home furnishings. The village is landscaped with magnolias, dogwoods, and azaleas. | 103 Saxon Ave. | 352/796–2415 | www.rogerschristmashouse.com | Daily 9:30–5.

ON THE CALENDAR

JAN.: *Brooksville Raid Festival.* One of Florida's largest Civil War battle re-enactments includes a parade, arts and crafts, mock battles, a Civil War encampment, and a Blue-Gray ball. | 352/799–0129.

JAN.–FEB.: *Hernando County Fair.* This old-fashioned county fair at the Hernando Fairgrounds includes a midway, corn dogs, cotton candy, candy apples, livestock exhibits, a rodeo, and live music. | 352/796–4552.

Dining

Papa Joe's Italian Restaurant. Italian. This family-friendly, family-run restaurant also has a catering service and meeting facilities. The zuppa di pesce and Roquefort steak are popular choices, as is the cheesecake. Other menu items include the seafood jambalaya and veal piccata. After dinner, you can browse in the gift shop and gourmet deli next door. | 6244 Spring Lake Hwy. | 352/799–3904 | $6–$15 | AE, MC, V.

Ye Olde Fireside Inn. American. This restaurant, located in a wooded area off the commercial street, is inside a 1908 inn filled with antiques from that era. The popular dishes include beef Wellington, chicken marsala, and prime rib. | 1175 S. Broad St. | 352/796–0293 | Closed Mon. | $12–$23 | AE, MC, V.

Lodging

Best Western Heritage Inn. This two-story motel was opened in 1999. A large outdoor pool has a small waterfall to one side. World Woods golf course, one of the state's top public courses, is 10 mi away; Croom Bike trail is 1 mi away. Restaurant, bar (with entertainment). In-room data ports. Cable TV. Pool. Video games. Laundry service. Business services. | 6320 Windmere Rd. | 352/796–9486 | fax 352/754–8721 | www.bestwestern.com | 118 rooms | $59–$79 | AE, D, DC, MC, V.

KODAK'S TIPS FOR PHOTOGRAPHING LANDSCAPES AND SCENERY

Landscape
- Tell a story
- Isolate the essence of a place
- Exploit mood, weather, and lighting

Panoramas
- Use panoramic cameras for sweeping vistas
- Don't restrict yourself to horizontal shots
- Keep the horizon level

Panorama Assemblage
- Use a wide-angle or normal lens
- Let edges of pictures overlap
- Keep exposure even
- Use a tripod

Placing the Horizon
- Use low horizon placement to accent sky or clouds
- Use high placement to emphasize distance and accent foreground elements
- Try eliminating the horizon

Mountain Scenery: Scale
- Include objects of known size
- Frame distant peaks with nearby objects
- Compress space with long lenses

Mountain Scenery: Lighting
- Shoot early or late; avoid midday
- Watch for dramatic color changes
- Use exposure compensation

Tropical Beaches
- Capture expansive views
- Don't let bright sand fool your meter
- Include people

Rocky Shorelines
- Vary shutter speeds to freeze or blur wave action
- Don't overlook sea life in tidal pools
- Protect your gear from sand and sea

In the Desert
- Look for shapes and textures
- Try visiting during peak bloom periods
- Don't forget safety

Canyons
- Research the natural and social history of a locale
- Focus on a theme or geologic feature
- Budget your shooting time

Rain Forests and the Tropics
- Go for mystique with close-ups and detail shots
- Battle low light with fast films and camera supports
- Protect cameras and film from moisture and humidity

Rivers and Waterfalls
- Use slow film and long shutter speeds to blur water
- When needed, use a neutral-density filter over the lens
- Shoot from water level to heighten drama

Autumn Colors
- Plan trips for peak foliage periods
- Mix wide and close views for visual variety
- Use lighting that accents colors or creates moods

Moonlit Landscapes
- Include the moon or use only its illumination
- Exaggerate the moon's relative size with long telephoto lenses
- Expose landscapes several seconds or longer

Close-Ups
- Look for interesting details
- Use macro lenses or close-up filters
- Minimize camera shake with fast films and high shutter speeds

Caves and Caverns
- Shoot with ISO 1000+ films
- Use existing light in tourist caves
- Paint with flash in wilderness caves

From *Kodak Guide to Shooting Great Travel Pictures* © 2000 by Fodor's Travel Publications

Best Western Heritage Inn. This modern two-story motel has a tropical pool and a cascading waterfall. Otherwise, the rooms are very modern and simple and only an hour's drive from Weeki Watchee, Walt Disney World, and Universal Studios. Restaurant, bar. Pool. Golf. Laundry service. Pets allowed (fee). | 6320 Windmere Rd. | 352/796–9486 | fax 352/754–8721 | www.bestwestern.com | 118 rooms | $60–$75 | AE, D, DC, MC, V.

Hampton Inn of Brooksville. This hotel is 10 mi east of Brooksville. Rooms are simple, and although it does not have many of its own facilities, you can use the Holiday Inn's pool and playground next door. Complimentary Continental breakfast. In-room data ports, some microwaves, some refrigerators. Cable TV. Business services. | 30301 Cortez Blvd. | 352/796–1000 or 800/426–7866 | fax 352/796–9170 | www.hamptoninn.com | 75 rooms | $74–$79 | AE, D, DC, MC, V.

Holiday Inn. This hotel is 10 mi from downtown Brooksville and one block from Croom Motor Park. Several golf courses are nearby, including World Woods, 18 mi from the property. Restaurant, bar, complimentary breakfast, room service. In-room data ports, some microwaves, some refrigerators. Cable TV. Pool, wading pool. 2 tennis courts. Playground. Laundry facilities, laundry service. Business services. Some pets allowed (fee). | 30307 Cortez Blvd. | 352/796–9481 or 800/465–4329 | fax 352/799–7595 | www.holiday-inn.com | 122 rooms | $79–$105 | AE, D, DC, MC, V.

CAPE CORAL

MAP 3, I8

(Nearby towns also listed: Captiva Island, Fort Myers Beach, Fort Myers, Matlacha, Sanibel Island)

Cape Coral, a planned city on the Caloosahatchee River peninsula next to Fort Myers, was incorporated in 1957, when the population was just 280. The largest concentration of earth-moving equipment ever amassed in the state was brought in to excavate over 400 miles of canals—more than in Venice, Italy—and prepare home sites. In terms of land size, Cape Coral became Florida's second-largest city, after Jacksonville. In terms of population growth, it remains one of the state's fastest-growing cities. In 1970 the population reached 11,000; by 1980 it was 32,000; in 1990 it was 74,000; and in 2000, the city's population exceeded 100,000. Affordable waterfront housing has made the city a haven for boating enthusiasts (ten percent of locals own boats). The city has another of the state's largest populations—Florida burrowing owls. Since the owls nest in vacant lots—a valuable commodity in town—the city has done much to protect the owls and to integrate them into developing neighborhoods.

Information: **City of Cape Coral** | 815 Nicholas Pkwy., Cape Coral, 33990 | 941/574–0401 | www.capecoral.net.

Attractions
Children's Science Center. How can kids resist bubble bins, mazes, optical illusions, mind-benders, and brain twisters? Outdoor fun at this center includes a nature trail, whisper dishes, and telescope viewing. Hands-on exhibits explore technology, math, and science. | 2915 N.E. Pine Island Rd. | 941/997–0012 | $4 | Weekdays 9:30–4:30, weekends 12–5.

Sun Splash Family Waterpark. Contains more than two dozen attractions, both wet and dry, including water slides, a Lilypad Walk (where you step from one floating "lily pad" to another), Squirtworks (a special play area for younger children), and Cape Fear (a fast, 15-second tube slide). | 400 Santa Barbara Blvd. | 941/574–0558 | $10.50 | Mar.–Apr., Fri.–Sun. 11–5; May, Wed.–Fri. 11–5; Jun.–Aug., daily 10–6; Sept., Sat.–Sun. 10–6.

OCT.: *Munich in Cape Coral.* The German-American Social Club of Cape Coral imports German bands and serves up large quantities of German food and beer the last two weeks in Oct. | 2101 Pine Island Rd. | 941/283–1400.

Dining

Ariani. Italian. This restaurant specializes in grilled northern Italian cuisine, such as veal scaloppine and filet mignon. The dining room has a terra-cotta ceiling and painted murals of Adriatic Italian life. | 1529 S.E. 15th Terr. | 941/772–8000 | Closed Sun. No lunch | $12.95–$18.95 | AE, D, MC, V.

Brigands. Seafood. A 38-ft sailboat directs the nautical theme at this popular steak and seafood restaurant. Try an aged Black Angus steak or the grouper Rockefeller. | 1708 Cape Coral Pkwy. W | 941/540–4665 | No lunch Sun. | $13–$21 | AE, MC, V.

Cape Crab and Steak House. Seafood. Designed after a Maryland steak house, you can enjoy casual dining within the nautical-theme wooden walls and tables. Maryland blue crabs are the specialty and are served steamed, in a garlic sauce, or sautéed. But you can also order prime rib any way you like it, in any size from 12 to 20 oz. Loosen your buckle. | Coral-wood Mall, Del Prado Blvd. | 941/574–2722 | fax 941/574–6073 | $10–$29 | AE, MC, V.

Iguana Mia. Mexican. A festive cantina popular for its fajitas and tacos. Aside from the main dining room, there is a bar and an outdoor patio that overlooks Cape Coral Parkway. | 1027 East Cape Coral Pkwy. | 941/945–7755 | $6–$15 | AE, D, MC, V.

Siam Hut. Thai. Within this urban shopping world, there thrives a special, spicy spot. Reasonably priced pad Thai combines rice noodles, peanut sauce, and shrimp or chicken; or you can try the sizzling shrimp platter, which comes to the table in a dramatic fashion. Traditional Thai art decorates the walls and soothes you away from the hustle and into your tom yum goong soup (shrimp, lemongrass, hot and sour). | Coral Pointe Shopping Center, 1873 Del Prado Blvd. | 941/772–3131 | fax 941/772–3131 | Closed Sun. | $8–$19 | AE, MC, V.

Venezia. Italian. This small, casual, family-oriented café decorated with white lights and red and white–checkered tablecloths serves such classic dishes as manicotti and linguine with garlic, broccoli, and oil. | 1515 S.E. 47th Terr. | 941/542–0027 | No lunch | $8–$16 | AE, D, MC, V.

Lodging

Casa Loma Motel. Rooms in this modest but pleasant motel face an attractive inlet that leads to the Caloosahatchee River. Picnic area. Kitchenettes, some microwaves, refrigerators. Cable TV. Pool. Dock, fishing. Laundry facilities. Business services. | 3608 Del Prado Blvd. | 941/549–6000 | fax 941/549–4877 | www.tropicaltravelers.com | 49 rooms | $70–$125 | AE, D, MC, V.

Quality Inn Nautilus. This tropically decorated five-story hotel has a poolside tiki bar and guest rooms with balconies. It is 15 mi from S.W. Florida Regional Airport, 10 mi from Fort Myers Beach, and 20 mi from Captiva Island. Restaurant, bar. Cable TV. Pool. Laundry facilities. Business services. Pets allowed (fee). | 1538 Cape Coral Pkwy. | 941/542–2121 | fax 941/542–6319 | 144 rooms | $100–$150 | AE, D, DC, MC, V.

Rainbow Motel Resort. This motel is on the Rainbow Canal, a 7-min boat ride to the Intracoastal Waterway. The rooms are spacious, with two beds, a sleeper sofa, and a separate living area. Kitchenettes, some microwaves, refrigerators. Cable TV, some in-room VCRs. Pool. Dock. Fishing. Laundry facilities. Business services. | 3817 Del Prado Blvd. | 941/542–0061 | fax 941/542–3678 | 15 rooms | $85 | AE, D, DC, MC, V.

CAPTIVA ISLAND

(Nearby towns also listed: Boca Grande, Cape Coral, Fort Myers, Fort Myers Beach, Bonita Springs, Matlacha, Sanibel Island)

This end-of-the-road island (pop. 3,000) just north of Sanibel and off the coast from Fort Myers, is known for its white clapboard cottages, good restaurants, pristine beaches, sea shells, and secluded serenity. Its most famous residents were aviator Charles Lindbergh and his wife, Anne, who wrote her woman's coming-of-age book, *Gift from the Sea,* here. The island's name is said to have originated in the 16th century, when Juan Ortiz was captured by the Calusa Indians and held captive here. Facing execution, he escaped with the help of the Indian chief's daughter. Vacationers can still see the remains of ceremonial shell mounds created by the Indians.

Information: Sanibel-Captiva Islands Chamber of Commerce | 1159 Causeway Rd., Sanibel Island, 33957 | 941/472–1080 | www.sanibel-captiva.org.

SIGHTSEEING TOURS/TOUR COMPANIES

Captiva Cruises. Tours include one- to three-hour nature and sunset cruises, four- and five-hour cruises to Cabbage Key, and five- and six-hour trips to Boca Grande. Departures are from South Seas Plantation Resort, at the far end of Captiva Island. | Captiva Dr. | 941/472–5300 | $17.50–$35.

Dining

Bellini's of Captiva. Italian. A large, airy restaurant in a gracious, old-island building with tropical themes serves northern Italian cuisine with a cutting-edge style. You can dine under the canvas canopy on the breezy patio, or listen to live piano music from the adjoining cocktail lounge. Try the chicken marsala, fettuccine carbonara, sausages with peppers over linguine, or grouper cooked with tomatoes, white wine, and garlic. | 11521 Andy Rosse La. | 941/472–6866 | No lunch | $11–$25 | AE, DC, MC, V.

Bubble Room. American. Waitstaff wearing scout uniforms race amid an array of colored Christmas lights, memorabilia from the '30s and '40s, and electric trains. The menu is just as eclectic, with dishes such as the Eddie Fisherman (poached fresh grouper) or the aged prime ribs Weissmuller. You can also start with dessert: the red velvet cake is an unforgettable meal in itself. | 15001 Captiva Dr. | 941/472–5558 | $15–$30 | AE, D, DC, MC, V.

Chadwick's Seafood. The menu at this friendly restaurant includes grilled salmon, grilled sirloin, and Jamaican barbecue chicken. A daily buffet has a changing selection of cuisines, such as New Orleans Cajun, Italian, and Caribbean. There's a dance floor and live music nightly. | Captiva Dr. | 941/472–7575 | $19–$25 | AE, D, DC, MC, V.

Green Flash. Seafood. Set at the edge of Pine Island sound at one of Captiva's narrowest sections, the views of tiny green islands peppered along the water make this restaurant extremely popular. Seafood is the specialty, but there's a bit of everything on the menu, from shrimp in beer batter to pork tenderloin Wellington to pasta primavera. | 15183 Captiva Dr. | 941/472–3337 | $14–$30 | AE, D, DC, MC, V.

Mucky Duck. Seafood. Imagine an English Pub along a sunny beach, and you have this casual shoreside spot. Fourteen beers are on tap; the menu includes such entrées as bacon-wrapped barbecued shrimp and duck à l'orange. The Key lime pie is overshadowed only by the homemade blueberry sour cream pie. | 11546 Andy Rosse La. | 941/472–3434 | fax 941/472–2388 | Closed Sun. | $13–$20 | AE, D, DC, MC, V.

Sunshine Café. American. This efficient, busy eatery is known for its great food. Sit out on the porch and start with the grilled portobello pita pizza with rosemary Gorgonzola sauce, artichokes, and chorizo sausage, followed by sesame seed–crusted tuna over greens tossed

with a wasabi and soy vinaigrette. | Captiva Village Square, Captiva Dr. | 941/472–6200 |
Tues. | $21–$27 | AE, MC, V.

Lodging

Jensen's Twin Palm Cottages and Marina. This collection of cottages on Captiva's bay side
are run by three brothers. Coconut palms and palmetto-thatched tiki huts line the beach.
The 1950s marina here is great for fishing and boating; you can rent boats or take a water
taxi to surrounding islands. The cottages have modern kitchens, screened-in porches, and
tin roofs to enjoy the sound of summer rains. Kitchenettes, microwaves, refrigerators. Cable
TV. Dock, boating, fishing. | 15107 Captiva Dr. | 941/472–5800 | fax 941/472–9263 | www.jensen-
captiva.com | 14 cottages | $135–$165 | AE, D, MC, V.

South Seas Plantation Resort and Yacht Harbor. This superb 330-acre resort has its own
private 2½-mile beach. Low-rise accommodations—from hotel rooms to villas, cottages,
and even some private homes—are tucked around the property in keeping with a peaceful spirit. A nature center, tracts of grassy dune and mangrove forest, and sea-turtle
patrols show the resort's sensitivity to nature while offering a complete range of recreational activities. Rates can drop as much as 40% off-season. 4 restaurants, 3 bars (with
entertainment), picnic area, room service. Some in-room data ports, in-room safes, some
kitchenettes, some microwaves, refrigerators. Cable TV, in-room VCRs. 8 outdoor pools. Barbershop, beauty salon, 3 hot tubs, massage, sauna. 9-hole golf course, putting green, 21
tennis courts. Gym, volleyball, beach, water sports, boating, fishing, bicycles. Shops, video
games. Baby-sitting, kids' program (ages 3–11), playground. Laundry facilities, laundry ser-
vice. Business services. | Captiva Dr. | 941/472–5111 or 800/237–3102 | fax 941/472–7541 |
www.south-seas-resort.com | 620 units | $185–$485 | AE, D, DC, MC, V.

Tween Water Inn. Luxury has a casual, breezy style at this sprawling island resort. The rooms
are each different, but all represent the Old Florida look and comfort. Though some of the
cottages are originals from the 1930s, most of the inn is more modern like the fitness center. You have your choice of several dining options, from casual to classy. 4 restaurants, complimentary Continental breakfast. Some kitchenettes, some microwaves, some refrigerators,
in-room safes. Pool, wading pool. Massage. Tennis. Gym. Water sports, kayaking, boating,
fishing, beach, dock. Laundry facilities. Pets allowed (fee). | 15951 Captiva Dr. | 941/472–5161
or 800/223–5865 | fax 941/472–0249 | www.tween-waters.com | 137 units | $105–$235 | AE,
D, MC, V.

CEDAR KEY

MAP 3, H4

(Nearby towns also listed: Chiefland, Crystal River, Homosassa Springs, Ocala)

Cedar Key (pop. 1,000) is actually the name of the only town on Way Key, one of about
100 low-lying keys among the marshes and scenic streams feeding the Gulf of Mexico
some 60 mi southwest of Gainesville. Way Key is the only island of this group connected
to the mainland. Town life is laid-back and centers around "The Dock," a Cannery
Row–style pier with art galleries, gift shops, and seafood restaurants. This downtown
area has become a favorite weekend jaunt for University of Florida students, who make
the one-hour trip from Gainesville. In the 1860s Cedar Key became the western termi-
nal of Florida's first trans-state railroad, and over the next few decades some of the
nation's top pencil factories logged the island's now-depleted red cedars. Besides
tourism, the island now survives on clamming and fishing.

Information: Cedar Key Area Chamber of Commerce | 480 Second St., Box 610, Cedar
Key, 32625 | 904/543–5600 | www.cedarkey.org.

Attractions

Cedar Key Historical Society Museum. Among photographs and exhibits displayed inside this 1871 home are maps and charts of early Florida, vintage photos, and Native American artifacts. | 609 2nd St. | 352/543–5549 | www.cedarkeymuseum.org | $1 | May–Oct., Sun.–Thurs. 2–5, Fri.–Sat. 11–5; Nov.–Apr., Mon.–Sat. 11–5, Sun. 2–5.

Cedar Key State Museum. The museum includes exhibits on the Timucuan Indians, antique glassware, old bottles, a very complete collection of sea shells, items from the pencil, fiber broom, and brush manufacturing days, and photographs of old Cedar Key. | 12231 S.W. 166th Ct. | 352/543–5350 | $1 | Thurs.–Mon. 9–5.

Cedar Key Scrub State Reserve. This reserve on Highway 24, 6 mi from Cedar Key, includes salt marsh, pine flatwoods, and sand pine scrub habitats. It's home to a variety of wildlife, including the Florida scrub jay, southern bald eagle, gopher tortoise, and the Florida mouse. You can fish, canoe, or picnic. | 12231 SW 166 Ct. | 352/543–5567 | www.dep.state.fl.us/parks | Free | Daily 9–sunset.

ON THE CALENDAR

APR.: *Sidewalk Arts Festival.* This two-day event in the city park at 2nd and A streets features works from Florida artists. There is also great seafood and live music. | 352/543–5600.

OCT.: *Seafood Festival.* Seafood dishes are sold along downtown's 2nd Street the third weekend of the month. There are also more than 200 regional artists exhibiting their works. | 352/543–5600.

Dining

Brown Pelican Restaurant. Seafood. Paintings with boat and ocean scenes line on walls of this laid-back spot. Try the Molly Brown, a combination seafood plate with shrimp, oysters, clams, and fish. The palm salad with ice-cream dressing is very popular. There's a kids' menu. | 490 Dock St. | 352/490–9466 | $15–$25 | AE, D, MC, V.

The Captain's Table. Seafood. Floor-to-ceiling sliding glass doors yield gulf views; in spring and fall the doors are opened to create an open-air dining room. The restaurant is known for its jambalaya, conch fritters, baked stuffed flounder, and char-grilled grouper. | 222 Dock St. | 352/543–5441 | $11–$29 | AE, D, MC, V.

Island Hotel. Seafood. The restaurant of this vintage inn was built in 1859 and has a pink interior ornamented with pictures of Paris. Specialty dishes include stuffed grouper topped with shrimp and cheese sauce, and the heart of palm salad, which is served over a bed of lettuce with seasonal fruits and a house ice cream and peanut butter dressing. Breakfast is available weekends. | 373 2nd St. | 352/543–5111 | Closed Tues. No lunch | $15–$25 | D, MC, V.

Island Room. Seafood. On the ground floor of the Cedar Cove Beach and Yacht Club, this upscale spot has great views of the Gulf of Mexico. Recommended dishes include the snapper piccata and the linguine vongole. The covered patio makes a nice spot for Sunday brunch. | 10 E. 2nd St. | 352/543–6520 | No lunch Mon.–Thurs. | $12–$24 | AE, D, MC, V.

Pat's Red Luck Café. Seafood. This obvious local favorite is also one of the best places to get a bite of some fresh fish or shrimp. The crab cakes are popular as is the shrimp casino (egg-dipped and fried shrimp served with sautéed vegetables). Homemade desserts are available daily, ranging from Key lime pie to chocolate mousse. | On the dock | 352/543–6840 | No dinner Mon.–Thurs. Breakfast also available | $10–$17 | MC, V.

Lodging

Cedar Key B&B. This B&B was built in 1880 entirely of native yellow pine by the Eagle Cedar Mill, as an employee and guest house. It was later operated as a boarding house by the daughter of David Levy Yulee, a U.S. senator for whom the county is named. The two-story house under the shade of an enormous oak is ideal for relaxing, romantic getaways.

Seven rooms with individual names and styles come with lace curtains, rattan furniture, and access to verandas and porches with gulf views. Complimentary breakfast. No room phones, no TV. Bicycles. No smoking. | 810 3rd St. | 352/543–9000 or 877/543–5051 | fax 352/543–8070 | www.cedarkeybedbreakfast.com | 7 rooms | $75–$120 | D, MC, V.

Gulf Side Motel. Some of the rooms at this single-story motel have views of the Gulf of Mexico. You can fish off the 180-ft pier or use the deck swing in the cool Gulf breeze. Restaurants, shops, and the historic downtown district are within walking distance. Some kitchenettes, some microwaves, some refrigerators. Cable TV. Fishing. Pets allowed (fee). | 552 1st St. | 352/543–5308 or 888/364–0477 | www.gulfsidemotel.com | 9 rooms | $50–$60 | D, MC, V.

Island Place. This modern condo-looking complex is filled with one- and two-bedroom apartments. Each is uniquely decorated and has a balcony overlooking the Gulf. You can utterly relax here and book a fishing trip or simply order out from the ringed binder provided in each unit, which lists the town's best restaurants. Washers and dryers are in each unit. Kitchenettes, microwaves, refrigerators. Cable TV. Pool. Hot tub. Laundry facilities. | 1st and C Sts. | 352/543–5306 or 800/780–6522 | fax 352/543–9141 | www.islandplace-ck.com | 27 1-bedroom suites, 3 2-bedroom suites | $85–$110 | MC, V.

Park Place Motel and Condominiums. This three-story motel offers standard rooms and condominiums. All the units have private balconies that overlook the city park or the gulf. There is an outdoor gazebo and barbecue. Picnic area. Kitchenettes, microwaves, refrigerators, in-room VCRs, cable TV. | 211 2nd St. | 352/543–5737 | fax 352/543–8011 | 31 rooms | $75–$85 | AE, D, MC, V.

CHATTAHOOCHEE

MAP 3, E2

(Nearby towns also listed: Blountstown, Marianna, Tallahassee)

Located on a high bluff overlooking the Apalachicola River and Lake Seminole on the Georgia border, this one-time Federal Arsenal during the Civil War has great fishing, boating, camping, and water sports. The lush rolling woodlands at one of Florida's highest elevations, bisected by I–10, 12 miles west of Tallahassee, make the town (pop. 3,913) popular with bikers. Nearby Lake Seminole is a huge lake (37,500 acres) with 500 miles of shoreline. Gadsden County's North Florida Art Trail follows roadways to art galleries, artists' studios, historic tobacco barns, bed and breakfast inns, bright outdoor murals, Victorian homes, and historic landmarks from Chattahoochee into surrounding towns.

The town's name is said to be from the Cherokee word for colored or marked stone. In 1819 General Andrew Jackson came to the area to establish civil government in northern Florida. In the early 1900s the area became known as River Junction and was incorporated in 1921, becoming Chattahoochee in 1938.

Information: Southwest Quarter Chattahoochee Chamber of Commerce | 201 N. Lumpkin St., Cuthbert, GA 31740 | 912/732–2683 | fax 912/732–6590.

ON THE CALENDAR
NOV.: *Chattahoochee Fall Festival.* Arts and crafts display, live music, a boat parade, and a fireworks display on the Apalachicola River highlight this fun fest the second Saturday in November at Riverfront Landing. | 850/663–4475.

Dining
The Homeplace Restaurant. American. Football plaques and early 1900s advertising signs decorate this restaurant, known for juicy hamburgers, fried chicken, and steaks. | 415 W. Washington St. | 850/663–4040 | $6–$9 | No credit cards.

Lodging

Admiral Benbow Morgan Lodge. This single-story lodge off Highway 90 has a 24-hr restaurant next door. Lake Seminole is just minutes away. Microwaves available, refrigerators available. Cable TV. Pets allowed (fee). | 116 E. Washington St. | 850/663–4336 or 800/451–1986 | fax 850/663–4336 | www.admiralbenbow.com | 43 rooms | $50–$55 | AE, MC, V.

CHIEFLAND

MAP 3, H4

(Nearby towns also listed: Cedar Key, Gainesville, Micanopy)

In this small town (pop. 2,000) 40 mi inland from Cedar Key in northern Florida, you can camp not far from the Suwannee River, or take a canoe trip on this stream, famous ever since composer Stephen Foster wrote about it more than a century ago (though he called it "Swanee"). Foster never actually set foot in Florida—he picked the name because he liked the sound of it. The surrounding terrain is now the 50,000-acre Lower Suwannee National Wildlife Refuge, home of more than 90 species of birds, including bald eagles.

Information: Chiefland Chamber of Commerce | 17 N. Main St., Box 1397, Chiefland, FL 32626 | 352/493–1849.

Attractions

Log Cabin Quilting Museum. The quilters among us will rejoice at this collection, which includes quilts dating back to 1857. There are also artifacts and crafts from Chiefland's earliest days. | 11050 NW 10th Ave. | 352/493–2801 | Free | By appointment.

Manatee Springs State Park. Springs gushing over 117 million gallons of crystalline water daily highlight this 2,300-acre preserve. A boardwalk near the springs overlooks a river swamp alive with cypress, gum, ash, and maple trees, and terminates at a pavilion and a floating boat dock on the scenic Suwannee River. You can picnic, fish, swim, canoe, camp, go boating, or hike and bike on an 8½-mi trail. | Hwy. 320 | 352/493–6072 | $3.75 per vehicle | Daily.

ON THE CALENDAR

DEC.: *Manatee Springs Christmas Festival.* Santa's workshop is surrounded by towering cypress, gum, ash, and maple trees decorated with Christmas lights at this yuletide fest at Manatee Springs State Park. | 352/493–6072.

Dining

Rhodes Real Pit Barbecue. Barbecue. Antique bowls and pots hang from the walls and birdhouses sit in the windows of this casual country restaurant known for its baby back ribs and steaks. There's an all-you-can-eat shrimp special Saturday night. | 1302 N. Young Blvd. | 352/490–9466 | $6–$12 | AE, D, MC, V.

Lodging

Best Western Suwannee Valley Inn. You'll know you're at this motel when you see the broad blue roof. It's 6 mi from Suwannee River and Manatee State Park, 26 mi from the Gulf of Mexico. Complimentary Continental breakfast. Some microwaves, some refrigerators. Pool. Laundry service. Some pets allowed. | 1125 N. Young Blvd. | 352/493–0663 | fax 352/493–0663 | www.bestwestern.com | 60 rooms | $55–$75 | AE, D, MC, V.

Holiday Inn Express. This is a slimmed-down version of bigger Holiday Inns. The motel is 7 mi from the Suwannee River and 5 mi from Manatee Springs State Park. Complimentary Continental breakfast. Some microwaves, cable TV. Pool. Hot tub. Business services. | 809 N.W. 21st Ave. | 352/493–9400 or 800/465–4329 | fax 352/493–4050 | www.holiday-inn.com | 65 rooms | $66–$72 | AE, D, DC, MC, V.

Manatee Springs Motel. This single-story motel is 5 mi from Manatee Springs State Park. A number of eateries are within walking distance. Some kitchenettes, microwaves, refrigerators. Cable TV. Some pets allowed. | 2226 Young Blvd. | 352/493–2991 | fax 352/493–2991 | 18 rooms | $40–$45 | AE, D, MC, V.

CHIPLEY

(Nearby towns also listed: De Funiak Springs, Marianna)

This Panhandle town of 4,100 on I–10, at the intersections of State Highways 77 and 90, is named for magnate William D. Chipley, who created one of the first major railroads in Florida. A plaque in front of the agricultural center on I–90 west reads "Kudzu Developed Here," in honor of Lillie and C. E. Pleas, locals who spent three decades developing and promoting the vine.

Chipley, the seat of Washington County, is 50 mi inland from the Gulf of Mexico, near the state's northern border. Two mi south on Highway 77 is Falling Waters State Recreation Area, famous for Falling Waters Sink, a waterfall visible from an observation deck. Ten miles northeast of Falling Waters (take U.S. 231 off I–10) is Florida Caverns State Park, which, besides stalactites and stalagmites, has canoeing and campsites on the Chipola River. You can also canoe, dive, and swim in Cypress Springs, a huge spring 15 miles south of Chipley in Vernon.

KUDZU: THE PLANT THAT ATE THE SOUTH

It seemed like a good idea at the time!

In 1876, the United States celebrated its 100th birthday with a Centennial Exhibition in Philadelphia, Pennsylvania. Foreign countries were invited to exhibit, and the Japanese government came through with a beautiful garden filled with plants native to Japan. One of these was the kudzu vine; with its large dark green leaves, small purple flowers that smell a little like sweet grapes, and easy cultivation it immediately became popular with American gardeners. And in no time at all, kudzu was out of control.

It grows at a phenomenal rate. Under the best conditions, kudzu vines can grow as much as 60 ft in a year and, in summer, a vine can grow as much as a foot each day. That works out to half an inch every hour. Think of it this way: A kudzu vine will grow the width of this book from dawn to dusk. At that rate, you can practically watch it grow!

The southeastern part of the U.S. turned out to be ideal for kudzu and, with root systems that can stretch 12 ft into the earth, kudzu settled in for a long stay. Today it covers more than seven million acres of the South and, because of the way it propagates, a single acre can have as many as 10,000 separate plants. And it won't go away. The best methods of eradicating it can take as much as three to ten years to show any results at all.

Although commonly used in foods and medicines in China and Japan, kudzu has no dignity in the United States. Over the years, kudzu has been promoted for a variety of uses, ranging from erosion control to fodder for animals, and a lady in Georgia markets kudzu blossom jelly and baskets made of dried kudzu. But only one really good and long-lasting use has been found for the vine so far in the United States. Free and fast-growing, kudzu makes a terrific ornament for outhouses.

© Corbis

Information: **Washington County Chamber of Commerce** | 685 N. 7th St., Chipley, 32428 | 850/638–4157 | www.washcomall.com.

Attractions

Falling Waters State Recreation Area. A 67-ft waterfall and a 100-ft-deep sink hole are the famous geological features of this park. You can hike the numerous short trails to see the many sink holes, a swimming lake, and a butterfly garden. | 1130 State Park Rd. | 850/638–6130 | www.dep.state.fl.us/parks | $3.25 per vehicle | Daily 8–sunset.

ON THE CALENDAR

JUNE: *Watermelon Festival.* Kids love the melon-rolling and seed-spitting contests at this lively festival the last Saturday in June at the Agricultural Center on Jackson Ave. There is also live bluegrass music and an antique car show. | 850/638–4157.

Dining

Coffee House Restaurant. Southern. This casual diner serves up tasty fried catfish and T-bone steaks. For dessert try the peach cobbler. | 1593 Main St. | 850/638–9781 | $6–$10 | MC, V.

Lodging

Holiday Inn Express. This motel is about 3 mi east of downtown Chipley. In-room data ports, refrigerators, some in-room hot tubs. Cable TV. Outdoor pool. Business services. Pets allowed (fee). | 1700 A Main St., #A | 850/638–3996 or 800/465–4329 | fax 850/638–4569 | www.hiexpress.com | 48 rooms, 2 suites | $62–$81 | AE, D, DC, MC, V.

CLEARWATER

MAP 3, H6

(Nearby towns also listed: Dunedin, Indian Rocks Beach, Redington Beach, Tampa, Tarpon Springs)

Pinellas County's largest city (pop. 106,000), Clearwater is located 12 mi north of St. Petersburg on Pinellas Peninsula. While there are many residential areas and sprawling shopping plazas, the city is more of a thoroughfare for the gorgeous beaches along the 30-mi strand of barrier islands offshore that make up the Pinellas Sun Coast. The northernmost of these islands, Clearwater Beach, belongs to Clearwater, and is connected to downtown via the 2-mi Memorial Causeway. There are nightly sunset celebrations on the beach here at Pier 60.

A state park on underdeveloped Caladesi Island, reachable only by ferry from Honeymoon Island (Dunedin), has a terrific beach and a self-guided nature trail that winds through the interior of the island. Spanish explorers arrived in Clearwater in 1528 and marveled at the area's clear springs; the name stuck. The first white settlers trickled in during the 1830s and the town was named Clear Water Harbor until the municipality was chartered Clearwater in 1915. The Philadelphia Phillies baseball team plays here during spring training.

Information: **Greater Clearwater Chamber of Commerce** | 1130 Cleveland St., Clearwater, 33755 | 727/461–0011 | www.clearwaterflorida.org.

Attractions

Clearwater Marine Aquarium. This aquarium rescues and rehabilitates marine mammals, sea turtles, and otters, while you learn about them through exhibits. Dolphins and sea turtles are on view in 350,000-gallon aquariums, and there is a beach holding tank with sharks and stingrays. | 249 Windward Passage, Clearwater | 727/441–1790 | www.cmaquarium.org | $6.75 | Weekdays 9–5, Sat. 9–4; Sun. 11–4.

Heritage Village. This 21-acre turn-of-the-20th-century Pinellas County village includes restored homes of local pioneers from the 1850s, the historic wooden Lowe Barn, a railroad depot, and ten other historical structures. The Pinellas Historical Museum traces the county's history from the Spanish-Indian period to contemporary times. | 11909 125th St. N, Largo | 727/582–2123 | Free | Tues.–Sat. 10–4, Sun. 1–4.

Moccasin Lake Nature Park. This 50-acre park preserves upland forest and wetlands and protects native plant and animal species. A 35-min walk takes you on a nature trail around Moccasin Lake. | 2750 Park Trail Lane, Clearwater | 727/462–6024 | $2 | Tues.–Fri. 9–5, weekends 10–6.

Pier 60. The 1,050-ft pier and New Pier 60 Park is a gathering spot for Key West–style sunset celebrations daily each summer, with tightrope walking, juggling, magic, and musicians. The park includes fishing, concessions, playground, and a covered pavilion for regularly programmed entertainment. | Pier 60 Park, Clearwater Beach | 727/461–7732 | Free | Mon.–Sat. 6–9, Sun. 5–8.

Ruth Eckerd Hall. This first-rate concert hall hosts ballet, opera, and pop, classical, and jazz music performances. The Florida Orchestra, one of Tampa Bay's leading performing arts institutions, performs a dozen concerts a year here. | 1111 McMullen Booth Rd., Clearwater | 727/791–7400.

SIGHTSEEING TOURS/TOUR COMPANIES

Captain Memo's Pirate Cruise. Cruise away into the fantasy world of swashbucklers and pirates aboard the *Pirate's Ransom*. The journey cruises within cannon range of Captain Memo's deserted island along Florida's Intracoastal Waterway, and out into the Gulf of Mexico along Clearwater Beach. | Clearwater Marina | 727/446–2587 | fax 727/447–3033 | www.captainmemo.com | $28–$30 | Daily.

Show Queen. The *Show Queen* is a 65-ft triple-decked riverboat specifically designed for harbor cruises on Clearwater Harbor. There are lunch and dinner cruises along the Intracoastal Waterway, and narrated sightseeing tours. Departure is from Clearwater Beach Marina. | 25 Causeway Blvd., Clearwater Beach | 727/461–3113 | www.showqueen.com | $8.95–$10.95 | Daily.

Starlight Majesty. This cruise boat sails from Clearwater Beach Marina for two-hour sightseeing and lunch trips in Clearwater Harbor and 3½-hour dinner-and-dancing cruises. There is a live house band on the dancing cruises. Departures from Clearwater Beach Marina, at the west end of State Road 60. | Clearwater Beach Marina | 727/462–2628 | $8.95 | Tues.–Sat. 12:30, evening cruise 6:30.

ON THE CALENDAR

MAR.– APR.: *Spring Training.* Jack Russell Memorial Stadium has been the winter home of the Philadelphia Phillies since 1955. You can watch the team work out during morning practices and against visiting teams. | 727/442–8496.

APR.–MAY: *Fun 'n Sun Festival.* This festival in Crest Lake Park, first staged in 1953, draws more than 100,000 annually. There are concerts, sports competitions, arts and crafts, and food. The main attraction is the illuminated Fun 'n Sun Night Parade. | 727/562–4800.

OCT.: *Jazz Holiday.* Top musicians play at this night of hot jazz and cool breezes in Coachman Park. | 727/461–5200 | www.clearwaterjazz.com.

NOV.: *Festival of Trees.* In anticipation of the coming holiday season, local restaurants and businesses decorate Christmas trees in Harborview Center. Bids are taken on the trees and the money is donated to charity. | 300 Cleveland St., Clearwater | 727/461–0011.

NOV.: *The Suncoast Dixieland Jazz Classic.* This weekend festival features live jazz and swing music performed by bands from all over the country. | Sheraton Sand Key Resort, 1160 Gulf Blvd. | 727/595–1611.

Dining

Alfano's Restaurant. Italian. This elegant restaurant serves wonderful northern Italian cuisine. The dining room is designed to look like the interior of an old Venetian hotel. There is a jazz pianist every Wednesday. Try the shrimp Milano or the roast duck. | 1702 Clearwater–Largo Rd. | 727/584–2125 | No lunch weekends | $11–$23 | AE, D, MC, V.

Arigato Japanese Steak House. Japanese. At this restaurant in the Ramada Inn Countryside, chefs prepare traditional meals directly at your table. All the chicken and shrimp dishes come with a "secret" dipping sauce. | 26508 U.S. 19 N, Clearwater | 727/799–0202 | No lunch | $12–$25 | AE, D, DC, MC, V.

Bob Heilman's Beachcomber. Seafood. This restaurant flies in some hard-to-find seafood, such as North Carolina trout, Boston scrod, and red snapper. There are three dining rooms, including one with high ceilings, a waterfall, and daily piano music. For more casual dining, there is a patio bistro run by the same owner behind the Beachcomber. | 447 Mandalay Ave., Clearwater Beach | 727/442–4144 | $13–$27 | AE, D, DC, MC, V.

Big Ben British Restaurant and Pub. English. British flags, miniature Big Ben towers, and the most extensive selection of British beer in the area make this the best place around to watch a soccer game. Traditional pub entrées include Abbey steak and mushroom pie and Southend fish and chips. | 731 Bayway Blvd., Clearwater Beach | 727/446–8809 | www.bigbenpub.com | Breakfast also available | $6–$15 | AE, D, MC, V.

Britt's Cafe. American. Anchors, fishing nets, and fishing poles are spread throughout this casual spot. A varied menu includes pastas, steaks, fish and chips, and hummus and tahini. Dining outdoors provides view of the Gulf. | 201 Gulfview Blvd., Clearwater Beach | 727/461–5185 | Breakfast also available weekends | No dinner weekends | $9–$29 | AE, D, MC, V.

Calico Jack's. Seafood. A bi-level dining room has Gulf views from this casual spot decorated with nautical paintings. A $20 seafood buffet includes shrimp, crab legs, and mussels. Prime rib is another popular selection here. There is a kids' menu. | 430 S. Gulfview Blvd., Clearwater Beach | 727/443–5714 | Breakfast also available | No lunch | $14–$22 | AE, D, DC, MC, V.

Carmelita's Mexican Restaurant. Mexican. Known for its all-you-can-eat tacos and homemade tamales, this restaurant has tables inlaid with ceramic tile (and, of course, oversized sombreros on the walls). | 5042 E. Bay Dr., Clearwater | 727/524–8226 | Reservations not accepted | $8–$10 | AE, D, MC, V.

Columbia Restaurant. Spanish. This family-owned eatery is a venerable Spanish restaurant—the first of six Florida Columbia eateries opened in 1905—serving classic dishes such as paella Valencia and snapper Alicante. Outdoor dining is on an uncovered patio overlooking the Intracoastal Waterway. | 1241 Gulf Blvd., Clearwater Beach | 727/596–8400 | $14–$23 | AE, D, DC, MC, V.

Cooter's Raw Bar & Restaurant. Seafood. Flags and license plates from all over decorate this casual spot. The grouper is fresh and the all-you-can-eat snow crab on Mondays and Tuesdays is very popular. There's a kids' menu. | 423 Poinsettia Ave., Clearwater Beach | 727/462–2668 | $9–$13 | AE, D, MC, V.

E&E Stakeout Grill. Southwestern. This lively restaurant has a waterfall cascading down the adobe wall of the lobby, a collection of cacti, two dining rooms, and Kokopelli's Bar. Try the grouper blackened, almond-crusted, or grilled, or the cut-to-order filet mignon. | 100 N. Indian Rocks Rd., Belleair Bluffs | 727/585–6399 | No lunch weekends | $11–$34 | AE, D, DC, MC, V.

Frenchy's Rockaway. Seafood. Owner Frenchy catches his own seafood, and serves it at his casual, beachside restaurant. Most of the tables have ocean views; the deck, a great spot to watch the sunset, is right on the sand. For lunch, try the "crabby shrimp" sandwich. Other popular dishes include stuffed grouper and Caribbean pork chops. | 7 Rockaway St., Clearwater Beach | 727/446–4844 | Reservations not accepted | $6–$14 | AE, MC, V.

Frenchy's Saltwater Cafe. Seafood. This very casual spot has bright Florida colors. The grouper sandwiches and she-crab soup are very popular with locals. There is outdoor dining on a covered patio. | 419 Poinsettia Ave., Clearwater Beach | 727/461–6295 | Reservations not accepted | $6–$12 | AE, MC, V.

G. Bellini's Ristorante. Italian. This trendy and upbeat spot in the Northwood Plaza mall is known for its veal scaloppine, roast duck, and 10 specialty pizzas from the homey brick oven. Kids will enjoy the Italian sodas. Earlybird specials are served from 4:30–6. There is also a full bar. | 2544 N. McMullen Booth Rd., Clearwater | 727/724–5716 | $11–$21 | AE, D, DC, MC, V.

Grill at Feather Sound. American/Casual. A stylish, casual restaurant with a menu of creative fare such as crabcakes and peppercorn seared tuna. There is a wine list with 250 selections and a front patio with five tables. | 2325 Ulmerton Rd., Clearwater | 727/571–3400 | Closed Sun. | $17–$26 | AE, D, DC, MC, V.

Seafood and Sunsets at Julie's. Seafood. This lively restaurant across the street from the ocean posts the time of sunset on a blackboard so you won't miss it. The upstairs dining room has huge windows, for views of the same. You can also eat at one of 12 umbrella-shaded tables on the wooden deck. Try the stuffed flounder, conch, or the grouper Oscar. | 351 S. Gulfview Blvd., Clearwater Beach | 727/441–2548 | Reservations not accepted | $8–$26 | AE, MC, V.

Kaiko Japanese Restaurant. Japanese. Step up to the counter or grab a table and try the traditionally prepared sushi and *makimono* (rolled sushi) specialties. Entrées, including teriyaki-grilled seafood, beef, and chicken, are accompanied by miso soup, a small salad, and rice. For dessert, try the fried ice cream. | 7245 McMullen Booth Rd., Clearwater | 727/791–6640 | Reservations not accepted | No lunch weekends | $10–$19 | AE, D, MC, V.

Key West Grill. Seafood. This restaurant has several different dining rooms with a Key West theme and nautical decorations. The blackened shrimp and scallops, coconut shrimp, and just about any dish with butter sauce are all very good. | 2660 Gulf-to-Bay Blvd., Clearwater | 727/797–1988 | $10–$18 | AE, D, DC, MC, V.

Krazy Bill's. Seafood. There is a decidedly nautical theme, with weathered wood walls, rope as an art form, and polyurethane-coated tables, at this casual spot. Popular dishes include grilled sea bass, Brazilian lobster tail, crab cakes, and shrimp Alfredo. | 37 Causeway Blvd., Clearwater Beach | 727/442–2163 | www.krazybills.com | $8–$29 | AE, MC, V.

Legends Grill. Steak. True to its name, this restaurant is adorned with pictures of all sorts of legends, from famous actors to international landmarks. The T-bone steaks and 16-oz lobster tail are popular. You can dine outdoors on a covered patio that overlooks the beach and the Gulf. | 309 S. Gulfview Blvd., Clearwater Beach | 727/445–1755 | $8–$30 | AE, D, DC, MC, V.

Le Tour Eiffel. French. The atmosphere is very casual in this corner spot at the end of a strip mall, but the delightful cuisine is decidedly French. Try the grilled lamb chops with cucumber-watercress sauce or the vegetable quiche. Daily and nightly specials are scrawled on a blackboard. For breakfast, try a buttery croissant, or a freshly made waffle. | 796 Indian Rocks Rd., Clearwater | 727/581–6530 | Closed Mon. | $17–$29 | D, MC, V.

Leverock's. Seafood. A wide variety of trendy menu items are available at this popular and well-established eatery. The onion-encrusted salmon and the seafood platter with shrimp, mahimahi, and a lobster tail are both very good. All the tables have views of the water, and evening appetizers and cocktails are served on the deck. | 551 Gulf Blvd. | 727/446–5884 | Reservations not accepted | $10–$26 | AE, D, DC, MC, V.

Marco Polo. Continental. Tuxedo-clad waiters here will place a linen napkin in your lap before you begin your meal, so be ready. The main dining room is very intimate and features such dishes as filet mignon and fire-roasted rack of lamb. Once you finish your dinner entrée, move to the adjacent bistro for coffee, dessert, and live entertainment. Tony

Thomas, former guitarist for Sammy Davis Jr., performs twice weekly. | 2516 McMullen Booth Rd., Clearwater | 727/791–7979 | $10–$23 | AE, D, DC, MC, V.

Panda. Cantonese. Decorated with wood carvings and Chinese lights, this restaurant is known for its chicken with garlic sauce and Hong Kong chicken. | 1201 Cleveland St., Clearwater | 727/447–3830 | No lunch Sun. | $6–$15 | AE, D, DC, MC, V.

Pepper Mill. Seafood. This casual and charming restaurant has wooden tables and a dining room that is fashioned after a garden. The fresh seafood selections are very good, and the crabcakes are one of the most popular dishes. | 1575 S. Fort Harrison Ave., Clearwater | 727/449–2988 | No lunch | $16–$25 | AE, D, DC, MC, V.

Shephard's Waterfront Restaurant. American. This family restaurant at the base of Shephard's Beach Resort is known for its beachfront views and breakfast, lunch, and dinner buffets. Popular à la carte dinner choices include beer-battered shrimp and seafood pasta. There is a tiki bar outside serving sandwiches and finger foods. | 601 South Gulfview Blvd., Clearwater Beach | 727/441–6875 | Breakfast also available | $12–$30 | AE, D, DC, MC, V.

Sukhothai. Thai. You can sit on the floor in traditional Thai style, or at one of a number of tables. The spring rolls make a great appetizer and chicken curry with coconut cream is a popular entrée. | 2569 Countryside Blvd., Clearwater | 727/724–2995 | No lunch weekends | $11–$20 | AE, D, DC, MC, V.

Sweetwater's. Seafood. Popular with seniors, this restaurant has fish tanks and a nautical theme. There is an earlybird special; popular dishes include salmon and Danish lobster tails. | 2400 Gulf-to-Bay Blvd., Clearwater | 727/799–0818 | $6–$19 | AE, D, DC, MC, V.

Tio Pepe Restaurante. Spanish. Although, in true Spanish style, it may be hard to hold a conversation over the loud chatter, the pompano and pork chops may make your visit worthwhile. The extensive wine list is also very good. | 2930 Gulf-to-Bay Blvd., Clearwater | 727/799–3082 | Closed Mon. No lunch Fri.–Sun. | $13–$24 | AE, MC, V.

Tommy Duff's Irish Aviation Pub. American. This lively pub is cluttered with miniature jets, plane pictures and other aviation knickknacks. There are a lot of TVs tuned to different sporting events, and 11 burgers and 15 different colorfully named sandwiches to choose from. Try the Blarney Burger, which is topped with Swiss cheese, jalapeños, and onions. | 126 Island Way, Clearwater Beach | 727/449–1366 | www.tommyduffs.com | $6–$11 | AE, D, DC, MC, V.

Lodging

Bay Queen Motel. This motel across the street from Clearwater Bay offers standard rooms and efficiencies with water views. Clearwater Beach is 2 mi away. Weekly and long-term rates are available. Kitchenettes, some microwaves, refrigerators. Cable TV. Pool. Laundry facilities. No pets allowed. | 1925 Edgewater Dr., Clearwater | 727/441–3295 | 18 rooms | $69–$79 | MC, V.

The Beachouse. This inn, 1½ blocks from the beach, has a blue brick courtyard. The spacious, modern rooms have king-size beds. Picnic area. Some kitchenettes, microwaves, refrigerators. Cable TV. Pool. No smoking. | 421 Hamden Dr., Clearwater Beach | 727/461–4862 | fax 727/446–4608 | www.thebeachouse.com | 5 rooms | $95–$185 | MC, V.

The Beach Place Motel. This affordable two-story motel is right across from the beach. Efficiencies have full kitchens. Picnic area. Microwaves, refrigerators. Cable TV. Pool. Beach. Business services. | 301 S. Gulfview Blvd., Clearwater Beach | 727/442–6714 or 800/393–2978 | fax 727/446–8944 | andrea@gate.net | 21 rooms | $69 | MC, V.

Bel Crest Beach Resort. A couple of blocks from the beach on the Intracoastal Waterway, Bel Crest offers cabins and condo suites on a nightly, weekly, or monthly basis (there is a three-night minimum stay off-season, and a five-night minimum in winter). Sleeper sofas and ceiling fans come with all units. Picnic area. In-room safes, microwaves, refrigerators. Cable TV, some in-room VCRs. Pool. Dock, boating, fishing. Laundry facilities. | 706 Bayway

Blvd., Clearwater Beach | 727/442–4923 | fax 727/442–7455 | www.belcrest.com | 18 units | $99–$171 | D, MC, V.

Belleview Biltmore Resort and Spa. This magisterial resort and spa was built in 1897 and is on the National Register of Historic Places. Situated on a high coastal bluff overlooking the Gulf of Mexico and surrounded by stately pine and oak trees, the Belleview Biltmore is thought to be the world's largest occupied wooden structure. A painstaking restoration has revived the feel of a century ago. Units, which vary from extra-cozy little rooms to spacious suites, are off creaky corridors that seem to extend for miles. Although the spa was recently constructed, it matches the rest of the hotel's Victorian opulence. Free transportation is offered to the Cabana Club and Gulf beaches. Restaurant, bar (with entertainment). Some in-room data ports. Cable TV. Pools. Barbershop, beauty salon, hot tubs, massage, sauna, spa, steam room. Driving range, golf privileges, 18-hole golf course, putting green, 4 tennis courts. Gym, volleyball, bicycles. Shops. Playground. Business services. | 25 Belleview Blvd., Clearwater | 727/442–6171 or 800/237–8947 | fax 727/441–4173 | www.belleviewbiltmore.com | 197 rooms, 47 suites | $109–$179 room, $159–$249 suite | AE, D, DC, MC, V.

Best Western Clearwater Central. This hotel is 6 miles from Gulf beaches and 18 mi from Busch Gardens. Many rooms look out over the pool, which is landscaped with palm trees and tiki hut umbrellas. The units on the second floor have balconies. Some microwaves, some refrigerators. Cable TV. Pool. Hot tub. 2 tennis courts. Volleyball. Laundry facilities. Business services. | 21338 U.S. 19 N, Clearwater | 727/799–1565 | fax 727/797–6801 | 150 rooms | $75–$85 | AE, D, DC, MC, V.

Best Western Sea Stone Resort. This resort offers elegant accommodations on the Intracoastal Waterway—the beach is across the street on the opposite side of the Clearwater Beach barrier island. The resort has a private marina and spacious rooms and suites in a seven-floor, Key West–style building. The pool has a sundeck with great views of the water. Restaurant, room service. Some In-room data ports, some microwaves, refrigerators. Cable TV. Pool. Beauty salon, hot tub. Dock, boating, fishing. Babysitting, children's programs (ages 5–12). Laundry facilities. Business services. | 445 Hamden Dr., Clearwater Beach | 727/441–1722 or 800/444–1919 | fax 727/461–1680 | www.bestwestern.com | 44 suites, 65 rooms | $109–$159 | AE, D, DC, MC, V.

Best Western Sea Wake Inn. This six-story hotel is located on its own 500-ft private beach. Most of the nicely decorated rooms have private balconies and ocean views. You can dry off from the ocean at the poolside bar. Restaurant, bars, room service. In-room data ports, microwaves, refrigerators. Cable TV. Pool. Volleyball, beach, fishing. Children's program (ages 5–12), playground. Laundry facilities. Business services. | 691 S. Gulf Blvd., Clearwater Beach | 727/443–7652 or 888/329–8910 | fax 727/461–2836 | www.bestwestern.com | 110 rooms | $159–$199 | AE, D, DC, MC, V.

Brightwater Inn on the Bay. This tidy one-story inn has views of Clearwater Bay and is two blocks from the beach. It has a fishing dock with umbrella-shaded tables, a sun deck, and an interior courtyard with a small, kidney-shaped pool. There are five nicely furnished one-bedroom apts. and two studio apts. Picnic area. Kitchenettes, microwaves, refrigerators. Cable TV. Hot tub. Dock, boating, fishing. | 124 Brightwater Dr., Clearwater Beach | 727/441–3001 | fax 727/447–7423 | www.brightwaterinn.com | 7 rooms | $75 | MC, V.

Clearwater Beach Hotel. This hotel has an attractive, five-story main complex flanked by smaller units on the way to its private beach. The middle ground is centered by a pool, with wide lawns dotted with palm trees. Many rooms have the relaxing balcony views of the hotel grounds, beach, and ocean. There is live music in the Schooner Lounge. Restaurant, bar (with entertainment), room service. Some kitchenettes, refrigerators. Cable TV, in-room VCRs available. Pool. Beach. Business services. | 500 Mandalay Ave., Clearwater Beach | 727/441–2425 or 800/292–2295 | fax 727/449–2083 | www.clearwaterbeachhotel.com | 200 rooms | $160–$220 | AE, DC, MC, V.

Comfort Inn Executive Center. This three-story hotel has a heated pool and a whirlpool in a landscaped courtyard. It's 2 mi south of St. Petersburg/Clearwater International Airport,

12 mi from Clearwater Beach, and ⅓ mi from the Airco Golf Course. Restaurant, complimentary Continental breakfast, room service. In-room data ports, some microwaves, some refrigerators. Cable TV. Pool. Hot tub. Laundry service. Business services. Airport shuttle. | 3580 Ulmerton Rd., Clearwater | 727/573–1171 | fax 727/572–8736 | www.comfortinn.com | 120 rooms | $89–$94 | AE, D, DC, MC, V.

Courtyard Saint Petersburg/Clearwater. This three-story hotel has standard rooms and one-bedroom suites with separate living areas. Feather Sound Country Club and Airco Golf Course are both a mile away; gulf beaches are 8 mi away. In-room data ports, some microwaves, some refrigerators. Cable TV, in-room VCRs. Pool. Hot tub. Gym. Laundry facilities, laundry service. Business services. | 3131 Executive Dr., Clearwater | 727/572–8484 or 800/331–3131 | fax 727/572–6991 | www.marriott.com | 149 rooms | $110–$140 | AE, D, DC, MC, V.

Dunes Motel. The Dunes offers spacious one-, two-, and three-bedroom suites overlooking Clearwater Bay and a good-size pool. The motel is ½ mi to the beach, convenient to dining and shopping, and a short drive to local attractions. In-room data ports, refrigerators. Pool. Dock. Fishing. Laundry services. Business services. | 514 S. Gulfview Blvd., Clearwater Beach | 727/441–4939 | fax 727/443–0490 | www.manningresorts.com | 36 rooms | $90–$172 | AE, D, MC, V.

Econo Lodge Beachfront Resort. This hotel is on a private beach. All rooms have balconies and two double beds; most have ocean views. Picnic area. In-room data ports, kitchenettes, refrigerators. Cable TV. Pool. Hot tub. Beach. Laundry facilities. Business services. | 625 S. Gulfview Blvd., Clearwater Beach | 727/446–3400 or 800/553–2666 | fax 727/446–4615 | www.econolodge.com | 64 rooms | $104–$124 | AE, D, DC, MC, V.

Falcon Motel. This simple, slightly older two-story motel is two blocks from the beach. It has a pool surrounded by many umbrella tables and chaises. Some kitchenettes, microwaves, refrigerators available. Cable TV, in-room VCRs available. Pool. Business services. | 415 Coronado Dr., Clearwater Beach | 727/447–8714 or 800/411–1977 | fax 727/461–3735 | www.internet-ad.com/falcon. | 42 rooms | $85 | D, MC, V.

Haddon House Inn. Done in 1890s Florida cracker style, with white lattice fences and balconies, this two-story inn is right on the Gulf of Mexico. Rooms alternate between Victorian, with redwood floors, and modern. Kitchenettes, refrigerators, microwaves. Cable TV. Outdoor pool. Beach, water sports, fishing. Laundry facilities. | 14 Idlewild St., Clearwater Beach | 727/461–2914 | fax 727/461–2914 | www.internet-ad.com/haddon | 13 suites | $79–$130 suites | AE, D, MC, V.

Hampton Inn Clearwater Central. This motel is 5 mi from St. Petersburg/Clearwater Airport and 13 mi from Tampa International Airport. The beautiful gulf beaches are 6 mi away, and Clearwater Mall is 1 mi away. Complimentary Continental breakfast. In-room data ports, some microwaves, some refrigerators. Cable TV. Pool. Hot tub. Putting green. Gym. Laundry facilities. Business services. | 21030 U.S. Hwy. 19 N, Clearwater | 727/797–8173 or 800/426–7866 | fax 727/791–7759 | www.hampton-inn.com | 118 rooms | $83–$111 | AE, D, DC, MC, V.

Hilton Clearwater Beach Resort. This luxurious, nine-floor, yellow hotel is on its own 4½-acre beach. Standard rooms and suites—including seven king gulf view suites and three executive suites—are available, and most of the units have balconies. There are two oceanfront pools. Restaurant, bar, room service. In-room data ports, in-room safes, some refrigerators. Cable TV. 2 Pools. Hot tub. Gym. Beach, water sports, fishing. Shops. Video games. Children's programs (3–12), playground. Laundry facilities. Business services. | 400 Mandalay Ave., Clearwater Beach | 727/461–3222 or 800/445–8667 | fax 727/446–2371 | www.hilton.com | 425 rooms | $182–$222 | AE, D, DC, MC, V.

Hi-Seas Motel. On the south end of Clearwater Beach, landlocked between the Gulf of Mexico and Clearwater Bay, this motel is a few blocks from the beach. About half the rooms have balconies that look onto the courtyard with its big, heated pool. Picnic area. In-room data ports, in-room safes available, some kitchenettes, microwaves, refrigerators. Cable TV.

Outdoor pool. Laundry facilities. | 455 South Gulfview Blvd., Clearwater Beach | 727/446–6003 | fax 727/443–3955 | www.hi-seas.com | 33 rooms | $95–$105 | AE, D, MC, V.

Holiday Inn Express. In the heart of the Clearwater business district, this hotel offers both standard rooms and suites that feature king-size beds and sleeper sofas. The gulf beaches are 10 mi away. Complimentary Continental breakfast. In-room data ports, some microwaves, some refrigerators. Cable TV. Pool. Hot tub. Business services. Some pets allowed. | 13625 ICOT Blvd., Clearwater | 727/536–7275 or 800/465–4329 | fax 727/530–3053 | www.holiday-inn.com | 127 rooms | $110–$135 | AE, D, DC, MC, V.

Holiday Inn Bayside/City Center. This motel is 4 mi from downtown Clearwater, 5 mi from Clearwater beaches, and 12 mi from Busch Gardens. A two-floor building has motel rooms and a three-story building has luxury suites. Restaurant, room service. In-room data ports, some microwaves, some refrigerators. Cable TV. Pool, wading pool. Hot tub. Gym. Playground. Laundry facilities. Business services. | 20967 U.S. 19 N, Clearwater | 727/799–1181 or 800/465–4329 | fax 727/797–8504 | www.holiday-inn.com | 180 rooms | $80–$95 | AE, D, DC, MC, V.

Holiday Inn Select. This hotel is in the Pinellas County Business District, a mile from the St. Petersburg/Clearwater International Airport. All rooms have a small living area, with a reading chair and full-size desk. Restaurant, bar (with entertainment), room service. In-room data ports. Cable TV. Pool. Hot tub. 2 tennis court. Gym. Laundry service. Business services. Airport shuttle. | 3535 Ulmerton Rd., Clearwater | 727/577–9100 or 800/465–4329 | fax 727/573–5022 | www.holiday-inn.com | 173 rooms | $109–$129 | AE, D, DC, MC, V.

Howard Johnson Express Inn. This simple two-story, pink motel overlooks the Intracoastal Waterway, and has a stretch of private beach 750 ft from the property. All rooms have either a king-size bed or two doubles, and most have a great view of the Waterway. Complimentary Continental breakfast. Some kitchenettes, some microwaves, some refrigerators. Cable TV. Pool. Laundry service. | 656 Bayway Blvd., Clearwater Beach | 727/442–6606 | fax 727/461–0809 | www.hojo.com | 40 rooms | $74–$109 | AE, D, DC, MC, V.

Island Queen Resort Motel. This comfortable, waterfront resort motel has sundecks, a grill, and a pier that juts into the Intracoastal Waterway. The hotel is on one of Clearwater Beach's pier-like, man-made perpendicular stretches; you have to walk a few blocks to the beach. Picnic area. In-room data ports, kitchenettes, microwaves, refrigerators. Cable TV. Pool. Dock, fishing. Laundry facilities. Business services. | 158 Brightwater Dr., Clearwater Beach | 727/442–8068 | fax 727/442-2412 | www.islandqueenmotel.com | 14 rooms | $72–$96 | AE, D, MC, V.

La Quinta Clearwater Airport. This Spanish-style, three-story hotel is a mile from the St. Petersburg/Clearwater Airport, 11 mi from the beaches. All suites have two queen-size beds. There is a second-floor deck where you can relax in a lounge chair. Complimentary Continental breakfast. In-room data ports, refrigerators. Cable TV. Pool. Hot tub, sauna. Gym. Laundry service. Business services, airport shuttle. Some pets allowed. | 3301 Ulmerton Rd., Clearwater | 727/572–7222 or 800/531–5900 | fax 727/572–0076 | www.laquinta.com | 118 rooms | $79–$110 | AE, D, DC, MC, V.

New Yorker Motel. This two-story motel is a block from the beach and is popular with families and couples. There is a barbecue grill, a balcony, and a patio that overlooks the pool. In-room data ports, kitchenettes, microwaves, refrigerators. Cable TV. Pool. Laundry facilities. | 332 Hamden Dr., Clearwater Beach | 727/446–2437 | fax 727/446–5818 | www.newyorkermotel.com | 15 rooms | $78–$97 | D, MC, V.

Patio Motel. Beach daisies are among the lush landscaping of the hotel's eponymous patio, which leads out to the wide gulf sands. Accommodations, which vary widely in prices, are furnished with rattan furniture. Some suites have vast beachfront views through glass doors. Some kitchenettes, some microwaves, refrigerators. Cable TV. Beach. Laundry facilities. | 15 Somerset St., Clearwater Beach | 727/442–1862 | fax 727/447–5825 | www.internet-ad.com/patiomotel | 14 units | $55–$93 | MC, V.

Porpoise Inn. Nestled in a quiet neighborhood on the northern part of Clearwater Beach, this simple, single-floor hotel is within steps of the Intracoastal Waterway and beautiful white sand beaches. There are many restaurants within walking distance. Picnic area. Kitchenettes, microwaves, refrigerators. Cable TV, in-room VCRs. Outdoor hot tub. Laundry facilities. No smoking. | 609 Cypress Ave., Clearwater Beach | 727/442–2022 or 888/441–2022 | fax 727/442–8396 | www.porpoiseinn.com | 6 apartments | $60 | No credit cards.

Quality Inn Beach Resort. This five-story hotel is on its own private beach. All rooms have a balcony or patio, and most of them have views of the ocean. There is a large waterfront deck and bar that often has live music. Restaurant, bar (with entertainment), picnic area, room service. In-room data ports, in-room safes, microwaves, refrigerators. Cable TV. Pool. Beach. Playground. Laundry facilities. Business services. | 655 S. Gulfview Blvd., Clearwater Beach | 727/442–7171 | fax 727/446–7177 | www.qualitybeachresort.com | 91 rooms | $159–$199 | AE, D, DC, MC, V.

Radisson Suite Resort on Sand Key. All units are suites in this 10-story resort overlooking the Intracoastal Waterway. All rooms have 2 TVs, a private balcony, and a sofa bed. The amorphous swimming pool is anchored by a 35-ft rock cascade. Sand Key Park beach, which is known for its natural environment and white sands, is only a 5-min walk from the property. 5 restaurants, 3 bars (with entertainment), room service. In-room data ports, kitchenettes, microwaves, refrigerators. Cable TV. Pool. Hot tub, massage, sauna, spa. Gym. Shops. Children's programs (ages 4–12), playground. Laundry facilities. Business services. | 1201 Gulf Blvd., Clearwater Beach | 727/596–1100 | fax 727/595–4292 | www.radisson-sandkey.com | 220 suites | $200–$319 | AE, D, DC, MC, V.

Ramada Inn Gulfview. This hotel overlooks Clearwater Pass in the Gulf of Mexico. All rooms have private balconies, and the beach is only 600 ft from the property. There is a sundeck by the pool, which has fantastic views of the water. The outdoor tiki bar offers live entertainment and great tropical drinks. Restaurant, 2 bars (with entertainment), room service. In-room data ports, in-room safes, some microwaves, some refrigerators. Cable TV. Pool, wading pool. Barbershop, beauty salon. Video games. Laundry service. Business services. | 521 S. Gulfview Blvd., Clearwater Beach | 727/447–6461 or 888/298–2054 | fax 727/443–5888 | www.ramada.com | 289 rooms | $109–$139 | AE, D, DC, MC, V.

Ramada Inn Countryside. This attractive five-story hotel offers both standard rooms and two-room suites with separate living areas. Downtown Dunedin, Pinellas Trail, and Caladesi State Park are all within 10 mi of the property; Clearwater beach is 20 mi away. Restaurant, bar (with entertainment). In-room data ports, some microwaves, some refrigerators, some in-room hot tubs. Cable TV. Pool. Hot tub. Tennis court. Laundry facilities. Business services. | 26508 U.S. 19 N, Clearwater | 727/796–1234 | fax 727/796–0452 | www.ramada.com | 125 rooms | $89–$109 | AE, D, DC, MC, V.

Ramada Limited. This three-story inn is 5 mi from the St. Petersburg/Clearwater airport and 10 mi from the gulf beaches. There are many restaurants and shops nearby. Refrigerators. Cable TV. Outdoor pool, indoor hot tub. Laundry facilities. Business services. | 16405 U.S. Highway 19 N, Clearwater | 727/535–0505 or 888/298–2054 | fax 727/535–0505 | www.ramada.com | 80 rooms, 2 suites | $65–$94 | AE, D, DC, MC, V.

Red Roof Inn. This chain inn has competitive prices and unobstructed views of the beach across the street. Motel rooms, one- and two-bedroom efficiencies, some with private balconies and gulf views. There are a number of gulfside efficiencies; many rooms have private balconies overlooking the ocean. Some in-room safes, some kitchenettes, some microwaves, refrigerators. Cable TV. Pool. Beach. Business services. | 421 S. Gulfview Blvd., Clearwater Beach | 727/447–3464 or 877/905–7663 | fax 727/446–7169 | www.redroof.com | 75 rooms | $125–$200 | AE, D, DC, MC, V.

Residence Inn by Marriott. This hotel has studios, suites, and loft units. Every room has a full kitchen and a fireplace. Gulf beaches are 8 mi away; the Airco and Feather Sound golf courses are within 4 mi. Complimentary Continental breakfast. In-room data ports, kitchenettes, microwaves, refrigerators. Cable TV. Pool. Hot tub. Laundry facilities, laundry service. Business services. Some pets allowed (fee). | 5050 Ulmerton Rd., Clearwater | 727/573–4444 or 800/331–3131 | fax 727/572–4446 | www.residenceinn.com | 88 rooms | $135–$149 | AE, D, DC, MC, V.

Safety Harbor Resort and Spa. The spa and hotel were originally built over natural hot springs on the western shore of Tampa Bay in 1926, but now it's much more modern, with on-site golf and tennis academies. But beside the 22 acres of sports and recreation facilities and luxury accommodations, visitors flock to experience the therapeutic effects of this resort's five natural mineral springs and the 50,000-square-ft spa. A few pleasant hours can be spent exploring the main street of Safety Harbor, a pleasant little hamlet with interesting gift shops and cafés. Restaurant, bar, room service. In-room data ports, some refrigerators. Cable TV. 3 pools. Beauty salon, 2 hot tubs, massage, sauna, spa, steam room. Driving range, putting green, 9 tennis courts. Basketball, gym, volleyball, bicycles. Shops. Laundry facilities, laundry services. Business services. Pets. | 105 N. Bayshore Dr., Safety Harbor | 727/726–1161 or 888/237–8722 | fax 727/726–4268 | www.safetyharborspa.com | 194 rooms | $119–$189 | AE, D, DC, MC, V.

Sea Captain Resort. Rooms in this two-story resort have panoramic views of Clearwater's bay and marina. The beach is 100 yards away. Picnic area. Some kitchenettes, some microwaves, refrigerators. Cable TV. Pool. Hot tub. Beach, dock, boating, fishing. Business services. | 40 Devon Dr., Clearwater Beach | 727/446–7550 or 800/444–7488 | fax 727/298–0100 | www.seacaptainresort.com | 28 rooms | $60–$95 | AE, D, MC, V.

Shephard's Beach Resort. Some rooms at this excellent six-story beachfront resort offer wonderful Gulf views. There is live musical entertainment every evening and there is a nightclub on premises. Restaurant (Shephard's Waterfront Restaurant), bar. In-room data ports, in-room safes, microwaves, refrigerators. Cable TV. Outdoor pool. Spa. Laundry facilities. Beach, water sports. | 619 Gulfview Blvd., Clearwater Beach | 727/442–5107 or 800/237–8477 | www.shephards.com | 48 rooms, 46 suites | $169–$375 | AE, D, DC, MC, V.

Sheraton Sand Key Resort. Set on 10 well-manicured acres, the nine-story, T-shape resort has its own white sand beach adjacent to Sand Key Park. Every room has a private balcony, and most have views of the Gulf or the Intracoastal Waterway. The hotel is considered one of the top corporate and convention spots in the Clearwater area. Restaurants, bars, room service. In-room data ports, refrigerators available. Cable TV. Pool, wading pool. Hot tub, massage. 3 tennis courts. Gym, volleyball. Beach, water sports. Children's programs (5–12), playground. Laundry facilities. Business services. | 1160 Gulf Blvd., Clearwater Beach | 727/595–1611 | fax 727/596–8488 | www.sheraton.com | 390 rooms | $195–$235 | AE, D, DC, MC, V.

Sunrise Resort Motel. Enjoy the sundeck and a barbecue cookout on the patio of this simple two-story motel a block from the beach. The patio also has a heated pool, attractively backed by the Intracoastal Waterway. Some kitchenettes, some microwaves, refrigerators. Cable TV. Outdoor pool. Laundry facilities. Business services. | 229 Coronado Dr. | 727/446–9911 or 800/269–9643 | fax 727/446–1891 | www.sunriseresortfla.com | 22 rooms | $55–$85 | MC, V.

Tropical Breeze. This modern two-story motel is 100 yards from the beach. The units vary from poolside suites to motel rooms. There is a barbecue grill and a shuffleboard alongside the Intracoastal Waterway. Microwaves, refrigerators. Cable TV. Pool. Beach. Fishing. Laundry facilities. Business services. | 333 Hamden Dr., Clearwater Beach | 727/442–6865 or 888/530–1088 | fax 727/443–4371 | www.tropicalbreezeresort.com | 36 rooms | $79–$92 | AE, D, MC, V.

Tropicana Resort Motel. Rooms in this two-story motel, just a block from the beach, are decorated in bright Florida colors, with bleached furniture and flowery curtains. The back side of this motel stretches to the Intracoastal with a small dock for fishing. Some kitchenettes, some microwaves, refrigerators. Cable TV. Outdoor pool. Spa. Beach, dock, fishing. Laundry facilities. | 350 Hamden Dr., Clearwater Beach | 727/442–9540 or 800/827–1602 | fax 727/443–6802 | www.internet-ad.com/tropicana | 32 rooms | $50–$70 | AE, D, DC, MC, V.

CLERMONT

(Nearby towns also listed: Lake Buena Vista, Orlando, Tavares, Walt Disney World)

This town of 10,000, whose population is largely retirees, is 22 miles west of Orlando. Because of its privileged rolling landscape—a rarity in Florida—it's often called the "Gem of the Hills." The town was christened by the New Jersey company that developed it in the late 19th century (Clermont was the French birthplace of the company's General Manager). Besides hills, another geographical allure to the town's setting is a series of 15 interconnected lakes surrounding it, good for water sports and fishing. Highway 50, which cuts through the middle of Clermont, has Lake Minneola to one side, and to the other, Lake Minnehaha.

Information: **Clermont Chamber of Commerce** | 691 W. Montrose St., Clermont, 34711 | 904/394–4191 | www.southlakechamber-fl.com.

Attractions
Citrus Tower. This 10-story structure on the northern outskirts of Clermont was constructed in 1956 when orange groves were abundant in the area. Now, if you go up to the observation deck you can see Lake County's numerous lakes, rolling hills, and, sure, a few orange groves. | 141 U.S. 27N | 352/394–4061 | www.citrustower.com | $3.50 | Daily 9–6.

Lakeridge Winery and Vineyards. This winery, in the rolling hills of South Lake County, is 7 mi from downtown Clermont. It produces Florida wines from grapes developed specifically for the state's climate. One-hour tours are available. | 19239 U.S. 27N | 352/394–8627 or 800/768–9463 | Free | Mon.–Sat. 10–5, Sun. 11–5.

ON THE CALENDAR
JUNE: *Harvest Festival.* Live music, arts and crafts booths, and free wine tasting highlight this event held annually at the Lakeridge Winery and Vineyards. Feel free to participate in the old-fashioned grape stomping. | 19239 U.S. 27N | 352/394–8627.

Dining
On the Corner Seafood Grill. Seafood. In historic Clermont, this casual spot is dressed up with paintings of ocean scenes. Try the shrimp and scallops Clermont, served with a special sauce over pasta. The mixed seafood grill, with your choice of fish, is another popular dish. | 801 W. Montrose St. | 352/394–6911 | No lunch Sat. | $10–$16 | AE, D, DC, MC, V.

Quincy Family Steakhouse. Steak. Book racks and wooden tables and booths give this eatery a country feel. The T-bone and rib-eye steaks are popular, along with standard American fare such as grilled chicken and pork chops. | 1000 E. Hwy. 50 | 352/394–4153 | $6–$13 | AE, D, DC, MC, V.

Lodging
Mulberry Inn Bed and Breakfast. In the downtown historic district you'll find the white picket fence that borders this B&B, built in 1890 by Archabald Gano, a sawmill owner and a Clermont founding father. The upstairs Carriage House is a fully furnished one-bedroom apartment with complete kitchen, living room, bedroom, bathroom and screened porch. Restaurant. In-room data ports. Bicycles. Business services. | 915 Montrose St. | 352/242–0670 | fax 352/242–9898 | www.mulberryinn.com | 4 rooms | $70–$95 | AE, D, DC, MC, V.

Ramada Inn. This two-story inn has an Olympic-size swimming pool. Walt Disney World is 25 mi away. Restaurant, bar. In-room data ports. Cable TV. Outdoor pool. | 20349 U.S. Hwy. 27 | 352/429–2163 or 888/298–2054 | fax 352/429–4994 | www.ramada.com | 200 rooms | $60 | AE, D, DC, MC, V.

Ramada Inn Orlando Westgate. This hotel is actually 20 mi south of Clermont, 6 mi from Walt Disney World. All rooms have two double beds. You can relax poolside and use one of the grills, or have a drink in the tiki hut bar. A free shuttle is provided to Disney World. Restaurant, bar, room service. In-room data ports, microwaves available, refrigerators available. Cable TV, in-room VCRs (and movies). Pool. Video Games. Laundry facilities. Business services. | 9200 W. U.S. Hwy. 192 | 863/424–2621 | fax 863/424–4630 | 198 rooms | $79 | AE, D, DC, MC, V.

Vacation Village. This vacation complex offers lofts and villas that can sleep up to eight people and come with full kitchens. Walt Disney World is a 20-min drive from the property, which is on Lake Louise. There is a private beach, and picnic areas and playgrounds dot the village. Picnic areas. Kitchenettes, microwaves, refrigerators. Cable TV. Pool, wading pool. Tennis courts. Basketball, volleyball. Beach. Playgrounds. Laundry facilities. | 10301 U.S. 27 | 352/394–4091 or 800/962–9969 | fax 352/394–4093 | 198 rooms | $391–427 per week (1–week minimum) | MC, V.

COCOA

MAP 3, K5

(Nearby towns also listed: Cocoa Beach, Melbourne, Titusville)

Cocoa (pop. 18,000), incorporated in 1895, has a quaint historic district, Olde Cocoa Village, with artsy antique shops, art shows, and restaurants. But it is most famously synonymous with NASA. The town has two causeways (Highway 528, and a few miles south, Highway 520) that extend over the Indian River onto Merritt Island, and back over the Banana River to Cocoa Beach. Merritt Island, an unincorporated area with 36,000 residents, is home to the United States space program. The northern half includes the Kennedy Space Center, where space shuttles take off; the space complex is in Titusville, but the best place to see a lift-off may be along Cocoa's waterfront on the Indian River facing Merritt Island. Cape Canaveral, a little town at the northern end of Cocoa Beach's island, is another popular spot for shuttle viewing. North of Cocoa, Playalinda Beach, part of the Canaveral National Seashore, is the longest stretch of undeveloped coast on Florida's Atlantic Seaboard. From May to August hundreds of giant sea turtles lay their eggs on these quiet shores.

No one knows exactly where the name Cocoa came from, though it was attached to the nascent settlement as early as 1884. With the development of the space program the population quadrupled in two decades, to 12,000 by 1960, and received its first influx of tourists.

Information: **Cocoa Beach Area Chamber of Commerce** | 400 Fortenberry Rd., Merritt Island, 32952 | 321/459–2200 | www.cocoabeachchamber.com.

Attractions

Astronaut Memorial Planetarium & Observatory. The observatory, inside Brevard Community College, features a 24-inch telescope through which visitors can view objects in the solar system and deep space—it's one of the largest public-access observatories in Florida. There are also two theaters that offer a choice of intergalactic movies. Travel 2½ mi east of I–95 exit 75 on Route 520, and take Highway 501 north for 1¾ mi. | 1519 Clearlake Rd. | 321/634–3732 | fax 321/634–3744 | www.brevard.cc.fl.us/~planet | Free; film $5 | Tues., Thurs.–Sat. 6:30 PM–9 PM.

Brevard Museum of History and Natural Science. Permanent exhibits in this museum reflect Florida's cultural history through hands-on discovery rooms and the Taylor collection of Victorian memorabilia. The nature center has 22 acres trails encompassing three distinct ecosystems—sand pine hills, lake lands, and marshlands. | 2201 Michigan Ave. | 321/632–

1830 | fax 321/631–7551 | www5.palmnet.net/~brevardmuseum | $4 | Tues.–Sat. 10–4, Sun. 1–4, closed Sun. Jun.–Sept.

Brevard Museum of Arts & Sciences. Children are engaged in hands-on activities at this museum, which also exhibits contemporary and decorative art. Photography and ethnographic works round out the collection. | 2201 Michigan Ave. | 321/632–1830 | $4 | Tues.–Sat. 10–4.

Historic Cocoa Village. Walking down the tree-lined streets, you will see a number of homes and buildings listed on the National Historic Register, some of which date as far back as the 1880s. Along the Indian Riverwalk, you can explore antiques stores, eat an old-fashioned ice cream cone, or rest in a Victorian-style coffee house. Guided tours of 14 historical sites and points of interest are available. | 430 Delannoy Ave. | 407/631–9075 | www.cocoavillage.com | Free | Daily.

Lone Cabbage Fish Camp. You can zoom through the grassy marsh and natural cypress swamp of the St. Johns River and Lake Poinsett at speeds of up to 45 mph at this old-style Florida Fish Camp at the Orange and Brevard county lines. You might see alligators, eagles, and several species of wading birds. Longer tours can be arranged, as well as nighttime rides. Popular menu items include gator tail, frog legs, turtle, and catfish. Every first and third Sunday there is a fish fry, with live country music. A bait and tackle shop and more than 300 ft of dock space are available. From I–95 take exit 75, and go west to the St. Johns River. | Rte. 520 and St. Johns River, Cocoa | 321/632–4199 | $15 boat rides | Daily.

ON THE CALENDAR

OCT.: *Fall Craft Fair.* This two-day event brings together more than 300 crafters to sell and show their wood, glass, and ceramic work. | Downtown Cocoa Village | 321/639–7551.

Dining

Black Tulip. Continental. This cozy, intimate restaurant in Cocoa Village is known for its roast duckling with apples and cashews, steak au poivre, and linguine with chicken in a garlic and white wine sauce. | 207 Brevard Ave. | 407/631–1133 | Reservations essential | Closed Sun. | $15–$24 | AE, D, MC, V.

Café Margaux. French. The menu at this small, intimate spot in Cocoa Village features an eclectic mix of classical French and Italian cuisines. Try the roast duck with berries, the fillet of beef with port wine sauce, or the pistachio- and walnut-encrusted sea bass. Dine in a beflowered dining room or in the charming outdoor courtyard. | 220 Brevard Ave. | 407/639–8343 | Closed Tues. | $16–$26 | AE, D, DC, MC, V.

Lone Cabbage Fish Camp. Seafood. This one-of-a-kind spot—note the gator souvenirs behind the bar, and the stuffed and mounted Swamp Monster caught by one of the owners—is 9 mi north of the Cocoa city limits. Local catches such as fried catfish, turtle, and alligator keep the crowds coming. Diners may also fish off the dock, buy bait, or enjoy an airboat ride through the St. Johns River marsh. | 8199 State Rd. 520 | 321/632–4199 | $5–$11 | AE, DC, MC, V.

Lodging

Best Western Cocoa Inn. This hotel has a covered deck with grills by the pool. Cocoa Village is 4 mi away. Picnic area, bar, complimentary Continental breakfast. Microwaves available, refrigerators available. Cable TV. Pool. Video games. Laundry facilities. Pets allowed (fee). | 4225 W. King St. | 407/632–1065 | fax 407/631–3302 | www.bestwestern.com | 120 rooms | $69–$79 | AE, D, DC, MC, V.

Cocoa Beach/Kennedy Space Center Super 8 Motel. This basic two-story motel is at exit 76 off I–95, 12 mi from the Kennedy Space Center and Cocoa Beach. Restaurant, picnic area, room service. In-room data ports, some microwaves, some refrigerators. Cable TV. Outdoor pool. Pets allowed (fee). | 900 Friday Rd. | 321/631–1212 or 800/800–8000 | fax 321/636–8661 | www.super8.com | 53 rooms | $62–$69 | AE, D, DC, MC, V.

Days Inn Space Coast. This simple two-story drive-up motel is 18 mi from Kennedy Space Center. Some microwaves, some refrigerators. Cable TV. Pool. Laundry service. Pets allowed (fee). | 5600 Hwy. 524 | 407/636–6500 or 800/544–8313 | fax 407/631–0513 | www.daysinn.com | 121 rooms | $75–$85 | AE, D, DC, MC, V.

Clarion Hotel Kennedy Space Center. The Kennedy Space Center is 14 mi away, and Cocoa Beach and Cocoa Village are both 5 mi from this hotel on Merritt Island. Every room has two double beds or a king-size. Restaurant, bar (with entertainment), room service. In-room data ports, some microwaves, some refrigerators. Cable TV. Pool. Tennis courts. Gym. Business service. | 260 E. Merritt Island Causeway | 321/452–7711 | fax 321/452–9462 | www.choice-hotels.com | 170 rooms | $80–$90 | AE, D, DC, MC, V.

Ramada Inn Cocoa-Kennedy Space Center. This hotel is on a 17-acre plot, with a private fishing lake and a jogging trail. Kennedy Space Center is 9 mi away. Restaurant, bar, room service. In-room data ports, microwaves, refrigerators. Cable TV. Pool, lake. Fishing. Laundry facilities. Pets allowed. | 900 Friday Rd. | 407/631–1210 | fax 407/636–8661 | www.ramada.com | 98 rooms | $79–$89 | AE, D, DC, MC, V.

COCOA BEACH

MAP 3, K5

(Nearby towns also listed: Cocoa, Melbourne, Titusville)

Just east from Cocoa, 50 mi south of New Smyrna Beach, this barrier island is a popular year-round escape for families in Central Florida. From the little town of Cape Canaveral at its northern shore, Cocoa Beach (pop. 13,000) extends 24 miles to the south to Sebastian Inlet. Motels and inexpensive restaurants line the beach, and the Kennedy Space Center is just a few minutes away. The 840-ft Cocoa Beach Pier is a central place to stroll, fish, shop, eat, drink, and dance. You can rent water sports equipment here, or at the landmark Ron Jon Surf Club on Highway A1A (you know surfing is big when a shop like this is open 24 hours).

Information: Cocoa Beach Area Chamber of Commerce | 400 Fortenberry Rd., Merritt Island, 32952 | 321/459–2200 | www.cocoabeachchamber.com.

Attractions

The Cocoa Beach Pier. Built in 1962, this 800-ft pier is one of the best places on the Space Coast to view a shuttle launch—or reel in a big one. It's lined with four unique restaurants, four tropical bars, souvenir shops, beach apparel boutiques, a small video arcade, and a bait-and-tackle shop. This is one of the best places on the central Florida coast to catch flounder, snapper, and trout. | 401 Meade Ave. | 321/783–7549 | www.l-n.com/cocoa.beach.pier or www.cocoabeachpier.com | Fishing $3.50 | Daily.

Port Canaveral. At the north end of Cocoa Beach, Port Canaveral has evolved into a major deep-water port and commercial area home to luxury cruise lines, some of the best deep sea fishing charters in Florida, and casino boats. Along Glen Creek Drive is a restaurant and entertainment area, Cove at Port Canaveral. Adjacent to the port is Jetty Maritime Park, a 35-acre park with a 1200-ft. fishing pier, 4½ acres of quiet beaches, 150 campsites, pavilions and picnic tables, a refreshment stand, and fish-cleaning tables. | 400 E. Jetty Rd., Cape Canaveral | 321/783–7111 | www.portcanaveral.org | Free | Daily.

Ron Jon Surf Shop. The most outlandish branch of the surf shop mecca (the original store opened in New Jersey in 1961) has swimwear, beach gear, and water sports equipment for rent and for sale. It's pink, two stories, and open 24 hours: you can't miss it. On A1A just south of the SR 520 intersection. | 4151 N. Atlantic Ave. | 321/799–8888 | www.ronjons.com | Free | Daily.

SIGHTSEEING TOURS/TOUR COMPANIES

Miss Cape Canaveral. This deep-sea fishing charter has been operating out of Port Canaveral since 1953. Yellowtail snapper and blue marlin are among the many species caught regularly. There's also shark fishing in summer. | 670 Glen Cheek Dr., Port Canaveral | 407/783–5274 | www.misscape.com | $45–$50 per person | Daily 8–5.

ON THE CALENDAR

MAR.: *Port Canaveral SeaFest.* The aroma of fried seafood floats in the air at this weekend festival that features 5,000 pounds of fresh catch, including flounder, Florida rock shrimp, blue crab claws, and 100 gallons of "gold medal" seafood chowder. There's also live music and carnival rides. | 321/459–2200.

APR.: *Easter Surfing Festival.* Thousands of people gather for this annual contest at the Cocoa Beach Pier that draws over 500 surfers on Easter weekend. There's also live entertainment, a bikini contest, and food vendors. | 321/783–7549.

NOV.: *Space Coast Art Festival.* This annual Thanksgiving weekend festival is a big draw in downtown Cocoa Beach, with a juried fine art show, food booths, and music. | 321/784–3322.

Dining

Alma's. Italian. This intimate stone building a block from the beach has a maze of dining rooms with stone floors, low lighting, and stained-glass windows. The fare is simple Italian dishes with a focus on local seafood; specialties include broiled fresh grouper, scallops Florentine, and homemade tiramisu. The family-run eatery boasts a cellar with over 200 imported wines, and live music weekends. | 306 N. Orlando Ave. | 321/783–1981 | No lunch | $7–$15 | AE, D, DC, MC, V.

Bernard's Surf. Seafood. Bernard's is an old-time family-owned restaurant that catches its own seafood and serves it up in a dining rooms full of autographed astronaut photos. The restaurant is one block from the beach in downtown Cocoa Beach. Try the grouper or the filet mignon with sautéed mushrooms. | 2 S. Atlantic Ave. | 321/783–8732 | No lunch | $13–$25 | AE, D, DC, MC, V.

Heidelberg. German. Dim lighting, wreath chandeliers, antique wood furnishings, and German music create a casual and festive atmosphere. The menu is full of German specialties such as bratwurst, Wiener schnitzel, and sauerkraut. You can also slip into Heidi's jazz club next door, a dark lounge with local and national acts playing late into the night. | 7 N. Orlando Ave. | 321/783–6806 | Closed Mon. No lunch Sun. | $13–$18 | AE, MC, V.

Grills. Seafood. Warm tropical breezes mix with the aroma of simmering seafood at this waterfront restaurant with a two-level deck and Polynesian tiki bar. Try the freshly grilled yellowfin tuna sandwich, sushi, blackened grouper, or Bahamian chowder. This is a popular spot for NASA workers. There is live music frequently. | 505 Glen Creek Dr., Cape Canaveral | 321/868–2226 | $6–$17 | AE, DC, MC, V.

Mango Tree. Continental. Dine in elegance at tables discreetly spaced amid orchid gardens, with piano music playing in the background. House favorites include fresh grouper with shrimps and scallops glazed in hollandaise sauce and veal *française* (scaloppine, very lightly breaded and glazed with a mushroom sauce). | 118 N. Atlantic Ave. | 321/799–0513 | Closed Mon. No lunch | $19–$29 | AE, MC, V.

The Pier House. Seafood. It would be hard to top the view of the Atlantic from this restaurant that rests 400 ft over the water at the Cocoa Beach Pier. The low-lit dining rooms, aquariums, compasses, and other nautical paraphernalia are downplayed to emphasize the view. You can have any of the fresh fish prepared four different ways. There is also a selection of chicken, steaks, and pastas. | 401 Meade Ave. | 321/783–7549 | No lunch Mon.–Sat., no dinner Sun. | $13–$25 | AE, D, DC, MC, V.

Roberto's. Cuban. In the morning, you'll find locals in flip-flops catching up on news over omelettes and pancakes. The lunch and dinner focus on Cuban sandwiches, rice and beans, plantains, and paella. | 26 N. Orlando Ave. | 321/784–1868 | Closed Mon. | $5–$11 | AE, MC, V.

Yen Yen. Hong Kong. The owner of this elegant Chinese restaurant in downtown Cocoa Beach greets each table. The large menu has such favorites as crab soup, chicken with mango sauce, roast duck, and spicy scallops. The large dining room is filled with authentic Chinese tapestries and carpets. | 2 N. Atlantic Ave. | 321/783–9512 | $8–$20 | AE, D, MC, V.

Lodging

Best Western Ocean Inn. Only one block from the beach and the Cocoa Beach Pier, this moderately priced two-story motel offers tropical decor in comfortable rooms. Some units have patios, balconies, and kitchenettes. Picnic area. In-room data ports, microwaves, some refrigerators. Cable TV. Pool. Gym. Laundry facilities. Some pets allowed. | 5500 N. Atlantic Ave. | 321/784–2550 or 877/233–9330 | fax 321/868–7124 | www.bestwestern.com | 103 rooms | $80–$90 | AE, D, DC, MC, V.

Cocoa Beach Hilton Oceanfront. Set back from busy A1A, adjacent to the Lori Wilson Park, this beachfront seven-story Hilton is one of the tallest on Cocoa Beach. Floor-to-ceiling windows really show off the scenery. Restaurant, 2 bars. In-room data ports. Cable TV. Pool. Gym. Water sports. Video games. Business services. | 1550 N. Atlantic Ave. | 321/799–0003 or 800/526–2609 | fax 321/799–0344 | www.hilton.com | 297 rooms | $119–$169 | AE, D, DC, MC, V.

Comfort Inn and Suite Resort. This resort occupies five acres, and is less than half a block from the beach. One-bedroom suites with oceanview balconies occupy the upper floors of the six-story tower; among the ground floor units are minisuites, and efficiencies with full kitchens. Restaurant, bars, picnic area. Some kitchenettes, refrigerators, microwaves in some rooms. Cable TV. Pool. Hot tub. Gym. Beach. Playground. Laundry facilities. Business services. | 3901 N. Atlantic Ave. | 321/783–2221 or 800/228–5150 | fax 321/783–0461 | www.comfortinn.com | 60 suites, 84 rooms | $77–$165 | AE, D, DC, MC, V.

Days Inn Oceanfront. Just steps away from the Cocoa Beach Pier, this hotel has clean, bright rooms and suites in two complexes: an off-ocean two-story building and an oceanfront seven-story tower. The former has 120 rooms around a courtyard with hibiscus and palm trees, plus a two-level sundeck around the pool. All 60 rooms in the oceanfront tour have private balconies overlooking the Atlantic. In-room data ports, microwaves. Cable TV. Pool. Gym. Beach. Playground. Laundry facilities. Business services. Pets allowed. | 5600 N. Atlantic Ave. | 321/783–7621 or 800/962–0028 | fax 321/799–4576 | www.daysinn.com | 180 rooms | $89–$239 | AE, D, DC, MC, V.

Discovery Beach Resort. These oceanfront condominiums are great for families who want lots of living space, full cooking facilities, and a terrific view of the beach and ocean. Each unit has a spacious private balcony facing the water. Each room is spacious with a modern, full-size kitchen, living area, bathroom, and one or two bedrooms. Lighted tennis courts are on top of a nearby parking garage. In-room data ports, microwaves. Cable TV. Pool. Business services. | 300 Barlow Ave. | 321/868–7777 or 800/228–2968 | 66 units | $110–$250 | AE, D, DC, MC, V.

Doubletree. This hotel consists of two buildings: an older, two-story motel near the highway and a more attractive six-story tower next to the beach. Rooms in the two-story building feature two double beds with mauve and green tropical print bedspreads, natural wood furniture, green carpet, and beige stucco walls. Rooms in the tower have private balconies; hand-colored black and white beach photographs hang on the walls. In-room data ports, microwaves. Cable TV. Pool. Business services. | 2080 N. Atlantic Ave. | 321/783–9222 or 800/552–3224 | fax 321/799–3234 | www.doubletree.com | 148 rooms | $95–$115 | AE, D, DC, MC, V.

Hampton Inn Cocoa Beach. This modern, eight-story hotel is 200 yards from the beach. Rooms are spacious, with floral prints and king-size beds. Restaurant, 2 bars, complimentary Continental breakfast. In-room data ports, microwaves, refrigerators. Cable TV. Pool. Gym. Water sports. Video games. Laundry facilities, laundry service. Business services. | 3425

N. Atlantic Ave. | 321/799–4099 | fax 321/799–4991 | www.hamptoninncocoabeach.com | 150 rooms | $119–$169 | AE, D, DC, MC, V.

Holiday Inn Cocoa Beach Resort. Tall palms line the entrance to this sprawling 30-acre motel resort, which has beige-and-aqua buildings stretching from A1A to the beach. Accommodations range from motel rooms to oceanfront suites and efficiencies. A two-story deck is open atop the hotel. Rooms are basic, with tropical print bedspreads and drapes, green carpet, and wooden furniture. Small coffeemakers and iron and ironing boards are provided in each room. Restaurant, bar. Some refrigerators. Beauty salon. Gym. Video games. | 1330 N. Atlantic Ave. | 321/783–2271 or 800/206–2747 | www.holiday-inn.com | 505 rooms | $80–$130 | AE, D, DC, MC, V.

Inn at Cocoa Beach. This oceanfront inn is home to spacious rooms, all with balconies and ocean views. Each room looks different, but all have reproduction 18th- and 19th-century armoires, four-poster beds, chairs, and sofas. In addition to the Continental breakfast with homemade bread, there is an evening spread of wine and cheese. Complimentary Continental breakfast. Some in-room hot tubs. Cable TV. Pool. | 4300 Ocean Beach Blvd. | 321/799–3460 or 800/343–5307 outside FL | fax 321/784–8632 | 46 rooms, 4 suites | $140 | AE, D, MC, V.

Ocean Landings Resort and Racquet Club. On 13 acres at the south end of the Cocoa Beach hotel strip, this resort offers six types of units catering to families. One- and two-bedroom units with spacious carpeted rooms, some with sofa beds, can sleep two to eight people. The decor is beige and white, with floral upholstery. The resort offers nature hikes and other activities for kids, and sometimes has wine and cheese parties at the gazebo. Restaurant, 2 bars. Microwaves, refrigerators. Cable TV. Sauna, stream room, hot tub. Pool. Basketball, racquetball, volleyball. Beach, water sports. Playgrounds. | 900 N. Atlantic Ave. | 321/783–9430 or 800/323–8413 | fax 321/783–1339 | www.oceanlandings.com | 228 units | $80–$200 | AE, D, DC, MC, V.

Ocean Suite. All units are two-room oceanfront suites with private balconies at this five-story building right next to the Cocoa Beach Pier. Each bedroom has a king-size or two double beds, with a sofa bed in the living room. Suites are bright and clean, with teal and peach upholstery and paintings. Restaurant, bar. Microwaves, refrigerators. Cable TV, some in-room VCRs. Pool. Exercise equipment. Laundry facilities. Business services. | 5500 Ocean Beach Blvd. | 321/784–4343 or 800/367–1223 | fax 321/783–6514 | 50 suites | $80–$110 suites | AE, D, DC, MC, V.

Radisson Resort. An upscale resort just down the road from Port Canaveral, this Radisson will get cruise-goers in the mood for the islands. The exterior is pink with a green roof and white trim. Inside the lobby, whirling ceiling fans and wicker furniture exude tropical elegance. Through the lobby's large windows, you can see the resort's centerpiece—a huge free-form pool with a 95-ft rocky waterfall. Restaurant, bar. In-room data ports, some microwaves, some refrigerators, room service. Cable TV. Pool, wading pool. Hot tub. Tennis court. Gym. Video games. Playground. Laundry facilities. Business services, airport shuttle. | 8701 Astronaut Blvd., Cape Canaveral | 321/784–0000 or 800/333–3333 | fax 321/784–3737 | 200 rooms | $99–$129 | AE, D, DC, MC, V.

Sea Esta Villas. Private balconies overlook a tropical courtyard with waterfalls and tall cacti in these apartments a block from the beach. Each two-room suite has a living room, kitchenette, floral decor, and wicker furnishings. Complimentary breakfast. In-room data ports, kitchenettes, microwaves. Cable TV, some in-room VCRs (and movies). Pool. Hot tub. Gym. Laundry facilities. No smoking. No kids. | 686 S. Atlantic Ave.; 7 mi south of SR 520 off A1A at 7th St. | 321/783–1739 or 800/872–9444 | fax 321/783–4969 | 8 suites | $125–$250 | AE, D, DC, MC, V.

Surf Studio Beach Resort. This friendly family-owned oceanfront motel in southern Cocoa Beach has a large sundeck facing quiet beaches with more local surfers than tourists. Rooms are small but clean and well-kept. In-room data ports, some kitchenettes, microwaves, refrigerators. Cable TV, in-room VCRs available. Pool. Beach, water sports, fishing, bicycles. Laundry facilities. Pets allowed (fee). | 1801 S. Atlantic Ave. | 321/783–7100 | fax 321/783–2695 | 11 rooms | $50–$145 | AE, D, DC, MC, V.

Wakulla Motel. This popular motel is clean and comfortable and just two blocks from the beach. Completely furnished five-room suites, designed to sleep six, are great for families; they include two bedrooms, a living room, dining room, and a fully equipped kitchen. Kitchenettes, microwaves. Cable TV. Pool, wading pool. Volleyball. Beach. Laundry facilities. | 3550 N. Atlantic Ave. | 321/783–2230 or 800/992–5852 | fax 321/783–0980 | Wakulla@travelbase.com | 116 suites | $96–$106 | AE, D, DC, MC, V.

COCONUT GROVE

(Nearby towns also listed: Coral Gables, Key Biscayne, Miami, Miami Beach)

South Florida's oldest settlement, the Grove (as it's known locally) is nestled about two miles southwest of downtown Miami, in a small area stretching from Biscayne Bay to U.S. 1. As a residential community, much of Coconut Grove (pop. 13,500) maintains a uniquely tropical identity, with dense, exotic trees and shrubs giving it a kind of bohemian jungle flair.

The city's commercial tone is contrastingly upscale and urban, with a mix of boutiques, galleries, and sidewalk cafés. At night, it's an energetic and chic spot for clubs, theaters, bars, and restaurants—especially at the neighboring malls and entertainment areas CocoWalk and Streets of Mayfair. After South Beach, the Grove is South Florida's nighttime hot spot, and parking is accordingly difficult.

While first settled in 1834, Commodore Ralph Middleton Monroe established Coconut Grove as a stylish neighborhood in the 1890s, before the railroad arrived. Bahamian immigrants were among the first to settle here, and the area around Charles Street still maintains a good-size Bahamian population. The community has also attracted artists, writers, and scientists, who established winter homes here. In the late 1960s, areas of the Grove drew hippies, and vestiges of their habitation can be seen in the present-day New Age shops that line Main Highway, a street that begins at the bay and ends at CocoWalk.

Information: Coconut Grove Chamber of Commerce | 2820 McFarlane Rd., Coconut Grove, 33133 | 305/444–7270 | www.coconutgrove.com.

Attractions

Barnacle State Historic Site. Dade County's oldest home in its original location is on Biscayne Bay, among five acres of native hardwood and landscaped lawns. Commodore Ralph Munroe built the house in 1891 from timber he salvaged from wrecked ships, giving it a broad, sloping room and verandas set deep to channel the sea breezes. Many of its original furnishings remain. The many old trees make the place appear much as it did in Munroe's day. Today, the property is one of the last places you can see the once vast Miami Hammock. Out of the original hammock, Commodore Munroe had cut only a winding buggy trail barely wide enough for one vehicle. There are no parking facilities. | 3485 Main Hwy. | 305/448–9445 | www.dep.state.fl.us/parks | $1 | Fri.–Mon. 9–4; tours at 10, 11:30, 1, 2:30.

Coconut Grove Playhouse. This Spanish Rococo–style playhouse began its life as a movie theater in 1926, and now stages everything from proven Broadway musicals to contemporary opera (*Don't Stop the Carnival*, written by by Jimmy Buffett and Herman Wouk, had its premier performance staged here). | 3500 Main Hwy. | 305/442–4000 | $25–$40 | Oct.–June, Tues.–Sat. 8 PM; matinees Wed., Sat., Sun. 2.

Miami City Hall. The nautical-style Art Deco trim on this government building is a reminder of its early years, when it served as the terminal for the Pan American Airways seaplane base on Dinner Key. A 1938 Pan Am menu on display lists filet mignon, petits pois au beurre, and Jenny Lind pudding. | 3500 Pan American Dr. | 305/250–5400 | Free | Weekdays 8–5.

Miami Museum of Science and Space Transit Planetarium. This museum is filled with hands-on gravity and electricity displays. There is also a wildlife center that houses native Florida snakes and birds of prey; it is famous for its rehabilitation facilities. Look through the telescopes or watch one of the laser shows at the planetarium. | 3280 S. Miami Ave. | 305/854–4247 | www.miamisci.org | $9 | Daily 10–6.

Plymouth Congregational Church. Built in 1917, this coral-rock structure resembles a Mexican mission church. The hand-carved walnut and oak door came from an early 17th-century monastery in the Pyrenees and has original wrought-iron fittings. You can also visit the first schoolhouse in Miami-Dade county, which is on the same 11-acre property. | 3400 Devon Rd. | 305/444–6521 | Free | Weekdays 9–4:30; Sun. service at 10 AM.

★ **Vizcaya Museum and Gardens.** This 1916 villa overlooking Biscayne Bay was the home of Chicago industrialist James Deering. Its 34 rooms open to the public are decorated in Renaissance, Baroque, Rococo, and Neoclassical styles. The 10-acre grounds are beautiful, with formal gardens, fountains, and an unusual indoor-outdoor pool. | 3251 S. Miami Ave. | 305/250–9133 | $10 | Daily 9:30–5.

ON THE CALENDAR
JUNE: *Miami/Bahamas Goombay Festival.* The largest black-culture fest in the country features a sailing regatta and Junkanoo bands—Bahamian folk groups that parade in elaborate garb while playing whistles and goat-skin drums. The fun takes place on Grand St., between 32nd and 37th streets. | 305/238–6186.

Dining
Café Tu Tu Tango. Spanish. This delightful little restaurant on the second level of CocoWalk is full of original oil paintings and easels set around the dining room. The menu consists of small-size dishes, meant to be shared; there's a little bit of everything to nibble at, from salads with smoked salmon and feta cheese to barbecued wings and pizzas. Try the Hurricane Shrimp (batter-fried shrimp with cayenne pepper sauce served over rice). | 3015 Grand Ave. | 305/529–2222 | Reservations not accepted | $4–$9 | AE, MC, V.

Chrysanthemum. Chinese. For years this Chinese restuarant was considered one of the best in Miami Beach. Now relocated to the Mayfair Mall in Coconut Grove, under new ownership, the place is less hectic and a little less formal. The new location is modern and elegant. You can dine on the patio if you want a view of the busy shoppers and pedestrians. The menu has changed, but some old favorites are still there, including a chicken breast with crispy spinach, moo shu pork, eggplant sauteed in balsamic vinegar, and ravioli in ginger and scallion sauce. | 2911 Grand Ave., Coconut Grove | 305/443–6789 | Closed Mon. | $12–$20 | AE, MC, V.

Green St. Cafe. Continental. This outdoor sidewalk café is perfect for people-watching. It serves innovative soups, salads, and sandwiches for lunch, and entrées such as red snapper and dolphin (mahimahi) for dinner. The indoor dining room has a big-screen TV for sports. | 3110 Commodore Plaza | 305/567–0662 | Reservations not accepted | Breakfast also available | $6–$20 | AE, MC, V.

Mayfair Grill. Contemporary. At this restaurant, which is part of the Mayfair House Hotel, the chairs are shaped like giant sea shells; roses and candles grace the tables. The chef, Frank Liberoni, uses USDA prime meat and fresh seafood to create Asian, French, Italian, and Caribbean-influenced dishes like onion-crusted Chilean salmon and pan-fried snapper with saffron roasted pepper pilaf. | 3000 Florida Ave. | 954/441–0000 | Breakfast also available | $17–$32 | AE, D, DC, MC, V.

Mezzanote. Italian. Located on the first floor of the Mayfair Shopping Center, this spacious restaurant dishes risottos, pizzas, and pastas served with veal, chicken, or seafood. Linen tablecloths, candles, and a high ceiling contribute to an elegant air. | 3390 Mary St. | 305/448–7677 | No lunch weekends | $10–$26 | AE, D, DC, MC, V.

Mykonos. Greek. A mural of the Aegean Sea adorns the exterior of this eatery. Inside are Greek travel posters. The menu is standard Greek fare of gyros, moussaka, and calamari and octopus sauteed in wine and onions. | 1201 Coral Way | 305/856–3140 | No lunch Sun. | $6–$12 | AE, D, DC, MC, V.

News Café. American. You can sit inside the restaurant, on the sidewalk beneath large umbrellas, or in a small smoke shop adjacent to the restaurant—just like the South Beach landmark hotspot of the same name. Expect filling steaks, hamburgers, and salads. The café is open late—till 1 AM weekdays, and 2 AM weekends. | 2901 Florida Ave. | 305/774–6397 | Reservations not accepted | Breakfast also available | $6–$16 | AE, DC, MC, V.

Pice. Italian. On the mezzanine level of the Grand Bay Hotel is this elegant restaurant anchored by two towering floral arrangements. A wide choice of Italian dishes include osso buco, served with a saffron risotto. | 2669 S. Bayshore Dr. | 305/860–0960 | Breakfast also available | $22–$37 | AE, D, DC, MC, V.

Senor Frog's. Mexican. Inside this large, bustling dining room, you'll find *mole poblano* (peppers and chocolate), *cochinito pibil* (sweet pork cooked in orange juice), and lots of different fajitas and enchiladas. Thursday nights DJs spin salsa music until the early morning. | 3480 Main Hwy. | 305/448–0999 | Reservations not accepted | $9–$16 | AE, D, DC, MC, V.

Lodging
Grand Bay Hotel. This 12-floor, stepped hotel embodies a contemporary, luxurious sense of Coconut Grove. Guests rooms are elegantly decorated with antique sideboards and woodwork. The hotel faces Biscayne Bay and Dinner Key Marina. Restaurant, 2 bars, room service. In-room data ports, some in-room hot tubs. Cable TV, in-room VCRs. Outdoor pool. Outdoor hot tub, massage, sauna, beauty salon. Laundry services. Business services. | 2669 S. Bayshore Dr. | 305/858–9600 or 888/472–6229 | fax 305/859–2026 | www.wyndham.com/coconutgrove | 232 rooms | $305–$429 | AE, MC, V.

Hotel Sofitel Miami. Part of the French chain, the hotel is 15 minutes from downtown, near the Vizcaya Museum and various golf courses. Glass dominates the 15-story high-rise, while the furnishings and amenities aim for a French tone. You will find fresh-cut flowers and handmade French soaps, as well as French music playing throughout the building. Many rooms have views of the Blue Lagoon, a pool with a waterfall, or the Miami skyline. Restaurant, bar (with entertainment). In-room data ports, refrigerators, cable TV, in-room VCRs (and movies). Pool. Tennis courts. Gym. Laundry facilites. Business services, free parking, airport shuttle. Pets allowed. | 5800 Blue Lagoon Dr. | 305/264–4888 | fax 305/262–9049 | 281 rooms | $170–$235 room, $220–$465 suite | AE, D, DC, MC, V.

Mayfair House Hotel. This European-style luxury hotel is within the upscale Streets of Mayfair complex. Rooms are decorated in fluid Art Nouveau patterns and feature either a Japanese hot tub on the balcony or a Roman tub inside. Restaurant, bar, room service. In-room data ports, minibars, in-room hot tubs. Cable TV, in-room VCRs. Outdoor pool. Outdoor hot tub, sauna. Laundry services. Business services. Some pets (fee). | 3000 Florida Ave. | 305/441–0000 or 800/433–4555 | fax 305/447–9173 | www.mayfairhousehotel.com | 179 suites | $269–$800 | AE, D, DC, MC, V.

CONCH KEY/DUCK KEY

MAP 3, D6

(Nearby towns also listed: Grassy Key/Crawl Key, Long Key, Marathon)

The economy of these two rustic islands, closely connected by canals, is dominated by fishing. Duck Key is home to a huge resort that boasts an interactive dolphin

CONCH KEY/
DUCK KEY

INTRO
ATTRACTIONS
DINING
LODGING

lagoon as well as a small, upscale community of a few hundred people. Many residents of Conch Key are descendants of the original settlers who came down from the mainland South.

Information: Greater Marathon Chamber of Commerce | 12222 Overseas Hwy., Marathon, 33050 | 305/743–5417 or 800/352–5397 | www.floridakeysmarathon.com.

Dining

Cantina. Mexican.Dishes at this poolside Mexican restaurant—tables under large umbrellas are just 10 ft from the edge of the main pool at Hawk's Cay Resort—include a fresh grilled mahimahi quesadilla. Interior decorations offer the popular, colorful view of Mexico—large straw sombreros, plants, wooden chairs and tables, and ceramics. | MM 61, OS, Duck Key | 305/743–7000 or 888/443–6393, ext. 1740 | $7–$19 | AE, D, DC, MC, V.

Water's Edge. Seafood. The most refined, yet still relaxed, of the restaurants at Hawk's Cay Resort offers a crab- and shrimp-stuffed chicken Key West, lobster and stone crabs in season, and, for dessert, homemade Key lime and mud pies. Soup and a 40-item salad bar are included with each dinner entrée. | MM 61, OS, Duck Key | 305/743–7000 or 888/443–6393, ext. 1751 | No lunch | $12–$30 | AE, D, DC, MC, V.

Lodging

Hawk's Cay Resort. After a $50 million renovation and expansion in 2000, this 60-acre resort provides a bit of Caribbean-style paradise in the Keys. Rooms are spacious, furnished with light, casual wicker and decorated in earthy colors. Sports and recreational activities—from

© Corbis

USEFUL EXTRAS YOU MAY WANT TO PACK

- ❏ Adapters, converter
- ❏ Alarm clock
- ❏ Batteries
- ❏ Binoculars
- ❏ Blankets, pillows, sleeping bags
- ❏ Books and magazines
- ❏ Bottled water, soda
- ❏ Calculator
- ❏ Camera, lenses, film
- ❏ Can/bottle opener
- ❏ Cassette tapes, CDs, and players
- ❏ Cell phone
- ❏ Change purse with $10 in quarters, dimes, and nickels for tollbooths and parking meters
- ❏ Citronella candle
- ❏ Compass
- ❏ Earplugs
- ❏ Flashlight
- ❏ Folding chairs

- ❏ Guidebooks
- ❏ Luggage tags and locks
- ❏ Maps
- ❏ Matches
- ❏ Money belt
- ❏ Pens, pencils
- ❏ Plastic trash bags
- ❏ Portable TV
- ❏ Radio
- ❏ Self-seal plastic bags
- ❏ Snack foods
- ❏ Spare set of keys, not carried by driver
- ❏ Travel iron
- ❏ Travel journal
- ❏ Video recorder, blank tapes
- ❏ Water bottle
- ❏ Water-purification tablets

*Excerpted from *Fodor's: How to Pack: Experts Share Their Secrets*
© 1997, by Fodor's Travel Publications

a sailing school to a saltwater lagoon—are extensive. Kids' programs are especially good and include an aquatic educational program that lets them interact with dolphins. 4 restaurants, 2 bars with entertainment, picnic area, room service. Some kitchenettes, some microwaves, some refrigerators. Cable TV, some in-room VCRs. 5 outdoor pools. Outdoor hot tub, sauna, spa, steam room. Putting green, 8 tennis courts. Basketball, health club, volleyball. Beach, dock, water sports, boating, fishing, bicycles. Shops, video games, library. Baby-sitting, children's programs (2–18), playground. Laundry facilities, laundry service. | MM 61, OS, Duck Key | 305/743–7000 or 888/443–6393 | fax 305/743–5215 | www.hawkscayresort.com | AE, D, DC, MC, V.

Conch Key Cottages. On tiny Walker's Island (one of the Conch Key Islands, between Conch and Duck Keys off Overseas Highway/U.S. 1), this is a relaxed conglomeration of unpretentious cottages and studios. Brightly flowered shrubs, palm trees, a beach, and ocean breezes evoke the spirit of the tropics. Units are furnished with rattan and wicker furniture; each of the eight freestanding cottages (five of which are oceanfront) also has hammocks. Picnic area. Kitchenettes, microwaves, refrigerators, some in-room hot tubs. Cable TV, some in-room VCRs. Outdoor pool. Beach, dock, water sports, boating, fishing. Laundry facilities. | MM 62.3, OS, 62250 Overseas Hwy./U.S. 1, Walker's Island | 305/289–1377 or 800/330–1577 | fax 305/743–8207 | www.conchkeycottages.com | 4 rooms, 4 1-bedroom apartments, 4 cottages | $110 room, $136 1–bedroom apartment, $151–$249 cottage | D, MC, V.

CORAL GABLES

MAP 3, E5

(Nearby towns also listed: Coconut Grove, Florida City, Homestead, Key Biscayne, Miami, Miami Beach)

Envisioned as an American Venice, with canals and gracious homes spreading across the community, Coral Gables was one of the world's first planned cities. The vision behind it all was that of George Merrick, whose ultimate plans were foiled by a hurricane and the Great Depression. Still, Coral Gables (pop. 41,000) is arguably South Florida's most attractive town, with magnificent entrances, lush landscaping, broad avenues, and gracious Mediterranean-style architecture. Streets in the city are named after places and monuments in Spain. Town leaders keep a careful eye on their City Beautiful, as it's sometimes called, restricting vertical growth and thoughtless construction. They also ticket regularly, so keep your parking meter well stuffed with quarters. Two of Florida's finest attractions are in Coral Gables: the Biltmore Hotel and the Venetian Pool. The University of Miami, Florida's largest private university, keeps the area's periphery full of youthful energy.

Information: Coral Gables Chamber of Commerce | 50 Aragon Ave., Coral Gables, 33134 | 305/446–1657 | www.gableschamber.org.

Attractions

Alhambra Water Tower. Back in 1924 this landmark stored water and looked like a lighthouse. It was restored in 1993 with a copper-rib dome and multicolored frescoes. It stands at the intersection of Greenway Ct. and Ferdinand St. | Alhambra Circle | 305/446–1657.

Biltmore Hotel. This richly ornamented hotel has made a grand comeback from its days an an army hospital. In 1992, it reopened after extensive renovations and went on to host the Summit of the Americas in 1994. Highlights include a 16-story replica of Seville's Giralda Tower and the Biltmore Country Club, a Beaux Arts–style structure that was reincorporated into the hotel. | 1200 Anastasia Ave. | 305/445–1926 | Free | Tours Sun. 1:30, 2:30, and 3:30.

Coral Gables City Hall. Built in 1928, this structure has a three-tier clock tower with a 500-pound bell. The second floor's dome ceiling contains a mural by Denman Fink, who was

George Merrick's uncle and artistic advisor and painted similarly to Maxfield Parrish. You can also see paintings, photos, and ads from Coral Gables in the 1920s. | 405 Biltmore Way | 305/446–6800 | Free | Weekdays 8–5.

Coral Gables Congregational Church. George Merrick, whose father was a Congregational minister, donated the land for this parish church. Organized in 1923, the church was first in the city. Its interior is still in good condition. | 3010 De Soto Blvd. | 305/448–7421 | Free | Weekdays 8:30–4:30; Sun. services at 9:15 and 10:45.

Coral Gables Merrick House. George Merrick founded Coral Gables in 1925. In 1976, the city acquired his boyhood home, and restored it to its 1920s appearance. The lush, tropical gardens suggest the inspiration for his planned community. | 907 Coral Way | 305/460–5361 | $2; grounds free | Wed.–Sun. 1–4; grounds daily 8–sunset.

★ **Fairchild Tropical Garden.** The magnificently landscaped botanical garden blooms throughout the year, offering breathtaking views, hidden passages, and winding paths through 83 acres of trees and lakes. The grounds include tropical flowers, lily pools, overlooks, vistas, and a sunken garden. Exotic plants from around the world can be enjoyed every season of the year. | 10901 Old Cutler Rd. | 305/667–1651 | www.ftg.org | $8 | Daily 9:30–4:30.

Granada Golf Course. This 9-hole golf course is one of the oldest in South Florida. It dates back to 1926 and was being constructed at the same time the Merrick House was built. Expert golfers will find it easy but it's ideal for beginners. | 2001 Granada Ave. | 305/460–5367 | Daily, 7–7.

Parrot Jungle and Gardens. Stop here to see flamingos other than the kind that used to stand on suburban front lawns. The 22-acre botanical gardens are home to more than 1,100 birds and other animals, and the gardens themselves contain more than 1,200 exotic plants. The waterfalls, streams, and lake lend a sense of tranquility. | 11000 S.W. 57th Ave. | 305/666–7834 | www.parrotjungle.com | $14.95 | Daily 9:30–6 (ticket booth closes at 4:30).

University of Miami. Founded in 1925, UM is the largest research university in the southeast. Its six campuses and facilities include the Coral Gables main campus, the medical campus in downtown Miami, the Rosenstiel School of Marine and Atmospheric Science campus on Virginia Key, the James L. Knight International Center, and the John J. Koubek Center. About 14,000 students attend UM. | 1301 Stanford Dr. | 305/284–3228 | www.miami.edu | Free | Daily.

Lowe Art Museum. The extensive permanent collection here has more than 8,000 works, including Renaissance and Baroque art, American paintings, and Latin American art. The museum also hosts traveling exhibitions. | Stanford Dr. | 305/284–3535 | www.lowemuseum.org | $5 | Tues.–Wed., Fri.–Sat. 10–5, Thurs. 12–7, Sun. 12–5.

★ **Venetian Pool.** Originally a rock quarry, the municipal pool was completed in 1924 and remains a popular spot due to its themed architecture, which was inspired by the lagoons of Venice. The pool, on the National Register of Historic Places, is in an attractive residential area of Coral Gables. | 2701 De Soto Blvd. | 305/460–5356 | Apr.–Oct. $8; Nov.–Mar. $5 | Nov.–Mar., Tues.–Sun. 10–4:30; June–Aug., weekdays 11–7:30, weekends 10–4:30; Apr.–May, Sept.–Oct., weekdays 11–5:30, weekends 10–4:30.

ON THE CALENDAR

MAR.: *Italian Renaissance Festival.* Celebrate Italy and enjoy performers, costumes, food, arts, and crafts at the Vizcaya Museum and Gardens, 10 min from downtown Miami. | 305/250–9133.

DEC.: *Junior Orange Bowl Parade.* This nighttime parade starts off at Biltmore Way and ends at Alhambra Circle. It is a junior version of the big Orange Bowl Parade held in downtown Miami. It features middle school marching bands and cheerleading groups. | 305/662–1210 | www.jrorangebowl.com.

Dining

Bangkok Bangkok. Thai. Cashews, lime, and pineapple are some of the ingredients that spice up the fish, beef, and duck dishes at this popular local restaurant. It can be quiet and intimate or loud and boisterous, depending on the night and the time. This charming restaurant has unique and delightful menu items. | 157 Giralda Ave. | 305/444–2397 | Reservations essential weekends | $9–$19 | AE, DC, MC, V.

Caffe Abbracci. Italian. This elegantly casual café is famous for its northern Italian specialties, whose preparation is personally supervised by the owner. It's known for its veal chop *tricolore* (a pound of grilled veal ground with marinated tomatoes, radicchio, and arugula), the red snapper fillet sautéed with white wine and fresh artichoke hearts, tomatoes, and basil, and its homemade gnocchi with bolognese sauce. | 318 Aragon Ave. | 305/441–0700 | Reservations essential | No lunch weekends | $14–$28 | AE, D, MC, V.

Caffe Buongiorno. Italian. Paintings of Venice ornament the walls at this eatery where pasta, veal, and fish entrées dominate the menu. Try the salmon with pistachio crust and orange sauce or the *triomfo di mare* (black and white linguine served with mixed seafood in a light and spicy marinara sauce). | 2271 Ponce de Leon Blvd. | 305/442–2033 | Reservations essential Fri.–Sat. | Closed Sun. | $15–$25 | AE, DC, MC, V.

Courtyard Cafe. Seafood. This open-air restaurant sits next to a large stone fountain in the Biltmore Hotel. The menu includes something for everybody (beef, chicken, and pasta dishes), but the specialty is the catch of the day and grilled seafood. For lunch there is also a buffet. Sunday brunch costs $52 and requires a reservation. | 1200 Anastasia Ave. | 305/445–1926 | Breakfast also available. No dinner Sun. | $11–$26 | AE, D, DC, MC, V.

John Martin's. Irish. Greens and dark woods dominate this traditionally flavored, slightly upscale Irish pub. Sit in a booth and enjoy an appetizer, like dolphin (mahimahi) fingers, and follow it up with a classic entrée—meatloaf, corned beef and cabbage, burgers, and the daily seafood special are all popular. The restaurant hosts Irish dancing and folk music Saturday nights. | 253 Miracle Mile | 305/445–3777 | www.johnmartins.com | $10–$18 | AE, D, DC, MC, V.

La Bussola. Italian. Roman columns and paintings of Italian notables ornament the walls at this elegant restaurant. The menu includes pastas, risottos, chicken, and fish dishes such as grilled tuna served with a white wine and anchovy sauce. | 270 Giralda Ave. | 305/445–8783 | Reservations essential | No lunch Fri.–Sun. | $14–$22 | AE, DC, MC, V.

Le Festival. French. Carved glass and mirror statues ornament the walls of this Art Deco dining room in which such classic dishes as filet mignon, rack of lamb, and Chateaubriand are served. Eye-catching antiques embellish this elegant restaurant. | 2120 Salzedo St. | 305/442–8545 | Closed Sun. No lunch Sat. | $16–$27 | AE, D, DC, MC, V.

Melody Inn. Swiss. Renaissance paintings hang above stained-wood wainscotting at this Swiss eatery. Classic Swiss dishes such as *raclette* (grilled cheese over potatoes) and *roesti* (sautéed shredded potatoes) are complemented by the variety of fish, veal, and beef entrées such as pan-seared salmon and mahimahi served with an almond and tomato pesto. | 83 Andalusia Ave. | 305/448–0022 | Closed Mon. No lunch | $12–$26 | AE, D, DC, MC, V.

Mozart Stube. Austrian. Pictures of Mozart and beer mugs decorate this popular spot. Start with some snails soaked in butter and garlic. For a main course try the roast duckling or veal shank, and end your meal with the Black Forest cake. | 325 Alcazar Ave. | 305/446–1600 | www.mozartstube.com | Reservations essential on weekends | No lunch | $14–$27 | AE, DC, MC, V.

★ **Norman's.** Contemporary. Some of Miami's most imaginative and most expensive meals are created by master chef Norman Van Aken at this restaurant that maintains a comfortable feel even when it's filled. Latin, North American, Caribbean, and Asian influences combine to deliver bold, fresh flavors in such dishes as grilled yellow tail snapper served with blanched asparagus in citrus butter, and the roasted pork tenderloin with 21st-cen-

CORAL GABLES

INTRO
ATTRACTIONS
DINING
LODGING

tury mole, black bean, and corn salsa. Considered by many to be among the top restaurants in the country. | 21 Almeria Ave. | 305/446–6767 | Closed Sun. No lunch | $26–$39 | AE, DC, MC, V.

Old Lisbon Restaurant. Portuguese. This pleasant restaurant in a Coral Gables shopping center is decorated with pictures of Portugal and filled with loyal, satisfied customers. Don't miss the codfish or the melt-in-your-mouth meringue, baked on the premises. | 1698 S.W. 22nd St. | 305/854–0039 | $9–$22 | AE, D, DC, MC, V.

Ortsnique on the Mile. Caribbean. French Caribbean food with a heavy Jamaican influence is served at this impressive restaurant. With mute sunset colors throughout, the multilevel dining area sits in a loftlike space with a tile floor on the main level and mahogany floors on the other two levels. Black grouper, Caribbean tuna, and jerk chicken penne pasta are all popular choices. | 278 Miracle Mile | 305/446–7710 | No lunch weekends | $15–$25 | AE, DC, MC, V.

Restaurant St. Michel. Contemporary. Located in the Hotel St. Michel, this restaurant evokes a whimsical aura with its combination of sculpted busts, circus posters, deco chandeliers, and a palm frond–shaped mosaic. The couscous chicken and pasta primavera are good light dishes, while the lemon-glazed fillet of salmon and sesame-coated loin of tuna are among the heartier menu options. There are sidewalk tables for outdoor dining. While this charming little establishment serves American cuisine, it offers both the flair and feel of the Mediterranean. | 162 Alcazar Ave. | 305/446–6572 | Breakfast also available | $18–$35 | AE, DC, MC, V.

Thai Orchid. Thai. This restaurant, known for its spicy fare, has sidewalk seating and a patio area available for dining, in addition to its statue-ornamented interior. Try the chicken masaman, a spicy curried chicken. | 317 Miracle Mile | 305/443–6364 | $9–$11 | AE, MC, V.

Two Sisters. Contemporary. This elegant yet casual spot is located on the ground floor of the Hyatt Regency hotel. If you're in the mood for seafood, try the marinated snapper with red onions and ginger butter, or just have one of their succulent steaks. | 50 Alhambra Plaza | 305/441–1234 | Breakfast also available | $12–$35 | AE, D, DC, MC, V.

Lodging

★ **The Biltmore Hotel.** This elegant Mediterranean-style grand hotel was built in the 1920s and overlooks the Coral Gables Golf Course. Much of the original decor remains, including hand-painted ceilings, marble floors, fireplaces, and spacious public rooms decorated with huge wooden bird cages home to many finches. The hotel is a living legend, the last word in city elegance. 4 restaurants (see Courtyard Cafe, above), 4 bars. In-room data ports, some microwaves, some refrigerators, room service. Cable TV. Pool. Barbershop, beauty salon, hot tubs, sauna. Driving range, 18-hole golf course, putting green, 10 tennis courts. Gym. Business services. | 1200 Anastasia Ave. | 305/445–1926 or 800/727–1926 | fax 305/442–9496 | www.biltmorehotel.com | 280 rooms | $269–$389 | AE, D, DC, MC, V.

Holiday Inn Coral Gables Business District. Only 3 mi from the airport and 5 mi south of downtown, this six-story hotel sits surrounded by the offices of over 250 multinational corporations. Restaurant, bar, complimentary Continental breakfast. In-room data ports, refrigerators. Cable TV. Pool. Equipment room. Laundry service. Business services, airport shuttle. | 2051 Le Jeune Rd. | 305/443–2301 or 800/465–4329 | fax 305/445–5523 | www.holiday-inn.com | 168 rooms | $109–$119 | AE, D, DC, MC, V.

Hotel Place St. Michel. Art Nouveau chandeliers suspended from vaulted ceilings grace the public areas of this intimate hotel that is within walking distance of Miracle Mile. Rooms are individually decorated with antiques imported from England, Scotland, and France. Restaurant, bar, complimentary Continental breakfast, room service. Cable TV. Laundry services. Business services. | 162 Alcazar Ave. | 305/444–1666 or 800/848–4683 | fax 305/529–0074 | www.hotelplacestmichel.com | 24 rooms, 3 suites | $150–$165 room, $185–$200 suite | AE, DC, MC, V.

Hyatt Regency. Colonnaded balconies and ornately sculpted stairways lend this 10-story hotel a vaguely Spanish character. Some rooms have balconies with large windows and balconies overlooking the pool. Restaurant (*see* Two Sisters' Restaurant, *above*), bar (with entertainment). In-room data ports, some microwaves, some refrigerators. Cable TV. Pool. Hot tub. Gym. Laundry services. Business services. | 50 Alhambra Plaza | 305/441–1234 | fax 305/441–0520 | www.hyatt.com | 242 rooms | $159–$290 | AE, D, DC, MC, V.

Omni Colonnade. Many of the original European flourishes of this hotel built in 1926 survive—mahogany armoires, tables and beds, as well as the lobby's marble floors and high ceilings. The hotel is located in the heart of Coral Gables. Restaurant, bar, room service. In-room data ports, minibars. Cable TV. Pool. Hot tub, beauty salon, sauna. Gym. Laundry service. Business services, parking ($10). | 180 Aragon Ave. | 305/441–2600 or 800/THE–OMNI | fax 305/445–3929 | 157 rooms | $185–$269 | AE, D, DC, MC, V.

Quality Inn, South. Official host of the Miami Metro Zoo, this two-story stucco motel has cozy, well-appointed rooms. It's 14 mi from downtown, but less than 10 mi from such attractions as the Miami Museum of Science, Monkey Jungle, and major shopping centers featuring Bloomingdale's and Macy's. Restaurant, bar. In-room data ports, microwaves, refrigerators, cable TV. Pool. Gym. Laundry facilites. Business services. Free parking. Pets allowed. | 14501 S. Dixie Rte. | 305/251–2000 or 800/228–5151 | fax 305/235–2225 | 100 rooms | $75–$125 | AE, D, DC, MC, V.

Terrace Inn. Formerly a Howard Johnson hotel, the Terrace Inn is situated in 2 buildings across the University of Miami campus and 8 mi from Miami International Airport. There is a restaurant adjacent to the hotel. Complimentary Continental breakfast. In-room data ports. Cable TV. Outdoor pool. Laundry services. Business services. | 1430 S. Dixie Hwy. | 305/662–8845 | fax 305/662–5562 | 80 rooms | $76–$85 | AE, D, DC, MC, V.

CRESTVIEW

MAP 3, B1

(Nearby towns also listed: De Funiak Springs, Destin, Fort Walton Beach, Niceville)

One of the highest towns in Florida is at the junction of I–10 and highways 90 and 85 (at 235 ft above sea level, residents say they're "on top of the mountain"). The town was a crossroads as far back as the Old Spanish Trail, when conquistadors passed through on trade routes.

Today, Crestview is one of the fastest-growing towns in northwest Florida. Its population has more than doubled since 1990, to 50,000. Much of that population is related to the three Air Force bases just outside of town. Eglin Air Force Base, with 724 square mi of land, is the largest air base in the world.

Information: Crestview Area Chamber of Commerce | 502 South Main St., Crestview, 32536 | 850/682–3212 | crestviewchamber@speedeenet.com.

Attractions

Blackwater River State Forest. The largest state forest in Florida, just northwest of Crestview, has over 190,000 acres of pine, oak, dogwood, and cedar trees. Three scenic rivers—the Blackwater, Shoal, and Yellow rivers—run through the forest, and a number of vendors rent canoes to paddle along the rivers and smaller creeks. Hikers can test the 21-mi Jackson Red Ground Trail. You can also fish, but a state license is required. | 11650 Munson Highway, Milton | 850/957–6140 | fax 850/957–6143 | Free | Daily.

Carver-Hill Museum. Displayed here are memorabilia from Carver-Hill Elementary and High School, which operated from 1954–1969 as a black-only school. When integration shut the school's doors, students petitioned for keepsakes, including band and sports trophies, to be saved, and the museum was set up as a place to store them. Graduates update their personal histories inside. | 901 McClellond St. | 850/682–3494 | Free | Weekdays 9–5; call for weekend hours.

Robert L.F. Sikes Public Library. Named for the former resident and U.S. Senator, the town library is housed in an impressive Greek Revival building, which holds over 44,000 volumes. | 805 James Lee Blvd. | 850/682–4432 | Free | Mon.–Tues. 10–8, Wed.–Thur. 10–6, Fri. 8:30–4:30, Sat. 10–4.

ON THE CALENDAR

APR.–MAY: *Old Spanish Trail Festival.* This one-week festival, which runs from the last weekend in April, commemorates the 16th-century trade route between Jacksonville and El Paso used by Spain, England, and France. Centered around Old Spanish Trail Park, events include a parade, rodeo, art and crafts, food vendors, a beauty pageant, live music, and a fair. | 850/689–6783.

Dining

Desi's. American. Specializing in pastas, steaks, and salads, this casual restaurant has golf decor on one side and animal prints on the other. The seafood fettucine has shrimp, scallops, and crab meat in a light Alfredo sauce with fettucine noodles, garlic bread, and a house salad. Friday is prime rib night. | 224 N. Main St. | 850/682–7477 | Closed weekends. No dinner Mon.–Wed. | $5–$11 | AE, MC, V.

Sonny's Real Pit BBQ. Barbecue. This primarily southern franchise restaurant is known for its grilled baby back ribs and sweet house BBQ sauce. The menu also includes barbecued hamburgers, sliced pork, sliced beef, and ribs. | 2680 S. Ferdon Blvd. | 850/683–0572 | $5–$11 | AE, D, MC, V.

Western Sizzlin'. Steak. The most popular choice at this inexpensive chain steakhouse is the buffet, which offers seven meats, seven vegetables, a complete salad bar, large selection of bakery items, and a dessert bar. | 2350 South Ferdon Blvd. | 850/682–7380 | $5–$17 | AE, D, MC, V.

Lodging

Comfort Inn. This motel is right off I–10, 5 mi from downtown Crestview. A marble, neo-Classical lobby has vases and columns, and a lighter pastel exterior features fountains. Rooms are standard motel-issue. Complimentary Continental breakfast. Some kitchenettes, some microwaves, some refrigerators, some in-room hot tubs. Outdoor pool. | 4040 South Ferdon Blvd. | 850/423–1200 | fax 850/423–1210 | www.comfortinn.com | 50 rooms | $80–$100 | AE, D, DC, MC, V.

Jameson Inn. This southeastern chain—which is found mostly in small towns—has hotels designed after elegant southern colonial mansions. Choose from one- and two-bedroom suites. From I–10, take exit 12 and follow Highway 85 south to Cracker Barrel Dr. Complimentary Continental breakfast. In-room data ports, some kitchenettes, some microwaves, some refrigerators. Cable TV, some in-room VCRs. Outdoor pool. Gym. Laundry facilities. Pets allowed. | 151 Cracker Barrel Dr. | 850/683–1778 or 800/526–3766 | fax 850/683–1779 | www.jamesoninns.com | 55 rooms | $59–$89 room, $159 suite | AE, D, DC, MC, V.

Crestview Holiday Inn. You'll find this simple stucco-and-sandstone motel at the intersection of Highway 85 and I–10. And you'll know you're in Florida when you see the shell-shape ceramic lamps, seashell-print bedspreads, and ocean-theme art on the walls. Restaurant, bar, room service. In-room data ports. Cable TV. Outdoor pool. Gym. Laundry facilities. Pets allowed (fee). | 4050 S. Ferdon Blvd. | 850/682–6111 or 800/465–4329 | fax 850/689–1189 | www.holiday-inn.com | 120 rooms | $74 | AE, D, DC, MC, V.

CRYSTAL RIVER

(Nearby towns also listed: Cedar Key, Chiefland, Homosassa Springs)

The Crystal River enters the Gulf of Mexico through Crystal Bay, where you'll find this uncommercialized town of 4,000, 70 mi north of Tampa. Most visitors are snorkelers and divers. A spring feeding warm water into the Crystal River draws one of the largest concentration of manatees in Florida—up to 300—between January and March. Manatees, also known as sea cows, are large, gentle vegetarian mammals threatened by development and speed boats; only about 2,600 still survive. The Crystal River National Wildlife Refuge harbors manatees but is only accessible by boat. If you have one, proceed slowly. The Crystal River State Archeological Site, which sits on a bluff over the river, protects six ceremonial mounds created by Indians who lived here as early as 200 BC.

Information: Citrus County Chamber of Commerce | 28 N.W. Hwy. 19, Crystal River, 34428 | 352/795–3149.

Attractions

Crystal River National Wildlife Refuge. This U.S. Fish and Wildlife Service sanctuary protects the endangered manatee. At the headwaters of Crystal River is King's Bay, which is fed by a number of freshwater springs that produce crystal-clear water at a consistent 72°F year-round. Manatees retreat to these waters for their warmth in the months between November and March. The refuge provides neither tours nor boat rentals, but dive shops and marinas in the town of Crystal River offer special manatee snorkeling tours. | 1502 S.E. Kings Bay Dr. | 352/563–2088 | Free | Weekdays 7:30–4, weekends Mar.–Nov., 7:30–4.

Crystal River State Archaeological Site. This 14-acre complex, built by a cultural group known simply as the Pre-Columbian Mound Builders, is considered one of the longest continuously inhabited sites in Florida. For 1,600 years, beginning around 200 BC, the site was an imposing prehistoric ceremonial center for Florida's Native Americans. A walk down the ½-mi paved loop trail at the site leads past six mounds, including temple, burial, and midden area mounds. An observation deck yields good views of the Crystal River, directly below. The site is located 2½ mi west of Highway 19 North. | 3400 N. Museum Point | 352/795–3817 | $2 per vehicle | Daily 9–5; grounds 8–sunset.

ON THE CALENDAR

JAN.: *Florida Manatee Festival*. The festival, held in the middle of January, is a tribute to this endangered marine mammal, with fine arts, entertainment, crafts, and seafood. | 850/942–6685.

NOV.: *Crystal River Jam*. This country music festival at Rock Crusher Canyon draws top performers from all over the nation. Tickets can be purchased for the entire weekend or for individual nights. | 352/795–1313 or 877/RC–CANYON.

Dining

Andre's. American. Huge windows overlook two golf courses at this low-key, comfortable restaurant located at the Citrus Hills Golf and Country Club. The extensive menu includes such treats as filet mignon, prime rib, and lobster; a large buffet, always available, complements this variety. Candles and linen tablecloths create a romantic environment in the evening. | 505 East Hartford St. | 352/746–6855 | $11–$20 | AE, D, DC, MC, V.

Charlie's Fish House Restaurant. Seafood. Sitting directly on a finger of the Crystal River, the spacious, no-frills eatery is busy and popular for its fantastic fresh seafood. The fried and broiled fish entrées include the crab meat–stuffed flounder, pre-breaded cod strips, and the cod burger. Grouper, catfish, and mullet are some of the other fish served. | 224 U.S. 19 N | 352/795–3949 | Reservations not accepted | $8–$12 | AE, D, MC, V.

Ray's Real Pit Bar-B-Q. Barbecue. A country setting, with mounted deer heads and horse reigns hanging on the wall. Popular barbecue dishes include the baby back ribs and turkey. Kids' menu. | 1935 S.E. U.S. Hwy. 19 | 352/795–2070 | $5–$15 | AE, D, MC, V.

Lodging

Best Western Crystal Resort. Directly on King's Bay, a spring-fed bay that leads into the Crystal River, this resort hotel offers rooms and efficiencies. It sits in the middle of Florida's "Nature Coast," a 150-mi stretch of coast along the state's western edge where eco-tourism dominates. The hotel is only mi south of the Crystal River Shopping Mall. Bar, picnic area. Some kitchenettes, some refrigerators. Cable TV. Pool. Hot tub. Dock, water sports, boating. Shops. Laundry facilities. Business services. Pets allowed (fee). | 614 N.W. Hwy. 19 | 352/795–3171 or 800/435–4409 | fax 352/795–3179 | 114 rooms | $78–$110 | AE, D, DC, MC, V.

Comfort Inn Crystal River. This three-story Comfort Inn is 3 mi east of the beaches and 10 mi south of Homosassa Springs Nature World. The Crystal River Mall is 1 mi south. Picnic area, complimentary Continental breakfast. In-room data ports. Cable TV. Pool. Tennis court. Laundry facilities. Business services. Pets allowed (fee). | 4486 N. Suncoast Blvd. | 352/563–1500 | fax 352/563–5426 | 66 rooms | $54–$65 | AE, D, DC, MC, V.

Crystal River Days Inn. This single-story Days Inn is off Highway 19. The on-site restaurant is open 24 hours. You can fish off the boat ramp. Restaurant. Some in-room hot tubs. Cable TV. Outdoor pool. Dock, fishing. Laundry services. Pets allowed (fee). | 2380 Suncoast Blvd. (Hwy. 19) | 352/795–2111 or 800/962–0028 | fax 352/795–4126 | www.daysinn.com | 107 rooms | $60–$70 | AE, D, DC, MC, V.

Econo Lodge. This simple, affordable single-story motel offers free local calling and has a restaurant and lounge next door. Complimentary Continental breakfast. Refrigerators available. Cable TV. Outdoor pool. Laundry facilities. Business services. Pets allowed (fee). | 2575 Suncoast Blvd. (Hwy. 19) | 352/795–9447 or 800/553–2666 | fax 352/795–6431 | www.econolodge.com | 44 rooms | $50–$65 | AE, D, DC, MC, V.

Plantation Inn & Golf Resort. White walls and green shutters together with tall white columns and manicured lawns evoke the charms of the Old South at this resort built in 1962. Located on the banks of the Crystal River, it sits on a 232-acre property that has two golf courses. Restaurant, bar, dining room, picnic area, room service. Some refrigerators. Cable TV. Pool. Hot tub. Driving range, 2 golf courses, putting green, tennis court. Dock, boating, fishing. Laundry facilities. Business services, airport shuttle. | 9301 West Fort Island Trail | 352/795–4211 or 800/632–6262 | fax 352/795–1368 | 131 rooms, 12 villas | $70–$210 for villas | AE, D, DC, MC, V.

DADE CITY

MAP 3, I5

(Nearby towns also listed: Brooksville, Clermont, Zephyrhills)

A half-hour north of Tampa is Dade City, a relaxed, friendly town of about 20,000. The downtown area has streets lined with oak trees and southern-style homes. The heart of this district, with its antiques, gift, and specialty stores, is marked by the 1909 Pasco County Courthouse. The town was originally founded in the 1840s as Fort Dade, but it was renamed in 1884. Just south of Dade City is St. Leo, which grows the bulk of America's kumquats.

Information: Dade City Chamber of Commerce | 14112 8th St., Dade City, 33525 | 352/567–3769 | www.dadecity.com.

Attractions

Dade Battlefield State Historic Site. This 40-acre park 25 mi north of Dade City is the site of the first battle of the Second Seminole War. Today, large oak and magnolia trees surround a museum and visitors center which exhibits the weapons and paraphernalia used in the war. The battle is reenacted annually on the weekend closest to the date of the battle, December 28. | 7200 Country Rd. 603, Bushnell | 352/793–4781 | $2 per vehicle | Daily 8–sunset; visitors center daily 9–5.

Dade City Historic District and Antique Center. As you stroll down the streets of this district in downtown Dade City, you will notice a number of buildings and homes that date back to the late 1800s and early 1900s and are on the National Historic Register. Notable buildings include the courthouse and original city hall, which is now home to a newspaper plant. There are also a number of charming antiques shops. | 352/567–3769 | Free | Daily.

Pioneer Florida Museum. At this museum located 1 mile north of Dade City (off Highway 301), you can visit a 1930s schoolhouse, an 1860s farmhouse, an 1878 church, and an 1896 railroad depot. | 15602 Pioneer Museum Rd. | 352/567–0262 | fax 352/567–1262 |:$5 | Tues.–Sun. 1–5.

ON THE CALENDAR

JAN.: *Kumquat Festival.* This large festival the last Saturday in January is held in honor of the small, tangy fruit. Highlights include live music, a craft show, and dinner theater. You can also sample a range of dishes made with kumquats. | Last Sat. in Jan. | 352/567–3769.

FEB.: *Pasco County Fair.* At this youth agricultural fair held annually at the county fairgrounds, you can see livestock, poultry, and animals raised by children, as well as exhibits of blue-ribbon quilts, canned goods, and arts and crafts. | 352/567–6678.

SEPT.: *Pioneer Florida Day.* The main act of this Labor Day weekend event held at the Pioneer Florida Museum is the reenactment of famous Civil War battles. You can also browse for arts and crafts, and antique cars and tractors; there is all-day live entertainment and kids' activities. | $6 | 352/567–0262.

DINING

Adrian's Grill. American/Casual. This relaxed eatery is housed in the oldest building in Dade City, which was constructed in the late 1800s. Blackened grouper, baby back ribs, and juicy burgers keep people coming back. | 37837 Meridian Ave. | 352/518–0990 | $5–$10 | AE, D, MC, V.

LODGING

Azalea House. The Azalea House is a beautifully restored 1906 home nestled amid moss-covered oak and azalea trees. All rooms are quite spacious and individually named and decorated. Guests may also visit the resident monkey, who stays in a private apartment adjacent to the garage. Dining room, complimentary breakfast. Cable TV, no room phones. Library. No kids under 5. No smoking. | 37719 Meridian Ave. | 352/523–1773 | www.floridasecrets.com/Bed&Breakfast/WCBeds/Azalea.htm | 3 rooms | $85–$95 | AE, D, MC, V.

DANIA BEACH

MAP 3, L9

(Nearby towns also listed: Davie, Fort Lauderdale, Hollywood)

Driving south a few miles from Ft. Lauderdale on I–95, it's hard not to notice Dania Beach (pop. 14,000). On the east side of the highway is the Hurricane, a 3,200-ft wooden roller coaster, part of an entertainment complex called Grand Prix Race-o-Rama. On the west side is the International Game Fish Association's World Fishing Center, an interactive fishing museum. Next door is a mammoth sporting goods store. Once

DANIA BEACH

INTRO
ATTRACTIONS
DINING
LODGING

you get off the highway, you can find the Graves Museum of Archaeology and Natural History, Dania Jai Alai, and a few minutes away, Port Everglades, the world's second-busiest cruise port. Federal Highway, the de facto Dania Beach Main Street, has over 100 antiques dealers. Inland on the Atlantic, the popular beach at John U. Lloyd State Park includes a 920-ft pier. The city used to be called simply Dania; a 1998 vote switched the name to reflect its breezy connection to the Atlantic.

Information: **Greater Dania Beach Chamber of Commerce** | 102 W. Dania Beach Blvd., Dania Beach, 33004 | 954/926–2323 | www.greaterdania.org.

Attractions

Dania Jai-Alai. The world's second-largest jai-alai court is host to some of the planet's best wicket talent. You can just sit and watch the world's fastest sport (one of Florida's top entertainment values), you can gamble on the action, or you can play cards in a large, attractive poker hall. Open all year. | 301 E. Dania Beach Blvd. | 954/927–2841 | $1.50–$7 | Games Sun. 1, Tues., Sat. noon and 7:15, Wed.–Fri. 7:15.

Fishing Museum and Hall of Fame. The International Game Fishing Association spent $32 million to develop this campus at Sportsman's Park, which also contains a marina, museum, and research library. The seven galleries have virtual-reality fishing, where you can cast off and try to reel in a marlin, sailfish, or bass. | 300 Gulfstream Way | 954/924–4310 | $9 | Daily 10–6.

Graves Museum of Archeology and Natural History. Bambiraptor, a recently discovered dinosaur, is part of this museum's 9,000-ft dinosaur hall. In addition, the museum has a large collection of pre-Columbian artifacts and crystals from the ancient Mediterranean world. | 481 S. Federal Hwy. | 954/925–7770 | $9.95 | Tues.–Sat. 10–4, Sun. 12–6.

John U. Lloyd Beach State Recreation Area. The park consists of 250 acres of barrier island with pine-shaded beach, a jetty pier where you can fish, a marina, and canoeing on the Whiskey Creek. It's also a great spot to watch cruise ships entering and departing Port Everglades, to the west across the waterway. Further inland you can explore subtropical coastal hammock along a quarter-mile long nature trail. | 6503 N. Ocean Dr. | 954/923–2833 | www.dep.state.fl.us | $4 per vehicle | Daily 8–sunset.

ON THE CALENDAR

FEB.: *Tomato Festival.* This event was started in the 1950s to commemorate the tomato harvest. There's a raft race, volleyball tournament, street party, and a big tomato fight held at venues across the city. | 954/924–3627.

Dining

Casa Bella. Continental. This elegant restaurant, complete with lace tablecloths and candlelights, is housed in a 1912 Victorian home. Popular dishes include the rack of lamb, veal shank, and a wide array of seafood selections. | 129 N. Federal Hwy. | 954/923–1000 | Reservations essential | No lunch. May–Sept. closed Sun.–Mon. | $14–$37 | AE, MC, V.

Lodging

Fort Lauderdale Airport Hilton. This hotel is located on I–95, a quarter-mile south of I–595 and only 1½ mi from the airport. Palm trees encircle the pool, which many rooms overlook. There are complimentary cocktails each evening. Restaurants, bar, complimentary Continental breakfast, room service. In-room data ports, some refrigerators. Cable TV. Pool. Hot tub. 2 tennis courts. Gym. Laundry service. Business services, airport shuttle. | 1870 Griffin Rd. | 954/920–3300 or 800/445–8667 | fax 954/920–3348 | www.hilton.com | 388 rooms | $179–$219 | AE, D, DC, MC, V.

Sheraton Fort Lauderdale Airport Hotel. You enter this hotel via a courtyard, which has a large stone fountain. The hotel is located just off I–95, 1½ miles from the airport terminals. The beach is 7 mi east. Restaurant, bar. In-room data ports, some refrigerators. Cable

TV. Pool. Hot tub, sauna. Tennis court. Gym. Laundry service. Business services, airport shuttle. Some pets allowed (fee). | 1825 Griffin Rd. | 954/920–3500 or 800/325–3535 | fax 954/927–2808 | www.sheraton.com | 250 rooms | $129–$149 | AE, D, DC, MC, V.

SpringHill Suites Ft. Lauderdale Airport. This seven-story hotel is just 1½ mi from Ft. Lauderdale Airport. All suites are spacious and offer separate sleeping, sitting, and work areas. There are a number of restaurants within walking distance. Complimentary Continental breakfast. In-room data ports, minibars, microwaves, refrigerators. Cable TV. Outdoor pool. Outdoor hot tub. Gym. Laundry facilities, laundry services. Business services. | 151 S.W. 18th Ct. | 954/920–9696 | fax 954/929–3577 | www.marriott.com | 168 suites | $95–$105 | AE, D, DC, MC, V.

DAVENPORT

(Nearby towns also listed: Haines City, Kissimmee, Lake Buena Vista, Lake Wales, Walt Disney World, Winter Haven)

If you want to save a little money on your Disney vacation, this town of 1,600 is only about 10 mi south of Walt Disney World on I–4. Otherwise, you won't find much there.

Information: **Davenport City Hall** | 1 S. Allapaha Ave., Davenport, 33836 | 863/422–4410.

ON THE CALENDAR

SEPT.: *Labor Day Festival.* This event is held on the Municipal Block in downtown Davenport and it usually brings out the entire town. There are a big outdoor barbecue and a number of interesting competitions, including the ugliest dog and pie eating contests. | Labor Day | 863/422–4410.

Dining

Green Leaf Restaurant. Chinese. Hawaii-fried shrimp and lobster and hot and spicy beef are among the more popular entrées at this casual eatery. | 4615 Hwy. 27 N | 863/420–0098 | $6–$12 | AE, D, MC, V.

Lodging

Comfort Inn Maingate South. This motel is off U.S. 27, only 5 mi from Walt Disney World, and allows visitors to avoid much of the traffic that surrounds the local attractions. There are two fast-food eateries within walking distance. Complimentary Continental breakfast. Some refrigerators. Cable TV. Outdoor pool, outdoor hot tub. Video games. Playground. Business services. Pets allowed (fee). | 5510 U.S. 27 N | 863/424–2811 | fax 863/424–1723 | www.comfortinn.com | 150 rooms | $59–$79 | AE, D, DC, MC, V.

Days Inn South of Magic Kingdom. This two-story inn is just 7 mi south of Walt Disney World. The heated pool is surrounded by palm trees. There are a handful of eateries within walking distance. In-room data ports, refrigerators. Cable TV. Outdoor pool. Outdoor hot tub. Video games. Laundry facilities. Business services. Pets allowed (fee). | 2524 Frontage Rd. | 863/929–3577 or 800/424–1880 | fax 863/420–8717 | www.daysinn.com | 122 rooms | $70 | AE, D, DC, MC, V.

Holiday Inn Express. Walt Disney World is 8 mi away from this two-story Holiday Inn, which is within walking distance of restaurants. Complimentary Continental breakfast. In-room data ports, some microwaves, some refrigerators. Cable TV. Outdoor pool, outdoor hot tub. Laundry facilities. Business services. | 5225 U.S. 27 N | 863/424–2120 or 800/465–4329 | fax 863/424–5317 | www.holiday-inn.com | 104 rooms, 20 suites | $79–$109 suites | AE, D, DC, MC, V.

DAVIE

MAP 3, L9

(Nearby towns also listed: Dania Beach, Fort Lauderdale, Hollywood)

The horse farms and estates all around this town of 72,000 make an unlikely portrait of South Florida as the Old West. Folks in western wear ride their fine horses through downtown, even ordering take out through "drive-through" windows that accommodate them, or you can even unsaddle in the corral that McDonald's provides out back. Although a town law requires kids on horseback to wear helmets, they can cut loose at the training rodeos that take place each Wednesday in town.

Information: **Davie-Cooper City Chamber of Commerce** | 4185 Davie Rd., Davie, 33314 | 954/581–0790 | www.davie-coopercity.com.

Attractions

Bergeron Rodeo Grounds. The Grounds holds free local rodeos every Wed. at 7 PM and five-star rodeos the last weekend of every month. From I–95 take Griffin Road west to Davie Road. | 4271 Davie Rd. | 954/384–7075 | $12 for five-star rodeo.

Flamingo Gardens. This 60-acre sanctuary includes a 25,000-square-ft aviary housing the largest collection of wading birds in America, a 30-min tram tour through groves, hammock, and wetlands area, an alligator lagoon, and butterfly and hummingbird gardens. | 3750 Flamingo Rd. | 954/473–2955 | www.flamingogardens.org | $10 | Open daily 9:30–5:30. Closed Mon. June–Sept.

Young at Art Children's Museum. Kids can play creatively at this non-profit museum designed for hands-on learning. Facilities include a "toddler's playspace" and art spaces including photography and ceramics studios. | 11584 Hwy. 84 | 954/424–0085 | www.youngatartmuseum.org | $4 | Mon.–Sat. 10–5, Sun. noon–5.

ON THE CALENDAR

FEB.: *Orange Blossom Festival and Parade.* The oldest parade in Florida—it began in 1936—marches on the last weekend in Feb. down Davie Road. The parade ends this down-home festival that includes a pie-baking contest, art and crafts, and a kids' carnival. | 954/581–0790.

Dining

★ **Armadillo Café.** Southwestern. This fun restaurant has been acclaimed for its inventive southwestern fare and is often cited in lists of Florida's top restaurants. A dish called seafood pasta *diabla* comes with shrimp, scallops, calamari, white water clams, tomatoes, and ancho chiles with fettucine. | 3400 South University Dr. | $15–$30 | AE, D, DC, MC, V.

Buca di Beppo. Italian. Items from the menu at this southern Italian restaurant chain (there's another branch in Fort Lauderdale) are served up family-style. The 300-seat restaurant is designed as a consciously kitschy replica of a 1940s Little Italy eatery. | 3355 S. University Dr. | 954/577–3287 | $10–20 | AE, D, DC, MC, V.

Vienna Cafe and Winebar. Continental. This restaurant is modeled after a European café-bistro, with a cottage-like exterior and wooden tables and chairs. The Austrian owner offers traditional dishes like *jaeger schnitzel* (veal medallions in a mushroom Madeira sauce). Also served are fresh seafood, pastas, and steaks. The extensive wine list includes 15 selections by the glass. | 9100 State Rd. 84 | 954/423–1961 | Closed Mon. | $10–18 | AE, MC, V.

Lodging

Rolling Hills Hotel and Resort. This seven-floor property features a 250,000-gallon heated pool with a rock waterfall, an atrium lobby, and complimentary shuttle service to Sawgrass Mills Mall and the airport. Inside, the Waterfall Café and Lounge has live entertainment, happy hour specials, and a Sunday champagne brunch. Off University Dr. in Davie. Restaurant, bar with entertainment, room service. In-room data ports, some in-room safes, some microwaves, some refrigerators. Cable TV. Outdoor pool. Outdoor hot tub. 2 tennis courts. Laundry facilities, laundry service. | 3510 W. Rolling Hills Circle | 954/475–0400 or 800/528–1234 | fax 954/474–9967 | www.bestwestern.com | 221 rooms | $69–$90 | AE, D, DC, MC, V.

Homestead Village Guest Studios. This hotel chain designs room with extended stays in mind. Studio rooms, which are tidy and modern, come equipped with kitchens and phones with both voice mail and data ports. In-room data ports, kitchenettes, microwaves, refrigerators. Cable TV. Gym. Laundry facilities, laundry service. Pets allowed (fee). | 7550 State Rd. 84 | 954/476–1211 | fax 954/476–0026 | www.stayhsd.com | 125 rooms | $60–$70 | AE, D, DC, MC, V.

DAYTONA BEACH

(Nearby towns also listed: DeLand, Flagler Beach, New Smyrna Beach, Ormond Beach)

Daytona Beach (pop. 62,000) is perhaps the most famous spring break destination in Florida; in fact, it bills itself as "The Most Famous Beach in the World." Certainly, it would be hard to find a beach more closely identified with fun; for decades, a reputation for hedonism has drawn university-age kids to the 23-mi stretch of sand, which is also the most built-up beach in Florida. In an effort to draw more families and change the place's reputation, city leaders have been tightening laws and cracking down on underage drinking.

One thing that will not change is the city's passion for automobiles. Since the early 1900s, folks such as Henry Ford and Louis Chevrolet have rocketed cars across the pavement-firm beach sands. Driving is still allowed on the shore here, although the speed limit is now 10 mph. From video games to theme restaurants and interactive attractions at the speedway, cars rule the town. The main event, of course, is the Daytona 500 race in February, luring race fans nationwide to the Daytona International Speedway.

Information: Daytona Beach Convention and Visitors Bureau | 126 E. Orange Ave., Daytona Beach, 32114 | 904/255–0415 or 800/854–1234 | www.daytonabeach.com.

Attractions

Adventure Landing. This large water park has 12 slides, an inner tube float, and other watery attractions. There are also 3 miniature golf courses, a go-cart track, and a large arcade on land. | 604 Earle St. | 904/258–0071 | www.adventurelanding.com | Water park $19.99, miniature golf $6, go-carts $6–$8 | Daily 10–8.

Daytona Beach. The beach itself was the city's first racetrack. Today cars cruise at a maximum 10 mph. | 904/239–7873 | www.volusia.org/beach | $5 per vehicle; Dec.–Jan. free | Daily.

Daytona Beach Kennel Club. The club has pari-mutuel wagering and greyhound racing throughout the year. | 2201 International Speedway Blvd. | 904/252–6484 | Races Mon.–Sat. 7:45 PM; Mon., Wed., Sat. 1 PM.

Daytona USA. You can change tires in a timed pit-stop competition, design and video-test your own race cars, and broadcast a famous race finish at this attraction in the Daytona International Speedway. "The Daytona 500" feature film presentation, starring some of NASCAR's finest drivers, puts guests in the driver's seat in a side-by-side race to the finish. Daytona USA also contains the 4th Turn Grill, the Pit Shop (a souvenir and apparel store), and the Sega Speedway (an electronic entertainment center). Daily speedway tours (weather and race schedule permitting) lead you on an exciting 30-min tram excursion. | 1801 W. International Speedway Blvd. | 904/254–2700 | Free | Daily 9–7.

Halifax Historical Museum. Housed in an old downtown bank building, this museum show-cases memorabilia from the early days of beach automobile racing, historic photographs, Native American artifacts, a postcard exhibit, and a video that details the city's history. | 252 S. Beach St. | 904/255–6976 | fax 904/255–7605 | www.halifaxhistorical.org | $3 | Tues.–Sat. 10–4.

Klassix Auto Museum. Driver Mark Martin has long been a friend to this museum that features a showroom filled with Corvettes, race cars, and motorcycles, with period murals as backdrops. | 2909 W. International Speedway Blvd. | 904/252–3800 or 800/881–8975 | www.klassixauto.com | $8.50 | Daily 9–6.

Museum of Arts and Sciences. One of the five largest museums in Florida, the Museum of Arts and Sciences has a large collection of pre-Castro Cuban art, Florida Native Ameri-can items, pre-Columbian art, Indian and Persian miniature paintings, and an eye-pop-ping complete skeleton of a giant sloth that is 13 ft long and 130,000 years old. | 1040 Museum Blvd. | 904/255–0285 | www.moas.org | $5 | Tues.–Fri. 9–4, weekends 12–5.

Ponce de León Lighthouse. This bright red, century-old lighthouse is an historic monument and museum. It marks the sleepy town of Ponce Inlet at the southern tip of Daytona Beach's barrier island. | 4931 S. Atlantic Ave. | 904/761–1821 | www.ponceinlet.org | $4 | May–Labor Day, daily 10–8; Labor Day–Apr., daily 10–4.

Southeast Museum of Photography. This museum at Daytona Beach Community College is just one of just a dozen photography museums in the country. It has changing exhibits. | 1200 W. International Speedway Blvd. | 904/254–4475 | fax 904/254–4487 | www.dbcc.cc.fl.us/dbcc/htm/smp/smphome.htm | Free | Mon., Wed., Thurs.–Fri. 9:30–4:30, Tues. 9:30–7, weekends 12–4.

Sugar Mill Gardens. These ruins of a 1763 English sugar mill, 4 mi south of Daytona Beach, are surrounded by 12 acres of botanical gardens. In the 1940s and '50s the park was an attraction known as Bongoland (after the monkey who greeted visitors); the huge con-crete dinosaurs you see around are left-overs from that era. | 950 Old Sugar Mill Rd., Port Orange | 904/767–1735 | Free | Daily dawn to dusk.

ON THE CALENDAR

FEB.: *Daytona 500.* A three-week celebration of auto racing, Daytona's Speed Weeks, culminates in the famous Daytona 500 auto race at Daytona International Speedway. | 904/254–2700.

MAR.: *Bike Week.* Some 500,000 motorcyclists descend on Daytona for 10 days of races, parades, and coleslaw wrestling. Begun in 1937, this event is held each year around the first week of March. Bikers crowd the bars and restaurants that line Main Street between the ocean and the Halifax River. | 904/255–0981.

JULY: *Florida International Festival.* The highlight of this biennial event, which occurs in the middle of July in venues across Daytona Beach, Palm Beach, and Stanford, is a series of London Symphony Orchestra concerts. Featured are chamber music and dance. | 904/257–7790.

Dining

Anna's Trattoria. Italian. Pink table linens, flowers, and low lighting set the scene for delightful Italian fare. Popular entrées include spinach ravioli, spaghetti with Italian sausage and onions, and angel-hair pasta with fresh chopped tomatoes and garlic. | 304 Seabreeze Blvd. | 904/239–9624 | Closed Mon. No lunch | $9–$17 | AE, D, MC, V.

Ashoka Indian Cuisine. Indian. This casual spot has two dining rooms decorated with tra-ditional Indian artwork. Specialties include tandoori dishes cooked in a clay oven. The shrimp curry and lobster masala are delicious. | 3218 S. Atlantic Ave. | 904/760–1535 | Reservations essential on weekends | Closed Mon. | $8–$16 | AE, D, MC, V.

Aunt Catfish's on the River. Seafood. This popular place is on the southwest bank of the Intracoastal Waterway, about 5 mi south of Daytona Beach. Enjoy the view of the Halifax River while enjoying freshly cooked seafood. Fried shrimp and fried catfish are specialties. Cinnamon rolls and hush puppies come with each entrée. | 4009 Halifax Dr., Port Orange | 904/767–4768 | $9–$28 | AE, D, MC, V.

Byron's Grill. American/Casual. Historical pictures of Daytona Beach's early racing days dress the dining area of this casual spot. In addition to traditional American fare such as rotisserie chicken and steaks, there are Greek and Italian specialties. The chicken kabobs and souvlaki are popular choices. | 701 N. Atlantic Ave. | 904/257–6606 | Reservations not accepted | $6–$15 | MC, V.

Crock Pot Fresh Seafood. Seafood. This nautical-theme restaurant is known for its steamed shrimp, conch salad, and a fried shrimp and fish combo plate. | 200 S. Martin Luther King Blvd. | 904/253–9696 | Closed Sun.–Mon. | $5–$11 | No credit cards.

Cruisin' Cafe Bar & Grill. American/Casual. Five booths made from cars that won the Daytona 500, and memorabilia donated by other drivers will let you know you could only be in Daytona Beach. Most all of the dishes have race-related names; the prime rib special and the Checkered Flag chicken Caesar salad are popular choices. | 2 S. Atlantic Ave. | 904/253–5522 | $13–$15 | AE, D, DC, MC, V.

Cuban Sandwich Shop. Cuban. Posters of Latin American nations await diners at this small, family-owned eatery. The grilled Cuban sandwich (roast pork, baked ham, and Swiss cheese on Cuban bread) is very popular, as is the black bean soup. | 722 Mason Ave. | 904/255–6655 | Closed Sun. | $3–$8 | No credit cards.

Daytona Hot Grill. Italian. If you're craving a late night sub or sandwich, this is your place—the grill is open until 4 AM nightly. The chicken parmigiana hero and lasagna are favorites. | 527 N. Atlantic Ave. | 904/255–3210 | No lunch | $7–$9 | No credit cards.

Gene's Steak House. Steak. This fine dining establishment first opened its doors in 1948, the same year that NASCAR races began. Consequently, racing pictures are featured in the two dining rooms. This is known as the best local steakhouse, and the filet mignon and porterhouse are top sellers. The wine list is one of the most comprehensive in the state. | 3674 W. International Speedway Blvd. | 904/255–2059 | Closed Mon. | $14–$36 | AE, DC, MC, V.

Hoho Restaurant. Mandarin. The General Tso's chicken, Mandarin shrimp, and an affordable, 70-item buffet make this Chinese restaurant popular with locals. | 149 Point Woods Dr. | 904/255–2395 | $5–$18 | AE, D, MC, V.

Lighthouse Landing. Seafood. Dine outdoors on picnic tables along the Atlantic, or in an interior dining room decorated with antiques and old pictures of Daytona Beach. The fried seafood platter comes with shrimp, scallops, oysters, and crabs. | 4940 S. Peninsula Dr., Ponce Inlet | 904/761–9271 | $6–$15 | AE, D, MC, V.

McK's Dublin Station. Irish. The fare at this tavern is simple but hearty—juicy burgers, shepherd's pie, London broil, and homemade meat loaf. There are a pool table and a dart league on Wednesdays. | 218 S. Beach St. | 904/238–3321 | www.dublinstation.com | $8–$15 | AE, DC, MC, V.

Park's Seafood. Seafood. Models of ships and paintings of seascapes ornament the walls of this low-key eatery where prime rib and chicken entrées complement the seafood selections. For a sampling, try the seafood platter with shrimp, oysters, and fresh fish. | 951 N. Beach St. | 904/258–7272 | Reservations not accepted | No lunch | $8–$25 | AE, D, MC, V.

Pottsie's Eatery. American. This casual spot in the Big Tree Shopping Center serves up simple American fare in a country setting. Pot roast and Philly cheese steak sandwiches are the most popular items on the menu. | 2032 S. Ridgewood Ave. | 904/756–1010 | Breakfast also available | No dinner Mon.–Wed., Sat. Closed Sun. | $4–$6 | No credit cards.

Riccardo's. Italian. Prints of Old Master paintings hang from the walls of this casually elegant family eatery. Veal is the specialty here, though shrimp dinners, parmigianas, and meatball pastas are also popular. | 610 Glenview Blvd. | 904/253–3035 | No lunch | $10–$22 | AE, MC, V.

Rosario's Ristorante. Italian. Chef Rosario Vinci shows off his talents in the charming candlelit dining room of the Live Oak Inn—Daytona's oldest home. The dining room overlooks the marina with antique Victorian settings. But the northern Italian fare is the draw: come for the veal marsala, *pollo peperonato* (chicken breast sautéed in wine with roasted peppers and onions), or fresh local grouper poached in white wine. | 488 S. Beach St. | 904/258–6066 | Closed Sun.–Mon. No lunch | $14–$25 | AE, MC, V.

St. Regis. Continental. Dining rooms in this restored wooden house built in the 1920s are individually named and decorated. The Sahara Room has zebra pattern tablecloths with red napkins, while the St. Regis Room has elegant settings, a double pedestal table, and French doors leading to a dining room along a porch. The fare includes duck à l'orange, rack of lamb, veal française, chicken marsala, pastas, and fresh fish specials. | 509 Seabreeze Blvd. | 904/252–8743 | No lunch Apr.–Sept. | $18–$25 | AE, MC, V.

Lodging

Acapulco Inn. All rooms in this white and orange beachfront hotel have views of the Atlantic from private balconies. Many rooms have complete kitchen facilities. The pool deck overlooking the ocean has two whirlpools and a kiddie pool. Restaurant, bar, picnic area. In-room safes, some kitchenettes, refrigerators. Cable TV. Pool. 2 hot tubs. Beach. Video games. Children's programs (ages 5–12). Laundry facilities. Business services. | 2505 S. Atlantic Ave. | 904/761–2210 or 800/245–3580 | fax 904/761–2216 | www.acapulcoinn.com | 133 rooms | $159–$173 | AE, D, DC, MC, V.

Adam's Mark Resort. Daytona's most luxurious high-rise hotel offers ocean views from each room. The beachfront, 15-story resort has a great pool and a spacious deck. Plans are in the works to double the size of the resort. Restaurant, bar. Minibars. Cable TV. Indoor pool. Hot tub. Gym. Beach. Shops. Laundry facilities. Business services. | 100 N. Atlantic Ave. | 904/254–8200 | fax 904/253–0275 | www.adamsmark.com/daytona | 437 rooms | $99–$184 | AE, D, DC, MC, V.

Aruba Inn. This clean, modern two-story, Mediterranean-style facility has modest prices for its beachfront location. Rooms are modern, and most have terrific glass door views out to the beach. | 32 rooms. Picnic area. Some kitchenettes, some refrigerators. Cable TV. Pool. Beach. Laundry facilities. Pets allowed. | 1254 N. Atlantic Ave. | 904/253–5643 or 800/241–1406 | fax 904/248–1279 | www.arubainn.com | $60–$75 | AE, D, DC, MC, V.

Bahama House. This 10-story hotel, which opened in 1994, has a two-tiered sun deck, a piano, and original art in the lobby. The colorful rooms are large and all have private balconies. Complimentary cocktails are offered in the evening. There are summer activities programs for all ages. Complimentary Continental breakfast. In-room data ports, in-room safes, kitchenettes, microwaves. Cable TV. Pool. Hot tub. Beach. Laundry facilities. Business services. | 2001 S. Atlantic Ave., Daytona Beach Shores | 904/248–2001 or 800/571–2001 | fax 904/248–0991 | www.daytonabahamahouse.com | 95 rooms | $179–$216 | AE, D, DC, MC, V.

Beachcomer Inn. Located at the northern end of the beach, this seven-story beachfront hotel has rooms with either ocean or street views. All rooms have balconies. There's a poolside restaurant and lounge. Restaurant, bar, picnic area, room service. In-room data ports, some kitchenettes, refrigerators. Cable TV. Pool, wading pool. Hot tub. Beach. Children's programs (2–18). Laundry facilities. Business services. | 2000 N. Atlantic Ave. | 904/252–8513 or 800/245–3575 | www.beachcomberinn.com | 174 rooms | $124–$144 | AE, D, DC, MC, V.

Beach Quarters Resort. The lobby of this beachfront five-story resort features a Victorian loveseat, an antique desk, and lush tropical greenery—separating it from a host of nearby mid-rise hotels. Baked goodies and coffee are served in the Galley, which overlooks the ocean and resembles a large family kitchen. All rooms here are suites with rich oak furnishings and a private balcony. Restaurant, room service. Kitchenettes, microwaves, refrigerators. Cable TV, in-rooms VCRs (and movies). Outdoor pool. Beach, fishing, bicycles. Laundry services. Business services. | 3711 S. Atlantic Ave. | 904/767–3119 | fax 904/760–7712 | www.the-beachquarters.com | 26 suites | $110–$180 | AE, D, MC, V.

Best Western Aku Tiki Inn. This Best Western inn, 1½ mi from the Daytona International Speedway, once sported a Polynesian theme. While no longer exotic-minded, it is still beachfront, and all rooms have balconies overlooking the Atlantic, and the large pool. Restaurant, bar (with entertainment), picnic area, room service. Some kitchenettes, some microwaves, refrigerators. Cable TV. Pool, pond, wading pool. Basketball. Beach. Shops, video games. Laundry facilities. Business services. Pets allowed. | 2225 S. Atlantic Ave. | 904/252–9631 or 800/258–8454 | fax 904/252–1198 | www.bestwestern.com | 132 rooms | $110–$120 | AE, D, DC, MC, V.

Best Western LaPlaya Resort. This formidable eight-story resort has terrific balcony views of the ocean. It's across the street from the Belair Plaza shopping center and 6 mi from the speedway. Restaurant, bar, picnic area. Some kitchenettes, microwaves, refrigerators. Cable TV. Indoor pool, wading pool. Hot tub, sauna, steam room. Gym. Beach. Shops, video games. Children's programs (ages 5–12). Laundry services. Business services. | 2500 N. Atlantic Ave. | 904/672–0990 or 800/874–6996 | fax 904/677–0982 | www.bestwestern.com | 239 rooms | $199–$270 | AE, D, DC, MC, V.

Best Western Mayan Inn. Only a block from the boardwalk and three blocks from the Convention Center, this eight-story hotel has direct access to the beach sands from its pool deck. Most rooms have private balconies with views of the Atlantic. Bar, complimentary Continental breakfast. In-room data ports, some in-room safes, some kitchenettes, some microwaves, some refrigerators. Cable TV. Pool, wading pool. Beach. Children's programs (ages 3–12). Laundry facilities. Business services. | 103 S. Ocean Ave. | 904/252–0584 | fax 904/252–8670 | www.bestwestern.com | 161 rooms | $128–$185 | AE, D, DC, MC, V.

Casa Marina Motel. While across the street from the beach, Casa Marina offers a variety of different styles of rooms, many with ocean views. Since it's run by the same management, you get access to the facilities at the Capri and Ocean View Motel across the street, including a 60-ft pool waterslide. Kitchenettes, microwaves, refrigerators. Cable TV. | 837 N. Atlantic Ave. | 904/252–4644 or 800/225–3691 | fax 904/255–7378 | www.casamarina.com | 23 rooms | $64–$89 | AE, D, DC, MC, V.

Coquina Inn Bed & Breakfast. This pristine inn, built in 1912 of local coquina rock (a mixture of coquina shells and limestone) and stucco, served as a parsonage for many years. It is on the National Register of Historic Places. There are four charming rooms, furnished with antiques including four-poster and canopy beds. Complimentary port and sherry are offered as well as fresh flowers in the rooms. Complimentary breakfast. Cable TV, no room phones. Hot tub. No kids under 16. No smoking. | 544 S. Palmetto | 904/254–4969 or 800/805–7533 | www.coquinainndaytonabeach.com | 4 rooms | $80–$110 | AE, D, MC, V.

Comfort Inn & Suites. This four-story hotel is just 9 mi from the Daytona International Speedway and 2½ mi from the Ocean Center. Suites, efficiencies, and spa rooms are available. Complimentary Continental breakfast. In-room data ports, some kitchenettes, some microwaves, some refrigerators, some in-room hot tubs. Cable TV. Outdoor pool. Laundry facilities. Business services. | 730 N. Atlantic Ave. | 904/255–5491 | fax 904/252–7188 | www.comfortinn.com | 96 rooms | $179–$219 | AE, D, DC, MC, V.

Days Inn Speedway. This three-story hotel is 4 mi from the beach and less than a mile from the Speedway. Prices skyrocket during race weeks. Restaurant. In-room data ports. Cable TV. Outdoor pool. Laundry services. Business services. Pets allowed (fee). | 2900 International Speedway Blvd. | 904/255–0541 or 800/544–8313 | fax 904/253–1468 | www.daysinn.com | 180 rooms | $69–$79 | AE, D, DC, MC, V.

Daytona Beach Days Inn. This four-story motel is right on the beach and features a spacious sundeck. There are a number of fishing and boating facilities nearby. Rooms are bright pink and turquoise; some have ocean views. Restaurant, bar, room service. Some kitchenettes, some microwaves, some refrigerators. Cable TV. Outdoor pool. Outdoor hot tub. Laundry facilities. Business services. | 1220 North Atlantic Ave. | 904/255–2745 or 800/452–0932 | fax 904/238–1646 | www.daysinn.com | 75 rooms | $50–$110 | AE, D, MC, V.

El Morocco Beach Motel. This two-story oceanfront motel commands a wonderful view of the Atlantic. Deep sea fishing charters and a few restaurants are within walking distance. Some kitchenettes, some microwaves, some refrigerators. Cable TV. Outdoor pool. Business services. | 817 S. Atlantic Ave. | 904/253–1643 | fax 904/253–4505 | 20 rooms | $120–$150 | AE, D, MC, V.

Flamingo Inn. Rooms in this beachfront, three-story motel all have balconies; most have ocean views. The motel is close to groceries and across the street from restaurants. Picnic area. In-room safes, some kitchenettes, some microwaves, refrigerators. Cable TV. Pool. Beach. Laundry facilities. | 2011 S. Atlantic Ave. | 904/252–1412 or 800/682–0919 | fax 904/252–1412 | 27 rooms | $69–$159 | MC, V.

Grand Prix. All rooms have ocean views at this moderately priced two-story motel. Many rooms have kitchens or kitchenettes, and all have private balconies. Shopping and restaurants are within walking distance. Picnic area. Some kitchenettes, some microwaves, some refrigerators. Cable TV. Pool. Beach. Laundry facilities. | 2015 S. Atlantic Ave. | 904/255–2446 or 800/456–2446 | fax 904/258–9084 | 41 rooms | $55–$65 | AE, D, DC, MC, V.

Grand Seas Resort. All condos at this lavish, fun beachfront resort have rooms with full kitchens and hot tubs. Kids will enjoy the pool slides and nine-hole miniature golf course. Restaurant, bar. In-room data ports, kitchenettes, microwaves, refrigerators. Cable TV. 3 outdoor pools, 1 indoor pool. 3 outdoor hot tubs. Gym. Beach, water sports. Baby-sitting, playgrounds. Laundry facilities. Business services. | 2424 N. Atlantic Ave. | 904/677–7880 or 800/982–9386 | fax 904/673–1991 | www.grandseas.com | 155 condominiums | $159–$219 | AE, D, DC, MC, V.

Hampton Inn Airport. Located 3 mi west of the beaches, this four-story hotel is surrounded by three landscaped acres across from Volusia Mall. Rooms have a bright tropical decor. Complimentary Continental breakfast. In-room data ports, some refrigerators. Cable TV. Pool. Hot tub. Business services, airport shuttle. | 1715 W. International Speedway Blvd. (Hwy. 92) | 904/257–4030 or 800/426–7866 | fax 904/257–5721 | www.hampton-inn.com | 122 rooms | $94 | AE, D, DC, MC, V.

Daytona Beach Hilton. This 11-story, beachfront hotel is popular with families. The pastel rooms are rather large and most have balconies; some have a kitchenette, patio, or terrace. Convenient touches include a hair dryer, lighted makeup mirror, and a bar with refrigerator. Restaurant, bar (with entertainment), room service. Microwaves, refrigerators. Cable TV. Pool, wading pool. Hot tub. Gym. Beach. Video games. Laundry facilities. Business services. | 2637 S. Atlantic Ave. | 904/767–7350 or 800/328–0122 | fax 904/760–3651 | www.hilton.com | 212 rooms | $80–$175 | AE, D, DC, MC, V.

Howard Johnson Oceanfront Resort Hotel. Rooms at this oceanfront retreat are tropically decorated with bright colors; they all have private balconies. Restaurants within walking distance. In-room data ports, some kitchenettes, some microwaves, refrigerators. Cable TV. Outdoor pool. Outdoor hot tub. Beach. Laundry services. | 2560 N. Atlantic Ave. | 904/672–1440 or 800/406–1411 | fax 904/677–8811 | www.hojo.com | 143 rooms | $99–$109 | AE, D, DC, MC, V.

Holiday Inn at Indigo Lakes. This two-story motel is 2 mi east of the Daytona International Speedway, 1 mi from Indigo Lakes Golf Course, and 6 mi from the beaches. Restaurant, room service. In-room data ports, refrigerators. Cable TV. Pool, wading pool. Tennis court. Gym. Laundry facilities. Business services, airport shuttle. | 2620 W. International Speedway Blvd. (Hwy. 92) | 904/258–6333 or 800/465–4329 | fax 904/254–3698 | www.holiday-inn.com | 151 rooms | $65–$85 | AE, D, DC, MC, V.

Howard Johnson's Oceanfront. All rooms in this eight-story structure contain kitchenettes and balconies; many have views of the ocean. In-room data ports, kitchenettes, microwaves, refrigerators. Cable TV. Pool, wading pool. Hot tub. Beach. Children's programs (ages 3–12). Laundry facilities. | 2560 N. Atlantic Ave. | 904/672–1440 or 800/446–4656 | fax 904/677–8811 | www.hojo.com | 143 rooms | $192–$210 | AE, D, DC, MC, V.

Holiday Inn Plaza Resort and Spa. All guest rooms have a balcony at this huge, 14-story beachfront hotel that was undergoing a $15 million renovation in 2000. The spacious sundeck has an Olympic-size pool, kiddie pool, and whirlpool looking out toward the Atlantic. Restaurant, bar, room service. In-room data ports, some kitchenettes, microwaves, refrigerators. Cable TV. Pool. Hot tub, massage, spa, beauty salon, sauna. Gym, beach, water sports. Video games. Children's programs (ages 4–12). Laundry facilities. Business services, parking ($7). | 600 N. Atlantic Ave. | 904/255–4471 or 800/767–4471 | fax 904/253–7543 | www.plazaresortandspa.com | 373 rooms | $149–$325 | AE, D, DC, MC, V.

Inn on the Beach. Most rooms at this beachside seven-story hotel face the ocean. The oceanside deck has a lounge next to the Olympic-size heated pool. Spacious oceanfront rooms, efficiencies, suites, and spa suites all have private balconies. Bar, complimentary Continental breakfast. Some kitchenettes, some microwaves, some refrigerators. Cable TV, in-room VCRs (and movies). Pool, wading pool. Sauna. Putting green. Gym. Beach. Video games. Laundry facilities. Business services. | 1615 S. Atlantic Ave. | 904/255–0921 | fax 904/255–3849 | www.innonthebeach.com | 195 rooms | $79–$150 | AE, D, DC, MC, V.

Live Oak Inn. This lovely bed and breakfast is in two restored homes next door to each other—Daytona's oldest buildings—both listed on the National Register of Historic Places. Some of the individually decorated guest rooms look from long porches out over the marina or onto gardens. In the first floor of one house is a fine restaurant, Rosario's (*above*), and a small lounge and reception area. Restaurant, complimentary Continental breakfast. Some in-room hot tubs. Cable TV, in-room VCRs. No smoking. | 488 S. Beach St. | 904/252–4667 | 10 rooms | $80–$90 | AE, MC, V.

Ocean Villa Motel. This contemporary two-story motel sits directly on the beach. Rooms come in all sizes, many with balconies and unrestricted ocean views. Some microwaves, refrigerators. Cable TV. Pool, wading pool. Beach. Video games. Laundry facilities. | 828 N. Atlantic Ave. | 904/252–4644 or 800/225–3691 | fax 904/255–7378 | 38 rooms | $89–$115 | AE, D, DC, MC, V.

Palm Plaza Oceanfront Resort. All rooms of this 11-story beachfront hotel have ocean views, full kitchens, and private balconies. Rooms are either efficiencies or one-bedroom suites. There are children's programs in the summer. Restaurant, complimentary Continental breakfast. In-room safes, kitchenettes, microwaves, refrigerators. Cable TV. Pool, wading pool. Hot tub. Beach. Video games. Laundry facilities. Business services. | 3301 S. Atlantic Ave. | 904/767–1711 or 800/329–8662 | fax 904/756–8394 | www.palmplaza.com | 98 rooms | $134–$229 | AE, D, DC, MC, V.

Perry's Ocean-Edge Resort. Perry's has several pools, 700 ft of beachfront, landscaped lawns and a real family atmosphere. Famous are the free homemade doughnuts and coffee served up each morning. The many children's activities include arts and crafts workshops, ice cream socials, and movies. Most rooms have kitchens and great ocean views. Restaurant, bar, picnic area, complimentary Continental breakfast. Some kitchenettes, some microwaves, some refrigerators. Cable TV. 2 outdoor pools, indoor pool, wading pool. Hot tub. Putting green. Volleyball. Beach. Video games. Children's programs (ages 5–12), playground. Laundry facilities. Business services. | 2209 S. Atlantic Ave. | 904/255–0581 or 800/447–0002 | fax 904/258–7315 | www.perrysoceanedge.com | 205 rooms | $94–$140 | AE, D, DC, MC, V.

Ramada Inn Speedway. The two-story motel is across the street from the Daytona International Speedway, next to the Volusia Mall, and less than a mile from the airport. There is a Pizzeria Uno restaurant inside the hotel. Rooms come with king-size or two double beds. Restaurant, bar. In-room data ports. Cable TV. Pool. Business services, airport shuttle. | 1798 W. International Speedway Blvd. | 904/255–2422 or 800/352–2722 | fax 904/253–1749 | www.ramadaspeedway.com | 128 rooms | $79–$249 | AE, D, DC, MC, V.

Royal Beach Motel. This two-story oceanfront motel has an Olympic-size swimming pool with a tiki bar. Most guest rooms have views of the ocean. Bar. Some kitchenettes, microwaves, refrigerators. Cable TV. Pool. Shops, video games. | 1601 S. Atlantic Ave. | 904/255–8341 | fax 904/258–0135 | 49 rooms | $46–$219 | AE, D, MC, V.

Seagarden Inn. All rooms at this friendly 10-story whitewashed hotel have private balconies with beach and ocean views. Some rooms have full kitchens. The large beachfront pool area has a good number of tables and chaises. Picnic area. In-room safes, some kitchenettes, some microwaves, some refrigerators. Cable TV. 2 pools, wading pool. Hot tub. Beach. Children's programs (ages 3–16), laundry facilities. Business services. | 3161 S. Atlantic Ave. | 904/761–2335 or 800/245–0575 | fax 904/756–6676 | www.daytonachamber.com/seagardn.htm | 144 rooms | $40–$140 | AE, D, DC, MC, V.

Sun Viking Lodge. This fun, family-friendly oceanfront motel has a 60-ft water slide in its heated outdoor pool. There is also an attractive indoor pool area, surrounded by trees. Restaurant, picnic area. Refrigerators. Cable TV, in-room VCRs (and movies) available. Indoor pool, outdoor pool, wading pool. Hot tub. Basketball, gym. Beach, water sports. Video games. Children's programs (3-16), playground. Laundry facilities. Business services. | 2411 S. Atlantic Ave. | 904/252–6252 or 800/874–4469 | fax 904/252–5463 | www.sunviking.com | 161 rooms | $97–$105 | AE, D, DC, MC, V.

Super 8 Speedway. Sitting just west of I–95, off exit 87, this two-story motel is 1½ mi west of the speedway and the airport, and 6 mi from the beach. Bar, complimentary Continental breakfast. Cable TV. Pool. Laundry facilities. Pets allowed. | 2992 W. International Speedway Blvd. (Hwy. 92) | 904/253–0643 or 800/800–8000 | fax 904/238–7764 | www.super8.com | 112 rooms | $45–$155 | AE, D, DC, MC, V.

Travelers Inn. Each room of this inexpensive motel is given its own personality through air-brushed murals and memorabilia. The King Room, for example, is dedicated to Elvis Presley, and another, to NASCAR racing. Some rooms have full kitchens. On Saturday evening the inn hosts a complimentary hotdog roast. Picnic area. Some kitchenettes, some microwaves, refrigerators. Cable TV. Pool. Laundry facilities. | 735 N. Atlantic Ave. | 904/253–3501 or 800/417–6466 | fax 904/441–5977 | www.visitdaytona.com/travelersinn | 21 rooms | $49–$59 | AE, D, MC, V.

Treasure Island Inn. Numerous plants give this beachfront family-friendly hotel a tropical feel. Most guest rooms have private balconies overlooking the Atlantic. The hotel

PACKING IDEAS FOR HOT WEATHER

- ❏ Antifungal foot powder
- ❏ Bandanna
- ❏ Cooler
- ❏ Cotton clothing
- ❏ Day pack
- ❏ Film
- ❏ Hiking boots
- ❏ Insect repellent
- ❏ Rain jacket
- ❏ Sport sandals
- ❏ Sun hat
- ❏ Sunblock
- ❏ Synthetic ice
- ❏ Umbrella
- ❏ Water bottle

© Corbis

*Excerpted from *Fodor's: How to Pack: Experts Share Their Secrets*
© 1997, by Fodor's Travel Publications

boasts the largest pool and deck in Daytona Beach, in addition to a pool-side restaurant and multi-tiered sun deck. 2 restaurants, bar, room service. In-room data ports, some kitchenettes, some microwaves, refrigerators. Cable TV. 2 pools, wading pool. 2 hot tubs. Beach. Shops, video games. Laundry facilities. Business services. | 2025 S. Atlantic Ave. | 904/255–8371 or 800/543–5070 | fax 904/255–4984 | www.treasureislandinn.com | 385 rooms | $120–$130 | AE, D, DC, MC, V.

Tropical Winds Oceanfront Resort. On the northern end of Daytona Beach, just south of Ormond Beach, this eight-story hotel has rooms with views of either the ocean or the city; all have balconies. Restaurant. Some kitchenettes, some microwaves, refrigerators. Cable TV. 2 pools. Beach. Video games. Laundry facilities. | 1398 N. Atlantic Ave. | 904/258–1016 | fax 904/255–6462 | 94 rooms | $67–$97 | AE, D, DC, MC, V.

DEERFIELD BEACH

MAP 3, L9

(Nearby towns also listed: Boca Raton, Dania Beach, Davie, Delray Beach, Fort Lauderdale, Pompano Beach)

Boca Raton's neighbor to the south has nice Atlantic beaches, pier fishing, and plenty of boating excursions to the area's reefs and shipwrecks. Deerfield Island Park, an 8½-acre island accessible by boat shuttle, contains a mangrove swamp that's a critical habitat for tortoises, foxes, raccoons, and armadillos. To the south of Deerfield Beach (pop. 47,000), Highway A1A traverses the so-called Hillsboro Mile (actually more than 2 mi), a millionaire's row of some of the most beautiful and expensive homes in Broward County. The road runs along a narrow strip of land between the Intracoastal Waterway and the ocean.

Information: **Greater Deerfield Beach Chamber of Commerce** | 1601 E. Hillsboro Blvd., Deerfield Beach, 33441 | 954/427–1050 | www.deerfieldchamber.com.

Attractions
Deerfield Island Park. This 56-acre island of urban wilderness along the Intracoastal Waterway contains an 8½-acre mangrove forest. There are two nature trails at the park: a ¾-mi trail leads through the mangrove swamp lands, the other half-mile trail goes through the upland habitat of gopher tortoises, raccoons, and armadillos. The island can only be reached by boat. Free ferries to the Island depart from Sullivan Park, at the end of Riverview Rd.; reservations are required. | 1720 Deerfield Island Park | 954/360–1320 | fax 954/360–1333 | Free | Park Wed.–Sun. 9–5; call for ferry times.

Quiet Waters Park. This 430-acre recreational park is especially suited for kids. Splash Adventure is a high-tech water-play system with swings, slides, and tunnels. The park also offers canoeing, paddleboating, swimming, windsurfing, camping, picnicking, and bicycling. | 401 S. Powerline Rd. | 954/360–1315 | Park $1 weekends and holidays, free weekdays; Splash Adventure $3 | Daily 8–7.

ON THE CALENDAR
OCT.: *Annual Golf Classic.* Fifty percent of the proceeds from this annual golf tournament at the Deer Creek Country Club benefit the Boys and Girls Club. | 2801 Country Club Blvd. | 954/427–1050.

Dining
Brooks. Continental. This popular, well-established restaurant serves such tastefully prepared entrées as red snapper in papillote, broiled pompano with seasoned root vegetables, and rack of lamb in its four large, often crowded, dining rooms decorated with antiques, Old Master reproductions, and floral wallpaper. For dessert, don't miss the souf-

flé. | 500 S. Federal Hwy. | 954/427–9302 | Closed Mon.–Tues. and early May–Oct. No lunch | $20–$36 | AE, D, MC, V.

Pal Charley's Crab. Seafood. Sitting directly on the Intracoastal Waterway, with views of the passing boats, this restaurant is popular not only for its crab specialties but also for its lobster and steak entrées. The melon-colored tables add a bright touch to the dining room. Don't miss Sunday brunch, served only in the winter high season. | 1755 S.E. Third Ct | 954/427–4000 | $12–$25 | AE, D, DC, MC, V.

Whale's Rib. Seafood. All types of memorabilia, from hats and license plates to stuffed fish, give this eatery its funky appeal. Since the early 1980s, the Williams family has been serving fresh fish specials, salads, fish sandwiches, and "Whale fries"—thinly sliced potatoes that look like potato chips. Selections from the raw bar and a fish dip are also popular. | 2031 N.E. 2nd St. | 954/421–8880 | Reservations not accepted | $12–$16 | AE, MC, V.

Lodging

Carriage House Resort Motel. Run by a French-German couple, this motel has two white, Colonial-style buildings with black shutters connected by a second-story sundeck. It is one block from the beach and is also close to restaurants and shops. Weekly rates are available. Some kitchenettes, some microwaves, refrigerators, cable TV. Pool. Laundry facilities. | 250 S. Ocean Blvd. | 954/427–7670 | fax 954/428–4790 | www.bocaraton.com/carriagehouse | 6 rooms, 14 efficiencies, 10 apartments | $105 rooms, $117 efficiency, $140–$195 apartment | AE, MC, V.

Comfort Suites Deerfield Beach. This hotel, located next to the Quality Suites in the Newport Center Corporate Park (just west of I–95 at exit 36C), is just 4 miles west of the beaches and 15 mi north of Fort Lauderdale Airport. Flower beds and well-maintained lawns add a colorful touch to this chain, which offers spacious rooms with separate sitting areas. Complimentary cocktails are offered in the evenings. Restaurant, bar, complimentary Continental breakfast. In-room data ports, refrigerators. Cable TV. Pool. Hot tub. Laundry facilities. Business services, free parking. Pets allowed. | 1040 E. Newport Center Dr. | 954/570–8887 or 800/538–2777 | fax 954/570–5346 | www.sunbursthospitality.com | 101 suites | $109–$179 suites | AE, D, DC, MC, V.

Hilton Deerfield Beach/Boca Raton. Just east of I–95 at exit 37 (37A if you are coming from the south), this hotel is 2½ mi west of the beaches, between the Fort Lauderdale and Palm Beach airports. Marble floors and a stone fountain give the lobby an air of luxury. A free shuttle service is provided for the beaches and attractions within a 5-mi radius of the hotel. Restaurant, bar. In-room data ports, in-room safes, some minibars, some microwaves. Cable TV. Pool. Hot tub. Gym. Laundry service. Business services, free parking. | 100 Fairway Dr. | 954/427–7700 or 800/624–3606 | fax 954/427–2308 | www.hilton.com | 221 rooms | $119–$189 | AE, D, DC, MC, V.

Quality Suites Deerfield Beach. Next to the Comfort Suites at the Newport Center Corporate Park, this hotel sits just west of I–95 at exit 36C, 15 mi north of the Fort Lauderdale Airport and 4 mi west of the beaches. Rooms are slightly larger than those of its next-door neighbor, and this hotel offers a few more amenities. Restaurant, bar, complimentary Continental breakfast. In-room data ports, microwaves, refrigerators. Cable TV, in-room VCRs (and movies). Pool. Hot tub. Laundry facilities. Business services, free parking. | 1050 E. Newport Center Dr. | 954/570–8888 or 800/538–2777 | fax 954/570–5346 | www.sunbursthospitality.com | 107 suites | $119–$189 suite | AE, D, DC, MC, V.

Ramada Inn Resort. Guests at this resort can relax in brightly colored rooms, a tropical garden courtyard, or the poolside lounge. The hotel is on the border of Deerfield Beach and Boca Raton and is midway between Fort Lauderdale and Palm Beach International Airports. It is also close to major highways and 1 mi from the beach. Bar. Complimentary Continental breakfast. Cable TV. Pool. Gym. | 1250 W. Hillsboro Blvd. | 954/427–2200 or 800/909–3297 | fax 954/421–1619 | www.ramadaboca.com | 151 rooms, 6 suites | $109 room, $169 suite | AE, D, DC, MC, V.

Seabonay Beach Resort. Directly on its own private beach, this six-story hotel has many units with full kitchens, some with balconies overlooking the ocean. The pool is only steps away from the beach. Picnic area. In-room data ports, some kitchenettes, some microwaves, some refrigerators. Cable TV. Pool. Beach. Children's programs (ages 2–12). Laundry facilities. Business services. | 1159 Hillsboro Mile, Hillsboro Beach | 954/427–2525 or 800/777–1961 | fax 954/427–3228 | www.seabonay.com | 80 units | $119 room, $159 studio, $179–$279 1–bedroom apt., $319–$349 2–bedroom apt | AE, D, MC, V.

Wellesley Inn Deerfield Beach. This four-story hotel with spacious rooms is 3 mi from the beach, among several office parks. Manicured lawns and many oak and palm trees help to add color to the corporate landscape. The hotel is just west of I–95, off exit 37. Complimentary Continental breakfast. In-room data ports, some microwaves, some refrigerators. Cable TV. Pool. Laundry facilities. Pets allowed. | 100 S.W. 12th Ave. | 954/428–0661 | fax 954/427–6701 | 79 rooms | $120–$145 | AE, D, DC, MC, V.

DE FUNIAK SPRINGS

MAP 3, C1

(Nearby towns also listed: Chipley, Crestview, Niceville)

Named for a prominent official of the Louisville and Nashville Railroad in the late 1800s, this Old Florida town of about 7,000 is midway between Alabama and the Gulf of Mexico in the panhandle. Walton County's seat is known for rich farmland and access to the white-sand beaches on the Gulf of Mexico, which are about 25 mi to the south. Thirty-five miles east of town, near Chipley, is Falling Waters State Recreation Area. The region's economy depends primarily on agriculture, but poultry and cattle are also raised and processed in the county.

Information: Walton County Chamber of Commerce | Chautauqua Bldg., Circle Dr., Box 29, De Funiak Springs, 32435 | 850/892–3191 | www.waltoncountychamber.com.

Attractions

Chautauqua Winery. Opened in 1990, Chautauqua gives free tours of its facilities, where you can learn about the wine-making process and the sample the vintages in the tasting room. The winery is off U.S. 331. | 364 Hugh Adams Rd. | 850/892–5887 | Free | Mon.–Sat. 9–5, Sun. 12–5.

Ponce de León Springs State Recreation Area. Some believe that Ponce de León Springs is the Spanish explorer's "fountain of youth." True or not, the sparkling 68°F water, which flows from a limestone cavity at the rate of 14 million gallons a day, is certainly refreshing. The spring flows into Sandy Creek and from there into the Choctawhatchee River, less than a mile to the south. A half-mile trail follows Sandy Creek, where you can picnic or fish. | 2860 Ponce de León Springs Rd., Ponce de León | 850/836–4281 or 850/638–6130 | $2 per vehicle | Daily.

Walton-De Funiak Public Library. One of Florida's oldest libraries, this wood-frame building opened its doors in 1887. Today it contains nearly 30,000 volumes and a collection of antique weapons. | 3 Circle Dr. | 850/892–3624 | Free | Mon.–Fri. 9–5, Sat. 9–3.

ON THE CALENDAR

FEB.: *Chautauqua Assembly.* Held on the last weekend in February, this festival offers musical and theatrical performances, arts and crafts classes, story-telling, heritage arts demonstrations, architectural walking tours, and a Victorian tea. | 850/892–0624.

Lodging

Best Western Crossroads Inn. Surrounded by eight acres of pecan groves, this motel sits halfway between Tallahassee and Pensacola at the junction of I–10 and Highway 331.

Restaurant, bar, complimentary breakfast, room service. Cable TV. Pool. Pets allowed. | 2343 Freeport Rd. | 850/892–5111 | fax 850/892–2439 | www.bestwestern.com | 100 rooms | $59–$79 | AE, D, DC, MC, V.

Hotel De Funiak. This tidy, old-fashioned hotel was built in 1920 and is now a B&B offering rooms furnished with period antiques, some the original furnishings. It's one of the nicer places to stay in this part of panhandle. Restaurant, complimentary Continental breakfast. Cable TV. Library. No smoking. | 400 E. Nelson Ave. | 850/892–4383 or 877/333–8642 | fax 850/892–5346 | www.hoteldefuniak.com | 8 rooms, 4 suites | $70 room, $120 suite | AE, D, MC, V.

DELAND

MAP 3, J4

(Nearby towns also listed: Daytona Beach, Leesburg, New Smyrna Beach, Sanford, Tavares)

This spacious, oak-filled town of 17,000, 21 mi southwest of Daytona Beach, was named by Henry DeLand, who sought to build an "Athens of the South." The main drag in town, Woodland Boulevard, is filled with a remarkable number of antiques and thrift stores, and charming cafés. The Volusia County seat is home to Stetson University, which is the oldest private university in the United States and a respected law program. DeLand established the school in 1886 together with hat magnate John Stetson—the school's nickname is the Stetson Hatters. The town hosts numerous festivals, and you can often catch sight of manatees in winter off the boardwalk at nearby Blue Springs State Park.

Information: **DeLand Area Chamber of Commerce** | 336 N. Woodland Blvd., DeLand, 32720 | 904/734–4331 | www.delandchamber.org.

Attractions

African American Arts Museum. This small museum is devoted to African-American and Caribbean-American culture and arts. It hosts six special exhibitions annually and has a collection of 150 art works in the permanent collection. | 325 S. Clara Ave. | 904/736–4004 | fax 904/736–4088 | Free | Wed.–Sat. 10–4.

Blue Spring State Park. This 3,000-acre park, 5 mi south of DeLand, plays a vital role in the survival of Florida's endangered manatee. You can learn more about these placid creatures at ranger programs held from November through March. There's also fishing, canoeing, and swimming in the Spring Run Creek, which feeds into the St. Johns River. Parking can be extremely tight on the weekends and during manatee season (November–March), often causing delays in entering the park. | 2100 W. French Ave., Orange City | 904/775–3663 | $4 per vehicle | Daily, 8–sunset.

DeLand Memorial Hospital Museum. Built in 1921, this former hospital at Bill Dreggers Park houses electrical and ice exhibits, an apothecary exhibit, a veterans museum, a restored 1920s operating room, and a display of model airplanes. In a second building, which was, as a result of segregation, originally the black hospital, there are collections of elephants and toys. | 230 N. Stone St. | 904/740–6813 | Free (donations encouraged) | Wed.–Sat. 10–3.

DeLand Museum of Art. The museum collects, exhibits, and preserves works of contemporary and traditional arts and crafts, and offers arts classes to the public as well. | 600 N. Woodland Blvd. | 904/734–4371 | Free | Tues.–Sat. 10–4, Sun. 1–4.

De León Springs State Recreation Area. Water is 72°F year-round. Swimming is not allowed during the spring run, but anglers will find bass and bream in abundance. De León Springs provides access to Lake Woodruff National Wildlife Refuge, where you can explore 21,500 acres of lakes, creeks, and marshes by canoe. A ½-mi nature trail showcases a floodplain forest and its varied plant and animal life. Boat tours are offered twice daily for an extra fee of $14. | Ponce de León Blvd. | 904/985–4212 | www.dep.state.fl.us/parks | $4 per vehicle | Daily.

Henry A. DeLand House. The West Volusia Historical Society gives tours of its headquarters, an 1886 Victorian complete with period furnishings, which was named for the founder of the city. DeLand owned the property that the house was built on, but never lived in it. The title of resident goes to George Hamlin who was the first attorney in DeLand, and was the propagator of Hamlin Oranges, which remain some of the most widely produced oranges to this day. | 137 West Michigan Ave. | 904/740–6813 | www.vis-arts.com/deland-house | Free (donations encouraged) | Tues.–Sat. 12–4.

Holly Bluff Marina. This marina, 10 mi west of DeLand, rents houseboats by the week or weekend for cruises on 90 mi of the St. Johns River from Palatka on the north to Lake Monroe at the south. | 2280 Hontoon Rd. | 800/237–5105 | www.hollybluff.com | $750–$1,500 per weekend, $1,250–$2,500 per week | Daily 8:30–5.

Hontoon Island State Park. First inhabited by the Timucuan Indians, the 1,650-acre island— still accessible only by boat—was a pioneer homestead, a boat yard, a commercial fishing center, and a cattle ranch before the state purchased it in 1967 and turned it into a state park. There are fishing, camping, hiking, boating, canoeing, and picnicking. The park runs a complimentary ferry between the parking lot and the island. | 2309 River Ridge Rd. | 904/736–5309 | $1 per person; $2 per group (up to 8 people) | Daily 8–sundown (ferry stops one hour before sundown).

Spring Garden Ranch. This standard-bred horse training center, 6 miles north of DeLand, welcomes visitors. Between October and May over 600 horses are trained at the ranch. From the restaurant, serving breakfast and lunch, you can watch the horses galloping around the two tracks below. | 900 Spring Garden Ranch Rd., De León Springs | 904/985–5654 | Free | Daily, 7 AM–2 PM.

Stetson University. Founded in 1883 by Henry DeLand (and named after the hat magnate John Stetson), this small liberal arts college, with about 2,300 students on its DeLand campus, is the cultural heart of the city. It was Florida's first private university. | Amelia and Michigan Aves. | 800/688–0101 | www.stetson.edu | Daily.

Duncan Gallery of Art. This gallery on the Stetson University campus hosts student and other art shows. | Sampson Hall, Michigan and Amelia Aves. | 904/734–4371 | www.stetson.edu | Free | Weekdays 10–4, weekends 1–4.

Gillespie Museum of Minerals. On the campus of Stetson University, the Gillespie Museum contains one of the largest private collections of gems and minerals in the world. Stetson's DeLand campus serves about 2,000 students in the College of Arts and Sciences, School of Music, and School of Business Administration. | Michigan and Amelia Aves. | 904/822–7330 | www.stetson.edu | Free | Weekdays 9–12 and 1–4 during the school year; weekdays 10–3 in summer.

Valentine Park. Five miles south of DeLand, this park has baseball diamonds and picnic areas. It is the site of the Blue Spring Manatee Festival. | 1511 W French Ave., Orange City | 904/775–2793 | Free | Daily.

ON THE CALENDAR

JAN.: *Blue Spring Manatee Festival.* For this event, held on the fourth weekend in January, there are arts and crafts and entertainment in Valentine Park as well as special buses that run the 1 mile to Blue Spring State Park, where you can watch the mammals and their offspring in the clear 72°F waters. | 904/775–2793.

DEC.: *St. Johns Boat Parade.* More than 25 boats are lighted and decorated in various themes for the waterborne parade down the St. Johns River. Music and costume dress complement the decorated craft and contribute to the outlandish festivities. | 904/734–4331.

NOV.: *Volusia County Fair and Youth Show.* This annual event, held at the Volusia County Fairgrounds, includes arts and crafts exhibitions, livestock competitions, live entertainment, food vendors, and carnival rides. | 904/734–9514.

Dining

Christo's and Eleni's. Italian. Ivy and prints grace the walls of this quaint eatery where the pastas, sauces, and desserts are all homemade. Try the chicken *Assiago* (a breast of chicken cooked with the sharp Italian cheese with sundried tomatoes and garlic) or the eggplant *à la Christo* (eggplant layered with ricotta cheese baked in a red and white sauce). Ambient music is performed on Monday nights. | 803 W. New York Ave. | 904/734–5705 | No lunch Sat. Closed Sun. | $6–$10 | D, MC, V.

Dublin Station. American. This large, dimly lit Irish pub has dark wood walls and wooden floors. With 24 beers on tap, they are known for lagers and ales. They are also known for meat pies, and fish and chips, but you'll still eat well if you pick the chops, steaks, burgers, or salads. Open-air dining on the sidewalk. Kids eat free Mon. and Thurs. nights with any entrée purchase. | 105 West Indiana Ave. | 904/740–7720 | $6–$13 | AE, MC, V.

Karlings Inn. American. Possibly the only Swiss chalet setting in Florida, this family-owned restaurant serves up a half roasted duck with bing cherry sauce or fried Bahamian lobster tails with a spicy honey-mustard sauce. The menu includes everything from steaks, seafood, and soups to a signature dessert, Key lime baked Alaska. | 4640 N. U.S. 17, De León Springs | 904/985–5535 | fax 904/740–9991 | Closed Sun.–Mon. No lunch | $14–$27 | MC, V.

Mom and Dad's Italian Restaurant. Italian. Italian restaurant from the old school, with lace curtains, red tablecloths, candles on the tables, and a few antiques. Some of the best things you can order are the spaghetti alla Bruzzi, or any of the pizzas with cheddar cheese. | 2184 U.S. 90 W | 850/892–5812 | No lunch Sun.–Mon. | $7–$13 | AE, D, MC, V.

Original Holiday House. American. Stained-glass windows from the original 1959 tea room complement the memorabilia that hang from the walls. The menu includes a limited array of steaks, seafood, and sandwiches, but the restaurant is best known for its buffets. It is so popular, in fact, that it inspired a small chain of Florida restaurants. | 704 N. Woodland Blvd. | 904/734–6319 | Reservations not accepted | $9–$11 | D, MC, V.

Pondo's. American. Built in 1921 as a lodging for rail travelers, this restaurant is a local landmark. The eatery's repertoire includes such dishes as rack of lamb, grilled salmon, and filet mignon. Both the lobster tail and duck are popular. There are also numerous homemade pastas. | 1915 Old New York Ave. | 904/734–1995 | No lunch. Closed Mon. | $11–$18 | AE, MC, V.

Lodging

Blue Spring State Park Cabins The cabins of the Blue Spring State Park sit approximately a half-mile from the St. Johns River. All cabins have full kitchens and full access to all the park's activities. Reservations are necessary. Picnic area. Kitchenettes, microwaves, refrigerators. No room phones, no TV. Hiking, water sports, fishing. | 2100 W. French Ave. | 904/775–3663 | 6 cabins | $55 per cabin per night (2–night minimum stay) | AE, D, MC, V.

Holiday Inn. This six-story hotel sits 2 mi north of downtown and Stetson University. Blue Spring State Park is 5 mi south. Restaurant, bar. In-room data ports, some microwaves, some refrigerators. Cable TV. Pool. Hot tub. Business services. Pets allowed (fee). | 350 E. International Speedway Blvd. | 904/738–5200 | fax 904/734–7552 | www.holiday-inn.com | 149 rooms | $80–$180 | AE, D, DC, MC, V.

Hontoon Landing Resort and Marina. The landscaped grounds with picnic tables, grills, and pool overlook the St. Johns River, as do most of the rooms, which are all bright and airy, with a tropical, Florida look. The resort is close to restaurants, shops, museums and Stetson University. Picnic area. Cable TV. Pool. | 2317 River Ridge Rd. | 904/734–2474 or 800/248–2474 | fax 904/738–9743 | www.hontoon.com | 14 rooms, 4 suites | $70–$100 rooms, $105–$195 suites | D, MC, V.

Quality Inn. Just off I–4 at exit 56 (on Highway 44), this two-story motel sits 4 mi east of DeLand and 1 mi west of the Volusia County Fairgrounds. The Daytona Speedway is 15 mi to the east. Restaurant, bar (with entertainment), complimentary Continental breakfast, room service. In-room data ports, some microwaves, some refrigerators. Cable TV. Pool, wading pool. Gym. Laundry facilities. Business services. Pets allowed (fee). | 2801 E. New York Ave. | 904/736–3440 | fax 904/736–7484 | www.qualityinn.com | 113 rooms | $50–$95 | AE, D, DC, MC, V.

University Inn. Across the street from Stetson University and about a mile away from downtown DeLand, the University Inn provides quality service and a few surprises in its traditional 2-story building, including eco-conscious rooms (with air and water filters) called Evergreen Rooms, and a nicely landscaped courtyard. Breakfast is served in the lobby. You can get your hair or nails done at the full-service salon. Complimentary Continental breakfast. Some microwaves, some refrigerators. Cable TV. Gym. Pool. Pets allowed (fee). | 644 N. Woodland Blvd. | 904/734–5711 or 800/345–8991 | fax 904/734–5716 | 60 rooms | $50–$60 | AE, D, DC, MC, V.

DELRAY BEACH

MAP 3, L8

(Nearby towns also listed: Boca Raton, Boynton Beach, Deerfield Beach, Lake Worth, Lantana, Pompano Beach)

Delray Beach (pop. 50,000) has learned much from the sophistication of its Atlantic neighbor 6 mi to the south, Boca Raton. Downtown's Atlantic Avenue runs east–west to Highway A1A at the beach, with a mile-long stretch of galleries, stores, and restaurants along brick sidewalks lined with palm trees. Another great pedestrian way begins across Northeast 8th Street, along the broad swimming beach off Atlantic Avenue, and reflects well on the town's historic preservation movement. The Morikami Museum and Japanese Gardens is a monument to the Japanese farmers who founded the town in 1905 as a farming community. A draw for divers is the offshore wreck of the S.S. *Inchulva,* which sank during a hurricane in 1903 and is now a state historical site.

Information: **Greater Delray Beach Chamber of Commerce** | 64A S.E. 5th Ave., Delray Beach, 33483 | 561/278–0424 | www.delraybeach.com.

Attractions

Cason Cottage. This restored house, now a museum, reflects how people in the Delray area lived between 1915 and 1935. It's furnished with period antiques, including a pipe organ donated by a descendant of one of the original Delray Beach settlers. Due to on-going restoration projects, the house is viewable by appointment only, but the gracious tour guide is happy to throw in the nearby Cornell Archives Room and a restored railway station to give you a complete look at the local history. | 5 N.E. 1st St. | 561/243–0223 | www.delraybeach-historicalsociety.org | Free | By appointment only.

★ **Morikami Museum and Japanese Gardens.** This well-loved local landmark is one of the only museums in the United States to focus exclusively on the culture of Japan; its collection includes painting, sculpture, pottery, and armor from the 19th and 20th centuries. There is also a Florida bonsai collection. Surrounding the museum are Japanese gardens, each one representative of a different period in Japanese gardening. Outside the gardens, you can hike a 1-mi nature trail that meanders through the property's many pine trees; several picnic pavilions dot the trail. | 4000 Morikami Park Rd. | 561/495–0233 | www.morikami.org | Park free; museum $4.25 | Grounds daily; museum Tues.–Sun. 10–5.

Old School Square Cultural Arts Center. Among the several historical structures of this center, the Cornell Museum of Art and History exhibits fine art by both international and local artists. It occupies a restored school building built in 1913; the Crest Theater, which hosts numerous performances at the center throughout the year, was built in 1926. | 51 N. Swinton Ave. | 561/243–7922 | Free | Tues.–Sat. 11–4; Oct.–Apr. also Sun. 1–4.

ON THE CALENDAR

FEB.: *Hatsume Fair*. Held on the last full weekend of February, the Morikami Museum's largest festival celebrates the coming of spring (*hatsume* means "first bud of the year"). Entertainment includes taiko drums and other cultural performances, martial arts demonstrations, children's activities, artisan booths, and crafts demonstrations. | 4000 Morikami Park Rd. | 561/495–0233.

APR.: *Delray Affair*. Since its modest beginnings in 1962, this three-day event has grown to become one of the region's largest festivals. More than a quarter-million people come to Swinton Avenue in downtown Delray Beach to enjoy works by more than 600 artists and craftspeople, rides and games, and music and dance on multiple stages. | 561/278–0424.

AUG.: *Bon Festival*. At this special evening held on the second Saturday of August at the Morikami Museum, floating lanterns and fireworks mark Obon, the Japanese holiday honoring deceased ancestors. You can also browse in stalls selling items from the gift shop, sample Japanese food, and watch Japanese games, folk dances, and taiko drum performances. | 4000 Morikami Park Rd. | 561/495–0233.

NOV.: *Delray Beach Garlic Festival*. This event, on the first weekend in November, features cooking and ice-carving demonstrations and competitions, and a celebrity cooking contest, which pits local newspaper, radio, and TV personalities against each other. | 561/274–4663.

YEAR-ROUND: *Roots Cultural Festival*. This year-round celebration of African-American history and culture in the Pompey Park Recreation Center began as a month-long festival in 1977 and is one of the oldest annual events in Palm Beach County. There are events now every month. | 561/274–0365.

Dining

Antonio's Mama Rosa. Italian. A local favorite, this restaurant has baby blue tablecloths, dark wood paneling, and gold-tinted windows. The menu includes pastas, fish, seafood, and lobster. Especially popular is the osso buco. | 1645 N. Federal Hwy. | 561/276–2569 | Closed Mon. from mid-Apr.–mid-Dec. No lunch | $11–$16 | AE, MC, V.

Blue Anchor. English. If the facade of this pub reminds you of a real English pub, that's because it is, or at least was before it was shipped from London, where it was once part of the Blue Anchor Pub, a bar frequented by such notables as Winston Churchill. The pub fare is decidedly British: steak-and-kidney pie, fish-and-chips, and bangers (sausage) and mash. Juicy burgers and wonderful salads complement these choices. English beers and ales are on tap. | 804 E. Atlantic Ave. | 561/272–7272 | $8–$12 | AE, MC, V.

Boston's on the Beach. Seafood. Across the street from the beach, this eatery has an ultra-casual dining room: The tables are old and made of wood; sports paraphernalia and traffic signs ornament the walls. New England clam chowder and lobster are two of the specialties here; you can also have fresh fish grilled, fried, or prepared in any other way. Live music nightly. | 40 South Ocean Blvd. | 561/278–3364 | Reservations not accepted | Breakfast also available | $12–$19 | AE, MC, V.

Fifth Ave. Grill. Steak. Exposed brick, stained-glass, and numerous brass fixtures give this steakhouse the appearance of an English pub. The menu focuses on its steak options, though other fare such as fish is also available. This is the kind of eatery that everyone loves to love, with its reliable service, professional preparation, and a reassuring menu with lots of freebies on the side. | 821 S. Federal Hwy. | 561/265–0122 | $16–$29 | AE, DC, MC, V.

Peter's Stone Crabs. Seafood. Murals of scuba divers, crabs, and fish ornament the walls of this eatery's large dining room. In season—from October to May—the specialty is

Florida stone crabs, served cold with a mustard sauce. The year-round menu offers a range of seafood, beef, and chicken entrées. | 411 E. Atlantic Ave. | 561/278–0036 | Closed Mon. No lunch | $13–$21 | AE, D, MC, V.

Splendid Blendeds Café. Eclectic. You can dine here on wide-ranging international cuisine either inside, where Haitian art decorates the dining room, or on the inviting patio. The menu includes such unusual dishes as *Pahoa* chicken (a Hawaiian preparation with a jerk marinade and mango preserves). On the slightly more traditional side, the roasted garlic–stuffed filet mignon or duck and wild mushroom quesadillas are good choices. | 432 E. Atlantic Ave. | 561/265–1035 | fax 561/265–1952 | Closed Sun. | $15–$25 | AE, MC, V.

Lodging

Breakers on-the-Ocean. Directly on the beach, the 22 one-bedroom units of this one- and two-story motel all have views of the ocean and full kitchens. Some of the rooms have balconies. Chairs and cabanas are provided on the beach. Complimentary Continental breakfast. Kitchenettes, refrigerators. Cable TV. Pool. Putting green. Beach. Business services. | 1875 S. Ocean Blvd. | 561/278–4501 | fax 561/276–6391 | 22 suites | $205–$235 suites | No credit cards.

Colony Hotel and Cabana Club. Delray's oldest hotel has an elegant, white Andalusian architectural style, with red domes atop twin four-story towers. The 1926 lobby maintains the original wood-burning fireplaces, with white wicker furniture and hardwood floors. The hotel's Cabana Club, 2 mi from the hotel, has 250 ft of private beach with complimentary cabanas and chaises, a heated saltwater swimming pool, and a restaurant. 2 restaurants, 2 bars, complimentary Continental breakfast. In-room data ports. Cable TV. Pool. No smoking. | 525 E. Atlantic Ave. | 561/276–4123 | fax 561/276–0123 | www.thecolonyhotel.com | 80 rooms | $165–$205 | Closed May 2–Oct. 31 | AE, MC, V.

Holiday Inn Highland Beach. One mile south of Delray Beach, rooms at this beach-side, five-story hotel have views of the ocean, the pool, or parking lot. The thatched-roof huts and tiki bar, together with the palm trees that surround the pool, give the property the feel of a tropical oasis. Restaurant, bar (with entertainment), room service. In-room data ports, some refrigerators, some in-room hot tubs. Cable TV. Pool, wading pool. Gym. Beach. Laundry facilities. Business services. | 2809 S. Ocean Blvd., Highland Beach | 561/278–6241 | fax 561/278–6241 | www.holiday-inn.com | 115 rooms | $199–$239 | AE, D, DC, MC, V.

Marriott Delray Beach. Across the street from the beach, the rooms of this five-story hotel have balconies, many with views of the water. The hotel is within easy walking distance of many restaurants and shops. It's the largest hotel in Delray Beach by far. Restaurant, bar, room service. In-room data ports, in-room safes, minibars, some refrigerators. Cable TV. Pool. Gym. Shops. Laundry facilities. Business service. | 10 N. Ocean Blvd. | 561/274–3200 or 800/627–7468 | fax 561/274–3202 | www.marriotthotels.com | 254 rooms | $109–$239 | AE, D, DC, MC, V.

The Parliament Inn. This modern, renovated inn consists of two one-story buildings with a courtyard and pool in the middle. The property has tropical landscaped grounds; young children are not allowed during the high season. Kitchenettes, microwaves, refrigerators. Cable TV. Pool. Laundry facilities. No kids under 12. | 1236 George Bush Blvd. | 561/276–6245 | fax 561/274–3939 | 8 apartments | $85–$180 | No credit cards.

Seagate Hotel and Beach Club. This two-story hotel, boasting 400 ft of private beach, has studios, one-, two-, and three-bedrooms units, all with full kitchens. It's one of the best garden hotels in Palm Beach County. And there's a private beach club for hotel guests. Restaurant, bar, complimentary Continental breakfast. In-room data ports, kitchenettes, microwaves, refrigerators. Cable TV. 2 pools. Beach, water sports. Business services. | 400 S. Ocean Blvd. | 561/276–2421 or 800/233–3581 | fax 561/243–4714 | 70 units | $119–$500 | AE, D, DC, MC, V.

DESTIN

(Nearby towns also listed: Fort Walton Beach, Niceville, Grayton Beach, Seaside)

If Destin's famed beaches (and those of its neighbor to the west, Fort Walton Beach) seem too white to be true, it's because they're actually made of powder-soft quartz, dropped here by glaciers eons ago. The town was named for its founder, Leonard Destin, a Connecticut sea captain who settled here with his family in the 1830s. Destin (pop 8,500) was a sleepy fishing village for 100 years, but when a bridge was built to this barrier island in 1935, amateur anglers soon discovered the fish-filled coves. Another radical transformation took place in the 1970s, when massive development along the coast made Destin and other Panhandle beach towns major tourist destinations and havens for family theme parks. But fishing is still big. In fact, more billfish are hauled in here each year than in all other Gulf fishing ports combined, accounting for the city motto, "World's Luckiest Fishing Village." You'll find a regular roster of fishing tournaments, including October's Destin Fishing Rodeo.

Information: **Destin Chamber of Commerce** | 1021 U.S. 98 E, Destin, 32541 | 850/837–6241 | www.destinchamber.com.

Attractions

Big Kahuna's Lost Paradise. When it gets too chilly for more than 50 water attractions, including crazy water slides to a man-made river built for tubing, the year-round attractions keep families coming. You'll find 54 holes of miniature golf, go-cart tracks, an arcade, and several thrill rides including the Wild Thing, where your seat flips as you go upside down in a Ferris wheel–type ride. You can grab a bite at either of the two eateries in the water park or the Kahuna Café, which has a variety of subs and sandwiches. | 1007 U.S. 98 E | 850/837–4061 | fax 850/837–7343 | www.big-kahuna.com | Grounds free, water park $29.50, miniature golf $6.50, go-carts $5.50 | Mid-Sept.–May, Fri.–Sat. 10–6; June–mid-Sept., daily 10–6. Water park closed mid-Sept.–April.

Eden State Gardens. Eden State Gardens, 16 mi east of Destin, was once home to the headquarters of the Wesley Lumber Company, one of many businesses involved in lumbering along the Gulf Coast between the 1890s and World War I. Today you can tour the Wesley family home and explore the 10½ acres of landscaped grounds, which are perfect for picnics. | 181 Eden Garden Rd., Point Washington | 850/231–4214 | $2 per vehicle, $1.50 for house tour | Grounds open daily; house tours Thurs.–Mon. 9–4.

ON THE CALENDAR

OCT.: *Anuual Destin Fishing Rodeo*. This rodeo has no horses and cowboys, but it is the ultimate fishing tournament for about 35,000 anglers of all kinds. There are daily, weekly, and over-all prizes. | 850/837–6241.

OCT.: *Destin Seafood Festival*. Held in what is described as the "world's luckiest fishing village," the festival is consistently chosen as one of the top ten by the Southeast Tourism Society. Area restaurants offer a sampling of seafood and other dishes. On the picturesque, waterfront setting of Harborwalk you'll find fine art exhibits and live entertainment. | Harborwalk | 850/837–6241.

Dining

AJ's Seafood. Seafood. This fun-filled restaurant offers fantastic steamed or raw oysters as patrons dine to the laid-back tunes of Jimmy Buffett and others. | 116 U.S. 98 E | 850/837–1913 | Reservations not accepted | $13–$21 | AE, DC, MC, V.

Back Porch. Seafood. Sea breezes will brush through your hair at this open wooden dining room overlooking the pristine white sand beaches and emerald green ocean. You can have just about any seafood dish prepared in the manner you desire: grilled, broiled, pan-fried, or steamed. The eatery is also known for its juicy charcoal-grilled hamburgers. | 1740 Old U.S. Hwy. 98E | 850/837–2022 | Reservations not accepted | $12–$20 | AE, D, DC, MC, V.

Elephant Walk. Seafood. At these open-air bungalows you are just off the beach, within easy sight of the Gulf of Mexico. The menu concentrates on seafood but also offers pork, steaks, and duck. Try the baked grouper with crab meat and hollandaise sauce. There is nightly live entertainment. | 9300 U.S. 98W | 850/267–4800 | No lunch Nov.–Feb. | $17–$29 | AE, D, DC, MC, V.

Flamingo Café. Contemporary. You can enjoy a casual evening on the outdoor patio or inside with starched white linens, but both afford you a view overlooking the Destin Harbor. Dishes are deluxe Florida and Caribbean blends, such as the oyster kebobs with button mushrooms and a clover honey–horseradish dipping sauce, or the potato-crusted grouper topped with crab meat. The snapper Napoleon, oven-roasted and wrapped in phyllo, is one of the house specialties, only to be topped by a killer dessert like the "heaven on earth" chocolate wafer and ice cream combo. | 414 U.S. Hwy. 98E | 850/837–0961 | fax 850/837–8890 | No lunch | $18–$26 | AE, D, MC, V.

Harry T's Boat House. Seafood. The dining rooms at this Destin Yacht Club restaurant overlook Destin Bay. The menu is mostly seafood, but there are also chicken and steak options. Try the grilled river grouper topped with crab and shrimp and served with a white wine and butter sauce, sprinkled with almonds. There are music and dancing here most nights. Tuesday is kids' night, when a clown entertains. This lively, fun restaurant was opened to honor the memory of trapeze artist "Flying Harry T." Babe. | 320 U.S. 98E | 850/654–4800 | Reservations not accepted | $11–$19 | AE, MC, V.

The Lighthouse. Seafood. This family restaurant sits beneath a 60-ft mock lighthouse. The menu, of course, includes a wide variety of seafood, including salmon, mussels, and lobster, as well as local favorites such as prime rib. | 878 U.S. 98 | 850/654–2828 | No lunch weekends | $10–$21 | AE, D, DC, MC, V.

Louisiana Lagniappe. Cajun. The floor-to-ceiling windows here provide spectacular views of Destin Harbor at sunset. The steaks, seafood, and lobster dishes are given a spicy Cajun flair, and the grouper Louisiana is a particular favorite: pan-seared grouper topped with sautéed crab meat with a lemon butter sauce. | 775 Gulfshore Dr., Sandpiper Cove | 850/837–0881 | Reservations not accepted | No lunch | $12–$23 | AE, D, DC, MC, V.

Marina Café. Contemporary. Marine tapestries and sea sculptures complement the Destin Harbor views at this restaurant, one of the Emerald Coast's best. Classic creole, Mediterranean, and Pacific Rim fare are given innovative treatment here, in order to render delectables such as the black pepper–crusted yellowfin tuna with braised spinach and spicy soy sauce. Service is impeccable, and the wine list is extensive. | 404 U.S. 98E | 850/837–7960 | Closed Jan. No lunch | $16–$29 | AE, D, DC, MC, V.

McGuire's Irish Pub. Steak. More than 225,000 single dollar bills, mementos from patrons, have been stuck to the bar and ceiling of this restaurant since it opened in 1977. USDA certified prime steaks and fresh seafood are the focus of the menu, though it also includes traditional Irish fare such as Irish lamb stew. Five house-made brews are on tap. The wine list includes over 350 bottles. Entertainment nightly. | 33 U.S. 98E | 850/650–0000 | $12–$21 | AE, D, DC, MC, V.

Porterhouse Grill. American. Locals and tourists alike are charmed by the fresh catch of the day and the unique breaded and fried green beans, a recipe the owner's mother created at this sports bar. Daring guys or sharing couples can attempt to eat the 2-lb porterhouse steak or sing karaoke upstairs in the dinner theater area. | 36000 Emerald Coast Pkwy. (Hwy. 98) | 850/837–9410 | fax 850/837–3390 | $10–$30 | AE, D, MC, V.

Lodging

Best Western Summerplace Inn. In the heart of Destin, this four-story chain hotel with bay windows and arched galleries is convenient to the town's famous white sand beaches and emerald waters (about ¼ mi away), as well as area attractions and recreational activities. Some of the rooms have balconies and views of the gulf. Complimentary Continental breakfast. In-room data ports, some microwaves, refrigerators, some in-room hot tubs. Cable TV. Indoor-outdoor pool. Outdoor hot tub, sauna. Gym. Laundry facilities. Business services. | 14047 Emerald Coast Pkwy. | 850/650–8003 or 888/232–2499 | fax 850/650–8004 | www.bestwestern.com | 72 rooms | $125– $179 | AE, D, DC, MC, V.

Club Destin Resort. This three-story, family-oriented resort is fairly close to Destin Beach (about 1,000 ft.), and has a private beachfront. Even the smallest rooms have both a bed and sleeper sofa, so they can accommodate a small family. Check out the grand 70,000-gallon heated pool surrounded by a three-story tropical atrium. None of the rooms has a water view, but all have kitchen facilities. Cable TV. Indoor pool. Hot tub. 9-hole putting green. Gym. Video games. Children's programs (ages 4–12). | 1085 U.S. 98 | 850/654–4700 or 888/983–3784 | www.clubdestin.com | AE, MC, V | 120 rooms | Efficiency $99, 1-bedroom $119, 2-bedroom $139.

Henderson Park Inn. Built in 1992 in Queen Anne style, this seaside B&B is a secluded, romantic retreat 2 mi west of Destin, at the eastern extreme of Henderson Beach State Park. The elegant rooms, appointed with reproduction period furnishings, all overlook the water; most have private balconies. There is a mile of secluded beach. Restaurant, complimentary breakfast. In-room safes, some microwaves, some refrigerators, some in-room hot tubs. Cable TV. Pool. Beach. Business services. No kids under 25. No smoking. | 2700 Scenic Hwy. 98E | 850/654–0400 or 800/336–4853 | fax 850/654–0405 | www.hendersonparkinn.com | 35 suites | $180–$289 suites | AE, D, MC, V.

Hidden Dunes Beach and Resort. This 27-acre resort offers a range of accommodations, including cottages, condos, and villas, overlooking Destin's snowy white beaches. All units are equipped with kitchens and washers and dryers. The popular Carolina-style beach cottages are tucked away by spacious and private screened porches, shaded walkways, reflecting pools, and fountains. Restaurant. Kitchenettes, microwaves, refrigerators, cable TV. 3 pools, lake. Hot tub. 6 tennis courts. Basketball. Beach. Laundry facilities. | 9815 Hwy. 98W | 850/837–3521 or 800/824–6335 | fax 850/654–9590 | www.hiddendunes.com | 133 units | $175–$395 (7-night minimum, summer; 3-night minimum, winter) | D, MC, V.

Hilton Sandestin. This all-suites hotel is on the grounds of the lush Sandestin resort. Hilton guests can use Sandestin's beachfront golf courses as well as the Hilton's many other amenities, which include its own trio of heated pools. The majority of guest rooms have views of the water; all have balconies. Restaurants, bar (with entertainment), room service. In-room data ports, in-room safes, minibars, microwaves, refrigerators. Cable TV, in-room VCRs (and movies). 3 pools, wading pool. 2 hot tubs, massage, sauna, steam room. Driving range, 4 golf courses, putting green, 13 tennis courts. Gym. Beach. Shops. Children's programs (ages 5–12). Business services. | 4000 Sandestin Blvd. S | 850/267–9500 or 800/367–1271 | fax 850/267–3076 | www.hilton.com | 598 suites | $245–$365 suites | AE, D, DC, MC, V.

Holiday Inn of Destin. This Holidome Holiday Inn sits directly on the beach in downtown Destin, close to area restaurants and shopping. Many rooms have views of the water. There are also both indoor and outdoor pools. Restaurant, bar, room service. In-room data ports, in-room safes, cable TV. 2 pools (1 indoor), wading pool. Hot tub. Gym. Beach. Children's programs (ages 5–12). Laundry service. Business services. | 1020 U.S. 98E | 850/837–6181 or 877/837–6181 | fax 850/837–1523 | www.holiday-inn.com | 233 rooms | $135–$185 | AE, D, DC, MC, V.

Sandestin. This 2,400-acre resort offers villas, condominiums, cottages, an inn, and a marina and is so large that it seems like a town unto itself. All rooms have some sort of pleasant view, either the gulf or Choctawhatchee Bay, a golf course, a lagoon, or a wildlife preserve. Accommodations run the gamut from simple to extravagant. You can also use the three swimming pools and other facilities of the Hilton resort, which is on the grounds. 4 restaurants, bar (with entertainment). Some in-room data ports, some kitchenettes, some microwaves, some refrigerators. Cable TV, some in-room VCRs. 10 pools, wading pool. Hot tub, beauty salon, spa. Driving range, 4 18-hole golf courses, putting green, 14 tennis courts. Health club, hiking. Beach, boating, bicycles. Shops. Children's programs (ages 4–12). Business services. | 9300 U.S. 98W | 850/267–8000 or 800/277–0800 | fax 850/267–8222 | www.sandestin.com | 175 rooms; 420 villas | $160–$215 rooms, $210–$285 1-bedroom villas, $250–$420 2-bedroom villas, $330–$590 3-bedroom villas, $410–$500 4-bedroom villas, $776 penthouse villa | AE, D, DC, MC, V.

Sea Oats Motel. Almost all rooms at this motel, 5 mi east of Destin, face the beach, which is right outside the door. Second-floor rooms have balconies. Picnic area. Some kitchenettes, some microwaves, some refrigerators, some in-room hot tubs. Cable TV. Pool. Beach. Laundry facilities. Business services. | 3420 Old Hwy. 98E | 850/837–6655 or 888/732–6287 | fax 850/654–8255 | www.seaoatsrentals.com | 80 rooms | $99–$120 | D, MC, V.

Seascape Resort and Conference Center. Across the road from the beach, this resort stands 6 mi east of Destin. The condos, all individually owned and appointed, do have balconies, though they do not have views of the ocean. A small lake on the large property allows you to fish (if you have a Florida license). Restaurant, bar. Kitchenettes, microwaves, refrigerators, some in-room hot tubs. Cable TV, in-room VCRs. 5 pools, wading pool. Driving range, 18-hole golf course, putting green, tennis court. Basketball, fishing, bicycles. Business services. | 100 Seascape Dr. | 850/837–9181 or 800/874–9106 | fax 850/837–4769 | www.seascape-resort.com | 115 condominiums | $105–$220 condominiums | AE, D, DC, MC, V.

Sleep Inn Destin. One mile north of the beach and 8 mi east of Destin, this two-story motel sits across the highway from the Silver Sands Outlet Mall and its 100 stores. Complimentary Continental breakfast. Some refrigerators. Cable TV. Pool. Laundry facilities. Business services. | 10775 W. Emerald Coast Pkwy. | 850/654–7022 | fax 850/654–7022 | www.choicehotels.com | 77 rooms | $92–$97 | AE, D, DC, MC, V.

Tops'l Beach and Racquet Club. Six miles east of Destin, this vast property, encircled by a nature preserve, occupies 53 acres on which there are three high-rise buildings (up to 15 stories tall). The resort is like a small town with shops, restaurants, and bars. Most condominiums have balconies overlooking the ocean. Restaurant. Kitchenettes, microwaves, refrigerators. Cable TV, in-room VCRs (and movies). 4 pools (1 indoor), wading pool. Hot tub, sauna, steam room. 12 tennis courts. Gym, racquetball. Beach. Business services. | 9011 Hwy. 98W | 850/267–9222 or 888/867–7535 | www.topsl.com | 300 units | $148–$236 1-bedroom condo, $210–$321 2-bedroom condo, $326–$475 3-bedroom condo, $230–$437 villas | AE, D, MC, V.

DUNEDIN

MAP 3, H6

(Nearby towns also listed: Clearwater, Indian Rocks Beach, Redington Beach, Tampa, Tarpon Springs)

North of Clearwater in the Tampa Bay area, Dunedin (pop. 35,000), named by two Scots in the 1880s, celebrates its heritage each spring with the Highland Games, as well as the yuletide Heather and Thistle holidays. A nicely restored five-block-long down-

DUNEDIN

INTRO
ATTRACTIONS
DINING
LODGING

town historic district is a one-stop shopping area for antiques, gift shops, and small eateries. Just west of town is Honeymoon Island, which prior to World War II was billed as a romantic post-nuptial getaway. There is a state park here now to protect nesting ospreys. A 15-min ferry from Honeymoon Island connects you to Caladesi Island, near Clearwater. Dunedin is the spring training home to the Toronto Blue Jays.

Information: **Dunedin Chamber of Commerce** | 301 Main St., Dunedin, 34698 | 727/733–3197 | www.dunedin-fl.com.

Attractions

Caladesi Island State Park. This park protects six of the state's few remaining undeveloped barrier islands, encompassing some 650 upland acres and more than 1,100 acres of surrounding mangroves and grass flats. Fishing, shelling, and nature study are the main pastimes. Most visitors arrive by private boat, tying up at Caladesi Island's 99-slip marina or anchoring offshore in calm weather; there are also scheduled passenger ferries from nearby Honeymoon Island. Picnic pavilions, bath houses, and a concession stand are on the island. | Honeymoon Island Ferry, No. 1 Causeway Blvd. | 727/469–5918 or 727/734–5263 (ferry) | Park free; ferry $7 | Daily 8–sunset; ferry hourly 10–5 in fair weather.

Honeymoon Island State Park. This landfall is another link in the chain of barrier islands that extends between Anclote Key on the north and Cape Romano to the south, protecting the Florida coast from tropical storms. Osprey and gopher tortoise are two of the many species of birds, amphibians, and mammals that call the park home. You can swim, sunbathe, or fish for flounder, snook, trout, redfish, snapper, whiting, sheepshead, or tarpon. In addition, the park boasts several nature trails, bird observation areas, and picnic pavilions. The park is 6 mi west of Highway 19, at the end of State Route 586 (also called Causeway Boulevard). | No. 1 Causeway Blvd. | 727/469–5942 | $4 per vehicle | Daily 8–sunset.

ON THE CALENDAR

MAR.: *Spring Training*. Grant Field has been the Spring home of the Toronto Blue Jays since the American League team's inception in 1977. | 800/707–8269.

APR.: *Highland Games and Scottish Festival*. Competitors from throughout the U.S. and Canada come to Highlander Park to compete in Scottish band competitions and contests in Highland dancing, piping, and drumming, and traditional Scottish athletics. | 727/733–6240.

Dining

Bon Appetit. Continental. Known for its imaginative cuisine, this restaurant changes its menu twice a month to include such delectable entrées as peppered quail, and scallops with figs and raisins on fettuccine. The restaurant sits directly on the Intracoastal Waterway and is a popular place to catch a sunset. | 148 Marina Plaza | 727/733–2151 | $12–$15 | AE, D, DC, MC, V.

Casa Tina. Vegetarian. The undying popularity of this restaurant is due to the excellent low-fat Mexican cuisine churned out nightly by chef-owner Javier Avila. The story goes that he wanted to help his wife stay slim, so he created dish after dish with spicy, exotic seasonings to keep her and the clients satisfied. There are a few chicken and fresh seafood dishes available such as the *pescado à la Veracruz*, which is the catch of the day grilled and topped with a vegetable sauce, or you can be adventurous and try the cactus soup. The enchiladas rojas or chiles rellenos are good standbys, but don't expect any of the beans to contain lard or any of the food to be deep-fried (except the fried ice cream dessert!). | 369 Main St. | 727/734–9226 | Closed Mon. | $10–$15 | AE, D, DC, MC, V.

Jesse's Dockside. Seafood. Sitting on the Intracoastal Waterway, this casual eatery offers water-side dining outdoors or a dining room decorated with nautical maps, barometers, and telescopes. The menu includes such favorites as grouper, among other seafood options, as well as steak, chicken, and pasta. | 345 Causeway Blvd. | 727/736–2611 | Reservations not accepted | $9–$24 | AE, D, MC, V.

Sea Sea Riders. Seafood. In a 1920s home in downtown Dunedin, this restaurant, with copper-top wooded tables and mounted fish on the walls, concentrates on fresh seafood dishes. Try the coconut shrimp or the mixed grill: tuna, mahimahi, grouper, shrimp, and scallops blackened and served over rice. | 221 Main St. | 727/734–1445 | $6–$16 | AE, MC, V.

Lodging

Best Western Yacht Harbor Inn and Suites. This two-story motor hotel has fine views of St. Joseph's Sound. Many of the rooms have balconies, and some have kitchens. The nearest beach is 3 mi away. Restaurant, bar. In-room data ports, some kitchenettes, some microwaves, some refrigerators. Cable TV. Pool. Business services. | 150 Marina Plaza | 727/733–4121 | fax 727/736–4365 | www.advantuscorp.com | 54 rooms | $119–$139 | AE, D, DC, MC, V.

Inn on the Bay. This four-story motel offers rooms for reasonable prices. Some rooms have wonderful views of the gulf; be sure to ask for one. Good beaches are only a 10-min drive away, and Caladesi Island State Park is only 5 mi north. Restaurant, bar, room service. Kitchenettes, microwaves, refrigerators. Cable TV. Pool. Dock, water sports, fishing, bicycles. Laundry facilities. Business services. | 1420 Bayshore Blvd./U.S. 19A | 727/734–7689 or 800/759–5045 | fax 727/734–0972 | 36 rooms | $45–$74 | AE, D, MC, V.

ENGLEWOOD

MAP 3, H8

(Nearby towns also listed: Boca Grande, Port Charlotte, Punta Gorda, Venice)

Relaxed Englewood, 28 mi south of Sarasota, is the northern gulf entrance to the Cape Haze peninsula. Since major thoroughfares pass the area by, traffic is minimal, and there's a real relaxed, small-town atmosphere here. Two causeways connect Englewood across Lemon Bay to Manasota Key, a barrier island with long beaches and parks with picnic areas, boat ramps, and fishing piers.

Englewood has several buildings on the National Register of Historic Places, including the 1906 Hermitage on Manasota Key, which is one of a few beachfront homesteads left in the state and is slated to become an artist's retreat.

The Englewood area (pop. 45,000) includes the residential areas of Rotunda, where you can kayak and take sunset cruises, and Placida, which has excellent galleries and restaurants, and is known for its white pelicans and bird watching. Night Island, Little Gasparilla Island, Don Pedro, and Palm Island have white sand beaches and lagoons, but are not connected by bridge to the mainland. However, connected to the mainland by a toll bridge is Gasparilla Island, where you'll find the charming town of Boca Grande.

Information: **Englewood Area Chamber of Commerce** | 601 S. Indiana Ave., Englewood, 34223 | 941/474–5511 | www.englewoodchamber.com.

Attractions

Cedar Point Environmental Park. This 88-acre park, nestled between creeks on the north and south sides and Lemon Bay Aquatic Preserve to the west, has walking trails for relaxed wandering and bird watching; you might spot eagles and their nests or possibly the mangrove cuckoo. Weekend guided walks are scheduled from October to May, and there are other activities throughout the year (call for a scheduled). | 2300 Placida Rd. | 941/475–0769 | fax 941/475–1899 | www.charlotte-florida.com/chec | Free | Park daily, guided walks Oct.–May, Sat–Sun at 10 AM.

Don Pedro Island State Recreation Area. One of the smaller barrier islands off the Cape Haze shoreline (near Placida) accessible only by private boat, Don Pedro has 1 mi of white sand beach as well as sea oat–covered dunes. There are picnic pavilions set up with grilling stations and rest rooms. This is a quiet place to sunbathe, collect shells, or possibly witness Loggerhead sea turtles climbing ashore to lay eggs in midsummer. | Don Pedro Island | 941/964–0375 | www.dep.state.fl.us/parks | $2 per boat | Daily 8 AM–sundown.

Island Bay National Wildlife Refuge. Wildlife photographers and bird-watchers will enjoy almost untouched landscapes of mangroves and sandbars. Island Bay is at the southern tip of Cape Haze and reachable only by private boat, which is a secret blessing for those who come with fishing gear and the prefer fighting fewer mosquitoes offshore. | Island Bay | 941/472–4061 | www.refuges.fws.gov | Free | Daily.

Lemon Bay Park. A relaxing, yet educational experience awaits you at Lemon Bay. You can wander through the well-marked trails, some of which have small bridges to cross the swampy parts, or flutter through the butterfly garden. The 196 acres are on the mainland, but have views of the nearby keys 1 mi off shore. Bird watching is always plentiful, and there is an accessible, paved trail. | 570 Bay Park Blvd. | 941/474–3065 | www.co.sarasota.fl.us | Free | Daily.

Manasota Beach. This beach's white sands are beckoning for you to relax here. There are both free parking and lifeguards during daylight, also a boat ramp, picnic area, and rest rooms. | Manasota Beach Rd., Manasota Key.

Myakka State Forest Park. This 8,500-acre state park, Florida's largest, has trails open to mountain biking, hiking, and horseback riding. Since the park is still being developed, you have the opportunity for some serious brushing with wilderness. The Myakka River, popular for canoeing, runs through the park. It's a popular bird-watching spot, and airboat tours are available on Myakka Lake. A canopy walkway, reminiscent of those in the rain forests of Costa Rica, is the only one of its kind in the state. | 13207 Hwy. 72 | 941/480–3145 | www.dep.state.fl.us/parks | $4 per vehicle | Daily 8 AM–sundown.

Stump Pass Beach State Rec. Area. One of the newer areas added to the family of state-run parks, Stump Pass is the name for the narrow channel that runs from Lemon Bay to the Gulf of Mexico, with Manasota Key to the North and Knight Key to the South. There are some picnic pavilions, rest rooms, and 1 mi of beach. The area at the southern tip of Manasota Key is accessible by car. | Beach Rd., Manasota Key | Free | Daily.

Dining

The Fishery Restaurant. Seafood. This casual, waterfront dining option along the Gasparilla Sound offers a menu of inventive seafood dishes. Especially popular are the Cajun spicy shrimp served with black beans and yellow rice; the "low tide" linguine topped with a creamy sauce, shrimp, scallops, and mushrooms; not to mention the homemade Key lime cheesecake or the orange Key lime pie, twists on the old standards. | 1300 Fishery Rd., Placida | 941/697–2451 | $10–$20 | AE, MC, V.

Flying Bridge II. American. Sitting above Rocky Creek, this casual eatery serves an assortment of seafood, steak, and pasta dishes. Specialties include the Danish lobster tails, baby back ribs, and a New York strip steak. | 2080 S. McCall Rd. | 941/474–2206 | $7–$14 | MC, V.

Johnny Leverock's Seafood House. Seafood. Almost all of the tables in this restaurant have views of the Intracoastal Waterway. The dining room is decorated with fishing memorabilia and local antiques. Start with the salmon fritters. The seafood harvest comes with Maine lobster tail, baked mahimahi, scallops, and shrimp. | 7092 Placida Rd., Cape Haze | 941/698–6900 | $8–$17 | AE, D, DC, MC, V.

Prime Time Steak and Spirits. American. You can order Mexican favorites such as enchiladas or chimichangas as well as four-square American fare such as prime ribs or seafood at this bustling restaurant. Seven televisions positioned strategically throughout the dining room give everyone a view of whatever sporting event is being televised. | 5855 Placida Rd. | 941/697–7799 or 941/697–7731 | www.primetimeflorida.com | No lunch Mon.–Sat. | $5–$16 | AE, D, DC, MC, V.

Ship's Lantern. American. This restaurant, sitting directly on the Intracoastal Waterway, allows you to dock your boat for free. An outdoor patio overlooks the water, though you can also eat inside on a screened-in porch. Porterhouse steaks, prime rib, broiled red snapper, and blackened mahimahi are some of the many items filling the menu. Thursday night offers an all-you-can-eat seafood buffet. If you would prefer to eat what you have pulled from the water yourself, the staff can prepare your catch for you. Entertainment nightly. | 8251 Esther St. | 941/697–2244 | Closed Mon. | $10–$22 | D, MC, V.

Lodging

Days Inn. This two-story motel sits 2 mi north of Englewood Beach and the gulf, in a quiet area off Route 776. Complimentary Continental breakfast. Some in-room data ports, some kitchenettes, some microwaves, some refrigerators. Cable TV. Pool. Playground. Laundry facilities. Business services. Pets allowed (fee). | 2540 S. McCall Rd./Hwy. 776 | 941/474–5544 800/ 887–5412 | fax 941/475–2124 | 84 rooms | $89–$99 | AE, D, DC, MC, V.

Palm Island Resort. One-, two-, and three-bedroom villas are available here, all with fully equipped kitchens, laundry facilities in the unit, and screened-in porches with views of the gulf. The expansive 2¼ mi of private beach means that you will feel all alone even when the resort is at capacity. This resort is south of Englewood, at the southern end of Cape Haze. 2 restaurants, bar, picnic area. Kitchenettes, microwaves, refrigerators. Cable TV. 5 pools. 5 hot tubs. 11 tennis courts. Basketball, volleyball. Beach, fishing, bicycles. Shops. Playground. Laundry facilities. Business services. | 7092 Placida Rd., Cape Haze | 941/697–4800 or 800/ 824–5412 | fax 941/697–0696 | www.palmisland.com | 87 villas | $290–$500 | AE, MC, V.

Pearl Beach Motel. On Manasota Key, this lodge sits in a secluded residential area. Because the next closest hotel is over a mile away, the beach here has little traffic. From the sun deck you can spy dolphins or watch the sun go down. All the rooms are equipped with kitchens and have gulf views. Picnic area. In-room data ports, kitchenettes, microwaves, refrigerators. Beach. Business services. | 7990 Manasota Key Rd. | 941/474–3316 | fax 941/ 474–3316 | www.pearlbeachmotel.com | 12 rooms | $100–$115 | D, MC, V.

Veranda Inn of Englewood. Located on the Intracoastal Waterway, 2 mi north of the beach, this two-story hotel (with elevator) has basic accommodations. The veranda on the second floor is furnished with chairs for lounging and offers full views of the waterway. In-room data ports. Cable TV. Pool. Laundry facilities. Pets allowed (fee). | 2073 S. McCall Rd./Hwy. 776 | 941/475–6533 or 800/633–8115 | 38 rooms | $85–$95 | AE, D, DC, MC, V.

EVERGLADES CITY

MAP 3, D4

(Nearby towns also listed: Everglades National Park, Marco Island, Naples)

This western gateway to the Everglades draws visitors who plan to canoe, fish, and bird-watch. The Wilderness Waterway, which extends 99 mi southeast to Flamingo, begins here. The town is just off the Tamiami Trail, which was built by Barron Collier, a wealthy advertising man, in the late 19th century. In fact, the town was created to house workers building the Trail and other of Collier's projects. The resident population fluctuates between 500 in the summer to 1,200 in the winter.

Information: **Everglades Area Chamber of Commerce** | Box 130, Everglades City, 34139 | 941/695–3941 | florida-everglades.com.

Attractions

Gulf Coast Visitors Center. This welcome center to Everglades National Park is a great place to rent canoes if you plan to explore the Ten Thousand Islands or the Wilderness Waterway. In winter park rangers lead canoe trips, and when staffing permits, rangers narrate boat tours around the islands. This is also where you pick up permits for backcountry exploring. | 815 S. Copeland Ave. | 941/695–3311 | www.nps.gov | Free | Mid-Nov–mid-Apr., daily 7:30–5; mid-Apr.–mid-Nov. daily 8:30–4:30.

Museum of the Everglades. The 2,000-year history of the human habitation of the south-western Everglades is represented in this museum, which is housed in the only remaining unaltered structure original to the town, then simply called Everglades. Changing exhibits include selections from the large collection of black-and-white photographs of the town circa 1920. The museum is a unit of the Collier County Museum, which is headquartered in Naples. | 105 W. Broadway | 941/695–0008 | www.colliermuseum.org | Free | Tues.–Sat. 11–4.

Smallwood's Store. This museum and gift shop was built in 1906 as a trading post raised on pilings in Chokoloskee Bay (4 mi south of Everglades City). It was re-opened in 1989 and features a museum showing some of the store's original goods, along with historic photographs and Indian clothing and furs. There's a small gift shop on the premises. | 360 Mamie St., Chokoloskee Island | 941/695–2989 | $2.50 | Daily May–Nov. 11–5; Dec.–Apr. 10–5.

SIGHTSEEING TOURS/TOUR COMPANIES

North American Canoe Tours. You can customize your Everglades tour from a simple sight-seeing powerboat ride to a camping and kayaking adventure that lasts a week. For overnight trips you must bring your own clothes and a sleeping bag, but food and other equipment are provided. At either end of your tour you can opt to spend a luxurious night at the Ivey House B&B and earn a 10% discount on your excursions. | Ivey House, 107 Camellia St., Everglades City | 941/695–3299 | fax 941/695–4155 | www.evergladesadventures.com | $40–$500 | Tours daily by appointment only.

ON THE CALENDAR

FEB.: *Seafood Festival.* About 60,000 people come to the three-day fest the first week-end in February on Broadway in the middle of town. A host of vendors compete in cooking a variety of seafood (and alligator meat); 150 vendors sell arts and crafts. | 941/695–3941.

Dining

Everglades Seafood Depot. Seafood. Seafood in this 1928 Spanish-style structure on Lake Placid ranges from lobster to frog's legs and alligator. Grouper comes fried, broiled, blackened, or grilled; or you can try the Island Grouper, which is baked in tin foil with onions, peppers, and lemon juice. | 102 Collier Ave. | 941/695–0075 | $10–$23 | AE, D, DC, MC, V.

Oar House Restaurant. Seafood. This wood-paneled eatery with picnic table–style booths and kitschy fishing and Everglades decor is a local favorite. A sampler dish will allow you to try frog's legs, gator, fresh fish, blue crab nuggets, and oyster. | 305 Collier Ave. | 941/695–3535 | $10–$16 | AE, D, MC, V.

Lodging

Rod and Gun Club. U.S. presidents, including Nixon, have stayed at this extremely laid-back (no room phones, for starters) landmark 1920s inn. The hotel once lodged wealthy hunters, anglers, and international yachting parties who came to winter in Florida. It was restored and reopened in January 2001, though rates and other details were unavailable at press time. Restaurant, bar. No room phones, no TV in some rooms. Outdoor pool. 2 tennis courts. Boating, fishing. Laundry service. | 200 Riverside Dr. | 941/695–2101 | 17 rooms | Rates unavailable at press time | No credit cards.

On the Banks of the Everglades. The name of this spacious B&B is a pun. The teal neo-classical facade reveals the teal inn to be the first bank in Collier County, built by Barron Collier in 1923. The inn keeps some original artifacts from the bank, including an old safe. A complimentary breakfast is served in the old vault. Picnic area, complimentary breakfast. No air-conditioning in some rooms, some kitchenettes, some microwaves, some refrigerators. Cable TV, TV in common area. Fishing, bicycles. Playground. Some pets allowed (fee). | 201 W. Broadway | 941/695–3151 or 888/431–1977 | fax 941/695–3335 | www.banksoftheeverglades.com | 10 rooms (5 with shared bath) | $55–$180 | Closed June–Oct. | A, DC, MC, V.

EVERGLADES NATIONAL PARK

(Nearby towns also listed: Everglades City, Florida City, Homestead, Marco Island, Naples)

Encompassing more than 1.5 million acres, sprawling across Miami-Dade, Monroe, and Collier counties, Everglades National Park is the largest subtropical wilderness in the country and the second-largest national park. The vast prairie and mangrove forest—the largest in the world—protects exotic flora, marvelous bird life, and alligators. It's home to more than 350 species of birds, 600 types of fish, and endangered species such as the Florida panther, manatee, and bald eagle.

Few backroads lead to the area; to see the Everglades, drive to access areas near the park's visitors centers, park your car, and hike, canoe, or bike out to the wetlands. The major entrance to the park from the west coast is at Everglades City, at the Gulf Coast Visitor Center, where you can often catch a ranger-guided narrative boat tour. A marked, 99-mi canoe trail, called the Ten Thousand Islands, snakes its way from here to the Flamingo Visitor Center at the southeast corner of the park. The islands in question are made of saltwater-rooting mangroves. The waters on this side are ideal for fishing, but not swimming—stingrays, sharks, and some alligators live here.

The main visitors center is southwest of Miami and Florida City, inside the park's eastern entrance. Inside the park are many interpretive trails along the main road, which eventually leads to the Florida City Visitor Center. For an easy day-trip from Miami, take Tamiami Trail (U.S. 41) 25 mi west to the Shark Valley Visitor Center. You can take a tram, walk, or rent a bike to ride along a 15-mi loop road that extends into sawgrass prairie topped by hardwood hammocks. The Gulf Coast Visitor Center, from which you can take canoe trips through the Ten Thousand Lakes, is in Everglades City. Alligators, though ubiquitous throughout the park, constantly lurk along the narrow waterways here and sunbathe along the loop. A warning: In summer, the heat, humidity, and mosquitoes can be overwhelming throughout the Everglades.

Information: Everglades National Park. | 40001 Hwy. 9338, Homestead, 33034 | 305/242–7700 | www.nps.gov/ever.

EVERGLADES
NATIONAL PARK

INTRO
ATTRACTIONS
DINING
LODGING

Attractions

Big Cypress Gallery. The photo gallery of Clyde Butcher is presented here in the middle of more than a million acres of national park. Large-format black-and-white film is the medium he uses to capture visions of grass, swamp, and the general beauty of nature, including some huge landscape prints. You can take a short hike on the nature trail behind the gallery, or check the website, which is kept up to date about upcoming events or lectures. The gallery is 37 mi west of Miami, 45 mi west of Naples. | 52388 U.S. 41 (Tamiami Trail) | 941/695–2428 | fax 941/695–2670 | www.clydebutcher.com | Free | Wed.–Sat. 10–5.

Big Cypress National Preserve. "Big" is the operative word here. This 729,000-acre preserve, 50 mi west of Miami, protects part of the Big Cypress Swamp, which includes marshes, dry prairies, hammocks, and pine woods. At the visitor center, you can watch a film and view exhibits that explain the natural habitat. Unlike many reserves, you can use this one for recreation—there are two scenic drives, three camp grounds, and a 30-mi hiking trial—including use of off-road vehicles and air boats. You can hunt (gun and bow, for deer and wild hog) in season: The two-month gun season begins in October and the archery season starts September 2. And go frogging, if that's your sport. Enter the preserve at the visitors center. | Visitors center, 33100 Tamiami Trail E (U.S. 41), Ochopee | 941/695–4111 | Free | Daily 8:30–4:30.

Ernest F. Coe Visitor Center. The Ernest F. Coe Visitor Center, one of five in the park, is at the main entrance, 10 mi west of Florida City and 11 mi southwest of Homestead. This is also the park's main headquarters. There are displays, audio programs, and orientation films. A shop sells books, postcards, and insect repellent, which you will definitely need if you are visiting in summer. | 40001 Hwy. 9336 | 305/242–7700 | Visitors center free; park admission $10 per vehicle | Daily 8–5.

Everglades Gator Park. If you're ready to touch a baby alligator, handle exotic birds, or play with a python, jump right in. The main emphasis is the 45-min narrated wildlife tour on an airboat that takes you through the Everglades. You pass a Miccosukee fishing village and see wildlife in its natural state. But there's also a wildlife show, where you can learn about reptiles, otters, birds of prey, alligator wrestling, you name it. The park is 12 mi west of Florida's Turnpike. | 24050 S.W. 8th St. (Tamiami Trail), Miami | 305/559–2255 or 800/559–2205 | fax 305/220–6611 | www.gatorpark.com | Park free, airboat tours $14 | Daily 9–5.

Everglades Safari Park. The 300-seat arena here is used for educational alligator shows and wrestling demonstrations. Also on the grounds is an alligator farm, a replica of an Indian village, and a small wildlife museum; you can also take an airboat ride through the

© Corbis

A COMPLEX ECOSYSTEM

Unlike in other national parks, where the goal is to protect beautiful scenery, the fight to maintain the Everglades is a constant struggle to protect a vast, one-of-a-kind ecosystem as a wildlife habitat. During the rainy season, a river inches deep and miles wide flows imperceptibly from Lake Okeechobee to the Gulf of Mexico. Marjorie Stoneman Douglas, the Everglades' most famous activist, called it "a river of grass."

In 1948, facing severe flooding in South Florida, Congress ordered the Army Corps of Engineers to reroute the flow of water. At one time the Everglades encompassed about four million acres in South Florida. Today it's roughly a third of its former size. As the build-up of South Florida intensifies, the canals, levees, and dikes have diverted water to land developments and Florida's $1.5-billion-a-year farming industry.

The restoration of the Everglades water supply system has been a cornerstone of the national environmental agenda heading into the 21st century. In 2000, the Congress passed an incredible $7.8-billion 36-year replumbing of the Everglades to restore its natural water flow, mainly by collecting and redirecting rain water. The measure will create what has been called the most complex environmental restoration project in the history of the world.

The original Everglades engineer—the alligator—cuts a mean picture, silently lurking, snout edged on the surface of water. And yet for countless animals and plants, the alligator is their most important friend, and an important factor in surviving Everglades drought. Alligators make holes around their nests that concentrate water in dry seasons, creating pools of life for wading birds, such as the roseate spoonbill, wood stork, white ibis, green-backed heron, anhinga, great blue heron, and a variety of egret. Everglades National Park, the southern tip of the Everglades, is home to as many as 68 plant and animal species fighting extinction, including the American crocodile (the Everglades is the only place in the world where alligators and crocodiles coexist), the bald eagle, the West Indian manatee, and the Florida panther.

swampy River of Grass. The park is 9 mi west of Krome Ave. | 26700 U.S. 41 (Tamiami Trail) | 305/226–6923 or 305/223–3804 | $15 | Daily 8:30–5.

Fakahatchee Strand State Preserve. The largest state preserve in Florida encompasses 70,000 acres and also has the largest community of native orchid species (43 at last count) in the state. The half-mile boardwalk takes you through part of the 215 acres of bald cypresses, some as old as 400 years, and through a rainforest filled with rare bromeliads and epiphytes. At the end of the boardwalk is the swampy home to a resident female alligator, who usually has babies viewable from September to March. If you move delicately, you might also get a look at a pair of bald eagles, white-tailed deer, raccoon, otter, numerous birds, reptiles, and amphibians, or possibly the rare ghost orchid. The ranger station is ¾ mi north of Tamiami Trail on Highway 29. | Hwy. 29 and U.S. 41 (Tamiami Trail), Copeland | 941/695–4593 | www.dep.state.fl.us/parks | Free | Daily 8–sunset.

Flamingo Visitor Center. This visitors center sits at the park's southern extreme, 38 mi south of the main entrance, and contains a lodge (the only accommodations within the national park), restaurant, post office, and marina. The exhibits focus on natural history. Boat tours and canoe rentals are available. Camping is located nearby, as are numerous hiking trails. Wildlife is plentiful here year-round. | 305/242–7700 | Visitors center free, park admission $10 per vehicle | Nov.–Apr., daily 7:30–5.

Long Pine Key Area Turnoff. At this campground and picnic area 6 mi west of the Ernest F. Coe Visitor Center there are grills, rest rooms, and numerous hiking trails. | 305/242–7700 | Area free, park admission $10 per vehicle | Daily.

Mahogany Hammock Trail. This ¼-mi boardwalk, 20 mi west of the main entrance, wanders through a dense, jungle-like hardwood forest filled with gumbo-limbo trees and air plants, and passes the largest living mahogany trees in the United States. | 305/242–7700 | Trail free, park admission $10 per vehicle | Daily.

Miccosukee Indian Village and Airboat Tours. A visit to the Miccosukee Indian Village is a good introduction to some of Florida's original inhabitants. You can see demonstrations and displays of woodcarving, patchwork, beadwork, basket weaving, and doll-making. Thrill to the world famous Indian Alligator Shows (basically, alligator wrestling). The Indian Museum includes a fashion film and historical artifacts, along with paintings by a tribal artist and a photo exhibit depicting contemporary Miccosukee society. The airboat—a flat-bottomed, propeller-driven boat—takes you through the vast "River of Grass" to a typical hammock-style Indian camp that has been owned by the same Miccosukee family for more than 100 years. The village is 25 mi west of Miami via U.S. 41 (Tamiami Trail). | U.S. 41 (Tamiami Trail) | 305/223–8380 or 305/223–8388 | Village $5, airboat tours $10 | Daily 9–5 | www.miccosukeetribe.com.

Ochopee Post Office. Don't miss (literally) the smallest post office in North America. It is also probably the only one without a street address. You can buy postcards bearing pictures of the office to send to one and all. Ochopee is 75 mi west of Miami. | U.S. 41 (Tamiami Trail 1), Ochopee | 941/695–4131 | Free | Weekdays 9:30–noon and 1–4:30, Sat. 9:30–11:30 AM.

Pa-Hay-Okee. Thirteen miles west of the main entrance and 9 mi south of the Royal Palm Visitor Center, sweeping towards the horizon, dotted by islands of cypress trees, you can see the park's characteristic vast expanses of sawgrass. A ⅛-mi boardwalk trail leads to a raised observation platform. | 305/242–7700 | Trail free, park admission $10 per vehicle | Daily.

Pineland Trail. Not many travelers venture onto this ½-mi trail, which meanders through pines, palmettos, and wildflowers. The trail begins 7 mi from the park entrance. It's paved but narrow and uneven, with potholes along the edges. | Trail free, park admission $10 per vehicle | Daily.

Royal Palm Visitor Center. Both the half-mile Anhinga Trail and the half-mile Gumbo-Limbo Trail begin here. The former is popular for herons, alligators, turtles, and other wildlife you see along your hike. The Gumbo-Limbo Trail wanders among, not surprisingly, gumbo-limbo

EVERGLADES
NATIONAL PARK

INTRO
ATTRACTIONS
DINING
LODGING

Cape Romano

Gullivan Bay

TO NAPLES

Ochopee

Monroe Station

Oasis Visitor Center

Barron River

Chokoloskee Bay

Everglades City

Ten Thousand Islands

Gulf Coast Visitor Center

Chokoloskee

Turner River

BIG CYPRESS NATIONAL PRESERVE

Loop Road Environmental Education Center

EVERGLADES NATIONAL PARK AND BIG CYPRESS NATIONAL PRESERVE

Wilderness

Waterway

Highland Point

EVERGLADES NATIONAL PARK

Broad River

Harney River

Shark River

Ponce de Leon Bay

KEY

Expressways
Highways
Minor Roads
Trail/Canoe Trail
Ranger Station
Campground
Primitive Camp
Picnic Area
Restaurant
Lodge

Whitewater Bay

Northwest Cape

Cape Sable

Middle Cape

East Cape

Flamingo Visitor Center

N

GULF OF MEXICO

0   10 miles

0   15 km

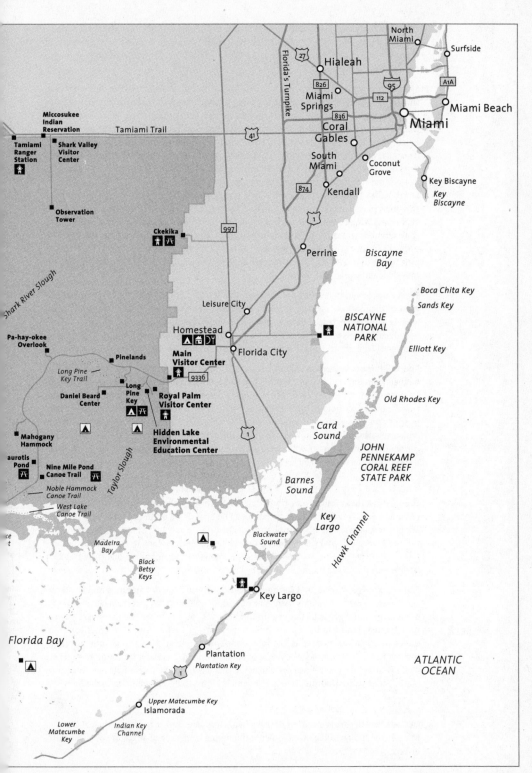

North
Miami

Surfside

Hialeah

27

826

Miami
Springs

I-95

112

A1A

Miami Beach

836

Coral
Gables

Miami

South
Miami

Coconut
Grove

Key Biscayne

Key
Biscayne

Florida's Turnpike

Tamiami Trail

41

Miccosukee
Indian
Reservation

Tamiami
Ranger
Station

Shark Valley
Visitor
Center

874

Kendall

1

Observation
Tower

Perrine

Biscayne
Bay

Ckekika

997

Boca Chita Key

Sands Key

BISCAYNE
NATIONAL
PARK

Elliott Key

Shark River Slough

Leisure City

Pa-hay-okee
Overlook

Homestead

9336

Main
Visitor Center

Florida City

Old Rhodes Key

Pinelands

Long Pine
Key Trail

Long
Pine
Key

Royal Palm
Visitor Center

Card
Sound

JOHN
PENNEKAMP
CORAL REEF
STATE PARK

Daniel Beard
Center

Hidden Lake
Environmental
Education Center

Mahogany
Hammock

1

aurotis
Pond

Nine Mile Pond
Canoe Trail

Taylor Slough

Barnes
Sound

Noble Hammock
Canoe Trail

West Lake
Canoe Trail

Key
Largo

Madeira
Bay

Blackwater
Sound

Hawk Channel

Black
Betsy
Keys

Key Largo

Florida Bay

Plantation

Plantation Key

1

Upper Matecumbe Key

Islamorada

ATLANTIC
OCEAN

Lower
Matecumbe
Key

Indian Key
Channel

trees. Inside the visitors center, displays illustrate the park's different ecosystems, and you can buy books, film, insect repellent, postcards, and sundries. Royal Palm is 4 mi west of the main entrance. | Hwy. 9336 | 305/242–7700 | Visitors center free, park admission $10 per vehicle | Daily 8–4:15.

★ **Shark Valley Visitor Center.** On U.S. 41 (the Tamiami Trail) at the park's northern extreme, this center has exhibits explaining the sawgrass marshes that make up this region. From the center, you can explore a 15-mi trail into the marshes or take a two-hour tram ride. At the halfway point, a concrete observation tower spirals upwards 50 ft., from which you'll be able to see that for miles around there's nothing but a river of grass. Bird watching is a popular pursuit out here, and you'll probably see alligators if you walk the trail. The visitors center is 24 mi west of Florida's Turnpike. | U.S. 41 (Tamiami Trail) | 305/242–7700 | Visitors center free, park admission $10 per vehicle | Daily 8:30–5:15.

Shark Valley Tram Tour. The Shark Valley area is a wildlife-rich freshwater ecosystem of sawgrass marsh and hammocks. The two-hr-long, 15-mi tram ride into the marsh is one of the best ways to see the Everglades' alligators and gives an overview of what the park is all about. If you want to explore on your own, you can hike the trail and walk or bike portions of the tram road. Get the tram at the Shark Valley Visitor Center. | U.S. 41 (Tamiami Trail) | 305/221–8455 | Tour $10, park admission $10 per vehicle | Dec.–Apr., daily 9–4; May–Nov, daily 9:30–3.

West Lake. Seven miles north of the Flamingo Visitor Center, which itself is 31 mi southwest of the main entrance to the park, West Lake consists of a series of large, open bodies of water connected by narrow, mangrove-edged creeks filled with alligators. A ½-mi boardwalk traverses a forest of mangroves and buttonwood trees leading to the Lake's edge. | 305/242–7700 | Lake free, park admission $10 per vehicle | Daily.

The Wilderness Waterway. Along this 99-mi waterway, numbered markers guide you between numerous islands filled with mangrove forests. Dolphins and manatees may accompany you part of the way on this seven-hour journey (by motor boat) or nine-day adventure (by canoe). Large craft (18 feet or longer) should not attempt this trip as there are many narrow channels with overhanging vegetation. You need a backcountry permit to camp, which you obtain at the Gulf Coast Visitor Center in Everglades City; nautical maps are a must. | Gulf Coast Visitor Center, Hwy. 29, Everglades City | 941/695–2591 | Waterway free, park admission $10 per vehicle | Daily.

SIGHTSEEING TOURS/TOUR COMPANIES

Everglades Airboat Tours. Three times daily, tours venture about 40 mi into the Everglades to view the native birds, fish, and alligators. The boats hold up to 12 people, and the sunset cruise offers a few nocturnal animal sightings. Bring bug spray. Reservations are required; once you make a reservation, you'll be given directions to the office. | Coopertown | 305/852–5339 or 305/221–9888 | $43 per person, $275 for a half-day trip of up to 5 people | Tours daily at 11, 2, and sunset, by reservation only.

Flamingo Lodge, Marina, and Outpost Resort Boat Tours. Nature abounds and so do the boat tours. A variety of boats carry 6 to 95 people on tours that last from 90 minutes to 4 hours around the Florida Bay or through the back country to see the mangrove ecosystem. The two-hour trip takes you through the swampy Everglades to see American crocodiles or alligators as well as the indigenous plant life such as the unique airplants (bromeliads). Reservations are strongly recommended. | 1 Flamingo Lodge Hwy. (Hwy. 9336), Flamingo | 941/695–3101, ext. 286 or 180 | fax 941/695–3921 | www.flamingolodge.com | Tours $10–$39, park admission $10 per vehicle | Tours daily (call for actual schedule).

CALENDAR OF EVENTS

DEC.–JAN.: *Miccosukee Indian Arts Festival.* This Miccosukee Indian festival at the Miccosukee Indian Village supplements the regular schedule of alligator wrestling and airboat rides. | 305/223–8380.

Dining

Coopertown Restaurant. American. This restaurant serves Old Florida–style cuisine centering around fried frog's legs and alligator tails. The less adventurous can try fried chicken or catfish or steak. You'll see an array of alligator paraphernalia, including skulls, stuffed heads, and a variety of catchy T-shirts and hats decorating the room. | 22700 S.W. 8th St. (Tamiami Trail), Miami | 305/226–6048 | fax 305/229–1260 | $10–$20 | AE, MC, V.

Flamingo Restaurant. American. Large picture windows look out onto Florida Bay and the abundance of seabirds as you dine on typical "Floribbean" cuisine at the only restaurant inside Everglades National Park. Coconut-fried shrimp is served with an orange marmalade–horseradish sauce, and a popular chicken dish is served topped with sautéed mushrooms, bacon, and melted Monterrey Jack. If you get lucky fishing, the restaurant will also clean and prepare your fish for your dinner. In summer, the Buttonwood Patio Café serves pizzas and salads in a more casual setting on a screened-in patio. | Flamingo Lodge, 1 Flamingo Lodge Hwy. | 941/695–3101 | fax 941/695–3921 | Closed May–Oct. | $12–$18 | AE, D, DC, MC, V.

Joanie's Blue Crab Café. Seafood. This 1950s-style swamp café has a country store to boot. You can't help but feel like you're in a southern movie while eating some local jumbo steamed blue crabs or the homestyle crab cakes. The screened-in patio-bar is a good place to unwind and decide how many pounds of crab you will be able to eat. It's right across the street from the Ochopee post office. | 39395 U.S. 41 (Tamiami Trail), Ochopee | 941/695–2682 | $7–$10 | AE, D, MC, V.

Miccosukee Restaurant. Native American. Murals of powwows and women gathered around the fire cooking help put you in the mood for some traditional Indian fry bread or deep-fried catfish and frog's legs. Occasionally buffets are served on weekend mornings, covering the gamut of traditional eggs and meats. The restaurant is on the Miccosukee Reservation, 25 mi west of Florida's Turnpike and 18 mi west of Krome Avenue. | U.S. 41 (Tamiami Trail) | 305/223–8380 | No dinner | $8–$15 | MC, V.

Pit Bar-B-Q. Barbecue. If you accidentally drive past this popular spot, you might want to make a U-turn and head right back for the ribs—they smell that good. Don't give into temptation because the fine for such an act is $85, but do make the legal turn so you can try some barbecued chicken or ribs with a tangy sauce. The old wooden structure has screened-in walls and ceiling fans. | 16400 S.W. 8th St. (Tamiami Trail) | 305/226–2272 | $8–$10 | AE, D, MC, V.

Lodging

Flamingo Lodge. The only home-away-from-home within Everglades National Park, this simple motel has the backdrop of grumbling alligators, raccoons, and a variety of chirping birds. The cottages are in a wooded area and can accommodate up to six guests. Florida Bay is nearby, but most rooms do not look out onto it. Reservations are mandatory in the winter. Restaurant (seasonal), bar, complimentary Continental breakfast (May–Oct.). Some kitchenettes, some refrigerators. No TV in some rooms. Pool. Gift shop. Laundry facilities. Some pets allowed. | 1 Flamingo Lodge Hwy. | 941/695–3101 or 800/600–3813 | fax 941/695–3921 | www.flamingolodge.com | 102 rooms, 24 cottages | $65–$95 lodge room, $115–$135 cottage | AE, D, DC, MC, V.

Miccosukee Resort and Convention Center. Providing one of the only points of interest besides the Everglades park itself is this huge complex bringing nightlife and luxury to a formerly desolate area of swampland. Rooms are large and modern, with little Indian touches in the decorations; some family suites are available. There are a full-service concierge, a shuttle to the mall, live entertainment in a 2,000-seat arena that has seen the likes of such popular performers as Santana and Bill Cosby, and a smoky 24-hour casino. 3 Restaurants. In-room data ports, in-room safes, minibars, some in-room hot tubs. Cable TV. Indoor pool and hot tub. Spa, sauna. Gym. Children's programs (ages 4 to 12). Laundry service. Business services, airport shuttle. | 500 S.W. 177 Ave. | 305/925–2555 or 877/242–6464 | fax 305/925–2556 | www.miccosukee.com | 302 rooms | $110–$129 | AE, D, DC, MC, V.

EVERGLADES
NATIONAL PARK

INTRO
ATTRACTIONS
DINING
LODGING

FLAGLER BEACH

MAP 3, J3

(Nearby towns also listed: Daytona Beach, Ormond Beach, Palatka, St. Augustine, St. Augustine Beach)

Midway between St. Augustine and Daytona Beach on Florida's northern Atlantic coast, this affluent Palm Coast town is well known for its unspoiled beaches. The town (pop. 4,000) is named for Henry Flagler, the Florida entrepreneur and railway magnate who ran the first railroad down the eastern shore of the state. Fishing is popular here; more than three dozen varieties of fish have been caught from the town's 800-ft pier. There are a number of quality tennis resorts, and Jack Nicklaus– and Arnold Palmer–designed golf courses.

Information: **Flagler Beach Chamber of Commerce** | 400C Ocean Shore Blvd., Flagler Beach, 32136 | 904/439–0995 | www.flaglercounty.com/fbcc.

Attractions

Flagler Pier. This historic 840-ft pier is open to the public year-round. It features a restaurant, a bait and tackle shop, and one of the area's most pristine beaches. | 123 Test St. | 319/555–1212 | Free | Daily until midnight.

Gamble Rogers Memorial State Recreation Area at Flagler Beach. This 144-acre park 12 mi north of town has 34 campsites on dunes overlooking the beach. On the west side of the park is a picnic area, a boat ramp and a nature trail. | 3100 Rte. A1A | 904/517–2086 | www.dep.state.fl.us/parks | $2 for beach, $3.25 per vehicle for nature trail | Daily 8–sunset.

Dining

Topaz Café & Porch. Contemporary. This charming seaside restaurant in the Topaz Hotel features a menu that utilizes fresh local seafood, quality meats, poultry, and vegetables for an ever-changing menu. Try Florida Keys lobster and conch cakes, or phyllo, feta, and spinach–stuffed roast chicken. Eat inside or out on the Victorian porch overlooking the ocean. | 1224 S. Oceanshore Blvd. | 904/439–3275 or 800/555–4735 | fax 904/439–1895 | Reservations essential | No lunch. Closed Sun.–Mon. | MC, V.

Lodging

Palm Coast Golf Resort. This 700-acre resort 18 mi south of St. Augustine caters primarily to golf and tennis enthusiasts. There are also 8 mi of biking and walking trails. The four three-story buildings all face the Intracoastal Waterway or the resort's marina. Restaurant, bar, room service. In-room data ports, some minibars, some refrigerators. Cable TV. 2 pools. Hot tub. 4 driving ranges, 4 golf courses, 4 putting greens, 18 tennis courts. Hiking. Beach, dock, boating, fishing, bicycles. Video games, playground. Laundry facilities. Business services. | 300 Clubhouse Dr., Palm Coast | 904/445–3000 or 800/654–6538 | fax 904/445–9685 | www.palmcoastresort.com | 154 rooms | $119–$300 | AE, D, DC, MC, V.

Whale Watch Motel. This small, quiet motel has only ten rooms spread over four low-rise buildings on a full acre of oceanfront. All rooms have ocean views. In winter you can even see whales. Cottage rooms have full kitchens and separate bedrooms. Some kitchenettes, some microwaves, some refrigerators. Cable TV. Pool. Beach, boating, fishing. Laundry facilities. | 2448 South A1A | 904/439–2545 or 877/635–5535 | www.whalewatchmotel.com | 10 rooms | $40–$65 | D, MC, V.

FLORIDA CITY

(Nearby towns also listed: Everglades National Park, Homestead, Key Largo)

This agricultural town of about 9,000 is surrounded by hundreds of acres of farmland west of Krome Avenue in Greater Miami. A huge farmer's market packs vegetables to be shipped around the country. You'll pass through Florida City if you take the Florida Turnpike to its southern end or if you are continuing down U.S. 1 towards the Keys. South of Florida City begins the miles of mangroves and water; as the last outpost of civilization, this stretch of U.S. 1 is lined with bars, dive shops, and restaurants.

Information: Greater Homestead/Florida City Chamber of Commerce | 43 N. Krome Ave., Homestead, 33030 | 305/247–2332 or 888/352–4891 | www.chamberinaction.com.

Attractions

Robert Is Here. People come to this fruit stand from miles around to taste the enormously popular fresh-fruit milkshakes, over 100 flavors of jams and jellies, and stands of fresh vegetables and fruits, including such tropical delights as soursop, carambola, monstera, and tamarind. Robert, the owner, has been selling at this site, which opened in 1960, since he was six. | 19200 Palm Dr. | 305/246–1592 | www.robertishere.com | Free | Daily 8–7.

ON THE CALENDAR

JAN.: *Super Chili Bowl Cook-Off.* Taste over 30 kinds of chili at this cooking contest held each January inside Prime Outlets mall courtyard. | 305/247–2332 or 888/352–4891.

Dining

Farmers Market Restaurant. Seafood. These seafood specialists are located in the farmers market, so they have great vegetable selections as well. In fact, the family-run restaurant opens at 5:30 AM, serving up jumbo eggs, pancakes, and omelettes with home fries or grits. At night try sirloin steaks, pork chops, the catch of the day, and conch. | 935 N. Krome Ave. | 305/242–0008 | $7–$13 | Breakfast also available | No credit cards.

Mutineer Restaurant. Seafood. This town classic (built in 1980) includes an indoor-outdoor fish and duck pond. The lobster shrimp Provençal dish comes with four 8-oz Florida lobster tails sautéed in garlic and a creamy white seafood sauce with linguine. | 11 S.E. 1st Ave. (U.S. 1 and Palm Dr.) | 305/245–3377 | $12–$27 | AE, D, DC, MC, V.

Richard Accursio's Capri Restaurant. Seafood. Opened in 1958, this is one of the oldest family-run restaurants in Miami-Dade County. Try the mussels or yellowtail snapper *française.* The slightly more formal King Richard Room within the restaurant has a dark-wood ceiling and heavy wooden furniture. | 935 N. Krome Ave. | 305/247–1544 | Closed Sun. | $6–$22 | AE, MC, V.

Lodging

Comfort Inn. This beige, two-story facility on the corner of U.S. 1 was renovated after Hurricane Andrew in 1992. The hotel has one- and two-bedroom suites, all with mini-refrigerators and microwaves. Complimentary Continental breakfast. In-room safes, microwaves, refrigerators. Cable TV. Pool. Laundry facilities. | 333 S.E. 1st Ave. | 248–4009 or 888/352–2489 | fax 305/248–7935 | www.comfortinnfloridacity.com | 83 rooms | $50–$99 | AE, D, DC, MC, V.

Everglades Motel. This simple, single-story motel is 2 mi south of Homestead; it's decorated with bright colors. Many restaurants are within walking distance. Cable TV. Outdoor pool. Laundry facilities. Pets allowed (fee). | 605 S. Krome Ave., Florida City | 305/247–4117 | 14 rooms | $32–$37 | AE, D, DC, MC, V.

Gateway to the Keys. This modern two- and three-story motel across the street from outlet stores and restaurants, was built in 1994. The tidy courtyard area has a pool and spa.

It's 1 mi south of Homestead, and the Keys are 20 mi away. Complimentary Continental breakfast. In-room data ports, some microwaves, some refrigerators. Cable TV. Pool. Outdoor hot tub. Laundry facilities, laundry service. Business services. Pets allowed (fee). No smoking. | 411 S. Krome Ave. | 305/246–5100 or 800/528–1234 | fax 305/242–0056 | www.bestwestern.com | 74 rooms, 40 suites | $89–$99 room, $94–$114 suite | AE, D, DC, MC, V.

Hampton Inn. If you can't make it all the way to the Keys, try this two-story motel on the corner of U.S. 1, which was built in 1990. Complimentary Continental breakfast. In-room data ports. Cable TV. Outdoor pool. Pets allowed. | 124 E. Palm Dr. | 305/247–8833 or 800/426–7866 | fax 305/247–6456 | www.hampton-inn.com | 123 rooms | $110 | AE, D, DC, MC, V.

FORT LAUDERDALE

MAP 3, L9

(Nearby towns also listed: Boca Raton, Dania Beach, Davie, Deerfield Beach, Hollywood, Lauderdale-by-the-Sea, Pompano Beach)

Up until a few years ago, if you were looking for a raucous time in Florida, this Broward County city of 150,000, about an hour north of Miami, was the place to go. During Spring Break, Fort Lauderdale was ground zero for the collegiate set, who came to party along the gorgeous 7-mi stretch of beach. It's a completely different story today. Upscale shops and restaurants now line the beachfront, where there were once T-shirt shops and fast food stands. Downtown Fort Lauderdale has been developed as more than a place for office-workers to trudge in and dash out. The tourists are now much more likely to be affluent families with children than partying students. If you ask the folks in Fort Lauderdale, no one seems to mind the change.

The first known white settler in the area, Charles Lewis, established a plantation along the New River in 1793, but it was the fort built by Major William Lauderdale at the river's mouth in 1838 that gave the town its name. Even after the Seminole wars, Fort Lauderdale was a sleepy place. Things began looking up in 1896 when the Florida East Coast Railroad reached the New River, and Fort Lauderdale was finally incorporated in 1911, with only 175 residents. But growth was still sluggish between the World Wars as a result of devastating hurricanes and the Great Depression.

The city's economic base has been largely rooted in tourism during the second half of the 20th century. Its fastest growth spurt came between the 1960s and 1980s, when Fort Lauderdale was popular as a spring break spot for vacationing college students. Although vacationers are still important to the economy, it has also become more diverse since the late 1980s due to the establishment of more manufacturing and international businesses in or near Las Olas Boulevard and the downtown area.

The town has been nicknamed the Venice of America for its 260-mi honeycomb of navigable waterways. It's almost as easy to get around here by boat as by car, and water taxis are popular with sightseers and bar-hoppers alike. A sizeable percentage of locals are boat owners. The Riverwalk, a pedestrian walkway bordering the New River, is charmed with restaurants, shops, and movie theaters. Tennis courts and golf courses abound, and jogging paths ribbon the many city parks. Stylish Las Olas Boulevard, the Galleria Mall, and the Coral Ridge Mall draw shoppers.

Information: Greater Fort Lauderdale Convention and Visitors Bureau | 1850 Eller Dr., Fort Lauderdale, 33316 | 954/765–4466 or 800/227–8669 | fax 954/765–4467 | www.co.broward.fl.us.

Attractions

Big Cypress Seminole Reservation. Although it's an hour's drive from Fort Lauderdale's tranquil beaches, this reservation is worth the trip for two very different attractions: swamp buggy tours and the Ah-Tha-Thi-Ki Museum of Seminole culture, which includes a re-creation of a Seminole village. There's a large citrus orchard and a campground on the reservation. | I–75, exit 14 | www.seminoletribe.com.

Ah-Tha-Thi-Ki Museum. In additional to viewing exhibits of artifacts from tribal history, some of them from the Smithsonian Institute, you can take a guided tour through a re-created Seminole reservation. There are also nature trails on the 60-acre property. The museum is 17 mi north of I–75 (exit 14). | Snake Rd. | 863/902–1113 | www.seminoletribe.com/museum | $6 | Tues.–Sun. 9–5.

Billie Swamp Safari. This wildlife center offers up information about the Everglades and its animal and bird inhabitants. You can take an airboat or swamp buggy tour into the wetlands and hammocks to see the wildlife up close. There are also a boardwalk nature trail and alligator and snake shows. The safari is 19 mi north of I–75 (exit 14). | Snake Rd. | 863/983–6101 or 800/949–6101 | fax 863/983–9396 | www.seminoletribe.com/safari | Airboat tours $10, swamp buggy tours $20–$25, shows $8, guided nature walk $20 | Daily 9:30–4:30.

Bonnet House This 35-acre oasis in the heart of the beach area was the winter residence of Frederic and Evelyn Bartlett, artists whose personal touches are evident throughout. The concrete mansion dates from the 1920s, and the natural gardens are filled mostly with orchids. | 900 N. Birch Rd. | 954/563–5393 | $9 | Wed.–Fri. 10–1:30, weekends 12–2:30.

Broward Center for the Performing Arts. The $55 million waterfront centerpiece of Fort Lauderdale's cultural arts district contains the 2,700-seat Au-Rene Theater and the 590-seat Amaturo Theater. Both present a variety of performing arts events, including Broadway musicals and pop and classical concerts. | 201 S.W. Fifth Ave. | 954/462–0222 | Ticket prices vary | Call for schedule.

Broward County Main Library. The library's stepped-glass windows and sturdy terraces designed by Marcel Breuer were completed in 1984, adding to the abundance of modern buildings in downtown Fort Lauderdale. Inside, you'll find a community computer lab with over a dozen computers and a 300-seat auditorium that hosts lectures and local theater productions, not to mention the books. | 100 S. Andrews Ave. | 954/357–7444 or 954/357–7384 for a guided tour | fax 954/357–7399 | www.broward.org/library | Free | Mon.–Thurs. 9–9, Fri.–Sat. 10–5, Sun. noon–5:30.

Everglades Holiday Park. This 30-acre park, 20 mi southwest of downtown Fort Lauderdale, provides a good overview of the Everglades. You can take an airboat tour, observe an 18th-century-style Native American village, and watch an alligator-wrestling show. A campground with RV hookups is on site. | 21940 Griffin Rd. | 954/434–8111 | Park free, airboat tour $14.50 | Daily; airboat tours 9–5 every 20 min.

Fort Lauderdale Beach. This 7-mi strip, which runs from 17th Street to Sunrise Boulevard, is famous from the *Where the Boys Are* era of spring break madness that is now a Fort Lauderdale memory. A $26 million renovation has given the beach new style with its wide brick walkways, lush plantings, and a "wave wall," a concrete barrier illuminated from within by neon lights. | Hwy. A1A | 954/761–5346 | ci.ftlaud.fl.us/aboutftlaud/see/water.htm | Free | Daily dawn to dusk.

Hall of Fame Aquatic Complex. This swimming center has two 50-m pools and a diving well, both open to the public, as well as a teaching pool, swimming flume (a small pool in which you swim but don't move because of the recirculating water), and a weight room. National and international swimming and diving meets are often held here, and the area's best swimmers often train here. | 954/468–1580 | $2 | Weekdays 8–4, 6–8, weekends 8–4.

International Swimming Hall of Fame. At this exhibition on the grounds of the Hall of Fame Aquatic Complex you see aquatic memorabilia such as Johnny Weissmuller's Olympic medals, Annette Kellerman's scandalous 1908 swimsuit (she was arrested for wearing it), and exhibits on Greg Louganis and Mark Spitz. The Hall of Fame's forerunner, the 1920s-era Casino Pool, was the first Olympic-size pool in Florida. | 1 Hall of Fame Dr. | 954/462–6536 | www.ishof.org | $3 | Weekdays 9–7, weekends 9–4.

Holiday Park. With 21 courts, 18 of them clay, this is Fort Lauderdale's largest public tennis facility. There are also baseball and softball diamonds, basketball courts, football and soccer fields, jogging trails, picnic pavilions, horseshoe pits, a playground, and racquetball, shuffleboard, and volleyball courts. | 730 N. Federal Hwy. | 954/761–5346 | ci.ftlaud.fl.us/aboutft-laud/see/parks.htm | Free; tennis $4 per hour | Daily sunrise–midnight; tennis 8 AM–9:15 PM.

Hugh Taylor Birch State Recreation Area. This 180-acre park contains several distinct native biological communities, including Broward County's last significant remnant of a tropical hardwood forest. You can rent canoes at the park entrance for short trips on a freshwater lagoon system that extends throughout the park. You can see wading birds, hawks, ducks, turtles, and other wildlife on one of two nature trails, and there are several shady picnic areas with playground equipment and barbecue grills. | 3901 E. Sunrise Blvd. | 954/564–4521 | $3 per vehicle | Daily.

Museum of Art Fort Lauderdale. The concrete, Edward Larrabee Barnes–designed building that houses this museum is Florida's largest art exhibition space; it opened in 1986. The permanent collection here is focused on 20th-century European and American art, and includes works by Picasso, Alexander Calder, Salvador Dalí, Robert Mapplethorpe, Andy Warhol, and Frank Stella. The museum sparked a revitalization of the downtown and nearby Riverwalk area. | 1 E. Las Olas Blvd. | 954/763–6464 | www.museumofart.org | $10 | Tues.–Sat. 10–5, Sun. 12–5.

Museum of Discovery and Science. You can discover more than 200 hands-on exhibits in this "playground for the mind" opposite Esplanade Park. There are seven themed areas (Florida EcoScapes, KidScience, Gizmo City, Space Base, Sound, Choose Health, and No Place Like

© Corbis

CARL HIAASEN, SOUTH FLORIDA'S OWN

Carl Hiaasen, a third-generation Floridian, grew up during the 1950s in Plantation Florida, then a rural suburb of Fort Lauderdale. As a boy, Hiaasen fought encroaching development by enlisting pals to help him saw down FOR SALE signs, and damming runoff canals.

Hiaasen obviously loves South Florida; he just hates what's happening to it (overdevelopment, crime, rampant tourism, and drugs).

Hiaasen will tell you there are certain advantages to working as a journalist in South Florida: "Being a journalist down here is like being a kid in a candy store." "Each day," he says, "is something colorful and wild and bizarre. I tell people it's Fellini, Peckinpah and Monty Python all rolled into one."

His contemporaries, John D. MacDonald, Edna Buchanan, and other Sunshine State mystery writers, have painted the state in the noir shades of a tarnished paradise. Hiaasen instead accentuates the vivid weirdness of present-day Florida as well as the weirdos who control and populate it. "That's the great thing about this place," he has said, "I can't keep up with the material."

His savagely funny novels are always set in Florida. Protecting Florida's environment (usually the job of the leading character), or at least standing off further damage to the state's eroding ethics and natural beauty are the recurring themes in Hiaasen's hilarious crime novels, which are generally ripe with bizzaro characters like Maximum Bob.

Built upon each novel's neat premise are mocking plots firmly established in the region, involving everything from the Florida Lottery, dognapping ecoterrorists, hurricane insurance, Disneyworld, sugar lobbyists, or bass fishing tournaments and alligators. Adding insane story gyrations and deluded influences, his end effect is a defective, yet extremely funny, strange world.

For example, his novel, *Tourist Season,* starts with a crazed newspaper columnist feeding a senior citizen snowbird to a crocodile. You get the idea.

Home) plus a hall devoted to changing exhibitions. Still other exhibits are outdoors on the esplanade. The museum's 3-D IMAX theater screens adventure films on a five-story-high screen. | 401 S.W. 2nd St. | 954/467–6637 | www.mods.org | $6; IMAX film $9 | Mon.–Sat. 10–5, Sun. noon–6.

Old Fort Lauderdale Museum of History. The historical society of Fort Lauderdale has acquired the King-Cromartie House, the New River Inn, and the Philemon Bryan House and restored them along with their new historical complex called Old Fort Lauderdale to create an interesting look at the city's history and several late 18th- and early 19th-century living quarters. The museum itself presents a look at the area from Seminole times to the present. | 231 S.W. 2nd Ave. | 954/463–4431 | fax 954/523–6228 | www.oldfortlauderdale.org | $5 | Tues.–Fri. 12–5, Sat. 10–5, Sun. 12–5.

Riverwalk Arts and Entertainment District. A wandering paved promenade along the north bank of the New River leads you along an exciting tour of shops, art and science museums, with ivy-hugged benches to relax on. It is the site of many small festivals and a farmer's markets on weekend mornings, concerts at night, and a jazz brunch on the first Sunday of every month. The district stretches from S.W. 7th Avenue to U.S. 1, between Broward Blvd. and the New River. | S.W. 2nd St. | 954/468–1541 | www.goriverwalk.com.

Sailboat Bend. For a nice walk, aside from the Riverwalk or the beach, there is the tropical neighborhood of Sailboat Bend. You can peek between willow and palm trees and old wood houses to see ivy-covered docks and small sailboats. Concentrated mostly in the area between Las Olas and the river, the houses here are reminiscent of Old Town of Key West or historical Coconut Grove in Miami. No shops or services are here, but you will enjoy the visuals.

Sawgrass Mills Mall. The alligator shape of the mall is only one of the lures making Sawgrass Mills the second-most visited tourist spot after Walt Disney World in Florida. You can plunge into shopping (Loehman's, Ann Taylor, Saks Fifth Avenue, Kenneth Cole, not to mention a few outlet stores and plenty of small, trendy spots). When you get tired, you can dine at the Hard Rock Café, Wolfgang Puck's restaurant, or any of a hundred restaurants. | 12801 W. Sunrise Blvd., at Flamingo Rd., Sunrise | 954/846–2300 or 800/FL–MILLS | fax 954/846–2312 | www.sawgrassmillsmall.com.

Sawgrass Recreation Park. For a swamp adventure extraordinaire you can jump into the thick of it by taking an airboat ride or renting a fishing boat. On solid ground, there is an alligator and reptile exhibit, a birds of prey demonstration, and a re-created 18th-century Seminole Indian village. If you donate a few dollars, you can get your picture taken with a baby alligator or possibly the park's panther. | U.S. 27, north of I–595 | 954/426–2474 or 800/457–0788 | fax 954/389–9425 | www.evergladestours.com | Park admission and airboat ride $15, boat rental $44, boat with fishing guide $175 for a half-day or $225 for a full day | Daily 7 AM–5 PM.

Snyder Park. This 93-acre park, 4 mi south of downtown Fort Lauderdale, has two spring-fed lakes in which you can swim, fish, or row a boat. You can also hike and play volleyball, basketball, or softball. | 3299 S.W. 4th Ave. | 954/468–1585 | www.ci.ftlaud.fl.us/cityparks/snyder/entrance.htm | Weekdays $1.50, weekends $2 | Weekdays 9–5, weekends 9–6.

Stranahan House. The birthplace of the city of Fort Lauderdale was here in the home of the entrepreneurial pioneer James Stranahan. He and his wife Ivy, who was the first school teacher in the area, befriended the Seminole Indians and began a trading post that also served as a post office and bank. In 2001, the museum celebrates its centennial with additional lectures, activities, and parties, as well as the regular tours of the house. | 335 S.E. 6th Ave. | 954/524–4736 | fax 954/525–2838 | www.stranahan.com | $5 | Wed.–Sat. 10–3, Sun. 1–3; guided tours hourly.

SIGHTSEEING TOURS/TOUR COMPANIES

Jungle Queen **Cruises.** On this sightseeing cruise up the New River from the Bahia Mar Yacht Basin, you stop off at a small island to observe monkeys, rare birds, and alligator wrestling. The four-hour dinner cruise, which includes all-you-can-eat barbecue ribs and shrimp, a variety show, and a sing-along, is a Fort Lauderdale classic. | 801 Seabreeze Blvd. | 954/462–5596 | Regular cruise $11.50, dinner cruise $25.95 | Daily 10 and 2; dinner cruise 7 PM.

Dive Trips. Although the main reefs are between 200 and 300 yards offshore, most charters sail about 20 or 30 minutes to find a spot. Among the most popular of the county's 80 dive sites is the 2-mi-wide, 2⅓-mi-long Fort Lauderdale Reef, the result of Florida's most successful artificial reef-building program. More than a dozen houseboats, ships, and oil platforms were sunk in depths from 10 to 150 ft. to provide a habitat for fish and other marine life. The most famous sunken ship is the 200-ft German freighter *Mercedes,* which was blown onto Palm Beach socialite Mollie Wilmot's pool terrace during a violent 1984 storm. The ship now rests a mile off Fort Lauderdale Beach. A number of dive shops offer regularly scheduled dives.

Lauderdale Diver. This outfitter arranges dive charters throughout the region. Dive trips typically last four hours. | 1334 S.E. 17th St. Causeway | 954/467–2822 | $45 for boat trip; $75 for boat package trip, which includes gear and two-tank dive | Mon.–Sat. 9–6, Sun. 10–3.

Pro Dive. This company operates a 60-ft boat that departs from the yacht basin at Radisson Bahia Mar Resort for four-hour dive trips off Fort Lauderdale Beach. Snorkeling trips are also available. | 5515 Seabreeze Blvd. | 954/761–3413 | Prices begin at $45; call for information | Dive trips depart Mon.–Sat at 1 PM and Sun. at 9 AM.

ON THE CALENDAR

FEB.–APR.: *Spring Training.* The Baltimore Orioles now train in Fort Lauderdale Stadium after five seasons in the Sarasota/St. Petersburg area. | 954/776–1921.

MAR.: *Las Olas Art Festival.* The Fort Lauderdale Museum of Art sponsors this Las Olas Boulevard event, one of South Florida's more popular outdoor art shows. The setting is Bubier Park, along the city's revitalized Riverwalk area, beside the New River. | 954/525–5500.

APR.: *Fort Lauderdale Seafood Festival.* More than 50 top local chefs offer samplings from their menus on Las Olas Boulevard in Bubier Park. Art displays, music, and children's activities round out the event. | 954/463–4431.

MAY: *Air and Sea Show.* South Florida's largest outdoor event draws 3 million spectators to its beaches, between Las Olas and Sunrise boulevards, to see aeronautic acts such as the Navy's Blue Angels and the U.S. Air Force Thunderbirds. The event usually takes place on the first weekend in May. | 954/467–3555 or 954/527–5600.

NOV.: *Promenade in the Park.* Numerous stages are built in Holiday Park for this popular event, held near Veteran's Day each year. Everything from circus acts to dance revues and musical performers fill the stages. There are also food vendors, antiques, jewelry artists, fine artists, and carnival rides. | 954/525–5500.

OCT.: *Fort Lauderdale International Boat Show.* The yachting capital's boat show is now one of the largest in the world. You'll see everything from a $1,200 inflatable to a 165-ft yacht with a price tag of $27 million. The five-day event at the Broward Convention Center begins in late October. | 954/764–7642.

OCT.–NOV.: *International Film Festival.* More than 100 independent films are screened at local theaters over two-plus weeks of this event, and there are seminars and galas galore. | 954/563–0500.

DEC.: *Winterfest.* Thousands of spectators line the Intracoastal Waterway to view the premier South Florida holiday boat parade. A hundred festively decorated boats cruise from Port Everglades to Lake Santa Barbara. | 954/767–0686.

Dining

Blue Moon Fish Company. Seafood. Both the view and the food will have you in awe. Most tables are in sight of the Intracoastal Waterway; the macadamia-crusted sea bass doused in red pepper butter will surely inspire your evening. Another favorite is the shellfish pan roast, a variety of lobster and shellfish cooked in spicey tarragon brandy cream sauce. | 4405 Tradewinds Ave. | 954/267–9888 | fax 954/267–9006 | $18–$34 | AE, MC, V.

Burt and Jack's. Steak. Heavy mission doors open to reveal a two-story, hacienda-style gallery with views of both Port Everglades and John U. Lloyd Beach State Recreation Area. Before your food is cooked, the waitstaff spreads the raw ingredients in front of you. Prime steaks, chops, and Maine lobster are the specialties. | Berth 23, Port Everglades | 954/522–5225 or 954/522–2878 | Jacket required | No lunch | $16–$37 | AE, D, DC, MC, V.

By Word of Mouth. Contemporary. Linen tablecloths and subdued lighting set the stage for this restaurant's gourmet fare, which might include Long Island barbecued duck in an apricot sauce, and the osso buco. The place is also known for a vegetarian pad Thai appetizer made with mascarpone cheese, basil pesto, and sundried tomatoes. The menu, however, changes daily. | 3200 N.E. 12th Ave. | 954/564–3663 | Closed Sun.–Mon. No dinner Tues. | $20–$37 | AE, D, DC, MC, V.

Canyon. Southwestern. The small, adobe-style dining room here has a few modern touches, including the light fixtures. Begin with the restaurant's famous prickly pear margarita or a choice from the extensive wine list. The menu sparkles with imaginative entrées such as ostrich skewers, smoked salmon tostadas, and Brie and wild-mushroom quesadillas. | 1818 E. Sunrise Blvd. | 954/765–1950 | No lunch | $16–$25 | AE, D, DC, MC, V.

The Caves. American. You get your very own cave, softened by pillows and mats, at this unique eatery, while the waitstaff serves you in animal-print garb. The menu's options include steaks, chops, and selections of fresh seafood. If you get the Maine lobster, you can eat with your fingers and feel like a cave-person, too. | 2205 N. Federal Hwy. | 954/561–4622 | No lunch | $11–$24 | AE, D, MC, V.

Charley's Crab. Seafood. At this local favorite, you eat outdoors on a covered patio overlooking the Intracoastal Waterway or inside among the ornate lamps and seascape paintings. The macadamia-crusted dolphin (mahimahi) and citrus-rum glazed grouper are two specialties that augment the full range of seafood options, including crab legs and lobster. | 3000 N.E. 32nd Ave. | 954/561–4800 | $20–$28 | AE, D, DC, MC, V.

Eduardo De San Angel. Mexican. You won't find burritos or tacos on the menu here, only classic dishes served in a Mexican style. Typical of the upscale fare are the beef tenderloin tips sautéed with portobello mushrooms and onions with a chipotle chili sauce, and the red snapper roasted with toasted almonds with a cilantro and garlic pesto. Original art and subdued lighting make this a good choice for a romantic evening. | 2822 E. Commercial Blvd. | 954/772–4731 | Closed Sun. No lunch Sat. | $19–$27 | AE, DC, MC, V.

Evangeline. Cajun/Creole. You can watch the ships drift past at this restaurant on the Intracoastal Waterway. The interior achieves its particular Acadian charm through the paneled wainscoting and plank floors. Among the many items on the menu are smoked rabbit gumbo, sautéed alligator in a meunière sauce topped with flash-fried oysters, jambalaya (clams, mussels, shrimp, and chicken andouille in a Creole sauce), and crawfish Caesar salad. Jazz nightly. | 211 S. Atlantic Blvd. | 954/522–7001 | $13–$19 | AE, D, MC, V.

Floridian. American. This place withstands time by serving hearty breakfasts and good old American lunches and dinners for reasonable prices. Stuffed omelettes, juicy hamburgers, grandma-style meatloaf and traditional sandwiches are fun and filling, and while you eat you get to gaze down Las Olas and watch the people pass by. There's a downhome-diner feel here, but with a definite gay flair. | 1410 E. Las Olas Blvd. | 954/463–4041 | $8–$15 | AE, D, DC, MC, V.

French Quarter. French. This elegant old Red Cross building from the 1920s is just off Las Olas and filled with antiques and plants. Traditional dishes such as bouillabaisse, crab cakes, and veal sweetbreads are all served with a fresh salad and a selection of homemade desserts ranging from chocolate mousse to crème brûlée. Entertainment Wed.–Sat. evenings. | 215 S.E. 8th Ave. | 954/463–8000 | fax 954/467–2308 | Closed Sun. No lunch Sat. | $18–$27 | AE, D, DC, MC, V.

Gibby's. Steak. Set among much greenery, this one-story brick and wood building has the appearance of an old Colonial mansion. The menu offers primarily steaks and chops, with some seafood selections. Especially popular are the rack of lamb and prime rib. | 2900 N.E. 12th Terr. | 954/565–2929 | No lunch | $15–$29 | AE, D, DC, MC, V.

Indigo. Pan-Asian. The more casual of the two restaurants at the Riverside Hotel, located along the New River in Fort Lauderdale's historic district, this eatery focuses on Southeast Asian cuisine and offers such dishes as *siap mepang gang* (coconut-grilled chicken) and Indonesian snapper baked on banana leaves topped with colo-colo and shallots. | 620 E. Las Olas Blvd. | 954/467–0045 | Breakfast also available | $9–$20 | AE, D, DC, MC, V.

La Coquille. French. Centered around a tropical garden with an Art Deco atmosphere, this restaurant is the perfect place to practice your French with the staff or chef-owner Jean Bert, who has operated the place since 1972. Time-proven favorites, including the foie gras appetizer and Maine lobster–stuffed ravioli, remain on the menu. There is always a special dessert soufflé or homemade *vacherin* (meringue) filled with vanilla ice cream with fresh raspberry coulis. | 1619 E. Sunrise Blvd. | 954/467–3030 | fax 954/565–9590 | Closed Mon. No lunch | $16–$22 | AE, MC, V.

La Reserve. French. Arrive by boat or by car at this romantic restaurant on the Intracoastal Waterway. Tables in the candlelit dining room are ornamented with flowers and overlook the water. The menu features fresh Florida fish as well as favorites such as beef tenderloin with a Beaujolais sauce and shallots. The lobster Cabourg is another favorite, served with a white wine, mushroom, and cognac sauce. | 3115 N.E. 32nd Ave. | 954/563–6644 | No lunch | $17–$32 | AE, D, DC, MC, V.

La Travernetta. Italian. Only the finest ingredients are used by the owner/chef at this charming bistro, where the fountains, imported ceramics, and soft Italian music make you feel as if you are dining in Tuscany. Seafood dishes are given northern Italian touches. Try the swordfish Ischia, in a light white wine tomato sauce over a bed of fettucine, served with mussels and scallops. | 926 N.E. 20th Ave. | 954/463–2566 | Closed Sept. and Sun.–Mon. No lunch | $16–$23 | AE, D, DC, MC, V.

Louie Louie. Italian. The best seafood and pasta are served up in a variety of homemade red or white sauces in this bistro-like sidewalk café setting. The menu has such enticing choices as *zuppa di pesce* (clams, mussels, shrimp, lobster, and calamari served atop linguine and your choice of sauce); rigatoni alla vodka, or any of the daily specials of fresh fish or pasta. Desserts, including tiramisu and strawberry cheesecake, are all house-made. Next door is the new Louie's Oyster, for all your sushi or raw bar desires. | 1103 Las Olas Blvd. | 954/524–5200 | fax 954/524–5224 | $10–$35 | AE, D, DC, MC, V.

Mai-Kai. Asian. Decorated as a Polynesian village, this restaurant has tiki torches and wooden statues to spare. Cantonese, Polynesian, and American influences combine to flavor the steak and seafood dishes such as lobster Pango Pango (Maine lobster and sliced pork tenderloin sautéed in a mushroom-lobster sauce, served over linguine). Twice nightly performers give a Polynesian Revue full of dance and theatrics. | 3599 N. Federal Hwy. | 954/563–3272 | No lunch | $15–$30 | AE, D, DC, MC, V.

Mark's Las Olas. Contemporary. A star among his Florida contemporaries, Mark Militello has built up a loyal following with his mixture of Caribbean, Southwestern, and Mediterranean cuisines. The menu changes daily, but typical items include gulf shrimp, dolphin (mahimahi), yellowtail snapper, Florida lobster, and callaloo (a West Indian dish made with spinach). Chayote, ginger, jicama, and plantain appear literally across the menu. A patio allows you to dine outside on Las Olas. | 1032 E. Las Olas Blvd. | 954/463–1000 | No lunch weekends | $18–$36 | AE, D, MC, V.

Primavera. Italian. Hidden in a humdrum shopping mall, this Fort Lauderdale treasure welcomes you with elegant floral arrangements and strums from a harp (three nights a week) or chords from a piano (four nights a week). Among the menu's highlights are the fresh catch of the day, prepared in a light, Pinot Grigio sauce with dried tomato and fried leeks, the homemade spinach-ricotta ravioli, and the osso buco. For dessert, try the chocolate mousse–stuffed banana in phyllo dough, served warm. Pastas are homemade at this Northern Italian restaurant. | 830 E. Oakland Park Blvd. | 954/564–6363 | www.restaurantprimavera.com | Closed Mon. No lunch | $17–$35 | AE, D, DC, MC, V.

Rainbow Palace. Chinese. Marble floors and walls punctuated by bursts of flowers set an elegant tone for this restaurant, where traditional dishes are given innovative and surprising flair. Try sea bass in lemon sauce or lobster-filled dumplings. To add extra charm to this place, an artist was hired to decorate a smaller dining room in a jungle theme. Reservations are a necessity weekends. | 2787 E. Oakland Park Blvd. | 954/565–5652 | No lunch Sat.–Wed. | $19–$40 | AE, D, DC, MC, V.

Rustic Inn Crabhouse. Seafood. Originally the McDonald family ran this joint as a roadhouse saloon serving up fresh seafood and Loraine's famous linguine. Fifty years later, you still get served on newspaper-covered tables and are given wooden mallets to crack your golden garlic crabs, which are the house specialty. If the frog's legs or fried gator don't excite you, there are about 150 menu items to choose from. You have a choice of sitting inside or out on a heated dock. They also ship seafood and sauces; check out their website, www.rusticinn.com. | 4331 Angler Ave. | 954/584–1637 | $10–$19 | No lunch Sun. | AE, D, DC, MC, V.

Sea Watch. Seafood. Sextants, seascapes, and nautical maps set the stage for the range of seafood delicacies served here, including a baked stuffed fillet of sole, and gulf shrimp with garlic. The Sea Watch Medley is a favorite among returning patrons—it includes lobster, shrimp, and scallops, all broiled. The restaurant sits directly on the beach, with lovely views of the Atlantic. | 6002 N. Ocean Blvd. | 954/781–2200 | $13–$30 | AE, DC, MC, V.

Shirttail Charlie's. Seafood. Named for a vagabond Seminole Indian from the early 1900s who wore his shirttails out, the legend lives on slightly more upscale in the outdoor seating area or in the more formal upstairs dining room, both of which look out onto the New River. After chowing down on some hearty hamburgers or your choice of blackened, broiled, or grilled swordfish, you can hop on the Shirttail Charlie's Express, a complimentary half-hour after-dinner cruise. | 400 S.W. 3rd. Ave. | 954/463–3474 | fax 954/463–4441 | www.shirttailcharlies.com | Reservations required for dining room | Closed Mon. May–Nov. | $10–$25 | AE, MC, V.

Shula's on the Beach. American. For steak or seafood and a view of the ocean, come aboard Shula's in the Sheraton Yankee Trader Hotel. Steak Mary-Anne will fill you up with two small filet mignons marinated in cognac and served with grilled peppers. Shula's is also known for sea bass and other fresh fish, all accompanied by vegetables and savory sauces. | 321 N. Atlantic Blvd. | 954/355–4000 | fax 954/462–2342 | $16–$37 | AE, D, DC, MC, V.

Tropical Acres. Steak. Dine in one of the cozy booths for an intimate meal at the county's oldest steakhouse, which opened in 1949. Of course, prime rib, steaks, and lamb chops grace the menu, but seafood and pasta are other options. For dessert, don't miss the chocolate mint mousse cake. Entertainment Tues.–Sun. nights. | 2500 Griffin Rd. | 954/989–2500 | www.eatattropicalacres.com | No lunch | $11–$16 | AE, DC, MC, V.

Yesterday's. American. Sitting on the Intracoastal Waterway, this popular restaurant offers views from every table, especially those dockside. The menu includes steaks, burgers, pastas, and, of course, seafood. Try the snapper Pontchartrain, pan-seared American snapper topped with shrimp and crabmeat in a lemon-lime beurre blanc with toasted almonds. Sun. brunch. | 3001 E. Oakland Park Blvd. | 954/561–4400 | No lunch Apr.–Sept. | $13–$29 | AE, D, MC, V.

Lodging

Bahia Cabana Beach Resort. This resort occupies 2½ acres across a busy street from the beach. Rooms in the five buildings overlook a courtyard, where there are pools and a hot tub. Approximately half the units are standard hotel rooms; the other half are either studios or one-bedroom apartments with kitchenettes. Restaurant, bar (with entertainment), picnic area. In-room safes, some kitchenettes, refrigerators. Cable TV. 3 pools. Hot tub, sauna. Video games. Laundry facilities. Business services. | 3001 Harbor Dr. | 954/524–1555 or 800/323–2244 | fax 954/764–5951 | www.bahiacabanabeachresort.com | 116 rooms in 5 buildings | $120–$170 | AE, D, DC, MC, V.

Banyan Marina Apartments. This eclectic mini-resort in a residential area offers several different types of apartments amid the yachts docked at the Banyan Marina. Each one is individually decorated, perhaps with silk drapes, an oak armoire, or french doors. All units have their own full kitchens. The complex has won several landscaping prizes for the tropical garden that has been developed around the central Banyan tree. The beach is 1 mi away. Data ports, in-room safes, kitchenettes, microwaves, refrigerators. Cable TV. Pool. Dock. Bicycles. Laundry facilities, laundry service. | 111 Isle of Venice | 954/524–4430 or 800/524–4431 | fax 954/764–4870 | www.banyanmarinaapartments.com | 10 apartments | $95–$225 | MC, V.

Best Western Marina Inn. Rooms at this four-story hotel, adjacent to the city's largest beach and two blocks from the Broward County Convention Center, have views of the Intracoastal Waterway, Port Everglades cruise port, or the pool. Restaurant, bar, complimentary Continental breakfast, room service. In-room data ports, in-room safes. Cable TV. Pool. Hot tub. Putting green. Boating. Laundry facilities. Business services, airport shuttle. | 2150 S.E. 17th St. Causeway | 954/525–3484 or 800/327–1390 | fax 954/764–2915 | www.bestwestern.com | 168 rooms | $119–$149 | AE, D, DC, MC, V.

Best Western Oceanside Inn. This five-story hotel is just south of the Bahia Mar Marina, 1 mi north of the Broward Convention Center, and two blocks from the Jungle Queen. Rooms here have wonderful views of the water from private balconies. Restaurant, bar, complimentary breakfast. In-room data ports, in-room safes, refrigerators. Cable TV. Pool. Beach. Laundry facilities. Business services. Pets allowed. | 1180 Seabreeze Blvd. | 954/525–8115 | fax 954/527–0957 | 101 rooms | $99–$139 | AE, D, DC, MC, V.

Best Western Pelican Beach Resort. Nine buildings occupy this property with 500 ft of private beach. Standard rooms, efficiencies, and one-bedroom units have views of the ocean or the landscaped courtyards. Complimentary Continental breakfast. In-room data ports, some kitchenettes, some refrigerators. Cable TV. 2 pools. Beach. Laundry facilities. Business services. | 2000 N. Atlantic Blvd. | 954/568–9431 or 800/525–6232 | fax 954/565–2622 | www.introweb.com/pelican | 110 rooms in 9 buildings | $130–$210 | AE, D, DC, MC, V.

Comfort Suites Airport-Convention Center. This seven-story all-suites hotel is only a mile north of the Broward Convention Center, and 2½ mi north of the airport. Complimentary Continental breakfast. In-room data ports, some microwaves, some refrigerators. Cable TV. Pool. Laundry facilities. Airport shuttle. | 1800 S. Federal Hwy. | 954/767–8700 | fax 954/767–8629 | 111 suites | $99–$189 suites | AE, D, DC, MC, V.

Courtyard Fort Lauderdale East. This five-story hostelry stands just north of the Coral Ridge Golf Course, 1 mi west of the beaches, and ½ mi from the Intracoastal Waterway. In-room data ports, some refrigerators. Cable TV. Pool. Hot tub. Gym. Laundry facilities. Business services. | 5001 N. Federal Hwy. | 954/771–8100 | fax 954/776–7980 | www.marriott.com | $120–$139 | AE, D, DC, MC, V.

Courtyard Ft. Lauderdale/Plantation. About 8 mi north of Ft. Lauderdale's downtown, this three-story hotel sits just 1 mi north of I–595 in the suburb of Plantation. In-room data ports, some microwaves, some refrigerators. Cable TV. Pool. Hot tub. Gym. Laundry facilities. Business services. | 7780 S.W. 6th St., Plantation | 954/475–1100 | fax 954/424–8402 | www.marriott.com | 149 rooms | $79–$129 | AE, D, DC, MC, V.

Doubletree Guest Suites. Towering 14 stories above the Intracoastal Waterway, this all-suites hotel is two blocks west of the beaches. The Galleria Mall, with its many boutiques, is next door. All rooms have full kitchens and views of either the Atlantic, the waterway, or the skyline. Restaurant, bar, room service. Kitchenettes, microwaves, refrigerators. Cable TV. Pool. Hot tub. Gym. Dock. Laundry facilities. Business services. Pets allowed (fee). | 2670 E. Sunrise Blvd. | 954/565–3800 | fax 954/561–0387 | www.doubletree.com | 239 suites | $189–$209 | AE, D, DC, MC, V.

Doubletree Ft. Lauderdale Oceanfront. This 12-story, box-like turquoise building stands across a busy street from the beach. All rooms have views of the Intracoastal Waterway or the Atlantic. Executive suites have wet bars and refrigerators. Restaurant, bar, room service. Some refrigerators, some in-room hot tubs. Cable TV. Pool. Hot tub. Gym. Dock, boating. Laundry service. Business services. | 440 Seabreeze Blvd. | 954/524–8733 | fax 954/467–7489 | www.doubletree.com | 244 suites | $199–$219 | AE, D, DC, MC, V.

Eighteenth Street Inn. A mile from the beach, just off the busy 17th St. Causeway, this secluded gay-friendly inn is in a quiet residential neighborhood. Each of the rooms is individually designed, but expect clean tile floors, wicker furniture, handmade crafts, local artwork, and luxurious beds. Each evening, you can join the other guests and the resident cocker spaniels for a drink around the pool. Complimentary Continental breakfast. In-room data ports, some kitchenettes, some microwaves, some refrigerators. Cable TV. Pool. Laundry service. | 712 S.E. 18th St. | 954/467–7841 or 888/828–4466 | fax 954/467–0309 | www.eighteenthstinn.com | 6 rooms | $135–$205.

Embassy Suites. Several small ducks make their home in this all-suites hotel's atrium in a waterfall beneath trees and flowers. The hotel is 2 mi west of the beach. Complimentary cocktails are provided in the evenings. Restaurant, bar (with entertainment), complimentary breakfast. In-room data ports, microwaves, refrigerators. Cable TV. Pool. Hot tub, sauna, steam room. Laundry facilities, laundry service. Business services, airport shuttle. | 1100 S.E. 17th St. | 954/527–2700 | fax 954/760–7202 | www.embassy-suites.com | 359 suites | $129–$189 | AE, D, DC, MC, V.

Fort Lauderdale Days Inn I–95/Broward Blvd. A convenient stop for those weary of travel, this motel, which was built in 1983, is just off I–95 (exit 29) and 4 mi from the beach. The five-story building is filled with spotless rooms, all with floral print bed spreads and framed art prints. Restaurant, complimentary Continental breakfast. In-room safes, some refrigerators. Cable TV. Pool. Beach, water sports, boating, fishing. | 1700 W. Broward | 954/463–2500 or 800/DAYSINN | fax 954/763–6504 | www.daysinn.com | 144 rooms | $79–$129 | AE, D, DC, MC, V.

Hampton Inn, Ft. Lauderdale-Cypress Creek. This four-story chain hostelry is located 2 mi west of the beaches and 9 mi north of downtown. Complimentary Continental breakfast. In-room data ports. Cable TV. Pool. Hot tub. Gym. Laundry service. Business services. | 720 E. Cypress Creek Rd. | 954/776–7677 | fax 954/776–0805 | 122 rooms | $129–$139 | AE, D, DC, MC, V.

Hyatt Regency Pier 66. Atop this 17-story luxury hotel, the trademark lounge revolves once every 66 minutes, offering views of the marina and the surrounding 22 acres of flowers and gardens along the Intracoastal Waterway. The beach is three minutes away by water taxi. 2 restaurants, 4 bars, room service. In-room data ports, in-room safes, minibars, some in-room hot tubs. Cable TV. 2 pools, wading pool. Beauty salon, hot tub, spa. 2 tennis courts. Gym. Dock, boating. Laundry facilities. Business services. | 2301 S.E. 17th St., Causeway | 954/525–6666 or 800/327–3796 | fax 954/728–3541 | www.hyatt.com | 388 rooms | $229–$389 | AE, D, DC, MC, V.

Ireland's Inn Beach Resort. Family-owned since 1965, this resort, which consists of three buildings, sits directly on 350 feet of private beach. Given its location on a dead-end, residential street, there is little tourist traffic. Most rooms overlook the water, some have balconies. There is a coral reef only 50 yards offshore. Restaurant, bar (with entertainment), room service. In-room data ports, some in-room safes, some kitchenettes, microwaves, refrigerators, some in-room hot tubs. Cable TV. Pool. Beach. Laundry facilities. Business services. | 2220 N. Atlantic Blvd. | 954/565–6661 or 800/347–7776 | fax 954/565–8893 | www.irelands.com | 75 rooms | $105–$249 | AE, MC, V.

La Casa del Mar. A proud addition to the Florida coast is this Mediterranean-style B&B that seems to capture the true spirit of relaxing. The inn is close to shopping on Sunrise or Las

Olas, not to mention the many activities along the beach. Rooms are individually decorated, most with colorful bedspreads and brightly painted walls. Complimentary breakfast. Some kitchenettes. Pool. Beach, water sports, bicycles. | 3003 Granada St. | 954/467–2037 | fax 954/525–9648 | www.lacasadelmar.com | 10 units | $110–$135 | AE, MC, V.

Lago Mar Resort and Club. Less a resort than a small town, this sprawling property occupies 14 acres of private beachfront and comes complete with shops. The luxuriant appeal of the lobby is produced by a coquina-rock fireplace and a huge saltwater aquarium. The beach is the broadest in the city. Restaurant, bar (with entertainment). In-room data ports, in-room safes, microwaves, refrigerators. Cable TV. 2 pools. Miniature golf, 4 tennis courts. Gym. Beach, dock. Shops, video games. Playground. Laundry service. Business services. | 1700 S. Ocean La. | 954/523–6511 or 800/255–5246 | fax 954/524–6627 | www.lagomar.com | 210 rooms | $100–$155 | AE, DC, MC, V.

La Quinta Inn-Cypress Creek. This four-story motel, not even a mile west of I–95, stands on the northeast corner of the Fort Lauderdale Executive Airport. It is 9 mi north of downtown and 2 mi west of the beaches. In-room data ports, refrigerators. Cable TV. Pool. Hot tub. Gym. Laundry facilities. Business services. Pets allowed. | 999 W. Cypress Creek Rd. | 954/491–7666 | fax 954/491–7669 | 144 rooms | $119–$134 | AE, D, DC, MC, V.

Marriott's Harbor Beach Resort. The 16 acres that make up this property, south of the public beaches, glimmer like so many jewels when seen from one of the hotel's top stories. Each room, done in tropical colors and floral patterns, wicker and wood, has a balcony and faces water, either the Atlantic or the Intracoastal Waterway. 3 restaurants, bar, room service. In-room data ports, microwaves, some refrigerators. Cable TV. Pool. Barbershop, beauty salon, hot tub. 5 tennis courts. Gym. Beach, water sports, boating, bicycles. Shops, video games. Children's programs (ages 5–12). Laundry facilities. Business services, parking (fee). | 3030 Holiday Dr. | 954/525–4000 or 800/222–6543 | fax 954/766–6152 | 624 rooms | $309–$369 | AE, D, DC, MC, V.

The Martindale. Enjoy privacy and tropical gardens in an efficiency or small apartment, one of which is considered the penthouse because of its size and commanding view of the beach. Each unit is a bit different, but they all have fine art (prints), tiled floors, wicker furniture, and a sea breeze since the beach is across the street. The gracious French-Canadian hosts offer charcoal for grilling around the pool and coffee in the morning served in the garden. In-room data ports, in-room safes, some kitchenettes, refrigerators. Cable TV. Pool. Laundry facilities. | 3016 Bayshore Dr. | 954/467–1841 or 800/666–1841 | fax 954/763–8109 | www.martindaleatthebeach.com | 21 units, ranging from rooms to two bedroom apartments | $75–$195 | AE, MC, V.

Motel 6 Fort Lauderdale. Just east of I–95 at exit 27, this two-story motel is 3 mi north of the Fort Lauderdale International Airport and 3 mi west of the Broward Convention Center. Cable TV. Pool. Laundry facilities. Pets allowed. | 1801 Hwy. 84 | 954/760–7999 | fax 954/832–0653 | 106 rooms | $48–$65 | AE, D, DC, MC, V.

Nina Lee Imperial House Motel. Once independent, the Nina Lee Motel and the Imperial House are now jointly owned and operated. The 15-unit Nina Lee Motel has efficiencies typical of 1950s-style lodgings found near the Fort Lauderdale Beach, while the 12-unit Imperial House has one- and two-bedroom apartments. Removed from the beach, the property is quiet. You also have use of the facilities at the Sheraton Yankee Clipper Hotel. Kitchenettes, refrigerators. Cable TV. Pool. | 3048 Harbor Dr. | 954/524–1568 | fax 954/763–2931 | 27 units | $79–$119 | AE, D, DC, MC, V.

The Pillars. This fresh new Florida version of a British Colonial plantation offers more than most top-notch hotels. In the rooms, you'll find fine bed linens and fluffy robes; or you can wander down to the library and read while the grand piano is being tickled by the former Grand Ole Opry star who is now the concierge. The hotel is a block from the beach and a few blocks north of Las Olas Boulevard. Complimentary Continental breakfast. In-room data ports, in-room safes, some kitchenettes, some refrigerators, some in-room hot tubs. Cable TV, in-room VCRs. Pool. Laundry service. No smoking. | 111 North Birch Rd. | 954/467–9639 |

www.pillarshotel.com | 19 rooms, 4 suites | $119–$249 rooms, $159–$369 suites | AE, D, DC, MC, V.

Radisson Bahia Mar Beach Resort. At the largest marina in North America, the Bahia Mar Yachting Center, this high-rise hotel sits across the street from the beach on 44 acres. You access the beach via a walkway over the road. Most rooms have either a marina or an Atlantic view. Restaurant, bar (with entertainment). In-room data ports, in-room safes, minibars. Cable TV. Pool. Beauty salon. 4 tennis courts. Gym. Dock, fishing, boating. Shops, video games. Laundry facilities. Business services. | 801 Seabreeze Blvd. | 954/764–2233 | fax 954/523–5424 | www.radisson.com | 297 rooms | $159–$229 | AE, D, DC, MC, V.

Radisson Resort Coral Springs. This golf resort is 24 mi northwest of Fort Lauderdale, a 10-min drive from the Sawgrass Mills Mall, and 20 min from the beach. The seven-story hotel has a sunlit atrium in the center and a tropical garden, complete with bright, fresh flowers. Golfers will be impressed with Heron Bay Golf Club, on the premises. Restaurant, bar. In-room data ports, some minibars. Cable TV. Pool, hot tub, 2 saunas. 18-hole golf course. Gym. Video games. Laundry facilities, laundry service. Some pets allowed (fee). | 11775 Heron Bay Blvd., Coral Springs | 954/753–5598 | fax 954/753–5598 | wwww.radisson.com | 224 rooms, 6 suites | $129–$189 room, $219 suite | AE, D, MC, V.

Ramada Plaza Beach Resort. This nine-story structure sits directly on the beach; the suites face the ocean directly while the other rooms all have a partial view of the water from their private balconies. Restaurant, bar, room service. In-room data ports, microwaves, refrigerators. Cable TV. Pool. Massage. Gym. Beach, water sports. | 4060 Galt Ocean Dr. | 954/565–6611 | fax 954/564–7730 | www.ramada.com | 225 rooms | $125–$159 | AE, D, DC, MC, V.

Residence Inn Plantation. Two mi west of the Florida Turnpike and 15 min west of downtown Fort Lauderdale, this Residence Inn is composed of two four-story, L-shape buildings. All units have full kitchens; the two-bedroom units have fireplaces. Bar, complimentary breakfast, room service. In-room data ports, kitchenettes, microwaves, refrigerators. Cable TV. Pool. Hot tub. Gym. Laundry facilities. Business services. Pets allowed (fee). | 130 N. University Dr., Plantation | 954/723–0300 | fax 954/474–7385 | www.marriott.com | 138 suites | $139–$159 | AE, D, DC, MC, V.

River Inn on the Water. The setting of this resort is secluded, right on the Middle River—you can fish off the hotel's dock, or stroll through its gardens, where wild parrots nest. Rooms in the two buildings have private balconies and views of the river. It's less than a mile from the beach and only a stroll away from the Galleria Mall. Picnic area, complimentary Continental breakfast. In-room data ports, some kitchenettes, some microwaves, some refrigerators. Cable TV. Pool. Dock, fishing. Laundry facilities. Business services. | 1180 N. Federal Hwy. | 954/564–6411 or 800/748–3716 | www.riverinnh2o.com | 77 rooms | $119–$125 | AE, D, DC, MC, V.

Riverside Hotel. This hotel along the New River in Fort Lauderdale's historic district has been entertaining guests since 1936. The lobby, paved with Mexican tile and accented with coral fireplaces and wicker sofas, opens onto a courtyard filled with flowering tropical plants. Rooms are appointed with antique oak furnishings, French prints, and European-style baths. The hotel is expanding and expects to have 235 rooms available by early 2002. 2 restaurants, bar, room service. In-room data ports, refrigerators. Cable TV. Pool. Dock. Business services. | 620 E. Las Olas Blvd. | 954/467–0671 or 800/325–3280 | fax 954/462–2148 | www.riversidehotel.com | 109 rooms | $169–$379 | AE, DC, MC, V.

Sheraton Yankee Clipper Beach Hotel. Of the four buildings that make up this resort, three stand on the beach side of A1A, with one across the street from the beach. Rooms overlook either the Atlantic, the Intracoastal Waterway, or the city. Only suites have balconies. Prices vary depending on the distance of the building from the beach and the view. The hotel is 1 mi north of the Broward Convention Center and a ½ mi south of the International Swimming Hall of Fame. Restaurant, bar (with entertainment), room service. In-room data ports, in-room safes. Cable TV. Pools. Gym. Beach. Shops. Baby-sitting. Laundry facilities. Business services. | 1140 Seabreeze Blvd. | 954/524–5551 or 800/958–5551 | fax 954/523–5376 | www.sheratonclipper.com | 502 rooms | $189–$229 | AE, D, DC, MC, V.

Sheraton Yankee Trader Beach Hotel. Both of this hotel's buildings, a 15-story and a 14-story tower, are connected to the beach by a skywalk across A1A. Rooms either have full ocean views, partial views of the water and city, or full views of the city. But no rooms have balconies. Restaurant, bar. In-room data ports. Cable TV, some in-room VCRs. Pools. Tennis. Gym. Beach. Children's programs (ages 4–12). Laundry facilities. Business services. | 321 N. Atlantic Blvd. | 954/467–1111 or 800/958–5551 | fax 954/462–2342 | www.sheratontrader.com | 463 rooms | $189–$229 | AE, D, DC, MC, V.

Tropi Rock Resort. The owner's artsy flare is apparent in the bright yellow tropical colors of the walls (both inside and out) and the unique art work you'll find everywhere in the building. Colored mosaic tiles lead you around the garden and up the stairs. The rooms are each decorated differently. You can sunbathe on the roof or head one block over to the beach. In-room data ports, some kitchenettes, some refrigerators. Cable TV. Pool. 2 tennis courts. Gym. Laundry facilities. | 2900 Belmar | 954/564–0523 or 800/987–9385 | fax 954/564–1313 | www.tropirock.com | 18 rooms, 11 efficiencies, 1 apartment | $85 room, $98 efficiency, $160 apartment | MC, V.

Wellesley Inn and Suites. Three mi west of the Fort Lauderdale Executive Airport and less than a mile east of the Sabal Palm Golf Club, this all-suites hotel is easily accessed from the highways. I–95 is 3 mi to the east (take exit 32), and the Florida Turnpike is less than 1 mi to the west (take exit 62). Complimentary Continental breakfast. In-room data ports, some microwaves, some refrigerators. Cable TV. Pool. Laundry facilities. Business services. Pets allowed (fee). | 5070 N St. Hwy. 7 | 954/484–6909 or 800/444–8888 | fax 954/731–2374 | 100 rooms | $79–$89 | AE, D, DC, MC, V.

The Westin, Fort Lauderdale. This 15-story hotel, just east of I–95 at exit 33A, towers above a three-acre lagoon around which you can jog. The hotel is just 1½ mi east of the Fort Lauderdale Executive Airport. Restaurant, bar, room service. In-room data ports, in-room safes, minibars, some microwaves. Cable TV. Pool. Hot tub, sauna. Gym, boating. Business services. Pets allowed. | 400 Corporate Dr. | 954/772–1331 or 800/937–8461 | fax 954/772–6867 | 293 rooms | $155–$225 | AE, D, DC, MC, V.

Wyndham Resort & Spa Fort Lauderdale. Tropical gardens, waterfalls, and golf courses fill the 23 acres of this resort, which is 2 mi west of I–75. The many amenities of this resort mean you will never be at a loss for something to do. But, if you feel you want to shop, the Sawgrass Mills Outlet Mall is only 1 mi northeast. Restaurant, bar, room service. In-room data ports, minibars. Cable TV. 5 pools. Barbershop, beauty salon, hot tub, massage. 2 18-hole golf courses, 15 tennis courts. Gym. Bicycles. Children's programs (ages 3–12). Business services. | 250 Racquet Club Rd. | 954/389–3300 | fax 954/384–1416 | 496 rooms in 9 buildings | $139–$259 | AE, D, DC, MC, V.

FORT MYERS

MAP 3, 18

(Nearby towns also listed: Bonita Springs, Cape Coral, Captiva Island, Fort Myers Beach, Matlacha, Punta Gorda, Sanibel Island)

Fort Myers (pop 45,000) was established in 1839 as a defensive post during the Seminole wars. A fort built here was later named for General Abraham Myers—though occupied by troops during the Civil War, the site was later dismantled even though the town took the name. Today, the downtown area covers the spot where the fort once stood.

In 1887, Fort Myers gained two prominent new part-time residents when Thomas Edison established a laboratory and winter residence in town; he was joined by Henry Ford, who also built an estate here when the town's population was still in the hundreds. Fort Myers began to grow after a severe 1898 freeze pushed citrus growers further south, though much of the city was not developed until the boom years of the

1920s. City planners had the foresight to plant rows of stately palms along many of the streets and boulevards; the Mediterranean Revival architecture in town is also the result of that early planning. Today, Fort Myers has a highly developed commercial center and several large city housing developments for retirees.

Information: **Greater Fort Myers Chamber of Commerce** | 6900 Daniels Parkway, Fort Myers, 33931 | 941/332–3624 | www.usa-chamber.com/fortmyers.

Attractions

Caloosahatchee National Wildlife Refuge. This branch of the J. N. Ding Darling National Wildlife Refuge is accessible by boat and best for wildlife photography or observation. There is no mooring or dock, but kayaks and canoes can oar around mangrove roots and boats can fish with a view. | 18500 N. River Rd., Alva | 941/472–1100.

Calusa Nature Center and Planetarium. This 105-acre complex is made up of a museum, planetarium, aviary, and nature trails. You can learn about many of Southwest Florida's reptiles—from venomous diamondback rattlesnakes to baby gopher tortoises—and local issues such as water resources and the plight of the endangered manatee. The planetarium offers star shows, laser-light shows, and Cinema-360 films. | 3450 Ortiz Ave. | 941/275–3435 | fax 941/275–9016 | www.calusanature.com/ | Nature center $4, planetarium $3 | Mon.–Sat. 9–5, Sun. 11–5.

Eden Vineyards Winery. Stop in at the southernmost winery in the continental U.S. to sample six local varietals including carambola (starfruit) wine. If the wine doesn't charm you,

THE WEST INDIAN MANATEE: FLORIDA'S LARGEST MAMMAL

Considering their enormous stature and phlegmatic nature, the West Indian manatee would not seem to be what ancient mariners had in mind when they described sightings of elusive "mermaids," even though some believe what the sailors actually saw were these huge sea creatures. Let's just say they won't win any beauty contests. The average adult male measures around 10 ft in length and weighs a bulky 1,000 pounds. Their size, in addition to their wrinkly gray skin, is evidence that the animal's closest cousin is the elephant. Manatees (also known as sea cows) are extremely docile, entirely herbivorous creatures who spend their days grazing along the ocean floor and surface of the water in search of aquatic greenery. And lots of it: Manatees can consume almost 15% of their body weight in plants each day.

Owing in part to their gentle nature, the mammals have no natural enemies and can live to be 60 years old. Despite this, they are an endangered species; only an estimated 2,600 of the creatures remain in the United States. As such, they are protected by several federal laws and special no-wake manatee boating zones. Still, many die each year from accidents with watercraft propellers, from consuming plastic and fish hooks, and from the depletion of their natural habitats by overdevelopment.

Manatees live in shallow, slow-moving waters, such as coastal canals, calm rivers, and bays. To see them, look along the Intracoastal Waterways on both coasts from spring to fall. In winter, they migrate to inland springs in search of warmer water. Since they typically travel together in a long line with their bodies mostly submerged, look for something resembling drifting coconuts.

There are several organizations intent on helping manatees, most notably the Save the Manatee Club, which allows for the "adoption" of a sea cow. For more information, contact the **Save the Manatee Club and Adopt A Manatee** (500 N. Maitland Ave. Maitland, | 800/432–5646).

© Corbis

the owners will. The winery is 10 mi east of I–75 on Highway 80. | 19709 Little Lane, Alva | 941/728–9463 | www.edenwinery.com | $2.50 | Daily 11–4.

★ **Edison/Ford Winter Estates.** Inventors Thomas Edison and Henry Ford were friends and neighbors in Fort Myers. You can visit Edison's home, research laboratory, and botanical garden, an artifact museum, and Ford's adjoining estate, all of which are now jointly administered. | 2350 McGregor Blvd. | 941/334–7419 | www.edison-ford-estate.com | $11 | Mon.–Sat. 9–5:30.

Edison Winter House and Botanical Gardens. Thomas Edison wintered in Fort Myers between 1886 and 1931. This 14-acre riverfront estate is a Southwest Florida must-see. Walking tours cover the inventor's winter home, laboratory, and botanical gardens, which have been maintained as they were at the time of Edison's death in 1931. The Edison-designed gardens contain a collection of rare and exotic tropical vegetation and trees from around the world. On display in the home are the electric chandeliers, called electroliers, designed and made in Edison's workshop. A collection of vintage automobiles and some two hundred Edison phonographs are in the museum. You can also take a river cruise on a replica of the *Reliance,* Edison's electric launch. | 2350 McGregor Blvd. | 941/334–7419 | www.edison-ford-estate.com | $11 | Mon.–Sat. 9–5:30.

Henry Ford Winter House. Henry Ford purchased this three-acre estate in 1916 to be closer to Edison. Now owned by the City of Fort Myers, it looks much as it did when Ford and his wife, Clara, lived there. The estate was opened to the public in 1990. It is said that the V-8 engine was primarily designed on the back porch here. Ford vehicles on display include a 1914 Model T, a 1929 Model A, and a 1917 Model T Truck. | 2350 McGregor Blvd. | 941/334–7419 | www.edison-ford-estate.com | $11 | Mon.–Sat. 9–5:30.

Fort Myers Historical Museum. Housed in a restored railroad depot, this museum showcases Fort Myers history dating to 800 BC. Displays showcase prehistoric Calusa Indian artifacts, a reconstructed chickee hut, canoes, clothing, and photos from Seminole settlements, and the Esperanza, a 1930s Pullman private rail car. | 2300 Peck St. | 941/332–5955 | fax 941/332–6637 | www.cityftmyers.com | $6 | Tues.–Sat. 9–4.

Imaginarium. This hands-on museum and aquarium has over 60 exhibits on environmental issues, physics, anatomy, weather, and animals. A new bee exhibit lets kids see honey being made. There are iguana and tortoise exhibits, the Hurricane Experience, a butterfly garden, a living-reef tank, an outdoor lagoon with an alligator exhibit, an area of model railroads, and a 3-D theater. Four mi west of I–75 at exit 23. | 2000 Cranford Ave. | 941/337–3332 | $6 | Tues.–Sat. 10–5.

Manatee Park. Florida's gentle sea creatures—a.k.a. manatees—congregate in warmer waters when the Gulf waters are too cold, November through March each year. There are three observation decks here to aid in spotting the animals (a hint: look for the bubbles that signal their rise to the surface). Guided walks are held Wed. and Sat. mornings during viewing season. The 16-acre site, a mile east of I–75, includes a lagoon, picnic shelters, canoe launch, fishing deck, gardens, and a seasonal visitors center and gift shop. | 10901 Hwy. 80 | 941/694–3537 | www.lee-county.com/parks&rec/regionalparks | Free | Daily Apr.–Sept. 8–8; Oct.–Mar. 8–5.

SIGHTSEEING TOURS/TOUR COMPANIES

JC Cruises. Cruises on the *Wofford* and a paddlewheeler take you along waterways filled with exotic birds, manatees, and alligators from the City Yacht Basin at the foot of Lee Street. You can take brunch, lunch, and dinner cruises, or eight different scenic cruises along the Caloosahatchee River. | 2313 Edwards Dr. | 941/334–7474 | $12–$40 | Mid.-Oct.–Apr.

ON THE CALENDAR

FEB.: *Edison Festival of Light.* One of southeast Florida's top annual events commemorates the birth of Fort Myers's most famous winter resident, Thomas Edison. Three weeks of activities include a spectacular parade of lights, one of the largest night parades in the country, with over 140 floats and marching bands downtown. | 941/334–2999 | www.edisonfestival.org.

MAR.–APR.: *Spring Training.* The Boston Red Sox have trained in Fort Myers since 1993. The Minnesota Twins play at the Lee County Sports Complex. | 2201 Edison Ave. (Red Sox), 1410 Six Mile Cypress Pkwy. (Twins) | 941/334–4700 (Red Sox), 941/768–4278 (Twins).

Dining

Bistro 41. Contemporary. Step away from the bustle of Bell Tower Mall for the steak au poivre (glazed with a cracked peppercorn sauce) or the seafood strudel (fresh shrimp and lobster wrapped with a delicate puff pastry shell). For dessert try the homemade chocolate bread pudding. | 13499 U.S. 41 SE | 941/466–4141 | fax 941/466–5592 | No lunch Sun. | $10–$30 | AE, MC, V.

Chart House. Steak. An extensive salad bar and the area's best prime rib draw diners to this large, relaxed restaurant and grill perched on pilings above the Caloosahatchee River. Five hundred French windows provide great views. Fresh fish dishes include a seared and peppered Ahi Tuna and grilled swordfish. | 2024 W. 1st St. | 941/332–1881 | Dinner only | $15–$36 | AE, D, DC, MC, V.

Chez le Bear. Mediterranean. This formal restaurant in Sanibel Harbor Resort and Spa is named for a modern art painting in the dining room. Tapered candles, white linen, crystal glassware, Versace showplates, and fine silver add a spark of romance. Appetizers include foie gras, Russian caviar, lobster bisque, and escargot. Entrées include Black Angus steak, Colorado rack of lamb, pheasant, Ahi tuna, yellowtail snapper, veal chop, and a 2-lb Maine lobster. Sorbet is served in between courses and hand-rolled truffles close the meal. | 17260 S. Harbour Pointe Dr. | 941/466–2136 | Closed Sun., Mon. No lunch | $25–$36 | AE, D, DC, MC, V.

Mel's Diner. American. Homestyle diner food is the name of the game here, served in a setting with black-and-white tiles on the floor and vinyl booths. Mashed potatoes and blue plate specials are complemented by fountain drinks and the popular mile-high pie. | 4820 Cleveland Ave. | 941/275–7850 | fax 941/274–3663 | $4–$9 | No credit cards.

Miami Connection. Deli. This kosher-style deli offers a little piece of New York. It's known for its homemade bagels, Reubens, choice chopped liver, and lean but tender corned beef. | 11506 Cleveland Ave. | 941/936–3811 | No dinner | $6–$8 | No credit cards.

Peter's La Cuisine. Continental. In the middle of downtown Fort Myers, two blocks off the river, is this charming restaurant in a restored, brick building. The dining room has high ceilings, exposed brick walls, dim lighting, and white linen tablecloths. Courtyard dining is available in milder seasons. A contemporary twist is evident in dishes such as roast duck with a blended berry and orange sauce and grilled salmon with roasted garlic served over spinach. There are live blues music and lighter fare upstairs. | 2224 Bay St. | 941/332–2228 | No lunch weekends | $26–$34 | AE, MC, V.

Prawnbroker Restaurant and Fish Market. Seafood. In the upscale Cypress Square shopping center is this very popular restaurant that boasts the freshest seafood in town. The large dining room has bright, tropical paintings, wood-paneled walls, and wood tables. Appetizers and drinks are available outdoors. Daily specials focus on the fresh catch of the day. Past examples include coco mahi—mahimahi coated in a crisp, shredded coconut, and barbecue sauce—or the local piccata trippletail. | 13451 McGregor Blvd. | 941/489–2226 | No lunch | $14–$21 | AE, MC, V.

The Veranda. Southern. Sconces and antique oil paintings line the pale yellow walls of this restaurant in a charming, turn-of-the-20th-century home. Dine inside or in a brick courtyard outdoors. The menu includes Bourbon Street filet mignon, rack of lamb with rosemary sauce, and a southern fried seafood sampler. | 2122 2nd St. | 941/332–2065 | Closed Sun. No lunch Sat. | $16–$27 | AE, DC, MC, V.

Lodging

Amtel Ramada Marina Hotel. This modern, 25-story high-rise on the Caloosahatchee River has a commanding spot in the downtown skyline, rising high above the river and yacht basin. Rooms have water or city views. Restaurants, shops, and Edison's winter home are all within walking distance. Restaurant, bar. In-room data ports, some microwaves, some refrigerators. Cable TV. 2 pools. Hot tub. Tennis court. Gym. Docks, boating. Video games. Laundry facilities. Business services. Airport shuttle. | 2500 Edwards Dr. | 941/337–0300 or 800/833–1620 | fax 941/337–0593 | www.amtelmarinahotel.com | 416 rooms | $125–$185 | AE, D, DC, MC, V.

Baymont Inn Fort Myers. This four-story, salmon-colored building is right in central Fort Myers. Rooms are designed in early American style, with maplewood furniture, contrasting with the Floridian lobby's pastels and tropical plants. A light breakfast is brought to your room each morning. Continental breakfast. Some in-room data ports, some microwaves, some refrigerators. Pool. Golf. Boating, fishing. Laundry service. Pets allowed (fee). | 2717 Colonial Blvd. | 941/275–3500 or 800/428–3438 | fax 941/275–5426 | www.baymontinn.com | 123 rooms | $60–$117 | AE, D, DC, MC, V.

Comfort Suites Airport. This simple, economic two-story motel is off I–75 at exit 21, 1 mi west of the airport and 2 mi east of the Minnesota Twins spring training site. Bar, complimentary Continental breakfast. In-room data ports, microwaves, refrigerators. Cable TV. Pool. Hot tub. Gym. Laundry facilities. Business services. Airport shuttle. Some pets allowed. | 13651 Indian Paint La. | 941/768–0005 | fax 941/768–5458 | www.comfortsuites.com | 65 rooms | $54–$89.

Courtyard Fort Myers. This three-story hotel has spacious rooms and a cozy lobby with fireplace, TV parlor, and a restaurant that serves breakfast only. It's a 5-min drive from downtown and 2 mi from the Fort Myers Golf Club. Bar. In-room data ports, some refrigerators. Cable TV, some in-room VCRs. Pool. Hot tub. Exercise equipment. Laundry facilities, laundry services. Business services. | 4455 Metro Pkwy. | 941/275–8600 or 800/321–2211 | fax 941/275–7087 | www.courtyard.com | 149 rooms, 12 suites | $119–$159 | AE, D, DC, MC, V.

Holiday Inn Select. This modern high-rise hotel is adjacent to the Bell Tower shops, restaurants, and movies. The hotel is 6 mi from the regional airport. A sports restaurant is inside the hotel. Restaurant, bar (with entertainment). In-room data ports, refrigerators, room service. Cable TV, some in-room VCRs. Pool. Exercise equipment. Laundry services. Business services, airport shuttle. | 13051 Bell Tower Dr. | 941/482–2900 or 800/664–7775 | fax 941/482–2900 | www.basshotels.com | 227 rooms | $107–$159 | AE, D, DC, MC, V.

Holiday Inn SunSpree Resort. This resort is on the Caloosahatchee River, with lush gardens right in downtown Fort Myers. It's just ½ mi from the Harborside Convention Center and 1 mi from the Edison and Ford Winter Estates. Restaurant, bar. In-room data ports, some microwaves, some refrigerators. Cable TV. Pool, wading pool. Beauty salon, hot tub. Exercise equipment. Docks, boating. Children's programs (ages 4–12), playground. Laundry services. Business services. Airport shuttle. | 2220 W. 1st St. | 941/334–3434 or 800/664–7775 | fax 941/334–3844 | www.sunspree.com | 146 rooms | $89–$189 | AE, D, DC, MC, V.

Homewood Suites Fort Myers. These suites come with separate bedrooms, fold-out couches, living rooms, two TVs, and kitchens. The three-story building has an enclosed courtyard with a pool and landscaped tropical plants. The central community lodge is busy with breakfast in the morning, and with hors d'oeuvres and drinks in the evening. Continental breakfast. In-room data ports, kitchenettes, microwaves, refrigerators. In-room VCRs. Pool. Outdoor hot tub, massage. Health club. Beach, boating, fishing. Babysitting. Laundry facilities, laundry service. Airport shuttle. | 3255 Big Pine Hwy. | 941/275–6000 or 800/225–5466 | fax 941/275–6601 | www.homewood-suites.com | 130 suites | $119–$199 | AE, D, DC, MC, V.

Howard Johnson. Many rooms in this two-story chain in North Fort Myers have views of the Caloosahatchee River. Rooms come with a king-size or two double beds. Complimentary Continental breakfast. In-room data ports. Cable TV. Pool. Exercise equipment. Laun-

6 "I'm thirsty"s, 9 "Are we there yet"s, 3 "I don't feel good"s,
1 car class upgrade.
At least something's going your way.

Hertz rents Fords and other fine cars. ® REG. U.S. PAT. OFF. © HERTZ SYSTEM INC., 2000/005-00

Make your next road trip more comfortable with a free one-class upgrade from Hertz.

Let's face it, a long road trip isn't always sunshine and roses. But with Hertz, you get a free one car class upgrade to make things a little more bearable. You'll also choose from a variety of vehicles with child seats, Optional Protection Plans, 24-Hour Emergency Roadside Assistance, and the convenience of NeverLost® the in-car navigation system that provides visual and audio prompts to give you turn-by-turn guidance to your destination. In a word: it's everything you need for your next road trip. Call your travel agent or Hertz at **1-800-654-2210** and mention PC# **906404** or check us out at **hertz.com** or AOL Keyword: **hertz**. Peace of mind. Another reason nobody does it exactly like Hertz.

Hertz
exactly.®

Find America *with a Compass*

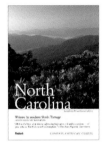
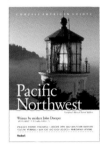
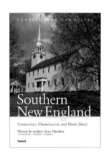

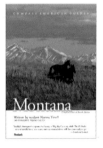

Written by local authors and illustrated throughout with images from regional photographers, Compass American Guides reveal the character and culture of America's most spectacular destinations. Covering more than 35 states and regions across the country, Compass guides are perfect for residents who want to explore their own backyards, and for visitors seeking an insider's perspective on all there is to see and do.

Fodor's Compass American Guides

At bookstores everywhere.

dry facilities. Business services. | 13000 N. Cleveland Ave. | 941/656–4000 or 800/406–1411 | fax 941/656–4000 | www.hojo.com | 87 rooms | $89–$129 | AE, D, DC, MC, V.

Inn at Sanibel Harbour. Within the Sanibel Harbour Resort is this newer seven-story building that's a bit more tranquil than the resort. Some of the rooms have a view of the harbor and the man-made beach along the edge. You have access to all the amenities at the resort, including all the water sports and spa facilities. The rooms are actually larger than at the resort and are splashed with pastel colors. Restaurant. Cable TV. Pool. Laundry service. | 17260 Harbour Pointe Dr., Fort Myers | 941/466–4000 or 800/767–7777 | fax 941/466–2150 | www.sanibel-resort.com | 107 rooms | $189–$269 | AE, DC, MC, V.

La Quinta Inn Fort Myers. This two-story chain hotel has a white exterior with teal trim and a Southwestern architecture. It is 10 mi west of the airport. Complimentary Continental breakfast. In-room data ports. Cable TV, some in-room VCRs (and movies). Pool. Video games. Laundry services. Business services. Free parking. Some pets allowed. | 4850 Cleveland Ave. | 941/275–3300 or 800/531–5900 | fax 941/275–6661 | www.laquinta.com | 130 rooms | $95–$115 | AE, D, DC, MC, V.

Radisson Inn Fort Myers. This Radisson off I–75 at exit 21 or 22 has two-story and five-story buildings. Rooms are spacious, and have a desk and reclining chair. Many have balconies. In the courtyard, palm trees surround a free form pool. Suites have two levels and come with a refrigerator and microwave. Restaurant, bar, room service. In-room data ports, some microwaves, some refrigerators. Cable TV. Pool. Tennis court. Volleyball. Laundry facilities. Business services. Airport shuttle. | 12635 Cleveland Ave. | 941/936–4300 or 800/333–3333 | fax 941/936–2058 | www.radisson.com | 192 rooms | $110–$169 | AE, D, DC, MC, V.

Radisson Inn Sanibel Gateway. This Radisson hotel uses Southwestern color schemes and artwork; the lobby has dark tiles and a fountain. The three-story inn is just across the bridge from Sanibel Island, in south Fort Myers. The Olympic-size pool has an underwater music system. Restaurant, bar, room service. In-room data ports, refrigerators. Cable TV. Pool. Hot tub. Laundry facilities. Bicycles (in season). Business services. Some pets allowed (fee). | 20091 Summerlin Rd. | 941/466–1200 or 800/333–3333 | fax 941/466–3797 | www.radisson.com | 158 rooms | $109–$199 | AE, D, DC, MC, V.

Sanibel Harbour Resort and Spa. This gorgeous resort overlooks Sanibel and Captiva Islands from an 80-acre complex. Its tennis complex was host to the Davis Cup tournament in 1989 and 1992. Free shuttles head to Sanibel Island 5 minutes away. The full-service spa offers over 60 treatments. Within the resort is a new 107-room boutique inn, The Inn at Sanibel Harbour, offering quieter, more secluded rooms. Both areas have rooms furnished in soft, pastel colors. | 408 rooms. 4 Restaurants (Chez le Bear), bar (with entertainment), room service. In-room data ports, minibars, some microwaves. Cable TV, some in-room VCRs. 4 outdoor pools, 1 indoor pool. Barbershop, beauty salon, 12 hot tubs, massage, sauna, spa, steam room. 13 tennis courts. Basketball, health club, racquetball. Beach, water sports, boating, bicycles. Video games. Children's programs (ages 5–12). Business services. | 17260 Harbour Pointe Dr. | 941/466–4000 or 800/767–7777 | fax 941/466–6050 | www.sanibel-resort.com | $189–$375 | AE, D, DC, MC, V.

Ta Ki-Ki. This relaxed motel has a private fishing pier with a covered pavilion on the Caloosahatchee River. It is within walking distance of downtown's historic district. Picnic area. Some kitchenettes. Cable TV. Pool. Dock, boating. Some pets allowed. | 2631 First St. | 941/334–2135 | fax 941/332–1879 | www.cyberstreet.com/takiki | 28 rooms | $42–$80 | AE, D, DC, MC, V.

Wellesley Inn and Suites. The portico and fountain at the entrance provide a stylish welcome to this four-story hotel 4 mi from downtown. There is a landscaped courtyard surrounding the heated pool, and barbecue grills. Continental breakfast. In-room data ports, some kitchenettes, some microwaves, some refrigerators. Cable TV. Pool. Golf, tennis. Health club. Laundry facilities, laundry service. Some pets allowed (fee). | 4400 Ford St. | 941/278–3949 or 800/444–8888 | fax 941/278–3670 | www.wellesleyinnandsuites.com | 105 rooms | $107–$119 | AE, D, DC, MC, V.

FORT MYERS BEACH

(Nearby towns also listed: Bonita Springs, Cape Coral, Captiva Island, Fort Myers, Matlacha, Sanibel Island)

Estero Island, a narrow, 7-mi-long crescent, is home to the laid-back, vacation-mad town of Fort Myers Beach (pop. 10,000). The town, 18 mi southwest of Fort Myers, is full of motels, hotels, and restaurants catering to travelers who flock here for the tranquil, warm gulf waters and white beaches. The marina at the more commercial north end of the island is the starting point for much boating, including sightseeing cruises and deep-sea fishing. Lover's Key State Park—connected by a causeway to the southern end of Estero Island—encompasses two islands and several uninhabited islets; it's great for biking, walking, bird watching, and shelling.

Information: **Fort Myers Beach Chamber of Commerce** | 17200 San Carlos Blvd., Fort Myers Beach, 33931 | 941/454–7500 | fax 941/454–7910 | www.fortmyersbeach.org.

ON THE CALENDAR

MAR.: *Shrimp Festival.* Shrimp boils, arts and crafts booths, a parade, and a 5K race are all part of this three-day celebration that takes place on and around the public beach and Lynn Hall Park. A bishop enacts a ceremonial blessing over the local shrimp fleet at the end of the festival. | 941/454–7500.

NOV.: *American Championship Sandsculpting Festival.* This three-day event takes over the beach between the Outrigger Beach Resort and the Holiday Inn, highlighted by a master sand-sculpting competition. | 941/454–7500.

Dining

Anthony's on the Gulf. American. This local favorite is set on stilts above the Gulf. You can dine indoors, with glassed-in views, or outdoors on the patio. There is also a beach bar with live reggae music Wednesday and Sunday. Early dinners are available with smaller portions. The menu includes everything from burgers and salads to veal and stuffed shrimp. | 3040 Estero Blvd. | 941/463–2600 | $13–$23 | AE, D, MC, V.

Ballenger's. Seafood. This casual spot has candlelight dining. It's known for its fish dishes, including Grouper Supreme (topped with white wine, rock shrimp, and bay scallops), Florida snapper served blackened or broiled, or Snapper Monte Carlo (broiled and topped with crab and béarnaise sauce). An unlimited salad bar is included with all entrées. Brunch is available Sunday. | 11390 Summerlin Square Dr. | 941/466–2626 | No lunch Mon.–Sat. | $11–$17 | AE, D, DC, MC, V.

Channel Mark. Seafood. This Italian restaurant ½ mi before the Fort Myers Beach bridge has tables that overlook Hurricane Bay. Though it's known for its seafood and pasta dishes, you can dine on chicken, veal, steak, and prime rib. There are two separate dining areas, one more casual than the other. There is live jazz weekend nights. | 19001 San Carlos Blvd. | 941/463–9127 | Reservations not accepted | $13–$25 | AE, D, DC, MC, V.

Charley Brown's. Continental. The glass-enclosed porch at this old-time favorite, part of a small family-owned chain, has views of the bay and Mangrove Canal. The menu includes fresh fish, shellfish, Grade A steaks, prime rib, barbecue baby back ribs, chicken, fresh baked bread, and an unlimited salad bar with over 50 items. | 6225 Estero Blvd. | 941/463–6660 | No lunch | $9–$22 | AE, D, DC, MC, V.

Mucky Duck. Seafood. This is a slightly more formal Mucky Duck that the one on the Captiva waterfront, but it scores just as highly at preparing fresh seafood. The bacon-wrapped barbecued shrimp is popular, as is the Grouper Café de Paris, which is prepared with a garlic herb butter. | 2500 Estero Blvd. | 941/463–5519 | No lunch | $9–$30 | AE, D, MC, V.

Pappa Mondo Ristorante. Italian. Italian cheeses and olive oil go into the dishes at this comfortable restaurant with gulf views. All pastas, including ravioli, are homemade: you'll believe it watching the chefs at work through glass windows. It's known for its risotto, salt-encrusted bass, and yellowtail snapper. | 1821 Estero Blvd. | 941/765–9660 | $9–$19 | AE, MC, V.

Lodging

Best Western Beach Resort. The white exterior of this five-story hotel blends with the beach beside it. All rooms have gulf views from private balconies and tropical prints. Picnic area, complimentary Continental breakfast. Kitchenettes, microwaves, refrigerators. Cable TV. Pool. Water sports. Playground. Laundry facilities. Business services. Some pets allowed (fee). | 684 Estero Blvd. | 941/463–6000 or 800/336–4045 | fax 941/463–3013 | www.bestwestern.com | 75 rooms | $199–$209 | AE, D, DC, MC, V.

Best Western Pink Shell. This 12-acre, beachfront resort caters to families looking for fun—highlights include social and recreational programs, three pools, and beach water sports. Rooms come in a five-story building or one-, two-, or three-bedroom cottages set on stilts. Bowditch Point Park is adjacent to the property. There's a poolside restaurant, and another that overlooks Estero Bay. 2 Restaurants, bar, picnic area. In-room data ports, some kitchenettes, microwaves, refrigerators. Cable TV, in-room VCRs (and movies). 3 pools, wading pool. 2 tennis courts. Volleyball. Beach, dock, water sports. Laundry facilities. Children's programs (ages 3–11), playground. Business services. | 275 Estero Blvd. | 941/481–3636 or 800/237–5786 | fax 941/463–1229 | www.pinkshell.com | 370 rooms, 49 cottages | $149–$259 room, $179–$419 cottage | AE, D, DC, MC, V.

Edison Beach House. On the western shore of Estero Island, the all-suites Edison Beach House, which opened in May 2000, fronts the Gulf of Mexico. The beach houses' architectural and interior designs are similar to an Old Florida–style home. The grounds have a courtyard grill for family cookouts. Just a short jaunt down the beach lies the Times Square area of intimate eateries, boutiques, surf shops and a popular fishing pier. In-room data ports, in-room safes, kitchenettes, microwaves, refrigerators, cable TV. Pool. Beach. Laundry facilities. No smoking. | 830 Estero Blvd. | 941/463–1530 or 800/399–2511 | fax 941/765–9430 | www.edisonbeachhouse.com | 24 suites | $250–$350 | AE, MC, V.

Lighthouse Island Resort. This resort has quaint one- and two-bedroom efficiencies or apartments clustered around heavy landscaping; an attractive little pool has a rock waterfall. It's 200 ft from the beach, and close to shopping, restaurants, a fishing pier, charter fishing, and casino boats. Bar, picnic area. Microwaves, some refrigerators. Cable TV, some in-room VCRs. 2 pools. Fishing. Laundry facilities. Business services. | 1051 5th St. | 941/463–9392 or 800/778–7748 | fax 941/765–5297 | www.lighthouseislandresort.com | 65 rooms | $72–$160 | AE, D, DC, MC, V.

Neptune Inn. This two-story complex has two pools, shuffleboard, and landscaping leading to 300 ft of beachfront. It's a short walk from Fort Myers Pier. All rooms have a full kitchen and are poolside or have a Gulf view. Best for fun-seeking families. Picnic area. Kitchenettes, microwaves, refrigerators. Cable TV. 2 Pools. Laundry facilities. Business services. | 2310 Estero Blvd. | 941/463–6141 or 800/333–2310 | fax 941/463–7503 | www.neptuneinn.com | 63 rooms | $127–$150 | D, MC, V.

Outrigger Beach Resort. This bright yellow four-story family resort has a wide stretch of Gulf front beach. There are six types of rooms to choose from, all decorated with bright prints. Views vary—some rooms overlook the beach—so ask when registering. There is a broad sundeck, tiki huts to escape the sun, sailboats, and a beautiful pool. Restaurant, bar, picnic area. In-room data ports, in-room safes, some kitchenettes, some microwaves, some refrigerators. Cable TV. Pool. Putting green. Exercise equipment, volleyball. Beach, bicycles. Laundry facilities. Business services. | 6200 Estero Blvd. | 941/463–3131 or 800/655–8997 | fax 941/463–6577 | www.outriggerfmb.com | 144 rooms | $110–$190 | D, MC, V.

Pointe Estero. On the quieter south end of the island, this beachfront 16-story tower has one- and two-bedroom suites with Gulf views from wide balconies. All suites have a

Jacuzzi tub, in-room laundry facilities, and a private screened balcony. Bedrooms have a king-size bed with a queen-size sleeper sofa. Picnic area. In-room data ports, kitchenettes. Cable TV, in-room VCRs (and movies). Pool. Hot tub. Tennis courts. Beach. Children's programs (ages 3–18). Business services. | 6640 Estero Blvd. | 941/765–1155 or 800 888/627–1595 | fax 941/765–0657 | www.pointeestero.com | 60 suites | $245–$255 1-bedroom suite, $280–$435 2-bedroom suite | D, MC, V.

Sandpiper Gulf Resort. This resort, family-owned and -operated since 1969, has four different size buildings with white exterior and private balconies. These are set around a pool, shuffleboard, and 315 ft of beachfront—come with a lighthearted family vacation mindset. Picnic area. Kitchenettes, microwaves, refrigerators. Cable TV. 2 Pools. Hot tub. Beach. Laundry facilities. Business services. | 5550 Estero Blvd. | 941/463–5721 or 800/584–1449 | fax 941/765–0039 | www.sandpipergulfresort.com | 63 suites | $75–$199 | D, MC, V.

Santa Maria Resort. This four-story tropical resort overlooks the Estero Bay, and is across the street from the beach. There is a center atrium with native foliage. One-, two-, or three-bedroom suites have balconies and in-room laundry facilities. Views are of the pool, spa, or marina. Picnic area. Kitchenettes. Cable TV, in-room VCRs available. Pool. Hot tub, sauna. Children's programs (ages 3–12). Business services. | 7317 Estero Blvd. | 941/765–6700 or 800/627–1595 | fax 941/765–6909 | www.santamariafl.com | 60 suites | $119–$169 1-bedroom suite, $159–$229 2-bedroom suite, 199–$279 3-bedroom suite | AE, D, MC, V.

FORT PIERCE

MAP 3, L7

(Nearby towns also listed: Jensen Beach, Port St. Lucie, Stuart, Vero Beach)

This community of 39,000 was named for Lt. Col. Benjamin Kendrick Pierce, who founded it in 1833 as a fort to defend settlers against the Seminoles. Early industries included water transportation and fishing, but gradually the economic focus shifted to citrus. Today, the presence of numerous ranches and groves gives Fort Pierce a somewhat rural feel. While it is the oldest city in the four-county area, Fort Pierce contin-

KODAK'S TIPS FOR NIGHT PHOTOGRAPHY

Lights at Night
- Move in close on neon signs
- Capture lights from unusual vantage points

Fireworks
- Shoot individual bursts using a handheld camera
- Capture several explosions with a time exposure
- Include an interesting foreground

Fill-In Flash
- Set the fill-in light a stop darker than the ambient light

Around the Campfire
- Keep flames out of the frame when reading the meter
- For portraits, take spot readings of faces
- Use a tripod, or rest your camera on something solid

Using Flash
- Stay within the recommended distance range
- Buy a flash with the red-eye reduction mode

From *Kodak Guide to Shooting Great Travel Pictures* © 2000 by Fodor's Travel Publications

ues to play an important part in the economic development of the Treasure Coast. The natural beauty of the landscape is the real attraction here.

Information: **St. Lucie County Chamber of Commerce** | 2200 Virginia Ave., Fort Pierce, 34982 | 561/595–9999 | www.stluciechamber.org.

Attractions
A.E. "Bean" Backus Gallery. As the home of the Treasure Coast Art Association, this gallery displays the works of one of Florida's foremost landscape artists, A. E. Backus. The gallery also mounts changing exhibits featuring the work of regional southeast artists. | 500 N. Indian River Dr. | 561/465–0630 | www.backusgallery.org | Free | Sept.–May, Tues.–Sat. 10–4, Sun. noon–4.

Fort Pierce Inlet State Recreation Area. Surfers and boaters flock to the 340 acres of beach, dunes, and coastal hammock on the north shore of Fort Pierce Inlet on North Hutchinson Island. Landlubbers can picnic or go biking. | 905 Shorewinds Dr. | 561/468–3985 | $3.25 per vehicle | Daily 8–sunset.

Jack Island Wildlife Refuge. Accessible only by a footbridge north of Fort Pierce Inlet State Recreational Area, this nature preserve is a hit with bird-watchers. You can spot roseate spoonbills, ibis, eagles, and many other species over 4 mi of trails. You can also picnic, or fish in the River Lagoon. | Hwy. A1A | 561/468–3985 | Free | Daily 8–sunset.

Heathcote Botanical Gardens. The 3½-acre gardens feature a Japanese garden and a palm walk. | 210 Savannah Rd. | 561/464–4672 | $3 | May–Oct., Tues.–Sat. 9–5; Nov.–Apr. Tues.–Sat. 9–5, Sun. 1–5.

St. Lucie County Historical Museum. A Seminole encampment, a reconstructed portion of a Spanish galleon, and mock-ups of the 1715 Spanish treasure fleet are among the exhibits exploring themes of local importance in this museum. A replica of a turn-of-the-20th-century train station includes a model of Henry Flagler's Florida East Coast Railway. | 414 Seaway Dr. | 561/462–1795 | $3 | Tues.–Sat. 10–4, Sun. 12–4.

Savannahs Recreation Area. The 550-acre semiwilderness park is back to its natural state after once serving as a reservoir. There are campsites, a petting zoo, botanical gardens, boat ramps, and trails. | 1400 E. Midway Rd. | 561/464–7855 | $1 per vehicle | Daily 8–6.

UDT-SEAL Museum. This museum in Pepper Park commemorates the site where more than 3,000 Navy frogmen trained during World War II. It focuses on the development of the elite Navy SEALs (Sea, Air, Land teams) and their forerunners. Displays include SEAL boats and artifacts from World War II, Korea, and Vietnam. Videos show SEAL training and operations. | 3300 N. Hwy. A1A | 561/595–5845 | www.udt-seal.org | $4 | Tues.–Sat. 10–4, Sun. 12–4.

ON THE CALENDAR
JAN.–APR.: *Jai-Alai.* Fort Pierce Jai Alai operates seasonally for live jai alai—it's one of only seven courts in the U.S. hosting the world's fastest game. The complex is open all year for horse racing simulcasts. | 561/464–7500.

MAR.: *Backus Art Festival.* Held along Melody Lane downtown the first weekend in March, this two-day event features a juried arts and crafts show and live bands. There are a rock climbing wall and interactive craft demonstrations for children. | 561/466–3880.

Dining
Harbortown Fish House. Seafood. This open-air restaurant overlooks Indian Lagoon. Try the baked African snook or the mahimahi. There is outdoor dining available on two patios. | 1930 Harbortown Dr. | 561/466–8732 | $14–$20 | AE, MC, V.

Kristi's. American. This casual eatery has lovely beach and ocean views as well a satisfying menu that features leg of lamb and prime rib. There is also a wide selection of seafood dishes. | 2400 S. Ocean Dr. | 561/465–4200 | Reservations essential | Closed Mon.–Tues. | $10–$26 | AE, MC, V.

Mangrove Mattie's. Seafood. This restaurant on Fort Pierce Inlet prides itself on the fresh fish dishes. Try the nut-crusted flounder. Outdoor dining on a small uncovered patio is available. | 1640 Seaway Dr. | 561/466–1044 | $12–$19 | AE, D, DC, MC, V.

P.V. Martin's. Seafood. This romantic restaurant has wood floors and wood beam ceilings. Try the snapper, fried rock shrimp, and fried oysters. | 5150 N. A1A | 561/569–0700 | $9–$20 | No lunch Mon.–Sat. | AE, MC, V.

Lodging

Comfort Inn. This Comfort Inn is 4 mi from the beach and 1½ mi from downtown. There are a number of restaurants within walking distance. Complimentary Continental breakfast. In-room data ports, some kitchenettes. Cable TV. Outdoor pool. Outdoor hot tub. Laundry facilities. Business services. Some pets (fee). | 3236 S. U.S. 1 | 561/461–2323 or 800/228–5150 | fax 561/464–5151 | www.comfortinn.com | 60 rooms | $69–$159 | AE, D, DC, MC, V.

Days Inn. This two-story motel is 8 mi from the beach. While there is no restaurant on property, there are many restaurants within a mile of the property. The motel is right off I–95 at exit 65. In-room data ports, some refrigerators, some microwaves. Cable TV. Outdoor pool. Laundry facilities. Business services. Pets allowed (fee). | 6651 Darter Ct. | 561/466–4066 or 800/544–8313 | fax 561/468–3260 | www.daysinn.com | 125 rooms | $55–$60 | AE, D, DC, MC, V.

Days Inn at Fort Pierce Beach. Some of the rooms in this single-story Days Inn have wonderful views of the Intracoastal Waterway. There are two restaurants and a few bars a short walk away. Picnic area, complimentary Continental breakfast. Some refrigerators, some microwaves. Cable TV. Outdoor pool. Fishing. Laundry facilities. Business services. | 1920 Seaway Dr. | 561/461–8737 or 800/544–8313 | fax 561/460–2218 | 36 rooms | $95–$135 | AE, D, DC, MC, V.

Dockside-Harbor Light Resort. This resort is spread out over an acre in six buildings along the Intracoastal Waterway. There are docks for boating and fishing, and two shuffleboard courts. Picnic area. Complimentary Continental breakfast. In-room data ports, some kitchenettes, microwaves, refrigerators. Cable TV. 2 outdoor pools. Outdoor hot tub. Four docks, fishing. Laundry facilities. | 1160 Seaway Dr. | 561/468–3555 or 800/286–1745 | fax 561/489–9848 | www.docksideinn.com | 65 suites | $45–$115 | AE, D, DC, MC, V.

Fort Pierce Super 8 Motel. This two-story budget motel on U.S. 1 is within walking distance of a few restaurants. Work on a tan by the pool or enjoy the cool shade provided by the towering palm and oak trees on the property. Complimentary Continental breakfast. Cable TV. Outdoor pool. Laundry facilities. Business services. | 612 U.S. Hwy. 1 | 561/466–8488 or 800/800–8000 | fax 561/466–8488 | www.super8.com | 40 rooms | $62–$69 | AE, D, DC, MC, V.

Garden State Motel. This single-story motel is on the southern tip of Fort Pierce, near Port St. Lucie. There is a shuffleboard court. At night the tall palm and oak trees are lit up. Some kitchenettes, microwaves, refrigerators. Cable TV, no room phones. Outdoor pool. Some pets allowed. | 5220 S. U.S. 1 | 561/461–7031 | fax 561/595–8896 | 17 rooms | $55–$70 | AE, D, MC, V.

Hampton Inn Fort Pierce. This two-story hotel is adjacent to a factory outlet mall and near a number of fast food restaurants. The jai alai court is 2 mi away. Take exit 65 off I–95. In-room data ports. Cable TV. Laundry services. Business services. | 2831 Reynolds Dr. | 561/460–9855 or 800/HAMPTON | fax 561/465–7117 | www.hamptoninn.com | 72 rooms | $80–$89 | AE, D, DC, MC, V.

Holiday Inn Express. This two-story motel is in the western part of town. The beach is 8 mi away and Fort Pierce Jai Alai is 1 mi away. There are restaurants within walking distance. Complimentary Continental breakfast. Cable TV. Pool, wading pool. Laundry facilities. Business services. Some pets allowed. | 7151 Okeechobee Rd. | 561/464–5000 or 800/664–7775 | fax 561/461–9573 | www.holiday-inn.com | 103 rooms | $69–$79 | AE, D, DC, MC, V.

Mellon Patch Inn. Across the street from a beach park and across a canal from the Jack Island Wildlife Refuge is this attractive B&B. It's decorated with Mexican tiles and features a cathedral ceiling living room with a wood-burning fireplace. All of the rooms have a unique theme and were decorated by a local artist. The resident parrot, Lowell, provides free entertainment. Picnic area, complimentary breakfast. Cable TV, some in-room phones. Beach, dock. Business services. No kids under 12. | 3601 N. A1A, North Hutchinson Island | 561/461–5231 or 800/656–7824 | fax 561/465–9841 | www.mellonpatchinn.com | 4 rooms | $85–$125 | AE, DC, MC, V.

FORT WALTON BEACH

(Nearby towns also listed: Crestview, Destin, Grayton Beach, Gulf Breeze, Niceville, Pensacola, Pensacola Beach, Seaside)

This popular beach Panhandle town of 22,000 is known for its gorgeous white beaches on the Gulf of Mexico. Fishing is also a big draw—the area calls itself the Billfish Capital of the World. Choctawhatchee Bay, one of the nation's largest inland bays, attracts many sailing enthusiasts. There are good restaurants, concert halls, theaters, and lively night clubs.

Indian tribes came here to perform ceremonial rites beginning in 500 BC. The town is named for Colonel George Walton, the acting governor of the territory of West Florida in the mid-1800s. During World War II, the area was home to Eglin Field, a focal point for Air Force armaments. To this day, Eglin—in nearby Crestview—remains the largest Air Force base in the world.

Information: Greater Fort Walton Chamber of Commerce | 34 Miracle Strip Pkwy. SE, Box 640, Fort Walton, 32459 | 850/244–8191.

Attractions

Air Force Armament Museum. This museum outside Eglin Air Force Base's west gate has restored aircraft and a collection of over 5,000 armaments from World Wars I and II, and the Korean and Vietnam wars. Uniforms, engines, weapons, flight simulators, and aircraft such as B-52 and B-17 bombers are among the exhibits. There's also a 32-min movie about Eglin's history. | 100 Museum Dr. | 850/651–1808 | www.eglin.af.mil | Free | Daily 9:30–4:30.

Gulfarium. The main attraction at this marine life park on Okaloosa Island is Living Sea, a 60,000-gallon tank that simulates conditions on the ocean floor. There are also sea lion shows, trained porpoise performances, and a dolphin interaction program. | 1010 Miracle Strip Pkwy. SE | 850/244–5169 | $16 | Daily 9–4.

Indian Temple Mound and Museum. This downtown museum tells the story of the prehistoric peoples who inhabited northwest Florida up to 10,000 years ago. Adjacent to the museum is the 600-yr-old National Historic Landmark Temple Mound, a large earthwork built over saltwater. | 139 Miracle Strip Pkwy. | 850/833–9595 | $2 | June–Aug., Mon.–Sat. 9–4:30, Sun. 12:30–4:30; Sept.–May, weekdays 11–4, Sat. 9–4.

Pleasure Island Waterpark. This water park has waterslides, wave runners, and volleyball and basketball in the activity pool. There's also a go-kart track. | 1310 Hwy. 98 E | 850/243–97387 | $15 | Mar.–Sept. daily 10–6.

ON THE CALENDAR
APR.: *Arts and Seafood Festival.* The Fort Walton Beach Art Museum hosts this weekend-long festival with live music, seafood tasting, and arts and crafts vendors at Fort Walton Beach Landing. | 800/322–3319.
JUNE: *Billy Bowlegs Pirate Festival.* Local pirate Billy Bowlegs battles local militia, seizes the city, and the fun begins at Fort Walton Beach Landing the first weekend in June. Live music, food, arts and crafts, a boat parade on the waterfront, and a torch-light parade down Eglin Parkway mark the celebratory festivities. | 850/244–8191.

SEPT.: *Greek Festival.* Belly dancers, traditional music, and Greek food are the spotlight of the fest at the Greek Orthodox Church. | 800/322–3319.

Dining

Caffé Italia. Italian. This charming restaurant is known for its cappuccino and desserts. The *maremonti* (a penne pasta with shrimp and covered in a white sauce) is a local favorite. | 189 Brooks St. | 850/664–0035 | Closed Mon. | $7–$17 | AE, D, DC, MC, V.

Kinfolks Bar-B-Q. Barbecue. This casual eatery prides itself on open fire pit cooking. Of the four dishes served, the ribs and chicken is most popular. There is an additional kids' menu. | 333 Racetrack Rd. NW | 850/863–5166 | Reservations not accepted | Closed Sun. | $5–$8 | No credit cards.

Pandora's Steak House. Steaks. This locally famous restaurant has copper chandeliers, ceiling beams, and intimate interior alcoves. You can order your prime rib regular or extra cut; steaks are cooked over a wood-burning grill. Try the char-grilled yellowfin tuna, bacon-wrapped and topped with Jamaican sauce. A lounge here has live music several nights a week. | 1120 Santa Rosa Blvd. | 850/244–8669 | No lunch | $12–$20 | AE, D, DC, MC, V.

Staff's Seafood. Seafood. Known for heaping baskets of hot, homemade wheat bread, this 1931 garage-turned-eatery serves a wonderful seafood skillet (a broiled seafood platter covered with melted cheese) and steaks broiled as you like them. Don't miss the cherry cheesecake at the desert bar. | 24 W. Miracle Strip Pkwy. | 850/243–3526 | Reservations not accepted | No lunch | $13–$28 | AE, MC, V.

Lodging

Carousel Beach Resort. This resort is only steps away from a great stretch of beach. Relax in the mid-beach gazebo or go fishing off the county pier a mile away. Bar. Some kitchenettes, some microwaves, refrigerators. Cable TV. Outdoor pool. Outdoor hot tub. Laundry facilities. Business services. | 571 Santa Rosa Blvd. | 850/243–7658 or 800/523–0208 | fax 850/244–4330 | www.carouselbeach.com | 107 rooms | $110–$170 | AE, D, DC, MC, V.

Days Inn. This two-story motel is in the middle of Fort Walton Beach, 2 mi from the beach. There is a restaurant next door. Complimentary Continental breakfast. Refrigerators, microwaves. Cable TV. Outdoor pool. Some pets allowed. | 135 Miracle Strip Pkwy. | 850/244–6184 or 800/544–8313 | fax 850/244–5764 | www.daysinn.com | 62 rooms | $68–$74 | AE, D, DC, MC, V.

Leeside Inn & Marina. On this Okaloosa Island inn you can watch porpoises at play or take in the sunset from the dock. A 94-slip marina is behind the complex, with a beach (and beachside bar) next door. Breakfast and dinner are served at the Jazz Café. Restaurant, bar. Some kitchenettes, some refrigerators. Cable TV. Outdoor pool. Dock, water sports, boating, fishing. Laundry facilities. Business services. | 1350 Miracle Strip Pkwy. SE | 850/243–7359 or 800/824–2747 | fax 850/243–2809 | www.leesideinn.com | 109 rooms | $75–$95 | AE, D, DC, MC, V.

Marina Motel. This motel across the street from Choctawhatchee Bay offer many rooms with excellent ocean views. Restaurants are within walking distance. Complimentary Continental breakfast. Some kitchenettes, microwaves, refrigerators. Cable TV. Outdoor pool. Docks, boating, fishing. Laundry facilities. Pets allowed (fee). | 1345 Miracle Strip Pkwy. | 850/244–1129 | fax 850/243–6063 | 36 rooms, 2 suites | $50–$125 | AE, D, DC, MC, V.

Radisson Beach Resort. This 15-acre resort has 800 ft of private white-sand beach property. The U-shape complex consists of a seven-story tower flanked by three-story wings. Rooms either face the gulf or one of the pools, though even poolside rooms have partial ocean views. Restaurant, 2 bars, room service. In-room data ports, some refrigerators. Cable TV. 2 outdoor pools, wading pool. 2 tennis courts. Gym, volleyball. Beach. Business services. | 1110 Santa Rosa Blvd. | 850/243–9181 | fax 850/243–7704 | www.radissonresort.com | 261 rooms, 26 suites | $89–$189 | AE, D, DC, MC, V.

Sea Isle Motel. Across the street from the beach is this six-story motel. Three restaurants are a short walk away. Complimentary Continental breakfast. Some kitchenettes, microwaves, refrigerators. Cable TV. Outdoor pool. Hot tub. Gym. Laundry facilities. | 1214 Miracle Strip Pkwy. | 850/243–5563 | fax 850/243–0166 | 60 rooms | $65–$95 | AE, D, DC, MC, V.

Super 8 Motel. The beach is only 1½ mi away from this two-story chain. The Intracoastal Waterway is directly across the street and there are a few restaurants within walking distance. Refrigerators, microwaves. Cable TV. Outdoor pool. No pets. | 333 Miracle Strip Pkwy. | 850/244–4999 | fax 850/243–5657 | www.super8.com | 34 rooms | $69–$89 | AE, D, DC, MC, V.

GAINESVILLE

MAP 3, I3

(Nearby towns also listed: Chiefland, Micanopy, Palatka, Starke)

The northern Florida city of Gainesville, founded in 1854, was named for Edmund Gaines, a hero of the Seminole Wars. Until the late 1800s, its economy was based on citrus farming, but when a site for the new University of Florida was chosen in 1906, its direction changed. Today, the university drives the economy of this city of 85,000. Almost 300 buildings have been preserved in the Northeast Historic District. Just outside of town, you can get a sense of the region's natural beauty at places like San Felasco Hammock State Preserve and Devil's Millhopper State Geological Site, the site of an amazing sinkhole. Florida's second-oldest town, Micanopy, is 13 mi away.

Information: Gainesville Area Chamber of Commerce | 235 S. Main St., Suite 206, Gainesville, 32602 | 352/334–7100 | fax 352/334–7141 | www.gainesvillechamber.com.

GAINESVILLE

INTRO
ATTRACTIONS
DINING
LODGING

Attractions

Bivens Arm Nature Park. This 57-acre urban park, close to the rim of Paynes Prairie, has a mature live-oak hammock and a freshwater marsh ringed by a 1,200-ft boardwalk where you can spot great blue herons, little blue herons, great egrets, cattle egrets, snowy egrets, and other wading birds. The marsh also attracts common moorhens, purple gallinules, aquatic turtles, and snakes. | 3650 S. Main St. | 352/334–2056 | Free | Daily 9–5.

Devil's Millhopper State Geological Site. This enormous sinkhole, a bowl-shaped cavity 120 ft deep, was formed when an underground cavern roof collapsed. Small streams tumble down its steep slopes, then disappear through crevices at the bottom. A boardwalk skirts the rim, and boardwalks and stairways allow access farther down. Many species of plants and animals here are more commonly found in the Appalachian mountains. | 4732 Millhopper Rd. | 352/955–2008 | www.dep.state.fl.us/parks/district_2/devilsmillhopper | $3.25 per vehicle, $1 per person | Daily 8–dusk.

Fred Bear Museum. This museum is dedicated to Fred Bear, a man who traveled the world with the hope of improving bow-hunting equipment and wildlife-management techniques. Exhibits focus on the history and lore of archery and bow-hunting. Near Archer Road at I–75. | 4600 S.W. 41st Blvd. | 352/376–2411 | $5 | Daily 10–6.

Ichetucknee Springs State Park. This 2,248-acre park, 35 mi northwest of Gainesville, preserves the Ichetucknee River, an oak hammock, and sand hills studded with long-leaf turkey oaks. Nine springs feed the river, which flows for 6 mi until it joins the Santa Fe River. Limpkin, wood duck, river otter, and beaver live along the river; rent a canoe or an inner tube from local vendors and float downstream. Or hike the 2.5 mi of trails through the oak hammock or the sand hills. | Hwy. 238, Fort White | 904/497–2511 | www.isgroup.net/issp | $3.25 per vehicle | Daily.

Kanapaha Botanical Gardens. This 62-acre complex on the shores of Lake Kanapaha includes 19 different gardens and encompasses both mature hardwood forests and rolling meadows. A path meanders through the woods, providing cool shade on hot days. | 4700 S.W. 58th Dr. | 352/372–4981 | fax 352/372–5892 | hammock.ifas.ufl.edu/kanapaha/about.html | $3 | Mon., Tues., Fri. 9–5; Wed. and weekends 9–dusk.

Matheson Museum. This museum is a tribute to the history of Alachua County. Highlights include a photo archive and artifacts that date back to the 1500s, and a re-creation of an early 19th-century general store. | 513 E. University Ave. | 352/378–2280 | Free | Tues.–Fri. 9:30–1:30, 2nd and 4th Sat. each month 10–4, Sun. 1–5.

Morningside Nature Center. Natural communities present on this 278-acre preserve include longleaf pine, wet flat woods, and depression marshes. There is also a barn that dates back to the 1880s and simple farm animals (sheep, pigs, mules) on the premises. | 3540 E. University Ave. | 352/334–2170 | www.natureoperations.org | Free | Daily 9–5.

O'Leno State Park. This 6,300-acre park, 30 mi northwest of Gainesville, lies along the Santa Fe River, a Suwannee tributary; it disappears in the park and flows underground for more than 3 mi before returning to the surface. The park also includes sinkholes, hardwood hammock, river swamp, and sand-hill communities that consist of pine and wire grass. Along two nature trails, you can see alligators and turtles. There's picnicking, camping, and horseback riding (bring your own horse) on land; and swimming, canoeing, and fishing in the Santa Fe River. | U.S. 441/41, High Springs | 904/454–1853 | $3.25 per vehicle | Daily.

University of Florida. Home of the University of Florida Gators, this 200-acre campus is worth visiting for its museums, architecture, and wildlife. The northeastern section of campus is on the National Register of Historic Places, and Lake Alice and environs is a wildlife

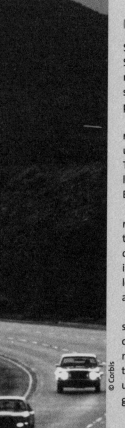

© Corbis

HANGING AROUND WITH SPANISH MOSS

Swaying palm trees in the tropics. Flat-topped baobab trees in southern Africa. Spiny cactus in the American southwest. Green things such as those have come to represent and instantly identify the areas where they are most common. And in the southern part of the United States, no plant seems more characteristic or atmospheric than Spanish moss.

Of course, there's nothing Spanish about it. Native Americans who lived in the region called it "tree hair." Early French explorers in the area adapted that name but used it as an opportunity to mock their Spanish counterparts in the New World. They called it "Spanish beard." The Spaniards, not to be outdone, also adapted the local name, but they called it "French hair." Over the years, and with a transfer into English, the name comes down to us as Spanish moss.

But it isn't moss either and is completely unrelated to the plant groups that include mosses. In fact, it's a bromeliad and therefore more closely related to the pineapple than any moss. Like tropical orchids, it's also an epiphyte, adhering to a host plant but drawing its own food and water from the air. The seeds of Spanish moss lodge securely in the rough bark of live oaks, set up shop, and start growing, sometimes reaching a length of 25 ft as they hang from a branch. And it only grows on trees, so if you see it on a telephone pole or elsewhere, it only got there courtesy of the wind.

With so much of it around—a large tree can yield as much as a ton of the stuff—human ingenuity has devised a number of uses for it: as an element in a caulking compound, as kindling and mulch, and in such commercial uses as packing material, saddle blankets, and stuffing for mattresses. It's useful, too, to the bats that love to make a home in it, and to the snakes that love to eat them. But its best use is no doubt in its natural state, lending an air of sleepy mystery and sedate gloom to the trees and forests of the South.

preserve. The Century Tower carillon, by the University Auditorium, chimes hourly. | W. University Ave. and 13th St. | 352/392–3261 | www.ufl.edu | Free | Daily.

Florida Museum of Natural History. This is the largest natural history museum in the southern United States, with many specimens of mammals, birds, reptiles, amphibians, fishes, mollusks, butterflies, vertebrate and invertebrate fossils, and recent and fossil plants. The main museum is in Powell Hall and the herbarium is in Rolfs Hall. The museum also manages the 9,000-acre Katharine Ordway Preserve, 26 mi east of Gainesville. | Powell Hall, 34th St. at Hull Rd. | 352/392–1721 | www.flmnh.ufl.edu | Free | Mon.–Sat. 10–5, Sun. 1–5.

Lake Alice Wildlife Preserve. This lush sanctuary edges the campus on the west. The main draws are the alligators, which can be seen crawling around. | Museum Rd. | 352/392–3261 | Free | Daily.

Samuel P. Harn Museum of Art. The permanent collection here contains more than 6,000 paintings, sculptures, prints, photographs, and artifacts of diverse cultures ranging from Europe and the Americas to Asia and Africa. | S.W. 34th St. and Hull Rd. | 352/392–9826 | fax 352/392–3892 | www.arts.ufl.edu/harn | Free | Tues.–Fri. 11–5, Sat. 10–5, Sun. 1–5.

University Art Gallery. This gallery has exhibitions of contemporary art in all mediums by regionally, nationally, and internationally recognized artists. Occasionally the work of students and faculty is shown. | 400 S.W. 13th St. | 352/392–0201 | Free | Tues.–Fri. 10–3, Sat. 1–5.

ON THE CALENDAR

FEB.: *Hogtown Medieval Fair.* This family-oriented event held the first two weeks of February at the Alachua County Fairgrounds is a throwback to Europe's medieval courts. Many people dress in traditional medieval garb, and there's a jousting competition. Children usually enjoy the juggling and puppet shows. | 352/334–5064.

FEB.: *The Gatornationals.* The National Hot Rod Association holds championship races each winter at the Gainesville Raceway. | 352/377–0046.

OCT.: *Celebration of the Autumn Moon.* Kanapaha Botanical Gardens is lighted with resident fireflies, *luminarias* (paper lanterns), floating candles, and the autumn moon. There is also live musical entertainment. | 352/372–4981.

NOV.: *Craft Festival.* Held in the Stephen C. O'Connell Center on the University of Florida campus, this is largest indoor craft show in north central Florida, with more than 260 booths. Santa Claus is known to show up. | 352/392–7238.

Dining

Amelia's. Italian. Amelia's is known for the best fine Italian food in town. With soft music, lace curtains, and flickering candles, it oozes with old-world charm. Be sure to try either the veal Sorrentino or chicken marsala. | 235 S. Main St., Suite 107 | 352/373–1919 | Reservations essential on weekends | No lunch weekends | $11–$32 | AE, D, MC, V.

Brasserie. Contemporary. The waiters at this formal restaurant wear tuxedos; the tables wear flowers and white cloths. Popular choices include grilled swordfish with sun-dried pimiento garlic oil, and filet mignon with roasted portobello mushrooms. The food is artistically presented. | 101 S.E. 2nd Ave. | 352/375–6612 | Closed Sun. No lunch | $15–$24 | AE, D, DC, MC, V.

Emiliano's Cafe. Caribbean. Paintings and sculptures of local artists adorn the walls and tables of this popular spot. Try the paella and malanga-encrusted snapper. There's sidewalk seating. Kids' menu. | 7 S.E. 1st Ave. | 352/375–7381 | Reservations not accepted | Closed Sun.–Mon. | $11–$19 | AE, D, MC, V.

Market Street Pub. American. This large British-style pub brews its own beer and serves homemade sausage, fish-and-chips, and hearty sandwiches. There's sidewalk seating. | 120 S.W. 1st Ave. | 352/377–2927 | Closed Sun. No lunch | $4–$7 | AE, D, MC, V.

Melting Pot. Eclectic. Sit downstairs or upstairs in the cozy loft at this fondue restaurant. No matter what you order, you do your own cooking here: dip slivers of fish or steak into sizzling hot oil or cubes of French bread into melted cheese. For dessert you can dip bits of fruit into chocolate. | 418 E. University Ave. | 352/372–5623 | No lunch | $11–$20 | AE, D, MC, V.

Napolatano's. Italian. This enormous restaurant has two indoor dining rooms and two outdoor patios. Abundant flora and pictures of the Italian countryside decorate the dining rooms. The lasagna and chicken parmigiana are delicious, and be sure to check the daily chef's specials. Kids' menu. | 606 N.W. 75th St. | 352/332–6671 | $8–$16 | AE, DC, MC, V.

Sovereign. Continental. This delightfully rustic local favorite is housed in a century-old brick building. The chef recommends the veal dishes and the ostrich. | 12 S.E. 2nd Ave., Gainesville | 352/378–6307 | www.sovereign-restaurant.com | Closed Sun. No lunch | $18–$33 | AE, D, DC, MC, V.

Steve's Cafe. American. In downtown Gainesville, Steve's makes its home in an historic structure that was built at the turn of the 20th century; it's popular with college students. Try the rack of lamb and rum-and-pepper-painted grouper with mango sauce. | 12 W. University Ave. | 352/377–9337 | No lunch | $11–$23 | MC, V.

Lodging

Best Western Gateway Grand. Built in 1998, this three-story hotel has a tranquil setting on a hill overlooking corn fields. There's a restaurant nearby, and the downtown Gainesville historic district is 12 mi away. Complimentary Continental breakfast. In-room data ports, some refrigerators, some microwaves. Cable TV. Pool. Outdoor hot tub. Gym. Laundry service. Business services. Some pets. | 4200 N.W. 97th Blvd. | 352/331–3336 | fax 352/331–3337 | www.bestwestern.com | 152 rooms | $79–$89 | AE, D, DC, MC, V.

Cabot Lodge. Rooms are spacious at this lodge, 12 mi from the airport and a mile from the university. Although the building dates to the mid-1980s, major renovations were made 1997–2000. A two-hour cocktail reception is held nightly. Complimentary Continental breakfast. In-room data ports. Cable TV, some in-room VCRs (and movies). Pool. Gym. Business services. | 3726 S.W. 40th Blvd. | 352/375–2400 or 800/843–8735 | fax 352/335–2321 | www.cabotlodge.com | 208 rooms | $77–$92 | AE, D, DC, MC, V.

Courtyard Gainesville. This three-story hotel sees a lot of business travelers and visitors to the University of Florida, which is only 4 mi away. There are a handful of restaurants within walking distance. Restaurant. In-room data ports. Cable TV. Pool. Outdoor hot tub. Gym. Laundry facilities. Business services. | 3700 S.W. 42nd St. | 352/335–9100 or 888/236–2427 | fax 352/335–1502 | www.marriott.com | 78 rooms, 3 suites | $81–$87; $131 suites | AE, D, DC, MC, V.

Econo Lodge. This inexpensive motel is six blocks from the University of Florida and 6 miles from the Gainesville Raceway. There are many restaurants within walking distance. In-room data ports. Cable TV. Pool. Pets allowed. | 2649 S.W. 13th St. | 352/373–7816 | fax 352/372–9099 | www.econolodge.com | 53 rooms | $47–$57 | AE, D, DC, MC, V.

Fairfield Inn. Five miles from the University of Florida and 15 mi from the airport, this three-story hotel often hosts visitors to the university. Complimentary Continental breakfast. In-room data ports. Cable TV. Pool. Gym. Laundry service. Business services. | 6901 N.W. 4th Blvd. | 352/332–8292 | fax 352/332–8292 | 135 rooms | $54 | AE, D, DC, MC, V.

Hampton Inn Gainesville. Built in 1995, this five-story hotel is a short drive away from many restaurants. Local attractions such as the Fred Bear Museum and the Florida Museum of Natural History are less than 5 mi away. In-room data ports, some microwaves, some refrigerators. Cable TV. Pool. Laundry service. Business services. | 4225 S.W. 40th Blvd. | 352/371–4171 or 800/HAMPTON | fax 352/371–4234 | www.hamptoninn.com | 96 rooms, 9 suites | $76–$80; $97 suites | AE, D, DC, MC, V.

Holiday Inn, University Center. This recently renovated six-story hotel is adjacent to the university. Guests can enjoy a swim in the Olympic-size rooftop pool and can sunbathe in the 12,000-square-ft tanning area. Rooms have desks and ergonomic chairs. Restaurant, bar. In-room data ports, room service. Cable TV. Pool. Gym. Laundry service. Business services, airport shuttle. | 1250 W. University Ave. | 352/376–1661 | fax 352/336–8717 | www.holiday-inn.com | 165 rooms | $97–$117 | AE, D, DC, MC, V.

La Quinta. Just 12 mi from the airport, this chain motel is across the street from a mall with shops and restaurants. Complimentary Continental breakfast. In-room data ports, some microwaves, some refrigerators. Cable TV. Pool. Pets allowed. | 920 N.W. 69th Terr. | 352/332–6466 | fax 352/332–7074 | www.laquinta.com | 131 rooms, 4 suites | $65–$69, $89–$99 suites | AE, D, DC, MC, V.

Magnolia Plantation Bed & Breakfast. This Second Empire Victorian home dates to 1885. The mansard roof, in addition to ten original fireplaces, contributes to the inn's elegance. Wine and snacks are served nightly. Complimentary breakfast. Refrigerators. Some in-room VCRs, some room phones, no TV in some rooms. Massage. Pets allowed (restrictions). No smoking. | 309 S.E. 7th St. | 352/375–6653 | fax 352/338–0303 | www.magnoliabnb.com | 5 rooms, 3 cottages | $90–$105, $135–$165 cottages | AE, MC, V.

Ramada Limited–Gainesville. This charming Ramada Inn is spread out over 4 wooded acres, next to I–75. A movie theater, shopping center, and restaurants are within walking distance. Complimentary Continental breakfast. In-room data ports. Cable TV. Pool. Business services. Pets allowed (fee). | 4021 S.W. 40th Blvd. | 352/373–0392 | fax 352/336–7855 | www.ramada.com | 114 rooms | $64–$74 | AE, D, DC, MC, V.

Residence Inn by Marriott. This luxurious hotel is ideally located, 4 mi from the university and 7 mi from the airport. Also, most local attractions are within 10 mi, and the Bivens Arm Nature Park is a half-mile away. Complimentary Continental breakfast. Kitchenettes, microwaves, refrigerators. Cable TV. Pool. Hot tub. Laundry service. Business services. Airport shuttle. Some pets allowed (fee). | 4001 S.W. 13th St. | 352/371–2101 or 888/236–2427 | fax 352/371–2247 | www.residenceinn.com | 80 suites | $90–$125 suites | AE, D, DC, MC, V.

Sweetwater Branch Inn. This 1885 Victorian inn is elegantly appointed with antiques. Most rooms have fireplaces and ornate Oriental rugs. You can relax on the patio or verandah. Complimentary breakfast. In-room data ports, some in-room hot tubs. Cable TV, in-room VCRs. Laundry facilities. Business services. No smoking. | 625 University Ave. | 352/373–6760 or 800/595–7760 | fax 352/371–3771 | www.sweetwaterinn.com | 14 rooms | $110–$175 | AE, MC, V.

GRASSY KEY/CRAWL KEY

MAP 3, D6

(Nearby towns also listed: Conch Key/Duck Key, Islamorada, Marathon)

Grassy Key (pop. 768) is a sleepy little key primarily inhabited by families that operate the handful of little motels and restaurants here. Most tourists who stop in are bound for the famous Dolphin Research Center. Although there are a few little motels, no one lives on Crawl Key, whose vegetation consists of shrubs and native trees.

Information: Greater Marathon Chamber of Commerce | 12222 Overseas Highway, Marathon, 33050 | 305/743–5417 or 800/352–5397 | www.floridakeysmarathon.com.

Attractions

Dolphin Research Center. The creator of the movie *Flipper* opened this not-for-profit home for dolphins and sea lions in the late 1950s. You can swim with dolphins (Dolphin Encounter, which requires at least a month's advance booking), interact from a submerged platform (Dolphin Splash), or watch from the water's edge (Tips on Training). | MM 59, Overseas Hwy. | 305/289–1121 | www.dolphins.org | Tours $12.50, Tips on Training $35, Dolphin Splash $60, Dolphin Encounter $110 | Daily 9–4, walking tours daily 10, 11, 12:30, 2, and 3:30.

Curry Hammock State Park. This 260-acre shoreline park is a birding paradise. Natives call the trails that run through the canopies of arching mangroves one of the Keys' top kayaking spots. The day-use facilities include a sandy beach and picnic areas on the ocean side.

GRASSY KEY/
CRAWL KEY

INTRO
ATTRACTIONS
DINING
LODGING

| MM 57, Overseas Hwy., Crawl Key | Long Key Recreational Area 305/664–4815 | www.dep.state.fl.us | Free | Daily 8–sunset.

Dining

Grassy Key Dairy Bar. Seafood. This family-owned restaurant has stood since 1959, though the old plastic ice cream cone that welcomed you to the "Dairy Bar" (the DB in the name) was knocked over by a hurricane in 1999. Besides seafood such as grilled dolphin (mahimahi) glazed with ginger and wasabi horseradish, the restaurant offers a wide variety of mud pies, including egg nog, praline, and black walnut cherry. | MM 58.5, Overseas Hwy. | 305/743–3816 | Closed Sun.–Mon. | $8–$20 | MC, V.

The Wreck. Seafood. This relaxed local hangout right off the highway serves up seafood, steaks, and burgers off the grill. There's a tiki hut patio outside, while wreckage from old ships that went down in the area, such as steering wheels and bells, hang on the walls of the interior. A popular dish is the fried, coconut-dipped jumbo shrimp; all meals come with baked potatoes or rice and vegetables. | MM 59, 58835 Overseas Hwy. | 305/743–8282 | $9–14 | MC, V.

Lodging

Valhalla Point. This very laid-back Crawl Key motel is superbly situated on the water, across from Curry Hammock State Park. On the water is a very nice small beach with hammocks and chaises, barbecue grills, kayaks, and canoes (loaned free to guests). You might spot manatees off the dock. Picnic area. Some kitchenettes, microwaves, refrigerators. Cable TV, no room phones. Beach, dock, water sports, boating, fishing. Laundry facilities. | MM 56.5, 56223 Ocean Drive, Crawl Key | 305/289–0614 | www.keysresort.com | 4 rooms | $75–$90 | MC, V.

Valhalla Beach Motel. This simple, secluded motel on the water offers gives free canoes to its guests, which you can use to get to mangrove trails of Curry Hammock State Park across the lagoon. You can also lounge in tiki huts under palm trees on the beach here and cook up dinner on the grill. Some kitchenettes, some microwaves, refrigerators. Cable TV. Beach, dock, water sports, boating, fishing. | MM 57.5, 56243 Ocean Dr., Crawl Key | 305/289–0616 | 10 units | $65–$145 | No credit cards.

GRAYTON BEACH

MAP 3, C2

(Nearby towns also listed: De Funiak Springs, Destin, Niceville, Seaside)

One of the oldest, simplest, and most charming of the 19 southern Walton County beach communities, Grayton Beach doesn't block its coastal views with built-up condominiums. Instead, it's easiest to rent individually owned Old Florida cottages from local real estate agencies. Shopping and great parks abound around here.

Information: South Walton Tourist Development Council | 25777 U.S. Hwy. 331S, Santa Rosa Beach, Santa Rosa Beach, 32459 | 850/267–1216 or 800/822–6877 | www.beachesofsouthwalton.com.

Attractions

★ **Grayton Beach State Recreation Area.** Swimming and fishing are popular in this 400-acre park with a mile of Gulf shoreline. In the dunes, what sometimes look like bushes are often full-size slash pines and southern magnolias buried up to their tops by drifting sand. Inland are pine flatwoods and scrub lands and the brackish Western Lake, ringed by salt marshes. The recreation area is 2 mi south of Highway 98. | 357 Main Park Rd. | 850/231–4210 | www.dep.state.fl.us/parks | $3.25 per vehicle | Daily 8–sunset.

Eden State Gardens. An antebellum mansion called the Wellesley House is situated amid moss-cloaked live oaks and surrounding gardens. Don't miss it if you're here in mid-March, when the dogwoods and azaleas are in full bloom. | Rte. 395, Point Washington | 850/231–4214 | $2 | Daily 8–sunset; tours of Wellesley House Thurs.–Mon. 9–4.

ON THE CALENDAR

MAY: *ArtsQuest*. This week-long fest in Eden State Gardens in early May has cultural events, live music, gallery tours, a 5K run, and parties culminating in a juried art show the final weekend. Vendors sell wares varying from food to jewelry. | 850/231–0885.

Dining

Criollas. Caribbean. The inventive menu here fuses Caribbean and Creole dishes. A Pueblo sun corn–crusted yellowfin tuna and mushroom-, pancetta-, and chayote-stuffed chimichanga is served on a blue corn *posole* with calamari and papaya salsa. | 170 E. Rte. 30A | 850/267–1267 | Reservations essential | Closed Sun. Sept.–Apr. Dinner only | $19–29 | AE, D, MC, V.

Picolo Restaurant & Red Bar. Mediterranean. Eclectic memorabilia cover every square inch of this lively beachfront favorite where a blackboard displays the day's five changing specials. On weekends, try the Louisiana jumbo long crab cakes with homemade mashed potatoes and mesclun salad greens. Live jazz bands play nightly all year, and the outdoor patio and bar is a hotspot on weekends. | 70 Hotz Ave. | 850/231–1008 | Reservations not accepted | $9–$15 | No credit cards.

Pandora's. Seafood. The thatched bamboo ceiling and outdoor tiki bar and deck with live music on weekends give Pandora's a real beach feel, though this casual family restaurant is a couple of blocks away from the water. Popular dishes include lobster snow crab, grouper, and six different cuts of steak. | 63 DeFuniak St. | 850/244–8669 | Closed Jan. 1–7 | $15–$32 | AE, D, DC, MC, V.

Lodging

Hibiscus Coffee & Guesthouse. Ten minutes from the beach is this quaint, two-story complex with gardens. The simple and very clean rooms are tastefully adorned with small artistic prints. The Art Deco room and Hibiscus rooms have claw-foot tubs. A café downstairs serves breakfast and lunch. Restaurant. Cable TV. Bicycles. Library. Laundry facilities. | 85 DeFuniak St. | 850/231–2733 | www.hibiscusflorida.com | 4 rooms | $95–$115 | MC, V.

GULF BREEZE

MAP 3, A2

(Nearby towns also listed: Pensacola, Pensacola Beach)

This pretty Florida Panhandle resort town of 5,000, at the tip of the peninsula that separates Pensacola Bay from its barrier islands, has miles of beaches on the Gulf of Mexico. The town can trace its history back to 1936, when the Gulf Breeze Cottages and store opened on the narrow peninsula. Today its economy relies on the presence of the U.S. Navy and a vast range of recreational activities including fishing, sailing, swimming, and diving, which draw tourists in large numbers.

Information: **Gulf Breeze Area Chamber of Commerce** | Box 337, Gulf Breeze, 32562 | 850/932–7888 | fax 850/934–4601 | www.gulfbreezechamber.com.

Attractions

The Zoo. Catch a ride on the Safari Line train for an up-close excursion through 30 acres of roaming animals in their natural habitat. You can see everything from orangutans to bears to alligators. | 5701 Gulf Breeze Pkwy. | 850/932–2229 | fax 850/932–8575 | www.the-zoo.com | $16 | Daily 9–5.

MAR.: *Gulf Breeze Celebrates the Arts Festival.* This festival usually brings out the entire town. The art on display is seemingly unlimited, from handcrafted objects to paintings and photography. There's a separate children's art exhibit. | Shoreline Park, 800 Shoreline Dr. | 850/432–9906.

Dining

Cancun Mexican Grill. Mexican. Note the large and realistic oceanfront mural as you enter this eatery known for chicken fajitas and quesadillas. There's outdoor dining on a patio. Kids' menu. | 1385 Shoreline Dr. | 850/916–4520 | $5–$11 | AE, D, MC, V.

Lodging

Holiday Inn Gulf Breeze Bay Beach. This hotel comprises three two-story buildings on Pensacola Bay. It's 6 mi from Pensacola Beach, and 5 mi from the zoo. Restaurant. In-room data ports, some microwaves, some refrigerators. Cable TV. Pool, wading pool. Laundry service. Business services. Pets allowed (fee). | 51 Gulf Breeze Pkwy. | 850/932–2214 | fax 850/932–0932 | www.holiday-inn.com | 160 rooms, 8 suites in 3 buildings | $89–$109, $129 suites | AE, D, DC, MC, V.

HAINES CITY

MAP 3, J6

(Nearby towns also listed: Davenport, Lake Wales, Winter Haven)

Set in the heart of central Florida's citrus country, this burgeoning town is a good jumping-off spot for a visit to Orlando, 45 miles to the northeast. At the northern end of the Lake Wales Ridge, the town has become a growing retirement community, seeing a shift from its traditional agriculture base. To that end, golf courses, condominiums, and shopping centers are popping up, along with the new Heart of Florida Hospital.

Information: Haines City Chamber of Commerce | Box 986 (908 U.S. 27), Haines City, 33845 | 863/422–3751 | fax 863/422–4704 | www.hainescity.com.

MAR.: *Heritage Days.* Food, games, and live music bring the residents of Haines City together for this celebration. Come and meet the oldest person in Haines City. | 863/422–3751.

Dining

El Ranchito. Mexican. Mariachi costumes and instruments and piñatas decorate this casual eatery. The tostadas and shrimp cocktail plate are popular. | 2555 U.S. 17/92 | 863/422–8920 | Breakfast also available | $7–$9 | AE, MC, V.

Hungry Howie's Pizza & Sub's. Fast food. Diners at this simple, mirrored spot can dine at a table or in a booth. As the name indicates, pizzas are the specialty, as is the combo sub, which comes with four different meats. | 117 N. 7th St. | 863/422–1111 | $4–$9 | MC, V.

Savanna Steak House. Steak. Top sirloins and the marinated (naturally, with a secret sauce) chicken are the top requests at this steak house. The decor is Western, with a mounted cow head and miniature rocking horses livening up the dining area. Kids' menu. | 608 U.S. 27 | 863/422–3910 | $6–$22 | AE, D, DC, MC, V.

Lodging

Best Western Lake Hamilton. Built in 1994 and just off U.S. 27, this Best Western has a quiet country setting and is surrounded by three fields. The famed Southern Dunes Championship Golf Course is only 3 mi away. Complimentary Continental breakfast. Some microwaves, some refrigerators. Cable TV. Pool. Tennis court. Laundry facilities. Business services. Pets allowed. | 605 B. Moore Rd. | 863/421–6929 | fax 863/422–0409 | www.best-western.com | 45 rooms, 5 suites | $55–$65, $75 suites | AE, D, DC, MC, V.

Grenelefe. This golf and tennis resort sprawls across 1,000 acres of manicured tropical gardens and oak trees. Rooms are in an Audubon Society preserve and have views of the woods, water, or golf course. Restaurant, bar, dining room, picnic area. Refrigerators. Cable TV, some in-room VCRs. Pool. Outdoor hot tub, massage, sauna. Driving ranges, 3 golf courses, miniature golf, putting green, 20 tennis courts. Gym. Dock, boating, fishing, bicycles. Video games. Children's programs (ages 4–12), playground. Laundry facilities. Business services. | 3200 Hwy. 546, Haines City | 863/422–7511 or 800/422–5333 | fax 863/421–5000 | www.grenelefe.com | 480 rooms, 370 suites | $190, $230–$420 suites | AE, D, DC, MC, V.

Howard Johnson–Haines City. This hotel was built in 1973 and remodeled in 1998. On U.S. 27, this two-story property is 20 mi from Walt Disney World. Restaurant, bar. Some microwaves, some refrigerators available. Cable TV. Pool. Laundry service. Business services. Some pets (fee). | 1504 U.S. 27 S | 863/422–8621 or 800/406–1411 | fax 863/421–4745 | www.hojo.com | 120 rooms | $59–$89 | AE, D, DC, MC, V.

State Motel. This single-story motel has spacious rooms and is within walking distance of a few restaurants. Cypress Gardens in Winter Haven is 12 mi away. Restaurant. Some kitchenettes, microwaves. Pool. | 905 U.S. 27N | 863/422–1331 | 28 rooms | $42–$48 | D, MC, V.

HIALEAH

MAP 3, E4

(Nearby towns also listed: Coral Gables, Hollywood, Miami, Miami Beach)

Florida's fifth-largest city (pop. 240,000) contains the world's largest Cuban population outside of Havana. It's home to lovely, landscaped Hialeah Park, famous for its thoroughbred racing and celebrity visitors, which have included the Kennedy family and J. P. Morgan. The flamingos that appeared in the opening credits of the 1980s TV series Miami Vice were filmed here.

It's also a Cuban exile political base with a hearty local scene. Long-time mayor Raul Martinez, the cause of much political scandal, threatened in 2000 to make Hialeah its own county, feuding with Miami-Dade mayor (and former Hialeah councilman), Alex Penelas.

Unlike those in most of the area's municipalities, the street grid in Hialeah follows its own pattern. The city is bounded roughly by the Palmetto Expressway (Highway 826) to the west, and by Le Jeune Road, called E. 8th Street (or 42nd St. on the Miami grid) on the east. The main thoroughfare is 49th Street (or 103rd Street).

Hialeah got started on its way to becoming a real metropolitan center in the roaring '20s. After the hurricane of 1926, the city was devastated but quickly rebounded and continued to see population and industrial growth. A major change came in the early 1960s, when Cuban immigrants fled Fidel Castro's Cuba for South Florida in large numbers, settling in to await his departure; they're still waiting. Today Hialeah (which means "high prairie" in the local Native American language) is a busy residential, mixed white- and blue-collar community. Telemundo, the country's largest Spanish-language television network, broadcasts from Hialeah. Although there are few tourist attractions, you can practice your Spanish while sipping *café cubano* from any of a hundred bakery cafés.

Information: **Hialeah Chamber of Commerce and Industries** | 1840 W. 49th St., Suite 700, Hialeah, 33012 | 305/828–9898 | www.hialeahchamber.com.

Attractions

Amelia Earhart Park. This 515-acre park at the city's northeast corner is alive with many exotic species of birds and fish. Kids love it, too: you can visit a farm village, rent a paddle boat, enjoy numerous elaborate playgrounds, or fish in any of five lakes. There's a 5K running track that wends around the park. | 401 E. 65th St. | 305/685–8389 | Free | Daily 9–dusk.

Hialeah Park. This beautiful 228-acre thoroughbred racetrack, built in 1925, is known for its meticulously landscaped grounds and gardens, its flock of Cuban pink flamingos, and its elegant design. Metrorail's Hialeah Station is nearby, should you wish to use public transport from downtown Miami. Racing takes place mid-March through May, though the grounds are open all year: You can count on seeing wedding photo shoots every day. The park is listed on the National Register of Historic Places. | 2200 E. 4th Ave. | 305/885–8000 | www.hialeahpark.com | Free | Daily 11–11.

ON THE CALENDAR

FEB.: *Hialeah Spring Festival.* This 10-day event usually brings out the entire town. The international food booths and musical performances are big draws. Children love the carnival-style rides. | 305/828–9898.

Dining

El Segundo Viajante. Spanish. Painted country scenes re-create the sense of a Spanish village at this restaurant across from Hialeah Park. The owners have been preparing the specialties taught them by their Cuban parents and Spanish grandparents since 1965. Try the paella, prepared traditionally with lobster, shrimp, clams, calamari, and chicken. Cuban

THE WORLD'S FASTEST SPORT

If children in arctic climes dream about Florida's wide, white-sand beaches, Basque boys must dream of Florida's long, sleek jai alai courts. After all, the sport that's synonymous with Spain's northeastern Basque region, where jai alai was born centuries ago, finds its professional apotheosis in Florida's frontons (the term for jai alai arenas). The biggest frontons in the world are here, attracting the best players from Spain and the rest of the globe—though most players in the sport are, in fact, Basque.

Jai alai resembles handball but with some special equipment. Players bounce a ball called a *pelota*—the hardest ball in all sports—and send it speeding across a 50-yard court with a *cesta* (a curved wicker scoop strapped to the right arm). (*Pelota* is also the name of the sport in the Basque Country.) The opposing player—or team of two players—must return the pelota after one bounce. It's a fast sport, the world's fastest according to the *Guiness Book of World Records* (the pelota travels upwards of 180 mph).

Gambling is a fundamental part of the jai alai experience, and bettors are often familiar with the stats of all the players. Miami Jai Alai, which has 6,500 seats, is the world's largest fronton and also the oldest one in the U.S., built in 1926. Dania Jai Alai, built in 1953, is the world's second-largest fronton, seating 5,600. Other frontons are in Ocala, Ft. Pierce, and Orlando. The city of North Miami has a jai alai training school. There are only two other frontons in the U.S.: in Newport, Rhode Island, and New Milford, Connecticut.

When it was imported to Cuba in 1900, jai alai was a big hit, but Fidel Castro banned it in the late 1950s, so the Cubans who fled from post-Castro Cuba brought it with them to Florida. A three-year strike beginning in 1988 set the sport's momentum back in the U.S. Perhaps because of this, jai alai is very affordable—general admission seating in Miami is $1—and the absence of advertising and theatrics is, to many, a welcome relief from other more heavily sponsored sporting events.

© Corbis

fare includes excellent *palomilla* (inside round cut) or *churrasco* (flank) steaks, grilled and served with black beans, rice, and fried plantains. | 2846 Palm Ave. | 305/888–5465 | Reservations not accepted | $8–$28 | AE, D, DC, MC, V.

La Carreta. Cuban. Experience the city's Cuban rhythms by sampling traditional staples like croquetas and black beans, and then heading upstairs for a peek of ongoing salsa classes. (You can join in for $7.) La Carreta is a popular, small local chain of large restaurants serving good *criolla* (homemade) Cuban cuisine. If you're in a rush, grab a few croquetas for 35 cents apiece at the takeout window. | 5350 W. 16th Ave. | 305/823–5200 | Reservations not accepted | $8–$15 | AE, D, MC, V.

Molinas Ranch. Cuban. One of three Molinas in the Miami area, this ranch-style restaurant packs in a crowds for lunch and dinner every day. The recipe is simple: good Cuban food with no fuss. Basic grilled steaks, pork, and Cuban stews fill the extensive menu. The restaurant is at the corner of Le Juene Road (in Miami terms, N.W. 42nd St., E. 8th St. for locals), 2 mi north of the airport. | 4100 E. 8th Ave. | 305/687–0008 | Reservations not accepted | $6–$20 | AE, D, DC, MC, V.

Lodging

Courtyard by Marriott–Miami Lakes. This four-story hotel draws a lot of business travelers. The hotel is near Don Shula's Steakhouse and Country Club, and a walk from the attractive Main Street conglomeration of shops, restaurant, and movies. Exit the Palmetto Expressway (Highway 826) at 154th Street. Restaurant. In-room data ports, some microwaves, some refrigerators. Cable TV. Pool. Outdoor hot tub, spa. Gym. Laundry facilities, laundry service. Business services. | 15700 N.W. 77th Ct. | 305/556–6665 or 888/236–2427 | fax 305/556–0282 | www.marriott.com | 139 rooms, 12 suites | $89–$104, $124–$134 suites | AE, D, DC, MC, V.

Miami Plaza Hotel. This attractive 10-story hotel is 8 mi northwest of Miami International Airport. There is a restaurant on the premises that doubles as a nightclub on the weekends. There are also seven banquet and meeting rooms. The hotel is directly west of the Palmetto Expressway (Highway 826) at the 103 Street/49th Street exit. Restaurant, bar, complimentary Continental breakfast. In-room data ports, some refrigerators. Cable TV. Pool. Laundry service. Business services, airport shuttle. | 7707 N.W. 103rd St., Hialeah Gardens | 305/825–1000 | fax 305/556–6785 | www.avistahotels.com/miami | 262 rooms | $69–$79 | AE, D, DC, MC, V.

Ramada Inn Miami Airport North. This four-story hotel is across from Hialeah's favorite shopping place, Westland Mall, and 10 mi north of Miami International Airport. The hotel offers shuttle service to the Sawgrass Mills Discount Outlet in Broward County. Access the hotel at the 103 Street/49th Street exit of the Palmetto Expressway (Highway 826). Restaurant, bar, room service. Some microwaves, some refrigerators. Cable TV. Pool, wading pool. Laundry facilities, laundry service. Business services, airport shuttle. | 1950 W. 49th St. | 305/823–2000 or 800/843–1334 | fax 305/362–4562 | www.ramada.com | 171 rooms | $85 | AE, D, DC, MC, V.

HOLLYWOOD

(Nearby towns also listed: Dania Beach, Davie, Hialeah, Miami, Miami Beach)

Hollywood was founded in 1921 by idealistic California entrepreneur Joseph W. Young, who aimed to make the area the tinseltown of the east. Today, at least, he seems to be getting his wish. The 2½-mile boardwalk along the beach is bustling with new shops, cafés, and people, who rollerblade by day and swoon at Harrison Street jazz clubs by night. The city of 125,000 is boosted with a healthy contingent of snowbirds and is slowly starting to resemble Miami's South Beach.

Information: **Greater Hollywood Chamber of Commerce** | 330 N. Federal Hwy., Hollywood, 33020 | 954/923–4000 or 800/231–5562 | fax 954/923–8737 | www.hollywood-chamber.org.

Attractions

Gulfstream Park. The nation's top thoroughbreds race here from January through mid-March. Gulfstream Park is also the venue for the famed Florida Derby in March. The park is a short drive south of Hollywood. | 901 S. Federal Hwy., Hallandale | 954/454–7000 or 800/771–8873 | www.gulfstreampark.com | $3 grandstand, $5 clubhouse | Jan.–mid-Mar., Wed.–Mon.

Seminole Native Village. You can pet a cougar, hold a baby alligator, and watch other wildlife demonstrations at this Seminole reservation. There's a daily snake demonstration and alligator-wrestling show. | 3351 N. U.S. 441/Hwy. 7 | 954/961–4519 | $5 | Mon.–Sat. 9–5; Sun. noon–5.

West Lake Park. With 1,500 acres along the Intracoastal Waterway, West Lake is one of Florida's largest urban parks, offering a wide range of recreational activities. The park's Anne Kolb Nature Center is great for kids with interactive displays about the inhabitants of the Mangrove Wetlands, a 3,500-gallon aquarium, and an ecology room where educational seminars are held. | 751 Sheridan St. | 954/926–2410 | Weekends $1, weekdays free; exhibit hall $3 | Daily 8–6.

ON THE CALENDAR

FEB.: *Canada Fest.* This two-day festival is held along the beach boardwalk from Johnson to Harrison streets. Many Canadians winter in and near Hollywood, hence the event's origins. Two stages with live entertainment, food vendors, and arts and crafts displays are the focal points. | 954/921–3404.

FEB.: *Seminole Tribal Festival.* Native Americans from many tribes come together for this four-day celebration. Highlights include singing and dancing competitions, animal exhibits, rodeos, arts and crafts, and live music. | 954/966–6300.

DEC.: *Hollywood Beach Candy Cane Parade.* This nighttime event is held along the Hollywood Beach boardwalk, starting at North Beach Park. The many floats are judged in different categories, and the parade ends with a social gathering. | 954/921–3404.

DEC.–MAY: *Dog Racing.* The Hollywood Greyhound Track has live racing nightly, and the track also simulcasts dog, thoroughbred, and harness racing from other locations. The famed Hollywood World Classic is held in March. | 954/454–9400.

DEC.–APR.: *Greater Hollywood Philharmonic Orchestra.* Classical music from every era is presented at the Hollywood Performing Arts Center. | 954/921–3408.

Dining

Bavarian Village. German. This restaurant has been serving excellent German cuisine since 1965. Popular items include sauerbraten and Wiener schnitzel. In summer there's live German music nightly except Monday. Kids' menu. | 1401 N. Federal Hwy. | 954/922–7321 | No lunch | $13–$24 | AE, D, DC, MC, V.

Giorgio's Grill. Mediterranean. White columns, flowing curtains, and Greek music give this eatery a refined, Grecian ambience. The chef recommends the filet mignon and lobster tails. | 606 N. Ocean Dr., Hollywood Beach | 954/929–7030 | Reservations essential on weekends | No lunch Mon.–Sat. No dinner Sun. | $12–$23 | AE, D, DC, MC, V.

Istanbul. Turkish. The owners of this Turkish spot take pride in making everything from scratch. The *adana kabab* (partially grilled lamb with yogurt and a hot butter sauce) and the phyllo-pie fingers filled with spinach or chicken are popular. There's outdoor dining under a covered patio. | 707 N. Boardwalk, Hollywood Beach | 954/921–1263 | Closed Tues. | $7–$14 | No credit cards.

Le Tub. American. Formerly a Sunoco gas station, this eatery along the Intracoastal Waterway is now a saloon teeming with hand-painted claw-foot bathtubs. Shrimp, burgers, and barbecue dishes dominate the menu. | 1100 N. Ocean Dr., Hollywood Beach | 954/921–9425 | $7–$12 | No credit cards.

Martha's Supper Club. Continental. For an incredible view of the Intracoastal Waterway, as well as excellent cuisine, indulge at this superb supper club. There are two dining rooms, one casual and the other more formal and with dancing. Popular dishes include the rack of Montana lamb and coconut shrimp. | 6024 N. Ocean Dr., Hollywood Beach | 954/923–5444 | $19–$40 | AE, D, DC, MC, V.

Sugar Reef. French. This casual beachside restaurant provides diners with a spectacular view of the ocean. The French fare has a Caribbean twist, providing for some very creative and tasty dishes. Try the Jamaican pork loin or seafood pasta. There's outdoor dining under umbrellas. Kids' menu. | 600 N. Surf Rd., Hollywood Beach | 954/922–1119 | Closed June–Sept. and Tues. No lunch Fri.–Sun. | $12–$21 | AE, DC, MC, V.

Sushi Blues Cafe. Japanese. Live blues on Friday and Saturday nights and an extensive menu keep the locals coming. Sushi, as the name would imply, is quite popular, as are a number of American items such as lamb chops and filet mignon. | 1836 Young Circle | 954/929–9560 | Reservations essential on weekends | No lunch | $11–$20 | AE, MC, V.

Lodging

Clarion Hotel Hollywood Beach. It's on the Intracoastal Waterway, but many rooms of this 10-story hotel face the Atlantic Ocean. Gulfstream Park is 2 mi west. Restaurant, bar, room service. In-room data ports, some microwaves, some refrigerators. Cable TV. Pool. Outdoor hot tub. Gym. Laundry service. Business services. | 4000 S. Ocean Dr. Hollywood Beach | 954/458–1900 | fax 954/458–7222 | www.choicehotels.com | 309 rooms | $96–$160 | AE, D, DC, MC, V.

Days Inn Airport South. This seven-story motel was renovated in 2000. The Ft. Lauderdale/Hollywood International Airport is minutes away, as are Hollywood Beach (3 mi) and the Broward County Convention Center. There is a handful of eateries within walking distance. Bar. Complimentary Continental breakfast. In-room data ports, some microwaves, some refrigerators. Cable TV. Pool. Outdoor hot tub. Gym. Laundry facilities. Business services, airport shuttle. Pets allowed (fee). | 2601 N. 29th Ave. | 954/923–7300 | fax 954/921–6706 | www.daysinn.com | 114 rooms | $89–$129 | AE, D, DC, MC, V.

Driftwood on the Ocean. This attractive resort dates back to the late '50s. Horse-racing, jai alai, and scuba diving are just minutes away. Rooms are spacious and most have balconies. Some kitchenettes, some microwaves, some refrigerators. Cable TV. Pool. Beach. Laundry facilities. Business services. | 2101 S. Surf Rd., Hollywood Beach | 954/923–9528 or 800/944–3148 | fax 954/922–1062 | www.driftwoodontheocean.com | 45 rooms, 4 suites | $80–$100, $130 suites | AE, D, MC, V.

Grand Palms Golf and Country Club. This sprawling resort is spread over 505 acres and has 27 holes of golf, a swimming pool, and six tennis courts. The beaches of Hollywood are 15 mi east. Restaurant, bar. In-room data ports, room service. Cable TV. Pool. Outdoor hot tub, spa. Driving range, 2 golf courses, putting green, 6 tennis courts. Gym. Laundry facilities. Business services. | 110 Grand Palms Dr., Pembroke Pines | 954/431–8800 or 800/327–9246 | fax 954/435–5988 | www.grandehotels.com | 101 rooms, 36 suites | $135–$145, $185–$200 suites | AE, D, DC, MC, V.

Greenbriar Beach Club. In a neighborhood known for its flowered streets, this oceanfront hotel retains its 1950s-style exterior. The hotel fronts a 200-ft stretch of semi-private beach, and there are restaurants and a casino within walking distance. Complimentary Continental breakfast. Kitchenettes, refrigerators. Cable TV. Pool. Beach, water sports, boating, fishing, bicycles. Laundry facilities. | 1900 S. Surf Rd., Hollywood Beach | 954/922–2606 or 800/861–4873 | fax 954/923–0897 | www.greenbriarbc.com | 49 suites | $169 | AE, D, DC, MC, V.

Hampton Inn & Suites–Fort Lauderale Airport. This five-story hotel is 4 mi south of downtown Ft. Lauderdale. It's 2 mi from many fast-food and more substantial restaurants and 3 mi from the beach. Complimentary Continental breakfast. Some in-room data ports, some microwaves, some refrigerators. Cable TV. Pool. Gym. Laundry service. Business services. | 2500 Stirling Rd. | 954/922–0011 or 800/HAMPTON | fax 954/929–7118 | www.hamptoninn.com | 79 rooms, 24 suites | $109–$119, $139 suites | AE, D, DC, MC, V.

Holiday Inn. This Holiday Inn is convenient to Fort Lauderdale–Hollywood International Airport, I–95, and the Tri-Rail station. Hollywood Beach is 3 mi away, and fast-food restaurants a short walk. Restaurant, bar. In-room data ports, some microwaves, some refrigerators. Cable TV. Pool. Outdoor hot tub. Gym. Laundry facilities. Business services, airport shuttle. Some pets allowed. | 2905 Sheridan St. | 954/925–9100 | fax 954/925–5512 | www.holidayinnfll.com | 140 rooms, 10 suites | $159–$170, $175–$250 suites | AE, D, DC, MC, V.

Howard Johnson Plaza. This high-rise has some rooms facing the Atlantic, and there are quite a few restaurants along the nearby boardwalk. | 242 rooms. Restaurant, bar. In-room data ports, room service. Cable TV. Pool, wading pool. Beach. Laundry facilities, laundry service. Business services. | 2501 N. Ocean Dr., Hollywood Beach | 954/925–1411 | fax 954/921–5565 | www.hojo.com | $124–$184 | AE, D, DC, MC, V.

Sea Downs. This two-story lodging is on the boardwalk. Most rooms offer outstanding views of the Atlantic. There are a number of specialty and international restaurants within walking distance. Picnic area. In-room data ports, kitchenettes, refrigerators, microwaves. Cable TV. Pool. Laundry facilities. | 2900 N. Surf Rd., Hollywood Beach | 954/923–4968 | fax 954/923–8747 | www.seadowns.com | 5 rooms, 8 apartments | $72–93, $106–$125 apartments | No credit cards.

HOMESTEAD

MAP 3, E5

(Nearby towns also listed: Coral Gables, Everglades National Park, Florida City, Key Largo)

Perched between Biscayne National Park, which covers 170,000 acres of water and beach, and Everglades National Park, the system's second-largest, Homestead is a gateway to both. But this city of 27,000 has had a rough time the past few years after having been virtually flattened by Hurricane Andrew in 1992. The devastation Andrew wrought, however, has ironically been a bit of a godsend. With a clean slate, the residents have set out to freshen up the town's image with plenty of good new restaurants, boutiques, and antiques shops. Today, billing itself as the "Gateway to the Keys," Homestead boasts new hotels, shopping centers, and residential communities. But the area's agricultural roots are still evident. Homestead is at the edge of agriculture country in Florida's warmest and most fertile region, so a large number of farm stands can be found on the outskirts of town.

Information: Homestead Chamber of Commerce | 43 N. Krome Ave., Homestead, 33030 | 305/247–2332 | www.chamberinaction.com.

Attractions

Biscayne National Park. This 180,000-acre park consists of mangrove forest, shallow Biscayne Bay, the upper Florida Keys, and coral reefs; 96% of the park is below water. The Convoy Point Visitor Center, 9 mi east of Homestead, offers glass-bottom boat trips and snorkel and scuba trips to the reefs. Biscayne National Park is home to a diverse population of fish and birds, and lobsters, sponges, crabs, and sea turtles; even the endangered manatee makes appearances in the warm, shallow waters of the bay. The park's boat-trip concessionaire offers glass-bottom boat tours ($20 per person), snorkel and scuba trips ($30–$45 per per-

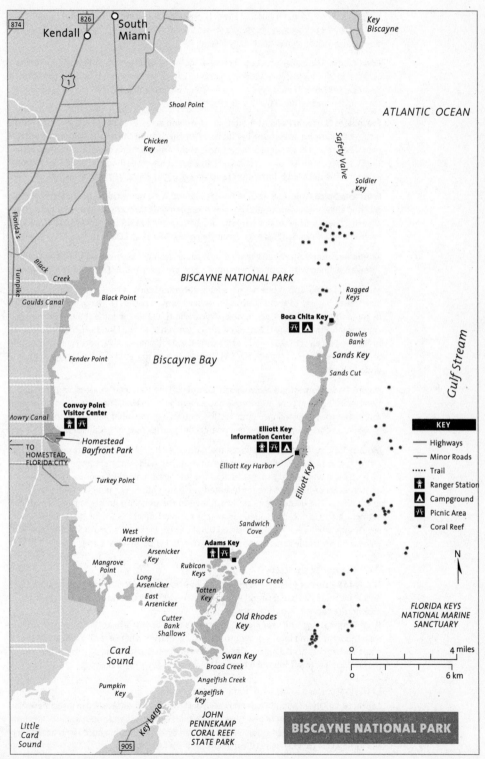

BISCAYNE NATIONAL PARK

Kendall
South Miami
874
826
1

Shoal Point

Chicken Key

ATLANTIC OCEAN

Safety Valve

Soldier Key

Key Biscayne

Florida's
Turnpike

Black Creek

Goulds Canal

Black Point

BISCAYNE NATIONAL PARK

Ragged Keys

Boca Chita Key

Bowles Bank

Sands Key

Sands Cut

Fender Point

Biscayne Bay

Mowry Canal

Convoy Point Visitor Center

Homestead Bayfront Park

TO HOMESTEAD, FLORIDA CITY

Turkey Point

Elliott Key Information Center

Elliott Key Harbor

Elliott Key

Gulf Stream

KEY

Highways
Minor Roads
Trail
Ranger Station
Campground
Picnic Area
Coral Reef

West Arsenicker

Arsenicker Key

Mangrove Point

Adams Key

Sandwich Cove

Rubicon Keys

Long Arsenicker

Caesar Creek

East Arsenicker

Totten Key

Cutter Bank Shallows

Old Rhodes Key

N

FLORIDA KEYS NATIONAL MARINE SANCTUARY

Card Sound

Swan Key

Broad Creek

Angelfish Creek

Pumpkin Key

Angelfish Key

Little Card Sound

Key Largo

JOHN PENNEKAMP CORAL REEF STATE PARK

905

0   4 miles

0   6 km

son), and canoe ($8 per hour) and kayak ($16 per hour). | Dante Fascell Visitor Center, 9700 S.W. 328th St. | 305/230–7275 or 305/230–1100 (boat tours) | www.nps.gov/bisc | Free | Park open daily; visitor center open daily 8–5:30.

Coral Castle. The castle was built between 1920 and 1940 by Latvian immigrant Edward Leekskalnin for his lost love. Working alone, he carved it from more than 1,100 tons of coral bedrock. | 28655 S. Dixie Hwy. | 305/248–6345 | www.coralcastle.com | $7.75; special rates for children and seniors | Daily 9–6.

Everglades National Park. At more than 1.5 million acres, Everglades National Park is the largest remaining subtropical wilderness in the United States. Its abundant wildlife includes rare and endangered species, such as the American crocodile and the Florida panther. Visitors may hike, camp, boat, and fish. See the town heading for Everglades National Park for more detailed information. | 40001 Hwy. 9336 | 305/242–7700 | www.nps.gov/ever.

Fruit and Spice Park. This 32-acre park is planted with more than 500 varieties of fruit, nut, and spice trees from around the world. You can walk through citrus and banana groves as well as herb and vegetable gardens, or have a picnic. | 24801 S.W. 187 Ave. | 305/247–5727 | www.co.miami-dade.fl.us/parks/fruitandspice.htm | $3.50 | Daily 10–5.

Krome Avenue. Homestead's main drag, Krome Avenue (Highway 997) with its redbrick sidewalk is lined with popular restaurants and antiques shops. | Krome Ave. | Daily.

Miami Metrozoo. This is one of only a few subtropical zoos in the United States. The 290-acre spread is home to about 1,000 animals that roam on islands (with no cages) surrounded by moats. Check out the Tiger Temple, African Plains exhibit, wildlife show, children's petting zoo, and the ecology theater. The zoo is $\frac{1}{2}$ mi west of the Florida Turnpike extension in Miami, 3 mi west of U.S. 1, and 20 mi from Miami International Airport. | 12400 S.W. 152nd St. (Coral Reef Dr.) | 305/251–0400 | $8 | Daily 9:30–5:30 (gates close at 4) | www.co.miami-dade.fl.us.com.

Miami-Dade Homestead Motorsports Complex. This state-of-the-art racing facility has two tracks: a $2\frac{1}{5}$-mi continuous road course and a $1\frac{1}{2}$-mi oval. There's a schedule of year-round manufacturer and race-team testing, club racing, and other national events. | 1 Speedway Blvd. | 305/230–7223 | www.racemiami.com | Varies by event | Call for hrs.

Monkey Jungle. The people, not the animals, are caged here. A tunnel-cage takes you through 20 acres of different exhibits where the animals run wild. Many endangered species live here and run wild through areas such as the "Cameroon Jungle," a gorilla habitat. A total of 30 species of primates are represented, including gibbons, guenons, spider monkeys, and colobus. The golden lion tamarin, native to the Brazilian jungle, is threatened with extinction; this facility participates in an international effort to save the tiny creature. Monkey Jungle is between Homestead and Coral Gables. | 14805 S.W. 216th St. | 305/235–1611 | www.monkeyjungle.com | $13.50 | Daily 9:30–5; ticket booth closes at 4.

ON THE CALENDAR

FEB.–MAR.: *Grand Prix of Miami.* The Miami-Dade Homestead Motorsports Complex hosts this major national Grand Prix race each year, with spectators and drivers from around the country. | 305/253–0063.

JULY: *Tropical Agricultural Fiesta.* Area chefs cook up a storm at the Goldcoast Railroad Museum using locally grown fruits and vegetables. There are also educational plant and agricultural displays. City-dwellers are particularly fond of this festival as they do not get to sample such tropical treats everyday. | 305/248–5533.

Dining

Capri. Italian. One of Miami-Dade County's oldest restaurants, established in 1958, this restaurant serves large portions of hearty red-sauce fare such as lasagna and spaghetti. Also note the extensive selection of traditional American dishes, including succulent steaks. | 935 N. Krome Ave. | 305/247–1542 | Closed Sun. | $13–$21 | AE, MC, V.

El Toro Taco. Mexican. This casual Mexican eatery is decorated with native pictures and murals. The *mole de pollo* (a chicken dish seasoned with chocolate and spices) and the fajitas are quite popular. | 1 S. Krome Ave. | 305/245–8182 | Reservations not accepted | Closed Mon. | $6–$12 | D, MC, V.

Tiffany's. American. What looks like a converted pioneer house with a high-pitched roof and lattice under a big banyan tree is really a cluster of shops, including this casual eatery. Frilly Victorian decor and floral placemats set the tone for such treats as crab au gratin, and asparagus rolled in ham with hollandaise sauce. Sunday brunch. | 22 N.E. 15th St. | 305/246–0022 | Closed Mon. No dinner | $6–$10 | MC, V.

Lodging

Homestead Days Inn. Every aspect of this motel has been updated in the past few years after it was ravaged by Hurricane Andrew. The lobby is a warm environment with comfy couches and is usually filled with guests reading newspapers. Rooms are bright with tropical colors on the bedspreads. Some rooms in the two-story building look out to the pool courtyard. Everglades National Park is 15 mi west. Bar, complimentary Continental breakfast. In-room data ports, refrigerators. Cable TV. Pool. Laundry facilities. Business services. Some pets. | 51 S. Homestead Blvd. | 305/245–1260 | fax 305/247–0939 | www.daysinn.com | 100 rooms | $89–$109 | AE, D, DC, MC, V.

Ramada Limited Homestead. This Ramada is 2 mi south of the famed Coral Castle and 4 mi from the Miami-Dade Homestead Motorsports Complex. Restaurants are across the street. Complimentary Continental breakfast. In-room data ports, some refrigerators. Cable TV. Pool. Laundry facilities. Business services. Some pets. | 990 N. Homestead Blvd. | 305/247–7020 | fax 305/247–7020 | www.ramada.com | 148 rooms | $69–$99 | AE, D, DC, MC, V.

HOMOSASSA SPRINGS

MAP, H5

(Nearby towns also listed: Brooksville, Crystal River, Pine Island)

Settled in the early 19th century, Homosassa Springs is one of the oldest residential communities on Florida's Gulf Coast. In its heyday before the Civil War, it was a major sugar center; thereafter, it became an important lumber center. With excellent fishing, the area has been promoted as a getaway for sportsmen since the early 1800s. That tradition continues today, as the shoals, channels, and Homosassa River still boast great catches of fish. Travelers also come to see the Homosassa Springs Wildlife Park, where animals roam in natural-looking settings, and the nearby Yulee Sugar Mill State Historic Site, which preserves the ruins of the 1851 mill built by David Yulee, one of Florida's first U.S. Senators. There are numerous restaurants and resorts in the area.

Information: **Homosassa Springs Area Chamber of Commerce** | 3495 U.S. 19, Homosassa Springs, 34448 | 352/628–2666 | www.homosassachamber.com.

Attractions

Chassahowitzka National Wildlife Refuge. About 7 mi south of Homosassa Springs, this refuge includes 31,000 acres of estuarine terrain and is accessible only by boat. It is home to a number of endangered species, including the Florida Black Bear. From U.S. 19, follow Hwy. 98/480 west 1 mi to the Chassahowitzka River Campground, which is the refuge's main boat ramp. | Off Hwy. 98/480 | 352/563–2088 | www.nccentral.com/fcnwr.htm | Free | Daily.

Homosassa Springs State Wildlife Park. At this 166-acre park, you can observe native plants and animals in their natural setting—and see manatees at close range. Daily ranger programs focus on manatees, alligators, crocodiles, snakes, and other wildlife topics. | 4150 U.S. 19 | 352/628–5343 | www.citrusdirectory.com/hsswp | $7.95 | Daily 9–5:30.

HOMOSASSA
SPRINGS

INTRO
ATTRACTIONS
DINING
LODGING

Yulee Sugar Mill Ruins State Historic Site. This small park contains ruins of a once prosperous sugar mill. Still standing are the steam boiler, the crushing machinery, the large cooking kettles used to process the cane, and stone chimney, well, and foundation. It's 2½ mi west of U.S. 19, off Hwy. 490. | Yulee Dr. | 352/795–3817 | www.citruscounty-fl.com/yulee.html | Free | Daily 8–dusk.

ON THE CALENDAR

NOV.: *Homosassa Arts and Seafood Festival.* Held in Old Homosassa, this festival is exactly what the title indicates. Arts and crafts booths show work in various mediums, and there's great seafood. | 352/628–2666.

Dining

K.C. Crump's Restaurant. Seafood. Housed in a converted 19th-century fishing lodge, this restaurant serves the area's freshest local shrimp and seafood. The fried shrimp and lobster dishes are quite popular. Kids' menu. | 11210 W. Halls River Rd. | 352/628–1500 | $11–$22 | MC, V.

Lodging

The Crown Hotel. This beautiful Victorian hotel dates to the early 1900s. The opulence is full-blown here, from the huge chandelier in the lobby to the elegant circular staircase. Replicas of England's famed Crown Jewels are in the lobby. It's 17 mi east of Homosassa Springs via Hwy. 44. Restaurant, bar, complimentary Continental breakfast. Cable TV. Pool. Business services. Some pets (fee). | 109 N. Seminole Ave., Inverness | 352/344–5555 | fax 352/726–4040 | www.thecrownhotel.com | 34 rooms | $50–$80 | AE, MC, V.

Homosassa River Retreat. On the banks of the Homosassa River, with two docks and nearby boat and pontoon rentals, this resort of one- and two-bedroom cottages with kitchens is well-situated for outdoor adventuring. Kitchenettes. Dock. Laundry facilities. | 10605 Hall's River Rd. | 352/628–7072 | 9 cottages | $59–$90 | MC, V.

Homosassa Riverside Resort. This two-story resort on the Homosassa River has rooms with great river views—you can watch the dolphins pass by and look out onto Monkey Island, with a small community of spider and squirrel monkeys. You can rent boats from the marina office to get a closer look, but you can't walk on the island. The resort has been around since 1960. Homosassa Springs Wildlife Park is 2 mi east. Restaurant, bar. Some kitchenettes, some microwaves, some refrigerators. Cable TV. Pool. Tennis. Boating. Laundry facilities. | 5297 S. Cherokee Way | 352/628–2474 or 800/442–2040 | fax 352/628–5208 | www.homosassariverside.com | 75 rooms | $45–$100 | D, MC, V.

Ramada Inn. This two-story Ramada Inn was built in 1970 and is adjacent to the Homosassa Springs State Wildlife Park. Restaurant, bar, room service. In-room data ports, some refrigerators. Cable TV. Pool. Tennis Court. Playground. Some pets. Business services, airport shuttle. | U.S. 19 at Hwy. 490A | 352/628–4311 or 888/298–2054 | fax 352/628–4311 | www.ramada.com | 103 rooms, 1 suite | $59–$69, $139 suite | AE, D, DC, MC, V.

INDIAN ROCKS BEACH

MAP 3, H6

(Nearby towns also listed: Clearwater, Clearwater Beach, Redington Beach, St. Petersburg, St. Pete Beach)

This friendly, lively resort community between the Gulf of Mexico and Boca Ciega Bay is one of several beach towns on the barrier islands off St. Petersburg. Originally developed as a resort for well-heeled Tampa Bay residents, it offers 2½ miles of quiet beaches lined with some of the area's best-known restaurants. Today the community of 4,200 residents make a life of golfing, fishing, and boating.

Information: **Gulf Beaches of Tampa Bay/Indian Rocks Beach Chamber of Commerce** | 105 5th Ave., Indian Rocks Beach, 33785 | 727/595–4575 or 800/944–1847 | www.gulf-beaches-tampabay.com.

Attractions

Indian Rocks Area Historical Society. Highlights of this small museum include a scrapbook and photographs chronicling the community's history. | 1507 Palm Bay Blvd. | 727/593–3861 | Free | By appointment.

Suncoast Seabird Sanctuary. This non-profit hospital cares for injured or orphaned birds. It was established by zoologist Dale Shields after he cared for a cormorant with a broken wing. Suncoast is the nation's largest wild-bird hospital and treats almost 25 patients daily, including cormorants, white egrets, and brown pelicans. | 18328 Gulf Blvd., Indian Shores | 727/391–6211 | webcoast.com/SeaBird | Free | Daily, 9–dusk.

ON THE CALENDAR

APR.: *Beauty and the Beach Festival.* Essentially a big outdoor party, this festival features an arts and crafts fair and live bands. There is also a big book sale. | 727/595–2517.
DEC.: *Indian Shores & The Redingtons Lighted Boat Parade.* This nighttime parade sails down the Intracoastal Waterway, beginning in Indian Shores and ending in Redington Beach. Various crafts, from speedboats to luxury yachts, adorn themselves with lights and participate in the parade. | 727/397–5538.

Dining

Blackstone's Tapas Café. Mediterranean. This bistro on a little peninsula near the Gulf of Mexico offers tapas, or tasters' portions, of almost every entree. In addition to three different paellas and endless pizza toppings, popular choices include baked oysters in garlic sauce and osso buco (a veal shank slow-roasted with tomatoes and olives). | 301 Gulf Blvd., Indian Rocks Beach | 727/517–7778 | No lunch. Closed Mon. | $10–$22 | AE, D, DC, MC, V.

Chateau Madrid Restaurant. Spanish. Imported chandeliers and pictures of the Spanish countryside give this elegant spot an authentic feel. Recommended are the paella, zarzuela (seafood combo plate), and the chicken and shrimp with lobster sauce. | 19519 Gulf Blvd. | 727/596–9100 | No lunch | $9–$19 | AE, D, DC, MC, V.

Crabby Bill's. Seafood. This informal spot is the first of what has become a Florida chain of fish houses. Popular are fried-oyster sandwiches, crab cakes, catfish, and the like—you dine at long picnic tables. | 401 Gulf Blvd. | 727/595–4825 | Reservations not accepted | $6–$25 | AE, MC, V.

Nadia's Restaurant & Bar. Continental. In addition to classic Continental dishes such as a rack of lamb with honey-rosemary demi-glace, the chef's Middle-Eastern background is the inspiration for dishes such as the grouper *tagine* (slow-cooked in Moroccan spices over couscous). Desserts, which are purely Continental, include a chocolate mousse with Grand Marnier. | 2721 Gulf Blvd., Indian Rocks Beach | 727/596–7222 | No lunch Sun. | $9–$25 | AE, DC, MC, V.

Slammers Crabhouse. Seafood. This seafood joint has a sporty atmosphere, with TV monitors showing sports and memorabilia hanging on the walls. More than 80 items are on the menu. The all-you-can-eat blue crab and numerous shrimp dishes are favorites. | 19703 Gulf Blvd. | 727/593–7733 | $6–$25 | MC, V.

Lodging

Holiday Inn. This Key West–style resort occupies 15 tropical harbor-side acres. Beautiful white-sand beaches are steps away and Tampa International airport is 18 mi east. 2 restaurants, 5 bars, room service. In-room data ports, some kitchenettes, some microwaves, some refrigerators, some in-room hot tubs. Cable TV. Pool. Outdoor hot tub. 1 tennis court. Gym, volleyball. Boating, fishing. Playground. Laundry service. Business services. | 401 2nd St. |

INDIAN ROCKS
BEACH

INTRO
ATTRACTIONS
DINING
LODGING

727/595–9484 or 800/726–0865 | fax 727/596–4825 | www.holiday-inn.com | 82 rooms, 82 suites | $109–$124, $189–$219 suites | AE, D, DC, MC, V.

Ramada Vacation Suites at Indian Shores. On the Intracoastal Waterway, this two-story, all-suites complex has water views from every unit. White-sand beaches where guests can windsurf and parasail are across the street. Kitchenettes, refrigerators, microwaves. Cable TV. Pool. Sauna. Fishing. Laundry facilities. Business services. | 19607 Gulf Blvd. | 727/596–7719 | fax 727/596–7819 | www.ramadavacationsuites.com | 32 suites | $80–$160 | AE, D, DC, MC, V.

ISLAMORADA

MAP 3, E6

(Nearby towns also listed: Conch Key/Duck Key, Grassy Key/Crawl Key, Key Largo, Marathon, Windley Key)

Legend tells us that this town on Upper Matecumbe Key, about 18 miles south of Key Largo gets its name from the early Spanish explorers who were reported to see flowery blue and purple flowers on the shores and who then named the area Islamorada, or "Purple Isles." Others will tell you that the literal translation actually means "Island Home." Either way, the island has some of the most beautiful beaches in the Keys, and is especially well known for its angling. Though the town's boast of being "Sportfishing Capital of the World" may be a bit overstated, Islamorada still attracts a well-heeled bunch who ply the waters and drop their lines. Former presidents Harry Truman, Jimmy Carter, and George Bush have all sought to land one of the many local species. For those who can't afford a full-service charter, you can often have good luck dropping a line from a bridge or the beach. The diving is also good, especially around the Underground Coral Gardens.

Information: Islamorada Chamber of Commerce | 116 Porto Salvo Dr., Islamorada, 33036 | 305/664–4503 or 800/322–5397 | www.islamoradachamber.com.

KODAK'S TIPS FOR PHOTOGRAPHING WEATHER

Rainbows
- Find rainbows by facing away from the sun after a storm
- Use your auto-exposure mode
- With a SLR, use a polarizing filter to deepen colors

Fog and Mist
- Use bold shapes as focal points
- Add extra exposure manually or use exposure compensation
- Choose long lenses to heighten fog and mist effects

In the Rain
- Look for abstract designs in puddles and wet pavement
- Control rain-streaking with shutter speed
- Protect cameras with plastic bags or waterproof housings

Lightning
- Photograph from a safe location
- In daylight, expose for existing light
- At night, leave the shutter open during several flashes

From *Kodak Guide to Shooting Great Travel Pictures* © 2000 by Fodor's Travel Publications

Attractions

Hurricane Monument. The site marks the grave of 423 persons who perished in a 1935 hurricane. Many were World War I veterans who had been working on the Overseas Highway. An Art Deco–style monument, built of Keys coral limestone, depicts wind-driven waves and palms bending in the storm's fury. | MM 81.6, Overseas Hwy. | Free | Daily.

Indian Key State Historic Site. Indian Key's colorful past is very much a part of early Florida history. In the 1830s, this landfall, accessible only by boat, was the seat of then-new Dade County. An observation tower, dock, and 1-mi hiking trail are highlights. Charters are available nearby. | MM 78.5, Overseas Hwy. | 305/664–2540 or 305/664–9814 (boat tours) | www.dep.state.fl.us | $3.25 | Daily 8–dusk.

Lignumvitae Key State Botanical Site. To step ashore here is to take a step back into the past, when the land and surrounding sea fulfilled most of the residents' needs. The virgin tropical forest here is typical of those that once covered most of Florida's Upper Keys. This key is accessible only by boats, which can be rented from nearby marinas, or by ferry service. | MM 78.5 Overseas Hwy. | 305/664–4815; 305/664–9814 or 305/664–4196 (ferry service) | www.dep.state.fl.us | $1 | Tours Thurs.–Mon. 10 and 2.

Long Key State Park. There are three nature trails at this 966-acre park 12 mi southwest of Islamorada. There are also picnic areas, campsites, and some of the best sport fishing in the Keys. Rangers run programs on birding, sea turtles, plants, history, and local marine ecology. | MM 67.5 Overseas Hwy. | 305/664–4815 | www.dep.state.fl.us | $3.25 per vehicle | Daily.

Somewhere in Time. Hundreds of interesting artifacts fill this small antiques and jewelry shop with an exhibit area, including objects from sunken merchant and slave ships. You'll find coins from the *Atocha,* which sank off Key West in 1622; original 18th-century maps; rare 16th-century ceramic containers and religious medallions; and much more. Most of the items on display are for sale. | MM 82.7 Overseas Hwy. | 305/664–9699 | fax 305/664–8010 | Free | Daily 7–5.

Theater of the Sea. At this marine park, you can pet a shark, kiss a sea lion, or enjoy a bottomless boat ride in the lagoon. You can also swim with the dolphins. In addition to the general admission, interaction programs cost $60 to $110 per person. | 87421 Overseas Hwy. | 305/664–2431 | fax 305/664–8162 | www.theaterofthesea.com | $17.25 | Daily 9:30–4.

ON THE CALENDAR

JAN.: *President's Sailfish Tournament.* Former President George Bush is traditionally on hand for this prestigious tournament. Fishermen from all over the world participate in this catch-and-release competition. | 305/664–4503.

Dining

Atlantic's Edge. Seafood. This elegant charmer serves novel and delicious fare such as onion-crusted Florida snapper and prime rib. Seating is by candlelight, with panoramic water views. Kids' menu. | 81801 Overseas Hwy. | 305/664–4651 | No lunch | $16–$29 | AE, D, DC, MC, V.

Coral Grill. American. Hearty portions are the norm at this large, popular restaurant. There's table service on the first floor, a buffet on the second. | 83532 Overseas Hwy. | 305/664–4803 | Closed Sept.–mid-Oct. and Mon. No lunch Tues.–Sat. | $9–$20 | AE, D, DC, MC, V.

Horizon Room. Caribbean. On top of the tallest building in the Upper Keys, the Holiday Isle Resort, this restaurant is a great place to take in a sunset. Specialties include a conch chowder served with sherry, and yellowtail almondine sautéed in butter sauce and flambéed in almond liquor and toasted almonds. | 84001 Overseas Hwy., Islamorada | 305/664–2321 or 800/327–7070 | $14–$28 | AE, DC, MC, V.

Islamorada Fish Company. Seafood. This fish house has the local vote locked up as *the* place for breakfast. Be sure to try the grouper Reuben. There's outdoor dining under umbrellaed tables. Kids' menu. | 81532 Overseas Hwy. | 305/664–9271 | Reservations not accepted | $8–$30 | AE, D, MC, V.

Lazy Days Oceanfront Bar and Seafood Grill. Seafood. The crowd digging into jumbo portions of steamed clams is loud and lively at this local favorite. Specialties include the hogfish *française* and the Mediterranean-style mahimahi. Outdoor dining is on the veranda. | MM 80, Overseas Hwy. | 305/664–5256 | Reservations essential | Closed Mon.–Tues. | $12–$20 | AE, D, MC, V.

Lorelei's. Seafood. This lively fish house, which is the home of the renowned Cabana Bar, is the place to go for live entertainment every night. The shrimp madness, with shrimp prepared seven different ways, is recommended. You can dine on the patio. Kids' menu. | 96 Madeira Rd., MM 82, Overseas Hwy. | 305/664–4656 | Breakfast also available | $9–$23 | AE, D, DC, MC, V.

Manny & Isa's. Cuban. The regular menu here is split between traditional Cuban dishes and local seafood, and there are several fish, chicken, and pork specials, all served with Cuban bread. The succulent fish fingers served with black beans and rice are delicious. Manny's Key lime pies are legendary. | MM 81.6, Overseas Hwy. | 305/664–5019 | Closed Labor Day–mid-Oct. and Tues. | $10–$20 | AE, D, MC, V.

Marker 88. Seafood. The waterfront location with views of the Gulf of Mexico all around makes this dining room filled with items from shipwrecks a real pleasure. Try the fish Rangoon, a sautéed fillet garnished with tropical fruits including mangos and papayas. Outdoor dining under a covered or uncovered patio is available. | MM 88, Overseas Hwy. | 305/852–9315 | Closed Mon. No lunch | $10–$35 | AE, D, DC, MC, V.

Morada Bay. Seafood. Conch architecture is enhanced by the black-and-white Everglades photos shot by Clyde Butcher, which line the walls. The shrimp bisque and cumin-seared snapper with roasted red peppers and a spinach quesadilla are heavenly. You can bring in your own catch and have the chefs cook it up. | MM 81, Overseas Hwy. | 305/664–0604 | Reservations not accepted | $16–$25 | AE, MC, V.

Pierre's. Eclectic. A decor that's equal parts colonial Indonesian, tribal African, and Louisiana plantation house sets the dramatic stage for sublime French and Mediterranean cooking, with more than a hint of Asian flavor. Voted by *South Florida Gourmet* magazine as the most romantic spots in the Keys, it's a place where you can cuddle up with your loved one under the Moroccan lights and taste the spicy Thai curry seared snapper served over a bed of green papaya slaw with garlic chili sauce. The roasted rack of lamb comes with a red onion tart tatin and sautéed artichoke bottoms and you can finish off your exotic meal with their tropical spin on an ice cream Napoleon. | MM 81.5, Overseas Hwy. | 305/664–3225 | $28–$48 | AE, MC, V.

Squid Row. Seafood. Seafood wholesalers own this casual restaurant. The bouillabaisse is very tasty. You can dine at the bar or on the covered patio. Kids' menu. | MM 81.9, 89901 Overseas Hwy. | 305/664–9865 | Closed Wed. June–Dec. | $9–$19 | AE, D, DC, MC, V.

Lodging

Cheeca Lodge. This beautifully landscaped 27-acre resort is on the Atlantic Ocean, with 1,100 ft of private, white-sand beach. There is a 500-ft-long private fishing pier. Activities include scuba diving and jet-skiing. 3 restaurants, 2 bars, dining room, picnic area. Some kitchenettes, some refrigerators, some microwaves. Cable TV. 2 pools. 5 outdoor hot tubs, spa. 9-hole golf course, 6 tennis courts. Gym. Water sports, boating, fishing, bicycles. Babysitting, playground. Laundry service. Business services. | 81801 Overseas Hwy. | 305/664–4651 or 800/327–2888 | fax 305/664–2893 | www.cheeca.com | 140 rooms, 63 suites | $280–$450, $500–$900 suites | AE, D, DC, MC, V.

Coral Bay Resort. This lavish resort is on the bay side of Islamorada, and all of the rooms have magnificent views. The grounds are lined with hibiscus and bougainvillea and the sunsets vistas are breathtaking. In-room data ports, some kitchenettes, some microwaves, some refrigerators. Cable TV. Pool. Beach, boating, fishing. Laundry facilities. Business services. | 75690 Overseas Hwy. | 305/664–5568 | fax 305/664–3424 | www.thecoralbayresort.com | 17 rooms | $109–$275 | MC, V.

El Capitan Holiday Isle. A secluded resort next to a hidden saltwater lagoon, El Capitan offers private cottages. It is part of the Holiday Isle community and numerous restaurants and bars are a stroll away. In-room data port, some microwaves, some refrigerators. Cable TV. Beach, dock, fishing. Laundry facilities. | 84001 Overseas Hwy. | 305/664–2321 | fax 305/664–2703 | 14 rooms | $165–$285 | AE, D, DC, MC, V.

Hampton Inn. This tropical escape fronts the ocean. Deep-sea fishing trips can be arranged and wave runners can be rented. Restaurant, bar, complimentary Continental breakfast. In-room data ports, some kitchenettes, some microwaves, some refrigerators. Cable TV, in-room VCRs. Pool. Outdoor hot tub. Dock, water sports, boating, fishing, bicycles. Laundry service. Business services. | 80001 Overseas Hwy. | 305/664–0073 or 800/426–7866 | fax 305/664–0807 | www.hamptoninn.com | 31 rooms, 48 suites | $289–$299, $389–$499 suites | AE, D, DC, MC, V.

Holiday Isle. This popular resort fronts white-sand beaches and offers myriad water sports, including parasailing and scuba diving. Rooms have either beach, harbor, garden, or ocean views. Restaurant, bar. In-room data ports, some kitchenettes, some refrigerators, some microwaves, some in-room hot tubs. Cable TV. Pool. Beach, dock, water sports. Laundry facilities. Business services. | 84001 Overseas Hwy. | 305/664–2321 or 800/327–7070 | fax 305/664–2703 | www.holidayisle.com | 60 rooms, 14 suites | $210–$285, $300–$475 suites | AE, D, DC, MC, V.

Howard Johnson at Holiday Isle. This oceanfront hotel in the world famous Holiday Isle resort community offers rooms with spectacular water views. The tiki bar is renowned for its frozen drinks and live entertainment. Bar. In-room data ports, some refrigerators, some microwaves. Cable TV. Pool. Beach, fishing. Playground. Business services. | 84001 Overseas Hwy. | 305/664–2711 | fax 305/664–2703 | www.hojo.com | 56 rooms | $160–$185 | AE, D, DC, MC, V.

Islander. This picturesque motel has 20 acres of tropically landscaped, oceanfront grounds, plus a pier. There are a few restaurants within walking distance and many more a short drive away. Some kitchenettes, some refrigerators. Cable TV. 2 pools. Fishing. Laundry facilities. Business services. | MM 82.1, Overseas Hwy. | 305/664–2031 | fax 305/664–5503 | info@islanderfloridakeys.com | www.islanderfloridakeys.com | 113 rooms, 1 suite | $119–$189, $275 suite | AE, D, DC, MC, V.

Key Islamorada Days Inn & Suites. This four-story hotel was built in the late 1980s. Rooms with ocean views are by far the most expensive. There are many restaurants within walking distance. In-room data ports, kitchenettes, some microwaves, refrigerators. Cable TV. Pool. Dock, fishing. | 82749 Overseas Hwy. | 305/664–3681 or 800/544–8313 | fax 305/664–9020 | www.daysinn.com | 36 suites | $159–$428 | AE, D, DC, MC, V.

Kon-Tiki Resort. This entertaining getaway on the Gulf of Mexico has a very laid-back, subtropical ambience. The private grotto is stocked with tarpon and tropical fish. Some rooms have porches or sundecks. Picnic area. Some kitchenettes, some microwaves, some refrigerators. Cable TV. Pool. Beach, dock, fishing. | 81200 Overseas Hwy. | 305/664–4702 | fax 305/664–5305 | www.thefloridakeys.com/kontiki | 25 rooms | $90–$210 | AE, D, MC, V.

Lime Tree Bay Resort. This intimate, welcoming resort is right along the Gulf of Mexico, in Long Key (12 mi southwest of Islamorada). Guests can participate in numerous activities, including snorkeling and kayaking. The rooms are cheerfully decorated with floral designs and patterns. Restaurant. In-room data ports, some kitchenettes, some microwaves, some refrigerators. Cable TV. Pool. Outdoor hot tub. Tennis court. Dock, boating. | 68500 Overseas Hwy., Long Key | 305/664–4740 or 800/723–4519 | fax 305/664–0750 | www.limetreebayresort.com | 30 rooms | $102–$235 | AE, D, DC, MC, V.

The Moorings Village. Halfway between Miami and Key West, this former coconut plantation is on 18 tropical acres. The cottages and houses have wicker and artistic African fabrics and pristine white kitchens. Rates rise according to the number of bedrooms per unit. Kitchenettes, refrigerators, microwaves. Cable TV. Pool. Tennis court. Beach, water sports. Laundry facilities. | 123 Beach Rd. | 305/664–4708 | fax 305/664–4242 | www.themooringsvillage.com | 6 cottages, 12 houses | $370–$460 cottage (2–night minimum), $2,625–$6,650 house (1–week minimum) | MC, V.

Pelican Cove Resort. This resort is secluded amid tropical island gardens along a white-sand beach on the ocean. Outdoors enthusiasts can enjoy a variety of water sports or visit the Theater of the Sea, which is next door. Restaurant, bar, picnic area, complimentary Continental breakfast. Some kitchenettes, some microwaves, refrigerators, some in-room hot tubs. Cable TV. Pool. Outdoor hot tub. Tennis court. Beach, docks, water sports, fishing. | 84457 Old Overseas Hwy. | 305/664–4435 or 800/445–4690 | fax 305/664–5134 | www.pcove.com | 63 rooms | $165–$285 | AE, D, DC, MC, V.

Ragged Edge Resort. Most downstairs rooms at this resort have screened porches, while upper units have wooden cathedral ceilings and Bahama fans. All of the rooms have ocean views, and there's a thatch-roof observation tower. There are barbecue pits, too. Picnic area. Some kitchenettes, refrigerators. Cable TV, no room phones. Pool. Dock, fishing, bicycles. | 243 Treasure Harbor Rd. | 305/852–5389 or 800/436–2023 | www.ragged-edge.com | 12 rooms | $80–$180 | AE, MC, V.

Sands of Islamorada. Spectacular sunrises, an extremely friendly staff, and macaws await you at this oceanfront resort. Some of the rooms have wraparound porches. Picnic area. In-room data ports, some kitchenettes, microwaves, refrigerators. Cable TV. Pool. Outdoor hot tub. Dock, boating, fishing. Pets allowed (fee). | 80051 Overseas Hwy. | 305/664–2791 | fax 305/664–2886 | www.florida-keys.fl.us/sandsislamorada | 9 rooms | $115–$185 | MC, V.

White Gate Court. Far from the crowds of Islamorada's business district, this resort consists of five wooden cottages laid out on 3 pretty, landscaped acres along 200 ft of white-sand beach. Barbecue grills and big palm trees contribute to the relaxing mood. Picnic area. Kitchenettes, microwaves, refrigerators. Cable TV. Beach, dock, boating, bicycles. Laundry facilities. Business services. Pets allowed. | 76010 Overseas Hwy. | 305/664–4136 or 800/645–4283 | fax 305/664–9746 | www.whitegatecourt.com | 7 rooms | $105–$180 | MC, V.

JACKSONVILLE

MAP 3, I2

(Nearby towns also listed: Amelia Island/Fernandina Beach, Atlantic Beach, Jacksonville Beach, Ponte Vedra Beach)

The skyline of Jacksonville seems to change almost every day. With a population of over 1 million and an increasing role as a center for business, culture, technology, and medicine—not to mention its role as a major port city and site of military bases—all roads seem to lead here. Since its name often appears on various lists of the best places to live in the U.S., more and more people are following those roads.

Jacksonville's history dates back to 1562, when the area was first settled by a small group of French Huguenots. Their settlement, named Fort Caroline, was on the banks of the St. Johns River. In 1821, the area was renamed for General Andrew Jackson, the first military governor of Florida and the seventh President of the United States.

The St. Johns River winds through the downtown area, and strolling along the Riverwalk is a favorite local pastime and also a great way for visitors to get a feel for the city. Jacksonville Landing has many good restaurants and entertainment venues, as well as a great selection of shops. Jacksonville Beach, 20 miles to the east, is a nice place to catch a sunrise.

Information: Jacksonville and the Beaches Convention and Visitors Bureau | 201 E. Adams St., Jacksonville, 32202 | 904/798–9111 or 800/733–2668 | www.jaxcvb.com.

Attractions

Alexander Brest Museum. This fine arts museum on the campus of Jacksonville University contains collections of Boehm, Royal Copenhagen, Bing, and Gröndahl porcelains. Also on display are Steuben glass, pre-Columbian artifacts, and an extensive collection of ivory. | 2800 University Blvd. N | 904/744–3950, ext. 7371 | www.ju.edu | Free | Weekdays 8:30–5.

Anheuser-Busch Brewery. From an open-air gallery overlooking the floor of the brew hall, and enormous structure constructed in 1969, you'll get a bubbly, step-by-step look at the Budweiser brewing process. | 111 Busch Dr. | 904/696–8373 | www.budweisertours.com | Free | Mon.–Sat. 9–4:30.

Cummer Museum of Art and Gardens. Nine galleries display more than 2,000 items from the museum's permanent collection covering more than 4,000 years of artwork. The collection is particularly rich in European and American fine and decorative arts and includes the Wark Collection of early 18th-century Meissen porcelain. | 829 Riverside Ave. | 904/356–6857 | fax 904/353–4101 | www.cummer.org | $6 | Tues., Thurs. 10–9, Wed., Fri., Sat 10–5, Sun 12–5.

Fort Caroline National Memorial. Spread across more than 600 acres along the north-flowing St. Johns River, 7 mi northeast of downtown Jacksonville, the fort is a replica of one built by Protestant French Huguenots, who settled here in the 1560s to escape religious persecution. This was the nation's first settlement, but Spanish soldiers annihilated it. This coastal hammock is a salt marsh that is home to hardwoods, scrub vegetation, and many bird species. A visitors center can fill you in on details of other northeast Florida estuarine environments. | 12713 Fort Caroline Rd. | 904/641–7155 | www.nps.gov/foca | Free | Daily 9–5.

Golf Club of Jacksonville. This 18-hole course, opened in 1989, challenges you to reach the course's large greens without visiting its numerous bunkers. | 10440 Tournament Ln. | 904/779–0800 | Year-round.

Huguenot Memorial Park. At this oceanfront city park, you can fish, swim, surf, sailboard, and enjoy nature on the shores of Fort George Inlet, the Atlantic Ocean, and the St. Johns River. You can camp (tent and RV), but there are no hook-ups. | 10980 Heckscher Dr., Northeast Jacksonville | 904/251–3335 | www.coj.net/fun | 50¢ | 8 AM–8 PM summer, 8–6 winter.

Jacksonville Historical Center. Along the riverwalk in a large pavilion is the small museum of local history and the visitors center. Exhibits trace the history from the days of the Timucuan Indians, using artifacts, photographs, and maps. You can watch an hour-long video on the history. Airplane buffs: look up and see the model planes hanging from the ceiling. The U.S. Navy has donated several, including a 10-ft model F-16 plane. | Southbank Riverwalk | 904/398–4301 | Free | Daily 11–5.

The Jacksonville Landing. Come here to watch fireworks across the water. The marketplace and mall area have retail shops, restaurants, and regularly scheduled live entertainment in the courtyard. Check the visitors center at the main entrance. Pep rallies, shuttles to football games, and bands keep the place lively with inside and outdoor entertainment. | 2 Independent Dr. | 904/353–1188 | Mon.–Thurs. 10–8, Fri.–Sat. 10–9, Sun. 12–5:30.

Jacksonville Maritime Museum. Model ships, photos, and artifacts display the maritime history of the area. The models include Columbus's three ships and a 17-ft model of the USS *Saratoga*, a former aircraft carrier that was based in Jacksonville. | 1015 Museum Cir., Unit 2 | 904/398–9011 | www.jaxmarmus.com | Free | Mon.–Thur. 10:30–3:30, Fri.–Sat. 10:30–5, Sun. 1–5.

Jacksonville Museum of Modern Art. Known as JMOMA, this museum showcases such contemporary artists as Helen Frankenthaler, Robert Rauschenberg, and Alexander Calder. Now operating in the 1931 Western Union Telegraph building, the museum has changing exhibitions on three floors. However, at press time, information about admission costs and hours in 2001 was unavailable. | 333 N. Laura St. | 904/398–8336 | fax 904/366–6911 | www.jmoma.org.

Jacksonville Zoological Gardens. Known for its collection of rare waterfowl, this zoo is home to more than 800 rare and exotic creatures and an isn't-that-cute animal nursery and petting zoo. In the African Veldt, elephants and white rhinos browse among African birds, and in the Great Apes of the World section, those big boys of the jungle play with their babies. | 8605 Zoo Rd. | 904/757–4462 | fax 904/757–4315 | info@jaxzoo.org | www.jaxzoo.org | $8; special rates for children and senior citizens | Daily 9–5.

Karpeles Manuscript Library Museum. This is one of seven Karpeles Museums in the nation that together house more than a million historic documents from Albert Einstein's letters to a copy of the Emancipation Proclamation and Mark Twain's discussion of his novel, *Tom Sawyer*. Exhibits here change frequently, although Florida history exhibits are usually available, along with a collection of antique books. | 101 W. 1st St. | 904/356–2992 | www.rain.org/~karpeles | Free | Mon.–Sat. 10–3.

JACKSONVILLE TO COCOA BEACH—THE SCENIC VIEW

"Florida's First Coast" encompasses the entire northeast corner of the state. Jacksonville is the hub, with a modern, international airport. Water is everywhere—the St. Johns River as the focal point downtown, and the Atlantic Ocean is just minutes away.

Downtown Jacksonville offers the picturesque Northbank and Southbank Riverwalk, where you can take in the beauty of the river and catch a performance at the Jacksonville Landing. History buffs will enjoy exploring Kingsley Plantation, the oldest remaining cotton plantation in the state.

Jacksonville is a good jumping-off place for side trips to peaceful inland towns such as Deland, home to Stetson University; Micanopy, the state's oldest inland town; and Gainesville, hometown of the University of Florida. The hub-city is a perfect place to start a trip north to Amelia Island Historic District and the beautifully preserved Civil War fort at Fort Clinch State Park. On the northern end of the island is quaint Fernandina Beach, a charming old seaport with an enchanting historic district featuring many exquisite examples of Queen Anne Victorian architecture.

Just over the Intracoastal Waterway are the Beaches of Jacksonville. Situated on one long barrier island, this area is composed of four separately incorporated small communities—Mayport, Atlantic Beach, Neptune Beach, and Jacksonville Beach—that share some of the state's whitest, widest, and prettiest fine sand beaches. Continue south of the Beaches, along the coast by the scenic main road A1A, to St. Augustine, the oldest city in the United States, with 144 blocks of historic houses listed on the National Register of Historic Places, Castillo de San Marcos, and a number of interesting tours of old town.

Outside of St. Augustine, the barrier islands with quaint beach side towns such as Crescent Beach, Palm Coast, and Flagler Beach continue on as far south as Daytona Beach, with a jog here and there back on to Highway 1. Daytona Beach is primarily known for spring break, the Daytona 500, and the drive-on sand.

You may want to spend a bit of time in the Cocoa Beach area and Titusville for a visit to the amazing Kennedy Space Center Visitor Complex or the Canaveral National Seashore, or you could continue to drive along the coastline toward the Treasure Coast.

Kingsley Plantation. Slave trader Zephaniah Kingsley owned this property, built in 1791, from 1813 to 1839 and flouted the social mores of the time by marrying a slave, Anna Madgigine Jai, said to have been a princess of her tribe, and freeing her. She was active in the management of this modest waterside plantation on Fort George Island, visiting the main house, a kitchen house, and barn. Stone slave cabins here are the best-preserved slave quarters in the nation. | 11676 Palmetto Ave., Fort George Island | 904/251–3537 | www.nps.gov | Free | Daily 9–5.

Little Talbot Island State Park. More than 5 mi of wide beaches, undisturbed salt marshes, and desert-like dunes are preserved at Little Talbot, an island unusual to this part of the Atlantic coast. River otters, marsh rabbits, bobcats, and shore birds live here. Surf fishing is good; and, in the tidal streams behind the island, bluefish, striped bass, redfish, flounder, mullet, and sheepshead are common catches. You can camp, hike, picnic, and swim at Little Talbot. | 12157 Heckscher Dr. | 904/251–2320 | www.dep.state.fl.us | $3.25 per vehicle | Daily 8–sunset.

Big Talbot Island State Park. Just across the Nassau Sound Bridge from Little Talbot Island is its bigger brother with 15 mi of hiking trails, a picturesque beach decorated with trees that erosion caused to fall, and a deep-water boat launch. It's a good place to fish, either along the 1½-mi fishing pier or in the surrounding waters. There are picnic areas with grills and rest rooms as well. | 904/251–2323 | www.dep.state.fl.us | $2 per vehicle, $3 per boat | Daily sunrise to sunset.

Mayport. This little fishing village dates back more than 300 years, officially settled by the French in 1530. Now it supports a small fishing community and several seafood restaurants, plus a fleet of shrimping boats. The Navy keeps its fourth-largest home port here. | 20 mi northeast of Jacksonville.

Kathryn Abbey Hanna Park. The only park grounds in Mayport consist of about 400 acres. You can hike the 5 mi of trails or bike the 10 mi of bike trails. Rent your bike at the camp store. There are also a beach, showers, rest rooms, snack bars, and 300 campsites ranging from tent spaces to RV electrical hook-ups. | 500 Wonderwood Dr. | 904/249–4700 | www.coj.net/fun | $1 per person, $13 tent, $18 for RV | Daily sunrise to sunset.

St. Johns River Ferry. This ferry operates between Mayport and Fort George Island. Your eight-minute cruise will be aboard either a 1990s-style ferry or *Blackbeard* from the 1950s. | 904/241–9969 | $2.75 car, $3 RV, 50¢ pedestrians or bicycles | Daily 6:20 AM–10 PM, every ½ hour.

Museum of Science and History. Permanent exhibits chronicle northeast Florida history, explain the ecology of the north-flowing St. Johns River, and entertain the kids with a Kidspace playground display of whales, dolphins, and manatees. The museum's Alexander Brest Planetarium has a 3-D laser show and ever-changing star shows. | 1025 Museum Cir. | 904/396–7062 | fax 904/396–5799 | www.jacksonvillemuseum.com | $6; special rates for children and seniors | Weekdays 10–5, Sat. 10–6, Sun. 1–6.

Museum of Southern History. Florida's prehistory and the local involvement with the Civil War are both well documented here. The research library has more than 2,500 books on the Civil War and many ways to research your Confederate ancestors and find out what battles and campaigns happened near you. The rest of the museum is filled with displays of clothing, medical artifacts, music, naval activities of the area, and several dioramas of major battles of the Civil War. | 4304 Herschel | 904/388–3574 | FLAdepot@aol.com | $1 | Tues.–Sat. 10–5.

Northbank Riverwalk. The north bank of the St. Johns River is anchored by the Jacksonville Landing and the riverfront. Historic street lamps, benches, docking facilities, and two Victorian-style gazebos make it a nice place for a stroll. Local government offices, commercial buildings, a few antiques stores, bookstores, a mini-mall, food court, and several restaurants now occupy this more commercial side of the river. From the Main Street Bridge, the Riverwalk runs about ¼ mi east and west.

Peterbrooke Chocolatier Production Center. This local chocolate factory specializes in chocolate-covered popcorn that is sold in seven of their family-owned stores. You can take an hour-long tour, then, should you choose to do so, pick up some chocolate bears,

JACKSONVILLE

INTRO
ATTRACTIONS
DINING
LODGING

cream-filled bon bons, or fresh-made chocolate-covered strawberries in their shop. | 1470 San Marco Blvd., San Marco | 904/398–2489 or 800/771–0019 | www.peterbrooke.com | $1 | Tour: Mon.–Fri. 10 AM.

Riverside and Avondale. The neighborhood of Riverside was created after the Civil War and named for the property that overlooked the St. Johns River. The architecture includes Colonial Revival, Georgian, Queen Anne/Victorian, and Tudor, plus, later, Prairie-style homes. By the 1920s the neighboring area was developed as Avondale and was originally advertised it as "Riverside's Residential Ideal," where only the "correct" and "well-to-do" people would live. The 3½-mi stretch now represents every architectural style in Florida. | 904/389–2449 | www.riverside-avondale.com.

San Marco. This up-and-coming area has some of the most elegant houses and trendy restaurants and cafés. The area around San Marco Square is known for its boutiques and cool stores. Most of the local architecture dates back to the 1920s, when the neighborhood was first formed. | South of downtown Jacksonville between Hendricks Ave. and San Marco Blvd.

Southbank Riverwalk. Friendship Fountain, restaurants, and a marina are all here on the south bank of the St. Johns River. The boardwalk, just over 1 mi long, is great for strolling, jogging, and picnicking near the Lone Sailor Monument. The boardwalk also has an excellent view of Jacksonville's downtown skyline and bridges. River taxis can take you on a tour of the area via the waterways. The Riverwalk stretches about ¾ mi in each direction from the Main Street Bridge.

Tree Hill. A 52-acre urban wilderness area in the heart of Jacksonville holds a hardwood forest, four nature trails, a natural history museum, meeting hall, garden, a live animal exhibit, science laboratory, guided tours, and gift shop. Locals come here to walk in the woods or to bird-watch along this migratory path. The pyramid-shaped and canvas-topped natural history museum lighted by the sun is a good place to see fossils and mastodon skulls found in the area. | 7152 Lone Star Rd. | 904/724–4646 | fax 904/724–9132 | www.tree-hill.org | $1 | Mon.–Sat. 8:30–5.

University of North Florida Nature Preserve. Hidden in the woodsy terrain of UNF are 12 mi of nature trails. You can use the jogging path, and there are adaptations for the physically handicapped. If you bring your own canoe or kayak, you can boat on Lake Oneida. | 4567 St. Johns Bluff Rd. S | 904/620–2998 | www.unf.edu | Free | Daily sunrise to sunset, closed in summer, depending on forest fire precautions.

Veterans Memorial Wall. The largest of its kind, this memorial wall was constructed of black granite and was dedicated November 1995, in "proud remembrance and humble tribute" to the veterans who fought in WWI, WWII, and the Korean, Vietnam, and Persian Gulf Wars and conflicts. Basically a replica of the Vietnam Memorial in Washington, D.C., this one lists only Jacksonville-area veterans. | 1145 E. Adams St.

Yellow Bluff Fort. This small fort was constructed in 1862 by Confederate troops to prevent Union gunboats from attacking Jacksonville. The fort saw little action during the war. Several cannons are on display. This state historic site is now within a residential area surrounded by a yard and benches. | Off New Berlin Rd. S, near Dames Point Bridge | 904/251–2323 | Free | Daily sunrise to sunset.

ON THE CALENDAR

MAR.: *Delius Festival.* This event celebrates composer Frederick Delius who lived just outside of Jacksonville in the late 1800s. Orchestras, soloists, and chamber groups perform his compositions and those of composers he influenced. | Jacksonville University, 2800 University Blvd. N | 904/745–7371.

APR.: *Historic Home Tour.* Homeowners in Jacksonville's 3-square-mi historic district are mighty proud of their property, much of it built between 1900 and 1930, by such prominent architects as Harold F. Saxelbye and Henry John Klutho. Here's a chance to see what's behind those 100-year-old walls. | 904/389–2449 | www.riverside-avondale.com.

SEPT.: *Riverside Art Festival.* Artists from all over the nation make their way here to exhibit their arts and crafts—and sell them—at this Riverside Park event. | Near Historic Five Points, at the intersection of College Park and Post Sts. | 904/389–2449 | www.riverside-avondale.com.

SEPT.–DEC.: *Jacksonville Jaguars.* From September through December, the NFL team plays home games at Alltel Stadium. (Alltel is also the site of the New Year's Day Gator Bowl, an annual Florida-Georgia gridiron clash that has been described as the world's largest outdoor cocktail party.) | 1 Alltel Stadium Pl. | 904/633–6000 (Jaguars) or 904/396–1700 (Gator Bowl) | www.jaguars.com | Prices vary | Call for schedule.

NOV.: *Light Boat Parade.* Boats decked out in Christmas motifs glide their holiday lights on the St. Johns River. Ingenuity and pocketbooks stretch wide to capture best-dressed-boat awards and a fireworks display caps the judging. | Downtown Riverfront, St. Johns River | The day after Thanksgiving | 904/798–9111.

NOV.: *Jacksonville Jazz Festival.* Jazz superstars take to the stage on the St. Johns riverfront, and pianists compete in the Great American Jazz Piano Competition. Superstar-wannabees line up for the jazz clinic. | 100 Festival Park Ave. | 904/353–7770 | www.wjtc.org.

DEC.: *Gator Bowl Festival.* Usually held in downtown Jacksonville on New Year's Eve, this festival salutes the region's blockbuster event, the Gator Bowl. Highlights include a parade and fireworks display and a great deal of Go Gators cheering. | 904/798–1700 | www.gatorbowl.com.

Dining

Biscotti's. American/Casual. Known for its exotic pizzas and huge, inventive salads, this neighborhood restaurant brings a taste of Southern California to northern Florida. Served in this brick-walled dining room are such selections as Thai chicken salad and mozzarella bruschetta. | 3556 St. Johns Ave. | 904/387–2060 | Reservations not accepted | Breakfast available Tues.–Sun. No supper Sun.–Mon. | $12–$20 | AE, D, MC, V.

Bombay Bicycle Club. American. Tassels, reflectors and antique bicycle memorabilia decorate this theme restaurant. Cajun grilled shrimp and steaks are among the options, and a dessert tray cradles a hot fudge chocolate cake. Kids' menu. | 8909 Baymeadows Rd. | 904/737–9555 | $10–$17 | AE, D, DC, MC, V.

Café Carmon. Seafood. After the theater, this little café makes a pleasant spot to dine on soft-shell crabs when they're in season, perhaps adding a peanut butter pie dessert. | 1986 San Marco Blvd. | 904/399–4488 | Reservations not accepted | $8–$16 | AE, D, MC, V.

Crawdaddy's. Seafood. You can dine on a patio overlooking the St. Johns River and Jacksonville Landing across the water. Big platters of crawfish or grilled shrimp are a favorite selection here. Kids' menu. | 1643 Prudential Dr. | 904/396–3546 | No lunch Sat. | $16–$23 | AE, D, DC, MC, V.

Huey's Restaurant at the Landing. Cajun/Creole. You can dine outside overlooking the river or inside in a cozy, redbrick and wood restaurant. Cajun/Creole sandwiches, gumbos, and seafood are favorites at Huey's, which sticks close to its New Orleans theme right down to jambalaya New Orleans style. Kids' menu. | 2 Independent Dr. | 904/356–5200 | $6–$16 | AE, D, MC, V.

Juliette's. American. This chic bistro features showy atrium architecture. Beef tenderloin and lemon-pepper sea bass are among the selections of note here. Kids' menu. | Omni Hotel, 245 Water St. | 904/355–7118 | Breakfast also available | $17–$26 | AE, D, DC, MC, V.

La Cruise Dockside. Seafood. This is one of the only places to eat in Mayport. It's in a very scenic spot on the docks next to the ferry. Tables look out onto the water, and you can dine on local seafood or good old American hamburgers. Specialties of the house are fried shrimp or catfish dishes. | 4738 Ocean St., Mayport | 904/246–8384 | $8–$13 | AE, D, DC, MC, V.

Mandarin Dragon. Chinese. This bi-level dining room, adorned with Oriental motifs and drawings, sports a murmuring waterfall for background music. Dress is casual, however.

Sesame Chicken is a jewel in the wide selection of Chinese cuisine. Kids' menu. | 11362-8 San Jose Blvd. | 904/260–4681 | $8–$15 | AE, D, DC, MC, V.

Marker 32. Continental. You can settle in here at waterfront tables overlooking the Intracoastal Waterway and watch the passing parade of yachts and small boats. Innovative culinary options include a warm spinach salad and oysters topped with spinach and pecorino cheese. | 14549 Beach Blvd. | 904/223–1534 | Reservations essential | No lunch | $13–$26 | AE, DC, MC, V.

Matthew's at San Marco. Eclectic. Renowned chef Matthew Madure, formerly of the Ritz–Carlton Amelia Island, now has his own kitchen here. In it, he creates innovative Southern, Mediterranean, and Asian selections that might include a grilled sea bass fillet with tomato eggplant caviar or grilled bison. | 2107 Hendricks Ave. | 904/396–9922 | Reservations essential on weekends | Closed Sun. No lunch | $19–$32 | AE, D, DC, MC, V.

Pagoda. Chinese. Cantonese, Mandarin, and Szechuan encompass the Chinese culinary styles served at this family-owned and -operated restaurant. Signature dishes include Mongolian beef and garlic chicken, served here since 1975. Kids' menu. | 8617 Baymeadows Rd. | 904/731–0880 | Reservations not accepted | Closed Sun. | $9–$19 | AE, D, DC, MC, V.

River City Brewing Company. American. Beautiful views of the river and the city's skyline are the strong point of this restaurant where diners vie for the tables in the riverside deck lounge. Prime rib and seared flounder are among an array of uncomplicated American-favorite culinary offerings. | 835 Museum Cir. | 904/398–2299 | Sunday brunch | $13–$40 | AE, DC, MC, V.

The Tree Steak House. Steak. Rib-eye steaks cut to order are the order of the day every day at this hunting club–style restaurant. Mounted deer, fish, and rabbits adorn the walls to keep the clubby atmosphere going. On the menu, New York strip is king. Kids' menu. | 11362-1 San Jose Blvd. | 904/262–0006 | No lunch | $12–$22 | AE, D, DC, MC, V.

Wilfried's 24 Miramar. Eclectic. You can see what's hidden in a "Beggar's Purse" when you dine at this Art Deco–style restaurant that serves some interesting options that are a bit off the beaten culinary path. That Beggar's Purse, by the way, is a medley of lobster, scallops, shrimp, and salmon, wrapped in pastry and topped with brandied lobster sauce. | 4446 Hendricks Ave. | 904/488–2424 | Reservations essential | Closed Sun. No lunch | $18–$30 | AE, D, DC, MC, V.

Wine Cellar. Continental. Candlelight teamed with classic Continental fare makes this restaurant a dining experience for special evenings. On the menu: grilled salmon with dill-mustard sauce and steak Diane (a fillet sauteed in butter, mushrooms, and brandy). | 1314 Prudential Dr. | 904/398–8989 | Reservations essential on weekends | Closed Sun. No lunch Sat. | $20–$30 | AE, D, DC, MC, V.

Workman's Deli and Bakery. American. The Deli opened way back in 1923 and has been serving its deli sandwiches to the hungry for all these years. Pictures of the Jacksonville of yesteryear and the Deli's early days are an intriguing diversion while you wait for the sandwich-makers to create your personalized sandwich. Those sandwiches are still the lure here, but the restaurant now also serves more elaborate fare, including beef Stroganoff and baked herb chicken. Kids' menu. | 5613 San Jose Blvd. | 904/739–9911 | Breakfast also available. No supper Sun. | $7–$15 | AE, D, DC, MC, V.

Lodging

Amerisuites. This six-story hotel is right off Baymeadows Road, 11 mi from Jacksonville Beach. All accommodations are one- and two-bedroom suites. There's no restaurant in the hotel, but there are several within walking distance. Complimentary Continental breakfast. In-room data ports, microwaves, refrigerators, some in-room hot tubs. Cable TV, in-room VCRs. Pool. Gym. Laundry facilities. Business services. Pets allowed. | 8277 Western Way Cir. | 904/737–4477 | fax 904/739–1649 | 112 suites | $79–$99 suites | AE, D, DC, MC, V.

Best Inns of America. This two-story chain hotel is a beacon to budget travelers. Restaurants are a short walk away. Picnic area, complimentary Continental breakfast. In-room data ports, some refrigerators. Cable TV. Pool. Business services. Some pets allowed. | 8220 Dix Ellis Tr. | 904/739–3323 | fax 904/739–3323 | 61 rooms | $51–$60 | AE, D, DC, MC, V.

Best Western Executive Inn. This two-story Best Western shows off with a heart-shape pool and hot tub. It is convenient to local attractions, including the Busch Brewery (2 mi) and the Jacksonville Zoo (5 mi). Restaurant, complimentary Continental breakfast. In-room data ports, microwaves, refrigerators. Cable TV. Pool. Outdoor hot tub. Laundry facilities. Business services. | 10888 Harts Rd. | 904/751–5600 | fax 904/757–4311 | 61 rooms | $55–$90 | AE, D, DC, MC, V.

Clarion Hotel Airport Conference Center. This six-story hotel on the grounds of Jacksonville International Airport boasts a comprehensive Biznet Business Center. A food court stays open late to provide sustenance to late arrivals. Downtown Jacksonville is nearby, but the beaches are about 20 mi east. Restaurant, bar. In-room data ports, some microwaves, some refrigerators, some in-room hot tubs. Cable TV. Pool. Outdoor hot tub. Gym. Business services, airport shuttle. | 2101 Dixie Clipper Dr. | 904/741–1997 | fax 904/741–5520 | www.hotelchoice.com/hotel/FL095 | 190 rooms, 10 suites | $109–$119, $139–$299 suites | AE, D, DC, MC, V.

Club Continental. This beautiful property 20 mi south of Jacksonville was once the Mediterranean-style villa estate of the Palmolive family. Built in 1923, the beautifully restored estate is today the centerpiece of a handsomely landscaped condominium development. Manatees play in the waters that lap at the edge of the property and an amazing variety of birds stop by to watch you. Dining room, complimentary Continental breakfast. In-room data ports, some microwaves, some refrigerators. Cable TV. Pool, wading pool. 7 tennis courts. Business services. | 2143 Astor St., Orange Park | 904/264–6070 or 800/877–6070 | fax 904/264–4044 | www.bbonline.com/fl/clubcontinental | 22 rooms | $85–$160 | AE, D, DC, MC, V.

Comfort Suites Baymeadows. Suites decorated in hues often described as 'tropical' are a feature of this hotel built in 1988. Offices of many corporations are based in the Baymeadows suburb, so this spot may be a good option for those on business trips. Complimentary Continental breakfast. In-room data ports, refrigerators, some microwaves. Cable TV, some in-room VCRs. Pool. Outdoor hot tub. Laundry facilities. Business services. Pets allowed. | 8333 Dix Ellis Tr. | 904/739–1155 | fax 904/731–0752 | www.comfortinn.com | 128 suites | $89–$119 | AE, D, DC, MC, V.

Courtyard by Marriott Mayo Clinc. This Courtyard by Marriott property offers a location close to the region's Mayo Clinic and about halfway between downtown Jacksonville and the beaches. Landscaped grounds and three ponds add a pleasant touch to this three-story hotel. Restaurant. In-room data ports, some refrigerators. Cable TV. Pool. Indoor hot tub. Gym. Laundry facilities. Laundry service. Business services. | 4600 San Pablo Rd. | 904/223–1700 or 888/236–2427 | fax 904/223–1026 | 134 rooms, 12 suites | $119–$129, $149–$169 suites | AE, D, DC, MC, V.

Days Inn Airport. Built in 1989 and remodeled in 1999, this two-story hotel offers spacious rooms and an airport location. Jacksonville Landing is just minutes away, and there are many restaurants within walking distance. Complimentary Continental breakfast. In-room data ports, microwaves, refrigerators. Cable TV. Laundry service. Business services, airport shuttle. | 1181 Airport Rd. | 904/741–4000 | fax 904/741–0609 | www.daysinn.com | 62 rooms | $79–$99 | AE, D, DC, MC, V.

Days Inn South. This two-story Days Inn was built in 1998 and is just off I-95 which may make it a convenient choice for you if you're touring the area's far-flung attractions or planning business meetings in several locations. Palm trees shade a swimming pool and you'll find restaurants just a short distance away. In-room data ports. Cable TV. Pool. Business services. Some pets. | 5649 Cagle Rd. | 904/733–3890 | fax 904/636–9841 | www.daysinn.com | 120 rooms | $65 | AE, D, DC, MC, V.

Embassy Suites. An alluring tropical atrium dominates the lobby of this seven-story, all-suites hotel. A complimentary breakfast and afternoon beverages are served daily here. Downtown Jacksonville is about 15 mi. Restaurant, bar, room service, complimentary Continental breakfast. In-room data ports, microwaves, refrigerators. Cable TV. Indoor pool. Hot tub, sauna. Gym. Laundry facilities. Business services. | 9300 Baymeadows Rd. | 904/731–3555 | fax 904/731–4972 | www.embassy-suites.com | 266 suites | $139–$169 suites | AE, D, DC, MC, V.

Fairfield Inn Jacksonville. This two-story, luxury hotel has some showy, two-level loft suites. Its location a mile from the highly rated Champions at Julington Creek Baymeadows golf course makes it a popular stop for golfers. For beach enthusiasts, the hotel is 12 mi east of the sand. Complimentary Continental breakfast. In-room data ports, some kitchenettes, some microwaves, some refrigerators, some in-room hot tubs. Cable TV. Pool. Tennis court. Laundry facilities. Business services. | 8050 Baymeadows Cir. W | 904/739–0739 | fax 904/739–3080 | www.marriott.com | 102 rooms, 18 suites | $79, $85–$129 suites | AE, D, DC, MC, V.

Hampton Inn Jacksonville-Orange Park. Orange Park is a popular enclave of shops and restaurants, and this Hampton Inn is close to all of those. A two-story hotel, the property is walking distance from a movie theater and many restaurants. Jacksonville Landing and Riverwalk are 12 mi northeast. Complimentary Continental breakfast. In-room data ports. Cable TV. Pools. Business services. | 6135 Youngerman Cir. | 904/777–5313 | fax 904/778–1545 | www.hamptoninn.com | 122 rooms | $78–$89 | AE, D, DC, MC, V.

Hampton Inn South. This four-story hotel is conveniently located just off I–95 on the south side of Jacksonville, making it a good spot if you're planning activities throughout this far-flung city. Rooms here were refurbished in 2000. Beaches are 13 mi to the east. Complimentary Continental breakfast. In-room data ports, microwaves, refrigerators. Cable TV. Pool. Laundry service. Business services. | 4690 Salisbury Rd. | 904/281–0443 | fax 904/281–0144 | www.hamptoninn.com | 128 rooms | $79 | AE, D, DC, MC, V.

Holiday Inn Baymeadows. This four-story Holiday Inn in the office park area of Jacksonville gets you in the tropical mood right in the lobby where tropical plants fill big urns and colorful fish zip about in large saltwater and freshwater aquariums. You'll find the hotel on the south side of Jacksonville about 10 mi from downtown. Restaurant, bar, room service. In-room data ports, some microwaves, some refrigerators. Cable TV, some in-room VCRs. Pool. Gym. Video games. Laundry facilities. Business services. Pets allowed. | 9150 Baymeadows Rd. | 904/737–1700 | www.holiday-inn.com | fax 904/737–0207 | 240 rooms, 9 suites | $69–$89, $79–$119 suites | AE, D, DC, MC, V.

Holiday Inn Commonwealth. Ongoing renovations keep this two-story Holiday Inn thoroughly modern. Alltel Stadium, home of the NFL's Jaguars and site of the Gator Bowl, is 13 mi away. Restaurant, bar, room service. In-room data ports, some microwaves, some refrigerators. Cable TV. Indoor pool. Hot tub. Gym. Laundry facilities. Business services. | 6802 Commonwealth Ave. | 904/781–6000 | fax 904/781–2784 | www.holiday-inn.com | 178 rooms | $75–$85 | AE, D, DC, MC, V.

Holiday Inn Express Hotel & Suites. This four-story hotel offers Holiday Inn amenities but no restaurant, although the hotel treats you to a complimentary breakfast that's a bit more extensive than the bagel and brew offered by some hotels. Just off I–95, it's a popular stop with passing-through travelers, and parents of University of North Florida students often settle in here to visit their offspring—the university is 8 mi away. In-room data ports, some microwaves, some refrigerators. Cable TV. Pool. Gym. Laundry facilities. Business services. Some pets. | 4675 Salisbury Rd. | 904/332–9500 or 888/610–3555 | fax 904/332–9222 | www.holiday-inn.com | 50 rooms, 38 suites | $109, $129 suites | AE, D, DC, MC, V.

Homewood Suites Jacksonville-Baymeadows. You'll find one- and two-bedroom suites here, some with fireplaces, which is definitely an unusual feature in a Florida hostelry. A number of restaurants are within walking distance; Jacksonville beaches are a short drive. Complimentary Continental breakfast. In-room data ports, kitchenettes, microwaves, refrigerators. Cable TV, in-room VCRs (and movies). Pool. Outdoor hot tub. Gym. Laundry facilities. Business services. Some pets allowed (fee). | 8737 Baymeadows Rd. | 904/733–9299 | fax 904/448–5889 | www.homewood-suites.com | 116 suites | $119–$175 suites | AE, D, DC, MC, V.

House on Cherry Street. In a 1909 Colonial-style house, this B&B is furnished with Oriental rugs, canopy beds, and antiques. Fresh flowers brighten rooms, most of which offer views of the St. Johns River. Complimentary breakfast. Cable TV, no room phones. Boating. No kids under 10. No smoking. | 1844 Cherry St. | 904/384–1999 | fax 904/384–5013 | houseoncherry@compuserv.com | 4 rooms | $85–$95 | AE, MC, V.

Inns of America. This three-story motel has a landscaped pool area with a pretty gazebo. The beach is 10 mi away, and there are a number of restaurants within 2 mi. Complimentary Continental breakfast. Some refrigerators, some microwaves. Cable TV. Pool. Laundry facilities. Pets allowed (restrictions). | 4300 Salisbury Rd. N | 904/281–0198 | fax 904/296–3580 | 124 rooms | $45–$55 | AE, MC, V.

Jacksonville Hilton Riverfront. This attractive, 10-story hotel occupies 3.8 acres along the south bank of the St. Johns River. It's within easy walking distance of the Museum of Science & History, San Marco, and a variety of restaurants. Restaurant, bar, room service. In-room data ports, some kitchenettes, some in-room hot tubs. Cable TV, some in-room VCRs. Pool. Outdoor hot tub. Gym. Laundry service. Business services. Airport shuttle. | 1201 Riverplace Blvd. | 904/398–8800 | fax 904/398–5570 | www.hilton.com | 275 rooms, 16 suites | $100–$119, $124–$148 suites | AE, D, DC, MC, V.

La Quinta Orange Park. Built in 1980, this two-story chain hotel has a 24-hr restaurant next door and is in the Orange Park area, home to a variety of restaurants and shops. The Orange Park Greyhound Track is just a mile to the east. Complimentary Continental breakfast. In-room data ports, microwaves available, refrigerators. Pool. Laundry facilities. Business services. Some pets. | 8555 Blanding Blvd. | 904/778–9539 | fax 904/779–5214 | www.laquinta.com | 121 rooms, 1 suite | $59–$77, $125 suite | AE, D, DC, MC, V.

La Quinta Baymeadows. This two-story La Quinta is in the suburban Baymeadows area where many corporations have headquarters in office parks. Beaches are 12 mi to the east; restaurants are nearby. Complimentary Continental breakfast. In-room data ports, some microwaves, some refrigerators. Cable TV. Pool. Laundry facilities, laundry service. Business services. Pets allowed. | 8255 Dix Ellis Tr. | 904/731–9940 | fax 904/731–3854 | www.laquinta.com | 104 rooms, 2 suites | $76–$93, $99–$106 suites | AE, D, DC, MC, V.

Jacksonville Marriott Hotel. This handsome downtown Jacksonville Hotel greets you with glowing marble floors and sports a showy, columned indoor swimming pool. All the upscale amenities from business center to fitness facilities are available at this nine-story hotel. Restaurant, bar, room service. In-room data ports, some refrigerators. Cable TV. Pool, indoor pool. Hot tub. Gym. Business services. Laundry service. | 4670 Salisbury Rd. | 904/296–2222 or 888/236–2427 | fax 904/296–7561 | www.marriott.com | 251 rooms, 5 suites | $150–$165, $174–$190 suites | AE, D, DC, MC, V.

Motel 6 Southeast. This single-story motel is a likely spot for budget travelers. Jacksonville Landing is 8 mi and Jacksonville International Airport 20 mi. Cable TV. Pool. Laundry facilities. Some pets. | 8285 Dix Ellis Tr. | 904/731–8400 | fax 904/730–0781 | www.motel6.com | 109 rooms | $41–$51 | AE, D, DC, MC, V.

Omni Jacksonville Hotel. This smart, 16-story hotel smack in the middle of downtown Jacksonville has a luxuriously decorated, four-story atrium lobby and a rooftop pool and sundeck overlooking the St. Johns River. Many rooms have attractive views of the city. Restaurant, bar, room service. In-room data ports, minibars. Cable TV. Pool. Gym. Laundry facilities. Business services, parking (fee). Pets allowed (fee). | 245 Water St. | 904/355–6664 | fax 904/791–4863 | www.omnihotels.com | 348 rooms | $159–$179 | AE, D, DC, MC, V.

Quality Inn & Suites. Alltel Stadium is 8 mi from this two-story property, making this a popular spot for sports fans. Both hotel rooms and small suites are available here. Picnic area. Complimentary Continental breakfast. In-room data ports, some microwaves, some refrigerators. Cable TV. Pool. Gym. Business services, airport shuttle. Pets allowed (fee). | 1153 Airport Rd. | 904/741–4600 | fax 904/741–4424 | www.qualityinn.com | 199 rooms, 25 suites in four buildings | $50–$55, $75–$80 suites | AE, D, DC, MC, V.

Radisson Riverwalk Hotel. Riverwalk is one of Jacksonville's prides and pleasures and this hotel is right in the middle of its restaurants and entertainment. A pleasant departure point for Riverwalk strolls, this five-story hotel on the south bank of the St. Johns has many rooms with views of the river and the downtown business district. Restaurant, bar. In-room data ports, some refrigerators, room service. Cable TV. Pool. 2 tennis courts. Gym. Laundry service. Business services. | 1515 Prudential Dr. | 904/396–5100 | fax 904/396–7154 | www.radis-oon.com | 303 rooms, 19 suites | $79–$149, $179–$500 suites | AE, D, DC, MC, V.

Ramada Inn Mandarin. This two-story property in the nearby town of Mandarin, which was once the home of author Harriet Beecher Stowe, was built in 1985. Today, the Comedy Zone resides here, luring comedians from across the nation. Restaurant, bar (with entertainment), complimentary breakfast, room service. In-room data ports, some microwaves, some refrigerators. Cable TV. Pool, wading pool. Laundry facilities. Business services. Some pets (fee). | 3130 Hartley Rd. | 904/268–8080 | fax 904/262–8718 | www.ramada.com | 149 rooms, 3 suites | $67–$80, $135–$150 suites | AE, D, DC, MC, V.

Ramada Inn Jacksonville Downtown. Built in 1984, this big hotel sprawls over 19 attractively landscaped acres. During football season, it's often packed with fans attending the games at Alltel Stadium, just steps away. Restaurant, bar, room service. In-room data ports, some microwaves, some refrigerators. Cable TV. Pool. Outdoor hot tub. Tennis court. Laundry service. Business services. Pets allowed (fee). | 5865 Arlington Expressway | 904/724–3410 | fax 904/727–7606 | www.ramada.com | 270 rooms in 5 buildings | $49–$89 | AE, D, DC, MC, V.

Red Roof Inn. This two-story motel is 17 mi southwest of downtown Jacksonville, off I–295. Several chain restaurants are a short distance away. In-room data ports. Cable TV. Pool. Business services. Some pets allowed. | 6099 Youngerman Cir. | 904/777–1000 | fax 904/777–1005 | www.redroof.com | 108 rooms | $65–$75 | AE, D, DC, MC, V.

Residence Inn by Marriott. In this two-story Residence Inn on the south side of Jacksonville, 28 of the units have lofts and/or fireplaces, a cozy touch on cool winter nights here. You'll find several restaurants nearby and the hotel offers complimentary area transportation. Complimentary Continental breakfast. In-room data ports, kitchenettes, microwaves, refrigerators. Cable TV. Pool. 3 outdoor hot tubs. Laundry facilities, laundry service. Business services. Pets allowed (fee). | 8365 Dix Ellis Tr. | 904/733–8088 or 888/236–2427 | fax 904/731–8354 | 112 suites | $130–$175 suites | AE, D, DC, MC, V.

JACKSONVILLE BEACH

MAP 3, J2

(Nearby towns also listed: Amelia Island/Fernandina Beach, Atlantic Beach, Jacksonville, Ponte Vedra Beach)

Twenty miles east of the Jacksonville city center, Jacksonville Beach is a lively Atlantic seacoast town. Home to 20,000 residents, it is the largest of the area's beach towns and has long been known to surfers, sunbathers, and shell collectors. Today it is in the throes of a major redevelopment program and has seen the arrival of several new restaurants, shops, and bars along the busy boardwalk, which tends to attract a fairly young crowd drawn to the amusements, concessions, and fishing pier.

Information: **Jacksonville and the Beaches Convention and Visitors Bureau** | 201 E. Adams St., Jacksonville, 32202 | 904/798–9111 or 800/733–2668 | www.jaxcvb.com.

Attractions

Adventure Landing. You can splash and splutter in Shipwreck Island water park, ram other boats in a watery version of bump-'em cars, putter through a mini-golf course, race go-carts on a two-level track, play laser tag, and try your batting skills at a "dry" park. | 1944 Beach Blvd. | 904/246–4386 | www.adventurelanding.com | $24; special rates for children | Daily 10–7.

Huguenot Memorial Park. An oceanfront city park for fishing, swimming, and experiencing nature on the shores of Fort George Inlet, the Atlantic Ocean, and the St. Johns River. Surfing, boardsailing, fishing, and swimming are popular activities. Camping is permitted, but there are no utility hook-ups. A store sells everything from firewood to lotion and food. You can actully drive onto the beach and set up camp. | 10980 Heckscher Dr., Northeast Jacksonville | 904/251–3335 | www.coj.net/fun | 50 ¢ per person | 8–8 summer, 8–6 winter.

Jacksonville Beach Fishing Pier. This pier was almost completely destroyed by Hurricane Floyd and is now in the process of being rebuilt. By spring of 2001 there should be a new park and a rebuilt pier running about 983 feet into the water for angling, surfing, and sightseeing. | 3 6th Ave. S | Free | Daily.

Pablo Historical Park. This open-air museum commemorates a turn-of-the-20th-century colony that sprang up around the railroad. Here you can visit an 1884 post office, a train depot, and one of the locomotives that once brought cypress logs to a local mill. A foreman's house exhibits American furniture dating from the early 1900s. | 425 Beach Blvd. | 904/246–0093 | Donations accepted | Mon.–Sat. 10–3.

ON THE CALENDAR

APR.: *Beaches Festival Weekend Celebration.* A sandcastle building competition, children's activities, parade, crafts, and food mark this April festival on the beach. | Jacksonville Beach Sea Walk Pavilion | Last weekend in April | 904/247–6236 | www.jacksonvillebeach.org.

MAY: *Cajun Crawfish Festival.* This event has everything from craft vendors to children's rides, but crawfish consumption is the big draw. | Seawalk Pavilion | 904/249–3972.

Dining

First Street Grille. Eclectic. Inside: vaulted ceilings; outside: ocean views and a thatched-roof tiki bar. Intriguingly eclectic, the culinary options here are based on seafood, prepared in a variety of ways and with several different sauces and accompaniments. Sauteed red snapper and black tuna Caesar salad are among the menu items. Kids' menu. | 807 N. 1st St. | 904/246–6555 | $11–$20 | AE, D, DC, MC, V.

The Homestead. American. This two-story log cabin built in 1934 is the backdrop for down-home cooking that features such Southern comfort foods as skillet-fried chicken and chicken and dumplings. Kids' menu. | 1712 Beach Blvd. | 904/249–5240 | Reservations essential for parties of 5 or more | Sunday brunch. No lunch | $7–$14 | AE, D, DC, MC, V.

Island Grille. Continental. You can dine here in an elegant, bi-level dining room or on an outdoor deck. Signature dishes include salmon tiki and pecan crusted tilapia, a Florida white fish. Kids' menu. | 981 N. 1st St. | 904/241–1881 | Reservations essential on weekends | No lunch Mon.–Thurs. | $12–$30 | AE, D, DC, MC, V.

Old Siam. Thai. Traditional Asian artwork covers the walls of this restaurant and provides an attractive backdrop for a menu that includes selections from a wide range of Asia cooking. Pad Thai or a whole fried red snapper introduce you to subtle Thai spices. | 1716 N. 3rd St. | 904/247–7763 | Reservations essential for 6 or more | No lunch | $9–$17 | AE, D, DC, MC, V.

Lodging

Comfort Inn Oceanfront. With the Atlantic as its front yard, this seven-story hotel offers ocean views from the private balconies of rooms decorated in pastel colors. Kids will enjoy playing in four waterfalls that cascade into the pool near an oceanfront garden grotto. Restaurant, bar. Complimentary Continental breakfast. In-room safes, microwaves available, refrigerators available. Cable TV. Pool. Spa. Gym. | 1515 N. 1st St. | 904/241–2311 or 800/654–8776 | fax 904/249–3830 | info@comfortinnjaxbeach.com | www.comfortinnjaxbeach.com | 165 rooms, 15 suites | $130–$150, $151–$170 suites | AE, D, DC, MC, V.

Sea Turtle Inn. Oceanview rooms at this eight-story inn have a Mediterranean look, redolent in dark woods. Near the hotel, numerous shops and nightclubs beckon. Restaurant, bar. In-room data ports, refrigerators. Cable TV, in-room VCRs (and movies). Pool. Laundry facilities, laundry service. | 1 Ocean Blvd. | 904/249–7402 or 800/874–6000 | fax 904/247–1517 | www.seaturtle.com | 190 rooms, 3 suites | $179–$239, $349–499 suites | AE, D, DC, MC, V.

JENSEN BEACH

MAP 3, L7

(Nearby towns also listed: Fort Pierce, Jupiter, Port St. Lucie, Stuart)

The white sand stretches for miles at Jensen Beach, a friendly community of 10,000 on the Intracoastal Waterway that separates mainland Florida from Hutchinson Island. Once known as the "Pineapple Capital of the World" during its late-1800s heyday, when over 1 million boxes of pineapples were shipped annually, Jensen Beach's largest employer was a pineapple cannery. That all ended with a devastating frost that killed off the pineapple fields, which were never able to recover. This pineapple legacy is not forgotten: The town still sports a pineapple logo and is also host to an annual pineapple festival. This is a pretty laid-back place, where many residents make a living in the agriculture or fishing industries. Between late April and August, more than 600 turtles come to roost on the town's Atlantic beach, which keeps the tourists coming.

Information: **Jensen Beach Chamber of Commerce** | 1910 N.E. Jensen Beach Blvd., Jensen Beach, 34957 | 407/334–3444 | www.jensenchamber.com.

Attractions

Bathtub Reef Beach. At the north end of Hutchinson Island, this beach has an intriguing name that describes its allure: a reef in waters so shallow and quiet that it forms a "bathtub," safe enough for children to explore. At low tide, you can walk out to the reef, where jellyfish, blue crabs, and wildly colorful parrot fish can be seen. There are rest rooms and showers here, too. | MacArthur Blvd. | 561/225–0505 | Free | Daily.

Coastal Science Center. Run by the Florida Oceanographic Society, this science center includes a coastal hardwood hammock and mangrove forest, a visitors center, a science center with interpretive exhibits on coastal science and environmental issues, and a ½-mi interpretive boardwalk. | 890 N.E. Ocean Blvd. | 561/225–0505 | www.fosusa.org | Mon.–Sat. 10–5, Sun. 12–4; nature walks Mon.–Sat. 10:30–4, Sun. 12–3 | $4.

Elliott Museum. Sterling Elliott was an inventor of note at the turn of the 20th century, creating an addressing machine, among other useful items. This museum salutes the inventor and displays an array of antiques from automobiles to dolls and toys. You can also visit an old-time blacksmith shop and an apothecary. | 825 N.E. Ocean Blvd. | 561/225–1961 | fax 561/225–2333 | $6 | Daily 10–4.

Environmental Study Center. Part of the school system, the center brings children here to study the sea, but everyone's welcome to visit. Saltwater aquariums give you a look at some of the odd and colorful creatures that inhabit the waters around Florida, and you can expand your knowledge of the state and its agriculture at a fruit tree grove, a native plant "slat" growing house, gift shop, and a marine museum. | 2900 N.E. Indian River Dr. | 561/219–1887 | fax 561/219–1889 | www.esc.sbmc.org | Free | Monday–Friday, 9–3; special guided tours 1st & 3rd Sat. from Oct.–May 19, 10–2. Closed to the public June 4–July 13.

Florida Power and Light Energy Encounter. Interactive displays explain the history of energy production at this Florida Power and Light nuclear power plant. You'll find an energy treasure hunt, videos about nuclear power, and a 1-mi looping nature trail at the facility. | 6501 S. Ocean Dr. | 561/468–4111 | www.fpl.com/encounter | Free | Sun.–Fri. 10–4.

House of Refuge Museum. The U.S. Life Saving Service, a predecessor of the Coast Guard, built this structure to aid stranded sailors. Today, it houses a model ship collection, aquariums of tropical and native fish, and changing exhibits related to the history of the building and of the Florida coast. On the grounds is a lookout tower built during WWII, as well as a hand-crafted replica of an 1840s surfboat, once used to rescue shipwreck victims. The boat house displays early lifesaving equipment and maritime artifacts. | 301 S.E. MacArthur Blvd. | 561/225–1875 | $4 | Daily 10–4.

Jensen Beach Turtle Watch. Big sea turtles lumber ashore in this region to lay eggs that later hatch into tiny turtles that make their way back to the sea. This attraction includes a slide presentation on the turtles' annual visit, sea turtle artifacts, and transportation to the beach to witness turtle nesting activities in July and July. | Jensen Beach Blvd. | 561/334–3444 | Reservations required, $5 fee | Daily May–early Aug.

Maritime & Yachting Museum of the Treasure Coast. This museums boasts an extensive collection of historic boats, maritime artifacts, ship models, and nautical paintings. | 3006 N.W. Federal Hwy., Jensen Beach | 561/692–1234 | fax 561/692–4045 | www.tcmall.com/mym/features.htm | Free | Mon.–Sat. noon–4, Sun. 1–5.

ON THE CALENDAR

JUNE–JULY: *Turtle Watch.* Hobe Sound National Wildlife Refuge organizes this annual event that offers visitors a chance to watch the arrival of more than 600 turtles, predominantly loggerheads and leatherbacks, who come ashore to dig a deep hole with their flippers and lay their eggs in nests that are carefully guarded by local environmentalists. Months later, tiny turtles exit those eggs and make their way back to the sea to complete the cycle. | 561/546–2067.

NOV.: *Pineapple Festival.* This weekend festival in downtown Jensen Beach has live music on multiple stages. The accompanying feast is based on pineapples prepared in some creative ways. | 561/334–3444.

Dining

11 Maple Street. Continental. The menu at this restaurant changes nightly, but the portions are consistently large. Salmon with leeks, porcini mushroom risotto, and blue-crab cakes are a few of the entrees that you might find on offer. For dessert, there is usually white-chocolate custard with blackberry sauce. Jazz plays softly in the background. | 3224 Maple Ave. | 561/334–7714 | Reservations essential | Closed Mon.–Tues. No lunch | $14–$21 | MC, V.

Conchy Joe's. Seafood. The layout is half the fun at this ultracasual spot filled with stuffed fishing trophies, gator-hides, and mounted snakeskins. The whole joint is on stilts, and a large palm tree grows straight through the roof. The menu changes nightly, but might feature grouper marsala or fried, cracked conch. Joe's also serves fruity rum drinks with exotic names. A steel-drum calypso band heats it up Wed.–Sun. nights. | 3945 N. Indian River Dr., Jensen Beach | 561/334–1130 | $7–$16 | AE, D, MC, V.

Longhorn Steakhouse. Steakhouse. Texas-style cooking, prepared with cowboy flair, is the fare here. "Flo's Fillet," a choice cut 9-oz tenderloin and the "Texas Tonion" appetizer—sweet, jumbo onions cut into "petals" and lightly battered then fried—are the specialties here. | 2901 N.W. Federal Hwy. | 561/692–7922 | $9–$18 | AE, D, DC, MC, V.

New England Fish Market. Seafood. This five-year-old restaurant began as a take-out and is now a 65-seat operation boasting a large selection of seafood from both Northern and Southern waters. Here's a sample offering: a "clambake for two" includes two lobsters, a dozen littleneck clams, a pound of mussels, two ears of corn, potatoes, and andouille sausage. Other fish entrees: salmon, grouper, haddock and clams. | 1419 N.E. Jensen Beach Blvd. | 561/334–7328 | fax 561/334–9957 | $13–$30 | D, MC, V.

Peter's Steakhouse. Steakhouse. Before opening his own restaurant, chef Peter Buchner spent 20 years working at New York's Peter Luger's Steak House. His menu is built around five cuts of steak, lamb chops, chicken, and a fresh fish of the day. Menu selections include onion-laced, crisply sautéed German potatoes and creamed spinach. A sizeable wine list completes the menu. | 3200 N.E. Maple Ave. | 561/225–2516 | fax 561/225–9667 | Closed Sun. | $11.95–24.95 | AE, D, DC, MC, V.

Lodging

Casa d'Este. This charming B&B opened in 1998 on the Indian River Lagoon, just a few minutes from the ocean and numerous recreational activities. Rooms are bright and tastefully decorated. Complimentary breakfast. Cable TV. Pool. Hot tub. | 4030 N.E. Indian River Dr., Jensen Beach | 561/225–2729 | fax 561/225–2729 | www.casadeste.com | 5 rooms | $75–$95 | AE, DC, MC, V.

Courtyard Hutchinson Island. A glass-walled elevator runs up the side of this two-story oceanside hotel built in 1993. The Elliott Museum is 4 mi away, and there are a number of restaurants nearby. In-room data ports. Cable TV. Pool. Gym. Beach. Laundry facilities, laundry service. Business services. | 10978 S. Ocean Dr. | 561/229–1000 or 888/236–2427 | fax 561/229–0253 | 108 rooms, 2 suites | $149–$189, $215 suites | AE, D, DC, MC, V.

Holiday Inn Oceanside. This four-story hotel was built in 1974 on a site that takes full advantage of ocean and Indian River views. Jet ski and boat rentals are 2 mi away. Restaurant, bar (with entertainment), room service. In-room data ports. Cable TV, in-room VCRs available. Pool. 3 tennis courts. Gym. Video games. Laundry facilities. Business services. | 3793 N.E. Ocean Blvd. | 561/225–3000 | fax 561/225–1956 | www.holiday-inn.com | 176 rooms, 3 suites | $189–$199, $525 suites | AE, D, DC, MC, V.

Hutchinson Inn. Decorated in soft shades of peach and teal and outfitted in wicker furniture, this inviting bed-and-breakfast inn nestles alongside white-sand beaches. Complimentary breakfast. Some kitchenettes, some microwaves, some refrigerators. Cable TV. Pool. Tennis court. Business services. No smoking. | 9750 S. Ocean Dr./Rte. A1A | 561/229–2000 | fax 561/229–8875 | www.hutchinsoninn.com | 21 rooms | $100–$225 | MC, V.

Hutchinson Island Marriott Beach Resort. This 200-acre resort attracts many families, with its many recreational activities, restaurants, swimming pool, and complimentary tram service to get around the sprawl. Many of the rooms are in three four-story buildings built around a central courtyard. The rest are in apartments tucked here and there throughout the property. 4 Restaurants, 2 bars. In-room dataports, some kitchenettes, some microwaves, refrigerators, cable TV. 4 pools. Hot tub. 18-hole golf course, putting green, 13 tennis courts. Health club, beach, water sports, dock, boating, fishing, bicycles. Babysitting, children's programs (ages 5–11), playground. Laundry facilities, laundry service. Business services. Pets allowed (fee). | 555 N.E. Ocean Blvd., Hutchinson Island, Stuart | 561/225–3700 or 800/775–5936 | fax 561/225–0033 | www.marriott.com | 298 rooms, 72 suites, 150 condos | $209–$219 room, $259–$299 suite, $349–$399 condo | AE, DC, MC, V.

Plantation Beach Club at Indian River Plantation. This condo property is part of the larger Indian River Plantation Resort, which is also home to the Marriott hotel. Secluded and spacious one- and two-bedroom units are rented weekly; some have screened-in porches and are surrounded by gardens and wild vegetation. Restaurant, bar with entertainment. In-room data ports, microwaves, refrigerators. Cable TV. Pool. 18-hole golf course, putting green, 13 tennis courts. Exercise equipment. Beach, water sports, boating, fishing, bicycles. Children's programs (ages 5–11), playground. Laundry facilities. Business services. | 329 N.E. Tradewinds La. | 561/225–0074 | fax 561/225–6318 | $180 1-bedroom condos, $255 2-bedroom condos | AE, MC, V.

River Palm Cottages & Fish Camp On the western bank of Indian River Lagoon, this 7¼-acre tropical spread has cottages, bungalows, and houses. You can fish in the ocean or go bird-watching on eco-tours, or simply relax in a *chickee* hut or hammock. Picnic area. Some kitchenettes, some microwaves, some refrigerators, cable TV. Pool. Fishing, boating, dock. Playground. Laundry facilities. Pets allowed (fee). | 2325 N.E. Indian River Dr., Jensen Beach | 561/334–0401 or 800/305–0511 | fax 561/334–0527 | www.riverpalmcottages.com | 25 units | $125–$159 | AE, D, DC, MC, V.

JUPITER

(Nearby towns also listed: Palm Beach Gardens, Palm Beach Shores, Riviera Beach, Stuart)

Jupiter is a town of about 25,000 residents, a mix of young professionals, retirees, and snowbirds. Set at the confluence of the Loxahatcheee River and Intracoastal Waterway, Jupiter and Jupiter Island are known for their relaxed lifestyle revolving around golf and water sports: there are 145 golf courses in the immediate area and beautiful beaches. And with the Gulf Stream flowing nearby, the area is rich in sportfish. Jupiter is also home to the spring training facilities of the St. Louis Cardinals and the Montréal Expos. Five mi north of Jupiter, Jupiter Island is home to the oldest structure in Palm Beach County, the Jupiter Lighthouse, built in 1860.

Information: Jupiter-Tequesta-Juno Beach Chamber of Commerce | 800 U.S. 1N, Jupiter, 33477 | 407/746–7111 | www.jupiterfl.org.

JUPITER

INTRO
ATTRACTIONS
DINING
LODGING

Attractions

Blowing Rocks Preserve. Within this 73-acre Nature Conservancy thrive plant communities native to beachfront dune, coastal strand (that's the landward side of the dunes), mangrove, and hardwood hammock environments. | 574 S. Beach Rd., Jupiter Island | 561/744–6668 | www.tncflorida.org | $3 | Daily 9–4:30.

Carlin Park. This park has beachfront picnic pavilions, a baseball diamond, 6 tennis courts, hiking trails, a playground, fishing sites, and, of course, a beach. There is a snack bar called the Park Galley, which is opened daily from 9–5. | 400 Rte. A1A | Free | Open daily 9–5.

Florida History Center and Museum. Permanent exhibits at this Burt Reynolds Park complex include 18th- and 19th-century photographs and artifacts that show how nature shaped the land and how it continues to affect development along the Loxahatchee River. On the grounds is a Seminole Living History Village and the Tindall House, built in 1892. | 805 U.S. 1N | 561/747–6639 | fax 561/575–3292 | www.gopbi.com/community/FLhistory | $5 | Tues.–Fri. 10–5, weekends noon–5.

DuBois Pioneer Home. Built in 1898 by pioneer Henry DuBois, who chose this spot atop a prehistoric Jeaga Indian shell mound, this historic house presents a look at early pioneer life in Florida and houses a collection of antique furnishings and memorabilia. | DuBois Park, Rte. A1A | 561/747–6639 | $5 | Closed Sept.–Oct.; Wed. 1–4 or by appointment.

Jupiter Inlet Lighthouse. Palm Beach County's oldest structure, this beacon was built in 1860 on a shell midden, a big mound of shells created by native tribes who tossed away their cast-off shells here. Overlooking Jupiter Inlet, the lighthouse was attacked and severely damaged by Seminole Indians during its construction. A museum at the base of the lighthouse tells the history of the structure and has other interesting exhibits outlining Florida history. | Capt. Armour's Way, U.S. 1 and Beach Rd. | 561/747–8380 | www.gopbi.com/community/groups/flhistory | $5 | Sun.–Wed. 10–4.

Hobe Sound National Wildlife Refuge. These 967 acres include three distinct plant communities: coastal dune, mangrove swamps, and sand pine-scrub forest. Among the numerous wildlife species you might spot here are brown pelicans, bald eagles, and American crocodiles. Sea turtle nesting beaches are a lure when the turtles swim in here each summer, and the carefully preserved ecosystem along these 3 mi of Jupiter Island offers a glimpse of old Florida. | 13640 S.E. Federal Hwy., Hobe Sound | 561/546–6141 | Mainland area free, $5 per vehicle on island area | Daily dawn to dusk.

Hobe Sound Nature Center. Baby alligators, baby crocodiles, a flying squirrel, and a scary-looking tarantula prowl the beach section of this nature center that also has interpretive exhibits detailing the ecosystem in the area. You can trek a short trail that winds through the sandhills. | 13640 S.E. Federal Hwy., Hobe Sound | 561/546–2067 | Free | Trail daily dawn to dusk; nature center weekdays 9–2:30.

Jonathan Dickinson State Park. About 20 percent of this 11,500-acre wildlife-rich park is covered in sand pine scrub, a biological community so rare that it has been designated as globally imperiled. Much of the rest is pine flatwoods and wetlands. A favorite camping and canoeing spot, the park also offers bicycling and picnicking along the banks of the Loxahatchee River which runs through the park. Freshwater and saltwater fishing may yield creels of mullet and snook. Canoes can be rented from the concession stand and paddled into the far reaches of the Loxahatchee River which eventually makes its way to Jupiter Inlet and the Atlantic Ocean. The 44-passenger *Loxahatchee Queen II* makes the trip upriver to the pioneer homesite of Trapper Nelson, who came to the area in the 1930s. The park is 5 mi north of Jupiter. | 16450 S.E. Federal Hwy., Hobe Sound | 561/546–2771 | www.dep.state.fl.us | $3.25 per vehicle | Daily 8–sundown.

ON THE CALENDAR

FEB., MAR.: *Spring Training.* Since 1991, when the Roger Dean Stadium opened, the St. Louis Cardinals have trained in Jupiter, along with the Montréal Expos. You can go out and watch them practice and get autographs from your favorite players. The Cardinals moved here from St. Petersburg; the Expos from West Palm Beach. | 561/775–1818 or 561/966–3309.

MAR.: *Art Fest By The Sea.* For more than a decade, hundreds of artists from across the nation have made their way each spring to the edge of the ocean in Juno Beach to present their work at this annual festival. Free. | 561/746–7111 or 800/616–7402.

NOV.–JUNE: *Promenade Concerts.* Classical and jazz performances are presented free on the second Sunday of each month on the Florida Atlantic University campus. | 561/848–9633.

Dining

Athenian Cafe. Greek. This storefront café specializes in Greek cuisine with a menu that includes such favorites as fresh spinach pie, moussaka, and antipasto at modest prices. A glass of Greek wine is available to add an authentic touch to a Greek meal. Kids' menu. | 6350 Indiantown Rd. | 561/744–8327 | Reservations not accepted | Closed Sun. | $7–$16 | AE, MC, V.

Charley's Crab. Seafood. Sporting a glass, three-tiered atrium overlooking the Intracoastal Waterway and Jupiter Inlet, this chic dining spot specializes in seafood but has some selections for landlubbers as well. Grouper and yellowfin tuna are popular options here. You can also dine outside on a covered patio. Kids' menu. | 1000 U.S. 1N | 561/744–4710 | Reservations essential | $16–$30 | AE, D, DC, MC, V.

Crabhouse Seafood Restaurant. Seafood. An outdoor deck overlooks Jupiter Inlet at this seafood restaurant that offers such options as crispy coconut shrimp with a tangy sauce or clam chowder flavored with bacon. Topping the old-favorites-with-a-twist list: broiled Maine lobster stuffed with crab Imperial, or Alaskan snow crab accompanied by roasted peppers. All entrees include a choice of Caesar or tossed salad. Chicken, pasta, and steak in similarly creative presentations are also available. Live music plays nightly. | 1065 Highway A1A N | 561/744–5559 | $10–$40 | AE, D, DC, MC, V.

Nick's Tomato Pie. Italian. Pictures of Frank Sinatra and paintings of Italian food set the tone at this big, casual dining spot. Portions are huge, and such interesting Italian selections as *zuppa di pesce* and roasted garlic appear on the menu. Kids' menu. | 1697 Indiantown Rd. | 561/744–8935 | Reservations essential for 6 or more | No lunch | $12–$19 | AE, D, DC, MC, V.

Lighthouse Restaurant. American. Chicken breast stuffed with sausage and fresh vegetables, burgundy beef stew, and king crab cakes are some of the offerings at this coffee shop-style restaurant with a menu that changes daily. | 1510 U.S. 1 | 561/746–4811 | $9–$13 | D, DC, MC, V.

Sinclair's Ocean Grill & Rotisserie. Seafood. Tall French doors look out on a pool and tropical greenery at this restaurant, which is part of the Jupiter Beach Resort. Cashew-encrusted Florida grouper, Cajun-spiced tuna, mahimahi with pistachio sauce, and filet mignon are some popular choices, as is the Sunday brunch. | 5 N. Hwy. A1A | 561/745–7120 | $16–$20 | AE, MC, V.

Lodging

Best Western Intracoastal Inn. This two-story, Spanish villa-style motel borders the Intracoastal Waterway so you can watch yachts glide by your waterside room. To get a gull's-eye view of the scenery, climb the observation tower here. Complimentary Continental breakfast. In-room data ports, some in-room hot tubs. Cable TV. Pool. Business services. | 810 U.S. 1S | 561/575–2936 | fax 561/579–9346 | www.bestwestern.com | 53 rooms | $109–$129 | AE, D, DC, MC, V.

Fairfield Inn & Suites Jupiter. An attractive brand in the Marriott chain of properties, this attractive hotel is a good spot to settle if you're planning a visit to Jonathan Dickinson Park which is about 10 mi from the hotel. Within 5 mi of the hotel are Jupiter Beach, the Intercoastal Waterway, and attractions like the Burt Reynolds Ranch. Restaurant, bar, complimentary Continental breakfast. Cable TV. Pool. Laundry facilities. Business services, free parking. | 6748 Indiantown Rd. | 561/748–5252 or 888/236–2427 | fax 561/748–5251 | www.marriott.com | 116 rooms | $69–$89 | AE, D, DC, MC, V.

Hampton Inn Juno Beach. Juno Beach's 7 mi of sandy shores are just minutes away from this two-story property built in 1995. There are restaurants within walking distance. Complimentary Continental breakfast. In-room data ports, some microwaves, some refrigerators. Cable TV. Pool. Outdoor hot tub. Laundry facilities, laundry service. Business services. | 13801 U.S. 1, Juno Beach | 561/626–9090 | fax 561/624–9936 | www.hamptoninn.com | 90 rooms | $119–$159 | AE, D, DC, MC, V.

Jupiter Beach Resort. You can select a room overlooking the ocean or choose one with a view of the sunset at this oceanside resort. Whichever view you prefer, you'll find rooms with marble baths and private balconies at this attractive resort hotel that offers entertainment in the lounge by night, bicycles and water sports by day. Restaurant, bar (with entertainment). In-room data ports, some kitchenettes, minibars, some microwaves, some refrigerators. Cable TV, in-room VCRs available. Pool. Gym. Beach, boating, bicycles. Laundry facilities, laundry service. Business services. | 5 Rte. A1A N | 561/746–2511 or 800/228–8810 | fax 561/744–1741 | www.jupiterbeachresort.com | 134 rooms, 20 suites | $195, $200–$1,000 suites | AE, D, DC, MC, V.

Jupiter Waterfront Inn. Located on the Intracoastal Waterway about 2 mi from the ocean, this pleasant hotel strives for an "inn" feeling with rooms that include a couch, wet bar, and, in some, whirlpool tubs. Some have views of the waterway and a 240-ft fishing pier that lures anglers and boaters. Complimentary Continental breakfast. Refrigerators, some in-room hot tubs. Cable TV. Pool. Outdoor hot tub. Fishing. Laundry facilities. Business services. | 18903 S.E. Federal Hwy., Tequesta | 561/747–9085 | fax 561/575–3374 | 36 suites | $140–$200 suites | AE, D, DC, MC, V.

Wellesley Inn. Adjacent to the Fisherman's Wharf Shopping Center, this three-story hotel is just 5 mi from the region's popular Jonathan Dickinson Park, where sports opportunities include canoeing and cycling. Complimentary Continental breakfast. In-room data ports. Cable TV. Pool. Laundry facilities. Business services. Pets allowed. | 34 Fisherman's Wharf | 561/575–7201 or 800/444–8888 | fax 561/575–1169 | www.wellesleyinnandsuites.com | 93 rooms, 11 suites | $109–179, $129–$189 suites | AE, D, DC, MC, V.

KEY BISCAYNE

MAP 5, J9

(Nearby towns also listed: Coconut Grove, Coral Gables, Miami, Miami Beach)

Key Biscayne is a barrier island 7 mi south of downtown Miami, accessible by the Rickenbacker Causeway over Biscayne Bay, with a population of about 9,000. Incorporated as a village in 1991, Key Biscayne is buffered by Bill Baggs Cape Florida State Recreation Area and Dade County's Crandon Park. Rich with golf courses, sports facilities, and long, winding roads that are perfect for biking and rollerblading, Key Biscayne attracts a fit, relaxed crowd. The mix of retirement housing, vacation resorts, and condominium complexes, combined with casual outdoor restaurants, boutiques, and galleries, makes this a great getaway from the bustle of Miami.

Information: **Key Biscayne Chamber of Commerce** | 87 W. McIntyre St., Key Biscayne, 33149 | 305/361–5207 | www.keybiscaynechamber.org.

Attractions

★ **Bill Baggs Cape Florida State Recreation Area.** Named after the late Miami newspaper editor who championed its creation, this tranquil park at the south end of Key Biscayne is part of the barrier island ecosystem that skirts the southeast Florida coast. Covered pavilions nestle around a lighthouse that looms over miles of tree-lined beaches. You'll find picnicking, fishing, and kayaking facilities here, too. | 1200 S. Crandon Blvd. | 305/361–5811 | www.dep.state.fl.us/parks | $1 | Daily 8–dusk.

Crandon Park. More than 3 mi of soft white sand frames the Atlantic's multi-hued waters at this 1,211-acre park on northern Key Biscayne. A favorite sunning spot that's often crowded on weekends, the park has an 18-hole golf course, 27 grass, clay, and hard tennis courts, a tennis center that's home to an annual professional tennis tournament, volleyball courts, a Family Amusement Center, and a 200-acre garden. Jet skis and other water sports equipment can be rented from concessionaires just outside the park. | 4000 Crandon Blvd. | 305/361–5421 | $3.50 per vehicle | Daily.

ON THE CALENDAR

JAN.: *Key Biscayne Art Festival.* On the last weekend of January each year, Key Biscayne shows its colors on the main street, Crandon Blvd., site of this annual showcase of art and craft works. | 305/361–0049.

MAR.: *The Ericsson Open.* The world's top professional tennis players face off in this 11-day tournament at Crandon Park Tennis Center which has a 14,000-seat stadium and grass, clay, and hard courts. | 305/442–3367.

NOV.: *Lighthouse Run.* Participants from all over the state join in this annual run that's been taking place here for 23 years on the second week of November. | 305/361–0049.

Dining

The Rusty Pelican. Continental. A mainstay of Key Biscayne dining, the Rusty Pelican nestles up to the water, offering diners a glittering view of Biscayne Bay and the Miami skyline. On the menu at this rustic, woodsy restaurant are such options as a Neptune platter laden with fish, lobster, and shrimp and a chargrilled chicken double breast. On the patio, three fire pits, blazing from September to May, add to the allure of panoramic views. Kids' menu. | 3201 Rickenbacker Causeway | 305/361–3818 | Reservations essential | $16–$29 | AE, D, DC, MC, V.

Stefano's. Italian. Patio dining is the lure at this indoor-outdoor restaurant that's been feeding a pasta-loving crowd here for many years. Such treats as risotto and ravioli de granchio provide their own allure, and on Friday and Saturday nights a DJ turns Stefano's into a nightclub that operates to the wee hours. Sunday brunch. Kids' menu. | 24 Crandon Blvd. | 305/361–7007 | Reservations essential on weekends | No lunch | $15–$26 | AE, D, DC, MC, V.

Sundays on the Bay. Seafood. Accessible by boat, car, and foot, this lively, waterside restaurant overlooks Crandon Marina, the bay, and Miami's skyline. Most of the tables are under a roof, but walls are open to the breezes. Shrimp scampi and snapper livornese are particular favorites here. Sunday brunch. | 5420 Crandon Blvd. | 305/361–6777 | Reservations essential | $15–$24 | AE, D, DC, MC, V.

Lodging

Silver Sands Beach Resort. Reclining lounges await at poolside, tropical foliage adds greenery to the sandy landscape, and a winding walkway at the water's edge beckons at this single-story, right-on-the-sand motel that's been a playground for locals and visitors alike for decades. A 15-min drive from downtown Miami, this sand-in-your-shoes resort has simply decorated rooms and a few cottages popular with families. Kitchenettes, microwaves, refrigerators. Cable TV. Pool. Laundry facilities. Playground. | 301 Ocean Dr. | 305/361–5441 | fax 305/361–5477 | www.key-biscayne.com/accom/silversands/ | 3 suites, 4 cottages | $169–$349 suite, $329 cottage | AE, D, DC, MC, V.

★ **Sonesta Beach Resort.** Another longtime resident of Key Biscayne, this showy hotel rises eight stories over the sands, and many rooms offer sea views. Rooms are outfitted in sand tones with emerald, purple, gold, and ruby accents. Sonesta's four dining spots include a restaurant at which Caribbean flavors prevail and the venerable Two Dragons, a longtime Miami favorite for upscale Asian cookery. Restaurant, bar, picnic area, room service. In-room data ports, minibars. Cable TV. Pool. Barbershop, beauty salon, outdoor hot tubs, massage. 9 tennis courts. Gym. Beach. Shops, video games. Children's programs (ages 5–13), playground. Laundry service. Business services. | 350 Ocean Dr. | 305/361–2021 or 800/766–3782 | fax 305/361–3096 | www.sonesta.com | 282 rooms, 14 suites | $365–$415, $825–$1,700 suites | AE, D, DC, MC, V.

KEY LARGO

INTRO
ATTRACTIONS
DINING
LODGING

KEY LARGO

MAP 3, E6

(Nearby towns also listed: Florida City, Homestead, Islamorada, Windley Key)

Home to Humphrey Bogart's movie of the same name, Key Largo is the first of the Keys that you cross as you head south from Miami on the Overseas Highway. Measuring 30 mi from tip to tip, it's also the longest of the islands. Its a laid-back place, and what with its dive shops, marinas, fishing boats, and bare feet, it feels like something out of a Jimmy Buffett song.

Key Largo considers itself the diving capital of the world. The John Pennekamp Coral Reef State Park is the first of the nation's undersea parks and can be visited on a dive or snorkel or by a glass-bottom boat tour. Classic movie buffs can check out the *African Queen*, the steamship Bogie and Katharine Hepburn rode in the famous film.

Information: The Florida Keys Visitor Center/Key Largo Chamber of Commerce | 10600 Overseas Hwy., Key Largo, 33037 | 305/451–1414 or 800/822–1088 | www.fla-keys.com.

Attractions

Dolphins Plus. Splish, splash, you're swimming with the dolphins. If Rex Harrison could talk with the animals, there's no reason you can't squeak with the dolphins while you're at this marine center that focuses on these intelligent marine mammals. You can swim with trained dolphins who will shake your hand . . .well, your flipper, offer you rides on their fins, and perform stunts for you, or you can tag along with untrained dolphins who just swim happily around in the pool with you. | MM 99 on U.S. 1 | 305/451–1993 | www.dolphinsplus.com | $10 to observe; $95–$125 for swims | Daily 8–5; swims at 8:45, 9, noon, 1:30, 3.

Florida Keys Wild Bird Rehabilitation Center. On the south end of Key Largo, you can get an up-close look at this facility dedicated to the care and repair of injured birds—hawks, ospreys, pelicans, cormorants—who get fishhooks caught in their bills or are injured by other accidents. Many of the recuperating birds have permanent injuries that will keep them grounded here forever, but others will recover and be set free. A video explains the center's mission. A short nature trail takes you into a mangrove forest similar to the ones in which many of these birds live. Bring bug spray, particularly between May and October. | 93600 Overseas Hwy., Tavernier | 305/852–4486 | $5 per vehicle (suggested) | Daily dawn to dusk.

John Pennekamp Coral Reef State Park. This park was the nation's first underwater preserve and, together with the adjacent Florida Keys National Marine Sanctuary, encompasses 178 nautical square mi of coral reefs, seagrass beds, and mangrove swamps that extend 3 mi out into the Atlantic and are 25 mi long. At the Visitor Center, you can get a video introduction to the fragile ecosystem that exists underwater here. Guided nature walks through the park's Mangrove and Wild Tamarind trails reveal how the land and water work together. Revered by scuba divers and snorkelers for the beauty of its ever-changing reefs, the park also has concessionaires who can get you down under for a look or take you on a glass-bottom boat trip that shows off the 'land' down under. | MM 102.5 on U.S. 1 | 305/451–1202 | www.pennekamppark.com | $3.25 per vehicle | Daily 8–dusk; guided walks from Dec.–Mar. or on request.

Spirit of Pennekamp. This high-speed, 149-passenger glass-bottom boat whisks you out for a look at the coral reef where a bevy of colorful fish play. | MM 102.5 on U.S. 1 | 305/451–1621 | www.pennekamppark.com | $18; special rates for children | Tours daily at 9:15, 12:15, and 3.

Key Largo Hammocks State Botanical Site. This 2,005-acre site on the northern end of Key Largo is the largest remaining stand of what was once a vast West Indian tropical hardwood hammock and mangrove wetland covering most of the Keys. Here, you can roam among 84 species of protected plants and animals, including the endangered Key Largo wood rat and the American crocodile. Self-guided tour information is available at the gate; guided tours are offered biweekly. | County Rd. 905, North Key Largo | 305/451–1202 | Free | Daily 8–5, tours Thurs, Sun. at 10.

Key Largo Harbor Marina. The boats moored at this marina may conjure up some Hollywood memories—the *African Queen* from the movie is on display, as is the *Thayer IV*, a 22-ft mahogany Chris Craft used by Katharine Hepburn and Henry Fonda in *On Golden Pond*. The marina is next to the Holiday Inn Key Largo Resort. | M.M. 99.7, OS | 305/451–4655 | Boat ride $15 | Daily by appointment.

Key Largo Underseas Park. A one-acre lagoon bordering the Atlantic, this underwater site is designed to showcase ocean ecology to diving and snorkeling enthusiasts of all skill levels. | 51 Shoreland Dr. | 305/451–2353 | $10 to snorkel and $25 to dive | Daily 8–4.

ON THE CALENDAR

APR.: *Break Away to Key Largo Bike Tour.* Hosted by the National Multiple Sclerosis Society, this annual two-day event brings together both recreational and serious cyclists intent on a scenic bike tour and the furtherance of a good cause. | 954/731–4224, 800/FIGHT-MS.

NOV.: *Island Jubilee.* Live music, carnival rides, clowns, and food keep this two-day festival at Rowells Marina lively. There's even a good 'ol docey-doe-your-partner square dance—and you just don't see those much at Florida festivals anymore! | 305/451–1414.

Dining

Alabama Jack's. Seafood. Conch fritters and crab cakes are two popular choices at this weathered, open-air seafood restaurant, which floats on two roadside barges in an old fishing community. Locals, including the occasional alligator in the canal, seem to love the place. | 58000 Card Sound Rd., Card Sound | 305/248–8741 | $8–$11 | MC, V.

Bayside Grill. American. A local gathering spot of significance, this grill and lounge is proud of the sunset it orchestrates—well, salutes—each evening, providing a moment of tranquility for the lively crowds that gather to watch it all happen. A casual spot, the grill offers simple cookery, with salads, sandwiches, and grilled selections, plenty of libations, and a pleasant indoor-outdoor setting to salute sundown. If you look really carefully, you might spot the famous "green flash," said to occur in the split second when the sun does this special trick . . . or is it the libations? | MM 99 Overseas Hwy. | 305/451–3380 | Reservations not accepted | $9–$23 | AE, MC, V.

Calypso's. Seafood. The chef at this casual seafood joint consistently gets awards at local cook-offs for his inventions, which include Nuts for Snapper, a local yellowtail snapper with macadamia nuts and orange Frangelica coulis. The wine list is a lot grander than the decor, which includes plastic outdoor furniture, paper napkins, and plastic cutlery. | MM 99.5, OS, 1 Seagate Blvd. | 305/451–0600 | Closed Tues. | $5–$11 | D, MC, V.

Café Largo. Italian. If you're steeping yourself in the Key Largo mystique, this may be a spot to combine a little of the film's *intime* atmosphere with a taste of the sea that is never far from sight in the Keys. Many of the pasta possibilities here add a touch of seafood to remind you where you are—a penne selection is topped with shrimp and broccoli, and lobster scampi melds Italian flavors with that favored crustacean. | MM 99, 99530 Overseas Hwy. | 305/451–4885 | Closed Wed. | $9–$23 | AE, MC, V.

Chad's Deli & Bakery. Delicatessen. First-timers at this four-table establishment often remark on the large sizes and low prices of the sandwiches here, which include everything from certified Angus roast beef to veggies. There are also salads, sides, soft drinks, and a choice of at least two 8-inch cookies. This is mostly a take-out place. | M.M. 92.3, BS | 305/853–5566 | No dinner | $5–$9 | No credit cards.

Coconuts Restaurant. Seafood. Lively and casual, this indoor-outdoor restaurant is best loved for its deck dining, but inside, historic photographs of the Keys in days long gone are entertaining. In keeping with its name, coconut shrimp is a specialty here, and oysters are shucked at the raw bar. Musical entertainment punctuates the night, every night, and draws crowds. | 528 Caribbean Dr. | 305/453–9794 | $9–$16 | AE, DC, MC, V.

The Fish House. Seafood. Huge portions of seafood and homemade Key lime pie are signature selections here at a restaurant that's fully focused on Keys' seafood from sauteed yellowtail snapper to fish Matecumbe, named for one of the local keys. Kids' menu. | 102401 Overseas Hwy. | 305/451–4665 | Reservations not accepted | $9–$25 | AE, D, DC, MC, V.

Frank–Keys Cafe. Eclectic. Moonlight dinners on the the veranda are a draw at this unusual Victorian-style café that is adorned with paintings by local artists. Signature dishes include roast duck and macadamia-crusted grouper. | 100211 Overseas Hwy. | 305/453–0310 | Reservations essential on weekends | No lunch. Jan.–May closed Mon.; June–Dec. closed Mon.–Tues. | $12–$38 | MC, V.

Hariette's Restaurant. American. A new mural and a bright, island-style paint job are the only things that have ever changed at this local breakfast favorite, which serves up comfort food like steak and eggs with hash browns or grits and toast and jelly, or old-fashioned hotcakes with butter, syrup, and sausage and bacon. | MM 95.7, BS | 305/852–8689 | No dinner | $4–$7 | No credit cards.

Mrs. Mac's Kitchen. American. This rustic, open-air, wood-paneled restaurant conjures up the 1950s, when the Keys were home to more fishermen than tourists. Burgers, barbecue, chili, traditional American sandwiches, and seafood are among the offerings. A popular choice is the T.J. Dolphin, which is a mahimahi fillet with spicy tomato sauce served with black beans and rice. The beer of the month is still $1.50 a bottle. | MM 99.4, BS | 305/451–3722 | Closed Sun. | $7–$20 | No credit cards.

Snooks Bayside. American. The terrace of this casual restaurant overlooks Florida Bay, making a change from ocean views. On the menu are such options as yellow-tail, conch steak—definitely an experience—and for traditionalists, filet mignon. | 99470 Overseas Hwy. | 305/453–3799 | $15–$26 | AE, D, DC, MC, V.

Lodging

Bay Harbor Lodge. A private, 2½-acre waterfront lodge, a hammock in the shade of a tiki hut, the Keys' watery wilderness waiting for exploration by complimentary boat, canoe, paddleboat, or kayak—life can only get worse. Cable TV. Pool. Beach, 2 docks. Free parking. | 97702 Overseas Hwy. | 305/852–5695, 800/385–0986 | fax 305/852–5695 | www.thefloridakeys.com/bayharborlodge | 7 rooms, 7 efficiencies, 7 cottages | $75–$105 room, $105–$145 efficiency, $125–$165 cottage | AE, D, MC, V.

Best Western Suites at Key Largo. All units here are bi-level suites with screened porches overlooking the marina and Intracoastal Waterway, making this among the more unusual accommodation choices in the Keys. You'll find restaurants, shops, and entertainment nearby, too. Picnic area, complimentary Continental breakfast. Kitchenettes, refrigerators. Cable TV. Laundry facilities. Pool. Business services. | 201 Ocean Dr. | 305/451–5081 or 800/462–6079 | fax 305/451–4173 | 40 suites | $100–$175 | AE, D, DC, MC, V.

Frank's Key Haven Resort. A residential neighborhood is home to this small, waterfront lodge, which does not advertise (and nonetheless is always busy). Towering gumbo-limbo trees surround the lodge, which was built in the 1930s to withstand hurricanes. Bird-watching, diving, fishing, kayaking, and eco-tours can all be arranged for guests, but you may be content to just read on the screened porch. The 14 units range from one-room efficiencies to two-bedroom apartments and family units. In the public area, there is a TV, half-kitchen, and seating. Kitchenettes. Cable TV. Pool. Boating. | MM 92, BS, 198 Harborview Dr., Tavernier | 305/852–3017 or 800/765–5397 | 14 units | $112 | MC, V.

Holiday Inn Resort and Marina. The *African Queen* that was one of the stars of the Humphrey Bogart–Katharine Hepburn movie is moored at the marina of this two-story hotel where the fun never seems to stop. Lively nightlife option here are joined by daytime diversions that include a deep-water marina where you can organize boating, fishing, snorkel, wave runners, and other water sports. Restaurant, bar, room service. In-room data ports, refrigerators. Cable TV. 2 pools. Outdoor hot tub. Gym. Fishing. Marina. Laundry service. Business services. | 99701 Overseas Hwy. | 305/451–2121 or 800/843–5397 | fax 305/451–5592 | www.holiday-inn.com | 132 rooms | $169–$189 | AE, D, DC, MC, V.

Howard Johnson Resort. Just a short distance from John Pennekamp Coral Reef State Park, this hotel is right on the ocean, has a private beach and fishing and snorkeling equipment. Restaurant, bar. In-room data ports, some microwaves, refrigerators. Cable TV. Pool. Beach, dock, fishing. Laundry facilities. Business services. Some pets allowed. | MM 102 on U.S. 1 | 305/451–1400 or 800/406–1411 | fax 305/451–3953 | www.hojo.com | 100 rooms | $189–$249 | AE, D, DC, MC, V.

Jules' Undersea Lodge. The only way to get into this lodge is by diving there—a former underwater research lab, the hotel is 30 ft below the surface. Guests must either be certified divers or take a 3-hour introductory course ($75) before check-in. Rates include diving gear, breakfast, dinner, snacks, and beverages. Rooms have a shower, galley, phone, VCR, and stereo, but there is no TV reception, and the lodge can sleep up to 6 people in two bedrooms. Once back on land, you can't fly or deep-dive for 24 hours because of the length of your underwater stay. Kitchettes, refrigerators. In-room VCRs. | MM 103.2, OS, 51 Shoreland Dr. | 305/451–2353 | fax 305/451–4789 | www.jul.com | 1 lodge | $225–$325 | MAP | AE, D, MC, V.

Kona Kai Resort. Beachfront hammocks, a heated pool, tropical furnishings, and lush landscaping contribute to the feeling of escape you get at this resort, which does not have room phones and provides maid service only every third morning. You can paddleboat or kayak, or just relax and perhaps visit the newly expanded art gallery with works by major South Florida and visiting artists. Cottages have CD players with music by local artists and toiletries made from fruits and flowers. Kitchenettes. Cable TV. Pool. Tennis court. Basketball, volleyball. Beach, boating. No kids under 16. No smoking. | MM 97.8, BS, 97802 Overseas Hwy. | 305/852–7200 or 800/365–7809 | fax 305/852–4629 | www.konakairesort.com | 11 units | $196 rooms, $257 suites | AE, D, MC, V.

Largo Lodge. A tropical garden of palms, sea grapes, and orchids hides this 1950s-style, adults-only lodge with 200 ft of Bay frontage. In the late afternoon, wild birds, including pelicans and herons, come to owner Harriet "Hat" Stokes for a snack. Cottages have kitchenettes, rattan furnishings, and screened porches. Kitchenettes, refrigerators. Cable TV, no room phones. Beach, dock. No kids under 16. | MM 101.5, BS, 101740 Overseas Hwy. | 305/451–0424 or 800/468–4378 | www.largolodge.com | 7 units | $115 | MC, V.

Marina Del Mar Bayside Resort. Spacious rooms with balconies overlooking the marina on Florida Bay or the resort's swimming pool are a pleasant day's-end spot to contemplate the beauty of these islands in the stream. Here, and at the Marina's sister property nearby, you can arrange fishing, snorkeling, and diving trips. Restaurant, bar, complimentary Continental breakfast. Some kitchenettes, some microwaves, refrigerators, some in-room hot tubs. Cable TV. Pool. Outdoor hot tub. 2 tennis courts. Dock, boating. Laundry facilities. Business services. | 527 Caribbean Dr. | 305/451–4107 or 800/451–3483 | fax 305/451–1891 | marinadelmar.com | 72 rooms, 4 villas | $99–$189, $199–$299 villas | AE, D, DC, MC, V.

Key Largo Bay Marriott Beach Resort. This resort is pleased with its tropical location and plays up that Keys ambience with rooms decorated in shades of pink, blue, and yellow. Occupying 17 waterfront acres overlooking Florida Bay, the resort also offers a dive shop ready to set you up for snorkeling or jet skiing. Restaurant, bar, room service. In-room data ports, in-room safes, some kitchenettes, minibars, some refrigerators. Cable TV, in-room VCRs available. Pool. Outdoor hot tub. 2 tennis courts. Gym. Beach. Children's programs (5–12). Laundry service. Business services. | 103800 Overseas Hwy. | 305/453–0000 or 888/236–2427 | fax 305/453–0093 | www.marriott.com | 153 rooms, 24 suites | $255–$285; $635 suites | AE, D, DC, MC, V.

Popp's Motel. The swings and sandy beach outside this 50-year-old motel attract families, who stay in units with efficiency kitchens, dark-wood panelling, and terrazzo floors. A high wall with stylized metal white herons marks the entrance of this family-run motel. Kitchenettes, refrigerators. Cable TV. Beach, dock. | MM 95.5, BS, 95500 Overseas Hwy. | 305/852–5201 | fax 305/852–5200 | 9 units | $120 | AE, MC, V.

Ramada Limited Key Largo Resort and Marina. Built in 1992, this three-story resort has its own marina to provide you with fishing, boating, and water sports opportunities. To get you started, a complimentary ticket to a Sun Cruz Casino Boat cruise awaits you at check-in. A shopping enclave with more than 60 discount designer shops and the Keys Gate Championship Golf course are only minutes away. Complimentary Continental breakfast, room service. Refrigerators. Cable TV. Pool. Dock, water sports. Laundry service. Business services. | 99751 Overseas Hwy. | 305/451–3939 or 888/298–2054 | fax 305/453–0222 | www.ramada.com | 83 rooms, 5 suites | $149–$189, $199–$229 suites | AE, D, DC, MC, V.

Sunset Cove Resort Motel. Oversized animal statues, Seminole Indian *chickee* huts and big rattan swing chairs add more than a touch of the tropics to this resort. Entertainment options are diverse: fish off the dock, rent a pontoon boat, fire up one of the facility's barbecue pits, or relax in a swing overlooking the water. A variety of accommodations include "diver dens," a series of three adjoining rooms for groups who can open up all the doors to make one big enclave. Pennekamp Coral Reef State park and area shops, just a short distance away, offer still more diversions. Complimentary Continental breakfast. Cable TV. Free parking. | MM 99.5 | 305/451–0705 | fax 305/451–5609 | digitalpark.com/suncove | 17 units | $80–$135 | AE, D, DC, MC, V.

Tavernier Hotel Built in 1935, this B&B inn is 8 mi south of Key Largo and 6 mi north of Islamorada. Inside, many of the furnishings reflect the motel's early days: lacy curtains and overflowing flower baskets adorn every room. A Copper Kettle restaurant here has an English-cottage motif but a contemporary menu. Complimentary Continental breakfast. Cable TV. Business services, free parking. | 91865 Overseas Hwy., Tavernier | 305/852–4131, 800/515–4131 | fax 305/852–4037 | tavhotel@aol.com | 17 | $50–70 | AE, D, DC, MC, V.

Westin Beach Resort, Key Largo. Nestled in a natural hardwood hammock right on Key Largo Bay, this four-story resort has rooms with private balconies and views over the water. So close is that water, in fact, that you can hear the waves lapping on shore, providing a lulling melody at night. Restaurant, bar, room service. In-room data ports, minibars, some microwaves, some in-room hot tubs. Cable TV. 2 pools. Outdoor hot tub. 2 tennis courts. Beach, dock, water sports, boating. Video games. Baby-sitting. Laundry service. Business services. | MM 97, 97000 Overseas Hwy. | 305/852–5553 | fax 305/852–8669 | www.westin.com | 190 rooms, 10 suites | $289–$369, $469 suites | AE, D, DC, MC, V.

KEY WEST

MAP 3, C7

(Nearby towns also listed: Big Pine Key, Little Torch Key, Sugarloaf Key, Summerland Key)

At the very tip of the Keys, Key West is the southernmost city in the continental United States. Originally called *Cayo Hueso,* Island of Bones, it is thought that the island was once a burial ground for the Caloosa Indians. The famous, including writers Ernest Hemingway, Tennessee Williams, Truman Capote, and Robert Frost, as well as presidents Eisenhower and Kennedy, found the same beauty and allure here that its hordes of residents and visitors find today.

It wasn't always so. From the time the U.S. acquired Florida from Spain in 1821, the big business in Key West was wrecking—rescuing people and salvaging cargo from ships that foundered on nearby reefs—until the government began building lighthouses in 1849, at least. Fishing, shrimping, sponge-gathering, and pineapple canning where important in the latter half of the 19th century, along with the military, which constructed Fort Taylor in 1845. But by 1929 the local government had begun to unravel, and when the Depression hit, the military moved out, leaving Key West hard hit. That's when it started promoting itself as a tourist destination, but a 1935 hurricane that wiped out the railroad also wiped out the tourist trade.

The resurgence of Key West started in the 1960s, when hippies flocked to the island for its lazy lifestyle and laissez-faire attitudes. Many of the restored Victorian "gingerbread" houses that now serve as accommodations for tourists were originally turned into gay guest houses during the mid-1970s, and about a fifth of locals are gay. But Key West has quite a diverse population, with large percentages of black Bahamians, Hispanics (primarily Cubans), recent refugees from the urban sprawl of mainland Florida, and long-time Key Westers, who can trace their ancestry back several decades. Overall, the island is very tolerant, and even somewhat flamboyant.

All kinds of people can be found down at Mallory Square for the evening revelry kicked off by the sunset over the Gulf. Musicians, jugglers, lovers, and vendors gather for the illustrious sunset and spend the next several hours strolling, shopping, dining, and carousing. Good restaurants are numerous, particularly along Duval Street, which is sadly losing a bit of charm with flashy new stores and T-shirt shops. Key West clubs are legendary, and the action goes on until sun-up.

Information: **Greater Key West Chamber of Commerce** | 402 Wall St., Key West, 33040 | 305/294–2587 | www.fla-keys.com.

Attractions

Audubon House and Tropical Gardens. In 1832 world-renowned ornithologist John Audubon visited the Florida Keys and the Dry Tortugas, to the west of Key West. When he left months later, he had sighted and drawn 18 new birds for his *Birds of America* folio. It is believed that many of those drawings were conceived in the gardens of this 1852 home, which was built by harbor pilot Captain John Geiger. | 205 Whitehead St. | 305/294–2116 | fax 305/294–4513 | www.audubonhouse.com | $8.50 | Daily 9:30–5.

C.B. Harvey Beach Park. This very well-equipped park and beach offer six picnic areas, dunes, and a bike path for use by wheelchairs as well. The site was named after former Key West mayor and commissioner Cornelius Bradford Harvey. | East side of White Street Pier | Free | Daily 7 AM–11 PM.

City Cemetery. In this 20-acre graveyard, a bronze statue resembling a ship's mast marks the graves of more than two dozen sailors who lost their lives on the battleship USS *Maine,* which sank in Havana Harbor in 1898. Elsewhere, there are a number of interesting (and frequently comical) headstones. Volunteers of the Historic Florida Keys Foundation conduct 90-min walking tours from the sexton's office (reservations requested). | Margaret and Angela Sts. | 305/292–6718 | Free, tour $10 (suggested) | Daily, tours Tues. and Thurs. 9:30.

Curry Mansion. William Curry, a penniless Bahamian immigrant who reputedly made his fortune as a salvager, preying on shipwrecked travelers in Florida's pirate-infested waters, was Key West's first millionaire. He began building this 25-room, wood Victorian mansion in 1855. It incorporates many styles and trends, ranging from the columns and colonnades of the Deep South to the ornate trellises of New Orleans. | 511 Caroline St. | 305/294–5349 or 800/253–3466 | fax 305/294–4093 | www.currymansion.com | $5 | Daily 10–5.

Dog Beach. This is the only beach where dogs are allowed in Key West. It is small and has a landscape of rocks and sand. It's next to Louie's Backyard (a restaurant). | N. Vernon and Waddell Sts. | Free | Daily sunrise–sunset.

PAPA'S PLACE—KEY WEST

Ernest Hemingway and second wife, Pauline Pfeiffer, came to Key West in 1928 from Paris via Havana at the urging of writer John dos Passos.

In 1931 Pauline's wealthy uncle Gus gave the couple the house at 907 Whitehead Street, now known as the Hemingway House and Museum. The Spanish Colonial–style home was constructed of native rock hewn from the grounds and boasted the first pool built in Key West—at a cost of $20,000. This price prompted Hemingway to take a penny from his pocket and press it into the wet cement of the surrounding patio and announce jokingly, "Here, take the last penny I've got!" That penny is still there. In 1935, when the visitor bureau included the house in a tourist brochure, an irate Hemingway built the high brick wall that surrounds it today.

The Key West home offered a calming atmosphere for this complex, restless man, and during his time in Key West, Hemingway penned some of his most important works, including *Death in the Afternoon, To Have and Have Not,* "The Snows of Kilimanjaro," *A Farewell to Arms,* and "Green Hills of Africa."

He kept a meticulous writing schedule, working almost every morning when the temperature was cool, in his adjacent second-story studio above the pool; descending the stairs at midday, he was ready for drinking and fishing with his cohorts.

The author's presence can still be felt in his studio; his quiet typewriter sits on the writing table. Many of the unique, original furnishings he collected during his visits to Europe stand throughout the home. Other personal touches, including his trophy mounts and skins from several African safaris and numerous hunting expeditions out west.

© Corbis

Dry Tortugas National Park. Ferries and seaplanes depart from Key West to make the 70-mi trip west to the Dry Tortugas archipelago, a national park consisting of coral reefs and seven small islands. Garden Key is home to the long-deactivated Fort Jefferson, the largest brick-and-masonry structure in the Western hemisphere. The pre–Civil War fort is most famous for the 1865 incarceration of Dr. Samuel Mudd, who set the broken leg of John Wilkes Booth after he assassinated President Lincoln. You can tour the fort, snorkel and dive, and picnic on the beach. Discovered in 1513 by Ponce de León, the islands were named for the turtles once found here, and because they have no potable water. More than 250 craft—from Spanish galleons to clipper ships—have been wrecked on the reefs here, a boon for divers today. Exploring the waters requires some skill, as there are powerful currents, fire coral, barracuda, and scorpion fish. Access is only via seaplane or boat, and there are no places to get food or water in the park. | Garden Key | 305/242–7700 | www.nps.gov/drto | Free | Daily.

Seaplanes of Key West. If you don't want to go the sea route, you can also fly to Dry Tortugas in a seaplane. On the four-hour trip, you fly on a low-altitude heading to Dry Tortugas National Park, where you'll have time to explore Fort Jefferson on your own and still have time for bird watching, snorkeling, or spotting sea turtles. Your price includes snorkeling equipment and a cooler of drinks. | Key West Airport, 3471 S. Roosevelt Blvd. | 305/294–0709 | fax 305/296–5691 | www.seaplanesofkeywest.com | $159 for 4-hr trip, $275 for 8-hr trip | Daily 8 AM–9 PM, call for exact schedule.

Sunny Days Catamarans. After a two-hour trip to Garden Key at Dry Tortugas National Park, you are treated to a tour of Fort Jefferson and then are free for some snorkeling. The trip includes a Continental breakfast, lunch, soft drinks during the day, and snorkeling gear. Advance reservations are recommended. | Greene and Elizabeth Sts. | 305/292–6100 or 800/236–7937 | www.sunnydayskeywest.com | $85 | Daily 8 AM.

Yankee Fleet. This company operates the *Yankee Freedom II*, a catamaran ferry, that takes you to Dry Tortugas National Park in about 2 hours, including breakfast, lunch, snorkel gear, and a 40-min tour of Fort Jefferson. | 240 Margaret St. | 305/294–7009 or 800/926–5332 | $95 | Daily at 8 AM.

East Martello Gallery and Museum. This brick and mortar Civil War fort at the southern end of Key West, built in 1862, now functions as an open-air museum where you can see photographs, sculptures, and artifacts depicting Key West as it was from the mid-19th century to the early 20th century. There are also changing art exhibitions. | 3501 S. Roosevelt Blvd. (Rte. A1A) | 305/296–3913 | fax 305/296–6202 | www.kwahs.com/martello | $6 | Daily 9:30–5.

Ernest Hemingway Home and Museum. Hemingway was the first important writer to discover Key West and make it his home. The Nobel Prize–winning author penned about 70 percent of his work here. His two-story, Spanish-colonial home was made of native rock hewn from the grounds and was built in 1851. It is now a National Historic Landmark; three months after Hemingway died in 1961 it became a museum. The pool, the hand-blown Venetian glass chandelier in the dining room, and the huge bed with a unique headboard are noteworthy, as is a ceramic cat made by Pablo Picasso and presented to the author by the artist as a gift. | 907 Whitehead St. | 305/294–1575 | www.hemingwayhome.com | $8 | Daily 9–5.

Fort Zachary Taylor State Historic Site. From this fort, built between 1845 and 1866, Union forces mounted their blockade of Confederate shipping during the Civil War; more than 1,500 Confederate vessels were detained in the harbor. Today you can take a 30-min tour and snorkel around an artificial reef. The beach is uncrowded, and there is a shady picnic area with grills. | Southard St. on Truman Annex | 305/292–6713 | www.dep.state.fl.us/parks/district_5/fortzacharytaylor | $2.50 per person for first two people in vehicle plus $0.50 each additional up to $8, $1.50 per pedestrian or bicyclist | Daily, tours noon and 2.

Harry S. Truman Little White House. President Harry S. Truman, a former Key West winter vacationer, stayed in this large, two-story wood frame house from 1946–1953. | 111 Front St. | 305/294–9911 | www.trumanlittlewhitehouse.com | $8 | Daily 9–5.

Higgs Beach. This picturesque park and 2,000-ft beach provides ample sunbathing sand as well as a grove of Australian pines for some shade. The ruins of the West Martello Tower, a Civil War–era fort now home to the Key West Garden Club, make an interesting addition to the landscape. Also nearby leading to the White St. Pier is a series of black granite monuments embedded in the walkway leading to the pier. Each one lists names of Key West residents who have fallen victim to the AIDS virus, totalling over 1,000. | Atlantic Blvd. between White and Reynolds Sts. | Free | Daily 7 AM–11 PM.

Historic Seaport at Key West Bight. This 8½-acre historic restoration project has grown into a huge complex of over 100 stores, restaurants, bars, a wedding chapel, and a marina. Highlights are bait and dive shops, the turtle museum, and the 2-mi waterfront walkway that takes you by sailboats, schooners, and ships, not to mention a variety of charter cruise companies. Most of the bars are dog-friendly and full of fresh seafood appetizers. | 201 Williams St. | 305/294–1100 | www.keywestseaport.com | Daily.

Key West Aquarium. Exhibits offer close-up views of area marine life. You can get a peek inside a conch shell, pet sharks, and feed turtles. | 1 Whitehead St. | 305/296–2051 | www.historictours.com | $8 | Daily 10–6; tours at 11, 1, 3, and 4:30.

Key West Museum of Art and History. The Key West Art and Historical Society runs the Museum with a strong emphasis on local artists, and the art and history of Key West, as well as tying their shows in with the local festivals. The building was begun in 1820 and served as a U.S. Custom House. By 1891 it was completed based on plans in the Richardsonian Romanesque style of architecture. The general plan provided various fireplaces throughout the building, obviously designed for a more northern structure. The 7 galleries of the museum have temporary exhibits changing almost every three months. The museum's exhibit on the USS *Maine* has stuck around the longest, showing the history of the ship that went down in the Havana Harbor and set off the Spanish–American War. Tours are available if requested ahead of time. | 281 Front St. | 305/295–6616 | fax 305/295–6649 | www.KWAHS.org | $6 | Daily 9–6.

Lighthouse Museum. This 90-ft-tall lighthouse was built in 1848. The views of Key West and the Atlantic Ocean from the top, which is accessible via a winding staircase, are well worth the trek. The keeper's quarters have been restored to resemble how it looked at the turn of the 20th century. | 938 Whitehead St. | 305/294–0012 | fax 305/296–6206 | www.kwahs.com/lighthouse | $8 | Daily 9:30–4:30.

Mel Fisher Maritime Heritage Society Museum. This nonprofit organization run by Mel Fisher has been excavating and diving for lost treasures since the 1960s. Their finds consist of numerous South American riches from two Spanish galleons that sank during a hurricane in 1622. The *Nuestra Señora de Atocha* and *Santa Margarita* were wrecked about 40 mi west of the Keys. Among the artifacts is a gold bar weighing 6.3 troy pounds and a 77.76-carat natural emerald crystal worth almost $250,000. There is a semi-permanent exhibit on a slave ship, the *Henrietta Marie*, which was wrecked in 1700 en route from Jamaica to England. Shackles, ivory from Africa, and beads are on display. You can wander through the museum at your own speed and catch a video on diving and excavation. | 200 Greene St. | 305/294–2633 | fax 305/294–5671 | www.melfisher.org | $6.50 | Daily 9:30–5:30, last video 4:30.

Nancy Forrester's Secret Garden. You can visit the last undeveloped land in Old Town Key West and enjoy the gardens developed by Nancy Forrester. She maintains the 1-acre lot filled with rare palms, ferns, bromeliads, bright ginger flowers, orchids, vines, and hundreds more species of plants. You might witness a wedding on the property, but if you bring your own lunch, you can eat at the picnic tables provided. Step into the art gallery to view botanical prints and environmental art. A cottage is available for overnight stays, 2 night minimum ($135–$179). | 1 Free School La. | 305/294–0015 | www.hurricanecenter.com/secretgarden | $6 | Daily 10–5.

San Carlos Institute. Founded in 1871 by Cuban immigrants, the institute exists to promote information on the history of 19th and 20th century Cuban exiles. There is a research library and museum full of interesting tidbits, such as how Cuban patriot José Martí delivered speeches from the balcony and Enrico Caruso sang opera in the Opera House. | 516 Duval St. | 305/294–3887 | $3 | Tues.–Sun. 11–5.

Smathers Beach. The beach stretches for nearly 2 mi and is one of the more popular beaches for the young folks. There are large trucks that come every day to rent Windsurfers, rafts, boogie boards, and other fun toys. | S. Roosevelt Blvd. | Free | Open 7 AM–11 PM.

Sunset Celebration—Mallory Square. Jugglers, mimes, palm readers, jewelers, and a variety of performers and visual artists gather at this waterfront venue one block from Duval Street for the nightly festival and bazaar. Watching sunset over the Gulf of Mexico from the dock with a cocktail is a local tradition. | Mallory Sq. | 305/292–7700 | www.sunsetkey .com | Free | Daily, 2 hrs before and after sunset.

West Martello Tower. Formerly a Civil War–era fort, now the remains are the site for the colorful flowers of the Key West Garden Club. Native and tropical plants are well groomed for art shows, orchid and flower shows, weddings, and private garden tours (in March). | Atlantic Blvd. and White St. | 305/294–3210 | Donations welcome | Tues.–Sat. 9:30–3.

Wrecker's Museum. This white frame structure, also known as the Oldest House Museum, was built in 1829. There are exhibits of the Keys' early maritime history. | 322 Duval St. | 305/ 294–9502 | $5 | Daily 10–4.

SIGHTSEEING TOURS/TOUR COMPANIES

Captain's Corner Charters. Captain's Corner, at the end of Green Street, operates snorkeling and dive trips, as well as dive classes in multiple languages (Czech, Japanese, Spanish). Diving trips range from 15 to 50 minutes (depending on how fast you're breathing!) as you hunt for treasure on a live reef in the Atlantic. Snorkeling tours can take up to 4 hours. | 125 Ann St. | 305/296–8865 | www.captainscorner.com | $25 for snorkeling including all equipment for 4 hrs, diving is $60 for two tanks, or $30 if you have your own equipment | Daily 9–6, dive and snorkeling charters leave at 9:30, 10, 1:30, 2.

Conch Tour Train. A 90-min ride on this train (it's really a bus) takes in 15 mi of Key West landmarks—including the Harry Truman Little White House and the Key West Aquarium. Catch it at Mallory Square depot, Roosevelt Boulevard depot, or Land's End Marina. Foreign charters are available. | 501 Front St. | 305/294–5161 | www.conchtourtrain.com | $14 | Daily 9–4:30.

GRM Enterprises. Guides on 2-hour narrated glass-bottom-boat cruises point out different kinds of fish, sponges, and sea fans in their delicate reef environments. There's a historical harbor tour and sunset and night trips. | 2 Duval St. | 305/296–6293 | www.seathereef.com | $20–$25 | Daily noon and 2; sunset tour after 4.

Island Aeroplane Tour. Go for a quick tour of the beaches and Old Town, or for a longer trip offshore over coral reefs to Little Palm Island. Tours are given in a two-seater 1941 Waco, a biplane with an open cockpit, and times range from 8 minutes to 1 hour and 15 minutes. | Key West Airport, 3469 Roosevelt Blvd. | 305/294–8687 | fax 305/294–3577 | www.islandaeroplanetours.com | $58–$367, for two people, prices range per tour | Daily.

Island City Strolls. Run by former state historian in Key West and the current owner of a historic-preservation consulting firm, Sharon Wells, you can get a serious walking tour in any number of realms. She has also written several guides, including *The Walking and Biking Guide to Historic Key West*, which offers 10 self-guided tours around Key West. The walking tours range from Architectural Strolls and Literary Landmarks, to Historic 1847 Cemetery Stroll. Wells will meet you at your hotel for the walking tour. | 305/294–8380 | fax 305/294–4233 | www.seekeywest.com | $20–$25 | Daily by appointment, two-person minimum.

Key West Nature Bike Tour. One of the best ways to view Key West is even better when you can bicycle around at a modest pace and discover the back roads and native plants of Key West. It is also a great way to get some exercise and check out some of the lesser viewed bits of architecture in the hidden neighborhoods. | Truman Ave. and Simonton St. | 305/ 294–1882 | $15 with your own bike, $18 without.

Mosquito Coast Island Outfitters and Kayak Guides. Full day tours are offered in guided sea-kayaks in and around the mangrove islands just east of Key West, including through an area called the Great Heron Natural Wildlife Refuge. Your price includes transportation to the kayak site, bottled water and a snack, snorkeling gear, supplies, and about 5 hours on the water. | 1107 Duval St. | 305/294–7178 | fax 305/292–2220 | moscoast@aol.com | $45 | Open daily by appointment.

Old Town Trolley. Fully narrated 90-min tours tell the history and lore of Key West with 14 stops at attractions and shopping and dining spots. Customers can spend time at an attraction and then board the next trolley from the same location. | 1910 N. Roosevelt Blvd. | 305/296–6688 or 800/868–7482 | www.oldtowntrolleytours.com | $18 | Daily 8:55–4:30, tours depart every 30 minutes.

Personalized Tours of Key West and the Keys. This firm operates an 85-mi scenic bus tour that weaves along the numerous bridges and islands of the Florida Keys. You can also hire a personal guide to either walk or drive around with you and point out items of interest. Tours accommodate varying numbers of people. Reservations are necessary. | 81 Bay Dr., Bay Point Island | 305/292–8687 | Prices vary by the individual tour requested | By appointment only.

ON THE CALENDAR

JAN.–MAY: *Old Island Days.* A variety of events—including flower shows, tours of historic homes, live concerts, antique toy exhibitions, and art fairs—serve to commemorate the early history of the island. The conch shell bowling contest is a lot of fun. | 305/294–2587.

OCT.: *Fantasy Fest.* Key West stages a no-holds-barred Halloween costume party, parade, and town fair. The gay community has a large presence. Children enjoy the pet masquerade. | 305/296–1817.

Dining

Alice's at La Te Da. Contemporary. Named one of South Florida's top ten chefs by *South Florida Gourmet,* chef/owner Alice and her team have created a unique bi-level tropical poolside environment adjoining the small La Te Da guest house. Expect a hearty wine list and a stunning array of new world fusion specials featuring fresh seafood, beef, pork, and poultry dishes, but don't expect anything typical; their potstickers have a southwestern flare. A good house standard is Key West yellowtail served with brown butter and capers or the coconut and macadamia–crusted shrimp served with a variety of sauces. Key lime pie and passion fruit shortcake are good dessert options. | 1125 Duval St. | 305/296–6706 | fax 305/296–3981 | Closed Mon. | $13–$30 | AE, D, MC, V.

Bagatelle. Seafood. This elegant, second-story restaurant overlooks Duval Street. The view from the veranda draws many diners. The seafood chowder and tuna *tataki* (rare tuna loin) are recommended. | 115 Duval St. | 305/296–6609 | Reservations essential | $16–$25 | AE, D, MC, V.

Bahama Mama's. Bahamian. Owner Cory Sweeting, a fourth-generation Conch, uses his grandmother's recipes. Dine indoors or outdoors. Specialties include the fried coconut shrimp with rum sauce, curried ginger chicken, and Mama's chicken. All platters include a salad, hush puppies, and a choice of side dishes such as cheese grits and collard greens. | Corner of Whitehead and Petronia | 305/294–3355 | $11–$13 | MC, V.

Banana Café. French. This popular spot on the main drag of Key West keeps the crêpes flying from breakfast through lunch. A tropical flair adds a colorful element to the food and the setting which has tables inside and out. Soups and salads offer the best in fresh seafood, while such entrées as the rack of lamb filled with foie gras and a Madeira wine sauce are prepared in traditional European style. An assortment of cheeses is available along with sorbets and homemade desserts. Live jazz on Thursday nights. | 1211 Duval St. | 305/294–3294 | $18–$24 | AE, D, MC, V.

★ **Café des Artistes.** French. This candlelit restaurant has two dining rooms and a rooftop deck shaded by a sapodilla tree, and it's one of the finest restaurants in South Florida. It's famous for lobster tango mango and delicious veal dishes. Desserts include the chocolat fondant (a flourless chocolate cake). | 1007 Simonton St. | 305/294–7100 | Reservations essential | No lunch | $25–$45 | AE, MC, V.

Cafe Marquesa. Contemporary. This sophisticated restaurant has a beautiful and lifelike mural of a kitchen. The chef recommends the grilled marinated Key West shrimp martini and the seared hand-harvested scallops. | 600 Fleming St. | 305/292–1244 | Reservations essential | No lunch | $25–$32 | AE, DC, MC, V.

Café Sole. French. You will be able to follow your nose to this restaurant, hidden in a residential neighborhood, for some serious cuisine utilizing the best of fresh seafood and Key West produce. The lobster bouillabaisse is an exquisite array of seafood and delicate broth; the grilled ostrich served with béarnaise sauce is a new treat. The setting of the café is quaint and casual, but offers award-winning zabaglione (a warm vanilla custard) and mixed berries for dessert, an extensive wine list, and outdoor seating to enjoy your artistically presented food. | 1029 Southard St. | 305/294–0230 | fax 305/296–7491 | No lunch | $21–$25 | D, MC, V.

Caribe Soul. Caribbean. Celebrating enough popularity to enable a move to a larger space, this tropical wonderland now houses a quirky casual side, a patio, and a more upscale dining room designed in British Colonial Caribbean style. The food remains the main draw with colorful soul dishes such as their famous crab cakes, mango chicken, and conch fritters. For dessert try the guava cream cake or peach and cherry cobbler, and peruse their small shopping section of salsas, relishes, spices, and several cookbooks including one they wrote called *Using What You've Got*. | 1202 Simonton St. | 305/296–0094 | fax 305/296–2950 | $10–$20 | AE, D, DC, MC, V.

Duffy's Steak and Lobster House. Steak/Seafood. President Truman frequented the restaurant during his Key West days. Though the place has gone through some remodeling to be modern and family style, the traditional surf and turf dishes are still the main draw. The prime rib is available from 10 to 16 oz. Fresh Maine and Florida lobsters are flown in daily and prepared steamed with butter or stuffed with crab and baked. | 1007 Truman Ave. | 305/296–4900 | fax 305/293–6964 | $15–$25 | AE, MC, V.

El Sibony. Cuban. You can get a real feeling of being at your Cuban relative's house because the setting is loud and full of great food prepared in a traditional and homestyle manner. One of the house specialties is the roast pork; if you've never tried Cuban pork, you're missing out. There are different specials every day, featuring anything from grilled garlic chicken to breaded shrimp and vanilla-rice pudding for dessert. | 900 Catherine St. | 305/296–4184 | Closed 2 weeks in June | $6–$16 | No credit cards.

Flagler's Steak House. Steak. With high ceilings, ornate archways, and dark woodwork, this restaurant is reminiscent of the 1920s. Try the Jack Daniels peppercorn fillet or the New York strip. Kids' menu. | 1500 Reynolds St. | 305/296–3535 | Breakfast also available | $16–$39 | AE, D, DC, MC, V.

Iguana Cafe. American. This 24-hr haunt with street-side bar stools and outdoor patio tables is perfect for people-watching. Breakfast, lunch, and dinner are served around the clock. Favorites include the Mexican-style spicy tenderloin tips, fish and chips, and the infamous alligator chowder. | 425 Greene St. | 305/296–6420 | $17–$28 | D, DC, MC, V.

Kelly's Caribbean Bar, Grill & Brewery. Contemporary. Actor Kelly McGillis owns this popular eatery with a wide deck and a canopy of tropical trees. The menu includes such Caribbean and local specialties as jerk chicken and camarones Curaçao—shrimp marinated in coconut milk, lime juice, ginger, and teriyaki, and served grilled with a citrus peanut sauce. There's a library with works of local writers. | 301 Whitehead St. | 305/293–8484 | $8–$18 | AE, D, DC, MC, V.

Lotsa Pasta. Italian. This northern- and southern-style Italian eatery is in a 1906 Victorian home. The house specialties are the thin-crust mini pizzas. The menu includes traditional pasta dishes and seafood. | 609 Duval St. | 305/294–7874 | $13–$20 | AE, D, DC, MC, V.

Louie's Backyard. American. Doric columns adorn the entrance of this restaurant in a 1909 Key West home. There are two outdoor decks that overlook the Atlantic Ocean. The grilled sirloin and conch chowder are heavenly. | 700 Waddell Ave. | 305/294–1061 | www.louies-backyward.com | $27–$33 | AE, D, DC, MC, V.

Mangia Mangia. Italian. One of Key West's best restaurants serves dishes such as rigatoni with jumbo shrimp and *funghi ai pomodori* (a mushroom-tomato dish). You can dine indoors or in the garden. | 900 Southard St. | 305/294–2469 | Reservations not accepted | $10–$15 | AE, MC, V.

Margaritaville Café. American. If you're in the mood to waste away dining on cheeseburgers and margaritas, this is the place. Owned by Key West resident and recording star Jimmy Buffett (who stops in occasionally), you can get the real vibe for his songs and views on life while chowing down on Key West pink shrimp prepared any way you want or the fresh fish of the day. | 500 Duval St. | 305/292–1435 | fax 305/294–9147 | $7–$16 | AE, MC, V.

Nicola. Seafood. Dine on the terrace facing the waves of the Atlantic or in the formal dining room. The seafood is always fresh, and the menu includes seafood pasta and spicy grilled shrimp. Kids' menu. | 601 Front St. | 305/296–9900 | Breakfast also available | Reservations essential on weekends | $13–$25 | AE, D, DC, MC, V.

Pepe's. American. Scenes of Old Key West cover the walls of this rustic, century-old restaurant. The baked oysters are popular with locals. | 806 Caroline St. | 305/294–7192 | Reservations not accepted | Breakfast also available | $13–$22 | D, MC, V.

Pier House. American. This casual restaurant on the Gulf of Mexico serves up American cuisine with an Italian and Caribbean twist. Dishes include West Indies curried chicken, jumbo shrimp, and scallops. You can dine outdoors on the partially covered patio. Kids' menu. | 1 Duval St. | 305/296–4600 | No lunch | $23–$36 | AE, D, DC, MC, V.

Rick's Blue Heaven. Contemporary. The outdoor seating area is filled with jungle vines and a history of cockfights and boxing matches refereed by Hemingway. Now you are more likely to see his cat's offspring wandering through as you dine on a variety of cuisines centering around West Indian foods. Entrée specials are offered nightly, but you can always count on a tasty seared tuna or grilled steak dish. The bar is open all day and be sure to check out the art gallery upstairs. | 729 Thomas St. | 305/296–8666 | No reservations accepted | $10–$23 | D, MC, V.

The Sands. Seafood. The terrace of this eatery has a view of the Atlantic. Inside, the walls are painted with seascapes. The herb-crusted grouper and fettuccine with Key West pink shrimp are delicious. | 1435 Simonton St. | 305/296–5000 | Breakfast also available. No lunch. No supper Sun.–Mon. | $12–$18 | AE, D, DC, MC, V.

The Seaport Tavern. Cuban. This diner and neighborhood tavern serves large portions of authentic Cuban-American dishes. Appetizers include the Tavern Flying Saucers (baked ham or Cuban pork, mustard, and cheese, and toasted). Entrées include the grilled skirt steak marinated in garlic and sour orange and topped with onions. All platters are served with yellow rice, black beans, plantain or yucca, and a tamale. | 610 Greene St. | 305/296–3002 | $10–$13 | AE, D, DC, MC, V.

Sloppy Joe's. American. This establishment, which opened the day Prohibition was repealed, was the infamous saloon beloved by Ernest Hemingway. Today it also has an upstairs speakeasy, where you can order lunch and dinner. The menu includes hand-pulled barbecue pork sandwiches, Key West coconut shrimp, and Conch fritters. | 201 Duval St. | 305/294–5717 | $8–$13 | AE, D, MC, V.

KEY WEST

INTRO
ATTRACTIONS
DINING
LODGING

Square One. American. This casually elegant spot, complete with fine china, candlelit tables, and a pianist, overlooks Duval Street. Dishes include the sautéed sea scallops and the New Zealand rack of lamb. | 1075 Duval St. | 305/296–4300 | No lunch | $16–$30 | AE, D, DC, MC, V.

Two Friends. Contemporary. This 32-yr-old family-owned business has an open-air patio. The bar has a large selection of frozen tropical drinks. Entrées include the stuffed mahimahi baked with shrimp, crab, and jack cheese, and the lobster combo house specialty (a half lobster tail, grilled shrimp, broiled scallops, and stuffed crab). Lighter fare includes the blackened chicken Caesar salad and seafood combo sampler. Breakfast is served. | 512 Front St. | 305/296–3124 | $18–$27 | AE, D, DC, MC, V.

Lodging

Artist House. Renowned Key West painter Gene Otto lived in this colonial Queen Anne–style mansion in the early 1900s. The lush garden has an in-ground heated spa and a fish pond. Rooms have ornate wall coverings. Complimentary Continental breakfast. Refrigerators. Cable TV, some in-room VCRs. Spa. No kids under 12. No smoking. | 534 Eaton St. | 305/296–3977 or 800/582–7882 | fax 305/296–3210 | www.artisthousekeywest.com | 7 rooms | $129–$289 | AE, D, DC, MC, V.

Best Western Hibiscus Motel. This two-story inn motel is three blocks from the southernmost point in the continental United States. The landscaped grounds have more than 100 varieties of exotic plants. Beaches, shopping, and nightlife are within walking distance. Complimentary Continental breakfast. Some kitchenettes, refrigerators. Cable TV. Pool. Outdoor hot tub. Business services. | 1313 Simonton St. | 305/294–3763 or 800/972–5100 | fax 305/293–9243 | www.bestwestern.com | 61 rooms | $219–$239 | AE, D, DC, MC, V.

Best Western Key Ambassador Resort Inn. The large rooms at this inn have Caribbean-style light-color furniture and coordinated linens in tropical colors. The 7-acre oceanfront grounds are surrounded by native trees. Restaurants are within walking distance. Picnic area, complimentary Continental breakfast. Refrigerators. Cable TV. Pool. Gym. Laundry facilities. Airport shuttle. | 3755 S. Roosevelt Blvd. | 305/296–3500 or 800/432–4315 | fax 305/296–9961 | www.bestwestern.com | 100 rooms | $89–$219 | AE, D, DC, MC, V.

Blue Marlin Motel. This motel is one block from famous Duval Street and the Atlantic Ocean. Rooms have contemporary oak furniture and overlook the pool and courtyard. Complimentary Continental breakfast. Some kitchenettes, refrigerators. Cable TV. Pool. Laundry facilities. Business services. | 1320 Simonton St. | 305/294–2585 or 800/523–1698 (outside FL), 800/826–5303 (FL) | fax 305/296–1209 | 62 rooms | $199–$219 | AE, D, DC, MC, V.

Coconut Mallory Resort and Marina. This small all-suites resort is in the heart of Old Key West, minutes from the airport. All of the rooms have private balconies, many with ocean views. Kitchenettes, refrigerators. Cable TV. 2 Pools. Outdoor hot tub. Laundry facilities. | 1445 S. Roosevelt Blvd. | 305/292–0017 | fax 305/292–5698 | www.coconutsuites.com | 34 suites | $250–$400 | AE, MC, V.

Center Court Historic Inn & Cottages. Only a block away from the touristy Duval street is this sprawling array of intimate lodgings. Each unit is uniquely designed with ceiling fans and some even have their own pools or Jacuzzis. The landscaped gardens complement the main Inn that was given an award by the Key West Historical Preservation Society. There are hammocks and a complimentary happy hour for proper relaxation, not to mention the love-seat within one of the pools for cuddling and sipping your drink surrounded by the tropical foliage. The attentive concierge can arrange anything from baby-sitting to bicycle deliveries—anything that will make your stay more pleasant. Complimentary breakfast. Some in-room data ports, in-room safes, some kitchenettes, some refrigerators. Cable TV. 2 pools. Outdoor hot tubs. Health club. Beach, bicycles. Laundry facilities. Pets allowed (fee). | 915 Center St. | 305/296–9292 or 800/797–8787 | fax 305/294–4104 | www.centercourtkw.com | 5 rooms, 17 cottages, 1 house | $138–$188 room, $188–$348 cottage, $358 house | AE, D, MC, V.

Cuban Club Suites (and La Casa de Luces). These two lodgings make up a private complex of rooms and town house–style suites overlooking Duval Street. The full concierge is able to set you up with tours, sports, you name it. With the beach only 3 blocks away and the 20-ft vaulted ceilings with skylights, you're sure to have a sunny disposition. The original building, built in 1860 as a social club for Cuban cigar makers, was later used as a gentlemen's club. After a fire in 1983 the building was rebuilt with modern luxuries including tiled counters, French doors, and balconies wrapping around the building in New Orleans style. Some units come with washer and dryer. Some in-room safes. Cable TV. Hot tub. Free parking. Pets allowed. | 1108 Duval St. (lobby at 422 Amelia St.) | 305/296–0465 or 800/432–4849 | fax 305/293–7669 | www.keywestcubanclub.com | 8 suites | $79–$349 | AE, MC, V.

Curry Mansion Inn. Nestled alongside the original 1899 Curry Mansion, this B&B has elegant rooms appointed with wicker furniture and handmade quilts. The pool is surrounded by lush foliage. Complimentary breakfast. Refrigerators. Cable TV. Pool. Beach. Library. Laundry facilities. Business services. Some pets. No smoking. | 511 Caroline St. | 305/294–5349 or 800/253–3466 | fax 305/294–4093 | www.currymansion.com | 28 rooms | $180–$325 | AE, D, DC, MC, V.

Duval House. Rooms of this early 1900s Victorian inn face the lush garden and have wicker furniture and European and early American antiques. Complimentary Continental breakfast. Some kitchenettes. Cable TV. Pool. No kids. | 815 Duval St. | 305/294–1666 or 800/223–8825 | fax 305/292–1701 | www.duvalhousekeywest.com | 33 rooms in 7 buildings | $160–$325 | AE, D, DC, MC, V.

Eaton Lodge. The inn's three buildings were built in the late 1800s. There are a courtyard garden, a fish pond, and resident parrots. Nightclubs are within walking distance. Complimentary Continental breakfast. Some kitchenettes, some refrigerators. Cable TV. Pool. Outdoor hot tub. No smoking. | 511 Eaton St. | 305/292–2170 or 800/294–2170 | fax 305/292–4018 | www.eatonlodge.com | 12 rooms, 3-bedroom house | $145–$195, $450 house | AE, D, DC, MC, V.

Eden House. A Hemingway retreat—and a location for Goldie Hawn's *Criss Cross* movie—this '20s-era Deco property is the oldest hotel in Key West. It has waterfalls, a hammock area, porch swings, and an elevated sundeck. Happy hour drinks are complimentary. Restaurant, bar. Pool. Bicycles. No smoking. | 1015 Fleming St. | 305/296–6868 | www.edenhouse.com | 42 rooms | $105–$195 | AE, MC, V.

Frances Street Bottle Inn. This B&B in an 1875 Conch house is named for the collection of rare antique bottles and marine articles scattered throughout the rooms. The porches of some rooms and the brick patio are shaded by poinciana trees—perfect places for spending a relaxing evening. Picnic area, complimentary Continental breakfast. Some refrigerators. Cable TV, no room phones. Outdoor hot tub. Bicycles. Business services. Pets allowed. No smoking. | 535 Frances St. | 305/294–8530 or 800/294–8530 | fax 305/294–1628 | www.bottleinn.com | 7 rooms | $135–$165 | AE, MC, V.

Galleon Resort and Marina. Most of the rooms of this five-story resort have two bedrooms, suites have three; many overlook the sunset-side of the Gulf of Mexico. There's an observation deck. Bar, picnic area. Kitchenettes, microwaves, refrigerators. Cable TV, in-room VCRs (and movies). Pool. Gym. Beach, water sports, fishing, bicycles. Laundry facilities. Business services. | 617 Front St. | 305/296–7711 or 800/544–3030 | fax 305/296–0821 | www.galleonresort.com | 88 rooms, 8 suites | $160–$410, $415–$515 suites | AE, D, DC, MC, V.

Hampton Inn. This hotel, now part of the Hilton family, is on the Gulf of Mexico. The pool and tiki bar have a sunset view. Rooms have two double beds or a king-size bed. Bar, complimentary Continental breakfast. In-room data ports, some refrigerators. Cable TV. Pool. Outdoor hot tub. Laundry facilities. Business services. | 2801 N. Roosevelt Blvd. | 305/294–2917 | fax 305/292–5222 | www.hamptoninn.com | 159 rooms in 2 buildings | $159–$229, $269 suite | AE, D, DC, MC, V.

Harborside Motel and Marina. Not your traditional motel, these units are clean and fresh with ceramic-tile floors and little patios. A 15-min walk to the beach and just off of Garrison Bight, the charter boat harbor. Several of the units are old houseboats that sleep four people each. Kitchenettes. Pool. Dock. Laundry facilities. | 903 Eisenhower Dr. | 305/294–2780 | fax 305/292–1473 | harbside@bellsouth.net | www.keywestharborside.com | 14 efficiencies | $79–$189 | AE, D, DC, MC, V.

Heron House. The houses that make up this tropically landscaped B&B in the center of Old Town were built in 1856. The owners have an orchid nursery. Wine and cheese are served in the evening. Complimentary Continental breakfast. Some minibars, some refrigerators, some in-room hot tubs. Cable TV. Pool. No kids under 17. | 512 Simonton St. | 305/294–9227 or 800/294–1644 | fax 305/294–5692 | www.heronhouse.com | 23 rooms in 4 buildings | $179–$349 | AE, DC, MC, V.

Hilton Key West Resort and Marina. The two traditional Key West Victorian buildings at this resort adjacent to Sunset Pier have comfortable rooms, many with balconies and Gulf views. The resort is a short walk from Old Town. Restaurant, bar. In-room data ports, in-roof safes, minibars, some refrigerators, some in-room hot tubs. Cable TV. Pool. Outdoor hot tub. Gym. Beach. Shops. Laundry facilities. Business services. | 245 Front St. | 305/294–4000 | fax 305/294–4086 | www.hilton.com | 147 rooms, 31 suites | $275–$550, $345–$995 suites | AE, D, DC, MC, V.

Holiday Inn, Beachside. Sunset Pier is nearby at this motel on the Gulf of Mexico. Suites have balconies that face the water. There's a lighted tennis court. Restaurant, bar, room service. In-room data ports, some refrigerators. Cable TV. Pool. Outdoor hot tub. 2 tennis courts. Beach, water sports. Laundry facilities. Business services. | 3841 N. Roosevelt Blvd. | 305/294–2571 or 800/292–7706 | fax 305/296–5659 | www.holiday-inn.com | 194 rooms, 28 suites | $160–$195, $215–$230 suites | AE, D, DC, MC, V.

Holiday Inn, La Concha. This seven-story hotel in the heart of Old Town dates back to the 1930s and is Key West's tallest building. The observation deck provides a panoramic view of the island. 3 restaurants, bar, room service. In-room data ports. Cable TV. Pool. Laundry service. Business services. Pets allowed. | 430 Duval St. | 305/296–2991 | fax 305/294–3283 | www.holiday-inn.com | 146 rooms, 14 suites | $179–$450, $525 suites | AE, D, DC, MC, V.

Hostelling International Key West. A fun alternative to paying high prices in this tourist destination is to share some of your privacy (kitchen and phone in common area) with other travelers. This hostel is well established and has all sorts of connections through the community to get you in your first kayak or snorkeling in the reefs nearby. The rooms are simple, but the setting is tropical and friendly with a super staff and common areas complete with a pool table and Internet access. They are only 2 blocks from the beach, and close to several others as well as the Fort Zachary State Park. The private motel rooms will sleep from 3–5 people. Some refrigerators. No room phones, TV in common area. Bicycles. Library. | 718 South St. | 305/296–5719 | fax 305/296–0672 | www.keywesthostel.com | 92 dorm beds, 14 motel rooms | $17–$20 dorm bed, $75 private room | MC, V.

Hyatt Key West Resort & Marina. This four-story resort is on the Gulf of Mexico within walking distance of Old Town restaurants and attractions. Rooms are beige and have plants. Parasailing, snorkeling, and windsurfing operators are on site. Restaurant, bar, complimentary Continental breakfast, room service. In-room data ports, in-room safes, refrigerators. Cable TV, in-room VCRs. Pool. Hot tub. Beach, boating, fishing, bicycles. Baby-sitting. Laundry facilities, laundry service. Business services, free parking. | 601 Front St. | 305/296–9900 | fax 305/292–1038 | www.hyatt.com | 120 rooms, 10 suites in 3 buildings | $309–$415, $600–$620 suites | AE, D, DC, MC, V.

Island City House Hotel. This hotel has three structures: a former gingerbread-trimmed carriage house that dates from the 1880s, a 1970s cypress-wood reconstruction of a cigar factory, and an 1880s three-story Victorian mansion known as the Island City House. The Cigar House is decorated in plantation style, with rattan furnishings and Bahama ceiling fans. The garden that fills the property has cactus, Spanish lime trees, and other tropical plants. Complimentary Continental breakfast. Kitchenettes, refrigerators. Cable TV, some in-room VCRs (and movies). Pool. Outdoor hot tub. Bicycles. | 411 William St. | 305/294–5702 or 800/634–8230 | fax 305/294–1289 | www.islandcityhouse.com | 24 suites | $175–$315 | AE, D, DC, MC, V.

Key Lime Inn. Not just another classy house on the National Register of Historic Places, this British/Bahamian style inn offers good service to all its adjacent cottages and cabanas. The rooms have a tropical breeze blowing through the bright, natural wood rooms. Some Continental breakfast delivered to rooms. Some in-room data ports, in-room safes, some refrigerators. Some in-room VCRs. Pool. Free parking. | 725 Truman | 305/294–5229 or 800/549–4430 | fax 305/294–9623 | 37 rooms | $98–$235 (during festivals) | AE, D, MC, V.

Key Lodge. This single-story lodge in Old Town is near Hemingway House. Rooms are basic motel. The Atlantic Ocean is within walking distance. Complimentary Continental breakfast. Some kitchenettes, refrigerators. Cable TV. Pool. Pets allowed (fee). | 1004 Duval St. | 305/296–9915 or 800/458–1296 | fax 305/292–5222 | www.keylodge.com | 22 rooms | $165–$180 | AE, D, MC, V.

Key West B&B. Constructed by Bahamian shipbuilders in 1898, this three-story Victorian house is full of Key West flavor. Rooms have high ceilings and are done in Caribbean style. Complimentary Continental breakfast. No room phones, no TV. Outdoor hot tub, sauna. No kids. No smoking. | 415 William St. | 305/296–7274 or 800/438–6155 | fax 305/293–0306 | www.keywestbandb.com | 8 rooms (4 with shared bath) | $110–$225 | AE, D, DC, MC, V.

Key West Harbor Inn. This three-story mansion, built in 1850, is near the boardwalk of the Historic Key West Seaport and two blocks from Duval Street. The grounds are surrounded by a tropical garden and include a boat house and carriage house. Rooms have four-poster beds, bamboo ceilings, French doors, and private verandas. Cable TV. Pool. Free parking. | 219 Elizabeth St. | 305/296–2978 or 800/608–6569 | fax 305/294–5858 | www.key-westharborinn.com | 14 rooms | $140–$300 | AE, D, MC, V.

La Mer Hotel and Dewey House. These two oceanfront B&Bs are joined by a lush tropical garden that is filled with palms and a fountain. Both houses are restored Queen Anne Victorians, and most rooms have ocean or garden views. Complimentary Continental breakfast. Some kitchenettes, minibars, some in-room hot tubs. Cable TV. Pool. Laundry facilities. Business services. No kids under 18. | 506 South St. | 305/296–5611 or 800/354–4455 | fax 305/294–8272 | www.oldtownresorts.com/lamerdewey.htm | 19 rooms | $220–$330 | AE, MC, V.

Marquesa Hotel. This elegant and austere hotel consists of four Greek Revival homes dating from the 1880s. The Marquesa combines European sophistication and Florida charm. Rooms have an eclectic mix of antiques, the Victorian-style lobby displays photographs of old Key West, and traditional English tea is served at the pools that are surrounded by lush foliage. Restaurant, bar, dining room, room service. Minibars. Cable TV. 2 Pools. Business services. No kids under 12. | 600 Fleming St. | 305/292–1919 or 800/869–4631 | fax 305/294–2121 | www.marquesa.com | 27 rooms | $260–$395 | AE, DC, MC, V.

The Merlinn Inn. Natural woodwork and sunny rooms bring this complex of rooms in and around the historic Simonton House to a stunning level of hospitality. The rooms are each unique with ceiling fans, four-poster beds, and they all surround the central pool and sundeck area. This private, tropical setting is only a block off Duval St. Even though there is only street parking available in the popular neighborhood, the inn's amenities make up for that ... not bad for a building that has a past history of being a bordello. Continental breakfast. Some kitchenettes, no room phones. Pool. | 811 Simonton St. | 305/296–3336 or 800/642–4753 | fax 305/296–3524 | www.merlinnkeywest.com | 10 rooms, 6 suites, 4 cottages | $135–$199 room, $159–$199 suite, $189–$235 cottage | AE, D, MC, V.

Ocean Key House Suite Resort. Adjacent to Mallory Square and the Sunset Pier, this five-story resort has rooms done in bright, bold colors. A daily narrated glass-bottom-boat cruise departs from here. Parasailing, diving, snorkeling, and deep sea fishing are nearby. Restaurant, bar, complimentary Continental breakfast, room service. In-room data ports, some kitchenettes, minibars, some in-room hot tubs. Cable TV. Free parking. | 0 Duval St. | 305/296–7701 or 800/328–9815 | www.oceankey.com | 21 rooms, 90 suites | $289–$329, $339–$549 suites | AE, D, DC, MC, V.

The Paradise Inn. Exactly as it sounds, you will be in the midst of tropical paradise (only 7 blocks away from the beach) and catered to by an attentive staff and all-knowing concierge. Some of the cottages are renovated cigar-makers' quarters; the rest were built 5 years ago and sport chic and stylish French doors, oak floors, balconies, plush robes, and antique furniture sure to inspire any romantic interlude. Complimentary Continental breakfast. In-room data ports, in-room safes, refrigerators. Cable TV. Pool, pond. Outdoor hot tub. Laundry service. Parking. No kids under 12. | 819 Simonton St. | 305/293–8007 or 800/888–9648 | fax 305/293–0807 | www.theparadiseinn.com | 15 suites, 3 cottages | $175–$270 suites, $220–$545 cottages | AE, D, DC, MC, V.

Pelican Landing. This four-story condominium complex is on Garrison Bight. Rooms are fully furnished and equipped. Tennis privileges across the street at Bayview Park are included. Picnic area. In-room data ports, in-room safes, kitchenettes, microwaves, refrigerators. Cable TV, in-room VCRs. Pool. Dock, boating. Laundry facilities. Business services. Pets allowed. | 915 Eisenhower Dr. | 305/293–9730 | fax 305/296–7792 | www.center-courthideaways.com | 16 units | $189–$324 | AE, D, MC, V.

Pier House. The four-story buildings that surround the lush courtyard at this Old Town resort are Key West at its most traditional. With its Caribbean-style architecture and festive furnishings, it's a perennial favorite. Harbor Front rooms have gulf views. Restaurant (Pier House), bar, room service. In-room data ports, minibars, some in-room hot tubs. Cable TV, some in-room VCRs. Pool. Beauty salon, massage. Gym. Beach, boating, fishing, bicycles. Laundry service. Business services. | 1 Duval St. | 305/296–4600 or 800/327–8340 | fax 305/296–7569 | www.pierhouse.com | 126 rooms, 16 suites in 4 buildings | $290–$460, $460–$1,600 suites | AE, D, DC, MC, V.

Quality Inn. This Quality Inn has a two-story and a four-story building. Mallory Square is 2 mi south and the entrance to Key West Beach is 1 mi southwest. Restaurant, bar, room service. In-room data ports, some kitchenettes, some refrigerators. Cable TV. Pool. Outdoor hot tub. Laundry facilities. Business services. | 3850 N. Roosevelt Blvd. | 305/294–6681 | fax 305/294–5618 | www.qualityinn.com | 148 rooms in 2 buildings | $189–$324 | AE, D, DC, MC, V.

Radisson Hotel. Rooms at this six-story hotel have either a view of the Gulf of Mexico or the pool area. The restaurant is open 24 hours. Restaurant, bar, room service. Some kitchenettes, refrigerators. Cable TV. Pool. Gym. Laundry facilities. Business services. | 3820 N. Roosevelt Blvd. | 305/294–5511 | fax 305/296–1939 | www.radisson.com | 154 rooms, 8 suites | $129–$199, $209–$319 suites | AE, D, DC, MC, V.

Santa Maria Motel. This two-story motel in Old Town is within walking distance of Duval Street restaurants and shops. The pool has a ship motif and is surrounded by stone. Room service. Some kitchenettes. Cable TV, some in-room VCRs (and movies). Pool. | 1401 Simonton St. | 305/296–5678 or 800/821–5397 | fax 305/294–0010 | 64 rooms | $150–$175 | AE, D, DC, MC, V.

Seascape Tropical Inn & Cottages. Built from native pine in the Bahamas in the 1840s and transported by ship to Key West in 1889, this B&B has been a private residence, a school house, a law library, and a brothel. Rooms have French doors, Bahama ceiling fans, and tropical furnishings. There are two secluded sundecks and a breakfast patio. Complimentary Continental breakfast. Cable TV. Pool. Free parking. | 420 Olivia St. | 305/296–7776 or 800/765–6438 | fax 305/296–6283 | www.seascapetropicalinn.com | 7 rooms, 4 cottage suites | $129–$189 room, $179–$269 cottage suite | AE, D, MC, V.

South Beach Motel. The Atlantic is at the doorstep of this Old Town motel. Rooms are appointed in florals and pastels and most have great views of the water and the beach. There is also an Olympic-size swimming pool and dive shop on the premises. Some kitchenettes, refrigerators. Cable TV. Pool. Water sports, bicycles. Laundry facilities. Business services. | 508 South St. | 305/296–5611 or 800/354–4455 | fax 305/294–8272 | www.oldtown-resorts.com/southbeach.htm | 47 rooms | $175–$275 | AE, MC, V.

Southernmost. The grounds of this Old Town motel are filled with palms and native flora. The rooms have a contemporary tropical theme. The Atlantic is directly across the street. Bar, some refrigerators. Cable TV. 2 Pools. Outdoor hot tub. Bicycles. Laundry facilities. Business services. | 1319 Duval St. | 305/296–6577 or 800/354–4455 | fax 305/294–8272 | www.old-townresorts.com/southernmost1.htm | 127 rooms in 6 buildings | $165–$240 | AE, MC, V.

Speakeasy Inn. With a rich history of rum-running and cigars, this inn has some of the most spacious and relaxing rooms in town. The Saltillo-tiled rooms and oak floors provide a cool refuge from the heat, but the bright artwork and throw rugs spice it up. The house was formerly owned by Raul Vasquez, who smuggled liquor in from Cuba during Prohibition. The current owner, Thomas Favelli, runs the small Key West Havana Cigar Company in the front lobby, the only place to smoke in the inn. The full concierge can arrange massages, water sport activities, or rooms at their other facility, the Casa 325 Suites, just down the block, with more classy rooms and a pool. Some microwaves, some refrigerators. Some room phones. Parking. Some pets (fee). | 117 Duval St. | 305/296–2680 or 800/217–4884 | fax 305/296–2608 | www.keywestcigar.com | 15 rooms in 2 buildings | $85–$250 | AE, D, MC, V.

Watson House. Rooms at this B&B blend Florida style with 1800s romanticism—paddle fans, wicker and rattan furniture, and floral patterns. The tropical garden is enhanced by the trickling waterfall in the pool. Complimentary Continental breakfast. In-room data ports, some microwaves, refrigerators. In-room VCRs. Pool. Outdoor hot tub. No kids. No smoking. | 525 Simonton St. | 305/294–6712 or 800/621–9405 | fax 305/294–7501 | www.key-westvacations.com | 4 rooms | $230–$370 | MC, V.

Wicker Guesthouse. This place is surrounded by swaying coconut palms, frangipani, and hibiscus flowers. There are several sundecks and a garden playhouse for the kids. Complimentary Continental breakfast. Cable TV. Pool. Free parking. | 913 Duval St. | 305/296–4275 or 800/880–4275 | www.wickerhousekw.com | 16 rooms | $85–$205 | AE, D, DC, MC, V.

Wyndham Reach Resort. Casual is the theme at this five-story resort with a white and peach exterior. All rooms have private balconies, most with ocean views. Restaurant, bar. In-room data ports, minibars, some refrigerators. Cable TV. Pool. Sauna, steam room. Beach, water sports, boating. Baby-sitting. Laundry service. Business services. | 1435 Simonton St. | 305/296–5000 or 800/874–4118 | fax 305/296–2830 | www.reachresort.com | 71 rooms, 79 suites | $299–$339, $339–$409 suites | AE, D, DC, MC, V.

Wyndham Casa Marina Resort. Heirs of railroad mogul Henry Flagler built this stylish hotel in 1921 at the end of the Florida East Coast Railway line. The elegant lobby has pine floors, new island French Provincial furniture, and a beamed ceiling. With 1,100 ft of pristine oceanfront, the Wyndham has the largest stretch of private beach in Key West. 2 restaurants, bar, room service. In-room data ports, in-room safes, minibars. Cable TV, some in-room VCRs. 2 Pools. Beauty salon, outdoor hot tub, massage, sauna. 3 tennis courts. Gym. Beach, water sports, boating. bicycles. Children's programs (ages 4–12). Business services. Airport shuttle. | 1500 Reynolds St. | 305/296–3535 or 800/626–0777 | fax 305/296–4633 | www.casamari-nakeywest.com | 240 rooms, 71 suites | $279–$429, $449–$799 suites | AE, D, DC, MC, V.

KISSIMMEE

MAP 3, J5

(Nearby towns also listed: Davenport, Haines City, Lake Buena Vista, Maitland, Orlando, Walt Disney World)

Kissimmee was originally a small trading post called Allendale on the banks of Lake Tohopekaliga, though in the late 1800s, when the town was incorporated, it changed its name to match that of the nearby river. From the late 1800s to the early 20th century, it was primarily a cattle and agricultural community. You can still see some of the historic parts of downtown Kissimmee, including the courthouse, which was built in 1890 and is the longest-serving such building in Florida. But most tourists don't see this part of the city. What Kissimmee is best known for today is being a gateway to Walt Disney World, which is just north and west of town. The U.S. 192 strip, which is also known as Irlo Bronson Memorial Highway, is crammed with every budget motel and tourist attraction you can imagine. If you are looking for anything remotely quaint, charming, or sophisticated, Kissimmee is not the place for you, but if you are looking for a decent room close to the mouse, then it's a wonderland.

Information: Kissimmee-St. Cloud Convention and Visitors Bureau | Box 422007, Kissimmee, 34742 | 800/327–9159 | www.floridakiss.com.

Attractions

Celebration. Set on 4,900 acres south of Walt Disney World, this residential area created and run by Disney is home to thousands of people. It's a carefully planned community, where every single blade of grass in every lawn is just right, but as life evolves, residents are finding that it's not such a bad life. The downtown area resembles a small town's main street and city square. There are shops and a hotel. Take I–4 exit 25A.

Flying Tigers Warbird Restoration Air Museum. The owners at this museum in an old hangar at Kissimmee Airport collect, refurbish, and sell old warplanes. Works in progress and more than 30 planes in the permanent collection are on display, from a wood and canvas 1909 "pusher" to an A-4 Skyhawk and a MiG-21. A few larger planes are also out on the tarmac. A ½-hour tour is available. Take I–4 exit 25A to U.S. 192. | 231 N. Hoagland Blvd. | 407/933–1942 | $8 | Mon.–Sat. 9–6, Sun. 9–5:30; tours 9:30–4.

Gatorland. This 70-acre nature-theme attraction in southern Orlando opened in 1949 as a roadside attraction and has endured despite competition from the major theme parks. Today it is home to 5,000 alligators. The main attractions are the three shows: gator feeding, gator wrestling, and a snake show. You can take a walk along the 2,000-ft boardwalk through cypress swamp and a 10-acre breeding marsh, including a three-story observation tower. There is also a zoo that houses many other reptiles and mammals. Free parking. Restaurant and picnic area. | 14501 S. Orange Blossom Tr. | 407/855–5496 or 800/393–5297 | $17.95 | Daily 9–dusk.

Green Meadows Petting Farm. Children love to milk cows and ride the ponies at this farm 6 mi from I–4. The 40-acre property is dotted with southern oaks and has almost 200 ani-

WHAT TO PACK IN THE TOY TOTE FOR KIDS

- ❏ Audiotapes
- ❏ Books
- ❏ Clipboard
- ❏ Coloring/activity books
- ❏ Doll with outfits
- ❏ Hand-held games
- ❏ Magnet games

- ❏ Notepad
- ❏ One-piece toys
- ❏ Pencils, colored pencils
- ❏ Portable stereo with earphones
- ❏ Sliding puzzles
- ❏ Travel toys

mals. A 2-hour guided tour lets kids chase chickens, pet pigs, and go on a tractor-powered hayride. There are also a mini-railway, pony rides, and a farm zoo with llama, buffalo, and ostriches. Lots of photo ops for parents. The general store has cold drinks. | 1368 S. Poinciana Blvd. | 407/846–0770 | $15 | Daily 9:30–4.

Jungleland. Smaller and less showy than its competitor, Gatorland, this similar attraction is home to more than 400 exotic animals, including lions, monkeys, tigers, reptiles, and birds. Get there for the gator show at 2 or 4, a half-hour of gator wrestling and education, folk lore, and trivia held in the 300-seat amphitheater. Then go on the ½-mi path where you are caged in on the boardwalk and the animals are peering in on you. You can even feed some of the animals. | 4580 U.S. 192W (Irlo Bronson Memorial Hwy.) | 407/396–1012 | $11.95 | Daily 9–6.

Medieval Times Dinner Show and Medieval Life Village. The large castle is hard to miss from the road at this restaurant attraction where you are transported back into the Middle Ages. Before dinner you can stroll through 12 cottages that make up the Medieval Life Village. There are demonstrations of antique blacksmithing, woodworking, and pottery making plus a dungeon and torture chamber. The dinner show takes place in a long, cavernous room with six tiers of seats flanking a 70-yard-long, sand-covered arena. The meal is soup, a whole roasted chicken, a pork rib, and a roasted potato. You eat with your fingers. The show includes equestrian demonstrations by six knights on Andalusian stallions, a tournament of sword fights, jousting matches, and other games on a good-versus-evil theme. Dinner show reservations are essential. | 4510 U.S. 192W (Irlo Bronson Memorial Hwy.) | 407/396–1518 or 800/229–8300 | $39.95 | Castle daily 9–4, village daily 4:30–8, performances usually daily at 8 but call ahead to check.

Old Town. Stroll down the pedestrian-only street lined with more than 70 specialty shops and restaurants, re-creating a turn-of-the-20th-century Florida village. You can buy a 25¢ Pepsi at the General Store, watch the taffy maker at Coffelt's Taffy & Chocolates or the candle maker at Kandlestix. While the grown-ups shop or take a break on one of the many benches, kids can enjoy the carnival midway rides, visit the Haunted Grimm House, or play laser tag. Every Saturday night there is a parade of 300–500 classic automobiles that winds down the main street and ends at the stage where live rock-n-roll is played. | 5770 U.S. 192W (Irlo Bronson Memorial Hwy., 1 mi east of I–4) | 407/396–4888 | Town free; rides extra | Daily 10 AM–11 PM.

Reptile World Serpentarium. Off the beaten track, this small stucco building houses more than 50 snakes from around the world including the Australian taipan, an 18-ft king cobra, an East African green mamba, an Eastern diamondback rattlesnake, and a monocled cobra. The snakes are housed in glass-fronted pens along a darkened corridor. There are also a 14-ft gator, iguanas, and a pond full of turtles. The daily venom show allows you to watch handlers extract the poison from the snakes to be shipped around the world for medical research. | 5705 E. Bronson Hwy., St. Cloud | 407/892–6905 | $4.55 | Tues.–Sun. 9–5:30; venom show 3 PM weekdays, 3 times daily on weekends.

Splendid China. This 76-acre outdoor theme-park displays 60 mini-replicas of China's wonders during the past 5,000 years. Its owners built it with the idea of bringing China to Americans. Highlights include a ½-mi-long Great Wall, the Forbidden City's 9,999-room Imperial Palace, and the Leshan Buddha. Live shows by acrobats, storytellers, martial artists, dancers, and puppeteers are presented all day. Little trams provide transportation around the park, with pick-up and drop-off at the bigger attractions. I–4 exit 25A. | 3000 Splendid China Blvd. | 407/396–7111 | $26.99 | Daily 9:30–6.

Water Mania. Surf a continuous simulated wave, plunge 300 ft down a watery abyss, or float on calmer waters at this 36-acre water park. There are a sandy beach, go-carts, an 18-hole miniature golf course, a picnic area, gift shops, and concerts. I–4 exit 25A | 6073 U.S. 192W (Irlo Bronson Memorial Hwy.) | 407/239–8448 or 407/396–2626 | $25.95; half price after 3; parking $5 | Nov.–Dec. 21 and Jan. 4–early Mar., Wed.–Sat. 11–5; Dec. 22–Jan. 3, daily 10–5; early Mar.–Aug., daily 9:30–6; Sept.–Oct., Wed.–Sat. 10–5.

MAR.: *Bluegrass Festival.* Bluegrass and gospel entertainers from across the country perform in this four-day event at the Silver Spurs Arena, along with The First Family of Bluegrass—the Lewis Family. | 800/473–7773.

MAR.: *Spring Training.* The Atlanta Braves have trained in the baseball stadium at Disney's Wide World of Sports since 1997. | 407/939–2200.

MAR.–APR.: *Spring Training.* The Houston Astros have been training in Kissimmee's Osceola County Stadium since 1985. | 407/933–2520 or 407/933–6500.

APR.: *Spring Fling.* Every spring the St. Cloud Lake Tohopekaliga lakefront comes alive with the rumble of offshore power boats as fans from around the state motor over for the three-day event that includes racing, food, and craft stands. | 407/847–5000.

OCT.: *Silver Spurs Rodeo.* Professional cowboys compete in bull and bronco riding and steer wrestling, and the Silver Spurs Quadrille perform square dancing on horseback at the Kissimmee Fairgrounds. | 407/847–4052.

Dining

Akbar Palace Indian Restaurant. Indian. This small low-lit restaurant serves good food at reasonable prices. The walls are covered with Indian art and memorabilia. Traditional dishes such as samosas, curry, and tandoori chicken are served in heaping portions. Beer and wine. | 4985 U.S. 192W (Irlo Bronson Memorial Hwy.) | 407/396–4836 | Reservations not accepted | No lunch | $5–$10 | MC, V.

Atlantic Bay Seafood Grill. Seafood. Across the street from the town of Celebration, this New England–theme eatery specializes in fresh fish. The dining area is bright with wood panels and nautical memorabilia. There's a choice of cooking methods for the catch of the day—broiled, grilled, blackened, Jamaican, or fried. Pastas, steak, chicken, and ribs are also on the menu. | 2901 Parkway Blvd. | 407/238–2323 | No lunch | $13–$21 | AE, D, MC, V.

Café d' Antonio. Italian. They keep the wood-burning oven and grill busy, and the mountain of hardwood they go through every week in the open kitchen at the rear of the dining room flavors most of the menu items—the pizza, the grilled fish and chicken, even the steaks and chops. Standouts include salmon from the grill and pizza Mediterranea. Desserts include hazelnut chocolate cake or ricotta cheesecake. Like the rest of Celebration's restaurants, this one has an awning-covered terrace overlooking the lagoon. | 691 Front St. | 407/566–2233 | $13–$36 | AE, D, MC, V.

Calabrisella. Italian. This pizza place is cozy with red-checkered tablecloths and red vinyl booths. The noise level is moderate. Beer and wine. | 3850 S. Orange Blossom Tr | 407/870–9242 | Reservations not accepted | Closed Sun. | $6–$11 | No credit cards.

Captain Nemo's. Seafood. Diners sit at long tables here. The all-you-can-eat seafood buffet includes lobster, crab, clams, shrimp, and mussels. Chicken and prime rib are also available. They also serve breakfast. It's in the Caribbean Village shopping center 2 mi east of I–4. Kids' menu. | 5469 U.S. 192W (Irlo Bronson Memorial Hwy.) | 407/396–6911 | Reservations not accepted | $10–$18 | MC, V.

Cattleman's. Steak. This steak house serves only USDA choice, aged, Midwestern corn-fed beef. The menu includes nine hand-cut steaks ranging from filet mignon to the house specialty—a 32-oz porterhouse. Salmon, fried or coconut shrimp, king crab, and Australian lobster tail are also on the menu. Kids' menu. | 2948 Vineland Rd. | 407/397–1888 | No lunch | $12–$27 | AE, MC, V.

Charley's Steak House. Steak. Polished mahogany, stained-glass, and splashy art work surround you as you dine on Seminole Indian dishes. Steaks are seared over a wood-burning pit, fired by three hardwoods. The 12-oz filet mignon and the New York strip sirloin are popular. | 2901 Parkway Blvd. | 407/396–6911 | No lunch | $21–$29 | AE, MC, V.

Columbias. Latin. This building looks like an old Spanish mansion, with gold stucco walls set off with dark wood and Spanish tile work. The menu includes two paellas—*paella à la Valenciana* (with clams, shrimp, scallops, chicken, pork, and even calamari mixed into tasty yellow rice), or the all-seafood version, *paella verde* (includes lobster in the mix). Desserts include a good Cuban flan and a credible Key lime pie. | 649 Front St. | 407/566–1505 | $23–$44 | AE, D, DC, MC, V.

Darryl's. American. Darryl's has an Old West theme from the wood-paneled walls to the swing bench on the wraparound porch outside. The menu includes burgers, barbecue, roast chicken, and cheesecake. | 5260 U.S. 192W (Irlo Bronson Memorial Hwy.) | 407/396–1901 | No lunch | $14–$23 | AE, DC, MC, V.

Francesco Italiano. Italian. The dining room walls are decked with murals of scenes of Rome at this intimate bistro. The menu includes lasagna, fettucine Alfredo, and chicken. | 4920 U.S. 192W (Irlo Bronson Memorial Hwy.) | 407/396–8899 | No lunch | $9–$16 | AE, DC, MC, V.

Front Street Grill. American. This urbane spot has dark wood paneling and a menu that includes bacon cheeseburgers, chicken pot pie, turkey meat loaf, chicken-salad sandwiches, and barbecued pork ribs. Maple-glazed salmon and crème brûlée are also served. There's a sidewalk seating area under an awning. | 721 Front St., Celebration | 407/566–1141 | $17–$46 | AE, D, MC, V.

Golden Chicken. Latin. Peruvian and Latin cuisine is served at this casual restaurant with a popular buffet. The menu specializes in seafood, especially spicy dishes. Beer and wine are served. Saturday evening there is dancing with a live band or DJ. | 1713 N. Main St. | 407/870–9988 | $13–$25 | AE, DC, MC, V.

Key W. Kool's. Steak. Balconies, wooden shutters, wrought iron, cute signs on the walls, and a ceiling painted like the sky are a mirror image of Key West. You can watch your dinner being grilled over an open flame. Hand-cut, prime steaks and seafood are the specialties. The 17-oz slice of boneless prime rib is more than 1-inch thick. Seating is at tables and bare booths. Kids' menu. | 7725 U.S. 192W (Irlo Bronson Memorial Hwy.) | 407/396–1166 | No lunch | $13–$25 | AE, DC, MC, V.

Little Italy. Italian. A pianist serenades at this friendly restaurant serving traditional Italian fare, including pasta primavera, stromboli, and lasagna. There is also a dinner buffet starting at 4 PM. | 3815 U.S. 192W | 407/847–4651 | $11–$17 | AE, D, DC, MC, V.

Logan's Roadhouse. Steak. Modeled after a 1940s honky-tonk roadside grill—with wooden floors, neon signs, and country music on the jukebox—this casual steak house serves country-flavored meals. Mesquite-grilled steaks are accompanied by sides such as baked sweet potatoes with cinnamon and brown sugar. | 5925 W. Irlo Bronson Memorial Hwy. | 407/390–0500 | $11–$17 | AE, D, DC, MC, V.

Max's Cafe and Coffee House. American. An Art Deco version of an American diner, Max's serves comfort food favorites such as meat loaf, roast chicken, and mashed potatoes in large portions. Veggie burgers and salmon sandwiches are also on the menu. Breakfast is served. I–4 exit 25A. | 701 Front St. | 407/566–1144 | $7–$13 | AE, D, DC, MC, V.

People's Place. American. Test the progress of a new generation of chefs at this restaurant in the Southeastern Academy Culinary Training Center. The weekday lunch menu might include *coq au vin* (chicken with wine), French oxtail soup, or seafood pasta primavera. On Thursdays the dessert buffet is free. Every five weeks the graduating class prepares an elaborate themed luncheon. | 219 Broadway | 407/870–9300 | Closed Sun. No lunch weekends; no dinner | $6–$12 | AE, D, DC, MC, V.

Roadhouse Grill. Steak. In a large, barnlike wooden building, this steak house has shades of black and red, with a cowboy motif upholstered across the chairs and booths. The menu focuses on steak, but includes a grilled catfish sandwich, grilled marinated chicken, and salads. | 4155 W. Vine St. | 407/932–4401 | $12–$19 | AE, D, DC, MC, V.

Romano's Macaroni Grill. Italian. This chain restaurant spins out popular pastas with toppings and sauces made with everything from sausage to eggplant. The specialty is *scaloppine di pollo Romano* (chicken with artichokes and capers and with angel-hair pasta). House wines are brought to the table in gallon bottles. You serve yourself and then report how many glasses you had. | 5320 W. Irlo Bronson Memorial Hwy. | 407/396–6155 | $12–$21 | AE, D, DC, MC, V.

Rosario's. Italian. This intimate restaurant with red interior serves traditional Italian favorites and seafood dishes. | 4838 U.S. 192W (Irlo Bronson Memorial Hwy.) | 407/396–2204 | No lunch | $16–$20 | AE, DC, MC, V.

Szechwan House. Chinese. This restaurant in the Fortune Mark Shopping Center has private tables providing intimate dining. Mandarin-style and spicy Szechuan dishes are served. Vegetarian selections and beer and wine are available. | 5489 U.S. 192W (Irlo Bronson Memorial Hwy.) | 407/396–1885 | $9–$16 | AE.

Twin Dragons Restaurant. Chinese. Upon entering Twin Dragons you walk across a wooden bridge that overlooks a school of goldfish. Inside, the restaurant resembles a palace, filled with wood carvings. Inside each dining room, a gigantic mural of pandas is displayed. The food is also extravagant, featuring Szechuan and Cantonese dishes, including General Tso's chicken, beef and broccoli, and sautéed shrimp. Buffet. | 4002 U.S. 192W (Irlo Bronson Memorial Hwy.) | 407/846–6161 | $8–$22 | AE, D, DC, MC, V.

Yoji's. Japanese. Japanese prints on the dining room walls and cherry blossom arrangements brighten this sushi–sashimi restaurant. The menu also includes traditional steak house items such as New York strip steak, chicken, and shellfish. | 4592 W. Irlo Bronson Memorial Hwy. | No lunch | 407/396–6858 | $16–$20 | MC, V.

Lodging

Best Western Kissimmee. Overlooking the greens of a 9-hole, par-3 executive golf course, this three-story motor inn attracts senior citizens and families. A white stone exterior with baby blue trim and palm trees dominates the landscape. Rooms have two king-size beds and a soft pastel color scheme with wood furniture. Rollaway beds available. Free Walt Disney World shuttle (12 mi away). Restaurant, bar, dining room, picnic area. In-room safes, microwaves, refrigerators. Cable TV. Pool. Basketball, volleyball. Laundry facilities. Business services. Airport shuttle. | 2261 U.S. 192E (Irlo Bronson Memorial Hwy.) | 407/846–2221 or 800/944–0062 | fax 407/846–1095 | www.orlandolodging.com | 282 rooms | $60–$100 | AE, D, DC, MC, V.

Best Western Suites & Resort Hotel on Lake Cecile. Of the all-suites hotels on U.S. 192, this complex of four-unit town houses is probably the best. One side of the complex faces the highway; the other overlooks an attractive lake, where you can sail, water ski, jet ski, and fish. (Water-sport rentals are operated by vendors next door.) Forty units are split-level suites that accommodate six and have kitchens, living rooms, loft bedrooms, and fireplaces. All others accommodate two and are similar to studio apartments but have full kitchens and fireplaces. Pool. Hot tub. Basketball. Playground. Laundry facilities, laundry service. | 4786 W. Irlo Bronson Memorial Hwy. | 407/396–2056 or 800/468–3027 | fax 407/396–2296 | www.bestwestern.com | 158 units | $90–$120 | AE, D, DC, MC, V.

Celebration Hotel. Like everything in the Disney-created town of Celebration, this three-story hotel weds the best of the 19th and 20th centuries in one concept. The lobby, modeled after a grand Victorian hotel, has hardwood floors and classic, decorative millwork on the walls and ceilings. The rooms have ceiling fans and furniture reminiscent of the early 1900s, three phone lines, and a stereo. A lighthouse tower overlooks the lake in the center of downtown. I–4 exit 25A. 2 restaurants, bar. Pool. Hot tub. Gym. Golf privileges. Laundry service. | 700 Bloom St., Celebration | 407/566–6000 | fax 407/566–1844 | www.celebrationhotel.com | 115 rooms | $175 | AE, D, DC, MC, V.

Clarion Hotel Maingate. The five-story brick Clarion Hotel Maingate has a tropical theme. It's 1½ mi from Walt Disney World. Various options for wining, dining, and recreation are available, including a breakfast restaurant, grill, poolside snack bar, lobby bar, and swimming pool. All rooms are painted in simple blues and whites. Each has two doubles or one king-size bed, a full-length mirror, and mini coffeemaker. I–4 exit 25B. Restaurant, bar. In-room data ports, in-room safes, microwaves, refrigerators. Cable TV. Pool. Gym. Baby-sitting. Children's programs. Laundry facilities. Business services. | 7675 U.S. 192W (Irlo Bronson Memorial Hwy.) | 407/396–4000 | fax 407/396–0714 | www.choicehotels.com | 198 rooms | $69–$135 | AE, D, DC, MC, V.

Clarion Suites Resort World. All units in this two-story town house–style complex 5 mi from Walt Disney World have one to three bedrooms, two baths, and a washer and dryer. The rooms are done in pink floral. Game house. Bike rental available. I–4 exit 25A, east 3 mi on U.S. 192. Restaurant, bar. Cable TV, in-room VCRs (and movies). Pool. Hot tub. Gym. Tennis. Laundry facilities. Business services. | 2800 Poinciana Blvd. | 407/396–8300 | fax 407/396–2986 | www.choicehotels.com | 311 rooms | $117–$185 | AE, D, DC, MC, V.

Best Inn Maingate. Standard rooms at this hotel 1 mi from Walt Disney World have a pastel color scheme as well as the outside, which is peach colored with a colonial Spanish theme. The deluxe rooms overlook a landscaped garden, have coffeemakers and hair dryers. Children 10 and under eat free. There is a free shuttle to all Disney theme parks. Restaurant. Refrigerators. Pool. Video games. Laundry facilities. | 7571 W. Irlo Bronson Memorial Hwy. | 407/396–7500 or 800/223–1628; 800/432–0887 in FL | fax 407/396–7497 | www.bestinn.com | 281 rooms | $45–$75 | AE, D, DC, MC, V.

Comfort Inn Maingate West. This two-story hotel is 6 mi from Walt Disney World. The guest rooms have contemporary furnishings and pastel colors. They're a little small but are large enough for a family and have sofabeds. I–4 exit 25B, west 6 mi on U.S. 192. Complimentary Continental breakfast. In-room data ports, microwaves, refrigerators. Cable TV. Pool. Video games. Children's programs. Laundry facilities. Business services. | 9330 U.S. 192W (Irlo Bronson Memorial Hwy.) | 407/424–8420 | fax 407/424–9670 | www.choicehotels.com | 73 rooms | $30–$140 | AE, D, DC, MC, V.

Comfort Suites Main Gate Resort. The suites at this three-story all-suites hotel are actually one oversized room with a separate sitting area and two queen-size or one king-size bed. Many have double sofa beds, allowing you to sleep six—great if you've got more than two kids. Free Disney shuttle. It's 10 mi from Walt Disney World. I–4 exit 25B, west 3 mi on U.S. 192. Complimentary Continental breakfast. In-room data ports, in-room safes, microwaves, refrigerators. Cable TV. Pool, wading pool. Beauty salon, hot tub. Video games. Laundry facilities. Business services. Pets allowed. | 7888 U.S. 192W (Irlo Bronson Memorial Hwy.) | 407/390–9888 or 800/228–5150 | fax 407/390–0981 | www.choicehotels.com | 150 rooms | $69–$139 | AE, D, DC, MC, V.

Days Inn, Eastgate. This two-story budget hotel 3½ mi from Walt Disney World has a peach exterior and a large courtyard. Rooms face the pool, a courtyard, or the parking lot. Each room, done in white and pink with floral patterns, has two double beds or one king-size bed and a double sleeper sofa. Rental cars on site. Free Disney shuttle. Restaurant. Microwaves, refrigerators. Cable TV. Pool. Video games. Laundry facilities. Business services. Airport shuttle. | 5245 U.S. 192W (Irlo Bronson Memorial Hwy.) | 407/396–7700 or 800/423–3684 | fax 407/396–0293 | www.daysinneastgate.com | 200 rooms | $49–$79 | AE, D, DC, MC, V.

Days Suites. Dense tropical vegetation and waterfalls highlight this two-story family resort 2½ mi from Walt Disney World and adjacent to Old Town shopping and entertainment complex. The apartment-style suites, done in beige with burgundy carpeting, have living rooms, dining areas, and kitchens with a dishwasher, stove, dishes, and utensils. Three pools and an expansive barbecue and picnic area give you plenty of room to spread out. All suites have a balcony or patio and sleep six. In-room safes, kitchenettes, microwaves, refrigerators. Cable TV. Pools. Video games. Playground. Laundry facilities. Business services. Pets allowed (fee). | 5820 U.S. 192W (Irlo Bronson Memorial Hwy.) | 407/396–7900 or 800/327–9126 | fax 407/396–1789 | 603 rooms | $79–$149 | AE, D, DC, MC, V.

Deluxe Florida Villas. This complex of condos and vacation homes 5 mi from Walt Disney World includes 1- to 3-bedroom units that can sleep up to eight. The two-story town houses, with blue, pink, and white interiors, have a private parking space in front, cathedral ceilings, a full kitchen, and a washer and dryer. Free Disney shuttle. In-room data ports. Cable TV, in-room VCRs (and movies). Pool. Hot tub, sauna. Tennis. Racquetball. Business services. Airport shuttle. | 2777 Poinciana Blvd. | 407/396–2744 | fax 407/396–8447 | 128 villas | $80–$200 | DC, MC, V.

Diplomat Resort Maingate. This four-story hotel with a tropical atrium and waterfall is 1 mi from Walt Disney World. Rooms have pink walls and red carpeting and accommodate up to four. There's a nightly magic show and karaoke in the food court. Free Disney shuttle. Restaurant, bar, room service. In-room safes, refrigerators. Cable TV. Indoor pool. Hot tub. Video games. Laundry facilities. | 7491 U.S. 192W (Irlo Bronson Memorial Hwy.) | 407/396–6000 or 800/66–WORLD | fax 407/396–7393 | 442 rooms | $99–$175 | AE, DC, MC, V.

Doubletree Guest Suites–Orlando Maingate. This property is modeled after a small village in Spain—stucco villas with red tile roofs. Walt Disney World is 4 mi away. The 1- to 3-bedroom bi-level suites sleep up eight and have two baths, a full kitchen, a living room, a dining room, and a patio. Free Disney shuttle. Restaurant. In-room data ports, in-room safes, microwaves, refrigerators. Cable TV. Pool, wading pool. Hot tub. Tennis. Basketball, gym, volleyball. Video games. Baby-sitting. Laundry facilities. | 4787 U.S. 192W (Irlo Bronson Memorial Hwy.) | 407/397–0555 or 800/222–TREE | fax 407/397–0553 | www.doubletree.com | 150 suites | $129–$229 | AE, D, DC, MC, V.

Doubletree Resort & Conference Center. This seven-story hotel is a few minutes from Walt Disney World. Rooms have large bathrooms. Two floors in each tower are reserved for nonsmokers. Free cookies for all guests. Restaurant, bar, room service. Pool. Hot tub. 2 tennis courts. Basketball, gym. Baby-sitting. Laundry facilities, laundry service. | 3011 Maingate Ln. | 407/396–1400 or 800/239–6478 | fax 407/396–0660 | 583 rooms in 2 buildings | $89–$169 | AE, D, DC, MC, V.

Econo Lodge Maingate–Hawaiian Resort. This property is 1 mi from Walt Disney World. The two-story pink and blue building surrounds a large courtyard and pool. Rooms have two double beds and white walls, blue carpet, and blue floral bedding. The pool bar and grill is open seasonally. Rollaway beds are available. I–4 exit 25B, 2 mi west on U.S. 192. Free Disney shuttle. Restaurant, bar. In-room data ports. Cable TV. Pool. Hot tub. Video games. Laundry facilities. Business services. Pets allowed (fee). | 7514 U.S. 192W (Irlo Bronson Memorial Hwy.) | 407/396–2000 or 800/365–6935 | fax 407/396–2832 | www.enjoyfloridahotels.com | 445 rooms | $59–$109 | AE, D, DC, MC, V.

Fantasy World Club Villas. Pink stucco villas, trimmed in green, make up this resort complex 3 mi from Walt Disney World. The two-story units have two bedrooms, a screened porch, a fully equipped kitchen, and a washer and dryer. Each sleeps up to six. Free Disney shuttle. Bar. In-room data ports, in-room safes, microwaves, refrigerators. Cable TV, in-room VCRs (and movies). 3 pools. Hot tub. Tennis. Volleyball. Playground. Laundry facilities. Business services. Airport shuttle. Pets allowed. | 2935 Hart Ave. | 407/396–1808 or 800/874–8047 | fax 407/396–6737 | 300 villas | $195 | AE, D, DC, MC, V.

Four Points Sheraton Lakeside. You can find a home away from a home in these 15 two-story buildings spread over 27 acres around a small lake. The rooms offer kid-friendly access to Disney movies and Sony playstations. If that's not enough, you can hop on the free shuttle service to any of the surrounding attractions, ranging from Walt Disney World to Water Mania. Universal Studios is the farthest away at 17 miles. The full concierge can set you up with a rental car or tickets to any of the nearby attractions. 2 restaurants. In-room data ports, in-room safes, some refrigerators. 3 pools, 2 wading pools. Miniature golf, 4 tennis courts. Basketball, exercise equipment. Fishing. Children's programs (4–12). Laundry facilities, laundry service. | 7769 W. Irlo Bronson Memorial Hwy. | 407/396–2222 or 800/848–0801 | fax 407/239–2650 | www.fourpointslakeside.com | 651 rooms | $54–$94 | AE, D, DC, MC, V.

Hampton Inn Maingate East. This four-story motel is set back from the road on a wooded property. The small rooms, done in white and mauve with floral patterns, have two double beds or one king-size bed. Several restaurants are nearby. I–4 exit 25A. Free Disney shuttle. Complimentary Continental breakfast. In-room safes. Cable TV. Pool. Gym. Tennis. Basketball. Babysitting. Business services. | 3104 Parkway Blvd. | 407/396–8484 or 800/HAMPTON | fax 407/396–7344 | www.hamptoninn.com | 164 rooms | $59–$95 | AE, D, DC, MC, V.

Hampton Inn Maingate West. One of the many newcomers springing up in the area, this five-story Hampton Inn is 1 mi from Walt Disney World. The property is simply landscaped, and the bright lobby has vaulted ceilings and earth tone furnishings. The rooms have large windows with plants, blue carpet, and floral bedding. Connecting rooms are also available. Car rentals on-site. I–4 exit 25B, west 2 mi on U.S. 192. Free Disney shuttle. Complimentary Continental breakfast. In-room data ports, microwaves, refrigerators. Cable TV. Pool. Laundry facilities. | 3000 Main Gate La. | 407/396–3600 or 800/HAMPTON | fax 407/396–0293 | 118 rooms | $79–$109 | AE, D, DC, MC, V.

Hampton Vacation Resort/Oak Plantation. This town house–style complex with gated access is set amid 16 acres of majestic oaks. The two-story villas surround a lake with a lighted fountain and gazebo. Each 1- or 2-bedroom villa has a living room with a sofabed, fully equipped kitchen, ceiling fan, and a washer and dryer. Interiors are done in soft yellow and blue hues with floral bedding. I–4 exit 25A, east 7 mi on U.S. 192. Complimentary Continental breakfast. In-room safes, microwaves, refrigerators. Cable TV, in-room VCRs (and movies). Pool, wading pool. Hot tub. Tennis (lighted courts). Basketball, gym. Fishing. Video games. Playground. Laundry facilities. Business services. Airport shuttle. | 4090 Enchanted Oaks Cir. | 407/847–8200 or 800/578–0140 | fax 407/847–7948 | www.vistanainc.com | 242 units | $79–$199 | AE, D, DC, MC, V.

Holiday Inn Express. This pink two-story motel has a grand lobby with chandeliers. Rooms, done in pastel colors, have two double beds or a king-size bed plus a sofabed. Connecting rooms are also available. Free Disney shuttle. Complimentary Continental breakfast. In-room data ports. Cable TV. Pool, wading pool. Laundry facilities. Business services. Airport shuttle. | 2145 U.S. 192E (Irlo Bronson Memorial Hwy.) | 407/846–4646 or 800/HOLIDAY | fax 407/932–2467 | 146 rooms | $109–$119 | AE, D, DC, MC, V.

Holiday Inn Hotel and Suites, Main Gate East. This family-friendly resort is 3 mi from Walt Disney World next to the Old Town shopping and entertainment complex. Standard rooms are done in shades of blue and mauve and overlook the pool courtyard or parking lot. Each has two double beds. Sleeping bags and rollaway beds are available. Standard rooms can be upgraded to a Kidsuite, a theme room inside the parents' room with bunk beds, Nintendo, CD player, phone, TV, and VCR. Complimentary tuck-in service is offered by the hotel's mascot—Holiday Hound. Free Disney shuttle. Restaurant, bar. In-room data ports, in-room safes, microwaves, refrigerators. Cable TV, in-room VCRs (and movies). Pool, wading pool. Hot tubs. Tennis court. Basketball, volleyball. Video games. Playground. Laundry facilities. Airport shuttle. Pets allowed. | 5678 U.S. 192W (Irlo Bronson Memorial Hwy.) | 407/396–4488 or 800/465–4329 | fax 407/396–1296 | www.holiday-inn.com | 614 rooms in 8 buildings | $109–$139 | AE, D, DC, MC, V.

Holiday Inn Nikki Bird Resort. Kidsuites at this family friendly resort include a brightly painted room-within-a-room furnished with bunk beds, Nintendo, a CD player, TV, and VCR. Rooms are yellow with floral bedding. There are three tropically landscaped recreation areas. Nikki's Nest has songs, puppet shows, magic shows, and games. I–4 exit 25B. Free Disney shuttle. 2 restaurants, bar (with entertainment). In-room data ports, in-room safes, microwaves, refrigerators. Cable TV. Pool, wading pools. Hot tubs. Tennis court. Video games. Playground. Laundry facilities. Airport shuttle. | 7300 U.S. 192W (Irlo Bronson Memorial Hwy.) | 407/396–7300 or 800/HOLIDAY | fax 407/396–7555 | 529 rooms | $99–$119 | AE, D, DC, MC, V.

Holiday Villas. The town house–style, two-story units at this complex 5 mi from Walt Disney World sleep six to eight people. Each has a king-size bed or two double beds, two baths, a fully equipped kitchen, and a living room. Rooms are done in blues and whites. Rte. 535 and U.S. 192. Microwaves, refrigerators. Cable TV, in-room VCRs (and movies). Pool. Hot tub, sauna. Tennis court. Gym. Video games. Laundry facilities. | 2928 Vineland Rd. | 407/397–0700 or 800/344–3959 | fax 407/397–0566 | www.holidayvillas.com | 255 rooms | $179–$249 | AE, DC, MC, V.

Homewood Suites Maingate at the Parkway. The grounds are immaculately landscaped at this two-story, pink condo-style hotel 1 mi from Walt Disney World. Rooms are done in white with blue carpet, and have large windows with plants. Some overlook the pool and courtyard. I–4 exit 25A. Restaurant, bar, complimentary Continental breakfast. In-room data ports, microwaves, refrigerators. Cable TV. Pool. Hot tub. Laundry facilities. Business services. | 3100 Parkway Blvd. | 407/396–2229 or 800/255–4543 | fax 407/396–4833 | www.home-woodmaingate.com | 156 units | $79–$179 | AE, D, DC, MC, V.

Howard Johnson Maingate Resort. A bright lobby with chandeliers and Victorian furnishings greets you at this two-story hotel set on 15 tropical acres. Each room has a balcony or patio that faces the pool courtyard and tiki pool bar. Rooms have maroon carpet, bright floral bedding, and wood furnishings. I–4 exit 25B. Free Disney shuttle. 2 restaurants, bar, room service. In-room data ports, in-room safes, microwaves, refrigerators. Cable TV, in-room VCRs (and movies). Pool. Hot tub. Tennis (lighted courts). Basketball, gym, volleyball. Video games. Playground. Laundry facilities. Airport shuttle. | 8660 U.S. 192W (Irlo Bronson Memorial Hwy.) | 407/396–4500 or 800/638–7829 | fax 407/396–8045 | 435 rooms in 2 buildings | $70–$90 | AE, D, DC, MC, V.

Howard Johnson Enchanted Land Resort Hotel. The flavor is fantasy at this ground-level kid-oriented resort 3 mi from Walt Disney World. Family-value rooms have fantasy themes with a sofa bed for the kids. Standard rooms with green carpet have a king-size or two double beds. The Action Theatre shows movies for kids. Barbecue and picnic area. I–4 exit 27. Free Disney shuttle. Restaurant, bar. In-room data ports, refrigerators, microwaves. Cable TV. Pool. Hot tub. Video games. Playground. Laundry facilities. | 4985 U.S. 192W (Irlo Bronson Memorial Hwy.) | 407/396–4343 or 800/446–4656 | fax 407/396–8998 | www.enchantedlandresort.com | 160 rooms | $99–$129 | AE, D, DC, MC, V.

Hyatt Orlando. You can jog on the 1⅓-mi trail or play tennis on one of three lighted courts at this two-story hotel set on 54 landscaped acres 1½ mi from Walt Disney World. Rooms face one of four courtyards each with a heated adult pool, hot tubs, and playground. Each room has a patio or balcony and is done in blue with floral bedding and wood furnishings. Guest privileges are provided at Falcon's Fire and Celebration golf clubs. The Trellis Court Lounge and Turtle Cove Activity Center are popular. I–4 exit 25A. Free Disney shuttle. Restaurants, 2 dining rooms, bar (with entertainment). In-room data ports, in-room safes, refrigerators. Cable TV. Pool, wading pool. Hot tubs. Beauty salon. Tennis. Gym. Video games. Playground. Laundry facilities. Business services. Airport shuttle. | 6375 U.S. 192W (Irlo Bronson Memorial Hwy.) | 407/396–1234 or 800/532–1496 | fax 407/396–5090 | www.hyatt.com | 922 rooms in 10 buildings | $154–$164 | AE, D, DC, MC, V.

Orange Lake Resort and Country Club. The two golf courses designed by Arnold Palmer are the big draw at this resort that stretches across 372 acres of fairways, lake, and woodlands. It's 4 mi from Walt Disney World. Units include 2- and 3-bedroom condominium villas and clubhouse studios, each decorated by the owners. On-property activities include Ping-Pong, tennis, water sports, canoes, and sunning by the 80-acre lake. The complex includes shops, six restaurants, and a 200,000-square-ft clubhouse with an arcade, pool tables, a children's activity area, and movie theater. A day of play can be extended into the evening on the lighted 9-hole, par-3 Legends Walk course. Car rentals are available on site. I–4 exit 25B. 2 restaurants, bar. In-room data ports. Cable TV, in-room VCRs. 4 pools, lake, wading pool. Hot tub. Driving range, 27-hole golf course, putting green, tennis. Basketball, health club, racquetball. Beach, water sports, fishing. Video games. Baby-sitting, playground. Laundry facilities. Business services. Airport shuttle. | 8505 U.S. 192W (Irlo Bronson Memorial Hwy.) | 407/239–0000 or 800/877–6522 | fax 407/239–5119 | www.orangelake.com | 140 units | $89–$225 | AE, D, MC, V.

Orbit One Vacation Villas. Rooms at this tropically landscaped town house–style resort are done in pastel hues with wicker furnishings. Each one- or two-story villa has a plush sofabed, fully equipped kitchen, washer and dryer, a screened terrace, and a hot tub. There are also a barbecue and picnic area and pre-arrival grocery service. I–4 exit 25B. Microwaves, refrigerators. Cable TV, in-room VCRs (and movies). Pool, wading pool. Hot tub, sauna. Tennis (lighted courts). Gym, racquetball, volleyball. Video games. Playground. Laundry facilities. Business services. | 2950 Entry Point Blvd. | 407/396–1300 | fax 407/396–0814 | 116 units | $114–$179 | AE, D, DC, MC, V.

Orlando/Kissimmee Maingate Knight's Inn. Budget lodgings in this area are hard to come by, but this is one of the few places that won't knock your wallet too hard before you walk into Walt Disney World. The rooms are simple, as is the motel centered around a small pool, but they still cart you to the attractions free of charge and offer a small buffet in the morning. See the website for weekend specials, even less than quoted. Free Disney shuttle. Continental breakfast. In-room safes, some kitchenettes. Pool. Laundry facilities. Free parking. | 7475 W. Irlo Bronson Memorial Hwy. | 407/396–4200 or 800/944–0062 | fax 407/396–8838 | www.knightsinn.com | 120 rooms | $44–$99 | AE, D, MC, V.

Orlando Sun Village. Each two-story blue town home at this gated property has two or three bedrooms that sleep up to nine, two or three bathrooms, a fully equipped kitchen, a living room with wooden furniture, a dining room, a breakfast bar, a patio, and a washer and dryer. Carpeting is green and bedding blue-violet. The tropical resort has two swimming pools and tropical landscaping throughout. Baby cribs are available upon request. I–4 exit 27. In-room data ports, microwaves, refrigerators. Cable TV, in-room VCRs. Pool. Tennis. Playground. Laundry facilities. | 4403 Sun Village Blvd. | 407/390–4000 | fax 407/390–9335 | www.orlandosunvillage.com | 28 units | $120–$210 | AE, D, DC, MC, V.

Park Inn International. You can enjoy lake activities while being a stone's throw away from all the Disney attractions. The hotel offers some rooms with views of Lake Cecile and jet-ski rentals to live on the wild side. The general architecture is Mediterranean, but the rooms lack any frills. They are under new management, so expect exciting changes in 2001. Free shuttle to Disney attractions. Complimentary Continental breakfast. Some microwaves, some refrigerators. Pool. Outdoor hot tub. Beach. Laundry facilities. | 4960 W. Irlo Bronson Memorial Hwy. | 407/396–1376 or 800/327–0072 | fax 407/396–0716 | www.parkinn.com | 192 rooms | $32–$89 | AE, D, DC, MC, V.

Parkside Record Inn. You'll find a piece of old Florida at this low-frills property. There are a few picnic tables. Complimentary Continental breakfast. Pool. Refrigerators, microwaves. Cable TV. | 4651 W. Irlo Bronson Memorial Hwy. | 407/396–8400 or 800/874–4555 | fax 407/396–8415 | 57 rooms | $34–$65 | AE, D, MC, V.

Parkway International. Each unit in this three-story condominium resort 1 mi from Walt Disney World has two bedrooms with canopy or poster beds, a Roman tub, a hot tub, a full kitchen, a balcony, and a washer and dryer. Rooms have high ceilings, pink carpet, and sleek gray bedding. Bar. In-room safes. Cable TV, in-room VCRs (and movies). Pool, wading pool. Hot tub. Tennis. Playground. | 6200 Safari Tr. | 407/396–6600 | fax 407/396–6165 | 144 units | $124–$188 | AE, D, DC, MC, V.

Poinciana Golf and Racquet Resort. Each unit in this condominium complex 20 mi from Walt Disney World has a washer and dryer. Restaurant, bar. Microwaves, refrigerators. Cable TV. Pool. 18-hole golf course, tennis. Playground. Laundry facilities. Business services. | 500 E. Cypress Pkwy. | 407/933–0700 | fax 407/870–5412 | 112 rooms | $70–$160 | AE, MC, V.

Quality Inn Lake Cecile. This five-story white pyramid-style hotel has a white-sand beach with water-skiing and jet-skiing. It's on the shores of Lake Cecile, 4 mi from Walt Disney World. Rooms are done in beige and mauve with floral bedding and sleep five. Free Disney shuttle. In-room safes, refrigerators. Cable TV. Pool. Dock, water sports, boating. Video games. Laundry facilities. Airport shuttle. | 4944 U.S. 192W (Irlo Bronson Memorial Hwy.) | 407/396–4455 or 800/864–4855 | fax 407/396–4182 | 222 rooms | $80–$139 | AE, D, DC, MC, V.

Quality Inn Maingate West. This three-story pink motel 1½ mi from Walt Disney World surrounds a courtyard and pool. The rooms have pink bedding and blue carpet and sleep five. Each has a king-size or two double beds. A large picnic area and playground is next to the lakeside tiki bar and dock. Free Disney shuttle. Restaurant. In-room data ports.

Microwaves, refrigerators. Cable TV. Pool, lake. Boating. Playground. Laundry facilities. | 7785 U.S. 192W (Irlo Bronson Memorial Hwy.) | 407/396–1828 or 800/634–5525 | fax 407/396–1305 | www.qualityinnorlando.com | 200 rooms | $39–$59 | AE, D, DC, MC, V.

Quality Suites Maingate East. The one- and two-bedroom suites at this four-story hotel 1½ mi from Walt Disney World sleep 6 or 10. One bedrooms have two double beds and a sleeper sofa. Two bedroom suites have four double beds and a sleeper sofa. Suites are done in yellow with wood furnishings. Free beer and wine are served poolside in the afternoon. Free Disney shuttle. Restaurant, bar, complimentary Continental breakfast. In-room safes, microwaves, refrigerators. Cable TV. Pool. Playground. Laundry facilities. Airport shuttle. | 5876 U.S. 192W (Irlo Bronson Memorial Hwy.) | 407/396–8040 or 800/848–4148 | fax 407/396–6766 | www.thhotels.com | 225 suites | $119–$249 | AE, D, DC, MC, V.

Radisson Resort Parkway. Amenities at this 10-story resort on 20 acres include a pool with waterfall and water slide, two outdoor hot tubs, an additional heated pool, and a wading pool for kids. There are also two lighted tennis courts, sand-based volleyball, a playground, and jogging areas. Rooms have a king-size or two double beds and are done in hues of white and blue with floral patterns. Rooms accommodate up to five. Free Disney shuttle (1½ mi). Restaurant. In-room data ports. Cable TV, VCR (movies). Hot tub, sauna. Tennis. Gym, volleyball. Video games. Playground. Laundry facilities. Business services. Airport shuttle. | 2900 Parkway Blvd. | 407/396–7000 or 800/333–3333 | fax 407/396–6792 | www.radissoninn.com | 718 rooms | $89–$149 | AE, D, DC, MC, V.

Ramada Inn Resort Maingate. This shady property spread out under a hammock of palm trees is 1 mi from Walt Disney World. The two-story pink-and-blue hotel's amenities include two tropical outdoor heated swimming pools, fitness center, and a game room. Rooms sleep up to 4, or 5 with a rollaway bed for an extra fee. Kids under 10 eat free. I–4 exit 25B. Free Disney shuttle. Restaurant, bar, room service. In-room data ports, in-room safes, microwaves, refrigerators. Cable TV. Pool, wading pool. Putting green, tennis court. Basketball, gym. Video games. Playground. Laundry facilities. Business services. Pets allowed (fee). | 2950 Reedy Creek Blvd. | 407/396–4466 or 800/365–6935 | fax 407/396–6418 | www.enjoyfloridahotels.com | 391 rooms, 3 suites | $69–$139 | AE, D, DC, MC, V.

Ramada Plaza Hotel and Inns, Gateway. The exterior and interior of this two-story hotel 1 mi west of Walt Disney World are pink and blue. Room have contemporary furnishings and tropical patterns. Rollaway beds. I–4 exit 25B. Free Disney shuttle. Restaurant, bar, room service. In-room data ports, microwaves, refrigerators. Cable TV. 2 Pools. Putting green. Basketball, gym. Video games. Playground. Laundry facilities. Business services. Pets allowed (fee). | 7470 U.S. 192W (Irlo Bronson Memorial Hwy.) | 407/396–4400 or 800/327–9170 | fax 407/397–4481 | 500 rooms | $55–$65 | AE, D, DC, MC, V.

Red Roof Inn. This three-floor hotel is close to it all. Among the millions of theme parks, these guys are also near the training camp for the Houston Astros and the Citrus Bowl. Rooms are standard, but the pool is landscaped in a nice tropical style. Free shuttle to Disney World. Continental breakfast. Pool. Hot tub. Laundry facilities. Pets allowed. | 4970 Kyng's Heath Rd. | 407/396–0065 or 800/843–7663 | fax 407/396–0245 | www.redroof.com | 102 rooms | $36–$89 | AE, D, DC, MC, V.

Residence Inn by Marriott on Lake Cecile. This is one of the best all-suites hotels on U.S. 192. It's 5 mi from Walt Disney World. The units done in violet and blue tones with wood furnishings have one or two bedrooms, large living areas, and fully equipped kitchens. Some suites in the two-floor hotel have lake views; some rooms have fireplaces. Complimentary Continental breakfast. In-room data ports, kitchenettes, microwaves, refrigerators. Cable TV, in-room VCRs. Water sports, fishing. Playground. Laundry facilities, laundry service. Business services. | 4786 U.S. 192W (Irlo Bronson Memorial Hwy.) | 407/396–2056 or 888/236–2427 | fax 407/396–2909 | www.residence-inn.com | 160 rooms in 4 buildings | $119–$199 | AE, D, DC, MC, V.

Ron Jon Resort Orlando. The atmosphere has Polynesian hints at this two-story resort with villa-style accommodations. It's 6 mi west of Walt Disney World. The 1- to 3-bedroom villas, which accommodate up to eight, have full kitchens and washers and dryers; some have hot tubs. Units are white with pink carpet, floral patterns, wicker furnishings, and lots of plants. All have queen-size beds and sofabeds, and large doors to a patio. The resort's lagoon has five water slides in the main pool, a wave pool with simulated ocean waves, an erupting volcano that shoots water and smoke, and a toddlers' area with an octopus swing set. There's also a small lake with paddleboats and a ½-mi nature trail. Complimentary Continental breakfast. In-room data ports, in-room safes, microwaves, refrigerators, some in-room hot tubs. Cable TV, in-room VCRs (and movies). Pools. Hot tubs, saunas. Tennis. Basketball, volleyball. Fishing. Video games. Laundry facilities. Business services. Airport shuttle. | 17777 Bali Blvd. | 407/239–5000 | fax 407/239–5092 | 308 rooms | $131–$230 | AE, D, DC, MC, V.

Sevilla Inn. This three-story stucco and wood inn has standard rooms. The pool area is surrounded by palm trees and tropical shrubs. Cable TV. Pool. Laundry facilities. | 4640 W. Irlo Bronson Memorial Hwy. | 407/396–4135 or 800/367–1363 | fax 407/396–4942 | www.sevillainn.com | 50 rooms | $45–$55 | AE, D, MC, V.

Sheraton Four Points Lakeside. The main lobby and connecting corridors are covered with wall murals depicting Caribbean village scenes at this two-story resort. Floors mock a cobblestone street. Rooms, done in beige with teal, blue, gold, and fuchsia, have two double beds. There's a recreation area with a large pool, kiddie pool, and tiki bar, all surrounded by a red stone patio. Free Disney shuttle. 2 restaurants, bar, room service. In-room data ports, in-room safes, refrigerators. Cable TV. Pool, 2 wading pools. Miniature golf, tennis court. Dock, boating. Video games. Baby-sitting, playgrounds. Laundry facilities. Business services. Airport shuttle. | 7769 U.S. 192W (Irlo Bronson Memorial Hwy.) | 407/396–2222 or 800/848–0801 | fax 407/239–2650 | www.sheraton.com | 651 rooms, 15 buildings | $100–$150 | AE, D, DC, MC, V.

Star Island Resort and Club. Villas at this Mediterranean-style resort and spa have three bedrooms and two baths. The three-story stucco buildings have red roofs. Every villa, some up to 1,350 square ft, has a marbled entryway and posh furnishings. There's a practice putting and driving range. It's 4 mi from Walt Disney World. Restaurant, bar. In-room data ports, in-room safes, microwaves. Cable TV, in-room VCRs (and movies). Pool. Hot tubs, massage, sauna, steam room. Tennis. Gym. Water sports, boating, bicycles. Business services. | 5000 Ave. of the Stars | 407/396–8300 | fax 407/396–2986 | 258 rooms | $125–$285 | AE, D, DC, MC, V.

Summer Bay Resort. Dancers and musicians don costumes and perform at this timeshare resort 6 mi from Walt Disney World. Two- and three-story buildings house one- and two-bedroom villas, and two- and three-bedroom condos. One-bedroom units sleep up to four. Each unit has blue carpet and floral pastel patterns. Some units also have a washer and dryer. Guest luau at the pool with tiki bar on Tuesdays. I–4 exit 25B, west 6 mi on U.S. 192. Restaurant. Microwaves, refrigerators. Cable TV, in-room VCRs (and movies). Pool. Tennis. Gym. Water sports, boating. Playground. Laundry facilities. Business services. | 17805 U.S. 192W (Irlo Bronson Memorial Hwy.) | 352/242–1100 or 877/STAYSBR | fax 352/242–0870 | www.summerbayresort.com | 182 rooms | $150–$360 | AE, MC, V.

Summerfield Resort. This resort has two-story blue town house–style units accommodating up to eight people each. The two-story units have two bedrooms, two baths, a washer and dryer, and fully equipped kitchens. The site has a swimming pool, club house, hot tub, wood sun deck, picnic tables, gas grills, and two equipped playground areas. I–4 exit 25A, east on U.S. 192. Kitchenettes, microwaves. Cable TV, in-room VCRs (and movies). Pool. Hot tub. Playground. Laundry facilities, laundry service. Business services. Pets allowed. | 2422 Summerfield Pl. | 407/847–7222 | fax 407/847–6774 | 37 units | $59–$179 | AE, D, DC, MC, V.

Travelodge Hotel Main Gate East. The first floor of this eight-story, twin-tower hotel holds a food court–style restaurant, convenience store, gameroom, and external pools. It's opposite Kissimmee's Old Town, 4 mi from Walt Disney World. Rooms have a king-size or two double beds, a couch, and large windows. Some rooms on upper floors have a view of the Magic Kingdom fireworks display. Free Disney shuttle. Restaurant, bar. In-room safes, refrigerators. Cable TV. Pool, wading pool. Hot tub, sauna. Volleyball. Video games. Playground.

Laundry facilities. Business services. Airport shuttle. | 5711 U.S. 192W (Irlo Bronson Memorial Hwy.) | 407/396–4222 or 800/327–1128 | fax 407/396–0570 | www.orlandotravelodge.com | 446 rooms | $48–$128 | AE, D, DC, MC, V.

Unicorn Inn English B&B. This two-story blue-shingled 1901 house in the heart of the Historical District is surrounded by tropical vegetation, allowing a quiet stay. All rooms have private baths. There's a public lounge, breakfast room, and deck. It's 20 minutes from Walt Disney World. I–4 exit 25A, east on U.S. 192. Complimentary breakfast. In-room data ports. Cable TV. Laundry facilities. | 8 S. Orlando Ave. | 407/846–1200 or 800/865–7212 | fax 407/846–1773 | 8 rooms | $75 | MC, V.

The Villages at Mango Key. These town house–style condos 4 mi from Walt Disney World are rented out on a weekly basis. The two-story buildings are white with red-tiled roofs. There's a large pool surrounded by palm trees. The two-bedroom units are white with green carpet and have lots of windows. They sleep seven. I–4 exit 25B, west on U.S. 192. In-room data ports, in-room safes. Cable TV, in-room VCRs (and movies). Pool. Hot tub. Tennis. Volleyball. Playground. Laundry facilities. | 3201 Lidifields Blvd. | 407/397–2211 | fax 407/397–2789 | 31 rooms | $525–$875 weekly | AE, MC, V.

Villas at Fortune Place. Villas in the 1-story blue houses with brown-shingled roofs have two bedrooms and two baths. They sleep up to six. A sparsely landscaped pool courtyard has a hot tub and a small playground. Lake Tohopekaliga is close by for fishing, boating, and other water sports. It's 15 mi from Walt Disney World. Microwaves, refrigerators. Cable TV, in-room VCRs (and movies). Pool. Tennis. Fishing. Playground. Laundry facilities. | 1201 Simpson Rd. | 407/348–0330 | fax 407/348–0232 | 100 rooms | $99–$159 | AE, MC, V.

Westgate Towers. Each master bathroom has a whirlpool tub at this five-floor complex 1 mi from Walt Disney World. Suites have a king-size bed, sleeper sofa, kitchen, washer and dryer, and entertainment center. Most have a hot tub. I–4 exit 25B, west 1 mi on U.S. 192. Restaurant. In-room safes, microwaves, refrigerators. Cable TV, in-room VCRs (and movies). Pool, wading pool. Hot tub. Tennis. Basketball, volleyball, boating. Bicycles. Laundry facilities. Business services. Airport shuttle (fee). | 7600 U.S. 192W (Irlo Bronson Memorial Hwy.) | 407/396–2500 or 888/808–7410 | fax 407/396–2096 | 178 units | $120–$400 | AE, D, DC, MC, V.

LAKE BUENA VISTA

MAP 3, J5

(Nearby towns also listed: Clermont, Davenport, Kissimmee, Orlando, Walt Disney World)

Unless you are staying in Walt Disney World itself, you can't get any closer than this area, just to the east of Downtown Disney. Just outside the park's northernmost entrance, the hotels tend to be sprawling, high-quality resorts catering to Walt Disney World vacationers. All of these are convenient.

Information: **Orlando/Orange County Convention and Visitors Bureau** | 1005 East Strawbridge Ave., Orlando, 32819 | 407/363–5871 | www.orlandoinfo.com.

Attractions
Crossroads at Lake Buena Vista. This mall is directly across from the Lake Buena Vista Village entrance to Walt Disney World. It's a group of more than 25 upscale and casual shops and 11 restaurants, plus a supermarket, post office, bank, and dry cleaner. Take I–4 Exit 27. | 12545–12551 Hwy. 535 | 407/827–7300 | Stores daily 10–10; restaurant hours vary.

Dining
Arthur's 27. Contemporary. The 27th floor of Wyndham Palace Resort provides a grand view of sunset over Walt Disney World. The innovative menu changes every two weeks. Specialties

might include roast loin of lamb with garlic sauce, beef tenderloin with cognac sauce, and crème brûlée for dessert. Prix-fixe menus are also available. | Wyndham Palace Resort and Spa, 1900 Buena Vista Dr. | 407/827–3450 | Reservations essential | No lunch | $24–$29 | AE, D, DC, MC, V.

The Black Swan. Contemporary. This establishment in the Hyatt Regency Grand Cypress is popular with golfers—it overlooks the 9th hole of the resort's golf course. The interior has a mountain-lodge theme, with a split level roof, fireplace, and cross-beamed ceiling. Floral arrangements are placed throughout the dining room. A pianist plays at a white baby grand piano. The menu includes corn-tortilla-crusted chicken with black beans and cilantro chili fettuccine, and roasted rack of lamb with mashed potatoes and rosemary jus. | 1 Grand Cypress Blvd. | 407/239–1999 | Reservations required | No lunch | $25–$34 | AE, D, DC, MC, V.

Chevy's. Mexican. This cantina-style restaurant is usually a bustle of activity due to the proximity to many tourist attractions and the many families that are lured by the margaritas and nachos. The menu is extensive and you can get anything from homemade tamales to sizzling fajitas. They offer a fish special daily as well as flan or sopapillas (fried pastry pillow) filled with ice cream for dessert. | 12547 Rte. 535 | 407/827–1052 | fax 407/827–1119 | $10–$12 | AE, MC, V.

La Coquina. French. On the fun side of French with a little Asian flair, La Coquina brings out the best in food. They make such combinations as lobster ravioli served with avocado and a citrus beurre blanc or mango-glazed duck breast thinly sliced on a shiitake risotto. You can look out onto the lake with black swans and relax to the baby grand's nightly pianist. | Hyatt Regency Grand Cypress, 1 Grand Cypress Blvd. | 407/239–1234 | Jackets, long pants, and collared shirts required for men. No jeans and proper attire for women | Closed Tues. and Wed. | $10–$35, $45 for Sun. brunch | AE, D, DC, MC, V.

Landry's Seafood House. Seafood. Also in the main Disney area is this warehouse-turned-restaurant. There are plenty of fresh catches of the day like the Pontchartrain broiled with Cajun spices, served with a creamy white-wine sauce and topped with lump crab meat. For fun, try the seafood-stuffed jalapeños or the grilled seafood platter to sample everything, and finish with flaming bananas Foster. | 8800 Vineland Ave. (Rte. 535) | 407/827–6466 | fax 407/827–6467 | $15–$20 | AE, D, DC, MC, V.

Pebbles. Contemporary. Part of a small California cuisine chain in southern Florida, these trendy restaurants have caught the attention of clients with their light and tasty food. Mediterranean salmon, herb-crusted baked chicken, smoked duck served over angel-hair pasta, burgers, and a variety of homemade desserts such as chocolate black-out cake or white chocolate mousse are examples of ways to be wooed by Pebbles. See their website at www.pebbleworldwide.com. | Crossroads of Lake Buena Vista | 407/827–1111 | fax 407/827–1070 | $10–$19 | AE, D, DC, MC, V.

Lodging

Blue Tree Resort at Lake Buena Vista. This complex of two-story peach town house–style condos set on 16 acres ½-mi from Walt Disney World has one- and two-bedroom suites that sleep six to eight. Each has a full kitchen and washer and dryer. The pool courtyard has a kids' pool and a barbecue area. Walk to restaurants and shopping in Downtown Disney. Free Disney shuttle. In-room data ports, microwaves, refrigerators. Cable TV, in-room VCRs (and movies). 4 pools, wading pool. Hot tub. Miniature golf, 2 tennis courts. Gym, basketball, volleyball. Video games. Playground. Laundry service. Business services. | 12007 Cypress Run Rd. | 407/238–6000 or 800/688–8733 | fax 407/239–0680 | www.bluetreeresort.com | 390 units | $119–$239 | AE, D, MC, V.

Bryan's Spanish Cove. All units in this two-story, red-tile roofed complex 1 mi from Walt Disney World have kitchens, a patio or balcony, and two bedrooms that sleep up to seven. Housekeeping units have washers and dryers and fireplaces. Bright and roomy units have yellow and mauve color schemes and plaid sofas. A waterfront recreation area has a barbecue and picnic tables. Recreation includes boating, canoeing, fishing, paddleboats, and horseshoes. Cribs and rollaways also available. In-room safes, kitchenettes, microwaves. In-room VCRs (and movies). Pool. Hot tub. Dock, water sports. Playground. Video games. Laundry service. | 13875 Rte. 535 | 407/239–4222 | fax 407/239–1886 | 44 units | $114–$179 | AE, D, MC, V.

Caribe Royale Resort Suites and Villas. Waterfalls and palm trees highlight this huge pink 10-story hotel that's popular with conferences. The two-room suites can sleep up to six and have a living room with a pullout double-bed sofa and a bedroom with two queen-size beds. A larger deluxe king suite has a king-size bed and a whirlpool spa tub. Suites are painted in neutral yellows, blues, and pinks. Villas have two-bedroom suites that sleep up to eight and have a kitchen, living room, and private balcony. The pool has a 65-ft water slide. Free Disney shuttle. 3 restaurants, complimentary breakfast, room service. In-room data ports, in-room safes, minibars, microwaves, refrigerators, in-room hot tubs. Cable TV, in-room VCRs. Pool, wading pool. 2 tennis courts. Gym. Video games. Playground. Laundry facilities, laundry service. Business services. | 8101 World Center Dr. | 407/238–8400 or 800/823–8300 | fax 407/238–8088 | www.cariberoyale.com | 1,218 suites, 120 villas, 3 buildings | $169–$189 suites, $269 villas | AE, D, MC, V.

Comfort Inn at Lake Buena Vista. This five-story white hotel on 23 acres less than 1 mi from Walt Disney World has a large, shady pool area. Rooms have two double beds, blue carpet, and blue floral bedding. Family suites sleep up to five and have bunk beds for kids and a queen-size bed for the adults. I–4 exit 27. Restaurant, bar. In-room safes, some microwaves, some refrigerators. Cable TV. 2 pools. Video games. Laundry facilities. Business services. Pets allowed (fee). | 8442 Palm Pkwy. | 407/239–7300 or 800/999–7300 | fax 407/239–7740 | www.comfortinnorlando.com | 640 rooms | $85–$110 | AE, D, MC, V.

Country Inn and Suites by Carlson. This five-story hotel with a yellow exterior and green roof is ½-mi from Walt Disney World. The lobby has plaid furnishings and a fireplace. Rooms have two double beds, blue carpet, and floral blue and pink bedding. Suites have a sofa and chair. Kid suites have bunk beds and VCR. Free Disney shuttle. I–4 exit 27. Complimentary Continental breakfast. In-room data ports, refrigerators, microwaves, some in-room hot tubs. Cable TV. Gym. Video games. Laundry service. Business services. | 12191 S. Apopka-Vineland Rd. | 407/239–1115 or 800/456–4000 | fax 407/239–8882 | www.countryinns.com | 120 rooms, 50 suites | $69–$79, $79–$89 suites | AE, D, MC, V.

Courtyard by Marriott at Vista Centre. This three-story hotel is 1 mi from Walt Disney World and within walking distance of Crossroads Shopping Center. The one-bedroom suites have yellow and peach tones with two double beds, blue carpet, and balconies. I–4 exit 27. Free Disney shuttle. Restaurant, bar, room service. Cable TV. 2 pools, wading pool. Hot tub. Gym. Video games. Playground. Laundry facilities. Business services. | 8501 Palm Pkwy. | 407/239–6900 or 888/236–2427 | fax 407/239–1287 | 222 rooms, 86 suites | $110–$130, $150–$180 suites | AE, D, MC, V.

Days Inn Lake Buena Vista Village. This eight-story brick motel is near International Drive and SeaWorld, 3 mi from Walt Disney World. Rooms are pink and blue and have large windows. Standard rooms sleep four. Connecting rooms and rollaway beds available. Free Disney shuttle. I–4 exit 27. Restaurant, bar. Microwaves, refrigerators. Cable TV, in-room VCRs (and movies). Pool, wading pool. Video games. Playground. Laundry facilities. Business services. Pets allowed. | 12490 Apopka-Vineland Rd. | 407/239–4646 or 800/521–3297 | fax 407/239–8469 | 203 rooms | $49–$125 | AE, D, MC, V.

Embassy Suites Resort, Lake Buena Vista. Each suite in this five-story all-suites hotel with an atrium courtyard is done in cream and pink hues and has a living room and a dining table. It's 1 mi from Walt Disney World. I–4 exit 27. Restaurant, bar, complimentary breakfast. In-room data ports, minibars, microwaves, refrigerators. Cable TV, in-room VCRs (and movies). Indoor-outdoor pool. Hot tub. Driving range, putting green, tennis. Gym. Video games. Children's programs (ages 4–12), playground. Laundry facilities. Business services. | 8100 Lake Ave. | 407/239–1144 or 800/362–2779 (reservations) | fax 407/238–0230 | www.embassy-suites.com | 330 suites | $48–$88 | AE, MC, V.

Holiday Inn SunSpree Resort. Kids have their own check-in area where they get a goodie bag upon arrival at this six-story hotel 1 mi from Walt Disney World. They also have their own dining area where they can eat with other kids and watch cartoons and movies. Camp Holiday has a free child-care center with magic shows, clowns, and arts and crafts. Half of the guest units include themed kid suites that sleep three or four kids, and have a semi-private divider wall, color TV, VCR, CD player, and Nintendo. The adult side has one or two queen-size beds and a kitchenette. Rooms have green carpet and blue and pink floral bedding. I–4 exit 27. Restaurant, bar, room service. In-room data ports, minibars, kitchenettes, microwaves, refrigerators. Cable TV, in-room VCRs (and movies). Pool, wading pool. Hot tub. Gym. Video games. Children's programs (ages 3–12). Laundry facilities. Business services. Some pets allowed. | 13351 Rte. 535 | 407/239–4500 or 800/465–4329 | fax 407/239–7713 | www.kidsuites.com | 507 rooms | $89–$173 | AE, D, MC, V.

Hotel Royal Plaza. Rooms are large in this pink tower hotel that's been serving Downtown Disney for more than 25 years. Everything here is pink. Rooms are furnished with light oak pieces. Free Disney shuttle. I–4 exit 27. 2 restaurants, 2 bars. Minibars. Cable TV, in-room VCRs (and movies). Pool. Hot tub. 4 tennis courts. Gym. Laundry facilities. Business services. | 1905 Hotel Plaza Blvd. | 407/828–2828 or 800/248–7890 | fax 407/827–6338 | www.royalplaza.com | 394 rooms | $109–$229 | AE, D, MC, V.

Hyatt Regency Grand Cypress Resort. This 1,500-acre resort has an 18-hole golf course, a golf school, a 45-acre nature preserve, and a pool with a 45-ft water slide. Villas have one-to four-bedroom suites with a kitchen. I–4 exit 27. 5 restaurants, 4 bars (with entertainment), room service. In-room data ports, minibars, microwaves, refrigerators. Cable TV, in-room VCRs (and movies). 2 pools. Hot tubs, massage. Driving range, 2 18-hole golf courses, putting green, 12 tennis courts. Hiking, horseback riding. Boating, bicycles. Baby-sitting, children's programs (ages 4–12). Laundry facilities, laundry service. Business services. | 1 Grand Cypress Blvd. | 407/239–4700 or 800/835–7377 | fax 407/239–7219 | www.grandcypress.com | 750 rooms | $220–$425 | AE, D, MC, V.

Orlando World Center Marriott. This 27-story resort hotel is set on 230 acres of gardens and lakes 2 mi from Walt Disney World. Rooms are done in soft hues and have bamboo furniture and balconies. They sleep up to five. Free Disney shuttle. 6 restaurants, room service. In-room data ports, in-room safes, minibars, refrigerators. 5 pools. Beauty salon, hot tub, massage, sauna. Driving range, 18-hole golf course, miniature golf, 2 tennis courts. Gym, volleyball. Baby-sitting, playground. Laundry facilities, laundry service. Business services. | 8701 World Center Dr. | 407/239–4200 or 888/236–2427 | fax 407/238–8777 | www.marriott.com | 1,503 rooms, 487 suites | $224–$269 room, $265–$2,400 suites | AE, D, DC, MC, V.

PerriHouse B&B Inn. Set on a 16-acre bird sanctuary with paths and a pond, this place is a bird-lover's paradise. Each unit has a private entrance. Some cottages have fireplaces, hot tubs, and king-size canopy beds. It's 3 mi from Walt Disney World. Complimentary Continental breakfast. Pool. Hot tub. Laundry service. | 10417 Centurion Ct. | 407/876–4830 or 800/780–4830 | fax 407/876–0241 | www.perrihouse.com | 8 rooms, 1 cottage | $99–$139, $225–$499 cottages | AE, D, MC, V.

Radisson Inn Lake Buena Vista. Each room in this six-floor hotel has two double beds, blue-gray carpet, pink floral bedding, light wood furnishings, and a patio or balcony. The pool has a 50-ft water slide. It's 1 mi from Walt Disney World. Free Disney shuttle. I–4 exit 27. Restaurant, bar. In-room data ports, minibars. Pool. Spa. Video games. Playground. Laundry facilities. | 8686 Palm Pkwy. | 407/239–8400 or 800/333–3333 | fax 407/239–8025 | www.radisson.com | 200 rooms | $99–$159 | AE, D, MC, V.

Residence Inn by Marriott, Lake Buena Vista. All of the one-and two-bedroom apartments in this hotel on 50 wooded acres 1 mi from Walt Disney World have a kitchen; some have washers and dryers. Suites sleep six and have large living rooms and country furnishings. Guests have privileges at the Orlando World Center Marriott. Free Disney shuttle. I–4 exit 27. Complimentary breakfast. In-room data ports, in-room safes, kitchenettes. Cable TV, in-room VCRs (and movies). Pool. Hot tub. Tennis courts. Basketball, volleyball. Video games.

Laundry facilities. Business services. Pets allowed. | 8800 Meadow Creek Dr. | 407/239–7700 or 888/236–2427 | fax 407/239–7605 | 688 apartments | $199–$239 | AE, D, MC, V.

Riu Orlando Hotel. This six-story brown brick hotel 1 mi from Walt Disney World overlooks a lake. It's across the street from Downtown Disney. Rooms are done in yellow, blue, and green and have sofas and big-screen TVs with Nintendo. Free Disney shuttle. Restaurant, bar, room service. In-room data ports, in-room safes, microwaves, refrigerators. Cable TV, in-room VCRs. Pool. Hot tub. Gym. Video games. Baby-sitting. Laundry facilities. Business services. | 8688 Palm Pkwy. | 407/239–8500 or 888/222–9963 | fax 407/239–8591 | www.riuhotels.com | 167 rooms | $80–$175 | AE, D, DC, MC, V.

Sheraton Safari Hotel. Jump into a different sort of environment that pumps out African music and is a very convincing portrayal of jungle living with tribal masks lining the bamboo walls and dense greenery, but at the same time you are safely and attentively cared for in your more tame rooms. The Casa Blanca restaurant offers finer dining throughout the day while the Outpost deli and Zanzibar provide quicker meals to enjoy on the way to the nearby Disney attractions or poolside when you get a chance to relax. Kids can slide through the giant snake-shape waterslide. Free shuttle to tourist parks. 3 Restaurants. In-room data ports, in-room safes, VCRs. Pool, wading pool. Outdoor hot tub. Gym. Video games. Baby-sitting. | 12205 Apopka–Vineland Rd., Orlando | 407/239–0444 or 800/423–3297 | fax 407/239–1778 | www.sheratonsafari.com | 496 rooms, 96 suites | $89–$259 | AE, D, DC, MC, V.

Summerfield Suites. One-bedroom suites sleep four and two-bedroom suites sleep eight at this three-story, all-suites complex 1 mi from Walt Disney World. Each suite has a kitchen and a living room. Rooms are done in bright hues of yellow, blue, and pink. Free Disney shuttle. I–4 exit 27. Restaurant, complimentary Continental breakfast. In-room data ports, in-room safes, kitchenettes, microwaves, refrigerators. Cable TV, in-room VCRs (and movies). Pool, wading pool. Hot tub. Gym. Video games. Laundry service. | 8751 Suiteside Dr. | 407/238–0777 or 800/830–4964 | fax 407/238–2640 | www.summerfield-orlando.com | 150 suites | $179–$319 | AE, D, MC, V.

Vistana Resort. Tennis is the draw at this resort with clay and all-weather courts. Villas and town houses are spread over 95-acres across the street from Downtown Disney. Each two-bedroom unit has a living room, kitchen, and washer and dryer. I–4 exit 27. 2 restaurants. Kitchenettes. Cable TV, in-room VCRs (and movies). 7 pools, wading pool. Hot tub, massage. Miniature golf, 13 tennis courts. Basketball, gym. Water sports, bicycles. Video games. Children's programs (ages 3–12), playground. | 8800 Vistana Center Dr. | 407/239–3100 or 800/877–8787 | fax 407/239–3062 | 1,539 units | $242–$350 | AE, D, MC, V.

LAKE CITY

MAP 3, H2

(Nearby towns also listed: Live Oak, Starke, White Springs)

This friendly and relaxed northern Florida town of 10,000 is quickly becoming a major tourist destination because of its location near the crossroads for I–75, I–10, and Highways 41 and 441. Almost midway between Tallahassee and Jacksonville, it makes a good stopping-point; its modern restaurants, good shopping, and proximity to Osceola National Forest are big draws, too.

Information: **Columbia County Tourist Development Council** | Box 1847, Lake City, 32056-1847 | 904/758–1366 | www.springs-r-us.org.

Attractions
Florida Sports Hall of Fame and Museum. View more than 40 exhibits and individual displays of each of the inducted players. A 50-seat theater runs sporting programs daily. | Hall of Fame Dr., U.S. 90 and I–95 | 904/758–1312 | Adults $3 | Mon., Thurs.–Sat. 9–4.

Osceola National Forest. When completed, the Florida Trail will run the length of Florida. Some 23 mi of the Florida Trail run through this flat 200,000-acre pine and oak forest named after the Seminole leader. There's more hiking on a shorter, scenic trail at the south end near the 1,800-acre Ocean Pond, and a boardwalk along parts of the Florida Trail and the swamp areas of Pinhook and Big Gum. Camping is available near the lake and can be accessed from U.S. 90, outside Olustee, 1 mi past the convenience store. The forest is 12 mi east of Lake City. There is a picnic and barbecue area in the south end near the beach. | Headquarters at U.S. 90, Olustee | 904/752–2577 or 904/942–9300 | Free; parking $2, camping $8 | Daily.

Olustee Battlefield State Historic Site. This park honors the memory of the 1,861 Union soldiers and 946 Confederates who died here on February 20, 1864—more than in any other Civil War battle in Florida. A re-enactment takes place in February, and exhibits in the interpretive center explain what happened. The battlefield is on U.S. 90, 15 mi east of Lake City. From I-10, take exit 45 to U.S. 90, then west 5 mi. | Box 40, Olustee | 904/758–0400 | Free | Daily 8–5.

Stephen Foster State Folk Culture Center. This 247-acre center on the banks of the famous Suwannee River is dedicated to the perpetuation of crafts, music, and legends of early and contemporary Floridians. Exhibits include dioramas that depict scenes described in Foster's most famous songs. Guided tours are available. | 17 mi north of Lake City in White Springs | 904/397–1920 | $3.25 | 7 AM–6:30 PM.

ON THE CALENDAR

FEB.: *Olustee Battle Festival.* This is the nation's second-largest Civil War battle reenactment, after the one in Gettysburg, Pennsylvania. | 904/752–3610.

OCT.: *Alligator Festival.* This event at a Seminole village takes you back to Lake City's inception, almost 200 years ago, when the chief of the village was Chief Alligator. Seminoles roamed the valleys and hills surrounding the village known as Alligator Town. The festival includes demonstrations of Native American life with dance, music, storytelling, and animal shows involving alligators and Florida panthers. | 904/719–9887.

Dining

El Potro. Mexican. American-style Mexican food is served at this casual restaurant in a strip mall. Tacos, enchiladas, burritos, fajitas, and chimichangas are the favorites. The full bar has margarita specials. Kids' menu. | 4290 U.S. 90W | 904/758–3100 | Reservations not accepted | $6–$11 | AE, MC, V.

Lodging

Best Western Inn. This two-story chain property is built around a pond liberally landscaped with palms. At the junction of I-75 and U.S. 90, exit 82. Complimentary Continental breakfast. Some refrigerators. Pool. Hot tub. Playground. Laundry facilities. | 4720 U.S. 90W | 904/752–3801 | fax 904/755–4846 | www.bestwestern.com | 80 rooms | $45–$63 | AE, D, DC, MC, V.

Lake City Knights Inn. This two-story motel is 1 mi from the Florida Sports Hall of Fame and local shopping. Fishing and area springs are nearby. Continental breakfast, picnic area. Cable TV. Pool. Putting green. Business services, free parking. Pets allowed. | Rte. 13, Box 201, | 904/752–7720 or 800/418–8977 | fax 904/752–7720 | www.knightsinn.com | 100 rooms, 3 suites | $40–$70 | AE, D, DC, MC, V.

LAKELAND

MAP 3, 16

(Nearby towns also listed: Bartow, Winter Haven, Zephyrhills)

Lakeland is a busy little city of about 79,000 in central Florida's Polk County. Surrounded by 600 lakes, rivers, and phosphate pits, whose mineral-rich waters attract the black bass, Lakeland is a prime destination for bass fishermen. Lakeland has a strong economy, buttressed by the county's six colleges, including the largest, Florida Southern University. The Lakeland Center Arena is also the training center for the Tampa Bay Lightning. The downtown area is well maintained and restored and features an antiques district perfect for browsing.

Information: **Lakeland Chamber of Commerce** | 35 Lake Morton Dr., Box 3607, Lakeland, 33802-3607 | 863/688–8551 | www.chamber.lakeland.net.

Attractions

Florida Southern College. Founded in 1885 by the United Methodist Church, this is one of the oldest private colleges in Florida. The campus is home to the largest collection of Frank Lloyd Wright buildings in the world—a dozen structures in all, revealing the styles in Wright's prolific body of work. Danforth Chapel, and next to it, the geometric, wrought-iron-topped Annie Pfeiffer Chapel, are noteworthy. | 111 Lake Hollingsworth Dr. | 863/680–4111 | www.flsouthern.edu | Free | Daily.

Polk Museum of Art. This museum has nine galleries, including an outdoor sculpture garden. The permanent collection focuses on pre-Columbian, contemporary American, and Asian art. One gallery exhibits the work of area students. | 800 E. Palmetto St. | 863/688–7743 | www.polkmuseumofart.org/ | Free | Mon. and Sat. 10–5, Tues.–Fri. 9–5, Sun. 1–5.

ON THE CALENDAR

FEB.: *Polk Museum Gala.* Annual black-tie fundraising event considered the county's most elegant party. The affair, boasting gourmet food and dancing, is held the last Saturday in February. | 863/688–7743.

MAR., APR.: *Spring Training.* The Detroit Tigers have trained in Lakeland since 1934, and in Joker Merchant Stadium since 1966. The team's association with Lakeland is the longest-lasting relationship between a major league team and their current spring training home. | 863/688–7911 or 863/603–6278.

APR.: *Orange Cup Regatta.* Two days of hydroplane races. A tradition since 1937, more than 100 boats in different classes participate at Lake Hollingsworth. | 863/688–3009.

APR.: *Sun and Fun EAA Fly-In.* This annual weeklong aviation convention at Lakeland Linder Regional Airport includes air shows, forums, workshops, displays, commercial exhibits, air races, and other aviation events. Some 2,000 special aircraft are on display. | 863/644–2431.

MAY: *Mayfaire by the Lake.* Held every Mother's Day weekend on the shores of Lake Morton in downtown Lakeland, this outdoor festival includes an art tent for kids, a crafts fair showcasing the work of more than 150 local artists, and an evening street party. | 863/687–3788.

Dining

The Grill at Terrace Hotel. Contemporary. In the upscale hotel you will find this award-winning restaurant overlooking Lake Mirror sporting a variety of dishes ranging from crab cakes with crispy potato garnish to Cajun rubbed rack of lamb served with roasted red pepper mashed potatoes, a jalapeño grit cake, and a tortilla shell. | 329 E. Main St. | 863/603–5420 | fax 863/688–0664 | $15–$30 | AE, DC, MC, V.

Pan Ye's. Chinese. Paintings, sculpture, and artifacts lend an Asian theme to this restaurant. There is one large dining area with four booths and about 40 tables. The seafood fantasy is a mix of shrimp, scallops, and crab. Also on the menu is the steak Polynesian served with stir-fried mixed vegetables. A lunch buffet is served Tues.–Fri. and Sun. | 743 E. Memorial Blvd. | 863/686–2052 | Closed Mon. | $5–$11 | AE, DC, MC, V.

Red Barn Steak House. American. Literally housed in a red barn, the fourth-generational southern hospitality will smother you with some down home goodness in their casual atmosphere. The porterhouse steak is the house specialty and you can order anywhere from 2–4 lbs of it! Sharing is thankfully allowed or you can opt for some grilled pork chops (also on the large side), a seafood special, or something from the children's or seniors' menu. Wash your meal down with some homemade turtle pie or strawberry shortcake. | 6150 New Tampa Hwy. (also U.S. 92) | 863/686–2754 or 800/688–STEAK | fax 863/688–6161 | $10–$30 | AE, D, DC, MC, V.

Reececliff. American. This traditional diner offers homecooked short ribs and a million sides ranging from mashed potatoes and turnip greens, to corn pudding. Milk shakes and sundaes come on the large side. | 940 S. Florida Ave. | 863/686–6661 | Closed Sun. | $7–$10 | AE, D, MC, V.

The Sago Grill. Contemporary. Owner Larry Ross describes his menu as Floribbean. The blackened Cancun chicken with melted jack and cheddar cheeses and roasted peppers gets to the heart of it. The Chilean lobster with Asiago cream sauce is an equally good choice. The Barbados Cajun gumbo or New Zealand green lip mussels are perfect for small appetites. | 2120 Harden Blvd. | 941/688–5522 | Reservations required at least two days in advance | $9–$17 | AE, D, DC, MC, V.

Lodging

Best Western Diplomat Inn. Rooms are bright at this two-story motel west of Lake Parker at the junction of U.S. 98 and I–4. It's near the antiques district (4 mi) and Florida Southern College (7 mi). The courtyard is landscaped with tropical plants. Live comedy club on weekends. Bar (with entertainment), complimentary breakfast. In-room data ports. Cable TV. Pool, wading pool. Laundry service. Free parking. | 3311 U.S. 98N | 863/688–7972 or 800/237–4699 | fax 863/688–8377 | www.bestwestern.com | 120 rooms | $79–$96 | AE, D, DC, MC, V.

Comfort Inn. This two-story motel is opposite Lake Parker on the town's main thoroughfare. The Detroit Tigers' winter home is nearby. Complimentary Continental breakfast. Some refrigerators. Cable TV, in-room VCRs (and movies) available. Pool. | 1817 E. Memorial Blvd. | 863/688–9221 | fax 863/687–4797 | www.comfortinns.com | 64 rooms | $54–$72 | AE, D, DC, MC, V.

Holiday Inn, South. This two-story hotel is in a corporate district, 2 mi south of Florida Southern College and the Sun N Fun Museum. Minisuites and poolside rooms are available. Restaurant, bar (with entertainment), complimentary Continental breakfast, room service. In-room data ports. Some microwaves, some refrigerators. Cable TV, some in-room VCRs. Pool. Hot tub. Gym. Laundry service. Business services. | 3405 S. Florida Ave. | 863/646–5731 or 800/833–4902 | fax 863/646–5215 | 172 rooms | $69–$86 | AE, D, DC, MC, V.

The Terrace Hotel. Originally opened in 1924, the facilities were restored in 1999 to boost the service and luxury. Mainly aimed at satisfying a traveling business-person, the hotel provides work desks and room service at a convenient ½ mi from the convention center. Families are welcome, too, and the hotel sits on Lake Mirror and is along a 200-mi chain of lakes, excellent for riding bikes around. Restaurant. In-room data ports, in-room safes. Cable TV, in-room VCRs. Gym. Laundry service. | 329 E. Main St. | 863/688–0800 | fax 863/688–0664 | www.terracehotel.com | 73 rooms, 15 suites | $119–$169 | AE, DC, MC, V.

Wellesley Inn and Suites. This six-story hotel is near the Lakeland Square Mall and restaurants. Standard rooms have a king-size or two double beds. Complimentary Continental breakfast. Some microwaves, refrigerators (in suites). Cable TV. Pool. Laundry facilities. Business services. Pets allowed (fee). | 3520 U.S. 98N | 863/859–3399 | fax 863/859–3483 | 106 rooms, 24 suites | $82–$92 | AE, D, DC, MC, V.

LAKE PLACID

MAP 3, J7

(Nearby towns also listed: Arcadia, Okeechobee, Sebring)

This area northeast of Lake Okeechobee was originally part of the territory set aside for the Seminole Indian Nation back in 1842. It was incorporated in 1928 and named

Lake Placid after New York's resort of the same name. Dr. Melvin Dewey spearheaded an effort to create a resort area here, which in its heyday attracted a sophisticated lot. The Depression squelched the visions of grandeur, however. The town managed to get some Depression-era public works projects underway, and those can be seen today. The town is surrounded by 27 freshwater lakes perfect for fishing and swimming and plenty of recreational facilities for golf and tennis. Agriculture is the major industry in the area, with citrus and cattle leading the way. Today the town of Lake Placid has a population of 1,427.

Information: Greater Lake Placid Chamber of Commerce | 18 N. Oak St., Box 187, Lake Placid, 33852 | 863/465–4331 or 800/557–5224 | www.lpfla.com.

Attractions

Cypress Knee Museum. Cypress knees, bulbous formations grown from the cypress tree root, resemble anything from animals to Groucho Marx. To see these oddly shaped natural sculptures, stop by this museum 25 mi south of Lake Placid. These unusual tree growths have been featured on the TV and at Ripley's Believe It Or Not! museum. There are also Seminole artifacts, vintage wood-carvings, and a $\frac{1}{2}$-mi walkway over a cypress swamp. | 6870 N. U.S. 27 at Rtes. 27 and 29, Palmdale | 863/675–0128 | Donations accepted | Daily 8–6.

Historical Society Museum. Dedicated to homesteaders who first settled the area in the 1890s, the Historical Society Museum is housed in a turn-of-the-20th-century railroad depot. The original Lake Placid jailhouse is on display, along with a Linotype printing press used to print the first local newspaper, an operator switchboard, and a replica of an early 1900s home. | 19 Park Ave. W | 863/465–1771 or 863/465–3712 | Donations accepted | Mon.–Sat. 1– 3:30 or by appointment; June–Aug. by appointment.

ON THE CALENDAR

AUG.: *Caladium Festival.* Artists and craftsmen display their work, and a large selection of hand-crafted arts and crafts are for sale. It also houses an essay contest, an antique car show, a floral competition, and a family county dance. | 800/557–5224.

Dining

The Tower. American. You can sit in one of their three dining rooms and enjoy the casual elegance of traditional homemade food. Crunchy grouper and shrimp or meatloaf with mashed potatoes are popular entrées which come with a cup of the soup of the day and a cornbread muffin. From 3 to 6 PM they offer an earlybird menu. | 461 U.S. 27N | 863/699– 9996 | Closed Sun. | $7–$12 | AE, MC, V.

Lodging

Ramada Inn Lake Placid Conference. This motel has a poolside tiki bar and grill, and an 18-hole golf course. The area's freshwater lakes are ideal for water-skiing, boating, and sailing. Bar, restaurant. Cable TV. Pool. Golf, tennis. Dock, fishing. Pets allowed. | 2165 U.S. 27S | 941/465– 3133 | fax 941/465–3354 | www.ramada.com | 100 rooms | $60–$140 | AE, D, DC, MC, V.

LAKE WALES

MAP 3, J6

(Nearby towns also listed: Bartow, Haines City, Sebring, Winter Haven)

In the heart of citrus country, this town of 10,000, directly east of Tampa and south and east of Orlando, is perched on a ridge and has the highest elevation in Florida, a whopping 295 ft. Surrounded by lakes and rolling hills, the town boasts of a relatively mild climate with low humidity. A major attraction is the 157-acre Bok Tower Gardens, anchored by a 200-ft carillon known as the Singing Tower, whose bells chime every half-hour. Lake Wales is primarily an agricultural town; on the outskirts you can get a whiff of oranges from the nearby groves.

Information: Lake Wales Area Chamber of Commerce | 340 W. Central Ave., Box 191, Lake Wales, 33859-0191 | 863/676–3445 | www.lakewaleschamber.com.

Attractions

Babson Park Audubon Center. This nature center, 7 mi south of Lake Wales in the Lake Wales Ridge ecosystem, has one of the most diverse plant colonies in the Northern Hemisphere. Walking tours and special programs are available. | 200 N. Crooked Lake Dr. | 941/638–1355 | Free | Grounds daily; museum Sept.–Apr., Tues.–Sat. 10–2.

Bok Tower Gardens. This 157-acre National Historic Landmark is 3 mi north of Lake Wales, atop 298-ft Iron Mountain, one of the highest points in Florida. The Bok Tower is made of pink and gray marble and stone with carvings and rises 205 ft. There is a 57-bell carillon on which recitals are performed daily. Thousands of plants flourish here, including 20 to 30 endangered species. More than 100 bird species and endangered animals reside here including the gopher tortoise and eastern indigo snake. There are gardening and craft workshops and lecture programs in the education and visitors center, plus guided nature walks. | 1151 Tower Blvd. | 863/676–1408 | fax 863/676–6770 | www.boktower.org | $6 | Daily 8–5.

Depot Museum. This museum in a railroad passenger station built in 1928 has become a center for the collection, conservation, exhibition, and study of materials pertaining to the history of Lake Wales. It houses a 1916 train car, a 1926 caboose, and other train artifacts. | 325 S. Scenic Hwy. | 863/678–4209 | fax 863/678–4180 | Free | Weekdays 9–5, Sat. 10–4.

Lake Kissimmee State Park. This 5,930-acre state park, 15 mi east of Lake Wales off Rte. 60, has fishing, bird watching, picnicking, and camping. The park is bordered by Lakes Kissimmee, Tiger, and Rosalie. There are boating on Lake Kissimmee and hiking on more than 15 mi of trails. Camping at 60 sites. | 14248 Camp Mack Rd. | 863/696–1112 | $3.25 per vehicle | Daily.

Kissimmee Cow Camp. This part of the park, 3½ mi from the entrance to Lake Kissimmee State Park, re-creates a Florida frontier cow camp in 1876. Cattlemen demonstrate cattle roundups, then share coffee and talk about their lives. The descendants of the original cows and horses brought to America by the Spanish in the early 1500s live here. | 14248 Camp Mack Rd. | 863/696–1112 | Weekends 9:30–4:30.

ON THE CALENDAR

OCT.: *Pinewood Estate Tours* Guides take you on a tour through a lavish 20-room mansion where 1930s furnishings give a bygone-era peek into the upscale lifestyle of America's rich and famous. Considered one of the finest examples of Mediterranean Revival–style architecture in the state. | 863/676–1408.

Dining

Boka-Vin Restaurant. Contemporary. This gourmet bistro-style eatery has frosted glass art panels, dark-wood private booths, and table seating under skylights. Favorites include the smoked salmon bruschetta appetizer and the honey Mandarin glazed chicken. | 253 E. Stuart St. | 863/678–3663 | Open for lunch Mon.–Sat. 11–2, dinner Tue.–Sat. 6–9. No breakfast | $15–$29 | AE, D, DC, MC, V.

Chalet Suzanne. American. Each of the five dining rooms in this restaurant has its own unique view of the inn's lake, where you can watch turtles and ibis. The rooms are filled with antiques, stained-glass windows, and old lamps. All meals are prix fixe, with six courses served on fine European china. Choose from 10 different entrées including lobster, crab, lamb chops, and filet mignon. Their signature soups are labeled and sold at the gift shop. Breakfast is served. | 3800 Chalet Suzanne Dr. | 863/676–6011. | $49–$79 prix–fixe | AE, D, DC, MC, V.

Vinton's New Orleans Restaurant. Cajun. This restaurant in an old arcade is a little bit of New Orleans in central Florida. Shrimp jambalaya and filet mignon are among the house specialties. Live music on Friday and Saturday. Wine cellar. | 229 E. Stuart Ave. | 863/676–8242 | Closed Sun., Mon. No lunch | $19–$23 | AE, MC, V.

Lodging

Chalet Suzanne. Switzerland meets Florida at this resort on 100 acres, resplendent with fountains, courtyards, balconies, and landscaped grounds. It's on the National Register of Historic Places and has been serving guests since 1931. The autograph garden is lined with ceramic tiles autographed by celebrities. The rooms are furnished with a mix of Scandinavian and Mediterranean antiques. There is a private lighted airstrip that can be used by guests and a restaurant with an extensive wine list. It's 6 mi north of Lake Wales. Restaurant, bar, complimentary breakfast. Cable TV. Pool, lake. Hot tub. Laundry facilities. Business services. | 3800 Chalet Suzanne Dr. | 863/676–6011 or 800/433–6011 | fax 863/676–1814 | www.chaletsuzanne.com | 26 rooms, 4 suites | $169–$229 | AE, D, DC, MC, V.

The G.V. Tillman House B&B. Across the street from Crystal Lake and around the corner from Lake Wales, this B&B offers two suites and three rooms with feather beds and lake views. A full home-cooked breakfast is served each morning and afternoon tea is served on the veranda or in the parlor. | 301 East Sessoms Ave. | 863/676–5499 or 800/488–3315 | www.tillmanbb.com | 5 rooms | $90 | AE, MC, V.

Noah's Ark B&B Inn. One of the oldest buildings in the city, this inn was formerly a speakeasy during Prohibition. The house is now furnished with 19th-century antiques, along with the owner's collection of Noah's Ark memorabilia from across the globe. There are several common areas, including a sitting room, drawing room, and terrace. Cable TV, complimentary breakfast. | 312 Ridge Manor Dr. | 800/346–1613 or 941/676–1613 | 10 rooms | $85–$100 | AE, D, DC, MC, V.

River Ranch. Activities at this dude ranch along the Kissimmee River on 1,500 wooded acres include cookouts, hay rides, rodeos, line dancing, horseshoes, and badminton. Some rooms have fireplaces and private patios. Bar, dining room, picnic area. Some kitchenettes, microwaves. Cable TV. 4 pools. Beauty salon. Driving range, 9-hole golf course, putting green, tennis court. Gym. Fishing, bicycles. Library. Laundry facilities. | 24700 Rte. 60 E, 25 mi east of Lake Wales | 863/692–1321 | fax 863/692–1303 | 340 rooms, 30 cottages | $100–$144, $156–$244 cottages | AE, MC, V.

LAKE WORTH

MAP 3, L8

(Nearby towns also listed: Boynton Beach, Delray Beach, Lantana, Palm Beach, West Palm Beach)

At the turn of the 20th century, the town of Lake Worth was named Jewel, and it's easy to see why, with beautiful beaches and perfect weather. Originally an area given to ex-slaves at the end of the Civil War, this very cosmopolitan city of 30,000 residents, just south of the Palm Beaches, is best known today for its proximity to its ritzier neighbors to the north and relatively inexpensive accommodations. You'll find everything from beaches to sunbathe on to one of the longest fishing piers in South Florida. On shore, the downtown area is loaded with boutiques, art galleries, and charming restaurants; and there are several golf courses, a jai alai arena, and polo fields for the sports-minded. With an environment catering to both upstart economics and long-retired relaxees, Lake Worth has a slow feel with high-end tastes.

Information: Greater Lake Worth Chamber of Commerce | 811 Lucerne Ave., Lake Worth, 33460 | 561/582–4401 | www.lwchamber.com.

Attractions

Hibel Museum of Art. Features the Small Gems exhibit of works by artist Edna Hibel. | 701 Lake Ave. | 561/533–1583 | Free | Mon.–Fri. 10–5.

Lake Worth Municipal Park. Known as Casino Park as well, this local hang-out has a beach, Olympic-size swimming pool, fishing piers, picnic areas, restaurants, shuffleboard, and shops. | Rte. A1A at end of lake Worth Bridge | 561/533–7367 | Pool $2, parking 25¢ for 15 min | Daily 9–5.

ON THE CALENDAR

JAN.–APR.: *Polo.* Lake Worth has two polo clubs. The Gulfstream Polo Field, established in the 1920s, has one of the oldest polo clubs in the Palm Beach area. It's 8 mi west on Lake Worth Road. There are six polo fields; games are December through April on Friday and Sunday afternoons. The second field is Palm Beach Polo in Wellington, 12 mi west of Lake Wales. This club has 2,200 acres, 13 fields, 45 holes of golf, 24 tennis courts, an equestrian club, and luxury accommodations. Polo matches are held on Sunday afternoons. | 561/965–2057 Gulfstream Polo Field, 561/798–7110 Palm Beach Polo.

MAY: *Memorial Weekend Sidewalk Sale Extravaganza.* Downtown merchants hold a marketplace at the City Annex; shops in the area also offer up great bargains. | 561/582–4401.

SEPT.: *Tropical Triathlon.* This annual mini-triathlon held on Labor Day weekend begins Sunday at 7 AM. | 561/582–4401.

Dining

Acapulco Grill. Mexican. This quiet restaurant caters mostly to an older crowd. The dining room has wooden tables. Popular entrées include grilled red snapper, shrimp scampi, and Mexican steak. | 3985 Jog Rd., Lake Worth | 561/432–1864 | $8–$15 | AE, D, MC, V.

Bohemian Garden. Continental. The owner is the artist of the oil paintings of various portraits displayed at this casual restaurant near the Gulfstream Polo Field and the Palm Beach golf course. The menu includes beef, seafood, duck, veal, pork, chicken, lobster, oysters, clams, and fresh fish dishes. Outdoor dining is also available. Early dinners. Kids' menu. | 5450 Lake Worth Rd. | 561/968–4111 | No lunch | $7–$20 | AE, D, DC, MC, V.

John G's. American. You will generally find the restaurant packed and pumping breakfast and lunch food up until the closing hour of 3 PM. Fruit platters, sandwiches, burgers, and omelettes fill your bellies in this casual ocean-side setting. Breakfast is served until 11 AM. | 10 S. Ocean Blvd. | 561/585–9860 | fax 561/585–2001 | No dinner | $3–$15 | Cash only.

Pizza Carnival. Italian. Brooklyn-born owner Rose has built a menu around thin-crust pizza. Her white pizza is famous. Entrées at this tiny family-run business include pasta dishes such as rigatoni Alfredo with bacon and broccoli. | 11 N. H St. | 561/533–6607 | Closed Sun. | $10–$13 | AE, D, MC, V.

Lodging

Holiday Inn West Palm Beach Turnpike. Rooms in this hotel set on 6 acres have armoires, and many overlook the courtyard and pool. It's adjacent to a shopping center and 9 mi east of the Palm Beach airport. Exit 93 of the Florida Turnpike. Restaurant, bar, room service. In-room data ports, some refrigerators. Cable TV. Pool. Tennis. Laundry service. Business services. | 7859 Lake Worth Rd. | 561/968–5000 | fax 561/968–2451 or 800/325–8193 | 114 rooms | $99–$105 | AE, D, DC, MC, V.

The Mango Inn B&B. Rosemary plants flank doorways and beds have monogrammed linens. The owners have a flair for detail, from the coral stone fireplace to the four-poster beds in every room. The inn is two blocks from restaurants and antiques shops. Complimentary breakfast. Cable TV. Pool. No smoking. | 128 N. Lakeside Dr. | 561/533–6900 or 888/626–4619 | www.mangoinn.com | 8 rooms, one small house | $90–$165 rooms, $225 house | AE, MC, V.

New Sun Gate Motel. The Art Deco style runs through the theme rooms named for famous movie stars. Cary Grant, James Dean, and Rita Hayworth can put you in the mood for some downtown fun. For those in need of quiet time, the pool area is tropical and suitable for stars. Restaurant, complimentary Continental breakfast. Some refrigerators, some microwaves. Pool. Sauna. Laundry facilities. | 901 S. Federal Hwy. | 561/588–8110 or 800/315–9050 | fax 561/588–8041 | www.new-sungate.com | 32 rooms | $41–$79, weekly rates available as well | AE, MC, V.

Sabal Palm House. You will find this two-story historic house close to the Intracoastal Waterway, the beach, antiques shopping, and restaurants. The rooms have all been updated and designed with artistic themes based on different artists. The Dalí room is pristine and white with oak wood floors, while the Chagall and Renoir rooms are more floral and romantic. You'll feel the intimate service in the gourmet breakfast, the tea and sweets served midday, and the appetizers and drinks served in the European courtyard or parlor in the evening. Complimentary breakfast. Some in-room data ports, in-room safes. No TV, TV in common area. Laundry service. No kids under 14. No smoking. | 109 N. Golfview Rd. | 561/582–1090 | fax 561/582–0933 | www.sabalpalmhouse.com | 7 rooms | $100–$180 | AE, D, MC, V.

LANTANA

MAP 3, L8

(Nearby towns also listed: Boynton Beach, Lake Worth, Palm Beach)

Lantana, a small town of 9,000, has nice picnic areas and a few casual eating options on its own local beach. The town includes Hypoluxo Island on the Intracoastal Waterway, a largely upscale community of boat owners. Across the bridge from town is the barrier island where ritzy Palm Beach is located to the north. To the south is a giant resort in the neighborhood community of Manalapan.

Information: **Greater Lantana Chamber of Commerce** | 212 Iris St., Lantana, 33462 | 561/585–8664.

ON THE CALENDAR
MAY: *Lantana Fishing Derby.* This Chamber of Commerce–run charity fundraiser is a catch-size tournament the first Saturday in May. Cash prizes are awarded to the largest catches in three categories: kingfish, wahoo, and dolphin (mahimahi). A maximum of 100 boats can register to enter. | 561/585–8664.

Dining
Old Key Lime House. Seafood. This informal Old Florida seafood house overlooking the Intracoastal Waterway specializes in Baltimore-style jumbo long crab cakes and homemade Key lime pie. The open-air nautical-theme dining rooms resemble a patchwork of shed-like spaces. | 300 E. Ocean Ave. | 561/533–5220 | $13–$25 | AE, D, MC, V.

Anchor Inn Seafood Restaurant. Seafood. Just west of I–95, this casual, tin-roofed restaurant is a local favorite for seafood and steaks. The restaurant, which opened in 1974, is adorned with paintings of lobsters and fish; diners sit in wooden captain's chairs. Try the fillet of salmon glazed with a Chablis mustard dill. | 2810 Hypoluxo Rd. | 561/965–4794 | Closed two weeks after Labor Day | $10–$30 | AE, MC, V.

Lodging
Ritz-Carlton, Palm Beach. Embrace total beachfront luxury at this triple-towered landmark. A double-sided marble fireplace graces the lobby, and a miniature forest of palm trees graces the courtyard. All rooms have balconies; most have ocean views. While technically on the same island as Palm Beach (and thus the swanky name), the resort is actually in Manalapan, which is closer to and can be reached more easily from Lantana. 4 restaurants, 2 bars (with

entertainment), room service. In-room data ports, in-room safes, minibars. Cable TV, some in-room VCRs. Pool. Beauty salon, outdoor hot tub, sauna, spa, steam room. 5 tennis courts. Basketball, health club, volleyball. Beach, water sports, bicycles. Shops, video games. Baby-sitting, children's programs (ages 5–12). Laundry facilities, laundry service. Business services. | 100 S. Ocean Blvd., Manalapan | 561/533–6000 or 800/241–3333 | fax 561/588–4555 | www.ritzcarlton.com | 270 rooms | $295–$485 | AE, D, DC, MC, V.

Super 8 Motel. This is a no-frills budget lodging—except for the tropical sheets and curtains in the rooms—at the Hypoluxo exit of I–95. Complimentary Continental breakfast. Kitchenettes, microwaves, refrigerators. Cable TV. Pool. | 1255 Hypoluxo Rd. | 561/585–3970 | fax 561/586–3028 | www.super8.com | 125 rooms | $53–$69 | AE, D, DC, MC, V.

LAUDERDALE-BY-THE-SEA

(Nearby towns also listed: Deerfield Beach, Fort Lauderdale, Pompano Beach)

This little, low-rise family resort town of about 5,000 is considerably mellower than Fort Lauderdale, its neighbor to the south. For one thing, buildings here are kept under three stories by law. The lassitude of its hyphenated, stretched-out name is matched by lawn-divided El Mar Drive, lined with garden-style motels a block east of Route A1A. The town is only half a mile wide and 3 miles long, and many visitors choose to walk or rent a bike in town rather than drive. A slew of good shops and restaurants are near the beach and hotels.

Lauderdale-by-the-Sea, the self-styled "Shore Diving Capital of Florida," is home to the closest living reef in the continental United States. You can scuba dive directly from the beach—100 yards out is the first of three tiers of coral reefs.

Information: **Lauderdale-by-the-Sea Chamber of Commerce and Visitor Center** | 4201 Ocean Dr., Lauderdale-by-the-Sea, 33308 | 954/776–1000 or 800/699–6764 | www.lbts.com.

Attractions

Anglin's Fishing Pier. This pier, which juts out 875 ft into the Atlantic, is open for fishing 24 hours. If nothing's biting, try some of the popular restaurants clustered around the seafront plaza. | E. Commercial Blvd. | 954/491–9403 | $4; tackle rental $5 (with $10 deposit); bait averages $2 | 24 hours.

ON THE CALENDAR

MAY: *Ocean Fest.* This beachfront festival offers three days of scuba lessons, a shore dive treasure hunt, nightly beach parties, seminars, live music, and the latest innovations displayed and offered for sale by diving equipment manufacturers. | 800/327–8150.

Dining

Aruba Beach Café. Caribbean. A casual, lively pier choice, serving up big plates of burgers, sandwiches, fresh tropical salads, seafood, and Caribbean conch chowder. Live reggae bands perform Thurs.–Sat. nights, and Sunday afternoons. | 1 E. Commercial Blvd. | 954/776–0001 | $7–$22 | AE, D, DC, MC, V.

Blue Moon Fish Co. Seafood. Specialties at this elegant waterside restaurant include a sautéed veal scaloppine with artichoke hearts, wild mushrooms, spring onions, and lemon garlic butter. The large wine list includes 26 selections by the glass. Sit in the fancy interior dining rooms or outside beside the dock overlooking the Intracoastal Waterway. | 4405 West Tradewinds Ave. | 954/267–9888 | $19–$29 | AE, D, DC, MC, V.

LAUDERDALE-BY-
THE-SEA

INTRO
ATTRACTIONS
DINING
LODGING

Sea Watch. Seafood. You may have to wait in a line a bit to dine at this beachfront nautical-theme restaurant, which offers daily specials that might include char-broiled dolphin fillet (mahimahi) marinated with soy sauce, garlic, black pepper, and lemon juice. Early-bird specials are offered from 5–6 PM, mid-May through Christmas. | 6002 N. Ocean Blvd. (Hwy. A1A) | 954/781–2200 | $14–$30 | AE, D, DC, MC, V.

Lodging

Blue Seas Courtyard. Innkeepers Christie and Marc Furth have decorated Blue Seas with great care, evident in the Mexican wood furniture, clay tile roofs, brick pool and walkways, fountained gardens, and warm-colored and stenciled interiors. Two rows (100 ft) off the beach. In-room data ports, some kitchenettes, some microwaves, some refrigerators. Cable TV. Pool. | 4525 El Mar Dr. | 954/772–3336 | fax 954/772–6337 | www.blueseascourtyard.com | 12 units | $64–$105 | MC, V.

A Little Inn by the Sea. Innkeeper Uli Brandt and his family maintain this bed-and-breakfast style inn with relaxed class; fountains and classical music at breakfast ease your way the few feet it takes to walk from your door to the shore. Many rooms have private balconies with ocean views. Efficiencies have full kitchens, while apartments have one or two separate bedrooms. Complimentary Continental breakfast. In-room data ports, some kitchenettes, some refrigerators. Cable TV. Pool. Beach. | 4546 El Mar Dr. | 954/772–2450 or 800/492–0311 | www.alittleinn.com | 10 rooms, 12 efficiencies, 7 apartments | $109–$189 | AE, D, DC, MC, V.

Tropic Seas Resort Inn. Directly on the beach, Tropic Seas offers units that are plain but comfortable, with rattan furniture, cool tiled floors, and ceiling fans. Complimentary Continental breakfast. Some kitchenettes, some microwaves, some refrigerators. Cable TV. Pool. Laundry facilities. | 4616 El Mar Dr. | 954/772–2555 or 800/952–9581 | fax 954/771–5711 | www.tropicseasresort.com | 16 rooms, 6 efficiencies, 7 apartments | $140–$205 | AE, D, DC, MC, V.

Villas-by-the-Sea. Paths between the six buildings of this resort run beneath canopies of tropical trees. Efficiencies, one-, and two-bedroom units, as well as hotel rooms, are available, all directly on the beach. Many rooms have private balconies with views of the water. Restaurant, bar, picnic area, complimentary Continental breakfast, room service. Some kitchenettes, some microwaves, refrigerators. Cable TV. 5 pools. Hot tub. Gym. Beach, water sports. Children's programs (ages ages 2½ to 15). Laundry facilities. Business services. | 4456 El Mar Dr., Lauderdale-by-the-Sea | 954/772–3550 or 800/247–8963 | fax 954/772–3835 | 132 rooms | $135–$150 | AE, D, DC, MC, V.

LEESBURG

MAP 3, I5

(Nearby towns also listed: Ocala, Tavares)

This small town is in the heart of Central Florida's lake country. It was incorporated in 1875 and today has a population of 16,000. Its economy is based primarily on citrus and other agriculture, with plenty of opportunities for outdoor recreation such as fishing and boating.

Information: Leesburg Chamber of Commerce | Box 490309, Leesburg, 34749-0309 | 352/365–2051 | www.lake-county.org.

Attractions

Lake Griffin State Recreation Area. Lake Griffin, the 13,000-acre body of water for which this 425-acre park is named, yields good creels of largemouth bass. But the only access to the lakeshore beyond the boat ramp is by boat. The park also includes woodlands and a freshwater swamp. There is a short (¼-mi) walking trail, a shaded picnic area, and boat rentals ($3/hr or $15/day). A variety of wildlife can be seen in a natural setting. The park, which is 4 mi north of Leesburg, also has a 40-site campground. | 3089 U.S. 441/27, Fruitland Park, | 352/360–6760 | www.dep.state.fl.us/parks | $3.25 per vehicle; $8–$10 camping; electricity $2 per night | Daily 8–sundown.

Venetian Gardens. This 80-acre park has bridges, miniature islands, flower gardens, a boat ramp, a ball field, and a picnic area. People often rent out the gazebo for weddings and the adjacent marina offers boat rides on Lake Harris. The gardens are not clearly marked, but you can't miss them when you find the community center. | 109 E. Dixie | 352/728–9885 | Free | Daily.

ON THE CALENDAR
OCT.: *Bike Fest* is an annual antique and custom bike show. | 352/365–0053.

Dining
Vic's Embers Supper Club. Steak. This friendly restaurant has a formally attired staff. The dining room has lots of wood, white linen tablecloths over old tables, silverware, and chandeliers. Focus is on steaks and chops. Caesar salad and fettucine are prepared tableside. The Sunday brunch has 15 entrées. Kids' menu. Jazz trio Thur.–Sat. | 7940 U.S. 441 | 352/728–8989 | No lunch Mon.–Sat., Sun. brunch | $13–$22 | D, MC, V.

Lodging
Microtel Inn & Suites Leesburg. This three-story inn is a half-mile from restaurants and less than 10 mi from a golf course. It's within 20 mi of Ocala National Forest and Lake Ridge Winery, and 45 mi from Walt Disney World, Universal Studios, and SeaWorld. Continental breakfast. Cable TV. Pool. Business services. | 9700 U.S. 441 | 352/315–1234 or 888/771–7171 | fax 352/315–1027 | www.microtelinn.com | 63 rooms, 18 suites | $49–$65 | AE, D, DC, MC, V.

LIDO KEY

MAP 3, H7

(Nearby towns also listed: Bradenton, Longboat Key, Sarasota, Siesta Key)

It's not hard to imagine why John Ringling had plans to turn this island into a major tourist attraction. Easy access to the mainland and perfect weather continue to make it a popular destination. With an average temperature of 75°F and easy access to bustling Sarasota, this small island boasts high-class restaurants and excellent shopping. Beach fans are happy here, too—the north Lido beach is a half-mile long.

Information: Sarasota Convention and Visitors Bureau | 655 N. Tamiami Tr., Sarasota, 34236 | 941/957–1877 or 800/522–9799 | www.sarasotafl.org.

Attractions
Lido Beach. This Gulf of Mexico beach on Lido Key sports dramatic soft, white sand. To get there from downtown, follow Gulf Stream Avenue across the Ringling Causeway and straight through St. Armand's Circle. | 941/957–1877 or 800/522–9799 | Free | Daily.

Mote Marine Aquarium. You can see more than 200 varieties of fish and marine invertebrates in this aquarium complex between Longboat Key and St. Armands Key. A 135,000-gallon shark tank lets you see the menacing creatures from above and below the water. In the 30-ft touch tank, you can handle rays, guitar fish, horseshoe crabs, and sea urchins. There's also an eco-barge tour. | 1600 Ken Thompson Pkwy. | 941/388–4441 | www.mote.org | $10 | Daily 10–5.

ON THE CALENDAR

FEB.–APR.: *Water-ski shows.* Weekly water-ski shows are held every Sunday afternoon in the Ski-A-Rees Ski Show Stadium, adjacent to the Mote Marine Aquarium in City Island Park. | 941/388–1666.

Dining

Cafe L'Europe. Continental. On fashionable St. Armand's Circle, this café is filled with greenery and engaging artwork. The menu changes regularly, but you might be able to luck into the fillet of sole Picasso, Dover sole with a choice of fruits, or Wiener schnitzel sautéed in butter and topped with anchovies, olives, and capers. | 431 St. Armand's Cir. | 941/388–4415 | $19–$27 | AE, DC, MC, V.

Columbia. Spanish. This restaurant on St. Armand's Circle pays homage to its 95-yr-old forebear of the same name in Ybor City. The menu here is essentially the same as that of the original, offering you phenomenal Spanish and Cuban dishes such as paella and black-bean soup. The outdoor patio hosts nightly entertainment and dancing. | 411 St. Armand's Cir. | 941/388–3987 | $16–$24 | AE, D, DC, MC, V.

Lodging

Half Moon Beach Club. This bright-white, two-story resort centers on a courtyard with two swimming pools and lanai with canvas umbrellas and deck chairs. There's a private beach of fine white sand. Guest rooms are done in a tropical aqua-and-salmon scheme, and second-floor rooms have balconies with stunning Gulf views. Restaurant, bar, picnic area, room service. Some kitchenettes, minibars, microwaves, refrigerators. Cable TV, some in-room VCRs (and movies). Pool. Volleyball, bicycles. Laundry facilities. Business services. | 2050 Benjamin Franklin Dr. | 941/388–3694 or 800/358–3245 | fax 941/388–1938 | www.halfmoon-lidokey.com | 127 rooms | $129–$259 | AE, D, MC, V.

Harley Sandcastle. This resort on Lido Beach has access to a spacious stretch of sand—some guest rooms open onto it; it also has a poolside bar and cabanas. Guest rooms are breezy and beach-themed, with shell art and tropical-looking airbrush prints on the walls. Restaurant, bar (with entertainment), room service. In-room safes, microwaves, refrigerators. Cable TV. Pool. Water sports, boating. Laundry facilities. Business services. | 1540 Benjamin Franklin Dr. | 941/388–2181 or 800/225–2181 | fax 941/388–2655 | 179 rooms | $159 | AE, D, MC, V.

Holiday Inn–Lido Beach. On the Lido Key barrier island, this hotel lies along a gorgeous stretch of public beach and is two blocks from the upscale restaurants, shops, and galleries of St. Armand's Circle. Guest rooms have huge windows that face either the Gulf or Sarasota Bay. Restaurant, 2 bars. In-room data ports, in-room safes, microwaves, refrigerators. Cable TV. Pool. Laundry facilities. Business services. Airport shuttle. | 233 Benjamin Franklin Dr. | 941/388–5555 or 800/892–9174 | fax 941/388–4321 | www.holiday-inn.com | 140 rooms | $119–$245 | AE, D, MC, V.

Radisson Lido Beach Resort. A graceful arched pavilion marks the entrance to this four-story resort property on Lido Key. Guest rooms all overlook big water of one kind or another and are decorated like beach cottages, with cozy sitting areas and floor-to-ceiling windows for enjoying the blazing sunsets over the Gulf of Mexico. Restaurant, bar. In-room data ports, in-room safes, microwaves, refrigerators. Cable TV, in-room VCRs (and movies). Gym. Water sports, boating, fishing. Laundry facilities. Business services, airport shuttle. | 700 Benjamin Franklin Dr. | 941/388–2161 or 800/333–3333 | fax 941/388–3175 | www.radisson.com | 116 rooms | $179 | AE, D, MC, V.

LITTLE TORCH KEY

MAP 3, F4

(Nearby towns also listed: Big Pine Key, Key West, Marathon, Sugarloaf Key, Summerland Key)

Located at Mile Marker (MM) 28–29 on the way into the Keys, this little island is more of a stopping-off spot on your way to other islands, unless you'd like to explore the Looe Key National Marine Sanctuary, one of the most beautiful coral reefs in the area; aficionados come from all over the world to dive here. There are also numerous charter operators who will take you out to catch "the big one."

Information: Florida Keys Visitor Center | 106000 Overseas Hwy., Key Largo, 33037 | 800/822–1088 | klchamber@aol.com.

Dining

Baby's Coffee. Café. Having withstood several hurricanes over the last ten years, Baby's has rebuilt (in cement) and remains the southernmost coffee roaster. You get a scentful experience as you walk through the art gallery or sit and try some fresh baked bread or treats. Among their coffee varieties is one called Baby's Private Buzz, the "last legal high," for the serious drinkers and you can always take some home with you or make orders from their Web site (www.babyscoffee.com). | 3178 U.S. 1, MM 15, Saddlebunch Keys | 305/744–9866 or 800/523–2326 | fax 305/744–9843 | 7 AM–6 PM | AE, MC, V.

Little Palm Island Restaurant. Contemporary. Tropical paradise is heightened by Chef Adam Votaw's cuisine—Floribbean, a combination of fresh Florida seafood, classical European meat dishes, pan-Asian touches, and Caribbean flair. You can dine on award-winning crab cakes served with baby vegetables, yellow snapper seared with a watermelon glaze, and lobster dumplings with tamarind and pineapple *jus*, either indoors or in your own wooden table set out at waterside. If you are not staying at the Little Palm Island hotel, check in at Little Torch Key, and then take a water taxi out to the island, which is 3 mi offshore. | Little Torch Key, MM 28.5 | 305/872–2524 | fax 305/872–4843 | Reservations required | $25–$50 | AE, D, DC, MC, V.

Lodging

★ **Little Palm Island.** Little Palm Island, the last island in the chain of islands known as the Newfound Harbor Keys, has long been a vacation spot for the nation's elite. Now the 5-acre landfall, which is littered with towering Jamaican coconut palms, is occupied by this luxury resort. It consists of the the Storm House, constructed with thick poured concrete in the 1960s, and 15 thatched-roof villa outbuildings with one- and two-bedroom suites adorned with British colonial, Caribbean, and oriental furnishings. Ferries run from Little Torch Key to Little Palm Island. Restaurant, bar (with entertainment), picnic area, room service. Minibars. Some in-room VCRs (and movies), no room phones, no TV. Pool. Massage. Gym. Beach, dock, water sports, boating, fishing. Business services, airport shuttle. No kids under 16. | 28500 Overseas Hwy., Little Torch Key | 305/872–2524 or 800/343–8567 | fax 305/872–4843 | www.littlepalmisland.com | 30 suites in 15 buildings | $850–$1,600 suites | AE, D, DC, MC, V.

Parmer's Resort. Sitting on the scenic Little Torch Key is this warm and friendly resort with 5 acres of gardens and 19 aviaries full of tropical birds. The owners earn many repeat customers by providing excellent service and sending out around 15,000 holiday cards each year. Rooms are modern and decorated with a light Florida style (pastels) and they vary in size to accommodate couples to families. Complimentary Continental breakfast. Some kitchenettes, microwaves. Cable TV. Pool. Dock, water sports, boating, bicycles. Laundry facilities. | MM 29, 565 Barry Ave., Little Torch Key | 305/872–2157 | fax 305/872–2014 | www.parmersplace.com | 18 rooms, 12 efficiencies, 13 apartments | $69–$115 room, $115–$150 efficiency, $115–$175 apartment | AE, D, MC, V.

LIVE OAK

(Nearby towns also listed: Lake City, Perry, White Springs)

This small North Florida community of 6,000 really has that Southern charm and feel, especially when the tobacco auctions come to town in July and August. Its proximity to Osceola National Forest makes it a convenient place to stop over for the night if you are seeking the great outdoors, and it's at a crossroads for anyone crossing the panhandle and heading to or from Jacksonville or Gainesville.

Information: **Suwannee County Chamber of Commerce** | Drawer C, Live Oak, 32064 | 904/362–3071.

Attractions

Suwannee River State Park. This preserve was one of the first parks in the Florida state park system. The original 300 acres was purchased in 1936; the park totals 1,843 acres today with 31 camping sites. The park's remoteness, 14 mi west of Live Oak off Rte. 90, ensures a thriving wildlife population. The park has fishing, canoeing, picnicking, and hiking on 11 mi of trails. | 20199 County Road 132, Live Oak | 904/362–2746 | $3.25 per vehicle | Daily.

ON THE CALENDAR

SEPT.: *Autumn Art Fest.* In this annual competition held at the Suwannee River Regional Library, artists submit works in a variety of mediums. | 904/362–3811.
OCT.: *Country Jam USA.* This weekend entertainment lineup attracts hundreds of thousands of concert-goers from all over the U.S. Held at the Suwannee Music Park. | Park 904/364–1683, tickets 800/530–3020.

Dining

R.L.'s Smokehouse Restaurant. Southern. This no-frills, line-style eatery specializes in country cooking for breakfast, lunch, and dinner. Try the surf and turf or the gargantuan smoked special: beef, fries, baked beans, coleslaw, and Texas toast. | 602 W. Howard | 904/362–3287 | fax 904/362–5255 | Closed Sunday | $6–$10 | No credit cards.

Lodging

Suwannee River Inn. This basic chain motel is 4 mi from the famed Suwannee River and the Spirit of Suwannee Music Park. Tubing and scuba diving activities are 25 mi away. Complimentary Continental breakfast. Cable TV. Pool. Pets allowed (fee). | 6819 U.S. 129 | 904/362–6000 | fax 904/364–1309 | 64 rooms | $60 | AE, D, DC, MC, V.

LONG KEY

MAP 3, D6

(Nearby towns also listed: Conch Key/Duck Key, Grassy Key/Crawl Key, Islamorada)

Though hurricanes flooded the ocean side in 1988 and 1999, Long Key is still rich in marine and bird life. An impressive, 2-mi bridge with 222 reinforced-concrete arches runs parallel to U.S. 1 as you cross Long Key Channel. The major attraction is natural, a tropical hardwood forest preserved in the Long Key Recreation Area.

Information: **Islamorada Chamber of Commerce** | Box 915, Islamorada, 33036 | 305/664–4503 or 800/322–5397 | islamoradachamber.com.

Attractions

Long Key State Park. You can fish, rent canoes, picnic, snorkel, and camp at this ecologically rich park. Golden Orb Trail leads to a boardwalk through a mangrove swamp alongside a waterbird-filled lagoon. Fishing for bonefish and tarpon is good in the near-shore flats. A park highlight is the Layton Nature Trail. | MM 67, Overseas Hwy. | 305/664–4815 | www.dep.state.fl.us | $3.25 per vehicle; canoe rental $4 per hr, $10 per day | Daily 8–sunset.

Layton Nature Trail. This gentle walk through a tropical hardwood forest takes 20–30 minutes, leading to a rocky Florida Bay shoreline overlooking shallow grass flats. The trail starts across the road from the entrance to Long Key State Park. | MM 67.6 BS | 305/664–4815 | www.dep.state.fl.us | Park admission $3.25 per vehicle | Park daily 8–sunset.

Dining
Little Italy. Italian. This island favorite, a traditional family-style Italian restaurant, serves up chicken, seafood, salads, snapper, steak, veal, and stone crabs in season. For dessert, ask for the rich chocolate-pecan pie. | MM 68.5, BS | 305/664–4472 | $9–$17 | AE, MC, V.

Lodging
Edgewater Lodge. Each room here comes with a private docking space for boats, just feet from the rooms. Tropical bedsheets and curtains enliven the bedrooms; large poolside cottages and second-floor balconies are available overlooking Florida Bay and southwesterly views of the Gulf sunsets. Picnic area. Some kitchenettes, some minibars, some microwaves, some refrigerators. Pool. Beach, dock. Laundry facilities. | MM 65.5 BS | 305/664–2662 | fax 305/664–9205 | www.edgewaterlodge.com | 24 rooms | $89–$205 | D, MC, V.

Lime Tree Bay Resort. This small, 2½-acre resort is on a small, quiet, sandy beach on Forida Bay. Rental boats, kayaks, and waverunners on premises. The best rooms, however, are those in the back, which lack bay views. Picnic area. In-room data ports, some kitchenettes, some microwaves, some refrigerators. Cable TV. Pool. Hot tub. Tennis courts. Water sports, boating, fishing. | MM 68.5 BS | 305/664–4740 or 800/723–4519 | fax 305/664–0750 | www.limetreebayresort.com | 30 rooms | $102–$235 | AE, D, DC, MC, V.

LONGBOAT KEY

(Nearby towns also listed: Bradenton, Lido Key, Sarasota, Siesta Key)

Longboat is one of the barrier islands that fronts the Gulf of Mexico off the shores of Sarasota. This 11-mi island slices its way along the coast, attracting 8,000 year-round residents and plenty of snowbirds, who come for the pristine, sugar-white beaches and recreation such as golf, fishing, and tennis. In season, this influx doubles the island's population. Longboat Key is peaceful and decidedly upscale, filled with snazzy boutiques, galleries, and shops, and plenty of dining options. There's a ten-mile bike path as well to help you keep trim. With an average household income of $150,000 and a mature population, you find a tasteful, neon-free, and very private key.

Information: **Longboat Key Chamber of Commerce** | 6854 Gulf of Mexico Dr., Longboat Key, 34228 | 941/383–2466 | www.longboatkeychamber.com.

Dining
Chart House Restaurant. Steak. This popular chain's specialty is aged, grain-fed Midwestern beef, hand-cut and grilled to order. Entrées include filet mignon, baby back ribs, New York strip, glazed lemon chicken, or Alaskan king crab legs. | 210 Gulf of Mexico Drive #12 | 941/383–5593 | $14–$28 | AE, D, MC, V.

Colony. Continental. Seafood is a specialty at this restaurant with a Gulf view in the Colony Beach and Tennis Resort. Dishes include Colorado lamb, pan-roasted red snapper, and filet mignon. Tables have white linen tablecloths; the room has dark-wood furniture and lots of windows. It is the more formal choice of the three restaurants in the resort. Sunday brunch. Live piano in the cocktail lounge. Breakfast is served. Kids' menu. | 1620 Gulf of Mexico Dr. | 941/383–5558 | Reservations required | www.colonybeachresort.com | $21–$33 | AE, D, DC, MC, V.

Euphemia Haye. Continental. This longtime favorite among locals has a loft serving desserts and light dinners. The menu downstairs ranges from hummus appetizers to Greek lamb steak, Gorgonzola fettucine, and Key West snapper. Tables have linen tablecloths and fine silver. The wine cellar houses the extensive wine list. | 5540 Gulf of Mexico Dr. | 941/383–3633 | www.euphemiahaye.com | Closed for 3 weeks after Labor Day. No lunch | $18–$34 | D, DC, MC, V.

Harry's Continental Kitchens. American. This fun and friendly restaurant serves dishes prepared with fresh herbs. They also have a gourmet take-out deli with fresh salads and sandwiches daily. Harry himself cooks up fresh seafood daily for the take-out or the quaint dining room that overlooks the backyard garden. The menu covers the gamut from deli sandwiches to any number of French, Italian, or traditional American dishes, and there's even a fine wine list. Specialties are soft shell crabs sautéed with lemon and garlic butter, or Harry's seafood cobb salad. | 525 St. Judes Dr. | 941/383–0777 | Closed Mon. in June–Aug. | $19–$29 | AE, MC, V.

Lynches Landing. Irish. The dining room of this restaurant is filled with pictures and memorabilia from Ireland. A patio overlooks the Gulf of Mexico, offering great sunset views. Irish dishes include cottage pie (ground beef with mashed potatoes and gravy); Irish stew made with lamb, potatoes, and rosemary; corned beef and cabbage; and Irish smoked salmon. Burgers, fried shrimp, and fish and chips are also on the menu. Live Maine lobsters are cooked up on weekends. The Key lime pie is also good. Live Irish bands perform on Friday and Saturday nights, Dixieland bands on Wednesday nights. | 4000 Gulf of Mexico Dr. | 941/383–0791 | Closed Sept. and the 1st two weeks of June; closed Sun. from Oct.–Dec. | $6–$17 | AE, D, DC, MC, V.

Moore's Stone Crab. Seafood. Sandwiches and salads are served all day at this casual bayfront restaurant on the Intracoastal Waterway, family-owned and in business since 1967. Stone crab in season, soft shell crab, lobster, snapper, and grouper are the specialties. | 800 Broadway | 941/383–1748 | Reservations not accepted | $10–$22 | DC, MC, V.

Poseidon. Seafood. This restaurant serves up contemporary dishes in a veranda room with a bay view. Tables have linens and silverware. The wine list has 250 varieties. The menu, which changes daily based on what is fresh, might include the Chilean sea bass with a miso honey glaze, roasted on cedar plank and served with wasabi mashed potatoes, or the 2½-lb lobster with grilled pesto corn. New York strip steak and filet mignon are served for meat lovers. | 3454 Gulf of Mexico Dr. | 941/383–2500 | No lunch | $19–$31 | AE, D, DC, MC, V.

Lodging

Colony Beach and Tennis Resort. This resort off the coast of Sarasota is the place to stay if tennis is your game. Instructors are USTPA-certified; there are 10 pros and numerous clinics and camps. There are 800 ft of beachfront and a health spa. All units, either one- or two-bedroom apartments, can sleep up to eight and have full kitchens, a living area, marble baths with a whirlpool, and private balconies. 3 Restaurants, bar, room service. Kitchenettes, microwaves, refrigerators. Cable TV, some in-room VCRs. Pool. Hot tub, massage. 21 tennis courts. Health club. Beach, water sports, boating, bicycles. Children's programs (ages 3–12). Laundry facilities. Business services, airport shuttle. | 1620 Gulf of Mexico Dr. | 941/383–6464 or 800/282–1138 | fax 941/383–7549 | www.colonybeachresort.com | 234 apartments (1- and 2-bedroom) | $395–$510 1–bedroom, $535–$670 2–bedroom | AE, D, DC, MC, V.

Diplomat Resort. This two-story resort is on the Gulf of Mexico and all rooms either face the beach or the pool. Studio, 1-bedroom, and 2-bedroom units are available. All have full kitchens. In-room data ports, kitchenettes, microwaves, refrigerators. Cable TV. Pool. Beach. Laundry facilities. Business services. | 3155 Gulf of Mexico Dr. | 941/383–3791 or 800/344–5418 | fax 941/383–0983 | diplomat@netsrq.com | 50 rooms, 1- and 2-bedroom | $133–$212, 2–night minimum stay | D, MC, V.

Harbour Villa Club at the Buccaneer. This three-story resort on Sarasota Bay overlooks the Harbour marina. Each villa is individually owned and has two bedrooms, two baths, a patio

KODAK'S TIPS FOR TAKING GREAT PICTURES

Get Closer
- Fill the frame tightly for maximum impact
- Move closer physically or use a long lens
- Continually check the viewfinder for wasted space

Choosing a Format
- Add variety by mixing horizontal and vertical shots
- Choose the format that gives the subject greatest drama

The Rule of Thirds
- Mentally divide the frame into vertical and horizontal thirds
- Place important subjects at thirds' intersections
- Use thirds' divisions to place the horizon

Lines
- Take time to notice lines
- Let lines lead the eye to a main subject
- Use the shape of lines to establish mood

Taking Pictures Through Frames
- Use foreground frames to draw attention to a subject
- Look for frames that complement the subject
- Expose for the subject, and let the frame go dark

Patterns
- Find patterns in repeated shapes, colors, and lines
- Try close-ups or overviews
- Isolate patterns for maximum impact (use a telephoto lens)

Textures that Touch the Eyes
- Exploit the tangible qualities of subjects
- Use oblique lighting to heighten surface textures
- Compare a variety of textures within a shot

Dramatic Angles
- Try dramatic angles to make ordinary subjects exciting
- Use high angles to help organize chaos and uncover patterns, and low angles to exaggerate height

Silhouettes
- Silhouette bold shapes against bright backgrounds
- Meter and expose for the background illumination
- Don't let conflicting shapes converge

Abstract Composition
- Don't restrict yourself to realistic renderings
- Look for ideas in reflections, shapes, and colors
- Keep designs simple

Establishing Size
- Include objects of known size
- Use people for scale, where possible
- Experiment with false or misleading scale

Color
- Accentuate mood through color
- Highlight subjects or create designs through color contrasts
- Study the effects of weather and lighting

© Artville

From Kodak Guide to Shooting Great Travel Pictures © 2000 by Fodor's Travel Publications

or balcony, a kitchen, and a stereo. It books early for high season. In-room data ports, microwaves, refrigerators. Cable TV, in-room VCRs (and movies). Pool. Hot tub. 4 tennis courts. Laundry facilities. Business services. | 615 Dream Island Rd. | 941/383–9544 or 800/433–5298 | fax 941/383–8028 | 38 suites | $1,895 (7–day minimum stay) | AE, MC, V.

Holiday Beach Hotel and Suites. This two- and three-story hotel on the Gulf of Mexico has an indoor Holidome recreation center with four tennis courts, a putting green, and volleyball. Kid suites have a standard room with two double beds and another room for the kids with two bunk beds, a TV, CD player, Nintendo, and microwave. The hotel has 750 ft of beachfront. 3 Restaurants, bar. In-room data ports, some microwaves, refrigerators. Cable TV. Hot tub, sauna. 2 pools (1 indoor), wading pool. Putting green, 4 tennis courts. Gym, volleyball. Beach, water sports. Laundry facilities, laundry service. Business services. | 4949 Gulf of Mexico Dr. | 941/383–3771 or 800/465–4436 | fax 941/383–7871 | 146 suites | $179–$239 suites | AE, D, MC, V.

Holiday Beach Resort. This motel has a private beach and several recreational options, including shuffleboard, a tennis court, and 12 mi of bike and hike paths. Cable TV. Pool. Laundry facilities. | 4765 Gulf of Mexico Dr. | 941/383–3704 | fax 941/383–0546 | holiday@travelbase.com | 25 rooms | $70–165 | MC, V.

Holiday Lodge. This small five-story hotel is on the Gulf of Mexico. Rooms have one bedroom and a combination living and kitchen area. Separate cottages have two bedrooms with one or two baths, and a porch. Some have water views. Microwaves. Cable TV, in-room VCRs. Pool. Hot tub. Putting green. Laundry facilities. | 4235 Gulf of Mexico Dr. | 941/383–3788 | fax 941/387–7966 | 29 rooms | $133–$173 | AE, D, DC, MC, V.

Longboat Key Hilton Beach Resort. One of the taller oceanfront resorts in the area, many rooms at this five-story, Caribbean-theme Hilton have water views. There are 400 ft of beachfront. Restaurant, bar, room service. Minibars, some microwaves, refrigerators. Cable TV. Pool. 1 tennis court. Water sports, boating, bicycles. Baby-sitting. Laundry facilities. Business services. | 4711 Gulf of Mexico Dr. | 941/383–2451 or 800/445–8667 | fax 941/383–7979 | www.hilton.com | 102 rooms | $215–$335 | AE, D, DC, MC, V.

The Resort at Longboat Key Club. This golf and tennis luxury resort is across the street from a nature preserve. All rooms have balconies, most have full kitchens. Kayaks, deep-sea charters, and ecology trips are also available. The 38 tennis courts are Har-Tru surfaced and many are lighted for night play. The resort also includes a 4,000-square-ft fitness center and spa. 4 restaurants, bar (with entertainment), room service. In-room data ports, minibars, microwaves, some refrigerators. Cable TV, some in-room VCRs. Pool. Hot tub, massage, sauna, spa. Driving range, 3 golf courses (45 holes), putting green, 38 tennis courts. Health club. Beach, water sports, boating, bicycles. Library. Children's programs (ages 5–12). Business services, airport shuttle. | 301 Gulf of Mexico Dr. | 941/383–8821 or 800/237–8821 | fax 941/383–0359 | www.longboatkeyclub.com | 232 rooms | $325–$410 room, $400–$525 club suite, $565–$850 1- or 2-bedroom suites | AE, D, DC, MC, V.

Riviera Beach Motel. Lush, landscaped walkways add intimacy to this waterfront motel. Garden on premises. Studio, 1-bedroom, or 2-bedroom apartments with full kitchens, living area, and dining room table. Most with 2 beds. Some price breaks for weekly rentals. Microwaves, refrigerators. Cable TV. Beach. Some pets allowed (fee). | 5451 Gulf of Mexico Dr. | 941/383–2552 | fax 941/383–2245 | 11 rooms | $113–$160 | AE, MC, V.

Sea Horse Beach Resort. This two-story resort stretched along the powdery Gulf of Mexico beach has studios and 1- and 2- bedroom apartments with water views. Kitchenettes, microwaves. Cable TV. Pool. Laundry facilities. Business services. | 3453 Gulf of Mexico Dr. | 941/383–2417 | fax 941/387–8771 | www.travelbase.com/destinations/sarasota/seahorse | 35 units | $140–$165 | D, MC, V.

Silver Beach Resort This family-run motel is nestled in a secluded haven on Longboat Key. Tropical foliage dots the 3½-acre landscape, and tennis courts are a half block from the grounds. Cable TV. Pool. Laundry facilities. | 4131 Gulf of Mexico Dr. | 800/414–0238 or 941/383–2434 | fax 941/383–8275 | 50 rooms | $70–$180 | D, MC, V.

MADEIRA BEACH

(Nearby towns also listed: Redington Beach, St. Pete Beach, St. Petersburg)

Some consider this to be one of the most beautiful beaches in all of Florida. A part of the Pinellas Sun Coast, this 30-mi strand of sand borders the Gulf of Mexico. It's easily accessible from St. Petersburg and known for its outstanding fishing. At John's Pass Village and Boardwalk you'll find marinas catering to deep-sea grouper boats.

Information: Gulf Beaches of Tampa Bay/Madeira Beach Chamber of Commerce | 501 150th Ave., Madeira Beach, 33708 | 727/391–7373 or 800/944–1847 | www.gulfbeaches-tampabay.com.

Attractions

Hubbard's Marina. Sitting in the middle of John's Pass Boardwalk community is the marina originally started by Wilson Hubbard. Now run by his son Mark Hubbard, their Sea Adventure company offers even more fishing trips, educational charters, and party boats. Their dolphin watching tours are run almost every hour Mon.–Sat. and 4 times daily on Sundays. A 6-hr trip to Shell Island is a great place to go shelling and join the other guests with a Florida-style beach-BBQ (Mon., Tue., Thu., and Sat. 10:30–4:30, $24.95 and optional $7 lunch). Snorkeling and wildlife viewing is available on the Egmont Key tour as you swim and wander through remains of Fort Dade, built during the Spanish–American War (Wed., Fri., Sun. 10:30–4:30 $30 plus $7 lunch). | 150 John's Pass Boardwalk | 727/393–1947 | fax 727/399–1934 | www.hubbardsmarina.com | Some metered parking, some free | Daily.

John's Pass Boardwalk & Village. John's Pass is named for the narrow pass between Treasure Island and Madeira Beach that a lost pioneer, John Levach, discovered after the landmarks were all rearranged by a terrible storm in 1848. Local entrepreneur Wilson Hubbard started a fishing company when he was a kid and later staged fishing contests in the area and built an 1,100-ft boardwalk to offer educational tours and fishing charters of John's Pass. The village now has plenty of gift stores (122 shops), eateries, and boating activities. The bait shop rents all the equipment you need to hang out on the jetty and fish, or you can just buy some pelican food and try for some fun photos. | 150 John's Pass Boardwalk | www.hubbardsmarina.com.

ON THE CALENDAR

OCT.: *John's Pass Seafood Festival.* More than 100,000 people consume tons of fish, shrimp, crabs, and other seafood specialties at this annual event, one of the state's largest seafood festivals. The celebration, which takes place at the end of the month, includes entertainment, arts and crafts, a haunted house, and lots of seafood from local restaurants. | 727/391–7373.

Dining

Apple Family Restaurant. American. This mom and pop place is beloved by tourists and locals because it's open 7 days a week from 7 AM to 11 PM and it's across the street from the beach. The omelettes and breakfast specials are followed by a super salad bar for lunch, and for dinner you can get fresh seafood specials or some old favorites like the grouper sandwich or the fisherman's platter. | 1500 Madeira Way | 727/391–1302 | $6–$8 | AE, D, MC, V.

The Friendly Fisherman. Seafood. Salty dogs of all ages and expertise are welcome to enjoy seafood platters brimming with fresh catches as they have been since being established by the Hubbards in 1976. The combination plates offer a variety of shellfish and heartier fish, while the grouper with hollandaise sauce is served broiled and with your choice of sweet potatoes, corn fritters, rice, and other sides. The theme is nautical with huge wooden tables and sea art on the walls, plus you can look out the windows to the marina. | 150 John's Pass Boardwalk | 727/391–6025 | fax 727/399–1934 | $11–$22 | AE, D, MC, V.

Lodging

Grey Gull Beach Resort. Just a few blocks away from the John's Pass Boardwalk on the Gulf of Mexico is this family-owned business providing efficiencies and apartments. The heated pool is steps away from the beach, but enclosed by a privacy fence; for even more of a hideaway, ask about the two-bedroom Starfish Cottage. Rooms are equipped with kitchen facilities and comfortable floral couches. Kitchenettes. Cable TV. Pool. Beach. Laundry facilities. | 13630 Gulf Blvd. #4 | 727/391–8949 or 800/473–3196 | fax 727/320–0526 | brights@mindspring.com | www.greygull.com | $55–$115 | MC, V.

Holiday Inn Madiera Beach. On 600 ft of beach, sunset views from the poolside Hardshells Tiki Bar or Maxie's Restaurant are very picturesque. Some of the tropical bright–colored rooms face poolside, some have beach views, and many have balconies. Restaurant, 2 bars. Cable TV, in-room data ports, in-room safes, some refrigerators. Pool. Beach. Laundry facilities and service. | 15208 Gulf Blvd. | 727/392–2275 or 800/360–6658 | fax 727/393–4012 | www.holiday-inn.com | 149 rooms | $89–$164 | AE, D, DC, MC, V.

Lighthouse B&B Motel. The three buildings were built around 1948 and are set around a common courtyard, secluding the goldfish pond and gazebo from the public. The main one, shaped like a lighthouse, is where a full breakfast is served and has several of the carpeted rooms. Each room is individually designed with floral to tropical patterns and tiled kitchen areas. They are only 2 blocks from the beach and 5 blocks from John's Path boardwalk. Complimentary breakfast. Some kitchenettes, some refrigerators, some microwaves. Cable TV, no phones in rooms. Bicycles. Laundry facilities. Some pets (fee). | 13355 2nd St. E | 727/391–0015 or 800/241–0334 | fax 727/393–7285 | lighthousebb@aol.com | bedandbreakfast.com | 6 rooms | $60–$95 | AE, D, MC, V.

My Cousin's Place. This woman-run facility has it all because of the mellow location on the water and proximity to so many wildlife areas, not to mention visiting herons. Rooms and suites are each designed individually with tropical and pastel patterns and well-supplied eat-in kitchens. Also available: fax machines, Internet access, picnic area, shuffleboard, and a grill by the seductive bayside pool. Kitchens, microwave. Cable TV, VCRs. Pool. Dock, fishing. Laundry facilities. | 215 144th Ave. E | 727/319–2507 or 877/854–2746 | fax 727/319–2507 | www.mycousinsplace.com | 2 apartments | 3–night minimum, $350–$450 | No credit cards.

MAITLAND

MAP 3, J5

(Nearby towns also listed: Altamonte Springs, Orlando, Sanford, Winter Park)

Maitland is one of the oldest incorporated municipalities in Central Florida, originally established as a U.S. army fort in 1838. The base was one of those guarding the Old Black Bear Trail, which ran from St. Petersburg all the way to Montréal, Canada. Maitland has seen relatively substantial growth in the last half-century, with the establishment of the new home of Lockheed Martin in Orlando, and, of course, the birth of Walt Disney World in 1971. It's now more of a northern Orlando suburb. Even with this growth, it's still a town of only 12,000 residents that is now giving itself a face-lift with improvements to parks, additional biking areas, burying of powerlines, and new landscaping and improved pedestrian areas.

Information: **Maitland-South Seminole Chamber of Commerce** | 110 N. Maitland Ave., Maitland, 32751 | 407/644–0741.

Attractions

Florida Audubon Society's Center for Birds of Prey. Having undergone some reconstruction until January of 2001, the programs are relatively new. The facilities provide a view into the lives of more than 20 species of birds, including hawks, owls, eagles, falcons, and vultures. Different exhibits represent different environments and you can also learn about their rescue program for injured birds. Tours, temporary exhibits, and special events are planned daily. | 1101 Audubon Way | 407/644–0190 | Suggested donation: $5 adults, $4 kids 2–11 | Tues.–Sat. 10–4.

Holocaust Memorial Resource and Education Center. A history of the Holocaust is displayed in multi-media and original art. Photographs and literature chronicle the events from 1933–1945 and the library and archives are available for perusal. Throughout the year special events, lectures, film series, and traveling exhibits add to the dramatic collection. A relaxing garden has a sculpture and benches. | 851 N. Maitland | 407/628–0555 | fax 407/628–1079 | www.holocaustedu.org | Free | Mon.–Thurs. 9–4, Fri. 9–1, Sun. 1–4.

Maitland Art Center. Originally started as an artist's community in the 1930s by artist and visionary Jules André Smith, the 22 buildings are themselves works of art. The outsides are covered with reliefs reminiscent of Mayan and Aztec, or Fantasy architecture. It is a popular spot for weddings and hiking on the nature trails and through the gardens. Art classes are offered throughout the year and you can often see classes working on the grounds. | 231 W. Packwood Ave. | 407/539–2181 | fax 407/539–1198 | www.maitartctr.org | Donations welcome | Weekdays 9–4:30, weekends noon–4:30, closed major holidays.

Maitland Historical Museum. This museum illuminates the area's history, from 1838 and the first Seminole War to the present, with photos, artifacts, and textiles. | 221 W. Packwood Ave. | 407/644–1364 | $2 | Thur.–Sun. noon–4.

ON THE CALENDAR

OCT., APR.: *Maitland Arts and Crafts Show.* Held on the third weekend of October and April, this event draws hundreds of arts and crafts vendors to Lake Lily Park at Orlando and Maitland Avenues. | 407/644–0741.

Dining

Antonio's La Fiamma. Italian. Offering traditional cooking from the old country, the downstairs café has lighter fare for lunch and the upstairs dining room has a wood burning oven to roast up many delicacies. Dinner specialties are *zuppa di pesce all'Antonio* (an assortment of shrimp, scallops, fish, mussels, octopus, clams, calamari, and lobster tail in a seafood broth) and *carré di agnello* (a rack of lamb sautéed with garlic and fresh herbs in a brandy demiglaze). For dessert the tiramisu heads off a list of rich Italian indulgences. | 611 S. Orlando Ave. | 407/645–5523 | fax 407/645–1052 | Dining room closed Sun. (café open) | $11–$27 | AE, MC, V.

Nicole St. Pierre. Contemporary. Sitting in its own garden of towering oaks, flowers, and ponds, this elegant restaurant concentrates on innovative dishes from the French tradition. Items on the menu include veal scaloppine with crab meat and asparagus, and grilled lamb chops with mushroom sauce and grilled tomato. The restaurant also serves fresh fish daily. | 1300 S. Orlando Ave. | 407/647–7575 | No lunch Sat. Closed Sun. | $20–$30 | AE, D, DC, MC, V.

Lodging

Thurston House B&B. Originally built as a winter getaway in 1885, the pine and cypress house sits opposite Lake Eulalia. Hardwood floors, mantels, and wainscoting are complemented by a tasteful selection of comfortable antiques. The five acres of wooded land on which the house sits are criss-crossed with walking trails. Complimentary breakfast (Continental weekdays, full weekends). In-room data ports. Cable TV. Library. No kids under 12. No smoking. | 851 Lake Ave. | 407/539–1911 or 800/843–2721 | fax 407/539–0365 | www.thurston-house.com | 4 rooms | $130–$140 | AE, MC, V.

MARATHON

(Nearby towns also listed: Big Pine Key, Conch Key/Duck Key, Grassy Key/Crawl Key, Little Torch Key, Windley Key)

With its central location in the Key archipelago, Marathon is the self-styled "Heart of the Keys." It's a great jumping-off point to explore destinations either to the north or south, and it has the only airport between Key West and the mainland. With several resorts, restaurants, and shopping, Marathon is itself becoming a popular destination. Retaining the charm of a 19th-century fishing village, it's home to quite a few attractions. The Crane Point Hammock is a 64-acre historical and archaeological site with pre-Columbian and Bahamian artifacts. There's also a dolphin research center and turtle hospital.

Information: Greater Marathon Chamber of Commerce | 12222 Overseas Hwy., Marathon, Florida Keys, 33050 | 800/262–7284 or 305/743–5417 | MarathonCC@aol.com | www.floridakeysmarathon.com.

Attractions

Dolphin Research Center. The DRC, a nonprofit education and research facility, shelters a pod of about 15 dolphins in a natural marine environment. Three-hour programs let you touch and communicate with these intriguing animals; a dolphin encounter program lets you join dolphins in the water. | MM 59, OS, Marathon Shores | 305/289–1121 | fax 305/743–7627 | $12.50 tours | Daily 9–4; Tours at 10 AM, 11 AM, 12:30 PM, 2, and 3:30.

Pigeon Key. You can reach this 5-acre island by walking or riding a tram across a 2⅕-mi section of the old bridge. Once on the island, 2 mi west of Marathon, you can tour on your own or with a guide. Once a workcamp and village for the workers that operated and maintained the Old Bridge, it is now an educational and research center on the culture and natural resources of the Florida Keys. You can take kayak trips in the mangroves, and rocky shoreline tidepool studies by way of educational programs, or do the ecotour on a catamaran with a box lunch, museum visit, and island tour. Concerts, art shows, and folk festivals are also held on the island. | 305/289–0025 or 305/743–7655 (ecotours) | 305/289–1065 | $7.50, ecotours $39.95 | Daily 10–5; ecotours Sun., Wed., Fri., noon–4.

Crane Point Hammock. The Museum of Natural History, the Florida Keys Children's Museum, and the Adderley Village Historic Site are on these 63 acres of virtually untouched hardwood hammock, in the heart of Marathon. You can hike the 1½ mi of trails that lead to a bay. | MM 50, U.S. 1, Marathon | 305/743–9100 | fax 305/743–0429 | $7.50 | Mon.–Sat. 10–5, Sun. noon–5.

Museum of Natural History of the Florida Keys. Cultural and natural history are central to this museum's exhibits, which cover a little bit of everything, from Keys geography to sea turtles and southeastern Native American culture. The museum grounds are home to 160 native plants, 50 exotic plants, and 10 endangered plant and animal species. Check out the re-created coral reef as well. | 5550 Overseas Hwy. | 305/743–9100 | fax 305/743–0429 | $7.50, included in entry to Crane Point Hammock | Nov.–May, Mon.–Sat. 10–5, Sun. 12–5.

ON THE CALENDAR

MAR.: *Seafood Festival.* At this event that draws more than 10,000 to the airport (9400 Overseas Hwy.), local fisherman set up booths to sell their fresh fish. Arts and crafts booths are also plentiful. | 305/743–5417.

Dining

Barracuda Grill. Eclectic. Come here once, and you'll come here again. On the main road to Marathon, this small, casual but elegant restaurant is in a free-standing old Conch building from the '50s. The floors have white tile, the walls are aqua blue. A sense of humor is evident in the furnishings: the votive candles on the tables use copper to simulate the open mouth and sharp teeth of a Barracuda. Menu favorites include a delicate pastry pouch filled with shrimp, veggies, and Thai seasonings—called Thai Money Bags. Grilled wahoo fish is sauteed with lobster tail, wine, and scallions. Or try the tortilla in lobster sauce or lobster enchilada. If you're feeling hungry for a standard dish, try a big cowboy Angus steak. The Key lime pie is good, as is the wine list, considering the size of the place. | 4290 Overseas Hwy. | 305/743–3314 | Reservations not accepted | Christmas–Apr., Mon.–Sat.; off-season Wed.–Sat. | No lunch | $13–$30 | AE, MC, V.

Hurricane Grille. Seafood. When there's not a band playing (Thursday through Sunday nights), the restaurant is abuzz with TVs broadcasting sporting events. The chicken, steak, and seafood dishes satisfy, but most popular are the shellfish. Clams are served raw or steamed; lobster, shrimp, crab, oysters come steamed. | 4650 Overseas Hwy. | 305/743–2220 | $13–$28 | AE, MC, V.

Island Tiki Bar and Restaurant. Seafood. Come here for dinner and you'll see an unbeatable sunset over the Gulf. The menu offers oysters Moscow and raw oysters with horseradish and sour cream. You can come by boat and dock at the private dock. | 12648 Overseas Hwy. | 305/743–4191 | $12–$36 | AE, D, MC, V.

The Quay Marathon. Seafood. On the Gulf of Mexico, this long-time favorite serves both steaks and a wide array of seafood. Dine outside on the deck to enjoy the sunset, best if you arrive for an early dinner. Kids' menu. | 12650 Overseas Hwy. | 305/289–1810 | $11–$33 | AE, D, DC, MC, V.

WatersEdge. Seafood. Historic photos of Duck Key during the railroad era and of the celebrities who visited at that time ornament the walls at this restaurant. Menu favorites include the spicy conch chowder, Florida stone-crab claws, mud pie, and coconut ice cream. Try the chicken Key West, chicken stuffed with crab and shrimp. | MM 61/61 Hawk's Cay Blvd. | 305/743–7000 | No lunch | $16–$44 | AE, D, DC, MC, V.

Lodging

Coral Lagoon. The pastel cottages here sit on a landscaped canal, and each has a private deck and hammock. You get free use of tennis rackets, fishing equipment, and dockage. A private beach, chartered fishing, and diving trips are available for an extra charge. Picnic area. In-room safes, kitchenettes, microwaves, refrigerators. Cable TV, in-room VCRs. Pool. Tennis court. Dock, boating. | 12399 Overseas Hwy. | 305/289–0121 | 18 cottages | $100–$125 | AE, D, MC, V.

Faro Blanco Marine Resort. Loyal guests return season after season to this resort with a topnotch and accommodating staff. You can stay in three-bedroom condominiums, cottages, and guest rooms. The guest rooms, like the condos and cottages, all have kitchens or kitchenettes. The condos, individually decorated, have wraparound screen porches; many have views of the water. 3 restaurants. Kitchenettes, microwaves, refrigerators. Cable TV. Pool. Dock, boating. Pets allowed. | 1996 Overseas Hwy. | 305/743–9018 | 100 units | $89–$327 | AE, MC, V.

Marathon Hotel and Marina. An on-site dive shop is one lure at this two-story oceanside hotel. You can also rent the charter boat to go deep-sea fishing or rent waverunners and pontoon boats. There's a boat ramp, too, if you arrive by water. Restaurant, bar. In-room data ports, some refrigerators. Cable TV. Pool, wading pool. Fishing. Laundry facilities. Business services. | 13201 Overseas Hwy., MM54, U.S. 1 | 305/289–0222 or 800/224–5053 | fax 305/743–5460 | www.keysdirectory.com/mhm | 134 rooms | $79–$89 | AE, D, DC, MC, V.

Marathon Wellesley Inn and Suites. This two-story resort is on the beach. In business since 1974, the owners completed major renovations in 2000. Rooms have one king-size or two double beds, with a desk. Nintendo is available. The restaurant next door is convenient. In-room data ports, microwaves, refrigerators. Cable TV, some in-room VCRs (and movies). Pool. Beach, water sports, boating. Laundry facilities. Business services. Some pets allowed. | 13351 Overseas Hwy. | 305/743–8550 | fax 305/743–8832 | www.wellesleyinnandsuites.com | 80 rooms | $129–$200 | AE, D, MC, V.

Royal Hawaiian Motel/Botel. Five of the eight rooms at this one-story motel have kitchens, and those without have refrigerators. All rooms have two double beds. You can take your boat to the shallow or deep waters of the Gulf, fishing all day, then come back to dock right behind your room and cook up your catch on the grills. Guests get free dockage and boat-ramp use. Picnic areas. Refrigerators. Pool. Cable TV. Dock. | 12020 Overseas Hwy. | 305/743–7500 | fax 305/289–0129 | 8 rooms | $95–$105 | AE, DC, MC, V.

Seascape Oceanfront Resort. The wrought-iron grills, faux-stone exterior, and barn lend the air of a villa in Provence. Each room is individually decorated by the owners, a painter and a photographer. You can relax on the lawn furniture scattered over the five tree-filled acres. Fresh fruit and flowers in the rooms are another nice touch. Some kitchenettes, refrigerators. Cable TV, no room phones. Pool. Beach, boating. No smoking. | 76th St. | 305/743–6455 | fax 305/743–8469 | www.thefloridakeys.com/seascape | 9 rooms | $135–$210 | AE, MC, V.

Valhalla Point Resort. Four of the five rooms here are efficiencies with kitchens. You can lounge around on the hammocks and chaises on the beach or use the resort's canoes and kayaks to explore the adjacent Curry Hammock Park. Look for the manatees that graze at the dock. Picnic area. Some kitchenettes, some microwaves, some refrigerators. Cable TV, no room phones. Beach, dock, boating. | 56223 Ocean Dr. | 305/289–0614 | www.keysresort.com | 5 rooms | $75–$94 | MC, V.

MARCO ISLAND

MAP 3, C4

(Nearby towns also listed: Everglades City, Everglades National Park, Naples)

Marco Island is the largest in Florida's Ten Thousand Islands group. It is south of Naples off its southwestern coast. It was originally two separate land masses, one of which was hand-raised by the Calusa Indians who inhabited the area until the arrival of Europeans. Notable artisans and fisherman, the Calusa also built giant mounds using fish bones and shells, which can still be seen in the Indian Hills area. Today the island's residents are a unique blend of bronzed millionaires and salty fishermen. High-end resorts and homes have traded a bit of serenity for luxury. There are plenty of beaches, parks, and romantic dining spots from which to experience the "mysterious allure" that has drawn many of its visitors to call it home.

Information: Marco Island Area Chamber of Commerce | 1102 North Collier Blvd., Marco Island, 34145 | 941/394–7549 | www.marco-island-florida.com.

Attractions

Collier-Seminole State Park. On the edge of the Everglades, 12 mi northeast on Hwy. 92 and 17 mi south of Naples, this 6,423-acre preserve has 13½ mi of trails where you can hike, plus another 5½ for biking. Visit the untouched mangrove swamp to see how this region looked when the first European explorers arrived. The Blackwater River flows through the park—you can rent canoes—and takes you to the Ten Thousand Islands and the Gulf of Mexico. For camping, choose from primitive, tent, or RV sites. You can fish and boat (motor boats are allowed); there's a boat ramp. | 20200 E. Tamiami Tr. | 941/394–3397 | $3.25 per vehicle, $1 for walk-ins | Daily.

Marco Island Trolley. The trolley stops at area hotels and attractions. | 941/394–1600 | $12 | May 1–Oct. 30, Mon.–Sat., call for scheduled stops and pick up points.

Tigertail Beach. The island's only public access beach, Tigertail is most interesting at low tide when birds feed between tidal pools on narrow sand bars. At the end of Hernando Drive, the beach looks much as it did before Europeans settled here. To the south, high-rises dominate the landscape. | Hernando Dr. | $3 fee for parking | 7 AM–sundown.

DEC.: *Christmas Island Style.* Each year the island celebrates the holiday season with a daytime boat parade and nighttime street parade, with the tides determining the time and date. Boats and floats are decorated to the hilt and are the site of many parties. | 941/394–7549.

Dining

Arturo's. Italian. White linens, dim lights, and fresh flowers lend a touch of class to this friendly and comfortable restaurant in the Lanai shopping plaza. The menu tends towards traditional American Italian entrées, with items such as veal parmesan, chicken piccata, baked clams, and escargot, all nicely presented. Locals favor Arturo's stuffed pork chops, which are done with a prosciutto, mozzarella, and mushroom stuffing with white wine sauce. Beer and wine only. | 844 Bald Eagle Dr. | 941/642–0550 | No lunch | $9–$19 | MC, V.

Bavarian Inn. Continental. Some German items vary the menu of this restaurant designed to resemble a German chalet: *Jung Schweinebraten* (tender roasted pork with caraway seeds, garlic, and spices) with mashed potatoes and braised Old World–style cabbage, and Bavarian bratwurst. If you favor American, try the prime rib, aged on site, duck, steaks, shellfish, and fresh fish. Tuesday is Duck Night. The four dining rooms make for ample space, and a bar serves several German and American beers and wines. Desserts are homemade. | 960 Winterberry Dr. | 941/394–7233 | Jan.–Apr. open 7 nights, closed Mon. in off-season | $9–$18 | AE, D, DC, MC, V.

Café de Marco. Seafood. This cozy, award-winning bistro with stained-glass panels in the three dining areas has been around for 18 years, on old Marco Island next to Snook Inn. The specialties here combine local seafood with the chef's original sauces, but don't overlook the crab cakes, the jumbo prawns served with saffron rice, or shrimp Lenny, stuffed with crab meat, wrapped in bacon, and covered with hollandaise sauce. The menu accommodates plainer tastes with New York strip steak, filet mignon, chicken, lamb, and pasta. Desserts are made on the premises. | 244 Palm St. | 941/394–6262 | Closed Sun. in the summer. No lunch | $16–$21 | AE, MC, V.

Konrad's. Continental. The menu at this little place is basic but substantial, with seafood, beef, lamb chops, and prime rib on offer. Even the salad bar is substantial, or you can opt for one of the in-house butchered steaks or the crab-stuffed grouper. If you tire of being indoors, you can eat on the patio, which sits on part of the Mission Plaza. | 599 S. Collier Blvd. | 941/642–3332 | No lunch Sun. | $24–$33 | AE, D, DC, MC, V.

Sandcastles. American. This restaurant, in the Marco Island Hilton, has a view of both the pool and the Gulf. The upscale, intimate room has linen tablecloths and plants, in a green and maroon color scheme. Specials include snapper encrusted in macadamia nuts and topped with a fruit salsa, or bourbon steak (a New York strip steak with a bourbon, mustard, and shallot sauce). Kids' menu. Large wine list. Nightly piano bar on the upper-level balcony. | 560 S. Collier Blvd. | 941/394–5000 | No lunch | $16–$28 | AE, D, DC, MC, V.

Snook Inn. Seafood. You can arrive at this restaurant by boat—and many people do. They head directly for the 200 outdoor seats that overlook the Marco River. The interior, furnished nautical style, is pleasant, too. The place is friendly and comfortable, and serves its fare fried, broiled, blackened, and sauteed—or in more exotic dishes. Grouper is prepared in a paper bag with crab and mushroom in a wine sauce. Known for steaks, pork chops, baby back ribs, and chicken. Seafood buffet on Thursday and Friday, and live entertainment nightly in the outdoor tiki bar. | 1215 Bald Eagle Dr. | 941/394–3313 | www.snookinn.com | Reservations not accepted | $12–$19 | AE, DC, MC, V.

Lodging

The Boathouse. For a great location at a good price, check into this modest but appealing motel at the north end of Marco Island. The two-story, white building trimmed in turquoise is on a canal very close to the mouth of the Gulf. Units are light and bright and

furnished with natural wicker and print fabrics. Each room has a balcony or terrace, and some have great water views. You can fish from the boat docks. Picnic area. Some microwaves. Cable TV. Pool. Dock. Laundry facilities. Business services. Some pets allowed (fee). | 1180 Edington Pl. | 941/642–2400 or 800/528–6345 | fax 941/642–2435 | www.theboathouse-motel.com | 20 rooms | $93–$105 | MC, V.

Eagle's Nest Beach Resort. Right on the beach, this 10-story all-suites resort has three buildings surrounding a landscaped courtyard and pool. Rooms have private patios or balconies. Picnic area. Kitchenettes, microwaves. Cable TV, in-room VCRs (and movies). Pool. Hot tub. Tennis court. Gym, sauna. Beach. Children's programs (ages 5–10). Business services. | 410 S. Collier Blvd. | 941/394–5167 or 800/448–2736 | fax 941/642–1599 | 96 suites | $199–$335 | AE, D, MC, V.

Lakeside Inn. The most affordable lodgings on the island, this two-story hotel sits on Marco Lake, 1 mi east of the beaches. Each unit has a private, screened-in porch with a view of the lake. Kitchenettes, refrigerators, microwaves. Cable TV. Pool. Shops. Laundry facilities. Pets allowed. | 155 First Ave. | 941/394–1161 | www.lakesideinnmarco.com | 12 suites, 26 efficiencies | $89–$119 | AE, D, DC, MC, V.

Marco Bay Resort. You can see out over Marco Bay from the five-story hotel at this all-suites resort. Condos of one or two bedrooms have full kitchens, a separate living area, and balconies. You can walk to a marina, shops, and restaurants. Restaurant, bar. Kitchenettes, microwaves, refrigerators. Cable TV. 2 Pools. Hot tub. 2 tennis courts. Laundry facilities. Business services. | 227 N. Collier Rd. | 941/394–8881 or 800/228–0661 | fax 941/394–8909 | www.marcobayresort.com | 75 suites (1–2 bedroom) | $700–$1000 per week (7–day minimum stay) | AE, MC, V.

Marco Island Hilton Beach Resort. The lobby's Oriental antiques and marble floors set a luxurious tone at this tasteful Gulf-front resort. A breakfast buffet is served on the large patio. This 11-story beachfront hotel has spacious rooms with private balconies and sleeper sofas, a sitting area, wet bar, and refrigerator, plus views of the Gulf. There is a huge 4,000-square-ft fitness and recreation facility, and theaters and a shopping mall are a block away. 2 Restaurants, bar. In-room data ports, minibars, some microwaves, refrigerators. Cable TV. Pool. Hot tub, massage. 3 tennis courts. Gym. Beach, water sports. Bicycles, video games. Valet or free parking. Children's programs (ages 3–14). Business services. | 560 S. Collier Blvd. | 941/394–5000 | fax 941/394–8410 | www.hilton.com | 264 rooms, 33 suites | $259–$349 | AE, D, DC, MC, V.

Marriott's Marco Island Resort and Golf Club. Rooms are spacious at this lovely 11-story resort on 3½ mi of Gulf beach on Marco Island. Enjoy a snack at the on-site pizzeria and ice cream parlor. Every room has a balcony, some with Gulf views. Choose from one king-size or two double beds in rooms; cribs and rollaway beds are free. 5 Restaurants, bar, room service. In-room data ports, minibars, refrigerators. Cable TV, some in-room VCRs. 3 Pools, wading pool. Barbershop, beauty salon, hot tub, massage. 18-hole golf course, 16 tennis courts. Gym. Beach, water sports, bicycles. Shops, video games. Playground. Laundry facilities, laundry services. Business services, free parking. | 400 S. Collier Blvd. | 941/394–2511 or 888/236–2427 | fax 941/642–2672 | www.marriott.com | 735 rooms | $275–$414 | AE, D, DC, MC, V.

Olde Marco Island Inn and Suites. The oldest part of the inn opened in 1883 as Captain Bill Collier's Inn, one of the oldest structures in this corner of the state. Inside, turn-of-the-20th-century prints of wildlife adorn the walls, above the 19th-century period furnishings. Each two-bedroom suite has a screened-in veranda; half the rooms overlook the garden, half overlook the bay. Restaurant. In-room data ports, microwaves, refrigerators. Cable TV, in-room VCRs. Pool. Beauty salon, spa. Business services. | 100 Palm St. | 941/394–3131 or 877/475–3466 | fax 941/394–4485 | www.oldemarcoislandinn.com | 27 suites | $275–$325 | AE, D, DC, MC, V.

Paramount Suite. All units are comfortable suites in this four-story hotel across the street from the Gulf of Mexico. Rooms, renovated and updated in 1999, all have full kitchens and balconies. Private beach access. Picnic area, complimentary Continental breakfast. In-room data ports, kitchenettes. Pool. Beach. Business services. | 901 S. Collier Blvd. | 941/394–8860 or 800/323–8860 | fax 941/394–3040 | 52 suites (47 with shower only) | $169–$215 suites | AE, D, MC, V.

Radisson Suite Beach Resort. A 12-story high-rise beachfront resort designed specifically for families, this lodging offers tasteful private master bedrooms, huge furnished balconies, and fully equipped kitchens. Some guest rooms have views of the Gulf or the pool. 3 restaurants, bar. In-room data ports. Cable TV, some in-room VCRs (and movies). Pool. Hot tub. Driving range, putting green, 1 tennis court. Basketball. Water sports, bicycles. Gym. Beach. Children's programs (ages 3–11). Laundry facilities. Business services. | 600 S. Collier Blvd. | 941/394–4100 or 800/333–3333 | fax 941/394–0262 | www.marcobeachresort.com | 55 rooms, 214 suites | $129–$419 | AE, D, DC, MC, V.

MARIANNA

MAP 3, E1

(Nearby towns also listed: Blountstown, Chattahoochee, Chipley)

Fifteen mi south of the Alabama border, this 10-square-mi town on the banks of the Chipola River is called home by about 6,200 residents. Marianna has been called one of the top 100 best small towns in America, the only Florida town to earn the distinction. With its proximity to Florida Caverns State Park, it makes a nice place to have lunch or grab a picnic before heading into the caves.

Information: Jackson County Chamber of Commerce | 2928 Jefferson St., Box 130, Marianna, 32447 | 850/482–8061.

MARIANNA

INTRO
ATTRACTIONS
DINING
LODGING

Attractions

Chipola River. Locals favor this north-south river for swimming, canoeing, rafting, and kayaking. You get to the river at Spring Creek Park along Highway 90E.

Florida Caverns State Park. Stalactites, stalagmites, soda straws, columns, rimstones, flowstones, and draperies are all within the caves at this site 3 mi north of Marianna, off Route 166. Only Florida Cavern is open to the public for tours; spelunkers can get permits to enter the others. At the 1,300-acre park, you can also picnic, camp, fish, swim, and canoe on Chipola River. The 7 mi of trails are good for hiking and horseback riding. | 3345 Cavern Rd. | 850/482–9598 or 850/482–1228 | www.dep.state.fl.us | $3.25 per vehicle; cavern admission $4 | Daily; tours daily 9–4:30.

Three Rivers State Recreation Area. The Chattahoochee and Flint rivers merge, becoming the Apalachicola River. You can wildlife-watch on the 2-mi nature trails of this 680-acre park; alligators and snapping turtles are commonly seen around Lake Seminole. Fishing, birding, and camping are popular. | Exit 23 off Rte. 10; 25 mi east on U.S. 90, then 2 mi north on Hwy. 271 | 850/482–9006 | $3.25 per vehicle | Daily.

Dining

Red Canyon Grill. Southwestern. Native American items and other southwestern artifacts furnish the interior at this restaurant, 2 mi north of Marianna. The antler chandelier adds a further rustic touch. Most dishes are cooked on an open flame on the pecan wood–fired grill. Try the pecan-and-sage crusted chicken breast, or wood-grilled rib-eye steak, along with wood-grilled vegetables and pasta. You can eat in the main dining room or the cantina, off to the side. | 3297 Caverns Rd. | 850/482–4256 | Closed Sun., Mon. No lunch | $9–$15 | AE, MC, V.

Tony's. Italian. With booths and checkered tablecloths, this place is inexpensive and fun for families and a hangout for locals. They serve a mix of traditional Italian dishes and local fare such as fried catfish with hush puppies and a side of candied yams. | 4133 W. Lafayette St. | 850/482–2232 | Open 11–8:30, Closed Sun. | $7–$16 | AE, D, MC, V.

Lodging

Comfort Inn. Just off I–10, this two-story motor inn is 4 mi south of Marianna. You're close to several restaurants and to the Florida Caverns State Park. Complimentary Continental breakfast. Cable TV. Pool. Laundry service. Business services. Pets allowed. | 2175 Hwy. 71; Exit 21 off I–10 | 850/526–5600 | fax 850/482–7899 | www.comfortinn.com | 80 rooms | $45–$54 | AE, D, DC, MC, V.

Hinson House B&B. Built in 1920, the house stands at the center of town where the Civil War Battle of Marianna was fought. Rooms and common areas both are furnished in period antiques. Wine and beverages are offered each evening. Complimentary breakfast. Cable TV. No smoking. | 4338 Lafayette St. | 850/526–1500 or 800/531–4786 (PIN 1500) | www.phonl.com/hinson_house | 5 rooms | $55–$85 | AE, D, MC, V.

MATLACHA

MAP 3, I8

(Nearby towns also listed: Boca Grande, Cape Coral, Captiva Island, Fort Myers, Fort Myers Beach, Pine Island, Sanibel Island)

Matlacha is a quiet, "old Florida" town in the center of Pine Island, a bucolic spot in the middle of the Intracoastal Waterway, 30 min from Fort Meyers. Pine Island isn't known for its beaches but rather for its mangrove-fringed coast, which keeps development to a minimum. Zoned against hi-rises and high-density construction, Matlacha has retained a laid-back feel, its shopping area trimmed with shops and boutiques. It boasts of having the "Fishingest Bridge in the World," the bridge over Matlacha Pass. There's plenty to do nearby, such as kayaking in the Pine Island Sound Aquatic Preserve, camping along the coast, or taking a charter to the one of the outer islands fishing grounds.

Information: **Greater Pine Island Chamber of Commerce** | Box 525, Matlacha, 33993 | 941/283–0888.

Attractions

Matlacha Bridge. The first bridge to connect Matlacha to the mainland was constructed in 1927—a wooden swing bridge. It was called the "fishingest bridge in the world" because of the large amount of fish caught from its sides. A modern bridge went up in 1968, and fishers still find it a perfect place to drop their lines.

ON THE CALENDAR

JULY: *Mango Picnic.* Held at the KOA Kampground in Saint James City, this festival includes arts and crafts boothes, food vendors, live entertainment, and, of course, plenty of mangos and mango trees. | 941/283–0888.

Dining

Lob Lolly. American/Casual. This place serves breakfast, lunch, and dinner seven days a week at affordable prices. The simple menu has grilled cheese sandwiches, burgers, and lots of seafood. Colorful murals line the walls. | Pine Island Rd. | 941/283–4567 | $4–$14 | No credit cards.

Moretti's Seafood Restaurant. Italian. The Italian chef of this local favorite serves up a delicious array of traditional dishes such as veal Marsala, pastas, and authentic Italian pizzas. The menu also includes many seafood entrées such as stuffed flounder and fried calamari. Especially popular, and available either as an appetizer or main course, are the clams in marinara sauce. One of the city's most fun dining spots, the owners are friendly in three languages— German, Italian, and English. | 4200 Pine Island Rd. | 941/283–5825 | $9–$18 | D, MC, V.

Lodging

Bayview B&B. You might glimpse manatees or dolphins from the 70-ft-long pier of this B&B in the historic fishing village of Matlacha. Rooms reflect the natural tropical setting with bright colors and wicker furniture. The staff is helpful with knowledge of area tours and especially bird-watching information. After you try the watermelon cake here, you might want to take home the recipe. Complimentary Continental breakfast. Some kitchenettes, refrigerators, some microwaves. Cable TV. Dock, boating, watersports, fishing. Some pets allowed (fee). | 12251 Shoreview Dr. | 941/283–7510 | www.webbwiz.com/bayviewbb | 4 rooms | $79–$149 | No credit cards.

Bridgewater Inn. The spectacular little inn is built directly on a pier, with efficiencies and motel-style rooms. Fresh seafood is available steps away where a small fleet of shrimpers dock. Most rooms have a view of the water—dolphins and manatees might swim by your front door—and the fishing docks of Matlacha. Picnic area. Some kitchenettes, some microwaves, some refrigerators. Cable TV, no room phones. Dock, boating, fishing. | 4331 Pine Island Rd. | 941/283–2423 | fax 941/282–8440 | www.bridgewaterinn.com | 12 rooms | $39–$139 | AE, MC, V.

The Sun and the Moon Inn. The rooms in the two stilt houses that make up this inn each have private decks or patios with views of the water and islands. The interiors are equally lovely, with four-poster beds and down pillows and comforters. You can use the inn's canoe and rowboat to look for wildlife from the Matlacha waters. Complimentary Continental breakfast. Refrigerators. Cable TV, no room phones. Pool. Hot tub. Beach, dock, boating. Pets allowed. No kids under 18. No smoking. | 3962 N.W. Pine Island Rd. | 941/283–3192 or 888/321–3192 | fax 941/283–6042 | www.sunandmoon.net | 6 rooms | $99–$250 (minimum stay may be required) | AE, D, MC, V.

MELBOURNE

MAP 3, K6

(Nearby towns also listed: Cocoa, Cocoa Beach, Sebastian)

This thriving Space Coast city of 60,000, a focal point for Florida's technology industry, is 5 mi from the Atlantic. Named after the Australian city, Florida's Melbourne was settled in the 1860s. Growth followed the arrival of the Flagler railroad in the 1890s. Nowadays, the Kennedy Space Center in nearby Titusville is the draw, along with beaches, the Brevard Zoo, and the Brevard Museum of Arts and Sciences.

Nearby Indialantic, a 1-square-mi strip of land tucked between the Indian River and Atlantic Ocean, is a community of about 3,000 people. With a strong local preservation movement (and strict zoning), the town was designated as a bird sanctuary in 1975, and makes natural resource conservation a top priority.

Information: **Melbourne-Palm Bay Area Chamber of Commerce** | 1005 E Strawbridge Ave., Melbourne, 32901 | 321/724–5400 | www.melpb-chamber.org.

Attractions

Archie Carr National Wildlife Refuge. This is considered to be the most important nesting area for loggerhead sea turtles in the western hemisphere. Head to the barrier island between Melbourne Beach and Wabasso Beach to discover this haven. | 1300 Rte. A1A, Melbourne Beach | 321/861–0667 | Free | Daily dawn to dusk.

Brevard Museum of Art and Science. One block from the Indian River in historic Eau Gallie, this small museum opened in 1978. The 7,000 square ft hold touring art exhibitions from major collections, contemporary art by regionally and nationally recognized artists, and showings of its permanent collection of island and local art. Another building across from the museum has hands-on science exhibits for children. | 1463 Highland Ave. | 321/242–0737 | www.artandscience.org | $5 | Tues.–Sat. 10–5; Sun. 1–5.

MELBOURNE

INTRO
ATTRACTIONS
DINING
LODGING

Brevard Zoo. More than 400 animals, including alligators, crocodiles, giant anteaters, jaguars, and eagles, represent 120 species at this 56-acre zoo. On the seven-minute train ride, guides take you past the Australian Aviary and around Lemur Island. Special shows include alligator and crocodile feedings, river otter feedings, and a jaguar show. You can also paddle a kayak into the new Wetlands Exhibit on a 20-min guided tour. Or try the Wild Side Tour—accompanied by a zookeeper, you have a one-hour guided, up-close, off-the-boardwalk, animal experience. Take I–95, Exit 73 | 8225 N. Wickham Rd. | 321/254–3002 | www.brevardzoo.org | $6.50 | Daily 10–5.

Florida Institute of Technology. Founded in 1958 as a high-tech space-oriented university, this 130-acre campus 1 mi from Melbourne now houses 4,000 students. The picturesque 30-acre botanical garden is the main attraction—a lush forest with more than 200 species of palm, water oaks, and tropical vegetation. The Evans Library dispenses maps outlining self-guided tours. On the first Wednesday of every month, you can take a special guided tour to learn the school's early history. | 150 W. University Blvd., | 321/674–8000 | www.fit.edu | Free | Daily.

Long Point Park. Otter, bobcats, birds, manatees, and other protected wildlife live at this park, which is also a major roosting site for wood storks. The 85-acre camping park on the Indian River Lagoon, 20 mi south of Melbourne, has 113 campsites along the shoreline convenient for fishing. There is a playground, several pavilions of varying sizes, picnic tables, a wading bird pond, and an unguarded swimming beach. If you favor primitive camping, you can stay on Scout Island, connected by a bridge, and hike the 1-mi nature trails. Other amenities include pavilions of several sizes, picnic tables and firepit, and a wading bird pond, and an unguarded swimming pond. Take Hwy. A1A S | 700 Long Point Rd. | 321/952–4532 | $1 per day per vehicle | Daily.

Wickham Park. Melbourne's answer to New York City's Central Park, this 391-acre regional park is 5 mi north of downtown Melbourne and adjacent to the Brevard Community College–Melbourne Campus. It has a championship horseshoe pitch, an archery range, two 10-acre swimming lakes, an 18-hole disc golf course, and more than a mile of nature and bike trails. Within the pine forest, you can stay at 88 campsites with water and electric hookups, as well as 23 rustic campsites. There are two swimming lakes (guarded in season), three small fishing lakes, volleyball courts, playgrounds, and soccer fields. You can ride the horse trails, with a horse stable and show ring at the southwest corner of the park for equestrians. A large pavilion with a banquet kitchen and seating for up to 1,500 people is at the north end of the park, and an amphitheater is near the campgrounds. Many festivals, concerts, and other performing arts events are held here throughout the year. Take I–95 exit 73, then go 8½ mi east on Wickham Road. | 2500 Parkway Dr. | 321/255–4307 | Free | Daily.

ON THE CALENDAR

MAR.: *Baseball Spring Training.* Built in 1993, Space Coast Stadium is the training home of Florida's first professional baseball team, the Florida Marlins. | 321/633–9200.
APR.: *Melbourne Harbor Festival.* This festival attracts nearly 40,000 people each year and includes a boat show, arts and crafts, live entertainment, and food stands. It's held on New Haven Avenue in downtown Melbourne. | 321/722–1964.
JULY: *Indialantic Crafts Festival.* This family-oriented event showcases local artists. There's also a garden and gourmet marketplace where spices and herbs are sold. | 321/724–5400.

Dining

Bella's. Italian. Small and simple, this downtown restaurant serves good food for reasonable prices. The specialty is Parmigiana (chicken, veal, or eggplant), as well as the baked clams Arreganata, and a wide selection of desserts. The dining room is furnished in traditional red, green, and white, with small café tables and dim lights. | 1904 Municipal La. | 321/723–5001 | $8–$13 | AE, MC, V.

Chart House. Seafood. You can watch passing boats, pelicans, and manatees at this local rendition of the national restaurant known for drawing on a region's natural features. Here this translates to a one-story, white building nestled among tropical vegetation and perched on the Indian River in downtown Melbourne. Wall-to-wall windows provide a panoramic view of the water, and the large dining room is simple, with fine wood furnishings and elegant light fixtures. The menu includes a wide selection of seafood and landlubber dishes, but the focus is on seafood. Among the most popular dishes are the grilled ahi tuna marinated in coconut-rum, mango relish, and crispy black beans, the chicken with peppercorn crust and kona onions, and the filet mignon au poivre. | 2250 Front St. | 321/729–6558 | $15–$30 | No lunch | AE, DC, MC, V.

Conchy Joe's Seafood. Seafood. Floridian and Bahamian seafood dishes are prepared daily using only the freshest fish from the Space Coast at this casual waterfront restaurant overlooking the Indian River. Bahamian knicknacks are well placed throughout the large, window-lined dining room. You can dine outdoors on the deck. The raw oyster bar and seafood buffet are popular, as is the Angus steak. Live reggae Thursday to Sunday. | 1477 Pineapple Ave. | 321/253–3131 | Reservations not accepted | $12–$20 | AE, DC, MC, V.

Denver's Banana Bay. American. This bright and open waterfront spot on the Indian River serves fresh seafood in a cozy dining room furnished in bright, tropical colors. Reopened in 2000, under a new owner and Miami chef Brian Nelson, the menu includes seafood, steak, and pasta dishes. Specialties include tangerine tuna, mahimahi stuffed with crabmeat, 10-oz filet mignon, or chicken teriyaki. For dessert, try cheesecake, apple and Key lime pies, and homemade bread pudding. Brunch. | 2425 Pineapple Ave. | 321/242–2401 | $10–$19 | AE, DC, MC, V.

Island Fish Grill. Seafood. Relaxing reggae music and bamboo chairs give this eatery a Caribbean flavor. Popular dishes include onion-crusted grouper and crab-and-herb-crusted swordfish. Kids' menu. | 111 5th Ave. | 321/956–0559 | Reservations essential | Closed Sun. No lunch | $11–$18 | AE, D, MC, V.

Stuart's Yellow Dog Cafe. Continental. Converted in 1997 to a relatively upscale restaurant, 5 mi south of Melbourne, this small, rustic building along the Indian River has three distinctive dining areas. One is indoors around the kitchen, another in the downstairs library that has many, many pictures of small yellow dogs, and a third on the upstairs porch. Menu highlights include baked Brie with cranberry, cherry sauce, and fresh fruit as an appetizer, and sesame-encrusted tuna and onion-encrusted duck for entrées. The chef also prepares well-known, hearty Australian dishes including kangaroo, rattlesnake, and emu steak. Wine and beer. | 905 U.S. 1, Malabar | 321/956–3334 | $15–$29 | Reservations required Fri.–Sat. | Closed Mon. | AE, DC, MC, V.

Lodging

Comfort Inn Imperial. Egyptian elegance, European marble, and a crystal chandelier dominate the lobby at this three-story hotel. Rooms are done in deep, rich reds and golds and have one king-size or two double beds. The top floor has the three-bedroom Imperial Suite with a plush living room and dining area large enough to to seat 12 people. Take I–95 exit 73. Restaurant, bar, complimentary Continental breakfast. Some microwaves, refrigerators. Cable TV, in-room VCRs. Pool. Driving range, putting green. Baby-sitting. Laundry facilities. Business services. Airport shuttle. | 8298 N. Wickham Rd. | 321/255–0077 | fax 321/259–9633 | www.comfortinn.com | 137 rooms | $70–$129 | AE, D, DC, MC, V.

Courtyard by Marriott. Built in 1987, this three-story hotel is 1 mi from downtown Melbourne and 5 mi from the beach, making it popular with both business travelers and tourists. The small, charming lobby is decorated in deep red with floral patterns, mahogany furnishings, and stained glass. Rooms surround a tropically landscaped courtyard, and are white and pale blue-grey with large windows, a sitting area, and light wood furnishings. Take I–95 exit 71, then go east 3 mi. Restaurant, bar, picnic area. Some refrigerators. Cable TV. Pool. Hot tub. Gym. Laundry facilities. Business services, airport shuttle. | 2101 W. New

Haven Ave. | 321/724–6400 or 888/236–2427 | fax 321/984–4006 | www.marriott.com | 146 rooms | $109–$119 | AE, D, DC, MC, V.

Hilton at Rialto Place. This contemporary eight-story glass high-rise hotel is across the street from the airport and in the center of the local high-tech district, making it a popular choice for business travelers. The lobby's Italian marble, a maze of waterfalls, and lush tropical decor contrast with the simple, elegant rooms, done in earth tones. Rooms are spacious and accommodating to business travelers, with desks and data ports. Car rental on-site. Restaurant, bar. In-room data ports, some microwaves. Cable TV, some in-room VCRs. Pool. Hot tub. Tennis (lighted courts). Gym. Business services, airport shuttle. | 200 Rialto Pl. | 321/768–0200 | fax 321/984–2528 | www.hilton.com | 237 rooms | $89–$119 | AE, D, DC, MC, V.

Hilton Oceanfront. Built in 1986 and renovated in 1995, this 11-story beachfront, upscale Hilton 5 mi from downtown Melbourne is on a quieter beach than that of Cocoa Beach. The small lobby has an open lounge and floor-to-ceiling windows overlooking the pool with tropical landscaping, tiki bar, and wooden sundeck. Rooms, done in green and mauve, have either two double beds or one king-size bed with a sofa. A sliding glass door opens up to a small balcony. Restaurant, bar (with entertainment), some microwaves. Cable TV. Pool. Gym. Beach. Business services. | 3003 Rte. A1A N, Indiatlantic | 321/777–5000 | fax 321/777–3713 | www.hilton.com | 118 rooms | $99–$159 | AE, D, DC, MC, V.

Holiday Inn. Rooms are bright and rates reasonable at this two-story chain property across the street from the Indian River and a few blocks from downtown Melbourne. Renovated in 1994, rooms feature white and blue decor with sailboat paintings, and wood furnishings. Three mi from beaches. Take I–95 exit 72 east to U.S. 1 S. Restaurant, bar, room service. Some microwaves. Cable TV. Pool. Baby-sitting. Airport shuttle. | 420 S. Harbor City Blvd. | 407/723–5320 | fax 407/724–0581 | www.holiday-inn.com | 100 rooms | $71–$89 | AE, D, DC, MC, V.

Holiday Inn Melbourne Oceanfront. Right on the ocean, this hotel has two eight-story towers 5 mi from downtown Melbourne. A large wooden sundeck wraps around the pool area and along the beachfront. Standard room decor features bright tropical bedspreads, dark burgundy carpet, and wood furniture. Private balconies have pool or ocean views. Restaurant, bar (with entertainment), room service. In-room data ports, refrigerators. Cable TV. Pool. Hot tub. Tennis. Gym. Video games. Business services, airport shuttle. | 2605 Rte. A1A N, Indialantic | 321/777–4100 | fax 321/773–6132 | 299 rooms | $109–$129 | AE, D, DC, MC, V.

Melbourne Oceanfront Quality Suites Hotel. Two nine-story towers with two-room suites, done in blue and mauve, make up this oceanfront hotel 5 mi from Melbourne. The living areas have a small dining table and sofabed. From the bedroom, a large sliding glass door opens to a private balcony or patio overlooking the ocean. A large sundeck around the pool overlooks the ocean. Restaurant, bar. Complimentary Continental breakfast. In-room safes, microwaves. Cable TV, in-room VCRs. Pool. Hot tub. Video games. Business services. | 1665 Rte. A1A N, Indialantic | 321/723–4222 or 800/876–4222 | fax 321/768–2438 | 208 suites | $79–$149 | AE, D, DC, MC, V.

Radisson Suite Oceanfront Hotel. This 16-story, all-suites hotel sits right on the beach with the other out-of-town beachfront lodgings. Around the pool, the upper level wooden sundeck offers a great view of the beach and the lower level has a gazebo. Each suite has contemporary furnishings with a sofabed, a dining table, and a sliding glass door that opens to a small private balcony overlooking the beach. Beware: views from the first and second floors are partially blocked by natural vegetation. Bedrooms have a king-size bed and a sliding glass door overlooking the beach. Restaurant, bar. In-room safes, kitchenettes, microwaves, refrigerators. Cable TV, in-room VCRs. Pool. Hot tub. Laundry facilities. Business services. | 3101 Rte. A1A, Indiatlantic | 321/773–9260 or 800/333–3333 | fax 321/777–3190 | www.radisson.com | 167 suites | $125–$200 | AE, D, DC, MC, V.

Ramada Oceanfront Resort. Ten mi north of Melbourne along the coast, this hotel is on a quiet strip of beach near Patrick Air Force Base—a great location if you want to bypass crowded beaches but still be close to the attractions. The lobby looks out onto the undisturbed dunes covered with sea grapes and sea oats. All rooms have private balconies with view of either the street, the pool, or the ocean. Restaurant, bar. In-room data ports, microwaves, refrigerators. Cable TV. Pool. Hot tub. Tennis. Business services. | 1035 Rte. A1A, Satellite Beach | 321/777–7200 or 800/345–1782 | fax 321/773–4608 | www.ramada.com | 108 rooms | $99–$119 | AE, D, DC, MC, V.

Super 8. Four mi from downtown Melbourne and 5 miles from the beach, this two-story budget motel, built in 1970 and renovated in 1997, is convenient and clean. Each room has large windows, a sitting area, and one king-size or two double beds. Complimentary Continental breakfast. In-room data ports, some microwaves, some refrigerators. Cable TV. Business services. | 1515 S. Harbor City Blvd. | 321/723–4430 | fax 321/723–4312 | www.super8.com | 56 rooms | $60–$66 | AE, D, DC, MC, V.

Windemere Inn by the Sea. Some rooms at this oceanfront B&B have balconies and ocean views; all have antiques and painted furniture reminiscent of the Victorian era. There's a gazebo on the beach. Complimentary breakfast. Some in-room hot tubs. TV in common area. Massage. Beach, fishing. Library. Business services. | 815 S. Miramar Ave. | 321/728–9334 or 800/224–6583 | fax 321/728–2741 | www.windemereinn.com | 8 rooms | $110–$195 | AE, D, DC, MC, V.

MIAMI

MAP 3, F4

(Suburbs and nearby towns also listed: Coconut Grove, Coral Gables, Hialeah, Hollywood, Key Biscayne, Miami Beach)

Miami is one of America's weirdest and most rewarding cities. It is one of the country's capitals of cultural diversity, with a majority Latin population that exhibits manic levels of energy and emotion on what amounts, geographically, to a paved swamp midway between the Everglades and the Atlantic Ocean.

A bit more than a hundred years ago, Miami (believed to be an Indian name for "sweet water") was a mosquito-infested swampland with an Indian trading post on the Miami River. Passenger train service to Miami began on April 22, 1896; the city was incorporated later that year. It wasn't until after WWI, however, that the first boom times began. Gambling and a resistance to Prohibition laws added to the allure of its weather and beaches. The Depression ended the fun, though the 1930s saw the creation of Miami Beach's Art Deco hotels. In the 1950s gamblers and gangsters continued to run between Miami and Havana.

After the Castro coup in 1959, Miami's Cuban population swelled, making it the city's majority group. In 1965 and in the late '70s, hundreds of thousands of Cubans arrived in a period of weeks into Miami. In the 1980s, the city gained notoriety as the major east coast entry port for drug smugglers, and the corollary lifestyles made a television smash in *Miami Vice*, bringing tourism and attention to the colorful city. Fashion and trendiness have since become bywords for Miami, and the city is now among the most popular tourist destinations in America.

With such little urban history behind it, Miami could be called a teenager among major cities. The city's growing pains—from hurricanes to riots—still make news, most recently on the international stage, when on Thanksgiving Day 1999, six-year-old Elian Gonzalez survived the trip to Miami from Cuba on a wooden raft. A fierce custody battle raged around his relatives' Little Havana home, covered step by step by media around the globe.

But to understand this phenomenon, one must realize that about half of Greater Miami's population of 2.1 million is Latin, and most of that Cuban. The fabric of modern Miami began to take shape in 1959, when Fidel Castro and a small band of *compañeros* took over the government and Fidel became dictator of Cuba. Thousands of refugees fled north to Miami, to wait out his political demise. They're still waiting (every few months, premature rumors of Castro's death still send a jolt of energy through the Latin community), though new generations of American-born Cubans feel more firmly rooted in the local soil.

For many tourists, these often-foreign aspects of daily life are a curious spectacle on the first leg of a Caribbean journey. The port of Miami is the cruise capital of the world, handling 3 million passengers a year with the world's largest year-round fleet. It also handles more megaships—vessels capable of transporting more than 2,000 people at a time—than any other port in the world.

For those who stay on land long enough to explore its different neighborhoods— where, in addition to Cubans, you can find populations from Brazil, China, Colombia, El Salvador, France, Germany, Greece, Haiti, Iran, Israel, Italy, Jamaica, Lebanon, Malaysia, Mexico, Nicaragua, Panama, Puerto Rico, Russia, Spain, Sweden, and Venezuela— Miami's distinctive, charming neighborhood enclaves are exciting ventures into cultural variation.

Miami is a proud professional sports town, home to the only NFL team to put together a perfect season, the Miami Dolphins. Its other professional teams include the Florida Marlins (baseball), Miami Heat (men's basketball), Miami Sol (women's basketball), and Miami Matadors (hockey). The University of Miami Hurricanes football and base-ball teams are perennially among the nation's best, and South Florida high school teams are considered to produce some of the nation's top pool of college football talent. Of course, with such brilliant weather, many people prefer to participate in aquatic activities such as boating and diving.

CUBAN CUISINE

If you're driving through neighborhoods of Miami and Hialeah on Christmas Eve with your windows open, you'll detect a mysterious, and delicious, scent wafting from backyards across the city. It's pork. And Cubans are doing the cooking, in an old-style roasting method that hearkens to the days when Cubans would prepare the *nochebuena* feast by slaughtering and roasting a pig and cooking it in an open-fire pit. Because of food shortages in Cuba, most of traditional Cuban cuisine is kept alive in Miami.

On Dec. 24, besides *lechón asado* (roasted pig), you'll find all the fixings typical of Cuban cuisine: *arroz con frijoles negros* (fluffy white rice with black beans, a staple often called *moros y cristianos*, or Moors and Christians, for the color contrast); *yucca con mojo* (a root vegetable cultivated by the Taíno people of Cuba, served with a typ-ical tangy marinade of sour orange juice and garlic); *tostones* (crunchy fried green plaintain patties); and sweet *platanos maduros* (sliced fried, ripe plantains).

Columbus arrived in Cuba in 1492 with a supply of beef and live pigs, and these still constitute the heart of Cuban cuisine—a Creole recasting of Spanish cuisine with Chinese, African, and Native Indian influences. Other traditional dishes *palomilla* (sirloin steak); *picadill* (ground beef served with a *sofrito* of sautéed onion, garlic, and green bell peppers with herbs and spices); and, perhaps most famous of all, *arroz con pollo* (chicken cooked with a moist yellow rice).

The hundreds of Cuban bakeries across the city constitute the backbone of Cuban social life, and present perhaps the best opportunity to practice a little Span-ish. Ask for un café, and you'll get a hard shot of Cuban coffee served in a thimble-sized plastic cup. Café con leche is three-quarters milk; this with pan cubano (Cuban bread is like French or Italian, but with a doughier middle) constitutes a true Cuban breakfast. Sample from a variety of pastelitos, flaky pastries stuffed with different ingredients. The classic *pastelito de guayaba* has guava marmalade filling.

If it weren't untrue in a literal sense, it would be fair to consider Miami Latin America's most important city. Greater Miami is the Latin American headquarters for more than 150 U.S. and multinational corporations. It's home to 40 foreign bank agencies, 11 Edge Act banks, 23 foreign trade offices, 31 bi-national chambers of commerce, and 53 foreign consulates. Miami International Airport is the world's principal Latin American hub.

Although tourists will probably never see any of the drugs-and-violence sizzle depicted in the 1980s TV show *Miami Vice*—the forum that earned the city much of its lingering notoriety and glitz—they don't need to get a sense of the color and emotional electricity of the city. Those residents who seek a quieter life move north to Broward County; those who remain, and tourists, can take in ocean breezes on immaculate beaches and sip *café con leche* in this strange paradise.

Information: **Greater Miami Convention and Visitors Bureau** | 701 Brickell Ave., Ste. 2700, Miami, 33131 | 305/539–3034 or 800/933–8448 | www.tropicoolmiami.com.

NEIGHBORHOODS

Coconut Grove. "The Grove," as locals call it, is South Florida's oldest settlement. Somehow, residents have been able to maintain a jungle-within-a-village feel over the decades. For many, it's a tropical version of New York City's once-bohemian Greenwich Village. At night, however, Coconut Grove is among the country's trendiest hotspots, an outpost from South Beach.

Coral Gables. This charming city tucked into southwest Miami was one of the world's first fully planned communities. George Merrick conceived of it as an American Venice, with canals and gracious homes. Built of stucco and quarried limestone in a Spanish Colonial Revival style, the city's clean, green streets gleam under the strict eyes of its leaders. Miracle Mile, the town's main commercial drag, and its surrounding streets exude subdued Mediterranean elegance and are lined with some of South Florida's best restaurants, boutiques, and homes.

Downtown. Downtown Miami dazzles from a distance. Its attractive, colorful skyline suggests a futuristic metropolis as rapid transit trains zoom across a Miami River bridge arched with neon, and colossal cruise ships hover in the background. The truth is, however, that besides good bayfront shopping, downtown is deserted at night, and good mainly for electronic goods and other cheap shopping in the daytime. Slightly north of downtown's handful of skyscrapers, at 40th St and N. Miami Ave., is an emerging gallery, restaurant, and club area known as the Design District.

Fisher Island. This gated residential community is home to wealthy Miami residents and is mostly private, though if you have a reservation at the Fisher Island Club, the island's only hotel, you can catch a glimpse of how the upper crust lives.

Key Biscayne and Virginia Key. You have to be wealthy to live on either of these two islands, but they remain popular stops among locals and tourists for a day's outing. Crandon Park is possibly Miami's best beach and is home to South Florida's oldest standing structure, the Cape Florida Lighthouse. All the trees on Key Biscayne were flattened by 1992's Hurricane Andrew, but replanting has restored much of the getaway atmosphere. Virginia Key is home to the Miami Seaquarium.

Little Havana. The original neighborhood where Miami's Cubans settled may seem now just like any other part of the city's Latin commercial dominion. If you look, though, you can still see old men in guayabera shirts tilting over dominos in little parks here in southwest Miami. Its role as the spiritual center of the Cuban community is especially evident when over a million people crowd Southwest 8th St., the heart of Little Havana, for a Carnival-like fete called *Calle Ocho* (8th Street).

Miami Beach. The town of Miami Beach lies on a barrier island 2 mi off Miami's mainland. Luxury hotels and first-rate beaches line its entire shoreline, but the southern tip, referred to as South Beach, is most remarkable. Its Art Deco District features a square-mile zone of about 800 pastel buildings constructed from the late 1920s to the early 1940s. Over the past two decades this district has increasingly drawn crowds of models, movie stars, artists, and clubgoers. Today it rates as possibly the world's hottest spot for people watching for the rich and famous.

North Miami/North Miami Beach. If you want to catch a glimpse of what Florida looked like to visitors in the 1950s and '60s, drive north along the stretch of A1A from the Sunny Isles Causeway at Northwest 163rd Street. Though this area is quickly being overrun by luxury condominiums and resorts that cater to the new Florida tourist, there are still a bevy of colorful neighborhood restaurants in these northern suburbs that reveal the city's diverse ethnic make-up, as well as a number of remarkably unspoiled natural enclaves.

TRANSPORTATION

Airports: The busy **Miami International Airport** is 7 mi west of downtown Miami. About 1,500 flights come in and out of Miami Airport every day. More than 33 million people pass through the airport every year, and more than half of them are international travelers. | 4200 N.W. 21 St. | 305/876–7000 | www.miami-airport.com.

Airport Transportation: Taxi, shuttle, Metrobus, and limousine service are available outside baggage claim areas on Level 1. A taxi to Downtown Miami will cost about $15–$18, including a $1 surcharge for trips originating at Miami International Airport or the Port of Miami. **SuperShuttle**'s blue vans (305/871–2000) will take you most anyplace in Downtown Miami or the Port of Miami for about $7–$9, to Miami Beach for about $11–$14.

Bus Lines: Greyhound (800/231–2222) serves several stations in Greater Miami. There are stations in Downtown (700 Biscayne Blvd. | 305/374–6160), the Airport (4111 N.W. 27th St. | 305/871–1810), and North Miami (16560 N.E. 6th Avenue | 305/945–0801).

Train Lines: Amtrak (8303 N.W. 37th Ave. | 800/872–7245) stops in downtown Miami.

Public Transportation: Elevated **Metrorail** (305/770–3131) trains run from downtown Miami northwest to Hialeah and south along U.S. 1 to South Dade, daily from 5 AM to midnight. The fare is $1.25.

The fun, elevated **Metromover** (305/638–6700) spans 4½ mi along two loops around downtown Miami. The fare is $.25.

Tri-Rail (800/874–7245) offers daily commuter service connecting Miami north to Broward and Palm Beach Counties, with 19 stops along a 71-mi route. Transfer from Metrorail at the Hialeah station. Fares range from $5.50–$9.25.

Metrobus (305/770–3131) stops have green and white signs with route info. The exact fare required is $1.25, $.60 for seniors and students.

DRIVING AND PARKING

Driving is the nearly unavoidable way to get through Miami's different neighborhoods. At rush hour, traffic is a problem nearly everywhere.

Within Miami, addresses fall into four quadrants: NW, NE, SW, and SE. The north–south diving line is Flagler Street, and the east–west line is Miami Avenue. Numbering starts with these axes and gets higher the farther away an address is from them. Avenues run north–south, streets east–west. Hialeah, Miami Beach, Coral Gables, and Key Biscayne have their own numbering systems.

From the northwest, I–75 is the major thoroughfare into Miami. From the north, Florida's Turnpike is a toll road. I–95 is free, and runs north–south along the coast, and turns into U.S. 1 after it is outside downtown Miami, which runs south to Key West. State road 836 is the primary east–west transverse, near downtown becoming the Julia Tuttle Causeway (395) to Miami Beach. This Causeway will drop you off in South Beach at 5th Street, ending at Ocean Drive at the water. The Palmetto Expressway (826) is the primary residential highway, running from I–95 west through Hialeah and south through Kendall and into South Miami. To head west through the Everglades from Miami, use Tamiami Trail (U.S. 41) and the Homestead Extension of Florida's Turnpike.

For parking in downtown Miami, attended lots are your best bet, and will give you a greater sense of security. Coral Gables meter maids expect a notoriously great degree of punctuality.

Attractions

ART AND ARCHITECTURE

Dade County Courthouse. From 1928, when it was built, until 1977, this 24-story building was the tallest structure in the United States south of Washington, DC. It is still used as a courthouse—and as a winter home by migrating vultures. The lobby has a grand atrium that was restored in 1999 to its original Neoclassical Revival style. | 73 W. Flagler St. | 305/375–5278 | Mon.–Fri. 8–5.

First Union Financial Center. Clocking in at a height of 55 stories, this is the tallest building in Miami. Though lacking an observation deck, it does have a one-acre plaza shaded by lofty palm trees. | 200 S. Biscayne Blvd.

Freedom Tower. Built in 1925 as the home of the *Miami Daily News,* this building was used in the 1960s to process some 500,000 Cuban immigrants seeking asylum from Fidel Castro's regime. Though vacant today, it was restored to its original splendor in 1988 and may be the future home for a Cuban museum. | 600 Biscayne Blvd.

U.S. Courthouse. Erected in 1931, this keystone building houses a large, Depression-era painting depicting many of the images which defined Florida during the epoch. Video cameras and audio recorders are not allowed inside the courthouse. | 300 N.E. 1st Ave., between N.E. 3rd and 4th Sts. | 305/536–3051 | Free | Building weekdays 8:30–5; security guards open courtroom on request.

BEACHES, PARKS, AND NATURAL SITES

Domino Park. Drop by to witness a scene lifted from the Cuba of yore: throngs of elderly *exilios,* men sporting guayaberas, passing the time playing dominos. | S.W. 8th St. at S.W. 15th Ave. | Daily.

Greynolds Park. This 185-acre expanse of woods in North Miami has bike and nature trails as well as picnic areas, a golf course, and paddleboat rental. There is also a rookery with roosting and nesting areas for wading birds and guided bird walks and owl prowls. | 17530 W. Dixie Hwy., North Miami Beach | 305/945–3425 | Free weekdays; $2 per vehicle on weekends and holidays | Daily dawn to dusk.

Mildred and Claude Pepper Bayfront Park. Stroll along Biscayne Bay and take in the views, grab a bite to eat, or take a boat ride from the pier in this 32-acre park. About five times a month you can catch live music in the evenings, though not for free. | 301 N. Biscayne Blvd. | 305/358–7550 | Free | Daily 7–6.

CULTURE, EDUCATION, AND HISTORY

Cuban Memorial Boulevard. The *Eternal Torch of the Brigade 2506* and a relief map of Cuba are among the monuments within this two-block area in Little Havana; it's a memorial to all of those who have fought for the island's freedom. | S.W. 8th St. at S.W. 13th Ave.

★ **Gusman Center for the Performing Arts.** Not to be confused with Gusman Concert Hall, this stunning hall in downtown Miami was built in the 1920s as a movie palace and is now the venue for Florida Philharmonic concerts and movie screenings during the Miami Film Festival. | 174 E. Flagler St. | 305/374–2444 or 305/372–0925 | Call for schedule.

Miami-Dade Community College. This is the downtown campus of the nation's largest community college. There are two excellent art galleries. | 300 N.E. 2nd Ave., between N.E. 3rd and 4th Sts. | 305/237–3278 | www.mdcc.edu | Free | Daily.

Centre Gallery. The larger of Miami-Dade Community College's two galleries, this third-floor space houses sculpture, painting, and photography exhibitions. | 300 N.E. 2nd Ave., between N.E. 3rd and 4th Sts. | 305/237–3278 | Free | Mon.–Thurs. 9–5.

Frances Wolfson Art Gallery. On the fifth-floor of Miami-Dade Community College, this gallery is home to smaller photo expositions. | 300 N.E. 2nd Ave., between N.E. 3rd and 4th Sts. | 305/237–3278 | Free | Mon.–Thurs. 9–5.

MUSEUMS

American Police Hall of Fame and Museum. Easy to identify thanks to the gravity-defying police car that adorns one of its outer walls, this museum is a collection of all things police, ranging from an electric chair and various weapons to a 400-ton marble memorial commemorating the 6,000 police officers who have died in action since 1960. | 3801 Biscayne Blvd. | 305/573–0700 | $6 | Daily 10–5:30.

Gold Coast Railroad Museum. In the Richmond area of Miami, this museum houses antique railroad cars and both steam and diesel engines. Famous steam engines include the #153 built in 1928 and the #113 built in the 1930s, both manufactured by Baldwin Co. You can see Presidential Car No. 1, built in 1948 for President Franklin D. Roosevelt and passed down to Presidents Truman, Eisenhower, and Reagan. | 12450 S.W. 152nd St. (Coral Reef Dr.) | 305/253–0063 | $5; $2 to ride link train on weekends | Weekdays 11–3, weekends 11–4.

Main Public Library. Miami's largest library contains almost 4 million books in addition to art exhibits in its second-floor lobby and auditorium. | 101 W. Flagler St. | 305/375–2665 | www.mdpls.org | Free | Mon.–Wed. and Fri.–Sat. 9–6, Thurs. 9–9, Sun. 1–5.

Historical Museum of Southern Florida. This facility lives up to its name by providing a look into the region's rich past, most notably the early days of the railroad and its impact on the area. | 101 W. Flagler St. | 305/375–3000 | www.historical-museum.org | $5 or $6 (including the Miami Art Museum) | Mon.–Wed. and Fri.–Sat. 10–5, Thurs. 10–9, Sun. noon–5.

Miami Art Museum. One of Miami's largest museums, this, along with the Miami-Dade Library, is the centerpiece for the Miami-Dade Cultural Center. It exhibits contemporary art of the western hemisphere with a focus on works from the 1940s to the present. In addition to 80 works in the permanent collection, the museum features provocative works by international artists. | 101 W. Flagler St. | 305/375–3000 | $5 or $6 (including the Historical Museum of Southern Florida) | Tues.–Fri. 10–5, weekends noon–5.

Miami Children's Museum. With its 45,000 square ft of exhibition space, this institution at Vizcaya Metrorail Station will be one of the country's ten largest children's museums when it opens in 2002. Kids will be able to learn with the "Mini-tropolis" where they can use the grocery store, bank, and other grown-up tools. The Museum will also feature an interactive music and art gallery. | 305/663–8800 (for further information).

★ **Miami-Dade Cultural Center.** This 3-acre compound comprises downtown Miami's three main cultural institutions, Miami Art Museum, Historical Museum of Southern Florida, and the Main Public Library. | 101 W. Flagler, between N.W. 1st and 2nd Aves | 305/275–2665 | Museums $5, library free | Daily.

Miami Museum of Science. Exhibits change every 8 to 12 weeks here, ranging from "Sports Challenge" and "Hunters in the Sky" to "Sharks!" The planetarium has good laser shows, and the wildlife center is fun. | 3280 S. Miami Ave. | 305/854–4247 | $10 planetarium, $9 wildlife center, $6 laser show | Daily 10–6 | www.miamisci.org.

Rubell Family Collection. This private collection of Don and Mera Rubell is a shrine of contemporary art, showcasing such works as paintings by Keith Haring and photography by Cindy Sherman. The works displayed in this 40,000-square-ft gallery rotate often, so you'll always find something new. | 95 N.W. 29th St. | 305/573–6090 | Free | June–Sept., Fri.–Sun. 11–4; Oct.–May, by appointment.

RELIGION AND SPIRITUALITY

Ancient Spanish Monastery. Randolph Hearst, never known for moderation, had this 12th-century Spanish monastery disassembled and moved to Florida in 1925. Built in Segovia, it is now one of the oldest buildings in the Western Hemisphere. The cloisters are embellished with the coats of arms of families who supported the monastery during its heyday. | 16711 W. Dixie Hwy., North Miami Beach | 305/945–1462 | www.spanishmonastery.com | $4.50 | Mon.–Sat. 10–4, Sun. 1–5.

Historic Gesu Church. The only old South Florida church still on its original site, this 1922, Venetian-style building has a three-story portico and a rose window, as well as other stained-glass windows. | 118 N.E. 2nd St. | 305/379–1424.

SHOPPING

Aventura Mall. With more 250 shops headed by powerhouse department stores such as Macy's and Bloomingdale's, this complex also has a 24-screen movie theater as well as dining choices ranging from the Cheesecake Factory to the Rainforest Cafe. | 19501 Biscayne Blvd., Aventura | 305/935–1110 | Daily.

Bayside Marketplace. If you're visiting Miami and feel homesick for familiar shopping, this is a good stop. The outdoor mall, bounded by Biscayne and Port Boulevards on Biscayne Bay, has many national stores, like The Gap, and Victoria's Secret, as well as specialty shops, gift shops, and more than 20 eateries. The view of the bay is good, too. | 401 N. Biscayne Blvd. | 305/577–3344 | Free | Mon.–Thurs., 10–10, Fri.–Sat. 10–11, Sun. 11–9; restaurant hours vary.

Calle Ocho. The pulsating heart of Little Havana, *Calle Ocho* (8th Street) is the place to capture the flavor of Cuba, from restaurants and cafeterias to shops.hawking hand-rolled cigars and guayaberas. | S.W. 8th St. | Daily.

Dolphin Mall. This new mall has more than 200 designer outlets, specialty stores, and entertainment venues, not to mention a 28-screen multiplex cinema. | Hwy. 836 at Florida's Tpke | 305/365–7446 | www.dolphinmall.com | Daily.

El Credito Cigar Factory. Though the tobacco leaves now come from the Dominican Republic and Mexico, this family-run outfit employs Cuban workers. Spanning three generations and dating back to the island nation's pre-revolutionary times, El Credito has served clients from Bill Clinton to Bill Cosby. | 1106 S.W. 8th St. | 305/858–4162 or 800/726–9481 | Weekdays 8–5:30, Sat. 10–6.

The Falls Shopping Center. One of the more upscale shopping malls in Miami, The Falls is named after the small waterfalls that enhance its common area. Two department stores (Macy's and Bloomingdale's), 50 specialty shops, a multiplex, and several restaurants round out the features. | 8888 S.W. 136th St., at U.S. 1, Kendall | 305/255–4570 | Daily.

Galleria International Mall. This indoor mall greets international visitors with a multiethnic food court, offering choices from India, Cuba, Brazil, and the United States. Stores include Marshall's and a variety of clothing, sporting goods, and electronics retailers. | 243 Flagler St., between N.E. 1st and 2nd Sts. | 305/371–4536 | Daily.

SPECTATOR SPORTS

Calder Race Course. You can go to the races seven months of the year at this Thoroughbred track in North Miami. One annual highlight is the Festival of the Sun, four major stakes races for Florida-bred horses, that takes place every October. | N.W. 27th Ave. (University Dr.), at 210th St. | 305/625–1311 | $2 grandstand, $4 clubhouse | May–Jan., daily; gates open at 11 AM, races start at 12:30. Wed. and Thurs. no live racing, TV only.

Flagler Greyhound Track. From June to November, dog racing takes place at this Little Havana track. Weekends you can stop by the Flagler Flea Market (50¢) and eat some ethnic cuisine while you peruse the stands or check out the live music. | N.W. 38th Court, at N.W. 37th Ave. and 7th St. | www.flaglerdogs.com | 305/649–3000 | Jun. 1–Nov. 30, Mon.–Sat. 8 PM, Tues., Thurs., Sat. 1 PM, Sun. 4 PM; flea market weekends year-round.

Florida Marlins. Winner of the 1997 World Series, this National League team plays home games at Pro Player Stadium. | 2267 N.W. 199th St. | 305/626–7400 | www.flamarlins.com | $2–$45 | Apr.–Oct., call for game schedule.

Miami Dolphins. This is the only NFL team ever to go undefeated for an entire season (17–0 in 1972). The Dolphins play in the 75,000-seat Pro Player Stadium, 16 mi northwest of downtown. | 305/620–2578 | www.miamidolphins.com | $37–$130 | Aug.–Jan., call for game schedule.

Miami Heat. This NBA team shoots hoops in the 20,000-seat American Airlines Arena, on the Miami waterfront. The Heat were the Atlantic Division Champs for the 1996–97 and 1997–98 seasons. | 601 Biscayne Blvd. | 786/777–4328 | www.nba.com/heat | $5–$250 | Nov.–Apr., call for game schedule.

Miami Jai Alai Fronton. Invented in the Basque region of Spain, jai alai is a mainstay of the Florida gambling scene. One mi east of the airport, this Miami *fronton* (court) established in 1926 is America's oldest. Spectators watch as two teams hurl a *pelota* (ball) along a 176-ft-long court at breakneck speeds, trying to catch it in their extended *cesta* (basket). You can wager on which teams you think will win or the order in which you think they'll finish. | 3500 N.W. 37th Ave. | 305/633–6400 | www.fla-gaming.com | $1; $2 for reserved seats; $5 for Courtview Club | Mon., Wed., and Fri.–Sat., noon–5 and 7–midnight; Thurs., noon–midnight; Sun. 1–6.

Miami Sol. This WNBA team brings women's professional basketball to American Airlines Arena. | 601 Biscayne Blvd. | 305/577–4328 | www.wnba.com/sol | $5–$25 | Jun.–Aug., call for game schedule.

SIGHTSEEING TOURS/TOUR COMPANIES

Celebration Charters. This company runs two popular bay cruises in Miami, both departing from the Bayside Marketplace. The "Bay Ex.Cape" is a bilingual (English/Spanish) sightseeing cruise aboard an air-conditioned boat that explores Millionaires' Row and the Venetian Islands. Their "Brunch Cruise" is only on weekends but includes a breakfast buffet. | 401 Biscayne Blvd. | 305/373–7001 | Bay Ex.Cape $12; Brunch Cruise $20 | Bay Ex.Cape daily at 11, 1, 3, 5, and 7; Brunch Cruise Sat.–Sun. at 11 and 1.

Heritage of Miami II. Beginning and ending at Bayside Marketplace, these tours are provided on an 85-ft schooner. The route loops around Biscayne Bay, the homes of some prominent celebrities, and Vizcaya. | 401 Biscayne Blvd. | 305/442–7001 | 1-hr tours $10, 2-hr tours $15 | Daily, call for schedules.

Island Lady and ***Pink Lady.*** You can tour Biscayne Bay, the Port of Miami, and Millionaires' Row on these 72-ft yachts. By day there are narrated 90-minute trips every hour from the Hyatt Regency Hotel; after dark the yachts become floating discos. | 41 Biscayne Blvd. | 305/379–5119 | $14 | Cruises, Mon.–Fri. 9 AM–10 PM, Fri–Sun 8 AM–9 PM.

OTHER POINTS OF INTEREST

American Airlines Arena. This stylish, ultramodern bay-front complex is the home of two professional basketball teams: the NBA's Miami Heat and the WNBA's Miami Sol. It also houses a slew of shops and restaurants, and it connects to the Bayside Marketplace via a pedestrian bridge. | 601 Biscayne Blvd. between N.E. 8th and N.E. 9th Sts. | 305/557–4328.

Plaza Bolivar. Punctuated with the colorful flags of Central and South American nations, the plaza centers around a statue of Ponce de León and a monument to those Cubans who left their homeland for this "land of endless opportunity". | Biscayne Blvd. between 2nd and 3rd Sts. | Daily.

Little Haiti. Signs in Creole and vividly painted buildings welcome you to this neighborhood, home to thousands of refugees from one of the western world's poorest countries. During daylight hours, the area is safe for tourists; at night it has little to offer visitors and can feel a bit unsafe. | North Miami Ave., 54th–59th Sts.

Caribbean Marketplace. Modeled after Port-au-Prince's Iron Market, this is a collection of crafts and goods kiosks and site of occasional live music performances. A few inexpensive restaurants serve up authentic Haitian treats such as goat stew, and small stores called botanicas sell potions to the many in the area who practice voodoo. | N. Miami Ave. between 54th and 59th Sts.

Miami Seaquarium. Killer whales, manatees, dolphins, sharks, sea lions, and tropical fish are on display in this zooquarium, on Biscayne Bay, in Virginia Key. You can visit a shark pool, a tropical reef aquarium, and West Indian manatees. Discover Bay, an endangered mangrove habitat, is home to indigenous Florida fish and rays, alligators, herons, egrets, and ibis. | 4400 Rickenbacker Causeway | 305/361–5705 | www.miamiseaquarium.com | $21.95 | Daily 9:30–6; ticket booth closes at 4, last series of shows begins at 3.

ON THE CALENDAR

NOV.–MAR.: *Florida Grand Opera.* A high-quality five-opera season produced by the Florida Grand Opera features internationally known performers. Performances are at the 2,300-seat Miami-Dade County Auditorium, just west of downtown; some are also held at the Broward Center for the Performing Arts in Fort Lauderdale. The season lengths vary from year to year. | 305/854–1643.

FEB.: *Miami Film Festival.* The Film Society of America and the Film Society of Miami sponsor this 10-day marathon of international, domestic, and locally made films. | 305/377–3456.

MAR.: *Carnaval Miami/Calle Ocho Festival.* This celebration of Cuban life and culture, Miami's biggest annual street festival, draws a half-million visitors to 8th Street in Little Havana on one Sunday in early March. You can sample Cuban food from more than 300 vendors and take in entertainment at the 25 stages. | 305/644–8888.

DEC.–JAN.: *Orange Bowl and Junior Orange Bowl Festival.* The Orange Bowl football game is the highlight of this event, which also includes the King Orange Jamboree Parade and more than 20 youth-oriented events. | 305/662–1210 or 305/371–4600.

NOV.: *Miami Book Fair International.* The largest book fair in the country is held on the Wolfson campus of Miami-Dade Community College. The highlights include talks by authors and book signings and sales. | 305/237–3032.

WALKING TOUR

A Walking Tour of Downtown Miami (approximately 3 hours)

Perhaps the best way to see downtown is on the 25¢ elevated rail system known as **Metromover.** Kids will love it, and it's hard for adults not to get excited by the small, comfortable cars that run without drivers above the city streets. After a preliminary tour of its two loops, get off at the Bayfront Park Metromover station at **Mildred and Claude Pepper Bayfront Park,** which extends east from busy, palm-filled Biscayne Boulevard to the bay. Before you is the heart of downtown Miami. The 55-story **First Union Financial Center** (200 S. Biscayne Blvd.) is the tallest building in Miami. Across the street is the **Hotel Inter-Continental Miami,** a 34-story monolith with *The Spindle,* a huge sculpture by Henry Moore, in the lobby. Rising up in the corner of the park is the white Challenger Memorial to the space shuttle that exploded in 1986; you'll also see the old Miami Memorial Library and the bandshell.

Walk north along Biscayne Boulevard to **Plaza Bolivar,** a tribute by Cuban immigrants to their adopted country. You'll reach the JFK Torch of Friendship, a plaza adorned with plaques representing all the South and Central American countries, except Cuba. Behind the torch is downtown's greatest tourist attraction, the **Bayside Marketplace,** an entertainment, dining, and retail complex that closely resembles, among others, New York City's South Street Seaport and Boston's Faneuil Hall. From Bayside, it will be hard not to notice **American Airlines Arena,** completed in 1999 for the NBA Miami Heat. A pedestrian footbridge links the two sites. On Biscayne Boulevard, at Northeast 6th Street, is the **Freedom Tower,** built in 1925 for the now-defunct *Miami Daily News.*

It was inspired by Seville's Giralda Tower. A Cuban-American museum is being installed within. Cross Biscayne Boulevard and walk up N.E. 3rd Street to N.E. 2nd Avenue, where you'll come to the downtown campus of **Miami-Dade Community College,** home of two worthy art galleries. One block further west stands the **U.S. Courthouse,** notable for the epic Depression-era mural inside that depicts Floridian prosperity.

Turn south on N.E. 1st Avenue, and walk one block to N.E. 2nd Street. On the corner stands the 1922 **Historic Gesu Church,** one of South Florida's oldest. Return to N.E. 2nd Avenue, then turn right. Before you is the architectural clutter that characterizes downtown Miami: a hodgepodge of gaudy outlet shops, homely storefronts, and the occasional gem of a building. One of these is the 1938 Art Moderne Alfred I. Dupont Building between N.E. 1st and Flagler Streets, notable for its distinctive facade and ornate marble floors. Another, across the street at 174 E. Flagler Street, is the landmark **Gusman Center for the Performing Arts,** a stunningly beautiful movie palace that now serves as a concert hall. If you feel like doing some shopping in a Latin American setting, **Galeria International Mall** is right next door.

Continue west on Flagler Street, downtown Miami's commercial spine. As you pass through a cluster of busy electronics, sporting goods, and shoe stores, you'll be in one of the first areas of Miami to be carved out of the pine woods and palmetto scrubs when Henry Flagler's railroad arrived in 1896. You'll see the 1936 Streamline Moderne **Burdines** department store. Continue up Flagler for one block until the **Dade County Courthouse** comes into view. Between October and March a huge flock of turkey vultures circles and circles the Courthouse's pyramidal crown. Crossing S.W. 1st Avenue, you'll reach the **Miami-Dade Cultural Center,** an impressive area that houses the Miami Art Museum, the Historical Museum of South Florida, and the Main Public Library. You can hop back on Metromover at the Government Center stop at N.W. 2nd Street and 1st Avenue and take the outer loop to the **S.E. 8th Street** stop along Brickell Avenue.

Here sleek high-rises and international banks have replaced the mansions of yesteryear. At this corner is the First Presbyterian Church, a 1949 coral-rock structure with a verdigris roof. Heading north along Brickell towards downtown you'll cross the Brickell Avenue Bridge over the Miami River. Notice the bridge's bronze plaques of native wildlife and its dramatic statue of a Tequesta Indian, one of Miami's original inhabitants, his arrow poised toward the sun. From the bridge, check out the parcel of riverfront land on the right, the site of the Miami Circle. A multimillion-dollar development was halted here when archeologists discovered a circular stone formation and other ancient artifacts, possibly the site of a Tequesta temple. After crossing the bridge, go left to the **Hyatt Regency Miami,** adjacent to the James L. Knight Convention Center. Walk down Southeast 4th Street to the old yellow frame house, the Flagler Palm Cottage, a 19th-century anachronism in this modern neighborhood.

Dining

INEXPENSIVE

Casa Panza. Spanish. The sign on the door says it all: Hasta que el cuerpo aguante (which means "until the body gives"). Feast on a bevy of authentic Spanish dishes, such as the traditional assortment of tapas, brimming tortillas, sautéed octopus, and fish seared with garlic. | 1620 S.W. 8th St. | 305/643–5343 | $6–$14 | AE, MC, V.

El Bodegon Gallego. Spanish. Don't consider this storefront's paltry exterior as a liability; it's one reason the prices are so ridiculously low. Enjoy heartily rationed appetizers such as chickpeas with Spanish sausage or yellow rice with shrimp, then move on to any number of tapas or sizable entrées. | 3174 N.W. 7th Ave. | 305/649–0801 | $6–$14 | No credit cards.

Giacomo Restaurant. Eclectic. Italian dishes dominate the menu here, but you can also get sushi at this small, cozy downtown eatery. Regulars favor the dragon rolls and chicken Alfredo with broccoli and pasta. | 1060 Brickell Ave. | 305/377–8820 | $8–$18 | AE, DC, MC, V.

Islas Canarias. Latin. As you admire the mural depicting a Canary Island street, munch on an order of homemade chips—you have your choice between potato, plantain, or malanga (the potato's tropical cousin). Baked lamb and tortilla Española top the list of low-priced dinner items. | 285 N.W. 27th Ave. | 305/649–0440 | $6–$15 | D, MC, V.

Las Delicias del Mar Peruano. Peruvian. Go for the exotic treats at this restaurant, such as the *papa a la huancaina* (a boiled potato appetizer topped with a chili pepper and white cheese sauce). For the more adventurous, there are *cau cau de los mariscos* (a seafood stew flavored with potatoes and mint), and *ahi* (a jalapeño-driven condiment supplied liberally). | 2937 Biscayne Blvd. | 305/571–1888 | $6–$13 | AE, MC, V.

Tobacco Road. American. This unassuming joint is one of a handful in the Miami area that presents live blues music. Enjoy such standard appetizers and main dishes as burgers, chili, chicken wings, and nachos, or if you visit in season, go all out with the Maine lobster special. | 626 S. Miami Ave. | 305/374–1198 | $6–$11 | AE, D, DC, MC, V.

MODERATE

Anacapri. Italian. A local institution, this casual restaurant in a mostly residential area of Pine Crest is decorated with rustic paintings and Italian sculpture. The regulars come for such dishes as linguine malasemina (seafood) and snapper de la casa. | 12669 S. Dixie Hwy., Pinecrest | 305/232–8001 | No lunch Sat. | $10–$18 | AE, D, DC, MC, V.

Basilico Ristorante. Italian. Just north of Miami International Airport, this restaurant is one of only a few places to dine in the neighborhood and is well worth seeking out. Insulated from the noise of air traffic, the dining room is quiet and inviting. The menu includes such dishes as linguine with seafood, ravioli stuffed with lobster, and veal with mashed potatoes. | 5879 N.W. 36th St., Virginia Gardens | 305/374–9449 | $10–$15 | AE, DC, MC, V.

Biscayne Wine Merchants. Contemporary. Though no longer on Biscayne Boulevard, this bistro lives up to the rest of its name by providing a vast selection of affordable wines to accompany the frequently changing menu selections. Specialties include portobello mushrooms in red wine sauce, brie in phyllo with a kumquat-jalapeño glaze, and a classic bouillabaisse. | 738 N.E. 125th St., North Miami | 305/899–1997 | $8–$20 | AE, D, MC, V.

Casa Juancho. Spanish. Brick, red tile, fabrics, and pottery from Spain give this atmospheric space an authentic ambience. Try *conejo al jenez* (a savory rabbit dish), or *cabrito meson* (baby goat baked in a casserole). Many wines are available. | 2436 S.W. 8th St. | 305/642–2452 | www.casajuancho.com | Reservations essential | $15–$34 | AE, D, DC, MC, V.

Casa Larios. Cuban. Co-owned in part by Gloria and Emilio Estefan, this Cuban has a similarly popular branch on Ocean Drive in South Beach. Roast pork loin is a favorite dish; *churrasco* (a boneless steak topped with chimichurri, a sauce of olive oil, vinegar, and herbs) tops the list of other specialties. For dessert, consider *natilla* (sweet custard covered with a layer of caramelized brown sugar). | 7705 W. Flagler St. | 305/266–5494 | $6–$22 | AE, MC, V.

Farolito. Peruvian. This small restaurant serves traditionally prepared, authentic Peruvian dishes. Try the ceviche or cilantro-flavored beef stew, or proceed straight to the shredded chicken served in a thick sauce of garlic, eggs, and minced walnuts. | 2885 Coral Way | 305/446–4122 | $5–$19 | AE, D, DC, MC, V.

Fleming. Danish. This fine dining establishment in southwest Miami is in a mostly residential area. Inside the walls are hung with Danish art and copper pans, with white linen tablecloths. Menu standouts include duck danoise and breaded sea bass with bread crust and walnuts. | 8511 S.W. 136th St. | 305/232–6444 | Closed Aug. and Mon. No lunch | $12–$21 | AE, MC, V.

★ **Hy-Vong Vietnamese Cuisine.** Vietnamese. Barbecued pork sliced thin and served in a sesame-and-peanut sauce draws crowds at this restaurant, which really fills up after 7 most nights (arrive early to avoid a wait). Other favorites include fish panfried whole in a garlic-lime sauce and a good selection of quality beer from the Far East. | 3458 S.W. 8th St. | 305/446–3674 | Reservations not accepted | Closed Mon. and 2 wks in Aug. No lunch | $7–$19 | No credit cards.

Los Ranchos. Latin. This successful, local chain of restaurants emulates the Managua original, concentrating on traditional Nicaraguan foods, such as spicy chorizo and *cuajada con maduro* (a skim cheese served with sweet fried plantains). However, the restaurant's stand-out selection is its *churrasco* steak. | Bayside Marketplace, 401 Biscayne Blvd. | 305/375–0666 | 125 S.W. 107th Ave., Sweetwater | 305/221–9367 | 2728 Ponce de León Blvd., Coral Gables | 305/446–0050 | The Falls, 8888 S.W. 136th St., Suite 303, South Miami | 305/238–6867 | Kendall Town & Country, 8505 Mills Dr., Kendall | 305/596–5353 | $12–$28 | AE, DC, MC, V.

Macau Chinese Bakery. Chinese. In the heart of a collection of Vietnamese, Korean, Japanese, and Chinese restaurants, this eatery functions as both a takeout bakery and a proper restaurant. Sit down and enjoy the shrimp with salty pepper flavor, and take home some almond cookies from the bakery. | 520 N.E. 167th St. | 305/947–5594 | $9–$27 | MC, V.

Mike Gordon. Seafood. Locals are regular patrons at this seafood spot on Biscayne Bay. Watercolors and lots of woodwork emphasize the Cape Cod theme. Favorites are pan-fried grouper and stuffed red snapper. | 1201 N.E. 79th St. | 305/751–4429 | $12–$21 | AE, D, DC, MC, V.

Paquito's. Mexican. In addition to traditional Mexican fare—enchiladas, burritos, chimichangas, and the like—this small storefront offers some more ambitious dishes, such as mahimahi cooked with capers, tomatoes, and green olives. Rich soups serve as solid starters, and for a sweet final act try the *sopaipillas* (bits of fried dough rolled in brown sugar and cinnamon). | 16265 Biscayne Blvd. | 305/947–5027 | $8–$27 | AE, DC, MC, V.

Patacón. Colombian. It's little surprise that this restaurant's specialty dish is its namesake, the *patacón pisao* (a bed of large, fried plantain topped with shrimp, chicken, meat, guacamole, and beans). Other specialties include hearty soups, such as the *sancocho* (a stew with oxtail, hen, tripe), and, if that isn't enough, corn on the cob. | 18230 Collins Ave., Sunny Isles | 305/931–3001 | 6734 Collins Ave., Miami Beach | 305/865–5695 | 7902 N.W. 36th St., Miami | 305/591–8866 | 13720 N. Kendall Dr., Kendall | 305/382–3717 | $5–$16 | MC, V.

Perricone's Marketplace. Italian. In a 120-yr-old Vermont barn, this popular spot stands out from the other Italian eateries south of the Miami River on Brickell Avenue. The recipes for such dishes as the homemade minestrone, linguine with sautéed jumbo shrimp, fresh asparagus, and tomatoes, and gnocchi with four cheeses have been handed down from grandmother to mother to daughter. The desserts are not to be missed, including the tiramisu, fruit tart, and six different flavors of homemade gelato, all made fresh every day. | 15 S.E. 10th St. | 305/374–9449 | $14–$18 | AE, MC, V.

Puerto Rico Restaurant. Latin. On weekends, the all-you-can-eat buffet is the main draw at this small eatery, featuring fresh soups and meats. Puerto Rican mementos adorn this eatery's walls, and if they sway you to patriotism you might try *mofongo*, the island's traditional dish. | 711 N.W. 27th Ave. | 305/642–6269 | $5–$22 | No credit cards.

Rosinella's. Italian. Run by owner Tonino Doino and his mother, Rosinella, this restaurant is stylish and authentic, and has spawned a busier sister restaurant on Lincoln Road in Miami Beach. Thin-crust pizzas, light vegetable soups, and gnocchi are all tasty, and the red-peppery *arrabbiata* pasta sauce excels. | 1040 S. Miami Ave. | 305/372–5756 | $10–$15 | AE, DC, MC, V.

Soyka. American. Upscale and stylish with chrome decorative accents, this eatery specializes in flavorful desserts and designer martinis. The dinner menu—sesame-seared salmon, calves' livers with caramelized onions—is more sophisticated (and naturally, more expensive) than the lunch menu, which features pizza, salads, and burgers. | 5556 Biscayne Blvd. | 305/759–3117 | $9–$32 | AE, D, DC, MC, V.

Tani Thai. Thai. Stark white walls hung with original Thai art and track lighting make for a pleasant place to enjoy good Thai food at this restaurant in south Miami-Dade's Pinecrest Village. Specialties include the volcano chicken and red snapper. | 12269 S. Dixie Hwy. | 305/253–3583 | $7–$19 | AE, MC, V.

Tropical Chinese. Chinese. This cozy restaurant in southeast Miami-Dade has walls lined with modern Chinese prints, paintings, and other artwork. The menu features various Szechuan specialties, including sizzling black bean chicken. | 7991 Bird Rd. | 305/262–7576 | $9–$50 | AE, DC, MC, V.

Tutto Pasta. Italian. With most entrées under $10, the kitchen here serves affordable Italian treats. Bruschetta, prosciutto and sundried tomatoes, and homemade soups are excellent starters, and options such as homemade ravioli with ricotta and spinach or the chicken fettuccine with tomatoes and mushrooms are main course highlights. | 1753 S.W. 3rd Ave. | 305/857–0709 | $7–$18 | MC, V.

Versailles. Cuban. If the idea of dining on *ropa vieja* (a shredded-beef dish translated literally as "old clothes") doesn't excite you, you simply haven't tried it at this famous Cuban restaurant. Other specialties include *arroz con pollo* (chunks of boneless chicken served with yellow rice) and *sopa de platano* (a velvety plantain soup). Also try the exceptionally strong Cuban coffee. | 3555 S.W. 8th St. | 305/445–7614 | $6–$20 | AE, D, DC, MC, V.

EXPENSIVE

94th Aero Squadron. American. Get a tarmac-side seat here, where the Wright brothers would have felt right at home. Old propellers and airplane photos line the walls, and the hum of take-offs and landings blends with dinner conversations. The food is fresh and flavorful, with a heavy emphasis on beef. Try the beer-cheese soup. You're just 5 min from the airport. | 1395 N.W. 57th Ave. | 305/261–4220 | $16–$35 | AE, D, DC, MC, V.

Firehouse Four. American/Casual. Renowned for its fabulous happy hour, this restaurant is set in the remnants of a 1930s firehouse. The food has global influences, with creative sandwiches at the core of the menu (the Euro-Cuban, for instance, is served on focaccia), but drinks are the most exciting part of a visit here. | 1000 S. Miami Ave. | 305/371–3473 | $15–$30 | AE, D, DC, MC, V.

Fishbone Grille. Seafood. An open kitchen dishes out fish prepared in a wide variety of styles: baked, blackened, broiled, and so on. Every meal is served with salad and jalapeño cornbread, and pizza is offered, too. | 650 S. Miami Ave. | 305/530–1915 | No dinner Sun. | $9–$25 | AE, MC, V.

Guayacan. Latin. This small, family-run restaurant offers counter service and traditional Nicaraguan fare, the hallmark of which is the churrasco steak and the most indulgent of which is *tres leches*, an impressively sweet dessert. All dishes come with red beans and rice and are heavily seasoned in true Nicaraguan fashion. | 1933 S.W. 8th St. | 305/649–2015 | $8–$25 | AE, MC, V.

Il Tulipano. Italian. The Rolls-Royces parked outside are a good barometer of the prices inside at this upscale Italian restaurant. Choose from almost 20 kinds of pasta or head straight for dishes such as tender lamb chops and broiled snapper, but either way, leave room for traditional desserts. | 11052 Biscayne Blvd., North Miami | 305/893–4811 | $15–$30 | MC, V.

Indigo. Contemporary. One of the Hotel Inter-Continental's remodeled eateries, Indigo is known amongst downtown employees for its reasonably priced brunches, lunch buffets, and happy hour. Try *tagine* (a Moroccan stew), and stone-crab *croquetas*, along with a selection from the impressive wine list. | 100 Chopin Plaza | 305/577–1000 | $13–$28 | AE, D, DC, MC, V.

La Paloma. Continental. Dine among a collection of European antiques at this Swiss Continental restaurant, where the menu ranges from Wiener schnitzel to local fish. Other specialties include veal chops with morel sauce, and the dessert with kick: lemon sherbet served with fresh kiwi and vodka. | 10999 Biscayne Blvd., North Miami | 305/891–0505 | No lunch weekends | $14–$35 | AE, MC, V.

Las Culebrinas. Spanish. You have to admire a place that will use a blowtorch to caramelize your *crema Catalana* right on your table. Start with this impressively presented dessert, or work your way up to the finale with a variety of tapas, such as garbanzos with sausage, ham, and oil, or a piece of Spanish tortilla. | 4700 W. Flagler St. | 305/445–2337 | $8–$25 | AE, MC, V.

Palm Grill. Contemporary. Nationally acclaimed and recently relocated from Key West, this restaurant has a full menu of exciting fusion dishes, such as the Cuban pork Wellington and portobello bear claws. A solid wine list rounds out the offerings. Another relocation is rumored to be in the works, so call first. | 16145 Biscayne Blvd., North Miami | 305/949–8448 | No lunch. Closed Sun.–Mon. | $10–$35 | AE, MC, V.

Porcao. Steak. Though a steak house by definition, this Brazilian restaurant offers a wide variety of entrées, from pickled quail eggs with chicken hearts to less adventuresome fare such as the filet mignon. There's also an impressive salad bar. | 801 S. Bayshore Dr. | 305/373–2777 | $21–$30 | AE, DC, MC, V.

Shula's Steak House. Steak. The main course menus are painted onto footballs ("pass" it around the table), and the various steaks (from a 48-oz porterhouse on down) and four-pound lobsters are displayed on a roll-around cart. The owner, former Miami Dolphins coach Don Shula, has adorned the dark wood–paneled walls with Miami Dolphins memorabilia and photos, representing the 1972 undefeated season. A cigar menu is available, but you may only smoke cigars in the smoking lounge. The staff is formal and attentive. New York sirloin, cowboy steaks, and filet mignon are popular as well as the 48-oz steak (which comes with a signed photograph of Don Shula). | 7601 N.W. 154th St., Miami Lakes | 305/820–8102 | Breakfast also available. No lunch weekends | $18–$65 | AE, DC, MC, V.

Tony Chan's Water Club. Chinese. At this restaurant off the lobby of the Doubletree Grand Hotel, choosing your meal can be quite the task—the menu lists some 200 appetizers and entrées. Seafood and meats get equal billing, with options such as steamed ginger and garlic sea bass or pork chops in a garlic and black bean sauce. | 1717 N. Bayshore Dr. | 305/374–8888 | No lunch weekends | $9–$24 | AE, D, DC, MC, V.

Villa Italia. Italian. Originally a pizza place, this restaurant has branched out into all aspects of Italian cuisine, serving a mean lasagna and tortellini Alfredo. For a more contemporary spin, try the broccoli and spinach sauté or an order of fried calamari. | 3058 Coral Way | 305/444–0206 | $7–$17 | AE, DC, MC, V.

VERY EXPENSIVE

Capital Grille. Steak. Home of executive power lunches and dinners, this elegant downtown restaurant offers a traditional steak-house menu. Consider steak au poivre, succulent porterhouse, and various fillets and sirloins. Other sure bets are the savory black bean soup, Caesar and spinach salads, and post-steak cheesecake. The waitstaff tends toward formal. | 444 Brickell Ave. | 305/374–4500 | $17–$30 | AE, D, DC, MC, V.

Casa Juancho. Spanish. Although the *tinajones* (large terra-cotta pots) that stand sentinel outside and the clientele dining inside are distinctively Cuban, the cuisine in this establishment hails from Spain. Try the *carabineros a la plancha* (a plate of jumbo red shrimp grilled with the head and shell intact). | 2436 S.W. 8th St. | 305/642–2452 | $16–$40 | AE, D, DC, MC, V.

★ **Chef Allen's.** American. A glass-enclosed kitchen entertains the people sitting in the formal dining area, who can watch their meals being made. The original artwork on the walls is for sale. Specialties include pistachio-crusted grouper and Tribeca veal chop. Consider coming on Friday, for "Chef's Table," when chef Allen comes out to a table of diners paying $100 a head and prepares a flashy and delicious dinner in front of their eyes. The restaurant is 30 min north of Miami, in a building constructed in 1985. | 19088 N.E. 29th Ave., Aventura | 305/935–2900 | No lunch | $20–$36 | AE, MC, V.

Lodging

INEXPENSIVE

Amerisuites Airport West. Catering to the business traveler, this is a business-oriented, high-rise, all-suites hotel. You're close enough to the Doral Golf Resort so that some rooms have views of the courses. There are three restaurants across the street and a 12,000-square-ft meeting space inside. Complimentary Continental breakfast. In-room data ports, microwaves, refrigerators. Cable TV, in-room VCRs (and movies). Pool. Gym. Laundry facilities. Business services, free parking. | 3655 N.W. 82nd Ave. | 305/718–8292 or 800/833–1516 | fax 305/758–8295 | www.amerisuites.com | 126 suites | $89–$149 | AE, D, DC, MC, V.

Best Western, Miami Airport Inn. This six-story hotel just outside the Miami International Airport is good for both between-flight overnights or longer stays. You're less than 15 minutes from the Merchandise Mart, downtown business district, Coral Gables, free trade zone, industrial parks, Port of Miami, beaches, Coconut Grove, Bayside, South Beach, and great shopping. Restaurant, bar. In-room data ports, refrigerators. Cable TV, in-room VCRs (and movies). Pool. Gym. Laundry facilities. Business services, airport shuttle, parking (fee). | 1550 N.W. Le Jeune Rd. | 305/871–2345 or 888/879–3578 | fax 305/871–2811 | www.best-western.com | 208 rooms | $89–$114 | AE, D, DC, MC, V.

Fairfield Inn by Marriott, Miami Airport South. Larger than its Miami West counterpart, this inn also gives you access to the facilities of the Airport Marriott and the other Fairfield Inn. | 285 rooms. Complimentary Continental breakfast. In-room data ports. Cable TV, in-room VCRs (and movies). Pool. Tennis. Laundry facilities. Business services, airport shuttle, free parking. | 1201 N.W. Le Juene Rd. | 305/643–0055 or 888/236–2427 | fax 305/649–3997 | $59–$89, $119 suite | AE, D, DC, MC, V.

Fairfield Inn by Marriott, Miami West. Designed for business travelers, the hotel is well equipped with workspace and business services. You may use all the facilities at the Miami Airport Marriott as well as another Fairfield Inn. Complimentary Continental breakfast. In-room data ports, refrigerators. Cable TV. Pool. Business services, airport shuttle, free parking. | 3959 N.W. 79th Ave. | 305/599–5200 or 888/236–2427 | fax 305/436–2935 | www.marriott.com | 135 rooms | $89 | AE, D, DC, MC, V.

Holiday Inn Miami-Calder/Pro Player Stadium. Stay here if you're a racing fan; the hotel is adjacent to Calder Race Course. The nine-story high-rise is halfway between Miami and Ft. Lauderdale international airports (13 mi from each). If you're an all-around sports fan, even better; you're 1 mi from Pro Player Stadium, home to the Miami Dolphins and Florida Marlins. Reserve early if you're coming during football or baseball season. Restaurant, bar. In-room data ports, some microwaves, some refrigerators. Cable TV. Pool. Gym. Laundry facilities. Business services, parking (fee). | 21485 N.W. 27th Ave. | 305/621–5801 or 800/HOLIDAY | fax 305/624–8202 | www.holiday-inn.com | 214 rooms | $79–$149 | AE, D, DC, MC, V.

Howard Johnson Hotel Miami International Airport. Convenience and relatively modest rates are the outstanding features here. Only $\frac{1}{4}$ mi from the airport and 6 mi from the downtown area with a free 24-hr shuttle to and from the airport. The white exterior with teal trim makes this four-story hotel look like pure Miami, and the landscaping is nicely done. Restaurant, bar. Refrigerators. Cable TV. Pool. Hot tub. Laundry facilities. Business services, airport shuttle. | 1850 N.W. Le Jeune Rd. | 305/871–4350 | fax 305/871–6810 | 254 rooms | $100–$149 | AE, D, DC, MC, V.

La Quinta Inn. This well-furnished and affordable three-story pseudo-southwestern stucco motel is noted for its clean guest rooms. You're a few minutes away from the International Mall, Mall of America, and the Doral Golf Resort. Kids under 18 free. Complimentary Continental breakfast. In-room data ports, some microwaves, refrigerators. Cable TV. Pool.

Gym. Laundry facilities. Business services, airport shuttle, free parking. Pets allowed. | 7401 N.W. 36th St. | 305/599–9902 | fax 305/594–0552 | 165 rooms | $69–$119 | AE, D, DC, MC, V.

Wellesley Inn Miami Airport West. Reasonable rates and proximity to the airport, malls, and golf are the lures at this four-story stucco hotel. The Doral Golf course is only ¼ mi away. Complimentary Continental breakfast. In-room data ports, microwaves, refrigerators. Cable TV. Pool. Laundry facilities. Business services, free parking. | 8436 N.W. 36th St. | 305/592–4799 or 800/444–8888 | fax 305/471–8461 | 106 rooms | $55–$100 | AE, D, DC, MC, V.

MODERATE

Club Hotel by Doubletree. This 10-story concrete Doubletree Club Hotel is 2 mi south of Miami International Airport and 7 mi from downtown, in the Waterford Park Business Complex. The facility overlooks the "Blue Lagoon," a 100-acre freshwater lake. Restaurant, bar. In-room data ports, microwaves, refrigerators. Cable TV. Pool. Laundry facilities. Business services, airport shuttle, free parking. | 1101 N.W. 57th Ave. | 305/266–0000 | fax 305/266–9179 | www.clubhotels.com | 264 rooms | $109 | AE, D, DC, MC, V.

Courtyard by Marriott–Miami Airport South. Renovated in 2000, this five-story stucco hotel was built in 1972 and is not too far from many area attractions. The rooms have views of the tennis courts, and there are 11,961 square ft of meeting space. Restaurant, bar. Refrigerators. Cable TV, in-room VCRs (and movies). Pool. Tennis court. Gym. Laundry facilities. Business services, airport shuttle, free parking. | 1201 N.W. Le Jeune Rd. | 305/642–8200 or 800/443–6000 | fax 305/644–1168 | www.marriott.com | 125 rooms | $89–$195 | AE, D, DC, MC, V.

Courtyard by Marriott–Miami West. Rooms at this four-story hotel designed by business travelers have desks with work lamps and key business amenities, including a free daily newspaper and voicemail. You're 1 mi from Doral Country Club, 5 mi from International Mall, and 2 mi from the Mall of Americas. Restaurant, bar. In-room data ports, in-room safes, microwaves, refrigerators. Cable TV. Pool. Hot tub. Exercise equipment. Laundry facilities. Business services, airport shuttle, free parking. | 3929 N.W. 79th Ave. | 305/477–8118 or 800/443–6000 | fax 305/599–9363 | www.marriott.com | 145 rooms | $99–$149 | AE, D, DC, MC, V.

Crowne Plaza Miami International Airport. Three floors of shopping, dining, and entertainment occupy half of this six-story stucco hotel that's a mile from the airport. The large, clean pool is especially nice, and the more than 5,000 square ft of event space accommodate up to 400 guests. You are within a few miles of many other restaurants and nightspots. Restaurant, bar. In-room data ports, refrigerators. Cable TV. Pool. Hot tub, sauna. Gym. Laundry facilities. Business services, airport shuttle, parking (fee). | 950 N.W. Le Jeune Rd. | 305/446–9000 | fax 954/441–0725 | www.crowneplaza.com | 304 rooms, 1 suite | $119–$179, $200 suite | AE, D, DC, MC, V.

Don Shula's Hotel & Golf Club. If you're looking just to relax, enjoy this hotel's light pastels and ask for a room away from the elevators for the best deal. However, if you like to hit the links, the golf club is your place, with championship and executive courses and even a golf school. 5 restaurants, 2 bars, room service. In-room data ports, some minibars, some microwaves, some refrigerators. Cable TV, some in-room VCRs. Pool. Sauna, steam room. Driving range, 18-hole golf course, 2 9-hole golf courses, putting green, 9 tennis courts. Basketball, health club, racquetball, volleyball. Laundry service. Free parking. | 6840 Main St., Miami Lakes | 305/821–1150 or 800/247–4852 | fax 305/820–8071 | www.donshula.com | 205 rooms, 22 suites | $119–$179 | AE, D, DC, MC, V.

Miami Airport Hilton and Towers. Junior suites (bedroom and sitting room) and deluxe suites (with parlor, too) make this a good choice for families, particularly given the many child-pleasing extras such as boating. Built in 1984, the 14-story hotel is on a private tropical peninsula in the heart of Blue Lagoon, a 100-acre freshwater lake. Rooms have views of the lagoon, airport, and city. You're just 4 mi west of downtown Miami, 2 mi from Miami International Airport. Restaurant, bar (with entertainment), room service. In-room data ports, minibars, refrigerators. Cable TV, in-room VCRs (and movies). Pool. Tennis court.

Gym. Water sports, boating, fishing. Laundry facilities. Business services, airport shuttle, parking (fee). | 5101 Blue Lagoon Dr. | 305/262–1000 or 800/916–2221 | fax 305/267–0038 | www.hilton.com | 500 rooms, 77 suites | $120–$265 | AE, D, DC, MC, V.

Miami Airport Marriott. Another airport hotel, this seven-story facility is 1 mi from the airport and within 10 mi of many golf courses and other attractions. Restaurant, bars. In-room data ports, refrigerators. Cable TV. Pool. Tennis court. Gym. Business services, airport shuttle, parking (fee). | 1201 N.W. Le Jeune Rd. | 305/649–5000 or 888/236–2427 | fax 305/642–3369 | www.marriott.com | 365 rooms | $125–$169 | AE, D, DC, MC, V.

Miami International Airport Hotel. Although you might not choose this as a vacation destination, this hotel, on the second floor of Concourse E, could be the right spot if you have a red-eye flight to catch. The rooms are all sound-proofed to assure a good night's sleep. Restaurant, 2 bars, room service. Cable TV. Pool. Gym. Business services. | Miami International Airport, Concourse E | 305/373–6000 or 800/284–2000 | fax 305/374–2279 | 260 rooms | $165–$179 | AE, D, DC, MC, V.

Miami Marriott, Dadeland. The hotel is the only one in the Miami area connected directly to the Metrorail system, so you can get almost anywhere easily. This 24-story hotel is in Kendall, a few miles south of downtown, in a commercial area. It's across the street from Dadeland Mall. Restaurant, bar. In-room data ports, in-room safes, minibars, refrigerators. Cable TV. Pool. Tennis court. Gym. Business services, airport shuttle, parking (fee). | 9090 S. Dadeland Blvd., Kendall | 305/670–1035 or 888/236–2427 | www.marriott.com | fax 305/670–7540 | 300 rooms, 2 suites | $139–$199, $300–$500 suites | AE, D, DC, MC, V.

Miami River Inn. The five restored clapboard buildings that make up this inn date from 1906 and are the last standing examples of Miami residential houses from this period. In a working-class neighborhood that is safe, despite its appearance, the inn is a sanctuary, only a 10-min walk from Miami's downtown. Rooms on the second or third stories overlook the river; guests have full use of a communal refrigerator. Complimentary Continental breakfast. Cable TV. Pool. Hot tub. Laundry facilities. | 118 SW South River Dr. | 305/325–0045 or 800/468–3589 | fax 305/325–9227 | www.miamiriverinn.com | 40 rooms (2 with shared bath) | $109–$159 | AE, D, DC, MC, V.

Radisson Mart Plaza Hotel. Next to the Miami International Merchandise Mart and Radisson Centre, this is a modern 12-story high-rise. You can shop at the mart (a wholesale trading center) for free by showing your room key. Restaurant, bars (with entertainment). In-room data ports, minibars, refrigerators. Cable TV. Pool. Hot tub, sauna. Tennis court. Gym, racquetball. Business services. Airport shuttle, free parking. | 711 N.W. 72nd Ave. | 305/261–3800 | fax 305/261–7665 | 334 rooms, 18 suites | $149–$169, $189–$399 suites | AE, D, DC, MC, V.

Wyndham Miami Airport. Overlooking the Melreese Golf Course and the Miami River, this nine-story hotel is only two min away from the airport, and 10 min from the downtown area. Restaurant, bar, room service. In-room data ports. Cable TV. Pool. Sauna. Golf course. Gym. Shops. Laundry service. Business services, airport shuttle. Parking (fee). | 3900 N.W. 21st St. | 305/871–3800 or 888/511–5317 | fax 305/871–0447 | www.wyndham.com | 408 rooms | $115–$169 | AE, D, DC, MC, V.

EXPENSIVE

Sheraton Biscayne Bay. A grove of oak trees stands outside the entrance of this Brickell Avenue hotel. The lobby is businesslike marble, but the back patio and surrounding green space face the bay. Restaurant, bar, room service. Pool. Health club. Shops. Business services. | 495 Brickell Ave. | 305/373–6000 or 800/284–2000 | fax 305/374–2279 | 598 rooms | $194–$209 | AE, D, DC, MC, V.

VERY EXPENSIVE

★ **Doral Golf Resort and Spa.** Among the many amenities of this sprawling 650-acre facility are the five championship golf courses, the Blue Lagoon Water Recreation Area, and the 148,000-square-ft spa. The most recent addition to the golf courses is the Great White

Course, a desert landscape designed by Greg Norman. The spa offers massages, European facials, aroma scrubs, hydrotheraphy, and many other treatments. 5 restaurants, 3 bars, room service. Minibars. Cable TV. 4 pools. Massage, spa. 5 golf courses, 11 tennis courts. Gym. Fishing. Shops. Children's programs (5–12). Free parking. | 4400 NW 87th Ave. | 305/592–2000 or 800/71–DORAL | fax 305/591–6630 | www.doralresort.com | 694 rooms | $339–$399 | AE, D, DC, MC, V.

Hotel Inter-Continental Miami. Towering above the rabble of the street, the rooms overlook Brickell Avenue, the port, the bay, and Key Biscayne. The marble lobby is complemented by palms and wicker furniture, while sunlight warms the atrium. For your health, the hotel has a fitness center on the fifth floor; for your wealth, it has 25 meeting and conference rooms. 3 restaurants, bar, room service. In-room data ports, minibars. Cable TV. Pool. Health club. Business services. | 100 Chopin Plaza | 305/577–1000 or 800/327–3005 | fax 305/577–0384 | 639 rooms | $259–$435 | AE, D, DC, MC, V.

Hyatt Regency Miami. Near the Port of Miami and the American Airlines Arena, this is the perfect place to stay if your vacation is centered on basketball, business, or boats. Rooms, some of which have views of the river or port, are done in surprising combinations of colors, such as avocado, beige, and blonde. You can reach the James L. Knight International Center, Metromover, and the Metrorail connection from inside the hotel. Restaurant, bar, room service. Cable TV. Pool. Health club. Business services. | 400 SE 2nd Ave. | 305/358–1234 or 800/233–1234 | fax 305/358–0529 | www.hyatt.com | 615 rooms | $284–$314 | AE, D, DC, MC, V.

★ **Turnberry Isle Resort and Club.** A large resort on 300 acres of bayfront property, Turnberry features two 18-hole golf courses and is subdivided into the Yacht Club (on the Intracoastal Waterway), the Marina and Country Club hotels, and a three-wing Mediterranean-inspired annex. The marina has moorings for 117 boats, and a new seven-story building was completed in 1999. 3 restaurants, 4 bars, dining room, room service. In-room safes, minibars, in-room hot tubs. Cable TV, some in-room VCRs. 4 pools. Beauty salon, hot tub, sauna, steam room. Driving range, 2 18-hole golf courses, 11 tennis courts. Health club, racquetball. Beach, dock, boating. Shops. Laundry service, parking (fee). | 19999 W. Country Club Dr., Aventura | 305/936–2929 or 800/223–6800 | fax 305/933–6560 | www.turnberry-isle.com | 369 rooms, 26 suites | $265–$360, $455–$745 suites | AE, D, DC, MC, V.

MIAMI BEACH

MAP 5, K1

(Nearby towns also listed: Coconut Grove, Coral Gables, Key Biscayne, Miami)

Most visitors to the Greater Miami area don't realize that Miami and Miami Beach are separate cities. But while Miami is Florida's commercial hub, Miami Beach is widely considered America's Riviera, luring refugees from winter with its warm sunshine, sandy beaches, graceful palms, and tireless nightlife. The great part of its nocturnal spark takes place at the southern end of Miami Beach's 7-mi-long barrier island, in a relatively small area known as South Beach.

There may be more photographs of South Beach than grains of sand on its much-praised shoreline. And for all its international fame, stylish allure, and glossy glamour, it's remarkable that South Beach remains essentially a mile-long stretch along three parallel avenues. In fact, Ocean Drive—which separates the most glamorous hotels and restaurants from the ocean—has pulled the great weight of Miami Beach's revival over the past two decades.

In the early 1920s a narrow strip of mangrove coast was transformed into Miami Beach, and tourists wasted no time. In just a few years, Miami Beach was a playground of the rich, and grand-themed hotels held sway. By the late 20s, however, shipping problems and a hurricane turned the boom to bust, and another approach was needed to attract tourists.

Enter the Art Deco hotels of the 1930s, the mostly three-story, cheerfully colored, sleek-looking structures that alluded to modern ships, cars, and ocean liners. In the 1950s, larger-than-life Deco hotels, such as the Fontainebleau and the Eden Roc, were built, and the days of the small Deco hotels were up. Most aged into flophouses or dirt-cheap homes for retirees. Now a worldwide synonym with glamour and the good life, Miami Beach is a study in urban renewal sparked through grass roots efforts, and a little fortuitous media exposure.

Things started to happen in the 1980s, when the hyperactive cop show *Miami Vice* played out against the pastel facades of Ocean Drive. A woman named Barbara Capitman proposed the buildings—which were set to be demolished—for the National Register of Historic Places. As bulldozers waited, the preservationist movement rolled forward, and investors began restoring the interiors and repainting the exteriors of classic South Beach buildings.

What followed was a mass influx of glamour industries and new fun-seeking residents and visitors. As recently as the late 1980s, Miami Beach was an ocean-side geriatric ward. Today's South Beach residents have the kind of hip that doesn't break. (The average age dropped from the mid-60s in 1980 to a youthful early 40s today.)

SoBe—a usefully terse newspaper condensation of South Beach, though a term probably never once casually uttered by a local—is now a shimmering condensation of upscale boutiques, trendy restaurants, hot nightclubs, and restored hotels with slick, avant-garde interiors. Miami Beach finds itself undergoing a seemingly never-ending process of beautification, making it perhaps the best place in the world for a people-watching getaway.

Information: Miami Beach Chamber of Commerce | 420 Lincoln Rd., Miami Beach, 33139 | 305/672–1270 | www.ci.miami-beach.fl.us.

Greater Miami Convention and Visitor Bureau | 701 Brickell Ave., Ste. 2700, Miami, 33131 | 305/539–3034.

NEIGHBORHOODS

South Beach Art Deco District. This 1-square-mi area—running roughly south–north from 5th to 15th streets, and east–west from Ocean Drive to Alton Road—is the largest preserved Art Deco district in the world. The preservation of its 800 buildings of the 1930s and '40s was the galvanizing force behind the entire revival of Miami Beach. The district is synonymous with South Beach, and covers nearly all its geographic lay.

Miami Beach. While South Beach continues to receive the lion's share of attention from global media, the city north of 23rd Street has its own set of glittering jewels. Multi-million dollar renovations have re-asserted the flamboyant glitz of 1950s landmark hotels like the Fontainebleau and the Eden Roc. Fronting these glamorous high-rise hotels and condominium communities are gorgeous, uncrowded beaches.

Surfside. North of Miami Beach, Collins Avenue (Hwy. A1A) winds through the little town of Surfside. This area from 87th Terrace to 96th Street is a sunny winter home to a bevy of French Canadians—in December, this is the best place in Florida to practice your French. The town's mile of wide public beach is backed by sand dunes and hotels.

Bal Harbour. North of Surfside, this planned community is the smallest, and one of the wealthiest, communities in South Florida. Luxury condos, the Sheraton Bal Harbor Beach Resort, and the Sea View and Beach House hotels rise along this stretch of palm-lined Collins Avenue. To most, however, the name Bal Harbour means one thing: ultra-swank shopping. Bal Harbour Shops welcomes those accustomed to luxuries of the highest order with white-helmeted guards at the door.

Sunny Isles. The Palmetto Expressway ends east on Sunny Isles Blvd. and Collins Avenue. This narrow stretch of land follows Collins north from Haulover Beach Park to the William Lehman Causeway at 191st St. Across the Intracoastal Waterway west of Sunny Isles is the Oleta River State Recreation Area. Just north of 191 St. is Golden Beach, a 2-mi-long enclave of private oceanfront homes. Though the beach is for residents only, the beautifully landscaped properties are a welcome relief after miles of high-rise condos to the south.

TRANSPORTATION

Transportation to Miami Beach: Visitors to Miami Beach should book their travel into Miami. From Miami International Airport, there are two convenient options into Miami Beach. If you take a taxi, there are flat-rate fares to five zones in Miami Beach; fares run $22–$41 per trip.

SuperShuttle (305/871–2000) will take you in one of their blue vans for about $11–$14.

Public Transportation: In Miami Beach, a free electric trolley service called **Electrowave** (305/535–9160) runs along Washington Avenue every few minutes from 5th to 17th streets, with turnabouts at the Lincoln Road Mall and South Pointe Park. The fare is 25¢.

DRIVING AND PARKING

The barrier island of Miami Beach is connected to the mainland by a series of free causeways. Venetian Causeway begins in downtown Miami, running parallel to the port and passing over a few small islands before arriving at 5th Street in the heart of South Beach. This one slows with weekend evening traffic into Miami Beach.

The Julia Tuttle Causeway (Hwy. 195) branches from I-95 in Miami and heads east to Miami Beach. The motor circulation along this wide highway is almost always light, and the views of downtown may be unsurpassed from this vantage. Taking the

© Corbis

ART DECO HOTELS: MIAMI NICE

Bikini-clad models and dazzling beaches aside, some of Miami's most recognizable icons are probably the Art Deco hotels of South Beach. In the 1920s, Miami Beach was a new winter playground of the rich, and grand hotels ruled. However, shipping problems and a hurricane toward the end of the decade turned the boom into a bust, and another approach to attract vacationers was needed. New, affordable hotels drew the middle class down south, and the architectural motif of choice for these lodgings became what we call Deco. Originally introduced in Paris in the 1920s, Art Deco was based on a sleek and cheerful look, with geometric designs and creative colors, a style that nicely complemented the beach's expansive ocean vistas.

In South Beach, architects borrowed from industrial designers and incorporated streamlined, aerodynamic forms based on trains, ocean liners, and automobiles. Geometric figures thrust out from facades and roofs and sharp edges were softened with wraparound windows and curved corners. To reflect the beach locale, elements of the seafaring life were added; portholes (frequently in sets of three) and oceanic symbols (starfish, marlin, and the classic rolling wave) often appeared on walls. Sunlight, an abundant commodity, was brought indoors through glass blocks, and, in the absence of air-conditioning, coolness was achieved by planting shady palms and laying terrazzo tile.

Eventually, the bold colors and creative accents became cliché, and ensuing decades saw owners hide their hotels beneath coats of plain white or beige paint. By the 1970s the vast majority of small Deco hotels were no longer welcoming tourists and had become dirt-cheap homes for retirees. Then in the 1980s, the Deco style was revitalized (via influences ranging from historical conservationists such as Barbara Capitman to the area's glamorization in television shows like Miami Vice), hotels were resurrected, and a new generation began to experience the tropical paradise enjoyed by travelers of the 1930s.

Julia Tuttle to Alton Road (exit right) and winding south is often the quickest way to get to South Beach from Miami.

Collins Avenue is the main north–south thoroughfare in Miami Beach. Doubling as Highway A1A, it runs north–south along all of Florida's east coast beaches. There are parking meters along the length of Collins Avenue.

South Beach parking, however, is a trickier issue. It's easy enough to find a metered spot weekdays along Washington Avenue, Collins Avenue, and their perpendicular numbered streets. But most roads west of Washington are reserved for residents, and tow trucks work hard to enforce that policy.

Weekends in South Beach, traffic moves inch by inch. Cars on Ocean Drive might as well be parked, so tight is the bumper-to-bumper cruising. Try your luck with the metered parking lots and pay lots behind the length of Lincoln Road's north side, catch the SuperShuttle from the airport, or walk—South Beach is just a square-mile area. Attended lots, the stress-free choice, charge $3–$10.

Attractions

ART AND ARCHITECTURE

The Carlyle. This 1941 Art Deco hotel and its neighbor, the Leslie, was featured in *The Birdcage,* starring Robin Williams and Nathan Lane. The hotel's mesmerizing blue neon, viewed from the beach at night, is the centerpiece of Ocean Drive's magical spectrum of light. | 1250 Ocean Dr.

The Cardozo. This hotel, owned by pop singer and Miami local Gloria Estefan, is a 1939 Hohauser-designed Streamline Moderne Classic. It was one of the first Art Deco hotels to be revived, beautifully restored inside and out, with wrought-iron furniture and hardwood floors. Note the eyebrows over the windows. | 1300 Ocean Dr. | 305/535–6500 | fax 305/532–3563 | www.cardozohotel.com | Free | Daily.

Casa Casuarina. Italian fashion designer Gianni Versace bought this ornate, three-story pre-Deco Spanish Mediterranean residence in the early '80s. It has a guest house, copper-dome rooftop observatory, and a pool. Tragically, Versace was shot to death here in 1997. | 1114 Ocean Dr.

Fontainebleau Hilton Resort and Towers. This group of hotels is an excellent example of Miami Beach's grandiose architecture from the Fabulous '50s. Even if you're not a guest, wander through the lobby and spectacular pool area just to feel the frenzy of bellhops, clerks, concierges, and travelers. | 4441 Collins Ave. | 305/538–2000 | fax 305/674–4607 | www.hilton.com.

South Beach: the Art Deco District. South Beach and the Art Deco District are almost synonymous, but not quite. This area, extending between 5th and 25th Streets, Alton Rd. and Ocean Drive is perhaps the hippest part of Florida. Art Deco as a design style developed in the 1920s, initially as a kind of Hollywood phenomenon, then making its way into American popular culture. From the district's Welcome Center, you can start audio or guided tours that describe the history of the now-restored buildings. You can dine outdoors, hang out on the beach, or shop at some of the world's top stores. | Welcome Center, 1001 Ocean Dr. | 305/672–2014 or 305/672–1270 | Welcome Center, free; audio tour $5, guided tour $10 | Daily 11–9; tours Thurs. 6:30 PM, Sat. 10:30 AM.

BEACHES, PARKS, AND NATURAL SITES

Haulover Beach Park. This county park is a throwback to the days before South Beach. You can picnic, cook on the barbecue grills, play volleyball, rent kites, and bike along trails. There are also a par-3, nine-hole golf course, and tennis. An underground path leads to Haulover Park Marina, home to the largest charter/drift fishing fleet in South Florida. There's a clothing-optional area at the north end of the beach. | 10800 Collins Ave., Sunny Isles | 305/947–3525 | $3.50 per vehicle | Daily dawn to dusk.

North Beach. If you want quiet, less crowded beaches, this section of public beach, on Ocean Terrace between 73rd and 75th streets, is a good spot. Metered parking is ample right behind the dune and a block behind Collins Avenue along a quiet, old shopping street. | Collins Avenue at 74th St.

South Pointe Park. This park, at the southernmost point of Miami Beach, provides public fishing from the 50-yard Sunshine Pier, which adjoins the 1-mi-long jetty at the mouth of Government Cut. Facilities include two observation towers, rest rooms, and volleyball courts—but no bait or tackle. | 1 Washington Ave.

CULTURE, EDUCATION, AND HISTORY

Holocaust Memorial. A bronze sculpture depicting refugees clinging to a 42-ft-tall arm, a granite memorial wall, and music from a children's choir honor the memory of the 6 million Jews killed by the Nazis. | 1933–1945 Meridian Ave. | 305/538–1663 | Donations accepted | Daily 9–7.

Jackie Gleason Theater of the Performing Arts. The original home of Gleason's *Honeymooners* series, this Art Deco theater stands on South Beach's northern fringe, and hosts blockbuster Broadway plays, concerts, and international ballet and modern dance companies. | 1700 Washington Ave. | 305/673–7300 | www.gleasontheater.com | Call for schedule.

The Wolfsonian-Florida International University Foundation Gallery. The Wolfsonian-FIU, a museum in South Beach, presents you with a fascinating collection of art and design, 1885–1945. Focusing on how art and design reflect and shape the human experience, the collection includes: decorative art, industrial design, sculpture, furniture, paintings, rare books, posters, machines, and more. Dedicated curators and staff bring these items alive, describing the context, making connections, and encouraging you to explore the material culture of the past and its relevance to the present. | 1001 Washington Ave. | 305/531–1001 | $5 | Tues.–Wed. and Fri.–Sat. 11–6, Thurs. 9–6, Sun. 12–5 | Closed Wed. | www.wolfsonian.org.

MUSEUMS

Bass Museum of Art. This fortress-like museum's permanent collection focuses on medieval and Renaissance European art and includes works of masters such as Rubens, Botticelli, Dürer, and Toulouse-Lautrec, as well as several 16th-century Flemish tapestries. Exhibits on Miami Beach design, architecture, and history add local flavor. The museum is now part of the Miami Beach Cultural Campus, which includes the Miami City Ballet, a new regional library, and a sculpture park. | 2121 Park Ave. | 305/673–7533 or 305/673–7530 | $5 | Tues.–Sat. 10–5, Sun. 1–4; 2nd and 4th Wed. of each month 1–9.

Sanford L. Ziff Jewish Museum of Florida. This museum chronicles 230 years of Jewish life in Florida through lectures, films, storytelling, walking tours, and special events. The building is the former Congregation Beth Jacob Synagogue. | 301 Washington Ave. | 305/672–5044 | fax 305/672–5933 | www.jewishmuseum.com | Adults $5 | Tues.–Sun. 9–5, closed Mon. and Jewish holidays.

SHOPPING

★ **Bal Harbour Shops.** In a tropical garden setting, this swank collection of 100 high-end shops, boutiques, and department stores includes such names as Chanel, Gucci, Bulgari, Jacques Dessange, Hermès, Bruno Magli, F. A. O. Schwarz, Neiman Marcus, and Florida's largest Saks Fifth Avenue. Local shoppers love its leafy outdoor corridors. | 9700 Collins Ave., Bal Harbour | 305/866–0311.

Lincoln Road Mall. A $16 million renovation has revitalized this pedestrian mall, known as the Fifth Avenue of the South during its heyday in the 1950s. The redesign has spruced up the futuristic 1950s vision of Fontainebleau designer Morris Lapidus and added a grove of 20 towering date palms and five linear pools. Lincoln Road now is second only to Ocean Drive for bustle, fun, and people watching. Diners sit amid hundreds of tables set out in the main pedestrian area. There's also a large number of boutiques, art galleries, stores, and cafés. The mall is between 16th and 17th streets from Collins Avenue to Alton Road. There's a Sunday morning farmers' market (Nov.–Mar.) that is becoming a must-visit event for antiques collectors. | Lincoln Rd.

SIGHTSEEING TOURS/TOUR COMPANIES

Deco Tours Miami Beach. Donna Zimo offers walking tours of the Art Deco District by reservation. Ninety-min tours depart from the National Hotel at 1677 Collins Avenue. | 420 Lincoln Rd., Ste. 412 | 305/754–0139 | fax 305/762–6080 | $15.

Jungle Queen **cruises.** Take a cruise on a river boat that loops through Biscayne Bay, along the Intracoastal Waterway, Millionaires' Row, and New River, before pausing on a private island inhabited by rare birds, monkeys, and alligators. Narrated day trips last three hours, and barbecue dinner cruises run four hours. Bayside Market trips are also available on Wednesdays and Saturdays; you take a three-hour trip each way to the market, with two hours for shopping in between. Departures are from the Haulover Park Marina. | 10800 Collins Ave. | 305/947–6597 | Sightseeing cruise $12.50, barbecue dinner cruise $26.95, Bayside Market cruise $15.50 | Sightseeing cruise 10 AM and 2 PM; dinner cruise at 7 PM; Bayside Market cruises Wed. and Sat. 9:15–5.

SeaKruz. These five-hour gambling cruises into international waters feature craps, roulette, blackjack, and pai gow. Cruises depart from the Miami Beach Marina daily at 1 and 7:30. | 1280 5th St. | 305/538–8300 | fax 305/538–4181 | $10–$15.

OTHER POINTS OF INTEREST

★ **Española Way.** This pleasing street, between 14th and 15th streets west of Washington Avenue, features Mediterranean Revival buildings constructed in 1925; artists and writers frequented the street over the years. The Clay Hotel, now an attractive youth hostel, had an especially spritely past: Al Capone ran his racket from upstairs in the mid-1920s, and Desi Arnaz played the congas here before his future fame as a band leader. The lane now has outdoor cafés, appealing restaurants, quaint shops, and a wonderful Sunday afternoon market. | Española Way.

WALKING TOUR

A Walking Tour of South Beach (approximately 3.5 hours)

Walking the streets of South Beach, with its Art Deco hotels, great restaurants, upscale shops, and beautiful people is half the fun of a trip to South Florida. Start this walk early (8 AM) if you want to watch the awakening city without distraction—at this hour you're also likely to see a fashion photo shoot in progress, since photographers like early morning light. But you might also want to repeat this walk at night, in the thick of the action.

The stretch of Ocean Drive from 5th to 15th Streets is the most talked-about beachfront in America, and possibly the world. A bevy of Art Deco jewels hugs the drive, while across the street lies palm-fringed **Lummus Park.** On the west side of the street, note the **Park Central Hotel** (no. 640), built in 1937 by Deco architect Henry Hohauser. Here begins a run of sidewalk cafés. The famous News Café (800 Ocean Dr.) is open 24 hours, and its outdoor spill-over tables are just about the beach's most famous spot to see and be seen. A block north, cross over to the beach side of Ocean Drive for the **Art Deco District Welcome Center** (1001 Ocean Dr., open daily 11–10) in the 1950s-era Oceanfront Auditorium. Inside, rent a taped walking tour of South Beach or arrange to take a bicycle tour.

Back across Ocean Drive notice the flying-saucer architecture of the **Clevelander** (no. 1020). On the next block you'll see the late Gianni Versace's Spanish Mediterranean mansion, **Casa Casuarina** (1114 Ocean Dr.). Versace was shot and killed in front of his home here in 1997. Graceful fluted columns stand at the **Leslie** (1224 Ocean Dr.), while the Gloria Estefan–owned **Cardozo** (1300 Ocean Dr.) stands as a streamlined Moderne classic.

The next block away from the beach, parallel to Ocean Drive, is Collins Avenue, which stretches north the length of Miami Beach. The hottest stretch of new hotels is here, starring the **Delano** (1685 Collins Ave.), where the three-story white drapes billow in the wind, and the backyard of oversized lawn furniture could double as a new Wonderland for Alice. The next parallel street away from the ocean, Washington Avenue, is the main strip for nightclubs. At 13th Street enter the 1937 Depression Moderne Miami Beach Post Office to see the rotunda and the WPA-era mural. Two blocks south is the unusual **Wolfsonian-FIU Foundation Gallery,** home to a collection of over 70,000 propaganda arts and modern design artifacts.

Return north along Washington past 14th Street, making a left at Española Way, a narrow, bohemian street of Mediterranean Revival buildings, eclectic shops, and a weekend market. Continue west down Española Way to Meridian Avenue, and head right three blocks to the sensational **Lincoln Road.** This open-air pedestrian mall runs between Alton Road at the west and Collins Avenue to the east. Its owner-operated boutiques offer a wonderful variety of clothing, furnishings, garden supplies, and art galleries. End-to-end open-air restaurants create a fun and stylish atmosphere that only Ocean Drive can compete with.

Two other stops in South Beach are worth an little extra walking. The **Holocaust Memorial** (1945 Meridian Ave.) will be recognizable by a 42-ft high bronze arm covered by sculptural depictions of tortured refugees. From here follow Dade Boulevard diagonally to 21st Street, where you can find a Maya-inspired temple filled with European masterworks at the **Bass Museum of Art** (2121 Park Ave.).

ON THE CALENDAR

JAN.: *Art Deco Weekend.* This four-day street party in the Deco district includes a sidewalk art show, entertainment, food, and tours. | 305/672–2014.

FEB.: *Festival of the Arts.* A pool of national and local artists display and sell their works alongside a variety of food stands at this oceanside festival along Ocean Terrace between 73rd and 75th Streets. | 305/672–1270.

FEB.: *International Boat Show.* One of two blockbuster boat shows held annually in South Florida (the other is in Fort Lauderdale), this mid-month event at the Miami Beach Convention Center draws some 150,000 people from 52 countries as well as all 50 states. You can buy anything from a $1 fishing lure to a $4.5 million mega-yacht. | 305/531–8410 | $12 | www.boatshows.com.

SEPT.–MAR.: *Miami City Ballet.* Led by director Edward Villella, Florida's first resident ballet company has achieved worldwide renown, thanks in large part to its world-class ensemble. Performances are primarily held at either the Jackie Gleason Theater of the Performing Arts in Miami Beach or the Broward Center for the Performing Arts in Fort Lauderdale. | 305/929–7000.

Dining

INEXPENSIVE

Arnie and Richie's. Delicatessen. This casual, family-run delicatessen features a delicious menu you can smell when you walk in: onion rolls, smoked whitefish salad, half-sour pickles, herring in sour cream sauce, chopped liver, corned beef, and pastrami. Service is brusque but quick. | 525 41st St. | 305/531–7691 | Closed Sat. | $5–$15 | AE, MC, V.

Balans. International. This eclectic sidewalk café has a free-spirited style that's in keeping with its wide-ranging menu. The black-and-white ceilings are crossed with multicolored beams. The simple, one-story brick building doesn't have the panache of its Art Deco neighbors, but the food does. Try the herb-crusted Chilean sea bass or the classic hoisin pork fillet. | 1022 Lincoln Rd. | 305/534–9191 | Breakfast also available | $8–$17 | AE, D, DC, MC, V.

Big Pink. American. This campy diner has a pink Lucite and stainless steel interior, and a menu so large it comes with a table of contents. The all-American fare features dozens of tasty sandwiches, pizzas, and burgers, all cooked with gourmet flair. | 157 Collins Ave. | 305/532–4700 | $6–$12 | AE, MC, V.

Café Efesus. Turkish. This South Beach hideaway features inexpensive, traditional cuisine from a varied menu. Turkish clientele drink beer and tell stories for hours. Grape leaves, hummus, and phyllo stuffed with feta are starters; chicken with garlic and tomato, or a gyro sandwich are popular main selections. | 1339 Washington Ave. | 305/674–0078 | Closed lunch | $12–$18 | AE, D, DC, MC, V.

Café Prima Pasta. Italian. Argentines, not Italians, run this cozy Italian restaurant in North Beach—a characteristic of many Italian restaurants in the area. The interior is standard Italian restaurant—checked tablecloths—with many photos of famous patrons of the restaurant. The specialties are *carpaccio di marzo pepperoni, arrostiti petto di pollo limone* (chicken with white wine and lemon butter sauce), or *vitello Milanese*. | 414 71st St. | 305/867–0106 | Reservations not accepted for parties under 6 | No lunch Sun. | $9–$15 | MC, V.

Charlie's Roast Beef. South American. Despite the down-home sound of the name, this is a branch of a South American fast food chain—in fact, the sole United States location. They sell sandwiches, including plump roast beef, salads, and ribs. Thick-cut, batter-dipped, deep-fried onion rings complement your meal. | 1570 Alton Rd. | 305/531–9555 | $4–$16 | AE, MC, V.

News Café. American. An Ocean Drive landmark, this 24-hr café attracts a crowd with snacks, light meals, drinks, and the people-parade on the sidewalk out front. Offering a little of this and a little of that—bagels, pâtés, chocolate fondue, sandwiches, and an impressive wine list—this place has something for everyone. | 800 Ocean Dr. | 305/538–6397 | Reservations not accepted | $7–$11 | AE, DC, MC, V.

Sport Café. Italian. This super-casual bistro is dominated by a giant TV inside and has many tables outside with a city view. The traditional Italian menu, dominated by pastas and pizza, is inexpensive and features other lighter items, like a spry salad of white beans, tuna, and red onion. | 538 Washington Ave. | 305/674–9700 | $8–$14 | AE, MC, V.

Taquerias el Mexicano. Mexican. Be warned: when these folks say "spicy," they mean it. Chicken fajitas, pork chops, enchiladas—everything at this restaurant is prepared with kick. Try a bowl of *posole* (a savory stew with beef broth and hominy). | 521 S.W. 8th St. | 305/858–1160 | 1961 S.W. 8th St. | 305/649–9150 | 6974 Collins Ave., Miami Beach | 305/864–5220 | $2–$9 | AE, MC, V.

Van Dyke Café. American. Rich wood–floored interior and a few French doors make a nice backdrop to the live jazz that takes center stage upstairs almost every night. If you decide to go during the day, dine at an outdoor table, and watch the kids make goo-goo eyes at all the dogs that seem to show up and hang out. Don't forget to eat—burgers, sandwiches, salads, omelettes, and delicious thin-crusted goat-cheese pizza are the standards. For dessert try the huge platter of assorted homemade cookies. | 846 Lincoln Rd. | 305/534–3600 | Breakfast also available | $8–$14 | AE, DC, MC, V.

Wolfie's. Delicatessen. If there's one place in Miami that screams New York, Wolfie's is it. A bakery featuring megacaloric desserts, steaming bowls of matzo ball soup, and sandwiches stacked high with pastrami and other deli meats. It's open 24 hours. | 2038 Collins Ave. | 305/538–6626 | $7–$21 | D, DC, MC, V.

MODERATE

Artichoke's. Contemporary. Specializing in dishes incorporating its green namesake, this restaurant offers a primarily vegetarian menu with a handful of seafood dishes thrown in for good measure. It's mostly frequented by health-oriented locals who come for the creative cuisine (would you like your artichokes with pasta, salad, or dunked in a zesty sauce?). One of their noteworthy dishes is the "chicken parrot" (a breaded chicken breast topped with scallops, shrimp, and vegetables). The place makes you feel at home and you can fulfill special diet requests like no salt or oil, since they cook each dish to order. | 3055 N.E. 163rd St., North Miami Beach | 305/945–7576 | No lunch | $9–$15 | AE, D, MC, V.

Caffe Sambuka. Italian. Locals consider this Italian restaurant their own: tucked in a corner of Lincoln Road Mall, this carpeted, quiet, and softly lighted restaurant features down-home Italian cooking in a family-friendly atmosphere. Featured dishes include home-made potato gnocchi in pesto sauce and chicken stuffed with goat cheese glazed with a sun-dried tomato reduction. There's also an extensive wine list. | 1233 Lincoln Rd. | 305/532–2800 | No Lunch | $12–$20 | AE, MC, V.

Crystal Cafe. Continental. This upscale restaurant has soft white walls, black chairs, smooth music, abstract art, and gentle light emanating from a crystal chandelier. Croatian-born chef/owner Klime Kovaceski creates specialties such as beef Stroganoff, Wiener schnitzel, and bouillabaisse. | 726 W. 41st St. | 305/673–8266 | Closed Mon., No lunch | $14–$25 | AE, D, DC, MC, V.

Dab Haus. German. This German eatery feels like the inside of a U-boat, with black-painted walls, scarred wood furniture, and a haze of persistent cigarette smoke. The menu is traditionally German, with spicy goulash, sauerbraten, schnitzels, homemade spaetzle, and sausages such as bratwurst and currywurst, as well as a fine selection of big draft beers and wine. | 852 Alton Rd. | 305/534–9557 | $7–$17 | AE, D, DC, MC, V.

11th Street Diner. American. This 1948 dining car was transported from Pennsylvania to 11th Street in 1992. It became an instant local favorite, a low-price, unpretentious hang-out for cherry cokes and milkshakes, blue plate specials, and regular diner fare. | 11th St. and Washington Ave. | 305/534–6373 | $10–$15 | AE, DC, MC, V.

El Rancho Grande. Mexican. This restaurant just off Lincoln Road is a local favorite and has the awards to prove it. Prices are reasonable for a wide selection of *flautas* (flute-shaped fried tortillas), enchiladas, *taquitas* (mini tacos), and an entire page of vegetarian dishes, served in a cantina-style setting. | 1626 Pennsylvania Ave. | 305/673–0480 | $12–$19 | AE, MC, V.

Grillfish. Seafood. This is the first Grillfish of five national locations, which opened in February of 1994. Everything seems large, from the mural on the wall, the stone bar, the many candles, and the open kitchen. Popular dishes include the grilled whole yellowtail and the grilled tuna. | 1444 Collins Ave. | 305/538–9908 | No lunch | $10–$19 | AE, D, DC, MC, V.

Kebab Indian Restaurant. Indian. Enjoy your mulligatawny or spicy shrimp vindaloo in private, curtained booths in this small restaurant. Choose from beef, lamb, or chicken tandoori, and gratify your sweet-tooth with a glass of *lassi* (a sweet yogurt drink). | 514 N.E. 167th St., North Miami Beach | 305/940–6309 | $11–$20 | AE, DC, MC, V.

Larios on the Beach. Cuban. Old Cuban newspapers and magazines line the walls of this festive spot co-owned by the singer Gloria Estefan. They serve up large classic Cuban dishes such as *ropa vieja* (a sort Cuban barbecued shredded beef) and *morros y cristianos* (black beans and rice). Have that classic Cuban drink, a Mojito, rum-based, with mint. Regulars come for the sidewalk scenery and clublike atmosphere. | 820 Ocean Dr. | 305/532–9577 | $7–$26 | AE, D, DC, MC, V.

Lemon Twist. French. Casual candlelight dining is the rule in this cozy and romantic restaurant with a lovely painted ceiling. The food is also impressive; favorites include lemon chicken, mussels with cream, and shrimp. | 908 71st St. | 305/868–2075 | No lunch | $9–$19 | AE, MC, V.

Maiko Japanese Restaurant and Sushi Bar. Japanese. Ever dependable for reasonably priced sushi standards, this popular Japanese restaurant hosts a lively crowd from club kids to models, all waiting to taste the sashimi and udon. House specialties include the kissing roll (made of crab, avocado, and cucumber with flying fish roe) and steamed dumplings with traditional ponzu sauce. | 1255 Washington Ave. | 305/531–6369 | $8–$19 | AE, D, DC, MC, V.

Noodles of Asia (NOA). Pan-Asian. This inexpensive house of noodles is proof that South Beach takes its style seriously. With decor that recalls a modern art museum—etched green glass, stained wood ceilings, brushed-metal chairs, and burlap-covered booths—NOA's menu features noodle dishes from Malaysia, China, Thailand, Vietnam, and Japan, among others. Most dishes are spicy, and house specialties such as smoky pork dumplings and Vietnamese-style grape leaves with beef and lemongrass are not to be missed. | 801 Lincoln Rd. | 305/925-0050 | $11–$15 | AE, MC, V.

Oasis Cafe. Mediterranean. This coolly tiled, breezy spot features traditional Mediterranean fare with an emphasis on health and natural food. Delicacies such as eggplant salads, hummus, grilled sesame tofu, and sautéed garlic with spinach are some of the starters; pan-seared turkey chop, roasted vegetable lasagna, grilled fresh fish on focaccia, or penne with turkey, tomato, saffron, and pine nuts are worthy entrées. | 976 41st St. | 305/674-7676 | No lunch Sun. | $7–$16 | AE, D, DC, MC, V.

Scandals. Seafood. This casual eatery is inside the Boulevard Hotel, an Art Deco building. Most of the diners are tourists. The interior is furnished with original paintings and sculptures. Favorites here are the lobster and the stone crabs. | 740 Ocean Dr. | 305/532-0376 | $12–$35 | AE, D, DC, MC, V.

Spiga. Italian. This small, pretty restaurant features modestly priced Italian standards cooked with flair. Homemade is the hallmark here, where pastas and bread are fresh daily. Carpaccio *di salmone* (thinly sliced salmon with mixed greens) is a typical appetizer, as is the *zuppa di pesce* (fish stew). Entrées include ravioli *di vitello ai funghi shitake* (homemade ravioli stuffed with veal and sautéed with shiitake mushrooms). | 1228 Collins Ave. | 305/534-0079 | $9–$20 | AE, D, DC, MC, V.

Sushi Hana. Japanese. Soothing fountains vie with giant TV screens blasting with music videos at this popular place; the contrast reflects the unusual menu combinations. The extensive list of rolls includes the French roll (shrimp, snow crab, avocado, cucumber, cream cheese, and roe), a combo that tastes like sushi in a crêpe. Take advantage of the sashimi by ordering *chirasi* (an assortment of raw fish on rice), or request a beautiful ark that, like Noah's, has two of just about everything. | 1131 Washington Ave. | 305/604-0300 | $13–$17 | AE, DC, MC, V.

Toni's Sushi. Japanese. Known for the freshest sushi in South Beach, Toni's kitchen also serves up a variety of Japanese foods from soba noodles to tempura. Tatami mats line a quiet enclosed room surrounded by fresh bamboo dividers, where patrons dine at "sunken" tables along the back wall. For dessert, try the fried cheesecake. | 1208 Washington Ave. | 305/673-9368 | No lunch | $12–$23 | AE, MC, V.

EXPENSIVE

★ **Blue Door.** French. This sleek French restaurant attracts an equally sleek and occasionally famous clientele to the private and candlelit dining room inside the stark white Art Deco high-rise, the Delano Hotel. With white curtains and white tablecloths, the environment is extremely—white. Start with an appetizer such as ravioli filled with a sugar pumpkin mousseline, then move on to the roasted lobster in soy, lime, and brown-butter sauce, or perhaps the rack of lamb. | 1685 Collins Ave. | 305/674-6400 | Breakfast also available | $19–$36 | AE, D, MC, V.

Carpaccio. Italian. This bustling Northern Italian eatery is casual and elegant at the same time. In one of the most popular area malls, this place attracts patrons dressed in dirty blue jeans to designer slacks, and has lines that sometimes spill outdoors. Eat outside in one of two patio areas looking out at other restaurants in the courtyard, or inside with a view of a festively painted wall of smiling and dancing women. Try the *carpaccio di pesce* and *carne* or one of the many weekly lobster specials. | 9700 Collins Ave. (at Bal Harbour Shops), Bal Harbour | 305/867-7777 | $15–$25 | AE, MC, V.

Cheeky Monkey. Contemporary. In the funky atmosphere of Merv Griffin's Blue Moon Hotel, this restaurant serves global cuisine with a contemporary spin. Popular appetizers include New Orleans barbecue shrimp, a roasted garlic cloud (biscuit), and blackened foie gras walnut brioche with a port wine fig sauce. For a main course, try the bacon-wrapped pork tenderloin with praline mashed potatoes and creole mustard sauce. | 944 Collins Ave. | 305/534-2650 | $5–$35 | AE, DC, D, MC, V.

Escopazzo. Italian. The staff is courteous and professional at this very popular and renowned northern Italian eatery. Don't overlook the risotto *del giorno* or the variety of excellent pastas. For something a little different, consider the guinea breast, veal in white wine and sage sauce, or red snapper baked in a balsamic bread shell. | 1311 Washington Ave. | 305/674–9450 | www.escopazzomiami.com | Reservations essential | Closed Wed. No lunch | $12–$30 | AE, DC, MC, V.

Joe Allen. American. This casual, upscale eatery, hidden away in an exploding neighborhood full of condos, is the creation of owner Joe Allen, who was reared in the kitchens and dining rooms of Manhattan. The atmosphere is friendly and family-oriented, and the menu has everything from pizza to calf's liver to steaks, as well as more metropolitan-inspired dishes such as arugula salad with pear, prosciutto, and Gorgonzola dressing. | 1787 Purdy Ave. | 305/531–7007 | Reservations recommended | $14–$24 | MC, V.

Joe's Stone Crab. Seafood. Family-owned and -operated since 1913, this Miami Beach oldtimer serves large portions of claws with "secret" mustard sauce and butter. The stone crabs are worth the wait, but you may have to wait for a while. Once you're in, don't forget your plastic bib; crabs get messy. Steaks, lamb chops, and chicken are also available. | 11 Washington Ave. | 305/673–0365 | www.joesstonecrab.com | Reservations not accepted | Closed mid-May–mid-Oct. No lunch Mon. | $18–$40 | AE, D, MC, V.

L'Entrecôte de Paris. French. An Art Deco interior in the Art Deco district. The tables are covered in white linen and a beautiful mural of Paris extends across an entire wall. It does get a bit noisy and busy at the high-energy bar, and after midnight the place takes on more of a nightclub atmosphere. Favorites include French steaks and the mussels. | 419 Washington Ave. | 305/673–1002 | No lunch | $15–$25 | AE, D, MC, V.

Macarena Tavern. Spanish. Spanish decor, woodwork, and pictures of bull fighters adorn the interior of this restaurant and club. During the early evening hours, enjoy pitchers of fruity sangria and tasty tapas such as shrimp, sauteed mushrooms, and roasted asparagus. At around 1 AM the tables disappear, dance music pours from hidden speakers, and droves of party people descend. | 1334 Washington Ave. | 305/531–3440 | $12–$24 | DC, MC, V.

★ **Pacific Time.** Pan-Asian. This restaurant is bustling and artful, with a changing menu of creatively conceived and masterfully prepared dishes by chef and proprietor Jonathan Eismann such as sake-roasted sea bass, wok-sauteed yellowfin tuna, and freshwater catfish in tempura batter, stuffed with ginger and served whole. There's modern decor to match the modern cuisine along the hyperactive Lincoln Road pedestrian mall. | 915 Lincoln Rd. | 305/534–5979 | No lunch | $18–$34 | AE, DC, MC, V.

Red Square. Russian. The management of China Grill has proven that Americans will happily dine at a Soviet-theme restaurant, even one that features a statue of Lenin in the foyer. Besides the selection of 100 types of vodka served on a bar made of ice, the wideranging menu of Frank Copestick is eclectic and only barely Russian. The fusion dishes include Siberian nachos, fried wontons topped with smoked salmon and crème fraiche, spicy Georgian chicken, and turkey–shiitake mushroom meatloaf. | 411 Washington Ave. | 305/672–0200 | Reservations essential | No lunch. Closed Sun.–Mon. | $20–$36 | AE, MC, V.

Tuscan Steak. Italian. Dark wood, mirrors, and green upholstery define this masculine, chic, expensive place, where big platters of meat and fish are served family-style. House specialties include a three-mushroom risotto with white truffle oil, gnocchi with Gorgonzola cream, and Florentine T-bone with roasted garlic puree. | 431 Washington Ave. | 305/534–2233 | Reservations essential | Closed lunch | $18–$60 | AE, DC, MC, V.

VERY EXPENSIVE

Astor Place. American. Astor Place is best known to Miami Beach diners for chef Johnny Vincencz, a.k.a. "Caribbean Cowboy," who prepares such dishes as barbecued shrimp martini and portobello mushroom shortstack. This gourmet eatery is in the Astor Hotel, one of the areas Deco buildings, and caters to Miami Beach's upscale singles' scene at night. The setting is sleek and modern with pastels. | 956 Washington Ave. | 305/672–7217 | Breakfast also available | $26–$36 | AE, D, DC, MC, V.

China Grill. Pan-Asian. This is a very busy spot with very good food located on a busy Miami Beach strip in an Art Deco–style building. As night comes the bar area transforms to night club status and oftentimes there is a wait. While you wait check out the mosaic floor and entertain yourself by reading the engraved excerpts from Marco Polo's diary. You can dine outside on the patio. The servings are huge and the menu is immense and vast with dishes such as crispy spinach, seared rare tuna in spicy Japanese pepper, and broccoli rabe dumplings. | 404 Washington Ave. at 5th St. | 305/534–2211 | No lunch Fri–Sun. | $21–$36 | AE, DC, MC, V.

The Forge. American. You might spot a famous face or two at this top-notch steak house. The chic restaurant is in a Victorian-style building and has a menu that specializes in meats and wine. Inside, the place has lots of stained glass and tall chairs. One favorite is the American grilled chicken, and for dessert, the well-known chocolate soufflé. | 432 41st St. | 305/538–8533 | No lunch | $21–$37 | AE, DC, MC, V.

Gaucho Room. Steak. Executive chef Frank Randazzo pulls out all the stops in this Argentinian-cowboy-theme room in the convention-friendly Loews hotel. Specialties include Chilean sea bass with boniato-ginger puree, seared turbot with pickled beet–brown butter escabeche, and supple *churrasco* (marinated skirt steak grilled and sliced table-side). | 1601 Collins Ave. | 305/604–5290 | Reservations essential | No lunch | $20–$60 | AE, D, DC, MC, V.

Nemo. Contemporary. Middle Eastern food meets Indian- and Asian-influenced New American Cuisine. Garlic-cured salmon rolls and the wok-charred salmon have been on the menu since the place opened in 1995; the grilled Indian-spice pork chop is also popular. The restaurant has a main room with bar, a banquet room, and an outdoor tree-lined courtyard featuring an Old Pigeon Plum Tree. Inside copper walls made to look like ostrich skin and a ceiling in the main room painted as a sky lend a distinctive air. Buffet-style Sunday brunch. | 100 Collins Ave. | 305/532–4550 | No lunch Sat. | $23–$32 | AE, MC, V.

Osteria del Teatro. Italian. This cozy northern Italian eatery features a panoramic view of the bustling nightlife thoroughfare of Washington Avenue. Nightly specials such as seafood baked with linguine, garlic, tomatoes, and olive oil sealed in a superb package of parchment paper and the homemade ravioli stuffed with scallops and crab keep the patrons coming back. | 1443 Washington Ave. | 305/538–7850 | Closed Sun. No lunch | $13–$42 | AE, D, MC, V.

Smith and Wollensky. Steak. From the moment this branch of the famed New York steak house opened in 1997, it's been packed with beef lovers. At the southern tip of South Beach, it overlooks the water and the exclusive Fisher Island. Pull up a stool at the waterfront raw bar and enjoy the sunset or watch the cruise ships pass by. All the dry-aged steaks are expertly prepared and tasty. The filet mignon is juicy, and the creamed spinach is perfect. The veal chop, notably, is of Flintstonian proportion. | 1 Washington Ave. | 305/673–2800 | $21–$31 | AE, D, DC, MC, V.

The Strand. Contemporary. This linen-draped restaurant sums up South Beach—hip, sophisticated, and just a little bit decadent. The opulent menu includes dishes such as cognac-soaked Hudson Valley foie gras, oysters topped with Osetra caviar, whole boneless squab stuffed with duck, and lamb chops filled with rabbit sausage. | 455 Ocean Dr. | 305/532–1200 | Closed Mon. | $24–$34 | AE, DC, MC, V.

Tantra. Contemporary. South Beach's reigning palace of sensuality appeals even to the world-weary, with decor and ambience reminiscent of a Middle Eastern hookah lounge, complete with rope hammocks and burning incense. Food is serious business here. The Tantra "love appetizer" is a Homestead (local) potato spiked with Laura Chenel goat cheese, set on a bed of watercress and dressed with fragrant basil oil and pomegranate seeds. | 1445 Pennsylvania Ave. | 305/672–4765 | Reservations essential | No lunch | $28–$65 | AE, DC, MC, V.

Wish. Contemporary. Designed by fashion designer Todd Oldham, this contemporary restaurant serves creative fusion fare by up-and-coming chef Andrea Curto. Check out favorites such as yellow-eye snapper with grilled shrimp and poblano chile risotto, and pan-roasted chicken with brie polenta. | 801 Collins Ave. | 305/674–9474 | Reservations essential | Closed Mon. | $25–$30 | AE, D, DC, MC, V.

Yuca. Latin. A bustling, upscale restaurant with large picture windows looking out on Lincoln Road, this is where the who's who of local power and politics dine; table-hopping is common. Try a crisp-plantain basket filled with shrimp and conch or pan-seared tuna with coconut curry rice, but do be warned—fat-free food this is not. | 501 Lincoln Rd. | 305/532–9822 | $20–$40 | AE, D, DC, MC, V.

© Artville

KODAK'S TIPS FOR PHOTOGRAPHING THE CITY

Streets
- Take a bus or walking tour to get acclimated
- Explore markets, streets, and parks
- Travel light so you can shoot quickly

City Vistas
- Find high vantage points to reveal city views
- Shoot early or late in the day, for best light
- At twilight, use fast films and bracket exposures

Formal Gardens
- Exploit high angles to show garden design
- Use wide-angle lenses to exaggerate depth and distance
- Arrive early to beat crowds

Landmarks and Monuments
- Review postcard racks for traditional views
- Seek out distant or unusual views
- Look for interesting vignettes or details

Museums
- Call in advance regarding photo restrictions
- Match film to light source when color is critical
- Bring several lenses or a zoom

Houses of Worship
- Shoot exteriors from nearby with a wide-angle lens
- Move away and include surroundings
- Switch to a very fast film indoors

Stained-Glass Windows
- Bright indirect sunlight yields saturated colors
- Expose for the glass not the surroundings
- Switch off flash to avoid glare

Architectural Details
- Move close to isolate details
- For distant vignettes, use a telephoto lens
- Use side light to accent form and texture

In the Marketplace
- Get up early to catch peak activity
- Search out colorful displays and colorful characters
- Don't scrimp on film

Stage Shows and Events
- Never use flash
- Shoot with fast (ISO 400 to 1000) film
- Use telephoto lenses
- Focus manually if necessary

From Kodak Guide to Shooting Great Travel Pictures © 2000 by Fodor's Travel Publications

Lodging

Bayliss Guest House. At both the Bayliss and its sister property, Nassau Suites, rooms, kitchens, sitting rooms, and baths are abnormally large, and surprisingly inexpensive. An easy three blocks west of the ocean, the Bayliss is in a residential neighborhood that's comfortably close to, but far away enough from, the din of the Art Deco district. In-room safes, some kitchenettes, some refrigerators, some microwaves. Cable TV. Laundry services. Free parking. | 500 14th St. | 305/531–3488 or 305/538–5620. | fax 305/531–4440 | www.thebayliss.com | 12 rooms, 7 suites | $55–$75 | AE, D, DC, MC, V.

Brigham Gardens. More than 100 tropical plants, a fountain, and colorful birds set the mood at this small hotel one block from the beach. Although the hotel is not immaculate, it offers functional rooms suited for budget travelers who need to dine in. Each room has a minifridge, microwave, and coffee maker; one-bedroom apartments have fully-equipped kitchens. Some in-room data ports, some kitchenettes, microwaves, refrigerators. Cable TV. Laundry facilities. Parking (fee). Pets allowed (fee). | 1411 Collins Ave. | 305/531–1331 | fax 305/538–9898 | www.brighamgardens.com | 9 rooms, 11 studios, 2 1-bedroom apartments | $100 room, $125 studio, $145 apartment | AE, MC, V.

Cadet Hotel. This Lincoln Road hotel is clean, friendly, and perfectly placed. The Cadet's modest decor features soft pastels in the lobby, and blues and creams in rooms. Complimentary breakfast. Refrigerators, Cable TV. | 1701 James Ave. | 305/672–6688 or 800/432–2338 | fax 305/532–1676 | www.cadethotel.com | 44 rooms | $80–$96 | AE, D, DC, MC, V.

The Claremont. Next door to the Cavalier, the Claremont offers similarly small rooms at a fair price without the free breakfast. Rooms are starkly simple and offer the necessities: soft beds, private baths, and color TVs. There is a small fee for parking, but the hotel is within walking distance of the Lincoln Road Mall, Ocean Drive, and other South Beach attractions. Some kitchenettes, refrigerators. Cable TV. Parking (fee). | 700 Collins Ave. | 305/538–4661 | fax 305/538–9631 | 70 rooms | $75–$95 | AE, D, DC, MC, V.

Days Inn Convention Center. Nothing flashy and nothing trashy, this chain hotel inhabits a happy middle ground. The lobby is bright and floral, with a fountain and a gift shop. Deluxe rooms have impressive views of the ocean. It's literally seconds from the beach, the boardwalk, and the new arts complex containing the Miami City Ballet and the Bass Museum. Restaurant, bar. In-room data ports, in-room safes, some refrigerators. Cable TV. Pool. Shops. Laundry facilities, laundry services. Parking (fee). Some pets. | 100 21st St. | 305/538–6631 or 800/451–3345 | fax 305/674–0954 | www.daysinn.com | 172 rooms | $119–$149 | AE, D, DC, MC, V.

Days Inn North Beach Hotel. Although the rooms and baths are small, the hotel itself is clean. It's on a quiet strip of Miami Beach, where you won't have to fight for parking or deal with traffic jams. The hotel also has a game room and bright breakfast room, a plus for families. Restaurant, bar. In-room data ports, in-room safes, refrigerators. Cable TV. Pool. Laundry facilities. Business services, free parking. | 7450 Ocean Terr. | 305/866–1631 | fax 305/868–4617 | www.daysinn.com | 93 rooms | $129–$149 | AE, D, DC, MC, V.

Kenmore. Utilitarian comfort is the theme of this hotel, which preserves the presence of 1930s Art Deco. With many inviting features such as a glass-block facade in the lobby, a courtyard bar, and patio furniture, Kenmore offers privacy with smallish tropical-theme rooms that have twin or king-size beds. Restaurant, bar, complimentary Continental breakfast. Minibars, refrigerators. Cable TV. Pool. Parking (fee). | 1020–1050 Washington Ave. | 305/532–1930 or 888/424–1930 | fax 305/972–4666 | www.parkwashingtonresort.com | 60 rooms | $129 | AE, D, DC, MC, V.

Monaco Oceanfront Resort. At the north end of Miami Beach is this two-story stucco motel directly on the ocean with a private beach and reasonable rates. The basic rooms have views of the garden, the pool/patio, or the ocean, and you can sit on the ground-floor deck to

MIAMI BEACH

INTRO
ATTRACTIONS
DINING
LODGING

gaze seaward. Restaurant, bar. Some kitchenettes, refrigerators. Cable TV. Pool, wading pool. Gym. Laundry facilities. Business services, free parking. | 17501 Collins Ave., Sunny Isles | 305/932–2100 | fax 305/931–5519 | www.monaco-resort.com | 112 rooms, 1 suite | $85–$115, $120 suites | AE, D, DC, MC, V.

Ocean Surf. This small, privately owned Art Deco hotel a block east of Collins Avenue, at 74th Street, is an affordable, quiet alternative. Rooms are generic hotel style, with double or queen-size beds. Complimentary Continental breakfast. In-room safes, refrigerators. Cable TV. Beach. Free parking. | 7436 Ocean Terr. | 305/866–1648 or 800/555–0411 | fax 305/866–1649 | www.oceansurf.com | 49 rooms | $99–$134 | AE, D, DC, MC, V.

Park Washington Hotel. This small hotel is part of the jungle-like community of lodgings collectively known as the Park Washington Resort. The feel is laid back and most activities are centered around the pie-shape pool and the tiki bar. Rooms are simple with 1930s Art Deco furnishings and powerful air-conditioners. The beach is two blocks away for more fun, and there is nearby parking for $3 all day. Complimentary Continental breakfast, picnic area. Refrigerators. Cable TV. Pool. | 1020–1050 Washington Ave. | 305/532–1930 or 888/424–1930 | fax 305/972–4666 | www.parkwashingtonresort.com | 30 rooms | $109 | AE, D, DC, MC, V.

Traymore. After the wall-to-wall hotels of South Beach, but before the wall-to-wall condos further north is this eight-story budget hotel. The back patio, pool area, and beach boardwalk make it a good value, although the rooms are plain. Complimentary Continental breakfast. In-room data ports, in-room safes, some minibars, some refrigerators, some in-room hot tubs. Cable TV. Pool. Beach. Business services. Parking (fee). | 2445 Collins Ave. | 305/534–7111 or 800/445–1512 | fax 305/538–2632 | 86 rooms, 2 suites | $75–$115 | AE, D, DC, MC, V.

Villa Paradiso. Less than a block from the beach, this place has studios and one-bedrooms that open onto a lush, tropical courtyard. Rooms all have full-size kitchens and living rooms with French doors and polished hardwood floors. The owners are friendly and accommodating. Kitchenettes, microwaves, refrigerators. Cable TV. Laundry facilities. Pets allowed. | 1415 Collins Ave. | 305/532–0616 | fax 305/673–5874 | www.villaparadisohotel.com | 14 studios, 3 1-bedrooms | $100–$125 | AE, DC, MC, V.

MODERATE

The Abbey Hotel. Designer Harry Schnaper has transformed this once-sleepy hotel into a tranquil retreat to soothe the senses, a chic enclave in the Deco District's serene north end. The lobby is modern and, like the exterior, done in Art Deco. Furnished in white and black, the room has large windows overlooking 21st Street and Collins Park. The rooms are also Deco and impressive. You're two blocks from the water, and close to Lincoln Road and Washington Avenue, home to many of Miami Beach's most popular restaurants and night clubs. Minibars. Cable TV, in-room VCRs. Gym. Laundry service. Parking (fee). | 300 21st St. | 305/531–0031 | fax 305/622–1663 | 50 rooms | $125–$195 | AE, D, DC, MC, V.

Bay Harbor Inn. The Inn's not on the ocean, but the tranquil Indian Creek flowing outside is sure to soothe. Rooms with king- and queen-size beds are large, and the front porches are perfect for relaxing or viewing the village of Bal Harbour, just a 5-min walk away. Restaurant, bar, complimentary Continental breakfast. In-room data ports, minibars. Cable TV. Pool. Dock. Business services, free parking. | 9660 E. Bayshore Dr., Bal Harbour Islands | 305/868–4141 | fax 305/867–9094 | www.bayharborinn.com | 22 rooms, 23 suites | $149–$179 | AE, MC, V.

Breakwater Hotel. Built in 1939 in the heart of the Art Deco District, this striking three-story hotel is in the middle of lots of action. Check out the live evening entertainment right outside the front door at The Breakwater Cafe. Restaurant, bar. In-room data ports. Babysitting. Cable TV. Laundry facilities. Business services, parking (fee). | 940 Ocean Dr. | 305/532–1220 or 800/454–1220 | fax 305/532–4451 | www.breakwater-hotel.com | 48 rooms, 1 suite | $149–$219, $375 suite | AE, D, DC, MC, V.

Cardozo Hotel. This elegantly restored Deco landmark is just across the street from the beach in the heart of South Beach. The spacious rooms have hardwood floors and leopard-print blankets, and many have ocean views. You're within walking distance of South Beach night clubs, restaurants, shopping, Lincoln Road Mall, and the Convention Center. Restaurant, bar. In-room data ports. Cable TV, in-room VCRs. Business services. Laundry service. Parking (fee). | 1300 Ocean Dr. | 305/535–6500 or 800/782–6500 | fax 305/532–3563 | www.cardozo-hotel.com | 44 rooms, 7 suites | $150–$195, $400–$620 suites | AE, D, DC, MC, V.

The Clevelander. It would be hard to talk about Ocean Drive nightlife without mentioning The Clevelander. Its series of courtyard bars loop around fountains and cascade with humanity. Inside the hotel, rooms have small double beds and medium-size baths. Restaurant, 5 bars, room service. Cable TV. Pool. Exercise equipment. Shops. Parking (fee). | 1020 Ocean Dr. | 305/531–3485 or 800/815–6829 | fax 305/531–3485 | 50 rooms | $140–$170 | AE, DC, MC, V.

Crest Hotel and Suites. This place is extremely clean, with streamlined furniture in the lobby and rooms as though it were a boutique hotel on the move. Simple rooms feature a king- or two full-size beds, and suites include kitchenettes and microwaves. Two separate buildings are joined by a small coffee bar and pool, and there is a rooftop solarium for those who need a little solitude. Restaurant, bar, room service. In-room data ports, some kitchenettes, some minibars, some microwaves, some refrigerators. Cable TV. Pool. Laundry service. Parking (fee). | 1670 James Ave. | 305/531–0321 or 800/531–3880 | fax 305/531–8180 | www.cresthotel.com | 41 rooms, 25 suites | $155 room, $195–$235 | AE, DC, MC, V.

Essex House Hotel. This three-story landmark hotel was designed by Henry Hohauser and built in 1938 in the Art Deco District. In the lobby, note the original polychrome mural of the Everglades, which was restored by the original artist, Earl LaPan, 50 years after he originally painted it. You're within walking distance of shops, restaurants, and night spots. Complimentary Continental breakfast. In-room data ports, some refrigerators. Cable TV. Pool. Hot tub. Laundry services. Business services, parking (fee). | 1001 Collins Ave. | 305/534–2700 or 800/553–7739 | fax 305/532–3827 | www.essexhotel.com | 61 rooms, 19 suites | $129–$149, $189–$209 suites | AE, DC, MC, V.

Greenview Hotel. Originally designed by Henry Hohauser, this 1939 Art Deco hotel now has an interior of such understated coolness, it seems straight out of a design magazine. In the Art Deco tradition, guest accommodations are simple, with queen-size beds and large baths. The lack of on-premise amenities is alleviated by the free access to the Albion, just a few steps away. Complimentary Continental breakfast. Some refrigerators. Cable TV. Laundry service. | 1671 Washington Ave. | 305/531–6588 or 887/782–3557 | fax 305/531–4580 | www.rubellhotels.com | 40 rooms, 2 suites | $155 room, $250 suite | AE, DC, MC, V.

Indian Creek Hotel. Not as busy as the Ocean Drive hotels, this 1936 Pueblo Deco gem has been thoroughly restored with Art Deco furniture, much of it original to the hotel. Restaurant, room service. Some in-room data ports, some refrigerators. Cable TV, some in-room VCRs. Pool. Laundry service. Business services. | 2727 Indian Creek Dr. | 305/531–2727 | fax 305/531–5651 | 61 rooms | $140–$240 | AE, D, DC, MC, V.

Kent. Although the rates have inched up over time, this is still a relative bargain when compared to other South Beach digs. Functional and basic, the hotel is clean and cheerful, with a bright and airy Jamaican feel. Rooms are equipped with minibars and CD players, and some have a view of the ocean. In-room safes, minibars, in-room VCRs. Business services. Parking (fee). | 1131 Collins Ave. | 305/604–5000 or 800/688–7678 | fax 305/531–0720 | www.islandoutpost.com | 50 rooms, 2 suites | $140–$210 room, $295 suite | AE, D, DC, MC, V.

Nassau Suite Hotel. Rooms in this 1937 hotel have been remodeled to create suites twice as large as the original rooms. Most have a sitting area, dining room table, and full kitchen. In-room data ports, in-room safes, kitchenettes. Cable TV, in-room VCRs. Laundry facilities, laundry service. Parking (fee). | 1414 Collins Ave. | 305/534–2354 | fax 305/534–3133 | www.nassausuite.com | 22 suites | $150–$210 | AE, D, DC, MC, V.

★ **Newport Beachside Hotel and Resort.** Stay right on the ocean and the 450-ft white sand beach with volleyball, private fishing pier, and a man-made reef. You can take lessons in snorkeling and diving. The pool area is shaded by palms and has thatch-roofed umbrellas, canvas cabanas, and poolside bar. Restaurant, bar, dining room. In-room data ports, microwaves, some refrigerators. Cable TV. Pool, wading pool. Beauty salon, hot tub. Gym, volleyball. Water sports, fishing. Video games. Children's programs (ages 3–12). Laundry facilities. Business services. | 16701 Collins Ave. | 305/949–1300 | fax 305/956–2733 | www.newportbeachsideresort.com | 300 rooms, 150 suites | $99–$159, $289 suites | AE, D, DC, MC, V.

Ritz Plaza Hotel. A friendly staff counterbalances the cold terrazzo tile in the Art Deco lobby at this hotel a few skips from the beach. Modern rooms come in muted colors; some have ocean views. Restaurant, 2 bars. In-room data ports, in-room safes, some refrigerators. Cable TV. Pool. Beach. Laundry service. Business service, parking (fee). | 1701 Collins Ave. | 305/534–3500 or 800/522–6400 | fax 305/531–6928 | www.ritzplaza.com | 132 rooms, 4 suites | $109–$259 room, $399–$699 suite | AE, D, DC, MC, V.

Seacoast Suites. An elegant all-suites, apartment-style hotel right on the beach, this place has spacious living and dining rooms and its own mini-market. The suites' terraces overlook the Atlantic or the exciting skyline of Miami. You're 15 minutes from the Bal Harbour shops, the Bayside Marketplace, and the Art Deco District. A private bus service runs from South Beach to Aventura Mall. Restaurant, bar. Minibars. Cable TV. Pool. Tennis court. Gym. Beach. Laundry facilities. Parking (fee). Pets allowed. | 5101 Collins Ave. | 305/865–5152 | fax 305/868–4090 | 73 1- to 2-bedroom suites | $119–$179 1–bedroom, $269–$359 2–bedroom | AE, D, DC, MC, V.

Suez Oceanfront Resort. Part of Sunny Isles' Motel Row, this family-run resort's rooms house Chinese-inspired furniture and eye-catching color schemes. Children's rates are offered. Restaurant, bar. Refrigerators, some kitchenettes. Cable TV. 2 pools. Tennis court. Volleyball. Beach. Playground. Laundry service. Free parking. | 18215 Collins Ave., Sunny Isles | 305/932–0661 or 800/327–5278 | fax 305/937–0058 | www.suezresort.com | 196 rooms | $130–$210 | AE, DC, MC, V.

Taft. Renovated and reopened in 1998, this hotel is part of the Park Washington Resort, an entire block of Art Deco accommodations. This one is furnished Deco style. You can lounge by a pool, drink at the tiki bar, and exchange stories with fellow guests. Bar, complimentary Continental breakfast. Refrigerators. Cable TV. Pool. Pets allowed. | 1020–1050 Washington Ave. | 305/532–1930 or 888/424–1930 | fax 305/534–6597 | www.parkwashingtonresort.com | 30 rooms | $159 | AE, MC, V.

Thunderbird. A breezy courtyard and Olympic-size pool highlight the outdoor aspects of this member of Sunny Isles' hotel row. You'll also find tennis courts and a tiki bar. Inside, rooms are tropically themed, and a few efficiencies are also available. There's a supermarket across the street. Restaurant, 2 bars. In-room safes, some kitchenettes, refrigerators. Cable TV. 2 pools. Tennis court. Gym. Parking (fee). | 18401 Collins Ave., North Miami Beach | 305/931–7700 or 800/327–2044 | fax 305/932–7521 | www.dezerhotels.com | 180 rooms | $120–$200 | AE, D, DC, MC, V.

EXPENSIVE

The Albion. This stylish 1939 Nautical-Deco building designed by Igor Polevitzky offers luxury with a minimalist touch. The two-story lobby is framed by an indoor waterfall, and the mezzanine-level pool has portholes that allow courtyard strollers an underwater view of the swimmers. Guest rooms are minimalist in design, but come with two phone lines, minibars, and stereos. 1 bar, room service. In-room data ports, in-room safes, minibars. Cable TV, some in-room VCRs. Pool. Massage. Exercise equipment, health club. Shops. Laundry service. Business services, parking (fee). | 1650 James Ave. | 305/913–1000 or 888/665–0008 | fax 305/674–0507 | www.rubellhotels.com | 96 rooms, 12 suites | $255 room, $325–$375 suite | AE, D, DC, MC, V.

Beacon Hotel. After a remodeling, this Ocean Drive gem reflects the grandeur of its 1937 design. In the frenzied heart of Ocean Drive, the Beacon offers moderately sized rooms, comfortable beds, fairly large closets, and an average-size bath. A restaurant with a sidewalk café provides plenty of people-watching, and the beach is a stone's throw away. Restaurant, bar. In-room safes, refrigerators. Cable TV. Laundry facilities. Parking (fee). | 720 Ocean Dr. | 305/674–8200 or 800/649–7075 | fax 305/674–8976 | www.beacon-hotel.com | 79 rooms, 2 suites | $170–$295 room, $345 suite | AE, D, DC, MC, V.

Cavalier. This is one of Chris Blackwell's six Island Outpost hotels (the others are Casa Grande, Kent, Leslie, Marlin, and the Tides). Rooms include a TV/VCR/CD player, queen-size bed, batik fabrics, requisite Deco-style furniture, vintage black-and-white photos, and access to the pool at the Tides. Suites get an ocean view and a king-size bed. 2 restaurants, 1 bar, room service. In-room data ports, in-room safes, minibars, refrigerators, some hot tubs. Cable TV, in-room VCRs. Pool. Massage. Shops. Laundry service. Business services, parking (fee). Some pets allowed. | 1320 Ocean Dr. | 305/604–5064 or 800/688–7678 | fax 305/672–5611 | www.thecavalierhotel.com | 45 rooms, 3 suites | $185–$210 room, $350–$395 suite | AE, D, DC, MC, V.

Fisher Island Club. William Vanderbilt's former mansion is the centerpiece of this ultra-exclusive resort hotel reachable only by ferry, and only for those with reservations. The resort features a top nine-hole golf course, the Spa Internazionale (an island market), two deep-water marinas, and a mile-long private beach with Bahamian sand. There are suites, villas, and cottages. 6 restaurants, 3 bars, picnic area, room service. In-room data ports, in-room safes, kitchenettes, minibars, microwaves, refrigerators, some in-room hot tubs. Cable TV, in-room VCRs. 2 pools. Barber shop, beauty salon, hot tub, massage, sauna, spa, steam room. Driving range, 9-hole golf course, 18 tennis courts. Exercise equipment, gym, health club, beach. Dock, water sports, boating, bicycles. Shops. Baby-sitting, children's programs (ages 4–12), playground. Laundry services. Free parking. Some pets allowed. | 1 Fisher Island Dr. | 305/535–6000 or 800/537–3708 | fax 305/535–6003 | www.fisherisland-florida.com | 30 rooms, 27 suites, 3 cottages | $385–$765 room, $765–$1,265 suite, $950–$1530 cottage | AE, D, DC, MC, V.

★ **Hotel Astor.** Just two blocks from the bustle of Ocean Drive, the rooms of this hotel (one of South Beach's best) have a relaxed and quiet tone thanks to double-insulated walls and soft lighting. Tasteful, muted colors complement these qualities, as do the eminently comfortable king beds with down pillows. The service is excellent. Restaurant, bar, room service. In-room data ports, in-room safes, minibars. Cable TV. Pool. Massage. Laundry service. Business services. | 956 Washington Ave. | 305/531–8081 or 800/270–4981 | fax 305/531–3193 | www.hotelastor.com | 40 rooms | $175–$420 | AE, MC, V.

★ **Hotel Impala.** This small Mediterranean Revival–style hotel has a tropical garden courtyard and rooms with Italian saturnier stone floors, and Spanish surrealist art. Ocean Drive is a block away, but it feels a lot further. Rooms are stocked with mineral water, CDs, and videos. Restaurant, bar, room service. In-room data ports, some refrigerators, some minibars. Cable TV, in-room VCRs (and movies). Laundry service. Business services. Pets allowed. No kids under 15. | 1228 Collins Dr. | 305/673–2021 or 800/646–7252 | fax 305/673–5984 | www.hotelimpalamiamibeach.com | 17 rooms | $215–$400 | AE, DC, MC, V.

Hotel Ocean. This luxury hotel is reminiscent of the French Riviera, complete with a shaded, bougainvillea-draped courtyard and complimentary breakfast at the hotel's brasserie. The comfortable rooms are highlighted by soft beds, authentic 1930s Art Deco pieces, large fold-out couches, and clean, spacious baths. Also offered are wet bars with refrigerators, TV/VCR/CD players, and two phone lines with data-port access, and well as soundproof windows. Restaurant, 1 bar, complimentary Continental breakfast, room service. In-room safes, minibars, refrigerators, some hot tubs. Cable TV, in-room VCRs. Shops. Baby-sitting. Laundry services. Parking (fee). Pets allowed. | 1230-38 Ocean Dr. | 305/672–2579 or 800/783–1725 | fax 305/672–7665 | www.hotelocean.com | 4 rooms, 23 suites | $215–$255 room, $275–$325 suite | AE, D, DC, MC, V.

Miami Beach Ocean Resort. Sea breezes flow through the moderate-size rooms with rattan furniture and sea prints. The hotel is far north along the main drag, so quiet beach times can be found waterside or around the tropical poolside bar. Restaurant, bar. In-room safes, in-room data ports. Cable TV. Pool. Beauty salon, massage, spa. Beach. Video games. Laundry service. Business services, parking (fee). | 3025 Collins Ave. | 305/534–0505 or 800/550–0505 | fax 305/534–0515 | www.mbor.com | 238 rooms, 5 suites, 1 penthouse | $220–$265 room, $325 suite, $1,200 penthouse | AE, D, DC, MC, V.

Park Central. Wraparound corner windows and a sunny roof deck draw the top names in the fashion industry to this seven-story blue-and-white Art Deco hotel. Rooms are pristine, with crisp whites and mahogany furniture. On the grounds are a juice bar and an open air sculpture garden, and a concierge can set you up with a massage by the beach. Restaurant, bar, complimentary Continental breakfast. In-room data ports, in-room safes, some refrigerators. Cable TV. Pool. Massage. Gym, volleyball. Beach. Shops. Laundry service. Business services, parking (fee). | 640 Ocean Dr. | 305/538–1611 | fax 305/534–7520 | www.theparkcentral.com | 116 rooms, 12 suites | $174–$225 room, $275–$325 suite | AE, D, DC, MC, V.

Pelican. At this Art Deco–inspired hotel, the rooms' imaginative titles (Leafforest, Cubarrean, and People from the 1950s) mirror their outrageous appointments. The Best Whorehouse, for instance, has black silk and red-flecked wallpaper, a heart-shaped red velvet chair, and statues of voluptuous griffins. Miami's most unusual hotel draws the hip and adventurous. Restaurant, bar, room service. In-room data ports, in-room safes, refrigerators. Cable TV, in-room VCRs. Laundry service. Business services. | 826 Ocean Dr. | 305/673–3373 or 800/773–5422 | fax 305/673–3255 | www.pelicanhotel.com | 26 rooms | $190 | AE, DC, MC, V.

Ramada Plaza Marco Polo Beach Resort. All rooms in this resort have at least partial ocean views (some have balconies as well), a mini-refrigerator, and two queen-size beds. The bottom level offers a convenience store, beauty salon, various shops, and, surprisingly, an art gallery. Restaurant, room service. In-room data ports, in-room safes, some kitchenettes, refrigerators. Cable TV. Beauty salon. Gym. Beach. Shops. Parking (fee). | 19201 Collins Ave., Sunny Isles | 305/932–2233 or 877/327–6363 | fax 305/935–5009 | www.ramada.com | 350 rooms, 20 suites | $155–$245 | AE, D, DC, MC, V.

Shelborne Beach Resort. This two-story Art Deco resort in the Deco district has both rooms and townhouses—nice if you're traveling with a family. The furnishings vary in style, from classic to neon. You're within walking distance of shopping, restaurants, and nightlife. Restaurants, bar. In-room data ports, minibars, refrigerators, microwaves. Cable TV, some in-room VCRs (and movies). Pool. Hot tub, massage. Gym. Business services. | 1801 Collins Ave. | 305/531–1271 | fax 305/531–2206 | www.shelborne.com | 220 rooms, 20 townhouses, 1 suite | $185–$400, $650 townhouses, $1000 suite | AE, D, DC, MC, V.

VERY EXPENSIVE

★ **The Alexander All-Suite Luxury Hotel.** On Miami Beach's famous Millionaires' Row, this is a four-star, full-service, beachfront resort with 150 spacious one- and two-bedroom suites. The suites have private balconies, complete living and dining rooms, two full bathrooms, and fully equipped kitchens. The Alexander's lush lagoon-shaped pools have a cascading waterfall and are the perfect backdrop for a barbecue or a cocktail reception. You can eat outside at the grill and rent pool-side cabanas for catered small gatherings. At the private beach, you can parasail, swim, go jet-skiing, or cruise on a hydrobicycle. Volleyball, paddleball, pool, and a fitness center are also available. Restaurants, bar. Kitchenettes, microwaves, refrigerators. Cable TV. 2 pools. Beauty salon, hot tub. Gym, water sports. Business services. | 5225 Collins Ave. | 305/865–6500 or 800/327–6121 | fax 305/864–8525 | www.alexanderhotel.com | 150 suites | $335–$775 1–bedroom suite, $485–$1100 2–bedroom suites | AE, D, DC, MC, V.

Beach House Bal Harbour. If the idea of a million-dollar oceanfront home appeals to you, you might enjoy a stay at this laid-back, luxurious hotel, which was taken over and renovated by Rubell Hotels in 2000. Spacious rooms are filled with Ralph Lauren furniture and

Nantucket-style wainscoting. Outdoors, there are screened-in porches, a pool-side spa, a hammock grove, a banquet tent for parties, and a white-sand beach leading up to the Atlantic. Restaurant, 2 bars, room service. Refrigerators. Cable TV, room phones. Pool. Beauty salon, massage, spa. Exercise equipment, gym, health club, beach. Dock, water sports, boating. Shops. Laundry service. Business services, parking (fee). | 9449 Collins Ave., Bal Harbour | 305/865–3551, 800/695–8284, or 800/327–6644 | fax 305/861–6596 | www.rubellhotels.com | 165 rooms, 5 suites | $250–$400 room, $420–$800 suite | AE, DC, MC, V.

Blue Moon. Recently acquired by one-time talk show host Merv Griffin, this hotel is designed to resemble a European estate rather than a 1930s box. The Blue Moon looks and feels like nothing else on Collins Avenue. The rooms, although not huge, are pleasant and airy, free of trendiness. Restaurant, bar, room service. In-room data ports, in-room safes, minibars, refrigerators. Cable TV. Pool. Massage, spa. Laundry services. Business services, parking (fee). | 944 Collins Ave. | 305/673–2262 or 800/724–1623 | fax 305/534–5399 | www.merv.com | 69 rooms, 5 suites | $249–$425 | AE, D, DC, MC, V.

Casa Grande. A Balinese theme dominates the luxury suites of this hotel: dhurrie rugs, Indonesian fabrics and artifacts, and two-poster beds. All rooms also have large baths (a rarity in the Art Deco District) and full kitchens; some include ocean views and terraces. Restaurant. In-room safes, kitchenettes, microwaves, refrigerators. Cable TV, in-room VCRs. Beach. Shops. Laundry service. Business services. Pets allowed. | 834 Ocean Dr. | 305/672–7003 or 800/688–7678 | fax 305/673–3669 | www.islandoutpost.com | 34 suites | $295–$1,500 | AE, D, DC, MC, V.

★ **Delano.** South Beach's chicest, trendiest hotel is a 15-story stark white Art Deco high rise. It opened on Collins Avenue in 1995 after a $20 million renovation, and now lures celebrities. The lobby has billowing gauze curtains hanging from 22-ft ceilings. The furnishings tend toward a Dali-esque surrealism. The pool has underwater music. Restaurant (Blue Door), bar, room service. In-room data ports, minibars. Cable TV, some in-room VCRs (and movies). Pool, wading pool. Sauna. Gym. Beach. Children's programs (ages 5–13), playground. Business services, parking (fee). | 1685 Collins Ave. | 305/672–2000 | fax 305/532–0099 | 194 rooms, 6 suites, 8 cottages | $375–$485, $695–$895 suites, $1,175 cottages | AE, D, DC, MC, V.

Eden Roc Resort. This Art Deco hotel, a classic 1950s resort designed by Morris Lapidus and now renovated, is a Miami landmark. On the ocean, it overlooks Miami Beach and the Intracoastal Waterway on the Golden Mile at 45th Street and Collins Avenue. The beautifully carved Italian marble and mahogany reception desk, the highly polished original terrazzo floors, and the stunning grand circular lobby offer a visually pleasing welcome. With 600 ft of white-sand beaches, you can either lounge or swim. You can walk to many night spots and restaurants. Game room with video games, pin ball, and pool table. Restaurants, bars. In-room data ports, minibars. Cable TV. 2 pools. Beauty salon. Gym. Beach. Business services, parking (fee). | 4542 Collins Ave. | 305/531–0000 or 800/327–8337 | fax 305/531–6955 | www.edenrocresort.com | 251 rooms, 98 suites | $334–$409, $434–$1,700 suites | AE, D, DC, MC, V.

Fontainebleau Hilton Resort and Towers. Perhaps the most recognizable landmark on the beach, the Fontainebleau Hilton Resort is on 20 lush tropical acres. Every president since Eisenhower has stayed here, as have many entertainers, some of whom performed here— Frank Sinatra, Elvis Presley, Bob Hope, Sammy Davis, Jr., and Lucille Ball. All the rooms are spacious and elegant; some are furnished in 1950s style, others are ultracontemporary. The half-acre lagoon-style rock-grotto pool with cascading waterfalls is surrounded by greenery; you can play night tennis on the seven lighted tennis courts. The 2-mi seaside boardwalk leads to the Art Deco District. Restaurants, bars. In-room data ports, some minibars, microwaves, some refrigerators. Cable TV. Pools. Barbershop, beauty salon, hot tub. 7 tennis courts. Gym. Dock, water sports, boating. Shops. Children's programs. Laundry service. Business services, airport shuttle. Some pets allowed. | 4441 Collins Ave. | 305/538–2000 | fax 305/531–9274 | www.hilton.com | 1,146 rooms, 60 suites | $240–$345 | AE, D, DC, MC, V.

The Hotel. It sounds generic, but this place has a sense of chic that's hard to top. This is due largely to the interior design of Todd Oldham, who brought the colors of the sea and sand indoors. Individually painted tiles, pale ash desks, and mosaic-patterned rugs are visual gems; minibars, bejeweled bathrooms with tie-dyed robes, TVs, VCRs, and minibars enlarge the smallish soundproof rooms. Restaurant, bar, room service. In-room data ports, in-room safes, minibar, refrigerators. Cable TV, in-room VCRs. Pool. Massage, steam room. Exercise equipment. Shops. Laundry services. Business services, parking (fee). | 801 Collins Ave. | 305/531–2222 or 888/877–8434 | fax 305/531–3222 | www.thehotelofsouthbeach.com | 48 rooms, 4 suites | $275–$295 room, $405 suite | AE, D, DC, MC, V.

Loews Miami Beach Hotel. This 18-story, 800-room hotel was built from the ground up with 99 ft of ocean frontage, 85,000 square ft of meeting space, an enormous ocean-view grand ballroom, a health spa, kids' programs, and more. Dining, too, is a pleasure thanks to the Argentinian-inspired Gaucho Room, Preston's South Beach Coffee Bar, and the Hemisphere Lounge. 3 restaurants, 2 bars, room service. In-room safes, minibars, refrigerators. Cable TV. Pool. Barbershop, beauty salon, hot tub, outdoor hot tub, massage, spa. Shops. Baby-sitting, children's programs (ages 4-12), playground. Laundry facilities, laundry services. Business services, parking (fee). | 1601 Collins Ave. | 305/604–1601 | fax 305/531–8677 | www.loewshotels.com | 743 rooms, 57 suites | $319–$439 | AE, D, DC, MC, V.

Marlin Hotel. This is one of the most photographed of South Beach hotels. Fun Jamaican art complements striking hand-painted furniture, woven grass rugs, batik-like shades, and rattan and mahogany furniture at this Island Outpost property. Every room is different; some have kitchenettes, but all are complete with VCRs, minibars, and orchid-theme embellishments. Each room also has Web-TV. Larger suites here are like villas. The Marlin Bar downstairs, a very hip spot, serves Jamaican appetizers like jerk chicken and coconut shrimp. Restaurant, bar. In-room data ports, in-room safes, minibars, kitchenettes. Cable TV, in-room VCRs. Laundry service. Parking (fee). Some pets allowed (fee). | 1200 Collins Ave. | 305/604–5063 or 800/688–7678 | fax 305/673–9609 | www.islandoutpost.com | 13 suites | $280–$395 | AE, D, DC, MC, V.

National Hotel. Originally opened in 1940, this 11-story luxury Art Deco hotel has the longest pool in Miami at 205 ft. The pool is the centerpiece for a chic backyard playground complete with fun lawn furniture leading to a sandy bar. The bars inside are among the hottest in South Beach. Restaurant, bar. In-room data ports, in-room safes, minibars. Cable TV, in-room VCRs. Beach. Gym. Laundry service. Business services, parking (fee). | 1677 Collins Ave. | 305/532–2311 or 800/327–8370 | fax 305/534–1426 | www.nationalhotel.com | 115 rooms, 5 suites | $279–$450 | AE, DC, MC, V.

Raleigh Hotel. Thick tropical foliage hides one of the nicest hotels in South Beach, with Victorian features. The hotel is popular among fashion photographers and production crews for its spacious and state-of-the-art accommodations. A breath-taking fleur-de-lis swimming pool and 300-ft beach give you ample room for swimming. The lobby has a coffee bar, martini bar, and restaurant. Restaurant, room service. In-room data ports, in-room safes, refrigerators. Cable TV, in-room VCRs. Pool. Massage. Gym. Beach. Laundry service. Business services. Pets allowed. | 1775 Collins Ave. | 305/534–6300 or 800/848–1775 | fax 305/538–8140 | www.raleighhotel.com | 107 rooms | $256–$1,500 | AE, D, DC, MC, V.

Sheraton Bal Harbour. The hotel sits on 10 acres of beach-front property, but you might not want to go much further than the bar patio that overlooks the beach. A sprawling lagoon-style pool drifts through the tropical backyard garden, complete with waterfalls and a 35-ft waterslide. Rooms have a light tropical feel with palm tree prints on the bed spreads. 3 restaurants, bar. Pool, wading pool. Beauty salon, 2 outdoor hot tubs, massage, spa. 2 tennis courts. Health club, volleyball. Water sports. Video games. Babysitting, playground. Laundry services. Business services, parking (fee). | 9701 Collins Ave. | 305/865–7511 or 800/999–9898 | fax 305/864–2601 | www.sheraton.com | 645 rooms, 53 suites | $329–$449 | AE, D, DC, MC, V.

The Tides. Some of the innovations introduced to this hotel when it was converted from 115 rooms to 45 suites are small, such as spyglasses in each room and blackboards for messages to maids, while others are large—each room has big closets, generous baths, and king-size beds. The Olympic-size swimming pool (Ocean Drive's only one), the terrace dining, and reading room are some of the features that will encourage relaxation. Restaurant, room service. In-room data ports, in-room safes, minibars. Cable TV. Pool. Gym. Beach. Baby-sitting. Laundry service. Business services. | 1220 Ocean Dr. | 305/604–5000 or 800/688–7678 | fax 305/604–5180 | www.islandoutpost.com | 45 suites | $450–$2,000 | AE, D, DC, MC, V.

★ **Wyndham Miami Beach Resort.** With the ocean on one side and the Intracoastal Waterway on the other, this 18-story high-rise Wyndham hideaway is a short distance from all of the hottest nightspots. You can lounge on the private beach, swim, and play tennis or volleyball. The resort's sports center has jet-skiing, scuba diving, and boating. Restaurant, bar, room service. In-room data ports, minibars. Cable TV. Pool. Tennis court. Water sports, boating. Baby-sitting. Laundry facilities. Business services, parking (fee). | 4833 Collins Ave. | 305/532–3600 | fax 305/534–7409 | www.wyndham.com | 352 rooms, 72 suites | $275–$375, $250–$1,030 suites | AE, D, DC, MC, V.

MICANOPY

MAP 3, I4

(Nearby towns also listed: Gainesville, Ocala)

Named after a Seminole chief, Micanopy was a hotbed of Seminole War activity in the mid-1800s. The town was established in 1821 as a trading post, a tradition that coincidentally survives today in a large annual fall antiques show. It's a beautiful town, which has streets lined with live oaks and which is still small enough, with 675 residents, that there's no mail delivery service; residents pick up their mail at the post office. Its most famous nearby resident was Marjorie Kinnan Rawlings, whose home is preserved as a state historic site.

Information: **Gainesville/Alachua County Visitors and Convention Bureau** | 30 E. University Ave., Gainesville, 32601 | 352/374–5260 | www.visitgainesville.net.

Attractions

Micanopy Historical Society Museum. Learn the history of the town and surrounding area, beginning with De Soto's 1525 visit, through artifacts, exhibits, and a video presentation. The museum is housed in a late 19th-century warehouse and former general store. | 607 Cholokka Blvd. | 352/466–3200 | www.afn.org/~micanopy | $2 donation | Daily 1–4.

Marjorie Kinnan Rawlings State Historic Site. This 12-acre park preserves the wood-constructed, shingled-roof house where author Marjorie Kinnan Rawlings made her home from 1928 until she was remarried in 1941. The place she wrote many of her books, including her well-loved novel *The Yearling*, the property is a microcosm of the Florida landscape, encompassing farmland, marsh, and a thriving hammock; listed on the National Register of Historic Places since 1970, it represents a side of rural Florida history, culture, and architecture that has all but vanished elsewhere. Cross Creek is about 10 mi east of Micanopy between Orange and Lochloose Lakes. | Rte. 325 | 352/466–3672 | www.dep.state.fl.us | Grounds free; Tours $3 | Grounds open daily 9–5; guided house tours Oct.–July, Thurs.–Sun. 10–4 on the hour.

★ **Paynes Prarie State Preserve.** This 21,000-acre wildlife preserve is a wintering area for migratory birds and home to alligators and a wild herd of American bison. You can swim, boat, picnic, and camp along the ponds, lakes, and trails here. There's also a visitors center and museum. | 100 Savannah Blvd. | 352/466–3397 | www.dep.state.fl.us | $3.25 per vehicle | Daily 8–sunset.

ON THE CALENDAR

OCT.–NOV.: *Fall Harvest Festival.* Since 1965 hundreds of antiques dealers and buyers have gathered yearly under the old oaks for this festival. Besides antiques, the event has music, arts, and crafts, and a Saturday afternoon auction. | 352/466–7026.

Dining

Colleen's Ice Cream Shop. Café. Besides homemade ice cream, this shop serves sandwiches and soups. The apple, peach, and cherry cobblers are also homemade. | 203 Cholokka Blvd. | 352/466–3839 | $2–$5 | No credit cards.

Old Florida Café. Café. Large, made-to-order sandwiches are served on a thickly sliced homemade bread. Cuban and Reuben sandwiches come off the grill. | 205 Cholokka Blvd. | 352/466–3663 | $4–$6 | No dinner | D, MC, V.

Wildflowers Café. American. White tablecloths and well-spaced tables create an appealing atmosphere at this very casual eatery, popular because of its reliable food: steaks, seafood, chicken marsala, spaghetti with meatballs, salads, and sandwiches. | 201 U.S. 441N | 352/466–4330 | Closed Mon. | $7–$14 | AE, MC, V.

Lodging

Herlong Mansion. Four two-story Corinthian columns pierce the wide veranda of this stately Greek Revival–style B&B. The classical touches were part of a 1910 renovation of a two-story 1845 Victorian house, still surrounded by old oak trees. Inside are 10 working fireplaces, mahogany inlaid oak floors, and suites decorated with period furniture, Oriental rugs, and

© Corbis

A SENSE OF PLACE—MARJORIE KINNAN RAWLINGS

"Cross Creek is a bend in a country road, by land, and the flowing of Lochloosa Lake into Orange Lake, by water. We are 4 mi west of the small village of Island Grove, 9 mi east of a turpentine still, and on the other sides we do not count distance at all, for the two lakes and the broad marshes create an infinite space between us and the horizon."

This is Marjorie Kinnan Rawlings' beginning to the story of her life in this rural Florida community. Arriving in Cross Creek, southeast of Gainesville, in 1928 with her husband, Charles Rawlings, she immediately felt an affinity for the remoteness, wildness, and simplicity of life here and made a lifelong commitment to it, observing: "When I came to the Creek, I knew the old grove and the farmhouse at once as home."

Three separate structures connected by screen porches, open verandas, tall ceilings, and floor-to-ceiling French doors comprise the eight-room house built of cypress and heart pine. The wide porch was her favorite writing spot—typewriter perched atop a cypress farmhouse table, where she would describe her life in the Florida county with a sharp ear for dialect, regional Cracker humor, and an uncanny ability to convey her deep feeling of connection to nature. These were impressions that would endear her to the world and capture forever the beauty of Florida farmland, wild marshland, and a culture that epitomizes a rural Florida that has all but disappeared.

The Yearling, winner of the Pulitzer Prize in 1938, is a bittersweet story of a backwater boy who adopts a fawn; it was made into a popular movie, and over the years has assumed the status of an American classic. *Cross Creek,* considered by many to be her best work, was published in 1942. This book is Rawlings's autobiography of her life at the Creek and the book in which she introduces readers to her favorite haunts, and to her Cracker friends and neighbors.

The rural territory and its people inspired her; her writings flowed into works that have placed her among the best known names in Florida and American literature.

armoires. Dining room, picnic area, complimentary breakfast. Some kitchenettes, some refrigerators, some in-room hot tubs. Some in-room VCRs, no TV in some rooms. Library. Some pets allowed. | 402 Cholokka Blvd. | 352/466–3322 or 800/437–5664 | fax 352/466–3322 | www.herlong.com | 5 rooms, 4 suites, 2 cottages | $80–$179 | AE, MC, V.

Shady Oaks B&B. This three-story inn has 14-ft-deep wraparound porches, which were designed to make the building resemble a 19th-century Florida mansion. A second-story screened veranda, with hammock, swing, and paddle fans, sits under a 400-yr-old live oak. Victoria's Suite is playfully decorated like an 1890s bordello, with purple velvet drapes, a hot tub, and a large stained-glass window (made by innkeeper Frank James) depicting a sensuous madame. Candlelight dinners are served in some rooms with 3-day advance notice. Restaurant, picnic area, complimentary breakfast. Some in-room hot tubs, some in-room VCRs (and movies). Pond. Shop. Laundry facilities. No smoking. | 209 Cholokka Blvd. | 352/466–3476 | fax 352/466–9233 | www.shadyoak.com | 9 rooms | $85–$175 | AE, D, MC, V.

NAPLES

MAP 3, C4

(Nearby towns also listed: Everglades City, Everglades National Park, Marco Island)

NAPLES

INTRO
ATTRACTIONS
DINING
LODGING

The rich and famous have flocked to the region ever since President Grover Cleveland's sister Rose became the first guest at the Naples Hotel in the late 19th century. The lovely historic buildings of that era have been preserved in a section of the city known as Old Naples.

Today, Naples is becoming the Palm Beach of Florida's west coast, with good shops and restaurants and great golf courses (in fact, more per capita than any other place in the country). Condominium towers and resorts are rising 20 stories or higher into the South Florida sky. The Gulf of Mexico, incredibly blue-green, laps the beaches. There's great fishing and sunbathing.

Be warned that, with all Naples has to offer, it can often be difficult to get a room or reservations during the popular winter months.

Information: **Naples Area Chamber of Commerce** | 895 5th Ave. S, Naples, 34102-6605 | 941/262–6141 | www.naples-online.com.

Attractions

Caribbean Gardens and Zoo. Originally a botanical garden planted in the early 1900s, this 52-acre junglelike educational park houses exotic wildlife, including African lions, mandrills, Bengal tigers, lemurs, antelope, and monkeys. The Primate Expedition Cruise takes you through islands of monkeys and apes living in their natural habitat. The Safari Canyon show has both live animals and stunning video footage. You can see elephants and watch alligators feeding. Kids can pet a young alligator. Call for show and tour times. | 1590 Goodlette Rd. | 941/262–5409 | $14.95 | Daily 9:30–5:30; last ticket sold at 4:30.

Collier County Museum. A steam logging locomotive and a permanent collection showcasing Collier County's historic past highlight this museum. Exhibits go back to the times when the Calusa Indians roamed the region. | 3301 Tamiami Tr. E (U.S. 41) | 941/774–8476 | fax 941/774–8580 | Free | Weekdays 9–5.

Conservancy of Southwest Florida. There's a wildlife rehabilitation center as well as boat rentals and short nature trails. Visit in the morning if you want to have time for boating. This park has 13 acres on the Gordon River. The center is on Merrihue Drive at 14th Ave. N, one block east of Goodlette-Frank Rd. | 1450 Merrihue Dr. | 941/262–0304 | fax 941/262–5872 | $5 | Mon.–Sat. 9–4:30.

Corkscrew Swamp Sanctuary. The sanctuary, 20 mi northeast of Naples and operated by the National Audubon Society, preserves the world's largest remaining subtropical old-growth bald-cypress forest. The 2-mi boardwalk trail meanders through towering 500-yr-old trees. Nearly 200 species of birds, including egrets, nesting wood storks, and wading birds, live here, as well as varieties of frogs, turtles, snakes, and lizards. You may see alligators, deer, or bobcat. | 375 Sanctuary Rd. | 941/657-3771 | www.naples-online.com | $6.50 | May–Nov., daily 8–5; Dec.–Apr., daily 7–5.

Naples Museum of Art. Southwest Florida's first full-scale art museum opened in Naples in November 2000, in a new 30,000-square ft building on the campus of the Philharmonic Center for the Arts. Two architectural highlights are a large glass sculpture, which was designed by Dale Chihuly, and the massive entrance doors, designed by artist Albert Paley. The permanent collection, housed in 15 galleries, focuses on American Modern and Chinese art; there is also a large collection of miniatures. | 5833 Pelican Bay Blvd., North Naples | 941/597-1900 | fax 941/597-7856 | $6 | Tues.–Sat. 10–4, Sun. noon–4.

Rookery Bay National Estuarine Research Reserve. Pristine mangrove forests surround the shallow waters of Rookery Bay at this site 5 mi south of Naples. Enjoy the mangrove, the manatees, and the alligators from the 2,500-ft-long boardwalk, and the butterfly garden at the Gulf Coast's largest wildlife sanctuary. If you're a bird watcher, this 8,000-acre reserve is a good stopping spot. | 300 Tower Rd.; Shell Rd. off Rte. 951 towards Marco Island | 941/417-6310 | fax 941/417-6315 | Free | Daily; headquarters open weekdays 8–5.

SIGHTSEEING TOURS/TOUR COMPANIES

Naples Trolley Tours. Guides point out local landmarks, from the magnificent estates to the beaches and other attractions during these tours. You can get on and off as often as you like. | 1010 6th Ave. S, Ste. 227A | 941/262-7300 | www.naples-trolley.com.htm | $14 | Daily 8:30–5:30.

ON THE CALENDAR

JAN.: *Collier County Fair.* Rides, concession stands, petting zoos, entertainment, and 4-H exhibits fill this quintessential fair at the Collier County Fairgrounds, 10 mi. east of Naples, off I–75, Exit 17 | 941/455-1444.

FEB.: *Naples National Art Festival.* More than 200 artists from throughout the nation display their work at this event in Cambier Park. | 941/262-6517.

MAY: *Tropicool Fest.* Thousands attend the more than 30 concerts and arts and sports events that make up this two-week festival. | 941/262-6141.

OCT.: *Swamp Buggy Championship Races.* The "Mile O' Mud" track at Florida Sports Park is the venue for this event, first run in 1949. | 941/774-2701 or 800/897-2701.

Dining

Bayside. Seafood. Two floors of dining overlooking Naples Bay, this restaurant is part of the Venetian Village shops. Eat downstairs for a more casual meal, with such menu favorites as barbecue shrimp and pizza, with live piano music in the background. Upstairs is a bit fancier, and the menu includes oak-grilled mahimahi in a honey-pepper glaze. Tropical artwork, columns, arches, and light blue wicker furniture fill the room. Kids' menu. | 4270 Gulfshore Blvd. N | 941/649-5552 | $21–$31 | AE, D, DC, MC, V.

Bill's Pier at 5th. Seafood. The former mayor of Naples owns this restaurant on the Gordon River, built in the 1920s. It's part of Tin City, a quaint shopping mall on the wharf. The dining is casual with a nautical theme. The indoor dining room is large, seating more than 200. In nice weather, you can eat outside. Seafood items include crab cakes, snapper, stuffed shrimp, Maine lobster. Also serving duck, prime rib, NY strip steak, and chicken. | 1200 5th Ave. S | 941/261-1811 | $12–$27 | AE, D, DC, MC, V.

Bistro 821. Contemporary. The long, narrow room is done mostly in black and white, and the lights are dim, but not too dim. The menu accommodates all appetites with small plates, big plates, and half portions. Try the leg of lamb marinated with basil and served with mashed potatoes or the snapper baked in parchment with wild mushroom pasta, vodka penne, or risotto. | 821 5th Ave. S | 941/261–5821 | Reservations essential on weekends | No lunch | $12–$23 | AE, D, MC, V.

Da Ru Ma. Japanese. Tepanyaki and sushi are the mainstays here. The architecture and decorations follow the Japanese theme, simple but elegant. The chef will prepare steak tableside on tepanyaki tables. | 241 N. Center | 941/591–1200 | No lunch | $11–$25 | AE, DC, MC, V.

The Dining Room. French. Big overstuffed chairs, polished silver, fine china, and white linen are the rule here at the Ritz Carlton hotel's signature restaurant. The menu changes but may include a pastilla of rabbit, escargot, and crab cocktail with avocado, as well as steak and fresh fish. Sunday jazz brunch. | 280 Vanderbilt Beach Rd. | 941/598–6644 | Jacket required | Closed Mon. No lunch Tues.–Sat., no dinner Sun.; also closed the last 2 weeks of August | $30–$50 | AE, D, DC, MC, V.

The Dock at Crayton Cove. Seafood. This open-air restaurant at the marina on Naples Bay serves the same menu for both lunch and dinner. They've been in business since 1976. Informal, with Caribbean influences, the menu includes grilled swordfish, Bahamian conch fritters, scallops, clams, tuna, snapper, mahimahi, mussels, and similar fare. They also serve burgers, steak, ribs, and pasta. Kids' menu. | 845 12th Ave. | 941/263–9940 | $8–$16 | AE, DC, MC, V.

The English Pub. English. Steak-and-kidney pie, fish and chips, and shepherd's pie fill the menu at this Tudoresque pub, which pours no fewer than 10 imports and an assortment of bottled imported beers. It's 1 mi from 5th Avenue in downtown Naples. | 2408 Linwood Ave. | 941/774–2408 | Reservations not accepted | Closed Sun. | $10–$15 | AE, D, DC, MC, V.

SWAMP BUGGY RACING

Anyone unfamiliar with Naples's automotive history might assume Cadillacs play a greater role than gritty swamp buggies. But the old-fashioned swamp buggy is practically the town's trademark—the vehicle was conceptualized and materialized in this Gulf Shore town. In the 1940s, Naples resident Ed Frank invented the quirky means of transportation in an attempt to design a vehicle suitable for use in the morass of the Florida Everglades. Basically, the buggy is a jeep-style vehicle with oversized wheels (although, since day one, designers have contributed their own trademarks to the conveyance, if sometimes only via decorative touches).

With the boggy wilderness of the Everglades in Naples's backyard, it was only a matter of time before innovative residents began modifying the swamp buggies for racing purposes, souping the awkward vehicles up for speed. The sport of buggy racing was born, and the first competitions, which coincided with the opening of hunting season, were not far off. With formalized races—and their prize incentives, usually turkeys and money for the winners—firmly in place, the clunky wooden buggies became sleeker and faster.

Today, swamp buggy races are held several times each year and are nationally televised at Florida Sports Park. Although the contraptions are by no means as popular as they once were, many long-time residents are stubborn to keep the buggy's good-ol'-boy tradition alive. "Must we become a new city and sacrifice our charm?" asks publisher Peter Stone. "I feel that the development of Naples needs to slow down long enough for the history of the area to catch up with it."

Tourists are not excluded from the nostalgic fun; some buggies are custom-built to accommodate up to a busload of sightseers eager for some backwoods adventure.

© Corbis

The Grill Room. American. Another Ritz-Carlton Hotel restaurant, this one recalls an English gentleman's club with dark mahogany walls and a fireplace. The menu features midwest-grown beef, with prime rib the specialty on Sundays and Wednesdays. Extensive wine cellar. Live entertainment (piano). | 280 Vanderbilt Beach Rd. | 941/598–6644 | Jackets required in season | No lunch | $32–$49 | AE, D, DC, MC, V.

Grouper House. Seafood. This restaurant in Grand Central Plaza, a strip mall, has a large seafood buffet with crab legs, hot or cold, grouper prepared about any way you could want it, fresh fish, oysters Rockefeller, and lots more, including some beef dishes. The buffet has salads and desserts. You can choose from the full menu similar items à la carte. Kids' menu. | 396 Goodlette-Frank Rd. | 941/263–4900 | No lunch | $9–$22 | D, MC, V.

Lafite. Continental. In the Registry Resort, just off the lobby, this restaurant attracts locals and visitors. The interior combines warmth, intimacy, and space. Fine crystal, chandeliers, beveled mirrors, and polished woods provide a special finish in the dining room. The à la carte menu includes filet mignon, sea bass, and Maine lobster. Try the lemon-roasted filet of yellowtail snapper. | 475 Seagate Dr. | 941/597–3232 | Reservations essential | Jacket required | Open Fri. and Sat. in summer, daily in season. No lunch | $28–$35 | AE, D, DC, MC, V.

Pacific 41. American. Cheerful and family-oriented, this restaurant on the edge of downtown Naples has a diverse menu that runs from corned beef and cabbage to shrimp stuffed with crab, to prime rib and roasted leg of lamb. The garden outside the restaurant has a pond and waterfall. The interior furnished in a tropical-nautical style, with large sharks and stuffed fish hanging up on the walls. | 173 9th St. S | 941/649–5858 | Breakfast also available | $10–$21 | AE, D, DC, MC, V.

Pippin's. Steak. Pippin's has four dining rooms, plus a lounge. The glassed-in orchid greenhouse is visible from three of the dining rooms. The menu lists steak and seafood with a choice of beef and fresh fish, including Florida grouper, tuna, swordfish, snapper, dolphin, and salmon. | 1390 9th St. N | 941/262–2880 | No lunch | $12–$25 | AE, D, DC, MC, V.

★ **Ristorante Ciao.** Italian. A northern Italian menu prevails at this downtown restaurant that's one block north of Fifth Avenue. The three dining rooms have white linen, china, and elegant paintings. Favorite starters include minestrone or Caesar salad. Try veal piccata, veal Parmesan, the nightly special, or the lobster fettucine with mushrooms and asparagus in a sherry cream sauce. The extensive wine list has some Italian selections. | 835 4th Ave. S | 941/263–3889 | Closed Sun. and Mon. No lunch | $13–$30 | AE, D, DC, MC, V.

St. George and the Dragon. Seafood. Antiques and wooden beams furnish the interior of this downtown establishment with four dining rooms. The house specialty is the almond-fried shrimp; conch chowder and broiled red snapper are also popular, as is the catch of the day. Strip steak, filet mignon, and prime rib are also served. | 936 5th Ave. S | 941/262–6546 | Jackets required in one dining area only | Mon.–Sat. 11–10; Open Sun. only Jan.–Mar., 5–9 | $11–$30 | AE, D, MC, V.

Seawitch. Seafood. Seafood comes baked, fried, or grilled at this pleasant, casual waterfront restaurant at the Marina and Vanderbilt Lagoon. The two-story converted marina is one of the older buildings in the area. The downstairs dining room has two walls of windows and a tropical mural of underwater marine life. The upstairs has three walls of windows and a lounge. It's known for yellowtail snapper, grilled, baked, or lightly blackened and drizzled with white wine beurre blanc sauce. Grouper with seafood stuffing, mahimahi, Florida lobster, New York strip steak, filet mignon, and chicken are also offered. Sunday brunch. | 179 Southbay Dr. | 941/566–1514 | Lunch only in season | $17–$23 | AE, D, DC, MC, V.

Sign of the Vine. Contemporary. In business for 17 years, this restaurant that's between downtown and south Naples is in an old fire marshal's house. The dim lighting, small chandeliers, and candlelit tables make the two-tiered dining room, which also has a two-tiered veranda, a romantic setting. All meals come in seven courses. Entrée selections include duck, peppered Ahi tuna, grilled lamb, a tenderloin encrusted in Vidalia onions, and fresh fish. Desserts are made to order. | 980 Solana Rd. | 941/261–6745 | Aug. 1–Oct. 15 closed Sun.–Wed.; Oct. 16–May 15 closed Sun. No lunch | $36–$44 prix fixe | AE.

Terra. Contemporary. Muted lighting, rattan chairs, and oak tables with inlaid terra-cotta tiles set the stage for wonderful food at this restaurant, one of the most popular in Olde Naples. A long bar on one side of the room and tables on the other, some lining a bank of sliding-glass doors, make it feel like a sunroom. Additional tables on an outdoor terrace overlook Third Street. The Mediterranean-inspired menu features such starters as seafood risotto cakes, sea scallops and prosciutto on grilled Tuscan bread, and a hearty bean soup. Grilled pork sausage, wild-mushroom lasagna, Mediterranean seafood stew, and herb-encrusted tuna are some of the excellent entrées, while tasty side dishes include tomato-basil polenta, roasted elephant garlic, and ratatouille. | 1300 3rd St. S | 941/262–5500 | $10–$22 | AE, DC, MC, V.

Lodging

Best Western Naples Inn and Suites. Although the busy thoroughfare Highway 41 speeds by in front of the property, the rooms of this two-story hotel are set within lush gardens, ponds, and waterfalls. The beach is less than a mile away, and shops and restaurants are nearby. Restaurant, bar, room service. In-room data ports, in-room safes, some kitchenettes, microwaves, refrigerators. Cable TV, in-room VCRs. 2 pools, pond. Hot tub. Laundry service. Business services. | 2329 9th St. N (Hwy. 41) | 941/261–1148 or 800/243–1148 | fax 941/262–4684 | 50 rooms, 30 suites | $129–$219 | AE, D, DC, MC, V.

Charter Club Resort on Naples Bay. This charming resort in historic Olde Naples has spacious bay-view units with screened porches in its 11 three-story buildings. You can walk to the Gulf beaches, only eight blocks away. Each unit has two bedrooms, two baths, full kitchen, and living and dining rooms, and sleeps six comfortably. Wednesdays and Fridays, you can go to the barbecue dinner in the lounge. Bar. In-room data ports, microwaves, refrigerators. Cable TV, in-room VCRs (and movies). Pool, wading pool. Dock, boating, fishing, bicycles. Laundry facilities. Business services. | 1000 10th Ave. S | 941/261–5559 or 800/494–5559 | fax 941/261–6782 | www.charterclubresort.com | 33 rooms | $139–$299 | AE, D, MC, V.

Comfort Inn Naples. Freshly baked cookies are served every afternoon in this four-story hostelry with a waterside lounge. The hotel, in the heart of the downtown Naples business district on the bay, is close to shops and restaurants in Tin City. You're ½ mi from the white sand of the Gulf beaches. Bar. Complimentary Continental breakfast. In-room data ports, refrigerators, microwaves. Cable TV. Pool. Hot tub. Laundry facilities. Business services. | 1221 5th Ave. S | 941/649–5800 | fax 941/649–0523 | www.comfortinnnaples.com | 101 rooms | $139–$149 | AE, D, MC, V.

Courtyard By Marriott. A four-story hotel in a quiet area offers spacious rooms and attentive service. It's 1 mi from Gulf beaches. The hotel serves breakfast on site, though it's not included in the room price. In-room data ports, microwaves, refrigerators. Cable TV. Pool. Hot tub. Gym. Laundry facilities, laundry service. Business services, free parking. | 3250 U.S. 41 N | 941/434–8700 or 888/236–2427 | fax 941/434–7787 | www.courtyard.com | 98 rooms, 4 suites | $74–$149 | AE, D, MC, V.

Edgewater Beach Hotel. At the north end of Gulf Shores Boulevard stands this compact, high-rise waterfront resort. The brightly decorated units have either one or two bedrooms, full kitchens, and either patios or balconies. Many have Gulf views. Dine by the pool or inside on the sixth floor. There's piano music in the lounge at Happy Hour, and shopping, golf, and tennis are nearby. 2 Restaurants, bar. In-room data ports, microwaves, refrigerators. Cable TV. Pool. Gym. Beach. Laundry facilities. Business services, free parking. | 1901 Gulf Shore Blvd. N | 941/403–2000 or 800/821–0196 (reservations) | fax 941/403–2100 | www.edgewaternaples.com | 124 suites | $270–$600 | AE, D, MC, V.

Hampton Inn. Spacious rooms and an attractive lobby mark this traditional chain hotel with a nearby restaurant. The Gulf beaches are 1½ mi west. Complimentary Continental breakfast. In-room data ports, microwaves, refrigerators. Cable TV. Pool. Video games.

Laundry facilities and services. Business services, free parking. | 3210 Tamiami Tr. N | 941/261–8000 or 800/426–7866 | fax 941/261–7802 | www.hamptoninn.com | 107 rooms | $69–$145 | AE, D, MC, V.

Holiday Inn. Because the rooms are located behind the restaurant, bar, and pool, away from the highway, quiet is maintained. You can lounge by the pool or enjoy the bar, well-populated during Happy Hour. Restaurant, bar, room service. In-room data ports. Cable TV. Pool. Gym. Laundry service. Business services. | 1100 9th St. N (Hwy. 41) | 941/262–7146 | fax 941/261–3809 | www.holiday-inn.com | 137 rooms | $129–$139 | AE, D, DC, MC, V.

Hotel Escalante. Opened in 2000, this hotel is really a compound of different buildings, the rooms of which encircle four separate courtyards. Around the compound stands a row of well-maintained bushes. Rooms have a Spanish-Colonial appearance with dark-wood furnishings and light-colored walls. Shuttle service is provided to 5th Avenue shops and restaurants. The hotel is very up to date and even rents laptops. Bar, complimentary Continental breakfast, room service. In-room data ports, in-room safes, minibars, refrigerators. Cable TV. Pool. Hot tub, spa. Laundry service. Business services. Pets allowed. | 290 5th Ave. S | 941/659–3466 or 877/GULF–INN | fax 941/262–8748 | www.hotelescalante.com | 65 rooms | $250–$600 | AE, D, DC, MC, V.

Inn at Pelican Bay. This six-story inn is built on the water's edge of a private lake, 1 mi from Gulf beaches. The architecture has a touch of Mediterranean, and the pool is ringed with palm trees. The rooms that face the pool and lake have private balconies. You're close to restaurants. Bar. Complimentary Continental breakfast. In-room data ports, microwaves, refrigerators. Cable TV, in-room VCRs (and movies). Pool, lake, wading pool. Hot tub, massage. Gym. Laundry service. Business services. | 800 Vanderbilt Beach Rd. | 941/597–8777 or 800/597–8770 (reservations) | fax 941/597–8012 | www.innatpelicanbay.com | 100 rooms | $100–$250 | AE, D, MC, V.

Inn by the Sea. This B&B, in the residential section of Old Naples, was built in 1937 and is on the National Register of Historic Places. It's 1/2 block from the shopping district and 21/2 blocks from the beach. The property has a garden and lots of palm trees, birds of paradise, and other tropical trees. Inside you will find fine wooden floors and ceilings. Rooms vary; some are furnished in wicker, some have Shaker-style furniture, and some four-poster beds. All have private baths and queen-size beds. Complimentary Continental breakfast. No room phones. TV in common area. Bicycles. Free parking. | 287 11th Ave. S | 941/649–4124 or 800/584–1268 (reservations) | fax 941/434–2842 | 2 rooms, 3 suites | $94–$189 | AE, D, MC, V.

Inn of Naples at Park Shore. This newly refurnished Mediterranean-style inn is in the center of Naples, on U.S. 41, 11/2 miles from the beach. Rooms are spacious, and the suites include refrigerators and microwaves. Two restaurants, bar, complimentary Continental breakfast, room service. In-room data ports, minibars, some microwaves, some refrigerators. Cable TV, in-room VCRs (and movies). Pool. Hot tub. Gym. Laundry service. Business services, free parking. | 4055 Tamiami Tr. N | 941/649–5500 or 888/627–1595 (reservations) | fax 941/430–0422 | 100 rooms | $132–$285 | AE, D, MC, V.

The Inn on 5th. This three-story boutique hotel is in Olde Naples. The fountains, courtyard, and gardens are in Mediterranean style. You can walk to the beach (six blocks away), or to cafés, art galleries and theaters. The rooms are also furnished in a Mediterranean motif and have either one king-size or two double beds. There is an Irish-style pub with Irish entertainment and Hemingway's Cigar Bar with jazz piano on the weekends. 2 restaurants, 2 bars (with entertainment). In-room data ports, some refrigerators. Cable TV. Pool. Laundry facilities. Business services. | 699 5th Ave. S | 941/403–8777 | fax 941/403–8778 | 76 rooms, 11 suites | $199–$209, $249–$349 suites | AE, D, MC, V.

La Playa Beach Resort. Directly on the beach, this resort has the Gulf on the west and the bay on the East, and was renovated extensively in the late 1990s, including the addition of a 14-story tower to go with the three-story original building. The colorful lobby is furnished in Spanish style and wicker furniture. The spacious rooms have crown moulding, marble bathrooms, and private balconies or patios. Suites are in the newer building.

Restaurant, bar. In-room data ports, minibars, microwaves, refrigerators. Cable TV. 2 Pools. Massage. Gym. Beach, dock, water sports, bicycles. Laundry service. Business services, free parking. | 9891 Gulf Shore Dr. | 941/597–3123 or 800/237–6883 (reservations) | fax 941/597–6278 | www.noblehousehotels.com | 191 rooms | $250–$365 | AE, D, MC, V.

Lemon Tree Inn. Built in 1948 as a one-story motel, this inn has been totally redone, and now offers more upscale accommodations with a Key West theme: fan-backed chairs and patios adjacent to every room. The surrounding grounds have lemon trees, as well as a pleasant gazebo in which to relax. Complimentary Continental breakfast. Some kitchenettes, microwaves, refrigerators. Cable TV. Pool. | 250 9th St. S | 941/262–1414 or 888/800–LEMO | fax 941/262–2638 | www.lemontreeinn.com | 35 rooms | $125–$145 | AE, D, MC, V.

The Naples Beach Hotel and Golf Club. A sports director and social director are on the premises at this resort hotel on the Gulf. The 125-acre complex has been run for more than 50 years by the Watkins family. The six buildings overlook either the Gulf or the golf course, and there is an Olympic-size free-form pool. 2 restaurants, bar (with entertainment), picnic area. In-room data ports, minibars, some microwaves, some refrigerators. Cable TV. Pool. Barber shop, spa, massage. Driving range. 18-hole golf course, putting green, 6 tennis courts. Beach, water sports, boating, bicycles. Children's programs (ages 5–12). Laundry service. Business services. | 851 Gulf Shore Blvd. N | 941/261–2222 or 800/237–7600 (reservations) | fax 941/261–7380 | www.naplesbeachhotel.com | 318 rooms | $115–$275 | AE, D, MC, V.

Park Shore Resort. Off the beaten path in a quiet residential neighborhood, this four-story, all-suites resort that opened in 1982 and was renovated in 1994 is 1 mi from the beach and 2 mi from the Caribbean Garden. All accommodations have large balconies that overlook the private lake and tropical island. The suites all have full kitchens, dining and living rooms, two baths, and one or two bedrooms. Restaurant, bar, room service, picnic area. In-room data ports, minibars, microwaves, refrigerators. Cable TV. Pool, pond. Hot tub. 4 tennis courts. Basketball, racquetball, volleyball. Laundry facilities. Business services. | 600 Neapolitan Way | 941/263–2222 or 800/548–2077 (reservations) | fax 941/263–0946 | www.sun-stream.com | 156 suites | $145–$220 | AE, D, MC, V.

The Registry Resort, Naples. This high-rise on 21 lush tropical acres is one of Naple's posh-est resorts. A two-story fountain stands in the atrium lobby, and swimming pools are free-form, with waterfalls. In the resort's backyard is a nature preserve. You can walk along the elevated boardwalk above the mangrove estuary to get to the beach or take a tram. Golf (arranged at area courses) and tennis are especially good at this resort. All the suites have Gulf views. 5 restaurants, bar (with entertainment), room service. In-room data ports, minibars, microwaves, refrigerators. Cable TV, in-room VCRs (and movies). 3 Pools. Hot tub. Barbershop, beauty salon, massage. Putting green. 15 tennis courts. Health club. Beach, water sports, boating, bicycles. Shops. Children's programs (ages 5–12). Laundry service. Business services. | 475 Seagate Dr. | 941/597–3232 or 800/247–9810 (reservations) | fax 941/597–3147 | www.registryhotels.com | 474 suites | $305–$395 | AE, D, MC, V.

Ritz-Carlton, Naples. You can find equally fabulous hotel rooms elsewhere, but this 14-story hotel is in a class by itself for the extensive network of lavishly appointed public rooms, including a dozen meeting rooms of varying sizes and an estimable collection of 19th-century European oil paintings. The gardens, fountains, courtyards, and arches evoke the Mediterranean. Rooms have marble baths. All rooms have balconies with a Gulf view. Afternoon tea served in the lounge. You have access to a nearby 27-hole golf course. 7 restaurants, bar (with entertainment), room service. In-room data ports, minibars, refrigerators. Cable TV, in-room VCRs. Pool. Hot tub. Barbershop, beauty salon, massage. 6 tennis courts. Gym. Beach, water sports, bicycles. Children's programs (ages 3–12). Laundry service. Business services, airport shuttle. | 280 Vanderbilt Beach Rd. | 941/598–3300 or 800/241–3333 (reservations) | fax 941/598–6690 | www.ritzcarlton.com | 431 rooms, 32 suites | $425–$525, $725–$1,775 suites | AE, D, MC, V.

Trianon Old Naples. This three-story pink stucco structure stands in a residential area, minutes away from restaurants and shopping. The lobby's high ceilings and working fireplace are nicely complemented by the antique appointments and chandeliers. Rooms are spacious with separate sitting areas and large baths. Bar, complimentary Continental breakfast. In-room data ports, some refrigerators. Cable TV. Laundry service. Business services. | 955 7th Ave. S | 941/435–9600 or 877/482–5228 | fax 941/261–0025 | www.trianon.com | 55 rooms, 3 suites | $140–$210 room, $250–$275 suite | AE, D, DC, MC, V.

NEW PORT RICHEY

MAP 3, H6

(Nearby towns also listed: Clearwater, Dunedin, Tarpon Springs)

This town of about 10,000 residents is just off the Gulf of Mexico, about 30 miles northwest of Tampa. The waterways around West Pasco, 5 mi to the north, are ideal for boating and fishing. The area was once a retreat for silent film stars.

Information: **West Pasco Chamber of Commerce** | 5443 Main St., New Port Richey, 34652 | 727/842–7651 | www.westpasco.com.

Attractions
Sims Park. Right on the Pithlachascoree River in downtown New Port Richey, this park with its bandstand and playground is perfect for family picnics. | 727/849–3733.

ON THE CALENDAR
MAR.: *Chasco Fiesta.* Florida's longest-running festival, first held in 1922, attracts more than 210,000 spectators during its 10-day run. Parades, a carnival, crafts, food, a pow-wow, and entertainment celebrate Native American tribes and traditions. | 727/817–1911 or 877/424–2726.
DEC.: *Downtown New Port Richey Festival Parade.* Five days of carnival celebrate the holiday season with Santa's workshops, craft booths, and carnival rides. | 727/849–3733.

Dining
Budapest Restaurant. Hungarian. The area's only authentic Hungarian food has been served here since 1976. Traditional favorites like goulash are mixed with other more American fare such as fish and steak courses. | 7411 U.S. 19N | 727/848–4437 | No lunch | $5–$11 | No credit cards.

Leverocks. Seafood. Moderately priced, casual dining on the Gulf. This large restaurant seats almost 500, on two levels with four dining rooms upstairs and a patio downstairs. There are multiple daily fresh catch choices, and usually swordfish and amberjack. If you like salmon, try it onion-crusted. Early dinner specials available. Kids' menu. | 4927 U.S. 19 | 727/849–8000 | $7–$22 | AE, D, DC, MC, V.

Lodging
Clarion Hotel and Conference Center. You can easily walk to shopping and restaurants from this two-story, exterior corridor hotel, while the beach is 3 mi to the east. Restaurant, bar, room service. In-room data ports, refrigerators. Cable TV. Pool, wading pool. Hot tub. Laundry service. Business services. | 5316 U.S. 19N | 727/847–9005 or 800/252–7466 | fax 727/844–3360 | 151 rooms | $69–$165 | AE, D, DC, MC, V.

Comfort Inn-Gateway. This two-story hotel in downtown New Port Richey is convenient to dining and shopping and 2 mi from the beach. Renovated in 1999, it has some rooms with kitchenettes. Complimentary Continental breakfast. In-room data ports, some microwaves, some refrigerators. Cable TV. Pool. Hot tub, sauna. Gym. Laundry facilities, laundry service. Business services. | 6826 U.S 19N | 727/842–6800 | fax 727/842–5072 | www.comfortinn.com | 66 rooms | $66–$98 | AE, D, MC, V.

NEW SMYRNA BEACH

MAP 3, K4

(Nearby towns also listed: Daytona Beach, DeLand, Ormond Beach, Sanford)

This getaway spot on the Atlantic coast, 15 miles south of Daytona Beach, is named for the area in Turkey where the wife of the town's founding father, Dr. Andrew Turnbull, was born. The beaches, long and dune-covered, are unspoiled and serene; you can surf, sun, or swim on what locals call the world's safest bathing beach, which is protected by the off-shore rocks that calm the tides and waves. There are plenty of shops along the beach, and the town is full of wide brick sidewalks punctuated by stately palm trees. Canal Street is also a popular shopping and dining street. The town is known for its international artists workshop, the Atlantic Center for the Arts.

Information: New Smyrna Beach Chamber Tourism | 115 Canal St., New Smyrna Beach, 32168 | 800/541–9621 or 904/428–2449 | www.newsmyrnabeachonline.com.

Attractions

Atlantic Center for the Arts. Gallery exhibits, which change every two months, feature the works of internationally known artists. Media includes sculpture, mixed media, video, drawings, prints, and paintings. Intensive three-week workshops are periodically run by visual, literary, and performing master artists such as Edward Albee, James Dickey, and Beverly Pepper. | 1414 Art Center Ave. | 904/427–6975 | www.atlantic-centerarts.org | Free | Weekdays 9–5, Sat. 10–2.

Arts on Douglas. This warehouse has been converted to a high-ceilinged art gallery that features a new exhibit each month. Many types of media are present and the gallery represents more than 50 local artists. Gallery talks are held periodically and openings are held the first Saturday of every month from 4–7 PM. Shows range from solo to group exhibitions and there are always interesting metal sculptures and colorful modern paintings around. | 123 Douglas St. | 904/428–1133 | Free | Tues.–Fri. 11–6 PM, Sat. 10–2.

★ **Canaveral National Seashore.** The park, established in 1975 to protect the largest stretch of undeveloped coastline on the east coast of Florida, is part of a barrier island with 24 mi of beach and wetlands encompassing more than 57,600 acres. It's a sanctuary for more than 1,000 species of plants, and 300 species of birds (including 14 that are threatened or endangered), as well as alligators, turtles, and manatees. At the north and south ends of the seashore you can swim, go boating, surf-fish, and try a hiking trail that leads to the top of a Native American shell midden at Turtle Mound. Remote Playalinda beach has pristine sands and is the site where hundreds of giant sea turtles come ashore from May through August to lay their eggs. I–95 exit 80 to Route 406, east across the Indian River, and Route 402 east for 12 mi. | 7611 S. Atlantic Ave. New Smyrna Beach | 321/428–3384 or 321/267–1110 | fax 321/264–2906 | www.nbbd.com/godo/cns/index.html | $5 per vehicle; $1 walk-ins and bicyclists | Apr.–Oct., daily 6–8; Nov.–Mar., daily 6–6. Sometimes closed for shuttle launches.

New Smyrna Speedway. Housed on the site of a former armadillo breeding ground, this high-banked ½-mi asphalt track draws stock car racing drivers and enthusiasts from around the country. | 3939 W. State Rd. 44 | 904/427–4129 | $10; $20 during Speed Week (early Feb.) | Races Sat. (nightly during Speed Week, in early Feb.).

New Smyrna Sugar Mill Ruins State Historic Site. This sugar mill was built in 1830 and then destroyed in 1835 during the Seminole War. It is constructed of coquina, a native rock consisting of shells and sand. You can walk through and see a "walking beam" from the steam engine that powered the mill and several cooking pots used to boil the sugar juice into sugar. The grounds are covered with a Live Oak canopy and there are hiking trails and picnic tables. | Mission Rd., just off State Rd. 44 | 904/428–2449 | Free | Daily 8–5.

ON THE CALENDAR

MAR.: *Images, A Festival of the Arts.* A judged and juried show at Riverside Park draws more than 250 artists. | 904/423–4733.

MAY: *Civil War Reenactment.* The Civil War comes alive at Old Fort Park on Riverside Drive. Held on a weekend in May, which changes annually, the reenactment includes children's events and programs on Friday, battles and camp reenactments on Saturday and Sunday. | 904/428–2449.

Dining

Chase's on the Beach. Seafood. The eatery's capacious deck allows you to stroll in from the beach and enjoy a hamburger or salad with a "loaded lemonade," before returning to the sand. Shoes are required only indoors. The dinner menu includes a lot of seafood—cashew-encrusted mahimahi, or fried shrimp. Reggae and calypso music is performed on weekends. | 3401 S. Atlantic Ave. | 904/423–8787 | $10–$20 | AE, D, MC, V.

New Smyrna Steakhouse. Steak. This busy restaurant draws both visitors and locals, who come for superb steaks and ribs. The room is dark and intimate. Try the 12-oz New York strip or sirloin, the 20-oz porterhouse, or a rack of tender ribs. | 723 Third Ave. | 904/424–9696 | $9–$15 | AE, MC, V.

Norwood's Seafood. Seafood. On the Causeway on the way to the beach, this nautical-theme establishment is family friendly. There is a very large seafood menu with a number of beef items as well. Seafood, pasta, and Black angus beef are covered. Early dinners. Kids' menu. | 400 E. 2nd Ave. | 904/428–4621 | $7–$23 | AE, D, DC, MC, V.

Patio Restaurant. Continental. This small Victorian-style house, about 100 years old, is on a main street, with large wrought-iron gated patio with jasmine and dangling vines and a Victorian fountain. The linen-covered, candle-lit tables are set up inside or on the patio. The favorites are the Lobster Chateaubriand for two, lobster served with filet mignon on a large platter, as well as lobster *fra diavolo,* shrimp and scallop fettucine, and *coq au vin* (a chicken breast with bacon, sweet onions, sliced mushrooms and wine). | 626 N. Dixie Fwy | 904/423–8355 | Closed Sun. | $8–$17 | AE, D, DC, MC, V.

Riverview Charlie's. Contemporary. Elegant and not touristy, this three-level restaurant draws both locals and out-of-towners from Orlando. The five dining rooms have exposed brick walls, and the covered patio is along the river's edge, where you can watch dolphins. The fresh-seafood-only menu includes eight or nine catches each day. Two favorites are peppercorn pan-seared tuna and lobster. If you don't feel like seafood, try the Black angus western beef. At tableside, the staff prepares Caesar salad, steak Diane, citrus coffee flambé, bananas Foster, crêpes Suzette, and cherries jubilee. A guitarist plays Sunday through Thursday, and a live jazz trio performs Friday and Saturday. | 101 Flagler Ave. | 904/428–1865 | $15–$20 | AE, D, DC, MC, V.

Toni and Joe's. American/Casual. Directly off the beach, you can stroll into this casual spot straight from the sand; shoes are definitely not required. Pizzas, hot dogs, hamburgers are served, but the specialty is the hoagies: long rolls filled with steak, sweet peppers, onions, and cheese. | 309 Buenos Aires St. | 904/427–6850 | $7–$10 | No credit cards.

Victor's Backstreet Cuisine. Contemporary. Small, neatly arranged wooden tables fill this small restaurant. The blackboard menu lists such innovative dishes as tuna seasoned with herbs and served in berry sauce and sirloin flavored with pepper salsa. You sit only feet from the open kitchen where Victor himself prepares your meal. | 103 S. Pine St. | 904/426–5000 | No lunch Sat.–Mon., no dinner Mon. | $7–$25 | No credit cards.

Vincenzo's. Italian. At this eatery, run by two, Vince prepares and cooks your meals, while Annie seats you. The large menu has something for everyone, but the specialties are the pizzas and pastas, the area's best. Try the angel-hair pasta with garlic, oil, and broccoli. | 410 Flagler Ave. | 904/423–4230 | No lunch. Closed Sun.–Mon. | $7–$16 | MC, V.

Lodging

Chadham by the Sea. This oceanfront hotel has two- and three-bedrooms units. The two five-story buildings are on the Atlantic Ocean and are divided by the pool and sundeck. Each unit has a full kitchen, laundry facilities, and balcony or patio. Microwaves, refrigerators. Cable TV, in-room VCRs. Pool. Tennis court. Laundry facilities. | 6713 Turtle Mound Rd. | 904/428–0513 | fax 904/428–8515 | 45 apartments | $200–$225 (3–day minimum stay) | MC, V.

Coastal Waters Inn. Units at this three-story oceanfront apartment hotel range from small apartments to multi-room suites. All have fully equipped kitchens and balconies or patios. Picnic area. Refrigerators. Cable TV. Pool, wading pool. Business services. | 3509 S. Atlantic Ave. | 904/428–3800 or 800/321–7882 (reservations) | fax 904/423–5002 | www.volusia.com | 40 rooms | $69–$149 | MC, V.

Coquina Warf B&B. This 1903 Dutch Colonial overlooking the Intercoastal Waterway is decorated with a combination of antiques and tasteful contemporary furnishings. Lace curtains and plates ornament the guest rooms, while the living room has a fireplace and pine floors. You can lounge on the two porches. Complimentary breakfast. Cable TV. Dock. Pets allowed. | 704 S. Riverside Dr. | 904/428–9458 | fax 904/409–9077 | www.coquinawarf.com | 3 rooms, 1 cottage | $75–$200 | No credit cards.

Holiday Inn Hotel and Suites. An oceanview motor inn offers airy studios and one- and two-bedroom units. All have balconies overlooking the ocean, fully-equipped kitchens, and living areas. The restaurant also overlooks the beach and ocean. Restaurant. In-room data ports, refrigerators. Cable TV. Pool. Beach. Laundry facilities, laundry services. Business services. | 1401 S. Atlantic Ave. | 904/426–0020 or 800/232–2414 | fax 904/423–3977 | www.holiday-inn.com | 102 rooms | $85–$225 | AE, D, DC, MC, V.

Islander Beach Resort. One tower of this seven-story beachside resort was renovated in the late 1990s. All suites offer a full kitchen, 90 of them have views. Choose from studio suites that sleep up to four, and one- or two-bedroom suites that accommodate up to six. You can play beach volleyball. Restaurant, bar, picnic area. Kitchenettes, microwaves. Cable TV. Pool, wading pool. Hot tub. Gym, volleyball. Beach. Video games. Children's programs (ages 5–12), playground. Laundry facilities. Business services. | 1601 S. Atlantic Ave. | 904/427–3452 or 800/831–1719 | fax 904/426–5606 | www.islanderbeachresort.com | 114 suites | $55–$150 (3–day minimum stay) | AE, D, MC, V.

Little River Inn B&B. This charming three-story B&B built in 1883 is on nearly two acres overlooking the Indian River Lagoon. The grounds feature gardens, a fountain, waterfall, reflecting pool, and a small citrus grove. Some of the oak trees are 300 years old. The home is painted white with some ironwork, with a courtyard in the works to enhance the New Orleans style. From the rocking chairs on the veranda, you can see the gardens; from the second-floor balcony, you can see the lagoon and nature preserve. The Garden Room is full of garden plants, and the Lighthouse Room has a nautical theme with a brass bed and rough-hewn wood paneling. The Parisian Room is often booked for anniversaries and romantic getaways. The Victorian Room features a four-poster bed and red wall covering. The Heritage room has a colonial theme, with an oak headboard and quilts. This inn is close to downtown antique shops and is 1½ mi from the beach. Complimentary breakfast. Some in-room hot tubs. Cable TV, TV in common area. Hot tub. Tennis. Bicycles. Library. | 532 N. Riverside Dr. | 904/424–0100 or 888/424–0102 | www.little-river-inn.com | fax 904/424–9350 | 6 rooms | $94–$159 | AE, D, DC, MC, V.

Night Swan Intracoastal B&B. This B&B on the Indian River about 1 mi from the Atlantic beaches is in a residential part of New Smyrna. There is a nice city park with a children's playground about two blocks south, and a church behind the property. The house has a wraparound porch, rocking chairs, and a porch swing. All rooms have private baths; some rooms overlook the Intracoastal Waterway. Some rooms have a sitting area. You can get breakfast in bed if you want. Complimentary breakfast. Refrigerators. Cable TV, in-room VCRs. Pool. Business services. | 512 S. Riverside Dr. | 904/423–4940 | fax 904/427–2814 | www.nightswan.com | 16 rooms | $85–$160 | AE, DC, MC, V.

Ocean Air. This small motel with a wooded front yard is 3 mi northwest of New Smyrna's beach and 12 mi from Daytona Speedway. Picnic areas. Refrigerators. Cable TV. Pool. | 1161 N. Dixie Freeway | 904/428–5748 | www.ocean-airmotel.com | 14 rooms | $40–$105 | AE, D, DC, MC, V.

Ocean Club North. Located directly on the beach, the three-story condo structure has 44 condos; all include two baths, two bedrooms, full kitchens, and dishwashers. Some units include balconies or patios with views of the ocean. Kitchenettes, microwaves, refrigerators. Cable TV. Pool, wading pool. Tennis courts. | 4821 Saxon Dr. | 904/428–2861 or 800/528–4790 | fax 904/428–2861 | oceanclubnorth@ucnsb.net | www.volusia.com/oceanclubnorth | 44 apartments | $150 (3–night stay minimum on weekends) | No credit cards.

Ocean Trillium Suites. Directly on the beach, this seven-story hotel has 30 suites all facing the Atlantic, each with its own private balcony, separate bedrooms, and full kitchens. Kitchenettes, microwaves, refrigerators. Cable TV. Pool. Beach. | 3405 S Atlantic Ave. | 800/321–7882 | fax 904/427–4301 | www.volusia.com/horizonresorts/trillum | 30 suites | $89 | D, MC, V.

Oceania Beach Club. All the suites in this ocean-front property have good views. Complimentary Continental breakfast. Kitchenettes. Cable TV. Pool. Gym. Beach. Business services. | 421 S. Atlantic Ave. | 904/423–8400 or 800/874–1931 | fax 904/423–0254 | 60 suites | $165 | AE, D, MC, V.

Riverview Hotel. This elegant refurbished inn, built in 1885, is on the Intracoastal Waterway. The exterior is red with white trim and rests on stilts. It's just a four-block walk to the beach, or you can borrow the hotel's bicycles. Explore the gift shops, boutiques and cafés just down the street on Flagler Avenue. Restaurant (Riverview Charlie's), complimentary Continental breakfast. Cable TV. Pool. Dock, bicycles. | 103 Flagler Ave. | 904/428–5858 or 800/945–7416 (reservations) | fax 904/423–8927 | www.volusia.com/riverview | 18 rooms | $80–$150 | AE, D, DC, MC, V.

Somerset B&B. The details are just right at this three-story 1916 home: fresh flowers in your room; wine at sunset; and homemade chocolates left in your room at night. French doors open onto the two spacious porches, which overlook the Intercoastal Waterway. Pine floors and wood details give the rooms extra charm. Complimentary Continental breakfast (weekdays), breakfast (weekends). Some in-room hot tubs. Cable TV, no room phones. Massage. Dock, bicycles. No kids under 6. No smoking. | 502 S Riverside Dr. | 904/423–3839 or 888/700–1440 | fax 904/423–2286 | www.somersetbb.com | 4 rooms, 1 carriage house | $124–$159 | D, MC, V.

CAR RENTAL TIPS

- ☐ Review auto insurance policy to find out what it covers when you're away from home.
- ☐ Know the local traffic laws.
- ☐ Jot down make, model, color, and license plate number of rental car and carry the information with you.
- ☐ Locate gas tank—make sure gas cap is on and can be opened.

- ☐ Check trunk for spare and jack.
- ☐ Test the ignition—make sure you know how to remove the key.
- ☐ Test the horn, headlights, blinkers, and windshield wipers.

*Excerpted from *Fodor's: How to Pack: Experts Share Their Secrets*
© 1997, by Fodor's Travel Publications

NICEVILLE

(Nearby towns also listed: Crestview, De Funiak Springs, Destin, Fort Walton Beach)

Niceville lives up to its name. It's close to Destin and Fort Walton Beach, and 12 miles north of the Gulf of Mexico. Both Niceville and its twin city, Valparaiso, were first settled at the beginning of the 20th century and were granted their charters in 1938 and 1921, respectively. Today, their combined populations are over 36,000. The surrounding forests provided a rich source for the logging industry, as well as the turpentine stills that flourished in the early 1900s. The other major industry was fishing, in the inland waterways around Choctawhatchee Bay. Now the largest employer is Eglin Air Force Base.

Information: Niceville-Valparaiso Bay Area Chamber of Commerce | 170 N. John Sims Pkwy., Valparaiso, 32580 | 850/678–2323 | www.niceville.net.

Attractions

Fred Gannon Rocky Bayou State Recreational Area. This 357-acre park, 5 mi east of Niceville, is relatively undiscovered, so you'll find some peace and quiet not far from civilization. You can hike, picnic, boat, and camp (sites available on a first-come first-served basis). Mountain bikers are welcome to try some of the difficult trails. | 4281 Hwy. 20 | 850/833–9144 | www.dep.state.fl.us | $2 per vehicle; camping $8–$10 per night | Daily 8–sunset.

Turkey Creek Walk. Travel this 5-mi boardwalk over the creek and through 20 acres of countryside to view wildlife and indigenous landscapes. | John Sims Parkway | 850/678–2323.

ON THE CALENDAR
OCT.: *Boggy Bayou Mullet Festival.* Held for three days on the third weekend in October, this event at the corner of College Boulevard and Highway 85N draws more than 100,000 people for the arts and crafts vendors, the food vendors, and the big-name entertainment. | 850/678–2323.

Dining

Brown Stones Grill. Contemporary. Numerous sandwiches, salads, and soups fill the lunch menu at this restaurant, ornamented with Warren Kimbele and Norman Rockwell prints. For dinner the restaurant serves a wide array of chicken, steak, seafood, and pasta dishes with innovative flair—sautéed shrimp and scallops over fettucine with vodka cream sauce and the pork tenderloin with apple juice over garlic mashed potatoes. | 540 E. John Sims Pkwy. | 850/729–0880 | $12–$16 | D, MC, V.

Lodging

Bluewater Bay Resort. On Choctawhatchee Bay, on Niceville's eastern side, this resort has hiking and biking trails that cut across the property. You can also play tennis and golf and swim. Only 10 minutes from the beach, the resort has a 120-slip marina. Restaurant, bar. Some kitchenettes, microwaves, refrigerators. Cable TV. 4 pools. 4 9-hole golf courses, 19 tennis courts. Dock, bicycles. Baby-sitting, playground. Laundry facilities. | 1950 Bluewater Blvd. | 850/897–3613 or 800/874–2128 | fax 850/897–2424 | www.bwbresort.com | 85 rooms | $75–$123 | AE, D, DC, MC, V.

OCALA

(Nearby towns also listed: Gainesville, Leesburg, Micanopy)

Horse farms spread across the rolling landscape and bluegrass fields of Ocala (pop 47,000), Florida's thoroughbred training center. The first farm was established in 1935, and horses are the major economic base of the county. Kentucky Derby winners have been raised in training centers here, and some of the farms are open to the public.

Offered free land after the Seminole Wars in 1842, white settlers flocked to the area, founding Ocala in 1846. The town lies at the western edge of the Ocala National Forest, a 366,000-acre wilderness with lakes, springs, and rivers. Nearby Silver Springs was the state's first tourist attraction.

Information: Ocala/Marion County Chamber of Commerce | 110 E. Silver Springs Blvd. (Hwy. 40), Ocala, 34470 | 352/629–8051 | www.ocalacc.com.

Attractions

Appleton Museum of Art. This collection of 6,000 pre-Columbian, Asian, African, and 19th-century objets d'art lives up to the surroundings—a three-building marble-and-granite cultural complex with a serene esplanade and reflecting pool. | 4333 E. Silver Springs Blvd. (Hwy. 40) | 352/236–7100 | fax 352/236–7137 | www.fsu.edu | $6 | 10–6.

Don Garlits Museum of Drag Racing. Legendary drag racer "Big Daddy" Don Garlits opened this museum to the auto sport in 1976. One building contains a classic car collection, featuring over 70 vintage cars dating from 1904; another building has a museum with exhibitions detailing the history of the sport, and the Drag Racing Hall of Fame. | 13700 S.W. 16th Ave. | 352/245–8661 | fax 352/245–6895 | www.garlits.com | $12 | Daily 9–5.

Marion County Museum of History. Displays in this McPherson Government Complex museum depict early life in the county with artifacts including Native American clothing and a 1,500-year-old canoe. | 307 S.E. 26th Terr | 352/629–2773 | Fri.–Sat. 10–2, or by appointment.

Ocala Jai-Alai. One of just seven jai alai courts in the country, Ocala has a roster of top players who compete here in the summer. Jai alai is the world's fastest sport. Betting is legal and an integral part of the jai alai experience. There are year-round simulcasts of Miami Jai-Alai, and other pari-mutuels. | Rte. 318, Orange Lake | 352/591–2345 | www.fla-gaming.com/ocala | $1 | Live jai alai June–Aug.: Mon., Thurs., Sun. 11:30–5; Wed., Fri.–Sat. 11:30–5 and 6:30 PM–midnight; simulcasting: daily 11:30–5 and Mon., Wed.–Sat. 6:30 PM–midnight.

Ocala National Forest. This delightful, 366,000-acre preserve is the home of Florida's largest stand of sand pine trees. There are three major recreational areas: Alexander Springs, which has a swimming lake and campground; Salt Springs, where Atlantic blue crabs spawn each summer; and Juniper Springs, the site of a picturesque stone water-wheel-house, a campground, and a natural-spring swimming pool. Also in the forest are hiking trails and a 22-mi bicycle trail, 30 campsites, and many lakes with fishing and boating opportunities. Alexander Springs is accessed off Route 40 via Route 445S, Salt Springs from Route 40 via Route 19N, and Juniper Springs from Route 40. | 10863 E. Rte. 40, Silver Springs | 352/625–2520 | www.r8web.com/florida/forests | Free | Daily.

Ocala Stud. This horse farm 2 mi west of Ocala off Route 200 has been selling horses since 1958, and is one of the most successful breeders in the area. By far the best time to visit is between 7:30 and 10 AM, when the horses are bathed and trained. | S.W. 27th Ave. | 352/237–2171 | fax 352/873–3223 | www.ocalastud.com | Free | Mon.–Sat. 7–10:30 AM, 2–3:30.

Silver Springs. Established as a tourist attraction in 1860 by steamboat captain James Burt, Silver Springs boasts the world's largest collection of (99.8% pure) artesian springs. Local entrepreneur Hullam Jones built the first glass-bottomed boat here in 1878, creating the state's first tourist attraction. Visitors would—and still do—take the boat ride to observe hundreds of fish and other marine life beneath the water's crystalline surface. Tourists weren't the only ones to take notice—Hollywood filmmakers shot the first six *Tarzan* films starring Johnny Weismuller here in the 1930s and '40s, as well as *The Creature from the Black Lagoon* in 1954. Today, the springs are the focal point of a 35-acre park with wild animals (including the endangered Florida panther) and a jungle cruise. Silver Springs is

3 mi east of Ocala, next door to Wild Waters aqua park. | 5656 E. Silver Springs Blvd. (Hwy. 40) | 352/236–2121 | www.silversprings.com | $16.95 | Daily 9–5:30.

Wild Waters. Have fun in the sun while you catch your thrills on the silver bullet, a 220-ft racing flume slide, or the thunderbolt, a 132-ft enclosed free-fall slide. If you're not up for anything that dramatic, try the 180-ft fan-shape wave pool or the sundecks with shady spots to relax in. | 5666 E. Silver Springs Blvd. | 352/236–2121 | $21.95 | Open daily April–Oct.

ON THE CALENDAR
AUG.: *Ocalifest.* Arts and crafts displays, live music, exotic animal demonstrations, and Native American dancers entertain at Tuscawilla Park. | 352/401–3900.

Dining
Arthur's. Contemporary. This restaurant inside the Ocala Silver Springs Hilton has three dining rooms with candlelight settings and dimmed lighting. One dining room has small, private corner booths; another a canopied back porch looking out over the pool and gardens. Steaks are the speciality, but there are also pork chops, lamb, chicken, salmon, and grouper, all served with a Cajun or Creole twist. The Sunday brunch is a must. | 3600 S.W. 36th Ave. | 352/854–1400 | No lunch | $14–$27 | AE, D, DC, MC, V.

Bella Luna Cafe. Italian. Offering an extensive wine list and an attractive seating area in a piazza with a fountain, Bella Luna does Italian specialties including pizza cooked in a wood-fired oven. The *Spiedino Pescatore* has scallops, mussels, clams, and shrimp in a white wine and plum tomato sauce served over arborio rice. There is brunch Sundays. | 3425 S.W. College Rd. | 352/237–9155 | No lunch weekends | Reservations essential | $9–$20 | AE, D, DC, MC, V.

Carmichael's. American. Floral tablecloths and fresh flowers and plants adorn the dining room and bar at this Italian-influenced restaurant. The restaurant is best known for its prime rib and daily chef's specials. | 3105 N.E. Silver Springs Blvd. (Hwy. 40) | 352/622–3636 | Breakfast also available | $7–$17 | AE, D, DC, MC, V.

Harry's Seafood. Cajun. This small, lively spot is filled with Mardi Gras spirit, with beads and masks on the wall and festive music in the background. The menu covers steak, chicken, pasta, and seafood, and features Southern classics such as red beans and rice with sausage, jambalaya, fried shrimp, and catfish. The front porch overlooks Ocala's main square. | 24 S.E. 1st Ave. | 352/840–0900 | www.hookedonharrys.com | $7–$18 | AE, MC, V.

Petite Jardin. Eclectic. In this cozy, romantic fine-dining restaurant, potted plants hang from the ceilings. Chef/owner John Bell specializes in cuisine from around the world, and the menu changes weekly. Still, you can usually count on wild game or fresh duck to appear on the menu. | 2209 E. Silver Springs Blvd. (Hwy. 40) | 352/351–4140 | Closed Sun.–Tues. | $20–$30 | AE, MC, V.

Lodging
Courtyard by Marriott. This three-story motel, just off I–75 at exit 68, is a 15–20 min drive to downtown. Some rooms have balconies. Restaurant, bar. In-room data ports, some microwaves, some refrigerators. Cable TV. Pool. Hot tub, exercise room. Laundry facilities. Business services. | 3712 SW 38th Ave. | 352/237–8000 | fax 352/237–0580 | www.marriott.com | 175 rooms, 8 suites | $89 | AE, D, DC, MC, V.

Days Inn. This two-story motel is ½ mi from Silver Springs. The lobby and rooms are simple and unassuming. Microwaves, refrigerators. Cable TV, in-room VCRs (and movies). Pool. Playground. Laundry facilities. Pets allowed. | 5001 E. Silver Springs Blvd. (Hwy. 40) | 352/236–2891 | fax 352/236–3546 | 56 rooms | $45–$75 | AE, D, MC, V.

Hampton Inn Ocala. This three-story motel is built around a courtyard planted with orange trees. The motel is two blocks from Paddock Mall, and 7 mi west of downtown Ocala. Complimentary breakfast. In-room data ports, some microwaves, some refrigerators. Cable

TV. Pool. Exercise equipment. Laundry facilities. Business services. | 3434 SW College Rd. | 352/854–3200 or 800/426–7866 | fax 352/854–5633 | www.hamptoninn.com | 147 rooms, 5 suites | $80 | AE, D, DC, MC, V.

Heritage Country Inn. Surrounded on all sides by horse pastures, this one-story country home was built and designed by the two proprietors, Harold and Lao, and their personal touches are noticeable throughout. The furniture, doors, and canopy beds are all hand-crafted; the large rooms (500 square ft) are sound-proof, with private entrances and individual whirlpools. The inn is 12 mi west of I–75 at exit 69. Complimentary breakfast. In-room hot tubs. No room phones. No smoking. | 14343 W. Hwy. 40 | 352/489–0023 or 888/240–2233 | www.heritagecountryinn.com | 147 rooms, 5 suites | $79–$104 | AE, D, MC, V.

Holiday Inn Express. Across the street from the Munroe Regional Medical Center, 4 mi west of I–75, is this simple three-story chain motel. The Ocala business district and Paddock Mall are 5 min away. Complimentary Continental breakfast. In-room data ports, some refrigerators, some microwaves, some in-room hot tubs. Cable TV. Pool. Laundry service. Business services. | 1212 S. Pine Ave. | 352/629–7300 | fax 352/629–3331 | www.holiday-inn.com | 47 rooms, 8 suites | $65–$75 | AE, D, DC, MC, V.

Holiday Inn Silver Springs. Directly across the highway from the entrance to Silver Springs, this single-story property has drive-up rooms and polyester curtains. The motel has a 24-hr restaurant. Restaurant, bar. In-room data ports, microwaves, refrigerators. Cable TV, in-room VCRs. Pool. Business services. Pets allowed. | 5751 E. Silver Springs Blvd. (Hwy. 40) | 352/236–2575 or 800/465–4329 | fax 352/236–2575 | www.holiday-inn.com | 104 rooms | $65–$90 | AE, D, DC, MC, V.

Ocala Silver Springs Hilton. A tree-lined road leads to this nine-story pink hotel in a forested area near the intersection of Highway 200 and I–75, a few minutes from downtown. The marble-floor lobby, with a piano bar, greets you before you reach the guest rooms, decorated in contemporary colors and prints. Restaurant, bar, room service. Some mini-bars, some refrigerators, some in-room hot tubs. Cable TV. Pool. Hot tub. Putting green, 2 tennis courts. Volleyball. Laundry service. Business services. Pets allowed. | 3600 S.W. 36th Ave. | 352/854–1400 | fax 352/854–4010 | 197 rooms | $89–$129 | AE, D, DC, MC, V.

★ **Seven Sisters Inn.** A picture-perfect 1888 Queen Anne mansion has been converted into this charming B&B with seven individually decorated rooms. One of the rooms is a converted loft, another, a Honeymoon Suite, features a spectacular four-poster bed draped in yards and yards of peach fabric. Rates include a gourmet breakfast and afternoon tea. Complimentary breakfast. Some in-room hot tubs. TV in common area. Bicycles. Laundry facilities. Business services. No kids under 13. | 820 S.E. Fort King St. | 352/867–1170 | fax 352/867–5266 | www.7sistersinn.com | 5 rooms, 2 suites | $115–$185 | AE, D, MC, V.

OKEECHOBEE

MAP 3, K7

(Nearby towns also listed: Fort Pierce, Lake Placid, Sebring)

Okeechobee, which meant "big water" to Seminole Indians, is named after the lake to its south, the second largest freshwater lake in the continental United States—only Lake Michigan is larger. The 733-square-mi lake is home to a fascinating variety of birds and other animals. The town is an outdoors center of 5,000 people centered on fishing, camping, air boat rides, and some rodeo.

Information: Okeechobee Chamber of Commerce | 55 S. Parrott Ave., Okeechobee, 34974 | 863/763–6464 or 800/871–4403.

Attractions

Kissimmee Prairie State Preserve. This grasslands sanctuary is home to much wildlife, including many fowl. | 33104 N.W. 192nd Ave. | 863/462–5360.

Lake Okeechobee. The second-largest freshwater lake in the United States extends over 730 square mi, and has perhaps the best bass fishing in North America. Curiously, most of the lake remains hidden from sight along the length of its circumference. It's girded by nearly 120 mi of roads, a 30-ft-high grassy levee (known locally as "the wall"), and the Lake Okeechobee Scenic Trail, a rough track that is part of the Florida National Scenic Trail. The lake's northern shore is 3 mi south of town.

ON THE CALENDAR
MAR.: *Speckled Perch Festival.* Arts and crafts are sold at this three-day event held in March and September in Flagler Park. | 863/763–6464.
SEPT.: *Labor Day Festival.* This weekend-long celebration includes arts and crafts vendors at Flagler Park, a downtown parade, and a rodeo at the Okeechobee Cattleman's Rodeo Arena. Rodeo events include steer wrestling, calf roping, bare-back riding, and bull fighting. | 863/763–6464 or 800/871–4403.

Dining

Lightsey's. Seafood. This restaurant overlooks the Kissimmee River at the Okee-Tantie Recreation Area. You can dine on an outdoor patio with river views or in the lodge-like interior. Seafood entrées come steamed, grilled, fried, and broiled. The restaurant is known for catfish, frog's legs, gator, and the freshwater turtle known as cooter. | 10430 Rte. 78W | 863/763–4277 | $12–$21 | MC, V.

Lodging

Budget Inn. Rooms are basic and economic at this single-story building surrounded by trees and shrubs. There are restaurants within walking distance. Complimentary Continental breakfast. Microwaves, refrigerators. Cable TV. Pool. Business services. Pets allowed (fee). | 201 S. Parrott Ave. | 863/763–3185 | fax 863/763–3185 | 23 rooms | $49–$89 | AE, D, DC, MC, V.

Holiday Inn Express. This two-story chain motel is ¼ mi north of Lake Okeechobee and within walking distance of shops and restaurants. Complimentary Continental breakfast. In-room data ports, microwaves, refrigerators. Cable TV, some in-room hot tubs. Outdoor pool. Laundry facilities. Business services. Pets allowed (fee). | 3975 U.S. 441S | 863/357–3529 | fax 863/357–3529 | www.holiday-inn.com | 43 rooms | $125–$150 | AE, D, DC, MC, V.

Pier II Resort. On the rim canal next to Lake Okeechobee's levee, this two-story motel has clean, well-maintained rooms. There is a five-story observation tower for views of the lake, as well as a 600-ft pier and a lakeside lounge—a place to play pool, watch TV, or chat with locals. Bar. Refrigerators. Cable TV. Outdoor pool. Fishing. | 2200 S.E. U.S. 441 | 863/763–8003 or 800/874–3744 | fax 863/763–2245 | 89 rooms | $59 | AE, D, DC, MC, V.

ORLANDO

MAP 3, J5

(Nearby towns also listed: Altamonte Springs, Clermont, Kissimmee, Lake Buena Vista, Maitland, Walt Disney World, Winter Park)

When most people think of Orlando, they think of theme parks—specifically Walt Disney World, SeaWorld, and Universal Orlando. But this fast-growing city of 165,000 is interesting in its own right, with its Spanish-moss draped parks, lovely gardens, sophisticated museums, wealth of cultural opportunities, and charming neighborhoods such as Winter Park, where tasteful houses rise along small lakes and waterways, and Span-

ORLANDO

INTRO
ATTRACTIONS
DINING
LODGING

ish moss festoons the trees. Suburban sprawl is endemic, however—and with it immense malls. In the visitor areas, there's outlet shopping to beat the band.

Downtown Orlando has its own entertainment center in Church Street Station, which was created in the 1970s by ex-Navy pilot Bob Snow, who transformed run-down buildings downtown into a complex of old-fashioned saloons, dance halls, dining rooms, and shopping arcades. Though not nearly as successful now as it was when Snow was at the helm, it played an important role in sprucing up the somewhat shabby downtown area in Orlando.

Because Walt Disney World visitors who arrive by air touch down at the huge, modern Orlando airport, the celebrated vacation kingdom is forever associated with Orlando. But Walt Disney World isn't in Orlando; actually, it is closer to the town of Kissimmee to the west. (See separate town listing for Walt Disney World.) Shady, four-lane, side-walk-edged International Drive in Orlando is the site of the huge Orlando Convention Center and most tourist hotels, and parts are as much as half an hour's drive from the Disney exits off I–4, the main north–south thoroughfare between Orlando and Walt Disney World. That half hour can as much as double when there's traffic—as there often is nowadays, given the swelling population of both visitors and residents.

Information: Orlando/Orange County Convention and Visitors Bureau | 6700 Forum Dr., Ste. 100, Orlando, 32821-8017 | 407/363–5800 or 407/363–5872 | www.go2orlando.com.

ORLANDO NEIGHBORHOODS

The city of Orlando is largely overshadowed by the area's numerous theme parks, even though most are actually located outside the city proper. The city, with a population

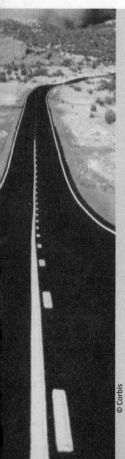

© Corbis

FLORIDA SPRING TRAINING: PLAY BALL!

In recent years, baseball has endured a shaky transition from its status as the national pastime to becoming somewhat of a mechanism for potential corporate sponsorship. For the devout who seek the simplicity and grace of the baseball of yesteryear, however, there is an alternative: every March, Central and South Florida play host to 20 major-league spring training camps, where the ambience brings baseball back to its roots. The games on the field don't have any effect on the regular season standings, but the stars still come to play. Here's a sampling of some of the better venues.

Atlanta Braves. Aside from being a sparkling new stadium (complete with towering archways and ballroom-style common areas), the sloping lawns that run alongside the first and third baselines are perfect for stretching out a blanket and watching the game. | Disney Baseball Stadium, 710 S. Victory Way, Kissimmee | 407/939–1500 | $10.50–$15.50.

Cleveland Indians. The upgraded seats notwithstanding, the feel this stadium evokes is of baseball's humble past, and provides a good deal for fans who want to watch the game in a bucolic Florida town. | Chain of Lakes Park, Cypress Gardens Blvd., Winter Haven | 941/293–3900 | $5–$13.

Detroit Tigers. The Detroit Tigers have been training in the Sunshine State each spring since 1934, and now call Joker Marchant Stadium their home. Named after the city's parks director, this slow-paced stadium is in a laid-back southern city conducive to the spring training vibe. | Joker Marchant Stadium, 2125 North Lake Ave., Lakeland | 941/688–7911 | $5–$10.

Kansas City Royals. Since there are only 6,000 seats in their quaint springtime home, you'll have a great view of the American League's Royals—even in February when guests are admitted free to watch the players limber up and practice for the following month's games. | Baseball City Stadium, 300 Stadium Way, Davenport. (15 minutes west of Walt Disney World) | 941/424–2500 | $6–$10.

of more than 1.5 million, is spread out, encompassing a hub of international business in its downtown area and a collection of lakes and parks. The rest of Orlando is made up of 111 residential neighborhoods, spread out over 101 square mi, though visitors to the Orlando area will never see most of these neighborhoods.

Downtown Orlando. Almost evenly spaced east and west of I–4 and radiating out a mile from the intersection of Toll Road 408 is the subtly progressive downtown area. City planners have recently installed several bike trails as well as bike lanes on the streets to help combat constant traffic woes, and several city parks are within easy reach, including Lake Eola with its trails and swan-shaped paddle boats. This area of the city thrives with commerce, the Orlando Arena (where the Magic play), and the nightlife center, Church Street Station.

International Drive. To the southwest of downtown is "I–Drive," anchored to the south by SeaWorld with Universal Orlando to the north. The road is lined with shops, restaurants, and hotels, and is sometimes called by locals the "beach without the ocean." The Orange County Convention Center sits along the central area of International Drive, which runs north–south.

Lake Buena Vista. Southwest of International Drive is the separate city of Lake Buena Vista, where most of the Disney family lives. Interstate 4 cuts through its southeast corner, with several Walt Disney World exits. The area is heavily built up with hotels and restaurants, which survive from the overflow of tourism.

Winter Park. Originally named by a group of neighbors from New Haven, Connecticut, who flocked south in the winter in the early 1900s to create this little bit of New England in the South, Winter Park is filled with quaint upscale stores, old estates, canal-linked lakes, tree-lined streets, and even Park Avenue. There are several museums here, and each spring there's a prominent arts festival. More than merely a neighborhood now, Winter Park has grown into its own city and encompasses the Princeton to Fairbanks exits east off of I–4. It's about 16 mi north of downtown Orlando.

Elsewhere Around Orlando. South of downtown Orlando and 10 mi southeast of Walt Disney World Resort is the more subdued city of Kissimmee, with its own parks, gardens, hotels and museums, a pleasant respite from the pumped-in theme music and pumped-up prices of the resort area. Walt Disney World dominates the landscape throughout most of the region from breakfast buffets and fun rides, to late night clubs and entertainment. Just north of the tree-canopied streets of Winter Park is the small town of Maitland, which offers fishing and hiking in its 34 lakes; Maitland is just off of I–4 between Lee Road to the south and Maitland Boulevard to the north, from State Road 434 to the west to State Road 436 to the east.

DRIVING AND PARKING

Traffic seems to be the general complaint anywhere you go in Orlando, in an area bustling with commerce and heavy with tourists year-round. Interstate 4 cuts through the region diagonally from southwest to northeast. Orange Street, running north to south, is the main thoroughfare through downtown, while Colonial Drive (State Rd. 50) is the main street from east to west. Most streets in the downtown grid run one way, and some are preserved brick roads. Several, including Magnolia Street, have clearly marked bus lanes, though they are very tempting to escape the traffic. Right turns are allowed on red as well as left turns onto one-way streets.

Traffic on the highways and major roads is at its worst from 6:30–9 AM and 4–6:30 PM. During these hours I–4 has a carpool lane for two or more people in a vehicle. If you are heading east to west, you can hop on Toll Road 408, which costs 75¢, but this can help you avoid some of the worst east–west traffic dilemmas. Driving to Disney from central Orlando can take up to an hour.

The popular International Drive is packed with as many tourists as restaurants and hotels, so it's best avoided if you don't want to feel like you are stuck in the "cruising" lane (meaning the slow lane used for cruising the sights).

Parking is becoming less of a problem with a few new parking garages in downtown Orlando over the past few years. You can expect to pay $1 an hour, up to $8 for the day. Although most hotels have plenty of spots, when major conventions are in town, parking can be a problem. There are coin-operated parking meters in operation weekdays from 9–6; a parking ticket averages $15.

TRANSPORTATION

Airports: Orlando International Airport (407/825–2001) is widely known, locally, as OIA. It's southeast of downtown, about 10 mi northeast of International Drive; about 20 mi from I–4 exit 26B, the nearest I–4 exit that accesses Walt Disney World; and about 24 mi from the center of the lodging area in Kissimmee. It is served by over 20 major airlines, not to mention 30 charter airlines; there are even direct flights from the UK.

Airport Transportation: Taxis are available at the airport and cost about $15–$25 per trip, depending on where you're going.

If your party includes one or two, a less expensive option than a taxi or renting a car may be **Mears Transportation Group** (407/699–9999), which meets you at the gate, helps you with your luggage, and drives you to your destination either in a van, town car, or limo. The cost is around $13 per person one way, depending on your destination. It is possible to use public buses operated by **Lynx** (407/423–5566) to travel from the airport if you're staying downtown. The cost is low at 75¢. However, you'll need a car if you are going anyplace else.

Rail Lines: Amtrak offers daily service to a station at Sligh Boulevard in Winter Park as well as Kissimmee, which is closer to Walt Disney World. | 1400 Sligh Blvd. | 407/425–9411 or 800/872–7245.

Bus: Greyhound operates daily service from destinations across the country. | 555 N. John Young Pkwy. | 407/292–3440 or 800/231–2222.

Attractions

PARKS, NATURAL AREAS, AND OUTDOOR ACTIVITIES

Harry P. Leu Gardens. The 50 peaceful acres showcase Florida as it used to be. Meandering paths, shaded by ancient oaks, lead to forests of camellias and giant camphors, a 50-foot floral clock, and the largest formal rose garden in the state. You can tour the 19th-century Leu House Museum, the restored family home that began life as a farmhouse and is now filled with furnishings and crafts. At the Garden House, take a quiet break to enjoy the view of Lake Rowena. Take I–4 exit 43 (Princeton Street), go east to Mills and turn right. Turn left on Virginia Drive. | 1920 N. Forest Ave. | 407/246–2620 | fax 407/246–2849 | $4 | Garden Nov.–Mar., daily 9–5; Apr.–Oct., daily 9–8; guided house tours daily on the hour and half-hour 10–3:30.

Lake Eola Park. Swan-shaped paddle boats decorate this eponymous lake that constitutes Orlando's premier park. Established in 1892 and revived as a family park since the 1970s, there is a playground as well as the Walt Disney Amphitheater—the site of the annual Shakespeare Festival in April and May, as well as many weekend concerts. | Rosalind and Robinson Sts. | 407/246–2827 | Park free; boats $7 per half-hour | Daily 7 AM–midnight; boats daily 11 AM–10 PM (to 6 PM in winter).

Lake Fairview Park. There is boating and sailing on 50-acre Fairview Lake in this 64-acre park. Playgrounds and picnic areas are also here. | Lee Rd. | 407/246–2649 | Free | Daily dawn to dusk.

Loch Haven Park. This large, grassy park in central Orlando is the home of several of Orlando's hallmark arts and science institutions, including the Orlando Museum of Art, the Orange County Historical Museum, the Edyth Busch Theater, the Orlando Science Center, and the Mennello Museum of American Folk Art. Shady paths with benches link the buildings. | Mills Ave. and Princeton St. | 407/246–2287 | Park free, museum admissions vary.

Turkey Lake Park. This 300-acre park has picnic tables, a 3-mi bicycle trail, 7 mi of hiking trails, two beaches (but no swimming lake), a swimming pool, a 200-ft wooden fishing pier, canoe rentals, a petting zoo, and a playground. All just a few minutes from Universal Studios. | 3401 Hiawassee Rd. | 407/299–5594 | $2 per vehicle | Daily.

MUSEUMS

Mennello Museum of American Folk Art. Florida's only museum devoted to folk art features the nation's most extensive permanent collection of Earl Cunningham paintings, Paul Marco sculptures, Virgil Norberg flat steel sculptures, and Gary Yost carvings of Uncle Sam. The Museum Shop features folk art books, toys, and unusual gifts. | 900 E. Princeton St. | 407/246–4278 | $2 | Tues.–Sat. 10–5, Sun. noon–5.

Orange County Historical Museum. This museum in Lake Eola Park offers a fascinating look back at the people and events that have shaped central Florida. Exhibit areas document how Native Americans lived when Florida was wilderness and how the citrus industry has affected the area around Orlando, among other things; Orlando's oldest fire station is also here. | 812 E. Rollins St. | 407/897–6350 | fax 407/897–6409 | $4 | Mon.–Sat. 9–5, Sun. noon–5.

Orlando Museum of Art. The American collection contains more than 688 works from the 19th century to the present; the Art of the Ancient Americas collection contains over 500 artifacts of pottery, jade, stone, cloth, gold, and silver from over 30 different cultural groups; and the African collection contains more than 70 ceremonial and utilitarian artifacts consisting of wood figures, masks, metal work, intricate beadwork, and carved ivory. | 2416 N. Mills Ave. | 407/896–4231 | fax 407/896–9920 | $4 | Tues.–Fri. 9–5, Sat. 9–5, Sun. noon–5.

Orlando Science Center. In this major Orlando attraction, four floors with 10 exhibition halls house hundreds of imaginative interactive exhibits ranging from a journey through the human body to an exploration of the solar system to electricity. Also here is the Dr. Phillips CineDome, the world's largest Iwerks Digistar planetarium, which presents large-format films and planetarium shows on an eight-story domed screen. OSC's Crosby Observatory houses Florida's largest publicly accessible refractor telescope. | 777 E. Princeton St. | 407/514–2000 | fax 407/514–2277 | $8; $12–$14 with movies | Mon.–Thur. 9–5, Fri.–Sat. 9–9, Sun. noon–5.

Ripley's Believe It or Not! Museum. A 10-square-ft section of the Berlin Wall, a pain and torture chamber, a Rolls Royce made entirely of matchsticks, and a 26- by 20-ft portrait of Van Gogh made from 3,000 postcards are among the 200-odd oddities this museum has on display. | 8201 International Dr. | 407/363–4418 or 800/998–4418 | $12.95 | Daily 9–midnight.

SHOPPING

Antiques Row. Orlando's small but thriving antiques row just north of downtown on North Orange Avenue will please antiques hunters. | Free.

Belz Factory Outlet World. This universe of shopping consists of over 180 outlet stores in two malls and four nearby annexes, plus a third set of shops, Belz Designers Outlet. This is a good place to find discount name-brand clothing. The complex includes such stores as Maidenform, Danskin, Calvin Klein, Van Heusen, Gap, OshKosh, Foot Locker, and Nike. | 504 W. Oak Ridge Rd. | 407/354–0126 or 407/352–9611 | www.belz.com | Free | Mon.–Sat. 10–9, Sun. 10–6.

Church Street Station. This three-story shopping mall in downtown Orlando has turn-of-the-20th-century Victorian elegance. A few of the 50-plus shops may be familiar, but most are boutiques. An International Food Court on the second level offers a less expensive alternative to the eateries to be found elsewhere in Church Street Station. Take I–4 exit 38. | 29 W. Church St. | 407/422–2434 | Free | Daily 11 AM–11 PM.

Florida Mall. When it first opened, this was the largest mall in Central Florida; when they tacked on an additional half-million square ft it became even larger. Now there's 1.6 million square ft of shopping action here: Burdines; Sears; JCPenney; Parisian; Dillard's; Saks Fifth Avenue; 250 specialty shops, kiosks, and carts; seven theaters; and a 17-restaurant food court as well as four sit-down restaurants including Ruby Tuesday, California Café, Paradise Bakery, and a Pebbles in Saks Fifth Avenue. The mall is 4½ mi east of I–4 and International Drive at the corner of Sand Lake Road and South Orange Blossom Trail. | 8001 S. Orange Blossom Trail | 407/851–6255 | www.simon.com | Mon.–Sat. 10–9:30, Sun. 11–6.

The Mercado. This "market" houses more than 60 specialty shops, such as American Cola Company, which offers Coca Cola and Anheuser-Busch memorabilia, and Earth Matters, a wildlife and environmental shop. There is also an international food court and seven restaurants. | 8445 International Dr. | 407/248–1166 | Daily 10–9.

Mount Dora. Founded by homesteaders in 1874, this quaint little town has 19th-century stores and houses tucked into rolling hills that overlook Lake Dora. Considered Florida's antique capital, this New England–style village is also known as Festival City for its art, antique, and craft shows that take place nearly every weekend in the fall, winter, and spring. Mount Dora is west of U.S. 441 on Old U.S. 441 or Route 44B. | 352/383–2165 | www.mount-dora.com.

Pointe*Orlando. This outdoor mall is the latest attempt to convert International Drive into Florida's version of Fifth Avenue. In addition to WonderWorks and the enormous Muvico Pointe 21 theater, the massive complex near the Peabody Orlando and the Orange County Convention Center is home to 70 specialty shops, including F. A. O. Schwartz, the famed toy store. | 9101 International Dr. | 407/248–2838 | www.pointeorlandofl.com | Free | Daily 10–11.

Renninger's Twin Markets. Antique lovers would do well to spend a weekend morning at this flea market, and an afternoon in Mount Dora. This is possibly Florida's largest conglomerate of antique and collectible dealers. At the top of the hill sit 400 flea market dealers; at the bottom, you'll find 200 more dealers selling antiques. Every third weekend of the month from March to October, however, the antiques market hosts the Antique Fair, attracting 500 dealers. | Hwy. 441 | 352/383–8393 | www.mount-dora.com | Free | Sat.–Sun. 9–5.

SPECTATOR SPORTS

Orlando Magic. The NBA's championship basketball team plays at the Orlando Arena. | 600 W. Amelia St. | 407/896–2442 | Oct.–Apr., call for game schedule.

Orlando Miracle. Orlando's WNBA team begins its summer basketball season in early June at the Orlando Arena. | 600 W. Amelia St. | 407/916–9622 | $8–$85 | June–Aug.

Orlando Predators. The Predators play arena football—a faster, indoor version of the sport—at the Orlando Arena. | 600 W. Amelia St. | 407/648–4444 or 407/872–7362 (season ticket information) | $5–$32 | May–Aug.

Orlando Rays. The Rays are the Tampa Bay Devil Ray's Class AA Southern League affiliate. They play 70 home games at Disney's Wide World of Sports Stadium April through August. | 700 W. Victory Way, Kissimee | 407/363–6600 | $5–$8 | Apr.–Aug.

Orlando-Seminole Jai Alai. This sport is the world's fastest game. The ticket prices are as superlatively cheap. Orlando's fronton is one of just seven jai alai courts in the country. You can bet on the players, or on horse simulcasts. The court at Fern Park is 20 min north of Orlando off I–4 at exit 48. | 6405 S. Hwys. 17/92, Fern Park | 407/331–9191 | $1–$2 | Games Thur., Sat. noon, 7:30; Fri. 7:30; Sun. 1; Mon. noon.

Orlando Solar Bears. Orlando's International Hockey League team began playing at the Orlando Arena in 1995. | 600 W. Amelia St. | 407/872–7825 | $6–$28 | Oct.–Apr.

THEME PARKS AND TOURIST ATTRACTIONS

Blazing Pianos. This large nightclub in the Mercado mall is usually crowded with a lot of out-of-town visitors singing at the top of their lungs to the childhood tunes being banged out by one of three piano players. Out of breath? On weekends, this may be the most active club in town. Sunday through Thursday the atmosphere is more PG than R. | 8445 International Dr. | 407/363–5104 | $5–$7 | Weekdays 7–12:30, weekends 7–1:30.

Church Street Station. This shopping, food and entertainment complex offers a turn-of-the-20th-century atmosphere for fun and music. There's amusement for the whole family in several clubs and restaurants, including live evening shows at Rosie O'Grady's Good Time Emporium, the Orchid Garden Ballroom, the Cheyenne Saloon and Opera House, Phineas Phogg's Balloon Works, Apple Annie's Courtyard, and Commander Ragtime's Midway of Fun, Food, and Games. Take the Anderson Street/Church Street exit 38 off I–4. | 129 W. Church St. | 407/422–2434 | www.churchstreetstation.com | $18 for pass to live show venues | Daily 11 AM–2 AM.

Guinness World Records Experience. Witness exhibits, film, and videos that reveal what it takes to be a record holder. In the Micro-Technology Playground, you can try your hand at setting your own Guinness World Record. Walk down the multimedia streetscape of Guinness Town and see the Big and Tall Shop, Rain Woman, Blasting Zone, and Lightning Man. | 8437 International Dr. | 407/248–8891 | $12.95 | Daily 10 AM–11 PM.

Mark Two. Orlando's first dinner theater stages complete Broadway shows and, during the winter season, musical revues chock-full of Broadway tunes. You eat a dinner buffet before the show, and dessert is brought out during intermission. | Edgewater Center, 3376 Edgewater Dr. | 407/843–6275 or 800/726–6275 | Reservations essential | Mon.–Tues. | $30–$43 | AE, D, MC, V.

Mystery Fun House. Explore the "Chambers of Surprises" 18-chamber maze, experience the ultimate laser-tag game Starbase Omega, or enjoy the video games areas and the 18-hole mini-golf course at this fun-plex just a few minutes from Universal Studios. Take I–4 exit 30B. | 5767 Major Blvd. | 407/351–3355 | $10.95 maze, $4.95 mini-golf, $9.95 laser-tag; $19.95 for all three | Daily 10–10.

Pirate's Cove Adventure Golf. At either of these two locations, you can immerse yourself in the miniature golf version of heaven. Each site offers an 18-hole course that winds around artificial mountains, meanders through caves, over waterfalls, and into lush foliage. For beginners, there is Captain Kidd's Adventure; pros can try their game on Blackbeard's Challenge. | 8501 International Dr. or Crossroads Center, I–4 exit 27 | 407/352–7378 (International Dr.) or 407/827–1242 (Crossroads) | $6.50–$11.50; all-day pass $15 | 9 AM–11:30 PM.

★ **SeaWorld Orlando.** SeaWorld, a 200-acre marine adventure park, manages to mix great fun with learning. Exhibit areas and trained-animal shows give you an intimate look at the animals who live near or in the sea, including whales, manatees, sea lions, penguins, dolphins, sharks, and more. Rides round out the mix, including Journey to Atlantis (a water ride and rollercoaster), Kraken (a new rollercoaster), and Wild Arctic (a helicopter flight simulator). Take I–4 exit 27A. | 7007 SeaWorld Dr. | 407/363–2200 | www.seaworld.org | $50.83 adults, $41.29 children | Daily 9–7; as late as 10 during peak periods.

Skull Kingdom. Across the street from Wet 'n Wild, this haunted house attraction on the International Drive tourist strip is housed in a huge castle with a skull-shaped entrance. Mechanical monsters and wild sound effects will keep you on your toes throughout the tour. You end in the Ghoulish Face Painting Gallery and the Haunted Toy Shop. | 5931 American Way, off International Dr. | 407/354–1564 | $12.50 | Daily 11 AM–midnight.

Sleuths Mystery Dinner Show. If Sherlock Holmes has always intrigued you, head here where your four-course meal is served up with a conspiracy. Each of the seven whodunit performances rotated throughout the year stops short of revealing the perpetrator. You get to question the characters and attempt to solve the mystery. | 7508 Universal Blvd. | 407/363–1985 or 800/393–1985 | www.sleuths.com | $38.95 | Mon.–Sat. at 6, 7:30, and 9, Sun. at 7:30 | AE, D, MC, V.

Titanic—Ship of Dreams, The Exhibition. This exhibition, which can be found in The Mercado shopping center, tells the story of the doomed ship and the passengers with actual artifacts pulled from the wreckage as well as props from the Hollywood movie set. | 8445 International Dr. | 407/248–1166 | $16.95 | Daily 10–9.

★ **Universal Orlando.** Within this complex on the north end of I-Drive, at I–4 exit 30B, you'll find a pair of outstanding theme parks, Universal Studios Florida and the newer Islands of Adventure, as well as the shopping, dining, and entertainment area CityWalk, and the Portofino Bay Hotel. Slightly off the property is the longtime favorite water park, Wet 'n Wild, which is now under the Universal umbrella. | 1000 Universal Studios Plaza | 407/363–8000 or 888/331–9108 | www.universalstudios.com | $46 for 1-day 1-park tickets; $84.75 for a 2-day pass.

Islands of Adventure. This park, opened in May 1999, is Universal Orlando's second theme park. And it truly gives Disney a run for its money, with its fanciful themes, wonderful detailing, magnificent special effects, and roster of enduring characters, including Marvel superheroes Spider Man and the Incredible Hulk; Dr. Seuss's the Cat in the Hat; classic cartoon characters such as Popeye, Dagwood, Betty Boop, and Rocky and Bullwinkle; and the Jurassic Park dinosaurs. One whole section is devoted to Dr. Seuss and is a favorite of younger kids. No other theme park world has anything as technically impressive as the *Amazing Adventures of Spider-Man*, a ride-through attraction that combines 3-D film with real fire and other special effects as well as the simulator technology originally used to train pilots. Two stunning roller coasters, the *Incredible Hulk Coaster* and *Dueling Dragons* (twin coasters that corkscrew gracefully within 12 inches of each other), are keeping thrill-seekers happy. | 1000 Universal Studios Plaza | 407/363–8000 or 888/331–9108 | Daily 9–7; as late as midnight during peak periods | www.universalstudios.com | $46 for 1-day, 1-park pass; $84.75 for a 2-day, 2-park pass.

Universal Studios CityWalk. This 30-acre entertainment, dining, and shopping complex is a part of the Universal Orlando complex. There are over a dozen clubs and restaurants to keep you occupied, plus a giant 20-screen movie theater. If you purchase a Party Pass, you pay no individual cover charges, and you can add movies onto that for $4 more. | Universal Blvd. at Hollywood Way | 407/363–800 (Universal main line) or 407/224–2684 or 407/224–2600 (CityWalk guest services) | www.universalstudios.com | CityWalk complex free; club cover charges vary; Party Pass $7.95, $11.95 including a movie pass; parking $7 (free after 6 PM) | CityWalk complex 11 AM–2 AM; individual club hours may vary.

Universal Studios Florida. The theme here is "Ride the Movies." You can experience action from *Jaws* (complete with a shark biting through an electrical cable and the ensuing pyrotechnics) and *Twister* (which involves a simulated tornado) among others. The Universal version of *Back to the Future* is one of its most popular attractions, drawing on pilot-training simulator technology; and *Terminator 2 3-D* mixes 3-D film and live action in another stunner. Meanwhile, *A Day in the Park with Barney* lets younger children sing along with their favorite purple dinosaur. And there's actually a working production studio on the premises. | 1000 Universal Studios Plaza | 407/363–8000 or 888/331–9108 | Daily 9–7; as late as midnight during peak periods | www.universalstudios.com | $46 for 1-day, 1-park pass; $84.75 for a 2-day, 2-park pass.

Wet 'n Wild. This 25-acre water park has some of the most popular water slides and rides in Orlando. On a hot day in Orlando, you can hop on the *Surge*, where five passengers take a tube ride through 600 ft of curves. Or try the Black Hole, a 500-ft ride through total darkness. Those looking for more relaxation can take it easy on the Lazy River. The park, off I–4 exit 30A, is convenient if you're staying on I-Drive. | 6200 International Dr. | 407/351–wild or 800/992–9453 | fax 407/363–1147 | www.wetnwild.com | $28.95 | Daily 10–5; as late as 11 PM during peak periods.

WonderWorks. There are 75 rightside-up interactive attractions. You can swim with the sharks, or experience a hurricane or an earthquake, or play in the largest laser tag arena in the world. | 9067 International Dr. | 407/352–8655 | $14.95 | Daily 9–midnight.

SIGHTSEEING TOURS/TOUR COMPANIES

Gray Line Bus Tours. Buses pick up passengers at most area hotels for trips to the Kennedy Space Center, Cocoa Beach, and Sterling Casino boats. | 4950 L. B. McLeod Rd. | 407/826–9999 | www.grayline.com | $30–$56 | Tours daily, call for schedule.

Scenic Boat Tour. An enduring and popular Orlando tradition is this boat tour in Winter Park, which leaves hourly from the dock at the end of Morse Boulevard. During the 1-hr tour you'll get to see homes of central Florida's rich and famous as the boat cruises by some of the area's most expensive homes. | 312 E. Morse Blvd., Winter Park | 407/644–4056 | $7 | Daily 10–4.

ON THE CALENDAR

JAN.: *Florida Citrus Bowl.* This nationally televised New Year's Day college football game pits the second ranked teams from the Southeastern Conference and the Big Ten Conference against each other. | 407/423–2476.
JAN., FEB.: *Zora Neale Hurston Festival of Arts and Humanities.* Theatrical performances, programs, and exhibits highlight the life and works of America's most celebrated collectors and interpreters of Southern rural African-American culture. In Eatonville. | 407/647–3307.
FEB., MAR.: *Central Florida Fair.* Central Florida's oldest and largest not-for-profit fair, held at the Orlando fairgrounds, showcases local diversity. | 407/295–3247 or 800/555–4361.
MAR.: *The Bay Hill Invitational.* This regular PGA Tour event takes place at the Arnold Palmer Bay Hill Golf and Country Club. | 407/876–2888.
JUNE: *Gay Weekend.* The first weekend in June has become known for attracting thousands of gay and lesbian travelers to Central Florida. An unofficial Gay Day is held at Walt Disney World, and other special events are organized throughout the city and attractions. | www.gayday.com.
OCT.: *Pioneer Days Folk Festival.* Rain or shine, the Pioneer Days is held annually on the grounds of the Pine Castle Folk Art Center, featuring craftspeople and musicians. | 407/855–7461.

Dining

INEXPENSIVE

Alfonso's Pizza & More. Italian. This neighborhood pizza parlor is about 60 yards from Edgewater High, so you might be competing with the football team for a table. The hand-tossed pizza is made with a variety of toppings, including pineapple and pepperoni. Calzones and pasta round out the menu. | 3231 Edgewater Dr. | 407/827–7324 | No lunch Sun. | $2–$12 | MC, V.

Amigo's. Mexican. There are those who say the best Tex-Mex food in central Florida is at Amigo's, a local chain of casual restaurants run by a family of transplanted Texans. They start with good basics, such as refried beans, that would play well in San Antonio. Go for the Santa Fe dinner, so big it almost takes a burro to bring it to your table; you'll be able to sample tamales, enchiladas, chiles rellenos, and those heavenly frijoles, and wash it all down with a Mexican beer. | 6036 S. Orange Blossom Trail | 407/857–3144 | $9–$16 | AE, MC, V.

Bahama Breeze. Caribbean. Lush palm trees and bright, island-style artwork keep things relaxed—a good thing, since your wait may be lengthy. You're issued a beeper on arrival and buzzed when your table is ready. Meanwhile, you can sip piña coladas and other West Indian delights on a big wooden porch. The food is worth the wait. Start with *tostones con pollo* (plantain chips topped with chicken and cheese), then consider either coconut curry chicken or paella. | 8849 International Dr. | 407/248–2499 | No lunch | $8–$16 | AE, D, DC, MC, V.

Beeline Diner. American. This slick, 1950s-style diner with red vinyl counter seats specializes in thick, juicy burgers with fries and milk shakes. It's in the Peabody Orlando, so it's not cheap, but the good griddle food is served up 24 hours. | 9801 International Dr. | 407/352–4000 | $8–$16 | AE, D, DC, MC, V.

Don Pablo's. Mexican. This restaurant in a big, barnlike building is known for its chicken enchiladas, made with slow-simmered chicken wrapped in corn tortillas, and beef fajitas with sides of frijoles, and rice and flour tortillas. | 4645 S. Semoran Blvd. | 407/208–0801 | Reservations not accepted | $8–$14 | AE, DC, MC, V.

Green Eggs and Ham Cafe. American. Dr. Seuss devotees will appreciate this eatery at the Seuss Landing section of Universal Studios Islands of Adventure—it resembles a slightly hallucinatory McDonald's. The most popular item here is the green egg and ham sandwich, but non-adventurous types can stick with a cheeseburger, fries, and "frings," a combo of fries and onion rings. | 6000 Universal Blvd. | 407/224–9255 | Reservations not accepted | $6–$8 | AE, D, MC, V.

La Piaza. Italian. This long-established restaurant is built around an enclosed piazza, with green carpet, wrought-iron railings, floral murals, and umbrellas. The pasta portion of the menu has 15 items covering the gamut of traditional and original combinations. Also try the mussels *fresca* (simmered in a buttery white wine-and-lemon sauce with mushrooms, black olives, basil, tomatoes, and artichoke hearts), or the combination platters, a choice of four, including shrimp alla Piaza, chicken scarpariello, and rollatini alla Piaza. | 4060 Town Center | 407/855–1170 | $8–$17 | AE, D, DC, MC, V.

Panera Bread. American. This informal eatery overlooking Lake Eola specializes in bread—everything from Asiago cheese bread to well-textured nine-grain loaf is made fresh daily, and used in a variety of sandwiches. Top picks include the Tuscan chicken on rosemary and onion focaccia, and roast beef and cheddar on an Asiago baguette. | 227 N. Eola Dr. | 407/481–1060 | Reservations not accepted | $4–$6 | AE, MC, V.

Straub's Fine Seafood. Seafood. The economically priced items at this unpretentious restaurant are broken down by their fat and calorie content on the menu. Owner Robert Straub fillets all his own fish and won't serve anything he can't get fresh. Specialties include a mesquite-grilled Atlantic salmon with béarnaise sauce and Cajun-style blackened dolphin. For dessert, there is a banana cream pie. | Straub's Boatyard, 743 Lee Rd. | 407/628–0067 | $7–$18 | AE, D, DC, MC, V.

Tiramisu Cafe. Italian. As the name implies, this small bistro on the edge of Lake Ivanhoe in the antiques and gallery district is a popular place to sit with an Italian pastry and a cappuccino. If you're in the mood for something a bit more substantial, the menu features focaccia pizzas, Italian soups, and grilled fish. | 399 Ivanhoe Blvd., at Orange Ave. | 407/228–0303 | $7–$17 | AE, MC, V.

Verona's. Italian. Northern Italian cuisine is the specialty at this restaurant. The dining room features a Broadway-style piano bar, where walls are plastered with photos of the owner with such celebrities as Frank Sinatra, Princess Diana, Liza Minnelli, and Shirley MacLaine. Try the *mussels fra diavolo* (a saucy presentation simmered in white wine, garlic, and crushed red peppers). Another good choice is "comboGamberoni," featuring chicken, jumbo shrimp, and artichokes sautéed with capers, garlic, and onions. | 2419 S. Hiawassee Rd. | 407/292–9228 | No lunch Sat. | $8–$16 | AE, D, DC, MC, V.

MODERATE

A Taste of Japan. Japanese. Although this is a small, brightly lit storefront in a shopping plaza, it manages to convey a quiet authenticity. The menu is only partially translated into English. Come prepared to explore outside-the-mainstream dishes—jelly fish, beef tongue, and octopus to name a few—as well as sushi and sashimi combos, teriyaki, and tempura. | 7637 Turkey Lake Rd. | 407/363–0360 | $12–$24 | AE, MC, V.

Bergamo's. Italian. This restaurant features fine cuisine and musical entertainment from talented singing waiters. When weather permits, enjoy seating outside on the patio. Try the tri-color farfalle with smoked salmon, fresh peas, and lemon cream; the whole yellowtail snapper with roasted potatoes, oven-dried tomatoes, and extra virgin olive oil; or the filet mignon wrapped in pancetta with fresh basil and porcini mushroom sauce. | 8445 International Dr. | 407/352–3805 | No lunch | $12–$20 | AE, D, DC, MC, V.

Bob Marley's. Caribbean. Jamaican patties and spicy jerk chicken on a stick are typical fare at this pulsating reggae club and restaurant at Universal Orlando's CityWalk. Bring ear plugs. | 6000 Universal Blvd. | 407/224–9255 | $9–$17 | AE, D, MC, V.

Cafe Tu Tu Tango. Contemporary. Multiple kitchens here bombard you with different courses, which arrive in waves if you follow the house custom and order a series of appetizers. Actually, you end up doing this anyway, since the entrées are appetizer-size. The menu gives the address—on International Drive—a new meaning. Try the Cajun chicken egg rolls, for instance, with blackened chicken, Greek goat cheese, Creole mustard, and tomato salsa if you want to get a compendium of world cuisines in one fell swoop. For added atmosphere, artists paint at easels while diners sip drinks like Matisse margaritas and Renoir rum runners. | 8625 International Dr. | 407/248–2222 | $13–$19 | AE, DC, MC, V.

Capriccio. Italian. Corporate executives and conventioneers, who make up much of the Peabody's clientele, like the relaxed atmosphere of this hotel restaurant. The marble-top tables are arranged so that everyone can view the open kitchen and the wood-burning pizza ovens, which turn out whole-wheat-flour pies ranging from pizza *margherita* (with sun-dried tomatoes and smoked mozzarella, fontina, provolone, and Parmesan cheeses) to pizza *blanca* (with mozzarella, goat cheese, and fresh thyme). If you're not in the mood for pizza, try one of the mesquite-grilled fish, beef, or chicken entrées, such as the *pollo gonzo* (chicken in a lemon sage sauce). | 9801 International Dr. | 407/352–4000 | Closed Mon. No lunch Tues.–Sat. | $13–$25 | AE, D, DC, MC, V.

Charley's Steak House. Steak. An ancient Seminole Indian cooking method—a red-hot wood-burning pit—distinguishes this steakhouse that is all about overindulgence. Everything is big here, from the perfectly cooked cuts of beef to the slices of Grand Marnier chocolate cake. Steaks are seared over a wood-burning pit at 1,100°, fired by three carefully chosen hardwoods. The result is a primordial thrill: charred outside, but succulent inside, 12-oz filet mignon. Also try the New York strip sirloin. | 6107 S. Orange Blossom Trail | 407/851–7130 | No lunch | $14–$20 | AE, MC, V.

Ciao Italia. Italian. This southern-Italian mom-and-pop restaurant serves dishes such as sweet New Zealand mussels with white garlic sauce and *pollo alla Tonino* (chicken breast with red and yellow peppers). For an appetizer, you might try Tony's special, with butterfly shrimp, a big mushroom stuffed with lobster, sauteed calamari and white beans with a white-wine sauce. | 6149 Westwood Blvd. | 407/354–0770 | fax 407/370–0124 | No lunch | $9–$19 | AE, D, DC, MC, V.

Confisco Grille. Contemporary. This eatery in the Port of Entry section at Universal Studios Islands of Adventure offers meals with the Dr. Seuss and Marvel comic characters from noon to 2. Entrées include pan-roasted pork chops, wood-grilled salmon steaks, and homemade macaroni and cheese with ham. For dessert, there is chocolate-banana bread pudding and crème brûlée. | 6000 Universal Blvd., Port of Entry section of Islands of Adventure | 407/224–9255 | $11–$17 | AE, D, MC, V.

Dan Marino's Town Tavern. American. This macho sports bar in the Pointe Orlando serves some beefed-up dishes, such as a 28-oz cowboy steak and hearty meat loaf. Culinary trends aren't ignored, either: There is a sesame-seared tuna and a wood-roasted, barbecued salmon. The giant-screen TV is always tuned to ESPN. | 9101 International Dr. | 407/352–4000 | $10–$25 | AE, MC, V.

Enchanted Oak Tavern. American. This restaurant is housed in a cavernous, fake oak tree at the Seuss Landing section at Universal Studios Islands of Adventure. You can get cafeteria-style meals such as chicken and spare ribs platters; most entrées are served with corn muffins. Universal's own brew, Dragon Scale Ale, is on tap here. | 6000 Universal Blvd. | 407/224–9255 | Reservations not accepted | $9–$17 | AE, D, MC, V.

ORLANDO

INTRO
ATTRACTIONS
DINING
LODGING

Forbidden City. Chinese. Hunan-style food is served at this restaurant in a reconstructed gas station. Start with the diced chicken with pine nuts in a package—icy lettuce cups wrapped around spicy chicken, which offers a delightful mix of cold and hot sensations. The sesame chicken—large chunks of sesame-coated chicken pieces sautéed in a sweet sauce—goes perfectly with bright-green broccoli in a subtle garlic sauce. The traditional 10-ingredient lo mein is full of fresh shrimp, chicken, beef, and pork. | 948 N. Mills Ave. | 407/894–5005 | $10–$21 | Closed Sun. No lunch Sat. | MC, V.

Gargi's Italian Restaurant. Italian. This mom-and-pop eatery across the street from a quiet Orlando lake specializes in old-fashioned spaghetti and meatballs, lasagna, and manicotti. Shrimp with marinara sauce and peppers over linguine are other popular dishes. | 1421 N. Orange Ave. | 407/894–7907 | Closed Sun. | $8–$16 | AE, MC, V.

Harvey's Bistro. Contemporary. Panelled walls and white tablecloths fill this club-like restaurant, which serves such dishes as oven-roasted saffron scallops, duck cassoulet with white and black beans, and a thin-crust pizza with carmelized onions, fresh spinach, and goat cheese. Red meat fans will appreciate the pot roast, pan-seared tenderloin, and porterhouse. | 390 N. Orlando Ave. | 407/246–6560 | $9–$19 | AE, D, DC, MC, V.

Hemisphere. Italian. You can watch planes take off and land from this elegant ninth-floor restaurant in the Hyatt Regency Orlando International Airport. The name doesn't give you a clue, but this airport restaurant specializes in northern Italian cuisine and does a good job of it. On the ninth floor, the restaurant overlooks a major runway, but it's far enough removed that you don't get any jet noise, just a nice air show. House specialties include sautéed shrimp and sea scallops on saffron risotto, rack of lamb with cannelloni and roasted potatoes, and an "everything-but-the-kitchen-sink" dish with shrimp, mussels, and scallops on linguine, with olives, capers, and tomatoes. | 9300 Airport Blvd. | 407/825–1234 | No dinner Sun. | $13–$22 | AE, D, DC, MC, V.

Jimmy Buffett's Margaritaville. American. A giant plastic replica of a seaplane hangs from the ceiling at this restaurant at Universal Orlando's CityWalk. The Ultimate Margarita and the cheeseburger will remind fans of "Wasting Away Again in Margaritaville," and "Cheeseburger in Paradise." The menu is extensive, with everything from fried fish and stone crab claws to quesadillas and steak. | Universal Studios Plaza | 407/224–9255 | $9–$18 | AE, D, MC, V.

Johnny Rivers Smokehouse and BBQ. Barbecue. Johnny Rivers spent years as the head chef at Disney before striking out on his own. The restaurant is known for smoked baby back ribs and the roasted tater quesadilla appetizer, which combines layers of smoked chicken, pork, and beef with slices of baked potato and jack cheese. | 5370 W. Colonial Dr. | 407/293–5803 | Closed Mon. | $9–$17 | AE, D, DC, MC, V.

La Fontanella da Nino. Italian. This lovely Neopolitan-style eatery was named after chef Nino's fountain in the quiet courtyard. It's known for dishes like *peperoni saltati* (roasted peppers sauteed with garlic, black olives and capers) and *vitello Marsala* (veal cutlet sauteed with mushrooms and wine). Service is slow, but it's worth the wait. | 900 E. Washington St. | 407/425–0033 | No lunch Sun. | $12–$17 | AE, MC, V.

Larry's Cedar River. Seafood. A few blocks from downtown, the fresh fish here comes both Southern-style and New England-style—grilled, broiled, sautéed, fried, or blackened. Try the Cedar River platter: captain's gulf shrimp, New Bedford scallops, select oysters, deviled crab, clam strips, and the freshest fish fillets; but you might also consider the 12-oz Delmonico steak or Alaskan split king crab legs. Take I–4 exit 29. | 7101 Orange Blossom Trail | 407/858–0525 | $9–$17 | AE, D, DC, MC, V.

★ **Le Coq Au Vin.** French. Although Louis Perrotte could run a stuffed-shirt kind of place—his food is as expertly prepared as any in town—he chooses to be self-effacing and to run a modest little kitchen in a small but charming house in south Orlando. Perrotte and his wife, Magdalena, who acts as hostess, make the place warm and homey, and it is usually filled with friendly Orlando residents, who appreciate the lovely traditional French fare: homemade chicken liver pâté, fresh rainbow trout with champagne sauce, and Long Island duck with green peppercorns. For dessert, try crème brûlée, and pat yourself on the back for discovering a place that few tourists know about. Ask to be seated in the main dining room— it's the center of action. Take I–4 exit 34. | 4800 S. Orange Ave. | 407/851–6980 | Reservations essential weekends | Closed Mon. No lunch weekends | $13–$26 | AE, D, MC, V.

Linda's La Cantina. Steak. This place takes beef very seriously, as you can tell by the disclaimer on the menu: "We cannot be responsible for steaks cooked medium-well and well done." Despite that stuffy-sounding caveat, this down-home eatery has been a favorite among locals since the Eisenhower administration. The menu is short and to the point, including about a dozen steaks and just enough ancillary items to fill up a page. Among the best is the La Cantina large T-bone—more beef than most can handle. With every entrée you get a heaping order of spaghetti or a baked potato. | 4721 E. Colonial Dr. | 407/894–4491 | $12–$25 | AE, D, MC, V.

Little Saigon. Vietnamese. As Orlando flourishes, so do its ethnic restaurants. The friendly folks here love to introduce novices to their healthy and delicious national cuisine. Sample the spring rolls or the summer rolls (spring-roll filling in a soft wrapper). Then move on to the grilled pork and egg, served atop rice and noodles, or the traditional soup, filled with noodles, rice, vegetables, and your choice of either chicken or seafood; ask to have extra meat in the soup if you're hungry, and be sure they bring you the mint and bean sprouts to sprinkle in. Beer and wine only. | 1106 E. Colonial Dr. | 407/423–8539 | $8–$18 | MC, V.

Ming Court. Chinese. Even though this place is on International Drive, a truly great wall designed to look like a dragon's back blocks out the hubbub and gives an enclosed courtyard-like serenity to this Chinese palace of a restaurant. A pool with carp greets you at the entrance, and the elegance continues inside, where you can look out through glass walls over a beautifully arranged series of floating gardens. The prices are probably a little higher than what you're used to paying at your local strip mall, but then the food is probably better, too. Ming Court is within walking distance of the Orange County Convention Center and can be quite busy at lunchtime. | 9188 International Dr. | 407/351–9988 | $11–$21 | AE, D, DC, MC, V.

Monty's Conch Harbor. Seafood. Whimsical, giant fiberglass sea creatures lurk above the dining area at this fish house at the Pointe Orlando. This is an offshoot of the classic Miami restaurant, known for dolphin with ginger glaze, swordfish with roasted-corn tomato salsa, she-crab soup, and, of course, conch chowder. The house specialty drink— called the Pain Killer—is priced on how much rum you can handle in your 16-oz glass. | 9101 International Dr. | 407/354–1122 | fax 407/354–1232 | $6–$18 | AE, MC, V.

Motown Café. Eclectic. This shrine to Motown music at Universal Orlando's CityWalk jumps by night to the sounds of the Jackson Five and Marvin Gaye. During the day, it's a quiet spot to try Smoky's ribs and fried chicken with Belgian waffles. | 6000 Universal Blvd. | 407/224–9255 | $8–$18 | AE, D, MC, V.

Mythos. Contemporary. This restaurant in Lost Continent at the Universal Studios Islands of Adventure looks like a giant rock formation from the outside, and a huge cave from the inside. Waiters wear names such as Plato and Adonis, but the cuisine is contemporary and eclectic. Try the blue corn–crusted mahimahi with sweet baby bell peppers and tomatillo salsa, the wood-roasted lobster with corn, or the wild mushroom risotto. For dessert, there's pumpkin cheesecake. | 6000 Universal Blvd. | 407/224–9255 | $10–$19 | AE, D, MC, V.

NASCAR Café Orlando. American/Casual. Race cars hang from the ceiling and NASCAR memorabilia crowds the walls at this loud restaurant at Universal Orlando's CityWalk. Dishes include the Thunder Road burger, with melted pimento cheese and sautéed onions, and chicken mushroom soup with grilled chicken and shiitake mushrooms. | 6000 Universal Blvd. | 407/224–9255 or 407/224–7223 (for reservations) | $9–$19 | AE, D, MC, V.

NBA City. American/Casual. The big-screen TV is always on at this basketball-obsessed restaurant at Universal Orlando's CityWalk. You can shoot computerized hoops, and look at

ORLANDO

INTRO
ATTRACTIONS
DINING
LODGING

court memorabilia, but the food is a winner as well. Try the house specialty, a BLT pizza; a 12-oz pork chop glazed with maple-mustard sauce; or a quesadilla stuffed with barbecued chicken, Monterey Jack cheese, and cilantro. | 6000 Universal Blvd. | 407/363–5919 or 407/363–5919 | $9–$20 | AE, D, MC, V.

★ **Numero Uno.** Cuban. To the followers of this long popular Latin restaurant, the name is quite appropriate. It bills itself as "the home of paella," and that's probably the best choice. If you have an hour and 15 minutes to wait and a good appetite, try the *paella Valenciana*, made with yellow rice, sausage, chicken, fish, and Spanish spices and served with a side order of plantains. If you don't have that long, go for traditional Cuban fare such as shredded flank steak or the dish that half of Latin America eats daily, *arroz con pollo*. Take I–4 exit 34. | 2499 S. Orange Ave. | 407/841–3840 | $12–$31 | AE, D, DC, MC, V.

Pastamore. Italian. The only theme at this Italian restaurant at Universal Orlando's City-Walk is good food and a creative menu. Huge sandwiches are filled with such ingredients as marinated chicken, peppers, and sun-dried tomatoes. It's also worth noting the wood-fire pizza, fresh pasta, and homemade gelato. Italian breakfast breads are also popular—the place opens at 8 AM. | 6000 Universal Blvd. | 407/224–9255 | $6–$19 | AE, D, MC, V.

Race Rock Restaurant. American. Racing memorabilia fills this loud restaurant, owned by 13 celebrity racing legends including Richard Petty, Mario Andretti, Jeff Gordon, and John Force. The menu includes burgers, sandwiches, and steaks. | 8986 International Dr. | 407/248–9876 | $7–$18 | AE, D, DC, MC, V.

Siam Orchid. Thai. One of Orlando's several elegant Asian restaurants, Siam Orchid occupies a gorgeous structure a bit off International Drive. Waitresses, who wear traditional Thai costumes, serve authentic fare such as Siam wings, a chicken wing stuffed to look like a drumstick, and *pla rad prik* (a whole, deep-fried fish covered with a sauce flavored with red chiles, bell peppers, and garlic). If you like your food spicy, say "Thai hot" and grab a fire extinguisher. | 7575 Universal Blvd. | 407/351–0821 | No lunch weekends | $11–$19 | AE, DC, MC, V.

Vito's Chop House. Steak. This classy restaurant seems to double as a wine cellar: literally hundreds of bottles are stacked in the dining room. If you don't mind shelling out $95 (at least) for two, try "Vito's Ultimate Surf n'Turf," a 50-oz porterhouse and 1½-lb lobster dinner. The T-bone, filet mignon, and rib eye, stone crabs, and wood-grilled pork chops di Vito (promised as 1½-inch thick) cost considerably less. | 6633 International Dr. | 407/354–2467 | No lunch | Reservations essential | $16–$95 | AE, D, DC, MC, V.

White Wolf Café. American. The centuries collide in this quaint restaurant hung with Tiffany lamps (all for sale) in Orlando's small but vibrant antiques and art gallery district. The fare is generally light and includes about a dozen salads. One solid choice is the Moroccan, made with chicken, almonds, raisins, and bananas tossed in honey curry mustard dressing on a bed of romaine. Sandwich mainstays include turkey clubs and BLTs as well as a strange but worthy pita sandwich called the Mighty Joe Mango, concocted with fresh fruit, vegetables, and mango salsa. Entrées change often but usually include a deep-dish lasagna; there's also an excellent lasagna variation baked into French bread instead of pasta. | 1829 N. Orange Ave. | 407/895–5590 | $16–$34 | AE, MC, V.

Wild Jack's Steaks and BBQ. American. A family place with a faux-rustic Western atmosphere serving chuck wagon grub. Entrees include smoked prime rib, filet mignon, and smokin' barbecue. | 7364 International Dr. | 407/352–4407 | Reservations not accepted | No lunch | $10–$19 | AE, D, DC, MC, V.

EXPENSIVE

Charlie's Lobster House. Seafood. Established in 1986, this is one of the area's premier seafood restaurants, with offerings from Florida's coast as well as the shores of the North Atlantic and Pacific. They also offer Angus steaks for the non-seafood lover, and six surf and turf combinations for those who want the best of both worlds. It's in the Mercado shopping center, with low lights and an elegant atmosphere. | 8445 International Dr. | 407/352–6929 | No lunch | $17–$27 | AE, D, DC, MC, V.

★ **Chatham's Place.** Contemporary. In Florida, grouper is about as ubiquitous as Coca-Cola, but to discover its full potential, try the grouper here, sautéed in pecan butter and flavored with cayenne. It's a strong contender for the best dish in Orlando today. A close second is another house specialty—pan-roasted rack of lamb flavored with rosemary. This place perennially appears on the "best" lists of virtually every Florida publication. The setting is a nondescript office building, so it's a good thing the food is worthy of a palace, and the service is as good as it gets in Central Florida. Take I–4 exit 29. | 7575 Dr. Phillips Blvd. | 407/345–2992 | No lunch | $18–$27 | AE, D, DC, MC, V.

Dux. Contemporary. Named for the Peabody's resident ducks that parade around the lobby, this restaurant's decor carries on the theme: ornate gold wallpaper backgrounds, mirrors, and framed duck watercolors line the walls. The menu changes with the seasons, but the food is consistently innovative and the service superb. Some recent entrées included Sonoma lamb chops glazed with Hunan barbecue sauce, and Florida black grouper marinated in West Indian spices with plantain-yam mash and tropical chutney. | 9801 International Dr. | 407/352–4000 | Closed Sun. in Aug. No lunch | $19–$45 | AE, D, DC, MC, V.

Everglades. American. This restaurant serves up thick, prime steak and ocean-fresh seafood. Or explore the incredible flavors of gator chowder, venison pepper steak, or other regional specialties. It's all impeccably presented with gracious service in a setting that captures the mysterious beauty of Florida's Everglades. A portion of all proceeds is donated to Florida's Save the Everglades Fund. | 9840 International Dr. | 407/996–9840 | No lunch | $18–$31 | AE, D, DC, MC, V.

Fishbones. Seafood. The fish and seafood selection includes 2-lb lobster tails, fresh Florida stone crabs (in season), hand-breaded colossal shrimp, swordfish, tuna, Dolphin (mahimahi), salmon, and red snapper, to name a few. Create your own fish of the day: oak-grilled, bronzed or blackened, topped with your choice of signature sauces and salsas. The unique menu also features aged steaks—USDA prime and choice, corn-fed beef, aged four to six weeks on the premises and hand-cut daily. | 6707 Sandlake Rd. | 407/352–0135 | No lunch | $15–$25 | AE, MC, V.

Haifeng. Chinese. Szechuan, Hunan, and Mandarin cuisines are the focus in this restaurant at the Renaissance Orlando Resort in an authentic oriental atmosphere. The specialty is Peking duck. | 6677 Sea Harbor Dr. | 407/351–5555 | Closed Mon. No lunch | $17–$27 | AE, D, DC, MC, V.

La Provence Bistro Francais. French. Besides the palm trees visible out the window, this charming two-story downtown restaurant might remind you of some out-of-the-way Parisian Left Bank bistro. Popular choices include the cassoulet *toulousain* (a hearty mixture of white beans, lamb, pork, and sausage) and the salade Niçoise (made with fresh grilled tuna, French string beans, and hard-boiled eggs). | 50 E. Pine St. | 407/843–1320 | Closed Sun. No lunch Sat. | $14–$28 | AE, DC, MC, V.

The Latin Quarter. Latin. The focus at this grottolike restaurant and club, at Universal Orlando's CityWalk, is on the music and cuisine of 21 Latin nations. Dishes such as *churrasco* (skirt steak), *puerco asada* (slow-roasted pork), and fried snapper with salsa are commonly found on a changing menu. For dessert, try the mango and guava cheesecakes. There is a wide selection of South American beers. | 6000 Universal Blvd. | 407/224–9255 | $11–$25 | AE, D, MC, V.

Pat O'Brien's Orlando. Cajun/Creole. This bayou-inspired watering hole and eatery is a replica of the famous New Orleans bar, complete with a brick-walled courtyard and outdoor tables. While known for such snacks as Cajun shrimp and crawfish nachos, you can chow on staple Louisiana French-bread sandwiches such as the po'boy, filled with tangy shrimp and sausage. There's live music at night. | 6000 Universal Blvd. | 407/224–9255 | $11–$24 | AE, D, MC, V.

Positano. Italian. If you're craving some New York–style pizza, look no farther. One side of this cheerful restaurant is a bustling pizza parlor; the other is a more formal dining room. The parlor side serves up some of central Florida's best New York–style pizza pies. Besides pizza, try the piquant *ziti aum* (mozzarella, Parmesan, eggplant, and basil in a tomato sauce). | Good Homes Plaza, 8995 W. Colonial Dr. | 407/291–0602 | $13–$29 | AE, D, DC, MC, V.

Ran-Getsu. Japanese. At this restaurant, you can sit at a curved, dragon tail–shaped sushi bar and order a matsu platter (nigiri- and maki-style sushi) or sit Japanese-style at low tables overlooking a carp pond and gardens. Specialties include kushiyaki (grilled skewers of shrimp, beef, chicken and scallops) and deep-fried alligator tail. | 8400 International Dr. | 407/345–0044 | No lunch | $14–$42 | AE, DC, MC, V.

Sam Snead's Tavern. American. The prototype for a golf-theme grill, this lively restaurant is a tribute to the venerable champion Sam Snead. The wood-paneled walls are chockablock with pictures and memorabilia of his illustrious career. The kitchen does well with an eclectic variety of foods ranging from hamburgers and grilled chicken to veal chops and fish. The Caesar salad is excellent, as are the barbecued spareribs. Chocolate sack sounds weird but isn't: it's pound cake, ice cream, strawberries, and whipped cream packed into what looks like a paper bag made of chocolate, but it's much too much for one person. This is one of the few restaurants in town open as late as 1 AM. Take I–4 exit 30. | 2461 S. Hiawassee Rd. | 407/295–9999 | $21–$29 | AE, D, DC, MC, V.

VERY EXPENSIVE

Atlantis. Seafood. Waiters bring entrées on silver-domed trays, and the dark-wood paneling, frescoes overhead, and plush green carpet underfoot in this dining room in the Renaissance Orlando Resort clearly imply that cut-offs belong back in your suitcase. Specialties include various lobster dishes and grilled fish such as yellowfin tuna and salmon. There are also worthy red meat dishes, including roast loin of lamb, and the obligatory surf-and-turf combo—a good sirloin served with scallops. Desserts include some fine soufflés, which must be ordered 30 min in advance. A harpist begins playing each evening at 7. | 6677 Sea Harbor Dr. | 407/351–5555 | Closed Sun. No lunch weekends | $26–$52 | AE, D, DC, MC, V.

The Butcher Shop. Steak. "Real beef" connoisseurs searching for a basic meat-and-potatoes outing need look no further. This chain restaurant not only promises "the biggest and best grain-fed beef direct from the Midwest," but invites patrons to grill their own selections over a brick hickory pit. No appetizers, no gourmet soups or salads, just the basics. Steaks range from an 8-oz filet mignon to a 28-oz T-bone. There are also rib eyes, top sirloins and Kansas City strips. Prime rib lovers may order a 16-oz boneless cut or a 32-oz king cut with bone. | 8445 International Dr. | 407/363–9727 | No lunch weekends | $21–$31 | AE, D, DC, MC, V.

Christini's. Italian. One of the city's best for northern Italian cuisine. As a result, the place always feels as if there's a party going on, particularly in the center of the room. Owner Chris Christini is on hand nightly to make sure that everything is perfect. Try the pasta with lobster, shrimp, and clams or the huge veal chops, perfumed with fresh sage. Note: This is no place to be in a hurry; dinner, with its various courses, will often take a couple of hours or more. Take I–4 exit 29. | 7600 Dr. Phillips Blvd. | 407/345–8770 | No lunch | $22–$34 | AE, D, MC, V.

★ **Emeril's.** Contemporary. Famed TV chef Emeril Lagasse has already nailed down a spot on every local critic's short list of the best restaurants in town for its rendition of the innovative Cajun cooking that Lagasse perfected in his New Orleans original, in a warehouse. At the Orlando version, in Universal Orlando CityWalk, the gleaming dark wood paneling and the crisp white napery are as polished as they come, though metal alloy chairs and an exposed-pipe ceiling recall the original. Not surprisingly, the Louisiana treats shine: smoked chicken and andouille sausage, gumbo, and shrimp remoulade. Even the wood-baked pizza is stellar, topped with wild and exotic mushrooms and a potato sauce spiked with chives and truffles. The desserts include a triple-chocolate cheesecake and a traditional New Orleans bread pudding. The cellar stocks 12,000 bottles. | Universal Orlando CityWalk, 6000 Universal Blvd. | 407/224–2424 | $15–$26 | AE, D, MC, V.

Lodging

INEXPENSIVE

Baymont Inn. Rooms at this motel are comfortably modern and have little extras like in-room coffeemakers and radios. It's 6 mi from Universal Orlando and 13 mi from Walt Disney World. Complimentary Continental breakfast. In-room data ports, microwaves, refrigerators. Cable TV. Pool. Laundry facilities. Business services. Pets allowed. Take I–4 exit 28. | 2051 Consulate Dr. | 407/240–0500 or 800/789–4103 (reservations) | fax 407/240–5194 | www.baymontinn.com | 128 rooms | $53–$75 | AE, D, DS, MC, V.

Best Western Airport Inn and Suites. Just over 1 mi from Orlando International Airport, this hotel (opened in spring 2000) is a good bet for experienced travelers who know the tricks of saving money on travel. The suites can easily sleep four, and have mini-kitchens. There's no in-house restaurant, but a Waffle House is next door and half a dozen other restaurants are within walking distance. The hotel is about 18 mi from International Drive and Universal Orlando, 20 mi from Walt Disney World. Take Highway 528 W exit 8. Cable TV. Pool. Laundry service. | 8101 Aircenter Ct., at McCoy Rd. | 407/581–2800 or 800/327–9742 | fax 407/581–2810 | www.bestwestern.com | 95 rooms | $69–$99 | AE, D, DC, MC, V.

Best Western, Florida Mall. Across the street from the Florida Mall and 5 mi from Orlando International Airport. Rooms have two double beds and are white with contemporary furnishings. Free Disney shuttle. It's about 6 mi from Universal Orlando and 5 mi from Walt Disney World. Restaurant, bar, room service. In-room data ports, in-room safes, refrigerators, microwaves. Cable TV. Pool. Video games. Laundry facilities. Business services. | 8421 S. Orange Blossom Trail | 407/855–6060 or 800/327–9742 (reservations) | fax 407/859–5132 | www.bestwestern.com | 204 rooms | $49–$89 | AE, D, MC, V.

Best Western Plaza International. This hotel 2 mi from SeaWorld and Universal Orlando offers many connecting rooms with large-screen TVs. Free Disney shuttle (about 10 mi away). Take I–4 exit 29. Bar. In-room data ports, in-room safes, microwaves, refrigerators. Cable TV. Pool, wading pool. Hot tub. Video games. Laundry facilities. | 8738 International Dr. | 407/345–8195 or 800/654–7160 (reservations) | fax 407/352–8196 | www.bestwestern.com | 672 rooms | $85–$105 | AE, D, MC, V.

Clarion Floridian Hotel. This eight-story peach hotel is right next to Wet 'n' Wild, 1 mi from Universal Orlando, and 9 mi from Walt Disney World. Rooms are average in size with two double beds, blue carpeting, and zig-zag blue, yellow, and red comforters. Restaurant, bar. In-room data ports, in-room safes, microwaves, refrigerators. Cable TV. Pool. 2 tennis courts. Basketball. Video games. Laundry facilities. Business services. | 7299 Universal Blvd. | 407/351–5009 or 800/445–7299 (reservations) | fax 407/363–7807 | www.clarionhotel.com | 303 rooms | $89–$129 | AE, D, MC, V.

Classic Inn and Suites. This motel is built around a courtyard. It offers large, up-to-date rooms as well as suites with two full baths and a sleeper sofa in the living room area. Take I–4 exit 29. The motel is 10 mi from Walt Disney World, 8 mi from Universal Orlando. Complimentary Continental breakfast. Microwaves, refrigerators. Cable TV. Pool, wading pool. Laundry facilities. Business services. | 8820 Orange Blossom Tr. | 407/851–8200 | fax 407/855–7153 | 141 rooms | $49–$99 | AE, D, MC, V.

Comfort Suites Orlando. This three-story all-suites hotel has a well-landscaped tropical courtyard. All suites have clock radios, sleeper sofas, and a spacious marble dressing vanity in the bathroom. The hotel is 10 mi from Walt Disney World, 2 mi from Universal Studios; there is a free shuttle to Universal Studios, SeaWorld, and Wet 'n' Wild. Bar, complimentary Continental breakfast. In-room safes, microwaves, refrigerators. Cable TV. Pool, wading pool. Hot tub. Playground. Laundry facilities. | 9350 Turkey Lake Rd. | 407/351–5050 or 800/277–

8483 (reservations) | fax 407/363–7953 | www.comfortsuitesorlando.com | 215 rooms | $79–$119 | AE, D, MC, V.

Country Hearth Inn. Reasonable rates, great location across from the Orlando County Convention Center, pretty rooms, plus a wine and cheese reception several times a week, all add up to a nice, low-key place to stay. The balcony with rocking chairs is a homey touch. French doors open onto patios, balconies, or courtyards. It's about 10 mi from Walt Disney World, 5 mi from Universal Orlando. Restaurant, bar, complimentary Continental breakfast. In-room data ports, in-room safes, microwaves, refrigerators. Cable TV. Pool. Laundry facilities. Business services. | 9861 International Dr. | 407/352–0008 or 800/447–1890 (reservations) | fax 407/352–5449 | www.countryhearth.com | 150 rooms | $79–$139 | AE, D, MC, V.

Courtyard Airport. Located south of downtown and 1½ mi from the airport, this hotel dates from 1989. Rooms are spacious with tropical decor and contemporary furnishings. It's about 12 mi from Universal Orlando and 20 mi from Walt Disney World. Restaurant, bar. In-room data ports, refrigerators. Cable TV. Pool. Hot tub. Gym. Laundry facilities. Business services, airport shuttle. | 7155 Frontage Rd. | 407/240–7200 or 800/443–6000 (reservations) | fax 407/240–8962 | www.courtyard.com | 149 rooms | $109–$139 | AE, D, MC, V.

Crosby's Motor Inn. This pleasant, two-story rural motel is off the beaten path in a small town 10 mi north of Orlando. Each room is uniquely decorated—most with antique mirrors, pink and green carpeting, and upholstery. Picnic area. In-room data ports, some kitchenettes, refrigerators. Pool. Laundry facilities. Some pets allowed. Walt Disney World is about 35 mi away, and Universal Studios is only 25 mi away. | 1440 W. Orange Blossom Trail (Hwy. 441N), Apopka | 407/886–3220 or 800/821–6685 | fax 407/886–7458 | 75 rooms | $50–$70 | AE, D, MC, V.

Fairfield Inn Orlando International Drive. This understated, few-frills, three-story hotel is a natural for single travelers or small families on a tight budget. It's squeezed between International Drive and the highway and doesn't have the amenities of top-of-the-line properties, but nice perks such as complimentary coffee and tea, free local phone calls, and cable TV give a sense of being at a much fancier place. It's 4 mi from Universal Orlando and 18 mi from Walt Disney World. Complimentary Continental breakfast. In-room data ports, in-room safes. Cable TV. Pool. Laundry facilities. | 8342 Jamaican Ct. | 407/363–1944 or 888/236–2427 (reservations) | fax 407/363–1944 | www.fairfieldinn.com | 134 rooms | $49–$69 | AE, D, MC, V.

Fairfield Inn Orlando South. This hotel has in-room movies, and radios. Take I-4 exit 29; it's 7 mi from Universal Orlando, 11 mi from Walt Disney World. Complimentary Continental breakfast. In-room data ports. Cable TV. Pool. Laundry facilities. | 1850 Landstreet Rd. | 407/240–8400 or 888/236–2427 | fax 407/240–8400 | www.fairfieldinn.com | 132 rooms | $69–$79 | AE, D, MC, V.

Hampton Inn Airport. This seven-floor hotel offers a convenient airport location within walking distance of several restaurants and night spots. Plus, there's a complimentary airport shuttle service. It's 15 mi from Universal Orlando, 20 mi from Walt Disney World. Complimentary Continental breakfast. In-room data ports, microwaves, refrigerators. Cable TV. Pool. Gym. Video games. Laundry facilities. Business services, airport shuttle. | 5767 T.G. Lee Blvd. | 407/888–2995 or 888/415–7356 (reservations) | fax 407/888–2418 | www.hamptoninn.com | 124 rooms | $74–$109 | AE, D, MC, V.

Hampton Inn at Universal Studios. Two blocks from Universal Orlando main entrance, this five-story hotel is in excellent condition. Rooms are clean and bright, with blue bedding and carpet, tropical paintings. Rooms are average in size. It's 10 mi from Walt Disney World. Complimentary Continental breakfast. In-room data ports, microwaves, refrigerators. Cable TV. Pool. Gym. Video games. Laundry facilities. Business services. | 5621 Windhover Dr. | 407/351–6716 or 888/415–7356 | fax 407/363–1711 | www.hamptoninn.com | 120 rooms | $59–$86 | AE, D, MC, V.

Hampton Inn Florida Mall. Located a half-mi off International Drive, this hotel built in 1998 is designed with a sophisticated and inviting decor, utilizing traditional mahogany furniture, including TV armoires with 25-inch remote control televisions. Take the Beeline Expressway West to U.S. 17/92/441N. It's 2 mi from Universal Orlando and 8 mi from Walt Disney World. Complimentary Continental breakfast. In-room data ports, microwaves, refrigerators. Cable TV. Pool. Gym. Video games. Laundry facilities. Business services. | 6101 Sand Lake Rd. | 407/363–7886 or 888/415–7356 (reservations) | fax 407/345–0670 | www.hamptoninn.com | 316 rooms | $52–$89 | AE, D, MC, V.

Hampton Inn, South of Universal Studios. This eight-story hotel is 1 mi from Universal Orlando, 10 mi from Walt Disney World. All rooms come complete with a refrigerator and microwave, which is convenient if you want to save money on meals. Take I–4 exit 30A. Free Walt Disney World shuttle. Complimentary Continental breakfast. Microwaves, refrigerators. Cable TV. Pool, wading pool. Gym. Video games. Laundry facilities. Business services. | 7110 S. Kirkman | 407/345–1112 or 888/415–7356 (reservations) | fax 407/352–6591 | www.hamptoninn.com | 170 rooms | $64–$89 | AE, D, MC, V.

Holiday Inn Express. This two-story hotel offers rooms that sleep up to four people. All rooms have two double beds. There's a large pool in a tropical courtyard. Free Walt Disney World shuttle. Walt Disney World is 18 mi away, while Universal Orlando is 1 mi. Complimentary Continental breakfast. In-room safes, microwaves, refrigerators. Cable TV. Pool. Video games. Laundry facilities. Business services. | 6323 International Dr. | 407/351–4430 or 800/365–6935 (reservations) | fax 407/345–0742 | www.enjoyfloridahotels.com | 218 rooms | $69–$139 | AE, D, MC, V.

Holiday Inn Express Orlando Airport West. This hotel is 3 mi from Orlando International Airport. Its suites have a separate living room with a Murphy bed, 2 color televisions, and 2-line phones with data ports. Walt Disney World is 20 mi away; Universal Orlando is 12 mi; shuttles are $20 per person with several drop-off times at each park throughout the day. Complimentary Continental breakfast. In-room data ports, microwaves, refrigerators. Cable TV. Pool. Hot tub. Laundry facilities. Business services, airport shuttle. | 1853 McCoy Rd. | 407/851–1113 or 800/228–2027 (reservations) | fax 407/438–5883 | www.orlandosuites.com | 168 rooms | $79–$99 | AE, D, MC, V.

Holiday Inn International Drive Resort. This tower hotel has an atrium, complete with tropical fish and waterfalls, all on 13 acres of landscaped grounds that center on a courtyard with a free-form heated pool. Rooms sleep up to four with one king or two double beds. It's 15 mi to Walt Disney World and 3 mi to Universal Orlando. Free shuttle to Universal and SeaWorld. Restaurant, bar, room service. In-room data ports, in-room safes, microwaves, refrigerators. Cable TV. Pool, wading pool. Hot tub. Gym. Playground. Business services. | 6515 International Dr. | 407/351–3500 or 800/465–4329 (reservations) | fax 407/351–5727 | 652 rooms | $89–$109 | AE, D, MC, V.

La Quinta Inn Airport. This hotel has three stories with a bright, new look that goes beyond the crisp white exteriors, including all new landscaping and lobbies. Rooms feature contemporary decor, floor-length draperies, built-in closets, ceiling moldings, and rich wood furniture. Expanded bathrooms have ceramic tile floors, designer vanities, and enhanced lighting. You'll also find an oversized workdesk and a dataport phone in every room. Walt Disney World and Universal Orlando are 20 mi from the hotel. Complimentary Continental breakfast. In-room data ports, refrigerators. Cable TV. Pool. Gym. Laundry facilities. Airport shuttle. Pets allowed. | 7931 Daetwyler Dr. | 407/857–9215 | fax 407/857–0877 | 128 rooms | $84–$116 | AE, D, MC, V.

La Quinta Inn, Orlando International Drive. This hotel features rooms with floor-length draperies, built-in closets, and expanded bathrooms. They have enhanced lighting, large desks and computer-friendly dataport telephones. There is a free shuttle to Universal Studios. Complimentary Continental breakfast. In-room data ports, microwaves, refrigerators. Cable TV. Pool. Laundry facilities. Pets allowed. | 8300 Jamaican Ct. | 407/351–1660 | fax 407/351–9264 | 200 rooms | $84–$109 | AE, D, MC, V.

Quality Inn, Plaza. Close to restaurants along International Drive, this motel offers rooms spread among five-, six-, and seven-story buildings. All rooms have two double beds. Built in 1983, the property is clean, but its furnishings are the bare minimum. Walt Disney World is 7 mi and Universal Orlando is 4 mi from the hotel. Restaurant, bar. In-room safes, refrigerators. Cable TV. Pool, wading pool. Hot tub. Kids programs (ages 2–12). Laundry facilities. Business services. Pets allowed. | 9000 International Dr. | 407/996–8585 or 800/999–8585 (reservations) | fax 407/996–6839 | www.tamarinns.com | 1,020 rooms | $35–$89 | AE, D, MC, V.

Quality Suites International Drive Area. Rooms are in a two-story building and seven-story tower. The hotel is 10 mi from Walt Disney World and provides free shuttles to all the Disney parks. Universal Orlando is 10 mi away. Complimentary breakfast. In-room data ports, microwaves, refrigerators. Cable TV. Pool. Hot tub. Gym. Video games. Playground. Laundry facilities. Business services. | 7400 Canada Ave. | 407/363–0332 or 800/228–2027 (reservations) | fax 407/352–2598 | www.orlandosuites.com | 154 rooms | $95–$119 | AE, D, MC, V.

Radisson Barcelo Hotel. Three blocks from Universal Studios and 15 mi from Walt Disney World, this hotel was renovated in 1997. Rooms have bright, tropical decor, two queen beds, and Nintendo-equipped televisions. Take I–4 exit 29. Restaurant, bar, complimentary breakfast. In-room data ports, in-room safes, microwaves, refrigerators. Cable TV. Volleyball. Video games. Laundry facilities. Business services. | 8444 International Dr. | 407/345–0505 or 800/333–3333 (reservations) | fax 407/352–5894 | www.radisson.com | 299 rooms | $89–$119 | AE, D, MC, V.

Sheraton Suites, Orlando International Airport. This three-story all-suites hotel is 1 mi from Orlando's International Airport, in Lee Vista Center. The hotel is 20 mi from Walt Disney World and 13 mi from Universal Orlando. Restaurant, bar. In-room data ports, refrigerators. Cable TV. Indoor-outdoor pool. Hot tub. Gym. Laundry facilities. Business services, airport shuttle. | 7550 Augusta National Dr. | 407/240–5555 or 800/222–8733 (reservations) | fax 407/240–1300 | www.sheraton.com. | 150 rooms | $89–$118 | AE, D, MC, V.

Wynfield Inn–Westwood. If you want a comfortable room with more than just the bare essentials, this two-story motel is a find. The rooms are comfy if not spectacular; most have two double beds. Children 17 and under stay free in their parents' room (with a maximum of four guests per room). The hotel is ¼ mi from SeaWorld, 4 mi from Universal Orlando, and 18 mi from Walt Disney World. Free shuttle to Universal Orlando and SeaWorld. Restaurant, 2 bars. Cable TV. 2 pools. Laundry facilities, laundry service. | 6263 Westwood Blvd. | 407/345–8000 or 800/346–1551 | fax 407/345–1508 | 299 rooms | $59–$109 | AE, D, DC, MC, V.

MODERATE

Adam's Mark Orlando. This 28-story hotel is connected to the south side of the Florida Mall, and guests get discounts at many mall stores. It is conveniently located between Orlando International Airport and International Drive. And if you like to shop in non-tourist-driven stores, there's a real bonus here. The hotel feels quite upscale with its polished marble floors and fountains in the lobby, a good in-house restaurant called Le Jardin, and a pleasant outdoor pool area that seems serene, even though the hotel complex is surrounded by the shopping center parking lot. Typical rooms have either two queen-size beds or a king-size and a fold-out sofa. Walt Disney World is 15 mi, Universal Orlando 8 mi. Theme park shuttle $15 per person. Restaurant, bar. In-room data ports, refrigerators. Cable TV. Pool. Hot tub, sauna. Gym. Laundry facilities. Business services. | 1500 Sand Lake Rd. | 407/859–1500 or 800/444–2326 (reservations) | fax 407/855–1585 | 496 rooms | $99–$169 | AE, D, MC, V.

Buena Vista Suites. All suites have two separate rooms (a bedroom and a living room with a fold-out sofa bed); a small kitchen area with microwave, sink, coffeemaker, and refrigerator; two TVs (one with a video player); and two phones. King suites feature a single king-size bed and an in-room whirlpool bath instead of a second bed. The hotel offers multi-night packages that include multi-day all-park passes to Disney, typically costing about $500 for four days, including lodging. You can stock your refrigerator 24 hours a day from the 7/Eleven across the street. Free Walt Disney World shuttle (the park is 1½ mi away); Universal Orlando is 10 mi. Restaurant, bar, complimentary breakfast, room service. In-room data ports, microwaves, refrigerators. Cable TV, in-room VCRs (and movies). Pool. Hot tub.

Tennis courts. Gym. Video games. Laundry facilities. Business services. | 14450 International Dr. | 407/239–8588 or 800/537–7737 (reservations) | fax 407/239–1401 | 280 suites | $129–$199 | AE, D, MC, V.

Castle Doubletree Hotel. Outside, this hotel looks like your standard I-Drive high-rise—but with turrets on top. Although popular with U.K. tourists, you won't necessarily think you're in Scotland despite the castle-like qualities. With purple carpets and drapes, medieval-style mosaics, and arched doorways, the hotel has a pleasant ambience that makes you feel as if you are playing Dungeons and Dragons. Of course, there is no dungeon, but there is a great rooftop terrace and an inviting courtyard with a big, round swimming pool. Because this property hosts a fair number of small-business meetings, it has such amenities as three phone lines in each room, data ports, and personal voice mail. Walt Disney World is 7½ mi, Universal Studios 3½ mi. Free shuttles to all Disney parks, Universal Orlando, and SeaWorld. 2 restaurants, bar (with entertainment). In-room data ports, in-room safes, microwaves, refrigerators. Cable TV. Pool, wading pool. Hot tub. Gym. Laundry facilities. Business services. | 8629 International Dr. | 407/345–1511 or 800/952–2785 (reservations) | fax 407/352–2991 | www.grandthemehotels.com | 216 rooms | $139–$179 | AE, D, MC, V.

Embassy Suites International Drive-Jamaican Court. This all-suites hotel has a central atrium with a lounge where a player piano sets a relaxing mood. Rooms are comfortably arranged—each unit has a bedroom and a full living room equipped with wet bar, refrigerator, pull-out sofa, and two TVs. Two-room suites can sleep up to six. An atrium is at the center of the lobby. Walt Disney World is 8 mi, Universal Orlando 2 mi; there is a free shuttle to Universal Orlando. Complimentary breakfast. In-room data ports, in-room safes, microwaves, refrigerators. Cable TV. Pool. Hot tub, sauna, steam room. Gym. Video games. Laundry facilities. Business services. | 8250 Jamaican Ct. | 407/345–8250 or 800/362–2779 (reservations) | fax 407/352–1463 | www.embassy-suites.com | 246 suites | $129–$209 | AE, D, MC, V.

Embassy Suites Orlando South. Another of the all-suites chain of hotels, this property has an expansive lobby with marble floors, pillars, hanging lamps, and old-fashioned ceiling fans. Tropical gardens with mossy rock fountains and palm trees add to the atrium's distinctive Southern ambience. Elsewhere, ceramic tile walkways and brick arches complement the tropical mood. The hotel offers a good number of little extras, like a health club with a fine steam room, free shuttle service to all four Disney parks (17 mi) and Universal Orlando (4 mi), and free hot breakfast. Restaurant, bar, complimentary breakfast. In-room data ports, in-room safes, microwaves, refrigerators. Cable TV. Pool. Gym. Video games. Laundry facilities. Business services. | 8978 International Dr. | 407/352–1400 or 800/EMBASSY (reservations) | fax 407/352–7315 | www.embassy-suites.com | 244 rooms | $129–$189 | AE, D, MC, V.

Enclave Suites at Orlando. With three 10-story buildings surrounding an office, restaurant, and recreation area, this all-suites property is less a hotel than a condominium complex. Here, what you would spend for a room in a fancy hotel gets you a complete apartment, with significantly more space than you'll find in other all-suites hotels. Accommodating up to six, the units have full kitchens, living rooms, two bedrooms, and small terraces with a view of a nearby lake. There's free transportation to SeaWorld, Wet 'n Wild, and Universal Orlando (7 mi), but Wet 'n Wild is an easy walk from the hotel. Walt Disney World is 25 mi. Kitchenettes, microwaves, refrigerators. Cable TV. 1 indoor pool, 2 outdoor pools, 2 wading pools. Hot tub. Tennis court. Gym. Playground. Laundry facilities, laundry service. | 6165 Carrier Dr. | 407/351–1155 or 800/457–0077 | fax 407/351–2001 | 352 suites | $89–$209 | AE, D, DC, MC, V.

Hawthorn Suites Hotel Orlando at SeaWorld. All units in this eight-story suite hotel, which opened in May 1999, have separate living areas and kitchens. In addition to breakfast, there's a free cocktail reception each evening. It's 10 mi from the Orlando International Airport, 4 mi from Walt Disney World Resort, 3 mi from Universal Orlando, 1 mi from SeaWorld, and a short walk to Wet 'n Wild. There is a free shuttle to Walt Disney World parks. Complimentary Continental breakfast. In-room data ports, kitchenettes, microwaves, refrigerators. Cable TV, in-room VCRs (and movies). Pool, wading pool. Hot tub. Gym. Video games. Playground. Laundry facilities. Business services. | 6435 Westwood Blvd. | 407/351–6600 or 800/527–1133 (reservations) | fax 407/351–1977 | www.hawthorn.com | 150 suites | $95–$165 | AE, D, MC, V.

Hilton Grand Vacations Club. Units of this timeshare at the SeaWorld International Center come with one, two, or three bedrooms, but you do have to be an owner to stay here. The provincial Bermudian seaside village design allows you to step back and enjoy life. Most units have screened balconies, and all have fully equipped kitchens, luxurious master baths with whirlpool spas, cable TV/VCR combos, washer/dryers. There are a few studios. Walt Disney World is 8 mi and Universal Orlando is 6 mi. Free shuttles to Universal, SeaWorld, and Wet 'n' Wild. In-room data ports, microwaves, refrigerators. Cable TV, in-room VCRs (and movies). Pool. Massage. Putting green. Gym. Video games. Children's programs (ages 4–12), playground. Laundry facilities. Business services. | 6924 Grand Vacations Way, | 407/239–0100 or 800/916–2221 (reservations) | fax 407/239–0200 | www.hilton.com | 224 units | $89–$199 | AE, D, MC, V.

Holiday Inn Hotel and Suites at the Main Entrance to Universal Studios. A 10-story hotel located at the entrance to Universal Orlando, less than a mile to SeaWorld, and 9 mi to Disney. There is a free shuttle to Universal Orlando, SeaWorld, and Wet 'n Wild. Rooms are average in size with two double beds, blue carpeting, and pink floral bedding. All rooms have a balcony. Restaurant, bar. In-room data ports, in-room safes, microwaves, refrigerators. Cable TV. Pool, wading pool. Hot tub. Gym. Playground. Laundry facilities. Business services. | 5905 S. Kirkman Rd. | 407/351–3333 or 800/327–1364 (reservations) | fax 407/351–3577 | www.holiday-inn.com | 220 rooms, 170 suites | $139, $159 suites | AE, D, MC, V.

Holiday Inn Select Orlando International Airport. Business facilities are the strong suit of this hotel 2 mi from the airport. Beautifully furnished guest rooms featuring work areas with data port telephones and TVs with free in-room movies. Suites come with a sofa bed and refrigerator. The hotel is about 20 mi from Walt Disney World and 12 mi from Universal Orlando. Restaurant, bar. In-room data ports, refrigerators. Cable TV. Pool. Hot tub, sauna. Tennis court. Basketball, gym, volleyball. Business services. Laundry facilities, airport shuttle. | 5750 T.G. Lee Blvd. | 407/851–6400 or 800/465–4329 (reservations) | fax 407/438–7297 | www.holiday-inn.com | 287 rooms | $129–$149 | AE, D, MC, V.

Orlando Airport Marriott. This nine-floor hotel has a resort-like setting and is 5 min from Orlando International Airport with easy access to major highways and attractions. You get complimentary coffee, a daily newspaper, and a free airport shuttle with your room. Walt Disney World is 12 mi from the hotel, Universal Orlando is 10 mi. Restaurant, bar (with entertainment), room service. In-room data ports, refrigerators. Cable TV. Indoor-outdoor pool, wading pool. Hot tub, massage, sauna, steam room. Basketball, gym, volleyball. Video games. Business services. Laundry facilities, airport shuttle. | 7499 Augusta National Dr. | 407/851–9000 or 888/236–2427 | fax 407/857–6211 | www.marriott.com | 484 rooms | $130–$179 | AE, D, MC, V.

Parc Corniche Resort. Each of the one- and two-bedroom suites is full of pastels and tropical patterns and has a patio or balcony with a golf course view, as well as a full kitchen. The largest accommodations, with two bedrooms and two baths, can sleep up to six. SeaWorld is only a few blocks away. Located on the newer section of I-Drive that's about 3 mi southwest of the Orlando Convention Center, the hotel is in a little less busy area than some of the properties closer to Orlando. A good bet for golf enthusiasts, the resort is framed by a Joe Lee–designed course. The hotel is 10 mi from Walt Disney World and 5 mi from Universal Orlando. There is a free shuttle service to Universal Orlando, SeaWorld, and Wet 'n' Wild. Complimentary Continental breakfast. Restaurant, bar. Kitchenettes, microwaves, refrigerators. Cable TV. Pool, wading pools. Hot tub. Video games. Playground. Laundry facilities. Business services. | 6300 Parc Corniche Dr. | 407/239–7100 or 800/355–4343 (reservations) | fax 407/239–8501 | www.parccorniche.com | 210 suites | $109–$199 | AE, D, MC, V.

Radisson Hotel Universal Orlando. When it opened in the mid-1970s, this was the largest convention hotel between Miami and Atlanta. It's undergone a lot of changes since then, including a major renovation completed in 1999. Still a hotbed of business-trippers, it's now mixed with a large percentage of theme-park visitors. Take I–4 exit 30B. Walt Disney World is 10 mi, Universal Orlando is across the street. There is a free shuttle to Universal Orlando, SeaWorld, and Wet 'n' Wild. Restaurant, bar, room service. Cable TV. Pool, wading pool. Hot tub. Gym. Baby-sitting, playground. Laundry facilities, laundry service. | 5780 Major Blvd. | 407/351–1000 or 800/327–2110 | fax 407/363–0106 | www.radisson.com | 742 rooms, 15 suites | $99–$199 | AE, D, DC, MC, V.

Ramada Resort and Conference Center. This five-story resort is 2 mi from Universal Orlando, 3 mi from SeaWorld, and 8 mi from Walt Disney World. There is a free shuttle to all local theme parks. Restaurant, bar. Microwaves, refrigerators. Cable TV. Indoor-outdoor pool. Beauty salon. Tennis court. Basketball. Video games. Playground. Laundry facilities. | 7400 International Dr. | 407/351–4600 or 800/327–1363 (reservations) | fax 407/363–0517 | 399 rooms | $125–$145 | AE, D, MC, V.

Residence Inn Orlando International Drive. Units in this two-story all-suites hotel accommodate up to five people, offering home-away-from-home comfort for families. Suites include full kitchen and living rooms. Most units have fireplaces and two full bathrooms. Walt Disney World is 9 mi, Universal Orlando is 2 mi. Free Walt Disney World shuttle. Complimentary Continental breakfast. In-room data ports, in-room safes, microwaves, refrigerators. Cable TV. Pool. Hot tub. Basketball, volleyball. Laundry facilities. Pets allowed. | 7975 Canada Ave. | 407/345–0117 or 888/236–2427 | fax 407/352–2689 | marriottresidenceinn.com | 176 rooms | $95–$205 | AE, D, MC, V.

Rosen Plaza. You'll see no shortage of wide-eyed conventioneers sporting name tags at this 12-story hotel alongside the Orange County Convention Center, but leisure travelers are gradually discovering both the hotel's prime location and its long list of amenities. Guest rooms are simple but large, with two queen-size beds and a nice little extra: a video-game unit hooked up to the TV. The presence of coin laundries on every floor is a big plus to families. Harris Rosen, the self-made millionaire who owns this and several other big Orlando hotels, got rich by saving money and figures you might want to as well. Walt Disney World is 10 mi, Universal Orlando 10 mi. Theme park shuttles are $8–$12 rountrip. Restaurant, bar (with entertainment). In-room data ports, in-room safes, microwaves, refrigerators. Cable TV. pool. Video games. Laundry facilities. Business services. | 9700 International Dr. | 407/352–9700 or 800/366–9700 | fax 407/351–9111 | www.rosenplaza.com | 810 rooms | $179 | AE, D, MC, V.

Sheraton World Resort. This quiet 30-acre townhouse complex on 28 acres features contemporary furnishings in all units and a sense of space. Families will enjoy the freedom of having a full kitchen to cook in—or not. Universal Orlando is 8 mi, Walt Disney World is 18 mi. There is a free Walt Disney World shuttle. Restaurant, bar, room service. In-room data ports, in-room safes, microwaves, refrigerators. Cable TV. Pool, wading pool. Hot tub, massage. Miniature golf, tennis court. Gym. Video games. Playground. Laundry facilities. Business services. | 10100 International Dr. | 407/352–1100 or 800/327–0363 (reservations) | fax 407/352–3679 | www.sheraton.com | 807 rooms | $130–$150 | AE, D, MC, V.

Sierra Suites Hotel. This all-suites hotel is designed for the business traveler: personal voice mail, two phone lines, speaker phone, and a good-size work table in each room, plus on-property copy and fax service. But the benefit for families is that you get a lot for your money. The full kitchen has everything you'll need to avoid restaurant tabs for as long as you like. The earth-tone decor is warm if not stunning, and the suites all have two queen- or one king-size bed, plus a sofa bed. Take I–4 exit 29. Walt Disney World is 5 mi, Universal Orlando is 2½ mi. There is a free shuttle to the Disney theme parks. In-room safes, kitchenettes, microwaves, refrigerators. Cable TV. Pool. Hot tub. Gym. Laundry facilities, laundry service. | 8750 Universal Blvd. | 407/903–1500 | fax 407/903–1555 | 137 suites | $69–$159 | AE, D, DC, MC, V.

Wyndham Orlando Resort. After a $36 million expansion, this hotel opened a children's entertainment center and an upscale shopping court. The most important fact, however, is its stone's throw-proximity to the new $2.6 billion Universal Orlando complex; 8 mi Disneyland and 3½ to Universal. There is a free shuttle to Universal Orlando, SeaWorld, and Wet 'n' Wild. 3 restaurants, 2 bars, room service. In-room dataports, in-room safes, some refrigerators, some in-room hot tubs. Cable TV. 3 pools, 2 wading pools. Outdoor hot tub, sauna, steam room. 4 tennis courts. Basketball, gym, volleyball. Video games, shops. Children's programs (ages 2–14), playground. Laundry facilities, laundry service. Free parking. Some pets allowed (fee). | 8001 International Dr. | 407/351–2420 or 800/996–3426 | fax 407/351–5016 | www.wyndham.com | 1,064 rooms | $99–$159 | AE, D, DC, MC, V.

EXPENSIVE

Hyatt Regency Orlando International Airport. If you have to catch an early morning flight, this hotel, inside the main terminal complex, is a good idea. Counting the time you spend waiting for the elevator, you're just a 5-min walk from your guest room to the nearest airline ticket counter. And for the bleary-eyed traveler, there's a Starbucks inside the terminal, about 50 yards from the front door of the hotel. Guest rooms have views of either the runways or a 10-story atrium area that's part of the terminal. (The terminal-side rooms all have balconies.) Considering the hotel's location it's amazingly quiet. Both Walt Disney World and Universal Orlando are about 18 mi. Restaurant, bar, room service. In-room data ports, microwaves. Cable TV. Pool. Hot tub, spa. Exercise equipment, laundry facilities. Business services, parking (fee). | 9300 Airport Blvd. | 407/825–1234 or 800/532–1496 (reservations) | fax 407/856–1672 | www.hyatt.com | 446 rooms | $200–$215 | AE, D, MC, V.

Rosen Centre Hotel. This 24-story high-rise tower of white concrete next to Convention Center is always bustling with meetings and conventions. Rooms are serviceable rather than posh, but the price is right. There's a massive pool area surrounded by tropical vegetation and a couple of good Caribbean restaurants. Microwaves don't come standard in the rooms, but are available for a fee. The hotel is 10 mi from Walt Disney World, 8 mi from Universal Orlando. 2 restaurants, 2 bars. In-room data ports, in-room safes, some microwaves, refrigerators. Cable TV. Pool. Beauty salon, massage, spa. 2 tennis courts. Health club. Laundry facilities. | 9840 International Dr. | 407/354–9840 or 800/800–9840 (reservations) | fax 407/248–0865 | www.rosencentre.com | 1,334 rooms | $165–$210 | AE, D, MC, V.

Ramada Inn and Suites by SeaWorld. All rooms at this family-oriented resort are suites with two bedrooms and two baths in this townhouse-style complex, each with a fully equipped kitchen. The contemporary two- and three-story story hotel building sits on 10 acres. Take I–4 exit 27A. The hotel is 14 mi from Walt Disney World and 5 mi from Universal Orlando. Free shuttles run to Sea World, Wet 'n' Wild, and Universal theme parks. Complimentary Continental breakfast. In-room safes, kitchenettes, microwaves, refrigerators. Cable TV. 2 pools. Hot tub. Basketball, gym, volleyball. Video games. Playground. Laundry facilities. Business services. | 6800 Villa de Costa Dr. | 407/239–0707 or 800/633–1405 (reservations) | fax 407/239–8243 | www.ramadaseaworld.com | 160 suites | $139–$209 | AE, D, MC, V.

Renaissance Orlando Resort. The hotel's 10-story atrium is full of waterfalls, goldfish ponds, and palm trees; as guests shoot skyward in sleek, glass elevators, exotic birds—on loan from SeaWorld across the street—twitter in a large, hand-carved, gilded Venetian aviary. It's nice to be greeted with a glass of champagne when you register, but the spacious guest rooms— Central Florida's largest—and luxurious marble bathrooms are even more pleasant. The place can sometimes seem like a busy convention hall, but it's in a section of International Drive that is not nearly as crowded (or tacky) as the hotels only a mile up the street. Walt Disney World is 8 mi from the resort, Universal Orlando is 6 mi; SeaWorld is across the street. 5 restaurants, bar (with entertainment), room service. In-room data ports, minibars, microwaves, refrigerators. Cable TV. Pool. Beauty salon, hot tub, massage, sauna, spa, steam room. 18-hole golf course, 12 tennis courts. Gym. Laundry facilities. Business services. | 6677 Sea Harbor Dr. | 407/351–5555 | fax 407/351–9991 | 780 rooms | $146–$216 | AE, D, MC, V.

The Seasons Resort. In this small townhouse complex, villas have full kitchens (complete with dishwasher, washing machine, and dryer). Opened in 1983, The Seasons is located near downtown shopping, restaurants, and nightlife. Take I–4 exit 32. Walt Disney World is 16 mi; Universal Orlando is 4 mi. In-room safes, microwaves, refrigerators. Cable TV. Pool, wading pool. Hot tub, sauna. 2 tennis courts, racquetball, exercise equipment. Video games. Playground. | 5736 S. Texas Ave. | 407/851–2278 | fax 407/438–1362 | www.west-gateresorts.com/wgseasons.html | 44 rooms | $140–$280 | AE, D, MC, V.

Sheraton Studio City. The most striking new feature of this former Quality Inn is a giant silver globe on the roof that makes it look like something suited for Times Square on New Year's Eve. But the hotel takes a Hollywood-theme approach, with ubiquitous movie posters and black-and-white art deco decor throughout. Because this 21-story building is round, the rooms are a little odd in shape, but everything above the fourth floor tends to have a great view. The 20th floor has plush luxury suites for those ready to spring for $300 a night for a good view of Universal Studios (directly across I–4) and International Drive (just out the front door). You can easily walk to Wet 'n Wild and half a dozen other International Drive attractions. Walt Disney World is 10 mi away and Universal is 2 mi away. The hotel offers a free shuttle to SeaWorld and Universal Orlando. 2 restaurants, 2 bars, room service. Cable TV. Pool, wading pool. Beauty salon, hot tub. Video games. Laundry service. | 5905 International Dr. | 407/351–2100 or 800/327–1366 | fax 407/248–0266 | www.sheraton.com | 302 rooms | $199–$299 | AE, D, DC, MC, V.

Summerfield Suites Hotel. Sleeping from four to eight people, the one- and two-bedroom units at the all-suites hotel are a great option for families. Parents relish the chance for a little peace, and youngsters enjoy the feeling of grown-up privacy and, more important, the chance to control their own TV fate—there's a set in each room. Two-bedroom units, the most popular, have fully equipped kitchens, plus a living room with TV and VCR. Plush landscaping manages to give the place a secluded feel even though it's on International Drive. The hotel frequently offers specials. Walt Disney World is 9 mi away, Universal Orlando 2 mi. Complimentary Continental breakfast. In-room safes, microwaves, refrigerators. Cable TV. Pool, wading pool. Hot tub. Gym. Video games. Laundry facilities. Business services. | 8480 International Dr. | 407/352–2400 or 800/833–4964 (reservations) | fax 407/352–4631 | www.summerfield-orlando.com | 146 suites | $249 | AE, D, MC, V.

VERY EXPENSIVE

★ **The Peabody Orlando.** At 11 AM, the celebrated Peabody ducks exit a private elevator into the marble-floor lobby and waddle across a red carpet to the little marble fountain where they pass the day. At 5, to the crowd's delight, the marching mallards repeat the ritual in reverse. Built by the owners of the landmark Peabody Hotel in Memphis, this 27-story structure looks like three high-rise offices from afar, but don't be put off by its austere exterior. The interior is impressive and handsome. The most panoramic of the oversized upper-floor rooms have views of Walt Disney World. Across from the Orange County Convention Center, the hotel attracts rock stars and other performers, conventioneers, and duck lovers. Walt Disney World is 14 mi from the hotel, and Universal Orlando is 5 mi. 3 restaurants, bar (with entertainment). In-room data ports, in-room safes, minibars, microwaves, refrigerators, room service. Cable TV. Pool, wading pool. Beauty salon, hot tub, massage, sauna, steam room. 4 tennis courts. Basketball, gym, volleyball. Video games. Children's programs (4–12), playground. Laundry facilities. Business services. | 9801 International Dr. | 407/352–4000 | fax 407/351–0073 | www.peabody-orlando.com | 891 rooms | $270–$330 | AE, D, MC, V.

Portofino Bay Hotel. At Universal's first on-property hotel (and 7 mi from Disney), there's a man-made lake, with a dozen faux fishing boats. You'll see the Italian "fishermen" (actually costumed actors) sitting around mending their nets, but they probably won't see fish anytime soon. The architecture of the resort will give you that Portofino feeling—it's an exact copy of the little Italian village, complete with the same brightly colored stucco buildings. One of the touches is a poolside water slide designed to look like a Roman aqueduct. If you want to be in a section of the hotel that is a little more kid-free than normal for a theme-park hotel, go for the more expensive villa section. Perks for staying here include one-hour early entry to Universal Orlando and Islands of Adventure and special VIP access to popular rides, plus free transportation around the resort. 3 restaurants, bar, room service. In-room data ports, in-room safes, some refrigerators. Some in-room VCRs. 3 pools. Beauty salon, spa, sauna, steam room. Health club. Video games. Children's programs (ages 4–14). Laundry service. Business services. Free parking. | 1000 Universal Studios Plaza | 407/224–7117 | www.loewshotels.com | 750 rooms | $392–$419 | AE, D, DC, MC, V.

Westgate Lakes Resort. All units are suites in this luxurious 110-acre hotel and time-share complex of six-story pink buildings less than a mile from a lakefront. Each suite sleeps four to eight people. Take I–4 exit 29A. Walt Disney World is 12 mi, and Universal Orlando is 1 mi. Restaurant, bar. In-room safes, microwaves, refrigerators. Cable TV. 2 pools, wading pool. Hot tub, sauna. Tennis court. Basketball. Dock, water sports, fishing, bicycles. Playground. | 10000 Turkey Lake Rd., | 407/345–0000 | fax 407/345–5384 | www.westgateresorts.com | 233 rooms | $230–$550 | AE, D, MC, V.

ORMOND BEACH

MAP 3, K4

(Nearby towns also listed: Daytona Beach, DeLand, Flagler Beach)

While Ormond Beach (pop. 35,000) is Daytona Beach's northern neighbor, it's hard to tell where one ends and the other begins. Originally established as a retirement colony by Connecticut's Corbin Lock Company, Ormond Beach saw its first hotel built in 1888. At the turn of the 20th century, a visitor made the most important discovery in town history: you could drive your car on the sand. Soon after, auto enthusiasts such as Alexander Winston, R. E. Olds, and Barney Oldfield were racing their cars along the firm sands here. The town is sometimes called the Birthplace of Speed. In the 1920s and 1930s it was the winter home of another famous name, John D. Rockefeller, whose estate is now a popular tourist attraction. And, of course, sun and surf seekers are still drawn by the town's Atlantic shoreline.

Information: Ormond Beach Chamber of Commerce | 165 W. Granada Blvd., Ormond Beach, 32174 | 904/677–3454 | www.ormondchamber.org.

Attractions

Bulow Plantation Ruins State Historic Site. In 1821, Major Charles Wilhelm Bulow acquired 4,675 acres of wilderness—land that eventually produced sugar cane, cotton, rice, and indigo. Today you can visit the coquina walls and chimneys of the sugar mill, 15 mi north of Ormond Beach. | 3501 S. Old Kings Rd., Bunnell | 904/517–2084 | www.dep.state.fl.us/parks | $2 per vehicle | Daily 9–5.

The Casements. The 1917–1937 winter residence of John D. Rockefeller got its name from diamond-paned casement windows throughout the estate. Listed on the National Register of Historic Places, it is now a cultural center and museum, and offers tours, classes, and various events throughout the year. Wander through the gardens and see displays of family memorabilia in the house, or visit the Boy Scout museum. The mansion is on the Halifax River, a mile from the Atlantic. | 25 Riverside Dr. | 904/676–3216 | fax 904/676–3363 | Donations accepted | Weekdays 9–5, Sat. 9–noon.

Ormond Beach Performing Arts Center. This 650-seat arts center stages both professional and non-profit productions throughout the year. | 399 U.S. 1N | 904/676–3378.

Ormond Memorial Art Museum and Gardens. This museum in a four-acre garden in downtown Ormond Beach focuses on work by Florida artists. Banana plants, sago palms, American elms, bamboos, and bromeliads fill the garden; waterfalls and gazebos punctuate the footpaths, along with a fountain and a pond with koi fish and turtles. The complex is three blocks west of Route A1A. | 78 E. Granada Blvd. | 904/676–3347 | fax 904/676–3244 | $2 (suggested donation) | Mon.–Fri. 10–4, weekends noon–4.

Tomoka State Park. This 900-acre state park, 3 mi north of Ormond Beach near the confluence of the Tomoka and Halifax rivers, is on the site of a Timucuan Indian settlement discovered in 1605 by Spanish explorer Alvaro Mexia. Live oaks, pines and palm trees shade campgrounds. You can also canoe, fish, hike, and go boating. A museum and visitor center houses exhibits on natural and cultural history. | 2099 N. Beach St. | 904/676–4050 | fax 904/676–4060 | www.dep.state.fl.us/parks | $3.25 per vehicle | Daily 8–sunset.

ON THE CALENDAR
JULY: *Fourth of July–Four Corners.* The independence holiday is livened by music, food, and fireworks off the corners of the bridge leading to the beach. | 904/677–3454.
NOV.: *Birthplace of Speed Antique Car Show.* Pre-1932 antique cars race down Ormond Beach and participate in a parade Thanksgiving weekend. | 904/677–3454.

Dining
Charlie Horse Restaurant. American. Known for spicy buffalo wings and snow crab legs, this family place has pool tables and a kids' menu. Baby back ribs, steaks, shrimps, and pastas are also on the menu. The wood-paneled restaurant and bar is open late each night. | 810 S. Atlantic Ave. | 904/672–4347 | $4–$18 | MC, V.

Chicago Stockyard Grill. Steak. Local art hangs from the walls, above the booths and tables of this restaurant at the Trails Shopping Center. Besides prime beef, the restaurant also has seafood choices including lobster tail. | 324 N. Nova Rd. | 904/671–9992 | No lunch Sun. | $12–$40 | AE, MC, V.

Delta Restaurant. American/Casual. Known for its large menu, this local favorite serves up everything from pancakes and pastas to steaks and sandwiches. Try a Greek specialty such as lamb shanks. | 790 S. Atlantic Ave. | 904/672–3140 | Breakfast also available | $9–$20 | AE, MC, V.

Frappes North. Contemporary. Owned and operated by the chef, this local favorite has a seasonal menu. Past dishes have included pepper-encrusted Ahi tuna with Neapolitan vinaigrette and mushroom risotto, or filet mignon with blue cheese, carmelized onions, and a port wine demi-glaze. The restaurant is divided into small dining rooms which combine traditionally elegant elements such as fresh flowers and finished wood, with contemporary notes like sculpted metal light fixtures. | 123 West Granada Blvd. | 904/615–4888 | No lunch Sat. Closed Sun. | $15–$25 | AE, MC, V.

Julian's. Seafood. A Polynesian-style thatched hut across the street from the Atlantic houses this 1967 steak-and-seafood restaurant. Inside, tropical plants and murals continue the Polynesian theme. On the menu are a wide variety of steak and seafood dishes, including prime western filet mignon, royal Alaskan salmon, and giant shrimp stuffed with deviled crabs, wrapped in bacon. There's live music daily. | 88 S. Atlantic Ave. | 904/677–6767 | www.juliansrest.com | Reservations not accepted | No lunch | $9–$18 | AE, D, DC, MC, V.

La Crêpe En Haut. French. A former crêperie, La Crêpe en Haut is now an elegant, upscale, classic French restaurant. Crêpes are still on the lunch and dessert menus, but dishes now include veal chop with black truffle sauce, crab cake with jumbo lump crabmeat, and roasted duck with berries. The wine list includes many top French labels. | 142 E. Granada Blvd. | 904/673–1999 | Reservations essential | Closed Mon. No lunch weekends | $25–$45 | AE, MC, V.

Stonewood Tavern and Grill. American/Casual. This new eatery is known for its chicken pot pie and herb-crusted rack of lamb, as well as pastas, sirloins, chicken, and burgers. There is a patio for outdoor eating, while the indoor dining room has wood and stone walls. | 100 S. Atlantic Ave. | 904/671–1200 | No lunch | $10–$20 | AE, D, DC, MC, V.

Lodging
Casa Del Mar Beach Resort. Two floors of this resort are hotel rooms; five are timeshare apartments. The late 1970s building directly faces the beach. All the rooms have private

balconies; many face the ocean. The rooms are decorated in light, sunny shades of blue, green, and yellow, accented by natural wood. Bar. In-room data ports, microwaves, refrigerators. Cable TV. Pool, wading pool. Hot tub. Beach. Laundry facilities. Business services. | 621 S. Atlantic Ave. | 904/672–4550 or 800/245–1590 | fax 904/672–1418 | www.vac-club.com | 115 rooms | $92–$154 | AE, D, DC, MC, V.

Comfort Inn Interstate. At exit 89 off I–95, this two-story motel is set back in the woods of Tomoka State Park, 7 mi northwest of the beach. There are 10 restaurants within walking distance. Complimentary Continental breakfast. In-room data ports, some microwaves, some refrigerators. Cable TV. Pool. Laundry facilities. Business services. Some pets allowed (fee). | 1567 U.S. 1N | 904/672–8621 | fax 904/677–9107 | www.comfortinn.com | 75 rooms | $70–$160 | AE, D, DC, MC, V.

Comfort Inn on the Beach. This four-story motel is, as the name boasts, right on the beach, with shopping, miniature golf, and tennis courts within a mile. The heart of Daytona Beach is 4 mi south. There are three one-bedroom apartments that sleep up to six, and standard rooms, which sleep four. Complimentary Continental breakfast. In-room data ports, in-room safes, some kitchenettes, microwaves, refrigerators. Cable TV. Pool, wading pool. Beach. Some pets allowed (fee). | 507 S. Atlantic Ave. | 904/677–8550 | fax 904/673–6260 | www.comfortinn.com | 49 rooms | $75–$165 | AE, D, DC, MC, V.

Coral Beach Motel. This seven-story beachfront resort hotel offers rooms, efficiencies, and suites. All rooms have private balconies with ocean view. There is a miniature golf course adjacent to the property, and shops, restaurants, and bars are all within walking distance. Complimentary Continental breakfast. In-room data ports, in-room safes, microwaves, refrigerators, some in-room hot tubs. Cable TV. Indoor pool, outdoor pool. Beach. Laundry facilities. | 711 S. Atlantic Ave. | 904/677–4712 or 800/553–4712 | fax 904/677–4712 ext. 151 | www.coralbeachmotel.com | 98 efficiencies, 12 suites | $85–$130 | AE, MC, V.

Coral Sands Inn and Seaside Cottages. This complex has restored 1920s cottages with Spanish barrel-tile roofs around a five-story inn overlooking the ocean. You can enjoy beachfront gazebos, sun patios, complimentary beach cabanas, a heated oceanfront pool, barbecues, and outdoor tables with umbrellas. Complimentary Continental breakfast. Some microwaves, some refrigerators, some kitchenettes. Cable TV. Pool. Beach. Laundry facilities. Business services. | 1009 Ocean Shore Blvd. | 904/441–1831 or 800/441–1831 | fax 904/441–1835 | www.coralsandsinn.com | 84 rooms, 36 cottages | $99–$150 | AE, D, DC, MC, V.

Driftwood Beach Motel. This beachfront motel has rooms, efficiencies, and one-bedroom units, some of which overlook the beach and water. There is an oceanfront shuffleboard court and heated outdoor pool. Picnic area. Some kitchenettes, some microwaves, some refrigerators. Cable TV. Pool. Beach. | 657 S. Atlantic Ave. | 904/677–1331 or 800/490–8935 | fax 904/677–0625 | www.driftwoodmotel.com | 44 rooms | $30–$180 | D, MC, V.

Hampton Inn Daytona-Ormond Beach. Sitting ¼ mi west of the I–95 and Route 40 junction, this four-story hotel is 5 mi west of the beach. Complimentary fresh cookies are served each evening in the lobby. Complimentary Continental breakfast. In-room data ports, some microwaves, some refrigerators, some in-room hot tubs. Cable TV. Pool. Gym. Laundry service. Business services. | 155 Interchange Blvd. | 904/627–9999 or 800/426–7866 | fax 904/677–0663 | www.hamptoninn.com | 84 rooms | $66–$94 | AE, D, DC, MC, V.

Ivanhoe Beach Resort. This oceanfront resort has basic rooms, efficiencies, and one-bedroom apartments that can sleep up to six people. Many of the rooms have ocean views and private balconies. Restaurant, bar. In-room data ports, in-room safes, some kitchenettes, some microwaves, refrigerators. Cable TV. Pool, wading pool. Beach. Laundry facilities. Business services. | 205 S. Atlantic Ave. | 904/672–6711 or 800/874–9910 | fax 904/676–9494 | www.ivanhoebeachresort.com | 147 rooms | $50–$145 | AE, MC, V.

Jameson Inn of Ormond Beach. This white-columned, three-story chain has motel rooms and one-bedroom suites. It is just off I–95 at exit 88. Complimentary Continental breakfast. In-room data ports, some minibars, some microwaves, some refrigerators. Cable TV.

Pool. Gym. Laundry service. Business services. Pets allowed. | 175 Interchange Blvd. | 904/672–3675 | 67 rooms | $65–$71 | AE, D, MC, V.

Mainsail Inn and Suites. This waterfront resort in the center of Ormond Beach has a nice pool deck only steps from the water. Room choices include penthouses, efficiencies, and two-bedroom suites. In-room data ports, in-room safes, some kitchenettes, some in-room hot tubs. Cable TV. Pool, wading pool. Beach. Laundry facilities. Business services. | 281 S. Atlantic Ave. | 904/677–2131 or 800/843–5142 | fax 904/676–0323 | www.bestwestern-mainsail.com | 42 rooms | $130–$140 | AE, D, DC, MC, V.

Makai Lodge Beach Resort. A Polynesian theme dominates the lobby of this owner-operated lodge, a mile north of the BelAir Shopping Plaza. Motel rooms, lodge rooms, and efficiencies are available; all are outfitted with new dark mahogany furniture. Half the units face the ocean. In-room data ports, in-room safes, some kitchenettes, some microwaves, refrigerators. Cable TV. Pool, wading pool. Hot tub. Beach. Video games. Laundry facilities. Business services. Pets allowed. | 707 S. Atlantic Ave. | 904/677–8060 or 800/799–1112 | www.makailodge.com | 110 rooms | $33–$130 | AE, D, DC, MC, V.

Quality Inn and Suites Resort. This attractive chain resort has a large swimming pool just feet from the beach. Individual touches include a chandelier and four-poster bed in the Honeymoon Suite, special golf and fishing packages, and tromp l'oeil murals in the lounge. There is a variety of rooms and suite choices; most have private balconies facing the Atlantic. Restaurant, bar (with entertainment). Some in-room data ports, in-room safes, some microwaves, some refrigerators. Cable TV. Indoor pool, outdoor pool, wading pool. Hot tub. Laundry facilities. | 251 S. Atlantic Ave. | 904/672–8510 or 800/227–7220 | fax 904/672–7221 | www.visit-daytona.com/quality | 130 rooms, 20 suites | $124–$169 | AE, D, DC, MC, V.

Sleep Inn. At exit 88 off I–95, this motel is 10 mi north of the Daytona International Speedway, next door to a shopping plaza, five restaurants, and a 12-screen movie theatre, and 5 mi west of the beach. Complimentary Continental breakfast. In-room data ports. Cable TV. Pool. Laundry facilities. Business services. | 170 Williamson Blvd. | 904/673–6030 or 800/753–3746 | fax 904/673–7017 | www.sleepinn.com | 83 rooms | $135–$150 | AE, D, DC, MC, V.

PALATKA

MAP 3, J3

(Nearby towns also listed: Flagler Beach, Gainesville, Micanopy, St. Augustine, St. Augustine Beach)

Old Florida lives on in this town of 11,000 just north of the Ocala National Forest. Palatka resident Judge Isaac Bronson proposed the act that led to Florida's statehood. Today his home is open to the public. The town is also the home of Ravine State Gardens.

Information: Putnam County Chamber of Commerce | 1100 Reid St., Box 550, Palatka, 32177 | 904/328–1503 | www.putnamcountychamber.org.

Attractions

Bronson-Mulholland House. Built in 1854 by Federal Judge Isaac Bronson, this three-story Greek Revival home was used as a post by both the Confederate and Union armies during the Civil War, and later served as a school where former slaves were taught to read and write. Furnishings are of the period, and guides on tours wear antebellum dress. | 100 Madison St. | 904/329–0140 | Free | Tues., Thurs., Sun. 2–5.

Palatka Railroad Preservation Society. The Society is dedicated to the preservation and perpetuation of the rail heritage of Palatka and surrounding communities, from the first railway in the 1800s to the present. A portion of the historic depot has already been established as the David Browning Railroad Museum and contains documents, photographs, maps, signs and other items donated or loaned by the public. | Union Depot, Reid St. | 904/328–1539 | First Sun. of every month, 1–4 PM.

Ravine State Gardens. Some 95,000 azaleas in 64 varieties were planted on this 59-acre tract, along with 11,000 palm trees and more than 250,000 other ornamental plants. Built in part by the WPA, this is one of nine Florida state parks with New Deal–era structures, and the only one with a formal garden. The park is 1 mi southeast of town, off Moseley Avenue. | 1600 Twigg St. | 904/329–3721 | fax 904/329–3718 | www.dep.state.fl.us | $1, $3.25 per vehicle | Daily 8–sunset.

Welaka National Fish Hatchery and Visitor Center Aquarium. Operated by U.S. Fish and Wildlife, this nature preserve has production ponds, wildlife observation areas, trails, and a freshwater fish aquarium. Visitors are likely to see sandhill cranes, native freshwater fish, woodstorks, a variety of heron and egrets, among other birds while touring the hatchery. | 723 County Road 309, Welaka | 904/467–2374 | fax 904/467–8108 | http://southeast.fws.gov/welaka | Free | Daily 7–3:30.

ON THE CALENDAR

MAR.: *Azalea Festival.* This celebration of spring is held in downtown Palatka along the banks of the St. Johns River. There are music, food, rides, a car show, a bass tournament, and a beauty pageant, along with monster trucks, arts and crafts, and blossoms galore. | 904/328–1503.

MAR.: *Putnam County Fair.* This is an all-American county fair with livestock, crafts, rides, and entertainment at the fairgrounds on Yelvington Rd. in East Palatka. | 904/328–1503.

APR.: *The Catfish Festival.* This festival features a championship catfish skinning contest, arts and crafts, a parade led by King Catfish, and a chance to indulge in southern delicacies such as fried fingerling catfish, crab, alligator tail, swamp cabbage, hush puppies, and strawberry shortcake. The fest takes place in Crescent City on the first Saturday in April. | 904/328–1503.

MAY: *Blue Crab Festival.* This Memorial Day weekend features crab boils and music along the St. John's River downtown. | 904/328–1503.

SEPT., OCT.: *Railfest.* A weekend-long celebration of Palatka's rail history features a tour of the Union Depot and the David Browning Museum. You can also buy railroad collectibles like model trains. | 904/328–1539.

Dining

Corky Bell's Seafood. Seafood. This busy restaurant has a large menu of fresh seafood, and fantastic views of St. Johns River. | 121 Comfort Rd. | 904/325–1094 | $8–$31 | AE, D, MC, V.

La Fiesta. Mexican. Friendly, efficient service and reasonable prices make this restaurant a favorite of locals, who return for enormous burritos, quesadillas, and fresh paella. | 2508 Crill Ave. | 904/328–5553 | $6–$15 | AE, MC, V.

Lodging

Azalea House B&B. This gracious yellow 1878 gingerbread Victorian is listed on the National Registry of Historic Places. The grounds are peaceful and elegant, with a pond, pool, lush gardens, flowering magnolias, and oak trees hung with Spanish moss. The individually named and decorated rooms feature period furniture. Aunt Esther's Room, on the third floor, has a tree top view and a reading alcove. Complimentary breakfast. Outdoor pool. Indoor hot tub. No kids under 12. No smoking. | 220 Madison St. | 904/325–4547 | 6 rooms | $85–$125 | AE, MC, V.

Holiday Inn Riverside. Half of the rooms here open onto the St. Johns River in this two-story hotel built in 1978. The hotel is in downtown Palatka, 5 mi from Ravine State Gardens. Restaurant, bar. In-room data ports, some refrigerators. Cable TV. Pool. Exercise equipment. Dock. Fishing. Laundry facilities. Business services. | 201 N. 1st St. | 904/328–3481 or 800/465–4329 | fax 904/329–9907 | www.basshotels.com | 131 rooms | $50–$100 | AE, D, DC, MC, V.

PALM BEACH

(Nearby towns also listed: Boynton Beach, Lake Worth, Lantana, Palm Beach Gardens, Palm Beach Shores, Riviera Beach, West Palm Beach)

In this fabulously wealthy town of 10,000, grandiose mansions hide behind high hedges and imposing fences. Exclusive stores line Worth Avenue, the Rodeo Drive of the East. The rich and famous have been coming here since the 1920s when developer Addison Mizner began building homes, stores, and public buildings in a Moorish-Gothic style.

Today's celebrity roster of residents includes rock star Rod Stewart; media mogul billionaire John Kluge; political talk-show host Rush Limbaugh; and musician and performer Jimmy Buffett. Mar-a-Lago, now a private club owned by Donald Trump, once belonged to cereal heiress Marjorie Meriweather Post. Resorts here also induce gasps, particularly The Breakers. Few of the opulent estates are open to the public; one exception is the museum in the former home of railroad magnate Henry Morrison Flagler.

Information: Palm Beach Chamber of Commerce | 45 Cocoanut Row, Palm Beach, 33480 | 561/655–3282 | www.palmbeachchamber.com.

Attractions

The Breakers. Built by Henry Flagler in 1895, this luxury hotel, which resembles an ornate Italian Renaissance palace, underwent a $100-million renovation in 1999. Be amazed by painted arched ceilings hung with crystal chandeliers and an ornate Florentine dining room with 15th-century Flemish tapestries. | 1 S. County Rd. | 561/655–6611 | www.thebreakers.com | Free | Daily.

The Church of Bethesda-by-the-Sea. This Spanish Gothic Episcopal church in the Cluett Memorial Gardens was built in the early 1800s. The church and cloisters were moved and restored several times before 1925, they settled in Palm Beach. | 141 South County Rd. | 561/655–4554 | fax 561/832–0140 | Free | Daily.

El Solano. This Spanish-style home was built by Addison Mizner as his personal residence in 1925, and has since been owned by the likes of Harold Vanderbilt and John Lennon and Yoko Ono. El Solano is not open to the public, but you can drive by and admire the architecture. | 721 S. County Rd.

★ **Henry Morrison Flagler Museum (Whitehall).** Henry Flagler founded Standard Oil in 1870, when he was 40. When he was in his 50s, Flagler became interested in Florida, and by the time of his death in 1913, his Florida East Coast Railway linked the state's entire east coast, from Jacksonville to Key West, establishing agriculture and tourism as Florida's leading industries. In 1902, Flagler built Whitehall for his wife, Mary Lily Kenan, in an opulent Beaux-Arts style, an elegant wedding cake with soaring columns fronting the two-story veranda framed by a palm-lined walkway. The house is is on the National Register of Historic Places. | 1 Whitehall Way | 561/655–2833 | fax 561/655–2826 | www.flagler.org | $8 | Tues.–Sat. 10–5, Sun. noon–5.

Mar-A-Lago. Donald Trump is the current owner of this estate, one of the grandest homes along Ocean Boulevard. Despite local opposition, Trump has turned Mar-a-Lago into a membership club and plans to subdivide the property. Italianate towers mark the silhouette of the estate once owned by breakfast-food heiress Marjorie Meriweather Post. | 1100 S. Ocean Blvd.

Mid-Town Beach. Directly east of Worth Avenue lies this small beach, which is especially popular because of its proximity to town. The only convenient meters for public beach access are found between Worth Avenue and Royal Palm Way. | 400 S. Ocean Blvd. | Parking 25¢ per 15 min | Daily 8–8.

Palm Beach Bicycle Trail. Nestled along the edge of Lake Worth, this flat, 10-mi-long palm-lined trail runs parallel to Lake Wayand allows glimpses into many local mansions. | Free | Daily.

Palm Beach Post Office. This 1932 National Historic Site building has a Spanish-style exterior. Inside, murals depict Seminole Indians in the Everglades. | 95 N. County Rd. | 800/275–8777 | Free | Weekdays 8:30–5.

Pan's Garden. This meticulously groomed half-acre garden on Hibiscus Avenue, adjacent to the Worth Avenue shopping area, has more than 75 varieties of native flowers and plants. A bronze statue of Pan stands at the entrance pool. | 386 Hibiscus Ave. | 561/832–0731 | Free | Open mid-May–mid-Nov., weekdays 10–2; mid-Nov.–mid-May, daily 9–5.

Phipps Ocean Park. Besides the beautiful beach, this park contains the Little Red Schoolhouse. Constructed in 1886, this was the first school built in what was then Dade County. Tours are given on weekday mornings. | 2145 S. Ocean Blvd. | 561/832–0731 | Free | Daily.

Society of the Four Arts. This complex dedicated to music, drama, literature, and art includes a library, the Philip Hulitar Sculpture Garden, and 13 other horticultural demonstration gardens (including an English Regency garden, a Chinese garden, and a tropical jungle). Exhibits, concerts, films, and lectures take place December to April at the Gallery Building. | 2 Four Arts Plaza | 561/655–7227 | fax 561/655–7233 | www.fourarts.org | Free | Library and gardens open weekdays 10–5, Sat. 9–1.

★ **Worth Avenue.** A stroll down this ¼-mi-long street of grand Moorish architecture takes in 250 of the most exclusive shops, boutiques, and ateliers in the world. A number of high-end automobiles, such as Mercedes and Bentleys, will be rolling next to you. | 561/659–6909 | fax 561/798–4905 | www.worth-avenue.com.

ON THE CALENDAR

JAN.–APR.: *Polo Championship Series.* Opening with the Millennium Cup in early January and concluding with the World Cup Final in mid-April, this series of Sunday matches at the Palm Beach Polo and Country Club is the sport at its finest. | 561/793–1440.

Dining

Amici's. Italian. Crowded, trendy, and visually exciting, Amici's serves northern Italian fare to demanding, wealthy clientele. If the six-figure cars pulling into valet outside is a worthy scene, so is the open kitchen, the archways separating dining areas, the large glass picture windows facing the street, and the contemporary Mediterranean design enhanced by sunflowers and bottles of herb-infused olive oil on each table. Entrées include gourmet pizzas and homemade pastas such as tagliolini with shrimp, asparagus, sun-dried tomatoes, and crushed red pepper; and white or red linguine with fresh clams, garlic, olive oil, crushed red pepper, and parsley in white wine. | 288 S. County Rd. | 561/832–0201 | www.amicipalmbeach.com | Reservations essential | No lunch Sun. | $18–$34 | AE, D, DC, MC, V.

Bice Ristorante. Italian. The aroma of basil, chives, and oregano fills the air at this Italian restaurant, where bright flower arrangements and lots of brass accent the interior's dark beige-and-yellow color scheme. House favorites include *Robespierre alla moda della Bice* (sliced steak topped with arugula salad) and *costoletta di vitello impanata alla milanese* (breaded veal cutlet with a tomato salad). | 313¼ Worth Ave. | 561/835–1600 | fax 561/835–1002 | Jacket required | $9–$36 | AE, D, DC, MC, V.

Café L'Europe. Continental. One of the most popular and elegant restaurants in Palm Beach features sumptuous oak panelling, dim lighting, refined service, and elaborate flower bouquets. Full-length arched windows open to create alfresco dining. The traditional menu has Italian, French, and touches of fusion, as in the Maryland lump crab cake with mango chutney and gingered vegetables, or the roasted duck marinated in soy and orange with oriental rice, orange confit, mini bok choy, and sweet and sour sauce. The wine list—with nearly 2,000 labels—is almost globally unbeatable. There is live jazz weekends and a piano bar nightly. | 331 S. County Rd. | 561/655–4020 | www.cafeleurope.com | Reservations essential | Closed Mon. No lunch weekends | $25–$36 | AE, D, DC, MC, V.

Charley's Crab. Seafood. The interior of this popular restaurant is airy and spacious with fish tanks and great ocean views. The menu emphasizes seafood, with traditional dishes such as shrimp cocktail, raw bar selections, fresh fish, lobster, and crab cakes. The Sunday brunch is a winner. | 456 S. Ocean Blvd. | 561/659–1500 | www.muer.com | Reservations essential | $13–$28 | AE, D, DC, MC, V.

Chuck and Harold's. Continental. Some of the country's biggest celebrities power-lunch on the palm-lined Royal Poinciana Way sidewalk café. The pots of red and white begonias mounted on the sidewalk rail here decorate the people-watching spot. Specialties include Bahamian conch chowder, terrific hamburgers, an onion-crunchy gazpacho, grilled steaks, and tangy Key lime pie. A big blackboard lists daily specials and celebrity birthdays. | 207 Royal Poinciana Way | 561/659–1440 | www.muer.com | Reservations essential | Breakfast also available | $14–$31 | AE, D, DC, MC, V.

Janeiro. French. The chocolate soufflé at this supremely elegant French restaurant is topped with an edible 24-carat gold leaf. The china is Versace, the crystal Riedel, the table-cloths black-on-black. Entrées, brought to the table under silver domes, include Mediterranean bouillabaisse; lemon sole fillets with tomato, black squid and spinach lasagna; boneless rack of lamb stuffed with spinach and wild mushrooms wrapped in puff pastry; and a beef fillet with green peppercorn sauce. | 191 Bradley Pl | 561/659–5223 | Reservations essential | Closed Mon. No lunch | $28–$48 | AE, D, DC, MC, V.

THE KENNEDYS OF PALM BEACH

The Kennedy family didn't discover Palm Beach, but they may have done as much for the town's reputation for fame and glitz as its founder, Addison Mizner. Boston mayor John Fitzgerald took his daughter Rose to Palm Beach for the first time when she was a young girl, in 1911. When Rose married Joe Kennedy, she introduced him to the elite vacation spot, and a Kennedy family tradition was born.

In 1933, Joe and Rose bought La Guerida, a Mediterranean Revival–style house designed by Palm Beach planner Addison Mizner at 1095 N. Ocean Drive—it was originally built in 1923 for department store owner Rodman Wanamaker. Joe, Rose, and three generations of Kennedys would winter in this house, dubbed the "Kennedy Compound." Future President John Fitzgerald Kennedy frequented the soda fountain at Green's Pharmacy, at 151 N. County Rd., as a child. Later, as President, Kennedy would duck his secret service agents for Green's chocolate shakes.

During Kennedy's presidential years, the Palm Beach home was known as "The Florida White House," drawing visiting dignitaries, heads of state, and celebrities. Jackie Kennedy regularly shopped on ritzy Worth Avenue.

On nearby Peanut Island, the secret service leased land for a presidential bomb shelter, completed ten months before the Cuban Missile Crisis (though no construction records exist). In the late sixties, RFK and JFK were assassinated, but tragedy did not visit the Kennedy family in Palm Beach until 1984, when David Kennedy, Robert F. Kennedy's son, died of an overdose at the nearby Brazilian Court Hotel. In 1991, William Kennedy Smith, son of Jean Kennedy Smith, was accused of raping a woman on the compound lawn. Smith was acquitted, but his trial damaged his family's Palm Beach standing. They sold the property in 1995 for a reported $4.9 million.

© Corbis

Leopard Lounge and Restaurant. Contemporary. The fabrics, carpeting, and wall-treatments of this Chesterfield Hotel restaurant are leopard-inspired; they exist against a background of black and lacquer red. The eclectic menu is globally influenced, with such dishes as lobster ravioli with sauternes-ginger sauce, Stilton soufflé over baby field greens, and nori-wrapped, sesame-seared ahi tuna over buckwheat soba noodles. | 363 Cocoanut Row | 561/659–5800 | fax 561/659–6707 | $15–$37 | AE, DC, MC, V.

The Restaurant at Four Seasons. Contemporary. This restaurant in the Four Seasons resort offers trend-setting cuisine with southeast American and Caribbean specialties. Ocean views, soft, muted colors, and fresh floral arrangements add to an opulent dining experience. Choose from yellowtail snapper with cilantro and melon relish, lemon thyme and Valencia orange, guava-braised short ribs of beef with chayote and minted pea essence, or macadamia rack of lamb with boniato and pineapple mash. | 2800 S. Ocean Blvd. | 561/533–3750 | Reservations essential | Jacket required | Closed Mon.–Tues. May–mid-Nov. No lunch | $30–$42 | AE, D, DC, MC, V.

Ta-boó. Contemporary. This Worth Avenue landmark is divided into discreet salons: one resembles an elegant living room with a fireplace, another a courtyard, a third a skylit gazebo. The Tiki Tiki bar makes an excellent salon for local patrons. Dinner entrées include steaks, prime rib, frog's legs, and chicken and arugula from the grill. A favorite is white pizza with goat and mozzarella cheeses, pesto, and sweet roasted red peppers. | 221 Worth Ave. | 561/835–3500 | $9–$24 | AE, DC, MC, V.

Testa's. Steak. This restaurant has been family-operated since 1921, the same year Flagler's railroad opened Palm Beach to the world. There's a popular, family-friendly sidewalk café and a tropical garden dining room with a sliding roof. It's known for its double center-cut sirloin steak (for two), and seafood specials such as mahimahi, tuna, and snapper. There's also a good selection of Italian choices, like veal marsala sauteed in wine with peppers and mushrooms. Sunday brunch and a kids' menu. | 221 Royal Poinciana Way | 561/832–0992 | www.testasrestaurants.com | Reservations essential | Breakfast also available | $13–$25 | AE, D, DC, MC, V.

TooJay's. Delicatessen. Wisecracking waitresses keep things moving at this New York–style deli with a California-style setting. The menu includes matzo-ball soup, corned beef on rye, roast chicken, and a cake with five different types of chocolate. | 313 Royal Poinciana Way | 561/659–7232 | $7–$12 | AE, DC, MC, V.

Lodging

The Beachcomber. The Beachcomber is a pink, two-story facility with a long lawn sloping down to the beach. There are economic motel rooms, efficiencies, and oceanfront apartments with private patios. You can use the large salt-water pool, and the sun deck that faces the Atlantic. Prices are halved off-season. Some kitchenettes, some refrigerators. Cable TV. Pool. Beach. Laundry facilities. Free parking. | 3024 S. Ocean Blvd. | 561/585–4646 | fax 561/547–9438 | 50 rooms | $95–$250 | AE, D, MC, V.

Brazilian Court. This sprawling Gatsby-era hotel ushers you back to a time of old Hollywood glamour with its yellow-stucco Mediterranean facade, red-tiled roof, stone fountains, and half a block of manicured gardens. The rooms and suites are on a large scale not often seen in modern hotels. Pets get their own room service menu. Restaurant, bar. Outdoor pool. Beauty salon. Exercise room. Library. Parking (fee). | 301 Australian Ave. | 561/655–7740 or 800/552–0335 (Canada 800/228–6852) | fax 561/655–0801 | www.braziliancourt.com | 63 rooms, 40 suites | $325–$360 room, $450–$675 1–bedroom suite, $775 2–bedroom suite | AE, D, DC, MC, V.

★ **The Breakers.** This legendary resort dates to 1926 and sprawls over 140 wonderfully manicured acres, making it the last word in Palm Beach luxury. The seven-story Italian Renaissance–style villa is surrounded by Venetian chandeliers, gold-leaf hand-painted ceilings, Florentine fountains, ballrooms, and numerous gardens (including a children's secret garden). A $100 million renovation added a fabulous spa and beach club and modernized the rooms. 5 restaurants, 4 bars, picnic area, room service. In-room data ports, in-room safes, minibars. Cable TV. Pool, wading pool. Barber shop, beauty salon, massage. Driving range, 18-hole golf course, putting green, 14 tennis courts. Gym. Water sports, bicycles. Shops. Children's programs (ages 3–12), playground. Laundry facilities. Business services, parking (fee). | 1 S. County Rd. | 561/655–6611 or 888/273–2537 | fax 561/659–8403 | www.thebreakers.com | 569 rooms | $405–$650 | AE, D, DC, MC, V.

The Chesterfield Hotel. Two blocks from Worth Avenue is this elegant four-story, white stucco Mediterranean palace cum boutique hotel. Rooms are individually decorated in rich colors, with marble bathrooms, antique desks, and potted plants. The pool is surrounded by lush foliage and all public areas, from the library to the dining room, exhibit extravagant luxury. Restaurant, bar (with entertainment), room service. In-room data ports, in-room safes, some refrigerators. Cable TV, some in-room VCRs. Pool. Hot tub. Library. Laundry service. Business services, free parking. Pets allowed (fee). | 363 Cocoanut Row | 561/659–5800 or 800/243–7871 | fax 561/659–6707 | 55 rooms, 12 suites | $229–$329 room, $429–$529 1–bedroom suite, $699–$799 2–bedroom suite | AE, D, DC, MC, V.

The Colony. This legendary pale-yellow Georgian-style hotel is just off Worth Avenue and 100 yards from the beach. The villas on the property share a private pool and run up to 3,000 square ft in size. Cool and classic guest rooms have fluted blond cabinetry, matching draperies, and bedcovers in deep floral prints. After charity balls at the Breakers, this is the scene for glitterati. Restaurant, bar (with entertainment), room service. In-room data ports, in-room safes, microwaves, refrigerators. Cable TV. Pool. Driving range, putting green. Bicycles. Laundry facilities. Business services, parking (fee). | 155 Hammon Ave. | 561/655–5430 or 800/521–5525 | fax 561/832–7318 | www.thecolonypalmbeach.com | 63 rooms, 39 suites, 7 villas | $255–$795 | AE, D, DC, MC, V.

The Four Seasons Resort. This six-acre beachside hotel at the south end of town has a serene atmosphere buoyed by marble, art, fanlight windows, swagged drapes, chintz, and palms. Every guest room has a private balcony and full marble bathroom. A number of poolside and beachfront restaurants add to the sense of luxurious relaxation. 3 restaurants, bar (with entertainment), room service. In-room data ports, in-room safes, minibars, some microwaves, some refrigerators. Cable TV, some in-room VCRs (and movies). Pool. Beauty salon, hot tub, massage, sauna, spa, steam room. 3 tennis courts. Gym. Beach, water sports, boating, fishing, bicycles. Baby-sitting, children's programs (ages 3–13). Laundry service. Business services, parking (fee). Pets allowed. | 2800 S. Ocean Blvd. | 561/582–2800 or 800/432–2335 | fax 561/547–1374 | www.fourseasons.com | 197 rooms, 13 suites | $375–$695 | AE, D, DC, MC, V.

Heart of Palm Beach Hotel. This European-style hotel is three blocks north of Worth Avenue and a 3-min walk from the beach. The two low, pink buildings date from 1960 and 1975. Rooms are spacious and sunny, with private balconies and terraces. A garden pavilion is the ideal place for drinks or outdoor dining. Restaurant, 2 bars. Refrigerators. Cable TV. Pool. Bicycles. Laundry facilities. Business services. Pets allowed. | 160 Royal Palm Way | 561/655–5600 or 800/523–5377 | fax 561/832–1201 | 88 rooms | $259 | AE, D, MC, V.

Palm Beach Hawaiian Ocean Inn. This two-story wood motel attracts families with reasonable prices and a beachfront location. The staff is laid-back and knowledgeable. A wide wooden sundeck surrounds the free-form pool and looks out to the sand, where you can rent umbrellas and rafts. An adjoining restaurant includes a bar and patio, and has live music most of the week. Restaurant, bar, room service. In-room data ports, in-room safes, some kitchenettes, some microwaves, refrigerators. Cable TV, some in-room VCRs. Pool. Beach, fishing. Laundry facilities, laundry service. Free parking. Some pets allowed. | 3550 South Ocean Blvd. | 561/582–5631 | fax 561/582–5631 | www.palmbeachhawaiian.com | 50 rooms, 8 suites | $150–$160 room, $180–$320 | AE, D, DC, MC, V.

Palm Beach Hilton Oceanfront Resort. This five-story Hilton is in quiet location, 6 mi south of Worth Avenue, surrounded by antique shops and art galleries in the primarily residential neighborhood. There are oceanfront rooms, oceanfront dining, and an oceanfront patio bar, stressing the Atlantic location. Restaurant, bar. In-room data ports, mini-bars, some in-room hot tubs. Cable TV. Pool. Hot tub, massage. Beach, water sports. Laundry service. Business services, parking (fee). | 2842 S. Ocean Blvd. | 561/586–6542 or 800/916–2221 | fax 561/585–0188 | www.hilton.com | 134 rooms | $129–$399 | AE, D, DC, MC, V.

Palm Beach Historic Inn. Tucked behind Town Hall and a seaside residential block, you'll be surprised to discover this delightful B&B in the heart of downtown. Built in 1923 in a Victorian style, the inn is just a block from the beach and two blocks from Worth Avenue. The two-story building is built around a garden courtyard. Guest rooms tend toward the frilly, with lots of lace, ribbons, and scalloped edges; there are Victorian antiques and reproductions throughout. Complimentary Continental breakfast. Refrigerators. Cable TV, in-room VCRs. Beach. Laundry service. Business services, free parking. Pets allowed (fee). No smoking. | 365 S. County Rd. | 561/832–4009 | fax 561/832–6255 | www.palmbeachhistoricinn.com | 9 rooms, 4 suites | $185–$275 | AE, D, DC, MC, V.

Plaza Inn. The three-story 1939 Art Deco building that houses this B&B-style hotel is fronted in pale pink stucco with light green trim. It is a block from the beach, and four blocks north of Worth Avenue. The French- and Italian-style rooms come with antique and high-quality reproduction furniture. Some have four-poster beds, hand-blown Murano glass chandeliers and French draperies. At the back is a secret garden, tropical plants set around a fountain, and the outdoor pool and Jacuzzi with waterfalls and plenty of room for sunbathing. Bar, complimentary breakfast. In-room data ports, refrigerators. Cable TV, some in-room VCRs. Pool. Hot tub. Laundry service. Business services, free parking. Pets allowed. | 215 Brazilian Ave. | 561/832–8666 or 800/233–2632 | fax 561/835–8776 | www.plazainnpalmbeach.com | 50 rooms | $205–$305 | AE, MC, V.

PALM BEACH GARDENS

MAP 3, L8

(Nearby towns also listed: Jupiter, Lake Worth, Palm Beach, Palm Beach Shores, Riviera Beach, West Palm Beach)

This relaxed upscale residential community of 23,000 is well known for its high-profile golf complex, the PGA National Resort and Spa, as well as good restaurants. From here, it's a 15-min drive to the ocean.

Information: **Northern Palm Beaches Chamber of Commerce** | Suite 104, 1983 PGA Blvd., Palm Beach Gardens, 33408 | 561/694–2300 | www.npbchamber.com.

Attractions

Loggerhead Park Marine Life Center of Juno Beach. This educational center 5 mi north of town focuses on the natural history of sea turtles, with exhibits on sharks, whales, and shelling. The center was founded by Eleanor N. Fletcher, known locally as the "Turtle Lady of Juno Beach" for her work with the animals. | 1200 U.S. 1, Juno Beach | 561/627–8280 | Free | Tues.–Sat. 10–4, Sun. noon–3.

Moroso Motorsports Park. This track is a year-round home to weekly ¼-mi drag racing, 2¼-mi, 10-turn road racing, and monthly AMA motorcycle road racing. | 17047 Beeline Hwy. | 561/622–1400 | www.morosomotorsportspark.com | $10 | Wed., Fri. 6–11, Sat. 4:30–11.

ON THE CALENDAR

FEB.: *Artigras.* This three-day outdoor event, held during President's Day weekend each year since 1975, features a juried exhibition of fine arts and crafts. | 561/694–2300.

APR.: *PGA Senior Championship.* The oldest (no pun intended) event on the professional senior golf circuit is held, as it has been since 1937, at the PGA National Resort & Spa. | 561/627–2000 or 800/633–9150.

Dining

Arezzo. Italian. This Tuscan Grill in the PGA National Resort & Spa is both casual (you can come right off the links in shorts) and elegant (you'll feel equally comfortable wear a jacket and tie). The dining room has a contemporary look, with slate floors and comfortable banquettes surrounding an herb garden. Choose from a dozen pastas and pizzas or one of the chicken, fish, or steak dishes that rounds out the menu. | 400 Ave. of the Champions | 561/627–2000 | Closed Mon. No lunch | $11–$20 | AE, MC, V.

River House. American. This waterfront restaurant is known for its large portions, fresh, slice-it-yourself breads, and a big salad bar. Entrées include the daily catch, steaks, chops, and seafood-steak combo platters. Since the wait on a Saturday night in season can be long, you may want to reserve one of the upstairs tables, which are a bit more formal. | 2373 PGA Blvd. | 561/694–1188 | No lunch | $7–$26 | AE, MC, V.

Lodging

Doubletree Hotel-Palm Beach Gardens. This hotel is a 15-min trip from the airport, and near the local mall, waterpark, and movie theater. Rooms feature a town or lake view. The beach is a 5-min drive. Restaurant, bar, complimentary Continental breakfast. In-room data ports, some minibars. Cable TV, in-room VCRs. Pool, outdoor hot tub. Gym. Laundry facilities, laundry service. Free parking. | 4431 PGA Blvd. | 561/622–2260 or 800/222–8733 | fax 561/624–1043 | www.doubletree.com | 280 rooms | $160–$215 | AE, D, DC, MC, V.

Marriott Palm Beach Gardens. This 11-story hotel is geared toward the business traveler, with 10 conference rooms. It's within 5 mi of many area businesses. Restaurant, bar, room service. In-room data ports. Cable TV. Outdoor pool. Hot tub. Exercise equipment. Laundry service. Business services. | 4000 RCA Blvd. | 561/622–8888 or 888/236–2427 | fax 561/622–0052 | 279 rooms, 6 suites | $69–$149 | AE, D, DC, MC, V.

PGA National Resort & Spa. This lavishly landscaped resort has six outdoor therapy pools, called "Waters of the World," joined by a collection of imported mineral salt pools; there are 22 private treatments. The 240-acre nature preserve is home to five golf courses and croquet courts. If you prefer, you can stay in two-bedroom, two-bath cottages with fully equipped kitchens. 8 restaurants, 4 bars, room service. In-room dataports, in-room safes, some kitchenettes, some refrigerators, minibars, cable TV. 9 pools, lake. Hot tubs, saunas, spa. 5 18-hole golf courses, 19 tennis courts. Health club, racquetball, boating, bicycles. Video games. Baby-sitting. Laundry service. Business services. | 400 Ave. of the Champions | 561/627–2000 or 800/633–9150 | fax 561/622–0261 | www.pga-resorts.com | 279 rooms, 60 suites, 80 cottages | $119–$319 | AE, D, DC, MC, V.

PALM BEACH SHORES

MAP 3, L8

(Nearby towns also listed: Jupiter, Lake Worth, Lantana, Palm Beach, Palm Beach Gardens, Riviera Beach, West Palm Beach)

The small southern end of Singer Island—only 10 blocks long and 3 blocks wide—faces the Lake Worth Inlet and the Atlantic Ocean. The mostly residential community of about 1,000 people is known for its proximity to beaches and parks, but there are some recommendable dining options and two large resorts here.

Information: Northern Palm Beaches Chamber of Commerce | 1983 PTA Blvd., Suite 104, Palm Beach Gardens, 33408 | 561/694–2300 | www.npbchamber.com.

Attractions

John D. MacArthur Beach State Park. The state park includes 2 mi of beach, and one of the finest examples of subtropical coastal habitat in southeast Florida. To learn more about native trees and wildlife, visit the Kirby Nature Center (closed Tues.) inside the park. | 10900 Hwy. A1A, North Palm Beach | 561/624–6950 | www.dep.state.fl.us | $3.25 per vehicle | Daily 8–5:30.

Dining

Sailfish Marina Restaurant. Seafood. After a $5 million renovation in 2000, this town favorite looks sharp, with vaulted wood ceilings and floor-to-ceiling windows that fold open for instant alfresco dining on the waterfront. Try the Gold Coast bouillabaisse, cooked with fresh local clams, mussels, calamari, and lobster. Intracoastal sightseeing water taxis depart from the restaurant dock. | 98 Lake Dr. | 561/842–8449 | Reservations not accepted | No dinner Mon. | $11–$27 | AE, MC, V.

The Buccaneer. Seafood. Shrimp, scallops, and clams served on linguini with a marinara sauce is a typical dish at this upmarket restaurant on the Intracoastal Waterway. Besides seafood, the menu features veal, spareribs, and lamb. In winter, there is live classical guitar music. | 142 Lake Dr. | 561/844–3477 | Closed first week in Sept. | $16–$29 | AE, D, MC, V.

Lodging

Radisson Palm Beach Shores Resort. This six-story, pink, oceanfront resort with a Spanish-tiled roof is a top family choice. Each suite has a separate bedroom, living room with sofa bed, full kitchen, and dining area. The Beach Buddies Kids Club has great kids programs. There are plans to turn this resort into a time-share by 2003. Restaurant, bar, room service. Some kitchenettes, microwaves, refrigerators. Cable TV. Outdoor pool. Outdoor hot tub, massage, spa. Gym, volleyball. Beach, water sports. Shops, video games. Baby-sitting, children's programs (ages 2–12), playground. Laundry facilities, laundry service. | 181 Ocean Ave. | 561/863–4000 or 800/328–2289 | www.radisson.com | 257 suites | $249–$509 | AE, D, DC, MC, V.

Sailfish Marina. With 24 boats, this hotel boasts the largest sports fishing fleet in the southeastern U.S. In short, people come here to fish. The thirty rooms and efficiencies—and a simple, three-bedroom, two-bath house with a private back yard and fishing dock on the Intracoastal Waterway—open onto landscaped grounds. Restaurant, bar (with entertainment), picnic area. Some kitchenettes, some microwaves, some refrigerators. Cable TV. Outdoor pool. Massage. Hiking. Dock, water sports, boating, fishing. Shops. Baby-sitting, children's programs (ages 5–16). Laundry facilities, laundry service. | 98 Lake Dr. | 561/844–1724 | fax 561/848–9684 | www.sailfishmarina.com | 30 rooms, 1 house | $99–$150 | AP available | AE, MC, V.

Sand Dunes Shore Resort. If you're looking for a small, laid-back, stay on the beach, try these older family-oriented one- and two-bedroom units and efficiencies. Simply furnished rooms in brown single-level buildings come with sleeper sofas. Kitchenettes, microwaves, refrigerators. Cable TV. Outdoor pool. Outdoor hot tub. Beach, bicycles. Laundry facilities. | 165 Ocean Ave. | 561/848–2581 | fax 561/848–2665 | sdshores@aol.com | 12 units | $650–$900/week (3–day minimum stay) | AE, MC, V.

PANAMA CITY

MAP 3, D2

(Nearby towns also listed: Destin, Grayton, Panama City Beach, Seaside)

This city of 38,000 on St. Andrew Bay in the Florida Panhandle is fast becoming one of the state's top vacation spots, thanks to its great beaches. But the area also has museums, marinas, and an interesting downtown area with good restaurants. The Navy's Coastal Systems Station and Naval Diving and Salvage Training Center employ 2,500 residents.

Information: Bay County Chamber of Commerce | 235 West 5th St., Box 1850, Panama City, 32402–1850 | 850/785–5206 | www.panamacity.org.

Attractions

Deer Point Dam. Built in 1961 to create a fresh water source for Bay County, this low-level dam 8 mi northeast of town channels 550,000 gallons of water a day between North Bay and the 5,000-acre Deer Point Reservoir. A catwalk on the saltwater side is a perfect vantage point on the 1,440-ft-long wall of water that pours over the dam. The adjacent Ira Hutchinson County Park has picnic areas, and swimming is allowed in the lake. | 4405 Hwy. 2321 | 850/784–4065 | Free | Daily.

Junior Museum of Bay County. Interactive programs and exhibits focus on science, history and the environment. The Pioneer Homestead has authentic buildings that evoke northwest Florida's pioneer days. A boardwalk leads you along a nature trail through a hardwood swamp. | 1731 Jenks Ave. | 850/769–6128 | fax 850/769–6129 | www.jrmuseum.org | $3 (suggested donation) | Weekdays 9–4:30, Sat. 10–4.

Visual Arts Center of Northern Florida. This non-profit school and museum houses two galleries—the 2,100-square-ft Main Gallery and the 750-square-ft Higby Memorial Gallery—in addition to several studios. | 19 E. 4th St. | 850/769–4451 | $2 | Mon.–Tues., Thur. 10–8, Wed., Fri. 10–4, weekends 1–5.

ON THE CALENDAR

MAY: *Spring Festival of the Arts.* Paintings and sculpture are on exhibit in McKenzie Park. | 850/913–0537.
JULY–AUG.: *Faces & Facets.* An annual photography competition and exhibition organized by the Visual Arts Center of Northern Florida. | 850/769–4451.
AUG.: *Open Spearfishing Tournament.* Contestants scuba-dive and sling spears at barracuda, flounder, red snapper, and other indigenous species during this competition, which also includes lobster-catching, photography, and sea shell–collecting events. At Tyndall Yacht Club, Beacon Beach Marina, Tyndall Air Force Base. | 850/871–4946.
OCT.: *Bay County Fair.* You'll find crafts, food stands, and rides at this small event at the Fairgrounds. | 850/769–2645.

Dining

Canopie's. Contemporary. This casually elegant restaurant, with white shutters and pretty landscaped grounds, overlooks St. Andrew's Bay. Favorite dishes include the cashew-crusted breast of chicken and trio of grilled grouper, salmon and tuna with a citrus beurre blanc, complemented by a selection from their well-edited wine cellar. There is also a martini menu. | 4423 U.S. 98W | 850/872–8444 | No lunch | $13–$30 | AE, MC, V.

House of Chan. Chinese. Mandarin, Szechuan and Cantonese dishes, as well as American-style steaks, are cooked at this restaurant overlooking St. Andrew's Bay. Specialities include General Tso chicken and Szechuan shrimp. In the basement there is a Mongolian buffet barbecue, where the ingredients you choose are cooked to order. | 4425 U.S. 98W | 850/769–9404 | Reservations not accepted | No lunch | $8–$13 | AE, D, MC, V.

Lighthouse Marina. Seafood. Most tables at this casual dining spot are outdoors with umbrella-shaded views of marina sailboats. Soups here have won local awards: try the sea crab and chowder boat. Other dishes include blackened tuna with crawfish. The restaurant's bar serves happy hour specials from 3 to 6. | 5325 N. Lagoon Dr. | 850/235–0000 | $15–$20 | D, MC, V.

Lodging

Bayside Inn. One mi from the heart of Panama City and 8 mi from Gulf beaches, this motel has rooms that look out over St. Andrew's Bay. There is a private beach with a sand volleyball court. Rooms are designed in a nuevo-Caribbean style with brightly colored prints and island art work on the walls; most have patios that lead right out to the water. Restaurant, bar. In-room data ports, some kitchenettes. Cable TV. Pool. Volleyball, fishing, dock. Playground. Laundry facilities, laundry service. Free parking. Pets allowed (fee). | 711 West

Beach Dr. | 850/763–4622 or 800/900–7047 | fax 850/747–9522 | www.bestwestern-baysideinn.com | 97 rooms, 3 suites | $75–$115 | AE, D, DC, MC, V.

Comfort Inn and Conference Center. In the heart of the business district, this hotel sees mostly business travelers as guests. The Panama City Mall, across the street, houses many shops and restaurants. The two-story building was built in 1987, and is constantly being renovated. The landscaping around the pool is all semi-tropical, with a wide array of native Florida plants such as sago palms and crape myrtle. Complimentary Continental breakfast. In-room data ports, some microwaves, some refrigerators. Cable TV. Pool. Exercise equipment. Laundry facilities. Business services. | 1013 E. 23rd St. | 850/769–6969 or 888/769–9696 | fax 850/763–4353 | www.comfortinn.com | 105 rooms | $52–$99 | AE, D, MC, V.

Comfort Inn and Suites. Built in 1997, this two-story motel has exterior corridors. The Panama City Mall is 2 mi to the east, and Panama City Beach is 4 mi to the west. All within 2 mi are the FSU campus, Gulf Coast Community College, Gulf Coast Hospital and the Naval Base. The Hathaway Bridge is also nearby. Complimentary Continental breakfast. In-room data ports, some microwaves, some refrigerators. Cable TV. Pool. Business services, free parking. | 4128 U.S. 98W | 850/763–0101 or 800/228–5150 | fax 850/763–4234 | www.comfortinn.com | 30 rooms, 10 suites | $75–$105 | AE, D, DC, MC, V.

Country Inn. This small two-story hotel opened in 2000 and has hard-wood floors in the lobby, and is 15 min from the beach. There are nearby restaurants and malls. Complimentary Continental breakfast. Some in-room data ports, some microwaves, some refrigerators, some in-room hot tubs. Cable TV. Pool. Gym. Laundry service. | 2203 Harrison Ave. | 850/913–0074 | fax 850/913–9970 | www.countryinns.com | 53 rooms | $75–$110 | AE, D, DC, MC, V.

Holiday Inn Select. The six-story building is set in 14 acres of landscaped gardens. The interior has an Old New Orleans theme, with 103 ceiling fans in the lobby and restaurant. The hotel is across the street from the Panama City Mall, in the center of downtown Panama City, 10 mi northeast of Panama City Beach. Restaurant, bar. In-room data ports, some microwaves, some refrigerators, some in-room hot tubs. Cable TV, some VCRs. Indoor pool. Hot tub, sauna. Exercise equipment, volleyball. Laundry facilities, laundry service. Business services, airport shuttle. | 2001 N. Cove Blvd. | 850/769–0000 or 800/465–4329 | fax 850/763–3828 | www.basshotels.com | 173 rooms | $89 | AE, D, DC, MC, V.

Howard Johnson Resort Inn-Panama City. This three-story motel has a private white-sand beach with volleyball and a 475-ft pier for boat docking. The building sits on nicely landscaped property surrounded by oaks, magnolias, and palms. The staff will also arrange charter fishing and diving reservations for guests. Restaurant, bar, complimentary Continental breakfast. In-room data ports, cable TV. Pool. Volleyball, beach, dock, fishing. Airport shuttle, free parking. Some pets allowed (fee). | 4601 Hwy. 98W | 850/785–0222 or 800/406–1411 | fax 850/769–3472 | www.hojo.com | 80 rooms | $50–$79 | AE, D, DC, MC, V.

La Quinta Inn and Suites. Three-quarters of the guests at this motel are business travellers, attracted by the location in the middle of the business district and reasonable prices. The six-story stucco building has modern and comfortably furnished rooms. Panama City Beach is 10 mi away, and Panama City Mall is next door. In-room data ports, some microwaves, some refrigerators. Cable TV. Pool. Exercise equipment. Laundry facilities. Business services. Pets allowed. | 1030 E. 23rd St. | 850/914–0022 or 800/687–6667 | fax 850/914–0027 | 119 rooms | $74–$109 | AE, D, DC, MC, V.

Ramada Inn at St. Andrew's Bay. This two-story hotel is 10 mi from the beach and 4 mi from St. Andrew's State Park. In addition to the outdoor pool, recreational options include nearby fishing and golf. Restaurant, bar, room service. In-room data ports, some refrigerators. Cable TV. Outdoor pool. Exercise room. Laundry service. | 3001 West 10th St. | 850/872–1100 or 888/298–2054 | fax 850/872–1725 | www.ramada.com | 149 rooms | $59–$129 | AE, D, DC, MC, V.

PANAMA CITY BEACH

(Nearby towns also listed: Destin, Grayton Beach, Panama City, Seaside)

Panama City Beach's 27 miles of sugary white sand have made this one of the most popular beaches in the country. Spurred by live MTV broadcasts in past years, college students descend on the area in March and April to cruise Front Beach Drive, work on their tans, and do a lot of drinking. Souvenir shops and nightclubs cater to the madness. With minigolf courses, arcades, amusements parks, cheap motels, condos, bars, restaurants, and recreation areas, there's no reason for any of this to change soon. The clear Gulf water is often an amazing emerald green, and the shelling is good—as is the fishing, whether you cast your line off one of the long piers or charter a deep-sea boat trip.

Information: Panama City Beach Convention and Visitors Bureau | 17001 Panama City Beach Pkwy., Box 9473, Panama City Beach, 32417 | 850/234–6575 or 800/722–3224 | www.800pcbeach.com.

Attractions

County Pier. You can catch anything from shark to flounder from this 1,000-ft wooden fishing pier. Rod and reel rentals are available, and the adjacent beach offers sailing, windsurfing, kayaking, swimming, and a marine mammal attraction. | 12213 Front Beach Rd. | 850/236–1009 | Free | Daily.

Gulf World. This attraction about 5 mi west of town includes a rainforest filled with birds as well as regular sea lion, dolphin, and parrot shows, and daily shark and turtle feedings. There are dolphin interaction programs and behind-the-scenes park tours. | 15412 Front Beach Rd. (U.S. 98A) | 850/234–5271 | www.gulfworldmarinepark.com | $19 | Daily 9–3.

Lagoon Legend Golf Course. Play 36 holes on this challenging course at Marriott's Bay Point resort, with the eponymous lagoon waiting at the 16th hole. This par-72 course has one of the highest slope ratings in the country and is consistently ranked among the best in the state. Tee times can be booked two months in advance. | 100 Delwood Beach Rd. | 850/235–6937 or 800/476–4101 | Green fees | Daily dawn to dusk.

Miracle Strip Amusement Park. This state fair-style amusement park has a host of mechanical rides, including a roller coaster, Ferris wheel and log flume. Hours of operation change year to year, so call ahead. | 12000 Front Beach Rd. | 850/234–5810 or 800/538–7395 | www.miraclestrippark.com | $5; $15 all-ride pass | Open June–mid-Aug., daily 10:30–5:30; Apr.–May, weekends 10:30–5.

Museum of Man in the Sea. This museum displays artifacts and documents relating to diving history, with exhibitions on shipwrecks in the Panama City Beach waters. | 17314 Panama City Beach Pkwy. | 850/235–4101 | $5 | Daily 9–5.

Shipwreck Island. This 6-acre water park next door to Miracle Strip Amusement Park has plenty of speed slides and aquatic fun. The Tree Top Drop slide starts slowly, and then drops into a long, near-vertical plummet. White Knuckle River Ride is a fast-paced tube ride for entire families. | 12000 Front Beach Rd. | 850/234–0368 | www.shipwreckisland.com | $20 | Open June–mid-Aug., daily 10:30–5:30; Apr.–May, weekends 10:30–5.

★ **St. Andrews State Recreation Area.** This 1,260-acre park at the eastern tip of Panama City Beach includes beaches, pinewoods, and marshes. There are two campgrounds with 176 sites. At the beach, you can swim, snorkel, dive, go fishing, walk the nature trails along the dunes, or have a picnic. There are also concessions renting canoes and kayaks for exploration of the lagoon and the channels around it. You can board a ferry to Shell Island, a pristine barrier island where you can pick up shells. | 850/233–5140 | fax 850/233–5143 | www.dep.state.fl.us/parks | $4 per vehicle | Daily 8–sunset.

Zoo World. This 7½-acre zoological preserve is known for allowing you to get close to the animals. You can, for example, feed the giraffes and llamas. | 9008 Front Beach Rd. | 850/230–1065 | fax 850/230–8500 | $10.95 | Tues.–Sun. 9–5, closed Mon. in winter.

SIGHTSEEING TOURS/TOUR COMPANIES

Shell Island Trips. Narrated 3-hr boat tours, from Capt. Anderson's Marina at Grand Lagoon, take you to deserted Shell Island. Along the way, you can look for dolphins; on the way-back, the boat cruises around St. Andrew's Bay. | 5550 N. Lagoon | 850/234–3435 | $12 | Mar.–Oct., daily 9–noon and 1–4.

ON THE CALENDAR

JAN.–OCT.: *Greyhound Racing.* Eight dogs tear around the Ebro Greyhound Track in these pari-mutuel races 15 mi north of Panama City Beach on Route 79. Racing schedules change monthly. | 850/234–3943.

JULY: *Bay Point Billfish Tournament.* Anglers from around the world compete for cash prizes in one of the largest invitational fishing tournaments on the Gulf Coast. Thursday night's Captain's Party is said to be Bay County's best fete, peaking with the fleet departure at midnight. | 3824 Hatteras La. | 850/235–6911 | www.baypointmarina.net.

SEPT.: *Treasure Island Mackerel Tournament.* A Friday night party with steaks and live music kicks off this Treasure Island Marina fishing contest the last full weekend in the month. An awards ceremony and fish fry takes place Sunday evening. | 850/234–6533.

OCT.: *Indian Summer Seafood Festival.* This seafood and country music festival in Aaron Bessant Park features live music, arts and crafts vendors, a parade, a pageant, and fireworks. | 850/234–6575 or 800/722–3224.

Dining

Angelo's Steak Pit. Steak. This western-style restaurant has been around since 1957. The 8–32 oz USDA choice corn-fed steer steaks are cooked on an open-pit hickory fire. There are N.Y. strip sirloin, baby back ribs, filet mignon, and rib eye, among other choice cuts. | 9527 Front Beach Rd. (Hwy. 98) | 850/234–2531 | www.angelos-steakpit.com | Reservations not accepted | Closed mid-Oct.–mid Mar. Closed Sun. mid-Mar.–Memorial Day. No lunch | $13–$23 | AE, D, MC, V.

Billy's Steamed Seafood Restaurant, Oyster Bar and Crab House. Seafood. Roll up your sleeves and dig into some of the gulf's finest blue crabs and shrimp seasoned by Billy's special recipe. There's also homemade gumbo, crawfish, sandwiches, burgers, and a daily catch. | 3000 Thomas Dr. | 850/235–2349 | $7–$16 | AE, D, MC, V.

Boar's Head. Continental. This restaurant and tavern has an exterior that resembles an oversize thatch-roof cottage. Fireplaces, beam ceilings, heavy wooden furniture, and boar heads on the walls create the idea of a medieval English hunting lodge. People have come here since 1978 for prime rib, but blackened seafood and dishes such as pepper-seared tuna and grouper Sonoma cooked in wine are popular, too. | 17290 Front Beach Rd. (Hwy. 98) | 850/234–6628 | Reservations not accepted | Closed Dec. 21–26. No lunch | $14–$26 | AE, D, DC, MC, V.

Capt. Anderson's. Seafood. People wait up to 3 hours for a table at this fixture on the beach. The restaurant is right on the marina dock, so you can watch boats come in with the day's catch. Famous dishes here (the house cookbook has gone through five editions) include the World's Finest Seafood Platter (stuffed deviled crab, golden fried shrimp, scallops and fried fresh fish) and whole broiled genuine South African lobster tail. There's an extensive wine list (which stretches to $4,000 a bottle) and a good selection of char-broiled steaks and pastas. | 5551 N. Lagoon Dr. | 850/234–2225 | www.captandersons.com | Reservations not accepted | Closed Sun. and Nov.–Jan. No lunch | $11–$38 | AE, D, DC, MC, V.

Hamilton's. Seafood. Hamilton's provides waterfront dining in a gorgeous Victorian-style complex overlooking Grand Lagoon, with antiques, stained glass and hardwood floors. The 5,000-square-ft second level deck is a great place to watch the sunset. Specialities include shrimp scampi, blackened tuna, shellfish with angel hair pasta, chicken teriyaki, and BBQ chicken. A mesquite grill cooks steaks and certain seafood dishes. | 5711 N. Lagoon Dr. | 850/234–1255 | www.hamiltonspcbeach.com | Reservations not accepted | No lunch | $14–$21 | AE, D, MC, V.

Lodging

Boardwalk Beach Resort. This resort covers four beachfront hotels along a mile-long stretch of sand: Four Points by Sheraton, Howard Johnson, Gulfwalk, and Beachwalk inns. If shorter on glitz than some of its neighbors, it's better on price. Each has its own pool, and the hotels regularly sponsor social events. 8 restaurants, 3 bars. Some microwaves, some refrigerators. Cable TV. 4 outdoor pools. Playground. | 9450 South Thomas Dr. | 850/234–3484 or 800/224–4853 | fax 850/233–4369 | www.boardwalkbeachresort.com | 628 units | $189–$289 | AE, D, DC, MC, V.

Dolphin Inn Motel at Pineapple Beach. Part of Pineapple Resorts, along with its sister property Pineapple Villas, the three-story Dolphin Inn is right on the beach with a Tiki bar, sun deck, and barbecue and picnic areas beside the beachfront pool. All rooms have ocean views. Kitchenettes, microwaves, refrigerators. Cable TV, some in-rooom VCRs. Pool. Beach, watersports. Laundry facilities. Free parking. Pets allowed (fee). | 19935 Front Beach Rd. (Hwy. 98) | 850/234–1788 or 800/234–1788 | www.pineapplebeachresort.com | 30 rooms | $49–$125 | AE, D, MC, V.

★ **Edgewater Beach Resort.** Each of the luxurious one-, two-, and three-bedroom units at this towering, 110-acre condominium complex has a washer and dryer and accommodates up to eight people. The three oceanfront towers are each 12 stories high; two six-story towers and a complex of golf and tennis villas overlook the Gulf. An 11,000-square-ft Polynesian-style lagoon pool has landscaped islands, reflecting ponds, waterfalls, footbridges, and over 20,000 species of tropical plants. Rooms are elegantly furnished with rattan and wicker, and decorated in pastel shades. Restaurant, bar. Kitchenettes, microwaves, refrigerators. Cable TV, in-room VCRs. 11 pools. Massage, sauna, spa. 9-hole golf course, 6 tennis courts. Health club, volleyball. Beach, water sports. Video games. Children's programs (5–12). Laundry facilities. Free parking. | 11212 Front Beach Rd. (Hwy. 98) | 850/235–4044 or 800/874–8686 | fax 850/233–7591 | www.edgewaterbeachresort.com | 510 rooms | $143–$231 | AE, D, DC, MC, V.

Holiday Inn Sunspree Resort. All rooms have ocean views at this 14-story resort. The curving building embraces the white sands of the beach and a huge heated pool with waterfalls, lush tropical planting, and many palm trees. A wide range of activities includes karaoke, live entertainment, and a Polynesian torch lighting ceremony every night at sunset, led by the resort's native warrior, Jomon. 2 restaurants, 2 bars. In-room data ports, in-room safes, microwaves, refrigerators, some in-room hot tubs. Cable TV. Pool. Hot tub, sauna, steam room. Gym. Driving range, putting green. Exercise equipment. Beach. Children's programs (ages 3–18). Laundry facilities. Business services. | 11127 Front Beach Rd. (Hwy. 98) | 850/234–1111 or 800/633–0266 | fax 850/235–1907 | www.basshotels.com | 337 rooms, 4 suites | $199 | AE, D, DC, MC, V.

Marriott's Bay Point Resort Village. This pink stucco resort complex is nestled in a 1,100-acre wildlife preserve overlooking St. Andrew's Bay. The property exudes sheer elegance, with wing chairs, camel-back sofas, Oriental carpets in the common areas, and Queen Anne guest-room furnishings. Rooms have balconies and patios overlooking golf or bay. The marina has 200 slips. Activities include bonfires on the beach, dolphin encounter tours, and aqua-aerobics. 5 restaurants, 4 bars, picnic area. In-room data ports, in-room safes, some microwaves, refrigerators. Cable TV. 3 outdoor pools, 11 indoor pools, wading pool. Hot tubs. Driving range, 2 18-hole golf courses, putting green, 4 tennis courts. Basketball. Exer-

cise equipment. Beach, water sports, boating, fishing, bicycles. Children's programs (ages 5–12), playground. Laundry service. Business services. | 4200 Marriott Dr. | 850/234–3307 or 800/874–7105 | fax 850/236–6153 | www.marriottbaypoint.com | 277 rooms, 78 suites | $99–$179 | AE, D, DC, MC, V.

Moonspinner Condominium. All the apartments in this resort are privately owned condominiums, but owners rent them when unoccupied. Each unit has two or three bedrooms, two bathrooms, a dining room, living room, kitchen, washer, dryer, dishwasher, and two decks with waterfront views, and sleeps up to eight people. Each condo is individually decorated; yearly renovations ensure a high standard of comfort. The resort is directly on the beach, adjacent to St. Andrew's State Park. Kitchenettes, microwaves, refrigerators, some in-room hot tubs. Cable TV, in-room VCRs (with movies). Pool, wading pool. Hot tub. 2 tennis courts. Basketball, exercise equipment. Beach. Video games. Laundry facilities. Business services. | 4425 Thomas Dr. | 850/234–8900 or 800/223–3947 | fax 850/233–0719 | www.moonspinner.com | 122 units | $170–$240 | MC, V.

Port of Call. This hotel, with a five-story and a three-story building, stretches parallel to 200 ft of private beach. It's next to the Gulf Coast's longest fishing pier. There are beachfront rooms, efficiencies and apartments available; though simply furnished, all are comfortable. 2 restaurants, bar. In-room data ports, some kitchenettes, refrigerators. Cable TV. 2 pools. Volleyball, beach, watersports. Free parking. | 15817 Front Beach Rd. | 850/234–6666 or 800/659–1213 | fax 850/234–2601 | www.portofcallmotel.com | 12 rooms, 152 efficiencies | $54–$184 | AE, D, DC, MC, V.

PENSACOLA

MAP 3, B2

(Nearby towns also listed: Destin, Fort Walton Beach, Gulf Breeze, Pensacola Beach)

Andrew Jackson finalized the purchase of Florida from Spain in 1821 in what is now Pensacola. This city of 60,000 on the western edge of the Florida Panhandle is sometimes called the City of Five Flags, since it has flown Spanish, French, British, and Confederate flags, in addition to the Stars and Stripes, over the centuries. Historic districts such as Seville, Palafox and North Hill are full of museums, galleries, and restored buildings. The Pensacola Naval Air Station is home of the famous Blue Angels precision flying team. And, of course, nearby Gulf of Mexico beaches—Santa Rosa Island contains the beach towns of Pensacola Beach and Navarre Beach—draw sun lovers from all over the country.

KODAK'S TIPS FOR USING LIGHTING

Daylight
- Use the changing color of daylight to establish mood
- Use light direction to enhance subjects' properties
- Match light quality to specific subjects

Dramatic Lighting
- Anticipate dramatic lighting events
- Explore before and after storms

Sunrise, Sunset, and Afterglow
- Include a simple foreground
- Exclude the sun when setting your exposure
- After sunset, wait for the afterglow to color the sky

From *Kodak Guide to Shooting Great Travel Pictures* © 2000 by Fodor's Travel Publications

Information: **Pensacola Convention & Visitors Bureau** | 1401 E. Gregory St., Pensacola, 32501 | 850/434–1234 or 800/874–1234 | www.visitpensacola.com.

Attractions

Big Lagoon State Recreation Area. This coastal park consists of 712 acres of sandy beaches and salt marshes. An observation tower gives visitors a bird's-eye view of local wildlife including great blue herons and brown thrashers. Year-round camping is available, as well as swimming, fishing, boating, nature exhibits, guided walks, and campfire programs. | 12301 Gulf Beach Hwy. | 850/492–1595 | www.dep.state.fl.us/parks | $3.25 per vehicle | 8–sunset.

Blackwater River State Park. The Blackwater River is considered one of the purest sand-bottom rivers in the world. The dark tannin waters contrast with large, white sandbars throughout the 590-acre park. You can camp, fish, canoe, and hike along trails. | 7720 Deaton Bridge Rd. | 850/983–5363 | www.dep.state.fl.us/parks | $2 per vehicle | 8–sunset.

Civil War Soldiers Museum. This must-see for Civil War buffs contains artifacts on wartime medicine as well as an impressive collection of Civil War books. | 108 S. Palafox St. | 850/469–1900 | $5 | Tues.–Sat. 10–4:30.

Historic Pensacola Village. This collection of historic houses, landmark buildings, museum exhibits, and archaeological sites interprets West Florida's heritage from the days of Spanish explorers. The village is on Pensacola Bay, in the heart of the Seville district, one of the oldest historic districts in the Southeast U.S. One ticket gets you into all the sites in the complex, which is maintained by the Historic Pensacola Preservation Board. | 120 East Church St. | 850/595–5985 | fax 850/595–5989 | www.historicpensacola.org | $6 | Mon.–Sat. 10–4.

Charles Lavallé House. This rare example of French Creole colonial architecture was built in 1810, during Florida's second Spanish period, and is furnished with 18th- and 19th-century pieces recreating Pensacola frontier life. | 205 E. Church St. | 850/595–5985 | fax 850/595–5989 | www.historicpensacola.org | Included in park admission of $6 | Mon.–Sat. 10–4.

Dorr House. Built in 1871 by the widow of a lumber tycoon, this is a unique example of Greek Revival architecture. Similar to the Double Gallery houses of New Orleans, it is West Florida's last known remaining example of this style. The house is completely furnished with pieces dating from the 1850s through the 1890s, including hair wreaths fashioned from the locks of family members. | 311 S. Adams St. | 850/595–5985 | fax 850/595–5989 | www.historicpensacola.org | Included in park admission of $6 | Mon.–Sat. 10–4.

Museum of Commerce. Occupying a turn-of-the-20th-century brick warehouse, this museum in Historic Pensacola Village houses a reconstructed 1890s streetscape complete with a toy store, pharmacy, hardware, music store, and print shop. The print shop contains one of the most complete collections of antique presses and type in the Southeast. | 201 E. Zaragoza St. | 850/595–5985 | fax 850/595–5989 | www.historicpensacola.org | Included in park admission of $6 | Mon.–Sat. 10–4.

Museum of Industry. This museum is housed in a turn-of-the-20th-century brick warehouse across the street from the Museum of Commerce in Historic Pensacola Village. It houses a series of exhibits depicting the major early industries of West Florida: lumber, maritime, and shipping. | 200 E. Zaragoza St. | 850/595–5985 | fax 850/595–5989 | www.historicpensacola.org | Included in park admission of $6 | Mon.–Sat. 10–4.

T. T. Wentworth Jr. Florida State Museum. This elaborate yellow brick Renaissance Revival building was the height of architectural fashion when it was built as Pensacola's City Hall in 1907. Now renovated as part of Historic Pensacola Village, it houses innovative exhibits showcasing West Florida history, architecture, and archaeology. The third floor is dedicated to hands-on exhibits. | 830 Jefferson St. | 850/595–5985 | fax 850/595–5989 | www.historicpensacola.org | Included in park admission of $6 | Mon.–Sat. 10–4.

Fort Barrancas. This restored pre-Civil War fort maintained by the National Park Service is on the grounds of the Pensacola Naval Air Station. Originally built by Spaniards, it was completed in 1844 by the U.S. Army. The 65-acre grounds include a restored 1797 Water Battery, as well as a picnic area, a visitor center, a ½-mi nature trail through part of a 40-acre

PENSACOLA

INTRO
ATTRACTIONS
DINING
LODGING

pine and oak forest. | Taylor Rd. | 850/455–5167 | Free | Nov.–Mar., daily 8:30–3:45; Apr.–Oct., daily 9:30–5. Tours weekends at 2.

National Museum of Naval Aviation. This is one of the world's largest air and space museums, with 250,000 square ft of exhibit space and 27 acres of grounds, displaying over 100 planes representing aviation in the Navy, the Marine Corps, and the Coast Guard at the Pensacola Naval Air Station. There are also aviators' mementos of historic battles, flight logs, vintage instruments, flight gear, a gift shop, and an IMAX theater. | 1750 Radford Blvd. | 850/452–3604 | fax 850/452–3296 | www.naval-air.org | Free, IMAX $5.50 | Daily 9–5.

Old Pensacola Lighthouse. This is the tallest and oldest lighthouse in Florida, standing on a bluff overlooking Pensacola Pass, across Radford Blvd. from the National Museum of Naval Aviation. The 191-ft-high structure was built in 1858 after Andrew Jackson recommended that the area be used for a deep water naval station. Its first-order lens (a term designating its large size) was sent from Paris in 1924 and still guides ships and freighters. Climb the 178 steps to the top for a magnificent view. | Radford Blvd. | 850/455–2354 | Free | Memorial Day–Oct., Sun. noon–4.

North Hill Preservation District. British and Spanish fortresses once stood in this 50-block residential district where well-to-do families built homes paid for by the timber boom. Cannonballs are still unearthed here, evidence of the area's military history. The district has 500 or so homes in Queen Anne Victorian, Tudor, neoclassical, and Mediterranean styles. | North Hill.

Palafox Historic District. Palafox Street is the main artery of this district, the commercial and governmental hub of old Pensacola. Highlights include Pensacola's old movie palace, the Spanish Renaissance–style Saenger Theater, and the Bear Block, a former wholesale grocery with wrought-iron balconies, a legacy of the city's Creole past. | Palafox St. | 850/434–1234.

Pensacola Greyhound Track. Greyhound racing offers speedy dogs and the promise of fast money through pari-mutuel wagering. | 951 Dog Track Rd. | 850/455–8595 | $2 | Wed.–Sat. 7 PM–10:30 PM, weekends 11–4.

Pensacola Museum of Art. The permanent collection of this museum, housed in the former city jail, features contemporary paintings and 19th- and 20th-century art glass. Rotating shows often have an experimental, interdisciplinary, or post-modern bent, with works by children and local artists. | 407 S. Jefferson St. | 850/432–6247 | fax 850/469–1532 | www.artsnwfl.org/pma | $2 | Tues.–Fri. 10–5, Sat. 10–4.

Pensacola Naval Air Station. President John Quincy Adams and Secretary of the Navy Samuel Southard selected this sight in 1825 to build a Navy Yard. The Naval Air Station is now most famous as the home of the Navy's precision flying team, the Blue Angels. In 1971, NAS was picked as the headquarters site for CNET (Chief of Naval Education and Training), a new command which controls all Navy education and training. Today, the complex employs more than 9,600 military and 6,800 civilian personnel. | Navy Blvd. | 850/452–2311 | www.cnet.navy.mil/naspcola | Free | Daily.

St. Michael's Cemetery. This late 18th-century cemetery contains 3,000 marked graves and monuments. | 6 S. Alcaniz St. | Free | Daily, dawn to dusk.

Scenic Highway. Atop the bluffs between Milton and Pensacola, Santa Rosa Island and Escambia Bay spread before you along this 20-mi stretch of U.S. 90. The best views are mostly between Nine Mile Rd. and 17th Ave.

ON THE CALENDAR

MAY: *Florida SpringFest.* Billed as "Pensacola's musical celebration," the annual four-day SpringFest on Spring St. has become the Gulf Coast area's premiere musical event, boasting an eclectic roster of well-known performers. | 850/469–1069.

JUNE: *Fiesta of the Five Flags.* Florida's oldest and largest festival honors Spanish Conquistador Don Tristan de Luna, who founded Pensacola in 1559. There are parades, treasure hunts, and a visit by a Spanish galleon. | 800/874–1234 or 850/434–1234.

OCT.: *Pensacola Interstate Fair.* The largest event on the Gulf Coast includes 11 days of shows, games, rides, and food, off Mobile Highway. | 850/944–4500.

NOV.: *Blue Angels Homecoming Air Show.* The Blue Angels fly at dozens of air shows all over the United States and Canada every year. At this November event in Pensacola, the group shows off its graceful aerodynamics at its home base Naval Air Station. | 850/452–2583 or 850/452–7469.

NOV.: *Great Gulfcoast Arts Festival.* Along with performing arts events and folk arts displays, this festival in Seville Square features one of the top juried art shows in the southeastern U.S. Over 2,000 artists exhibit paintings, sculpture, pottery, jewelry, photography, and mixed media. | 850/432–9906.

DEC.: *Pensacola Christmas Parade.* More than 50,000 people gather downtown to watch this parade of marching bands and floats ablaze in Christmas lights. | 850/434–5371.

Dining

China Star. Chinese. Families love this restaurant for its all-day buffet of Mandarin and Szechuan dishes. | 505 E. Brent La. | 850/477–6163 | Reservations not accepted | $6–$16 | AE, D, DC, MC, V.

Grouper Seafood and Steak. Seafood. This nautical-theme restaurant has many influences; dishes display Southern, Cajun, Italian, and Greek touches. Grouper is popular and comes cooked in many ways. The Greek-style grouper is baked and broiled with basil and oregano and topped with feta cheese, shrimp, crabmeat, tomatoes and olives. There is a Sunday brunch. | 830 E. Gregory St. | 850/438–3141 | Breakfast also available | $10–$19 | AE, D, DC, MC, V.

★ **Jamie's Restaurant.** French. An 1879 framed cottage in historic Pensacola was converted into this tiny restaurant. The cuisine is haute French, with light sauces and innovative flavor pairings. Start with a platter of smoked salmon and asparagus with a Dijon dill vinaigrette, or sautéed shrimp served on avocado with Cajun remoulade. For the main course, try roasted veal chop with shiitake mushroom and Madeira veal stock sauce or the black walnut-crusted rack of New Zealand lamb with caramelized pears and a port wine reduction sauce. | 424 E. Zaragoza St. | 850/434–2911 | www.jamies.pensacola.com | Reservations essential | Closed Mon. No lunch Sun. | $20–$30 | AE, MC, V.

McGuire's Irish Pub and Brewery. American. Care for a $100 hamburger? It comes with caviar and champagne. If cheddar will do, the price is much closer to fast-food. You can try the usual Irish pub fare: steaks, ribs, chicken, fish, sandwiches and burgers. With the money you'll save you can add to the collection of over 225,000 signed dollar bills on the walls. | 600 E. Gregory St. | 850/433–6789 | www.mcguiresirishgifts.com | Reservations not accepted | $9–$25 | AE, D, DC, MC, V.

Mesquite Charlie's. Steak. A huge selection of paintings and sculptures with a Southwestern, desert theme decorates this Western-style establishment. All the steaks are grilled over mesquite. The cowboy (24 oz) and cowgirl (16 oz) steaks are the most popular, and the seafood platter with fried oysters, scallops, shrimp, and fish also goes down well. | 5901 N. West St. | 850/434–0498 | $9–$17 | AE, D, MC, V.

1912 Restaurant. Seafood. A converted 1912 train station houses this restaurant, which adjoins the soaring modern glass block of the Pensacola Grand Hotel. The chandeliers, flowers, candles, low classical music, and dim lighting create a romantic atmosphere. Specialities include steak, and a fish filet broiled in white wine and butter, topped with crab and shrimp in a béarnaise sauce. | 200 E. Gregory St. | 850/433–3336 | Breakfast also available | No dinner Sun. | $12–$20 | AE, D, DC, MC, V.

Skopelos On the Bay. Seafood. This 1959 restaurant, named after the Greek isle of the owners' birth, specializes in seafood, steak, veal, and lamb. A Grecian platter comes with moussaka, dolmades (stuffed vine leaves), spanakopita, lamb, and Greek salad. Scamp—a flaky, white deep water fish—is served with lump local blue crabmeat in a cream reduction. Grouper margarita comes breaded with a margarita sauce. Take in ocean views from the backyard patio deck, which rests 25 ft above the bay. | 670 Scenic Hwy. | 850/432–6565 | Closed Sun.–Mon. Lunch Fri. only | $14–$20 | AE, D, MC, V.

Lodging

Best Western Village Inn. This motel occupies four buildings around a courtyard pool. Some rooms have balconies or patios. The motel is across the street from West Florida Hospital, 4 mi from the airport, and 2 mi from West Florida University. Complimentary Continental breakfast. In-room data ports, some microwaves, some refrigerators. Cable TV. Pool. Laundry service. Business services. | 8240 N. Davis Hwy. | 850/479–1099 or 888/879–3578 | fax 850/479–9320 | www.bestwestern.com | 142 rooms | $59–$87 | AE, D, DC, MC, V.

Civic Inn. This white-stucco building with grey columns and royal blue doors had its origins as a 1950's travel lodge. It is a 10-min walk to Pensacola's historic district, and convenient to the trolley system, which you can use to get to museums and sights. Some refrigerators, some microwaves. Cable TV. Pool. Laundry facilities. Free parking. Some pets allowed (fee). | 200 N. Palafox St. | 850/432–3441 | fax 850/438–5956 | 48 rooms | $40–$68 | AE, D, MC, V.

Comfort Inn N.A.S.-Corry. This three-building motel is the entrance to Corry Field military base. The airport is 7 mi away, and the Historic District is 3 mi away. There are nearby hiking and jogging trails, fishing, and tennis facilities. Bar (with entertainment), complimentary Continental breakfast. In-room data ports, microwaves, refrigerators. Cable TV. Pool. Laundry facilities. Business services. Pets allowed (fee). | 3 New Warrington Rd. | 850/455–3233 or 800/554–3206 | fax 850/453–3445 | www.comfortinn.com | 101 rooms | $70 | AE, D, DC, MC, V.

Days Inn. This motel was renovated in 2000. It's an easy walk to restaurants, museums, art galleries, and shops and two blocks from the trolley stop. Restaurant, bar, room service. In-room data ports. Outdoor pool. Beauty parlor. Baby-sitting. Laundry service. Pets allowed. | 710 N. Palafox St. | 850/438–4922 or 800/544–8313 | fax 850/438–7999 | 146 rooms | $58–$100 | AE, MC, V.

Econo Lodge. This small, motel is 10 mi from the beach, 2 mi from University Mall, and 5 miles from the University of West Florida. Rooms, decorated in a contemporary style, come with either a queen or king bed. Complimentary Continental breakfast. Cable TV. Pool. Laundry facilities. Free parking. Some pets allowed (fee). | 7194 Pensacola Blvd. | 850/479–8600 or 800/553–2666 | fax 850/479–8600 | 60 rooms | $30–$49 | AE, MC, V.

Fairfield Inn by Marriott. This motel is on the same block as University Mall, which has restaurants, shops, and a movie theater. West Florida University is 3 mi away, Marcus Point and Scenic Hills golf courses are 5 mi away, and the airport is 5 mi away. Complimentary Continental breakfast. In-room data ports, some microwaves, some refrigerators. Cable TV. Indoor pool. Business services. | 7325 N. Davis Hwy. | 850/484–8001 or 800/228–2800 | fax 850/484–6008 | www.marriott.com | 55 rooms, 8 suites | $62 | AE, D, DC, MC, V.

Hampton Inn. Palm trees rise around this three-story hotel at the entrance to University Mall, which has 80 shops as well as a food court and movie theater. To reach it from I–10, get off at exit 5 onto Highway 291, turn left at the bottom of the ramp and go on for ½ mi. The hotel is in the primary business district of Pensacola. The pool is shared with the Holiday Inn next door. Complimentary Continental breakfast. In-room data ports. Cable TV. Pool. Laundry service. Business services, airport shuttle. | 7330 Plantation Rd. | 850/477–3333 or 800/426–7866 | fax 850/477–8163 | www.hamptoninn.com | 124 rooms | $65–$99 | AE, D, DC, MC, V.

Holiday Inn Express. Just 1 mi south of exit 5 on I–95 is this basic motel fronting the Marcus Pointe Golf Course. The rooms are basic but comfortable with standard chain-motel decor. Complimentary Continental breakfast. In-room data ports, some microwaves, some refrigerators. Cable TV. Pool. Laundry facilities. Business services. | 6501 Pensacola Blvd. (Hwy. 29) | 850/476–7200 or 800/465–4329 | fax 850/476–1277 | www.basshotels.com | 214 rooms | $60–$100 | AE, D, DC, MC, V.

Holiday Inn University Mall. Next door to the Hampton Inn, this two-story, four-building motel is also at the entrance to the University Mall in a commercial/business district of Pensacola. The motel offers reliable if unshowy quality, comfortable and clean rooms with nondescript decor, and of course convenient shopping opportunities. The hotel wraps around a shaded courtyard containing the pool. Restaurant, bar (with entertainment). In-room data ports. Cable TV. Pool. Laundry facilities. Business services, airport shuttle. | 7200 Plantation Rd. | 850/474–0100 or 800/465–4329 | fax 850/477–9821 | www.basshotels.com | 150 rooms | $49–$99 | AE, D, MC, V.

Howard Johnson Express Inn. This is a no-frills motel with basic, comfortable rooms, and a small breakfast area. The motel is 2 mi from downtown Pensacola and 1 mi from the Navy base. Complimentary Continental breakfast. Microwaves, refrigerators, cable TV. Pool. | 4126 Mobile Hwy. | 850/456–5731 or 800/406–1411 | fax 850/456–5731 | www.hojo.com | 67 rooms | $30–$100 | AE, D, DC, MC, V.

Howard Johnson Inn. This motel is a step up in comfort from the Howard Johnson Express in town. Some guest rooms come with kitchenettes and pool views. The motel is ¼ mi south of I–10, off exit 3A, about 12 mi from the beach. Restaurant, complimentary Continental breakfast, room service. In-room data ports, in-room safes, microwaves, refrigerators. Cable TV. Pool. Laundry service. Free parking. Pets allowed (fee). | 6911 Pensacola Blvd. | 850/479–3800 or 800/406–1411 | www.hojo.com | 97 rooms, 24 suites | $45–$70 | AE, D, DC, MC, V.

La Quinta Inn. Like most properties in the La Quinta chain, this three-story motel has a white exterior with teal trim, and a sharp, vaguely southwestern-style look. The beach and Historic District are 7–8 mi away; the airport is 3 mi from the motel. Complimentary Continental breakfast. In-room data ports, some microwaves, some refrigerators. Cable TV. Pool. Laundry facilities. Pets allowed. | 7750 N. Davis Hwy. | 850/474–0411 or 800/531–5900 | fax 850/474–1521 | www.laquinta.com | 128 rooms, 2 suites | $59–$72 | AE, D, DC, MC, V.

★ **New World Landing.** This charming B&B-style inn is two blocks from Pensacola Bay in Pensacola's historic district. The five periods of the city's past are reflected by antiques and reproductions in Spanish, French, early American, antebellum, and Victorian styles. Individually decorated rooms are named after historical figures from Pensacola history. The two-story inn, a former box factory, is over 100 years old. If the photos of famous guests displayed in the front hall are any indication, the inn has attracted a bevy of celebrities over the years. Complimentary Continental breakfast. In-room data ports, cable TV. Business services. | 600 S. Palafox St. | 850/432–4111 | fax 850/432–6836 | www.newworldlanding.com | 14 rooms, 1 suite | $75 room, $125 suite | AE, MC, V.

Pensacola Grand Hotel. You enter this downtown hotel through the restored 1912 Louisville & Nashville train depot. The hotel still has old railway signs, ticket and baggage counters. Twenty-first century rooms are in the attached 15-story modern tower; some have huge picture windows and wooden spiral staircases. Restaurant, bars. In-room data ports, some refrigerators. Cable TV. Pool. Exercise equipment. Library. Laundry facilities. Business services, airport shuttle. Pets allowed (fee). | 200 E. Gregory St. | 850/433–3336 or 800/348–3336 | fax 850/432–7572 | www.pensacolagrandhotel.com | 201 rooms, 11 suites | $90–$100 | AE, D, DC, MC, V.

Pensacola Suites. This inexpensive, family-owned all-suites hotel opened in 2000 with rooms in soothing peach, blue, and crimson touches. All rooms come with full kitchens, plus coffee machines, ironing boards, and pull-out love seats. The hotel is 1 mi off I–10 at exit 3A. Complimentary Continental breakfast. In-room data ports, kitchenettes, minibars, microwaves, refrigerators, some in-room hot tubs. Cable TV. Pool. Exercise equipment. Laundry facilities. Business services. | 6703 Pensacola Blvd. | 850/484–5451 | fax 850/484–4327 | 50 rooms | $50–$70 | AE, D, DC, MC, V.

Pensacola Victorian. This blue-grey Queen Anne home, complete with a turret and wraparound porch, was built for the ship captain William Northup, who later founded Pensacola's first philharmonic orchestra. The B&B has hardwood floors and paneling throughout. The homemade breakfast includes fresh fruit salad, waffles, omelets, or quiche and homemade breads. The inn is a 5-min walk from downtown. Complimentary breakfast. Cable TV. Kitchenettes. No room phones. No kids. No smoking. | 203 W. Gregory St. | 850/434–2818 | fax 850/429–0675 | www.pensacolavictorian.com | 4 rooms | $75–$120 | AE, MC, V.

Ramada Inn Bayview. This hotel, off I–10 at exit 6, 5 mi from downtown, contains several buildings surrounding a landscaped courtyard with a pool and gazebo. The hotel, on a cliff overlooking the bay, offers Atlantic views from the restaurant and lounge. Rooms do not have views. Restaurant, bar (with entertainment). Complimentary Continental breakfast. In-room data ports, some microwaves, some refrigerators. Cable TV. Pool. Hot tub. Exercise equipment. Laundry facilities, laundry service. Business services, airport shuttle. Pets allowed. | 7601 Scenic Hwy. | 850/477–7155 or 800/212–1212 | fax 850/477–7198 | www.ramada.com | 150 rooms | $70–$78 | AE, D, DC, MC, V.

Residence Inn by Marriott. Units in this all-suites, two-story facility come with a kitchen and a fireplace, and sleep up to six people. The hotel is on the same block as University Mall, in a business and commercial area of Pensacola. It's good for families interested in Pensacola's historical attractions. Complimentary Continental breakfast. In-room data ports, kitchenettes. Cable TV. Pool. Hot tub. Laundry facilities, laundry service. Business services. | 7230 Plantation Rd. | 850/479–1000 or 800/331–3131 | fax 850/477–3399 | www.marriott.com | 64 suites | $97–$125 | AE, D, DC, MC, V.

Shoney's Inn and Suites. This motel curls around a pool courtyard. There are rooms and two kinds of suites, which come with a refrigerator and microwave. It is 8 mi from downtown, off I–10 at exit 5, within walking distance of University Mall. A Shoney's restaurant is next door. Complimentary Continental breakfast. In-room data ports, some microwaves, some refrigerators. Cable TV. Pool. Laundry facilities, laundry service. Airport shuttle. Pets allowed (fee). | 8080 N. Davis Hwy. | 850/484–8070 or 800/222–2222 | fax 850/484–3853 | www.shoneysinn.com | 111 rooms, 4 suites | $67–$79 | AE, D, DC, MC, V.

The Yacht House Bed & Breakfast. This B&B is just west of downtown, across from the prestigious Pensacola Yacht Club, and a 5-min walk to Sanders Beach. Each of the three upper level rooms—the Shanghai, Nairobi, and Sahara suites—has an outdoor hot tub on a private deck. Guests can borrow a telescope for stargazing, or test their fortune with a daily tarot reading. Complimentary Continental breakfast. In-room data ports, in-room safes, some refrigerators, in-room hot tubs. Cable TV, some in-room VCRs. Pond. Gym. Laundry facilities. Pets allowed (fee). | 1820 Cypress St. | 850/433–3634 | www.yachthouse.com | 6 rooms | $65–$125 suites | AE, D, MC, V.

PENSACOLA BEACH

MAP 3, B2

(Nearby towns also listed: Destin, Fort Walton Beach, Gulf Breeze, Pensacola)

Six years before the founding of St. Augustine, America's oldest city, Spanish explorer Don Tristan de Luna established the first settlement in North America, on Santa Rosa Island. The island towns of Pensacola Beach (pop. 5,000) and Navarre Beach (pop. 2,000) are separated by pristine beaches that constitute part of Gulf Islands National Seashore. A 40-mi bicycle loop finished in 2000 gives you the complete tour of the island. The finely ground, dazzling white quartz sand along the shore will make you want to sing, as it audibly squeaks beneath your feet.

Information: **Pensacola Beach Chamber of Commerce** | 735 Pensacola Beach Blvd., Pensacola Beach, 32561 | 800/635–4803 | www.pensacolabeachchamber.org.

Attractions

Gulf Islands National Seashore. While the national seashore includes 150 miles of coastline between Fort Walton Beach and Ocean Springs, Mississippi, the area that separates

Pensacola Beach and Navarre Beach consists of 7 mi of virgin, white-sand beach. The Opal Beach Day Use Area has 20 picnic shelters. Nature trails take you via wooden boardwalks over marshland waters. Special tours include full moon walks. | Headquarters, 1801 Gulf Breeze Pkwy., Gulf Breeze | 850/934–2600 | www.nps.gov/guis | $6 per vehicle | 8–sunset.

Fort Pickens. At the western end of Santa Rosa Island is this area of the Gulf Islands National Seashore. A once-proud fort constructed in 1834 overlooks lush beaches, bicycle paths, and a fishing pier inside this park. A Union outpost during the Civil War, Geronimo and other Apaches were held at the fort in 1886. Guided tours are weekdays at 2 PM and weekends at 11 and 2. | 1400 Fort Pickens Road | 850/934–2623 | www.nps.gov/guis | $6 per vehicle | Open daily 8–sunset.

USS *Massachusetts*. You can find this 1896 battleship—the oldest such American vessel—26 ft under the Gulf of Mexico in the Fort Pickens State Aquatic Preserve, 1½ south-south-west of Pensacola Pass. Following its decommission in 1919, the USS *Massachusetts* was used for artillery practice. Today, the ship is an artificial reef popular with divers, its 350-ft hulk partially buried in a white sandy bottom. | 850/434–1234 | www.dos.state.fl.us/dhr/bar.

ON THE CALENDAR

FEB.–MAR.: *Mardi Gras*. A big street parade along Via de Luna highlights this downtown festival, held the Sunday before Mardi Gras Tuesday. | 850/473–8858.
JULY: *Red White and Blues Week*. Fireworks kick off this 10-day summer celebration that includes concerts on the beach and aerobatics by the Blue Angels and the Army's Golden Knights parachute team. | 850/932–1500 or 932–2259.
JULY: *Pensacola Beach Air Show*. On a weekend in the middle of July, 200,000 to 300,000 people gather to watch parachuting, aerial fly-bys and stunt plane aerobatics along the shore. The main draw is the Blue Angels, the Navy's precision jet team, who are based in the nearby Pensacola Naval Air Station. | 800/635–4803.

Dining

Bayside Grill. Cajun/Creole. This beachfront grill attracts locals starting at 6:30 each morning for breakfast. At night, top choices include coconut-breaded shrimp. | 14 Via de Luna | 850/932–9898 | $7–$21 | AE, MC, V.

Chan's Gulfside. Seafood. This restaurant has a café, a saloon overlooking Casino Beach, and two indoor dining areas. The casual downstairs area is decorated with stuffed fish. Popular entrée choices include grouper, mahimahi, and a BBQ tuna sandwich cooked to order. | 2½ Via de Luna | 850/932–3525 | Reservations not accepted | $10–$20 | AE, D, DC, MC, V.

Flounder's Chowder and Ale House. Seafood. Dining rooms at this restaurant have maps under glass on the tables, and lots of antiques—the owner is an avid collector. One room has a library theme, complete with a fireplace, and another is decorated like a wine cellar. The seafood platter comes with grouper, shrimp, and oysters, and the stuffed flounder is served with peppers, celery, onions, and shrimp topped with Monterey Jack. There is a pirate ship playground for kids and live entertainment nightly April through October. | 800 Quietwater Beach Rd. | 850/932–2003 | Reservations not accepted | $15–$18 | AE, D, DC, MC, V.

Jubilee. Seafood. Topside is the formal half of this restaurant complex, with stained glass, antiques, 1930s photographs of Pensacola, and a view of Quietwater Sound. The menu here has dishes such as smoked gouda shrimp, Cajun-fried artichoke hearts, carrot raisin Ahi, and soft shell crabs with honey-roasted nuts. Downstairs, a more casual café called Beachside serves sandwiches of such items as BBQ chicken and fried oysters. There's live entertainment weekends. | 400 Quietwater Beach Rd. | 850/934–3108 | www.jubileefun.com | Beachside: reservations not accepted. Topside: reservations essential | $7–$25 | AE, D, DC, MC, V.

Peg Leg Pete's Oyster Bar. Seafood. This funky, fun place—there's a volleyball court and gift shop on the ground level—overlooks LaFitte Cove Marina. You can bring your boat and dock behind the restaurant. Try the fried grouper or the chargrilled mahimahi. There is a kids' menu. | 1010 Fort Pickens Rd. | 850/932–4139 | $5–$18 | AE, MC, V.

Lodging

Best Western Resort Pensacola Beach. This modern, two-building complex on the beach is in the middle of the Pensacola Beach nightlife scene. On the bay side, you can go parasailing, and rent boats and jet skis. Each room comes with a full kitchen, 27-inch TV, coffee makers, hair dryers, and ironing boards. Complimentary Continental breakfast, bar. In-room data ports, minibars, microwaves, refrigerators. Cable TV. 2 pools. Beach, boating. Playground. Laundry facilities. Business services. | 16 Via De Luna, Pensacola Beach | 850/934–3300 or 800/934–3301 | fax 850/934–4366 | www.bestwestern.com | 123 rooms | $119–$159 | AE, D, DC, MC, V.

Hampton Inn Pensacola Beach. This hotel in pink and blue was built in 1995. Most rooms have a gulf view and are rather large. The hotel is within walking distance of many restaurants and shops. Complimentary Continental breakfast, room service. In-room data ports, some minibars, microwaves, refrigerators. Cable TV. 2 outdoor pools. Gym. Beach. Laundry facilities, laundry service. | 2 Via de Luna, Pensacola Beach | 850/932–6800 or 800/320–8108 | fax 850/932–6833 | www.hamptonbeachresort.com | 181 rooms | $129–$169 | AE, D, DC, MC, V.

Perdido Sun. This high-rise is the perfect expression of high-rise living. The hotel offers the choice of one-, two-, and three-bedroom decorator-furnished units. All have seaside balconies with wonderful water views and fully equipped kitchens. Maid service is optional. Kitchenettes, microwaves, refrigerators, some in-room hot tubs. Cable TV, in-room VCRs. Indoor pool, outdoor pool. Outdoor hot tub, spa, sauna, steam room. Health club, beach, volleyball. Video games. Laundry facilities. Business services. | 13753 Perdido Key Dr., Pensacola Beach | 850/492–2390 or 800/227–2390 | fax 850/492–4125 | www.perdidosun.com | 93 units | $90–$150 | AE, D, MC, V.

Sabine Yacht and Racquet Club. This family-run, high-rise offers balconies that run the length of each one- or two-bedroom unit. Rooms have views of Little Sabine Bay in back or the Gulf of Mexico in front, across the street. All units come with full-size kitchen and sleeper sofas. Picnic area. Kitchenettes, microwaves, refrigerators, some in-room hot tubs. Cable TV. Outdoor pool. Sauna. 2 tennis courts. Exercise equipment. Beach, dock, boating, fishing. Laundry facilities. | 330 Ft. Pickens Rd. | 850/932–7290 or 800/343–0344 | fax 850/932–7647 | www.sabinecondo.com | 81 units | $155–$190 | AE, D, MC, V.

The Dunes. All rooms face the Gulf of Mexico with private balconies in this eight-story, U-shape complex directly on the beach. Except for four one-bedroom penthouses, all units are simple studios. Restaurant, bar (with entertainment), room service. In-room safes, some minibars, some refrigerators, some in-room hot tubs. Cable TV. Outdoor pool. Massage. Beach, water sports. Baby sitting. Laundry service. | 333 Fort Pickens Rd., Pensacola Beach | 850/932–3536 or 800/833–8637 | fax 932–7088 | www.theduneshotel.com | 76 rooms | $150 | AE, D, MC, V.

PERRY

MAP 3, G2

(Nearby towns also listed: Live Oak, Tallahassee)

The Florida National Scenic Trail runs 17 miles south of this rural community of 7,000. The surrounding area is thickly wooded; camping, fishing, and hiking are popular. The Forest Capital State Museum explores the history of the local forest industry.

Information: Perry-Taylor County Chamber of Commerce | 428 N. Jefferson St., Box 892, Perry, 32348 | 850/584–5366 | www.gulfnet.com/chamber.

Attractions

Forest Capital State Museum and Cracker Homestead. Long-leaf pines grow on the 13-acre grounds of this museum and homestead, which celebrates the local timber industry and early settlers. Inside the museum, exhibit cases are made of different native woods, including redwood, ash, and magnolia; and a 5-ft map of Florida outlines the state's 67 counties with 67 different types of local wood. The exhibits themselves cover timber issues past and present, from animal species in hammock areas to reasons for prescribed burning. The Cracker Homestead is the best remaining example of a dog trot–style of housing favored by early settlers, who were called "crackers" for their use of the bull whip in cattle driving. The house features big porches, with a breezeway running through the house leading to a backyard kitchen. The complex is 1 mi south of town. | 204 Forest Park Dr. | 850/584–3227 | $1 | Thur.–Mon. 9–noon, 1–5.

Mayo Blue Springs. In Mayo, 20 mi southeast of Perry along U.S. 27, are these crystal-clear springs on the Suwannee River. You can swim, picnic, hike along nature trails, and use the boat ramps. | Highway 27 Extension 251b, Mayo | 904/294–1617 | $1.50 | Weekdays 8:30–8:30, weekends 8–8:30.

ON THE CALENDAR

OCT.: *Florida Forest Festival.* The world's largest free fish fry is the highlight of this festival, which has been celebrating forests and the forestry industry since 1957. You can browse through more than 150 arts and crafts booths, take in live music, go on rides, study forestry exhibits, attend a beauty pageant, and watch a bed race, fireworks, and a parade. | 850/584–8733.

OCT.: *Pioneer Day.* This festival, which takes place the second Saturday in October in Mayo, is headed by an elected "Granny and Pappy" who must be third-generation Mayo residents. Arts and crafts, local food, and a reenacted gunfight round out the activities witnessed by about 15,000 people. | 904/294–2705.

Dining

Downtown Café of Perry. American. This Main Street restaurant is in the middle of other shops and cafés, but people come here for the all-you-can-eat, $5.49 buffet featuring heavy country biscuits, fried chicken, pork chops, soups, and salads. Hamburgers are the biggest sellers. | 108 E. Main St. | 850/584–2232 | $4.50–$5.50 | Closed Sat. No dinner | No credit cards.

Pouncey's Restaurant. American/Casual. This comfortable restaurant has a friendly staff and down-home menu classics like country-fried steak and fried chicken. Servings are generous and the prices are low. | 2186 S. Byron Butler Pkwy. | 850/584–9942 | $4–$10 | AE, MC, V.

Lodging

Perry Days Inn. This small two-story motel is in the center of rural Perry and is a popular place to stay if you're in the area for fishing or hunting. Some in-room data ports, in-room safes, some microwaves, some refrigerators. Cable TV. Pool. Laundry facilities, laundry service. Some pets allowed (fee). | 2277 S. Byron Butler Pkwy. | 850/584–5311 or 800/544–8313 | www.daysinn.com | 60 rooms | $40–$70 | AE, D, DC, MC, V.

Villager Lodge. This basic motel is surrounded by fast-food chains and a retail area with a huge laundromat. This two-story red brick building takes up only a portion of the 4 acres it owns, so there is a touch of nature around. While not big on charm, you can't beat the price. Complimentary Continental breakfast. Some kitchenettes, some microwaves, some refrigerators. Cable TV. Pool. Pets allowed (fee). | 2238 S. Byron Butler Pkwy. | 850/584–4221 | fax 850/838–1718 | 66 rooms | $40 | AE, MC, V.

PINE ISLAND

MAP 3, H5

(Nearby towns also listed: Boca Grande, Cape Coral, Captiva Island, Ft. Myers, Matlacha, Sanibel Island)

Two miles wide and 17 miles long, Pine Island is the largest island on the west coast of Florida. Although it's just 10 mi west of Cape Coral, there's a sense of seclusion here—

strict zoning laws prohibit high-rise construction, and the island coast is fringed with mangroves. The island consists of the small, self-sufficient communities of Matlacha (pronounced mat-la-SHAY, this Calusa Indian name means "water to the chin"), Pine Island Center, Bokeelia, Pineland, and St. James City.

After the Calusa Indians were wiped out by Spanish-imported diseases, the island was "rediscovered" in 1873 by Captain John Smith who felt it would be a safer place for his ships than Sanibel and Captiva islands, which are more susceptible to hurricanes.

Information: Greater Pine Island Chamber of Commerce | Box 525, Matlacha, 33993 | 941/283–0888.

Attractions
Museum of the Islands. This tiny museum has exhibits on Pine Island pioneers, featuring artifacts from archaeological research on the island and a Calusa Indian dugout canoe. | 5728 Sesame Dr. | 941/283–1525 | $1.

Tropic Star Cruise. On this African Queen–style boat, you can get an all-day narrated nature cruise with stops at Cabbage Key Island for lunch at an historic inn, two bird rookery islands, and a manatee hole. | Knight's Landing, 16499 Portobello St., Bokeelia | 941/283–0015 | fax 941/283–7255 | www.tropicstarcruises.com | $25 | Daily 9:30–4.

ON THE CALENDAR
JULY: *Mangomania*. At this weekend-long tropical fruit fair, taste mango and tropical concoctions at the KOA Campgrounds south of Pine Island Center. There are gifts and novelties for sale, presentations on planting, growing, and harvesting, live entertainment, and arts and crafts. | 941/283–0888.

Dining
Waterfront Restaurant & Marina. Seafood. This restaurant has paper place mats and crayons on the table—some of the more memorable creations are displayed on the walls. They'll also trade your "interesting" T-shirt for one of the ones on display. In short, this is a loose place. The baked clam chowder and the Mariner's Platter are house specialties, but its known locally for its great 10-oz hamburgers. There's a back deck, and views of Sanibel Island. | 2131 Oleander St. | 941/283–0592 | fax 941/283–0932 | $6–$16 | AE, D, MC, V.

POMPANO BEACH
MAP 3, L9

(Nearby towns also listed: Boca Raton, Deerfield Beach, Fort Lauderdale, Lauderdale-by-the-Sea)

The popular local fish, the pompano, gave its name to this city of 75,000 on Florida's Atlantic coast 8 mi north of Fort Lauderdale. After low-rise Lauderdale-by-the-Sea, the high-rises start up once again. Sportfishing is the big draw here, as you might expect from the town's name.

Information: Greater Pompano Beach Chamber of Commerce | 2200 E. Atlantic Blvd., Pompano Beach, 33062 | 954/941–2940 | www.pompanobeachchamber.com.

Attractions
Butterfly World. You can walk amid butterflies from around the world in this giant walk-through aviary, 2 mi west of Pompano Beach. The surrounding park also includes a botanical garden, a rainforest exhibit, English rose gardens, a museum, an insectarium, and a hummingbird aviary. | 3600 W. Sample Rd., Coconut Creek | 954/977–4400 | fax 954/977–4501 | www.butterflyworld.com | $12.95 | Mon.–Sat. 9–5, Sun. 1–5.

Fern Forest Nature Center. This 254-acre forested island contains a visitor center, Cypress Boardwalk and Prairie Overlook Trail, and an arboretum. Native to the area are black-and-yellow striped zebra longwing butterflies and orange ruddy daggerwings, as well as songbirds, red-shouldered hawks, and gray squirrels. | 201 Lyons Rd. S | 954/970–0150.

Gold Coast Ice Arena. Weary of the warmth? Lace up a pair of skates at one of the arena's morning, afternoon, or evening skating sessions. This is the site of the NHL Florida Panthers practice facility. | 4601 North Federal Hwy. | 954/943–1437 | $5–$5.50; $2 skate rental | Sun.–Mon., Wed.–Thurs. 8:30–4, Tues. 8:30–10 PM, Fri.–Sat. 8:15–11.

Goodyear Blimp Visitor Center. If your timing's right, you can view the enormous *Stars and Stripes* zeppelin at its Pompano Beach home. A public viewing area in the hangar lets you observe the blimp at rest or lugging lazily about the sky. The blimp is usually on the ground Mondays and Tuesdays half of the year. | 1500 N.E. 5th Ave. | 954/946–8300 | Free | Daily 9–5.

Lowrance Artificial Reef. Since 1983, 25 ships have been sunk off the coast of Pompano Beach to serve as artificial reefs, attracting different varieties of fish and sea life. *Lowrance*, a 435-ft freighter was the first to be sunk; it remains the area's largest artificial reef. It lies 210 ft under the Atlantic, about 1½ mi from shore. You can charter a boat to the site to fish or dive to the wreck. Shallower wrecks also offer prime fishing and diving. | 954/942–4513.

Pompano Park. This 1964 circuit has hosted more Breeders Crown harness races than any other track. Take the Atlantic Blvd. exit west off I–95. Races take place at 7:30; there is simulcasting daily all year. | 1800 S.W. 3rd St. | 954/972–2000 | Racing Oct.–Mar., Mon., Wed., Fri.–Sat.; Apr.–Aug., Wed., Fri.–Sat.

Pompano Pier. This pier extends 1,080 ft into the Atlantic. You can rent rods and bait 24 hours a day. | 222 Pompano Beach Blvd. | 954/943–1488 | $2, $10 equipment and bait | Open daily 24 hours.

ON THE CALENDAR
APR.: *Seafood Festival.* Booths offering fresh squid, calamari, and other Florida seafood are the main draw at this 3-day beachside event. Live entertainment, arts and crafts exhibits, and children's rides round out the festivities. | 954/942–4513.
MAY: *Pompano Beach Fishing Rodeo.* South Florida's largest saltwater sport-fishing tournament draws anglers and spectators from around the region. Prizes are awarded for the most pounds of fish "wrangled up" during the contest. | 954/971–0818.
SEPT.: *Fine Food and Wine Festival Auction.* Since 1983, this festival has attracted expert and amateur oenologists and gourmands. Eat, drink, and be merry. | 954/941–2940.
DEC.: *Boat Parade.* Over 80,000 people line up along the Intracoastal Waterway to witness this festive procession of decorated and brightly lit boats. | 954/941–2940.

Dining
Café Arugula. Contemporary. This restaurant has culled influences from the Mediterranean and the southwest. Innovative dishes include a free-range loin of venison with juniper–wild mushroom sauce, quesadilla, and stir-fried vegetables, and seabass with capers and shaved almonds over fettuccine. Velvet booths and steamboat wheel windows give the dining room a warm elegance. | 3110 N. Federal Hwy. | 954/785–7732 | No lunch | $24–$41 | AE, D, DC, MC, V.

★ **Café Maxx.** Contemporary. New-wave epicurean dining had its South Florida start here in the early 1980s, and Café Maxx remains popular among regional food lovers. The setting is ordinary, in a little strip of stores, but inside both food and atmosphere are festive. The menu showcases the tropics: jumbo stone-crab claws with honey-lime mustard sauce and black-bean and banana pepper chili with Florida avocado. Desserts also reflect a tropical theme, from praline macadamia mousse over chocolate cake with butterscotch sauce to candied ginger with pears poached in muscatel and sun-dried cherry ice cream. More than 200 wines are offered by the bottle, another 20 by the glass | 2601 E. Atlantic Blvd. | 954/782–0606 | No lunch | $36–$50 | AE, D, DC, MC, V.

Cap's Place. Seafood. This restaurant has an illustrious pedigree: Winston Churchill, FDR, and JFK all ate here. It was named for Captain Theodore Knight who, along with Al Hasis, floated the barge on which the restaurant sits to the place where it rests today–and it is run by Hasis's descendents. Baking is done on the premises and you can't miss with the wahoo steaks and fries. Save room for the classic Florida dessert, Key lime pie, which Cap's does very well. | 2765 N.E. 28th Ct; Located on Cap's Dock | No lunch | $20–$30 | AE, MC, V.

Vesuvio's. Italian. Cozy and popular, with an attentive waitstaff, this southern Italian restaurant is decorated with Mediterranean murals, wine racks, plants, and paintings. The culinary focus is on chicken, veal, and fish in light sauces, often wine-based, as in Chicken Vesuvio, which is sauteed with white wine, artichoke hearts, and asparagus. Another favorite is snapper with clam juice and olive oil. | 2715 E. Atlantic Blvd. | 954/941–1594 | Closed mid-May–late Dec. Closed Mon. No lunch | $12–$25 | AE, D, DC, MC, V.

Lodging

Best Western Beachcomber Hotel and Villas. This oceanfront hotel offers accommodations ranging from standard rooms to Mediterranean-style villas. The eight-story building towers above the beach, with palm trees, pools, and tropical landscaping. Wraparound balconies provide amazing views of the Atlantic Ocean. The complex includes a poolside tiki bar and barbecue, beachfront cabanas, and glass-enclosed sundecks. The beach location is central to most Broward County attractions. Boat and jet ski rentals, and a fishing pier are within walking distance. Restaurant, bar. In-room data ports, in-room safes, some kitchenettes. Cable TV. 2 pools. Putting green. Volleyball. Beach. Playground. Laundry facilities. | 1200 S. Ocean Blvd. | 954/941–7830 or 800/231–1234 | fax 954/942–7680 | www.bestwestern.com | 147 rooms, 4 suites, 9 villas | $169–$275 | AE, D, DC, MC, V.

Holiday Inn on the Ocean. Rooms at this three-story motel face the ocean, with 200 ft of private beach, or the Spanish River. Restaurant, bar. In-room data ports, some refrigerators. Cable TV. Pool. Putting green, 3 tennis courts. Beach, water sports. Laundry facilities. Business services. | 1350 S. Ocean Blvd. | 954/941–7300 or 800/465–4329 | fax 954/941–7300 | www.basshotels.com | 111 rooms, 22 suites | $139–$215 | AE, D, DC, MC, V.

Howard Johnson Plaza Resort. This nine-story resort is across the road from the beach. Rooms have views toward the city, the pool, or the ocean; all have private balconies. The center of Pompano Beach is within walking distance, with shops and restaurants in easy reach. Restaurant, bar. In-room data ports, in-room safes, some kitchenettes, some microwaves, some refrigerators. Cable TV. Pool. Gym. Laundry facilities. Business services. | 9 N. Pompano Beach Blvd. | 954/781–1300 or 800/223–5844 | fax 954/782–5585 | www.hojo.com | 96 rooms, 8 efficiencies | $135–$189 | AE, D, DC, MC, V.

Ocean Palms Resort. At the end of a quiet, one-way street, this small 17-unit resort is decorated with rattan chairs and floral patterns. Rooms have full kitchens and most sit on the beach with their own patios. There is a video-lending library with plenty of movies. Kitchenettes, microwaves. Cable TV, in-room VCRs. Pool. Beach. Laundry facilities. | 700 Briny Ave. | 954/942–2470 | fax 954/782–2444 | $70–$90 | No credit cards.

Palm-Aire Resort and Spa. This luxurious, 750-acre resort has a 40,000-square-ft spa with 40 different treatment rooms. Separate men's and women's pavilions have private sunken Roman baths, Swiss showers, and experienced massage therapists. Five top golf courses surround the resort; guests get 50% off. The one- and two-bedroom condos are very spacious: all have separate dressing rooms, and some have two baths. Bar. Kitchenettes. Cable TV, some in-room VCRs (and movies). Pool. Hot tub, massage, sauna, spa, steam room. 5 18-hole golf courses, 37 tennis courts. Gym. Kids' programs (ages 5–15). Laundry facilities. Business services. | 2601 Palm-Aire Dr. N | 954/972–3300 or 800/725–6247 | fax 954/968–2711 | www.premiervacationrentals.com/palmair.htm | 203 suites | $139–$199 | AE, D, DC, MC, V.

Ramada Inn Paradise Beach Resort. This beachfront resort between Pompano Beach and Ft. Lauderdale has spacious rooms, oceanfront dining, a tiki bar, pool, tennis, and water sports. A fishing pier, charter boats and scuba diving shops are all within a mile. Restaurant, bar, room service. Cable TV. Outdoor pool. Laundry service. | 1380 S. Ocean Blvd. | 954/785–3300 or 888/298–2054 | fax 954/785–8031 | www.ramada.com | 102 rooms | $65–$415 | AE, D, DC, MC, V.

Sands Harbor Hotel & Marina. This eight-story downtown hotel has balconies overlooking the Intercoastal Waterway and a yacht-filled marina. It's an easy walk to restaurants and shops; the ocean is two blocks away. The hotel provides dockage for boats up to 100 ft. 3 restaurants, bar, Continental breakfast. In–room safes, some microwaves, some refrigerators, some kitchenettes. Cable TV, some in-room VCRs. Pool. Dock, fishing, boating, watersports, volleyball. Video games. | 125 N. Riverside Dr. | 954/942–9100 or 800/227–3353 | fax 954/785–5657 | www.sandsharbor.com | 60 rooms | $99–$199 | AE, MC, V.

Villamar Inn. This oceanfront inn has rooms, efficiencies, and one-bedroom suites with patio entrances, private balconies, and Italian ceramic tile floors. Every room is decorated differently. Views are of the ocean or the pool. In-room data ports, in-room safes, some kitchenettes, some microwaves, some refrigerators. Cable TV. Pool. Putting green. Beach. Laundry facilities. Business services. | 740 N. Ocean Blvd. | 954/941–3530 | fax 954/782–2778 | www.villamar.com | 18 units | $89–$149 | MC, V.

PONTE VEDRA BEACH

MAP 3, J2

(Nearby towns also listed: Atlantic Beach, Jacksonville, Jacksonville Beach)

This beach town of 29,000 borders Jacksonville Beach to the south. It is known for its Atlantic surf and sand. Some historians believe that Guana River State Park is where the famed explorer Ponce de León first landed on the shores of America.

Information: **Ponte Vedra Beach Chamber of Commerce** | Four Sawgrass Village, Suite 104F, Ponte Vedra Beach, 32082 | 904/285–0666 | www.pvbchamber.org.

Attractions
Guana River State Park. You can go biking, canoeing, swimming, and hiking on nature trails at this park. | 2690 S. Ponte Verda Blvd. | 904/825–5071 | Free | Daily, dawn to dusk.

ON THE CALENDAR
MAR.: *Tournament Players Club Championship.* See a field of the world's top golfers compete for a share of the $6 million purse on this PGA circuit event. The course is one of the most challenging and scenic in the country. | 904/273–3383.

Dining
Aqua Grill. Continental. A plant-filled dining room overlooks a pond at this restaurant popular with guests of the nearby Marriott hotel. Aqua Grill features daily fresh seafood, vegetarian dinners, certified Angus steaks, unique chicken entrées and pasta dishes. There are four tanks of exotic fish. Outdoor seating is available. | 950 Sawgrass Village Dr. | 904/285–3017 | Reservations essential | $14–$23 | AE, D, DC, MC, V.

Gio's Café. Italian. This upscale Art Deco restaurant with black and white interiors has elegant dining areas arranged on different levels. The menu is primarily Italian but also serves beef Wellington with a smoked lobster filling; seafood; and a roasted rack of lamb. Save room for a wild-berry fruit tart, the most popular dessert. | 900 Sawgrass Village Dr. | 904/273–0101 | $20–$37 | AE, D, DC, MC, V.

Lodging
Marriott at Sawgrass. This large hotel is luxuriously appointed, with immaculately maintained and spacious rooms. It is surrounded by meticulously landscaped grounds. Five cham-

pionship golf courses are within a 5-mi radius of the hotel. 3 restaurants, 2 bars, dining rooms, room service. In-room data ports, some kitchenettes, minibars, some microwaves, some refrigerators. Cable TV, some in-room VCRs. 4 outdoor pools, 4 ponds, wading pool. 3 outdoor hot tubs, spa. Miniature golf, putting greens, tennis court. Gym, horseback riding. Beach, boating, bicycles. Children's programs (ages 3–12). Laundry services. Business services. | 1000 PGA Blvd. Ponte Vedra Beach, | 904/285–7777 or 800/453–4653 | fax 904/285–0906 | www.marriotthotels.com/jaxsw | 324 rooms, 160 villas, 24 suites | $210–$700 | AE, D, DC, MC, V.

Ponte Vedra Lodge and Club. White stucco and Spanish roof tiles give this elegant beach-front resort a Mediterranean villa feel. Spacious rooms have a private terrace or patio; some have fireplaces. You also have access to 36 holes of golf, 15 tennis courts, and a full service spa that belongs to the lodge's larger sister resort, the Ponte Vedra Inn and Club, 1½ mi up the road. 3 restaurants, 2 bars, room service. Some kitchenettes, minibars, some microwaves, some refrigerators, some in-room hot tubs. Cable TV. 3 outdoor pools. 2 outdoor hot tubs. Beach. Gym. Baby-sitting, children's programs (ages 3–12). Laundry services. Business services. | 607 Ponte Vedra Blvd. | 904/273–9500 or 800/243–4304 | fax 904/273–0210 | www.pvresorts.com | 43 rooms, 23 suites | $300–$380 | AE, D, DC, MC, V.

Ponte Vedra Inn and Club. This 300-acre oceanfront resort on the Atlantic was established in 1928. Nine, low-rise, orange-tiled, Florida-style buildings pepper the shoreline, with their backs to water-fringed gold courses. Rooms are comfortably luxurious. Most have ocean views. 4 restaurants, 2 bars (with entertainment), dining room, picnic area, room service. In-room data ports, some kitchenettes, minibars, some microwaves, refrigerators. Cable TV. 4 outdoor pools, wading pool. Beauty salon, outdoor hot tub, spa. Driving range, 2 18-hole gold courses, putting green, 15 tennis courts. Gym. Beach, boating, bicycles. Baby-sitting, children's programs (ages 4–12), playground. Business services. | 200 Ponte Vedra Blvd. | 904/285–1111 or 800/234–7842 | fax 904/285–2111 | www.pvresorts.com | 158 rooms, 64 suites | $240–$380 | AE, D, DC, MC, V.

PORT CHARLOTTE

MAP 3, 18

(Nearby towns also listed: Arcadia, Englewood, Fort Myers, Punta Gorda, Venice)

Port Charlotte (pop. 44,000) is an unincorporated area within Charlotte county, half way between Fort Myers and Sarasota. There are about 38 mi of shoreline in the area and numerous golf courses which keeps the mainly retirement community busy year-round. There's actually no port to speak of; the town is set on the Peace River, set just back from Charlotte Harbor.

Information: **Charlotte County Chamber of Commerce** | 2702 Tamiami Trail (U.S. 41), Port Charlotte, 33952 | 941/627–2222 | www.charlotte-florida.com.

Attractions

Charlotte Harbor Environmental Center. Supported in part by the Peace River Audubon Society, this center is dedicated to environmental education, recreation, research, and preservation management. You can hike along 4 mi of nature trails. Free guided walks are offered November through April. | 10941 Burnt Store Rd. | 941/575–5435 | fax 941/575–5437 | www.charlotte-florida.com/diningandentertainment/chec.htm | Free | Daily 7–7.

Port Charlotte Beach. At the southeast end of Harbor Boulevard in Port Charlotte, this beach complex offers a beach club, fishing pier, tennis, volleyball, and basketball courts, horseshoe pits, a pool, a snack bar, boat ramps, and barbecue grills. | 4500 Harbor Blvd. | 941/627–1628 | Beach free, pool $2.68 | Daily 10–4:45.

FEB.: *Peace River Seafood Festival and Boat Show.* This seafood festival in Laishley Park attracts 15,000 people, 100 boats, and several varieties of crustaceans. Seafood vendors, over 50 arts and crafts booths, live music, and a local water ski show complete the fest. | 941/639–1188.

MAR.: *Baseball Spring Training.* Charlotte County Stadium has been the Texas Rangers' spring home since 1987. You can watch the team practice and take on other major league teams. | 2300 El Jobean Rd. | 941/625–9500.

JULY: *Independence Day Fireworks, July 3.* Start your holiday celebrations early: after the Charlotte Rangers (a Texas Rangers minor league affiliate) baseball game on July 3, there's an Independence Day fireworks display at Charlotte County Stadium. | 941/625–9500.

Dining

Cap'n and the Cowboy. Steak. The mixed nautical and western theme is elaborated by collectibles—fishing poles and saddles—displayed on the walls. There are seafood dishes, such as lobster and macadamia nut–encrusted grouper, but most come for the prime rib, filet mignon, and other steaks. | 2200 Kings Hwy. (U.S. 41) | 941/743–3969 | Closed Mon. | $11–$25 | AE, D, MC, V.

Chantalle's. French. This romantic restaurant has white interiors, intimate, candlelit booths, and a garden view. The menu features innovative dishes such as duck *Jombano* (duck stuffed with ground veal, peppers, herbs, and black beans atop lingonberries and bourbon sauce) or fresh bay scallops tossed in a mix of cracked peppercorn, herbs, and pistachio nuts. | 3822 Tamiami Trail | 941/766–1251 | No lunch | $16–$25 | AE, D, DC, MC, V.

Harbour Tea Room. Tea. Decorated in turn-of-the-20th-century style, this pink-shingled house, part of the Harbor Inn, has a wide selection of teas, scones, tea sandwiches, and fresh-baked desserts. There's a view of Charlotte Harbor from most of the dining area. | 5000 Tamiami Trail (U.S. 41) | 941/629–5996 | Closed Sun.–Mon. | $10 | MC, V.

Ming Court. Chinese. You can get Hunan, Mandarin, or Szechuan cooking at this very popular restaurant in the Carousel Shopping Center. Among the menu favorites are the hot and spicy shrimp (you can request mild, spicy, or 911), orange chicken, and Ming Court steak, but the most popular choice is the 60-item New York Chinatown buffet. | 1900 Tamiami Trail (U.S. 41) | 941/625–0300 or 941/625–0373 | $6–$16 | AE, MC, V.

Lodging

The Coffey House B&B. This bed-and-breakfast in a wooded area of Port Charlotte has two rooms for those searching for a little quiet. Enclosed porches overlook an herb garden and a fish pond. The rooms are in a two-bedroom guest home and decorated from private travels; one has a collection of Moroccan brass, the other has Scottish handiwork. Complimentary breakfast. No room phones, TV in common area. Pool. Hot tub. Bicycles. Library. No kids under 12. | 2379 Sunninglow | 941/624–4215 | fax 941/624–5733 | www.bbonline.com/fl/coffeyhouse | 2 rooms | $95–$125 | No credit cards.

Days Inn of Port Charlotte. This is an affordable, simple three-story motel, off U.S. 41 at exits 31 and 32. It is in a commercial area, across the street from several strip malls, and next door to a restaurant. There are century-old oak trees covered in Spanish Moss nearby. In-room data ports, refrigerators, some microwaves. Cable TV. Pool. Exercise equipment. Laundry facilities. Business services. Some pets allowed (fee). | 1941 Tamiami Trail (U.S. 41) | 941/627–8900 or 800/329–7466 | fax 941/743–8503 | www.daysinn.com | 122 rooms, 4 suites | $99–$109 | AE, D, DC, MC, V.

Econo Lodge. Rooms have been designed in modern motel style with green carpeting. There are several restaurants nearby and a laudromat across the street, but you can still see miles of forest and it is 2 mi from fishing, golf, and Thomas Edison's house. Restaurant, complimentary Continental breakfast, bar. Some in-room data ports, some refrigerators, some microwaves. Cable TV. | 4100 Tamiami Tr. (U.S. 41) | 941/743–2442 or 800/553–2666 | fax 941/743–6376 | www.econolodge.com | 60 rooms | $35–$95 | AE, D, DC, MC, V.

Hampton Inn. This three-story motel overlooks Lake Suzie. It is set back a bit in the woods so that the noise from I–75 (take exit 31) doesn't reach the motel. Restaurants are nearby. Complimentary Continental breakfast. In-room data ports, some microwaves, some refrigerators. Cable TV. Pool. Laundry facilities. Business services. | 24480 Sandhill Blvd. | 941/627–5600 or 800/426–7866 | fax 941/627–6883 | www.hamptoninn.com | 73 rooms | $65–$119 | AE, D, DC, MC, V.

Litchfield Inn. Across from Promenades Mall in downtown Port Charlotte is this complex of three two-story, landscaped buildings. Most of the rooms overlook a central garden-filled courtyard, and others have exterior entrances for easy unloading from the car. Many of the rooms have small, separate living room areas and some have bars. Restaurant, bar (with entertainment). Some microwaves, some refrigerators. Cable TV. Pool. Laundry facilities, laundry service. Business services. Pets allowed (fee). | 3400 Tamiami Tr. (U.S. 41) | 941/625–4181 or 800/933–9987 | fax 941/629–1740 | 104 rooms, 13 suites | $59–$149 | AE, D, DC, MC, V.

Port Charlotte Motel. This cheerful blue-tiled, white stucco motel on Charlotte Harbor has its own boat and fishing dock, and a coffee bar. The rooms are basic but comfortable, with carpeting and wall-mounted TVs. Complimentary Continental breakfast. Some kitchens, refrigerators, cable TV. Pool, outdoor hot tub. Dock, boating, fishing, water sports. Laundry facilities. | 3491 Tamiami Tr. (U.S. 41) | 941/625–4177 or 800/559–5561 | fax 941/624–5591 | www.portcharlottemotel.com | 52 rooms, 7 efficiencies | $43–$75 | D, DC, MC, V.

PORT ST. LUCIE

MAP 3, L7

(Nearby towns also listed: Fort Pierce, Jensen Beach, Stuart, Vero Beach)

This rapidly growing city of 80,000 on the Atlantic Coast sports some of the best boating and fishing in the eastern seaboard. There are plenty of shops, restaurants, and attractions, including the Fort Pierce Inlet State Recreation Area.

Information: **Port St. Lucie Chamber of Commerce** | 1626 S.E. Port St. Lucie Blvd., Port St. Lucie, 34952 | 561/398–1469 | www.stluciechamber.org.

Attractions

St. Lucie Inlet State Preserve. This barrier island park, accessible only by boat, is a nesting ground for sea turtles, especially loggerheads, greens, and leatherbacks. Visitors can swim, dive, fish, or walk the boardwalk through mangrove forests and coastal hammocks filled with native trees such as cabbage palms, paradise trees, live oaks, wild limes, ferns, and cocoa plums. | 16450 S.E. Federal Hwy., Hobe Sound | 561/744–7603 | Free | Daily dawn to dusk.

ON THE CALENDAR

MAR.–APR.: *Spring Training.* The New York Mets have trained in St. Lucie West at Thomas J. White Stadium since 1988. | 525 N.W. Peacock Blvd., Port St. Lucie | 561/871–2100.

APR.–SEPT.: *St. Lucie Mets.* The Florida State League affiliate of the New York Mets baseball team plays home games at Thomas J. White Stadium (the spring training home of the major league Mets). | 561/871–2115.

NOV.: *Annual Antique & Classic Boat Rendezvous.* Boats 6–80 ft in length parade at Northside Marina in the nearby town of Stuart. | 561/692–1234.

Dining

Le Brittany. French. This small, bistro-style restaurant offers traditional French fare. It's known for its rack of lamb. Though close to commercial shops, the setting inside is welcoming. | 897 E. Prima Vista Blvd. | 561/871–2231 | Reservations essential | Closed Mon. | $13–$19 | MC, V.

R.J. Gator's. American/Casual. This Florida-based chain has a typically family-oriented menu. Try the Caribbean conch chowder or a heaping plate of the Garbage Nachos loaded with cheese and salsa—at bargain prices. | 7950 U.S. 1 | 561/878–3338 | $4–$12 | AE, MC, V.

Lodging

Best Western Port St. Lucie. Hibiscus trees add bright splashes of color on the grounds of this two-story hotel. Only minutes from the ocean and close to the New York Mets spring training facility, the hotel is 10 mi north of Jensen Beach. Complimentary Continental breakfast. In-room data ports, some microwaves, some refrigerators. Cable TV. Pool. Outdoor hot tub. Laundry facilities. Business services. | 7900 S. U.S. 1, Port St. Lucie | 561/878–7600 | fax 561/340–0422 | www.bestwestern.com | 98 suites | $59–$99 suites | AE, D, DC, MC, V.

Holiday Inn Port St. Lucie. A free-form pool, complete with a lovely cascading waterfall, highlights this five-story hotel. It fronts on Port St. Lucie's main thoroughfare, and beaches are 8 mi away. Restaurant, bar, room service. Some microwaves, some refrigerators, some in-room hot tubs. Cable TV. Pool. Outdoor hot tub. Laundry facilities. Business services. | 10120 U.S. 1S | 561/337–2200 | fax 561/335–7872 | www.holiday-inn.com | 142 rooms, 72 suites | $149–$169, $189–$200 suites | AE, D, DC, MC, V.

PUNTA GORDA

MAP 3, I8

(Nearby towns also listed: Cape Coral, Englewood, Fort Myers, Port Charlotte)

Punta Gorda, the only incorporated city in Charlotte County, is at the mouth of the Peace River, where it empties into Charlotte Harbor. Like its slightly larger neighbor, Port Charlotte, Punta Gorda is on the water, but not the ocean: beaches are about 20 min away. Half of the town's 13,000 residents are senior citizens. Come here to escape the crowds, and get up close to the region's flora and fauna by trudging through swamps in old buggys at a huge ranch, or paddling up the Peace River.

Information: Charlotte County Chamber of Commerce | 2702 Tamiami Trail (U.S. 41), Port Charlotte, 33952 | 941/627–2222 | www.charlotte-florida.com.

Attractions

Fishermen's Village. This unique waterfront area includes a 98-slip marina and a shaded shopping area where you can browse for crafts, jewelry, gifts, and clothing. There are also restaurants with outdoor dining and good views. Depart here for fishing, sailing, and sightseeing trips. You'll also find water sports, live entertainment, and gorgeous sunsets. | 1200 W. Retta Esplanade | 941/639–8721 | Free | Mon.–Sat. 10–6, Sun. noon–5.

Florida Adventure Museum. The Florida military heritage room in this former Museum of Charlotte County contains uniforms, ammunition, weapons, and soldiers' personal belongings dating to the Civil War. Exhibits on local natural history change every few months. Hands-on activities are available for kids. | 260 W. Retta Esplanade | 941/639–3777 | $2 | Weekdays 10–5, Sat. 10–3.

Peace River Wildlife Center. A non-profit organization runs this rescue, rehabilitation, and release facility for locally injured or orphaned wildlife. At the wildlife center you can often see bald eagles, herons, and egrets. The center is inside Ponce de León Park, a 16-acre recreation area with a ½-mi nature trail and picnic facilities. | 3400 W. Marion Ave. | 941/637–3830 | www.charlotte-florida.com/chec | Free | Open Wed.–Mon. 11–3.

SIGHTSEEING TOURS/TOUR COMPANIES

Babcock Wilderness Adventures. Midway between Punta Gorda and Fort Myers, the 90,000-acre Babcock Crescent Ranch gives you a chance to see what Florida was like centuries ago. You hop in a swamp buggy (converted school buses mostly) and embark on a 90-min tour through a variety of ecosystems, including Telegraph Cypress Swamp. Experienced guides ask you to spot hogs, bison, panthers, alligators, birds, and the cattle and horses that are raised on the ranch. You can also opt for a 3-hr bike tour. | 8000 Rte. 31 | 941/637–0551 or 800/500–5583 | fax 941/637–4611 | $17.95 | Tours daily by reservation only.

ON THE CALENDAR

JULY: *Hot Summer Days.* This weekend arts and crafts show in Fishermen's Village also includes wildlife displays, food, and entertainment. | 941/639–8721.

Dining

Aquí Está Diner. American/Casual. Like most diners, the menu here is large, and breakfast is served all day. This family restaurant tries to go a step above other diners by having other fresh specials such as lobster tail. The Greek owner took the name from the street that intersects U.S. 41 at the corner near them, it translates as "here it is." | 3105 Tamiami Trail (U.S. 41) | 941/639–6667 | No dinner Sun. | $7–$19 | MC, V.

Captain's Table. Seafood. This upscale restaurant in Fishermen's Village sits on a pier overlooking Charlotte Harbor, with enormous plate glass windows seemingly designed for sunset watching. There is a nautical theme, and a laid-back atmosphere. Choose from fusion dishes such as blackened Ahi tuna with wasabi and ginger, or Continental classics such as Dijon-crusted rack of lamb with a rosemary cream sauce. There is a Sunday brunch and a Friday night buffet. | 1200 W. Retta Esplanade | 941/637–1177 | www.smugglers.com | $9–$19 | AE, D, MC, V.

Harpoon Harry's Restaurant and Raw Bar. American/Casual. Appetizers, sandwiches, and barbecue are served all day, but the draw is location and a party atmosphere. A patio overlooks Charlotte Harbor, the choice spot for sunsets. There is live music evenings, with dancing and karaoke. Women drink free Wednesday nights. | 1200 W. Retta Esplanade | 941/637–1177 | $4–$10 | AE, MC, V.

Salty's Harborside. Seafood. Fresh seafood is what Salty's is known for, but other dishes, such as rosemary chicken and filet mignon, are also worth a try. You can watch boats in Charlotte Harbor and the Burnt Store Marina from the dining room. | Burnt Store Rd. | 941/639–3650 | $14–$21 | AE, D, DC, MC, V.

Lodging

Best Western Waterfront. A great pool area looks out over a few palm trees to Charlotte Harbor. Adjacent to the hotel is Gilchrist Park, with tennis courts, bicycle paths, and playgrounds. Fishermen's Village is just 1 mi away. The hotel restaurant is on a large covered deck 3 ft from the water. Restaurant, bar. In-room data ports, some microwaves, some refrigerators. Cable TV. Pool. Exercise equipment. Dock, fishing. Laundry facilities. Business services. Pets allowed (fee). | 300 W. Retta Esplanade | 941/639–1165 or 800/525–1022 | fax 941/639–8116 | www.bestwestern.com | 176 rooms, 7 suites | $89–$145 | AE, D, DC, MC, V.

Days Inn Punta Gorda. This standard two-story motel is just off I–75 at exit 28, 3 mi from downtown Punta Gorda. It's close to some chain restaurants. Picnic area, complimentary Continental breakfast. In-room data ports, some refrigerators, some in-room hot tubs. Cable TV. Pool. Hot tub. Playground. Laundry facilities. Business services. | 26560 N. Jones Loop Rd. | 941/637–7200 or 800/329–7466 | fax 941/639–0848 | www.daysinn.com | 74 rooms | $44–$94 | AE, D, DC, MC, V.

Fishermen's Village Resort. This resort is part of a large waterfront shopping and dining destination beside a 98-slip marina. Fully furnished villas sleep up to six people and feature complete kitchens and balconies. 7 restaurants, bar, picnic area. Kitchenettes, microwaves, refrigerators, cable TV. Pool. Beauty salon. Tennis. Dock, boating, fishing, water sports. Shops. laundry facilities. | 1200 W. Retta Esplanade | 941/639–8721 | fax 941/637–1054 | www.fishville.com | 47 rooms | $85–$100 | AE, MC, V.

Gilchrist B&B. This restored turn-of-the-20th-century Florida Cottage is in the historical district of Punta Gorda, within walking distance of Fishermen's Village. The house features pine floors, tongue and groove ceilings, a tin roof, and finely manicured lawns. | 115 Gilchrist St. | 941/575–4129 | fax 941/575–9666 | www.all-florida.com/gilchrist | 2 rooms | $65–$85 | MC, V.

Holiday Inn Harborside. This centrally located motel is next to the bridge over the Peace River. Fishermen's Village, the nearest attraction, is 2 mi away. Restaurant, bar (with entertainment), room service. In-room data ports, some kitchenettes, some refrigerators. Cable TV. Pool. Gym. Dock, fishing. Laundry facilities, laundry service. Business services. Some pets allowed (fee). | 33 Tamiami Trail (U.S. 41) | 941/639–2167 or 877/639–9399 | fax 941/639–1707 | www.holiday-inn.com | 100 rooms | $67–$109 | AE, MC, V.

Marina Inn. In the popular Burnt Store Marina and Country Club, each one- or two-bedroom suite is individually owned and decorated. Walk-ins are accepted if a suite is available. The two-story brown and yellow stucco building is by the marina, 9 mi south of Punta Gorda, and about 30 min from Fort Myers Beach. The largest units sleep six. Restaurant, bar. Kitchenettes, microwaves, refrigerators. Cable TV, some in-room VCRs. Pool. Driving range, 18-hole golf course, putting green, 6 tennis courts. Exercise equipment. Dock, boating, fishing, bicycles. Laundry facilities. Business services. | 3160 Matecumbe Key Rd. | 941/575–4488 or 800/859–7529 | fax 941/575–7968 | 40 suites | $150–$275 | AE, D, DC, MC, V.

Motel 6. This one-story, no-frills motel is clean, comfortable, and inexpensive. There are several restaurants within a mile. In-room data ports. Cable TV. Pool. Laundry facilities. Some pets allowed. | 9300 Knights Dr. | 941/639–9585 or 800/466–8356 | fax 941/639–6820 | www.motel6.com | 114 rooms | $35–$50 | AE, MC, V.

REDINGTON BEACH

MAP 3, H6

(Nearby towns also listed: Clearwater, Indian Rocks Beach, Madeira Beach, St. Petersburg, St. Pete Beach, Tampa, Treasure Island)

Redington Beach, outside St. Petersburg, is famous as the site of Sand Key, a Gulf of Mexico barrier island on the famed Pinellas Peninsula. This beach is very popular and has everything from swimming to sunbathing, as well as lodging and restaurants that serve seafood fresh from the gulf.

Information: Gulf Beaches of Tampa Bay Chamber of Commerce | 6990 Gulf Blvd., St. Pete Beach, 33706 | 800/944–1847 | www.gulfbeaches-tampabay.com.

Attractions
Redington Pier. Built in 1963, this is the only wooden fishing pier on the West Gulf Coast. Standing 1,021 ft long, it is a popular spot to catch snook, tarpon, kingfish, mackerel, flounder, redfish, and more. Rental equipment is available. | 17490 Gulf Blvd. | 727/391–9398 | $1, fishing $6 | daily 24-hr pass issued.

Dining
Leverock's Seafood House. Seafood. The catch phrase here about the seafood is "any fresher, and it would still be swimming." The interior is simple and casual, preferring to emphasize the view of the water that surrounds most of the diners. Everyday, a list of catches is posted in the restaurant and on the menu. | 565 150th Ave. | 727/393–0459 | $17–$25 | AE, D, DC, MC, V.

The Lobster Pot. Seafood. The specialty of the house is, of course, lobster of all types. Maine lobster and South African lobster are flown in daily, and local spiney lobsters from the Keys are rushed over from the docks. You can get your lobster with a variety of sauces, and can also try escargots or raw oysters. | 17814 Gulf Blvd. | 727/391–8592 | No lunch | $15–$46 | AE, DC, MC, V.

The Wine Cellar. Continental. This family-owned (and -run) restaurant offers professional, attentive service, an extensive wine list (no surprise, given the name), and a warmly elegant dining room. Menu highlights include broiled Georgia farm-raised quail or the classic Dover sole meuniére, but save room for their crème brûlée or their freshly baked hazelnut torte. | 17307 Gulf Blvd. | 813/393–3491 | $15–$27 | AE, MC, V.

Lodging

Hilton Tampa Bay / North Redington Beach Resort. This hotel's spacious guest rooms and private balconies overlook the Gulf of Mexico and the Boca Ciega Intracoastal Waterway. There is an excellent restaurant, where guests can dine oceanside on the veranda or watch the sunsets from the beachside bar. The Suncoast Seabird Sanctuary is 2 mi away, and a car-rental desk is available. Restaurant, bar. In-room data ports. Outdoor pool. Business services. | 17120 Gulf Blvd., North Redington Beach | 727/391–4000 or 800/445–8667 | fax 813/397–0699 | www.hilton.com | 125 rooms | $160–$190 | AE, D, DC, MC, V.

RIVIERA BEACH

MAP 3, L8

(Nearby towns also listed: Jupiter, Palm Beach, Palm Beach Gardens, Palm Beach Shores, West Palm Beach)

The 47 miles of beach stretching up and down the Treasure Coast here include some pretty swank places. Riviera Beach, just north of West Palm Beach, is one of them. With plenty of golf, tennis, shopping, fine restaurants, and hip night spots, it's a nice place to come, meander, and relax. And with the rich Gulf Stream waters coming as close to shore here as anywhere on the coast, you'll find top-prize sport fish to be caught just 100 yards from shore. Nearby is the Port of Palm Beach, where casino cruises disembark.

Information: **Palm Beach County Convention and Visitors Bureau** | 1555 Palm Beach Lakes Blvd., Ste. 204, West Palm Beach, 33401 | 561/471–3995 | pbccvb@flinet.com | www.palmbeachfl.com.

Attractions

Peanut Island. In 1999 the 79-acre island opened as a county park for camping, fishing, and picnicking. | 6500 Peanut Island Rd. | 561/845–4445 | Free | Sunrise–sunset for non-campers.
Palm Beach Maritime Museum. On Peanut Island, this small museum's star attraction is the "Kennedy Bunker," a bomb shelter prepared for President John F. Kennedy in several restored Coast Guard buildings. | 6500 Peanut Island Rd. | 561/842–8202 | Bunker tours daily at 10:45, 11:45, 1:15, and 2:45 | $7.

Phil Foster Park. The pier has day-use boat slips and a boat ramp, so you may want to pack your water skis and inner tubes and don't forget your fishing rod. You can also bask on the beach. There are picnic pavilions, barbecue pits, concession stands, and outdoor showers. | 900 E. Blue Heron Blvd. | 561/966–6600 | Park free | Daily sunrise to sunset.

Dining

Ocean's Eleven North. American. Not for the faint of heart, this oceanside bar and grill serves big portions, and the happy hour lasts "all day and all night" because it doesn't close until five in the morning! You will be surrounded by 17 TVs and saturated with sporting events.

Between beers or steamers you can play pool or throw darts. Menu items include seafood steaks, ribs, and burgers. | On the beach, north end ocean mall | 561/840–1812 | $5.50–$11.95 | AE, MC, V.

Lodging

Hilton Singer Island Ocean Front Resort. Right across the bridge from Riviera Beach is Singer Island. Each room in this hotel has at least partial views of the Atlantic. Room configurations determine whether your deck will be a "stand out," "sit out," or a "wraparound sit out." You can bask in the sunshine on the resort's private beach strip. There is no lifeguard. A complimentary breakfast buffet comes with some packages. Restaurant. In-room data ports, refrigerators. Outdoor pool. Exercise equipment. Beach, water sports, fishing. Laundry facilities. Business services. No pets. | 3700 N. Ocean Dr. | 561/848–3888 | fax 561/848–4299 | www.hilton.com | 223 rooms | $189–$249 | AE, D, DC, MC, V.

ST. AUGUSTINE

MAP 3, J3

(Nearby towns also listed: Flagler Beach, St. Augustine Beach)

St. Augustine is the oldest continuously occupied European-settled city in the U.S, founded by Spanish settlers in 1565. In truth, the city was founded by Pedro Menéndez de Avilés under orders of King Phillip II in order to protect important Spanish trading routes in Florida, which was originally colonized by the French in 1562 in the area now known as Jacksonville. The site of their Fort Caroline is now a national memorial. But, as the Spanish ultimately prevailed over the French, it is St. Augustine that is best remembered.

The late 1880s saw the birth of the city as a tourist destination. The beautiful climate and unique feel attracted Henry Flagler, fellow industrialist and co-founder of the Standard Oil Company with John D. Rockefeller. Sinking his vast fortune into the area, he built two grand hotels, the Alcazar and the Ponce de León, and the tourists followed.

Today, St. Augustine has a formidable restoration movement, and it has become a center for colonial Spanish culture and architecture. Golf, yachting, and resorts—as well as the more than 60 historic sites and attractions and 144 blocks of houses listed on the National Register of Historic Places—attract visitors from around the world. Its 43 mi of beaches on two barrier islands can be easily reached by causeway.

Information: **St. Johns County Visitors and Convention Bureau** | 88 Riberia St., Ste. 400, St. Augustine, 32084 | 904/829–1711 or 800/653–2489 | www.visitoldcity.com.

Attractions

Anastasia State Recreation Area. One of Florida's busiest state parks, this preserve 3 mi south of St. Augustine occupies 17 acres of beach, lagoon, and marshes. You can swim, surf, windsurf, and sunbathe on 4 mi of beach, and there's a primitive 139-site campground on the coast, as well as ½ mi of trails. | 1340A Hwy. A1A S | 904/461–2033 | fax 904/461–2006 | www.dep.state.fl.us/parks/district_3/anastasia | $3.25 per vehicle | Daily 8–sundown.

Basilica Cathedral of St. Augustine. The oldest record of mass in Florida was held in 1594 on nearby shores, making this cathedral the country's oldest parish. The building dates back to 1797, but was restored after a fire in 1887. | 40 Cathedral Pl. | 904/824–2806 | Donations welcome | Open weekdays 7–5, weekends 7–7.

★ **Castillo de San Marcos National Monument.** This imposing fort, built from 1672–1695, overlooks Matanzas Bay and defended the city of St. Augustine for many years. Inside the Castillo, there are exhibits that display period artifacts and a few restored fort rooms. With St. Augustine itself, the Castillo is a reminder of the Spanish territories in the New World. | 1 S. Castillo Dr. | 904/829–6506 | www.nps.gov/casa | $4 | Daily 8:45–4:45.

Flagler College. The centerpiece of this school's 19-acre campus is the grand Ponce de León Hall, a luxurious structure that was a hotel until 1968 and is now on the National Register of Historic Places. The structure, a masterpiece of Spanish Renaissance architecture, was the dream of Henry Flagler, an industrialist, oil magnate, and railroad pioneer. Today the school has a student body of almost 2,000. | 74 King St. | 904/829–6481 | www.flagler.edu | Free | Daily 10–4.

Fountain of Youth Archeological Park. On April 3, 1513, Spanish explorer Ponce de León discovered what he believed to be the legendary Fountain of Youth. The park contains foundations and artifacts of the first St. Augustine colony. Other highlights include the Landmark Spring, the first North American Christian Indian burial sites, a globe depicting Spanish discoveries, and a planetarium. | 11 Magnolia Ave. | 904/829–3168 | www.fountainofyouthflorida.com | $5.50 | Daily 9–5.

Gonzalez-Alvarez House. Known to generations of tourists and residents as the Oldest House, the Gonzalez-Alvarez House is one of the country's most-studied and best-documented historic homes. Built in 1727, the house was occupied by various European and American families until 1918, when it was acquired by the St. Augustine Historical Society and opened to the public. Inside, you can see period furniture, and a tour highlights the old way of life and the history of the building. | 14 St. Francis St. | 904/824–2872 | fax 904/824–2569 | www.oldcity.com/oldhouse | $5 | Daily 9–5.

Lightner Museum. The former Alcazar Hotel, commissioned by Henry Flagler and designed by architects Carrere and Hastings, now displays an extensive collection of crystal, many examples of Tiffany glass, and exhibits of natural history and antique mechanical musical instruments. The three-floor Spanish Renaissance structure dates from 1887. | 75 King St. | 904/824–2874 | fax 904/824–2712 | www.lightnermuseum.com | info@lightnermuseum.org | $6 | Daily 9–5.

Memorial Presbyterian Church. Designed by Henry Flagler and built in 1889, this Venetian Renaissance structure has a dome that's more than 100 ft high and is topped by a 20-ft Greek cross. Eighty-six 20-ft-tall stained-glass windows showing the Apostle's creed line the walls. Take a guided tour, then explore further on your own. | 36 Sevilla St. | 904/829–6451 | Free | Daily 8:30–4:30.

Mission of Nombre de Dios. This mission, overlooking the Intracoastal Waterway, was founded in 1565 and was possibly America's first permanent Catholic mission. The 208-ft cross that stands here is visible to ships, day and night. The mission is three blocks north of the Visitor Information Center. | San Marco Ave. | 904/824–2809 | Free | Daily dawn to dusk.

Museum of Historic St. Augustine Government House. The collection here covers more than five centuries of local St. Augustine history. You can see displays of archaeological finds and Spanish shipwreck remnants, all presented along a timeline. The cultural, economical, architectural, and social changes are visible in the collection. The building still houses government offices. | 48 King St. | 904/825–5033 | $2.50 | Daily 9–6.

North American Top Gun Rides. Take an instructional flight in authentic two-seater 1940's Warbirds. You actually fly the plane for 10 to 60 minutes while the instructor sits behind you. If that isn't enough, take the 5-hr air combat course, then dogfight a buddy. | 270 Estrella Ave. | 904/823–3505 | www.natg.com | 10 min $99; up to 1 hr $590; combat course is $1,345 for 2 dueling people | Daily.

Old Florida Museum. This hands-on museum with a self-guided tour transports you through three significant historic Florida periods, from pre-European through 1926: Timucuan Indian, Spanish Colonial, and Florida Cracker Pioneer. A home representing each era lets you experience different aspects of life unique to each period. You can write with a quill pen, drill a hole with a Colonial pump drill, or grind corn in an old mill. Group tours, directed by guides in period costumes, need to be arranged in advance. | 245 D San Marco Ave. | 904/824–8874 or 800/813–3208 | $5 | Daily 10–5.

Oldest Store Museum. St. Augustine's Oldest Store Museum, once an operating general store, displays more than 100,000 vintage items that stocked the original site, including bikes, tools, guns, household goods, medicines, and hardware dating from the turn of the 20th century. A 1927 Model-T truck, frontier-era Conestoga wagon, and a steam tractor are also among the treasures. | 4 Artillery La. | 904/829–9729 | www.oldcity.com/oldstore | $5 | Daily 10–4.

Oldest Wooden Schoolhouse. One of the nation's oldest schoolhouses, this small building was built of cypress and cedar in 1804 and served as a guardhouse and sentry shelter during the Seminole wars. | 14 St. George St. | 904/824–0192 | www.oldschoolhouse.com | $2.50 | Sun.–Thurs. 9–6, Fri.–Sat. 9–7.

Peña-Peck House. This historic house, built in the 1740s as the home of the Royal Spanish Treasurer, was later the home of the Peck family for 90 years. You can see priceless 18th-century American antique furniture. | 143 St. George St. | 904/829–5064 | $4.50 | Weekdays, Sat. 12:30–4:30, Sun. noon–4:30; Jun.–Sept. closed Sun.

Potter's Wax Museum. The first wax museum in the United States, Potter's is recognized for its realism and the accurate period costuming of the likenesses of more than 150 famous people. | 17 King St. | 904/829–9056 | www.potterswax.com | $6.95 | Sept.–May, daily 9–5; mid-June–Aug., daily 9–9.

Ripley's Believe It or Not! Museum. A fixture near the City Gate since 1950, the first Ripley's ever opened has more than 500 exhibits—including a shrunken head, a replica of the Tower of London made from 264,345 matches, a mask covered with skin flayed from

KODAK'S TIPS FOR PHOTOGRAPHING PEOPLE

Friends' Faces
- Pose subjects informally to keep the mood relaxed
- Try to work in shady areas to avoid squints
- Let kids pick their own poses

Strangers' Faces
- In crowds, work from a distance with a telephoto lens
- Try posing cooperative subjects
- Stick with gentle lighting—it's most flattering to faces

Group Portraits
- Keep the mood informal
- Use soft, diffuse lighting
- Try using a panoramic camera

People at Work
- Capture destination-specific occupations
- Use tools for props
- Avoid flash if possible

Sports
- Fill the frame with action
- Include identifying background
- Use fast shutter speeds to stop action

Silly Pictures
- Look for or create light-hearted situations
- Don't be inhibited
- Try a funny prop

Parades and Ceremonies
- Stake out a shooting spot early
- Show distinctive costumes
- Isolate crowd reactions
- Be flexible: content first, technique second

© Artville

From Kodak Guide to Shooting Great Travel Pictures © 2000 by Fodor's Travel Publications

prisoners of war, a giant prehistoric jaw with more than 200 teeth, and lots more. | 19 San Marco Ave. | 904/824–1606 or 904/824–1607 | www.ripleys.com | $9.95 | Memorial Day–Labor Day 9–8; Labor Day–Memorial Day 9–9.

St. Augustine Alligator Farm. At this attraction on Anastasia Island, 2 mi south of the Bridge of Lions, you can explore the habitat of crocodiles, giant tortoises, alligators, and snakes. Established in 1893, it's the world's only complete alligator farm, with 23 species from all over the world. | 999 Anastasia Blvd. | 904/824–3337 | $11.95 | Daily 9–5.

St. Augustine Lighthouse and Museum. This Anastasia Island museum displays artifacts that have been collected from the numerous shipwrecks on St. Augustine inlet. Inside the adjacent St. Augustine lighthouse, built in 1870, you can climb the 219 steps to view downtown St. Augustine, the Historic District, and the beaches. | 81 Lighthouse Ave. | 904/829–0745 | fax 904/829–0745 | www.stauglight.com | $2.75 for museum; $5.50 for lighthouse | Daily 9–6.

San Sebastian Winery. Though the vineyards are in Claremont and Prosperity, you can taste the final product and tour the East Coast Railway Building, where the winery makes and sells its twelve varieties of wine. Tours leave every 15 or 20 minutes. There is a shop on the premises, so you can take home your favorite port, cream sherry, or sparkling wine. | 157 King St. | 904/826–1594 or 888/352–9463 | Free | Mon.–Sat. 10–6, Sun. 11–6.

Spanish Quarter. This nine-building complex in downtown St. Augustine re-creates a typical mid-18th-century Spanish garrison town. Here you can see Spanish and Spanish-Colonial artifacts, fine and decorative arts, and craft demonstrations. One entrance fee admits you to all the structures in the complex. | www.oldcity.com/spanishquarter | $6.50 | Daily 9–6.

Blacksmith Shop. At the historically reconstructed shop in the Spanish Quarter you can see the artisan working with his wrought-iron tools. | 29 St George St. | 904/825–6830 | www.oldcity.com/spanishquarter | Included in complex admission of $6.50 | Daily 9–6.

De Mesa-Sanchez House. Extensive excavation in the shellstone of this historic house in the Spanish Quarter has provided a great deal of information about the history of St. Augustine from the first Spanish period to later American times. | www.oldcity.com/spanishquarter | Included in complex admission of $6.50 | Daily 9–6.

Gallegos House. This two-room house in the Spanish Quarter is a typical mid-18th-century family home. The front room was used for sleeping and indoor activities; meals were prepared in the rear room. | www.oldcity.com/spanishquarter | Included in complex admission of $6.50 | Daily 9–6.

Gomez House. The small store inside this Spanish Quarter home provided extra income for the soldier and his family who lived here. This was how many soldiers, especially privates, helped make ends meet on their small salaries. | www.oldcity.com/spanishquarter | Included in complex admission of $6.50 | Daily 9–6.

Peso de Burgo and Pellicer House. These wooden Spanish Quarter homes are reconstructions of a Minorcan family house and separate kitchen on the site during the British Period (1763–1783), when control of the area was surrendered to Britain after the French-Indian War. | 55 St. George St. | 904/825–6830 | www.oldcity.com/spanishquarter | Included in complex admission of $6.50 | Daily 9–6.

Visitor Information Center. The entertaining film shown here covers St. Augustine's beginnings. | 10 Castillo Dr. | 904/825–1000 | Free; parking $3 | Jun.–Aug., daily 8–7:30; Apr.–May, Sept.–Oct., daily 8:30–6:30; Nov.–Mar., daily 8:30–5:30; film shown hourly 9–4.

Whetstone Chocolate Factory. In business since 1966, when Mrs. Whetstone started making fudge in her kitchen, this factory a few minutes from downtown produces sweets most days between 10 AM and 2 PM. The newest addition of the family-owned business is the chocolate orange, which splits into 18 slices. After the 15-min introductory video, you take a self-guided tour and see some of the 25,000 lbs of chocolate being produced (every eight hrs). At the end you get a free sample of chocolate and can shop in the factory store. | 2 Coke Rd. (Hwy 312E and Coke Rd., just off of U.S. 1S) | 904/825–1700 | Free | Mon.–Sat. 10–5.

World Golf Village. This complex contains two 18-hole golf courses, including The King & the Bear, a collaboration between Arnold Palmer and Jack Nicklaus. There's also a golf academy, a resort, and a convention center. | 21 World Golf Pl. | 904/940–4123 | www.wgv.com | Daily.

World Golf Hall of Fame. The central institution of World Golf Village pays tribute to the game. Highlights include a replica of Swilcan Burn Bridge at St. Andrews, an 1880s-style putting green, and a swing analyzer that tells you which professional your swing resembles. An IMAX theater screens films about everything from athletics to nature. | $10; IMAX film $9 | Daily 10–6.

Ximenez-Fatio House. Andres Ximenez, a Spanish storekeeper, built this house in 1797 from native coquina shellstone, using Spanish and English design principles. The late-18th-century kitchen, which has a brick baking oven, is the only original example in St. Augustine. The house is on the National Register of Historic Places. | 20 Aviles St. | 904/829–3575 | Oct.–Aug., Thurs.–Mon. 11–4, Sun. 1–4, closed Weds.

SIGHTSEEING TOURS/TOUR COMPANIES

Historical Tours. This narrated 7-mi trolley tour gives you an overview of St. Augustine, from the arrival of Ponce de León in 1513 to the present. Your ticket, good for three days, entitles you to hop on and hop off at major points of interest and park at no charge in the ticket office's parking lot. | 167 San Marco Ave. | 904/829–3800 | $12 | Daily 8:30–5:30.

Scenic Cruise. This 75-min cruise on Matanzas Bay, leaving from the Municipal Marina, is narrated by third and fourth generation members of the Usina family, Minorcan pioneers, who first came to St. Augustine in 1768. | 4125 Coastal Hwy. | 904/824–1806 or 800/542–8316 | www.scenic-cruise.com | $9.50 | Daily 11, 1, 2:45, 4:30, 6:15, 8:30.

Sightseeing Trains. Sightseeing Trains take you on a tram ride to a number of sites, including Castillo de San Marcos, Flagler College, and the Fountain of Youth Archaeological Park. Tickets are for sale at the company's eight stations, some of which provide free parking; packages including discounted admissions to historical attractions are available. | 170 San Marco Ave. | 904/829–6545 or 800/226–6545 | www.redtrains.com | $12 | Daily 8:30–5.

Stroll with the Spirits. Guides on these after-dark walking tours, which start at the Old Jail Complex parking lot, regale you with ghostly tales of St. Augustine's past as you stroll through the Huguenot Cemetery, call on the spirit that haunts the Old Jail, and stand in front of the gallows where, some say, the ghost of sheriff Sam Jackson still hangs out. | 167 San Marco Ave. | 904/826–4218 | $8 | Daily 7:30 PM.

Tour St. Augustine. This company offers a different walking tour each morning, lasting 1½ hours. "The Bloody Sunset Tour" examines the still unsolved 1974 brutal machete killing of Broadway actress/model Athalia Lindsley. Other tours include "The Gilded Age of Henry Flagler," a tour of stately homes, and "It's Not a Building," which looks at local landmarks, monuments, and bridges and discusses their historic significance. All tours meet in the lobby of Casa Monica. | 95 Cordova St. | 904/825–0087 or 800/797–3778 | $10 | Daily.

Voyager Sailing Cruises. Captain Paul likes when you take the wheel and experience the joys of sailing firsthand. He takes four-hour trips with no more than six people on his three-hulled trimaran, which has 700 square ft of deck space. You can take a dip or simply enjoy the wind at your sails and the lilt of dolphins frolicking. Both lunch or sunset trips are available. | Downtown City Municipal Marina, 111 Avenida Menendez | 904/347–7183 | $35 | By appointment.

ON THE CALENDAR

MAR.–APR.: *Blessing of the Fleet.* Each year on Palm Sunday, the Bishop of St. Augustine blesses commercial and pleasure craft. | 904/829–5681.

JUNE: *Greek Landing Day Festival.* This event at the St. Photios National Greek Orthodox Shrine celebrates the landing of the first colony of Greeks in North America with Greek folk dancing, food, and music. | 904/829–8205.

JUNE: *Spanish Night Watch.* Costumed actors assemble in the Government House to re-enact a Spanish night watch, giving you a feel for 18th-century life in St. Augustine. A torchlight procession in the Spanish Quarter is the highlight of the festivities. | 904/ 829–5681.

SEPT.: *Founder's Day Celebration.* This Spanish fiesta, downtown next to the Visitor Information Center, celebrates the founding of St. Augustine with arts and crafts, entertainment, games, music, and food. The first Catholic Mass of America is commemorated at the Mission of Nombre de Dios. | 904/825–1010.

DEC.: *Christmas Tour of Homes.* Unusual and historic homes throughout St. Augustine are decorated for the Christmas holidays and opened to the public for tours. | 904/ 826–0242.

Dining

Cortesse's Bistro. Continental. This cafe is located in a charming turn-of-the-20th-century house. You can eat inside or in the oak tree-shaded courtyard, and there is live jazz Wed.–Sun. Popular dishes include the veal oscar and Angus beef tenderloin. | 172 San Marco Ave. | 904/825–6775 | Reservations essential on weekends | $9–$25 | AE, D, MC, V.

Columbia. Spanish. This bustling, popular restaurant, decorated with pictures of the owner and a statue of Cortez, serves time-honored Cuban and Spanish dishes. Try the arroz con pollo or the filet salteado. Sun. brunch. | 98 St. George St. | 904/824–3341 or 800/227–1905 | Reservations essential | $11–$19 | AE, D, DC, MC, V.

The Conch House. Seafood. With tiki torches and palm trees, this eatery has a real island feel, and diners may also eat outdoors on individual thatched-roof pods on the water. Try the conch fritters or the conch chowder. Many of the dishes also have a Caribbean flavor—the Jamaican chicken is especially good. Kids' menu. | 57 Comares Ave. | 904/829–8646 | Breakfast also available | $14–$18 | AE, MC, V.

95 Cordova. Eclectic. In the historic Casa Monica Hotel, this contemporary dining room gets funky with Floridian and Asian cuisine. For starters you can have alligator and smoked sausage fritters or seafood crêpes, then move on to the seared tuna on lo mein noodles or the grilled duck with raspberry hoisin sauce. The decadent desserts include such items as St. John's mud cake. Champagne brunch on Sunday is a good deal. | 115 Cordova St. | 904/810–6810 | $10–$35 | AE, MC, V.

Florida Cracker Café. Continental. Works by local artists adorn the walls of this popular café in the heart of the Historic District. You can dine inside or on the shaded patio and enjoy fresh local seafood, pastas, salads, and hamburgers. Daily specials can include fried shrimp stuffed with crab or seafood pasta salad. Key lime pie is the dessert of choice here. | 81 St. George St. | 904/829–0397 | $17–$29 | D, MC, V.

Gypsy Cab Co. Contemporary. Local artwork, including streetscapes and glassware, decorate this casual eatery. They like to call their cuisine "urban," because it blends styles from various locales. The specialty is the breaded and marinated Gypsy chicken. Leave room for dessert—the key lime pie is great. Kids' menu. | 828 Anastasia Blvd. | 904/824–8244 | www.gypsycab.com | $9–$18 | AE, D, MC, V.

Hooked on Henry's. Cajun. Once you step inside and get a whiff of the spicy Cajun cooking, you might think you're on Bourbon Street. Red beans with rice and sausage, shrimp and crab étouffée, and jambalaya are the house specialties, but the menu also includes po'boys, burgers, fried oysters, blackened shrimp, and several spicy pastas. | 46 Avenida Menendez | 904/824–7765 | $9.99–$23.99 | AE, D, DC, MC, V.

King's Head British Pub. English. Dark wood walls and a bar featuring a superb selection of fine English beers on tap lend an authentic touch to this English pub. Bangers and mash, fish and chips, steak and kidney pie, and other English pub fare are the order here. | 6460 U.S. 1N | 904/823–9787 | Closed Mon. | $5–$9.75 | AE, MC, V.

★ **La Parisienne.** French. This tiny place is in a white stucco building with a little flower-filled courtyard. Try the roasted duck or chicken Provençal, but save room for the delicious pastries. Weekend brunch. | 60 Hypolita St. | 904/829–0055 | Closed Wed. | $19–$32 | AE, D, MC, V.

Raintree. Continental. Antiques fill this restaurant in an 1860s Victorian house. There's also a splendid garden and gazebo on the premises. Try the rainbow trout, filet of salmon, or the oven-roasted duck with raspberry sauce. | 102 San Marco Ave. | 904/829–5953 | Reservations essential on weekends | No lunch | $15–$30 | AE, DC, MC, V.

White Lion Restaurant and Tavern. American. In this Old English–style café and pub, you can eat indoors or on the patio overlooking the Castillo de San Marcos. White lion statues and stained-glass windows emphasize the theme of the restaurant. The grilled mahimahi and the T-bone steaks are recommended. Kids' menu. | 20 Cuna St. | 904/829–2388 | $8–$18 | MC, V.

Zaharias. Greek. A short drive from downtown across the Bridge of Lions, this big, busy restaurant buzzes with an air of open hospitality. You can serve yourself from an enormous buffet instead of, or in addition to, ordering from the menu. Greek and Italian specialties include homemade pizza, a big gyro dinner served with spaghetti, shish kebabs, steaks, seafood, and sandwiches. | 3945 Rte. A1A S | 904/471–4799 | No lunch | $8.95–$12.95 | AE, D, MC, V.

Lodging

Agustin Inn. This contemporary B&B is in charming, historic downtown St. Augustine. Rooms are decorated with antiques and some feature private balconies. Just follow the cobblestone streets for a short block to reach many wonderful restaurants and shops. Dining room, complimentary breakfast. Many in-room hot tubs, no room phones, TV in common area. No pets. | 29 Cuna St. | 904/823–9559 or 800/248–7846 | fax 904/824–8685 | agustin@aug.com | www.agustininn.com | 7 rooms | $89–$135 | D, MC, V.

Alexander Homestead. Vintage furniture and European paintings fill this B&B in a Victorian home dating from 1888. The elegant parlor is perfect for spending an intimate evening by the fireplace with a glass of wine. Dining room, complimentary breakfast. Some in-room hot tubs. Cable TV, some room phones. No pets. No smoking. | 14 Sevilla St. | 904/826–4147 or 888/292–4147 | fax 904/823–9503 | bonnie@aug.com | www.alexanderhomestead.com | 4 rooms | $125–$175 | AE, D, MC, V.

Bayfront Inn. This motel is ideally situated for touring historic St. Augustine. Just outside the door is Matanzas Bay where guests can watch boats and the occasional dolphin pass under the Bridge of Lions. Restaurants, fine shops, and museums are all within walking distance. Complimentary Continental breakfast. In-room data ports. Cable TV. Outdoor pool. Outdoor hot tub, spa. No pets. No smoking. | 138 Avenida Menendez | 904/824–1681 or 800/558–3455 | fax 904/829–8721 | info@bayfrontinn.com | www.bayfrontinn.com | 37 rooms, 2 suites in 2 buildings | $150, $225–$250 suites | AE, D, MC, V.

Best Western Historical Inn. This two-story hotel is six blocks north of St. Augustine's Historic District and is decorated in traditional Spanish architectural style. There are a number of local attractions and excellent restaurants within walking distance. Complimentary Continental breakfast. In-room data ports, some kitchenettes, microwaves, refrigerators. Cable TV. Outdoor pool. Outdoor hot tub. Laundry facilities. Business services. | 2010 Ponce de León Blvd. | 904/829–9088 or 800/528–1234 | fax 904/829–6629 | www.bestwestern.com | 38 rooms, 1 suite | $89, $180 suite | AE, D, DC, MC, V.

★ **Carriage Way Bed and Breakfast.** This Victorian home built in 1883, lies within walking distance of the old town. It features an upper and lower veranda, where you can relax after a long day of exploring the historic sites. Most of the rooms have clawfoot tubs and all are furnished with antiques or replicas. There is a guest cottage three doors down from the main home, in which you can rent just one room or the entire home. The owners offer special-occasion breakfasts and let you borrow bikes to get around town. Complimentary

Continental breakfast. Some kitchenettes, some microwaves, some refrigerators, some in-room hot tubs. TV in common area. No pets. No kids under 8. | 70 Cuna St. | 904/829–2467 or 800/908–9832 | fax 904/826–1461 | www.carriageway.com | 9 rooms in the main home, 2 rooms in the cottage | $69–$175 | D, MC, V.

Casa Monica Hotel. The towers and turrets here have been turned into suites that resemble town homes and have views of downtown St. Augustine. The 112-yr-old Spanish-style building, once owned by Henry Flagler, was closed from 1932 to 1962, when it was restored to its luxurious state. You can get the concierge to set you up on a tour, fishing adventure, or with a baby-sitter, and the beach is only about 15 min away. Rooms are elegant with white mesh draped on wrought-iron bed posts and marble tile bathrooms. Restaurant, bar. In-room safes, some kitchenettes. Cable TV. 1 in-room hot tub. Pool. Outdoor hot tub. Gym. Business services. Laundry service. | 95 Cordova St. | 904/827–1888 or 800/648–1888 | fax 904/827–0426 | www.grandthemehotels.com | 120 rooms and 11 suites | $139–$219 | AE, DC, MC, V.

Casablanca Inn on the Bay. This restored 1914 Mediterranean-style home overlooks Matanzas Bay and is listed on the National Register of Historic Places. Rooms are decorated with fine antiques and local artwork, and fresh-baked cookies are served every afternoon. Dining room, complimentary breakfast. Some in-room hot tubs. Some room phones, no TV in some rooms. Bicycles. No pets. No kids under 12. No smoking. | 24 Avenida Menendez | 904/829–0928 or 800/826–2626 | fax 904/826–1892 | innkeeper@casablancainn.com | www.casablancainn.com | 18 rooms, 2 suites | $139–$189, $199–$225 suites | AE, D, MC, V.

Casa de la Paz Bayfront B&B. This B&B in a 1915 Mediterranean-style structure sports a view of Matanzas Bay. Attractions such as the Castillo de San Marcos and the Bridge of Lions are just steps away. The interior of the home is decorated with antique furnishings and lush plants. Dining room, complimentary breakfast. Cable TV. No pets. No kids under 15. No smoking. | 22 Avenida Menendez | 904/829–2915 or 800/929–2915 | fax 904/824–6269 | delapaz@aug.com | www.casadelapaz.com | 6 rooms | $120–$225 | D, MC, V.

Casa de Solana B&B Inn. Family heirlooms, including Oriental rugs and chandeliers, fill this 1763 Spanish Colonial house. Some rooms afford guests a view of Matanzas Bay, and there is a lush garden out front featuring a beautiful Spanish fountain. Dining room, complimentary breakfast. Cable TV. No pets. No kids under 12. No smoking. | 21 Aviles St. | 904/824–3555 | fax 904/824–3316 | www.oldcity.com/solana | 4 rooms | $125–$175 | AE, D, MC, V.

Casa de Suenos B&B. This B&B is in a beautiful turn-of-the-20th-century Mediterranean-style inn that is on the romantic Carriage Route. Rooms are decorated with antiques and some feature crystal chandeliers and balconies. Dining room. In-room data ports, some refrigerators, some in-room hot tubs. Cable TV, in-room VCRs. Bicycles. No pets. No kids under 13. No smoking. | 20 Cordova St. | 904/824–0887 or 800/824–0804 | fax 904/825–0074 | www.casadesuenos.com | 4 rooms, 2 suites | $85–$160, $160–$190 suites | D, MC, V.

Cedar House Inn. Great pains were taken to preserve the original floors and woodwork in this 1893 Victorian home when it was restored in the 1990s. All the rooms are named after the innkeepers' grandparents and feature private balconies. Dining room, complimentary breakfast. In-room data ports, some refrigerators, some in-room hot tubs. Cable TV, some in-room VCRs. Bicycles. No pets. No kids under 13. No smoking. | 79 Cedar St. | 904/829–0079 or 800/233–2746 | fax 904/825–0916 | www.cedarhouseinn.com | 6 rooms | $109–$174 | AE, D, MC, V.

Centennial House. Just steps from Flagler College, this two-story home was completely renovated in 1998. The innkeeper's intent is to combine 19th-century living with 20th-century luxury. Some rooms have gas fireplaces and vaulted ceilings, and there is one first-floor room suitable for the physically disabled. Each of the uniquely themed rooms has down pillows, blankets, and Egyptian cotton towels. There is a garden courtyard where you can sit and bask in the historic surroundings. Complimentary breakfast. Some in-room data ports, some in-room hot tubs. In-room VCRs. Business services. No kids under 16. | 26

Cordova St. | 904/810–2218 or 800/611–2880 | fax 904/810–1930 | www.centennialhouse.com | 7 rooms | $135–$205 | AE, MC, V.

Edgewater Inn. This single-story motel is on Matanzas Bay and overlooks the St. Augustine skyline. The attractions and restaurants of downtown St. Augustine are within walking distance. In-room data ports. Cable TV. Outdoor pool. Business services. No pets. | 2 St. Augustine Blvd. | 904/825–2697 | fax 904/825–4698 | 18 rooms | $150 | AE, D, MC, V.

Hampton Inn Historic. Nearby are a number of museums and the Spanish Historic District. Complimentary Continental breakfast. In-room data ports, some microwaves, some refrigerators, some in-room hot tubs. Cable TV. Outdoor pool. Outdoor hot tub. Business services. No pets. | 2050 N. Ponce de León Blvd. | 904/829–1996 or 800/426–7866 (reservations) | fax 904/829–1988 | 48 rooms, 4 suites | $75–$185 | AE, D, DC, MC, V.

Holiday Inn Express. This two-story motel is just 5 mi from St. Augustine's Historic District. There are a handful of eateries within walking distance. In-room data ports, some microwaves, some refrigerators, some in-room hot tubs. Cable TV. Outdoor pool. Laundry facilities. Business services. No pets. | 2310 Rte. 16 | 904/823–8636 or 800/HOLIDAY (reservations) | fax 904/823–8728 | www.holiday-inn.com | 51 rooms | $69–$79 | AE, D, DC, MC, V.

Kenwood Inn Bed and Breakfast. For more than a century, this stately Victorian inn has welcomed travelers, and the Constant family continues the tradition. In the heart of the Historic District, the inn is near restaurants and sightseeing. Rooms have hardwood floors and sitting areas; some have fireplaces and access to wraparound porches. Complimentary Continental breakfast. Outdoor pool. | 38 Marine St. | 904/824–2112 | www.oldcity.com/kenwood | 10 rooms, 4 suites | $110–$145 | D, MC, V.

Monterey Inn. The fact that it's right across from the Castillo de San Marcos National Monument and across the street from Matanzas Bay is the draw of this modest two-story motel. Most rooms overlook the bay, but the efficiency units are in back and offer no scenic relief. There is a sun deck, and if you can ignore the car exhaust from the street, you'll have a lovely view of the bay. Restaurant. In-room data ports, some kitchenettes, some microwaves, some refrigerators. Outdoor pool. No pets. | 16 Avenida Menendez | 904/824–4482 | fax 904/829–8854 | www.themontereyinn.com | 59 rooms | $59–$89 | AE, D, DC, MC, V.

Old City House Inn. This Colonial-style inn in the heart of downtown St. Augustine was built in 1873. Some rooms are decorated with floral tones, some with Victorian pastels, and some with natural-wood accents. The restaurant serves eclectic cuisine with a Mediterranean flare. Restaurant, picnic area, complimentary breakfast. Some in-room hot tubs. Cable TV. Bicycles. No smoking. | 115 Cordova St. | 904/826–0113 | fax 904/823–8960 | www.oldcityhouse.com | 7 rooms | $75–$145 | AE, D, DC, MC, V.

Old Powder House Inn. This turn-of-the-20th-century Victorian home sits right in the path of the horse-drawn carriages that parade through the Historic District. You can sit on the shady veranda and enjoy complimentary afternoon lemonade or an evening glass of wine. Some rooms have four-poster cherry beds, whirlpools, fireplaces, or private libraries. Some even come with a split of champagne! With dishes such as baked apple pecan pancake, you won't want to oversleep and miss breakfast. Bikes and TVs are also available upon request. There is a two-night minimum stay on weekends. Complimentary breakfast. Some minibars, some in-room hot tubs. No room phones, TV in common area. Outdoor hot tub. Business services. No kids under 8. No smoking. | 38 Cordova St. | 904/824–4149 or 800/447–4149 | fax 904/825–0143 | www.oldpowderhouse.com | 9 rooms | $65–195 | AE, D, MC, V.

Quality Inn Alhambra. The Castillo de San Marcos and the Lightner Museum are just 1 mi to the south of this two-story hotel. Guests can board the Sightseeing Train just behind the hotel. Restaurant, room service. Some in-room hot tubs. Cable TV. Outdoor pool. Outdoor hot tub. Business services. No pets. | 2700 N. Ponce de León Blvd. | 904/824–2883 | fax 904/825–0976 | www.qualityinn.com | 72 rooms, 5 suites | $99–$175, $225–$300 suites | AE, D, DC, MC, V.

Radisson Ponce de León Golf and Conference Center Resort. Sprawled across 350 acres and bordering the marshlands of the Intracoastal Waterway, this resort is almost like a small city. The 18-hole championship golf course was designed by Donald Ross and is a focal point of the resort. Restaurant, bar, room service. In-room data ports, some microwaves, some refrigerators. Cable TV. Outdoor pool. Driving range, 18-hole golf course, miniature golf, 6 tennis courts. Business services. No pets. | 4000 U.S. 1N | 904/824–2821 or 800/333–3333 | fax 904/824–8254 | www.radisson.com | 186 rooms, 7 suites | $129–$159, $169 suites | AE, D, DC, MC, V.

★ **Sheraton Visitana Resort at World Golf Village.** You can watch the action on the 17th and 18th holes from many rooms at this golfer's haven. There are one- and two-bedroom units in the 134 villas in the World Golf Village, on the northwest corner of town, off of I–95. Richly appointed rooms are painted in deep shades of green or ochre and decorated with framed prints and earth-tone fabrics. Each unit has a separate living room, a full kitchen, and a washer and dryer. The units can be rented nightly, weekly, or monthly. In-room data ports, kitchenettes, in-room hot tubs. Cable TV, in-room VCRs. Outdoor pool. Outdoor hot tub. Golf courses. Exercise equipment. Laundry facilities. No pets. | 1 Front Nine Dr. | 904/940–2000 | www.sheraton.com | 134 units | $239–$329 | AE, D, DC, MC, V.

St. Francis Inn. Constructed with native coquina limestone in 1791, this B&B is decorated with antique and replica furniture. The courtyard and garden are shaded by banana trees, jasmine, and other exotic flora—ideal for spending a relaxing afternoon with a book. Dining room, complimentary breakfast. Some kitchenettes, some refrigerators, some in-room hot tubs. Cable TV. Outdoor pool. Bicycles. No pets. No smoking. | 279 St. George St. | 904/824–6068 or 800/824–6062 | fax 904/810–5525 | innceasd@aug.com | www.stfrancisinn.com | 11 rooms, 4 suites, 1 cottage | $99–$149, $189 suites, $219 cottage | AE, D, DC, MC, V.

Westcott House. This B&B in a Victorian house built in the late 1880s overlooks Matanzas Bay. Rooms are decorated with lovely American and European antiques and most offer panoramic bay views. The Westcott House is within walking distance of many fine restaurants and quaint shops. Complimentary breakfast. Cable TV. No pets. No smoking. | 146 Avenida Menendez | 904/824–4301 or 800/513–9814 | fax 904/824–4301 | info@westcotthouse.com | www.westcotthouse.com | 9 rooms | $95–$175 | AE, D, MC, V.

World of Golf Village Renaissance Resort. Adjacent to the World Golf Hall of Fame and the bordering PGA tour golf course, the nine-story building has large rooms overlooking either the central atrium or out onto the 6,000 acres of property. Next door is a convention center and a whole complex of shopping, restaurants, and even an IMAX theater. Restaurant, bar. In-room data ports, in-room safes, some kitchenettes, refrigerators. Cable TV. Pool. Massage, sauna, spa. 36-hole golf course, tennis. Gym, health club. Bicycles. Baby-sitting. Laundry facilities. | 500 S. Legacy Trail | 904/940–8000 or 800/228–9290 | fax 904/940–2092 | www.renaissancehotels.com; Golf: www.wgv.com | 300 rooms | $139–$199 | AE, D, DC, MC, V.

ST. AUGUSTINE BEACH

MAP 3, J3

(Nearby towns also listed: Flagler Beach, St. Augustine)

Just east of St. Augustine on the northern end of 18-mi long Anastasia Island is St. Augustine Beach. The island, nestled between the Atlantic and the Intracoastal Waterway, sports wide, white-sand beaches and is a popular spot for outdoors lovers. Camping, hiking, fishing, picnics, nature walks, and a 1,700-acre bird sanctuary with 4 mi of lagoons and plenty of wildlife are within easy reach.

Information: St. Johns County Visitors and Convention Bureau | 88 Riberia St., Ste. 400, St. Augustine, 32084 | 904/829–1711 or 800/653–2489 | www.visitoldcity.com.

Attractions

Fort Matanzas National Monument. This Spanish fort was built from 1740–1742 to defend St. Augustine from enemies approaching from the south. The park, which is spread out over 300 acres, provides a natural habitat rich in wildlife. You can get to the monument by ferry from the visitor center. | 8635 Hwy. A1A S | 904/471–0116 | www.nps.gov/foma/ | Free | Daily 8:30–5:30.

Marineland of Florida. Opened in 1938, this marine attraction was one of the first of its kind in the United States. There are 10 dolphin shows daily at the two dolphin tanks, where you can watch divers swim with these sensitive mammals, or scuba and snorkel among them yourself. During these 90-min Dolphin Encounters, you can feed and play with a dolphin. Marineland is also home to penguins, sea lions, and a shell museum. | 9600 Oceanshore Blvd. | 904/460–1275 | www.marineland.net | $12 | Wed.–Sun. 9:30–4:30; Dolphin Encounter Mon., Tues. 10:30, 1:30 by reservation.

St. John's County Pier. This 600-ft pier is open for fishing or strolling. There is a bait and tackle shop on the pier, so you don't have to carry too much gear. The fish really bite in cooler weather; you might catch whiting, flounder, or tarpon. | 350 A1A Beach Blvd. | 904/471–1596 | $2 to fish, 50¢ to stroll | The pier is never closed; shop hours 6–10.

Washington Oaks State Gardens. This 389-acre preserve, 22 mi south of St. Augustine Beach, just north of Palm Coast, is planted with azaleas, camellias, exotic bird of paradise plants, and more. About 3 mi of hiking trails allow visitors to explore a mature coastal maritime hummock. | 6400 N. Oceanshore Blvd., Palm Coast | 904/446–6780 | www.dep.state.fl.us | $3.25 per vehicle | Daily 8–sundown.

ON THE CALENDAR

JAN.–DEC.: *Farmers Market.* Every Wednesday, rain or shine, in the parking lot of St. John's County Pier, local produce and house-plant vendors gather to sell their goods. The market is open 7–noon. | 370 A1A Beach Blvd. | 904/471–8267 or 800/OLD–CITY.

Dining

Barnacle Bill's Beachside. Seafood. One of three Barnacle Bill's in town and a St. Augustine institution since 1981, this beachside branch is right across from the Hampton Inn. Famous for its Dat'l Do-It sauce (which can garnish seafood, steaks, chops, or chicken) as well as its mouth-watering fried shrimp. You can order Dat'l Do-It fried shrimp for the complete experience. | 451 A1A Beach Blvd. | 904/471–2434 | No lunch | $11–$13 | AE, D, DC, MC, V.

Oasis Deck and Restaurant. American. It seems like there's always a party at the Oasis, where the two-story beach shack in pink and blue and the 24 beers on tap put you in a carefree state of mind. For breakfast, people love the eggs Benedict, served with the homemade biscuits. Later in the day, those ready to adventure beyond the raw bar can try the conch fritters or the fresh Florida gator tail. | 4000 A1A South and Ocean Trace Rd. | 904/471–3424 restaurant; 904/471–2451 deck | Breakfast also available | $8–$14 | AE, D, DC, MC, V.

Salt Water Cowboys. Seafood. Snake and alligator skins decorate this casual spot. Popular dishes include fried shrimp, soft-shelled crab, alligator tail stew, and the jambalaya. Kids' menu. | 299 Dondanville Rd. | 904/471–2332 | Reservations not accepted | No lunch | $7–$15 | AE, D, DC, MC, V.

Sunset Grille. American/Casual. Despite the party vibe at this beachfront spot, the food is better than you would expect. TVs throughout the dining room keep you in touch with sporting events, but there is outside seating if you want to worship the sun as you dine. There is either a band or a DJ most nights. You could accompany, Buffett's namesake, the *Cheeseburger in Paradise,* with a house special, Sunset Margarita. Besides burgers, a popular choice is the Sunset Shrimp (sautéed in garlic with white wine, bacon, mushrooms, tomatoes, Parmesan, and mozzarella, served over pasta). | 421 A1A Beach Blvd. | 904/471–5555 | $3.95–$16.95 | AE, D, MC, V.

ST. AUGUSTINE
BEACH

INTRO
ATTRACTIONS
DINING
LODGING

Lodging

Best Western Ocean Inn. This two-story hotel is near beautiful beaches, 3 mi from the St. Augustine Alligator Farm, and 10 mi from Marineland of Florida. Restaurant, complimentary Continental breakfast. Cable TV. Outdoor pool. Laundry facilities. Business services. Pets allowed. | 3955 Hwy. A1A S | 904/471–8010 or 888/879–3578 (reservations) | fax 904/460–9124 | www.bestwestern.com | 33 rooms, 2 suites | $99–$149, $119–$169 suites | AE, D, DC, MC, V.

Comfort Inn. Your 1980s-style room, with colorful bedspread and sandy-colored walls, is just a two-block walk from the beach at this hotel with a palm tree–lined canopy. Unfortunately, there is a closed community right across the street (with direct access to the beach), so there are no ocean views. The closest beach access is about ¼ mi away. Complimentary Continental breakfast. In-room data ports, some kitchenettes, some microwaves, some refrigerators, some in-room hot tubs. Outdoor pool. Outdoor hot tub. Beach. Laundry facilities. Business services. | 901 A1A Beach Blvd. | 904/471–1474 | fax 904/460–1160 | www.comfortinn.com | 70 rooms | $91–$111 | AE, D, DC, MC, V.

Days Inn, St. Augustine Beach. Decorated in an Old Spanish-style setting, this three-story hotel was built in 1991 and renovated in 1998. There are a number of restaurants within walking distance. Complimentary Continental breakfast. In-room data ports, some microwaves, some refrigerators. Cable TV. Outdoor pool. Outdoor hot tub. Laundry facilities. Business services. No pets. | 541 Rte. A1A S. Beach Blvd. | 904/461–9990 or 800/544–8313 | fax 904/471–4774 | www.daysinn.com | 48 rooms, 2 suites | $90–$130, $169–$189 suites | AE, D, DC, MC, V.

Econo Lodge. Exit 93 off of I–95 brings you to this two-story chain on a strip of other chain hotels. This spot for the thrifty is just across from the beach and close to the fishing pier and some restaurants. Picnic area, complimentary Continental breakfast. Some kitchenettes, some minibars, some in-room hot tubs. Outdoor pool. Outdoor hot tub. Beach. | 311 A1A Beach Blvd. | 904/471–2330 | 50 rooms | $49–$189 | AE, D, DC, MC, V.

Hampton Inn, St. Augustine Beach. This four-story oceanside hotel was built in 1997, just 4 mi from St. Augustine's Historic District, and there are a number of restaurants within walking distance. In-room data ports, some microwaves, some refrigerators, some in-room hot tubs. Cable TV. Outdoor pool. Exercise equipment. Beach. Laundry facilities. Business services. No pets. | 430 Rte. A1A Beach Blvd. | 904/471–4000 or 800/HAMPTON | fax 904/471–4888 | www.hamptoninn.com | 87 rooms, 13 suites | $89–$154, $199–$259 suites | AE, D, DC, MC, V.

Hilton Garden Inn, St. Augustine Beach. Off of State Road 312, this is an extremely business-friendly hotel. Rooms come in many configurations, including a jacuzzi suite and a family suite, which is much like a one-bedroom apartment. Facilities include a pantry store for any forgotten food items and a restaurant that serves breakfast only. The beach across the street disappears when the tide comes in, but two blocks up is the full sun-bathing experience. Restaurant. In-room data ports, some kitchenettes, microwaves, refrigerators, some in-room hot tubs. Outdoor pool. Outdoor hot tub. Exercise equipment. Beach. Shops. Laundry facilities, laundry service. Business services. No pets. | 401 A1A Beach Blvd. | 904/471–5559 | fax 904/471–7146 | www.hilton.com/hiltongardeninn | 83 rooms | $99–$214 | AE, D, DC, MC, V.

Holiday Inn, St. Augustine Beach. Built in the late 1960s, this five-story motel offers guests access to a private beach. Restaurant, bar. In-room data ports. Cable TV. Outdoor pool. Exercise equipment. Beach. Video games. Laundry facilities. Business services. Some pets allowed. | 860 A1A Beach Blvd. | 904/471–2555 or 800/626–7263 | fax 904/461–8710 | www.holiday-inn.com | 151 rooms | $110–$130 | AE, D, DC, MC, V.

La Fiesta Oceanside Inn. This two-story inn offers rooms with either a poolside or oceanfront view. There is an 18-hole miniature golf course and an Olympic-size swimming pool on site. Restaurant. Some in-room data ports, some microwaves, some refrigerators. Cable

TV. Outdoor pool. Miniature golf. Beach. Laundry facilities. No pets. | 810 A1A Beach Blvd. | 904/471–2220 or 800/852–6390 (reservations) | fax 904/471–0186 | www.lafiestaocean-side.com | 32 rooms, 5 suites | $79–$149, $199–$259 suites | D, MC, V.

Ramada Limited, at the Beach. This three-story hotel is just ½ mi from beautiful sandy beaches. Complimentary Continental breakfast. In-room data ports, some microwaves, some refrigerators, some in-room hot tubs. Cable TV, in-room VCRs (and movies). Outdoor pool. Laundry facilities. Business services. No pets. | 894 A1A Beach Blvd. | 904/471–1440 | fax 904/471–2922 | www.ramada.com | 32 rooms, 6 suites | $59–$99, $120–$150 suites | AE, D, DC, MC, V.

ST. PETERSBURG

MAP 3, H6

(Nearby towns also listed: Clearwater, Dunedin, Indian Rocks Beach, Madeira Beach, Redington Beach, St. Pete Beach, Tampa, Treasure Island)

St. Petersburg was founded in 1875, when John C. Williams, an early pioneer snowbird from Detroit, came down and decided to buy some land to call home. Working in conjunction with exiled Russian nobleman Pietr Dementieff, who helped build a railroad into the area and named the town after his own home in Russia, the two slowly turned this peaceful coastal area into a mecca for ailing Northerners.

Today St. Petersburg is a bustling city of 266,000 with a lively feel and an up-tempo development scheme. There are two distinct parts of St. Petersburg: its downtown area with six major museums and popular sports arenas; and the beaches ringing it, including separate communities such as Treasure Island and Madeira Beach.

Residents appreciate the outdoors, and the town boasts 102 parks and 7 mi of waterfront. The 47-mi Pinellas hiking/biking trail and five public beaches provide plenty of opportunities to get outdoors.

Information: **St. Petersburg Area Chamber of Commerce** | 100 Second Ave. N., Ste. 150, St. Petersburg, 33701 | 727/821–4069 | www.stpete.com.

Attractions

Florida International Museum. Visitors here can stroll through life-size re-creations of the Rose Garden, Oval Office, and other famous scenes as they view this extensive collection of artifacts from the Kennedy era. This museum is affiliated with the Smithsonian Institution in Washington and receives many exhibits on loan from that renowned collection. | 100 2nd St. N | 727/822–3693 or 800/777–9882 | fax 727/898–0248 | www.floridamuseum.org | $13.95 | Mon.–Sat. 9–6, Sun. noon–6.

Florida's Sunken Gardens. Established in the 1910s, this is one of the area's oldest attractions. Sunken Gardens contains four acres of lush gardens and features daily trained-bird shows as well as a butterfly garden on the property's northern perimeter. | 1825 4th St. N | 727/551–3100 | www.sunkengardens.com | $4 | Wed.–Sun. 10–4.

Fort De Soto Park. Two 1890 British rapid-fire cannons stand on display outside Fort De Soto, which dates back to the late 1800s. This 900-acre Pinellas County park, made up of six interconnected islands, is in the southeast corner of Mullet Key. There are beaches, fishing, about 7 mi of trails, camping, boating, and more. | 3500 Pinellas Bayway S., Tierra Verde | 727/866–2484 | fax 727/866–2485 | Free | Daily dawn to dusk.

Friendship Trail. The former Gandy Bay Bridge has been turned into a pedestrian walkway with fishing decks along the side. The only amenities are the few portable toilets placed every ¾ mi. You can use the 2½ mi of car-free territory for biking, roller blading, walking, or fishing. | 13000 Gandy Blvd. | 727/549–6099 | Free | Daily.

Great Explorations. A big hit with children, this hands-on museum lets them play veterinarian on a stuffed animal, crawl through the belly of a giant snake, and get close to the "Animal of the Day," among other attractions. | The Pier, 800 2nd Ave. NE, 3rd Fl. | 727/821–8992 | www.greatexplorations.org | $4 | Mon.–Sat. 10–8, Sun. 11–6.

Holocaust Memorial Museum and Education Center. The museum is a living memorial in every last detail: The eleven eternal flames on the exterior of the building symbolize the 11 million victims of the Holocaust; the triangular entrance to the 27,000-square-ft structure represents the shape of the badges worn by concentration camp inmates. The museum houses exhibits, archives, a memorial center, and a meditation court where you can go to try to come to terms with this poignant reminder of the horrifying, historic experience. | 55 5th St. S | 727/820–0100 | $6 | Mon.–Fri. 10–4, Sat.–Sun. noon–4.

Municipal Marina. It's fun to stroll around the Municipal Marina, right on Tampa Bay. It's huge, with more than a thousand transient and permanent ships. | 300 Second Ave. SE | 727/893–7329 | Weekdays. 8–6, weekends 8–4.

Museum of Fine Arts. Since it was founded in 1965, the Museum of Fine Arts has become one of the best of its type in the Southeast. The more than 4,000 objects in the collection span the centuries from antiquity to the present, and include works by Fragonard, Vigée-Lebrun, Corot, Cézanne, Monet, Morisot, Gauguin, Renoir, and Rodin, as well as such American painters as Moran, Inness, Henri, Bellows, and O'Keeffe. There are lectures, tours, classes, films, and performing arts events. | 255 Beach Dr. NE | 727/896–2667 | fax 727/894–4638 | www.fine-arts.org | $6 | Tues.–Sat. 10–5, Sun. 1–5, closed Mon.

Pinellas County Historical Museum. This open-air, 21-acre historical village and museum in the St. Petersburg suburb of Largo includes 23 structures, some of which date to the middle of the 19th century. The on-site museum tells the story of Pinellas County back to Spanish colonial times. | 11909 125th St. N., Largo | 727/582–2123 | fax 727/582–2455 | www.co.pinellas.fl.us/bcc/heritag.htm | Free | Tues.–Sat. 10–4, Sun. 1–4.

The Pier. Sparkling water views surround you at this pyramid-shaped five-story structure. Attractions include numerous retail shops, an aquarium, a hands-on museum, and restaurants. Feel free to go fishing in Tampa Bay. | 800 2nd Ave. NE | 813/821–6164 | www.stpete-pier.com | Mon.–Thurs. 10–9, Fri.–Sat. 10–10, Sun. 11–7.

YOUR FIRST-AID TRAVEL KIT

- ❏ Allergy medication
- ❏ Antacid tablets
- ❏ Antibacterial soap
- ❏ Antiseptic cream
- ❏ Aspirin or acetaminophen
- ❏ Assorted adhesive bandages
- ❏ Athletic or elastic bandages for sprains
- ❏ Bug repellent
- ❏ Face cloth

- ❏ First-aid book
- ❏ Gauze pads and tape
- ❏ Needle and tweezers for splinters or removing ticks
- ❏ Petroleum jelly
- ❏ Prescription drugs
- ❏ Suntan lotion with an SPF rating of at least 15
- ❏ Thermometer

© Artville

*Excerpted from *Fodor's: How to Pack: Experts Share Their Secrets*
© 1997, by Fodor's Travel Publications

St. Petersburg Junior College Planetarium. Stars, planets, and constellations surround you in this 47-seat planetarium at St. Petersburg Junior College. On Fridays, more than 2,500 celestial bodies are projected in the 13-meter dome during star shows, and you can look at larger stars and planets through telescopes on the rooftop observatory. | St. Petersburg Junior College, 6605 5th Ave. N., 2nd Fl. of the Natural Science Bldg. | 727/341–4320 | Free | Sept.–Apr., Fri. 7 PM, 8:15 PM.

St. Petersburg Museum of History. Since 1920, this waterfront museum has been collecting, preserving, and presenting St. Petersburg history through exhibitions and special programs. Highlights include the multimedia learning center and the Flight One Gallery, where visitors can attempt to pilot the historic Benoist airboat by using the gallery's flight simulator. | 335 2nd Ave. | 727/894–1052 | fax 727/823–7276 | www.ij.net/spmh/ | $5 | Mon.–Sat. 10–5, Sun 1–5.

Salvador Dali Museum. This waterfront museum is home to the world's largest collection of the late Spanish surrealist's works. The collection includes the renowned *Portrait of My Dead Brother,* purchased in 1995. | 1000 3rd St. S | 727/823–3767 or 800/442–3254 | fax 813/894–6068 | www.daliweb.com | $9 | Mon.–Wed., Sat. 9:30–5:30, Thurs. 9:30–8, Sun. noon–5:30, closed Fri.

Science Center of Pinellas County. The center, which takes a hands-on approach to the study of science, features laboratories, workshops, field studies, and exhibits. Shows of interest include an inventors exhibit and a Florida archaeology display. | 7701 22nd Ave. N | 727/384–0027 | Free | Weekdays 9–4, closed weekends.

★ **Sunshine Skyway.** The 4-mi skyway bridge hangs up to 183 ft above Tampa Bay and has views of several small islands if you are heading southeast and of St. Petersburg Beach if you're heading northwest. The span runs from Pinellas and Manatee counties along a section of I–275. It costs $1 per car. It's the best view in the entire Tampa Bay Area. | I–275 | $1 | Daily.

ON THE CALENDAR

MAR.: *Antiquaria Book Fair.* National and international vendors and bibliophiles gather for a three-day extravaganza of selling, buying, and swapping paper collectibles. Most booths have antique books, but scripts and postcards are also for sale. | 727/892–5202.

MAR.: *International Folk Fair.* St. Petersburg's ethnic groups are honored with food and folk dancing. | 727/821–4069.

MAR., APR.: *Renaissance Festival.* Along with stage shows, jugglers, magicians, fire-eaters, and other specialty acts perform here and there around the festival village, which is about 15 mi north of St. Petersburg. Twice daily, there's jousting, while more than 125 shops sell handmade jewelry, pottery, leather, artwork, footwear, glassware, clothing, furniture, and sculpture. | 727/586–5423.

MAR.: *Sunshine Festival of States.* The South's largest civic celebration, going strong since 1921, includes three major parades as well as concerts, sporting events, and other activities. Music is the focal point, with bands from around the country competing during the two-week competition in downtown St. Petersburg. | 727/898–3654.

SEPT.–MAY: *Concerts.* Each year, Jahja Ling directs the professional 88-member Florida Orchestra and guest artists in some 150 concerts around the area, some focusing on pops and classics and others designed for kids. | 813/286–1170.

Dining

Arigato Japanese Steakhouse. Japanese. You can watch your dinner being prepared at the Teppanyaki grill at this Japanese steak house. Lots of red Japanese artwork provide the setting. Succulent steaks are served with fried rice. Kids' menu. | 3600 66th St. N | 727/343–5200 | No lunch | $8–$23 | AE, D, DC, MC, V.

Carmelita's Mexican Restaurant. Mexican. Landscape murals and maps of Mexico line the walls of this casual spot. Try the chicken chimichangas or the enchiladas. Kids' menu. | 5211 Park St. N | 727/545–2956 | $6–$10 | AE, D, MC, V.

Casual Clam. Seafood. Miniature sailboats, ship helms, and mounted fish provide for a truly nautical theme at this eatery. Popular dishes include the blackened grouper sandwich and the fish and chips. Outdoor dining on a patio overlooking 9th St. is available. Kids' menu. | 3336 9th St. N | 727/895–2526 | Reservations not accepted | $6–$12 | MC, V.

Chateau France. French. The quaint Victorian house dates to 1910, and the restful dining room is lighted by candles. Some of the specialties are *canard a l'orange* (duck sautéed in Grand Marnier sauce) or filet mignon Roquefort. Entrées come with the house "Eiffel Tower" salad, and you can choose from the extensive wine list that's more than half vintage French wines. Dine on the veranda in nice weather. The desserts include crêpes suzette and bananas flambé. | 136 4th Ave. NE | 727/894–7163 | Reservations required | No lunch | $18–$29 | AE, D, DC, MC, V.

The Firehouse Bar and Grille. American. Good burgers and chili are a staple at this eatery, which is decorated with pictures of fire stations and fires. The ribs are also very popular with the locals. | 260 1st Ave. S | 727/895–4716 | Reservations not accepted | Closed Sun. No lunch Sat. | $6–$14 | DC, MC, V.

The Garden Bistro. Mediterranean. Such dishes as grilled garlic and basil–marinated grilled shrimp as well as inventive salads are served in this lively restaurant, which is fitted out with surreal artwork. Be sure to check out the large 100-yr-old tree in the garden. Kids' menu. | 217 Central Ave. | 727/896–3800 | $13–$19 | AE, MC, V.

Grand Finale. Eclectic. This trendy restaurant in an art gallery is always buzzing with music from a DJ or a live jazz band. Seared halibut comes with black truffle risotto, and filet mignon gets dressed up with portobello mushrooms and stone-ground grits. The place lives up to its name and serves dinner up to 1 AM. They specialize in great desserts such as the chocolate macadamia nut soufflé drenched in a caramel and coconut emulsion. | 1101 1st Ave. N | 727/823–9921 | fax 727/894–3397 | No lunch, closed Sun. | $14–$22 | AE, MC, V.

Julian's at the Heritage. Steak. Wood furnishings and paintings depicting hunting scenes give this spot a very traditional and masculine feel. The filet mignon and tuna steak are recommended. | 256 Second St. N | 727/823–6382 | No lunch | $19–$40 | AE, D, DC, MC, V.

The Keystone Club. Steak. Pictures of vintage cars from the early 1900s line the walls of this elegant spot, while Frank Sinatra can be heard in the background. Although you don't need to wear a jacket, a collared shirt is required. The two most popular dishes are the pork chops and the prime rib. | 320 4th St. N | 727/822–6600 | No lunch | $12–$27 | AE, D, DC, MC, V.

Limey's. English. Traditional English fare, such as shepherd's pie or bangers and mash, is accompanied by a roster of imported draft beers. Replicas of London Underground signs and Scottish ornaments give the place an authentic feel. Kids' menu. | 1492 4th St. N | 727/895–2049 | $5–$13 | AE, D, MC, V.

★ **Marchand's Grill and the Terrace Room.** Mediterranean. In the Renaissance Vinoy Resort, first opened in 1925, this wonderful eatery has frescoed ceilings and a spectacular view of Tampa Bay and the nearby boat docks. Happily, the atmosphere is matched by the great food, prepared by Tom Chin, named 1999 Chef of the Year by the Tampa Bay chapter of the American Culinary Federation. The imaginative menu contains lobster quesadillas with roasted tomato salsa and sweet pea guacamole as well as macadamia nut–crusted grouper with citrus papaya salsa. The wine list is quite extensive. | 501 5th Ave. NE | 727/894–1000 | Breakfast also available | $12–$23 | AE, D, DC, MC, V.

Native Seafood and Trading Company. Seafood. With a herb garden and lush tropical plants scattered about, the setting at this eatery recalls a rain forest. Popular items include the giant sea scallops and various grilled and baked shellfish. Outdoor dining under a covered patio is available. Kids' menu. | 5901 Sun Blvd. | 727/866–8772 | Reservations essential | No lunch | $9–$19 | AE, D, DC, MC, V.

Pepin. Spanish. Red terra-cotta tiles and many Dali prints set the scene at this Spanish eatery, which has three dining rooms. Be sure to try the shrimp suprema or pompano à la Fal. Kids' menu. | 4125 4th Street N | 727/821–3773 | Reservations essential on weekends | Closed Mon. No lunch weekends | $14–$30 | AE, D, DC, MC, V.

Saffron's. Caribbean. This casual yet elegant spot is on the Intracoastal Waterway and offers outdoor dining under a covered patio. The signature dish is the jerk chicken, while the appleton steak with rum is also very popular. Kids' menu. | 1700 Park St. N | 727/522–1234 | $8–$20 | AE, D, DC, MC, V.

The Steak Joint. Steak. The Mediterranean flare brings some greenery to the otherwise typical steak house. You can get anything from ribs to seafood or chicken, or any cut of steak grilled or broiled. The house specialty is the steak joint sirloin. | 4871 Park St. | 727/545–9481 | No lunch | $12–$19 | AE, D, MC, V.

Ted Peters Famous Smoked Fish. Seafood. These guys have been smoking fish and serving it up for 51 years in this same outdoor picnic table area. Fishermen drop by to fill up on the smoked salmon, mackerel, or mullet. You can also pick some up to go along with heaping quantities of German potato salad. | 1350 Pasadena Ave. S, Pasadena | 727/381–7931 | Closed Tues. | $11–$15 | No credit cards.

Lodging

Bayboro House B&B on Tampa Bay. This B&B in a 1907 Victorian home on Tampa Bay is filled with period antiques and comfortable wicker furniture. Downtown is just 2 mi away, and the beach is adjacent to the house. Complimentary Continental breakfast. In-room data ports, some microwaves, some refrigerators. Cable TV, in-room VCRs (and movies). Outdoor pool. Outdoor hot tub. Laundry facilities. No pets. No kids under 12. No smoking. | 1719 Beach Dr. SE | 727/823–4955 or 877/823–4955 | fax 727/823–4955 or 877/823–4955 | www.bayborohousebandb.com | 7 rooms | $125–$249 | AE, D, DC, MC, V.

Bayboro Inn and Hunt Room B&B. Each room has a theme in this inn, which was built in 1914: the Renaissance, Egypt, Santa Fe, Key West, Art Deco, and the Victorian era. It's just four blocks from the waterfront and downtown. Complimentary breakfast. No room phones, TV in common area. Laundry facilities. Business services. No pets. No kids under 10. No smoking. | 357 3rd St. S | 727/823–0498 | www.bayboroinnhuntbb.com | 6 rooms | $75–$110 | MC, V.

Claiborne House. This three-story Key West–style home is hidden behind a tranquil garden featuring a gazebo. There are a number of restaurants, museums, and shops within walking distance. Complimentary refreshments and cookies are served every afternoon. Complimentary Continental breakfast. In-room data ports, some kitchenettes, some microwaves, some refrigerators. Cable TV. Laundry facilities. Business services. No pets. No smoking. | 340 Rowland Ct. | 727/822–8855 or 800/281–4090 | fax 727/824–7223 | 5 rooms, 4 suites | $95, $115 suites | AE, D, MC, V.

Days Inn St. Petersburg Central. This three-story inn is a short walk from a number of eateries, while St. Petersburg Beach is just 10 mi away. Complimentary Continental breakfast. In-room data ports, some kitchenettes, some microwaves, some refrigerators. Cable TV. Outdoor pool. Laundry facilities. Business services. No pets. | 650 34th St. N | 727/321–2958 or 800/544–8313 | fax 727/327–1625 | www.daysinn.com | 28 rooms | $66–$78 | AE, D, DC, MC, V.

Dickens House B&B. Built by some of the first settlers in St. Petersburg, this arts and crafts–style home is in the town's historic Old Northwest Section. The common areas in the three-story bungalow have wood floors and white walls with wood trim and are airy and refreshingly sparse. Each room is wholly unique in character, ranging from a Victorian room with a brass and porcelain bed to a suite with a hand-crafted bent willow bed. Complimentary Continental breakfast. In-room data ports, refrigerators, some in-room hot tubs. Cable TV, in-room VCRs. Library. Laundry services. Business services. No kids under 9. | 335 8th Ave. NE | 727/822–8622 or 800/381–2022 | fax 727/822–6312 | www.dickenshouse.com | 3 rooms, 2 suites | $70–$210 | AE, D, MC, V.

Holiday Inn Sunspree Resort Marina Cove. This two-story resort is spread out over four buildings on 18 acres. Many of the rooms offer views of the lush tropical garden, pool area, or the beach. Restaurant, bar (with entertainment). In-room data ports, in-room safes, microwaves, refrigerators. Cable TV. 2 outdoor pools. Outdoor hot tub. 5 tennis courts. Exercise equipment. Beach, dock, water sports, boating, fishing. Video games. Children's programs (ages 5–16), playground. Laundry facilities. Business services. | 6800 Sunshine Skyway La. | 727/867–1151 or 800/227–8045 | fax 727/864–4494 | www.holiday-inn.com | 146 rooms, 11 suites | $99–$174, $169–$189 suites | AE, D, DC, MC, V.

Inn at the Bay B&B. This bright yellow home, equidistant to St. Petersburg and Tampa, has been serving as a B&B since 1910. Each of the spacious rooms has its own color scheme and either a queen- or king-size bed. Each room has a private bath, while the common areas are airy and inviting. Complimentary Continental breakfast. In-room data ports, some in-room hot tubs, cable TV. | 126 4th Ave. N | 727/822–1700 or 888/873–2122 | fax 727/896–7412 | www.innatthebay.com | 5 rooms | $65–$85 | AE, MC, V.

La Quinta Inn. This two-story hotel is built around a courtyard. St. Petersburg Beach is just 10 mi away and there is a 24-hr restaurant across the street. Complimentary Continental breakfast. In-room data ports. Cable TV. Pool. Exercise equipment. Laundry facilities. Business services. Some pets allowed. | 4999 34th St. N | 727/527–8421 | fax 727/527–8851 | www.laquinta.com | 120 rooms | $69–$110 | AE, D, DC, MC, V.

Lee Manor Inn. Right in the heart of the downtown business district lies this hotel, built in 1937. Adorned with period antiques and treasures, it has been restored to its personality of yesteryear. Rooms are individual in style and straddle the line between dorm room and a room at your best friend's house. Complimentary Continental breakfast. In-room data ports, some microwaves, refrigerators. Laundry facilities. | 342 3rd Ave. | 727/894–3248 | fax 727/895–8759 | www.leemanorinn.com | 21 rooms | $63–$99, weekly rates also available | AE, D, MC, V.

Mansion House. The Carriage House, one of a dozen guest accommodations at this B&B, is perfect for a romantic getaway. For a fee, the owner will take you out in his six-passenger, 23-ft sport cruiser, just for a ride or to nearby Barrier Islands, where you can snorkel or swim. Mansion House is an excellent example of Craftsman-style architecture. Complimentary breakfast. In-room data ports. Cable TV. Outdoor pool. Outdoor hot tub. Bicycles. Library. Laundry facilities. Business services. No pets. No smoking. | 105 5th Ave. NE | 727/821–9391 | fax 727/821–9391 | www.mansionbandb.com | 12 rooms | $110–$185 | AE, D, DC, MC, V.

Renaissance Vinoy Resort. This seven-story 1925 landmark resort, now on the National Register of Historic Places, sits on 14 acres, with a 74-slip marina and tropical gardens. The Terrace Room and Marchand's Grill (*see* Dining) are on the property, and the hotel is 15 min from the beach. 5 restaurants, bar (with entertainment), room service. In-room data ports, minibars, refrigerators. Cable TV. Outdoor pool. Beauty salon, outdoor hot tub, massage, sauna, spa, steam room. 18-hole golf course, 12 tennis courts. Gym, dock. Children's programs (ages 4–13). Laundry facilities. Business services. No pets. | 501 5th Ave. NE | 727/894–1000 | fax 727/894–1970 | www.renaissancehotels.com | 338 rooms, 22 suites | $289–$349, $510–$1,520 suites | AE, D, DC, MC, V.

St. Petersburg Bayfront Hilton. Rooms have a view of Tampa Bay in this 15-story hotel on exit 9 of I-275. The St. Petersburg-Clearwater Airport is 20 min away. Restaurant, bar. In-room data ports, some refrigerators. Cable TV. Outdoor pool. Outdoor hot tub. Gym. Laundry facilities. Business services. Pets allowed (fee). | 333 1st St. S | 727/894–5000 or 800/916–2221 (reservations) | fax 727/894–7655 | www.hilton.com | 315 rooms, 18 suites | $189, $190–$315 suites | AE, D, DC, MC, V.

Sunset Bay Inn. This B&B is housed in a 1911 Georgia Colonial Revival home. The elegant sunroom is ideal for relaxing and enjoying a day, and there are numerous restaurants within walking distance. Complimentary Continental breakfast. In-room data ports, refrigerators, some in-room hot tubs. Cable TV, in-room VCRs (and movies). Bicycles. Laundry facilities. Business services. No pets. No kids under 8. No smoking. | 635 Bay St. NE | 727/896–6701 or 800/794–5133 | fax 727/898–5311 | www.sunsetbayinn.com | 5 rooms, 3 suites | $160–$240, $250 suites | AE, D, DC, MC, V.

ST. PETE BEACH

MAP 3, H7

(Nearby towns also listed: Clearwater, Dunedin, Indian Rocks Beach, Madeira Beach, Redington Beach, St. Petersburg, Tampa, Treasure Island)

Show what a savvy traveler you are by referring to this Tampa Bay beach town by its proper name, by city ordinance, St. Pete Beach. Located on the southern tip of St. Petersburg's barrier island, this town of 9,200 has over 35 miles of white sandy beaches stretching from St. Pete to Clearwater. There's plenty to do, including parasailing, surfing, scuba diving, and, for the landlubber, dining and shopping.

Information: Gulf Beaches of Tampa Bay Chamber of Commerce | 6990 Gulf Blvd., St. Pete Beach, 33706 | 727/360–6957 or 800/944–1847 | www.gulfbeaches-tampabay.com.

Attractions

Gulf Beaches Historical Museum. This museum, a satellite of the Pinellas County Historical Museum in Largo, is in the first church built on Pinellas County's barrier islands. Exhibits trace the island's history back to the 1500s. The museum is in the Pass-A-Grille Beach historical district. | 115 10th Ave. | 727/360–2491 | Free | Thurs. and Sat. 10–4, Sun. 1–4.

ON THE CALENDAR
APR.–MAY: *Beach Goes Pops.* Sunset concerts by the Florida Orchestra are held on Passagralle Beach as members of the Tampa Bay Orchestra and Opera join locals for a pops concert. | 727/367–8590.

Dining

Brunello's. Italian. Northern Italian fare is the specialty of this smart, casual spot; white linen tablecloths and red roses adorn the tables. Grilled beef tenderloin stuffed with Gorgonzola and veal Sorrentino are recommended. Kids' menu. | 3861 Gulf Blvd. | 727/367–1851 | Closed Sun.–Mon. No lunch | $16–$26 | AE, MC, V.

Fetishes. Contemporary. In this intimate eatery with just 10 tables, savor such delicacies as Jamaican prawns seared in spices with a passion fruit–cognac–mango sauce. The dining room has black–on–light pink color scheme, with nautical art. Extensive wine list. | 6690 Gulf Blvd., 33706 | 727/363–3700 | Reservations essential | Closed Sun. No lunch | $14–$21 | AE, D, MC, V.

Hurricane. Seafood. The Hurricane has been going strong since the 1960s. Dine in the wood-paneled dining room or sit out on the shaded wraparound veranda on the second floor. Try blackened grouper or grilled salmon, sip cocktails as the sun sets. | 807 Gulf Way | 727/360–9558 | Reservations not accepted | Breakfast also available | $10–$17 | AE, MC, V.

Johnny Leverock's. Seafood. This local favorite is named after the original owner, who opened the restaurant in the 1940s. Enjoy the fried grouper or onion-crusted salmon while taking in magnificent views of Boca Ciega Bay. Kids' menu. | 10 Corey Ave. | 727/367–4588 | Reservations not accepted | $10–$23 | AE, D, DC, MC, V.

Maritana Grill. American. This elegant spot at Don CeSar Resort is spruced up with tanks of tropical fish. Try Atlantic salmon with shrimp or venison. Kids' menu. | 3400 Gulf Blvd. | 727/360–1882 | Reservations essential | No lunch | $25–$35 | AE, D, DC, MC, V.

Palm Court. Continental. French doors and a floral decor set a relaxed yet classy tone at this restaurant in the Tradewinds Resort. Recommended are grilled and marinated lamb and the beef bocaccini. Dine outdoors on an uncovered porch overlooking the courtyard. Sun. brunch. Kids' menu. | 5500 Gulf Blvd. | 727/367–6461 | Reservations essential | $14–$23 | AE, D, DC, MC, V.

Sea Porch Cafe. American. This bright, airy café at the Don CeSar Resort fronts the beach. More casual than the other dining options at the resort, the restaurant specializes in salads, pastas, and burgers. There's outdoor dining. Kids' menu. | 3400 Gulf Blvd. | 727/360–1884 | Breakfast also available | $13–$21 | AE, D, DC, MC, V.

Skidder's. Continental. This casual, friendly spot offers little in the way of decor, but the food is terrific. Broiled whole red snapper and steak Diane are recommended. There's patio dining. Kids' menu. | 5799 Gulf Blvd. | 727/360–1029 | Reservations not accepted | Breakfast also available | $8–$17 | AE, D, DC, MC, V.

Lodging

Alden Beach Resort. Just 15 mi from St. Petersburg/Clearwater International Airport, this hotel is spread over 5 acres on the Gulf of Mexico. All units have either pool or gulf views. Bar. In-room safes, microwaves, refrigerators. Cable TV, in-room VCRs (and movies). 2 outdoor pools. Outdoor hot tub. 2 tennis courts. Volleyball. Beach. Video games. Laundry facilities. Business services. No pets. | 5900 Gulf Blvd. | 727/360–7081 or 800/237–2530 | fax 727/360–5957 | www.aldenbeachresort.com | 143 suites | $161–$211 | AE, D, DC, MC, V.

Bay Street Villas. These one- and two-bedroom villas face the gulf and have queen-size beds and French doors that open to the waterfront, pool, or gardens. There are two gas grills on the pool-side sundecks. From the dock you can snorkel and boat. Kitchenettes, microwaves, refrigerators. Outdoor pool. Beach, dock, water sports, boating, fishing, bicycles. Laundry facilities. | 7201 Bay St. | 727/360–5591 or 800/566–8358 | fax 727/360–9626 | www.stpetebeach.com/baystreet | 20 units | $90–$110 (3–day minimum stay) | MC, V.

Crystal Sands Motel Apartments. At this small beachside resort you'll find one-bedroom and efficiency villas with brightly colored furnishings. Nightly happy hour—with free food and drinks in season—is held by the landscaped, lagoonlike pool. Picnic area. In-room data ports, kitchenettes, microwaves, refrigerators. Outdoor pool. Laundry facilities. | 601 71st Ave. | 727/360–7822 | fax 727/360–1040 | 8 units | $64–$74 | AE, MC, V.

The Don CeSar Beach House. This five-story, all-suites hostelry provides shuttle service to and from its sister property, the Don CeSar Beach Resort, which is ¼ mi south—guests can use the facilities at both places. Units have living rooms and sleeper sofas. There's no room service, but hotel staff can grocery-shop for you by request. In-room data ports, microwaves, refrigerators. Cable TV. Outdoor pool. Massage. Gym. Beach, water sports, boating. Children's programs (ages 4–12). Laundry facilities. Business services. No pets. | 3860 Gulf Blvd. | 727/360–1881 or 800/227–0007 | fax 727/367–7597 | www.doncesar.com | 70 suites | $294–$389 | AE, D, DC, MC, V.

The Don CeSar Beach Resort and Spa. This pink, gulf-side resort hotel anchors 3 acres of lawn and flower gardens. It's hosted the likes of F. Scott and Zelda Fitzgerald during its illustrious history. Be sure to explore and rejuvenate yourself at the spa. The Maritana Grill and Sea Porch Cafe restaurants are well regarded. 3 restaurants, 3 bars, room service. In-room data ports, in-room safes, minibars. Cable TV. 2 outdoor pools. Outdoor hot tub, massage, sauna, spa. Gym. Beach, water sports, boating, fishing. Shops. Video games. Children's programs (ages 4–12). Laundry facilities. Business services. No pets. | 3400 Gulf Blvd. | 727/360–1881 or 800/637–7200 | fax 727/367–7597 | www.doncesar.com | 232 rooms, 23 suites | $299–$389, $404–$824 suites, $2,000 penthouse suites | AE, D, DC, MC, V.

Holiday Inn Hotel and Suites Beachfront Resort and Conference Center. Fronting the beach, this resort has beautifully landscaped grounds with palm trees. The view is breathtaking from the revolving rooftop restaurant. The hotel is a mile north of Pinellas Bayway.

Restaurant, bar (with entertainment). In-room data ports, in-room safes, some microwaves, refrigerators. Cable TV. Outdoor pool. Exercise equipment. Beach, water sports. Fishing. Laundry services. Business services. No pets. | 5250 Gulf Blvd. | 727/360–1811 or 800/448–0901 | fax 727/360–6919 | www.holiday-inn.com | 140 rooms, 16 suites | $208–$258, $318 suites | AE, D, DC, MC, V.

Howard Johnson St. Pete Beach Resort Inn. This five-story hotel on the gulf is within walking distance of a shopping mall and several restaurants. Restaurant, bar (with entertainment). In-room data ports, in-room safes, some kitchenettes, some microwaves, refrigerators, some in-room hot tubs. Cable TV. Outdoor pool. Beach. Laundry facilities. Business services. No pets. | 6100 Gulf Blvd. | 727/360–7041 or 800/406–1411 | fax 727/360–8941 | www.hojo.com | 117 rooms, 16 suites | $100–$130, $200 suites | AE, D, DC, MC, V.

Island's End Cottages. The cottages are in a secluded spot on the Gulf of Mexico beach, and the individually designed rooms have water views. Three mornings a week you can have fresh-squeezed orange juice and croissants with other guests in the central gazebo. Complimentary Continental breakfast three times a week. One cottage has a pool. In-room safes, kitchens, some in-room hot tubs. Cable TV. Beach, fishing. Laundry facilities. | 1 Pass-A-Grille Way | 727/360–5023 | fax 727/367–7890 | jzgpag@aol.com | www.islandsend.com | 6 cottages | $75–$195 | MC, V.

Lamara Motel Apartments. On the beach side of the island, these economical accommodations, family owned and operated, occupy three pink buildings with aqua trim. The outdoor heated pool is nestled among the buildings. Efficiency and one-bedroom units are painted and decorated in white with black accents. Kitchenettes, some microwaves, refrigerators. Outdoor pool. | 520 73rd Ave. | 727/360–7521 or 800/211–5108 | fax 727/363–0193 | 16 units | $65–$75 | AE, MC, V.

Pasa Tiempa B&B. This Mediterranean B&B on Boca Ciega Bay has an alluring tropical courtyard and rooms done with plush antiques and newer pieces. Complimentary Continental breakfast. In-room data ports, some refrigerators. Cable TV. Dock, fishing. Business services. No pets. No kids under 16. No smoking. | 7141 Bay St. | 727/367–9907 | fax 727/367–9906 | www.pasa-tiempo.com | 8 rooms | $110–$150 | AE, MC, V.

Sandpiper Beach Resort. This seven-story resort has standard hotel rooms, plus one- and two-bedroom suites. Many units offer courtyard, gulf, and beach views. Guests can use the dining and recreational facilities at the nearby Sirata and Tradewinds Resorts. Restaurant, bar. In-room data ports, in-room safes, some kitchenettes, microwaves, refrigerators. Cable TV. Pool. Gym, racquetball. Beach, water sports, boating. Fishing. Children's programs (3–11). Laundry facilities. Business services. No pets. | 6000 Gulf Blvd. | 727/360–5551 or 800/237–0707 | fax 727/562–1812 | www.tradewindsresort.com | 67 rooms, 142 suites | $169–$229, $259–$524 suites | AE, MC, V.

Snowden Resort and Apartments. Built in 1958 and renovated in 1999, this complex has studio, one-bedroom, and two-bedroom apartments, which flank the pool on either side. Each has a terrace. There's weekly maid service and direct beach access. Complimentary Continental breakfast. Kitchenettes. Outdoor pool. Beach, dock, water sports, boating, fishing. Laundry facilities. | 5353 Gulf Blvd. | 727/367–1444 | fax 727/360–1175 | 50 units | $85–$160 | AE, D, MC, V.

Tradewinds Resort on St. Pete Beach. Spanning 18 lush, tropical acres, this waterfront resort is spread among six buildings. There's a $\frac{1}{4}$-mi waterway that meanders through the resort attracting swans, ducks, and egrets. Complimentary paddleboats are available, and nightly gondola cruises offered. 4 restaurants, bar (with entertainment), picnic area, room service. In-room safes, some kitchenettes, some microwaves, refrigerators. Cable TV. Outdoor pool, wading pool. Barber shop, beauty salon, hot tub, sauna. Putting green, 4 tennis courts. Gym. Water sports, boating, fishing. Video games. Children's programs (ages 5–16), playground. Laundry facilities. Business services. No pets. | 5500 Gulf Blvd. | 727/367–6461 or 800/237–0707 | fax 727/562–1222 | www.tradewindsresort.com | 370 rooms, 207 suites | $209–$325, $299–$399 suites | AE, MC, V.

Tradewinds Sirata Beach Resort. This resort and conference center lies along a long stretch of white-sand beach along the gulf. Rooms are spacious and comfortably decorated with wood furnishings; large windows provide ample sunlight. Restaurant, bar, room service. In-room data ports, in-room safes, some kitchenettes, some microwaves, refrigerators. Cable TV. 3 outdoor pools. Outdoor hot tub. Exercise equipment. Beach, water sports. Laundry facilities. Business services. No pets. | 5390 Gulf Blvd. | 727/367–2771 or 800/344–5999 | fax 727/367–8082 | www.siratabeachresort.com | 210 rooms, 170 suites | $177–$257, $237–$379 suites | AE, MC, V.

SANFORD

MAP 3, J5

(Nearby towns also listed: Altamonte Springs, DeLand, Maitland, Winter Park)

The town 22 mi north of Orlando called itself the celery capital of the world in the 1900s. Today the population is about 35,000, many of them Orlandoans seeking a respite from the burgeoning urban sprawl. There are good restaurants, shopping, and entertainment, but the town is perhaps best known as the stopping-off point for Amtrak's Auto Train.

Information: **Sanford and Seminole County Chamber of Commerce** | 400 E. 1st St., Sanford, 32771-1408 | 407/322–2212 | www.sanfordchamber.com.

Attractions

The Big Tree. This giant cypress on General Hutchinson Parkway, also known as "The Senator," is said to be one of the largest in the country and is estimated to be 3,500 years old. | General Hutchinson Pkwy. | 407/788–0405.

Central Florida Zoological Park. Clouded leopards, hyacinth macaws, and cotton-top tamarinds are among the endangered species who live among the lofty oaks and pines in this 21-acre park, just off exit 52 of I–4. You can get close-up views of crocodiles and venomous snakes, and also pet and feed various domestic animals. | 3755 U.S. 17/92 | 407/323–4450 | www.centralfloridazoo.org | $7 | Daily 9–5.

Henry Shelton Sanford Museum. Named after influential U.S. diplomat Henry Sanford, this museum houses his official papers and letters and his mid-19th-century library, and displays an eclectic mix of local, European, and Native American artifacts, including a 1,000-yr-old Timucuan Indian canoe. European furniture, paintings, and family portraits reflect Sanford's 30-odd years in Brussels. Photographs and memorabilia from local businesses document the area's 19th-century celery industry. | 520 E. 1st St. | 407/302–1000 | fax 407/330–5666 | Free | Tues.–Fri. 11–4, Sat. 1–4.

Sanford-Orlando Kennell Club. About 6 mi north of Altamonte Springs, this track offers live greyhound racing from November through May 2. Simulcast racing is offered year-round. | 301 Dog Track Rd. | 407/831–1600 | $1 | Nov.–early May, Mon.–Sat. 7:30 PM, matinees Mon., Wed., Sat. 12:30 PM.

SIGHTSEEING TOURS/TOUR COMPANIES

Rivership *Romance*. Three- and four-hour cruises, full-day cruises, moonlight dinner-and-dancing cruises, and other excursions run along the St. Johns River. | 433 N. Palmetto Ave. | 407/321–5091 or 800/423–7401 | fax 407/330–7043 | www.rivershipromance.com | $35–$50 | Lunch cruises Wed. and weekends 11–2; Mon.–Tues. and Thurs.–Fri. 11–3; dinner cruises Fri., Sat. 7:30.

St. Johns River Cruises. As you travel along the St. Johns and Oklawaha rivers, look for birds, sunning alligators, and frolicking otters. One to eight passengers per trip. You can also rent pontoon boats for your own trip. | Floridian Sports Club, 114 Floridian Club Rd., Welaka | 904/467–2030 | www.ecocruising.com | $125 for rental, $150 for guided tour | Daily 8–6.

Toon Tours at Gator's Landing. You can take a ride down the St. Johns River on this pontoon boat. Each of the 2-hr trips is narrated. Four-person minimum. | 4255 Peninsula Point | 407/330–3803 | $18 | Tues.–Sat., 10 AM and 1 PM.

ON THE CALENDAR
NOV.: *Sanford Heritage Festival.* Big-name bands help celebrate Sanford in all of its glory at this event that also features local artists, food vendors, craft booths, and street entertainers. Sunday, the end of the three-day festival, is family day so you may hear some high school bands. You can also try your hand at the karaoke contest. | 407/322–2212.

Dining

Angelina's. Italian. Pictures of Sicily and the Italian countryside dress up this casual eatery. Popular dishes include chicken and eggplant Parmesan and chicken marsala. For dessert try a homemade cannoli. Kids' menu. | 3109 S. Orlando Dr. | 407/321–6524 | Closed Sun. | $7–$13 | AE, D, DC, MC, V.

Billy Boy's Famous Chili Dogs. Fast Food. This classic stand for burgers, hot dogs, shakes, and ice pleases the masses of Sanford. There's seating for just ten inside, but you can take your chili dog, chicken-fried steak, or kraut dog, baked beans, slaw, and shake across the street and picnic at Fort Mellon Park. | 401 E. 1st St. | 407/321–0833 | $1–$2.50 | No credit cards.

Lodging

Best Western Marina Hotel and Conference Center. Set on its own small, man-made island, this two-story hotel is just 2 mi from the Central Florida Zoological Park. The Rivership *Romance* tour boat departs from here. 2 restaurants, bar. In-room data ports, some microwaves. Cable TV. Outdoor pool, lake. Dock, water sports, boating, fishing. Laundry facilities. Business services. Pets allowed (fee). | 530 N. Palmetto Ave. | 407/323–1910 or 800/290–1910 | fax 407/322–7076 | www.bestwestern.com | 96 rooms | $79–$89 | AE, D, DC, MC, V.

Days Inn. This two-story motel is across the street from the Seminole Towne Center Mall. There's a 24-hr restaurant on premises and several additional eateries within walking distance. In-room data ports, some refrigerators. Cable TV. Outdoor pool. Laundry facilities. Business services. Pets allowed. | 4650 Hwy. 46W | 407/323–6500 or 800/544–8313 | fax 407/323–2962 | www.daysinn.com | 119 rooms | $60–$105 | AE, D, DC, MC, V.

The Higgins House B&B. This Victorian B&B was built in 1894. This two-story structure features patterned wood shingles, bay windows, and an upstairs veranda. It's in Sanford's Historic District and a short walk from downtown. Complimentary Continental breakfast. Some kitchenettes, some microwaves, some refrigerators. Some in-room VCRs, some room phones, no TV in some rooms, TV in common area. Outdoor hot tub. Bicycles. No pets. No smoking. | 420 S. Oak Ave. | 407/324–9238 or 800/584–0014 | www.higginshouse.com | 4 rooms | $80–$150 | AE, MC, V.

Holiday Inn Express–Sanford/Lake Mary. South of Sanford, in the direction of Orlando, is this chain property built in 1999. Single rooms come with either two twins or a king-size bed, and suites have pull-out couches in addition to king-size beds and separate sitting rooms. In-room data ports, some refrigerators, some in-room hot tubs. Exercise equipment. Laundry facilities, laundry service. Business services. | 3401 S. Orlando Dr. | 407/320–0845 or 800/465–4329 | fax 407/328–6306 | www.holiday-inn.com | 64 rooms, 8 suites | $84–$100 | AE, D, MC, V.

The Martin House Bed and Breakfast. Rooms in this Colonial Revival home each have their own character, from formal Victorian to country wicker—fresh flowers and seasonal fruit spruce things up. You can relax either on the front porch, where you might catch glimmers of breezes from Lake Monroe, or on the back courtyard. A block away from Centennial Park. Complimentary Continental breakfast. Airport shuttle. | 305 S. Park Ave. | 407/330–9013 or 877/807–2194 | www.martinhouse.net | 3 rooms | $95 | AE, MC, V.

SANIBEL ISLAND

(Nearby towns also listed: Cape Coral, Captiva Island, Fort Myers, Fort Myers Beach, Matlacha, Pine Island)

This barrier island on the Gulf of Mexico lies 15 mi southwest of Fort Myers, via the Sanibel Causeway. Locals and environmentalists have worked hard to preserve the island's spectacular natural beauty, and many residents favor bicycles and mopeds over cars to get around. The J. N. "Ding" Darling National Wildlife Refuge preserves 6,000 acres on the north side of the island, and another 1,500 acres are protected by the Sanibel-Captiva Conservation Foundation. It's one of the premier places in the nation for collecting seashells—to find the choicest pickings arrive just as the tide is going out or just after a storm. Resort and residential development, although brisk since the causeway was constructed, is less intense than on Captiva Island, which is just north. Still, there are plenty of good restaurants and resorts, plus many shops and entertainment venues.

Information: **Sanibel-Captiva Islands Chamber of Commerce** | 1159 Causeway Rd., Sanibel Island, 33957 | 941/472–1080 | www.sanibel-captiva.org.

Attractions

Bailey-Mathews Shell Museum. One million shells from around the world are displayed in this museum. The centerpiece, a globe 6 ft in diameter, pinpoints the origins of shells in the collection. Local species are labeled, so it's easier to identify your own finds. | 3075 Sanibel-Captiva Rd. | 941/395–2233 | www.shellmuseum.org | $5 | Tues.–Sun. 10–4.

Bowman's Beach. At the northwest tip of Sanibel is perhaps the most unsung and least developed beach in the area. You're not in the middle of a bunch of condos, parking is plentiful, and you even get showers and rest rooms, as well as picnic areas with grills. | Bowman Beach Rd. | 941/472–6477 | Parking $3.

Care and Rehabilitation of Wildlife (C.R.O.W.). This 10-acre sanctuary is dedicated to the rescue and rehabilitation of sick, orphaned, and injured wildlife. Because of the delicate state of its patients, C.R.O.W. offers just one tour daily. | 3883 Sanibel-Captiva Rd. | 941/472–3644 | $3 | Weekdays 11 AM.

Gulfside City Park. A short strip of beach looks out on the ocean. Inland a bit are some Australian pine trees for shade. There are also picnic tables and a handicapped-accessible sidewalk area. | Algiers La., off Casa Ybel Rd. | 941/472–6477 | Parking 75¢ per hour.

J. N. "Ding" Darling National Wildlife Refuge. This refuge is one of the best spots in Florida for viewing wildlife. The visitor center gives an overview of the area. You can see it on your own along 4 mi of foot trails, two 2-mi and 4-mi canoe trails, and a 5-mi wildlife drive; or take an open-air tram ride. Nearly 300 bird species, more than 50 species of reptiles and amphibians, and some 32 mammals live here for at least part of the year. Sunrise, sunset, and low tide are the best times to observe resident wildlife, particularly shorebirds and wading birds, including many roseate spoonbills. Alligators (and occasionally an American crocodile) often bask in the sun alongside the wildlife drive. There are also ranger tours. A $1.5 million educational center was added in 2000. | 1 Wildlife Dr. | 941/472–1100 | www.fws.gov | $5 per vehicle, $1 for pedestrians and bicyclists, $8 tram ride | Daily; visitor center Nov.–Apr., Sat.–Thurs. 9–5; May–Oct., Sat.–Thurs. 9–4.

Old Lighthouse Beach. An ideal spot for shell-collecting, this beach adjacent to historic, wooden Sanibel Lighthouse draws a mix of families, shellers, and singles. The lighthouse dates to 1884, back when the whole island was a nature preserve; it's not open to the public. Rest rooms are available. | Periwinkle Way | 941/472–6477 | Parking 75¢/hr | Daily.

Sanibel-Captiva Conservation Foundation. This foundation has acquired and preserves over 1,500 acres of environmentally sensitive land, including wildlife habitats, rare and unique plant communities, and freshwater wetlands along the Sanibel River. Without the foundation's protection, most of these areas would have been lost forever. In the reception center, you can join a guided tour along the foundation's nature trails and view exhibits about the area's ecology. | 3333 Sanibel-Captiva Rd. | 941/472-2329 | www.sccf.org | $3 | Nov.–Apr., Mon.–Sat. 8:30–4; May–Oct., weekdays 8:30–3.

★ **Sanibel Historical Village and Museum.** This cracker-style Florida pine home built in the 1890s chronicles the island's pioneer days through vintage documents and old photographs. Nearby are a 1927 general store and gas station and a 1926 post office, both moved from elsewhere and restored. | 950 Dunlop Rd. | 941/472-4648 | Donation suggested | Dec.–July, Wed.–Sat. 10–4, Sun. noon–4.

Sanibel Lighthouse Beach. Known as a good place to collect shells, the beach is a welcoming place with its picturesque lighthouse landmark, built in 1884. Rest rooms are available. | Periwinkle Way | 941/472-6477.

Tarpon Bay Road Beach. Parking is a short walk from the small, secluded beach, which makes it an ideal spot for a quiet family day. There are rest rooms and handicapped-accessible facilities. | Tarpon Bay Rd. | 941/472-6477 | Parking 75¢/h.

ON THE CALENDAR

FEB.: *Rotary Arts and Crafts Fair.* Proceeds from this two-day festival fund scholarships for local youth. Artists come from across the nation to set up tents in the elementary school playground. A traveling minstrel show weaves between the booths. | 941/472-6368.

MAR.: *Sanibel Shell Fair.* Shell displays and crafts at the Sanibel Community Center. | 941/472-2155.

Dining

Gilligan's. Seafood. This friendly neighborhood bar is strewn with fishing nets and buoys. There are usually about ten daily fish specials. Create-a-plate allows you to choose a fish, pick a way it's cooked (Cajun, blackened, bronzed, fried, or grilled) and select two sides from a list of dishes that includes red bliss potatoes, black beans, and rice. | 2163 Periwinkle Way | 941/472-0606 | Closed Sun. | $10–$20 | AE, D, DC, MC, V.

Happy Shrimp Company. Seafood. The more than 45 ways to eat shrimp of all sizes here should make you happy, if not the shrimp, the mural on the wall that depicts happy, dancing shrimp notwithstanding. Popular dishes are shrimp Diane (prepared with a garlic, shallot, chardonnay, and cream sauce) or the Sanibel salad (mixed greens topped with sautéed shrimp, sweet and sour sauce, and fresh grapes). Open for breakfast as well. | 630 Tarpon Bay Rd. | 941/472-6300 | $12–$16 | AE, D, MC, V.

Jacaranda. Continental. Enjoy the live nightly entertainment, which varies from reggae to jazz, as you chow away on grouper stuffed with crab, or the Florida snapper en papillote. Abundant greenery and local watercolors help set a relaxed mood. There's outdoor dining on a screened patio. Kids' menu. | 1223 Periwinkle Way | 941/472-1771 | No lunch | $17–$28 | AE, D, DC, MC, V.

Jean-Paul's French Corner. French. Food critics have been praising this long-time favorite ever since it opened its doors in 1979. The food here is finely seasoned with everything but the highfalutin' attitude sometimes dished up in haute French establishments. Excellent onion soup, salmon in creamy dill sauce, veal medallions in a cream sauce with mushrooms, and roast duckling in fruit sauce are among the few but well prepared choices on the menu. | 708 Tarpon Bay Rd. | 941/472-1493 | Closed Sun. and mid-Dec.–Apr. No lunch | $20–$30 | MC, V.

Lighthouse Café. American. Sanibel's oldest restaurant is within its most notable historical landmark, and the breakfasts are heartwarming. Lacquered navigational charts on the tables and lighthouse photos on the wall lend further authenticity. You get huge quantities of food for modest prices. For breakfast, try whole wheat pancakes and fresh baked muffins; lunch and dinner might be grilled burgers or fresh fish. | 362 Periwinkle Way | 941/472–0303 | No dinner Easter through Dec. | $5–$10 | MC, V.

Mad Hatter. American. Flavors of various regions and the innumerable ethnic groups of the United States mingle in the dishes served here. Recommended are sesame-crusted Thai-barbecued yellowfin tuna and pan-seared jumbo sea scallops. Time your visit to take in the amazing sunset views over the gulf. | 6467 Sanibel-Captiva Rd. | 941/472–0033 | Reservations essential | Closed Sun. No lunch | $20–$30 | AE, MC, V.

McT's Shrimphouse and Tavern. Seafood. Shrimp comes in every imaginable form in this informal pub—from fried to grilled to broiled. For dessert, try the Sanibel mud pie, a delicious concoction heavy on Oreos. | 1523 Periwinkle Way | 941/472–3161 | Reservations not accepted | No lunch | $13–$22 | AE, D, DC, MC, V.

Morgan's Forest. Seafood. With mechanical animals and sounds of rain in the background, you might think that you are in a rain forest. Popular dishes include the broiled grouper and pollo de Peru. Kids' menu. | 1231 Middle Gulf Dr. | 941/472–3351 | Reservations not accepted | Breakfast also available | $14–$24 | AE, D, DC, MC, V.

Pippin's Bar and Grill. Seafood. Fish tanks and lots of cedar dress up this dome-shaped, casual eatery. Locals like the shellfish trio—lobster, king crab, and shrimp, and the "as much as you like" prime rib. Kids' menu. | 1975 Periwinkle Way | 941/395–2255 | No lunch | $10–$24 | AE, D, DC, MC, V.

Sunset Grill. Contemporary. The small, quaint dining room overlooks the Gulf of Mexico and has a surprisingly large wine list. The mesquite-burning stove is a great beginning for your steak or crab cakes. The place has won awards for years for the homemade sauced ribs as well as the warm spinach salad with pancetta dressing. | 6536 Pine Ave. | 941/472–2333 | $15–$20 | AE, D, MC, V.

Tarpon Bay Café. Japanese. The decor is predictably Eastern and spare in this excellent, authentic Japanese restaurant and sushi bar. Sashimi and sushi are available, plus seaweed salad, fried dumplings, seafood, vegetable tempura, and sukiyaki salmon. Try the green-tea ice cream or banana tempura for dessert. | 630 Tarpon Bay Rd. | 941/472–6300 | $5–$21 | AE, DC, MC, V.

Thistle Lodge Waterfront Restaurant. Seafood. A taste of old Sanibel at Casa Ybel Resort, in a 19th-century Victorian Mansion. Outdoor dining is available. Inside sports a jungle theme, with leopard carpeting, wildlife prints on the walls, wicker furniture, and plants galore. The bronzed snapper is a hit as is the lobster Thermador. | 2255 W. Gulf Dr. | 941/472–9200 | $17–$29 | AE, D, DC, MC, V.

Windows on the Water. American. The views of the gulf from all tables are wonderful at this restaurant in the Sundial Resort. Specialties include seared grouper with garlic and red wine sauce, and the Sundial salmon (a fillet topped with peanut sauce). Kids' menu. | 1451 Middle Gulf Dr. | 941/395–6014 | Breakfast also available | $18–$25 | AE, D, DC, MC, V.

Lodging

Anchorage Inn of Sanibel. Just two blocks from the Gulf of Mexico is this relatively affordable accommodation. The central pool area is palm-shaded for privacy. There is also a large deck for sunning. Available are standard rooms, one-room efficiencies, two-room efficiencies, and A-frames with sleeper sofas. Refrigerators, some kitchenettes. Pool. | 1245 Periwinkle Way | 941/395–9688 | fax 941/395–2411 | 12 rooms | $99–$150 | AE, D, MC, V.

Best Western Sanibel Island Beach Resort. This two-story resort occupies 4½ acres on the beach; rooms offer either gulf or garden views. There are a number of restaurants 2 mi away. Complimentary Continental breakfast. In-room data ports, microwaves, refrigerators. Cable TV. Outdoor pool. 1 tennis court. Beach, fishing, bicycles. Laundry facilities. Business services. No pets. | 3287 W. Gulf Dr. | 941/472–1700 or 800/645–6559 | fax 941/

472–5032 | www.bestwestern.com | 41 rooms, 4 suites | $235–$309, $315–$395 suites | AE, D, DC, MC, V.

Blind Pass Condominium. Choose a two- or three-bedroom unit at this condo resort; each has a living room and dining area. This complex is on the western end of the island, which is more conservation-conscious, so guests are more likely to see native animals. Picnic area. Kitchenettes, microwaves, refrigerators. Cable TV, some in-room VCRs. Outdoor pool. Sauna. 2 tennis courts. Beach, boating, fishing. Laundry facilities. No pets. | 5117 Sea Bell Rd. | 941/472–6981 or 800/852–2038 | fax 941/472–1489 | www.blind-pass.com | 65 apartments | $207–$235 (7–night minimum) | MC, V.

Brennen's Tarpon Tale Inn. Built in the early 1960s, this B&B offers five charming attached bungalows and—two blocks away—a cottage with two units (each with full gourmet kitchens). Accommodations are decorated in whitewash wicker and rattan and have antique oak furniture. Complimentary Continental breakfast (for inn guests). Some kitchenettes, microwaves, refrigerators. Cable TV, in-room VCRs (and movies), some room phones. Bicycles. Library. Laundry facilities. Pets allowed (restrictions). | 367 Periwinkle Way | 941/472–0939 | fax 941/472–6202 | www.tarpontale.com | 5 rooms, 2 cottage units | $159–$289, $209–$299 cottages | D, MC, V.

Buttonwood Cottages on Sanibel. Guests at this small, well-maintained resort have two-bedroom or efficiency units with king-size beds and screened-in porches; plus complimentary use of bikes, beach chairs, umbrellas, fishing equipment, barbecue grills, and hammocks nestled in palms. The tranquil and spacious accommodations are in earth tones. Kitchenettes, in-room VCRs. Outdoor hot tub. Beach, water sports, boating, fishing, bicycles. | 1234 Buttonwood La. | 941/395–9061 | fax 941/395–2620 | 8 cottages | $125–$220 | AE, D, DC, MC, V.

Casa Ybel Resort. This condominium complex is on 23 acres and fronts the beach. Feel free to collect seashells on the shore or play tennis by day. The restaurant is quite elegant and serves Caribbean-inspired seafood. Restaurant, bar. In-room data ports, in-room safes, microwaves, refrigerators. Cable TV, in-room VCRs (and movies). Outdoor pool, wading pool. Outdoor hot tub, massage. 6 tennis courts. Beach, water sports, boating, bicycles. Laundry facilities. Business services. No pets. | 2255 W. Gulf Dr. | 941/472–3145 or 800/276–ISLE | fax 941/472–2109 | www.casaybelresort.com | 114 suites | $400–$475 (7–night minimum Jan.–Apr.) | AE, D, MC, V.

Driftwood Inn. These fully stocked, light-pink and hot-pink efficiency cottages with turquoise doors, have two bedrooms and two bathrooms units, plus multiple beds and pull-out couches—it's ideal for groups of friends traveling together. Each cottage has a full kitchen, dining, and living room areas, as well as a screened-in porch, complete with dining-room table for eating alfresco. Most amenities including sheets, beach chairs, and umbrellas are included; you just provide your own beach towels. Microwaves, refrigerators. Beach, water sports. Pets allowed. | 711 Donax St. | 941/395–8874 | fax 941/472–6935 | www.driftwoodsanibel.com | 4 units | $150–$175 | MC, V.

Hilton Sanibel Cottages. Waterfalls and a gazebo are on the grounds of this complex of cottages on the beach. Apartment decor recalls the early 1900s, with gingerbread-Victorian accents. Kitchenettes, microwaves, refrigerators, in-room hot tubs. Cable TV, some in-room VCRs (and movies). Outdoor pool. Spa. 2 tennis courts. Beach, fishing. Laundry facilities. Business services. No pets. | 2341 W. Gulf Dr. | 941/472–1868 | fax 941/472–8711 | www.hgvc.com | 28 apartments | $365 (7–night minimum) | AE, D, DC, MC, V.

Holiday Inn Beach Resort–Sanibel Island. This resort overlooks sandy white beaches and swaying palm trees, and is designed with a tropics-meets-the-Mediterranean aesthetic. Morgan's Forest restaurant is quite popular. Restaurant, bar. In-room data ports, in-room safes, refrigerators. Cable TV. Outdoor pool. 2 tennis courts. Beach, bicycles. Laundry facilities. Business services. No pets. | 1231 Middle Gulf Dr. | 941/472–4123 or 800/HOLIDAY | fax 941/472–0930 | www.holidayinnsanibel.com | 98 rooms | $229–$269 | AE, D, DC, MC, V.

SANIBEL ISLAND

INTRO
ATTRACTIONS
DINING
LODGING

Hurricane House. This resort is situated on 3 acres right on the gulf. Rooms are decorated with bright vibrant colors, and some feature water views. There are a number of restaurants 1 mi away. Picnic area. Kitchenettes, microwaves, refrigerators. Cable TV, in-room VCRs (and movies). Outdoor pool. Spa. Tennis court. Beach. Laundry facilities. | 2939 W. Gulf Dr. | 941/472–1696 | fax 941/472–1718 | www.hgvc.com | 15 rooms, 2 buildings | $345 | AE, MC, V.

Kona Kai Motel. A taste of the Hawaiian Islands on Sanibel. Meaning "garden place," the Kona Kai encourages guests to sing, rest, and play. Dinner cruises and shell trips are available for an additional fee. Motel rooms, efficiencies, and suites (with two beds, a sleeper sofa and fully equipped kitchens) are offered. Some kitchenettes, some microwaves, some refrigerators. Outdoor pool. | 1539 Periwinkle Way | 941/472–1001 or 800/820–2385 | fax 941/472–2554 | www.konakaimotel.com | 12 units | $109–$149 | AE, D, MC, V.

Ocean's Reach Condominiums. This complex is on the eastern end of Sanibel Island, right on the Gulf. There is a washer, dryer, and dishwasher in each room. Restaurants are a short 1-mi drive away. Picnic area. Kitchenettes, microwaves, refrigerators. Cable TV, in-room VCRs. Outdoor pool. Tennis court. Beach, bicycles. Laundry facilities. No pets. | 2230 Camino del Mar | 941/472–4554 or 800/336–6722 | fax 941/472–5087 | www.oceansreach.com | 57 apartments in 4 buildings | $231–$271 (7–day minimum stay) | No credit cards.

Pelicans Roost. Each apartment at this beachfront condominium complex has a screened-in porch with a view of the water. The Darling National Wildlife Refuge and an 18-hole golf course are a long walk or short bike ride away. Kitchenettes, microwaves, refrigerators. Cable TV, some in-room VCRs. Outdoor pool. 2 tennis courts. Beach, bicycles, fishing. Laundry facilities. | 605 Donax St. | 941/472–2996 or 877/757–6678 | www.pelicansroost.com | 21 apartments | $310 (7–day minimum stay) | MC, V.

Sanibel Beach Club II. Each unit in this condo complex has two bedrooms and two baths, and has its own screened-in balcony with a view of the gulf. Sanibel Island Lighthouse is within walking distance, and restaurants are 1 mi away. In-room data ports, microwaves, refrigerators. Cable TV, some in-room VCRs. Outdoor pool. Tennis court. Beach, bicycles. Playground. Laundry facilities. Business services. No pets. | 205 Periwinkle Way | 941/472–5772 or 800/456–0009 | fax 941/472–3790 | 29 apartments | $295 (7–day minimum stay) | AE, MC, V.

The Sanibel Inn. Hummingbird and butterfly gardens dot this 8-acre beachfront retreat, and hundreds of native plants and flowers bloom year-round. Rooms have eco-style decors, each with a native plant motif and a screened-in balcony. Restaurant, bar. In-room data ports, in-room safes, some kitchenettes, microwaves, refrigerators. Cable TV, in-room VCRs. Outdoor pool. Tennis courts. Beach, boating, bicycles. Laundry facilities. Business services. No pets. | 937 E. Gulf Dr. | 941/472–3181 or 800/237–1491 | fax 941/472–5234 | www.sanibelinn.com | 96 units | $290–$480 | AE, D, DC, MC, V.

Sanibel Moorings. Some 600 plant species grow on this 6-acre property, which is bordered by the beach and a lagoon. Each unit has a full kitchen and living room. In high season there's a seven-night minimum; the rest of the year it's four nights. Microwaves, refrigerators. Cable TV, in-room VCRs (and movies). 2 outdoor pools. 2 tennis courts. Beach, dock, fishing. Laundry facilities. Business services. | 845 E. Gulf Dr. | 941/472–4119 or 800/237–5144 | fax 941/472–8148 | www.sanibelmoorings.com | 110 rooms | $220–$310 (7–night minimum Feb.–Apr.) | MC, V.

Sanibel's Seaside Inn. Each room here has either a porch or a balcony that overlooks the central pool, garden, or the beach. You can borrow videos or books from the lending library and have access to a local health club. Rooms are bright and colorful with tropical prints and white rattan furniture, and you get a basket of breakfast treats delivered to your door. Complimentary Continental breakfast. In-room data ports, in-room safes, some kitchenettes. Cable TV, VCRs. Pool. Beach, bicycles. Library. Laundry facilities. No smoking. | 541

E. Gulf Dr. | 941/472–1400 or 800/831–7384 | fax 941/481–4947 | www.seasideinn.com | 32 units | $159–$319 | AE, D, DC, MC, V.

Shalimar. Quaint and pristine white rooms await you in tropical beachfront property, and shorebirds loiter in the morning around the courtyard pool. Some of the cottages are only 70 ft from water while the tide is rising. Five-night minimum in cottages. Kitchenettes, refrigerators, microwaves. Cable TV. Pool. Basketball, volleyball. Beach, fishing. Laundry facilities. | 2823 W. Gulf Dr. | 941/472–1353 or 800/645–4092 | fax 941/472–6430 | shalimar-cottage@att.net | www.shalimar.com | 21 efficiencies, 11 1-bedroom units, 2 2-bedroom units | $123–$143 | DC, MC, V.

Signal Inn Beach and Racquetball Club. Each of these elevated, bedecked cottages has cross ventilation and lets in plenty of sunlight. The upscale accommodations range from one- to four-bedroom units. The resort is eco-friendly—the pool and each unit's water is solar-heated. The beach is famous for shelling. Kitchenettes. In-room VCRs. Hot tub, sauna. Hiking, racquetball. Beach, water sports. Laundry facilities. Some pets (fee). | 1811 Olde Middle Gulf Dr. | 941/472–4690 or 800/992–4690 | fax 941/472–3988 | www.signalinn.com | 19 cottages | $195–$395 (7–night minimum) | AE, MC, V.

Song of the Sea. Guests at this romantic seaside inn are greeted with a bottle of wine, fresh flowers, and bottled water. Rooms have luxurious Thomasville pine furniture and bright Florida colors. Picnic area. Complimentary Continental breakfast. In-room data ports, in-room safes, microwaves, refrigerators. Cable TV, in-room VCRs (and movies). Outdoor pool. Outdoor hot tub. Beach, fishing, bicycles. Laundry facilities. Business services. No pets. | 863 E. Gulf Dr. | 941/472–2220 or 800/931–6600 | fax 941/472–8569 | www.songofthe-sea.com | 30 rooms | $330–$410 | AE, D, DC, MC, V.

Sundial Beach and Tennis Resort. Apartments in this 33-acre resort are airy and right on the beach. Polish your tennis game on the soft or hard courts, or take part in some of the best shelling in the world. Windows on the Water is the hotel restaurant. Restaurant, bar (with entertainment). In-room data ports, in-room safes, kitchenettes, microwaves, refrigerators. Cable TV, in-room VCRs (and movies). Outdoor pool. Hot tub. Driving range, 6 tennis courts. Exercise equipment, volleyball. Beach, water sports, fishing, bicycles. Shops, video games. Children's programs (ages 3–11), laundry facilities. Business services. No pets. | 1451 Middle Gulf Dr. | 941/472–4151 or 800/965–7772 | fax 941/472–8892 | www.sundialresort.com | 271 apartments | $305–$635 | AE, D, DC, MC, V.

Tortuga Beach Club. These time-share condominiums are connected to the beach via walkways that are bordered by lush tropical landscaping. Feel free to relax in the poolside gazebo. Kitchenettes, microwaves, refrigerators. Cable TV, in-room VCRs (and movies). Outdoor pool. Outdoor hot tub. 4 tennis courts. Volleyball. Beach. Laundry facilities. No pets. | 959 E. Gulf Dr. | 941/472–0400 or 800/448–2736 | fax 941/472–6540 | 54 apartments | $370 (7–night minimum) | AE, D, DC, MC, V.

Waterside Inn on the Beach. Accommodations at the Waterside are in clusters and consist of condo units, beach cottages, and efficiencies. Rooms are in an airy, island motif; some have a private patio. There are two outdoor pools, and the property fringes the gulf. Some kitchenettes, some microwaves, some refrigerators, some in-room hot tubs. 2 outdoor pools. Beach, water sports, boating, fishing. Laundry facilities. Small pets allowed. | 3033 W. Gulf Dr. | 941/472–1345 or 800/741–6166 | fax 941/472–2148 | www.watersideinnonthe-beach.com | 4 rooms, 10 efficiencies, 8 cottages | $218–$346 | AE, D, MC, V.

West Wind Inn. Many of the rooms and the pool at this beachfront resort overlook the Gulf of Mexico. The Darling National Wildlife Refuge is within 8 mi. Restaurant, bar. In-room data ports, in-room safes, some kitchenettes, microwaves, refrigerators. Cable TV. Outdoor pool, wading pool. 2 tennis courts. Beach, water sports, bicycles. Laundry facilities. Business services. No pets. | 3345 W. Gulf Dr. | 941/472–1541 or 800/824–0476 | fax 941/472–8134 | www.westwindinn.com | 104 rooms | $228–$288 | AE, D, DC, MC, V.

SARASOTA

MAP 3, H7

(Nearby towns also listed: Bradenton, Lido Key, Longboat Key, Siesta Key, Venice)

Sarasota had been a popular resort area since the beginning of the 20th century, but it came into its own when John Ringling picked the town as the winter home of his circus in 1927. He transformed Sarasota, investing a great deal of his fortune buying chunks of local real estate, and his legacy shapes the city to this day. Ringling's magnificent estate, now the home of the John and Mable Ringling Museum of Art complex, has drawn a sophisticated group of snowbirds to Sarasota, and they support the arts in a big way—music, ballet, opera, theater, and more. The Downtown Cultural District contains the Sarasota Opera House, also home to the Sarasota Ballet, and numerous theaters and night clubs, all within walking distance of excellent restaurants and superb art galleries. Just over the causeway from Sarasota are a number of barrier islands, including Lido Key and Longboat Key.

Information: **Sarasota Convention and Visitors Bureau** | 655 N. Tamiami Trail, Sarasota, 34236 | 941/957–1877 or 800/522–9799 | www.sarasotafl.org.

Attractions

★ **John and Mable Ringling Museum of Art:** *Ca'd'Zan.* The centerpiece of Ringling's 66-acre estate along Sarasota Bay is this Italian Renaissance–style palazzo, built in 1926 at a cost of $1.5 million. Ringling's world-renowned collection of ornate 17th-century Baroque paintings, including a vast number of works by artist Peter Paul Rubens, fill his former home. Ornate decorative sculptures fill the courtyard outside. The landscaped grounds contain more than 400 species of Florida trees, plants, flowers, and Mable Ringling's rose garden. One ticket admits you to both the residence and the Circus Museum. | 5401 Bay Shore Rd. | 941/359–5700 | www.ringling.org | $9 (combined with Circus Museum); grounds free | Daily 10–5:30.

Circus Museum. This is one of only four museums of its kind in the world. The collection includes rare handbills, posters, sequined costumes, miniature circuses, and elaborately carved wagons. | 5401 Bay Shore Rd. | 941/359–5700 | www.ringling.org | $9 (combined with Ca'd'Zan); grounds free | Daily 10–5:30.

Marie Selby Botanical Gardens. This 11-acre bay-front garden estate, with a graciously restored mansion, is known for its collection of more than 6,000 orchids, but there are some 20,000 colorful plants in all. Many were collected on scientific expeditions by the gardens' research staff. Selby's seven greenhouses contain botanical research and plant-identification facilities for which the organization is internationally recognized. | 811 S. Palm Ave. | 941/366–5730 | fax 941/366–9807 | www.selby.org | $8 | Daily 10–5.

Museum of Asian Art. Dedicated to the exhibition and education of the arts and cultures of Asia, this museum, which opened its door in April 2000, places the art within a cultural context through a comprehensive lecture series. The museum is intimate and the collection quite stunning. A photo ID is required. | 640 S. Washington Blvd. | 941/954–7117 | Free | Wed.–Fri. 11–5.

Myakka River State Park. This 28,900-acre park, about 17 mi southeast of town, offers you unparalleled opportunities for bird watching and gator sighting. To see it all, you can hop aboard one of the world's two largest airboats—the *Myakka Maiden* or the *Gator Gal*—which cruise Upper Myakka Lake. You can take a tram ride into the backcountry, rent a mountain bike, canoe through the park on your own, or climb up a stairway to a 100-ft-long swinging bridge that lets you walk through the subtropical and pine-forest canopy. Park rangers offer beginning birding classes and other programs. | Hwy. 72 | 941/365–0100 | Vehicles $4, pedestrians $2, guided tours $7 | Airboat tours 10, 11:30, 1, 2:30; grounds daily 8–sunset.

Sarasota Classic Car Museum. This automobile museum across U.S. 41 from the Ringling Museum houses circus tycoon John Ringling's personal automobile collection, plus 175 Rolls-Royces, Pierce Arrows, Auburns, and other antique vehicles. More than 1,200 old-time music makers—hurdy-gurdies, calliopes, music boxes—are also on display. | 5500 N. Tamiami Trail | 941/355–6228 | $8.50 | Daily 9:30–5:30.

Sarasota Jungle Gardens. The 10 acres of gardens, crossed with footpaths, make for leisurely strolling. You'll find bird and reptile shows, animal exhibits, a shell and butterfly museum, and a petting zoo and playground. It's about 1 mi south of the local airport. | 3701 Bayshore Rd. | 941/355–5305 | fax 941/355–1222 | $9 | Daily 9–5.

Sarasota Visual Art Center. The center displays touring exhibitions of contemporary art, both regional and national, and there's a sculpture garden and a gallery with works for sale. | 707 N. Tamiami Trail | 941/365–2032 | fax 941/366–0585 | Free | Daily 10–4.

Van Wezel Performing Arts Hall. This hard-to-miss purple building in the shape of a clam shell mounts performances of everything from local ethnic dance groups to touring companies of Broadway shows. | 777 N. Tamiami Trail | 941/953–3366 or 800/826–9303 | Call for schedule.

SIGHTSEEING TOURS/TOUR COMPANIES

Le Barge **Cruises.** Narrated cruises on Sarasota Bay show off the area's historic homes and its wildlife. There's live music aboard the sunset cruise, and special events are scheduled year-round. | 2 Marina Jack Plaza | 941/366–6116 | $15 | Dolphin cruise, Tues., Thurs., Sat. 11 AM; sightseeing, Tues.–Sun. 2 and sunset.

ON THE CALENDAR

JAN.: *Sarasota Film Festival.* This five-day film festival continues to gain in international reputation. The festival features indie, documentary, foreign, and student films, focusing on the films of a particular country each year. | 941/364–9514.

FEB.–MAR.: *Sarasota Opera Association.* Housed in the beautifully renovated 1926 Sarasota Opera House, the Opera Association presents dozens of shows ranging from full-on major productions to smaller, more experimental works. | 941/366–8450.

MAR.: *Medieval Fair.* The Ringling Museum of Art hosts this popular annual event with period costumes, jousting, arts and crafts, music, food, and entertainment. | 941/359–5700.

MAR.: *Sarasota Jazz Festival.* This jazz event runs at the Van Wezel Performing Arts Hall. | 777 N. Tamiami Trail | 941/366–1552.

MAR.–APR.: *Sailor Circus.* Students from the area's public schools perform full-scale circus acts, including acrobatics, high-flying, and unicycling. | 941/361–6350.

MAR.: *Baseball Spring Training.* The Cincinnati Reds have been training at Ed Smith Stadium in Sarasota since 1998, when they moved here from Plant City. | 2700 12th St. | 941/954–4101 or 813/287–8844.

JUNE: *Sarasota Music Festival.* The Florida West Coast Symphony Center hosts this three-week festival, which features world-renowned musicians, composers, and conductors joining forces with talented young students to perform symphonic and chamber concerts. Shows are held either at the Symphony Center or at the Sarasota Opera House. | 941/952–9634 or 800/287–9634.

SEPT.–JUNE: *Asolo Theatre Company.* The Asolo Theatre Company, Florida's official theatrical troupe, performs everything from Shakespeare classics to edgy new works in the Asolo Center for the Performing Arts, next to the Ringling Museum. The theater itself was moved from its original home in Asolo, Italy, by John Ringling and is a gorgeous example of Baroque architecture. | 941/351–8000.

SEPT.: *Sarasota Sailing Squadron Labor Day Regatta.* This Sarasota Bay regatta is the largest all-class, saltwater regatta in the Southeast, drawing more than 300 boats each year. There's a grilled chicken/sloopburger cookout with musical entertainment onshore throughout the day. | 941/388–2355.

OCT.–JUNE: *Concert Series.* The Van Wezel Performing Arts Hall concert season brings national and international names to perform in theatrical events as well as classical, pop, and country music concerts. | 941/953–3366.

NOV.: *Sarasota Comedy Festival.* This ten-day funny fest benefits both the United Way of Sarasota and the Child Protection Center. Events include a comic-strip competition, a downtown cartoon walk, a golf classic, headline and aspiring stand-up comedians, comedy dinners, kids' comedy, and more. Events happen all over town but the main events are held at the Sarasota Opera House and Van Wezel Performing Arts Hall. | 941/954–2006.

Dining

Bijou Café. Continental. A gas station in the '20s, this building is now decked in classy wood and brass accents, and acres of green carpeting. Chef-owner Jean Pierre Knagg's specialties include fierce crab cakes with remoulade sauce and crispy roast duckling with orange-lingonberry-and-port-cherry glaze. Top things off with the stellar crème brûlée. There's an extensive wine list. | 1287 1st St. | 941/366–8111 | Closed Sun. May–Dec. | $12–$22 | AE, D, MC, V.

Cafe Campestre. Mexican. The walls of the cantina-like space are painted in deep-ochre tones and hung with ornate crucifixes and bejeweled folk-art mirrors. There is one large dining area and several smaller, more intimate rooms. The café's carefully prepared Mexican food is authentically rendered: try the unusual *uchepos* (corn tamales stuffed with shredded chicken, served with hot spices and pico de gallo). | 3589 Webber St. | 941/923–5356 | $9–$15 | AE, D, DC, MC, V.

Fred's. Eclectic. This restaurant lies within a cluster of historic buildings around Sarasota's Hillview Street. The menu focuses on American-bistro fare with global, often pan-Asian, influences. High, inlaid-copper ceilings, hardwood floors, deep-red plaster, and marble walls set an elegant tone. Try wok-seared veggies with basil and lemongrass broth, and shrimp-and-mango spring rolls. Sun. brunch. | 1917 S. Osprey Ave. | 941/362–9463 | $13–$24 | AE, DC, MC, V.

Les Saisons. French. The dining room here is small and relaxed, the menu reasonably priced. Try coq au vin, any of the bountiful salads, and chocolate mousse. | 4785 Swift Rd. | 941/925–3385 | $10–$20 | AE, D, MC, V.

Marina Jack. Seafood. Either dine inside overlooking Sarasota Bay, or hop aboard the *Marina Jack II*, the restaurant's paddle-wheel boat, which offers romantic 2-hr dinner cruises with live entertainment. Fresh seafood rules the roost at both the onshore and floating venues. | 2 Marina Plaza | 941/365–4232 or 941/366–9225 (for dinner boat) | Reservations essential for dinner cruise | $14–$28 | MC, V.

Michael's on East. Contemporary. Despite the elegant setting and sophisticated food, prices are fair at this downtown favorite. Recommended are penne with grilled summer vegetables and black olives, and grilled fillet of beef with garlic-mashed potatoes. Live piano nightly. | 1212 East Ave. S | 941/366–0007 | $13–$29 | AE, D, MC, V.

Patrick's. American/Casual. A longtime locals' favorite, this upscale sports bar and eatery draws after-work types for steak sandwiches, juicy cheeseburgers, meat loaf, pizza, pasta, and char-grilled steaks. Weekends are also busy. Sun. brunch. | 1400 Main St. | 941/952–1170 | $6–$18 | AE, D, DC, MC, V.

Phillippi Oyster Bar. Seafood. This is an excellent choice for a meal if you're traveling with kids: There's ample open-air, waterfront seating at rustic picnic tables on Phillippi Creek. Favorites include creek combo pot, which overflows with steamed-shellfish, corn-on-the-cob, and fresh veggies. There are chicken and pasta dishes, too. | 5353 S. Tamiami Trail | 941/925–4444 | $6–$13 | AE, D, DC, MC, V.

Siam Orchid Thai. Thai. You can enjoy simple, well-prepared food in this tasteful, Asian-inspired eatery. Siam specializes in spicy seafood dishes but also offers many vegetarian choices. The staff wears traditional Thai dress. | 4141 S. Tamiami Trail | 941/923–7447 | Reservations not accepted | $7–$15 | AE, DC, MC, V.

Sugar and Spice. American. Though Amish handicrafts and country-home decor may seem a bit out of place in a beach community, this place serves tasty comfort food that fits with the old-fashioned ambience. If you're not planning on hitting the beach any time soon, try the spaghetti with homemade sauce, or the turkey with dressing. The chocolate cake is legendary. | 4000 Cattleman Rd. | 941/342–1649 | Reservations not accepted | Closed Sun. | $6–$14 | DC, MC, V.

Trolley Station. American. With a train-station motif that borrows from its former location by a trolley depot, this traditional American eatery has a long salad and baked-potato bar, and serves roast beef, fish, chicken, and pasta. | 3550 Clark Rd. | 941/923–2721 | $5–$11 | MC, V.

Walt's Raw Bar. Seafood. This casual restaurant, one of several owned by the eponymous Walt, serves sea critters in just about every form—from on the half-shell to cooked several different ways. | 560 N. Washington Blvd. | 941/365–1735 | Reservations not accepted | $8–$18 | DC, MC, V.

Wild Eats. Vegetarian. This bright, airy little spot specializes in vegetarian and vegan fare, but does offer an occasional fish or chicken dish. The interior is filled with art and antiques. Try poached salmon, the veggie burger, or Portobello mushroom sandwich. | 325 John Ringling Blvd. | 941/388–3948 | $14–$24 | AE, D, DC, MC, V.

Yoder's. American. Owned and operated for more than 25 years by the same Amish family, the restaurant gives you friendly service and downhome food. The hearty breakfasts are followed by lunches and dinners of meat loaf or southern-fried chicken served with a side of "real" mashed potatoes. They are known for their pies, so don't miss out on the seasonal fruit pies, such as the strawberry cream or peach pie. | 3434 Bahia Vista St. | 941/955–7771 | Closed Sun. | $8–$12 | No credit cards.

Lodging

Best Western Midtown. This two-story motel is seashell-pink stucco and surrounded by palms. The motel surrounds a spacious outdoor pool. Rooms have big windows with balconies or sliding doors. Complimentary Continental breakfast. In-room data ports, microwaves, refrigerators. Cable TV. Pool. Laundry facilities. Business services. | 1425 S. Tamiami Trail | 941/955–9841 or 888/879–3578 | fax 941/954–8948 | www.bestwestern.com | 100 rooms | $49–$99 | AE, D, MC, V.

The Cypress–A B&B Inn. Overlooking Sarasota Bay, and beneath palms, mangos, and moss-draped oaks, this tin-roofed, two-story retreat has rooms with hardwood floors, Oriental rugs, fresh flowers, and American and European antiques. One room has a balcony on the bay. The inn is across the street from Bayfront Park, a block south of the Marie Selby Botanic Gardens, and 200 yards from a marina. Complimentary breakfast. Some in-room hot tubs. No room phones. No kids. | 621 Gulfstream Ave. S | 941/955–4683 | 4 rooms | $140–$230 | AE, D, MC, V.

Hampton Inn I-75. This hotel has its own private white-sand beach and is less than 10 minutes from the Asolo Theatre and Ringling Museum complex and Myakka River State Park. Guest rooms connect to each other and are comfortable, if basic; all have recliner sofas. In-room data ports, microwaves, refrigerators. Cable TV, in-room VCRs (and movies). Pool. Exercise equipment. Laundry facilities. Business services. | 5995 Cattleridge Rd. | 941/371–1900 | fax 941/371–0241 | 121 rooms | $89–$119 | AE, D, MC, V.

Hampton Inn–Sarasota/Bradenton. This hotel is conveniently situated between Sarasota and Bradenton. It's only ½ mi from the Circus and the Sarasota Classic Car museums and within 5 minutes of many popular eateries. Free coffee and cookies in the lobby. Complimentary Continental breakfast. In-room data ports, microwaves, refrigerators. Cable TV, in-room VCRs (and movies). Pool. Exercise equipment. Laundry facilities. Business services, airport shuttle. | 5000 N. Tamiami Trail | 941/351–7734 | fax 941/351–8820 | 97 rooms | $64–$119 | AE, D, MC, V.

Holiday Inn–Downtown by the Bay. This hotel is within easy walking distance of the marina and the downtown shopping and business center. It's about 6 mi from Sarasota's main beaches and museums, and 5 to 7 mi from many golf courses. Bay-side guest rooms have water views, and city-side rooms look out onto downtown Sarasota. Restaurant, bar. In-room data ports, microwaves, refrigerators. Cable TV. Pool. Exercise equipment. Laundry facilities. Business services. | 1 N. Tamiami Trail | 941/365–1900 or 800/465–4329 | fax 941/365–1900 | www.holiday-inn.com | 100 rooms | $69–$129 | AE, D, MC, V.

Hyatt Sarasota. This hotel's lobby and guest rooms are done in a sleek, contemporary style, overlooking either the marina or Sarasota Bay. The property is across from the Van Wezel Performing Arts Hall. Restaurant, bar. In-room data ports, microwaves, refrigerators. Cable TV, in-room VCRs (and movies). Pool. Exercise equipment. Boating, fishing. Laundry facilities. Business services, airport shuttle. | 1000 Blvd. of the Arts | 941/953–1234 or 800/532–1496 | fax 941/952–1987 | 297 rooms | $164–$229 | AE, D, MC, V.

Quayside Inn. A B&B atmosphere prevails here at this downtown property. Rooms in this two-story building are adorned with standard motel furnishings, such as matching bedside and sitting-area tables. Light-wood furnishings and soft colors help brighten things up. Some refrigerators, some microwaves. Outdoor pool. Pets allowed. | 270 N. Tamiami Trail | 941/366–0414 or 877/294–3265 | fax 941/954–3379 | www.quaysideinn.com | 26 rooms | $65–$85 | AE, D, MC.

Sarasota/Bradenton Courtyard by Marriott. This three-story, upscale business property is ½ mi from Circus Museum and 3 mi from the Van Wezel Performing Arts Hall. Unlike many of the area's lodgings, this hotel is a few blocks back from the beach, which makes it a bit quieter and less touristy. Restaurant, bar. In-room data ports, microwaves, refrigerators. Cable TV, in-room VCRs (and movies). Pool. Exercise equipment. Laundry service. | 850 University Pkwy. | 941/355–3337 | fax 941/355–5518 | 81 rooms | $84–$124 | AE, D, MC, V.

Sarasota Super 8 Motel. Built in 1989, this two-story, sandy-pink chain motel is dotted with palm trees and is equidistant from downtown and the airport. Outdoor pool. Laundry facilities, laundry service. | 4309 N. Tamiami Trail | 941/355–9326 | fax 941/355–5285 | www.super8.com | 50 rooms | $75–$150 | AE, D, DC, MC, V.

Sleep Inn. This budget mid-priced property is across from the airport, exit 40 off of I–75. Complimentary Continental breakfast. In-room data ports, some microwaves, some refrigerators. Outdoor pool. Laundry facilities. Airport shuttle. | 900 University Pkwy. | 941/359–8558 | fax 941/359–8558 | www.sleepinn.com | 76 rooms, 4 suites | $79–$99 | AE, D, DC, MC, V.

Sunset Lodge Motel. The sundeck and shuffle board here might help you forget the 1-mi walk to Crescent Beach. The ground-floor efficiencies have recliner or sleeper sofas. Kitchenettes, microwaves, refrigerators. Swimming pool. Laundry facilities. | 1765 Dawn St. | 941/925–1151 or 888/669–6782 | fax 941/925–8168 | 6 efficiencies | $55–$95 | AE, D, MC, V.

Timberwoods Vacation Villas. This resort is actually a sprawling, rambling compound of two-bed, two-bath bungalows with screened-in porches and garages. The grounds are covered with towering pine trees and several ponds that harbor swans by day and chirping frog-choruses at night. A wine-and-cheese party is held Friday evenings. In-room data ports, kitchenettes, microwaves, refrigerators. Cable TV. Pool. Hot tub. Tennis. Basketball. Library. Laundry facilities. Business services. | 7964 Timberwood Cir. | 941/923–4966 or 800/824–5444 (reservations) | fax 941/924–3109 | 110 villas | $595–$875 | AE, D, MC, V.

Wellesley Inn. This independently run motel is a dependable choice for basic, no-frills accommodations. It has interior corridors, an elevator to the second floor, connecting rooms, and is about 5 mi from local museums and restaurants. Complimentary Continental breakfast. In-room data ports, microwaves, refrigerators. Cable TV. Pool. Business services, airport shuttle. Pets allowed. | 1803 N. Tamiami Trail | 941/366–5128 or 800/444–8888 | fax 941/953–4322 | 106 rooms | $60–$130 | AE, D, MC, V.

SEASIDE

(Nearby towns also listed: Grayton Beach, Panama City, Panama City Beach)

You may recognize Seaside as the perfect community depicted in the 1998 film *The Truman Show,* starring Jim Carrey. The town is indeed perfect in its own way, designed to promote a neighborly, old-fashioned lifestyle. The first home of the pre-planned town was finished in 1981. Now there are about 350 expensive, Victorian-style cottages, complete with white picket fences and front-porch rockers, all on redbrick streets. The majority of residents (only about 15 families live here year-round) use their cottages as vacation retreats, and the rest of the year rent out the cottages—including, yes, Jim Carrey's movie house—to tourists.

Information: Seaside Community Development Corporation | Box 4730, Seaside, 32459 | 800/277–8696 | www.seasidefl.com.

Attractions

Ruskin Place Artist Colony. In the heart of Seaside is this quaint collection of galleries and small craft shops. | 800/277–8696 | www.seasidefl.com/merchants/ruskin | Free | Apr.–Oct., daily 10–7; Nov.–Mar., daily 10–5.

ON THE CALENDAR
MAY: *White Wine Festival.* Purveyors of wine converge on Seaside the first weekend in May, centered around the town amphitheater, though tasting tables and tents are set up around town. A similar Red Wine Festival takes place the first weekend in November. | 850/231–5424.

Dining

Bud & Alley's. Seafood. The only restaurant in town that's directly on the beach offers a few different sunset-viewing options: there's a roof deck bar, 6-ft wraparound windows on the first floor porch, or an outdoor gazebo, in addition to the main dining room, which looks out onto an herb garden. You'll find a daily changing menu of salads, soups, pastas, and grilled fish such as dolphin (mahimahi) with a Florida salsa and cilantro dressing. | Hwy. 30A | 850/231–5900 | Closed Jan. and Tuesdays Oct.–Feb. | $18–$30 | MC, V.

Cafe Thirty-A. Eclectic. It's worth the mile drive east of Seaside to dine inside this beautiful Florida-style home or on its wide veranda. The service is impeccable, with a menu that changes daily and features such entrées as Thai red-curry shellfish steam pot with coconut-milk broth. They also have a wide salad selection and a 122-bottle wine list. | 3899 E. Scenic Hwy. 30A, Seagrove Beach | 850/231–4196 | fax 850/231–2128 | Closed Sun. and Jan.1–14 | $20–$30 | AE, D, DC, MC, V.

Shades. American/Casual. Shades is the most relaxed of Seaside's restaurants—kids' dishes come served on a Frisbee—and you can get a good half-pound burger here, beside a variety of fresh fish, calamari, salads, and other inexpensive fare. Perhaps Shades is best known for its homemade seafood sauces, including a Jack Daniels tangy mustard sauce for grouper and dolphin (mahimahi) fish bites, and a sweet barbecue sauce for shrimp. Outdoor dining is available in a big deck outside this converted century-old house. | 83 Central Sq. | 850/231–1950 | Reservations not accepted | $8–$20 | AE, MC, V.

Lodging

Josephine's Inn. This is the only B&B in Seaside. A very nice breakfast is offered in the ground-floor restaurant run by the same owners. Restaurant, picnic area, complimentary breakfast. In-room data ports, kitchenettes, microwaves, refrigerators. Cable TV. Library. No kids under 10. No smoking. | 38 Seaside Ave. | 850/231–1940 or 800/848–1840 | fax 850/231–2446 | www.josephinesfl.com | 7 rooms, 2 suites | $200–$240 | AE, MC, V.

Seaside Cottage Rental Agency. A great majority of town residents rent out their Victorian-style, one- to six-bedroom vacation cottages. They come complete with all furnishings, the style of which reflects the owners' tastes. A centralized booking service handles reservations. | 850/231–1320 or 800/277–8696 | www.seasidefl.com | 270 cottages | $150–$1,000 per night | AE, D, DC, MC, V.

SEBASTIAN

MAP 3, K6

(Nearby towns also listed: Fort Pierce, Melbourne, Vero Beach)

This little fishing village of 15,000, occupying 3 mi of Atlantic coastline, is possibly the most remote of any town from Jacksonville to Miami Beach. This adds to the pleasure of exploring the miles of quiet beaches along the state park around Sebastian Inlet. For surfing enthusiasts, one of Florida's most consistent wave breaks is at Sebastian Inlet's first peak, next to the north jetty.

Information: **Sebastian River Area Chamber of Commerce** | 700 Main St., Sebastian, 32958 | 561/589–5969 | http://sebastian.fl.us/chamber.

Attractions

Mel Fisher's Treasure Museum. Booty from the *Atocha,* which was recovered in 1985 along with other wrecks from the hurricane of 1715, are on display here, as in a similar museum run by Mel Fisher in Key West. | 1322 U.S. 1 | 561/589–9875 | www.melfisher.com | $5 | Mon.–Sat. 10–5, Sun. noon–5.

Sebastian Inlet State Recreation Area. This is one of Florida's most visited state parks due to its productive fishing waters. At the north end of Orchid Island, the 578-acre site also has great beaches, some of the best surfing waves in the state, and memorable views from both sides of a high bridge that spans the inlet. | 9700 S. Hwy. A1A, Melbourne Beach | 321/984–4852 | www.dep.state.fl.us | $3.25 per vehicle | Daily.

McLarty Treasure Museum. This historical museum is a National Historic Landmark on the spot where 1,500 hurricane survivors camped in 1715. The hurricane sank 11 ships of a Spanish fleet, and 700 people died in the storm. Inside you'll find artifacts from the wrecks and a 45-min A&E video. | 13180 Rte. A1A N | 561/589–2147 | www.dep.state.fl.us | $1 | Daily 10–4:30.

ON THE CALENDAR

NOV.: Taste and Treasures of Sebastian. This fishing and aquatic festival at Riverview Park on the Indian River Lagoon is usually held the second weekend of Nov. It includes an on-shore fishing contest, canoes races, and a fish fry. | 561/589–5969.

Dining

Captain Hiram's. Seafood. This fun waterfront restaurant has wooden booths, stained glass, and umbrellas on an open deck. Try Capt. Jim's Maryland blue crab cakes, cooked, fried, or sautéed. Kids will like Capt. Hiram's Sandbar out back, while parents drink from a beached boat. There's live music all year on weekends, including a swing band on Sundays. | 1606 N. Indian River Dr. | 561/589–4345 | $11–$17 | AE, D, MC, V.

Finn's Grill and Raw Bar. Seafood. Jutting 150 ft into the Indian River on a dock off Semblers Marina, Finn's is an open-air deck restaurant and bar on stilts, with views of Sebastian Inlet. From the oak fire grill, try the "crunchy" grouper, oysters, or shrimp, with a cornflake batter. | 1660 Indian River Dr. | 561/589–3828 | $6–$18 | AE, D, DC, MC, V.

Hurricane Harbor. Continental. First a garage, later a Prohibition smugglers' den, Hurricane Harbor has waterfront window seats on the Indian River. Besides steaks, pastas, and variations on Florida grouper, you can have Continental dishes such as Wiener schnitzel with lemon butter, and veal St. Moritz. | 1540 Indian River Dr. | 561/589-1773 | Closed Mon. | $10-$15 | AE, D, DC, MC, V.

Lodging

Captain's Quarters Riverfront Motel. Five units—four overlooking the Indian River Lagoon and the marina at Capt. Hiram's Restaurant and one two-room suite—are all Key West cute. Painted in bright colors with matching fabrics, the rooms have pine and white-wicker furniture and pine plank floors with grass rugs. The adequate bathrooms have large stall showers. Glass doors open to a plank porch, but the porches are all within sight of each other. Restaurant. Complimentary Continental breakfast. Air-conditioning, in-room data ports. Cable TV, room phones. Beach, dock, water sports, boating, fishing. Laundry facilities, laundry service. | 1606 Indian River Dr. | 561/589-4345 | fax 561/589-4346 | 4 rooms, 1 suite | $134-$144 | AE, D, DC, MC, V.

Davis House Inn. Owner Steve Wild designed this simple, clean, and comfortable inn after the clubhouse at Augusta National. There are wraparound porches shaded by overhung roofs, and rooms are huge. Picnic area. Kitchenettes, microwaves, refrigerators. Cable TV. Laundry facilities. No smoking. | 607 Davis St. | 561/589-4114 | fax 561/589-1722 | www.davishou-seinn.com | 12 rooms | $69-$89 | AE, D, MC, V.

Ferndale Lodge. This 1948 one-story efficiency motel offers simple rooms on two heavily wooded acres directly on the river. From Jan. to Mar., rentals are available by the month. Picnic area. Kitchenettes, microwaves, refrigerators. Cable TV. Dock, fishing. No smoking. |

© Archive

THE TREASURE COAST—COASTLINE GEMS

Situated on Florida's east coast about midway down the peninsula, these 60 mi of immaculate, picturesque, stretches of beach run from Sebastian Inlet to Jupiter Inlet just north of Palm Beach.

Dotted with small, laid-back hamlets that are seriously committed to strict zoning standards and the fragile ecosystem, this part of Florida is definitely not lined with wall-to-wall high-rises that blot out the horizon. Energies of the townfolk are dedicated to preserving their charming, historic, downtown areas.

The beach is sandwiched between the shimmering Atlantic Ocean on the east—legendary for surfers and deep seas sportsmen—and the Indian River lagoon to the west, a pristine waterway rich with hundreds of species of fish, plants, and animals. Some of the major communities and travel destinations are Sebastian, Vero Beach, Port St. Lucie, Fort Pierce, Jensen Beach (Hutchinson Island), and Jupiter.

You might well call this area a wonderful "critter land," as the beaches along this region are sought out by nesting sea turtles and are a protected species; you can join organized watches, which go out to view the turtles laying their eggs in the sand between late April and August. The much beloved sea cow (manatee), so ugly it's cute, travels inland (from mid-November to early April) to the warm waters of Moore's Creek in Fort Pierce, where the Manatee Observation and Education Center is located. One of the few areas within the state of Florida that permits horseback riding is available on the scenic beach at Hutchinson Island's Fredrick Douglas Memorial Park.

Heading south to Palm beach is a journey from the sublime to the extreme— the playground of the wintering rich and famous. Famous Worth Avenue is exclusive and pricey. Cartier, Charles Jourdan, and Giorgio Armani are just a few of the fashionable names you'll find on storefronts on this quarter-mile-long street. Other defining landmarks are The Breakers Hotel, Flagler Museum, Mar-A-Lago, and the amazing mansions on Shore Road (A1A).

11450 Indian River Dr. | 561/589–5247 | fax 561/388–6035 | www.ferndalelodge.com | 12 rooms | $45–$65 | No credit cards.

Key West Inn at Captain Hiram's. This blue three-story Key West Victorian-style hotel opened in March 2000, keeping five older units a block away—four of which overlook the Indian River and the marina. The surfboard collection in the otherwise Victorian lobby hints at fun. Complimentary Continental breakfast. In-room data ports, some kitchenettes, some minibars, some microwaves, some refrigerators. Cable TV, some in-room VCRs. Outdoor pool. Dock, water sports, boating, fishing, bicycles. Video games. Laundry facilities, laundry service. | 1580 U.S. 1 | 561/388–8588 | fax 561/388–3118 | www.keywestinn.net | 56 rooms | AE, D, DC, MC, V.

SEBRING

MAP 3, J7

(Nearby towns also listed: Lake Placid, Okeechobee)

This town in the middle of the state was founded in 1911 by transplanted Ohio pottery manufacturer G. E. Sebring. The town, centered around historic Circle Park, is surrounded by citrus groves and is famous for its annual stock-car endurance race. About 1,000 lush acres make up Highlands Hammock State Park, filled with trees nearly 1,000 years old. Outdoor activities are a popular local pastime.

Information: **Highlands County Chamber of Commerce** | 309 South Cir, Sebring, 33870 | 863/385–8448 | www.sebringflchamber.com.

Attractions

Highlands Hammock State Park. Someone sees white-tail deer and alligators almost every day in this 4,896-acre park, about 4 mi south of town. There are nine hiking trails: Three are ramped boardwalks bordering cypress swamps and a virgin hardwood forest; the others are packed dirt, meandering through the park's plant communities. Otters and Florida scrub jays make frequent appearances, as do bears and the rare Florida panther. | Hwy. 27 | 863/386–6094 | $3.25 per vehicle | Daily.

Sebring International Raceway. Home of the famed 12-Hour Endurance Race of Sebring, and adjacent to the Sebring Regional Airport off U.S. 98, the raceway has been around since 1950. Other events include a Sports Car Classic and an Endurance Classic. | 113 Midway Dr. | 863/655–1442 or 800/626–RACE | Prices vary by event | Call for schedule.

ON THE CALENDAR

MAR.: *Sebring 12-Hour Endurance Race.* Sebring is known around the world for this auto-racing event, held annually during the third week of the month. Thousands return every spring to see it. | 863/655–1442.

NOV.: *Highlands Fine Arts Festival.* On the second Saturday of November, more than 100 local and national artists gather around the town circle to show their work. You can get food, hear music, and walk through the artists' booths. An inspiring and thoroughly enjoyable afternoon. The festivities begin around 9 and start winding down at 4. | 863/385–5312.

Dining

Lakeside Tea Room. Café. Each of this tearoom's three rooms is filled with light and decorated with a floral motif. Views are of Lake Sebring and a courtyard with a butterfly garden and fountain. The prix-fixe lunches come with an entrée, side dishes, a beverage, and homemade dessert. Try any of the quiches, seafood au gratin, the grilled chicken Caesar, or the seafood and chicken salads. | 500 Lake Sebring Dr. | 863/385–7113 | Closed Aug. and Sun. No dinner | $10 | AE, D, MC, V.

Lodging

Chateau Elan Hotel and Spa. The Chateau is close to Sebring International Raceway, with a number of guest rooms and all the meeting areas overlooking action. An on-site spa offers beauty treatments and massages. Restaurant, bar. Microwaves, refrigerators. Cable TV, in-room VCRs. Pool. Hot tub, massage, spa. Exercise equipment. Laundry facilities. Business services. Pets allowed. | 150 Midway Dr. | 863/655–6252 | fax 863/655–6303 | 161 rooms | $88–$125 | AE, D, MC, V.

Quality Inn and Suites Conference Center. About 10 mi from the track, this is the official host of the Sebring International Raceway, and many of the drivers, staff, and spectators stay here. Both the spacious lobby and the guest rooms are furnished in dark cherry-wood antique reproductions. Restaurant, bar (with entertainment). Microwaves, refrigerators. Cable TV, some in-room VCRs. Pool, wading pool. Massage, sauna. Laundry facilities. Business services. | 6525 U.S. 27N | 863/385–4500 | fax 863/382–4793 | www.choicehotels.com | 148 rooms | $64–$94 | AE, D, MC, V.

Sebring Lakeside Golf Resort Inn and Tea Room. This scenic resort has a fountain courtyard, pavilion, fishing dock, and sandy white beach on Lake Sebring. The inn is built around a 1920s Spanish Mission–style home with a bell tower. Guests range from honeymooners to families. There's a short nine-hole golf course. Some kitchenettes, some minibars, some microwaves, some refrigerators, some in-room hot tubs. Outdoor pool. 9-hole golf course. Beach, dock, water sports, boating, fishing. | 500 Lake Sebring Dr. | 863/385–7113 or 888/2–SEBRING | fax 863/385–9471 | 18 units | $75–$200 | AE, MC, V.

SIESTA KEY

MAP 3, H7

(Nearby towns also listed: Bradenton, Lido Key, Longboat Key, Sarasota, Venice)

Established in 1846, the community of Siesta Key lies along an 8-mi-long barrier island connected to Sarasota on the mainland by two long bridges. The island is covered with lush foliage, tropical flowers, and mangrove swamps that shelter manatees and hundreds of bird species. Siesta Key's beaches are 99% pure quartz, which makes them white as snow and soft as powdered sugar. The Key is an intriguing mix of natural beauty and touristy development.

Information: Siesta Key Chamber of Commerce | 5100 Ocean Blvd., Ste. B, Siesta Key, 34242 | 941/349–3800 | www.siestachamber.com.

Attractions

Siesta Beach. This 40-acre park has nature trails, a concession stand, soccer and softball fields, picnic facilities, a playground, rest rooms, a fitness trail, and tennis and volleyball courts. Free spirits gather on Sunday evenings (an hour before sunset) to partake of a bonfire and drum circle, to which all are welcome. | 600 Beach Rd. | Free | Daily.

Turtle Beach. On 14 acres, this beach park is popular with families. It has boat horseshoe pits in town, plus picnic and play facilities, a recreation building, rest rooms, and a volleyball court. | Turtle Beach Rd. | Free | Daily.

ON THE CALENDAR

NOV.: *Sand Fest.* The party starts Friday night and ends late Saturday night. Saturday is family day with sand and water games, sand-sculpture competitions, and a climbing wall. Saturday night the innocence of the day's events turn into an evening of debauchery on the beach with live music, cocktails, and a buffet sponsored by local restaurants. Daytime events are free but there is a charge for the nighttime fiesta. | 941/349–3800.

Dining

Captain Curt's Crab and Oyster Bar. Seafood. This crustacean feast is just off of the Stickney Point Road Bridge. Specialties are fried-seafood baskets, hot pots filled with steamers or oysters, and raw-bar treats. Captain Curt bottles his hot sauce. | 1200 Old Stickney Point Rd. | 941/349–3885 | $7–$21 | AE, D, MC, V.

Chez Daniel. French. Choose from the extensive by-the-glass wine list as you savor old French standards including escargots with garlic butter, steak au poivre, duck à l'orange, and grilled salmon on spinach with champagne sauce. | 6621 Midnight Pass Rd. | 941/346–9228 | Closed Aug. | $15–$23 | AE, MC, V.

Ophelia's on the Bay. Seafood. Consistently voted the most romantic restaurant in the area, this place has candle-lit tables overlooking Sarasota Bay. You can also dine in the tropical garden. Try the Szechuan crusted tuna served with seaweed salad. The menu changes nightly, but you can usually find the pinenut-covered salmon stuffed with mascarpone and roasted peppers served with a lemon dill sauce or the Colorado rack of lamb cooked in grain mustard and covered with a cognac demi-glace. The in-house pastry chef serves up mean white chocolate mousse in a chocolate covered almond twill cup floating over raspberry coulis. | 9105 Midnight Pass Rd. | 941/349–2212 | No lunch | $18–$28 | AE, D, DC, MC, V.

The Summerhouse. Continental. Often cited as greater Sarasota's most romantic restaurant, the Summerhouse has a multi-level atrium dining room with glass walls and a jungle of lush greenery illuminated with sparkling lights. Consider chicken *chasseur* (grilled and topped with sautéed mushrooms and shallots in a dry sherry sauce). Finish with the key lime pie, served chilled with real cream and fresh lime juice. | 6101 Midnight Pass Rd. | 941/349–1100 | No lunch. Mon.–Sat. | $12–$26 | AE, D, DC, MC, V.

Turtles. American. This casual, touristy spot, with nautical/beach–theme decor, is ideal if you've got kids in tow. Watch herons and the occasional pod of dolphins from the waterfront deck or in the air-conditioned interior confines. Either is perfectly nice. Try crab-stuffed mushroom caps or spicy veal meat loaf. | 8875 Midnight Pass Rd. | 941/346–2207 | Reservations not accepted | $10–$15 | AE, D, DC, MC, V.

Lodging

Anchor Down. This family-owned and -operated establishment provides economical accommodations on a canal, 50 yards from the beach and 100 ft from a boat ramp. An outdoor pool is flanked by two-story structures on all sides, which contain studio, one-bedroom, and two-bedroom units. There's a tiki hut for barbecuing. Microwaves, refrigerators. Outdoor pool. Dock, water sports, boating, fishing, bicycles. Laundry facilities. | 9004 Midnight Pass Rd. | 941/349–5556 | 10 units | $90–$120.

Banyan Tree Beach Resort. This ever-expanding resort comprises seven buildings, some of them stand-alone units with private pools and private laundry facilities. Studio, two-bedroom, and three-bedroom town houses have brightly colored furnishings. There are barbecue pits. Microwaves, refrigerator. 5 outdoor pools. Dock, fishing, bicycles. Laundry facilities. | 5053 Ocean Blvd. | 941/346–0651 or 800/732–7231 | fax 941/346–1694 | www.siestakeybanyanresort.com | 22 units | $455–$185 (7–night minimum) | AE, D, MC, V.

Best Western Siesta Beach Resort. This cheerful, blue-and-white two-story motel lies across the street from the gulf, its pool and lanai ablaze with tropical plants and equipped with shaded tables and lounge chairs. Siesta Village shopping area is steps away, and a courtyard has shuffleboard. Complimentary Continental breakfast. In-room data ports, microwaves, refrigerators. Cable TV. Pool. Hot tub. Laundry facilities. Business services. | 5311 Ocean Blvd. | 941/349–3211 or 800/223–5786 | fax 941/349–7915 | www.bestwestern.com | 53 rooms | $149–$209 | AE, D, MC, V.

Captiva Beach Resort. Short- and long-term rates are offered at this apartment hotel 400 ft from a gorgeous stretch of white sand. Private bungalows are airy and cool, with ceiling fans, French doors, and flowers and greenery on the well-tended grounds. Microwaves, refrigerators. Cable TV. Pool. Boating, fishing. Laundry facilities. Business services. | 6772 Sara Sea Cir. | 941/349–4131 or 800/349–4131 | fax 941/349–8141 | www.captivabeachresort.com | 20 apartments | $170 (3–night minimum) | AE, D, MC, V.

Crescent Beach Villas. These three buildings of beachfront duplexes and triplexes rent only by the week—all have pull-out couches, terra-cotta floors, full kitchens, and upscale decor, plus screened-in porches and grill areas. Microwaves, refrigerators. In-room VCRs. Outdoor pool. Hot tub. Bicycles. Laundry facilities. | 1104 Crescent St. | 941/927–7322 or 941/376–0093 | fax 941/924–2806 | 6 villas | $110–$140 (7–night minimum) | AE, D, MC, V.

Crescent View Beach Club. This all-suites property has bright, sea-sand-and-sun-theme furnishings and fabrics. Guest rooms have high ceilings and either water views or golf-course views, with balconies or decks. Microwaves, refrigerators. Cable TV. Pool. Hot tub. Laundry facilities. | 6512 Midnight Pass Rd. | 941/349–2000 or 800/344–7171 | fax 941/349–9748 | www.crescentviewbeachclub.com | 26 suites | $205–$350 | AE, D, MC, V.

Palm Bay Club. This gulf-front resort offers an array of accommodations: an 11-story tower whose units have floor-to-ceiling windows, ocean-theme decor, and great sunset views from many units; club-side condos close to tennis and a short walk from the beach; and bay-side condos facing pool and marina. The grounds are well maintained and landscaped with palms, hyacinths, and orchids. Kitchenettes. Cable TV, in-room VCRs (and movies). 2 pools. Spa. Exercise equipment. Tennis. Beach, docks, fishing. Laundry facilities. | 5960 Midnight Pass Rd. | 941/349–1911 or 800/725–6229 | fax 941/349–1034 | www.palmbayclub.com | $240–$350 | 145 rooms | MC, V.

Sara Sea Inn at the Beach. This small property, built around a lush courtyard of fountains and koi ponds, has attractive but unfancy rooms with wicker, marine colors, and flower-and-palm motifs. In-room data ports, microwaves, refrigerators. Cable TV, in-room VCRs (and movies). Pool. Hot tub. Beach, water sports, boating, fishing. Laundry facilities. Business services. | 6760 Sara Sea Cir. | 941/349–3244 | fax 941/349–4999 | www.sarasea.com | 27 rooms | $169–$269 | AE, MC, V.

Siesta Breakers. Condos in this five-story building a stone's throw from the gulf can be rented only for a week or more. Units have screened-in lanais and water views; they also overlook a pool and palm-shaded grounds traversed by walking paths. Kitchenettes, microwaves, refrigerators. Cable TV, in-room VCRs (and movies). Pool. Tennis court. Laundry facilities. Business services. | 6480 Midnight Pass Rd. | 941/349–6505 or 800/853–0999 | fax 941/349–6552 | 42 rooms | $195–$220 (7–night minimum) | MC, V.

Tropical Shores Beach Resort. This Key West–style resort has a whimsical tiki-hut barbecue area and 2 acres of tropical gardens. Rooms have large windows looking out toward the beach. In-room data ports, microwaves, refrigerators. Cable TV. Pool. Laundry facilities. Business services. | 6717 Sara Sea Cir. | 941/349–3330 or 800/235–3493 | fax 941/346–0025 | www.tropicalshores.com | 30 apartments | $225 | AE, MC, V.

Turtle Beach Resort. This is a small, cozy waterfront property—on Siesta Key's less-touristy southern tip—consisting of eight private cottages themed differently (Victorian, Caribbean, etc.) and with hot tubs and beach chairs. Ophelia's on the Bay restaurant is next door, and Turtle's is across the street. Microwaves, refrigerators, in-room hot tubs. Cable TV, in-room VCRs. Pool. Laundry facilities. Pets allowed. | 9049 Midnight Pass Rd. | 941/349–4554 | 10 units | $155–$315 | AE, MC, V.

STARKE

MAP 3, I3

(Nearby towns also listed: Gainesville, Lake City, St. Augustine)

This predominantly Southern Baptist north Florida town of 5,000 is home to five prison compounds, including the Florida State Penitentiary. On a more inviting note, the town also claims to raise the "sweetest strawberries this side of heaven," which you can pick yourself at many roadside farms and pickin' patches. The town is also home to Camp Blanding, a major military training center during World War II, which along with the prisons and E. I. Dupont mining operations now forms the town's economic backbone. Fishing and hunting are popular local pastimes.

Information: **Starke-Bradford County Chamber of Commerce** | 202 S. Walnut St., Box 576, Starke, 32091 | 904/964–5278 | www.techcomm.net/starkenet/chamber.html.

Attractions

Camp Blanding Museum. Uniforms, weapons, photographs, and other World War II artifacts are on display at this museum on a military installation 8 mi east of Starke. Also check out the Sherman tank and C-47 bomber. | Hwy. 16, Building 3040 | 904/533–3196 | Free | Daily noon–4.

Mike Roess Gold Head Branch State Park. This 1,562-acre park 20 mi southeast of Starke comprises the rolling sandhills that make up the central ridge of Florida. It was developed by the Civilian Conservation Corps (CCC) during the 1930s, and the organization's exceptional craftsmanship is still in evidence in the park's roads, paths, and picnic shelters. The area is bisected by a deep ravine, where several springs form the Gold Head Branch River. Nearby marshes, lakes, and scrub provide a habitat for a wide variety of wildlife. You can swim, fish, and canoe in the Gold Head Branch or in a trio of small park lakes. Primitive camping and well-maintained hiking trails are also available. | 6239 Hwy. 21, Keystone Heights | 352/473–4701 | www.dep.state.fl.us | $3.25 per vehicle | Daily.

ON THE CALENDAR

APR.: *Bradford County Fair.* With auctions, booths from local businesses, rides, agricultural shows, and live entertainment. | 904/964–5278.

Dining

Cedar River Seafood. Seafood. This family-dining chain eatery serves fresh dishes such as striker's haul (fried or broiled shrimp) and seafarer's treasure (a combo platter of any two seafood items on the menu) at very reasonable prices. | 900 S. Walnut St. | 904/964–8282 | $7–$43 | AE, MC, V.

Lodging

Best Western Motor Inn. This simple, two-story motel has basic rooms but rather bleak grounds. Complimentary Continental breakfast. Refrigerators. Cable TV. Pets allowed. | 1290 N. Temple Ave. | 904/964–6744 | fax 904/964–3355 | 51 rooms | $53–$115 | AE, D, MC, V.

Starke Days Inn. This basic motel has a tropical courtyard, large airy rooms, and a Denny's restaurant and Winner's Pub. Pets allowed. | 1101 N. Temple Ave. | 904/964–7600 or 800/544–8313 | fax 904/964–5201 | www.daysinn.com | 100 rooms | $49–$99 | AE, DC, D, MC, V.

STUART

MAP 3, L7

(Nearby towns also listed: Jensen Beach, Port St. Lucie)

Stuart is on a little peninsula that juts out between the Atlantic Ocean and the St. Lucie River, which makes it a good base for bass-fishing and, on nearby Jensen Beach, for observing sea turtles nesting. The city also has a charming downtown historic district, with numerous shops and eateries. Sport-fishing charters and tourism are staples of the local economy.

Information: **Stuart/Martin County Chamber of Commerce** | 1650 S. Kanner Hwy., Stuart, 34994-7199 | 561/287–1088 | www.stuartmartinchamber.org.

Attractions

Cultural Courthouse Center. The Martin County Council for the Arts is housed in this courthouse built in 1937. The building is on the National Register of Historical Places and has Art Deco styling. The several galleries change their exhibits every six to eight weeks. | 80 E. Ocean Blvd. | 561/288–2542 | www.martinarts.org | Free | Mon.–Fri. 10–4.

Historic Downtown Stuart. Strict architectural and zoning standards guide civic renewal projects in the city's historic downtown, which has several antiques shops and restaurants, plus more than 50 specialty shops within a two-block area. Highlights include the renovated Lyric Theatre, which was built as a silent-film cinema in 1925 and now presents performing and community events. | Stuart Main Street Office, 151 S.W. Flagler Ave. | 561/286–2848 | Free | Mon.–Fri. 9–4.

Lyric Theater. This impressive theater sits in the midst of historic Stuart and presents shows ranging from children's plays to big names. The theater was started as a silent movie house in 1926, and Tuesday nights you can catch some cabaret action with food and drinks while local performers strut their stuff during an open mike show. | 59 S.W. Flagler Ave. | 561/220–1942 | www.lyrictheatre.com | Box office open Mon.–Sat. 10–4.

Stuart Heritage Museum. In the former general store (also the feed store) of Martin County, the Heritage Society maintains tradition with displays of artifacts from early residents. You can take their tours of the surrounding historical buildings as well as of their collection. A large diorama of downtown Stuart Beach from the early 1900s is notable. | 101 S.W. Flagler Ave. | 561/220–4600 | Donations requested | Mon.–Sat. 10–3.

Stuart Main Street Office. Stop in here as you tool around town to learn about all the upcoming events and anything you want to know about the city. The most popular event is Dancing in the Streets held in September (reportedly to celebrate the kids going back to school!), when 16,000 people get funky on the main streets of Stuart Beach. | 201 S.W. Flagler Ave. | 561/286–2848 | Mon.–Fri. 9–4.

ON THE CALENDAR

FEB., MAR.: *Martin County Fair.* Livestock shows, rides, food, and live music. | 561/287–1088.

Dining

The Ashley. Continental. This swank restaurant is housed in a vintage bank building downtown—the bank was robbed three times by the Ashley Gang in the early 1900s, hence its present name. The plant-filled dining room is a lovely space to sample traditional Continental fare, with an emphasis on fresh seafood: try scallops in butter sauce with a salad of tossed greens. | 61 S.W. Oceola St. | 561/221–9476 | Reservations not accepted | Closed Mon. in Apr. and Dec. | $9–$25 | AE, MC, V.

The Emporium. American. This is a charming little coffeehouse-cum-bistro adjacent to the sprawling Indian River Plantation Marriott Beach Resort. There's an old-fashioned soda fountain inside, and a grill that turns out excellent breakfasts and deli sandwiches. | 555 N.E. Ocean Blvd. | 561/225–3700 | Breakfast also available | $6–12 | AE, DC, MC, V.

The Jolly Sailor Pub. American. Like the Ashley, this restaurant occupies a former bank building downtown. "The Pub," however, is a little more relaxed and casual, with nautical murals, models of big ships, and a brass-railed bar. Of course, being a pub, the Jolly Sailor specializes in salty-dog dishes such as fish-and-chips and cottage pie, plus juicy burgers and crisp salads, and Guinness and Double Diamond beers on tap. | 1 S.W. Oceola St. | 561/221–1111 | $10–$18 | AE, MC, V.

Scalawags. American. Despite the name, this restaurant is quite gentrified, with planta-tion-tropical charm created with coach lanterns, wicker furnishings, and lazy overhead pad-dle-fans. The buffet-style dining area offers a Wednesday night, all-you-can-eat Seafood Extravaganza with a bounty of jumbo shrimp, Alaskan crab legs, clams on the half shell, and a featured fresh catch. This window-filled dining room on the second floor of the Indian River Marriott Beach Resort overlooks the Indian River. | 555 N.E. Ocean Blvd. | 561/225–6818 | $16–$26 | AE, D, DC, MC, V.

Lodging

Harborfront Bed and Breakfast. This intimate inn sits on a quiet lot that slopes down to the St. Lucie River. The Harborfront is decorated both with antiques and sturdy wicker pieces, some with a Victorian sensibility and others decked in tweedy prints and plaids. A few rooms have private decks, and a yard has a hammock. The inn also owns a 33-ft sailboat avail-able for full- or half-day sails. Cable TV. Hot tub. Dock, boating, fishing. No pets. No kids under 12. | 310 Atlanta Ave. | 561/288–7289 | fax 561/221–0474 | www.harborfrontinn.com | 6 rooms, 2 suites, 1 cottage, 2 apartments | $75–$175 | MC, V.

Holiday Inn–Downtown. This is one of the few hotels in the area away from the beach. Rooms are attractive despite the dull location; they feature lush plants and tropically themed decor. Beaches and shopping are 1 mi away. Restaurant, bar. In-room data ports, microwaves, refrigerators. Cable TV. Pool. Gym. Laundry facilities. Business services. | 1209 S. Federal Hwy. | 561/287–6200 | fax 561/287–6200 | www.holiday-inn.com | 119 rooms | $82–$120 | AE, D, MC, V.

SUGARLOAF KEY

MAP 3, C3

(Nearby towns also listed: Big Pine Key, Key West, Little Torch Key, Summerland Key)

This landfall in the lower keys was named for the sugarloaf pineapples that were once grown here. One landmark is the unusual Sugarloaf Bat Tower, built by a resort owner in 1929 to attract bug-eating bats to combat the island's mosquitos. The bats never came, the mosquitoes never went away, and the 45-ft-tall pyramid stands empty. But it's worth seeing—mostly because you won't find anything like it anywhere else.

Information: **Florida Keys Visitor Center/Key Largo Chamber of Commerce** | 106000 Overseas Hwy., Key Largo, 33037 | 305/451–1414 or 800/822–1088 | info@floridakeys.org | www.floridakeys.org.

Dining

Mangrove Mama's Restaurant. Caribbean. Exotic and enticing aromas drift through the surrounding banana groves that lead to this laid-back dining spot. There's always a fresh catch of the day prepared several different ways, as well as the popular baked crab-stuffed shrimp and coconut-fried shrimp with a teriyaki-pineapple dipping sauce. Vegetarian dishes are also offered. The key lime pie is here is locally famous. | MM 20, Overseas Hwy. | 305/745–3030 | fax 305/745–3076 | Closed much of Sept. | $15–$20 | AE, MC, V.

Sugarloaf Lodge Restaurant. Seafood. Tall open-glass windows face the water from this large, casual family-dining restaurant. Try the key lime–pepper mahimahi, or the coconut fried shrimp with a pineapple-mango sauce. | MM 17, Overseas Hwy. | 305/745–3211 | $12–$24 | AE, D, DC, MC, V.

Lodging

Sugarloaf Lodge. All rooms at this resort face the sparkling blue-green waters off the keys. Rooms in the older building have a fishing-lodge feel with dark-wood paneling and bright bedspreads. The rooms in the new building have light walls and light-wood furniture. Restaurant, bar (with entertainment), room service. Some kitchenettes, some refrigerators, cable TV. Pool. 2 tennis courts, miniature golf. Dock, water sports, boating, fishing, bicycles. Laundry facilities. Pets allowed (fee). | MM 17, Overseas Hwy. | 305/745–3211 or 800/553–6097 | www.sugarloaflodge.com | 55 rooms | $130 | AE, D, DC, MC, V.

Sugarloaf Key KOA Resort. Camp at the southernmost KOA in the US, 20 mi from Key West. You can hang out on the beach, boat, swim, and all the rest. New RV efficiency rentals are available with kitchenettes and air-conditioning. Great snorkeling, diving, and fishing are available nearby. Some sites are beachfront. Bar. Pool. Outdoor hot tub. Miniature golf. Volleyball. Beach, boating, fishing, bicycles. Playground. Laundry facilities. Pets allowed. | MM 20, cross Bow channel bridge, immediately on left | 305/745–3549 or 800/KOA–7731 | fax 305/745–9889 | sugarloaf@koa.net | www.koa.com | 200 sites plus tent area | $43–$83 | AE, D, MC, V.

SUMMERLAND KEY

MAP 3, C6

(Nearby towns also listed: Big Pine Key, Key West, Little Torch Key, Sugarloaf Key)

Summerland Key is one of the many small but luxe islets on the way to Key West. There are no guest accommodations, but you can still find plenty of opportunities to enjoy yourself. Try "gunk-holing"—local for boating or kayaking around the Keys' inland waterways and mangrove wetlands to observe native water birds, fish, and marine mammals. For an even closer look at local wildlife, try scuba diving or snorkeling among the offshore coral reefs.

Information: Florida Keys Visitor Center/Key Largo Chamber of Commerce | 106000 Overseas Hwy., Key Largo, 33037 | 305/451–1414 or 800/822–1088 | info@floridakeys.org | www.floridakeys.org.

Dining
Monte's Restaurant. Seafood. At this seafood restaurant, try the super combo, which includes the catch of the day, shrimp, oyster, scallops, and more. Also on the menu in season is stone crab served hot or cold. If you arrive prior to stone crab season, try the broiled lobster tail. | 924 Flagship Dr., MM 25 | 305/745–3731 | $12–$17 | No credit cards.

SUN CITY CENTER

MAP 3, I6

(Nearby towns also listed: Bradenton, St. Petersburg, Sarasota, Tampa)

Sun City Center, between Tampa and Sarasota, was developed as a retirement community in the 1960s, which it remains. Although it has some of the amenities of larger cities—public pools, tennis courts, and a community center—it has a relaxed pace and feels smaller. The population consists mostly of senior citizens who have come here to escape from cold winters up north.

Information: Sun City Center Chamber of Commerce | 1651 Sun City Center Pl, Sun City Center, 33573-5303 | 813/634–5111.

Lodging
Comfort Inn. This standard chain property is 6 mi southwest of Tampa Bay Beach, ½ mi from tennis courts, and has an outdoor pool and hot tub. Complimentary Continental breakfast. Microwaves, refrigerators. Cable TV. Pool. Hot tub. Laundry facilities. Business services.

| 718 Cypress Village Blvd. | 813/633–3318 | fax 813/633–2747 | www.comfortinn.com | 74 rooms | $70–$80 | AE, D, DC, MC, V.

Sun City Center Inn. Tropical plants and a putting green might drive you to dance to the oldies with some older golf-lovers in the bar. This motel is 9 mi from the boating activities on the bay and about 25 mi to the Gulf beach. Rooms have two double beds, and some open directly onto the pool patio. Restaurant, bar (with entertainment). Cable TV. Pool. Putting green, tennis. Business services. Pets allowed. | 1335 Rickenbacker Dr. | 813/634–3331 or 800/237–8200 | fax 813/634–2053 | 100 rooms | $49–$79 | AE, MC, V.

TALLAHASSEE

MAP 3, F2

(Nearby towns also listed: Chattahoochee, Live Oak, Perry)

When Florida was a British-ruled territory, from 1763 through 1783, it had two administrative capitals, Pensacola and St. Augustine. This arrangement continued even after Florida became a United States territory in 1821, but the dangers and time associated with travel between the two cities made the system unworkable in the long run. In 1824 legislators settled on a new spot—Tallahassee—almost midway between the two former capitals. According to legend, envoys rode out from both Pensacola and St. Augustine, and they met in Tallahassee. At the time, the new townsite was just a hill overlooking a flower-filled meadow. Soon, it became both a government and mercantile center for the surrounding cotton lands.

Unlike many more popular Florida destinations, Tallahassee isn't a sun-and-surf town. Instead, it continues to reflect its ties to the Old South. Glorious gardens are filled with azaleas and magnolias. Many roads are lined with antebellum houses shaded by majestic, Spanish moss–draped trees. It's a tranquil atmosphere, where vestiges of the city's colorful past can be found around almost every corner. Like many state capitals, it's hardly the most exciting vacation destination, yet one shouldn't so quickly resist its many charms.

The city's historical roots run deep, and you'll find that its antebellum architecture and downtown are particularly well preserved. Perhaps this is because it was the only Confederate state capital not taken by Union troops during the Civil War. Or perhaps it's because the town's economy slowed after the war, and its population increased little more than 1,000 people in the next hundred years. Today Tallahassee is undergoing a boom and is home to about 130,000 people.

Government is the major business here, but two local colleges, Florida A&M University and Florida State University, keep things lively. Tallahassee is in the middle of a fertile farming area and also has an industrial base that includes lumber and wood products, processed foods, printed materials, and gunpowder. The city is also home to the National High Magnetic Field Laboratory, a state-of-the-art physics research institution.

Visitors are charmed by the city's tree-lined streets and its five roads canopied by live oaks. Each of these roads is lined with country stores and antebellum plantation houses. They are among the Top 10 scenic byways in the U.S. Residents prefer to think of their hometown as "Florida with a Southern accent."

Information: Tallahassee Area Convention and Visitors Bureau | 200 W. College Ave., Box 1369, Tallahassee, 32302 | 850/413–9200 or 800/628–2866 | www.co.leon.fl.us/visitors/index.htm.

TRANSPORTATION
Airports: Tallahassee Regional Airport (3300 Capitol Circle SW | 850/891–7800 or 800/354–9822) is serviced by national and regional airlines.

Airport Transportation: Many hotels in town offer free airport shuttle service. **Yellow Cab** (850/580–8080) operates 24 hours a day, accepts Visa and MasterCard, and charges about $12–$15 to or from downtown.

Bus Lines: There is daily service by **Greyhound** (112 W. Tennessee St. | 850/222–4249 or 800/231–2222) to and from points nationwide.

Rail Lines: Amtrak's transcontinental *Sunset Limited* connects Tallahassee with Los Angeles, New Orleans, Jacksonville, Orlando, and points beyond from the railway depot (918½ Railroad Ave. | 850/224–2779 or 800/872–7245).

Public Transportation: The **Taltran** city bus (850/891–5200) has 31 routes in and around the city.

The free **Old Town Trolley** (850/891–5200 or 850/413–9200), with hand-crafted slat seats and brass handrails, runs along a downtown commuter route weekdays from 7 AM to 6 PM.

DRIVING AND PARKING

Interstate 10 cuts through Tallahassee from west to east, with the downtown area to the south of the interstate. Lake Jackson is north of town. Traffic is rarely the problem that it is in a larger city, but you should still avoid rush hours, 7–9 AM and 5–6:30 PM. Parking is also rarely a problem. If you have difficulty finding metered parking, there are lots that charge reasonable rates.

Attractions

ART AND ARCHITECTURE

Brokaw-McDougall House. This house combines Greek Revival and Italianate architectural styles. You can climb up to the cupola to see the neighborhood. In the back yard is an old smoke house where they used to smoke meats, and on the rest of the property are several stunning 150-yr-old oak trees. | 329 N. Meridian | 850/891–3900 | Free | Mon.–Fri. 9–3.

Governor's Mansion. The residence of Florida's chief executive is a Georgian-style Southern mansion styled after President Andrew Jackson's Hermitage. A one-hour tour highlights the home's collection of French Impressionist paintings, antique furnishings, and gifts from foreign dignitaries. | 700 N. Adams St. | 850/488–4661 | Free | Mar.–May, daily 10–noon.

New Capitol. Tallahassee is busy during the legislative session, and March to May is the best time to visit the Capitol. You can watch legislators in the Senate and House chambers in action, visit the art gallery and tiny coquina shell–lined chapel, and get a view of Tallahassee's spring blossoms from the Capitol's glass-walled 22nd floor. There's a 1-hr free tour. | S. Duval St. | 850/488–6167 | Free | Visitor center weekdays 8–5, weekends 9–3.

Old Capitol. The current building, constructed in 1902, is splendidly restored, with red-and-white striped awnings and combination gas-electric lights. Inside, the historically accurate exhibits of the House and Senate chambers, the governor's suite, Supreme Court, and rotunda offer an interesting peek into Florida's past. | 400 S. Monroe St. | 850/487–1902 | Free | Weekdays 9–4:30, Sat. 10–4:30, Sun. noon–4:30.

CULTURE, EDUCATION, AND HISTORY

Florida Agricultural and Mechanical University. One of the three oldest schools in the Florida State University system, this land grant university was founded in 1887. Florida A&M's 419 rolling acres are home to the Lee Hall Auditorium, a performing arts center, and the Black Archives Research Center and Museum, among other structures. | Martin Luther King Blvd. and Wahnish Way | 850/599–3000 or 850/599–3020 | Free | Weekdays.

Black Archives Research Center and Museum. Oral history tapes, manuscripts, art works, photographs, and artifacts document the history and culture of Africans and African-Americans at this archive and museum. The complex is in the university's 1907 Carnegie Library. | Gamble St. and Martin Luther King Blvd. | 850/599–3020 | Free | Weekdays 9–4.

Florida State University. The university's School of Music regularly hosts concerts and recitals, performances by the Tallahassee Symphony Orchestra, and a number of productions by its top-rated theater program. | 132 N. Copeland St. | 850/644–4774 | Free | Daily.

Lake Jackson Mounds State Archaeological Site. This ceremonial Indian site dates back to AD 1000. You can see six earth mounds and walk through the woods on a nature trail to see remnants of an old grist mill, used to grind corn and grains. The 19th-century plantation of Colonel Robert Butler, who served under General Andrew Jackson during the siege of New Orleans, was also here, and a few ruins remain. You can request a guided tour from the park service two weeks in advance. | 3600 Indian Mounds Rd. | 850/562–0042, for tours call 850/922–6007 | www.dep.state.fl.us/parks | $2 per car, $1 per person on foot or bicycle | Daily 8–sunset.

Natural Bridge State Historic Site. The site commemorates the Battle of Natural Bridge, which took place here on March 6, 1865. The battle in which Confederates prevented Union troops from capturing Tallahassee is reenacted every year in March. During the weekend reenactment you can view Confederate and Union encampments. | Natural Bridge Rd., Woodville | 850/922–6007 | Free | Daily 8–sunset.

San Marcos de Apalache State Historic Site. The Spanish governor of Florida began constructing a fort here in 1678, at the junction of the Wakulla and St. Marks rivers. In 1821 the fort was returned to the U.S. government; 35 years later a federal marine hospital was built on the site of stones salvaged from the old Spanish fort. Today exhibits and artifacts covering the area's history are on display in a visitor center built on the foundation of the old marine hospital. The site is 24 mi south of Tallahassee via Route 363. | Old Fort Rd., St. Marks | 850/925–6216 | Free; museum $1 | Thurs.–Mon. 9–5.

© Corbis

LIVE-OAK CANOPY ROADS

Frank Lloyd Wright would have been proud of mother nature. Tallahassee's celebrated "canopy roads," breathtaking tunnels of towering, verdant oak trees overhung with Spanish moss, incorporate nature's beauty into modern living with an effect that is at once ethereal and awe-inspiring.

Five of Tallahassee's live-oak passageways are among the Top Ten Scenic Byways in America. Meandering out through the countryside reverberating with echoes of plantation life, a drive on the canopy roads should be a part of any visit to the Tallahassee area. Here's a description of some of the finest.

Old St. Augustine Road. Dating back to the 1600s, the oldest of the canopy roads travels southeast from Tallahassee and once connected the Franciscan missions built in this area with St. Augustine on the Atlantic Coast. The road became part of Florida's first American roadway, the Pensacola–St. Augustine Highway, which was constructed in part by the slaves of a local planter. The nicest stretches of the drive are between Capitol Circle and Williams Road.

Meridian Road (Highway 155). This road starts in Tallahassee—at the Prime Meridian Marker downtown (the starting point for all land surveys in the state)—and heads north, past lakes and the old farms and across the Georgia border.

Centerville Road (Highway 151) and Miccosukee Road (Route 146). These roads travel roughly parallel one another, both running northeast from town. Sights along the way include the Goodwood Plantation and Bradley's Country Store, where homemade sausage has 'em coming in from miles around. Miccosukee Road was once a footpath that lead to an Indian village, and it later served cotton plantations.

Old Bainbridge Road (Highway 361). Once an Indian trail, this road runs northwest toward Lake Jackson and ancient Indian mounds.

MUSEUMS

LeMoyne Art Foundation. Once a field hospital during the Civil War, the historic Meginnis–Monroe House is now the local gallery, featuring rotating shows that range from local student artwork to professional local and national artists. The permanent collection is diverse and includes a tranquil sculpture garden. Educational art programs are held weekly as well. | 125 Gadsden St. | 850/222–8800 | www.lemoyne.org | $2 | Tues.–Sat. 10–5, Sun. 1–5, Closed Nov. 1–24.

Museum of Florida History. This museum, the repository for the state's some 44,000 historical artifacts, documents the lives of Floridians. | 500 S. Bronough St. | 850/488–1484 | fax 850/921–2503 | www.dos.state.fl.us/museum/ | Free | Weekdays 9–4:30, Sat. 10–4:30, Sun. noon–4:30.

Tallahassee Museum of History and Natural Science. Exhibits about history, nature, and wildlife tell the story of the Big Bend area of Florida. Highlights include an 1880s farm complex and the Natural Habitat Zoo, which has Florida panthers, black bears, red wolves, otters, and other animals. There are also hands-on activities such as soap-making and blacksmithing. | 3945 Museum Dr., off Rankin Rd. | 850/576–1636 | fax 850/574–8243 | www.tallahasseemuseum.org | $6 | Mon.–Sat. 9–5, Sun. 12:30–5.

PARKS, NATURAL SITES, AND OUTDOOR RECREATION

Apalachicola National Forest. The state's largest forest, with 564,000 acres, is full of rivers, creeks, lakes, sink holes, and savannahs—excellent habitats for rare and endangered plants and animals. The forest, which has several interpretive hiking trails, extends west from 30 mi southwest of Tallahassee to the Apalachicola River. U.S. 319 at Sopchoppy is a main entrance to the forest. To get to the closest forest service office, take Highway 20 south to Bristol, about a 45-min drive. | Forest office: Hwy. 20, Bristol | 850/643–2282 | www.co.leon.fl.us/forest.htm | Free | Daily.

Edward Ball Wakulla Springs State Park. One of the world's largest and deepest sweetwater springs is a highlight of this 2,860-acre park, which is 15 mi south of Tallahassee on Route 61. Famed explorer Ponce de León thought these springs were his long sought-after "fountain of youth" when he discovered them in 1513. The park retains the wild and jungle-like beauty it had in the 1930s, when *Tarzan* movies were filmed here. You can have a picnic and hike on 6 mi of trails. There are daily boat tours. | 250 Wakulla Park Dr. | 850/922–3632 | $3.25 per vehicle | Daily.

Maclay State Gardens. New York financier Alfred B. Maclay created a masterpiece of garden design on the rolling hills overlooking Lake Hall, some 5½ mi north of Tallahassee via U.S. 319. Maclay began developing the property in 1923 as his family's southern retreat. In spring the grounds are abloom with azaleas, dogwood, and other flowers. You can have a picnic, or, in Lake Hall, go swimming, boating, or fishing for largemouth bass, bream, and bluegill. | 3540 Thomasville Rd. | 850/487–4556 | $3.25 per vehicle | Park daily 8 AM–sunset; gardens daily 9–5.

St. Marks National Wildlife Refuge. The salt marshes, hardwood swamps, pine flatwoods, and pine and oak uplands bordering Apalachee Bay make up this 64,934-acre refuge, which is 25 mi south of Tallahassee, via Route 363. Diked impoundments attract wintering waterfowl. There are 75 mi of trails for hiking, and you can bicycle on the refuge roads. Fort San Marcos de Apalachee was built here in 1639, and stones salvaged from the fort were used in the lighthouse, which is still in operation. On the beach and pilings nearby look for shorebirds, gulls, and terns. The visitor center has a small retail shop. | 1255 Lighthouse Rd., St. Marks | 850/925–6121 | fax 850/925–6930 | www.dep.state.fl.us | $4 per vehicle | Daily dawn to dusk; visitor center weekdays 8–4:15, weekends 10–5.

RELIGION AND SPIRITUALITY

First Presbyterian Church. This Greek Revival church was completed in 1838, and stands at the heart of Tallahassee's Park Avenue Historic District. It's Florida's oldest public building still used for its original purpose. The tall white columns, steeple, and Gothic windows reflect building styles that prevailed all over Florida at the beginning of the 19th century. | 110 N. Adams St. | 850/222–4504 | Free | Mon.–Thurs. 8:30–5, Fri. 8:30–1, Sun. 9–10:45.

WALKING TOUR
Walking Tour of Tallahassee (2 to 3 hours)
Tallahassee has made it easy to be a dutiful tourist; most of the historical sites in town, as well as the modern new buildings of downtown, are compacted into a few blocks. You can also take a free trolley to most of these sites.

A good place to start is at the **Old Capitol** (South Monroe Street at Apalachee Pkwy.), which you can tour either on your own or with a guide. Here you will find the local visitor information office with free maps. It's easy to find the **New Capitol** building, whose 22 stories loom above it. On the top floor of the New Capitol building there is an observation deck where you can see the flat countryside all the way to Georgia; you can also visit an art gallery displaying local artists' work. Across the street from the Old Capitol is the restored Union Bank Building. Two blocks to the west, on South Bronough Street, you will encounter the **Museum of Florida History,** where you'll learn about the past 12,000 years of local history.

A good way to see the rest of downtown Tallahassee is by following the **Downtown Tallahassee Historic Trail,** which winds its way from the Capitol complex through several of the city's historic districts. The trail, which runs 8 miles, takes you through the **Park Avenue** and **Calhoun Street** historic districts to see preserved Greek Revival, Italianate, and Prairie-style homes. The **Brokaw–McDougall House** and the Meginnis–Monroe House (now an art gallery) are open for the public to get a feel for Old Tallahassee. Pick up a self-guiding tour map at the New Capitol visitor center.

ON THE CALENDAR
MAR.: *Natural Bridge Battle Reenactment.* The famous Civil War battle that took place at what is now Natural Bridge State Historic Site is reenacted each year on a weekend near the anniversary date, with complete Confederate and Union encampments. | Natural Bridge Rd., Woodville | 850/922–6007.
MAR.: *Springtime Tallahassee.* Tallahassee's premiere event celebrates the blossoming of the city with parades, arts and crafts, entertainment, and contests. | 850/224–5012.
APR.: *Flying High Circus.* Collegians perform under Florida State University's big top. | 850/644–4874.
MAY: *Southern Shakespeare Festival.* A medieval fair, with entertainment and costumed craftspeople, culminates in performances of works by the Bard. | 850/413–9200.
JULY: *Summer Swamp Stomp.* Sounds of bluegrass, folk, and acoustical music blend with folk tales and cloggers alongside the Southern Cypress Swamp outdoor exhibit at the Tallahassee Museum of History and Natural Science. | 850/575–8684.
OCT.: *North Florida Fair.* Nearly 225,000 people show up at the Fairgrounds during the 11-day run of North Florida's largest event. | 850/878–3247.
DEC.: *December on the Farm.* Weaving, candlemaking, cane-grinding, and blacksmithing demonstrations highlight activities at the 1880s farm area at the Tallahassee Museum of History and Natural Science. | 850/575–8684.

Dining

INEXPENSIVE
Banjo's Smokehouse. Steak. Savory meat slow-cooked and covered with thick barbecue sauce is the specialty here. The menu includes chicken, pork, and beef selections. The baby back ribs and the USDA prime Black Angus steaks are popular. The dining area is cavernous and woody and accented with down-home knickknacks. | 2335 Apalachee Pkwy. | 850/877–8111 | Reservations not accepted | Sun.–Thurs. 11–9, Fri.–Sat. 11–10. Closed Labor Day | $6–$17 | AE, D, DC, MC, V.

Barnacle Bill's. Seafood. This casual restaurant has an Ark-size menu with fresh seafood of all descriptions. Entrées come with fresh veggies on the side. This is a popular local hangout and can get a little loud at peak times. Children eat free on Sundays. | 1830 N. Monroe St. | 850/385–8734 | Reservations not accepted | $8–$17 | AE, DC, MC, V.

Monroe St. Grille. American. This restaurant in a Ramada Inn is casual yet polished. The Grille's claim to fame is its 100-item salad bar, which includes everything from garbanzo beans to chocolate mousse. The menu includes prime rib, steaks, and seafood selections. | 2900 N. Monroe St. | 850/386–1027 | Reservations not accepted | Breakfast also available | $8–$16 | AE, D, DC, MC, V.

Nicholson's Farmhouse. American. This is a friendly, down-home kind of place. The kitchen and grill are both outside, and you can pick your favorite cut of meat and have it grilled or roasted to order. | From U.S. 27, follow Rte. 12 toward Quincy and look for signs | 850/539–5931 | Closed Sun.–Mon. No lunch. BYOB | $6–$12 | AE, D, MC, V.

Nino. Italian. You can dine outdoors on the big front deck at this restaurant surrounded by trees. The *scampi all'aglio* is a handful of jumbo shrimp lightly dredged in flour then sautéed in olive oil with lemon, white wine, and garlic. | 6497 Apalachee Pkwy. | 850/878–8141 | Closed Sun.–Mon. No lunch | $8–$18 | AE, D, DC, MC, V.

On the Border. Mexican. Saddles and bull's heads give this place a cowboy feel. You can dine indoors or out on the covered patio, or sip your margaritas at the bar (draft beer and margaritas are always 2 for 1). The house specialty is the "Ultimate Fajitas," which features steak, chicken, ribs, shrimp, and roasted red potatoes on a sizzling platter. The pico shrimp and chicken dish is topped with a spicy pico de gallo sauce and melted jack cheese. | 1650 N. Monroe St. | 850/521–9887 | $8–$12 | AE, D, MC, V.

MODERATE

Andrew's Capital Bar & Grill. American. This restaurant across from city hall has a touch of elegance. Upstairs choose from the main menu, which includes New York strip steak, or downstairs at Andrew's Second Act, dine on a five-course meal. | 228 S. Adams St. | 850/222–3444 | $10–$22 | AE, DC, MC, V.

★ **Andrew's 2nd Act.** American. The food is excellent at this elegant restaurant that plays host to many suited local politicos. Andrew's is known for its tournedos St. Laurent and peppered New York strip steak. The menu also includes a fresh catch of the day. | 228 S. Adams St. | 850/222–3444 | Reservations recommended | No lunch | $14–$19 | AE, DC, MC, V.

Bahn Thai. Thai. This restaurant has a simple dining area with pale gold walls and brick archways between seating areas, creating a warm mood. The streetside buffet includes tasty pan-Asian dishes including coconut-milk soup and minced avocado salad. The menu includes such favorites as beef with snow peas and shrimp with golden rice. Bahn Thai also stocks a number of Asian beers and wines. | 1319 Monroe St. | 850/224–4765 | Closed Sun. No lunch Sat. | $7–$16 | AE, DC, MC, V.

Kool Beanz Café. Eclectic. In the heart of downtown Tallahasee is this trendy spot where the menu changes nightly. You can expect a seafood, meat, pasta, and vegetarian dish. Desserts featuring seasonal fresh fruit or other delicacies. The space is small, centered on the open kitchen and bar area, and the walls are hung with bright, modern art. | 921 Thomasville Rd. | 850/224–2466 | fax 850/224–1233 | Closed Sun., no lunch Sat. | $12–$15 | AE, D, MC, V.

Longhorn Steaks. Steak. This casual steak house just across the street from the Tallahasee Mall is a good place to rest your feet at the shotgun-style bar or a large wooden table. "Cowboy" style fare means a lot of beef, all of which is cut fresh in house. If you like something lighter, try the grilled salmon marinated in a Bourbon sauce. | 2400 N. Monroe St. | 850/385–4028 | fax 850/383–0466 | $15–$20 | AE, D, DC, MC, V.

Samrat. Indian. Occupying a former fast-food joint, Samrat is nothing fancy. But chefs turn out good tandoori chicken (bright-crimson chicken bits dusted with turmeric and other savory spices). For a slightly less throat-grabbing dish, the *paneer masala* consists of home-made cottage cheese tossed in butter and cultured yogurt and served with creamy red sauce and rice. | 2529 Apalachee Pkwy. | 850/942–1993 | Closed weekdays 2:30–5 | $9–$20 | AE, DC, MC, V.

EXPENSIVE

Albert's Provence. French. Garden and other outdoor seating, an extensive wine list, and an eclectic menu distinguish this place. The menu features mainly fresh local seafood in deluxe dishes such as the red snapper Marseillaise (stuffed with crabmeat, baked with chablis, sour cream, and saffron, and topped with lobster sauce). On the meaty side is the roasted leg and rack of lamb Provençale, served with garlic mashed potatoes, fresh sautéed vegetables, and flageolet beans. | 1415 Timberlane Rd. in Market Square | 850/894–9003 | Closed Sun., no lunch Sat. | $15–$29 | AE, D, MC, V.

Chez Pierre. French. This little restaurant serves up Southern hospitality while paying homage to the great French bistros of Paris and New Orleans with its intimate seating and complex dishes. The *saumon aux huitres* is a Florida citrus–roasted salmon fillet topped with fried oysters and lime-ginger sauce. The *blanc de poulet fumé* is a smoked breast of chicken with spinach, apples, and tomatoes tossed in a pesto cream sauce and served over tender penne pasta. | 1215 Thomasville Rd. | 850/222–0936 | Closed Sun. | $10–$20 | AE, DC, MC, V.

The Melting Pot. Eclectic. The booths have high backs for privacy, and the candlelight makes for romantic fondue dipping. You cook most dishes over a flame and dip them in your chosen sauce. The "French Quarter" meal comes with andouille sausage, shrimp, beef tenderloin, and chicken and a variety of sauces such as the Gorgonzola-port sauce or the lemon-pepper dip. For dessert you can get a platter of fruit and cakes to be dipped in chocolaty amaretto or Bailey's Irish Cream sauce. | 2727 N. Monroe St. | 850/386–7440 | fax 850/386–8410 | No lunch | $12–$22 | AE, D, MC, V.

Mori Japanese Steakhouse. Japanese. Bamboo plants and watercolors on the wooden walls evoke Japan. The sushi ranges from fresh seafood to vegetables or you can try the hibachi menu, for which a chef comes to your table and prepares your meal. | 2810 Charer Rd. | 850/386–8449 | No lunch | $12–$25 | AE, MC, V.

Silver Slipper. Steak. A number of U.S. presidents, including John F. Kennedy and George Bush, have enjoyed this hallowed establishment. Founded in 1938, the Slipper caters to a largely political clientele. A crystal chandelier lights the lobby. Curtained booths for two are off the main dining area. The 2-inch-thick filet mignon practically melts under its crispy charred crust. There is a large wine list. Desserts include white chocolate mousse cake. | 531 Scotty's La. | 850/386–9366 | Closed Sun. No lunch | $20–$40 | AE, D, DC, MC, V.

The Tree Steak House. Steak. There are candles and white linens on the tables, an extensive wine list, and a platter of raw beef is brought to your table so that you may select your cut of meat. You can then watch the meat being prepared in the open kitchen. House specials are the rib-eye and prime rib, although you can also get fresh seafood. The white chocolate bread pudding is not to be missed | 3540 Mahan Dr. | 850/942–7117 | fax 850/942–5658 | Dinner only | $12–$26 | AE, DC, MC, V.

Lodging

INEXPENSIVE

Howard Johnson Express Inn. This chain property is 3 mi north of the Capitol and ½ mi south of the Tallahassee Mall. Some of the rooms face the pool. Complimentary Continental breakfast. Business services. | 2726 N. Monroe St. | 850/386–5000 or 800/406–1411 | fax 850/386–5000 | www.hojo.com | 51 rooms | $50 | AE, DC, D, MC, V.

Microtel Inn & Suites. This motel 20 min from downtown caters mostly to a business crowd. Complimentary Continental breakfast. Exercise room. | 3216 N. Monroe St. | 850/562–3800 or 888/771–7171 | fax 850/562–8611 | www.microtelinn.com | 61 rooms, 20 suites | $45–$65; higher on football weekends Sept.–Nov. | AE, D, DC, MC, V.

Shoney's Inn. This two-story motel is built around a courtyard with a landscaped pool. Rooms are done in Spanish-mission style. Complimentary Continental breakfast. Refrigerators. Cable TV. Pool. Laundry facilities. Pets allowed. Free parking. | 2801 N. Monroe St. | 850/386–8286 | fax 850/422–1074 | www.shoneysinn.com | 112 rooms | $85–$125 | AE, D, MC, V.

Tallahassee Best Inn. This motel 10 min from downtown is a reasonable option for both business travelers and tourists. The rooms are basic. Complimentary Continental breakfast. Pool. Cable TV. | 3090 N. Monroe St. | 850/562–2378 or 800/BESTINN | fax 850/562–2378 | www.bestinn.com | 75 rooms | $47–$79 | AE, D, DC, MC, V.

MODERATE

Cabot Lodge-North. This motel on six quiet acres feels more like a B&B or a resort lodge than a motel. The huge, wraparound porch overlooks shaded grounds and walking paths. Rooms have homey charm with antique reproduction furnishings and wooden beds. Complimentary Continental breakfast. In-room data ports. Cable TV. Pool. Laundry facilities. Business services, free parking. | 2735 N. Monroe St. | 850/386–8880 or 800/223–1964 (reservations) | fax 850/386–4254 | www.cabotlodge.com | 160 rooms | $72–$78 | AE, D, MC, V.

Comfort Inn. Rooms at this three-story, green-and-white motel have deep ochre and sage hues. Sleeping areas are separated from sitting areas by high arched doorways. The motel is 1 mi from the Capitol and within 5 mi of most museums and galleries. In-room data ports, microwaves, refrigerators. Pool. Laundry facilities. Free parking. | 2727 Graves Rd. | 850/562–7200 | fax 850/562–6335 | www.comfortinn.com | 100 rooms | $51–$76 | AE, D, MC, V.

Comfort Suites. This three-story all-suites hotel is ½ mi from the Capitol and less than 2 mi from Florida State University and Florida A&M University. Rooms are done in earth tones; some have whirlpool tubs. Complimentary Continental breakfast. In-room data ports, in-room safes, refrigerators, microwaves. Cable TV. Exercise equipment. Business services. | 1026 Apalachee Pkwy. | 850/224–3200 or 888/224–1254 | fax 850/224–2206 | www.comfortinn.com | 64 suites | $90 | AE, D, DC, MC, V.

Hilton Garden Inn Tallahassee. Wrapped around a palm-shaded pool area, this four-story lodging has a comfortable lounge with a view of swimmers and sunbathers outside. Rooms are done in a breezy, tropical style with lots of pale colors and airbrushed wall art. Restaurant, bar. In-room data ports, microwaves, refrigerators. Cable TV. Pool. Hot tub. Exercise equipment. Laundry facilities. Business services, free parking. | 3333 Thomasville Rd. | 850/385–3553 or 800/916–2221 | fax 850/385–4242 | www.hilton.com | 100 rooms | $74–$94 | AE, D, MC, V.

Holiday Inn Downtown. This hotel is a few blocks from the Capitol and within a 2-mi radius of Florida State University and Florida A&M University. Restaurant. Pool. | 316 W. Tennessee St. | 850/222–9555 or 800/648–6135 | fax 850/224–8410 | www.holiday-inn.com | 164 rooms | $139–$250 | AE, D, DC, MC, V.

Holiday Inn, Northwest. This two-story hotel has a covered drive and pale stucco exterior. Rooms are done in dark pine greens and earthy browns. It's within walking distance of shops and restaurants and 5 mi from the Governor's Square Mall. Restaurant, bar. In-room data ports, microwaves, refrigerators. Cable TV. Pool. Laundry facilities. Business services, free parking. Pets allowed. | 2714 Graves Rd. | 850/562–2000 | fax 850/562–8519 | www.holiday-inn.com | 179 rooms | $66–$89 | AE, D, MC, V.

Quality Inn and Suites. Located 3 mi from both Florida A&M and Florida State, this is a good choice for those in town for a football game. Rooms are basic motel. The Governor's Square Mall is 1 mi away, the Capitol 2 mi. In-room data ports, microwaves, refrigerators. Cable TV. Pool. Exercise equipment. Laundry facilities. Business services, free parking. | 2020 Apalachee Pkwy. | 850/877–4437 or 800/786–7446 (reservations) | fax 850/878–9964 | www.qualityinn.com | 94 rooms | $64 | AE, D, MC, V.

Shoney's Inn. The central courtyard is filled with fountains and a huge moss-covered oak tree. Rooms are also a little Spanish with autumn colors and views of the courtyard. Your Continental breakfast is served at the adjacent Shoney's restaurant. Complimentary Continental breakfast. In-room data ports, some microwaves, some refrigerators, some in-room hot tubs. Cable TV. Pool. Laundry facilities. Free parking. Pets allowed. | 2801 N. Monroe St. | 850/386–8286 | fax 850/422–1074 | www.shoneysinn.com | 112 rooms | $67–$99 | AE, D, DC, MC.

Wakulla Springs Lodge and Conference Center. The lodge was completed in 1937, and most of the rooms reflect this era. Furnishings are simple, and there's a large fireplace in the lobby. You can hike in the surrounding Wakulla Park and swim year-round in the 70 degree Wakulla Springs. They also offer educational tours on their glass-bottom boats. Restaurant. No TV. Playground. | 550 Wakulla Park Dr. | 850/224–5950 | fax 850/561–7251 | www.dep.state.fl.us/parks/district_1/wakulla | 27 rooms | $69–$90 | MC, V.

EXPENSIVE

Cabot Lodge, Thomasville Rd. This stately five-story, pale-vanilla stucco building sits on a little rise amid pruned evergreen shrubbery. Rooms are somewhat stark, with almost-bare white walls and dark carpet. All have generous work spaces and upholstered lounge chairs. Complimentary Continental breakfast. In-room data ports. Cable TV, in-room VCRs (and movies). Pool. Laundry facilities. Business services, free parking. | 1653 Raymond Diehl Rd. | 850/386–7500 or 800/223–1964 (reservations) | fax 850/386–1136 | www.cabot-lodge.com | 135 rooms | $84 | AE, D, MC, V.

Doubletree Hotel Tallahassee. This property two blocks from the Capitol is the preferred lodging for visiting politicos and for FSU football fans in the fall. The lobby has a lounge area off the reception desk, and rooms have cherrywood antique reproductions. Valet parking. Restaurant, bar. In-room data ports, microwaves, refrigerators. Cable TV. Pool. Exercise equipment. Laundry facilities. | 101 S. Adams St. | 850/224–5000 or 800/222–TREE (reservations) | fax 850/513–9516 | www.doubletree.com | 242 rooms | $79–$119 | AE, D, MC, V.

Hampton Inn. Rooms are basic at this frill-free motel north of downtown off I–10. In-room data ports, microwaves, refrigerators. Cable TV. Pool. Laundry facilities. Business services, free parking. | 3210 Monroe St. | 850/562–4300 | fax 850/562–6735 | www.hamptoninn.com | 93 rooms | $82 | AE, D, MC, V.

La Quinta Inn-North. Rooms in this three-story motel in a colonnaded Mission-style building have large, white-tiled bathrooms with huge mirrors. Most have comfortable sitting areas with tables and love seats. In-room data ports, microwaves, refrigerators. Cable TV. Pool. Laundry facilities. Business services, free parking. Some pets allowed. | 2905 N. Monroe St. | 850/385–7172 | fax 850/422–2463 | www.laquinta.com | 154 units | $76–$96 | AE, D, MC, V.

La Quinta Inn, Tallahassee South. This motel has a crisp, white exterior with teal trim and well-maintained grounds. The outdoor pool has an expansive deck area with chaise longues for sunbathing and umbrellaed tables for shade. Rooms are basic but comfortable. In-room data ports, refrigerators. Cable TV. Pool. Laundry facilities. Business services, free parking. Some pets allowed. | 2850 Apalachee Pkwy. | 850/878–5099 | fax 850/878–6665 | www.laquinta.com | 134 rooms | $72–$92 | AE, D, MC, V.

Ramada Inn, North. Situated on 13 acres of landscaped grounds, this motel has a pleasant lobby with high ceilings. Rooms are done in mauve. Restaurant, bar. Microwaves, refrigerators. Cable TV, in-room VCRs (and movies). Pool. Business services, airport shuttle, free parking. Pets allowed. | 2900 N. Monroe St. | 850/386–1027 | fax 850/422–1025 | www.ramada.com | 200 rooms | $79–$102 | AE, D, MC, V.

TownePlace Suites Marriott. These roomy town house–style Marriott suites come in studio, one-bedroom, and two-bedroom varieties. Rooms are beige with green carpet. All have full kitchens. The hotel is 5 mi from the Capitol and the Tallahassee Museum of History and Natural Science, and 20 mi from Wakulla Springs State Park. Pool. Exercise room. Laundry facilities. Business services. Pets allowed. | 1876 Capital Circle, NE | 850/219–0122 | fax 850/219–0133 | www.towneplace.com | 95 suites | $84–$110.

Courtyard by Marriott. This four-story property 2 mi from Florida A&M and Florida State and 1 mi from the Capitol is on Tallahassee's motel strip. Rooms have large, well-lit work spaces and sitting areas. Restaurant, bar. In-room data ports, refrigerators. Cable TV. Pool. Hot tub. Exercise equipment. Laundry facilities. Business services. | 1018 Apalachee Pkwy. | 850/222–8822 or 800/443–6000 (reservations) | fax 850/561–0354 | www.courtyard.com | 141 rooms, 13 suites | $109 | AE, D, MC, V.

★ **Governors Inn.** This hotel occupies a restored historic warehouse in downtown Tallahassee one block from the Capitol. Rooms are richly appointed with lots of mahogany, brass, and classic art prints. The VIP package includes breakfast, cocktails, robes, shoe-shines, and a daily paper. Valet parking. Bar. In-room data ports. Cable TV. Business services, airport shuttle. | 209 S. Adams St. | 850/681–6855 or 800/342–7717 (reservations) | fax 850/222–3105 | 40 rooms | $149 | AE, D, MC, V.

Radisson Hotel Tallahassee. The lobby of this stately, seven-story white masonry building is naturally illuminated during daylight hours by large bay windows looking out onto well-tended grounds. Rooms are large and furnished with antique reproductions in dark cherrywood veneer. Restaurant, bar. In-room data ports, refrigerators, in-room hot tubs (in most suites). Cable TV, in-room VCRs (and movies). Exercise equipment. Laundry facilities. Business services, airport shuttle, free parking. | 415 N. Monroe St. | 850/224–6000 | fax 850/224–6000 | www.radisson.com | 112 rooms, 7 suites | $105–$129, $150 suites | AE, D, MC, V.

TAMPA

MAP 3, H6

(Nearby towns also listed: Clearwater, Dunedin, Indian Rocks Beach, Madeira Beach, Reddington Beach, St. Petersburg, St. Pete Beach, Sun City Center)

For many years Native Americans were the sole inhabitants of the Tampa Bay area. (Tampa is a Native American word meaning "sticks of fire.") Spanish explorers Juan Ponce de León, Panfilo de Narvaez, and Hernando de Soto passed through here in the mid-1500s, but the U.S. Army and the first settlers didn't arrive until 1824. The town remained slow and sleepy, growing to about 1,500 residents by the early 1880s. But in 1884 railroad magnate Henry Plant built a narrow-gauge rail extension to the Hillsborough River, which provided access to new areas and a conduit for goods and materials from the river to town. Plant also built several beautiful hotels along the rails to attract visitors—and they came in great numbers. His Tampa Bay Hotel, built in 1891, is now a museum and part of the University of Tampa.

In 1866 another important Tampa figure arrived from Key West. Vincente Martinez Ybor brought with him thousands of Cubans to make cigars in his cigar factory in what is now Ybor City. By the 1890s this factory employed almost 20 percent of the town's residents. Though the cigar factory no longer operates, the Cuban influence does, and Ybor City has been reborn as Tampa's favorite Latin-flavored entertainment and dining district, with fashionable galleries, nightclubs, and restaurants replacing the lofts where Cubans once rolled tobacco leaves.

The Spanish-American War was good to Tampa, sparking an economic momentum that has seldom abated since then. Today booming Tampa is the center of the second-largest metropolitan area in Florida, with a population of more than 2 million. It is a cultural center as well as a business center, with good theater, concerts, and museums. The U.S. Operations Command maintains a military presence at Tampa's MacDill Air Force Base.

Though international banking and communications firms have set up shop in the gleaming, glass skyscrapers of downtown Tampa, funding an urban resurgence, most of Tampa's real industry is centered on Tampa Bay, which serves as a major shipping center for locally mined phosphates and locally caught shrimp. A pleasure cruise line also operates out of the bay. The city has a few theme parks, which the kids will enjoy.

Information: **Tampa/Hillsborough Convention and Visitors Association** | 400 N. Tampa St., Ste. 1010, Tampa, FL 33602 | 800/44–TAMPA or 813/223–2752 | www.gotampa.com.

TAMPA BAY AREA

Downtown Tampa. Tampa's sprawling downtown area is made up of 8 separate districts enclosed by the Ybor channel to the east, Palm Boulevard to the north, North Boulevard to the west, and Harbor Island to the south. Upscale shops and restaurants, as well as the local aquarium and cruise terminals, are found along the channel side. You might find some of the city's helpful ambassadors walking around the city to help with directions in their white safari outfits.

Ybor City. One of the more popular sections near downtown Tampa, Ybor City is a National Historic Landmark District encompassing many ethnicities. It's filled with stores and restaurants that trade on the early Cuban influence in the area. The cigar industry was brought here from Cuba in the mid-1800s, but now most of the factories have been turned into lively night spots or trendy boutiques. Ybor City is found between Nuccio Parkway and 22nd Street, from 7th to 9th avenues.

St. Petersburg. Twenty-one mi west of Tampa is the dangling peninsula that holds St. Petersburg. The downtown is mainly commercial with a few restaurants and Tropicana Field (home of the Tampa Bay Devil Rays), although the action is along the coast, where there is a huge pier complex full of shops and restaurants. The nearby barrier islands are linked by causeways to St. Petersburg. Highway 19 borders the downtown area to the west, with the Gulf of Mexico to the east, 5th Avenue to the north, and 10th Avenue to the south.

Sarasota/Bradenton. South of Tampa and St. Petersburg, the artistic community of Sarasota originally prospered under the wealth and vision of John Ringling. The main sights to see are still the Ringling circus, mansion, and museum. Along the white-sand beaches you can find large sculptures and plenty of quiet hotels and restaurants. Bradenton is the town to the north, with around 20 mi of beaches; Sarasota/Bradenton has one of the busiest airports in the area.

Beaches. From Tarpon Beach in the north to St. Pete Beach in the south, St. Petersburg is ringed with white-sand, barrier island beaches. Along the way you will pass through Bellaire Beach and Shore, Redington Beach and Shore, Madeira Beach, and Treasure Island, to name a few.

Clearwater. Holding a state record for the most days of sunshine (with 361), this island community off the west coast of St. Petersburg is full of restaurants, motels, and a large charter fishing fleet. Fishing and sunset-viewing off the main pier or parasailing won't hurt your sunny disposition here, either, and you can always hop aboard the Jolley Trolley for 50¢ to transport you around the island. Two drawbridges link Clearwater to the mainland.

TRANSPORTATION

Airports: St. Petersburg-Clearwater International Airport (State Highway 686, Roosevelt Boulevard, just west of I–275 | 727/535–7600 | www.stpete-cwairport.com) provides regional and some national service. A big plus here is that there's free parking for up to 14 days and plenty of car rentals. It's 6 mi east of Clearwater and 5 mi north of St. Petersburg on the western shore of Old Tampa Bay, accessed via Hwy. 688 or Highway 686.

Most of the region's visitors arrive at **Tampa International Airport** (813/870–8700 | www.tampaairport.com), the Tampa Bay Area's busiest airport, which is 5 mi west of downtown Tampa on the eastern shore of Old Tampa Bay, accessed by Hwy. 589.
Sarasota Bradenton International Airport (941/359–5200 | www.srq-airport.com) lies just north of Sarasota off U.S. 41 or I–75 exit 40. It is one of central Florida's rapidly growing airports. It is served by American, Continental, Delta, Northwest, TWA, United, and USAirways, as well as some low-cost airlines.
Airport Transportation: The **Limo** (727/572–1111 or 800/282–6817) provides service to and from both the St. Petersburg-Clearwater and Tampa airports. The average cost is $15.
Yellow Cab (727/799–2222) operates taxi service at both the St. Petersburg-Clearwater and Tampa airports. Expect taxi fares to be about $12–$25 for a destination in the city where the airport is located and twice that for other destinations.
Diplomat Taxi (941/355–5155) is the contracted taxi provider at the Sarasota-Bradenton International Airport. The average cab fare between the airport and downtown is $16–$25.
Bus Lines: Greyhound (180 N. Ninth St. | 727/898–1496 or 800/231–2222 | www.greyhound.com) offers daily service across the country.
Train Lines: Amtrak (800/872–7245) trains arrive at the Tampa station (601 Nebraska Ave.).

DRIVING AND PARKING

Since driving is the only possible option for residents in the sprawling Tampa Bay area, with many workers living in St. Petersburg and the Gulf beach cities and working in

YBOR CITY—A BIT OF CUBA IN FLORIDA

By the time Theodore Roosevelt's Rough Riders arrived in Tampa en route to Cuba in 1898, Ybor City—then its own town, east of Tampa—was home to the largest Cuban population outside the island nation. In the 15 years since its founding, Ybor City had welcomed over 3,000 Cuban expatriates, and Tampa's Latin roots began here. The great Cuban leader and poet, José Martí made regular trips to Tampa to garner support for the independence cause. When war did break out between Spain and the United States in 1989, the army stationed thousands of men in Ybor City.

The Cuban cigar factories in Tampa had quickly become the biggest in the world. The very biggest belonged to the town's founder, Vincente Martinez Ybor, who re-located from Cuba via Key West to the Tampa area when he learned of Henry B. Plant's new railroad line and steamship service into Tampa in 1884. A year later, Ybor obtained 40 acres of land—then just palmettos and scrub pines—and began construction of houses, stores for workers. The idea of workers owning their homes, as opposed to renting them from their company, was a unique one at the time, and it instilled workers with a sense of independence and self-respect. Cubans, trained from a young age in the art of hand-rolling cigars, were joined by Spanish, German, Jewish, and Italian immigrants who brought communal medical care and aid societies. Prosperity, marked by opera houses, ball rooms, and hotels, lasted 50 years. At peak times, nearly 12,000 workers worked in more than 200 cigar factories, producing 400 million cigars a year.

After World War II, factories closed and residents moved into new suburbs. In 1990 Ybor City was designated a National Historic Landmark District, and renovated redbrick streets, wrought-iron balconies, and antique street lamps brought back much old charm. Today, the area is Tampa's greatest public space and principal entertainment hotspot.

Tampa, or vice versa, you will also have no alternative but to drive. During weekday rush hours (7–9 AM and 5–7 PM), traffic on I–275 between Tampa and St. Petersburg, as well as the Courtney Campbell Parkway (Highway 60) and the Gandy Bridge (U.S. 92), backs up eastbound in the morning and westbound in the afternoon.

Another trouble spot for motorists is I–4, the major eastern approach to Tampa and the primary route from Orlando to both Tampa and St. Petersburg. Construction on I–4 between Lakeland (about 30 mi east) and Tampa has been non-stop for several years, with no end in sight. Consequently, travel on I–4 during rush hours should be avoided if possible. Traffic on I–275, which is the central conduit between the two cities, backs up near the downtown areas of both periodically throughout the day, but delays are usually minimal during non-rush hours.

The Tampa Bay area suffers from a lack of highways between the downtown areas and the suburbs. Consequently, you must often take traffic light–laden routes such as State Road 597 (Dale Mabry Boulevard) to reach the north central portion of Hillsborough County (Tampa) or another traffic nightmare, U.S. 19, to reach the northern part of Pinellas County (St. Petersburg).

North-south travel on I–75, which runs up and down the west coast of Florida, is one of the Tampa Bay area's few highway success stories. If you are bound from northern Florida to Fort Myers or Naples, south of Tampa Bay, you can skirt around metro Tampa completely without leaving the interstate. Or, if you're headed through the Tampa downtown area or St. Petersburg, I–275 via the Sunshine Skyway Bridge ($1 toll) takes you easily to the south, where I–275 and I–75 merge.

Parking is not the problem in the downtown areas of Tampa Bay that it is in most urban areas of the U.S. The central business districts are not quite as crowded as they are in Atlanta or Miami. It's not out of the question to find a parking meter in either downtown Tampa or St. Petersburg, where it will cost from 25 to 50 cents an hour to park. Both cities also have plenty of commercial parking garages that charge from $1 to $2 an hour, or $5 to $12 a day.

Attractions

CULTURE, EDUCATION, AND HISTORY

Tampa Bay Performing Arts Center. The Southeast's largest performing arts center occupies nine acres along the Hillsborough River. The four-theatre complex stages Broadway shows and dance, opera, music, drama, and comedy performances. | 1010 N. MacInnes Place | 813/286–2403.

Tampa Theatre. Built in 1926 as a venue for silent films, this theater has dramatic vaulted ceilings, arches, murals, and tapestries. Legend has it that the restless ghost of a longtime projectionist haunts the place. Concerts, movies, and special events take place here; guided tours are available by appointment. | 711 Franklin St. | 813/274–8981.

University of South Florida. A contemporary art museum and botanical gardens are notable features of the 1,700-acre northeast Tampa campus of this state-funded university with more than 35,000 students. | 4202 E. Fowler Ave. | 813/974–2235 or 813/974–2011 (campus tours) | Free | Weekdays 9–5; tours by appointment.

University of Tampa. This private university, established in 1933, occupies 40 buildings on 80 acres along the Hillsborough River in downtown Tampa. The 3,500 undergraduate and graduate students choose from more than 60 academic programs, from liberal arts to business. Though the student body is relatively small, more than 80 nations are represented in the student body, 65% of which lives on campus. | 401 W. Kennedy Blvd. | 813/253–6220 | Free | Daily; tours Sept.–May, Tues., Thurs. 1:30.

Henry B. Plant Museum. The centerpiece of the University of Tampa is the former Tampa Bay Hotel, built in 1891 by Henry B. Plant, a force in the reconstruction of the postwar South, and the entrepreneur behind the Hillsborough rail line. The 13 silver minarets atop the Spanish-Moorish-Turkish structure represent the months in the Muslim calendar. Now called Plant Hall, the building has been the university's main building since 1933. Occupying the first floor of the south wing is the Henry B. Plant Museum, which is devoted to area history with displays of some of the old hotel's furnishings and art as well as artifacts, photos, and memorabilia relating to tourism in early Tampa. The Henry B. Plant Memorial Fountain sits in the middle of a circular drive on the east side of the building, and is thought to be the oldest piece of outdoor sculpture in Tampa, created circa 1900. | 401 W. Kennedy Blvd. | 813/254–1891 | $3 | Tues.–Sat. 10–4, Sun. noon–4.

MUSEUMS

Museum of Science and Industry. At the Southeast's largest science center you can experience 74 mph hurricane winds, be a Top Gun fighter, watch a film projected on a 360°, eight-story dome in the IMAX theater, and more. There are some 450 interactive exhibits in all. MOSI is about 2 mi west of I–75 exit 54. | 4801 E. Fowler Ave. | 813/987–6000 | Museum $8, Imax theater $6, combo ticket $11 | Sept.–May, Sun.–Thurs. 9–5, Fri., Sat. 9–7; Jun.–Aug., daily 9–7.

Tampa Bay History Center. See the history of Florida from the end of the Ice Age to the present. Exhibits have focused on the neighborhoods that sprang up around Henry Plant's railroad endeavors, telling their stories through photos, personal testimonials, and artifacts from day-to-day life around 1900. The Center also has a library with information on genealogy, journals, photos, and historical documents. The museum is 1½ mi east of I–275 exit 25. | 225 S. Franklin St., adjacent to the Tampa Convention Center | 813/228–0097 | Free | Tues.–Sat. 10–5, Sun. 1–5.

Tampa Museum of Art. An ultra-modern building composed of smooth planes of masonry blended with glass walls and punctuated with exposed metal girders houses the Tampa Museum of Art. The permanent collection of some 7,000 items includes the most comprehensive collection of Greek, Roman, and Etruscan antiquities in the Southeast. Also on display are 20th-century American paintings, works on paper, and photography. Works by well-known and emerging local artists are shown in the Florida Gallery. There is a lively program of changing exhibits and a sculpture garden on the grounds. | 600 N. Ashley Dr. | 813/274–8130 | fax 813/274–8732 | $5 | Mon.–Tues., Thurs.–Sat. 10–5, Wed. 10–9, Sun. 1–5.

Ybor City State Museum. The history of the cigar industry is profiled through three restored cigar workers' houses, one of which is a mini-museum unto itself. You can tour the adjacent La Ferlita Bakery, which produced most of Ybor City's bread during its heyday as Cigar Capital of the World. Free tours are available of the museum complex and ornamental garden. | 1818 E. 9th Ave. | 813/247–2807 | $2 | Tues.–Sat. 9–noon, 1–5.

PARKS, NATURAL SITES, AND OUTDOOR ACTIVITIES

Weeki Wachee Springs Waterpark. This attraction has long been famous for its live mermaid shows. The spring flows at a rate of 170 million gallons of water a day, with a constant temperature of 74°F. A nature trail threads through the subtropical wilderness, and a jungle boat cruise provides views of local wildlife. Other attractions include a birds-of-prey show, an exotic bird show, and a petting zoo. It's 45 min north of Tampa on U.S. 19 at the intersection of Route 50. | 352/596–2062 or 800/678–9335 | $14.95 (includes admission to Buccaneer Bay) | Nov.–Feb., weekdays 10–3, weekends 10–4; Mar.–Oct. daily 10–5.

Buccaneer Bay. Adjacent to Weeki Wachee Springs is a family water park where you can relax on a white-sand beach, brave the Pirate's Revenge water slide, or plummet three stories in the dark, down the cannonball flume. | 6131 Commercial Way | 352/596–2062 or 800/678–9335 | $14.95 (includes admission to Weeki Wachee Spring) | Mar.–Oct., daily 10–5.

SHOPPING

Ybor City. In the 1800s, Cubans brought their cigar-making skills to this area of Tampa, about 2 mi east of downtown. Ybor City (pronounced ee-bore) quickly became known as the Cigar Capital of the World. You can still see artisans at work in smoke shops, hand-rolling cigars following time-honored methods, and the rich smell of cigars still wafts through the air. Today the neighborhood is brimming with galleries, ethnic eateries, and clubs. By day you can grab a Cuban pork sandwich for lunch, browse a vintage clothing store, or admire a local artist's crafts. After dark (particularly on weekends) Seventh Avenue is packed with restaurant- and club-goers. There are several annual weekend festivals celebrating Ybor history or culture. The area is bordered by I–4, 5th Ave., Nebraska Ave. and 22nd St. | 813/248–3712.

Ybor Square. The impressive brick building known as Ybor Square was built by Vincente Martinez-Ybor as the home of the V. M. Ybor Cigar Company. Today it houses several stores and restaurants. Historic markers note that Teddy Roosevelt's Rough Riders passed through Ybor Square during the Spanish American War. Walking tours of Ybor City begin at the information counter. | 1901 13th St. | 813/247–4497 | Free | Daily.

SPECTATOR SPORTS

Tampa Bay Buccaneers. This NFL team plays at Raymond James Stadium. | 4201 N. Dale Mabry Hwy. | 813/879–2827 | $35–$60 | Aug.–Dec.

Tampa Bay Lightning. Winter brings hockey to Florida. This NHL team hits the ice in the Ice Palace, a huge sporting complex designed for hockey games but used for everything from basketball to major concerts. | 401 Channelside Dr. | 813/223–6100 | $10–$80 | Oct.–Mar.

SIGHTSEEING TOURS/TOUR COMPANIES

Around The Town. If you're traveling with a group, or would like to meet like-minded travelers, Tampa-based Around The Town Travel operates senior bus tours to attractions and sites all over the United States. Reservations are necessary, and singles and pairs are integrated into tour groups. | 3450 Buschwood Park Dr. | 813/932–7803 | Tours range upward from $20 | Reservations available weekdays 9–5:30.

OTHER POINTS OF INTEREST

Adventure Island. Adventure Island, 1 mi north of Busch Gardens Tampa (and one of that park's corporate cousins) is 36 acres of water slides, swimming areas, and more. The two artificial wave pools have continuous 5-ft swells perfect for floating on an inner-tube. Key West Rapids sends you down 6 stories over 700 ft of turns and pools interspersed by "water mines" strategically placed to soak you. There's a championship volleyball complex, cafés, snack bars, changing rooms, and video games. I–75 exit 33, at Busch Blvd. | 1001 Malcolm McKinley Dr. | 813/987–5660 | www.adventureisland.com | $24.45 | Feb.–Mar., weekends 10–5; Apr.–Oct., daily 9:30–6.

★ **Busch Gardens.** Tampa's most popular attraction is like a zoo and theme park rolled into one. More than 3,400 animals roam the manicured 335-acre grounds in sections designed to capture the spirit of Africa a hundred years ago. A monorail ride provides sky-high views of zebras, giraffes, rhinos, lions, and other animals. Busch Gardens is also home to some of the largest and fastest roller coasters in the Southeast. The park is 8 mi northeast of downtown Tampa, and 2 mi east of I–75 exit 33. | 3000 E. Busch Blvd. | 813/987–5082 | $41.55, parking $4–$6 | Park opens at 9, closing hours vary.

★ **Florida Aquarium.** With its 83-ft glass-and-steel dome, this building more resembles a huge, glittering seashell than a state-of-the-art, hands-on aquatic science center. It is home to more than 10,000 types of aquatic plant and animal life. You can pet sharks, feed stingrays, and learn about the waters that cover 75% of our planet. The plants and animals represent a cross-section of Florida's native ecosystems, but many are from other parts of the globe. A man-made coral reef in a 500,000-gallon tank is the aquarium's centerpiece. It's on the river, next to the Convention Center. I–75 Exit 25 (Scott St.) or Exit 26 (Jefferson St.). | 701 Channelside Dr. | 813/273–4000 | $11.95 | Daily 9:30–5.

Lowry Park Zoo. This midsize zoo has 41 acres of natural habitats in five distinct exhibit areas with hundreds of animals from four continents—many of them threatened or endangered. You can see Siberian tigers lounging on rocky outcroppings and seals and sea lions in their pool, or take a guided tour. The Florida Wildlife Center has alligators, Florida panthers, bears, and rare red wolves. The Manatee and Aquatic Center gives you a close look at the endangered Florida mammals. There's also a petting zoo, with goats, exotic sheep, and other domesticated animals. It's 2 mi from downtown Tampa. I–275 exit 31. | 7530 North Blvd. | 813/932–0245 | www.lowryparkzoo.com | $8.50 | Daily 9:30–5.

Seminole Indian Casino. Gaming options include poker, high stakes bingo, and slot machines. Next door the Seminole Indian Museum and Cultural Center has demonstrations of Seminole skill in beadwork and carving, with many craft items for sale. | 5223 N. Orient Rd. | 813/621–1302 | Free | Casino daily 24 hrs; museum Mon.–Sat. 9–5, Sun. 10–4.

WALKING TOUR
A Walk Down Seventh Avenue (2–3 hours including stops for food and shopping)
A ten-block stretch of brick-paved East Seventh Avenue between 22nd Street and Nick Nuccio Parkway represents a combination of a 21st-century Noah's Ark of commerce (there are at least two of everything) and a living anthropological exhibit of everything Tampa has been in the past 105 years. At one end of the 10-block strip you'll find the 95-year-old Cuban dining palace Columbia Restaurant (in a building that dates back to 1895), and as you walk west down Seventh Avenue, you'll find everything from a Steven Spielberg–designed interactive game arcade to historic museums to art galleries to a cavernous female-impersonator bar. (Don't let the latter worry you about the demeanor of the neighborhood, it's definitely G-rated and quite safe, one of the most thriving tourism and entertainment districts in Florida.)

  Columbia Restaurant (2117 E. 7th Ave.) makes a good place to start; step inside and gander at the classic Spanish colonial architecture, or sit down and sample the *arroz con pollo* as well. The next good spot to get a bite is only two blocks down the street, Cha Cha Coconuts (2029 E. 7th Ave.), where you will find good Caribbean food and tropical libations. A couple of doors down, step into the El Molino Gourmet Coffee Shop (2012 E. 7th Ave.), which includes a cigar store, café, and barber shop. (Of course, you can get your hair cut while smoking a cigar and drinking coffee—they love that here.)

  The 1900 block of East Seventh Avenue is particularly eclectic, with a good sushi bar (Sushi on Seventh, 1919 E. 7th Ave.), a country-and-western bar (Spurs, 1915 E. 7th Ave.), and a great art gallery (Hoffman Porges Gallery, 1907 E. 7th Ave.), where you will find everything from antique French posters to impressionist paintings.

  If you care to venture a couple of blocks to the north of Seventh Avenue, stop at the **Ybor City State Museum,** 1818 E. 9th Ave., where, for a $2 admission, you can learn about Ybor's history as a cigar factory district where thousands of Cuban immigrants turned out millions of hand-rolled stogies. And if you're up for hiking another six blocks north, try the Ybor City Brewing Co. (1812 N. 15th Ave.), a working micro-brewery in a historic building, where you'll find a tasting room and a good informal eatery.

  Back on Seventh Avenue, a couple of spots in the 1700 block may merit your attention. The Blue Devil Tattoo Gallery (1717 E. 7th Ave.) seems to earn good marks from those who like that sort of thing. And if you like to browse in strange emporiums, a must-try is The Spitting Gargoyle (also 1717 E. 7th Ave. in the same building complex as the tattoo shop), which offers a huge collection of stone and masonry gargoyles, the kind you might see on Dracula's castle or an old building—great for yard art.

  The entire 1600 block of Seventh Avenue is occupied by the biggest thing to hit Ybor in decades, **Centro Ybor** (16th Street at E. 7th Ave.), a two-square-block mega-center that opened in October 2000 with a wide variety of offerings. You'll find GameWorks, a Steven Spielberg–designed, interactive game emporium; Dish, a trendy restaurant where they grill your lunch while you watch; Starbucks coffee; Brainfood!, a bookstore; and a **Victoria's Secret** store, among others. The new center also has a 20-screen **Muvico** movie theater complex and its own parking garage, where you can park a few hours for $1 or overnight for $5. (Parking is only a problem on nights and weekends in this area.)

Finding East Seventh Avenue in Ybor City is easy. Take I–4 exit 1, and go south a few blocks. Ybor is alive from 6 AM, when some of the coffee shops open, until 3 AM, when the majority of the trendy bars close.

ON THE CALENDAR

JAN.: Outback Bowl. This New Year's Day football classic matches teams from the Big Ten Conference and the Southeastern Conference. | Raymond James Stadium | Jan. 1 | 813/874–BOWL.

FEB.: Florida State Fair. This annual event at the Florida State Fairgrounds showcases the state's agricultural industry. The midway is one of the largest in the country, and there's plenty of live entertainment and food. | 4800 U.S. 301N, off I–4 exit 6A | 813/621–7821.

FEB.: Gasparilla Festival of Tampa Bay. For three days the city commemorates a mythical pirate, José Gaspar, with a parade, arts and crafts, local and national entertainment, and fireworks downtown. | 813/353–8108.

MAR.: Florida Strawberry Festival. Plant City, about 15 mi northeast of Tampa, calls itself the strawberry capital of the United States. Its two-week-long festival is themed around that claim, with farmer's markets, food booths, and every tasty thing anyone's ever thought to make out of strawberries for sale. There's also country music and rides. | 813/752–9194.

MAR.–APR.: Baseball Spring Training. The Yankees have been practicing at Legends Field every spring since 1995. Its dimensions are, interestingly enough, identical to those of Yankee Stadium. | I–275 to Martin Luther King, west to Dale Mabry | 813/879–2244.

JULY–DEC.: Greyhound Racing. Greyhounds race at Tampa Track. | 8300 Nebraska Ave. | 813/932–4313.

DEC.–MAY: Horse Racing. Tampa Bay Downs is the only Thoroughbred horse racing venue on Florida's West Coast. Route 580 to Oldsmar. | Race Track Rd. | 813/855–4401.

Dining

INEXPENSIVE

Cafe Winberie. Eclectic. This is a sophisticated little café with sidewalk seating under a big red awning. The menu includes authentic Thai dishes and familiar fare such as char-grilled sirloin and light salads. The stand-out is the salmon baked in parchment. The key lime pie is excellent. The outdoor patio can be a little hot and sticky from May to November. | 1610 W. Swann Ave. | 813/253–6500 | Reservations not accepted | $7–$14 | AE, D, DC, MC, V.

Dong Phuong. Vietnamese. This is one of those strip-mall restaurants that doesn't look like much from the road but serves good food. Dong Phuong will tone down the normal spice-load of the authentic Vietnamese dishes at your request. Entrées come with rice noodles or white rice and vegetables. The lemongrass chicken with curry is popular. | 3638 Henderson Blvd. | 813/874–2919 | $5–$10 | AE, D, MC, V.

Kojak's House of Ribs. Barbecue. For more than 20 years, the same family has been pumping out good old-fashioned barbecue ribs and meat on the grill, as well as corn on the cob. Try the heaping servings of cole slaw and potato salad, then some of the locally baked pies or cakes. The scene is casual and you can dine inside or out on the patio. | 2808 Gandy Blvd. | 813/837–3774 | fax 813/837–2179 | Closed Mon. | $9–$111 | No credit cards.

Whiskey Joe's. American. You'll find expansive bay views, peanut shells on the plank floors, and a wraparound deck at this casual restaurant and bar serving sandwiches, platoons of oysters and crabs, and daily fresh fish selections. | 2500 N. Rocky Point Dr. | 813/281–0577 | $6–$12 | AE, D, MC, V.

Ybor City Diner. Diner. The portions are massive at this all-American joint in a storefront in historic Ybor City. The interior is a rich blue, and booths have high backs for privacy. You can sit at a classic lunch counter complete with twirly-chairs or at formica-topped tables.

The menu includes burgers and an open-faced beef sandwich with gravy. On the sweet side, you can stand a fork up in the diner's malts or split a caramel-drenched hot brownie sundae. | 1724 7th. Ave. | 813/248–2828 | No breakfast Mondays | $5–$10 | D, MC, V.

MODERATE

The Cactus Club. Southwestern. This restaurant specializes in Southwestern fare with a Floridian twist. Shrimp fajitas and the Texas Pie—crispy-crust pizza—are favorites, but they also serve burgers. Patio dining is available. | 1601 Snow Ave. | 813/251–4089 | Reservations not accepted | $9–$16 | AE, D, MC, V.

Café Creole. Cajun/Creole. The Mardi Gras bar is always decked out here, and a jazz band plays Tuesday through Saturday. Menu specialties include grouper Bienville (topped with a shrimp and crab stuffing and coated in a mushroom, sherry wine sauce and then baked). Crab cakes, crawfish étouffée, jambalaya, gumbo, red beans and rice, and bread pudding soaked in a whiskey brandy sauce are staples. | 1330 9th Ave. | 813/247–6283 | fax 813/248–3041 | No lunch Sun. | $12–$18 | AE, MC, V.

The Castaway. Seafood. This rustic bay-front eatery has a panoramic bay view with an outdoor deck for watching the sunset. Seafood—grilled, broiled, and blackened—is the specialty, but you can order grilled steak or pasta dishes. | 7720 Courtney Campbell Causeway | 813/281–0770 | Reservations not accepted | No lunch Sun. | $12–$20 | AE, D, DC, MC, V.

★ **Columbia.** Spanish. High, arched doorways, vaulted ceilings, and ornate railings adorn this eatery open since 1905. It occupies an entire block in Ybor City and has a sunny atrium. The paella and the famous 1905 salad (with ham, olives, cheese, and garlic) are standouts. Flamenco dancers entertain nightly in the main dining room, and a walk-in humidor holds hundreds of hand-rolled cigars. | 2117 E. 7th Ave. | 813/248–4961 | $13–$20 | AE, D, DC, MC, V.

Crawdaddy's. Cajun. This New Orleans–inspired eatery has lots of wood, some brass, and the odd piece of river-city wall art. The menu includes gator tail, crawfish pancakes, chicken chipotle phyllo, and steak. | 2500 Rocky Point Dr. | 813/281–0407 | No lunch | $12–$21 | AE, D, DC, MC, V.

Damon's. American. This dim, cavernous establishment is popular with sports fans. This outpost of the national chain has four huge TV screens projecting basketball, football, and pay-per-view boxing events. There are interactive trivia and sports video games at the tables. The service can be slow. The menu includes barbecued ribs, burgers, and sandwiches. | 7700 Courtney Campbell Causeway | 813/281–0566 | No lunch | $9–$19 | AE, D, DC, MC, V.

Jasmine Thai. Thai. The 110-plus choices on the menu outshine the spare, Asian-inspired dining area. You can have your chosen dish made from tame to hot. The menu includes mee-krob (crispy noodles) and piquant Panang chicken. | 13248 N. Dale Mabry Hwy. | 813/968–1501 | Reservations not accepted | $7–$19 | AE, DC, MC, V.

Rice and Co. Asian Bistro. Japanese. This bright restaurant occupies a building adjacent to the Town Center Mall. A railed, outdoor patio welcomes you to dine alfresco and enjoy the sun. Indoors the main dining area follows a circular floorplan around the central sushi bar. Everything is smooth blond wood, with the mulberry walls and deep periwinkle ceiling both bearing whimsical gold swirlies. Dishes are meant for sharing. A popular dish is the black bean garlic chicken with tri-colored peppers and black beans stir-fried in the chef's secret sauce. There's live jazz on the patio Friday and Saturday nights. | 7982 Citrus Park | 813/920–7423 | Reservations not accepted | $8–$15 | AE, DC, MC, V.

Sam Oh Jung. Korean. Two huge aquariums stocked with bright tropical fish burble in the background in this good restaurant with an unassuming exterior. Rice-paper screens add to the relaxing mood. The menu includes spicy teriyaki chicken, which is served on a lacquered tray with rice, pickled ginger, and hot horseradish. | 602 N. Dale Mabry Hwy. | 813/871–3233 | $6–$20 | AE, D, DC, MC, V.

Seabreeze Restaurant by the Bay. Seafood. This restaurant has been serving fresh fish since it opened in 1929. It's south of Ybor City near the docks. The air can get a little fishy when it's hot or the wind blows just right. The fresh-grilled grouper sandwich served on dense Cuban bread is a good choice. | 3409 22nd St. (Causeway Blvd.) | 813/247–2103 | Reservations not accepted | $7–$19 | AE, D, DC, MC, V.

Taj. Indian. The food can be either mild or ferocious at this small eatery popular with FSU students. Fans order their dishes hot. To cool off, the lassi is a chilled yogurt drink that comes in four different fruit flavors. | 2734B E. Fowler Ave. | 813/971–8483 | Reservations recommended | Closed Mon. | $9–$16 | AE, MC, V.

Valencia Gardens. Spanish. Walls in the dining areas are covered with old photos, Spanish art, and bits and pieces of Tampa history. Specialties include Cuban-style roast pork and potatoes stuffed with shredded beef, breaded, and fried. Guavas with cream cheese are a nice finish. | 811 W. Kennedy Blvd. | 813/253–3773 | Closed Sun. No lunch Sat. | $10–$18 | AE, D, DC, MC, V.

EXPENSIVE

Bernini Restaurant. Italian. A bit of homage to sculptor Giovanni Bernini, this trendy spot is filled with copies of Old Masters' works. The meals are mostly modern versions of the traditional. You can choose the slow-cooked osso buco, but you can also spice things up with the mixed grill of pork chops, beef fillet, and duck served with a trio of sauces. The pan-seared sea scallops drizzled with a sauce of 35-yr-old balsamic vinegar is another interesting choice. | 1702 E. 7th Ave. | 813/248–0099 | fax 813/247–4546 | $17–$26 | AE, MC, V.

Bill's Sundowner. American. On the far Western edge of the city, this upscale urban eatery has a distinctly sporty feel with the dozens of pieces of jock memorabilia on the walls. Steaks and chops are the specialties here, but there are also hearty appetizers such as crab cakes and wood-smoked corn chowder. The menu also includes veal Toscana sautéed in cognac with pine nuts. | 5401 W. Kennedy Blvd., Ste. 100 | 813/636–8686 | Reservations recommended | No lunch Sat. | $10–$30 | AE, D, MC, V.

CK's. Continental. This revolving restaurant in the Tampa Airport Marriott hotel gives you a 360° view of arriving and departing planes. Tables are sedately draped. Steaks and prime-rib are staples of the menu, but neither are particularly opulent or painstakingly prepared for the prices. | 813/878–6500 | No lunch, no supper Sun. | $14–$27 | AE, D, DC, MC, V.

Colonnade. Seafood. Across the street from Hillsboro Bay, this fourth-generation family-style seafood house has a nautical style. The menu consists of dishes that are at the same time traditional and inventive. You can create your own meal by choosing several types of seafood—or chicken—and specifying how you'd like it prepared. Or try the rainbow trout, broiled whole to order. For dessert look for a fresh fruit pie or a chocolate or peanut butter indulgence. | 3401 Bayshore Blvd. | 813/839–7558 | fax 813/837–1312 | $8–$34 | AE, DC, MC, V.

Donatello. Italian. Donatello was established in 1984 and has been serving good northern Italian fare ever since. The dining area has gold-leaf ceilings and sandy stucco walls bathed in diffuse, rosy light. There are lots of plants, fresh flowers, and framed paintings. The menu includes *osso buco Milanese* (a veal shank with marrow bone slowly braised in a wine-and-cream sauce), chicken, and seafood. For dessert, the soufflé Grand Marnier is available if requested when making a reservation. | 232 N. Dale Mabry Hwy. | 813/875–6660 | No lunch weekends | Reservations recommended | $16–$29 | AE, D, DC, MC, V.

Harbourview. American. The window seats here are the best in the house, particularly for the Sunday brunch. The restaurant is casual. The menu includes a grilled pork chop in balsamic glaze and herb-crusted beef tenderloin. | 725 S. Harbour Island Blvd. | 813/229–5001 | Reservations recommended for brunch | Breakfast also available | $15–$25 | AE, D, DC, MC, V.

Le Bordeaux. French. This is an intimate spot with six small dining areas. In the evenings the space doubles as a jazz club. The menu changes daily. The grilled salmon drizzled with ginger sauce is a standout. | 1502 S. Howard Ave. | 813/254–4387 | No lunch | $15–$35 | AE, D, MC, V.

Oystercatchers. Seafood. This is the place for you if you want to dine on the deck in the salty air and aren't in a rush. The menu includes mesquite-grilled salmon steak and a bowl of the soup-of-the-day with a chunk of homemade sourdough bread. | 6200 Courtney Campbell Causeway | 813/281–9116 | No supper Sun. | $13–$25 | AE, D, DC, MC, V.

The Rusty Pelican. Seafood. Perched on stilts over the waters of Tampa Bay, this restaurant has a fabulous view. Waterbirds are common visitors, and many other aquatic and semi-aquatic wildlife make the surrounding rushes and reeds their home. Appetizers include escargot in puff pastry; entrées include grouper *Grenoblaise* (a lightly battered fish fillet with lemon-caper sauce). | 2425 Rocky Point Dr. | 813/281–1943 | No lunch | $18–$28 | AE, D, DC, MC, V.

Shula's Steak House. Steak. Owned by former Miami Dolphins coach Don Shula, this place is popular with football fans and football widows alike. The restaurant is in the elegant, pillared atrium of the Wyndham Westshore Hotel, with a view onto a courtyard with palms and lush ferns. The filet mignon weighs almost a pound, the Porterhouse 48 oz. There's also grilled breast of chicken, Maine lobster, and fresh Florida snapper. | 4860 W. Kennedy Blvd. | 813/286–4366 | No lunch weekends, no supper weekdays | $18–$34 | AE, D, DC, MC, V.

Trattoria Lauro Ristorante Italiano. Italian. Despite the long-winded name, this is a basic, down-to-earth Italian eatery that serves simple, no-frills dishes. The dining area is casual, with large tables and several more intimate booths. The menu includes cannelloni *pulcinella* (pasta stuffed with veal and drizzled with tomato-cream sauce) and breast of chicken sautéed in mustard. | 3915 Henderson Blvd. | 813/281–2100 | No lunch | $17–$23 | AE, D, DC, MC, V.

VERY EXPENSIVE

Armani's. Italian. Both the food and the view are wonderful at this restaurant atop the Hyatt Regency Westshore, overlooking the bay. Low, golden light suffuses the main dining area, which is done in blond wood and black lacquer. Service is efficient and unobtrusive. The ever-changing antipasto bar is almost a feast in and of itself. The restaurant's signature dish is veal Armani (a tender cut of veal topped with mushrooms, cream, and cognac in black and white truffle sauce). | 6200 Courtney Campbell Causeway | 813/281–9165 | Reservations essential | Jacket and tie | Closed Sun. No lunch | $25–$30 | AE, D, DC, MC, V.

★ **Bern's Steak House.** Steak. The dining area of this Florida landmark is a warren of small, intimately draped rooms filled with historical and pop-culture memorabilia. Dinners come with a side of Bern's own organically grown vegetables. The restaurant's 212-page wine list includes some 7,000 selections ranging in price from $10 to $10,000. After dinner, relocate to a private, glass-walled room upstairs for dessert. | 1208 S. Howard Ave. | 813/251–2421 | No lunch | $24–$36 | AE, D, DC, MC, V.

Mise En Place. Contemporary. This comfortable-yet-elegant restaurant turns out such unusual yet wildly successful dishes as shrimp, manchego cheese, and chorizo grits with Puerto Rican red-bean salsa. The menu also includes roast duck and rack of lamb. The owners of the restaurant also operate the ultra-hip jazz club next door. | 442 W. Kennedy Blvd. | 813/254–5373 | Closed Sun. No lunch Sat. | $25–$40 | No reservations for parties of fewer than 6 | AE, D, DC, MC, V.

Lodging

INEXPENSIVE

Amerisuites. This all-suites property has accommodations with large sleeping and sitting areas and mini-kitchens. Busch Gardens and the University of South Florida campus are less than 1 mi away. Picnic area, complimentary Continental breakfast. In-room data ports, microwaves, refrigerators. Cable TV, in-room VCRs (and movies). Pool. Gym. Laundry facilities. Business services, free parking. Pets allowed. | 11408 N. 30th St. | 813/979–1922 or 800/

833–1516 (reservations) | fax 813/979–1926 | www.amerisuites.com | 128 suites | $79–$109 | AE, D, MC, V.

Baymont Inn, Tampa/Busch Gardens. This well-maintained property is 2 mi west of Busch Gardens' main gate. The three-story inn is finished in pale, cream-colored stucco with white trim. The rooms have large windows. Complimentary Continental breakfast. In-room data ports, in-room safes, microwaves, refrigerators. Cable TV. Pool. Business services, free parking. Pets allowed. | 9202 30th St. N | 813/930–6900 or 800/789–4103 (reservations) | fax 813/930–0563 | www.baymontinn.com | 149 rooms | $56–$96 | AE, D, MC, V.

Baymont Inn, Tampa Fairgrounds. This chain motel across from the state fairgrounds has large rooms. It's 7 mi from downtown. Complimentary Continental breakfast. In-room data ports, microwaves, refrigerators. Cable TV. Pool. Business services, free parking. Pets allowed. | 4811 U.S. 301 N | 813/626–0885 or 800/789–4103 (reservations) | fax 813/623–3321 | www.baymontinn.com | 102 rooms | $54–$90 | AE, D, MC, V.

Baymont Inn, Tampa Southeast. This lodging is within 2 mi of a dozen popular chain restaurants. The rooms are large. Complimentary Continental breakfast. In-room data ports, microwaves, refrigerators. Cable TV. Pool. Laundry service. Business services, free parking. Pets allowed. | 602 S. Falkenburg Rd. | 813/684–4007 or 800/789–4103 (reservations) | fax 813/681–3042 | www.baymontinn.com | 102 rooms | $57–$82 | AE, D, MC, V.

Best Western Tampa. This small three-story motel is 2 mi north of MacDill Air Force Base. Complimentary Continental breakfast. Pool. Hot tub. Exercise room. Business services. | 734 S. Dale Mabry | 813/490–2378 | fax 813/490–2380 | www.bestwestern.com | 40 rooms, 5 suites | $95 | AE, DC, MC, V, D.

Best Western Weeki Wachee Resort. This motel is across from the Weeki Wachee Springs and Buccaneer Bay water parks. Rooms in the two-story building have bright, tropical prints, balconies, and floor-to-ceiling windows. The resort can set you up with golf packages at area courses. Local nature paths offer good hiking and biking. Picnic area, complimentary Continental breakfast. Pool, wading pool. Cable TV. Business services, free parking. Some pets allowed. | 6172 Commercial Way, Weeki Wachee | 352/596–2007 | fax 352/596–0667 | www.bestwestern.com | 122 rooms | $65–$78 | AE, D, DC, MC, V.

Comfort Inn. This motel angles around an outdoor pool area. Rooms are done in pale colors, and all have whirlpool baths. There are more than 25 restaurants within 4 mi of the motel, and the Florida Aquarium and Fairgrounds are within 6 mi. Refrigerators. Cable TV. Pool. Business services, free parking. Some pets allowed. | 9373 Cortez Blvd., Weeki Wachee | 352/596–9000 or 800/228–5150 | fax 352/597–4010 | www.comfortinn.com | 68 rooms | $55–$70 | AE, D, MC, V.

Courtyard by Marriott Tampa Brandon. This three-story hotel is in the suburb of Brandon, within 10 mi of Busch Gardens and the Florida State Fairgrounds. Rooms are bright and have sitting areas. Restaurant, bar. Complimentary Continental breakfast. In-room data ports, microwaves, refrigerators. Cable TV. Indoor pool. Exercise equipment. Laundry facilities. Business services, free parking. | 10152 Palm River Rd. | 813/661–9559 or 800/443–6000 (reservations) | fax 813/661–4583 | www.courtyard.com | 83 rooms, 7 suites | $99–$129 | AE, D, MC, V.

Courtyard by Marriott Tampa Westshore. Each bright room has a sitting area in this three-story hotel. It's 10 mi to Busch Gardens. Restaurant, bar. In-room data ports, microwaves, refrigerators. Cable TV, in-room VCRs (and movies). Pool. Exercise equipment. Laundry facilities. Business services, airport shuttle, free parking. | 3805 W. Cypress St. | 813/874–0555 or 800/443–6000 (reservations) | fax 813/870–0685 | www.courtyard.com | 145 rooms | $80–$139 | AE, D, MC, V.

Courtyard by Marriott Tampa North. Rooms have large work spaces and lots of light. The three-story hotel is 5 mi from Busch Gardens and the University Square Mall. Restaurant, bar. In-room data ports, microwaves, refrigerators. Cable TV. Indoor pool. Exercise equipment. Laundry facilities. Business services, free parking. | 13575 Cypress Glen La. | 813/978–

9898 or 800/443–6000 (reservations) | fax 813/978–1835 | www.courtyard.com | 81 rooms | $89–$115 | AE, D, MC, V.

Days Inn Airport Stadium. Raymond James Stadium and the Yankees' spring training facility are within walking distance of this two-story motel. The building wraps around a central courtyard with two pools. The motel has a Hawaiian theme, with a tropical garden and a palms-and-hyacinths motif in the lobby and rooms. Complimentary Continental breakfast. Pools. Cable TV. Laundry facilities. Business services, free parking. Pets allowed. | 2522 N. Dale Mabry Hwy. | 813/877–6181 or 800/448–4373 | fax 813/875–6171 | www.daysinn.com | 285 rooms | $70–$84 | AE, D, MC, V.

Days Inn Rocky Point Island. The lobby of this motel on the bay has a domed atrium and white wicker furniture. Large windows look out onto the grounds in one direction, and onto the bay in the other. Rooms have high ceilings and some have bay views. Restaurant, bar. In-room data ports, in-room safes, microwaves, refrigerators. Cable TV. Pool. Exercise equipment. Beach, dock, water sports, boating, fishing. Laundry facilities. Business services, free parking. | 7627 Courtney Campbell Causeway | 813/281–0000 or 800/237–2555 | fax 813/281–1067 | www.daysinn.com | 144 rooms | $65–$170 | AE, D, MC, V.

Doubletree Guest Suites Tampa/Busch Gardens. This all-suites hotel is housed in a Spanish Mission–style building. The property has landscaped courtyards with fountains and streams. Rooms have large sleeping areas and adjacent parlors with lounge chairs, work desks, and comfortable mini-sofas. Breakfast is served in the main courtyard on sunny mornings. In-room data ports, microwaves, refrigerators. Cable TV, in-room VCRs (and movies). Pool. Hot tub. Exercise equipment. Laundry facilities. Airport shuttle, free parking. | 11310 N. 30th St. | 813/971–7690 | fax 813/972–5525 | www.doubletree.com | 129 suites | $79–$129 | AE, D, MC, V.

Fairfield Inn by Marriott. Rooms have dark wood-veneer furnishings and floral-print bedspreads. The motel is 3 mi from Ybor City, a 15-min drive from Busch Gardens, and within 10 mi of five major golf courses. Complimentary Continental breakfast. In-room data ports, microwaves, refrigerators. Cable TV. Pool. Free parking. | 10150 Palm River Rd. | 813/661–9719 or 800/228–2800 | fax 813/661–0416 | www.fairfieldinn.com | 107 rooms | $59–$99 | AE, D, MC, V.

Gram's Place. Smack in the middle of Tampa, this "Bohemian-eclectic" bed and breakfast looks more like a shady bungalow in the Keys. The decor is inspired by the love of music, from the recording studio in the basement to the themed rooms. The name itself pays homage to singer/songwriter Gram Parsons. The inn is surrounded by dense foliage. The flagstone pool area is shady and walled for quiet and privacy. Each room reflects a distinct musical genre: The Jazz Room has bold colors and is hung with framed concert posters and related instruments. Pool. Hot tub. Cable TV, in-room VCRs. Laundry facilities. Business services, free parking. | 3109 N. Ola Ave. | 813/221–0596 | gramspl@aol.com | 6 rooms | $48–$95 | AE, MC, V.

Hampton Inn and Suites. This four-story hotel occupies a quiet corner of a fast-developing business district. Rooms are basic and uncluttered, with modular furnishings. In-room data ports, microwaves, refrigerators. Cable TV. Pool. Exercise equipment. Laundry service. Business services, free parking. | 8210 Hidden River Pkwy. | 813/903–6000 | fax 813/977–3343 | www.hamptoninn.com | 127 rooms | $75–$95 | AE, D, MC, V.

Hampton Inn Airport, Westshore. A covered drive shades the lobby entrance, and the meticulously maintained grounds surround the outdoor pool and sun deck. Complimentary fresh-baked cookies are served in the lobby every evening. In-room data ports, microwaves, refrigerators. Cable TV. Pool. Laundry facilities. Business services, airport shuttle, free parking. | 4817 W. Laurel St. | 813/287–0778 | fax 813/287–0882 | www.hamptoninn.com | 134 rooms | $83–$93 | AE, D, MC, V.

Holiday Inn Busch Gardens. This hotel's lobby area has Crayola-bright color schemes in the lobby and rooms. Kids' Suites have separate sleeping areas for kids, cordoned off from the main room by screens emblazoned with wildlife images. The minirooms have three-tiered bunkbeds, TVs, and pay-per-play video games. It's next to Busch Gardens and across from Tampa's largest shopping mall. Restaurant. In-room data ports, minibars, microwaves, refrigerators. Cable TV, in-room VCRs (and movies). Pool. Exercise equipment. Laundry facilities. Business services, free parking. Pets allowed. | 2701 E. Fowler Ave. | 813/971–4710 | fax 813/977–0155 | www.holiday-inn.com | 395 rooms | $90–$109 | AE, D, MC, V.

Holiday Inn Express. This motel with sparse-but-neat landscaping is on the waterfront. Rooms are geared toward business travelers and have large work spaces. Some have views of Tampa Bay. Complimentary Continental breakfast. In-room data ports, microwaves, refrigerators. Cable TV. Pool. Gym. Laundry facilities. Business services, free parking. | 3035 N. Rocky Point Dr. | 813/287–8585 | fax 813/287–8484 | www.holiday-inn.com | 83 suites | $77–$87 | AE, D, MC, V.

Holiday Inn Express. The rooms here are basic but pleasant, with modular, wood-veneer furnishings and a muted, mauve-and-teal color scheme. Complimentary Continental breakfast. In-room data ports, microwaves, refrigerators. Cable TV. Pool, wading pool. Laundry facilities. Business services, free parking. Pets allowed. | 100 E. Bears Ave. | 813/961–1000 | fax 813/961–5704 | www.holiday-inn.com | 154 rooms | $80–$100 | AE, D, MC, V.

La Quinta Inn Airport. Mission-style architecture characterizes this motel, with its clay tiles and arches. The airport generates some noise. Rooms are comfortable. In-room data ports, microwaves, refrigerators. Cable TV. Pool. Exercise equipment. Laundry service. Free parking. Pets allowed. | 4730 Spruce St. | 813/287–0440 | fax 813/286–7399 | www.laquinta.com | 122 rooms | $84–$119 | AE, D, MC, V.

La Quinta Inn State Fair. The State Fairgrounds and Expo Park are directly across the highway, and Busch Gardens is about 5 mi away. The rooms have a Southwestern theme with floral bedspreads. In-room data ports, microwaves, refrigerators. Cable TV. Pool. Laundry service. Pets allowed. | 2904 Melbourne Blvd. | 813/623–3591 | fax 813/620–1375 | www.laquinta.com | 128 rooms | $49–$76 | AE, D, MC, V.

La Quinta Inn and Suites USF. This motel sports La Quinta's hallmark Hacienda-style architecture—vanilla stucco, terra-cotta tiles, and palm trees. Rooms are sedate with lots of cream and teal accents in both the sleeping and sitting areas, which are separated by arched doorways. In-room data ports, microwaves, refrigerators. Cable TV. Pool. Exercise equipment. Laundry service. Free parking. Pets allowed. | 3701 E. Fowler Ave. | 813/910–7500 | fax 813/910–7600 | www.laquinta.com | 109 rooms | $99–$109, $129 suites | AE, D, MC, V.

Radisson Hotel at Sabal Park. The facade of this sleek hotel is held aloft by granite pillars accented with neon strips, and the lobby is dominated by a three-story cascading waterfall. Rooms are done in sandy neutrals, with sophisticated, Shaker-style furnishings and tasteful, unobtrusive flower arrangements. Restaurant, bar. In-room data ports, microwaves, refrigerators. Cable TV, in-room VCRs (and movies). Pool. Beauty salon, hot tub. Gym. Laundry facilities. Business services, free parking. | 10221 Princess Palm Ave. | 813/623–6363 or 800/333–3333 (reservations) | fax 813/621–7224 | www.radisson.com | 265 rooms | $105–$116 | AE, D, MC, V.

Sailport Resort. All suites in this sophisticated four-story bay-front hotel have full kitchens. Cable TV, in-room VCRs. Pool. Tennis. Beach. Shop. Laundry facilities. Free parking. | 2506 Rocky Point Dr. | 813/281–9599 or 800/255–9599 | fax 813/281–9510 | www.sailport.com | 214 suites | $100 | AE, D, MC, V.

Shoney's Inn. Rooms are basic at this chain motel. Restaurant, complimentary Continental breakfast. In-room data ports, microwaves, refrigerators. Cable TV. Pool. Laundry facilities. Business services, free parking. | 8602 Morris Bridge Rd. | 813/985–8525 or 800/222–2222 (reservations) | fax 813/988–3552 | www.shoneysinn.com | 122 rooms | $59–$78 | AE, D, MC, V.

Tahitian Inn. This smallish motel bills itself as "the last independently owned and operated motel in the Tampa area." The service is personal and the accommodations are non-generic. The pool area has deck chairs shaded by thatched awnings. Rooms have understated furnishings, track-lighting, and patio/courtyard views via glass sliding doors. The Tahitian is quiet and pleasantly removed from the crowded tourist areas. In-room data ports, refrigerators. Cable TV. Pool. Exercise equipment. Laundry facilities. Business services, free parking. Pets allowed. | 601 S. Dale Mabry Hwy. | 813/877–6721 or 800/876–1397 (reservations) | fax 813/877–6218 | www.tahitianinn.com | 79 rooms | $55–$61 | AE, D, MC, V.

Wildlife on Easy Street. This unique lodging on 40 acres is a nonprofit wildlife sanctuary that is home to 144 large exotic cats. Three cabins are in the middle on a lake and one at the entrance to the sanctuary. All have air-conditioning, indoor plumbing, a private bathroom with shower, and a basic kitchenette with a stove. This place is a cross between a rustic B&B and a couple of shacks in the woods. Residents include lions, tigers, and leopards, as well as caracals, kodkods, and Chinese mountain cats. After a mandatory 2-hr tour and orientation, you may move into one of four rustic cabins adjacent to a "cat-i-tat", or cat habitat, wherein lives one of the preserve's large, tame felines. Though friendly, the cats are not domesticated, and you must be supervised while interacting with them. But you *can* interact with them. Refrigerators. Free parking. No kids under 18 overnight. | 12802 Easy St. | 813/920–4130 | fax 813/920–5924 | www.wildlifeeasyst.com | 4 private cabins | $100 | AE, D, MC, V.

MODERATE

Amerisuites, Tampa Airport. This all-suites hotel is 2 mi from Raymond James Stadium and 5 mi from the Tampa Performing Arts Center, the Florida Aquarium, and the Convention Center. Picnic area, complimentary Continental breakfast. In-room data ports, microwaves, refrigerators. Cable TV, in-room VCRs (and movies). Pool. Gym. Laundry facilities. Business services, airport shuttle, free parking. Pets allowed. | 4811 W. Main St. | 813/282–1037 or 800/833–1516 (reservations) | fax 813/282–1148 | www.amerisuites.com | 126 suites | $129–$189 | AE, D, MC, V.

Crowne Plaza Tampa, Westshore. In the Westshore business district, about 5 mi from downtown Tampa, this hotel caters to business travelers. The lobby has wood trim, expanses of marble, and artfully arranged cut flowers. Rooms are done in understated antique reproductions with deep burgundy carpet and coordinating window treatments. Restaurant, bar. In-room data ports, microwaves, refrigerators. Cable TV, in-room VCRs (and movies). Pool. Hot tub. Exercise equipment. Laundry service. Business services, airport shuttle, free parking. | 700 N. Westshore Blvd. | 813/289–8200 | fax 813/289–9166 | www.crowneplaza.com | 272 rooms | $79–$159 | AE, D, MC, V.

Doubletree Guest Suites Tampa Bay. This all-suites hotel is on Old Tampa Bay 2½ mi from the airport. Each two-room suite has a separate living room and bedroom. The building's V-shape design provides water views from all suites. Restaurant, bar. In-room data ports, minibars, microwaves, refrigerators. Cable TV, in-room VCRs (and movies). Pool. Hot tub, sauna. Exercise equipment. Laundry facilities. Airport shuttle, free parking. | 3050 N. Rocky Point Dr. W | 813/888–8800 | fax 813/888–8743 | www.doubletree.com | 203 suites | $129–$209 | AE, D, MC, V.

Embassy Suites, USF Campus. This all-suites hotel is on the campus of the University of South Florida. Rooms are in a circular configuration around a central, skylit atrium with artificial brooks and fountains. Rooms are upscale but very home-like, with table lamps, separate sitting areas with overstuffed sofas, and live plants. Restaurant, bar, complimentary breakfast. In-room data ports, microwaves, refrigerators. Cable TV. Pool. Exercise equipment. Laundry facilities. Business services, free parking. | 3705 Spectrum Blvd. | 813/977–7066 | fax 813/977–7933 | www.embassysuites.com | 247 suites | $159–$179 | AE, D, MC, V.

Embassy Suites Hotel, Tampa/Airport/Westshore. This white tower looms over the adjacent pool area. Most rooms look out into the multistory atrium, which is full of live plants and fountains. All rooms have dark wood antique reproductions. Restaurant, bar, complimentary full breakfast. In-room data ports, minibars, microwaves, refrigerators. Cable TV, in-room VCRs (and movies). Pool. Hot tub, saunas. Exercise equipment. Laundry facilities. Airport shuttle, free parking. Pets allowed. | 555 N. Westshore Blvd. | 813/875–1555 | fax 813/287–3664 | www.embassysuites.com | 221 rooms | $129–$199 | AE, D, MC, V.

Hilton Garden Inn Tampa/Ybor Historic District. The rooms at this well-manicured, three-story property are comfortable. It's within walking distance of Ybor City restaurants and nightlife. Refrigerators. Cable TV. Pool. Exercise room. Business services, airport shuttle, free parking. | 1700 E. 9th Ave. | 813/769–9267 | fax 813/769–3299 | www.hiltonybor.com | 84 rooms, 11 suites | $149–$189 | AE, D, DC, MC, V.

Holiday Inn City Centre. Stars booked at the Tampa Bay Performing Arts Center stay at this hotel on the Hillsborough River. They occasionally gather around the lobby piano bar. The comfortable rooms are done in mauve with floral prints and have views of the skyline and bay. The lobby has a sunny atrium with polished wood and marble. Restaurant, bar. In-room data ports, microwaves, refrigerators. Cable TV. Pool. Exercise room. Laundry facilities. Business services, airport shuttle, free parking. | 111 W. Fortune St. | 813/223–1351 or 800/513–8940 | fax 813/221–2000 | www.holiday-inn.com | 312 rooms | $93–$160 | AE, DC, MC, V.

Marriott, Tampa Westshore. Tampa's largest indoor/outdoor pool is found at this Marriott. The hotel overlooks the Westshore business district. Rooms are well-lit with floor-to-ceiling windows. Restaurant, bar. In-room data ports, microwaves, refrigerators. Cable TV, in-room VCRs (and movies). Indoor-outdoor pool. Exercise equipment. Laundry service. Business services, airport shuttle, free parking. | 1001 N. Westshore Blvd. | 813/287–2555 | fax 813/289–5464 | www.marriott.com | 310 rooms | $120–$149 | AE, D, MC, V.

Marriott Hotel, Tampa Airport. This eight-story, crescent-shaped hotel is connected to the airport. There's a revolving restaurant on the top floor. Rooms are soundproofed, so jet noise is not a problem. Restaurant, bar. In-room data ports, microwaves, refrigerators. Cable TV, in-room VCRs (and movies). Pool. Exercise equipment. Laundry service. Business services, airport shuttle, free parking. | Tampa International Airport | 813/879–5151 | fax 813/873–0945 | www.marriott.com | 296 rooms | $125–$184 | AE, D, MC, V.

Radisson Bay Harbor Inn. Each of this hotel's rooms has a private balcony with a view of Old Tampa Bay or the city. Restaurant, bar. In-room data ports, microwaves, refrigerators. Cable TV, in-room VCRs (and movies). Pool. Hot tub. Exercise equipment. Laundry facilities. Business services, free parking. | 7700 Courtney Campbell Causeway | 813/281–8900 or 800/333–3333 (reservations) | fax 813/281–0189 | www.radisson.com | 256 rooms | $135–$190 | AE, D, MC, V.

Saddlebrook Resort. This is a good choice for golfers, with the 36-hole course; for those who like to fish, there's a stocked pond. The rooms, done in restfully neutral colors, usually have patios or balconies. Most rates include breakfast at one of the resort's restaurants; some also cover dinner. You can hike, swim, and play games. The helpful staff will (for a fee) arrange most things from transport to recreation. 4 restaurants, 2 bars. In-room data ports, some kitchenettes, minibars. Cable TV. Pool, pond, wading pool. Sauna, spa. Driving range, 2 18-hole golf courses, 45 tennis courts. Health club, fishing, bicycles. Playground. Laundry services. | 5700 Saddlebrook Way, Wesley Chapel | 813/973–1111 or 800/729–8383 | fax 813/773–4504 | www.saddlebrookresort.com | 790 units | $120–$185, per person | AE, DC, MC, V.

Sheraton Tampa Airport. Rooms are done in a clean, understated style with distressed-wood cupboards and armoires, wrought-iron end tables, and soft, diffused lighting. Restaurant, bar. In-room data ports, some kitchenettes, microwaves, refrigerators, room service. Cable TV. Pool. Hot tub, sauna, steam room. Exercise equipment. Laundry facilities. Business services, free parking. | 4400 W. Cypress St. | 813/873–8675 | fax 813/879–7196 | www.sheraton.com | 260 suites | $109–$159 | AE, D, MC, V.

Tampa Hilton Garden Inn Ybor Historic District. This hotel in the heart of the Ybor City Historic District has a sunlit courtyard with plants, trees, pool, and whirlpool. The comfortable rooms have lots of space for families and big work desks for business people. Restaurant, bar. In-room data ports, microwaves, refrigerators. Cable TV. Pool. Hot tub. Tennis. Exercise equipment. Business services, airport shuttle, free parking. | 2225 N. Lois Ave. | 813/877–6688 or 800/916–2221 | fax 813/879–3264 | www.hilton.com | 238 rooms | $174 | AE, D, MC, V.

Wyndham Harbour Island. On the north shore of Harbour Island, a 177-acre development separated from Tampa proper by the Garrison Channel, this huge concrete structure looks out over the bay on one side and across to the city skyline on the other. The lobby is done in toned-down neutrals punctuated with sprays of tropical flowers and ornate Chinese urns. Rooms follow suit, with lots of tans and rich browns. Some have sunset views. Restaurant, bar, complimentary Continental breakfast. In-room data ports, minibars, microwaves, refrigerators. Cable TV. Pool. Exercise equipment. Dock. Children's programs (ages 5–16). Laundry facilities. Business services, airport shuttle, free parking. | 725 S. Harbour Island Blvd. | 813/229–5000 or 800/WYNDHAM (reservations) | fax 813/229–5322 | www.wyndham.com | 300 rooms | $119–$179 | AE, D, MC, V.

EXPENSIVE

Hyatt Regency Tampa. One of Tampa's largest hotels, this Hyatt connects to office and shopping complexes and has a multilevel courtyard with benches, minimalist waterscape-type fountains, and well-tended greenery overhanging every ledge. The lobby has thick Persian carpets. Rooms are done in muted, powdery colors and have views of downtown. Shaker-style pencil-post beds and floor-to-ceiling windows give the rooms an understated, sunny demeanor. Restaurant, bars, room service. In-room data ports, refrigerators. Cable TV, in-room VCRs (and movies). Pool. Hot tub, massage, saunas. Exercise equipment. Laundry facilities. Business services, airport shuttle, free parking. | 2 Tampa City Center | 813/225–1234 or 800/532–1496 (reservations) | fax 813/273–0234 | www.hyatt.com | 518 rooms | $169–$210 | AE, D, MC, V.

Hyatt Regency Westshore. Rooms here are Scandinavian-minimalist with blond wood, pillared sitting areas, huge windows, and a sage-and-sand color scheme. Deluxe suites have chandeliers and separate living areas. The elaborately landscaped hotel on Tampa Bay is surrounded by 35 acres of unspoiled natural vegetation. The building is fronted by a courtyard fountain. 3 restaurants, bar (with entertainment), room service. In-room data ports, minibars, refrigerators. Cable TV, in-room VCRs (and movies). 2 pools. Hot tub, massage. Tennis. Exercise equipment. Dock. Baby-sitting. Business services, airport shuttle, free parking. | 6200 Courtney Campbell Causeway | 813/874–1234 or 800/532–1496 | fax 813/281–9168 | www.hyatt.com | 445 rooms | $204–$240 | AE, D, MC, V.

Wyndham Westshore. This Wyndham hotel is connected to the Tampa Urban Center via two 11-story atriums with fountains, and streams. The lobby is cavernous, with polished black-marble floors and huge pillars. Rooms have muted taupes and mauves. Most have panoramic skyline views. Restaurant, bar (with entertainment), complimentary breakfast, room service. In-room data ports, minibars, refrigerators. Cable TV, in-room VCRs (and movies). Pool. Massage. Exercise equipment. Laundry facilities. Business services, airport shuttle, free parking. | 4860 W. Kennedy Blvd. | 813/286–4400 or 800/WYNDHAM (reservations) | fax 813/286–4053 | www.wyndham.com | 324 rooms | $174–$204 | AE, D, MC, V.

TARPON SPRINGS

MAP 3, H6

(Nearby towns also listed: Dunedin, Clearwater, Indian Rocks Beach, New Port Richey)

The city of Tarpon Springs was born in the 1890s when banker John K. Cheyney began to develop the area. What he discovered in the process was going to alter the face of the village forever: sponges, and lots of them. In no time at all, professional sponge divers arrived from Greece in search of profit, wearing hulking 200-lb dive suits and collecting sponges. The Greek influence is strongly felt here to this day. In fact, Dodecanese Boulevard, named for the original spongers' Greek home, looks quite like a quintessential Greek village with white-washed buildings, cafés and sponge shops. The Epiphany ceremony, an ancient Greek Orthodox rite, is still held every January 6.

Large scale sponging was halted in the 1940s by a fungal outbreak and the introduction of the artificial sponge. It's been revived today, but mainly as a show for tourists.

Information: **Greater Tarpon Springs Chamber of Commerce** | 11 E. Orange St., Tarpon Springs, 34689 | 727/937–6109 | www.tarponsprings.com.

Attractions

Dodecanese Boulevard. Greek bakeries and sponge markets line waterside Dodecanese Boulevard, Tarpon Springs' main thoroughfare. The street is named after the Greek islands from which most of the spongers immigrated. Spongers still bring their wares to the docks on the Anclote River after weeks of sponging on the Gulf. Off U.S. 19. | 727/937–9165 | Daily 10–5.

Fred Howard Park. This beach has lifeguards, picnic shelters, barbecue grills, rest rooms, and clear, inviting Gulf waters. | Sunset Dr. | 7–sunset.

Spongeorama Exhibit Center. This museum/cultural center spotlights the contribution the creature from the phylum *porifera* made in building Tarpon Springs. The gift shop sells a bounty of natural sponges and loofahs. | 510 Dodecanese Blvd. | 727/943–9509 | Free | Mon.–Sat. 10–5, Sun. noon–5.

St. Nicholas Greek Orthodox Cathedral. A replica of St. Sophia's in Istanbul, this magnificent New Byzantine–style cathedral is the most memorable building in Tarpon Spring's downtown historic district. Ornate icons and stained-glass windows line the gold-hued walls, which rise into a huge dome and tower above the resplendent altar. | 36 N. Pinellas Ave. | 727/937–3540 | Free | Mon.–Sat. 10–4.

Sunset Beach. Another welcoming Gulf beach with lifeguards, picnic shelters, barbecue grills, and rest rooms. | Gulf Rd. | 727/942–5610 | Sunrise–10 PM.

Unitarian Universalist Church. Known for his unique use of light and color, Paris-raised George Inness, Jr., spent the latter years of his life in Tarpon Springs painting many works specifically for this church. Among the 11 paintings you can see are the triptych *Promise, Realization, and Fulfillment,* made to cover windows damaged by a hurricane in the 1920s, and *Centurion,* which won the Gold Medal Award from the International Academy of Design in Paris in 1897. | 57 Reed St. | 727/937–4682 | $1 (suggested) | Oct.–May, Tues.–Sun. 2–5.

ON THE CALENDAR

JAN.: *Festival of the Epiphany.* A January 6th Greek Orthodox celebration at the St. Nicholas Cathedral and nearby includes a morning service, a dive for the cross in Spring Bayou, the releasing of a white dove of peace, Greek foods, music, and dancing. | 727/937–3540.

NOV.: *Annual Downtown Tarpon Springs Festival of the Arts.* Head to Court St. for this outdoor showcase of artisans, musicians, and gourmet food. | 727/944–3364.

Dining

Hellas Restaurant and Bakery. Greek. The menu at this casual Greek restaurant includes the Greek combo platter, which comes with *pastitsio* (Greek lasagna), *moussaka* (layers of eggplant, meat sauce and potatoes topped with cheese custard cream sauce), *dolmades* (grape leaves stuffed with ground beef, rice, onions, and Greek herbs and topped with egg-lemon sauce), a *gyro with tzatziki sauce* (beef, lamb, tomatoes, and onions), plus vegetables, rice, Greek potatoes, and fruit. | 785 Dodecanese Blvd. | 727/943–2400 | $8–$14 | AE, D, DC, MC, V.

Louis Pappas' Riverside Restaurant. Mediterranean seafood. This restaurant is on the main waterfront of the Alcote River. The restaurant has views of the shrimp and sponge-diving boats. The Greek salad is a popular item. | 10 W. Dodecanese Blvd. | 727/937–5101 | $8–$29 | AE, MC, V, D.

Martini's. American. Formerly known as Tarpon Avenue Grill, this eclectic restaurant is in an old brick building near the Westin Innisbrook Golf Resort. The specialty of the house is fresh grouper. You can dine outdoors on a wooden deck. | 200 E. Tarpon Ave. | 727/942–3011 | $15–$25 | AE, DC, MC, V.

Lodging

Holiday Inn Hotel and Suites. This hotel has a contemporary exterior, a landscaped pool area, and large rooms all with a balcony. It is 2 mi west of Fred Howard Park and 2 mi from downtown Tarpon Springs. Kids under 12 receive a free meal with a paying adult in the dining room. Suites have full kitchens. Restaurant, bar. Some kitchenettes, some refrigerators. Cable TV. Outdoor heated pool. Hot tub, steam room. Gym. Playground. Free parking. No pets. | 38724 U.S. 19 N | 727/934–5781 | fax 727/934–1755 | www.holiday-inn.com | 79 rooms, 33 suites | $95–$105 | AE, D, DC, MC, V.

Tarpon Shores Inn. Some of the rooms at this family-owned motel have king-size beds. The furnishings are nothing fancy. There's a courtyard pool area. Kids under 12 stay free. It's 3 mi west of Fred Howard Park. Microwaves, refrigerators. Cable TV. Outdoor pool. Hot tub, sauna. Laundry facilities. Business services, free parking. No pets. | 40346 U.S. 19N | 727/938–2483 or 800/633–3802 | fax 727/938–2486 | www.tarponshoresinn.com | 51 rooms | $60–$70 | AE, DC, MC, V.

DIVING FOR SPONGES

The sponge may not have pizzazz—or like its local underwater mate, the devil ray, a pro baseball team named after it—but it remains a major player in the Tampa area ecosystem. In fact, the town of Tarpon Springs, 10 mi northwest of Tampa, owes its success to the humble sponge.

Sponge diving predates the birth of Christ, and for the past millennium or so, most spongers have been Greek Orthodox males. Greeks initially partook in the practice as an homage to the god Poseidon, and it is not uncommon for modern-day divers' boats to carry a small shrine to St. Nicholas, the patron saint of mariners.

In Florida, gathering sponges was first undertaken in the Keys during the mid-1800s and gained momentum in the Tampa area 50 years later. The implementation of Florida's first mechanical diving apparatus (which enabled divers to remain submerged for a couple hours at a time) served as a tremendous boon to the industry and soon led to the discovery of the Rock Island wool sponge, a profitable variety named after its abundant source and its semblance to delicate wool.

Serendipitous as it was, the discovery led to a westward emigration of Greek sponge-diving families, and within a few years, Tarpon Springs was the home to a population of several thousand Greeks. Over time, the town's charm has proved to lie more in its Hellenic culture than its sponging industry, and now Tarpon Springs boasts a lovely tourist district filled with Greek restaurants, Greek pastry shops, and Greek art galleries.

For the record, sponges actually consist of only one cell; the form which divers retrieve is in fact a colony of the organisms clumped together to form a soft, airy mass. When you scrub your dishes or reach for something to lather up with in the shower, you are holding a veritable colony of the creatures.

© Corbis

★ **Westin Innisbrook Resort.** Guest suites at this 600-acre resort are in 28 two-story lodges tucked in the trees between golf courses. All units are roomy, and all have kitchens; some have balconies or patios as well. A massive new pool and water-slide complex helps make what was once considered a corporate-meeting-and-golf retreat more family friendly. Grounds are beautifully maintained. 6 restaurants, 5 bars, room service. In-room data ports, kitchenettes, microwaves, refrigerators. Cable TV. 6 outdoor swimming pools, lake. Massage. 4 18-hole golf courses, 11 tennis courts. Health club, racquetball. Fishing, bicycles. Shops, video games. Baby-sitting, children's program (ages 4–12). Laundry service. Business services. | 36750 Hwy. 19N | 727/942–2000 or 800/456–2000 | fax 727/942–5576 | www.westin-innisbrook.com | 1,000 rooms | $160–$400 | AE, D, DC, MC, V.

TAVARES

MAP 3, I5

(Nearby towns also listed: Altamonte Springs, Leesburg, Orlando)

The city of Tavares was founded in 1880 by Major St. Clair Abrams. Though his hope that the town would become the state capital was not realized, it did become the county seat. Tavares, which means "hub" in Portuguese is an apt name, for Tavares sits at the heart of Lake County. Mainly a residential community, the town also has excellent camping and fishing, the main recreational pastimes of the city's 8,000 residents. Its proximity to Ocala National Forest makes it a nice place to stock up before, or relax in, after a few days in the woods.

Information: **Tavares Chamber of Commerce** | 912 Sinclair Ave., Box 697, Tavares, 32778 | 352/343–2531.

Attractions
Lake Dora. Boat launching, docking, and fishing are available on the city-owned public pier, which juts into Lake Dora. It's at the south end of St. Clair Abrams Ave. | Municipal pier | Free | Daily.

ON THE CALENDAR
DEC.–JAN.: *Lights of Lake Festival.* An illuminating trail of more than 3 million decorative lights are hung in Tavares and several surrounding towns during the Christmas season. | 800/798–1071.

Lodging
Inn on the Green. This motel has a man-made lake behind the property and a 3-hole chipping and putting green. The rooms are done in earth tones and have king-size beds and walk-in closets. Some have lake views. Picnic area. Microwaves, refrigerators. Cable TV, in-room VCRs (and movies). Volleyball. Laundry facilities. Pets allowed. | 700 E. Burleigh Blvd. | 352/343–6373 or 800/935–2935 | fax 352/343–7216 | www.innonthegreen.net | 77 rooms, 4 suites | $79 | AE, D, DC, MC, V.

TITUSVILLE

MAP 3, K5

(Nearby towns also listed: Cocoa, Cocoa Beach, Sanford)

Titusville is the gateway to the Kennedy Space Center, earning the city of 40,000 the nickname "Space City USA." Cape Canaveral, on which the space center is situated, is directly across the Indian River from the town that's also known for its citrus and seafood. Also on the cape are the 140,000-acre Merritt Island National Wildlife Refuge, home to 16 species of endangered or threatened mammals including the Florida manatee, and the Canaveral National Seashore with its 24 mi of beach. The town is named after Confederate Col. Henry Theodore Titus who in 1873 won a dominoes match for the right to name the town, which had been known as Sand Point. He built a hotel, donated land for the first courthouse, and laid out many of the town's streets.

Information: **Titusville Chamber of Commerce** | 2000 S. Washington Ave., Titusville, 32781 | 321/267–3036 | www.titusville.org.

Attractions

★ **Kennedy Space Center Visitor Complex.** This 140,000-acre megaplex built along the pristine shores of the Atlantic Ocean might be the best entertainment value in Florida. Although only 6,000 acres are used for space operations—the rest is a wildlife sanctuary—it takes at least six hours to see the three main attractions: the Visitor Center exhibits, the IMAX movies, and a bus tour. Begin your visit at the United States Astronaut Hall of Fame, which recounts the milestones and personal stories of the astronauts. It includes a replica of the shuttle *Explorer,* the Astronaut Encounter, and the Rocket Garden, with its collection of authentic rockets. Then head into one of the extraordinary IMAX movies that will make you think you're at an actual shuttle launch. The most popular, *The Dream is Alive,* is shown hourly on a 5½-story-high screen in the Galaxy Theater; it takes you from astronaut training, through a thundering launch, and into the cabins where the astronauts live while they're in space. You can buy an access badge at the Visitor Complex and take an official bus tour of restricted areas. The narrated, three-hour tour visits the Launch Complex 39 Observation Gantry, which has unprecedented views of the twin space shuttle launch pads; the Apollo/Saturn V Center, which has multimedia shows, hands-on displays, and the 6.2 million-lb Saturn V rocket; and the Space Station Center, where you can see recreated space station modules. From Route 528, follow the well-marked signs to Route 417 until it becomes Route 405. | NASA Parkway (Rte. 405) | 321/452–2121 | fax 321/452–3043 | www.kennedyspacecenter.com | $24 (includes IMAX movies) | Daily 9–6:30.

Cape Canaveral: Then and Now Tour. For an additional fee at the Visitor Complex entrance, you can add the Cape Canaveral: Then and Now Tour to your visit. This tour takes you to Cape Canaveral Air Force Station, where early models of unmanned rockets and launch pads illuminate the history of the space program. The tour includes visits to the old Apollo, Mercury, and Gemini launch pads, where Alan Shepard and John Glenn began America's space age, and to the Cape Canaveral Lighthouse. | $44 (includes regular admission) | Daily 9–6:30.

Merritt Island National Wildlife Refuge. This 140,000-acre preserve, including the Kennedy Space Center and adjoining the Canaveral National Seashore, gives you an opportunity to see migratory waterfowl, manatees, and other wildlife among the salty estuaries and dense marshes. In addition to the ¼-mi trail at the visitors center, three other trails are offered: Oak Hammock Trail (½ mi), Palm Hammock Trail (3 mi), and Cruickshank Trail (5 mi). Or take a self-guided, 7-mi driving tour along the Black Point Wildlife Drive. The Cruickshank Tower at Stop 8 has a view of the surrounding marshes from a 10-ft tower. It's possible to combine a tour of Kennedy Space Center with a guided tour of the wildlife refuge for a fee in addition to the regular Space Center admission, which is purchased at the Kennedy Space Center. | Rte. 402, across Titusville Causeway 4 mi east of Titusville | 321/861–0667 | www.nbbd.com/godo/minwr | Free; guided tour combined with Kennedy Space Center admission $44 | Daily 9–6:30; Closed Sun. Apr.–Oct.

United States Astronaut Hall of Fame. At the north entrance to Kennedy Space Center, this attraction lets you lose your breath from the 3-G pull of a mock G-force trainer, or experience the Astronaut Adventure, which includes a simulated liftoff, a hair-raising simulated jet aircraft dogfight complete with 360° barrel rolls, then carefully guide the space shuttle to a smooth landing. Exhibits include videotapes of historic moments in the space program such as the crew selection for Apollo 11 and the Soviet Union's role in the space race. This is also home to U.S. Space Camp, which gives young people a hands-on learning environment that budding astronauts will love. I–95 exit 79. East on U.S. 50 to Route 405. Follow Route 405 past U.S. 1. | 6225 Vectorspace Blvd. | 321/269–6100 | www.astronauts.org | $13.95 | Daily 9–5.

ON THE CALENDAR

MAR.: *Valiant Air Command Air Show.* Restored military aircraft and high-tech jets, including vintage C-47s and sophisticated 400 mph F-86 Saber jets, are the draw at this Space Center Regional Airport event, next to the Kennedy Space Center. There are also exhibits, simulated dogfights, and skydiving. | 321/268–1941.

APR.: *Indian River Festival.* This weekend event at Sand Point Park includes an arts-and-crafts show, car shows, a petting farm, pig races, helicopter rides, a fishing contest, and live entertainment. | 10 E. Max Brewer Causeway | 321/267–3036.

Dining

Dixie Crossroads. Seafood. Owned and operated by a native fisherman, this popular spot is nestled under spreading old live oak trees and is constructed in the old Florida Cracker tradition with tin roof, wood siding, and Bahamas-style shutters. The outer entrance has two large open-air gazebos joined by a bridge over two fish ponds filled with Japanese koi and other tropical fish and turtles. Across the parking lot is a large garden area with three more fish ponds. On the inside, six dining rooms display artwork from various local artists. The interior walls are covered with a 150-ft mural depicting the variety of ecosystems and seashore recreational activities found in the Titusville area. A glass bubble wall

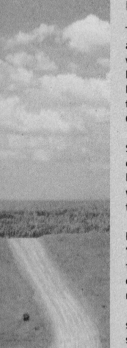

© Corbis

FROM MARSH TO THE MOON

The Merritt Island Wildlife Refuge was a quiet area speckled with orange groves and stocked with wild pigs, bobcats, and alligators in the 1950s. In 1961, the calm was throttled by the roar of massive engines when the Kennedy Space Center, home to NASA, was constructed. The site was chosen both for its climate and the low population of east-central Florida. Tourists began to visit this coast for the first time because of the space center, and it is now a popular stopover for visitors to Orlando theme parks, and a major destination in its own right.

The years after the center's construction saw the Cold War intensified by Russia's Sputnik launch. American Mercury astronauts John Glenn and Scott Carpenter quickly certified the feasibility of manned space travel, and NASA's objective to reach the moon became solidified. Their first challenge—deployment of massive Saturn V rockets—was met with the Vehicle Assembly Building. This structure, three times the height of the Statue of Liberty, was so large personnel reported lightning occurring on its inside.

After Kennedy's 1963 assassination, authorities renamed the Space Center to honor the president, but efforts to rename the bordering city of Cape Canaveral "Cape Kennedy" failed in heavily Republican Florida. NASA troubles increased in 1967 when three astronauts died during a launch pad fire. Vindication came, however, when Apollo 11 landed on the moon on July 20, 1969. Fourteen astronauts returned to the moon between 1969 and 1973.

Despite the deaths of seven astronauts in the Challenger explosion in 1986, the space shuttle program, begun in 1979, has been a success, weathering Congressional debate on NASA funding. Preparations are underway for the launch of final pieces of the International Space Station in 2004 or 2005.

The portions of the Kennedy Space Center open to the public are funded solely by visitor entry fees, and a recently completed 5-yr, $130-million overhaul has assured its continuing popularity.

includes a large replica of the Cape Canaveral lighthouse and a coral reef scene. The lines outside on the weekend are for the rock shrimp. Also available are char-crust steak, prime rib, chicken, crab legs, and lobster. Live entertainment. I–95 exit 80, 2 mi east. | 1475 Garden St. | 321/268–5000 | Reservations not accepted | $9–$28 | AE, D, DC, MC, V.

Paul's Smokehouse Restaurant. Steak. For an alternative to all of the fresh seafood in the area, head to this casual restaurant on the Indian River that specializes in steak. It's a good spot to view a shuttle launch. The menu includes prime rib, beef burgundy, and New York strip. Seafood dishes such as rock shrimp and scallops are available as well. | 3665 S. Washington Ave. | 321/267–3663 | Reservations not accepted | Closed Mon. | $11–$17 | AE, D, DC, MC V.

Renaissance Grill. Steak. This restaurant in downtown Titusville has brick walls with Renaissance art reproductions and period mirrors. The menu includes Jamaican rum–glazed mahimahi served with fried plantains and pineapple mango salsa, and the duck *à la Chambord* (a crispy roasted duck half with a Chambord blackberry sauce). Pasta Michelangelo is grilled chicken strips and broccoli served over penne pasta with a blue-cheese and bacon sauce. | 336 S. Washington Ave. | 321/385–0730 | Closed Sun. No lunch Sat.; No dinner Mon.–Tues. | $14–$20 | AE, D, DC, MC V.

Steamers Riverside. Seafood. Popular with boaters, this rustic restaurant on the waterfront has a view of the hundreds of boats at the Titusville marina and the Indian River. The walls are covered with fish hooks and sea murals. Chowders, rock shrimp, scallops, and mahimahi are the specialties. | 801 Marina Rd. | 321/269–1012 | $9–$19 | AE, MC, V.

Lodging

Best Western Space Shuttle Inn. This two-story motel is on the Indian River. The pool has a large screened porch adjacent to the pool area. There's also a picnic/barbecue area and a fishing dock. Rooms have king-size or two double beds, light wood furnishings, a lounge chair, and a balcony. Evergreen Rooms are odor- and allergen-free and have purified water. I–95 exit 79. Restaurant, bar, complimentary Continental breakfast. Picnic area. In-room data ports, microwaves, refrigerators. Cable TV. Pool. Sauna. Basketball, exercise equipment, volleyball. Fishing. Playground. Laundry facilities, laundry service. Children's programs (up to age 12). Business services. Pets allowed. | 3455 Cheney Hwy. | 321/269–9100 | fax 321/383–4674 | www.spaceshuttleinn.com | 125 rooms | $59–$99 | AE, D, MC, V.

Days Inn, Kennedy Space Center. Rooms are done in yellow, green, and pink with floral bedding and have queen- or king-size beds and a sitting area. The two-story motel sits on the Indian River. Restaurant, bar. Microwaves, refrigerators. Cable TV. Pool, wading pool. Hot tub. Laundry facilities. Pets allowed. | 3755 Cheney Hwy. | 321/269–4480 | fax 321/383–0646 | www.daysinn.com | 150 rooms | $54–$69 | AE, D, MC, V.

Holiday Inn, Kennedy Space Center. The Titusville outpost of this chain overlooks the Kennedy Space Center launch pads from across the Indian River. Rooms in the two-story hotel are comfortable with balconies overlooking the river or pool. Restaurant, bar (with entertainment), room service. In-room data ports, refrigerators. Cable TV. Pool. Gym, volleyball. Beach, fishing. Laundry facilities. Business services. Pets allowed. | 4951 S. Washington Ave. | 407/269–2121 or 800–HOLIDAY | fax 407/267–4739 | www.holiday-inn.com | 118 rooms | $69–$129 | AE, D, MC, V.

Indian River B&B. This two-story motel-style B&B on the Indian River has an Olympic-size pool surrounded by a tropically landscaped courtyard. There's also a well-stocked library and a Florida room with a large screen TV. A light breakfast and afternoon tea are served in the Florida room daily. Rooms are done in pastel colors. Each has a king-size or two double beds. Some adjoining rooms are also available. I–95 exit 79. Route 50 2½ mi east to U.S. 1/Washington Ave., then north 1 mi. Restaurant, bar, complimentary breakfast. Cable TV. Pool. Library. Laundry facilities. Business services. | 3810 S. Washington Ave. | 321/269–5945 or 888/420–3044 | fax 321/269–1054 | 105 rooms | $54–$59 | AE, D, MC, V.

Ramada Inn, Kennedy Space Center. The lobby of this two-story peach stucco motel is bright with a tropical theme. Rooms have a king-size or two double beds and a sitting area with large windows. I–95 exit 79. Restaurant, bar, room service. In-room data ports. Cable TV.

Pool. Hot tub, sauna. Exercise equipment. Video games. Playground. Laundry facilities. Business services. | 3500 Cheney Hwy. | 321/269–5510 or 800/292–1192 | fax 321/269–3796 | www.ramada.com | 96 rooms, 28 suites | $89–$146, $110–$170 suites | AE, D, MC, V.

Riverside Inn. This motel with views of the Indian River is nothing fancy, but has a small pool area with lounge chairs and sparse tropical landscaping. Rooms, which are small and show some wear, have wood furnishings and dark hues of maroons and blues. I–95 exit 80. Restaurant, bar. Microwaves, refrigerators. Cable TV, in-room VCRs (and movies). Pool. Exercise equipment. Dock. Laundry facilities. Business services. Pets allowed. | 1829 Riverside Dr. | 321/267–7900 | fax 321/267–7080 | 119 rooms | $45–$79 | AE, D, MC, V.

Royal Oak Resort and Golf Club. This busy country club has an 18-hole course, a lodge, and a clubhouse with a large dining room, lounge, snack bar, and golf shop. The lodge, a two-story structure adjacent to the clubhouse, has rooms that overlook either the Olympic-size pool and tropical courtyard, or the ninth fairway and green. Restaurant, bar. Refrigerators. Cable TV. Pool. Golf. Laundry facilities. Business services. | 2150 Country Club Dr. | 321/269–4500 or 800/884–2150 | fax 321/383–9666 | 40 rooms | $40–$80 | AE, D, MC, V.

TREASURE ISLAND

MAP 7, B5

(Nearby towns also listed: Indian Rocks Beach, Madeira Beach, Redington Beach, St. Petersburg, St. Pete Beach)

Treasure Island, with a resident population of nearly 7,500, is made up of five separate barrier islands north of the larger St. Pete Beach. Its 4 mi of beaches have been nicknamed "Jewel of the Beaches." Tourists find plenty of things to do, including excellent fishing and boating to an annual kite-flying competition, and a week-long Pirate Days fair.

Information: **Gulf Beaches of Tampa Bay Chamber of Commerce** | 152 108th Ave., Treasure Island, 33706 | 800/944–1847 or 727/367–4529 | www.gulfbeaches-tampabay.com.

Attractions
St. Petersburg Municipal Beach. This Treasure Island public beach has dressing rooms, metered parking, and a snack bar. | 11260 Gulf Blvd. | Free.

ON THE CALENDAR
SEPT.: *Taste of the Beaches.* This annual weekend event, which draws local restaurants and musicians, is held on the beach at Treasure Island, about 6 mi from downtown. Headline bands perform weekend nights, and the whole event attracts over 70,000 people. Call to confirm specific dates. | 727/360–6957.

Dining
Beach Nutts Bar & Grill. American/Seafood. Sunset views are available at this casual restaurant on the water. There is live classic rock music every night. The speciality of the house is blackened grouper nuggets on a bed of long grain wild rice with Caesar salad and sautéed veggies. | 9600 W. Gulf Blvd. | 727/367–7427 | fax 727/360–7894 | $6–$12 | MC, V.

Lodging
Bilmar Beach Resort. This three-building resort sits on 550 ft of Gulf Beach. It has a beachfront bar with live entertainment. The rooms are bright and have views of the beach. Restaurant, bar. Pool. | 10650 Gulf Blvd. | 727/360–5531 | fax 727/360–2362 | www.gotampabay.com/bilmar | 172 rooms | $128–148 | AE, D, MC, V.

Holiday Inn-Treasure Island Beach. Each room at this nine-story beach hotel has a balcony with a view of the beach. There's a rooftop restaurant where children under 12 eat free and a tiki bar and grill near the outdoor heated pool. It's 1 mi north of Central Avenue.

In-room data ports. Hot tub. Gym. | 11908 Gulf Blvd. | 727/367–2761 | fax 727/367–9446 | www.holiday-inn.com | 117 rooms | $159 | AE, D, DC, MC, V.

The Sea Chest. This sprawling resort-like motel has apartments, studios, and guest rooms with contemporary furnishings. It's 10 mi west of I–275. Refrigerators, some kitchenettes. Cable TV. Pool. Laundry service. No pets. | 11780 Gulf Blvd. | 727/360–5501 | fax 727/360–8453 | www.gotampabay.com/seachest | 22 rooms | $82–$119 | AE, MC, V.

Shifting Sands Vacation Cottages. The units at this small property on the Gulf of Mexico are well maintained and roomy. A sundeck is right outside your door. There is a 3-day minimum stay. Pool. | 10232 Gulf Blvd. | 727/360–7777 | fax 727/367–7945 | www.beachdirectory.com/shiftingsands | 7 units | $65–$90 | DC, MC, V.

VENICE

(Nearby towns also listed: Englewood, Port Charlotte, Punta Gorda, Sarasota, Siesta Key)

This small city of 19,000 on the Gulf of Mexico between Sarasota and Fort Myers is crisscrossed with more canals than its namesake. You'll also see quickly that there are other similarities with Italy's famous tourist center, including an Italian Renaissance architectural style for most of the historic downtown buildings. Unusual for the west coast of Florida, Venice is not separated from the Gulf by a barrier island, but the city's commercial area is still on an island, created when the Intracoastal Waterway was cut through the area in 1963.

The town started out as a planned retirement community in 1916, designed by well-known planner John Nolen. Its name was chosen by settler Frank Higel, who felt the area reminded him of the original Venice, which is at the same latitude.

One of the favorite pastimes of residents and visitors alike is shark-tooth hunting. With mesh baskets attached to poles, they ply the beach hoping to find teeth or fossils that wash up, as they often do from ancient shark burial grounds just offshore. But traditional shell collectors also will not be disappointed, as the beaches are almost as rich in shells as those of Sanibel and Captiva islands to the south.

Information: **Venice Chamber of Commerce** | 257 N. Tamiami Trail (U.S. 41), Venice, 34285 | 941/488–2236 | www.venicechamber.com.

Attractions

Caspersen Beach. Sarasota County's largest park has a nature trail, fishing, picnicking, rest rooms, and lots of beach for those who prefer space to a wealth of amenities. It's known as a place for great shelling; the persistent may find shark teeth. | Harbor Dr., South Venice.

Nokomis Beach. This is the oldest beach in Sarasota County. Just north of North Jetty Park, it has year-round lifeguards, rest rooms, a concession stand, picnic equipment, play areas, two boat ramps, a volleyball court, and fishing. | Albee Rd., Casey Key.

Oscar Scherer State Recreation Area. Bald eagles, bobcats, river otters, and alligators are often seen in this 1,384-acre park on the Myakka River, which also has a small population of Florida scrub jays, an endangered species. There's swimming, fishing, canoeing, and camping. It's about 5 mi from Venice and 6 mi south of Sarasota, in Osprey. I–75 Exit 35-A northbound, Exit 36 southbound. | U.S. 41 | 941/483–5956 | $3.25 per vehicle | Daily.

Warm Mineral Springs. This resort and spa 7 mi southeast of Venice in North Port is the site of natural warm springs whose temperature is a relaxing 87°F. The resort has developed around the springs, but there are still public springs available for lollygagging. I–75 Exit 34. | 941/426–1692 | Daily.

ON THE CALENDAR

AUG.: *Sharks Tooth and Seafood Festival.* You can sink your own teeth into seafood at this festival built around a local beach find. There are displays of prehistoric shark teeth, arts and crafts, entertainment by local bands, and kids events. | 941/412–0402.

OCT.: *Venetian Sun Fiesta.* This festival draws a huge crowd. There's a parade, an antique car show, more than 100 crafts booths, food stands, games, and entertainment. | 941/429–4939.

Dining

The Crow's Nest. Seafood. The specialty of this restaurant on the water is the fresh grouper Key Largo with sautéed shrimp, scallops, mushrooms, and lobster in a hollandaise sauce. The bi-level restaurant has large windows and an open air deck for watching the sunset over the Gulf of Mexico. No smoking. Bar. | 1968 Tarpon Center Dr. | 941/484–9551 | $11–$24 | AE, DC, MC, V.

Purple's. American. This offbeat restaurant is housed in a hard-to-miss bright purple building with a rather chaotic, art deco–inspired decor. The menu varies considerably, with Virginia ham, steak au poivre, and veal with peppers, mushrooms, and a sauce of veal broth, lemon, garlic, and wine. Top your dinner off with a slab of death by chocolate. | 385 N. Tamiami Trail (U.S. 41) | 941/485–6277 | No lunch weekends | $8–$20 | AE, D, MC, V.

Sharky's. Seafood. This is the only restaurant in the area directly on the Gulf of Mexico. You can dine outdoors facing the beach. The catch-of-the-day menu includes grouper, mahimahi, and salmon. | 1600 S. Harbor Dr. | 941/488–1456 | $8–$28 | AE, DC, MC, V.

Lodging

Best Western Sandbar Beach Resort. This is the only hotel in Venice on the beach. Rooms are white with gray carpet and tropical patterns. Some rooms face the gulf. It's 6 mi west of I–75. Some kitchenettes, microwaves. Cable TV. Pool. Volleyball. Beach. Laundry facilities. Business services. | 811 The Esplanade North | 941/488–2251 or 800/822–4853 | fax 941/485–2894 | www.sandbarbeachresort.com | 44 rooms | $169–$239, $349–$399 suite | AE, D, DC, MC, V.

Days Inn. This motel is less than 3 mi from Venice Beach and 2 mi from I–75. Rooms are basic motel. Restaurant. Microwaves, refrigerators. Cable TV. Pool. Laundry service. Business services. Pets allowed. | 1710 S. Tamiami Trail | 941/493–4558 or 800/DAYS–INN | fax 941/493–1593 | info@daysinnvenice.com | 72 rooms | $56–$99 | AE, D, MC, V.

Hampton Inn and Suites. Rooms have king-size, queen-size, or two double beds and contemporary furnishings. Suites have living rooms and separate bedrooms. I–75 exits 35, 36. In-room data ports, microwaves, refrigerators. Cable TV, in-room VCRs (and movies). Complimentary Continental breakfast. Pool. Exercise equipment. Laundry facilities. Business services. | 881 Venetia Bay Blvd. | 941/488–5900 or 888/945–9161 | fax 941/488–6746 | www.hisvf.com | 76 rooms, 34 suites | $99–$119, $159 suites | AE, D, MC, V.

Holiday Inn Venice. Rooms at the Venice outpost of this chain are beige with floral patterns. Each has a king-size or two double beds. This hotel is built around a courtyard. In-room data ports, microwaves, refrigerators. Cable TV. Pool. Hot tub. Gym. Laundry facilities. Business services. | 455 U.S. 41 Bypass N | 941/485–5411 or 800/237–3712 | fax 941/484–6193 | www.holiday-inn.com/venicefl | 160 rooms in 4 buildings | $109–$139 | AE, D, MC, V.

Inn at the Beach. Across from the beach, this resort is popular with families. The suites have gulf views, and the rooms face the palm trees on Venice Avenue. There is a courtyard and a garden. It's 3½ mi east of I–75. Pool. | 725 W. Venice Ave. | 941/484–8471 or 800/255–8471 | fax 941/484–0593 | www.inn-at-the-beach.com | 35 rooms, 14 suites | $166–$188 | AE, D, DC, MC, V.

VERO BEACH

(Nearby towns also listed: Fort Pierce, Jensen Beach, Port St. Lucie, Sebastian, Stuart)

Vero Beach in Indian River County, is considered one of the crown jewels of Florida's Treasure Coast. The town retains a tranquil sense of ease, well in alignment with the artsy and ecologically minded residents. Though the population doubles in winter with northern vacationers, it still has an exclusive feel. The downtown is undergoing a thorough restoration, as homes built in the 1920s are polished to their former luster. The downtown, in fact, has been named a Florida Main Street Community.

Information: **Indian River County Chamber of Commerce** | 1216 21st St., Vero Beach, 32960 | 561/567–3491 | www.vero-beach.fl.us/chamber.

Attractions

Center for the Arts. In Riverside Park's Civic Arts Center, this site hosts a full schedule of exhibitions, art movies, lectures, workshops, and other events, with a focus on Florida artists. | 3001 Riverside Park Dr. | 561/231–0707 | Free | Fri.–Wed. 10–4:30, Thurs. 10–8.

Environmental Learning Center. This 51-acre preserve displays aquariums filled with Indian River Lagoon life, and a 600-ft boardwalk takes you through the mangrove area along the shore. You can also canoe through mangroves along a 1-mi trail. | 255 Live Oak Dr. | 561/589–5050 | Free | Apr.–Jan., Tues.–Fri. 10–4, Sat. 9–noon, Sun. 1–4; Feb–Mar., Tues.– Fri. 10–4, Sat. 9–4, Sun. 1–4.

Humiston Park. This is just one of many beach-access parks along the east edge of town with boardwalks. It also has a large children's play area and picnic tables. | Ocean Dr. below Beachland Blvd. | Free | Daily 7–10.

Indian River Citrus Museum. The museum re-creates a time when family fruit stands dotted the Florida roadsides and colorful packing labels enticed Northerners to visit Florida. A video takes visitors back in time to the pre-industrial farming era and displays of photos and farm tools resonates its existence. You can also book tours of nearby citrus groves. | 2140 14th Ave. | 561/770–2263 | Donations accepted | Tues.–Sat. 10–4, Sun. 1–4.

Riverside Children's Theatre. This venue hosts a series of local and professional touring productions, as well as acting workshops at the Agnes Wahlstrom Youth Playhouse. Shows are usually weekends at 1:30. | 3280 Riverside Park Dr. | 561/234–8052 | $6–$10 | Call for exact showtimes.

ON THE CALENDAR

FEB.–MAR.: *Baseball Spring Training.* The Los Angeles Dodgers are fixtures at Holman Stadium, known as Dodgertown; they've been here since 1948, when Bud Holman invited them to train at a converted Vero Beach naval air station. The stadium is old, so the dugout is not enclosed or underground allowing the players to interact with the visitors before and after practice. | 4000 126th St. | 561/569–4900.
OCT.: *Fall Fest.* This annual Chamber of Commerce event includes arts and crafts, music, kids activities, a car show, and food stands. | 561/567–3491.

Dining

Beachside. American. Specialities at this restaurant near the beach include home-cooked meals such as chicken pot pie, turkey, meat loaf, lasagna, and fresh seafood. | 3125 Ocean Dr. | 561/234–4477 | No dinner | $5–$7 | AE, D, DC, MC, V.

Black Pearl. Continental. This restaurant serves many original dishes, including the kitchen's signature onion-crusted mahimahi with caramel-citrus glaze. | 2855 Ocean Dr. | 561/234– 4426 | No lunch weekends | $13–$23 | AE, D, DC, MC, V.

Café Du Soir. French. This French country restaurant's signature dishes include rack of lamb, Dover sole, and fresh snapper. It's on the Indian River and has a garden patio. | 21 Royal Palm Point | 561/569–4607 | Reservations required | No lunch | $18–$28 | AE, D, MC, V.

Chez Yannick. French. There are three rooms (the Piano Room, the Fireplace Room, and the Chandelier Room) at this upscale restaurant. Diners are wowed by a crystal chandelier the size of a Volkswagen that hangs in the main dining room. This large establishment also has a rooftop terrace. The Dover sole is popular. | 1605 S. Ocean Dr. | 561/234–4115 | Reservations required | Closed Sun. No lunch | $16–$29 | AE, MC, V.

★ **Ocean Grill.** Seafood. Driftwood paneling, Tiffany lamps, and chandeliers give this restaurant on the ocean a rustic and elegant feel. Popular dishes include the crab au gratin and the seafood casserole. | 1050 Sexton Plaza | 561/231–5409 | No lunch weekends; closed for 10 days after Labor Day | $15–$27 | AE, D, DC, MC, V.

Pearl's Bistro. Jamaican. Come for island-style cuisine at this more laid-back and less expensive sister restaurant to the Black Pearl. For starters, try the pasta Rasta, the seafood chowder, or the Jamaican jerk shrimp. Then move on to grilled Yucatan-spiced local fish, barbecued ribs, Bahamian shrimp, and grouper pepper pot. | 56 Royal Palm Blvd. | 561/778–2950 | No lunch | $12–$20 | AE, MC, V.

Tangos. American. This upbeat, casual restaurant near the beach has two outside dining patios. Signature dishes include lobster quesadillas with pineapple and papaya salad, and roasted barbecue pork tenderloin with country-style grits and Jack Daniels sauce. There is live entertainment on the weekends and an open kitchen. | 925 Bougainvillea La. | 561/231–1550 | Closed Sun. No lunch | $18–$28 | AE, D, DC, MC, V.

Lodging

Aquarius Oceanfront Resort Motel. This motel on South Beach has a sun deck in front with tiki huts and a barbecue grill that overlooks the ocean. It's 8 mi east of I–95. Picnic area. Kitchenettes, refrigerators. Cable TV. Outdoor heated pool. Laundry facilities. | 1526 S. Ocean Dr. | 561/231–5218 | 27 rooms | $95–$140 | AE, D, DC, MC, V.

Best Western Vero Beach. This motel is ¼-mi from I–95 and 10 mi from the beach. Cable TV. Pool. Laundry service. Business services. | 8797 20th St. | 561/567–8321 | fax 561/569–8558 | www.bestwestern.com | 114 rooms | $59–$79 | AE, D, DC, MC, V.

Disney's Vero Beach Resort. This Disney resort, 12 mi from Dodgertown, has a nature trail around a man-made lake, miniature golf, character breakfasts, and organized activities (such as "Disney Discovery Club") for all ages. Restaurant, bar. Pool. | 9250 Island Grove Terr. | 561/234–2000 | fax 561/234–2030 | www.dvcresorts.com | 208 rooms | $255–$345 | AE, D, DC, MC, V.

Doubletree Guest Suites. The comfortable suites in this oceanfront hotel have a living room and bedroom and a balcony with an ocean view. 2 restaurants. In-room data ports, microwaves, refrigerators. Cable TV, in-room VCRs (and movies). Pool, wading pool. Hot tub. Beach. Business services. | 3500 Ocean Dr. | 561/231–5666 | fax 561/234–4866 | www.doubletree.com | 55 suites | $235–$325 | AE, D, DC, MC, V.

Great American Inn & Suites. The hotel is ½ mi away from Outlet Mall and Indian River Mall, 8 mi west of Vero Beach, and near fishing, boating, and wildlife areas. It has a restaurant that serves breakfast and an outdoor pool. Cable TV. Laundry service. Pets allowed. | 8800 20th St. | 561/562–9991 or 800/960–7707 (reservations) | fax 561/562–0716 | 225 rooms, 4 suites | $57–$69 | AE, D, DC, MC, V.

Holiday Inn Vero Beach Oceanside. The rooms at this hotel on Orchid Island have two double beds or a king-size bed. Some have ocean views. Suites and efficiencies are available with kitchenettes. Restaurant. Pool. Exercise equipment. | 3384 Ocean Dr. | 561/231–2300 or 888/670–7470 | fax 561/234–8069 | www.holiday-inn.com | 106 rooms | $129–$189 | AE, D, DC, MC, V.

ONE LAST TRAVEL TIP:

Pack an easy way to reach the world.

Wherever you travel, the MCI WorldCom Card℠ is the easiest way to stay in touch. You can use it to call to and from more than 125 countries worldwide. And you can earn bonus miles every time you use your card. So go ahead, travel the world. MCI WorldCom℠ makes it even more rewarding. For additional access codes, visit **www.wcom.com/worldphone**.

EASY TO CALL WORLDWIDE

1. Just dial the WorldPhone® access number of the country you're calling from.
2. Dial or give the operator your MCI WorldCom Card number.
3. Dial or give the number you're calling.

Canada	1-800-888-8000
Mexico	01-800-021-8000
United States	1-800-888-8000

EARN FREQUENT FLIER MILES

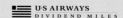

Howard Johnson Express Inn. This chain property is behind the Outlet Mall, ½ mi from I–95 and 8 mi west of Vero Beach. Complimentary Continental breakfast. Refrigerators, microwaves. Cable TV. Laundry facilities. Business services. | 1985 90th Ave. | 561/778–1985 | fax 561/778–1998 | www.hojo.com | 60 rooms | $69–$89 | AE, D, DC, MC, V.

Howard Johnson Lodge, Downtown. This family-owned and -operated Howard Johnson is 1½ mi east of Vero Beach fishing and boating, and 3 mi from Dodgertown. Complimentary Continental breakfast. In-room refrigerators. Cable TV, in-room VCRs (and movies). Pool. Laundry facilities. | 1725 U.S. 1 | 561/567–5171 or 800/406–1411 (reservations) | fax 561/567–5194 | www.hojo.com | 52 rooms | $54–$75 | AE, D, DC, MC, V.

The Islander Inn. The rooms at this well-maintained motel are painted in a festive Caribbean style with wicker furniture and have two double beds. Efficiencies have kitchenettes. Picnic area. Refrigerators. Pool. | 3101 Ocean Dr. | 561/231–4431 or 800/952–5886 | www.theislanderinn.com | 16 rooms | $105 | AE, DC, MC, V.

Palm Court Resort. A beachfront sister resort to the Doubletree, this hotel has several efficiency suites that are a good bet for families. Many rooms have stunning ocean views. The pool looks out over the water and pink shade umbrellas and blue-and-white striped cabanas line the beach. Restaurant. Some kitchenettes, some microwaves, some refrigerators. Cable TV. Outdoor pool. Gym. Laundry facilities. | 3244 Ocean Dr. | 561/231–2800 or 800/245–3297 | fax 561/231–3446 | www.palmcourtvero.com | 107 rooms | $145–$225 | AE, D, MC, V.

Vero Beach Comfort Inn. This motel is 5 minutes from the beach. Bar, complimentary Continental breakfast. In-room data ports, refrigerators. Cable TV, in-room VCRs (and movies). Pool. Laundry service. | 950 U.S. 1 | 561/569–0900 | fax 561/569–5502 | www.comfortinn.com | 66 rooms | $99 | AE, D, DC, MC, V.

WALT DISNEY WORLD

MAP 3, J5

(Nearby towns also listed: Clermont, Davenport, Haines City, Kissimmee, Lake Buena Vista, Orlando)

Few people could have guessed the colossal hold that Walt Disney World would have on a collective imagination when its first theme park, the Magic Kingdom, opened its gates in 1971. Millions of visitors later, the original park continues to enchant with its unique attractions—rides that tell a story—like Pirates of the Caribbean and Space Mountain. But now, on this vacation kingdom's 43 square mi, you'll find not one theme park but four, plus water parks, resort hotels, shopping, golf courses, restaurants, and clubs and other entertainment venues, not to mention the cast of thousands both real and animated. This is definitely no "small world."

Walt Disney didn't have enough money to buy up a lot of extra land in Anaheim when he was planning Disneyland, but he learned from his mistakes. Not wanting cheap, tacky tourist attractions and hotels sprouting up in the immediate vicinity of his new park in Florida, he started buying up land in central Florida during the mid-1960s. When the story behind the purchases finally leaked out in 1965, Walt was ready to make the formal announcement of his plans. Although he died the next year, in 1966, his brother Roy carried on and opened up the Magic Kingdom, two resort hotels, and a campground in 1971. Although the park was popular, growth in attendance stagnated. When Epcot opened in 1982 the park's future was still not very bright.

That changed beginning in 1984, when Michael Eisner took charge of the Disney Company. And the growth in the late 1980s and throughout the 1990s has made Orlando one of the vacation capitals of the entire world. The third theme park, Disney–MGM Studios, opened in 1989, and the fourth, Disney's Animal Kingdom, opened in 1998.

Today hotels and villa complexes cover more than 2,500 acres alone. After that, the 98-acre Magic Kingdom seems a drop in the bucket.

A bewildering array of options awaits you in Walt Disney World. There are several ticketing options—from single-day tickets to multi-park, multi-day passes. Some allow you to hop between parks on the same day; others don't, so keep that in mind when making your plans. And prices change several times a year.

Information: Walt Disney World Resort Guest Relations (407/824–4321 | www.disney.com). **Dining reservations at Walt Disney World restaurants** (407/939–3463). **Accommodations and shows reservations** (407/934–7639).

TRANSPORTATION

Transportation to Walt Disney World: The international airport in Orlando is the touchdown point for travelers who arrive by air. Bus lines also serve Orlando, and Amtrak serves Orlando, Winter Park, and Kissimmee.

Walt Disney World Resort Transportation: The resort has its own transportation network, which can get you wherever you need to go. If you are staying in one of the Disney hotels, transportation is included in the price of your multiday pass. Allow at least an hour to travel between sites on the Disney property. All transportation usually operates from early in the morning until at least midnight unless you visit during one of the early closing periods.

By Boat: Motor launches operate between Epcot resorts—except the Caribbean Beach Resort—and Disney–MGM Studios; between Bay Lake and the Magic Kingdom; and between Fort Wilderness, the Wilderness Lodge, and the Polynesian, Contemporary, and Grand Floridian resorts.

By Bus: You'll find bus service between all major and minor theme parks, and express buses go between the major parks. You can go directly from or make connections at Downtown Disney, Epcot, and the Epcot Resorts, as well as Disney's Animal Kingdom and Animal Kingdom Resort. Buses to the Magic Kingdom serve the Ticket and Transportation Center, where you have to change for a monorail or boat to get you to the turnstiles.

By Monorail: The monorail operates in two loops: one links the Magic Kingdom, Ticket and Transportation Center, and a handful of Magic Kingdom resorts; another loops from the Ticket and Transportation Center directly to Epcot.

DRIVING AND PARKING

Walt Disney World has four exits off I–4. For the Magic Kingdom, Disney–MGM Studios, Disney's Animal Kingdom, Fort Wilderness, and the rest of the Magic Kingdom resort area, take the one marked **Magic Kingdom–U.S. 192 (exit 25).** From here it's a 4-mi drive along Disney's main entrance road to the toll gate, and another mile to the parking area. During peak vacation periods be prepared for bumper-to-bumper traffic on I–4 nearing the U.S. 192 exit and on U.S. 192. A more direct and less-congested route to the theme parks and other Disney venues is via the exit marked **Disney World/Animal Kingdom/Epcot/MGM/Wide World of Sports (exit 24D),** 4 mi west of exit 25. If I–4 traffic is not too heavy, it's worth it to go the extra distance.

For access to Downtown Disney (including the Marketplace, Pleasure Island, and Disney's West Side), as well as to Typhoon Lagoon, the Crossroads Shopping Center, and the establishments on Hotel Plaza Boulevard, get off at **Route 535–Lake Buena Vista (exit 27).** The exit marked **Epcot–Downtown Disney (exit 26)** is the one to use if you're bound for those destinations or for hotels in the Epcot and Downtown Disney resort areas; you can also get to MGM from here.

Each theme park has a parking lot—and all are huge. Sections are named and numbered. Make note of which section you park in. Trams make frequent trips between the parking area and the turnstile areas. Although valet parking is available at Downtown Disney ($8), it's congested. At Disney's BoardWalk you park in the hotel lot, where valets are available as well (free). There is no valet parking available at theme parks.

At all major theme-park lots parking costs $6 for cars, $7 for RVs and campers, and is free for Walt Disney World resort guests with ID. Save your receipt; if you want to visit another park the same day, you won't have to pay to park twice. Parking is free at the three water parks.

Resort Areas

There are four major resort areas within Walt Disney World. **Animal Kingdom Resort Area.** Disney's newest theme park, Disney's Animal Kingdom, is here, as is its newest resort hotel, Disney's Animal Kingdom Lodge. Nearby, you'll also find the various All-Star resorts as well as the Coronado Springs Resort and the Blizzard Beach water park. It's in the southwest corner of Disney World and is the least developed of the resort areas.

Downtown Disney. Bristling with activity, this commercial area on the east edge of Walt Disney World is an open-air complex of shops and restaurants with outdoor vendors and a computer-animated fountain. Connecting Walt Disney World to the real world beyond is shady Hotel Plaza Boulevard, a four-lane street divided by a verdant median and bordered by spreading lawns dominated by tall chain hotels. Spreading away from the Marketplace to the west is Pleasure Island, an after-dark complex. Adjoining Pleasure Island is Disney's West Side, where brand-name retailers mix with fast, young, and hip nightspots and restaurants; this is also the site of the entertainment complex DisneyQuest. Downtown Disney is also home to a number of Disney hotels,

14 ROMANTIC THINGS TO DO AT WALT DISNEY WORLD

Disney isn't just for kids. Here's a things-to-do list that will make romance the heart of your trip.

1. Have dinner at the very grand Victoria and Albert's restaurant in the Grand Floridian.

2. Have dinner at the California Grill and watch the Magic Kingdom fireworks.

3. Rent a boat to take a cruise on the Seven Seas Lagoon or the waterways leading to it. Bring champagne, and glasses.

4. Take a nighttime whirl on Cinderella's Golden Carousel in Fantasyland. The sparkling lights make it magical.

5. Ride the Skyway in the Magic Kingdom—either direction is fine. Line up a half an hour ahead to ensure being seated about five minutes before the fireworks start. Ride operators stop you midway to let you have a spectacular view.

6. Sit on the beach at the Grand Floridian at sunrise or at dusk—a special time.

7. Buy a faux diamond ring at the Emporium on Main Street in the Magic Kingdom. Propose to your sweetheart at your favorite spot in the World.

8. Sit by the fountain in front of Epcot's France pavilion and have some wine or pastry and a coffee.

9. Rent a hot-air balloon for a magical tour of Walt Disney World.

10. Have dinner at Alfredo's in Epcot, right after IllumiNations—request an 8:55 reservation. After dinner, since the park is officially closed, it's quiet and lovely.

11. Every night is New Year's Eve at Pleasure Island. Declare your love amid confetti and fireworks.

12. Take a walk on the BoardWalk. Watch IllumiNations from the bridge to the Yacht and Beach Club. Then boogie to Atlantic Dance.

13. Have a drink at the cozy Yachtsman's Crew bar at the Yacht Club hotel.

14. After dinner at Narcoosee's in the Grand Floridian, watch the Electrical Water Pageant outside.

© Corbis

including The Villas at the Disney Institute, Disney's Old Key West Resort, and Disney's Dixie Landing Resort. Typhoon Lagoon is also in this area.

Epcot Resort Area. The pathway out of the International Gateway, between France and Canada in Epcot's World Showcase, leads to a number of evocative resort hotels, including the aptly named Disney's Yacht and Beach Hotels and the Swan and Dolphin hotels. Beyond these is Disney's BoardWalk, a spit-and-polished version of turn-of-the-20th-century Atlantic City (before casinos). The BoardWalk includes two hotels, Disney's Boardwalk Inn and Disney's Boardwalk Villas. The hotels' grounds are expansive and green. Disney–MGM Studios is directly south of Epcot.

Magic Kingdom Resort Area. Walt Disney World's original theme park is the heart of this part of the resort. The futuristic monorail links a number of Disney's top resorts here, including the Polynesian Village, the Grand Floridian, and the huge, A-frame Contemporary. Secluded and a bit away from the Polynesian is Shades of Green, a resort open only to members of the armed forces and their families, flanked by a couple of championship golf courses. About 1 mi from the Contemporary—but a million miles away in feeling—is Disney's Wilderness Lodge Resort. Some 2 mi away from the Wilderness Lodge is Fort Wilderness, with cabins and 784 private campsites, where you can pitch your own tent or park your own RV—or rent one of Mickey's. On the grounds here is River Country, one of Disney World's trio of water parks.

Imagine taking a trip to Disney and avoiding most of the lines. **FASTPASS** is your ticket to this terrific scenario, and it's included in regular park admission. You insert your theme park ticket into a special FASTPASS turnstile. Out comes a FASTPASS ticket, complete with the time you should return to the attraction. In the meantime you are free to enjoy the other attractions in the park. At the appointed time you return to the attraction, head for the FASTPASS entrance, and proceed to the preshow or boarding area with little or no wait. (Note: You must use one FASTPASS ticket before trying to make your next FASTPASS appointment.)

Attractions

THEME PARKS AND TOURIST ATTRACTIONS

Blizzard Beach. You might rub your eyes when you see an alpine ski lift dangling above the live oaks as you drive along Buena Vista Drive. But in Blizzard Beach, the Alps do seem to come to the tropics—well, almost. The park's centerpiece is rocky Mt. Gushmore; Disney's melting snow runs through the water slides that stripe its slopes: Summit Plummet, Slush Gusher, and Snow Stormers. You ride some as a family, in a huge raft; others are curvy shots in pitch darkness—scary but still fun. Summit Plummet is simply terrifying. Tike's Peak, a toddler-sized version of the park, delights little ones. | I–4 exit 25B | 407/560–9283 | $27.95 | Daily 10–5; June–Aug. 9–8; Closed Jan.

★ **Disney–MGM Studios.** Disney's third theme park has a motion picture theme, and its lands recall the Hollywood of the 1920s and '30s. Attractions vary from rides that are purely entertaining—such as *Star Tours*, which uses flight-simulator technology to take you on a star-crossed journey into outer space, and *Rock 'n Roller Coaster starring Aerosmith*, a pretty fast limousine coaster—to attractions that are also informative, such as *The Magic of Disney Animation*, where you can learn about how Disney creates its animated features and actually see animators at work. Every day at 3 there is a parade. | I–4 exit 25B | 407/560–4651 | $46 | Daily 9–7; as late as 10 during peak periods.

★ **Disney's Animal Kingdom.** At 500 acres, Disney's fourth theme park in Orlando, opened in spring 1998, is the largest of all (five times the size of the Magic Kingdom). Part wildlife park, part entertainment complex, it showcases animals real, imaginary, and extinct via carefully re-created landscapes, musical shows, and other themed attractions. The centerpiece of the park is the Tree of Life, an immense, spectacular Disney-made tree whose trunk and every branch is carved with animal faces and forms. Inside this is a theater that screens *It's Tough to Be a Bug*, a 3-D film with some funny and startling special effects. The

Kilimanjaro Safari is more up-close than anything you'd find in a zoo. The park is home to lions, hippos, rhinos, giraffes, and many far less familiar creatures. Don't miss the two Safari Village nature trails; here Disney makes wildlife-watching even more entertaining. I–4 exit 25B. | 407/938–2784 | $46 | Daily 8–6; as late as 8 during peak periods.

Downtown Disney. Downtown Disney is really three entertainment areas in one featuring attractions, theaters, nightclubs, shopping, and dining. First, there's **Downtown Disney West Side** with restaurants, shows, entertainment and a terrific lineup of shops and boutiques. Then, there's **Downtown Disney Pleasure Island,** which is primarily an evening entertainment complex geared towards adults. Finally, there's **Downtown Disney Marketplace,** which is home to a variety of shops and restaurants.

Cirque du Soleil. The daring artistry and acrobatic spectacles of the French-Canadian troupe Cirque de Soleil, now has a permanent tent-home in Downtown Disney West Side. *La Nouba,* a circus of fanciful and brightly colored performers, including trapeze acts, is accompanied by a live modern orchestra. There are two shows a night at 6 and 9, and the theater is small enough that every seat in the house is a good one. I–4 exit 27. | 407/939–7600 | $62 | Shows Thurs.–Mon. 6 and 9.

DisneyQuest, the first indoor, interactive, virtual reality theme park, is brought to you by the imaginative folks at Disney. Inside the massive 50-story, 100,000-square-ft windowless structure on Disney's West Side in Downtown Disney you can shoot the rapids in a virtual prehistoric world, hop into a simulator and ride a roller coaster that you design, or fly a magic carpet through an ancient city. I–4 exit 27. | 407/828–4600 | www.disneyworld.com | $27 | Daily 10 AM–midnight.

Disney's West Side. Adjacent to Pleasure Island, in Downtown Disney, the West Side is a laid-back waterside entertainment, shopping, and dining promenade. It's here you'll find the House of Blues, DisneyQuest, a Virgin Megastore, and Cirque du Soleil, among many others. | Downtown Disney | 407/824–4500 or 407/824–2222 | Free | Daily 11–2.

Downtown Disney Marketplace. For pure shopping pleasure, nothing else in Disney's world matches this complex of lakeside shops. This third of Downtown Disney has shops selling chocolates and pastries, Disney housewares and artwork, silver and gold, as well as quiet cafés. | Downtown Disney | 407/828–3870 | Daily 11:30–10:30.

Pleasure Island. This after-dark entertainment complex, part of Downtown Disney, is flanked by Disney's West Side to the west and Downtown Disney Marketplace to the east. Seven clubs are here; single admission price services all of the clubs, which have become some of Orlando's most popular nightspots. Children under 18 are not admitted without a parent or guardian when the clubs are open, but free admission for all to shop and dine during the day. | 1550 Buena Vista Dr. | 407/560–9283 | Free 11–7; $18.86 7 PM–2 AM | Shops daily 11 AM–2 AM; clubs daily 7 PM–2 AM.

★ **Epcot.** Epcot, whose name is an acronym for "Experimental Prototype Community of Tomorrow," was inspired by Walt Disney's dream of the technologically advanced community of the future where thousands could live and work in comfort and harmony. The theme park built on this dream, which is something like a very well-executed world's fair, but is not a true community in any sense of the word. Epcot does showcase technology in many ways, and it does take a look at how it's being used in daily life and at the many nations of the world. There are two sections, Future World and World Showcase.

The huge golf ball–shape building known as Spaceship Earth, the geosphere that is Epcot's icon, guards the entrance to **Future World,** a collection of rides and displays that show how progress and technology has shaped, and will continue to shape, human life. In the Energy pavilion, Ellen's Energy Adventure, starring comedienne Ellen Degeneres, gives you a crash course about energy. In the Wonders of Life pavilion, Body Wars and Cranium Command take you through the inner workings of the circulatory and neural systems. Body Wars is an imaginative use of flight simulator technology. The Land and the Living Seas pavilions offer discovery programs about the environment and human exploration.

The pavilions of **World Showcase** celebrate the culture, cuisine, and architecture of America, Canada, China, France, Germany, Italy, Japan, Mexico, Morocco, Norway, and the United Kingdom. Natives staff each one, sell handicrafts and food, perform in alfresco shows, and staff exhibit areas, theaters, and the occasional ride-through attraction. A scaled-down Eiffel Tower tops France, which screens the stunning film, *Impressions de France*. China has its own film, *Wonders of China*, as does Canada with *O! Canada*—both visually splendid. In the *American Adventure*, evocative sets, orchestral music, and life-like robots powered by Disney's trademark AudioAnimatronics speak to the patriot in every American visitor. There are appropriately themed shops in every pavilion; the United Kingdom pavilion is mainly shops. Most have a restaurant, and some of these are among the top restaurants in the Orlando area. Every night there's a wonderful parade, Tapestry of Nations, which reflects the talent of Broadway's *Lion King* creator and director Julie Taymor. Before closing, Epcot presents *IllumiNations*, an extravaganza that includes fountains, stirring orchestral music, and lasers, lights, fireworks, and other effects that are not soon forgotten. The best and least obstructed views are from the bridges between France and the United Kingdom, and between Germany and China, as well as on the promenade in front of Canada and Norway. | I–4 Exit 26B | 407/938–2784 | $46 | Future World daily 9–9, as late as 10 during peak periods; World Showcase daily 11–9, as late as 10 during peak periods.

★ **Magic Kingdom.** This 98-acre park, the smallest of the four major theme parks at Walt Disney World, was the original here, and is similar to Walt's first theme park, Disneyland. It's still the soul of the entire Disney operation in Florida. The centerpiece is the Cinderella's Castle, elegantly turreted, spired, and gilded. From this hub extend various lands, each with a theme. Every afternoon at 3 there's the Disney's Magical Moments Parade, which stars well-scrubbed, lip-syncing singers and dancers, Disney characters, and small floats on a seasonal theme. After dark during busy periods there's a spectacular Spectro Magic parade and afterward a fireworks display, heralded by a flying Tinkerbell, who emerges in a pouf of pixie dust from the top of the Castle.

The gateway into the Magic Kingdom is **Main Street U.S.A.,** a promenade lined with perfect storefronts. The 4/5-scale and use of a set designers' technique known as forced perspective make things feel at once very real yet unusually intimate. Inside every building is a shop, and the merchandise makes the shopping almost as entertaining as the attractions.

A "rickety" bridge transports you from the Hub area, fronting the Cinderella Castle, to bougainvillea-draped, palm-filled **Adventureland.** Infused with the spirit of the Caribbean, Africa, Polynesia, and Thailand, it is the home of great attractions such as the Swiss Family Treehouse, cradled in a 50-ft high man-made tree; the Jungle Cruise, where many a comic gets his start; and the classic Pirates of the Caribbean, a tongue-in-cheek boat tour of an imaginary Caribbean island in the middle of a pirate attack.

Walt's "timeless land of enchantment," as he called it, **Fantasyland** takes you into the worlds of Snow White, Peter Pan, Cinderella, Dumbo, Tigger and Pooh, and many other characters made famous by Disney animators. Fantasyland is also the site of It's a Small World.

Characters such as Tom Sawyer and Br'er Rabbit occupy **Frontierland.** Fiddle music is in the air, and mesquite, cacti, and slash pines surround unpainted clapboard buildings, complete with wooden sidewalks. Along with the requisite saloon, the Diamond Horseshoe, there's the Country Bear Jamboree, with wise-cracking AudioAnimatronics bears; leafy Tom Sawyer Island, with barrel bridges and caves to explore; Splash Mountain, one heck of a flume ride; and Big Thunder Mountain Railroad, a tame roller coaster styled to look like a runaway mine train—the thrills are largely in the scenery along the way.

The frontier segues gently into **Liberty Square,** where everything has an elegant and prosperous Bostonian quality. At its heart are the Liberty Tree, an impressive 150-yr-old live oak, and the Hall of Presidents, which tells the story of the United States' founding and climaxes with a roll call of AudioAnimatronic versions of every president. On the fringe of Liberty Square is the Haunted Mansion, a Gothic-style brick mansion filled with imaginative special effects. It's one of the park's best attractions.

Diminutive houses evoke a cartoon world in **Mickey's Toontown Fair,** devoted to the little mouse who became the soul of the kingdom. Here you can visit Mickey and Minnie's homes, Goofy's farm, and Donald Duck's boat, all interminably cute, and ride a pint-sized roller coaster. Toddlers and young children love this area.

Tomorrowland, not far away, looks like the future as envisioned by people in the past. Space Mountain, a roller coaster that's entirely in the dark, is famously scary albeit relatively tame as these rides go nowadays. ExtraTERRORestrial Alien Encounter is terrifying, even though you sit in an auditorium chair for the duration. | I–4 exits 25B, 26B | 407/934–7639 | $46 | Daily 9–6; as late as 12 midnight during peak periods.

River Country. The smallest and oldest of the Disney water parks, this one in Fort Wilderness, a lively corner of Disney's Bay Lake, officially in the Magic Kingdom Resort Area, is also the most charming. It's generally less crowded than the other two, and with its surrounding pines and maples, its red-rock cliffs, and its non-chlorinated lake water, it lives up to everyone's image of an old-fashioned swimming hole from the good old days—except in this case, it comes with an unobstructed view of Cinderella Castle. Whoop 'n Holler Hollow is the huge main pool; all the water slides dump their riders here, and there are a number of other ways to fly through the air and land with a splash. White Water Rapids, which you ride in jumbo inner tubes, is the slip-sliding leisurely way down the mountain. I–4 Exit 26B. | 407/560–9283 | $15.95 | Daily 10–5; later closing in summer months.

Typhoon Lagoon. Typhoon Lagoon, in the Downtown Disney Resort Area, is four times the size of River Country. The 2,100-ft Castaway Creek rings the park, and allows you to get an overview of the park's attractions while floating tranquilly amid typical subtropical vegetation. The eponymous lagoon, the size of two football fields, is the focal point. Every hour or so, *Miss Tilly,* a tugboat perched atop the adjacent mountain, gives a couple of toots and waves large enough for surfing competitions start rolling in toward the shore. Humunga Kowabunga, the Storm Slides, and Mayday Falls are the water slides, which plummet down the side of the mountain at various speeds and angles. Smaller versions of it all are off to one side of the action, at Ketchakiddie Creek. I–4 exit 27. | 1195 Buena Vista Dr. | 407/560–9283 | $27.95 | Sept.–May, daily 10–5; June–Aug., daily 9–8; Closed in Jan. for maintenance.

DINNER SHOWS

The Hoop-Dee-Doo Revue. This revue staged at Fort Wilderness's rustic Pioneer Hall may be corny, but it is also the liveliest dinner show in Walt Disney World. A troupe of jokers called the Pioneer Hall Players stomp their feet, wisecrack, and otherwise make merry while the audience chows down on barbecued ribs, fried chicken, corn on the cob, strawberry shortcake, and all the fixins. | Fort Wilderness Resort | 407/939–3463 | $46 | Daily 5, 7:15, 9:30.

Polynesian Luau. This is an outdoor barbecue with entertainment appropriate to its colorful South Pacific setting at the Polynesian Resort. Its fire jugglers and hula-drum dancers are entertaining for the whole family. The hula dancers' navel maneuvers are something to see. | Polynesian Resort | 407/939–3463 or 407/824–1593 | $46 | Tues.–Sat. 5:15, 8.

SPORTS AND RECREATION

Bay Lake Fishing Trips. You can take 2-hr fishing excursions on regularly stocked Bay Lake and Seven Seas Lagoon. Cruises depart from Fort Wilderness, Wilderness Lodge, Contemporary, Polynesian, and Grand Floridian resort marinas. Yacht and Beach Club and Disney's Boardwalk Hotel guests fish on Crescent Lake. Trips include equipment, coffee and pastries, and a guide for up to five anglers. | 407/939–7529 | 2-hr trip $171, $51 per additional hour | Daily 8, 11:30, 3.

Captain Jack's Guided Bass Tours. Two-hour fishing expeditions on Lake Buena Vista for up to five anglers depart from Downtown Disney's Marketplace Marina. | 407/828–2461 | $68.50, $137 per group of 2–5 | Daily 6:30, 9.

Golf Courses. Where else would you find a sand trap shaped like the head of a well-known mouse? Walt Disney World has 99 holes of golf on five championship courses—all on the

PGA Tour route—plus a nine-hole walking course. Eagle Pines and Osprey Ridge are new-comers, flanking the Bonnet Creek Golf Club just east of Fort Wilderness. They join the WDW's original courses, the Palm and the Magnolia, which flank the Shades of Green resort, to the west, and the Lake Buena Vista course, near Downtown Disney's Marketplace. All courses are full-service facilities, including driving range, pro shop, locker room, snack bar-restaurant, and PGA-staffed teaching and training program. | 407/939–4653.

Eagle Pines. One of the two newer courses, this 18-hole course was designed by course archi-tect Pete Dye. Greens are small and undulating and fairways are lined with pines and punc-tuated by bunkers that broaden the challenge. The par-72 course is 6,772 yards, with a USGA rating of 72.3. | Bonnet Creek Golf Club.

Lake Buena Vista. This 18-hole course winds among Downtown Disney–area town houses and villas. Greens are narrow—straight drives are important since errant balls risk end-ing up in someone's bedroom. The par-72 course is 6,819 yards, with a USGA rating of 72.7. | Lake Buena Vista Dr.

The Magnolia. Played by the pros in the Disney/Oldsmobile Golf Classic, this 18-hole course is long but forgiving, with extra-wide fairways. The par-72 course is 7,190 yards, with a USGA rating of 73.9. | Shades of Green Resort.

Oak Trail. This 9-hole, par-36 walking course near the Magnolia was designed by Ron Garl for families, with small, undulating fairways. Shades of Green Resort.

Osprey Ridge. Designer Tom Fazio leavened the challenge of this course with a relaxing tour into Walt Disney World forest. However, tees and greens high above the fairways keep you from getting too comfortable. The par-72 course is 7,101 yards, with a USGA rating of 73.9. | Bonnet Creek Golf Club.

The Palm. One of WDW's original courses, the Palm has been confounding the pros as part of the annual Disney/Oldsmobile Classic for years. It's not as long as Magnolia, or as wide, and there are more trees. And don't go near the water! This 18-hole course is 6,957 yards, with a par of 72 and a USGA rating of 73. | Shades of Green Resort.

Sammy Duvall's Water Sports Centre. This water sports center, part of Disney's Contempo-rary Resort, offers waterskiing, wakeboarding, and parasailing on Bay Lake. Waterskiing and wakeboarding include boat and equipment rental, plus the services of an expert instruc-tor. | Disney's Contemporary Resort, 4600 N. World Dr. | 407/939–7529 | Parasailing $75–$145 per hour, watersports $125–$150 per hour (up to 5 people) | Daily 9–5 (7–7 in summer).

Walt Disney Speedway. This speedway adjacent to Disney's Wide World of Sports Complex, has a 1-mi tri-oval track and accommodates 51,000 fans. | 407/939–7810 | Call for schedule.

Richard Petty Driving Experience. If you need to take your NASCAR obsession to the next level, you can ride a real stock car on the Walt Disney Speedway. The cheapest thrill ($89) involves three passenger laps on the 1½-mi track. For much more money you can take 1½ days of lessons, and go it alone. | Walt Disney Speedway | 800/237–3889 | www.disney.com | $89 for 3-lap ride, $1,199 for individual instruction | Daily by appointment only.

Winter Summerland and Fantasia Gardens Miniature Golf Courses. Walt Disney World has carved out 72 holes of miniature golf in two complexes. At the Winter Summerland course, putt around sand castles and snow banks. The course is close to Disney's Animal Kingdom and the Coronado Springs and All-Star Resorts. The Fantasia course is adjacent to the Swan and Dolphin Resort complex, near the Disney-MGM studios. | 407/939–7529 | $9.25 | Daily 10–11.

OTHER POINTS OF INTEREST

Disney's Boardwalk. Across Crescent Lake from Disney's Yacht and Beach Club Resorts, WDW has created its own version of turn-of-the-20th-century shoreline amusement areas. It's cleaner than Atlantic City, and complete with restaurants, bars, clubs, souvenir sellers, sur-rey, saltwater taffy vendors, and shops. When the lights go on after sunset, the mood is festive—a nostalgic setting for plentiful diversions and a romantic stroll. | Across Crescent Lake | 407/939–3492 | Free | Daily.

Disney's Wide World of Sports. At this 200-acre, state-of-the-art complex you can see football, baseball, softball, and track and field competitions among amateurs, as well as professionals such as the Atlanta Braves who use the complex for spring training. I–4 exit 25B. | 407/828–3267 | $9 | Daily 10–5; later for some events.

WALKING TOUR

The Magic Kingdom: A Blitz Tour (more than 10 frenetic hours)

Arrive at the park 45 min before the scheduled opening, and once in the park, head for the **Walt Disney Railroad,** getting off at Frontierland to claim an early FASTPASS time for **Splash Mountain.** After you've received your ticket head over for **Big Thunder Mountain Railroad.** Then, catch the next **Country Bears Jamboree** show. By now your FASTPASS ticket should be valid to ride Splash Mountain. Next, head over to Adventureland to the **Jungle Cruise** and pick up another FASTPASS. Use the 35-min time allotment to do **Pirates of the Caribbean** and the **Swiss Family Treehouse.**

When you've finished at the Jungle Cruise, sprint over to Tomorrowland and pick up your next FASTPASS, this time for **Space Mountain.** Take in the **Carousel of Progress,** where there is seldom a wait, and then ride the **Tomorrowland Transit Authority (TTA).** Experience the **ExtraTERRORestrial Alien Encounter** and, if there's time, **The Timekeeper.** By now, it should be time for you to ride Space Mountain. Then it's time for another FASTPASS, this one for **Buzz Lightyear's Space Ranger Spin.** If you haven't yet had your fill of Tomorrowland, you'll have time to revisit some favorites or squeeze in one or two other attractions that you might have missed—such as the **Astro-Orbiter** or **Tomorrowland Indy Speedway.**

Grab the next FASTPASS for **The Many Adventures of Winnie the Pooh.** Then treat yourself to a snack or a more substantial late lunch, and it should be time for the 3 PM parade. If the crowds are not too thick, a nice viewing spot is the second floor of the train station.

After the parade, take the train to **Mickey's Toontown Fair.** Take a ride on **Snow White's Scary Adventures,** then see the **Legend of the Lion King.** It should be about time for your Pooh FASTPASS. (This attraction is so popular that when you retrieve your FASTPASS appointment, you could have as much as a seven-hour wait to use it.)

Now, it's time to wind down and take in the other Fantasyland attractions. **Cinderella's Golden Carousel** is magical at night. Then, wind up at **It's a Small World.**

Meander over to Liberty Square. Take in the next **Hall of President's** show and then do the **Haunted Mansion.** See if there's another performance of the **Diamond Horseshoe Saloon Revue.** During the off-season the last show is usually at 5, but during holidays there is almost always an evening show. You can stick around for the evening parade or wait for the fireworks at Main Street.

Epcot: A Blitz Tour (8 to 9 strenuous hours)

Plan to arrive at the parking lot 45 minutes before the official opening. As soon as you arrive, race over to **Test Track.** Get your FASTPASS appointment and backtrack to **Spaceship Earth.**

On the way, don't bother stopping at the Universe of Energy or the Living Seas pavilions for now; just head for the **Wonders of Life** and go directly from **Body Wars** to *The Making of Me* to **Cranium Command.** But save the Fitness Fairground for later.

Take your Test Track ride. Afterward, head to Future World's western pavilions. Visit **Imagination!** and pick up another FASTPASS for *Honey, I Shrunk the Audience.* Visit **Journey into Your Imagination,** and if you have some time left, go to **Image Works** before returning for your FASTPASS appointment.

Now enter The Land, and take the **boat ride,** see **Circle of Life,** and **Food Rocks.** There may be a line at **Living Seas,** but it's worth it.

Head counterclockwise into World Showcase, toward **Canada.** Then see **France** and the **American Adventure.** Head for **Norway,** but if there are lines, move on to **Innoventions,** the Image Works (if you didn't see it before), and Wonders of Life's **Fitness Fairground.**

After dinner, see any World Showcase attractions you missed, plus the **Universe of Energy.** (Parts of Future World sometimes close ahead of the rest of the park.) End the evening at **IllumiNations.**

ON THE CALENDAR

APR.: *Easter Parade.* This parade down Main Street shows a whole new side to Mickey Mouse. | 407/939–7814.

JULY: *Fourth of July.* Special fireworks fill the skies over the various Walt Disney World theme parks for Independence Day. The Magic Kingdom launches a fireworks spectacular over Cinderella Castle, while Epcot adds an explosive finale to IllumiNations that nearly triples the number of pyrotechnics. The festivities extend to Disney–MGM Studios, Typhoon Lagoon, River Country, and Downtown Disney. | 407/824–2222 or 407/939–7814.

OCT.: *Walt Disney World Oldsmobile Golf Classic.* A PGA Tour tradition since Jack Nicklaus's final round scores of 68, 64, and 67 earned him victories in 1971–73, this tournament drew the 8th strongest tour field in 1999. | 407/824–2729.

OCT.–NOV.: *Epcot Food and Wine Festival.* Culinary masters from around the world gather at the Epcot pavilions for this three-wk-long celebration devoted to the pleasures of the palate. You can watch cooking demonstrations and sample food and wine from all over the world. | 407/824–4500.

NOV.: *Festival of the Masters.* This is a three-day art show during the second weekend of November at Disney's Village Marketplace. The show includes art, photography, and crafts from juried art shows throughout the United States. | 407/824–4321.

DEC.: *Disney Christmas.* Once the last Thanksgiving turkey is eaten, the Yuletide season cranks up all over Walt Disney World, and there are festivities everywhere. The Magic Kingdom celebrates with a Christmas-theme daily parade throughout December. The Walt Disney World's Very Merry Christmas Party is a special after-hours event from 8 PM–1 AM for 7 nights in December. Epcot traditionally holds a Candlelight Processional and Holidays Around the World. | 407/824–4321.

Dining

INEXPENSIVE

'50s Prime Time Café. American. Step back in time to the perfect world of meat loaf, pot roast, and fried chicken served on Formica table tops. Fountain shakes and "I Love Lucy" on the tube keeps the place packed, so come early. | Disney–MGM Studios | 407/939–3463 | $6–$10 | AE, MC, V.

Aunt Polly's. American. The arrival to Tom Sawyer's aunt's house is an adventure; you have to take the raft ride in Frontierland and float over to the riverside eatery. The menu revolves around American favorites such as fried chicken, "PB&J" sandwiches, on up to apple pie. | Magic Kingdom, Frontierland | 407/939–3463 | $6–$8 | AE, D, DC, MC, V.

Chef Mickey's. American. One of the many photo opportunities with Mickey, Minnie, and Goofy is in front of this boisterous, buffet-style restaurant. Oven-roasted prime rib, pasta, and Parmesan mashed potatoes are some of the specialties you'll find for lunch and dinner. There is also a kids' menu—with such delicacies as macaroni & cheese and pizza—and an all-you-can-eat dessert bar complete with ice cream sundaes. | Contemporary Resort | 407/939–3463 | $7–$12 | AE, D, DC, MC, V.

Crystal Palace. American. This glass atrium restaurant is a heavenly oasis, where the air-conditioning is turned high in the summer, so you can rest your bones in a place exempt from the Florida heat. The buffet-style meal includes a wide range of items, from roasted meats to soups of the day, with pasta, fresh-baked breads, and ice cream sundaes as part of the package. There's also a kids-only buffet. | Magic Kingdom, Main Street USA | 407/939–3463 | $5–$11 | AE, D, DC, MC, V.

Gulliver's Grill at Garden Grove. American. Supposedly founded by Gulliver of the Jonathan Swift novel, this restaurant is housed in a giant greenhouse. The menu varies from grilled salmon to sandwiches, and on Tuesdays and Saturdays expect visits from the *Legend of the Lion King* characters. | Walt Disney World Swan | 407/934–3000 | $6–$14 | AE, D, DC, MC, V | No lunch.

Hollywood & Vine. American. The buffet and the menu keep you deciding what you're in the mood for because they are both filled with too many options. Smoked salmon or oven-roasted pork are good entrées, but you can also be adventurous with the roasted sweet potatoes with root beer and bourbon glaze. | Disney–MGM Studios | 407/939–3463 | $5–$9 | AE, MC, V.

Hollywood Brown Derby. Contemporary. This re-creation of the famous Hollywood restaurant from the 1940s is lined with movie star caricatures and potted palms, just as the original was. The Cobb salad is a specialty, or try the hearty pan-roasted veal chop. The rotisserie chicken with sweet potatoes and a maple-whiskey glaze is another stand-out. | Disney–MGM Studios | 407/939–3463 | $7–$13 | AE, MC, V.

Sci-Fi Dine-In Theater Restaurant. American. This is probably the only faux drive-in restaurant in existence, but you can sit in the back of a fake car and dine on cheeseburgers or even grilled yellowfin tuna here. Old classics such as *Attack of the Fifty-foot Woman* keep the mood going, but this isn't the place to attempt any steamy windows. | Disney–MGM Studios | 407/939–3463 | $6–$13 | AE, MC, V.

Tubbi's Buffeteria. American. The all-day and all-night service here is a blend of hearty goods on the buffet table and a few blue plate specials such as barbecued chicken or meat loaf. You can also get kid-friendly sandwiches or pizza. | Walt Disney World Dolphin | 407/934–4000 | $6–$17 | AE, D, DC, MC, V.

Whispering Canyon Cafe. American/Casual. Though lacking the serene aspects that the name suggests, this friendly family spot will give you a warm and friendly service while you enjoy huge servings of pancakes or spare ribs. The bargain meal is the $21, all-you-can-eat dinner that includes pork ribs, beef brisket, smoked sausage, and smoked turkey. Kids can enjoy the "Worms in the Dirt" dessert of chocolate cake with gummy worms protruding. | Wilderness Lodge | 407/939–3463 | $6–$14 | AE, D, DC, MC, V.

Wild Horse Saloon. American/Casual. Country dancing and barbecue are on the menu here, so don't be shy. Steaks and seafood are all thrown on the grill, but don't miss the white bean chili. Live country music keeps the place lively. | Downtown Disney Marketplace | 407/939–3463 | $6–$14 | AE, MC, V.

MODERATE

Biergarten. German. An oompah band slinks around at this popular beer hall and eatery in the German section of the Epcot World Showcase. It always feels like Oktoberfest here, and the long communal tables are filled with jovial patrons, feasting on the buffet that includes bratwurst, sauerkraut, Wiener schnitzel—plus there's lots of beer. | Epcot, World Showcase | 407/824–3200 | $13–$19 | AE, MC, V.

Big River Grille and Brewing Works. American. At Disney's BoardWalk in the Epcot Resort Area, this is one of a handful of breweries in central Florida. The interior is industrial and minimal throughout, with cubist seating arrangements, graphic murals of factory scenes, and copper vats where the beers are crafted. Some of the entrées are infused with brews including a drunken rib eye in Iron Horse stout. Grilled apple chops is another popular item. | Disney's BoardWalk | 407/560–0253 | Reservations not accepted | $10–$19 | AE, V.

Boatwright's Dining Hall. Cajun. At Disney's Dixie Landings Resort, this 1800s-style boat factory–theme restaurant has the hull of a fishing boat suspended from the ceiling, wood floors,

and fireplaces. The menu includes pan-sautéed crawfish with mushrooms and tomatoes in mustard cream sauce, bouillabaisse, and blackened seafood over pasta in garlic sauce. Breakfast is also available. | Disney's BoardWalk | 407/939–3463 | $11–$19 | AE, MC, V.

Bongos Cuban Café. Cuban. This two-story pineapple-shape restaurant on Disney's West Side is designed in the style of the golden age of Havana. Owned by singer Gloria Estefan and her husband, leopard-skin motifs are offset with bongo-shape bar stools. Desi Arnaz look-a-likes play live music. On the menu you'll find dishes such as roasted meat, skirt steak, paella, Cuban sandwiches, and hamburgers. | Disney's West Side | 407/828–0999 | Reservations not accepted | $9–$25 | AE, D, DC, MC, V.

Cap'n Jack's Oyster Bar. Seafood. Enjoy a cup of New England clam chowder in this nautical-theme restaurant—unless you want to go for the raw oysters or steamed clams. Aside from the lobster, the dishes are reasonably priced, so you can afford the pumpkin cheesecake for dessert. | Downtown Disney Marketplace | 407/939–3463 | $6–$19 | AE, MC, V.

Cinderella's Royal Table. American. High up in the trademark castle is where Cinderella and her sisters make their appearances to a packed crowd. Reservations are definitely required if you desire one of their fine meals, which get somewhat more sophisticated at night. There are good standards such as ribs, pasta, or even cheeseburgers, but don't be surprised if spice-crusted salmon or Thai barbecue tuna steak show up on the dinner menu. | Magic Kingdom, Fantasyland | 407/939–3463 | Reservations essential | $8–$22 | AE, D, DC, MC, V.

Concourse Steak House. Steak. With the monorail running above, you can ponder electricity to a steak or mango-glazed barbecue pork ribs. Thanks to technology, the place is not too noisy and the marbled cheesecake is also a worthy societal advance. | Contemporary Resort | 407/939–3463 | $8–$18 | AE, D, DC, MC, V.

Coral Reef. Seafood. Tables are centered around a 5 million–gallon aquarium filled with all kinds of sea-specimens, and classical music plays in the background at this restaurant in Epcot's Future World. To go along with the Living Sea theme of the pavilion it is housed in, the menu is mostly seafood. The menu includes sautéed mahimahi in lemon-caper butter sauce, shrimp satay with red pepper pasta, but a hearty steak is available as well. | Future World, Living Seas Pavilion | 407/939–3463 | $13–$25 | AE, MC, V.

ESPN Sports Club. American. This popular spot for catching a big game is on Disney's Board-Walk in the Epcot Resort Area. It has sports art on the walls, dozens of sports-tuned TV monitors scattered about, and part of the wall and ceiling are designed to resemble concrete bleachers, so it looks as though you are dining under a stadium. The menu includes burgers, the tail-gate barbecue pork sandwich, and a marinated tuna sandwich. | Disney's BoardWalk | 407/939–5100 | Reservations not accepted | $9–$16 | AE, MC, V.

House of Blues. Cajun/Creole. Looking like a rusted old factory from the outside, the place has been converted into a bizarre church-like setting for Southern cooking and live blues music. One of the house specialties is the Elwood (as in Blues Brothers) sandwich (blackened chicken with chili garlic mayonnaise and sour cream). Be sure to make reservations for the righteous gospel Sunday brunch. | Downtown Disney West Side | 407/934–2583 | $8–$18 | AE, D, MC, V.

Juan and Only's Bar and Jail. Tex-Mex. Dedicated to the Tex-Mex banderos who once ravaged the southwest, this restaurant offers you a chance to go to a pretend jail and have fun food while you're there. The lobster and papaya quesadilla is one of the more exotic dishes, but the house specialties such as the chiles rellenos and margaritas also deserve attention. | Walt Disney World Dolphin | 407/934–4000 | $8–$19 | AE, D, DC, MC, V.

Kimonos. Japanese. Popular with Japanese tourists, this sushi restaurant is in the Walt Disney Swan Resort in the Epcot Resort Area. Bamboo and paper lanterns adorn the dining room, and the chef prepares special Florida sushi with soft-shell crab. Other Japanese dishes such as steamed dumplings and beef or chicken teriyaki are also available. I–4 exit 26B. | Walt Disney World Swan | 407/934–1621 | No lunch | $15–$23 | AE, D, DC, MC, V.

Kona Cafe. Contemporary. Coffee and desserts are specialties here since the pastry Chef continually proves his talents by winning gold medal awards from the American Culinary Federation for such creations as his white chocolate guava cake and his Kahlúa torte. One entrée comes to your table filled with fish, clams, pork, and vegetables in a roasting bag, which is sliced open and served by your server. | Polynesian Resort | 407/939–3463 | $8–$13 | AE, D, DC, MC, V.

Le Cellier Steakhouse. Canadian. Step through the stone arches into the old wine cellar setting of this restaurant and enjoy tenderloin and prime ribs; or you can opt for something more exotic such as venison or glazed salmon. Maple Butterfinger mousse with raspberry sauce is a dessert stunner. | Epcot World Showcase, Canada Pavilion | 407/939–3463 | $8–$16 | AE, D, DC, MC, V.

Liberty Tree Tavern. American. Colonial period comfort food such as roast turkey, honey-cured Virginia ham, and beef brisket are mainstays here. The menu now includes some more interesting dishes such as a crêpe with thin-sliced, pan-seared steak and a brandy cream sauce. No alcohol. | Magic Kingdom, Liberty Square | 407/939–3463 | $12–$20 | AE, D, DC, MC, V.

Marrakesh. Moroccan. For a bit of the unusual, try some of the reasonably priced cous cous or kebab dishes. Chef Abrache Lahcen was personally recommended by the late King Hassan II of Morocco, so you know the food is authentic. The *bastilla* (an appetizer made of alternating layers of sweet-and-spicy pork and a thin pastry, redolent of almonds, saffron, and cinnamon) is a good way to start your meal, which comes complete with belly dancers and a traditional band. | Epcot World Showcase, Morocco Pavilion | 407/939–3463 | $12–$20 or $17.25 prix–fixe | AE, D, DC, MC, V.

Mitsukoshi. Japanese. Several little restaurants actually make up this tranquil garden area. At the Yakitori House, get simple and fast meals such as the teriyaki basted chicken skewers to-go from the tea house–style building. At Tempura Kiku you can sit around a central table and watch the sushi chefs in action. The larger Teppanyaki Dining Rooms have different stations with chefs stir-frying meats and vegetables to order. Nearby is the Motsu No Ma Lounge with seriously strong *saketinis* (martinis made with sake rather than vermouth). | Epcot World Showcase, Japan Pavilion | 407/939–3463 | $12–$22 | AE, D, DC, MC, V.

Narcoosee's. Seafood. Named after a small central Florida town, the food here is a tribute to local fare, especially seafood. Pan-fried grouper, grilled shrimp, and crab with potato cakes are some good standards, but you can also get fancy with focaccia served with duck pastrami and tiramisu. This casual spot also overlooks the Seven Seas Lagoon and is a good place to catch the Electric Water Pageant in the evening. | Grand Floridian Resort | 407/939–3463 | $12–$22 | AE, D, DC, MC, V.

Nine Dragons Restaurant. Chinese. Cantonese cuisine is the specialty with such dishes as *moo goo gai pan* (a stir-fried chicken or vegetable dish), but the Chinese style ranges from Szechuan and Hunan to Kiangche as well. To the common man, the seafood and meat dishes come served with sautéed vegetables and a variety of sauces, some of which are spicy. The lobster and sea treasure casserole is a combination of lobster tail, scallops, squid, and shrimp served with a ginger and scallion sauce on a bed of Chinese cabbage. | Epcot World Showcase, China Pavilion | 407/939–3463 | $9–$18 | AE, D, DC, MC, V.

Olivia's Café. American/Casual. This pleasant restaurant offers a wide variety of selections ranging from seafood to Mexican to good old fried chicken with mashed potatoes and gravy. The slow-roasted prime rib is especially good followed up with the chocolate chip pecan pie. You can sit outdoors and overlook the water when it's not too hot. | Old Key West Resort | 407/939–3463 | $6–$12 | AE, D, DC, MC, V.

Planet Hollywood. American/Casual. Memorabilia donated by Schwarzenegger, Stallone, and Willis, among other big names, keeps the place packed with curious tourists. Burgers, smoked and grilled meats, and contemporary salads can satisfy most appetites. There's an indoor waterfall and 20,000 square ft of movie memorabilia to keep you occupied. It's right outside the entrance to Pleasure Island. | Downtown Disney West Side | 407/827–7827 | Reservations not accepted | $8–$19 | AE, D, DC, MC, V.

Rainforest Café. Eclectic. A smoking volcano that erupts every few minutes and jungle animal calls entertain in this jungle-theme restaurant. People line up even before it opens to snag a table. The cool and damp jungle dining room "inside" the volcano is inviting if you've been out in the hot sun all day. The menu focuses on American dishes with funky names, such as Eyes of the Ocelot meat loaf, Rasta Pasta, and Mojo Bones tender ribs. The bar has fresh vegetable juices in addition to alcohol. | Downtown Disney Marketplace | 407/827–8500 | Reservations accepted on-site only | $6–$18 | AE, DC, MC, V.

Restaurant Akershus. Scandinavian. Seafood and cold meat dishes help compose the *koltbord* (Norwegian buffet), but you won't be confused for long because your hosts will carefully explain and suggest food options to you. Gravlax, or cured salmon, is served with mustard sauce and the traditional flatbread, *lefse,* is good to sop up your leftover gravy from some of the hot lamb or venison dishes. | Epcot World Showcase, Norway Pavilion | 407/939–3463 | $19 prix fixe | AE, D, DC, MC, V.

Rose and Crown. English. Traditional fish-and-chips and meat pies are served up in the jolly pub setting along with ale and beer. To get the full liquid effect, try the sampler, five 4-oz glasses of ale and beer for $8.25. Tea is served at 4 PM, and you'll find this one of the favorite employee hang-outs towards the end of the day because of the amiable crowd (and the fact that it is one of the more economical drinking venues in Epcot). | Epcot World Showcase, United Kingdom Pavilion | 407/939–3463 | $8–$20 | AE, D, DC, MC, V.

San Angel Inn. Mexican. Tropical surroundings envelop you while marimba music fills the air as you sit at the candlelit tables. Dinners such as the *mole poblano* (chicken simmered until tender in a rich sauce of different kinds of chilies, green tomatoes, ground tortillas, cumin, and 11 other spices mixed with cocoa), or any of the more common enchiladas or fajitas are good choices. | Epcot World Showcase, Mexico Pavilion | 407/939–3463 | $7–$16 | AE, D, DC, MC, V.

Seasons Dining Room. Eclectic. Every day brings a new season and menu to this interesting environment. It could be New Orleans night, with jambalaya, or Polynesian night, with grilled mahimahi. This is a good spot for those who are tired and want a change of pace, away from the crowds. | Disney Institute | 407/939–3463 | $7–$14 | AE, MC, V.

Wolfgang Puck Café. Contemporary. Pizzas and pastas are simple yet elegant lunch and dinner choices that will not require you to spend a fortune. Some of the pasta sauces contain hidden treasures such as lobster, salmon, or chicken, and there is always a fresh ravioli of the day. This is one of several Puck enterprises located around Walt Disney World. | Downtown Disney West Side | 407/938–9653 | $7–$24 | AE, MC, V.

EXPENSIVE

★ **Artist Point.** American. Northwest-style steaks and chops are cooked over a hardwood fire at this restaurant in Disney's Wilderness Lodge. Overlooking a waterfall and lake, the dining room is modeled after an early 20th-century national park lodge, with Rocky Mountain mural scenes. An outdoor terrace is also available. Although the menu changes seasonally, entrées might include smoked duck breast, pan-fried rainbow trout, and trail dust shortcake—a buttermilk biscuit with vanilla-bean ice cream, whipped cream, and strawberries. Pacific Northwest wines keep with the theme. | Wilderness Lodge | 407/824–3200 | Breakfast also available. No lunch | $17–$26 | AE, MC, V.

★ **Bistro de Paris.** French. This trés-cool and well-hidden bistro is around the back of Les Chefs de Paris and upstairs. The chic menu changes regularly and keeps up with the foremost in French cuisine and wines. A window seat late in the evening gets you a great view of the IllumiNations light show. | Epcot World Showcase, France Pavilion | 407/939–3463 | $16–$19 | AE, D, DC, MC, V.

California Grill. Contemporary. The 15th floor of the Contemporary Hotel Resort provides a dramatic view of the Magic Kingdom. This restaurant is a favorite of many a Disney exec for its imaginative, well-prepared cuisine by chef Clifford Pleau—dishes such as braised lamb shank with wild chanterelle risotto and orange sauce, pan-roasted grouper with herb dumplings, and cappuccino quake dessert. The menu changes seasonally. The dining room has a cove ceiling and black granite tables, but all eyes are on the open kitchen with a big wood-burning stove and rotisserie in the center. | Contemporary Resort | 407/824–1576 | No lunch | $15–$27 | AE, MC, V.

Flying Fish Cafe. Seafood. Along Disney's 1940s Atlantic coast waterfront, this upscale restaurant has whimsical touches including a faux Ferris wheel and postmodern fish sculptures dangling from the ceiling. Blue and aquamarine green walls set a soothing, relaxed mood. Chef John State changes the menu daily to reflect in-season fare in the United States. Specials might include peeky toe crab cakes, red snapper wrapped in a crisp potato casing and served with leek fondue and cabernet sauvignon reduction, and the oak-grilled scallops with corn-bacon risotto and chive blossoms. | Disney's BoardWalk | 407/939–3463 | No lunch | $20–$27 | AE, MC, V.

Fulton's Crab House. Seafood. This fish house fills three decks of the *Empress Lilly,* a replica of a 19th-century Mississippi riverboat docked in the lagoon between Downtown Disney Marketplace and Pleasure Island. The interior is filled with nautical memorabilia and there are views of the Marketplace. The menu includes Florida stone crab claws, tuna filet mignon with lemongrass sauce, and pan-fried oysters with spinach and bacon. Kids' menu. | Pleasure Island | 407/934–2628 | No lunch | $9–$50 | AE, MC, V.

Les Chefs de France. French. Operated by three of France's culinary masterminds, you can imagine the deluxe fare that is put forth here. The chicken and duck pâté or the *canard à l'orange* (duck roasted with sweet and sour orange sauce) are traditional choices, though there is always a vegetarian option of the day as well as other specials. Desserts are always winners with delicate pastry touches. | Epcot World Showcase, France Pavilion | 407/939–3463 | $15–$22 | AE, D, DC, MC, V.

L'Originale Alfredo di Roma Ristorante. Italian. The restaurant created in part by the descendants of Alfredo (the namesake to the creamy sauce) still upholds family traditions such as flying in butter from Italy. Pasta lovers will have trouble choosing between the many varieties and sauces, while the grouper is a good contender baked in a zesty sauce flavored with garlic. Cannoli or ricotta cheesecake are good meal enders. | Epcot World Showcase, Italy Pavilion | 407/939–3463 | $16–$26 or $33 prix–fixe | AE, D, DC, MC, V.

Mama Melrose's Ristorante Italiano. Italian. Tucked away in a corner of MGM-Studios, this casual spot has typical red-checkered tablecloths and red vinyl booths. The portions of Italian classics such as lasagna, spaghetti, and tiramisu are large. | Disney MGM-Studios | 407/934–3463 | $15–$23 | AE, MC, V.

'Ohana. Hawaiian. Meaning "family" in Hawaiian, 'Ohana has thatched roofs, carved Polynesian columns, and an open kitchen with a wood-burning, 18-ft grill. The prix-fixe feast includes steamed dumplings, salad, herb bread, grilled chicken, smoked sausage, marinated turkey breast, mesquite beef, teriyaki ribs, jumbo shrimp, stir-fried vegetables, and pineapple with caramel sauce. There are coconut races, storytellers, and singing and dancing. | Polynesian Resort | 407/939–3463 | No lunch | $21 | AE, MC, V.

Palio. Italian. This lively restaurant in the Walt Disney World Swan is the Orlando branch of the New York original, where good northern Italian fare is the specialty. Strolling musicians keep you entertained until the entrées arrive, such as red snapper, swordfish, and veal. | Walt Disney World Swan | 407/934–1610 | No lunch | $17–$30 | AE, MC, V.

Portobello Yacht Club. Italian. Northern Italian cuisine is featured here. Start off with sourdough bread and roasted garlic. *Spaghettini alla Portobello* is a good hearty meal choice because the sauce is filled with scallops, clams, shrimp, mussels, tomatoes, garlic, Portobello mushrooms, and herbs. The wood-oven pizza is made to order, and the desserts are creamy and delicious, including Crema Cotta Caramellata (a white chocolate custard with a baked sugar glaze and fresh wild berries). | Pleasure Island | 407/934–8888 | $12–$26 | AE, MC, V.

Spoodles. Mediterranean. The name is a twist on "noodles" and "spoons" at this restaurant on Disney's BoardWalk. The dining room centers around the open-air kitchen stage, and there are rainbow ceramics on every table. Dishes are inspired by the flavors of the Mediterranean Coast including the braised lamb shank prepared osso buco style, garnished with a gremolata of crumbled garlic toast, parsley and lemon zest, and the spice-crusted salmon with potato-fennel gratin and truffle oil. The fillet of yellowfin tuna is seared and drizzled with a saffron-scented aioli. | Disney's BoardWalk | 407/939–3463 | $16–$23 | AE, MC, V.

VERY EXPENSIVE

Citricos. Contemporary. While the restaurant's menu focuses on southern French cuisine, chefs include international influences. It's on the second floor of Disney's Grand Floridian Resort & Spa. The dining room has earth tones throughout. The kitchen is open so you can watch chefs create entrées such as roasted loin of lamb, Maine lobster ratatouille, or pork tenderloin with basil pesto and scalloped potatoes. | Grand Floridian Resort & Spa | 407/939–3463 | No lunch | $22–$36 | AE, MC, V.

★ **Victoria and Albert's.** Continental. This elaborate restaurant in Disney's Grand Floridian hotel has a gimmick: Every table is served by a maid (named Victoria at every table) and a butler (always an Albert), as well as a wandering harpist. The place is lavish and Victorian, complete with a domed ceiling and faux marble columns. Each table has leather chairs and Victorian lamps. Dinner is a seven-course prix fixe that changes nightly. The menu might include sautéed Peking duck with wild rice and cranberry chutney or jumbo sea scallops with shallot-chive sauce. There are two seatings each evening, the first beginning between 5:45 and 6:30, the second between 9 and 9:45. The special chef's table is also available nightly for up to six people. | Grand Floridian Resort & Spa | 407/939–3463 | Reservations essential | Jacket and tie | $85; $30 additional for Royal Wine Pairing; $115–$160 chef's table | AE, MC, V.

Yachtsman's Steak House. Steak. The beef on the tables at this restaurant in Disney's Yacht Club Resort is aged and grain-fed. You can check out the cuts for yourself in the glass beef-aging room, and watch the chefs prepare them in the open kitchen. The wood-paneled dining room with leather chairs has nautical memorabilia and western landscape murals. The menu includes the 18-oz Kansas City strip steak served on the bone and the mixed grill of a fillet of beef, lamb chop, and chicken breast. Kids' menu. | Yacht and Beach Club | 407/939–3463 | No lunch | $22–$29 | AE, MC, V.

Lodging

INEXPENSIVE

Disney's All-Star Movie Resort. The third All-Star Resort to go up, this themed budget hotel has smallish rooms. It's on Walt Disney World property in the Animal Kingdom Resort Area. The movie theme extends mostly to animated Disney movies, making this a good choice for the under 10 set. Blizzard Beach water park is next door. I–4 exit 25B. Restaurant, bar, room service. Cable TV. Pool, wading pool. Playground. Laundry facilities, laundry service. Baby-sitting, playground. Business services. | 1991 W. Buena Vista Dr. | 407/939–7000 | fax 407/939–7111 | www.disneyworld.com | 1,900 rooms | $74–$104 | AE, MC, V.

Disney's All-Star Music Resort. This huge, music-theme resort hotel has large images of music icons such as a walk-through-jukebox stationed at every stairway. Its 10 buildings on 246 acres of pine forest have musical themes from jazz to country to calypso. Rooms are small with two double beds with musically themed bedspreads, an armoire, and a desk. I–4 exit 25B. Restaurant, bar, room service (pizza only). Cable TV. 2 pools, wading pool. Video games. Playground. Laundry facilities. Business services. | 1801 W. Buena Vista Dr. | 407/939–6000 | fax 407/939–7222 | www.disneyworld.com | 1,920 rooms | $74–$104 | AE, MC, V.

Disney's All-Star Sports Resort. At this 82-acre hotel, giant sports motifs from football, basketball, and tennis, to surfing are stationed at every stairway. One of the pools is shaped like a baseball diamond, with the outfield as the sundeck. Rooms with sports-theme bedspreads sleep four on two double beds. I–4 exit 25B. Restaurant, bar, room service (pizza only). Cable TV. Pool, wading pool. Video games. Playground. Laundry facilities. Business services. | 1701 W. Buena Vista Dr. | 407/939–5000 | fax 407/939–7333 | www.disneyworld.com | 1,920 rooms | $74–$104 | AE, MC, V.

MODERATE

Best Western Lake Buena Vista Resort Hotel. Rooms accommodate up to four people at this 18-floor resort hotel on 12-acres on Lake Buena Vista. Throughout, the tropical landscaping is almost overwhelming, but a nice touch is the rain-forest look of the patio restaurant, which is even screened-in for the full effect. The rooms, though overwhelmed by their bright tropical print decor, are comfortable and include furnished balconies to enjoy the lake view. In-room Nintendo is an extra perk. Free Walt Disney World shuttle. Take I–4 exit 27. Restaurant, bar, room service. In-room data ports, in-room safes, refrigerators. Pool, wading pool. Video games. Playground. Laundry facilities, laundry service. | 2000 Hotel Plaza Blvd. | 407/828–2424 | fax 407/828–8933 | www.orlandoresorthotel.com | 325 rooms | $103–$179 | AE, D, DC, MC, V.

Courtyard by Marriott Downtown Disney. A 14-floor atrium, accented by glass elevators, overlooks the garden courtyard with a colorful cabana-covered lounge at this 14-story hotel ½ mi from Walt Disney World and within walking distance of Downtown Disney. Rooms are moderate in size and have two double beds, contemporary wood furnishings, in-room Nintendo, and most have balconies. Free Walt Disney World shuttle. I–4 exit 27. Restaurant, 2 bars. In-room data ports, refrigerators. Cable TV. Hot tub. Exercise equipment. Video games. Laundry facilities. Business services. | 1805 Hotel Plaza Blvd. | 407/828–8888 | fax 407/827–4623 | www.courtyardorlando.com | 323 rooms | $79–$169 | AE, D, MC, V.

Disney's Fort Wilderness Resort and Campground. Each wilderness home or cabin is surrounded by lush wilderness. Each of the one-bedroom units sleeps six and has one double bed and a set of bunk beds, a Murphy bed in the sitting area, a fully equipped kitchen, and a dining table that seats six. Each cabin has an outdoor patio-deck with a picnic table, charcoal grill and parking for one vehicle. In addition, Creekside Meadows is available for group tent camping in a more primitive section of the campground. Groups require a minimum of 20 people. Petting farm. Restaurants, bar, room service. In-room data ports, minibars. Cable TV, in-room VCRs (and movies). 2 pools, wading pool. Hot tub. Golf privileges, 2 tennis courts. Basketball, gym, horseback riding, volleyball. Beach, water sports, boating, fishing. Video games. Baby-sitting. Laundry facilities. Business services. | 4401 Floridian Way | 407/824–3000 | fax 407/824–3186 | www.disneyworld.com | 900 wilderness homes, 784 campsites | $184–$299 wildnerness home, $34–$77 campsite | AE, MC, V.

EXPENSIVE

Disney's Animal Kingdom Lodge. Rooms here overlook a savanna where giraffes, zebras, and other exotic animals roam about a spacious wildlife reserve. Rooms have hand-crafted furnishings, including a table and chairs, and are done in an African theme with bold gold hues. Sleeping areas have two queen-size beds, a king-size bed, or a queen-size bed and bunk beds. All have a private balcony, some with a savanna or pool view. I–4 exit 25B. 3 restaurants, bar, room service. In-room data ports, in-room safes. Cable TV. 2 pools, wading pool. Massage. Gym. Video games. Baby-sitting, playground. Laundry facilities, laundry service. Business services. | 1991 W. Buena Vista Dr. | 407/939–7000 | fax 407/939–7111 | www.disneyworld.com | 1,900 rooms | $199–$385 | AE, MC, V.

Disney's Caribbean Beach Resort. The seven buildings that make up this resort in the Epcot Resort Area are designed to look like a Caribbean village. Each structure wraps around its

own quiet swimming pool; a faux stone wall that looks like part of a colonial fortification, complete with booming cannon, borders one end of the communal pool, which has a water slide. The promenade that connects it all borders a placid lagoon, and the island in the middle, Parrot Cay, has a playground with soft white sand underfoot. Rooms are done in beige and olive. All have two double beds or one king-size bed, a table and chairs, and a ceiling fan. Some rooms have water views. I–4 exit 26B. 4 restaurants, bar, picnic areas. In-room safes, minibars. Cable TV. 7 pools, lake, wading pool. Hot tub. Golf privileges. Boating, bicycles. Shops, video games. Playground. Laundry facilities. Business services. | 900 Cayman Way | 407/934–3400 | fax 407/934–3288 | www.disneyworld.com | 2,112 rooms | $129–$209 | AE, MC, V.

Disney's Coronado Springs Resort. This hotel, close to Epcot and Disney's Animal Kingdom, has a Southwestern theme. Two-story peach buildings surround a lake. A Mayan pyramid sits in the center of a pool area. Rooms have turquoise and sand colors and sleep up to four people in two double beds; king-size beds are available. Some have water views. There is also a large playground surrounded by a nature walk. I–4 exit 25B. 4 restaurants, 2 bars, room service. In-room data ports, in-room safes, refrigerators. 4 pools, wading pool. Hot tub, massage, sauna. Tennis. Golf privileges. Gym, volleyball. Beach, boating, bicycles. Video games. Playground. Laundry facilities. Business services. | 1000 W. Buena Vista Blvd. | 407/939–1000 | fax 407/939–1001 | www.disneyworld.com | 1,967 rooms | $129–$209 | AE, MC, V.

Disney's Dixie Landings Resort. Louisiana-style Dixie Landings, which adjoins the Port Orleans resort, re-creates the plantation dwellings of Southern mansions. The bayou accommodations line a Mississippi-style waterway on the Disney canal system, so you can get to Downtown Disney by boat. Rooms are beige with quilts, poster beds, and have two double beds or one king-size bed, a table and chairs, and a ceiling fan. Some have water views. 3 restaurants, bar (with entertainment). In-room data ports, refrigerators. Cable TV, in-room VCRs. 6 pools, wading pool. Hot tub. Golf privileges. Boating, bicycles. Video games. Playground. Laundry facilities. Business services. | 1251 Dixie Dr. | 407/934–6000 | fax 407/934–5777 | www.disneyworld.com | 2,048 rooms | $129–$209 | AE, MC, V.

Disney's Port Orleans Resort. Reminiscent of the French Quarter in New Orleans, this impeccably manicured resort in the Downtown Disney Resort Area is complete with cobblestone streets and flat-bottom boat rides. Rooms can accommodate up to four and have green carpet, teal and pink bedding, with two double beds or one king-size bed, a table and chairs, and a ceiling fan. Some have water views. 2 restaurants, bar, room service (pizza only). In-room safes, cable TV, in-room VCRs. Pool, wading pool. Hot tub. Golf privileges. Boating, bicycles. Video games. Playground. Laundry facilities. Business services. | 2201 Orleans Dr. | 407/934–5000 | fax 407/934–5353 | www.disneyworld.com | 1,008 rooms | $129–$209 | AE, MC, V.

Grosvenor Resort. This 19-story peach stucco hotel across the street from Downtown Disney and ½ mi from Walt Disney World is on 13 tropically landscaped acres. The theme is British colonial, but the spacious rooms are simple with floral bedding in soft colors and have a view of Downtown Disney or the pool courtyard. Each sleeps up to 4 people. Kid-suites offer a separate sleeping area with bunk beds. I–4 exit 27. Restaurant, bar (with entertainment). In-room data ports. Cable TV, in-room VCRs (and movies). 2 pools, wading pool. Hot tub. 2 tennis courts. Exercise equipment, volleyball. Shops, video games. Playground. Laundry facilities. Business services. | 1850 Hotel Plaza Blvd. | 407/828–4444 or 800/624–4109 (reservations) | fax 407/827–8230 | www.grosvenorresort.com | 626 rooms | $170–$220 | AE, D, MC, V.

Hilton at Walt Disney World Resort. This 10-story hotel is the closest to Downtown Disney and only ½ mi from Walt Disney World. Waterfalls, fountains, and ponds filled with tropical fish adorn the lobby. At Vacation Station you can park your kids and enjoy a good adult dinner at one of the restaurants on property. Rooms are done in bright yellow and mauve hues and sleep up to four. I–4 exit 27. 9 restaurants, bar, room service. In-room data ports, minibars, microwaves, refrigerators. Cable TV. 3 pools, wading pool. Barbershop, beauty salon, hot tubs, sauna. Gym. Video games. Baby-sitting, children's programs (3–12).

Laundry facilities, laundry service. Business services. | 1751 Hotel Plaza Blvd. | 407/827–4000 or 800/916–2221 | fax 407/827–6369 | www.hilton.com | 814 rooms | $190–$270 | AE, D, MC, V.

Villas at the Disney Institute. This is a cluster of five villas within walking distance of Downtown Disney and 1 mi from Walt Disney World that share a single check-in point. The villas—Bungalows, Fairway Villas, Grand Vista Homes, Townhouses, and Treehouse Villas—range from one-story bungalows to two-story town houses that sleep four to eight people. Restaurant, bar. In-room data ports, microwaves, refrigerators. Pool. Hot tubs, massage. 4 tennis courts. Basketball, exercise equipment. Boating, bicycles. Playground. | 1960 N. Magnolia Way | 407/827–1100 | fax 407/827–4101 | 585 rooms | $204–$450 | AE, MC, V.

VERY EXPENSIVE

Disney's Beach Club Resort. Rising above a 25-acre man-made lake that's connected by a waterway to the lagoon at the center of Epcot, this hotel is designed to look like a classic late 19th-century New England summer resort. Stormalong Bay is a water recreation area with a 3-acre mini–water park with water slides and pool, white sand beaches, river, and bridges. Green and pink rooms have two queen-size beds or one king-size bed, table and chairs, ceiling fan, minibar, private balcony, vanity area with two sinks, and bath. Many rooms have water views. Refrigerators are available upon request. I–4 exit 26B. 2 restaurants, 2 bars, room service. In-room data ports, in-room safes, minibars, microwaves. Cable TV, in-room VCRs. Pool, wading pool. Hot tub. Barbershop, beauty salon, hot tub, massage, sauna. Volleyball. Bicycles. Video games. Children's programs (ages 4–12). Laundry facilities. Business services. | 1700 Epcot Resorts Blvd. | 407/934–7000 | fax 407/934–3450 | www.disneyworld.com | 1,213 rooms | $279–$480 | AE, MC, V.

Disney's BoardWalk Inn. In the Epcot Resort Area, this resort recalls Atlantic shore hotels of the 1920s to 1940s. The pool's 200-ft Keister Coaster waterslide is reminiscent of classic roller coasters. Rooms are pink and blue with two queen beds, a sofa, and a table. I–4 exit 26B. 2 restaurants, bar, room service. In-room data ports, in-room safes, refrigerators, in-room hot tubs. Cable TV, in-room VCRs (and movies). 2 pools, wading pool. Hot tub, massage, sauna. Driving range, golf privileges, 2 tennis courts. Gym. Boats, fishing, bicycles. Video games. Baby-sitting. Laundry facilities. Business services, airport shuttle. | 2101 N. Epcot Resorts Blvd. | 407/939–5100 | fax 407/939–5150 | www.disneyworld.com | 378 rooms | $279–$480 | AE, MC, V.

Disney's BoardWalk Villas. These units—from studios to three-bedroom villas—are done in red and beige with wood furnishings. Studio rooms have one queen-size bed and a double sleeper sofa, dining table with two chairs, and a balcony. The one-bedroom villa has a fully equipped kitchen, dining area, washer and dryer, and balcony. Many units have garden or water views overlooking Crescent Lake. I–4 exit 26B. In-room data ports, refrigerators, microwaves, in-room hot tubs. Cable TV, in-room VCRs (and movies). 2 pools, wading pool. Hot tub, massage. Golf access, mini-golf access. 2 tennis courts. Gym, bicycles, fishing, dock. Video games. Children's programs (ages 4–12). Laundry facilities. Business services, airport shuttle. | 2101 N. Epcot Resorts Blvd. | 407/939–5100 | fax 407/939–5150 | www.disneyworld.com | 532 apartments | $279–$415 studio; $375–$540 1–bedroom | AE, MC, V.

Disney's Contemporary Resort. The monorail to the Magic Kingdom runs right through the center of this A-shaped high-rise in the Magic Kingdom Resort Area. The swimming pool is immense, and there's a video game room. The hotel's California Grill is one of Disney's premier restaurants. The rooms done in pink and gray have large sliding doors and balconies. All have two queen-size beds or one king-size bed, a day bed, a table and chairs, and a ceiling fan. Many rooms have garden views. I–4 exits 25B, 26B. 6 restaurants, bar, room service. In-room data ports, in-room safes, refrigerators. Cable TV, in-room VCRs. Pool, wading pool. Golf privileges. Barbershop, beauty salon, hot tub, massage, sauna. 6 clay tennis courts. Gym, volleyball. Beach, water sports, fishing. Video games. Children's programs (ages 3–12), playground. Laundry facilities. Business services. | 4600 N. World Dr. | 407/824–1000 | fax 407/824–3539 | www.disneyworld.com | 1,041 rooms | $224–$445 | AE, MC, V.

Disney's Grand Floridian Resort and Spa. This sprawling, bright-white Victorian-style resort is on the monorail, alongside Seven Seas Lagoon, a quick ride from the Magic Kingdom. It's Disney's most luxurious hostelry and the site of two of its best restaurants, Victoria and Albert's and Citrico's. The Victorian-style rooms are done in white and have two queen-size beds or one king-size bed, a table and chairs, and a ceiling fan. Most rooms have a daybed and a balcony with a garden or water view. 8 restaurants, 2 bars, room service. In-room data ports, in-room safes, minibars. Cable TV, in-room VCRs (and movies). Pool, wading pool. Barbershop, beauty salon, hot tub, massage, sauna. Golf privileges, 2 clay tennis courts. Gym, volleyball. Beach, water sports, boating, fishing. Video games. Baby-sitting. Laundry facilities. Business services. | 4401 Floridian Way | 407/824–3000 | fax 407/824–3186 | www.disneyworld.com | 900 rooms | $304–$480 | AE, MC, V.

Disney's Old Key West Resort. With 60 buildings on 150 acres, this hostelry is modeled after a Key West resort circa 1900. Accommodations sleep from 4 (studios) to 12 (3-bedroom villa) guests. Rooms are done in peach with tropical highlights and have a patio or a balcony. I–4 exit 25B. Restaurants, bar. In-room data ports, in-room safes, refrigerators. Cable TV, in-room VCRs. 4 pools, wading pool. Hot tubs, massage. Golf privileges, 3 tennis courts. Basketball, gym, volleyball. Boating, bicycles. Video games. Playground. Laundry facilities. | 1510 N. Cove Rd. | 407/827–7700 | fax 407/827–7710 | www.disneyworld.com | 761 rooms | $244–$349 studio, $330–$480 villa | AE, MC, V.

Disney's Polynesian Resort. The South Seas provides the theme for this well-loved hotel, one of Walt Disney World's originals. Rooms, which accommodate up to six, are in dark-wood longhouses, which are angled along winding paths fringed by tropical vegetation. It's in the Magic Kingdom Resort Area, on the monorail, less than ¼ mi from the Magic Kingdom turnstiles. Or you can walk home from the theme park. Rooms have four-poster canopy beds, in creme and mauve hues, with two queen-size beds and a day bed, a table and chairs, and a ceiling fan. Most have a balcony or patio with a garden or water view. 5 restaurants, bar, room service. In-room data ports. Cable TV, in-room VCRs. 2 pools, lake, wading pool. Massage. Golf privileges. Volleyball. Beach, water sports, boating, fishing. Video games. Children's program (ages 3–11), playground. Laundry facilities. | 1600 Seven Seas Dr. | 407/824–2000 | fax 407/824–3174 | www.disneyworld.com | 853 rooms | $289–$520 | AE, MC, V.

Disney's Wilderness Lodge. This rustic lodge in the Magic Kingdom Resort Area looks like something out of the Pacific Northwest with its fir-and-pine landscaping, Native American motifs, park lodge furniture, and balconied lobby columned with tall timbers. Rooms are done in red with mahogany furnishings and have two queen-size beds, one queen-size bed and bunk beds, or one king-size bed, table and chairs, a writing table, a ceiling fan, and a balcony or patio. Many rooms have courtyard views. 3 restaurants, bar, room service, picnic area. In-room data ports, microwaves, refrigerators. Cable TV, in-room VCRs. 7 pools, wading pool. Hot tubs. Boating, beach, bicycles. Video games. Children's programs (ages 4–12), playground. Laundry facilities. Business services. | 901 W. Timberline Dr. | 407/824–3200 | fax 407/824–3232 | www.disneyworld.com | 724 rooms, 4 suites | $188–$355 | AE, MC, V.

Disney's Yacht and Beach Club Resorts. This resort in the Epcot Resorts Area, just a stroll from the park's International Gateway, adjoins Disney's Beach Club and shares its water recreation area, which includes a complex of pools, water slides, and bridge-crossed streams. Rooms, which sleep up to four, are white and bright with blue-and-white-checkered bedspreads and gray carpet. Each has two queen-size beds or one king-size bed, a table and chairs, a ceiling fan, a minibar, and a balcony. Many rooms have water views. 2 restaurants, bar, room service. In-room data ports, in-room safes, minibars, microwaves. Cable TV, in-room VCRs. 3 pools, wading pool. Barbershop, beauty salon, hot tub, massage, sauna. Golf privileges, 2 tennis courts. Gym, volleyball. Beach, boating, bicycles. Video games. Children's programs (ages 4–12). Laundry facilities. Business services. | 1700 Epcot Resorts Blvd. | 407/934–7000 | fax 407/934–3450 | www.disneyworld.com | 1,213 rooms | $279–$480 | AE, MC, V.

Walt Disney World Dolphin. Renowned postmodern architect Michael Graves designed two elegant hotels at Walt Disney World, and this pyramid-shape tower in the Epcot Resorts Area, dominated by a pair of surreally large dolphins, is one of them. The huge pool has a water slide. You can see Epcot's nighttime IllumiNations from rooms that face the park, and *Palio* is one of the many restaurants. Rooms are tropical Florida with pink and blue florals, and have a king-size or two double beds. Other rooms have Japanese, Southwestern, Oriental, Mediterranean, and Egyptian themes. There's a 3-acre grotto pool with white-sand beach. 6 restaurants, bar, room service. In-room data ports, in-room safes, minibars. Cable TV, in-room VCRs. 4 pools, wading pool. Hot tub, massage, sauna. 4 tennis courts. Gym, volleyball. Beach, water sports, boating, fishing. Video games. Playground. Business services, airport shuttle. | 1500 Epcot Resorts Blvd. | 407/934-4000 | fax 407/934-4499 | www.swandolphin.com | 1,369 rooms, 140 suites | $295–$425, $410–$3100 suites | AE, D, MC, V.

Walt Disney World Swan. In the Epcot Resort Area, two 46-ft swans rise above the roof of this polished Michael Graves–designed hotel, a 12-story tower with a pair of seven-story wings that faces the Dolphin across Crescent Lake. Guests share all the facilities with the Dolphin. 5 restaurants, 3 bars, room service. In-room data ports, minibars. Cable TV, in-room VCRs. 4 pools, wading pools. Hot tub, massage, sauna. Golf privileges, 4 tennis courts. Gym, volleyball. Beach, water sports, boating, fishing. Video games. Playground. Business services, airport shuttle. | 1200 Epcot Resorts Blvd. | 407/934-3000 | fax 407/934-4499 | www.swandolphin.com | 649 rooms, 109 suites | $295–$425, $410–$3100 suites | AE, D, MC, V.

WEST PALM BEACH

MAP 3, L8

(Nearby towns also listed: Belle Glade, Boynton Beach, Delray Beach, Lake Worth, Lantana, Palm Beach, Palm Beach Gardens, Palm Beach Shores, Riviera Beach)

When oil baron Henry Morrison Flagler built his dream city for the rich and famous in Palm Beach in the 1890s, West Palm was set aside for the middle-class fishermen and laborers he had uprooted. For long, the town was considered Palm Beach's impoverished cousin, untouchable across the Intracoastal Waterway.

However, capital improvements such as the Kravis Center for the Performing Arts, the Norton Museum, and a revitalized downtown area have turned West Palm Beach into the county's cultural, entertainment, and business center. Flagler Drive and Rosemary Avenue, the cornerstones of this rebirth, are filled with sculpted palm trees, bustling cafés, and galleries. Thursday nights the streets are closed to traffic, and crowds spill with music, open air dining, and reverie.

Information: **Palm Beach County Tourist Information Center** | 8020 West Indiantown Road, Jupiter, 33478 | 561/575-4636 | www.palmbeachfl.com.

Attractions

Ann Norton Sculpture Gardens. You'll find seven English-style granite figures and six brick megaliths on these three-acre grounds. The gardens are a monument to the late American sculptor and environmentalist Ann Weaver Norton, the second wife of Norton Museum founder Ralph H. Norton. The plantings, designed by Norton, were designed to attract native bird life. | 253 Barcelona Rd. | 561/832-5328 | fax 561/835-9305 | annorton@bellsouth.net | $5 | Mid-May–Oct., Wed.–Sun. 11–4.

Clematis Street. As good as the malls are, they're sterile compared to the in-the-midst-of-things excitement—the mix of food, art, performance, landscaping, and retailing—that has renewed downtown West Palm around Clematis Street. Water-view parks, outdoor performing areas, and attractive plantings and lighting—including fanciful palm tree sculptures—add to the pleasure of browsing, window-shopping, and resting at an outdoor cafe. | Clematis St.

Lion Country Safari. More than 1,300 wild animals roam free in this 500-acre wildlife preserve, the nation's first cageless zoo. Residents include zebras, ostriches, and rhinoceri. There are also an aviary; an alligator moat; a nursery; a petting zoo; Pelican Island, a refuge for injured pelicans; and Safari World, which includes a 10-min boat cruise around Siaming and Spider Monkey islands on the *Safari Queen*. | 2003 Lion Country Safari Rd., Loxahatchee | 561/793–1084 | $15.50; car rental $6 per 90 min | Daily 9:30 –5:30.

Mounts Botanical Gardens. This little-known horticultural center, across the street from Palm Beach International Airport, has more than 14 acres of rare trees, serene gardens, native plants, and butterfly and rainforest gardens. | 531 N. Military Trail | 561/233–1749 | www.mounts.org | Free | Mon.–Sat. 8:30–4:30, Sun. 1–5.

Norton Museum of Art. Steel magnate Ralph H. Norton built this museum in 1941 to showcase his extensive collection of 19th- and 20th-century American and European paintings, with special emphasis on French Impressionism. Nine galleries feature traveling exhibits and art from the permanent collection. | 1451 S. Olive Ave. | 561/832–5194 | www.norton.org | $6 | Tues.–Sat. 10–5, Sun. 1–5.

Okeeheelee Nature Center. You can explore 2½ mi of paved and shallow rock trails amid 100 acres of native pine–flat woods and wetlands. The center holds regular special events, and guided walks daily except Mondays. | 7715 Forest Hill Blvd. | 561/233–1400 | Free | Visitor center open Tues.–Fri. 1–4:45, Sat. 8:15–4:45.

Old Northwood Historic District. Sundays you can take walking tours of this 1920s-era neighborhood on the National Register of Historic Places. | 26th and 35th Sts. west of Flagler Dr.

Palm Beach Kennel Club. Greyhounds have been racing here since 1932. There are simulcasts of jai alai and horse racing all year. | 1111 N. Congress Ave. | 561/683–2222 | $1 | Races Mon. 12:30, Wed.–Thurs., Sat. 12:30 and 7:30; Fri. 7:30; Sun. 1.

Palm Beach Zoo at Dreher Park. You can see 500 animals representing 100 species at this 22-acre zoo, including the endangered Florida panther, two Bengal tigers, and red kangaroos. You can also tour the reptile house, walk along a nature trail, and make friends at the children's zoo. | 1301 Summit Blvd. | 561/533–0887 | www.palmbeachzoo.org | $6 | Daily 9–5.

Pine Jog Environmental Education Center. The draw here is 150 acres of mostly undisturbed Florida pine flat woods with two self-guided ½-mi trails. Formal landscaping around the five one-story buildings features an array of native plants, and dioramas of native ecosystems. Trails are open to the public Sunday afternoons. | 6301 Summit Blvd. | 561/686–6600 | Free | Daily 9–5, trails Sun. 2–5.

Raymond F. Kravis Center for the Performing Arts. Named for a prominent geologist and philanthropist who wintered in Palm Beach, this $60 million center hosts over 800 events a year. The 35-ft-high twin steel spires on the roof pay allude to the Breakers and Biltmore hotels. | 701 Okeechobee Blvd. | 561/832–7469 | Weekdays 8:30–5.

Robert and Mary Montgomery Armory Arts Center. Built by the WPA in 1939, the facility is now a complete visual arts center. Its gallery hosts rotating exhibitions, and classes are held throughout the year. | 1703 S. Lake Ave. | 561/832–1776 | Free | Weekdays 9–5, Sun. 10–2.

South Florida Science Museum. In addition to interactive science exhibits, you'll find planetarium shows and aquarium displays with touch tanks at this museum. Friday nights you can look at the stars through South Florida's most powerful telescope. The museum is off Summit Blvd., behind the Palm Beach Zoo at Dreher Park. | 4801 Dreher Trail N | 561/832–1988 | $6; planetarium $2 | Mon.–Thurs. 10–5, Fri. 10–10, Sat. 10–6, Sun. noon–6.

ON THE CALENDAR

JAN.–FEB.: *South Florida Fair and Exposition.* This 17-day event at the South Florida Fairgrounds has everything you'd expect from an old-fashioned county fair: live entertainment, arts and crafts, animals, a midway, a circus, and lots of food. | 9067 Southern Blvd. | 561/793–0333.

APR.–MAY: SunFest. With over 40 bands and over 400,000 people, this festival, along Flagler Dr. downtown, is one of Florida's largest. Beside music, there's a judged art show, fireworks, waterfront activities, and a youth park. | 561/659–5980 or 800/SUN–FEST.

Dining

391st Bomb Group. American. This franchise at the airport allows you to watch planes taking off over pasta, lobster tails, crab cake, prime rib, or fish specials. The restaurant, founded by World War II vets, is decorated with battlefield memorabilia. | 3989 Southern Blvd. | 561/683–3919 | $16–$35 | AE, D, DC, MC, V.

Aleyda's Tex-Mex Restaurant. Tex-Mex. Since 1981, this casual family-style favorite has offered classic Mexican dishes such as fajitas and chimichangas. The bar claims the best margaritas in town. | 1890 Okeechobee Blvd. | 561/688–9033 | $8–$11 | AE, DC, MC, V.

Café Protégé. Contemporary. At this restaurant at the Florida Culinary Institute, diners can watch chefs chopping, dicing, and slicing in the unique observation kitchen. Try the lavender herb- and Gorgonzola-encrusted rack of lamb served with cabernet mashed potatoes, sautéed mushrooms and bok choy ragout in a balsamic reduction. Another superb dish is the Floridian bouillabaisse, with shrimp, scallops, clams, mussels, and whitefish. | 2400 Metrocentre Blvd. | 561/687–2433 | Reservations essential | No lunch weekends. Closed Sun. | $16–$32 | AE, MC, V.

Don Ramone. Cuban. Low ceilings with wood beams give this wonderful three-room restaurant a cozy, warm ambiance. Try the *bistec de pollo* (marinated chicken breast grilled with sauteed onions), or *ropa vieja* (shredded beef in a tomato base). | 7101 S. Dixie Hwy. | 561/547–8704 | $7–$19 | AE, D, MC, V.

Great Texas Land and Cattle Co. Steak. Fifteen min from the beach, this casual local favorite serves prime rib, NY strip, rib eye, and other great steaks. Seafood choices include Alaskan king crab legs. | 6000 N. Military Trail | 561/840–1511 | Reservations not accepted | No lunch | $10–$19 | AE, D, DC, MC, V.

Morton's of Chicago. Steak. This steakhouse is in the classic Chicago style, with a dimly lit, dark-wooded, warm interior. The two most popular dishes are the double cut filet mignon with a béarnaise sauce, and the live Maine lobster. | 777 S. Flagler Dr. | 561/835–9664 | Reservations essential | $20–$33 | AE, D, MC, V.

No Anchovies. Italian. "The kids don't like anchovies," according to one of the owners, "and that's how the restaurant got its name." This casual family restaurant's specialties include rigatoni a la vodka, capellini with chicken and artichokes, and brick oven pizzas. | 771 Village Blvd. | 561/684–0040 | Reservations not accepted | No lunch Sun. | $11–$16 | AE, D, DC, MC, V.

Rain Dancer Steak House. Steak. Since 1975, this dark and cozy restaurant has served thick and juicy filet mignons, giant 24-oz porterhouse steaks, sizzling sirloins for two, and grilled lean flank steaks. | 2300 Palm Beach Lakes Blvd. | 561/684–2811 | www.raindancer-steakhouse.com | Reservations not accepted | No lunch | $17–$40 | AE, D, DC, MC, V.

Pescatore Seafood and Oyster Bar. Seafood. There's a sophisticated bustle beyond the handsome French doors of this trendy spot across from the fountain in Centennial Square. Enjoy *pescatore* for two (shrimps, scallops, clams, mussels, calamari, and lobster on a bed of linguini in a light marinara sauce), Maine lobster, grilled shrimp, and fresh grilled fish such as mahimahi, tuna, and salmon. | 200 Clematis St. | 561/837–6633 | $10–$32 | AE, D, DC, MC, V.

Roxy's. Continental. This kid-friendly favorite is decorated with mahogany and forest green leather booths, with an 1890s mahogany bar from Spalding Co. (a name you might recognize on bowling pins). Signature dishes include the Roxy Burger, made with beef and veal, and the chicken marsala. | 309 Clematis St. | 561/833–2402 | $9–$18 | AE, MC, V.

Lodging

Best Western Palm Beach Lakes Inn. Three mi from the beaches and across the street from Palm Beach Mall, this hotel has a 60-ft heated pool in the courtyard. There are shuffleboard and a lounge. Restaurant, bar, complimentary Continental breakfast. In-room data ports. Some microwaves, some refrigerators, cable TV. Pool. Airport shuttle. | 1800 Palm Beach Lakes Blvd. | 561/683–8810 or 800/331–9569 | fax 561/478–2580 | www.bestwestern.com | 132 rooms, 3 suites | $89–94 | AE, D, DC, MC, V.

Blossom's Otahiti. After a summer 2000 renovation, this B&B has a casual dining area, a bright family room, and an elegant living room. There is a screened-in pool and patio area, a lush garden, and a pond with water lilies and tropical fish. Complimentary breakfast, dining room. TV in common area. Laundry facilities. Some pets allowed (fee). | 3169 Horseshoe Circle W | 561/640–9295 | fax 561/640–9542 | www.blossoms-otahiti.com | 4 rooms | $95 | AE, MC, V.

Comfort Inn. This six-story budget motel is 3 mi south of West Palm Beach International Airport, and 20 min from the beaches. Most of the rooms have patios or balconies that overlook the pool area. A new in-house restaurant opens in 2001, but there are plenty within walking distance. You can also hit the gym at a nearby health club with which the motel is affiliated. Complimentary Continental breakfast. In-room data ports, in-room safes, some microwaves, some refrigerators, cable TV. Pool. Video games. Laundry facilities, laundry service. Business services. Pets allowed (fee). | 1901 Palm Beach Lakes Blvd. | 561/689–6100 or 800/228–5150 | fax 561/686–6177 | www.comfortinn.com | 162 rooms | $120 | AE, D, DC, MC, V.

Courtyard by Marriott. Five mi from beaches and golfing, and 1 mi from Rapids Water Park, this hotel features comfortable rooms with balconies. The restaurant serves only a breakfast buffet ($7.95 per person). A complimentary car service is available for nearby travels. A private courtyard area has a pool, whirlpool, and exercise room. Restaurant. In-room data ports. Cable TV. Pool. Hot tub. Gym. Laundry facilities. Business services. | 600 Northpoint Pkwy. | 561/640–9000 or 800/321–2211 | fax 561/471–0122 | www.courtyard.com/pbich | 149 rooms | $109–$134 | AE, D, DC, MC, V.

Crowne Plaza Hotel. This luxurious four-story hotel features an atrium with skylight windows, a gift shop, and a fitness room. The hotel is about 8 mi from the beach. Restaurant, bar, room service. In-room data ports, some refrigerators. Cable TV. Pool. Outdoor hot tub. 2 tennis courts. Gym. Laundry service. Airport shuttle. | 1601 Belvedere Rd. | 561/689–6400 | fax 561/683–7150 | www.crowneplaza.com | 109 rooms, 110 suites | $160–$229 | AE, D, DC, MC, V.

Days Inn West Palm Beach/Airport North. A lush tropical courtyard garden creates a colorful tropical atmosphere at this motel. Rooms are basic, but have balconies. Restaurant. Some in-room data ports, in-room safes, some microwaves, some refrigerators. Cable TV. Pool. Outdoor hot tub. Laundry facilities. Airports shuttles. Pets allowed (fee). | 2300 45th St. | 561/689–0450 or 800/544–8313 | fax 561/686–7439 | www.daysinn.com | 214 rooms | $52–$70 | AE, D, DC, MC, V.

Fairfield Inn West Palm Beach. The rooms are basic at this hotel and face either the road or the parking lot. This four-story building is 6 ½ mi from the beach. Complimentary Continental breakfast. In-room data ports. Cable TV. Pool. Gym. Business services, airport shuttle. | 5981 Okeechobee Blvd. | 561/697–3388 or 800/228–2800 | fax 561/697–2834 | 114 rooms | $99 | AE, D, DC, MC, V.

Hampton Inn Palm Beach/International. This hotel is ¼ mi west of I–95, 10 minutes from downtown. Rooms are comfortable, but the only views are of the parking lot. Complimentary Continental breakfast. In-room data ports. Cable TV. Pool. Gym. Business services, airport shuttle. | 1505 Belvedere Rd. | 561/471–8700 or 800/888–0175 | fax 561/689–7385 | 135 rooms | $119 | AE, D, DC, MC, V.

Hibiscus House. Built in 1922 by Mayor David Dunkle during the Florida land boom, this Cape Cod–style B&B began the beautification trend that landed the neighborhood on the National Register of Historic Places. Rooms are individually decorated with antiques the owner collected during his career as an interior designer. Each room of this residential B&B has a terrace view of the attractive poolside covered in tropical Florida foliage. Complimentary breakfast. In-room data ports, microwaves. Cable TV. Pool. Airport shuttle. Pets allowed. | 501 30th St. | 561/863–5633 or 800/203–4927 | fax 561/863–5633 | www.hibiscushouse.com | 5 rooms, 2 suites, 1 apartment, 1 cottage | $95–$170 | AE, D, MC, V.

Holiday Inn Palm Beach Airport. Rooms at this 11-story hotel are basic. Some have poolside views (others face I–95). The hotel is 15 min from the beach and 2 min from the airport. Restaurants, bar, room service. In-room data ports, refrigerators. Cable TV. Pool. Exercise equipment. Business services, airport shuttle. | 1301 Belvedere Rd. | 561/659–3880 | fax 561/655–8886 | www.holiday-inn.com | 199 rooms | $99–$129 | AE, D, MC, V.

Knights Inn. This efficient motel is popular with business travelers. Each room is carpeted, and comes with either two double, a queen-, or a king-size bed. There are plenty of palm trees and tropical landscaping around the property, and the beach is about 20 mi away. In-room safes, some microwaves, some refrigerators. Cable TV. Pool. Business services. Airport shuttle. | 2200 45th St. | 561/478–1554 or 877/309–5225 | fax 561/478–7183 | www.knightsinn.com | 120 rooms | $49 | AE, D, DC, MC, V.

Palm Beach Airport Hilton. Three mi west of the beach, this 10-story hotel underwent a complete renovation in December 1999. The hotel is between the airport and Lake Cloud, where you can fish or water ski. The rooms are luxurious; many overlook the lake. Restaurant, bar, room service. In-room data ports, some in-room safes, some refrigerators. Cable TV. Pool. Outdoor hot tub. Tennis. Gym. Dock, fishing, boating, water sports. Laundry service. Business services. Airport shuttle. | 150 Australian Ave. | 561/684–9400 or 800/916–2221 | fax 561/689–9421 | www.hilton.com | 244 rooms, 2 suites | $184–$525 | AE, D, DC, MC, V.

Parkview Motor Lodge. This beautifully landscaped motel is 1½ mi from the beach. The carpeted rooms, some with private balconies, are comfortable and well kept. It's a simple but comfortable place. Complimentary Continental breakfast. In-room data ports, refrigerators. Cable TV. | 4710 S. Dixie Hwy. | 561/833–4644 or 800/523–8978 | fax 561/833–4644 | 27 rooms, 1 suite | $76–$88 | AE, D, DC, MC, V.

Red Roof Inn. This chain motel is 20 min from the beach and Palm Beach Mall. Rooms are basic with pastel walls and carpeting, and wood furniture, but the pool area and the landscaping around the building are lush, with tropical foilage and blooming flowers. In-room data ports, some microwaves, some refrigerators, cable TV. Pool. Some pets allowed (fee). | 2421 Metro Center Blvd. E | 561/697–7710 or 800/843–7663 | fax 561/697–1728 | www.redroof.com | 129 rooms | $84 | AE, D, DC, MC, V.

Royal Palm House B&B. This tastefully decorated and well-maintained Dutch colonial–style B&B was built in 1925. It has five individually decorated rooms and the Date Palm Cottage, which has a full kitchen, two queen-size beds, and a Jacuzzi tub and shower. The hosts serve a complimentary home-cooked breakfast, and there are complimentary cocktails in the evening. Complimentary breakfast, dining room. Some in–room data ports, some kitchenettes, some microwaves, some refrigerators. Cable TV, some in-room VCRs. Pool. No kids under 14. | 3215 Spruce Ave. | 561/863–9836 or 800/655–3196 | fax 561/863–9836 | www.royalpalmhouse.com | 4 rooms, 1 cottage | $75–$125 | AE, D, DC, MC, V.

Sheraton. This 10-story hotel caters to short-term business customers, with luxurious rooms and marble bathrooms. Some rooms have balconies. The hotel is two blocks from downtown, and 3 mi from the beach. Restaurant, bar (with entertainment), room service. In-room data ports. Cable TV. Pool. Hot tub. 2 tennis courts. Exercise equipment. Laundry service. Business services, airport shuttle. | 630 Clearwater Park Rd. | 561/833–1234 or 800/325–3535 | fax 561/833–4689 | www.sheraton.com | 349 rooms | $150–$170 | AE, D, DC, MC, V.

Tropical Gardens B&B. This cozy cottage-style B&B has a colorful Key West atmosphere, more informal than its Old Northwood neighbors. The white picket fence, French doors, and bright yellow paint create a tropical, relaxed mood. Rooms are distinct, but the poolside Carriage House and Cabana House are most adorable. Complimentary breakfast. Some kitchenettes. Cable TV, in-room VCRs (and movies). Pool. Bicycles. Laundry service. No kids under 21. Pool. Bicycles. | 419 32nd St. | 561/848–4064 or 800/736–4064 | fax 561/848–2422 | www.tropicalgardensbandb.com | 2 rooms, 2 cottages | $75–$125 | AE, MC, V.

Wellesley Inn. This six-story building is 4 mi from the beach. Standard rooms come with views of the city. Complimentary Continental breakfast. In-room data ports, refrigerators. Cable TV. Pool. Laundry service. Business services. Pets allowed. | 1910 Palm Beach Lakes Blvd. | 561/689–8540 or 800/444–8888 | fax 561/687–8090 | www.wellesley.com | 93 rooms, 13 suites | $67–$110 | AE, D, MC, V.

WHITE SPRINGS

MAP 3, H2

(Nearby towns also listed: Lake City, Live Oak)

White Springs is on the legendary Suwannee River, made famous by Steven Foster's song "Old Folks at Home." The river is a federally protected waterway, and White Springs abuts the Osceola National Forest, so nature is part of local life and lore.

White Springs has a long history of Indian settlement, and it's here that local tribes congregated with freed slaves, creating the Seminole tribe. Much of the local development centered around White Sulphur Springs which had been used by natives for centuries as a healing grounds and mutual territory. During the Civil War, the area became a refuge for coastal residents fleeing Yankee invaders. Many never left, and by the late 1800s there were 14 hotels and all the trimmings of a major town.

Today, an 88-structure historic district on the National Register of Historic Places has preserved much of the feel of that period. The town is also surrounded by thousands of acres of public lands, making it a great area for recreational activities.

Information: **Suwannee County Chamber of Commerce** | 601 Howard St. E, Live Oak, 32060 | 904/362–3071.

Attractions

Stephen Foster State Folk Culture Center. This 247-acre complex on the Suwannee River honors the memory of early 19th-century songwriter Stephen Foster, whose song, "Old Folks at Home," immortalized the waterway. A museum houses dioramas with scenes from Foster's most famous songs, along with rare pianos and musical instruments. In the crafts area, you can watch artisans at work, and buy their products. There is a new campground with 45 sites, and 3 mi cycling and walking trails. Wildlife includes deer, possums, raccoons, and snakes. There are daily guided tours at the complex, off I–75 at exit 84. | U.S. 41 N | 904/397–2733 | fax 904/397–4262 | $3.25 per vehicle | Daily 8–dusk, exhibits 9–5.

ON THE CALENDAR

MAY: *Florida Folk Festival.* Since 1952, the Stephen Foster State Folk Culture Center has run this Memorial Day weekend event, with musicians, dancers, arts and crafts, folk games, and food. | 850/488–1484 or 800/847–7278.

Lodging

Suwannee Valley Campground. Located on the high banks of the Suwannee River, this scenic and tranquil site offers fully equipped cabins, in addition to campsites. Each cabin sleeps four, and has air-conditioning, a microwave, a refrigerator, and a porch. Hiking trails run through the property. Pool. TV in common area. Hiking. Dock, water sports, fishing. Playground. Laundry facilities. Pets allowed. | Rt. 1 Box 1860 | 904/397–1667 | fax 904/397–1560 | www.isgroup.net/camping | 12 cabins | Cabin $39.

WINDLEY KEY

MAP 3, E6

(Nearby towns also listed: Islamorada, Key Largo, Long Key)

Windley Key was originally two small keys, but the gap was filled in with fossilized coral to accommodate railroad tracks. The quarried rock subsequently became popular as a substitute for marble in some of the more opulent homes in Miami. The quarry filled with sea water and today is the home of the Theater of the Sea, where you can take glass bottom boat tours or swim with dolphins. Windley Key has the highest point above sea level of any key—16 ft—and it is considered the first island of the Middle Keys.

Information: Florida Keys Visitor Center/Key Largo Chamber of Commerce | 106000 Overseas Hwy., Key Largo, 33037 | 305/451–1414 or 800/822–1088 | www.floridakeys.org.

Attractions

Theater of the Sea. Dolphins, sea lions, stingrays, and tropical fish swim—and you can swim with them, for an extra fee—in the blasted holes of the 1907 Windley Key railroad quarry. The park features marine mammal shows, sea life interaction programs, snorkel eco-tours, and glass-boat cruises. Reservations are required. | MM 84.5, OS | 305/664–2431 | $17.25; snorkel ecotours $55; dolphin swim $110, sea lion swim $75, stingray swim $35 | Daily 9:30–4.

Windley Key Fossil Reef State Geologic Site. Some 125,000 years ago, this coral reef was living submerged beneath the Atlantic Ocean and the Gulf of Mexico. Its fossilized coral rock was quarried by Flagler's railroad workers, whose old tools and equipment still remain on site. You can take rubbings of fossilized brain and star coral, or try one of five color-coded trails leading through the key. The Alison Fahrer Environmental Education Center houses geological, biological, and historic displays. | MM 85.5, BS | 305/664–2540 | Free; quarry trails $2.50 | Thurs.–Mon. 8–5.

CALENDAR OF EVENTS
MAR.: *Rain Barrel Annual Arts Festival.* Browse through 100 juried art exhibitors and listen to live jazz and blues music at this festival at bayside mile marker 86.7. | 305/852–3084.

WINTER HAVEN

MAP 3, I6

(Nearby towns also listed: Bartow, Davenport, Haines City, Lakeland, Lake Wales)

This town of 25,000 in the geographic heart of the state, half an hour from Orlando and Tampa, is surrounded by some of Florida's best citrus groves. It's perhaps better known, though, as the home of the state's first theme park, Cypress Gardens. Dick Pope, a real estate promoter, and his wife Julie, a southern belle with a green thumb, carved the place out of snake- and alligator-infested swamp on the shores of Lake Eloise during the Depression. It's been open ever since, famous for the antebellum-style hoop skirts of its female staff, and for its water ski shows, which have been imitated at theme parks all over the country. This largely retiree community is known for its system of 12 linked lakes, with good fishing and boating.

Information: Winter Haven Chamber of Commerce | Box 1420, Winter Haven, 33882 | 863/293–2138 | www.winterhavenfl.com.

WINTER HAVEN

INTRO
ATTRACTIONS
DINING
LODGING

Attractions

Cypress Gardens. Since 1936, Florida's first theme park has entertained with botanical gardens, amusement rides for adults and children, and a famous waterskiing show. The first of these aquatic performances was staged by park co-founder Julie Pope, who skied during World War II to entertain soldiers at a nearby military base. Today's extravaganza features human pyramids, backward and barefoot skiing, flips, pivots, jumps, and other stunts.

Some 8,000 varieties of plants, gathered from 75 countries, are landscaped on over 200 acres. Over the years, various other attractions have sprung up on the grounds: a small exhibit building devoted to electricity and radios, an immense model train layout, a 153-ft-high revolving platform, a butterfly conservatory, and a complement of shops and mostly southern-theme restaurants. The park, now owned by Anheuser-Busch, is affiliated with Tampa's Busch Gardens and Orlando's SeaWorld. | Rte. 540, off U.S. 27 | 941/324–2111 or 800/237–4826 (800/282–2123 in FL) | www.cypressgardens.com | $31.95, parking $4 | Feb.–Mar., daily 9:30–8; Apr., daily 9:30–9; May–Nov., daily 9:30–5.

Water Ski Museum and Hall of Fame. The world's largest collection of water ski photos, displays, and equipment is housed in this museum off U.S. 27, at the Haines City exit. Featured exhibits include a display highlighting every U.S. Water Ski Team since 1949, vintage photographs of waterskiing pioneers, and—believe it or not—the very first water skis, designed by Ralph Samuelson, who created the sport at Lake Pepin, Minnesota, in 1922. | 799 Overlook Dr. | 863/324–2472 | fax 863/324–3996 | Free | Weekdays 10–5.

ON THE CALENDAR

AUG.: *World Precision Hang Gliding Tournament.* Top athletes from around the world participate in this sporting tournament at Cypress Gardens. | 941/324–2111.
NOV.: *Cypress Gardens Mum Festival.* Enjoy the vibrant colors and arrangement of 3 million blooms on display, as well as the centerpiece 35-ft mum waterfall at the world's largest chrysanthemum festival. | 941/324–2111 or 800/237–4826 (800/282–2123 in FL).

Dining

Christy's Sundown. Greek. This restaurant opened as a drive-in in 1952. The new owner, Nicholas Christy, added his name to the old. Popular dishes include prime rib, and Athenian grouper seasoned with light Greek seasonings. | 1100 3rd St. SW (Hwy. 17) | 863/293–0069 | Closed Sun. | $10–$30 | AE, D, DC, MC, V.

Harborside. Seafood. At this casual family restaurant, try the stemmed or raw oysters served with butter, lemon, and homemade cocktail sauce, or the NY strip grilled then baked with tomato and fresh basil. | 2435 7th St. SW | 863/293–7070 | $9–$23 | AE, D, DC, MC, V.

Johnny's Restaurant. American. This restaurant, a former Shoney's, maintains a casual, family-style atmosphere. Good, inexpensive entrées include pot roast, and chicken strips with a side of vegetables, potatoes, or cranberry sauce. | 6005 Cypress Gardens Blvd. (Hwy. 540) | 863/324–2089 | $6–$8 | AE, D, DC, MC, V.

Outback Steakhouse. Steak. This family chain restaurant has an Australian theme. Try the Outback Special—center cut sirloin served with a choice of potatoes or vegetables and salad—or 4-oz steamed Maine lobster tails served with lightly salted butter. | 170 Cypress Gardens Blvd. | 863/295–9800 | $6–$25 | AE, D, DC, MC, V.

Shells Seafood Restaurant. Seafood. This casual, family restaurant is decorated with nautical gear. The catch of the day is grilled and served with rice and vegetables; shrimp pasta comes in a light cream sauce. | 1551 3rd Street SW | 863/299–7393 | $9–$21 | AE, D, MC, V.

Lodging

Best Western Admiral's Inn. Adjacent to Cypress Gardens, and 1 mi from Lake Eloise, this luxury hotel has a heated Olympic-size pool, and a lounge with a comedy club. Restaurant, bar, complimentary Continental breakfast. Refrigerators. Cable TV. Pool. Beauty salon.

Business services, airport shuttle. Pets allowed. | 5665 Cypress Gardens Blvd. (Hwy. 540) | 863/324–5950 or 888/879–3578 | fax 941/324–2376 | www.bestwestern.com | 157 rooms | $95–$105 | AE, D, DC, MC, V.

Budget Host Driftwood. This budget motel is 1½ mi from Cypress Gardens, and ¼ mi from the Cleveland Indians' spring training facility. Complimentary Continental breakfast. Refrigerators. Cable TV. Pool. Pets allowed. | 970 Cypress Gardens Blvd. (Hwy. 540) | 863/294–4229 or 800/283–4678 | fax 863/293–2089 | 23 rooms | $38–$68 | AE, DC, MC, V.

Chain of Lakes Beach Resort. This resort is on Lake Roy, which is connected to 11 other lakes by navigable canals. The resort also has 350 ft of private beach, fishing, and waterskiing. It is 2 min from Cypress Gardens. | 1823 Cypress Gardens Blvd. (Hwy. 540) | 863/324–6320 | fax 863/324–0373 | www.chain-of-lakes.com | 28 rooms | $169–$199 | AE, D, DC, MC, V.

Cypress Motel. This family retreat, 2 mi east of Cypress Gardens on a quiet side road, has a 50-ft pool surrounded by two acres of lush greenery. The rooms are basic, but tastefully decorated, with views of the pool and garden. There are four mobile homes behind the motel, and eight efficiencies. Lake Fox is 200 yards away. Picnic area, complimentary Continental breakfast. In-room data ports, some kitchenettes, some microwaves, some refrigerators. Cable TV, some in-room VCRs (with movies). Pool. Playground. Laundry facilities. Pets allowed. | 5651 Cypress Gardens Blvd. (Hwy. 540) | 863/324–5867 or 800/729–6706 | fax 941/324–5867 | www.cypressmotel.com | 21 rooms | $70–$80 | AE, D, DC, MC, V.

Holiday Inn Cypress Gardens, Winter Haven. This hotel is 1 mi west of Lake Shipp, in a quiet area with fishing, waterskiing, and boating. There is a Country Kitchen restaurant on the premises which serves breakfast, and a courtyard with a heated outdoor pool and a lounge area. Restaurant, room service. In-room data ports, refrigerators. Cable TV. Pets allowed. | 1150 3rd St. SW (Hwy. 17) | 863/294–4451 or 800/465–4329 | fax 863/293–9829 | www.holiday-inn.com | 223 rooms, 2 suites | $119–$139 | AE, D, DC, MC, V.

Winter Haven-Days Inn Cypress Gardens. Next door to the Cleveland Indians training complex, this Days Inn features rooms with either two queen- or one king-size bed. Complimentary Continental breakfast. Cable TV. Pool. | 200 Cypress Gardens Blvd. (Hwy. 540) | 863/299–1151 or 800/329–7466 | fax 863/297–8019 | www.daysinn.com | 105 rooms | $60–$100 | AE, D, DC, MC, V.

WINTER PARK

MAP 3, J5

(Nearby towns also listed: Altamonte Springs, Maitland, Orlando, Sanford)

Winter Park, an upscale residential suburb of 24,000, is only 5 mi north of downtown Orlando, but you'd never know it. Brick-paved Park Avenue, the main thoroughfare, is lined with boutiques, cafés, restaurants, and art galleries; cozy alleyways lead to more shops and restaurants. Lovely Central Park is the town's central gathering point. Nearby, side streets are lined with live oaks draped in Spanish moss, and stately homes punctuate the stores of canal-linked lakes.

Information: Winter Park Chamber of Commerce | 150 N. New York Ave., Box 280, Winter Park, 32790 | 407/644–8281 | www.winterparkcc.org.

Attractions

The Albin Polasek Galleries. This gallery is housed in the studio home and gardens of the late Czech-American sculptor Albin Polasek. The luxurious home overlooking Lake Osceola was designed by Polasek himself and built in 1950. It houses some 200 works. | 633 Osceola Ave. | 407/647–6294 | Free | Wed.–Sat. 10–noon and 1–4, Sun. 1–4. Closed July–Aug.

Central Park. This lush park, across the street along the popular Park Avenue shopping area, has fountains and shady sidewalk trails. | Park Ave. | Free | Daily 8–dusk.

The Charles Hosmer Morse Museum of American Art. The museum boasts the world's most comprehensive collection of the works of Louis Comfort Tiffany. There are over 4,000 lamps, watercolors, desk sets, and immense stained-glass windows. A breathtaking chapel, built for the 1893 World's Fair, has been painstakingly reassembled here. The museum also displays a major collection of American art and pottery, and representative collections of late 19th- and early 20th-century American painting, graphics, and decorative arts. | 445 Park Ave. N | 407/645–5311 | fax 407/647–1284 | $3 | Tues.–Sat. 9:30–4, Sun. 1–4.

Mead Gardens. The 55 acres in this unusual park have been left intentionally wild. Joggers use the trails that wind around a creek. A boardwalk offers perspectives of wetlands. | S. Denning Ave. | 407/599–3334 | Free | 8–sunset.

Rollins College. Founded in 1885, this is the oldest recognized college in Florida. The Spanish Mediterranean–style, 67-acre lakefront campus is two blocks from downtown. On campus are the Knowles Memorial Chapel, built in 1932, and the Annie Russell Theater, a 1931 building used in local theatrical productions. | 1000 Holt Ave. | 407/646–2233 | Free | Daily.
Cornell Fine Arts Museum. This museum in a Spanish-style villa on the Rollins College campus, houses a 6,000-object collection of 19th- and 20th-century American and European paintings, decorative arts, and sculpture. Quiet gardens surround the building. | 1000 Holt Ave. | 407/646–2526 | Free | Tue.–Fri. 10–5, Sat.–Sun. 1–5.

Winter Park Historical Association Museum. This historical museum next to Central Park displays photographs of now-vanished buildings and changing exhibits of antique furniture and local artifacts. | 200 W. New England Ave. | 407/647–8180 | Free | Thurs. 11–3, Sat. 9–1, Sun. 1–4.

SIGHTSEEING TOURS/TOUR COMPANIES
Winter Park Scenic Boat Tour. This hour-long pontoon boat tour begins on Lake Osceola and moves through the narrow canals to Lake Virginia, site of the Rollins College waterfront, and Lake Maitland. Hourly departures provide glimpses of private canalside homes and lakefront mansions. | 312 E. Morse Blvd. | 407/644–4056 | $7 | Daily 10–4.

ON THE CALENDAR
MAR.: *Winter Park Sidewalk Art Festival*. This huge, weekend festival in Central Park features more than 260 artists working in clay, fiber, leather, glass, metal, mixed media, painting, photography, sculpture, watercolor, and wood. There is also a children's art show, food kiosks, and continuous live music. The fest draws 350,000 people. | 407/644–8281.

Dining
Antonio's La Fiamma. Italian. There's a second-floor view of shimmering Lake Lily at this upscale restaurant a mile from downtown. The dining area glows with candlelight, crisp white linens, and china. Sauces are the heart of Sicilian chef Sebastian Santangelo's menu—catch a glimpse of him at work behind the kitchen counter, visible from most seats in the dining area. Try the ravioli *al funghetto* (stuffed with shiitake mushrooms in a pink sauce of cream and tomatoes), the veal chop with cognac sauce enhanced with lemon and fresh herbs, or the *zuppa di pesce* (shrimp, calamari, scallops, fish and langostino in a broth of tarragon, basil, garlic, and a touch of marinara). | 611 S. Orlando Ave., Maitland | 407/645–1035 | Closed Sun. No lunch Sat. | $15–$23 | AE, D, DC, MC, V.

Brazilian Pavilion. Brazilian. This fine, authentic Brazilian restaurant in downtown features a large dining room, with flowers, linens, and soft Brazilian music. The menu focuses on spicy Brazilian dishes, including heart of filet mignon in mushroom sauce; shrimp flavored by a piquant blending of onions, tomatoes, peppers, garlic and olive oil; and fillet of red snapper with shrimp and tomatoes au gratin. | 140 W. Fairbanks Ave. | 407/740–7440 | Closed Sun. | $12–$20 | AE, D, MC, V.

Café de France. Continental. This established Park Avenue restaurant offers a range of international flavors. Taste Asian inspiration in the grilled sesame-scented yellowfin tuna with tahini-peanut sauce and wasabi ponsu, or Latin spices in the New York strips with garlicky *mojo* sauces. An old favorite is the slow-cooked, crispy mallard duck, with braised leeks and a glaze of lavender and lime. | 526 S. Park Ave. | 407/647–1869 | Closed Sun.–Mon. | $15–$23 | AE, D, DC, MC, V.

Captain Mary's Bar and Grill. Seafood. This small restaurant near Rollins College has only 12 tables, but the mix of interesting sketches, black-and-white photographs, New England memorabilia, and 1940s music makes this a memorable stop. Specialties include fried green tomato sandwiches, black and blue burgers, grouper, and oysters. | 1881 Fairbanks Ave. | 407/599–9269 | Closed Sun. | $5–$11 | AE, D, DC, MC, V.

Chez Vincent. French. This 15-table fine-dining restaurant is on the first floor of a two-story brick building on the renovated Hannibal Square, two blocks west of Park Avenue. The interior is colored in olives, taupes, and cremes, with candles and flowers creating an intimate mood. The chef, Vincent Gagliano, formerly of Café de France, offers specialties such as Gulf shrimp sautéed in cream dill sauce, venison with sun-dried cherries in port wine sauce, rack of lamb with blue cheese sauce, and poached salmon with a sherry wine raspberry sauce. | 533 W. New England Ave. | 407/599–2929 | No lunch | $15–$23 | AE, D, DC, MC, V.

Dexter's. American. The menu changes monthly at this always-packed restaurant one block off of Park Avenue. The dining area is filled with low, cherry-wood tables with Art Deco chairs, and oversized French doors that open to the street. Past dishes include hickory-smoked tuna tartar, chicken tortilla pie, veggie peanut pasta, and garlic buccatini with fresh pesto. The bar offers 30 wines by the glass, or choose a bottle from the white-washed Chicago-brick vault. | 558 W. New England Ave. | 407/629–1150 | Reservations not accepted | $10–$18 | AE, D, DC, MC, V.

El Potro. Mexican. This small restaurant near the Winter Park Mall offers large portions of south-of-the-border favorites. The dining room features exposed brick walls, very low lighting, and festive tables decked with rainbow-colored Mexican throws. Beyond the basic tacos, burritos, and quesadillas, try the *taquitos mexicanos* (deep-fried corn tortillas stuffed with beef or chicken), or Maria's burritos (filled with beef and topped with nacho cheese). | 501 N. Orlando Ave. | 407/975–9132 | Reservations not accepted | $5–$10 | AE, D, DC, MC, V.

Houston's. Barbecue. All seats in the dining room have a view of Lake Killarney at this upscale restaurant. The dining room is all wooden, with old west memorabilia. The small menu features pork, steak, chicken, and fish. Try the fork and knife ribs, prime rib, New York strip, or salmon. | 215 S. Orlando Ave. | 407/740–4005 | Reservations not accepted | $9–$16 | AE, MC, V.

P.F. Chang's. Chinese. Two huge, stone Ming dynasty–style statues of horses stand guard outside this restaurant; inside are replicas of sculptures found in the ancient Chinese city of Xi'an, and a big mural depicting 12th-century China over the bar. Try the Cantonese duck, Chang's spicy chicken, and salt and pepper shrimp. There's a lengthy wine list. | 423 N. Orlando Ave. | 407/622–0188 | $8–$13 | AE, MC, V.

Pannullo's. Italian. Casual and friendly, this is the only Italian restaurant on Park Avenue. Specialties include bruschetta, ravioli *terracina* (crescent-shaped pasta pockets stuffed with wild mushrooms), and seafood-stuffed shrimp. Ask for one of the few tables that overlooks Central Park. | 216 S. Park Ave. | 407/629–7270 | $9–$15 | AE, D, DC, MC, V.

Park Avenue Grill. American. This mainstay overlooking bustling Park Avenue is charming, with wood furnishings and simple marble-top tables. Yet much of its appeal comes from its busy social pace; the restaurant, including the sidewalk café, is often full. Try the grouper Oscar (grilled and topped with lump crabmeat, grilled asparagus and a dollop of béarnaise sauce); or the grilled salmon Parisian (bathed in a sauce of Brie cheese and green onions). | 358 N. Park Ave. | 407/647–4556 | Reservations not accepted | $10–$17 | AE, D, DC, MC, V.

WINTER PARK

INTRO
ATTRACTIONS
DINING
LODGING

Park Plaza Gardens. Contemporary. This upscale restaurant in the center of Park Ave. has an ever-evolving kitchen that creates with Cajun-Creole, Chesapeake Bay, New England, and Florida regional influences. The dining room is a New Orleans–style patio with brick floors, and ficus trees with white lights. Specialties include a simple Amish roasted corn chowder, fire-roasted rack of lamb, and Atlantic blue crab cakes with mustard sauce. | 319 Park Ave. S | 407/645–2475 | Reservations essential | $15–$30 | AE, D, DC, MC, V.

Saikyo Sushi Bar and Grill. Japanese. Taking its name from a combo of "Saigon" and "Tokyo," this sushi restaurant 2 mi east of downtown offers sashimi and sushi plus sukiyaki, teriyaki, and tempura. A wooden footbridge over a fish pond leads to the front door; a small *tatami* seating area and sushi bar are set against soft colors and subdued lighting. Try the French roll (with shrimp, crab, avocado, cucumber and cream cheese); or the Sanibel roll (with salmon, asparagus, and cream cheese). | 2522 Aloma Ave. | 407/673–8294 | $5–$13 | AE, D, MC, V.

Trastevere Ristorante. Italian. Named after a neighborhood on the Tiber River, this fine restaurant has a dark dining room decorated with dark wood, pots, pans, and paintings on deep yellow walls. Opera music and comfortable small wood tables with white linens make this the sort of place for a romantic dinner. Specialties include the *pollo al formaggio* (chicken breast simmered in chicken broth and white wine, topped with mozzarella) and *vitella piccata* (thinly sliced veal sautéed in butter). | 400 S. Orlando Ave. | 407/628–1277 | Closed Sun. | $10–$15 | AE, D, DC, MC, V.

Varina's. Pan-Asian. One block west of Park Ave., this Thai and fusion restaurant is, with the addition of a Tokyo chef, quickly becoming known for Japanese sushi. The dining room is small and subtle, with soft overhead lighting, and simple well-spaced wooden tables. Over-size sushi rolls are a specialty, as well as seasoned red and green seaweed salads, and minced meats glazed with lemongrass and ginger soy sauce. | 601 S. New York Ave. | 407/628–5912 | $10–$17 | AE, DC, MC, V.

Village Bistro. Contemporary. French, Italian, American, and Mediterranean dishes are served at this café-style bistro along Park Avenue. A place to go when you're not in a hurry, the dining room is intimate and warm, with the tables close together and soft lighting. Try the grouper with saffron sauce, the penne *Portofino* (topped with chicken and diced apples in Parmesan sauce), or the crab cakes. | 326 S. Park Ave. | 407/740–7573 | $13–$24 | AE, D, DC, MC, V.

Lodging

Best Western Mt. Vernon Inn. Set back from the road on a quiet, wooded property, this two-story hotel is 1 mi from downtown Winter Park. The main building is modeled after Washington's colonial style mansion; rooms have wooden armoires and carved headboards, lace curtains, and several antique lamps. The pool courtyard is filled with tropical vegetation, and there is also a small fountain out front. Restaurant, bar (with entertainment), room service. Some refrigerators. Cable TV. Pool. Business services. | 110 S. Orlando Ave. | 407/647–1166 or 800/992–3379 | fax 407/647–8011 | www.bestwestern.com | 143 rooms | $59–$99 | AE, D, MC, V.

Days Inn of Winter Park. Rooms at the two-story hotel, across from the Winter Park Village Shopping Mall, come with a king-size or two double beds, light wood furnishings, blue carpet and floral pink-and-blue bedding. A shady pool courtyard is surrounded by high pink stucco walls. Complimentary Continental breakfast. Some microwaves, some refrigerators. Cable TV. Pool. Beauty salon. Laundry service. Business services. | 901 N. Orlando Ave. | 407/644–8000 or 800/611–6575 | fax 407/644–0032 | 105 rooms | $70–$100 | AE, D, MC, V.

Fairfield Inn Winter Park. Open for over 60 years, this three-story white Marriott hotel is less than 1 mi from downtown Winter Park. Spacious guest rooms have well-lit work desks; however, the decor is brown, orange, and creme—seemingly un-updated since the 1970s. Each room has a king-size or two double beds, wood furnishings, and large windows.

Complimentary Continental breakfast. Cable TV. Pool. Laundry facilities, laundry service. Business services. | 951 N. Wymore Rd.; I–4 Exit 46/Lee Rd. | 407/539–1955 or 800/228–2800 | fax 407/539–1955 | 135 rooms | $59–$79 | AE, D, MC, V.

Holiday Inn Orlando North at Winter Park. This five-story hotel on the edge of Winter Park and downtown Orlando has a warm, inviting country style. Rooms are decorated in rich blue and red plaids, with mahogany furnishings, and a desk with a rolling high-back chair. Each room has a king-size or two double beds, and connecting rooms and roll-away beds are available. Restaurant, bar. In-room data ports. Cable TV. Pool. Exercise equipment. Video games. Laundry facilities, laundry service. Business services. | 626 Lee Rd. | 407/635–5600 | fax 407/740–7912 | 200 rooms, 4 suites | $80–$110 | AE, D, DC, MC, V.

Park Plaza Hotel B&B. The Park Plaza, an up-scale European-style hotel built in 1922, overlooks Park Avenue and the rose gardens of Central Park. Antiques, wicker furniture, and plants grace the lobby and guest rooms. Each room has a queen-size antique brass bed and hardwood floors; some rooms have sofa beds, sitting areas, desks, and balcony views of the park or street. Aim for the front garden suite. Restaurant, bar, complimentary Continental breakfast, room service. In-room data ports. Cable TV. Exercise equipment. Laundry facilities. Business services. No kids. No smoking. | 307 Park Ave. S | 407/647–1072 | 27 rooms | $91–$226 | AE, D, DC, MC, V.

ZEPHYRHILLS

MAP 3, I6

(Nearby towns also listed: Dade City, Lakeland)

Zephyrhills bills itself as the city of pure spring water. It's in the rolling hills of southeastern Pasco county, in central Florida's citrus and lake country. Its famed Zephyrhills Natural Spring Water comes from one of the deepest water sources in Florida, in a naturally filtered aquifer. The spring is known for its good mineral content and is protected by 500 acres of preserved land. The majority of the surrounding area is used for cattle farming and citrus cultivation. The town received its name when Captain H. B. Jeffries, a Civil War veteran from Pennsylvania, heard someone remark about the "zephyr-like breezes" that rolled across the hills. Zephyrhills Municipal Airport is home base for one of the largest parachuting centers in the U.S.

Information: Zephyrhills Chamber of Commerce | 38550 Fifth Ave., Zephyrhills, 33540 | 813/782–1913 | www.zephyrhills.net.

Attractions

Fort Foster Historic Site. This was a key fortification along the Hillsborough River during the Second Seminole War. Abandoned in 1938, the fort has been reconstructed and is now an historic site. Tours are available. It's 6 mi south of Zephyrhills. | 15402 U.S. 301, North Thonotosassa | 813/987–6771 | $3.25 per vehicle | Daily.

Hillsborough River State Park. Developed by the Civilian Conservation Corps (CCC) in 1936, the 3,950-acre park, 6 mi south of town, was opened to the public in 1938. The river has one of Florida's only sections of class II rapids. You can fish and canoe in the stream. Some 8 mi of nature trails meander through hammocks of live oaks, sabal palms, and hickories, along the water's edge. There is a 103-site campground with electricity and water, and a swimming pool. | 15402 U.S. 301 N, Thonotosassa | 813/987–6771 | $3.25 per vehicle | Daily.

ON THE CALENDAR

NOV.: *Thanksgiving Skydiving Competition.* Hundreds of skydivers from around the world get a jump on the Thanksgiving holiday at this event in Skydive City, Florida's top skydiving center. | 813/783–9399.

Lodging

Best Western Zephyrhills. This motel is set in a small town atmosphere where travelers can enjoy a reprieve from the chaos of central Florida's attractions. The rooms are standard, but the building is U-shape, so they have views of the large pool and garden area. Picnic area. In-room data ports, refrigerators. Cable TV. Pool. Business services. | 5734 Gall Blvd. | 813/782–5527 or 888/879–3578 | fax 813/783–7102 | www.bestwestern.com | 52 rooms | $69–$89 | AE, D, DC, MC, V.

Index

Notes

Notes

Notes

TALK TO US

Fill out this quick survey and receive a free *Fodor's How to Pack* (while supplies last)

---

1 Which Road Guide did you purchase?
(Check all that apply.)

❑ AL/AR/LA/MS/TN ❑ IL/IA/MO/WI
❑ AZ/CO/NM ❑ IN/KY/MI/OH/WV
❑ CA ❑ KS/OK/TX
❑ CT/MA/RI ❑ ME/NH/VT
❑ DE/DC/MD/PA/VA ❑ MN/NE/ND/SD
❑ FL ❑ NJ/NY
❑ GA/NC/SC ❑ OR/WA
❑ ID/MT/NV/UT/WY

2 How did you learn about the Road Guides?
❑ TV ad
❑ Radio ad
❑ Newspaper or magazine ad
❑ Newspaper or magazine article
❑ TV or radio feature
❑ Bookstore display/clerk recommendation
❑ Recommended by family/friend
❑ Other:_____

3 Did you use other guides for your trip?
❑ AAA ❑ Insiders' Guide
❑ Compass American Guide ❑ Mobil
❑ Fodor's ❑ Moon Handbook
❑ Frommer's ❑ Other:_____

4 Did you use any of the following for planning?
❑ Tourism offices ❑ Internet ❑ Travel agent

5 Did you buy a Road Guide for (check one):
❑ Leisure trip
❑ Business trip
❑ Mix of business and leisure

6 Where did you buy your Road Guide?
❑ Bookstore
❑ Other store
❑ On-line
❑ Borrowed from a friend
❑ Borrowed from a library
❑ Other:_____

7 Why did you buy a Road Guide? (Check all that apply.)
❑ Number of cities/towns listed
❑ Comprehensive coverage
❑ Number of lodgings ❑ Driving tours
❑ Number of restaurants ❑ Maps
❑ Number of attractions ❑ Fodor's brand name
❑ Other:_____

8 Did you use this guide primarily:
❑ For pretrip planning ❑ While traveling
❑ For planning and while traveling

9 What was the duration of your trip?
❑ 2-3 days ❑ 11 or more days
❑ 4-6 days ❑ Taking more than 1 trip
❑ 7-10 days

10 Did you use the guide to select
❑ Hotels ❑ Restaurants

11 Did you stay primarily in a
❑ Hotel ❑ Hostel
❑ Motel ❑ Campground
❑ Resort ❑ Dude ranch
❑ Bed-and-breakfast ❑ With family or friends
❑ RV/camper ❑ Other:_____

12 What sights and activities did you most enjoy?
❑ Historical sights ❑ Shopping
❑ Sports ❑ Theaters
❑ National parks ❑ Museums
❑ State parks ❑ Major cities
❑ Attractions off the beaten path

13 How much did you spend per adult for this trip?
❑ Less than $500 ❑ $751-$1,000
❑ $501-$750 ❑ More than $1,000

14 How many traveled in your party?
___ Adults ___ Children ___ Pets

15 Did you
❑ Fly to destination ❑ Rent a van or RV
❑ Drive your own vehicle ❑ Take a train
❑ Rent a car ❑ Take a bus

16 How many miles did you travel round-trip?
❑ Less than 100 ❑ 501-750
❑ 101-300 ❑ 751-1,000
❑ 301-500 ❑ More than 1,000

17 What items did you take on your vacation?
❑ Traveler's checks ❑ Digital camera
❑ Credit card ❑ Cell phone
❑ Gasoline card ❑ Computer
❑ Phone card ❑ PDA
❑ Camera ❑ Other

18 Would you use Fodor's Road Guides again?
❑ Yes ❑ No

19 How would you like to see Road Guides changed?

☐ More ☐ Less Dining
☐ More ☐ Less Lodging
☐ More ☐ Less Sports
☐ More ☐ Less Activities
☐ More ☐ Less Attractions
☐ More ☐ Less Shopping
☐ More ☐ Less Driving tours
☐ More ☐ Less Maps
☐ More ☐ Less Historical information
☐ Other:_____

20 Tell us about yourself.

☐ Male   ☐ Female

Age:
☐ 18-24   ☐ 35-44   ☐ 55-64
☐ 25-34   ☐ 45-54   ☐ Over 65

Income:
☐ Less than $25,000   ☐ $50,001-$75,000
☐ $25,001-$50,000   ☐ More than $75,000

Name:_____   E-mail:_____

Address:_____   City:_____ State:_____ Zip:_____

Fodor's Travel Publications
Attn: Road Guide Survey
280 Park Avenue
New York, NY 10017

Atlas

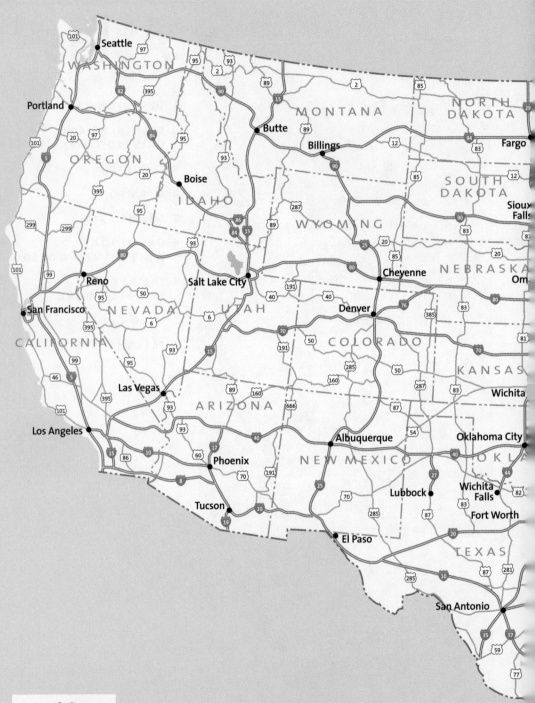

U. S. Highways

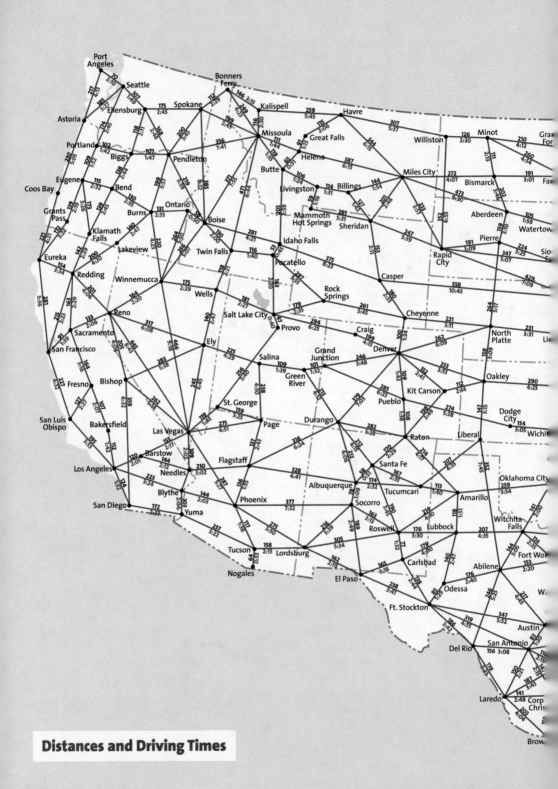

Distances and Driving Times

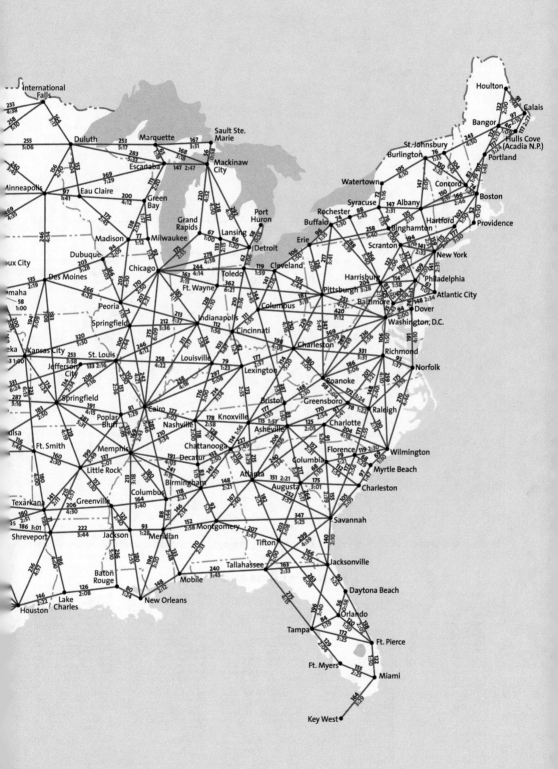

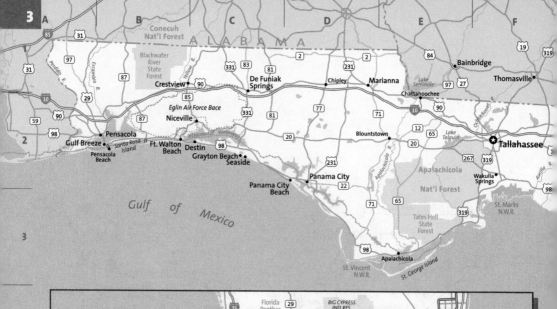

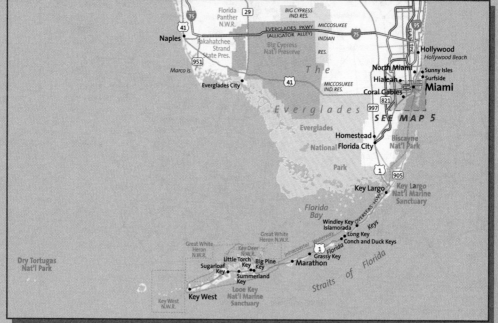

Florida – Cities and Towns

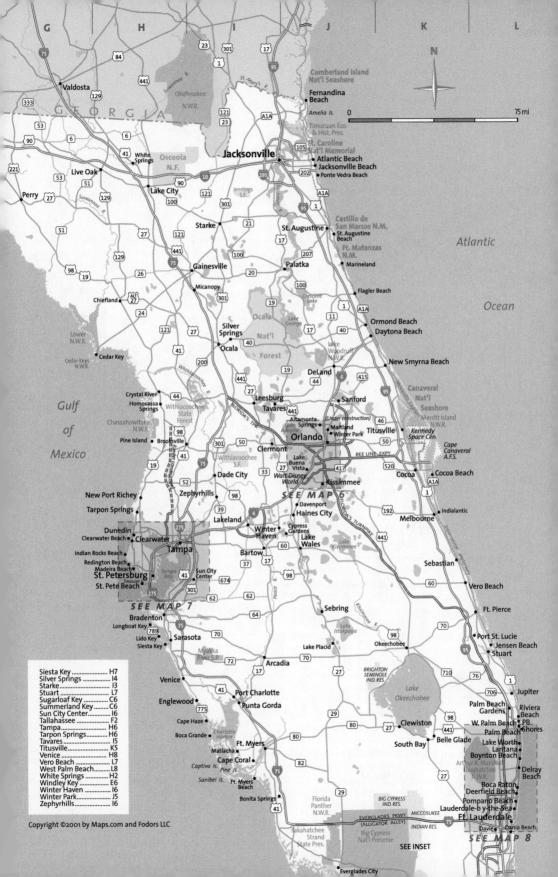

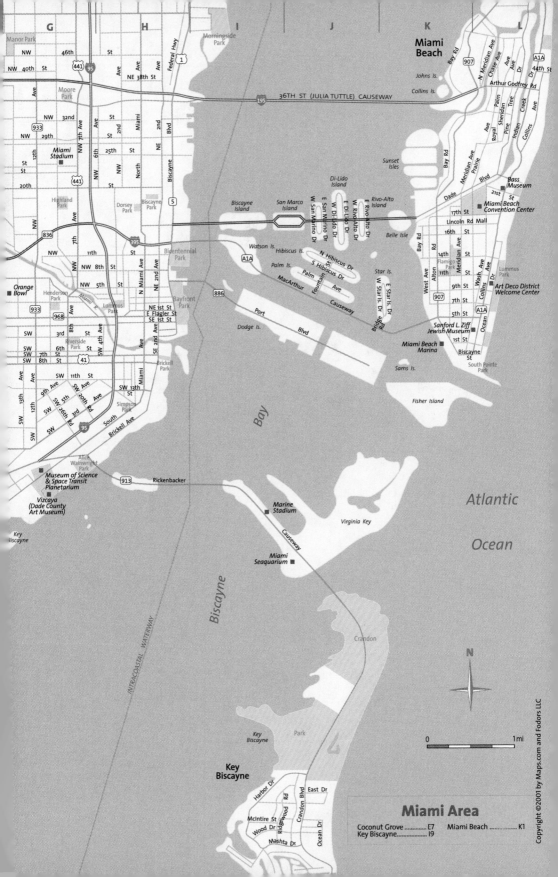

Miami Area

G **H** **I** **J** **K** **L**

Manor Park

NW 46th St
NW 40th St

NE 38th St

Federal Hwy

Morningside Park

Miami Beach

Johns Is.

Bay Rd

907

A1A
N Meridian Ave
Chase Ave
44th St
Arthur Godfrey Rd

36TH ST (JULIA TUTTLE) CAUSEWAY

Collins Is.

Palm
Royal
Sheridan
Pine Tree
Indian Creek
Collins

NW 32nd St
NW 29th St

Miami
NE

Biscayne Blvd

Sunset Isles

Meridian Ave
Prairie

Miami Stadium

NW 25th St
North

Di-Lido Island

Bass Museum

Dade Blvd

21st St

Highland Park

Dorsey Park
Biscayne Park

Biscayne Island

San Marco Island

Rivo-Alto Island

17th St

Miami Beach Convention Center

Lincoln Rd Mall

W San Marino Dr
E San Marino Dr
W Di-Lido Dr
E Di-Lido Dr
W Rivo-Alto Dr
E Rivo-Alto Dr

16th St
15th St

NW 11th St

Belle Isle

14th St

Bay Rd

Flamigo Park

Alton Rd

West Ave

Washington Ave

Meridian Ave

Bicentennial Park

Watson Is.

Hibiscus Is.
N Hibiscus Dr

Star Is.

11th St
9th St

Collins

Orange Bowl

Henderson Park
Lummus Park

A1A

S Hibiscus Dr
Palm Is.
Palm Ave
Fountain

W Star Is. Dr
E Star Is. Dr

7th St
5th St

A1A

MacArthur Causeway

NE 1st St
E Flagler St
SE 1st St

886

Bridge Rd

907

Sanford L. Ziff Jewish Museum

1st St

Port Blvd

Miami Beach Marina

Biscayne St

Dodge Is.

Sams Is.

South Pointe Park

Brickell Park

Simpson Park

Fisher Island

Bay

Museum of Science & Space Transit Planetarium

913
Rickenbacker

Marine Stadium

Atlantic

Virginia Key

Ocean

Vizcaya (Dade County Art Museum)

Causeway

Miami Seaquarium

Key Biscayne

Biscayne

Crandon

INTRACOASTAL WATERWAY

N

Key Biscayne
Park

Key Biscayne

Harbor Dr
McIntire St
Wood Dr
Redwood Rd
Crandon Blvd
East Dr
Ocean Dr
Mashta Dr

0   1mi

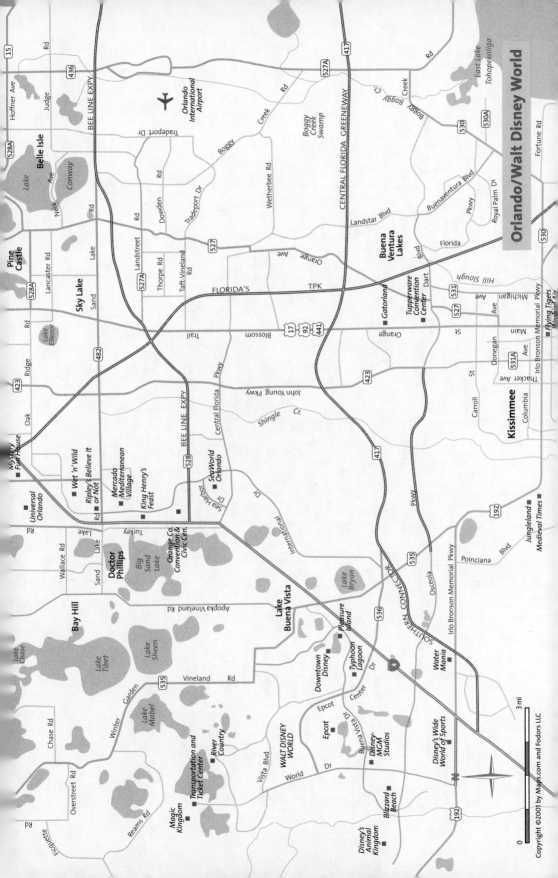

Orlando/Walt Disney World

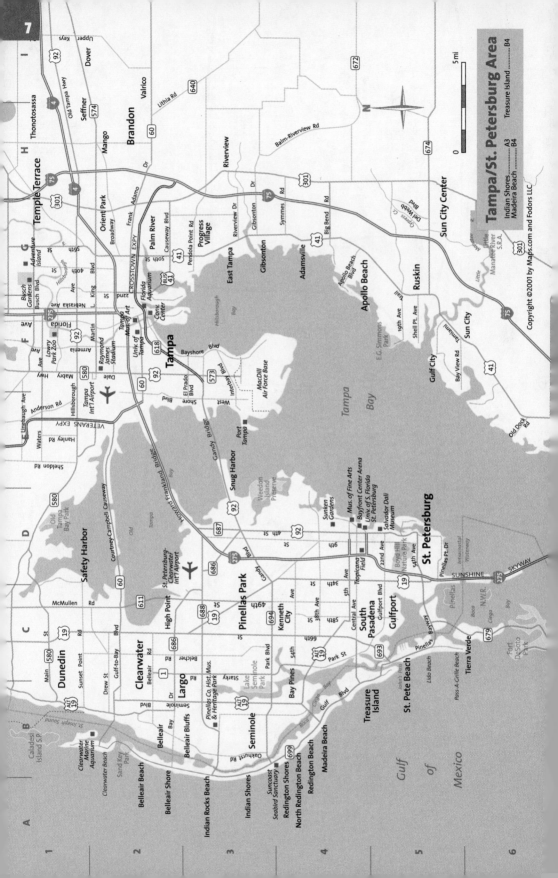

Tampa/St. Petersburg Area

Indian Shores A3
Madeira Beach B4
Treasure Island B4

0   5 mi

N

Copyright ©2001 by Maps.com and Fodors LLC

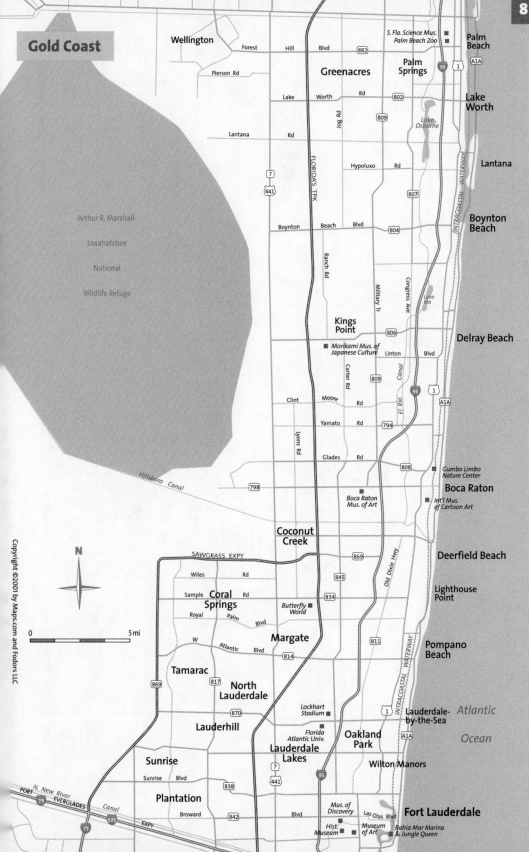

Gold Coast

Wellington

S. Fla. Science Mus.
Palm Beach Zoo

Palm Beach

Forest   Hill   Blvd   882

Palm Springs

Greenacres

Pierson Rd

Lake   Worth   Rd   802

Lake Worth

809

Lake Osborne

Lantana   Rd

Hypoluxo   Rd   807

Lantana

7
441

FLORIDA'S TPK

Boynton Beach

Ranch Rd

Boynton   Beach   Blvd   804

Arthur R. Marshall-
Loxahatchee
National
Wildlife Refuge

Military Tr

Congress Ave

Lake Ida

Kings Point

806

Delray Beach

Morikami Mus. of
Japanese Culture

Linton   Blvd

Carter Rd

809

95   1

A1A

El Rio Canal

Clint   Moore   Rd

Lyons Rd

Yamato   Rd   794

Glades   Rd   808

Gumbo Limbo
Nature Center

Hillsboro Canal

798

Boca Raton
Mus. of Art

Boca Raton

Int'l Mus.
of Cartoon Art

Coconut Creek

SAWGRASS EXPY

869

Old Dixie Hwy

Deerfield Beach

Wiles   Rd

845

Lighthouse Point

Sample   Rd

Coral Springs

834

Royal   Palm   Blvd

Butterfly World

INTRACOASTAL WATERWAY

Pompano Beach

W   Atlantic   Blvd

Margate

814

811

Tamarac

817

North Lauderdale

869

870

Lockhart Stadium

1

Lauderdale-by-the-Sea

Atlantic

Lauderhill

Florida
Atlantic Univ.

A1A

Ocean

Sunrise

Lauderdale Lakes

Oakland Park

Wilton Manors

95

7
441

N. New River

PORT
EVERGLADES

75

Sunrise   Blvd

838

Plantation

Broward   Blvd

Canal

595

EXPY

842

Mus. of
Discovery

Hist.
Museum

Museum
of Art

Las Olas Blvd

Fort Lauderdale

Bahia Mar Marina
& Jungle Queen

N

0   5 mi

Copyright ©2001 by Maps.com and Fodors LLC

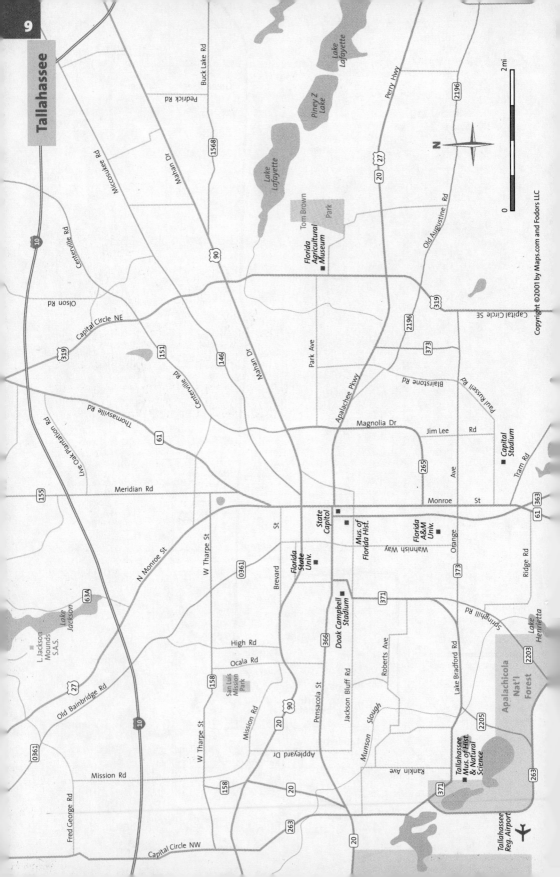

2 mi

N

0

Buck Lake Rd

Pedrick Rd

Mahan Dr

Miccosukee Rd

Centerville Rd

1568

Lake Lafayette

Lake Lafayette

Piney Z Lake

Lake Lafayette

Perry Hwy

2196

20

27

Old Augustine Rd

Tom Brown Park

Florida Agricultural Museum

90

Olson Rd

Capital Circle NE

319

151

146

Mahan Dr

Park Ave

2196

Capital Circle SE

319

373

Thomasville Rd

Centerville Rd

61

Blairstone Rd

Paul Russell Rd

Apalachee Pkwy

Magnolia Dr

Jim Lee Rd

Capital Stadium

Tram Rd

Live Oak Plantation Rd

155

Meridian Rd

Monroe St

265

Ave

61 363

Lake Jackson

63A

N Monroe St

W Tharpe St

0361

Brevard St

St

State Capitol

Mus. of Florida Hist.

Florida State Univ.

Florida A&M Univ.

Wahnish Way

Orange

373

Ridge Rd

L.Jackson Mounds S.A.S.

27

High Rd

Ocala Rd

158

San Luis Mission Park

Mission Rd

20

90

Pensacola St

Dook Campbell Stadium

366

Jackson Bluff Rd

371

Roberts Ave

Munson Slough

Lake Bradford Rd

Springhill Rd

Lake Henrietta

2203

Apalachicola Nat'l Forest

Old Bainbridge Rd

10

0361

Mission Rd

W Tharpe St

158

Appleyard Dr

20

Rankin Ave

2205

Tallahassee Mus. of Hist. & Natural Science

371

263

Fred George Rd

Capital Circle NW

263

20

Tallahassee Reg. Airport